PREFACE

This Evidence Rules and Statute Supplement can be used with Cases and Materials on Evidence by Weinstein, Mansfield, Abrams and Berger (9th ed. 1997) or any other set of Evidence teaching materials. It will also provide the basis for teaching through the problem method with the aid of a Treatise.

Included are the Federal Rules of Evidence with amended notes and the California Evidence Code with excerpts from the comments to that Code. We have also included the version of the Uniform Rules of Evidence adopted in 1999 with comments.

As of January 1, 2007, forty–two states and Puerto Rico had adopted the Federal Rules of Evidence in various forms. They are as follows: Alabama (1996), Alaska (1979), Arizona (1977), Arkansas (1976), Colorado (1980), Conneticut (1999), Delaware (1980), Florida (1979), Hawaii (1980), Idaho (1985), Indiana (1994), Iowa (1983), Kentucky (1992), Louisiana (1989), Maine (1976), Maryland (1994), Michigan (1978), Minnesota (1977), Mississippi (1986), Montana (1977), Nebraska (1975), Nevada (1971), New Hampshire (1985), New Jersey (1993), New Mexico (1973), North Carolina (1984), North Dakota (1977), Ohio (1980), Oklahoma (1978), Oregon (1982), Pennsylvania (1998), Puerto Rico (1979), Rhode Island (1987), South Carolina (1995), South Dakota (1978), Tennessee (1990), Texas (1983 and 1986), Utah (1983), Vermont (1983), Washington (1979), West Virginia (1985), Wisconsin (1974) and Wyoming (1978). Military Rules of Evidence which apply in courts-martial and are based on the Federal Rules of Evidence were prescribed by Executive Order in 1980.

The Federal Rules as proposed by the Supreme Court were not adopted by Congress but were modified in a number of relatively minor respects. In addition, all of the individual privilege rules were dropped, except Rule 501, which was substantially changed. Congress has recently enacted Rule 502. In these materials we have published the rules on privileges as proposed by the Supreme Court with the notes originally provided by the Advisory Committee since these provisions are widely relied upon and furnish useful models for classroom discussion.

After Congress modified the Rules, a set of amended notes was provided by the Federal Judicial Center. These constituted revisions, primarily by Professor Edward W. Cleary, Reporter to the Advisory Committee on Rules of Evidence, of the notes prepared for the Supreme Court's version. In a number of cases, there were subsequent amendments by Congress. These amendments have been noted in the materials that follow.

We have thought it useful to include the California Evidence Code, since it represents a much more detailed codification than does the Feder-

PREFACE

al Rules and thus provides a useful tool for comparison and study. The comments to this codification however, have been cut heavily, since they are somewhat repetitive of other materials. The California Code was relied upon heavily by the Advisory Committee that drafted the Federal Rules of Evidence and, from time to time, there are references in the notes to California's practice. Thus, the California Code will prove particularly useful if it is available in the same volume as the Federal Rules and notes. The California Evidence Code has been brought up-to-date, and all amendments approved through June 30, 2011 are included in this Supplement.

The comments to the 1999 version of the Uniform Rules have been included because they explain why the Commissioners on Uniform State Laws were unwilling to accept the Federal Rule on point. Thus these comments provide valuable insights into issues that arise in connection with the Federal Rules. Furthermore, the ability easily to compare the California Rules, the Uniform Rules and the Federal Rules enables the student of evidence to evaluate different solutions to the same problem.

We have also included excerpts from the Delaware Lawyers' Rules of Professional Conduct, which are nearly identical with the ABA Model Rules of Professional Conduct. Having the pertinent ethical rules and comments thereto available in one location should make it easier to integrate these materials into the Evidence course.

While there have been many earlier attempts to codify and revise the Anglo-American Rules of Evidence in the United States, a new chapter was written when the American Law Institute's Model Code of Evidence was adopted on May 15, 1942 by the American Law Institute. This codification under the general direction of Edmund M. Morgan as Reporter, had an eminent group of advisors and committees, including the leading professors of evidence law at the time, among them Mason Ladd, John M. Maguire, Charles T. McCormick, John H. Wigmore, Judson F. Falknor, Jerome Michael, and many other luminaries of the bench, bar and teaching profession. With its extensive notes, it proved highly useful in much the same way as the Restatements of the Law of the American Law Institute. But it did not succeed in its goal of providing a basis for codification by the states. In 1948 the Commissioners on Uniform State Laws authorized a revision based upon the ALI's Model Code. That revision was more modest in its changes and shorter in length. It was adopted in 1954 by the Commissioners and was widely relied upon in interpreting the common law. It was adopted *in toto,* however, only in Kansas and it provided the basis for the New Jersey Rules which followed it closely in text and format.

Earlier editions of the casebook included the ALI Code of Evidence or the 1954 Uniform Rules of Evidence. There appears to be no reason to include them now that the Federal Rules are available. Where relevant, there will be references to the text and theory of the Model Code of Evi-

EVIDENCE
Rules, Statute and Case Supplement

Includes:

Federal Rules of Evidence, with Excerpted Notes

California Evidence Code, with Excerpted Comments

Uniform Rules of Evidence, with Comments

Excerpts from Rules of Professional Conduct

Comparative Table of Federal Rules and
California Evidence Code Sections

Selected Cases and Notes

By

JACK B. WEINSTEIN
Senior Judge, United States District Court for the
Eastern District of New York

JOHN H. MANSFIELD
John H. Watson, Jr. Professor of Law Emeritus, Harvard University

NORMAN ABRAMS
Distinguished Professor of Law Emeritus
University of California, Los Angeles

MARGARET A. BERGER
Trustee Professor of Law
Brooklyn Law School

This supplement may be used in conjunction with materials in any Evidence course. It was prepared to accompany the Ninth Edition of Weinstein, Mansfield, Abrams, Berger, Cases and Materials on Evidence.

FOUNDATION PRESS
2011

THOMSON REUTERS™

© 1981, 1984, 1987–1990, 1992, 1993, 1996–2004 FOUNDATION PRESS

© 2005-2010 THOMSON REUTERS/FOUNDATION PRESS

© 2011

By

THOMSON REUTERS/FOUNDATION PRESS

1 New York Plaza, 34th Floor
New York, NY 10004
Phone Toll Free 1–877–888–1330
Fax 646–424–5201
foundation-press.com

Printed in the United States of America

ISBN 978–1–60930–001–2

[No claim of copyright is made for official U.S. government statutes, rules or regulations.]

This publication was created to provide you with accurate and authoritative information concerning the subject matter covered; however, this publication was not necessarily prepared by persons licensed to practice law in a particular jurisdiction. The publisher is not engaged in rendering legal or other professional advice and this publication is not a substitute for the advice of an attorney. If you require legal or other expert advice, you should seek the services of a competent attorney or other professional.

Nothing contained herein is intended or written to be used for the purposes of 1) avoiding penalties imposed under the federal Internal Revenue Code, or 2) promoting, marketing or recommending to another party any transaction or matter addressed herein.

Mat #41135290

PREFACE

dence and the Uniform Rules of Evidence (1954) in the main volume of the current casebook and the notes in this Supplement.

At its April 22-23, 2010, meeting, the Advisory Committee on Evidence Rules approved the comprehensive style amendments to the Federal Rules of Evidence. It is not intended that this will effect any substantive changes in the Federal Law of Evidence. The Advisory Committee will then transmit the revised style amendments to the Committee on Rules of Practice and Procedure for consideration at its June 2010 meeting.

A detailed history of the Federal Rules, amendments and state adaptations, with cases, will be found in J.B. Weinstein and M.A. Berger, "Weinstein's Evidence" (1983).

J.B.W.
J.H.M.
N.A.
M.A.B.

July 2011

TABLE OF CONTENTS

	Page
PREFACE	iii
COMPARATIVE TABLE—FEDERAL RULES OF EVIDENCE AND CALIFORNIA EVIDENCE CODE SECTIONS	ix

FEDERAL RULES OF EVIDENCE FOR UNITED STATES COURTS AND MAGISTRATES ... 1

Article I. General Provisions	7
Article II. Judicial Notice	17
Article III. Presumptions in Civil Actions and Proceedings	24
Article IV. Relevancy and Its Limits	25
Article V. Privileges	62
Article VI. Witnesses	71
Article VII. Opinions and Expert Testimony	103
Article VIII. Hearsay	120
Article IX. Authentication and Identification	172
Article X. Contents of Writings, Recordings, and Photographs	182
Article XI. Miscellaneous Rules	189

APPENDIX OF DELETED MATERIALS ... 196

CALIFORNIA EVIDENCE CODE ... 232

Division 1. Preliminary Provisions and Construction	248
Division 2. Words and Phrases Defined	250
Division 3. General Provisions	255
Division 4. Judicial Notice	270
Division 5. Burden of Proof; Burden of Producing Evidence; Presumptions and Inferences	278
Division 6. Witnesses	295
Division 7. Opinion Testimony and Scientific Evidence	320
Division 8. Privileges	330
Division 9. Evidence Affected or Excluded by Extrinsic Policies	377
Division 10. Hearsay Evidence	397
Division 11. Writings	429

UNIFORM RULES OF EVIDENCE ... 446

Article I. General Provisions	452
Article II. Judicial Notice	457
Article III. Presumptions	458
Article IV. Relevancy and Its Limits	460
Article V. Privileges	468
Article VI. Witnesses	477
Article VII. Opinions and Expert Testimony	484
Article VIII. Hearsay	488
Article IX. Authentication and Identification	500

TABLE OF CONTENTS

Article X. Content of Record, Writing, Recording, Photograph, Image, and Other Record 505
Article XI. Miscellaneous Rules 508

DELAWARE LAWYERS' RULES OF PROFESSIONAL CONDUCT 509

SELECTED CASES 541

COMPARATIVE TABLE—FEDERAL RULES OF EVIDENCE AND CALIFORNIA EVIDENCE CODE SECTIONS

(according to Evidence Topics)

The following Table indicates the sections in the Federal Rules and California Evidence Code that deal with the same general Evidence topics. Because the two codes adopt different approaches to many issues it is not possible to match their provisions on a one-to-one basis. Nor does the Table refer to all provisions of either code. Only those sections directly related to the major topics usually covered in an Evidence course are included. Where one of the codes does not contain a provision on a subject, this is indicated by the word "none" in the Table. In those instances where there is no corresponding provision in one of the codes but the subject is dealt with in a Comment or Note or obliquely in other provisions, the Comment, Note or principal other provision(s) are indicated.

Topics	Federal Rules	California Evidence Code
1. Relevancy—In General		
Definition	401	210, 140
Relevant evidence admissible	402	350, 351
Probative value v. prejudice	403	352
Evidence erroneously admitted or excluded	103	353, 354
Limited admissibility	105	355
Contextual parts of admitted statements	106	356
Polygraph evidence	none	351.1
2. Witnesses and Testimony		
Competency	601	700, 701
Personal knowledge	602	702
Oath	603	710
Opinion—lay	701	800
Qualifying the expert	none	720
Subject of expert testimony	702	801(a)
Sources of information; expert opinion	703	801(b)
Stating basis for expert opinion—hypothetical	705	802
Expert opinion based upon opinion of another	none	804
Opinion on ultimate issue	704	805
Opinion as to sanity	704	870
Opinion as to value of property	none	810–822

COMPARATIVE TABLE

Topics	Federal Rules	California Evidence Code
2. Witnesses and Testimony—Continued		
Court appointment of experts and compensation	706	730–732, 722
Judicial control—in general	611(a)	765, 320
Court calling witnesses	614	775
Judge as a witness	605	703, 703.5
Juror as a witness	606	704
Exclusion of witnesses	615	777
Leading questions	611(c)	764, 767
Adverse witness	none	776
Refreshing recollection—writings	612	771, 250
Prior statements of a witness	613(a)	769, 768
Prior inconsistent statements—extrinsic evidence	613(b)	770
Scope of cross-examination	611(b)	760, 761, 772, 773
Cross-examination of expert	none	721
Hypnosis of witness	none	795
3. Credibility—Impeachment and Support		
Relevant factors—in general	none	780
Impeachment—own witness	607	785
Collateral matters	403	352, 780 (Comment)
Relevant character trait	608(a)	786
Reputation	608(a)	1100, 1101(c)
Opinion	608(a)	780 (Comment) 1100, 1101(c)
Specific acts	608(b)	787
Impeachment—prior sexual conduct	none (but see 412)	782, 783
Prior convictions	609	788
Support—character	608	790
Support—prior consistent statements	none	791
Religious belief	610	789
4. Hearsay		
Definitions—statement	801(a)	225
conduct	none	125
declarant	801(b)	135
hearsay	801(c)	1200(a)
General rule of inadmissibility	802	1200(b)
Unavailable—defined	804(a)	240
Admission	801(d)(2)(A)	1220
Adoptive admission	801(d)(2)(B)	1221

COMPARATIVE TABLE

Topics	Federal Rules	California Evidence Code
4. Hearsay—Continued		
Agent's statement	801(d)(2)(C), (D)	1222
Co-conspirator's statement	801(d)(2)(E)	1223
Party's liability or interest based on declarant's	none	1224, 1225
Prior inconsistent statement	801(d)(1)(A)	1235
Prior consistent statement	801(d)(1)(B)	1236
Past recollection recorded	803(5)	1237
Prior identification	801(d)(1)(C)	1238
Former testimony	804(b)(1)	1290, 1291, 1292, 1293
Declaration against interest	804(b)(3)	1230
Dying declaration	804(b)(2)	1242
Statement of unavailable minor	none	1228
Present sense impression	803(1)	none, but see 1241
Excited utterance	803(2)	1240
Then existing state of mind, bodily condition	803(3)	1250, 1252
Statement regarding making of will	none	1260
Statement for purpose of medical diagnosis or treatment	803(4)	none, but see 1251
Business records	803(6), (7)	1270, 1271, 1272
Decedent's statement—action against his estate	none	1261
Public records	803(8), (9), (10), (12), (14)	1280, 1281, 1282, 1283, 1284, 1316
Family history	803(11), (13), (19), 804(b)(4)	1310, 1311, 1310, 1311, 1314, 1315
Judgments	803(22), (23)	1300, 1301, 1302
Dispositive instruments	803(15)	1330
Ancient writings	803(16)	1331
Reputation relating to community history, public interest in property, boundaries	803(20)	1320, 1321, 1322
Statement concerning boundary	none	1323
Reputation concerning character	803(21)	1324

COMPARATIVE TABLE

Topics	Federal Rules	California Evidence Code
4. Hearsay—Continued		
Market reports, commercial lists	803(17)	1340
Learned treatises, scientific publications	803(18)	1341
General residual exception	807	1350 and see 2
Child abuse, elder abuse, physical injury to declarant	none	1360, 1370, 1380
Multiple levels of hearsay	805	1201
Credibility of hearsay declarant	806	1202, 1203
5. Character Evidence		
Types of character evidence	405	1100
Character in issue	405(a), (b)	1100
To prove conduct—general prohibition	404(a)	1101(a)
Character of witness	404(a)(3)	1101(c)
Proving motive, intent, plan, etc.	404(b)	1101(b)
To prove conduct—character of criminal defendant	404(a)(1)	1102(a), (b)
To prove conduct—character of victim	404(a)(2)	1103(a)
Prior sexual behavior of victim—rape prosecution	412	1103(b), 1106
Character for care or skill	none	1104
Habit or custom	406	1105
Similar crimes, sexual assault, molestation	413, 414, 415	see 1108
Intimate partner battering	none	1107
Domestic violence	none	1109
Evidence regarding validity of verdict	none	1150
Subsequent remedial conduct	407	1151
Offers to compromise	408	1152
Offer to plead guilty or withdrawn guilty plea	410	1153
Offer for civil resolution of crimes against property	none	1153.5
Offer to discount claim	none (but see 409)	1154
Payment of medical expenses	409	none (but see 1154)
Liability insurance	411	1155

COMPARATIVE TABLE

Topics	Federal Rules	California Evidence Code
6. Authentication		
Requirement of authentication	901(a)	1400, 1401
Methods		
Knowledge	901(b)(1)	1413
Handwriting	901(b)(2), (3)	1415, 1416, 1417, 1418, 1419
Voice identification	901(b)(5)	none
Content	901(b)(4)	1421
Written reply	none	1420
Telephone conversations	901(b)(6)	none
Ancient documents	901(b)(8)	none (but see 1419)
Public records	901(b)(7)	none
Admissions	none (but compare 1007)	1414
Process or system	901(b), (9)	none
Non-exclusivity of listed methods	901(b)	1410
Writing	none	1410.5
Altered writing	none	1402
Necessity for subscribing witness' testimony	903	1411, 1412
Presumptions and self-authentication		
Presumptions	902(10)	1450
Acknowledged writings	902(8)	1451
Official seals	902(1)	1452
Domestic official signatures	902(1), (2)	1453
Foreign official signatures	902(3)	1454
Certified copies of public records	902(4)	none
Official publications, newspapers, trade inscriptions, commercial paper	902(5), (6), (7), (9)	none
7. Original and Secondary Writings (The Best Evidence Rule)		
Definitions		
Writing	1001(1), (2)	250
Original	1001(3)	255
Duplicate	1001(4)	260
Requirement of original	1002	1500, 1511, 1550, 1551
Admissibility of duplicates	1003	
Copy preferred	none (see 1004 and compare 1005)	1505 (also see 1501

COMPARATIVE TABLE

Topics	Federal Rules	California Evidence Code
7. Original and Secondary Writings (The Best Evidence Rule)—Continued		
Where original unavailable through court process	1004(2)	1502
Where original under opponent's control	1004(3)	1503
Collateral writing	1004(4)	1504
No degrees of secondary evidence after copy	none	1505
Voluminous writings	1006	1509
Proof of contents by opponent's admission	1004	none (but compare 1414)
Writing produced at hearing	none	1510
Public records	1005	1506, 1507, 1508, 1530–32
Hospital records	none	1560–1566
Writings affecting property	none	1600–1605

8. Privileges

[Note: The Federal Rules as originally drafted contained detailed provisions relating to privileges, but these were deleted from the Rules as finally promulgated, with the exception of Rule 501 which provides that issues of privilege are governed by the principles of the common law, or in certain specified contexts, by state law. Subsequently, in September 2008, Congress enacted Rule 502, which addresses limitations on waiver by disclosure relating to the attorney-client privilege and work product. Accordingly, these two rules, 501 and 502, are the only provisions in the Federal Rules themselves that address privilege issues.

In this part of the Table, most of the references to Federal Rules provisions are therefore references to the superseded rules that were not exacted. To highlight this fact, superseded Federal Rule references are marked with an asterisk. Where the word "none" appears in the Federal column, it signifies that there was no provision dealing with the subject in the superseded rules.]

Topics	Federal Rules	California Evidence Code
General Provisions		
Applicability	none	910, 901
Statutory privileges only	501*	911
Waiver	511*, 502	912
Comment upon	513*	913
Contempt as penalty	none	914
Disclosure of privileged information in ruling on claim	104(a)	915

COMPARATIVE TABLE

Topics	Federal Rules	California Evidence Code
8. Privileges—Continued		
Power of presiding officer to exclude evidence in absence of claimant	none	916
Presumption of confidentiality	none	917
Who may claim error	none	918
Disclosure erroneously compelled	512*	919
Lawyer-client Privilege		
Definitions		
Lawyer	503(a)(2)*	950
Client	503(a)(1)*	951
Lawyer's representative	503(a)(3)*	none
Confidential communication	503(a)(4)* 503(b)*	952
Holder	none	953
Invocation of the privilege	503(c)*	954, 955
Exceptions		
Crime-fraud	503(d)(1)*	956
All parties claim through deceased client	503(d)(2)*	957
Relating to breach of lawyer-client relationship	503(d)(3)*	958
Lawyer as attesting witness	503(d)(4)*	959
Deceased client-writing affecting property interest	none	960, 961
Joint clients	503(d)(5)*	962
Spousal Privileges		
Privilege not to testify against	none	970
Privilege not to be called as a witness against		971
Waiver of "against" privilege		973(a)
Exceptions to the "against" privilege	972(a)g, 973(b)	
Marital communications privilege	none	980
Exceptions to the marital communications privilege		981–987
Criminal accused's privilege to prevent spouse from testifying against	505(a)*	none
Who may claim accused's privilege	505(b)*	
Exceptions to accused's privilege	505(c)*	
Physician-patient Privilege		
Invocation of the privilege	none	994, 995

xv

COMPARATIVE TABLE

Topics	Federal Rules	California Evidence Code
8. Privileges—Continued		
Definitions		990–993
Exceptions		996–1007
Psychotherapist-patient		
Privilege Definitions		
Psychotherapist	504(a)*	1010, 1010.5
Patient	504(a)(1)*	1011
Confidential communication	504(a)(3)*	1012
Holder	none	1013
Application of privilege	504(b), (c)*	1014, 1015
Exceptions		
Patient-litigant	504(d)(3)*	1016
Examination by order of judge	504(d)(2)*	1017
Breach of duty	none	1020
Crime or tort	none	1018
Parties claiming through deceased patient	none	1019
Deceased patient-writing affecting property interest	none	1021, 1022
Sanity proceeding—criminal defendant	none	1023
Proceedings for hospitalization—psychotherapist initiated	504(d)(1)*	none
Dangerous patient	none (but see 504(d)(1)*)	1024
To establish patient's competence	none (but see 504(d)(1)*)	1025
Required reports	none	1026
Child under 16—crime victim	none	1027
Clergyman-penitent Privilege		
Definitions		
Clergyman	504(a)(1)*	1030
Penitent	none	1031
Confidential communication	506(a)(2)*	1032
Scope of privilege	506(b)*	1033, 1034
Who may claim	506(c)*	1033, 1034
Newsman's Immunity from Contempt	none	Art. I, 2(b) California Constitution (1070, Evidence Code)
Official Information	509*	1040

COMPARATIVE TABLE

Topics	Federal Rules	California Evidence Code
8. Privileges—Continued		
Informer's Identity	510*	1041, 1042
Political Vote	507*	1050
Trade Secrets	508*	1060
Peace Officer Personnel Records	none	1043–1045
Required Reports Privileged by Statute	502*	none
Sexual Assault Counselor Privilege	none	1035–1036.2
Domestic Violence Counselor Privilege	none	1037–1037.7
Human Trafficking Caseworker Privilege	none	1038–1038.2
9. Preliminary Fact Determinations		
Preliminary fact—defined	none	400 (also see 401)
Procedure for determining	104(c)	402
Preliminary facts involving relevancy, personal knowledge or authenticity	104(b)	403
Other types of preliminary facts	104(b)	405
Applicability of rules of evidence to preliminary fact determinations	104(a)	none (but compare 454(2) and see 915)
Testimony by accused	104(d)	none
Evidence affecting weight and credibility	104(e)	406
10. Judicial Notice		
No judicial notice unless authorized by law	none	450
Judicial notice of adjudicative facts	201	451, 452
Judicial notice of law	none	451, 452
List of specific items which must be judicially noticed	none	451
List of specific items which may be judicially noticed	none	452
General type of facts subject to be judicially noticed	201(b)	451(e), (f), 452(g), (h)
Sources of information	none	454, 460
Compulsory judicial notice on request	201(d)	453

COMPARATIVE TABLE

Topics	Federal Rules	California Evidence Code
10. Judicial Notice—Continued		
Procedures	201(e), (f), (g)	455, 456, 457
Judicial notice by trial court in subsequent proceedings in same action	none	458
Judicial notice by reviewing court	none	459

11. Presumptions, Burden of Proof and Burden of Production

[Note: The California Evidence Code contains some 40 provisions dealing with different kinds of presumptions and affecting a variety of evidentiary subjects (600–669). Similarly, it contains a number of provisions dealing with burdens of proof (500–502, 520–522) and burden of producing evidence (550). As enacted, the Federal Rules contain only two provisions on presumptions, Rule 301 which describes the effect of a presumption in a civil action where otherwise not provided for and Rule 302 which defines when the effect of a presumption is to be determined in accordance with state law. Additionally, Rule 303* which was not enacted treats the subject of presumptions in criminal cases. Given the diversity in approaches to these topics in the two Codes, it was not practicable to treat them in the Table.]

12. Applicability of Code	101, 1101	300

EVIDENCE
Rules, Statute and Case Supplement

FEDERAL RULES OF EVIDENCE FOR UNITED STATES COURTS AND MAGISTRATES

TABLE OF RULES

Article I. General Provisions

Rule			Page
101.	Scope		7
102.	Purpose and construction		7
103.	Rulings on evidence		7
	(a)	Effect of erroneous ruling	7
		(1) Objection	7
		(2) Offer of proof	8
	(b)	Record of offer and ruling	8
	(c)	Hearing of jury	8
	(d)	Plain error	8
104.	Preliminary questions		12
	(a)	Questions of admissibility generally	12
	(b)	Relevancy conditioned on fact	12
	(c)	Hearing of jury	12
	(d)	Testimony by accused	12
	(e)	Weight and credibility	12
105.	Limited admissibility		16
106.	Remainder of or related writings or recorded statements		17

Article II. Judicial Notice

201.	Judicial notice of adjudicative facts		17
	(a)	Scope of rule	17
	(b)	Kinds of facts	17
	(c)	When discretionary	17
	(d)	When mandatory	17
	(e)	Opportunity to be heard	17
	(f)	Time of taking notice	18
	(g)	Instructing jury	18

Article III. Presumptions in Civil Actions and Proceedings

301.	Presumptions in general in civil actions and proceedings	24
302.	Applicability of State law in civil actions and proceedings	24

Article IV. Relevancy and Its Limits

401.	Definition of "relevant evidence"		25
402.	Relevant evidence generally admissible; irrelevant evidence inadmissible		27
403.	Exclusion of relevant evidence on grounds of prejudice, confusion, or waste of time		29
404.	Character evidence not admissible to prove conduct; exceptions; other crimes		30
	(a)	Character evidence generally	30
		(1) Character of accused	30
		(2) Character of alleged victim	30

FEDERAL RULES OF EVIDENCE

Rule		Page
	(3) Character of witness	30
	(b) Other crimes, wrongs, or acts	30
405.	Methods of proving character	36
	(a) Reputation or opinion	36
	(b) Specific instances of conduct	36
406.	Habit; routine practice	37
407.	Subsequent remedial measures	39
408.	Compromise and offers to compromise	41
	(a) Prohibited uses	41
	(b) Permitted uses	41
409.	Payment of medical and similar expenses	45
410.	Inadmissibility of pleas, offers of pleas, plea discussions, and related statements	45
411.	Liability insurance	49
412.	Sex offense cases; relevance of alleged victim's past sexual behavior or alleged sexual predisposition	50
	(a) Evidence generally inadmissible	50
	(b) Exceptions	50
	(c) Procedure to determine admissibility	50
413.	Evidence of similar crimes in sexual assault cases	60
414.	Evidence of similar crimes in child molestation cases	61
415.	Evidence of similar acts in civil cases concerning sexual assault or child molestation	61

Article V. Privileges

501.	General rule	62
502.	Attorney-client privilege and work product; limitations on waiver	64

Article VI. Witnesses

601.	General rule of competency	71
602.	Lack of personal knowledge	72
603.	Oath or affirmation	73
604.	Interpreters	74
605.	Competency of judge as witness	74
606.	Competency of juror as witness	75
	(a) At the trial	75
	(b) Inquiry into validity of verdict or indictment	75
607.	Who may impeach	78
608.	Evidence of character and conduct of witness	79
	(a) Opinion and reputation evidence of character	79
	(b) Specific instances of conduct	79
609.	Impeachment by evidence of conviction of crime	83
	(a) General rule	83
	(b) Time limit	83
	(c) Effect of pardon, annulment, or certificate of rehabilitation	83
	(d) Juvenile adjudications	84
	(e) Pendency of appeal	84
610.	Religious beliefs or opinions	92
611.	Mode and order of interrogation and presentation	92
	(a) Control by court	92
	(b) Scope of cross-examination	92
	(c) Leading questions	93
612.	Writing used to refresh memory	96
613.	Prior statements of witnesses	99

FEDERAL RULES OF EVIDENCE

Rule			Page
	(a)	Examining witness concerning prior statement	99
	(b)	Extrinsic evidence of prior inconsistent statement of witness	99
614.		Calling and interrogation of witnesses by court	100
	(a)	Calling by court	100
	(b)	Interrogation by court	100
	(c)	Objections	100
615.		Exclusion of witnesses	101

Article VII. Opinions and Expert Testimony

701.		Opinion testimony by lay witnesses	103
702.		Testimony by experts	105
703.		Bases of opinion testimony by experts	112
704.		Opinion on ultimate issue	114
705.		Disclosure of facts or data underlying expert opinion	117
706.		Court appointed experts	118
	(a)	Appointment	118
	(b)	Compensation	118
	(c)	Disclosure of appointment	118
	(d)	Parties' experts of own selection	118

Article VIII. Hearsay

801.		Definitions	124
	(a)	Statement	124
	(b)	Declarant	124
	(c)	Hearsay	124
	(d)	Statements which are not hearsay	124
		(1) Prior statement by witness	124
		(2) Admission by party-opponent	125
802.		Hearsay rule	133
803.		Hearsay exceptions; availability of declarant immaterial	134
	(1)	Present sense impression	134
	(2)	Excited utterance	134
	(3)	Then existing mental, emotional, or physical condition	135
	(4)	Statements for purposes of medical diagnosis or treatment	135
	(5)	Recorded recollection	135
	(6)	Records of regularly conducted activity	135
	(7)	Absence of entry in records kept in accordance with the provisions of paragraph (6)	135
	(8)	Public records and reports	135
	(9)	Records of vital statistics	136
	(10)	Absence of public record or entry	136
	(11)	Records of religious organizations	136
	(12)	Marriage, baptismal, and similar certificates	136
	(13)	Family records	136
	(14)	Records of documents affecting an interest in property	136
	(15)	Statements in documents affecting an interest in property	136
	(16)	Statements in ancient documents	137
	(17)	Market reports, commercial publications	137
	(18)	Learned treatises	137
	(19)	Reputation concerning personal or family history	137
	(20)	Reputation concerning boundaries or general history	137
	(21)	Reputation as to character	137
	(22)	Judgment of previous conviction	137

FEDERAL RULES OF EVIDENCE

Rule		Page
803.	Hearsay exceptions; availability of declarant immaterial	134
	(23) Judgment as to personal, family, or general history, or boundaries	137
804.	Hearsay exceptions; declarant unavailable	158
	(a) Definition of unavailability	158
	(b) Hearsay exceptions	159
	(1) Former testimony	159
	(2) Statement under belief of impending death	159
	(3) Statement against interest	159
	(4) Statement of personal or family history	159
	(6) Forfeiture by wrongdoing	160
805.	Hearsay within hearsay	168
806.	Attacking and supporting credibility of declarant	169
807.	Residual exception	171

Article IX. Authentication and Identification

Rule		Page
901.	Requirement of authentication or identification	172
	(a) General provision	172
	(b) Illustrations	172
	(1) Testimony of witness with knowledge	172
	(2) Nonexpert opinion on handwriting	172
	(3) Comparison by trier or expert witness	172
	(4) Distinctive characteristics and the like	172
	(5) Voice identification	172
	(6) Telephone conversations	172
	(7) Public records or reports	172
	(8) Ancient documents or data compilation	172
	(9) Process or system	173
	(10) Methods provided by statute or rule	173
902.	Self-authentication	176
	(1) Domestic public documents under seal	176
	(2) Domestic public documents not under seal	176
	(3) Foreign public documents	176
	(4) Certified copies of public records	177
	(5) Official publications	177
	(6) Newspapers and periodicals	177
	(7) Trade inscriptions and the like	177
	(8) Acknowledged documents	177
	(9) Commercial paper and related documents	177
	(10) Presumptions under Acts of Congress	177
	(11) Certified domestic records of regularly conducted activity	177
	(12) Certified foreign records of regularly conducted activity	178
903.	Subscribing witness' testimony unnecessary	181

Article X. Contents of Writings, Recordings, and Photographs

Rule		Page
1001.	Definitions	182
	(1) Writings and recordings	182
	(2) Photographs	182
	(3) Original	182
	(4) Duplicate	182
1002.	Requirement of original	183
1003.	Admissibility of duplicates	184
1004.	Admissibility of other evidence of contents	185
	(1) Originals lost or destroyed	185

FEDERAL RULES OF EVIDENCE

Rule		Page
1004.	Admissibility of other evidence of contents	185
	(2) Original not obtainable	185
	(3) Original in possession of opponent	185
	(4) Collateral matters	186
1005.	Public records	187
1006.	Summaries	187
1007.	Testimony or written admission of party	188
1008.	Functions of court and jury	188

Article XI. Miscellaneous Rules

1101.	Applicability of rules	189
	(a) Courts and judges	189
	(b) Proceedings generally	189
	(c) Rule of privilege	189
	(d) Rules inapplicable	189
	(1) Preliminary questions of fact	190
	(2) Grand jury	190
	(3) Miscellaneous proceedings	190
	(e) Rules applicable in part	190
1102.	Amendments	194
1103.	Title	194

APPENDIX OF DELETED MATERIALS

105.	Summing up and comment by judge	196
303.	Presumptions in criminal cases	196
	(a) Scope	196
	(b) Submission to jury	196
	(c) Instructing the jury	196
406.	Habit; routine practice	199
	(b) Method of proof	199
501.	Privileges recognized only as provided	200
502.	Required reports privileged by statute	204
503.	Lawyer-client privilege	205
	(a) Definitions	205
	(b) General rule of privilege	205
	(c) Who may claim the privilege	205
	(d) Exceptions	206
	(1) Furtherance of crime or fraud	206
	(2) Claimants through same deceased client	206
	(3) Breach of duty by lawyer or client	206
	(4) Document attested by lawyer	206
	(5) Joint clients	206
504.	Psychotherapist-patient privilege	210
	(a) Definitions	210
	(b) General rule of privilege	210
	(c) Who may claim the privilege	210
	(d) Exceptions	210
	(1) Proceedings for hospitalization	210
	(2) Examination by order of judge	210
	(3) Condition an element of claim or defense	211
505.	Husband-wife privilege	213
	(a) General rule of privilege	213
	(b) Who may claim the privilege	213
	(c) Exceptions	213
506.	Communications to clergymen	216
	(a) Definitions	216
	(b) General rule of privilege	216

FEDERAL RULES OF EVIDENCE

Rule			Page
506.	Communications to clergymen		216
	(c)	Who may claim the privilege	217
507.	Political vote		218
508.	Trade secrets		219
509.	Secrets of state and other official information		220
	(a)	Definitions	220
		(1) Secret of state	220
		(2) Official information	220
	(b)	General rule of privilege	221
	(c)	Procedures	221
	(d)	Notice to government	221
	(e)	Effect of sustaining claim	221
510.	Identity of informer		224
	(a)	Rule of privilege	224
	(b)	Who may claim	224
	(c)	Exceptions	224
		(1) Voluntary disclosure; informer a witness	224
		(2) Testimony on merits	224
		(3) Legality of obtaining evidence	225
511.	Waiver of privilege by voluntary disclosure		227
512.	Privileged matter disclosed under compulsion or without opportunity to claim privilege		228
513.	Comment upon or inference from claim of privilege; instruction		229
	(a)	Comment or inference not permitted	229
	(b)	Claiming privilege without knowledge of jury	229
	(c)	Jury instruction	229
804(b)(2).	Statement of recent perception		230

Editorial Note

Changes have been incorporated which make the Rules gender neutral. These changes took effect on October 1, 1987. The following rules have been affected: Rules 104(c) and (d); 106; 404(a), (a)(1) and (b); 405(b); 411; 602; 603; 604; 606(a) and (b); 607; 608(b); 609(a); 610; 611(c); 612; 613(a) and (b); 615; 701; 703; 705; 706(a); 801(a), (d)(1) and (d)(2); 803(5), (18), (19), (21), (24); 804(a)(1), (a)(2), (a)(3), (a)(4), (a)(5) and (b)(2), (3), (5); 806; 902(2), (3); 1004(3); 1007.

As to all of these changes, the Advisory Committee stated that: "The amendments are technical. No substantive change is intended."

Changes have also been incorporated that correct a number of technical errors in the 1987 amendments. These changes took effect on November 1, 1988.

The Supreme Court of The United States has already approved a stylistic revision of the Federal Rules of Evidence, and if Congress does not act by December 1, 2011, it will become law.

ARTICLE I. GENERAL PROVISIONS

Rule 101.

SCOPE

These rules govern proceedings in the courts of the United States and before the United States bankruptcy judges and United States magistrate judges, to the extent and with the exceptions stated in rule 1101.

Advisory Committee Note to 1993 Amendment

This revision is made to conform the rule to changes made by the Judicial Improvements Act of 1990.

Note by Federal Judicial Center

The rule enacted by the Congress is the rule prescribed by the Supreme Court without change.

Advisory Committee's Note

Rule 1101 specifies in detail the courts, proceedings, questions, and stages of proceedings to which the rules apply in whole or in part.

Rule 102.

PURPOSE AND CONSTRUCTION

These rules shall be construed to secure fairness in administration, elimination of unjustifiable expense and delay, and promotion of growth and development of the law of evidence to the end that the truth may be ascertained and proceedings justly determined.

Note by Federal Judicial Center

The rule enacted by the Congress is the rule prescribed by the Supreme Court without change.

Advisory Committee's Note

For similar provisions see Rule 2 of the Federal Rules of Criminal Procedure, Rule 1 of the Federal Rules of Civil Procedure, California Evidence Code § 2, and New Jersey Evidence Rule 5.

Rule 103.

RULINGS ON EVIDENCE

(a) Effect of erroneous ruling. Error may not be predicated upon a ruling which admits or excludes evidence unless a substantial right of the party is affected, and

(1) Objection. In case the ruling is one admitting evidence, a timely objection or motion to strike appears of record, stating the specific ground of objection, if the specific ground was not apparent from the context; or

(2) Offer of proof. In case the ruling is one excluding evidence, the substance of the evidence was made known to the court by offer or was apparent from the context within which questions were asked. Once the court makes a definitive ruling on the record admitting or excluding evidence, either at or before trial, a party need not renew an objection or offer of proof to preserve a claim of error for appeal.

(b) Record of offer and ruling. The court may add any other or further statement which shows the character of the evidence, the form in which it was offered, the objection made, and the ruling thereon. It may direct the making of an offer in question and answer form.

(c) Hearing of jury. In jury cases, proceedings shall be conducted, to the extent practicable, so as to prevent inadmissible evidence from being suggested to the jury by any means, such as making statements or offers of proof or asking questions in the hearing of the jury.

(d) Plain error. Nothing in this rule precludes taking notice of plain errors affecting substantial rights although they were not brought to the attention of the court.

Advisory Committee's Note to 2000 Amendment to Rule 103

The amendment applies to all rulings on evidence whether they occur at or before trial, including so-called "*in limine*" rulings. One of the most difficult questions arising from *in limine* and other evidentiary rulings is whether a losing party must renew an objection or offer of proof when the evidence is or would be offered at trial, in order to preserve a claim of error on appeal. Courts have taken differing approaches to this question. Some courts have held that a renewal at the time the evidence is to be offered at trial is always required. *See, e.g., Collins v. Wayne Corp.*, 621 F.2d 777 (5th Cir.1980). Some courts have taken a more flexible approach, holding that renewal is not required if the issue decided is one that (1) was fairly presented to the trial court for an initial ruling, (2) may be decided as a final matter before the evidence is actually offered, and (3) was ruled on definitively by the trial judge. *See, e.g., Rosenfeld v. Basquiat*, 78 F.3d 84 (2d Cir.1996) (admissibility of former testimony under the Dead Man's Statute; renewal not required). Other courts have distinguished between objections to evidence, which must be renewed when evidence is offered, and offers of proof, which need not be renewed after a definitive determination is made that the evidence is inadmissible. *See, e.g., Fusco v. General Motors Corp.*, 11 F.3d 259 (1st Cir.1993). Another court, aware of this Committee's proposed amendment, has adopted its approach. *Wilson v. Williams*, 182 F.3d 562 (7th Cir.1999) (en banc). Differing views on this question create uncertainty for litigants and unnecessary work for the appellate courts.

The amendment provides that a claim of error with respect to a definitive ruling is preserved for review when the party has otherwise satisfied the objection or offer of proof requirements of Rule 103(a).When the ruling is definitive, a renewed objection or offer of proof at the time the evidence is to be offered is more a formalism than a necessity. See Fed.R.Civ.P. 46 (formal exceptions unnecessary); Fed.R.Cr.P. 51 (same); *United States v. Mejia–Alarcon,* 995 F.2d 982, 986 (10 Cir.1993) ("Requiring a party to renew an objection when the district court has issued a definitive ruling on a matter that can be fairly decided before trial would be in the nature of a formal exception and therefore unnecessary."). On the other hand, when the trial court appears to have reserved its ruling or to have indicated that the ruling is provisional, it makes sense to require the party to bring the issue to the court's attention subsequently. *See, e.g., United States v. Vest,* 116 F.3d 1179, 1188 (7th Cir.1997) (where the trial court ruled *in limine* that testimony from defense witnesses could not be admitted, but allowed the defendant to seek leave at trial to call the witnesses should their testimony turn out to be relevant, the defendant's failure to seek such leave at trial meant that it was "too late to reopen the issue now on appeal"); *United States v. Valenti,* 60 F.3d 941 (2d Cir.1995) (failure to proffer evidence at trial waives any claim of error where the trial judge had stated that he would reserve judgment on the *in limine* motion until he had heard the trial evidence).

The amendment imposes the obligation on counsel to clarify whether an *in limine* or other evidentiary ruling is definitive when there is doubt on that point. *See, e.g., Walden v. Georgia–Pacific Corp.,* 126 F.3d 506, 520 (3d Cir.1997) (although "the district court told plaintiffs' counsel not to reargue every ruling, it did not countermand its clear opening statement that all of its rulings were tentative, and counsel never requested clarification, as he might have done.").

Even where the court's ruling is definitive, nothing in the amendment prohibits the court from revisiting its decision when the evidence is to be offered. If the court changes its initial ruling, or if the opposing party violates the terms of the initial ruling, objection must be made when the evidence is offered to preserve the claim of error for appeal. The error, if any, in such a situation occurs only when the evidence is offered and admitted. *United States Aviation Underwriters, Inc. v. Olympia Wings, Inc.,* 896 F.2d 949, 956 (5th Cir.1990) ("objection is required to preserve error when an opponent, or the court itself, violates a motion *in limine* that was granted"); *United States v. Roenigk,* 810 F.2d 809 (8th Cir.1987) (claim of error was not preserved where the defendant failed to object at trial to secure the benefit of a favorable advance ruling).

A definitive advance ruling is reviewed in light of the facts and circumstances before the trial court at the time of the ruling. If the relevant facts and circumstances change materially after the advance ruling has been made, those facts and circumstances cannot be relied upon on appeal unless they have been brought to the attention of the trial court by way of a renewed, and timely, objection, offer of proof, or motion to strike. *See Old Chief v. United States,* 519 U.S. 172, 182, n. 6 (1997) ("It is important that a reviewing court evaluate the trial court's decision from its perspective when it had to rule and not indulge in review by hindsight."). Similarly, if the court decides in an advance ruling that proffered evidence is admissible subject to the eventual introduction by the proponent of a foundation for the evidence, and that foundation is never provided, the opponent cannot claim error based on the failure to establish the foundation unless the opponent calls that failure to the court's attention by a timely motion to strike or other suitable motion. *See Huddleston v. United States,* 485 U.S. 681, 690, n. 7 (1988) ("It is, of course, not the responsibility of the judge *sua sponte* to ensure that the foundation evidence is offered; the objector must move to strike the evidence if at the close of the trial the offeror has failed to satisfy the condition.").

Nothing in the amendment is intended to affect the provisions of Fed. R.Civ.P. 72(a) or 28 U.S.C. §§ 636(b)(1) pertaining to nondispositive pretrial rulings by magistrate judges in proceedings that are not before a magistrate judge by consent of the parties. Fed.R.Civ.P. 72(a) provides that a party who fails to file a written objection to a magistrate judge's nondispositive order within ten days of receiving a copy "may not thereafter assign as error a defect" in the order. 28 U.S.C. §§ 636(b)(1) provides that any party "may serve and file written objections to such proposed findings and recommendations as provided by rules of court" within ten days of receiving a copy of the order. Several courts have held that a party must comply with this statutory provision in order to preserve a claim of error. See, e.g., Wells v. Shriners Hospital, 109 F.3d 198, 200 (4th Cir.1997) ("[i]n this circuit, as in others, a party 'may' file objections within ten days or he may not, as he chooses, but he 'shall' do so if he wishes further consideration."). When Fed.R.Civ.P. 72(a) or 28 U.S.C. §§ 636(b)(1) is operative, its requirement must be satisfied in order for a party to preserve a claim of error on appeal, even where Evidence Rule 103(a) would not require a subsequent objection or offer of proof.

Nothing in the amendment is intended to affect the rule set forth in *Luce v. United States*, 469 U.S. 38 (1984), and its progeny. The amendment provides that an objection or offer of proof need not be renewed to preserve a claim of error with respect to a definitive pretrial ruling. *Luce* answers affirmatively a separate question: whether a criminal defendant must testify at trial in order to preserve a claim of error predicated upon a trial court's decision to admit the defendant's prior convictions for impeachment. The *Luce* principle has been extended by many lower courts to other situations. See *United States v. Dimatteo*, 759 F.2d 831 (11th Cir.1985) (applying *Luce* where the defendant's witness would be impeached with evidence offered under Rule 608). See also *United States v. Goldman*, 41 F.3d 785, 788 (1st Cir.1994) ("Although *Luce* involved impeachment by conviction under Rule 609, the reasons given by the Supreme Court for requiring the defendant to testify apply with full force to the kind of Rule 403 and 404 objections that are advanced by Goldman in this case."); *Palmieri v. Defaria*, 88 F.3d 136 (2d Cir.1996) (where the plaintiff decided to take an adverse judgment rather than challenge an advance ruling by putting on evidence at trial, the *in limine* ruling would not be reviewed on appeal); *United States v. Ortiz*, 857 F.2d 900 (2d Cir.1988) (where uncharged misconduct is ruled admissible if the defendant pursues a certain defense, the defendant must actually pursue that defense at trial in order to preserve a claim of error on appeal); *United States v. Bond*, 87 F.3d 695 (5th Cir.1996) (where the trial court rules *in limine* that the defendant would waive his fifth amendment privilege were he to testify, the defendant must take the stand and testify in order to challenge that ruling on appeal).

The amendment does not purport to answer whether a party who objects to evidence that the court finds admissible in a definitive ruling, and who then offers the evidence to "remove the sting" of its anticipated prejudicial effect, thereby waives the right to appeal the trial court's ruling. See, e.g., *United States v. Fisher*, 106 F.3d 622 (5th Cir.1997) (where the trial judge ruled *in limine* that the government could use a prior conviction to impeach the defendant if he testified, the defendant did not waive his right to appeal by introducing the

GENERAL PROVISIONS Rule 103

conviction on direct examination); *Judd v. Rodman,* 105 F.3d 1339 (11th Cir.1997) (an objection made *in limine* is sufficient to preserve a claim of error when the movant, as a matter of trial strategy, presents the objectionable evidence herself on direct examination to minimize its prejudicial effect); *Gill v. Thomas,* 83 F.3d 537, 540 (1st Cir.1996) ("by offering the misdemeanor evidence himself, Gill waived his opportunity to object and thus did not preserve the issue for appeal"); *United States v. Williams,* 939 F.2d 721 (9th Cir.1991) (objection to impeachment evidence was waived where the defendant was impeached on direct examination).

Note by Federal Judicial Center

The rule enacted by the Congress is the rule prescribed by the Supreme Court, amended by substituting "court" in place of "judge," with appropriate pronominal change.

Advisory Committee's Note

Subdivision (a) states the law as generally accepted today. Rulings on evidence cannot be assigned as error unless (1) a substantial right is affected, and (2) the nature of the error was called to the attention of the judge, so as to alert him to the proper course of action and enable opposing counsel to take proper corrective measures. The objection and the offer of proof are the techniques for accomplishing these objectives. For similar provisions see Uniform Rules 4 and 5; California Evidence Code §§ 353 and 354; Kansas Code of Civil Procedure §§ 60–404 and 60–405. The rule does not purport to change the law with respect to harmless error. See 28 U.S.C. § 2111, F.R.Civ.P. 61, F.R.Crim.P. 52, and decisions construing them. The status of constitutional error as harmless or not is treated in Chapman v. California, 386 U.S. 18, 87 S.Ct. 824, 17 L.Ed.2d 705 (1967), reh. denied, 386 U.S. 987, 87 S.Ct. 1283, 18 L.Ed.2d 241.

Subdivision (b). The first sentence is the third sentence of Rule 43(c) of the Federal Rules of Civil Procedure [1] virtually verbatim. Its purpose is to reproduce for an appellate court, insofar as possible, a true reflection of what occurred in the trial court. The second sentence is in part derived from the final sentence of Rule 43(c).[1] It is designed to resolve doubts as to what testimony the witness would have in fact given, and, in nonjury cases, to provide the appellate court with material for a possible final disposition of the case in the event of reversal of a ruling which excluded evidence. See 5 Moore's Federal Practice § 43.11 (2d ed. 1968). Application is made discretionary in view of the practical impossibility of formulating a satisfactory rule in mandatory terms.

Subdivision (c). This subdivision proceeds on the supposition that a ruling which excludes evidence in a jury case is likely to be a pointless procedure if the excluded evidence nevertheless comes to the attention of the jury. Bruton v. United States, 389 U.S. 818, 88 S.Ct. 126, 19 L.Ed.2d 70 (1967). Rule 43(c) of the Federal Rules of Civil Procedure [1] provides: "The court may require the offer to be made out of the hearing of the jury." In re McConnell, 370 U.S. 230, 82 S.Ct. 1288, 8 L.Ed.2d 434 (1962), left some doubt whether questions on which an

---

1. Rule 43(c) of the Federal Rules of Civil Procedure was deleted by order of the Supreme Court entered on November 20, 1972, 93 S.Ct. 3073, 3075, 3076, 3077, 34 L.Ed.2d lxv, ccv, ccviii, which action was affirmed by the Congress in P.L. 93–595 § 3 (January 2, 1975).

offer is based must first be asked in the presence of the jury. The subdivision answers in the negative. The judge can foreclose a particular line of testimony and counsel can protect his record without a series of questions before the jury, designed at best to waste time and at worst "to waft into the jury box" the very matter sought to be excluded.

Subdivision (d). This wording of the plain error principle is from Rule 52(b) of the Federal Rules of Criminal Procedure. While judicial unwillingness to be constricted by mechanical breakdowns of the adversary system has been more pronounced in criminal cases, there is no scarcity of decisions to the same effect in civil cases. In general, see Campbell, Extent to Which Courts of Review Will Consider Questions Not Properly Raised and Preserved, 7 Wis.L.Rev. 91, 160 (1932); Vestal, Sua Sponte Consideration in Appellate Review, 27 Fordham L.Rev. 477 (1958–59); 64 Harv.L.Rev. 652 (1951). In the nature of things the application of the plain error rule will be more likely with respect to the admission of evidence than to exclusion, since failure to comply with normal requirements of offers of proof is likely to produce a record which simply does not disclose the error.

Rule 104.

PRELIMINARY QUESTIONS

(a) Questions of admissibility generally. Preliminary questions concerning the qualification of a person to be a witness, the existence of a privilege, or the admissibility of evidence shall be determined by the court, subject to the provisions of subdivision (b). In making its determination it is not bound by the rules of evidence except those with respect to privileges.

(b) Relevancy conditioned on fact. When the relevancy of evidence depends upon the fulfillment of a condition of fact, the court shall admit it upon, or subject to, the introduction of evidence sufficient to support a finding of the fulfillment of the condition.

(c) Hearing of jury. Hearings on the admissibility of confessions shall in all cases be conducted out of the hearing of the jury. Hearings on other preliminary matters shall be so conducted when the interests of justice require, or when an accused is a witness and so requests.

(d) Testimony by accused. The accused does not, by testifying upon a preliminary matter, become subject to cross-examination as to other issues in the case.

(e) Weight and credibility. This rule does not limit the right of a party to introduce before the jury evidence relevant to weight or credibility.

Note by Federal Judicial Center

The rule enacted by the Congress is the rule prescribed by the Supreme Court, amended by substituting "court" in place of "judge," with appropriate pronominal change, and by adding to subdivision (c) the concluding phrase, "or when an accused is a witness, if he so requests." [2]

Advisory Committee's Note

Subdivision (a). The applicability of a particular rule of evidence often depends upon the existence of a condition. Is the alleged expert a qualified physician? Is a witness whose former testimony is offered unavailable? Was a stranger present during a conversation between attorney and client? In each instance the admissibility of evidence will turn upon the answer to the question of the existence of the condition. Accepted practice, incorporated in the rule, places on the judge the responsibility for these determinations. McCormick § 53; Morgan, Basic Problems of Evidence 45–50 (1962).

To the extent that these inquiries are factual, the judge acts as a trier of fact. Often, however, rulings on evidence call for an evaluation in terms of a legally set standard. Thus when a hearsay statement is offered as a declaration against interest, a decision must be made whether it possesses the required against-interest characteristics. These decisions, too, are made by the judge.

In view of these considerations, this subdivision refers to preliminary requirements generally by the broad term "questions," without attempt at specification.

This subdivision is of general application. It must, however, be read as subject to the special provisions for "conditional relevancy" in subdivision (b) and those for confessions in subdivision (c).

If the question is factual in nature, the judge will of necessity receive evidence pro and con on the issue. The rule provides that the rules of evidence in general do not apply to this process. McCormick § 53, p. 123, n. 8, points out that the authorities are "scattered and inconclusive," and observes:

> "Should the exclusionary law of evidence, 'the child of the jury system' in Thayer's phrase, be applied to this hearing before the judge? Sound sense backs the view that it should not, and that the judge should be empowered to hear any relevant evidence, such as affidavits or other reliable hearsay."

This view is reinforced by practical necessity in certain situations. An item, offered and objected to, may itself be considered in ruling on admissibility, though not yet admitted in evidence. Thus the content of an asserted declaration against interest must be considered in ruling whether it is against interest. Again, common practice calls for considering the testimony of a witness, particularly a child, in determining competency. Another example is the requirement of Rule 602 dealing with personal knowledge. In the case of hearsay, it is enough, if the declarant "so far as appears [has] had an opportunity to observe the fact declared." McCormick, § 10, p. 19.

If concern is felt over the use of affidavits by the judge in preliminary hearings on admissibility, attention is directed to the many important judicial determinations made on the basis of affidavits. Rule 47 of the Federal Rules of Criminal Procedure provides:

---

2. The effect of the amendment was to restore language included in the 1971 Revised Draft of the Proposed Rules but deleted before the rules were presented to and prescribed by the Supreme Court.

> "An application to the court for an order shall be by motion.... It may be supported by affidavit."

The Rules of Civil Procedure are more detailed. Rule 43(e), dealing with motions generally, provides:

> "When a motion is based on facts not appearing of record the court may hear the matter on affidavits presented by the respective parties, but the court may direct that the matter be heard wholly or partly on oral testimony or depositions."

Rule 4(g) provides for proof of service by affidavit. Rule 56 provides in detail for the entry of summary judgment based on affidavits. Affidavits may supply the foundation for temporary restraining orders under Rule 65(b).

The study made for the California Law Revision Commission recommended an amendment to Uniform Rule 2 as follows:

> "In the determination of the issue aforesaid [preliminary determination], exclusionary rules shall not apply, subject, however, to Rule 45 and any valid claim of privilege." Tentative Recommendation and a Study Relating to the Uniform Rules of Evidence (Article VIII, Hearsay), Cal.Law Revision Comm'n, Rep., Rec. & Studies, 470 (1962).

The proposal was not adopted in the California Evidence Code. The Uniform Rules are likewise silent on the subject. However, New Jersey Evidence Rule 8(1), dealing with preliminary inquiry by the judge, provides:

> "In his determination the rules of evidence shall not apply except for Rule 4 [exclusion on grounds of confusion, etc.] or a valid claim of privilege."

Subdivision (b). In some situations, the relevancy of an item of evidence, in the large sense, depends upon the existence of a particular preliminary fact. Thus when a spoken statement is relied upon to prove notice to X, it is without probative value unless X heard it. Or if a letter purporting to be from Y is relied upon to establish an admission by him, it has no probative value unless Y wrote or authorized it. Relevance in this sense has been labelled "conditional relevancy." Morgan, Basic Problems of Evidence 45–46 (1962). Problems arising in connection with it are to be distinguished from problems of logical relevancy, e.g. evidence in a murder case that accused on the day before purchased a weapon of the kind used in the killing, treated in Rule 401.

If preliminary questions of conditional relevancy were determined solely by the judge, as provided in subdivision (a), the functioning of the jury as a trier of fact would be greatly restricted and in some cases virtually destroyed. These are appropriate questions for juries. Accepted treatment, as provided in the rule, is consistent with that given fact questions generally. The judge makes a preliminary determination whether the foundation evidence is sufficient to support a finding of fulfillment of the condition. If so, the item is admitted. If after all the evidence on the issue is in, pro and con, the jury could reasonably conclude that fulfillment of the condition is not established, the issue is for them. If the evidence is not such as to allow a finding, the judge withdraws the matter from their consideration. Morgan, supra; California Evidence Code § 403; New Jersey Rule 8(2). See also Uniform Rules 19 and 67.

GENERAL PROVISIONS — Rule 104

The order of proof here, as generally, is subject to the control of the judge.

Subdivision (c). Preliminary hearings on the admissibility of confessions must be conducted outside the hearing of the jury. See Jackson v. Denno, 378 U.S. 368, 84 S.Ct. 1774, 12 L.Ed.2d 908 (1964).[3] Otherwise, detailed treatment of when preliminary matters should be heard outside the hearing of the jury is not feasible. The procedure is time consuming. Not infrequently the same evidence which is relevant to the issue of establishment of fulfillment of a condition precedent to admissibility is also relevant to weight or credibility, and time is saved by taking foundation proof in the presence of the jury. Much evidence on preliminary questions, though not relevant to jury issues, may be heard by the jury with no adverse effect. A great deal must be left to the discretion of the judge who will act as the interests of justice require.

Report of the House Committee on the Judiciary

... Although recognizing that in some cases duplication of evidence would occur and that the procedure could be subject to abuse, the Committee believed that a proper regard for the right of an accused not to testify generally in the case dictates that he be given an option to testify out of the presence of the jury on preliminary matters.

The Committee construes the second sentence of subdivision (c) as applying to civil actions and proceedings as well as to criminal cases, and on this assumption has left the sentence unamended.

Advisory Committee's Note

Subdivision (d). The limitation upon cross-examination is designed to encourage participation by the accused in the determination of preliminary matters. He may testify concerning them without exposing himself to cross-examination generally. The provision is necessary because of the breadth of cross-examination [possible] under Rule 611(b).

The rule does not address itself to questions of the subsequent use of testimony given by an accused at a hearing on a preliminary matter. See Walder v. United States, 347 U.S. 62, 74 S.Ct. 354, 98 L.Ed. 503 (1954); Simmons v. United States, 390 U.S. 377, 88 S.Ct. 967, 19 L.Ed.2d 1247 (1968); Harris v. New York, 401 U.S. 222, 91 S.Ct. 643, 28 L.Ed.2d 1 (1971).

Report of Senate Committee on the Judiciary

... This rule is not, however, intended to immunize the accused from cross-examination where, in testifying about a preliminary issue, he injects other issues into the hearing. If he could not be cross-examined about any issues gratuitously raised by him beyond the scope of the preliminary matters, injustice might result. Accordingly, in order to prevent any such unjust result, the committee intends the rule to be construed to provide that the accused may

---

3. At this point the Advisory Committee's Note to the 1971 Revised Draft contained the sentence, "Also, due regard for the right of an accused not to testify generally in the case requires that he be given an option to testify out of the presence of the jury upon preliminary matters." The statement was deleted in view of the deletion from the rule, mentioned in the preceding footnote.

subject himself to cross-examination as to issues raised by his own testimony upon a preliminary matter before a jury.

Advisory Committee's Note

Subdivision (e). For similar provisions see Uniform Rule 8; California Evidence Code § 406; Kansas Code of Civil Procedure § 60–408; New Jersey Evidence Rule 8(1).

Rule 105.

LIMITED ADMISSIBILITY

When evidence which is admissible as to one party or for one purpose but not admissible as to another party or for another purpose is admitted, the court, upon request, shall restrict the evidence to its proper scope and instruct the jury accordingly.

Note by Federal Judicial Center

The rule enacted by the Congress is the rule prescribed by the Supreme Court as Rule 106, amended by substituting "court" in place of "judge." Rule 105 as prescribed by the Court, which was deleted from the rules enacted by the Congress, is set forth in the Appendix hereto, together with a statement of the reasons for the deletion.

Advisory Committee's Note

A close relationship exists between this rule and Rule 403 which ... [provides for] exclusion when "probative value is substantially outweighed by the danger of unfair prejudice, confusion of the issues, or misleading the jury." The present rule recognizes the practice of admitting evidence for a limited purpose and instructing the jury accordingly. The availability and effectiveness of this practice must be taken into consideration in reaching a decision whether to exclude for unfair prejudice under Rule 403. In Bruton v. United States, 389 U.S. 818, 88 S.Ct. 126, 19 L.Ed.2d 70 (1967), the Court ruled that a limiting instruction did not effectively protect the accused against the prejudicial effect of admitting in evidence the confession of a codefendant which implicated him. The decision does not, however, bar the use of limited admissibility with an instruction where the risk of prejudice is less serious.

Similar provisions are found in Uniform Rule 6; California Evidence Code § 355; Kansas Code of Civil Procedure § 60–406; New Jersey Evidence Rule 6. The wording of the present rule differs, however, in repelling any implication that limiting or curative instructions are sufficient in all situations.

Report of House Committee on the Judiciary

... The Committee adopted this Rule without change on the understanding that it does not affect the authority of a court to order a severance in a multi-defendant case.

Rule 106.

REMAINDER OF OR RELATED WRITINGS OR RECORDED STATEMENTS

When a writing or recorded statement or part thereof is introduced by a party, an adverse party may require the introduction at that time of any other part or any other writing or recorded statement which ought in fairness to be considered contemporaneously with it.

Note by Federal Judicial Center

The rule enacted by the Congress is the rule prescribed by the Supreme Court as Rule 107 without change.

Advisory Committee's Note

The rule is an expression of the rule of completeness. McCormick § 56. It is manifested as to depositions in Rule 32(a)(4) of the Federal Rules of Civil Procedure, of which the proposed rule is substantially a restatement.

The rule is based on two considerations. The first is the misleading impression created by taking matters out of context. The second is the inadequacy of repair work when delayed to a point later in the trial. See McCormick § 56; California Evidence Code § 356. The rule does not in any way circumscribe the right of the adversary to develop the matter on cross-examination or as part of his own case.

For practical reasons, the rule is limited to writings and recorded statements and does not apply to conversations.

ARTICLE II. JUDICIAL NOTICE

Rule 201.

JUDICIAL NOTICE OF ADJUDICATIVE FACTS

(a) Scope of rule. This rule governs only judicial notice of adjudicative facts.

(b) Kinds of facts. A judicially noticed fact must be one not subject to reasonable dispute in that it is either (1) generally known within the territorial jurisdiction of the trial court or (2) capable of accurate and ready determination by resort to sources whose accuracy cannot reasonably be questioned.

(c) When discretionary. A court may take judicial notice, whether requested or not.

(d) When mandatory. A court shall take judicial notice if requested by a party and supplied with the necessary information.

(e) Opportunity to be heard. A party is entitled upon timely request to an opportunity to be heard as to the propriety of taking judicial notice and the tenor of the matter noticed. In the absence of prior notification, the request may be made after judicial notice has been taken.

(f) Time of taking notice. Judicial notice may be taken at any stage of the proceeding.

(g) Instructing jury. In a civil action or proceeding, the court shall instruct the jury to accept as conclusive any fact judicially noticed. In a criminal case, the court shall instruct the jury that it may, but is not required to, accept as conclusive any fact judicially noticed.

Note by Federal Judicial Center

The rule enacted by the Congress is the rule prescribed by the Supreme Court with the following changes:

In subdivisions (c) and (d) the words "judge or" before "court" were deleted.

Subdivision (g) as it is shown was substituted in place of, "The judge shall instruct the jury to accept as established any facts judicially noticed." The substituted language is from the 1969 Preliminary Draft. 46 F.R.D. 161, 195.

Advisory Committee's Note

Subdivision (a). This is the only evidence rule on the subject of judicial notice. It deals only with judicial notice of "adjudicative" facts. No rule deals with judicial notice of "legislative" facts. Judicial notice of matters of foreign law is treated in Rule 44.1 of the Federal Rules of Civil Procedure and Rule 26.1 of the Federal Rules of Criminal Procedure.

The omission of any treatment of legislative facts results from fundamental differences between adjudicative facts and legislative facts. Adjudicative facts are simply the facts of the particular case. Legislative facts, on the other hand, are those which have relevance to legal reasoning and the lawmaking process, whether in the formulation of a legal principle or ruling by a judge or court or in the enactment of a legislative body. The terminology was coined by Professor Kenneth Davis in his article An Approach to Problems of Evidence in the Administrative Process, 55 Harv.L.Rev. 364, 404–407 (1942). The following discussion draws extensively upon his writings. In addition, see the same author's Judicial Notice, 55 Colum.L.Rev. 945 (1955); Administrative Law Treatise, ch. 15 (1958); A System of Judicial Notice Based on Fairness and Convenience, in Perspectives of Law 69 (1964).

The usual method of establishing adjudicative facts is through the introduction of evidence, ordinarily consisting of the testimony of witnesses. If particular facts are outside the area of reasonable controversy, this process is dispensed with as unnecessary. A high degree of indisputability is the essential prerequisite.

Legislative facts are quite different. As Professor Davis says:

"My opinion is that judge-made law would stop growing if judges, in thinking about questions of law and policy, were forbidden to take into account the facts they believe, as distinguished from facts which are 'clearly ... within the domain of the indisputable.' Facts most needed in thinking about difficult problems of law and policy have a way of being outside the domain of the clearly indisputable." A System of Judicial Notice Based on Fairness and Convenience, supra, at 82.

An illustration is Hawkins v. United States, 358 U.S. 74, 79 S.Ct. 136, 3 L.Ed.2d 125 (1958), in which the Court refused to discard the common law rule that one spouse could not testify against the other, saying, "Adverse testimony given in criminal proceedings would, we think, be likely to destroy almost any marriage." This conclusion has a large intermixture of fact, but the factual aspect is scarcely "indisputable." See Hutchins and Slesinger, Some Observations on the Law of Evidence—Family Relations, 13 Minn.L.Rev. 675 (1929). If the destructive effect of the giving of adverse testimony by a spouse is not indisputable, should the Court have refrained from considering it in the absence of supporting evidence?

> "If the Model Code or the Uniform Rules had been applicable, the Court would have been barred from thinking about the essential factual ingredient of the problems before it, and such a result would be obviously intolerable. What the law needs at its growing points is more, not less, judicial thinking about the factual ingredients of problems of what the law ought to be, and the needed facts are seldom 'clearly' indisputable." Davis, supra, at 83.

Professor Morgan gave the following description of the methodology of determining domestic law:

> "In determining the content or applicability of a rule of domestic law, the judge is unrestricted in his investigation and conclusion. He may reject the propositions of either party or of both parties. He may consult the sources of pertinent data to which they refer, or he may refuse to do so. He may make an independent search for persuasive data or rest content with what he has or what the parties present.... [T]he parties do no more than to assist; they control no part of the process." Morgan, Judicial Notice, 57 Harv.L.Rev. 269, 270–271 (1944).

This is the view which should govern judicial access to legislative facts. It renders inappropriate any limitation in the form of indisputability, any formal requirements of notice other than those already inherent in affording opportunity to hear and be heard and exchanging briefs, and any requirement of formal findings at any level. It should, however, leave open the possibility of introducing evidence through regular channels in appropriate situations. See Borden's Farm Products Co. v. Baldwin, 293 U.S. 194, 55 S.Ct. 187, 79 L.Ed. 281 (1934), where the cause was remanded for the taking of evidence as to the economic conditions and trade practices underlying the New York Milk Control Law.

Similar considerations govern the judicial use of non-adjudicative facts in ways other than formulating laws and rules. Thayer described them as a part of the judicial reasoning process.

> "In conducting a process of judicial reasoning, as of other reasoning, not a step can be taken without assuming something which has not been proved; and the capacity to do this with competent judgment and efficiency, is imputed to judges and juries as part of their necessary mental outfit." Thayer, Preliminary Treatise on Evidence 279–280 (1898).

As Professor Davis points out, A System of Judicial Notice Based on Fairness and Convenience, in Perspectives of Law 69, 73 (1964), every case involves the use of hundreds or thousands of non-evidence facts. When a witness in an automobile accident case says "car," everyone, judge and jury included, furnishes, from non-evidence sources within himself, the supplementing information that the "car" is an automobile, not a railroad car, that it is self-propelled, probably by an internal combustion engine, that it may be assumed to have four wheels with pneumatic rubber tires, and so on. The judicial process cannot construct every case from scratch, like Descartes creating a world based on the postulate *Cogito, ergo sum*. These items could not possibly be introduced into evidence, and no one suggests that they be. Nor are they appropriate subjects for any formalized treatment of judicial notice of facts. See Levin and Levy, Persuading the Jury with Facts Not in Evidence: The Fiction–Science Spectrum, 105 U.Pa.L.Rev. 139 (1956).

Another aspect of what Thayer had in mind is the use of non-evidence facts to appraise or assess the adjudicative facts of the case. Pairs of cases from two jurisdictions illustrate this use and also the difference between non-evidence facts thus used and adjudicative facts. In People v. Strook, 347 Ill. 460, 179 N.E. 821 (1932), venue in Cook County had been held not established by testimony that the crime was committed at 7956 South Chicago Avenue, since judicial notice would not be taken that the address was in Chicago. However, the same court subsequently ruled that venue in Cook County was established by testimony that a crime occurred at 8900 South Anthony Avenue, since notice would be taken of the common practice of omitting the name of the city when speaking of local addresses, and the witness was testifying in Chicago. People v. Pride, 16 Ill.2d 82, 156 N.E.2d 551 (1959). And in Hughes v. Vestal, 264 N.C. 500, 142 S.E.2d 361 (1965), the Supreme Court of North Carolina disapproved the trial judge's admission in evidence of a state-published table of automobile stopping distances on the basis of judicial notice, though the court itself had referred to the same table in an earlier case in a "rhetorical and illustrative" way in determining that the defendant could not have stopped her car in time to avoid striking a child who suddenly appeared in the highway and that a nonsuit was properly granted. Ennis v. Dupree, 262 N.C. 224, 136 S.E.2d 702 (1964). See also Brown v. Hale, 263 N.C. 176, 139 S.E.2d 210 (1964); Clayton v. Rimmer, 262 N.C. 302, 136 S.E.2d 562 (1964). It is apparent that this use of non-evidence facts in evaluating the adjudicative facts of the case is not an appropriate subject for a formalized judicial notice treatment.

In view of these considerations, the regulation of judicial notice of facts by the present rule extends only to adjudicative facts.

What, then, are "adjudicative" facts? Davis refers to them as those "which relate to the parties," or more fully:

> "When a court or an agency finds facts concerning the immediate parties—who did what, where, when, how, and with what motive or intent—the court or agency is performing an adjudicative function, and the facts are conveniently called adjudicative facts...."
>
> "Stated in other terms, the adjudicative facts are those to which the law is applied in the process of adjudication. They are the facts that normally go to the jury in a jury case. They relate to the parties, their activities, their properties, their businesses." 2 Administrative Law Treatise 353.

Subdivision (b). With respect to judicial notice of adjudicative facts, the tradition has been one of caution in requiring that the matter be beyond reasonable controversy. This tradition of circumspection appears to be soundly based, and no reason to depart from it is apparent. As Professor Davis says:

> "The reason we use trial-type procedure, I think, is that we make the practical judgment, on the basis of experience, that taking evidence, subject to cross-examination and rebuttal, is the best way to resolve controversies involving disputes of adjudicative facts, that is, facts pertaining to the parties. The reason we require a determination on the record is that we think fair procedure in resolving disputes of adjudicative facts calls for giving each party a chance to meet in the appropriate fashion the facts that come to the tribunal's attention, and the appropriate fashion for meeting disputed adjudicative facts includes rebuttal evidence, cross-examination, usually confrontation, and argument (either written or oral or both). The key to a fair trial is opportunity to use the appropriate weapons (rebuttal evidence, cross-examination, and argument) to meet adverse materials that come to the tribunal's attention." A System of Judicial Notice Based on Fairness and Convenience, in Perspectives of Law 69, 93 (1964).

The rule proceeds upon the theory that these considerations call for dispensing with traditional methods of proof only in clear cases. Compare Professor Davis' conclusion that judicial notice should be a matter of convenience, subject to requirements of procedural fairness. Id., 94.

This rule is consistent with Uniform Rule 9(1) and (2) which limit judicial notice of facts to those "so universally known that they cannot reasonably be the subject of dispute," those "so generally known or of such common notoriety within the territorial jurisdiction of the court that they cannot reasonably be the subject of dispute," and those "capable of immediate and accurate determination by resort to easily accessible sources of indisputable accuracy." The traditional textbook treatment has included these general categories (matters of common knowledge, facts capable of verification), McCormick §§ 324, 325, and then has passed on into detailed treatment of such specific topics as facts relating to the personnel and records of the court, id. § 327, and other governmental facts, id. § 328. The California draftsmen, with a background of detailed statutory regulation of judicial notice, followed a somewhat similar pattern. California Evidence Code §§ 451, 452. The Uniform Rules, however, were drafted on the theory that these particular matters are included within the general categories and need no specific mention. This approach is followed in the present rule.

The phrase "propositions of generalized knowledge," found in Uniform Rule 9(1) and (2) is not included in the present rule. It was, it is believed, originally included in Model Code Rules 801 and 802 primarily in order to afford some minimum recognition to the right of the judge in his "legislative" capacity (not acting as the trier of fact) to take judicial notice of very limited categories of generalized knowledge. The limitations thus imposed have been discarded herein as undesirable, unworkable, and contrary to existing practice. What is left, then, to be considered, is the status of a "proposition of generalized knowledge" as an "adjudicative" fact to be noticed judicially and communicated by the judge to the jury. Thus viewed, it is considered to be lacking practical significance. While judges use judicial notice of "propositions of generalized knowledge" in a variety of situations: determining the validity and meaning of statutes, formulating common-law rules, deciding whether evidence should be admitted, assessing the sufficiency and effect of evidence, all are essentially nonadjudicative in nature. When judicial notice is seen as a significant vehicle for progress in the law, these are the areas involved, particularly in developing fields of scientific knowledge. See McCormick 712. It is not believed that judges now instruct juries as to "propositions of generalized knowledge" derived from encyclopedias or other sources, or that they are likely to do so, or, indeed, that it is desirable that they do so. There is a vast difference between ruling on the basis of judicial notice that radar evidence of speed is admissible and explaining to the jury its principles and degree of accuracy, or between using a table of stopping distances of automobiles at various speeds in a judicial evaluation of testimony and telling the jury its precise application in the case. For cases raising doubt as to the propriety of the use of medical texts by lay triers of fact in passing on disability claims in administrative proceedings, see Sayers v. Gardner, 380 F.2d 940 (6th Cir.1967); Ross v. Gardner, 365 F.2d 554 (6th Cir.1966); Sosna v. Celebrezze, 234 F.Supp. 289 (E.D.Pa.1964); Glendenning v. Ribicoff, 213 F.Supp. 301 (W.D.Mo.1962).

Subdivisions (c) and (d). Under subdivision (c) the judge has discretionary authority to take judicial notice, regardless of whether he is so requested by a party. The taking of judicial notice is mandatory, under subdivision (d), only when a party requests it and the necessary information is supplied. This scheme is believed to reflect existing practice. It is simple and workable. It avoids troublesome distinctions in the many situations in which the process of taking judicial notice is not recognized as such.

Compare Uniform Rule 9 making judicial notice of facts universally known mandatory without request, and making judicial notice of facts generally known in the jurisdiction or capable of determination by resort to accurate sources discretionary in the absence of request but mandatory if request is made and the information furnished. But see Uniform Rule 10(3), which directs the judge to decline to take judicial notice if available information fails to convince him that the matter falls clearly within Uniform Rule 9 or is insufficient to enable him to notice it judicially. Substantially the same approach is found in California Evidence Code §§ 451–453 and in New Jersey Evidence Rule 9. In contrast, the present rule treats alike all adjudicative facts which are subject to judicial notice.

Subdivision (e). Basic considerations of procedural fairness demand an opportunity to be heard on the propriety of taking judicial notice and the tenor of the matter noticed. The rule requires the granting of that opportunity upon request. No formal scheme of giving notice is provided. An adversely affected party may learn in advance that judicial notice is in contemplation, either by virtue of being served with a copy of a request by another party under subdivision (d) that judicial notice be taken, or through an advance indication by the judge. Or he may have no advance notice at all. The likelihood of the latter is enhanced by the frequent failure to recognize judicial notice as such. And in the absence of advance notice, a request made after the fact could not in fairness be considered untimely. See the provision for hearing on timely request in the Administrative Procedure Act, 5 U.S.C. § 556(e). See also Revised Model State Administrative Procedure Act (1961), 9C U.L.A. § 10(4) (Supp.1967).

Subdivision (f). In accord with the usual view, judicial notice may be taken at any stage of the proceedings, whether in the trial court or on appeal.

Uniform Rule 12; California Evidence Code § 459; Kansas Rules of Evidence § 60–412; New Jersey Evidence Rule 12; McCormick § 330, p. 712.

Subdivision (g). Much of the controversy about judicial notice has centered upon the question whether evidence should be admitted in disproof of facts of which judicial notice is taken.

The writers have been divided. Favoring admissibility are Thayer, Preliminary Treatise on Evidence 308 (1898); 9 Wigmore § 2567; Davis, A System of Judicial Notice Based on Fairness and Convenience, in Perspectives of Law 69, 76–77 (1964). Opposing admissibility are Keeffe, Landis and Shaad, Sense and Nonsense about Judicial Notice, 2 Stan.L.Rev. 664, 668 (1950); McNaughton, Judicial Notice—Excerpts Relating to the Morgan–Whitmore Controversy, 14 Vand.L.Rev. 779 (1961); Morgan, Judicial Notice, 57 Harv.L.Rev. 269, 279 (1944); McCormick 710–711. The Model Code and the Uniform Rules are predicated upon indisputability of judicially noticed facts.

The proponents of admitting evidence in disproof have concentrated largely upon legislative facts. Since the present rule deals only with judicial notice of adjudicative facts, arguments directed to legislative facts lose their relevancy.

Report of House Committee on the Judiciary

... Being of the view that mandatory instruction to a jury in a criminal case to accept as conclusive any fact judicially noticed is inappropriate because contrary to the spirit of the Sixth Amendment right to a jury trial, the Committee adopted the 1969 Advisory Committee draft of this subsection, allowing a mandatory instruction in civil actions and proceedings and a discretionary instruction in criminal cases.

Editorial Note

Uniform Rules of Evidence, Rule 201 (1974) provides:

(g) Instructing jury. The court shall instruct the jury to accept as conclusive any fact judicially noticed.

Note on Judicial Notice of Law (by the Advisory Committee)

By rules effective July 1, 1966, the method of invoking the law of a foreign country is covered elsewhere. Rule 44.1 of the Federal Rules of Civil Procedure; Rule 26.1 of the Federal Rules of Criminal Procedure. These two new admirably designed rules are founded upon the assumption that the manner in which law is fed into the judicial process is never a proper concern of the rules of evidence but rather of the rules of procedure. The Advisory Committee on Evidence, believing that this assumption is entirely correct, proposes no evidence rule with respect to judicial notice of law, and suggests that those matters of law which, in addition to foreign-country law, have traditionally been treated as requiring pleading and proof and more recently as the subject of judicial notice be left to the Rules of Civil and Criminal Procedure.

ARTICLE III. PRESUMPTIONS IN CIVIL ACTIONS AND PROCEEDINGS

Rule 301.

PRESUMPTIONS IN GENERAL IN CIVIL ACTIONS AND PROCEEDINGS

In all civil actions and proceedings not otherwise provided for by Act of Congress or by these rules, a presumption imposes on the party against whom it is directed the burden of going forward with evidence to rebut or meet the presumption, but does not shift to such party the burden of proof in the sense of the risk of nonpersuasion, which remains throughout the trial upon the party on whom it was originally cast.

Note by Federal Judicial Center

The bill passed by the House substituted a substantially different rule in place of that prescribed by the Supreme Court. The Senate bill substituted yet a further version, which was accepted by the House, was enacted by the Congress, and is the rule shown above.

Conference Report

The House bill provides that a presumption in civil actions and proceedings shifts to the party against whom it is directed the burden of going forward with evidence to meet or rebut it. Even though evidence contradicting the presumption is offered, a presumption is considered sufficient evidence of the presumed fact to be considered by the jury. The Senate amendment provides that a presumption shifts to the party against whom it is directed the burden of going forward with evidence to meet or rebut the presumption, but it does not shift to that party the burden of persuasion on the existence of the presumed fact.

Under the Senate amendment, a presumption is sufficient to get a party past an adverse party's motion to dismiss made at the end of his case-in-chief. If the adverse party offers no evidence contradicting the presumed fact, the court will instruct the jury, that if it finds the basic facts, it may presume the existence of the presumed fact. If the adverse party does offer evidence contradicting the presumed fact, the court cannot instruct the jury that it may *presume* the existence of the presumed fact from proof of the basic facts. The court may, however, instruct the jury that it may infer the existence of the presumed fact from proof of the basic facts.

The Conference adopts the Senate amendment.

Rule 302.

APPLICABILITY OF STATE LAW IN CIVIL ACTIONS AND PROCEEDINGS

In civil actions and proceedings, the effect of a presumption respecting a fact which is an element of a claim or defense as to which State law supplies the rule of decision is determined in accordance with State law.

Note by Federal Judicial Center

The rule enacted by the Congress is the rule prescribed by the Supreme Court, amended by adding "and proceedings" after "actions."

Advisory Committee's Note

A series of Supreme Court decision in diversity cases leaves no doubt of the relevance of Erie Railroad Co. v. Tompkins, 304 U.S. 64, 58 S.Ct. 817, 82 L.Ed. 1188 (1938), to questions of burden of proof. These decisions are Cities Service Oil Co. v. Dunlap, 308 U.S. 208, 60 S.Ct. 201, 84 L.Ed. 196 (1939), Palmer v. Hoffman, 318 U.S. 109, 63 S.Ct. 477, 87 L.Ed. 645 (1943), and Dick v. New York Life Ins. Co., 359 U.S. 437, 79 S.Ct. 921, 3 L.Ed.2d 935 (1959). They involved burden of proof, respectively, as to status as bona fide purchaser, contributory negligence, and nonaccidental death (suicide) of an insured. In each instance the state rule was held to be applicable. It does not follow, however, that all presumptions in diversity cases are governed by state law. In each case cited, the burden of proof question had to do with a substantive element of the claim or defense. Application of the state law is called for only when the presumption operates upon such an element. Accordingly the rule does not apply state law when the presumption operates upon a lesser aspect of the case, i.e. "tactical" presumptions.

The situations in which the state law is applied have been tagged for convenience in the preceding discussion as "diversity cases." The designation is not a completely accurate one since *Erie* applies to any claim or issue having its source in state law, regardless of the basis of federal jurisdiction, and does not apply to a federal claim or issue, even though jurisdiction is based on diversity. Vestal, Erie R.R. v. Tompkins: A Projection, 48 Iowa L.Rev. 248, 257 (1963); Hart and Wechsler, The Federal Courts and the Federal System, 697 (1953); 1A Moore, Federal Practice ¶ 0.305[3] (2d ed. 1965); Wright, Federal Courts, 217–218 (1963). Hence the rule employs, as appropriately descriptive, the phrase "as to which state law supplies the rule of decision." See A.L.I. Study of the Division of Jurisdiction Between State and Federal Courts, § 2344(c), p. 40, P.F.D. No. 1 (1965).

Presumptions in Criminal Cases

Note by Federal Judicial Center

The rules prescribed by the Supreme Court included Rule 303, Presumptions in Criminal Cases. The rule was not included in the rules enacted by the Congress.

Editorial Note

See Appendix of Deleted Materials, infra.

ARTICLE IV. RELEVANCY AND ITS LIMITS

Rule 401.

DEFINITION OF "RELEVANT EVIDENCE"

"Relevant evidence" means evidence having any tendency to make the existence of any fact that is of consequence to the determination of the action more probable or less probable than it would be without the evidence.

Note by Federal Judicial Center

The rule enacted by the Congress is the rule prescribed by the Supreme Court without change.

Advisory Committee's Note

Problems of relevancy call for an answer to the question whether an item of evidence, when tested by the processes of legal reasoning, possesses sufficient probative value to justify receiving it in evidence. Thus, assessment of the probative value of evidence that a person purchased a revolver shortly prior to a fatal shooting with which he is charged is a matter of analysis and reasoning.

The variety of relevancy problems is coextensive with the ingenuity of counsel in using circumstantial evidence as a means of proof. An enormous number of cases fall in no set pattern, and this rule is designed as a guide for handling them. On the other hand, some situations recur with sufficient frequency to create patterns susceptible of treatment by specific rules. Rule 404 and those following it are of that variety; they also serve as illustrations of the application of the present rule as limited by the exclusionary principles of Rule 403.

Passing mention should be made of so-called "conditional" relevancy. Morgan, Basic Problems of Evidence 45–46 (1962). In this situation, probative value depends not only upon satisfying the basic requirement of relevancy as described above but also upon the existence of some matter of fact. For example, if evidence of a spoken statement is relied upon to prove notice, probative value is lacking unless the person sought to be charged heard the statement. The problem is one of fact, and the only rules needed are for the purpose of determining the respective functions of judge and jury. See Rules 104(b) and 901. The discussion which follows in the present note is concerned with relevancy generally, not with any particular problem of conditional relevancy.

Relevancy is not an inherent characteristic of any item of evidence but exists only as a relation between an item of evidence and a matter properly provable in the case. Does the item of evidence tend to prove the matter sought to be proved? Whether the relationship exists depends upon principles evolved by experience or science, applied logically to the situation at hand. James, Relevancy, Probability and the Law, 29 Calif.L.Rev. 689, 696, n. 15 (1941), in Selected Writings on Evidence and Trial 610, 615, n. 15 (Fryer ed. 1957). The rule summarizes this relationship as a "tendency to make the existence" of the fact to be proved "more probable or less probable." Compare Uniform Rule 1(2) which states the crux of relevancy as "a tendency in reason," thus perhaps emphasizing unduly the logical process and ignoring the need to draw upon experience or science to validate the general principle upon which relevancy in a particular situation depends.

The standard of probability under the rule is "more ... probable than it would be without the evidence." Any more stringent requirement is unworkable and unrealistic. As McCormick § 152, p. 317, says, "A brick is not a wall," or, as Falknor, Extrinsic Policies Affecting Admissibility, 10 Rutgers L.Rev. 574, 576 (1956), quotes Professor McBaine, "... [I]t is not to be supposed that every witness can make a home run." Dealing with probability in the language of the rule has the added virtue of avoiding confusion between questions of admissibility and questions of the sufficiency of the evidence.

The rule uses the phrase "fact that is of consequence to the determination of the action" to describe the kind of fact to which proof may properly be directed. The language is that of California Evidence Code § 210; it has the advantage of avoiding the loosely used and ambiguous word "material." Tentative Recommendation and a Study Relating to the Uniform Rules of Evidence (Art. I. General Provisions), Cal.Law Revision Comm'n, Rep., Rec. & Studies, 10–11 (1964). The fact to be proved may be ultimate, intermediate, or evidentiary; it matters not, so long as it is of consequence in the determination of the action. Cf. Uniform Rule 1(2) which requires that the evidence relate to a "material" fact.

The fact to which the evidence is directed need not be in dispute. While situations will arise which call for the exclusion of evidence offered to prove a point conceded by the opponent, the ruling should be made on the basis of such considerations as waste of time and undue prejudice (see Rule 403), rather than under any general requirement that evidence is admissible only if directed to matters in dispute. Evidence which is essentially background in nature can scarcely be said to involve disputed matter, yet it is universally offered and admitted as an aid to understanding. Charts, photographs, views of real estate, murder weapons, and many other items of evidence fall in this category. A rule limiting admissibility to evidence directed to a controversial point would invite the exclusion of this helpful evidence, or at least the raising of endless questions over its admission. Cf. California Evidence Code § 210, defining relevant evidence in terms of tendency to prove a disputed fact.

Rule 402.

RELEVANT EVIDENCE GENERALLY ADMISSIBLE; IRRELEVANT EVIDENCE INADMISSIBLE

All relevant evidence is admissible, except as otherwise provided by the Constitution of the United States, by Act of Congress, by these rules, or by other rules prescribed by the Supreme Court pursuant to statutory authority. Evidence which is not relevant is not admissible.

Note by Federal Judicial Center

The rule enacted by the Congress is the rule prescribed by the Supreme Court, with the first sentence amended by substituting "prescribed" in place of "adopted", and by adding at the end thereof the phrase "pursuant to statutory authority."

The provisions that all relevant evidence is admissible, with certain exceptions, and that evidence which is not relevant is not admissible are "a presupposition involved in the very conception of a rational system of evidence." Thayer, Preliminary Treatise on Evidence 264 (1898). They constitute the foundation upon which the structure of admission and exclusion rests. For similar provisions see California Evidence Code §§ 350, 351. Provisions that all relevant evidence is admissible are found in Uniform Rule 7(f); Kansas Code of Civil

Procedure § 60–407(f); and New Jersey Evidence Rule 7(f); but the exclusion of evidence which is not relevant is left to implication.

Not all relevant evidence is admissible. The exclusion of relevant evidence occurs in a variety of situations and may be called for by these rules, by the Rules of Civil and Criminal Procedure, by Bankruptcy Rules, by Act of Congress, or by constitutional considerations.

Succeeding rules in the present article, in response to the demands of particular policies, require the exclusion of evidence despite its relevancy. In addition, Article V recognizes a number of privileges; Article VI imposes limitations upon witnesses and the manner of dealing with them; Article VII specifies requirements with respect to opinions and expert testimony; Article VIII excludes hearsay not falling within an exception; Article IX spells out the handling of authentication and identification; and Article X restricts the manner of proving the contents of writings and recordings.

The Rules of Civil and Criminal Procedure in some instances require the exclusion of relevant evidence. For example, Rules 30(b) and 32(a)(3) of the Rules of Civil Procedure, by imposing requirements of notice and unavailability of the deponent, place limits on the use of relevant depositions. Similarly, Rule 15 of the Rules of Criminal Procedure restricts the use of depositions in criminal cases, even though relevant. And the effective enforcement of the command, originally statutory and now found in Rule 5(a) of the Rules of Criminal Procedure, that an arrested person be taken without unnecessary delay before a commissioner or other similar officer is held to require the exclusion of statements elicited during detention in violation thereof. Mallory v. United States, 354 U.S. 449, 77 S.Ct. 1356, 1 L.Ed.2d 1479 (1957); 18 U.S.C. § 3501(c).

While congressional enactments in the field of evidence have generally tended to expand admissibility beyond the scope of the common law rules, in some particular situations they have restricted the admissibility of relevant evidence. Most of this legislation has consisted of the formulation of a privilege or of a prohibition against disclosure. 8 U.S.C. § 1202(f), records of refusal of visas or permits to enter United States confidential, subject to discretion of Secretary of State to make available to court upon certification of need; 10 U.S.C. § 3693, replacement certificate of honorable discharge from Army not admissible in evidence; 10 U.S.C. § 8693, same as to Air Force; 11 U.S.C. § 25(a)(10), testimony given by bankrupt on his examination not admissible in criminal proceedings against him, except that given in hearing upon objection to discharge; 11 U.S.C. § 205(a), railroad reorganization petition, if dismissed, not admissible in evidence; 11 U.S.C. § 403(a), list of creditors filed with municipal composition plan not an admission; 13 U.S.C. § 9(a), census information confidential, retained copies of reports privileged; 47 U.S.C. § 605, interception and divulgence of wire or radio communications prohibited unless authorized by sender. These statutory provisions would remain undisturbed by the rules.

The rule recognizes but makes no attempt to spell out the constitutional considerations which impose basic limitations upon the admissibility of relevant evidence. Examples are evidence obtained by unlawful search and seizure. Weeks v. United States, 232 U.S. 383, 34 S.Ct. 341, 58 L.Ed. 652 (1914); Katz v. United States, 389 U.S. 347, 88 S.Ct. 507, 19 L.Ed.2d 576 (1967); incriminating statement elicited from an accused in violation of right to counsel, Massiah v. United States, 377 U.S. 201, 84 S.Ct. 1199, 12 L.Ed.2d 246 (1964).

Report of House Committee on the Judiciary

Rule 402 as submitted to the Congress contained the phrase "or by other rules adopted by the Supreme Court". To accommodate the view that the Congress should not appear to acquiesce in the Court's judgment that it has authority under the existing Rules Enabling Acts to promulgate Rules of Evidence, the Committee amended the above phrase to read "or by other rules prescribed by the Supreme Court pursuant to statutory authority" in this and other Rules where the reference appears.

Rule 403.

EXCLUSION OF RELEVANT EVIDENCE ON GROUNDS OF PREJUDICE, CONFUSION, OR WASTE OF TIME

Although relevant, evidence may be excluded if its probative value is substantially outweighed by the danger of unfair prejudice, confusion of the issues, or misleading the jury, or by considerations of undue delay, waste of time, or needless presentation of cumulative evidence.

Note by Federal Judicial Center

The rule enacted by the Congress is the rule prescribed by the Supreme Court without change.

Advisory Committee's Note

The case law recognizes that certain circumstances call for the exclusion of evidence which is of unquestioned relevance. These circumstances entail risks which range all the way from inducing decision on a purely emotional basis, at one extreme, to nothing more harmful than merely wasting time, at the other extreme. Situations in this area call for balancing the probative value of and need for the evidence against the harm likely to result from its admission. Slough, Relevancy Unraveled, 5 Kan.L.Rev. 1, 12–15 (1956); Trautman, Logical or Legal Relevancy—A Conflict in Theory, 5 Van.L.Rev. 385, 392 (1952); McCormick § 152, pp. 319–321. The rules which follow in this Article are concrete applications evolved for particular situations. However, they reflect the policies underlying the present rule, which is designed as a guide for the handling of situations for which no specific rules have been formulated.

Exclusion for risk of unfair prejudice, confusion of issues, misleading the jury, or waste of time, all find ample support in the authorities. "Unfair prejudice" within its context means an undue tendency to suggest decision on an improper basis, commonly, though not necessarily, an emotional one.

The rule does not enumerate surprise as a ground for exclusion, in this respect following Wigmore's view of the common law. 6 Wigmore § 1849. Cf. McCormick § 152, p. 320, n. 29, listing unfair surprise as a ground for exclusion but stating that it is usually "coupled with the danger of prejudice and confusion of issues." While Uniform Rule 45 incorporates surprise as a ground and is followed in Kansas Code of Civil Procedure § 60–445, surprise is not included in California Evidence Code § 352 or New Jersey Rule 4, though both the latter otherwise substantially embody Uniform Rule 45. While it can scarcely be doubted that claims of unfair surprise may still be justified despite procedural requirements of notice and instrumentalities of discovery, the granting of a continuance is a more appropriate remedy than exclusion of the evidence. Tentative Recommendation and a Study Relating to the Uniform Rules of Evidence (Art. VI. Extrinsic Policies Affecting Admissibility), Cal.Law Revision Comm'n, Rep., Rec. & Studies, 612 (1964). Moreover, the impact of a rule excluding evidence on the ground of surprise would be difficult to estimate.

In reaching a decision whether to exclude on grounds of unfair prejudice, consideration should be given to the probable effectiveness or lack of effectiveness of a limiting instruction. See Rule 106[105] and Advisory Committee's Note thereunder. The availability of other means of proof may also be an appropriate factor.

Rule 404.

CHARACTER EVIDENCE NOT ADMISSIBLE TO PROVE CONDUCT; EXCEPTIONS; OTHER CRIMES

(a) Character evidence generally. Evidence of a person's character or a trait of character is not admissible for the purpose of proving action in conformity therewith on a particular occasion, except:

(1) Character of accused. In a criminal case, evidence of a pertinent trait of character offered by an accused, or by the prosecution to rebut the same, or if evidence of a trait of character of the alleged victim of the crime is offered by an accused and admitted under Rule 404(a)(2), evidence of the same trait of character of the accused offered by the prosecution;

(2) Character of alleged victim. In a criminal case, and subject to the limitations imposed by Rule 412, evidence of a pertinent trait of character of the alleged victim of the crime offered by an accused, or by the prosecution to rebut the same, or evidence of a character trait of peacefulness of the alleged victim offered by the prosecution in a homicide case to rebut evidence that the alleged victim was the first aggressor;

(3) Character of witness. Evidence of the character of a witness, as provided in Rules 607, 608, and 609.

(b) Other crimes, wrongs, or acts. Evidence of other crimes, wrongs, or acts is not admissible to prove the character of a person in order to show action in conformity therewith. It may, however, be admissible for other purposes, such as proof of motive, opportunity, intent, preparation, plan, knowledge, identity, or absence of mistake or accident, provided that upon request by the accused, the prosecution in a criminal case shall provide reasonable notice in advance of trial, or during trial if the court excuses pretrial notice on good cause shown, of the general nature of any such evidence it intends to introduce at trial.

Advisory Committee's Note to 2006 Amendment

The Rule has been amended to clarify that in a civil case evidence of a person's character is never admissible to prove that the person acted in conformity with the character trait. The amendment resolves the dispute in the case law over whether the exceptions in subdivisions (a)(1) and (2) permit the circumstantial use of character evidence in civil cases. *Compare Carson v. Polley*, 689 F.2d 562, 576 (5th Cir. 1982) ("when a central issue in a case is close to one of a criminal nature, the exceptions to the Rule 404(a) ban on character evidence may be invoked"), *with SEC v. Towers Financial Corp.*, 966 F.Supp. 203 (S.D.N.Y. 1997) (relying on the terms "accused" and "prosecution" in Rule 404(a) to conclude that the exceptions in subdivisions (a)(1) and (2) are inapplicable in civil cases). The amendment is consistent with the original intent of the Rule, which was to prohibit the circumstantial use of character evidence in civil cases, even where closely related to criminal charges. *See Ginter v. Northwestern Mut. Life Ins. Co.*, 576 F.Supp. 627, 629–30 (D. Ky. 1984) ("It seems beyond peradventure of doubt that the drafters of Fed.R.Evid. 404(a) explicitly intended that all character evidence, except where 'character is at issue' was to be excluded" in civil cases).

The circumstantial use of character evidence is generally discouraged because it carries serious risks of prejudice, confusion and delay. *See Michelson v. United States*, 335 U.S. 469, 476 (1948) ("The overriding policy of excluding such evidence, despite its admitted probative value, is the practical experience that its disallowance tends to prevent confusion of issues, unfair surprise and undue prejudice."). In criminal cases, the so-called "mercy rule" permits a criminal defendant to introduce evidence of pertinent character traits of the defendant and the victim. But that is because the accused, whose liberty is at stake, may need "a counterweight against the strong investigative and prosecutorial resources of the government." C. Mueller & L. Kirkpatrick, *Evidence: Practice Under the Rules*, pp. 264–5 (2d ed. 1999). See also Richard Uviller, *Evidence of Character to Prove Conduct: Illusion, Illogic, and Injustice in the Courtroom*, 130 U.Pa.L. Rev. 845, 855 (1982) (the rule prohibiting circumstantial use of character evidence "was relaxed to allow the criminal defendant with so much at stake and so little available in the way of conventional proof to have special dispensation to tell the factfinder just what sort of person he really is"). Those concerns do not apply to parties in civil cases.

The amendment also clarifies that evidence otherwise admissible under Rule 404(a)(2) may nonetheless be excluded in a criminal case involving sexual misconduct. In such a case, the admissibility of evidence of the victim's sexual behavior and predisposition is governed by the more stringent provisions of Rule 412.

Nothing in the amendment is intended to affect the scope of Rule 404(b). While Rule 404(b) refers to the "accused," the "prosecution," and a "criminal case," it does so only in the context of a notice requirement. The admissibility standard of Rule 404(b) remain fully applicable to both civil and criminal cases.

Advisory Committee's Note to 2000 Amendment to Rule 404

Rule 404(a)(1) has been amended to provide that when the accused attacks the character of an alleged victim under subdivision(a)(2) of this Rule, the door is opened to an attack on the same character trait of the accused. Current law does not allow the government to introduce negative character evidence as to the accused unless the accused introduces evidence of good character. *See, e.g., United States v. Fountain*, 768 F.2d 790 (7th Cir.1985) (when the accused offers proof of self-defense, this permits proof of the alleged victim's character trait for peacefulness, but it does not permit proof of the accused's character trait for violence).

The amendment makes clear that the accused cannot attack the alleged victim's character and yet remain shielded from the disclosure of equally relevant evidence concerning the same character trait of the accused. For example, in a murder case with a claim of self-defense, the accused, to bolster this defense, might offer evidence of the alleged victim's violent disposition. If the government has evidence that the accused has a violent character, but is not allowed to offer this evidence as part of its rebuttal, the jury has only part of the information it needs for an informed assessment of the probabilities as to who was the initial aggressor. This may be the case even if evidence of the accused's prior violent acts is admitted under Rule 404(b), because such evidence can be admitted only for limited purposes and not to show action in conformity with the accused's character on a specific occasion. Thus, the amendment is designed to permit a more balanced presentation of character evidence when an accused chooses to attack the character of the alleged victim.

The amendment does not affect the admissibility of evidence of specific acts of uncharged misconduct offered for a purpose other than proving character under Rule 404(b). Nor does it affect the standards for proof of character by evidence of other sexual behavior or sexual offenses under Rules 412–415. By its placement in Rule 404(a)(1), the amendment covers only proof of character by way of reputation or opinion. The amendment does not permit proof of the accused's character if the accused merely uses character evidence for a purpose other than to prove the alleged victim's propensity to act in a certain way. *See United States v. Burks*, 470 F.2d 432, 434–5 (D.C.Cir.1972) (evidence of the alleged victim's violent character, when known by the accused, was admissible "on the issue of whether or not the defendant reasonably feared he was in danger of imminent great bodily harm"). Finally, the amendment does not permit proof of the accused's character when the accused attacks the alleged victim's character as a witness under Rule 608 or 609.

The term "alleged" is inserted before each reference to "victim" in the Rule, in order to provide consistency with Evidence Rule 412.

Committee Note to 1991 Amendment

Rule 404(b) has emerged as one of the most cited Rules in the Rules of Evidence. And in many criminal cases evidence of an accused's extrinsic acts is viewed as an important asset in the prosecution's case against an accused. Although there are a few reported decisions on use of such evidence by the defense, see, e.g., United States v. McClure, 546 F.2d 670 (5th Cir.1977[sic])(acts of informant offered in entrapment defense), the overwhelming number of cases involve introduction of that evidence by the prosecution.

The amendment to Rule 404(b) adds a pretrial notice requirement in criminal cases and is intended to reduce surprise and promote early resolution on the issue of admissibility. The notice requirement thus places Rule 404(b) in the mainstream with notice and disclosure provisions in other rules of evidence. See, e.g., Rule 412 (written motion of intent to offer evidence under rule), Rule 609 (written notice of intent to offer conviction older than 10 years), Rule[s] 803(24) and 804(b)(5) (notice of intent to use residual hearsay exceptions).

The Rule expects that counsel for both the defense and the prosecution will submit the necessary request and information in a reasonable and timely fashion. Other than requiring pretrial notice, no specific time limits are stated in recognition that what constitutes a reasonable request or disclosure will depend largely on the circumstances of each case. Compare Fla.Stat.Ann[.] § 90.404(2)(b) (notice must be given at least ten days before trial) with Tex. R.Evid. 404(b) (no time limit).

Likewise, no specific form of notice is required. The Committee considered and rejected a requirement that the notice satisfy the particularity requirements normally required of language used in a charging instrument. Cf. Fla.Stat. Ann[.] § 90.404(2)(b) (written disclosure must describe uncharged misconduct with particularity required of an indictment or information). Instead, the Committee opted for a generalized notice provision which requires the prosecution to apprise the defense of the general nature of the evidence of extrinsic acts. The Committee does not intend that the amendment will super[s]ede other rules of admissibility or disclosure, such as the Jencks Act, 18 U.S.C. § 3500, et seq. nor require the prosecution to disclose directly or indirectly the names and addresses of its witnesses, something it is currently not required to do under Federal Rule of Criminal Procedure 16.

The amendment requires the prosecution to provide notice, regardless of how it intends to use the extrinsic act evidence at trial, i.e., during its case-in-chief, for impeachment, or for possible rebuttal. The court in its discretion may, under the facts, decide that the particular request or notice was not reasonable, either because of the lack of timeliness or completeness. Because the notice requirement serves as [a] condition precedent to admissibility of 404(b) evidence, the offered evidence is inadmissible if the court decides that the notice requirement has not been met.

Nothing in the amendment precludes the court from requiring the government to provide it with an opportunity to rule in limine on 404(b) evidence before it is offered or even mentioned during trial. When ruling in limine, the court may require the government to disclose to it the specifics of such evidence which the court must consider in determining admissibility.

The amendment does not extend to evidence of acts which are "intrinsic" to the charged offense, see United States v. Williams, 900 F.2d 823 (5th Cir.1990)(noting distinction between 404(b) evidence and intrinsic offense evidence). Nor is the amendment intended to redefine what evidence would otherwise be admissible under Rule 404(b). Finally, the Committee does not intend through the amendment to affect the role of the court and the jury in considering such evidence. See Huddleston v. United States, 485 U.S. 681, 108 S.Ct. 1496, 99 L.Ed.2d 771 (1988).

Note by Federal Judicial Center

The rule enacted by the Congress is the rule prescribed by the Supreme Court, with the second sentence of subdivision (b) amended by substituting "It may, however, be admissible" in place of "This subdivision does not exclude the evidence when offered."

Advisory Committee's Note

Subdivision (a). This subdivision deals with the basic question whether character evidence should be admitted. Once the admissibility of character evidence in some form is established under this rule, reference must then be made to Rule 405, which follows, in order to determine the appropriate method of proof. If the character is that of a witness, see Rules 608 and 609 for methods of proof.

Character questions arise in two fundamentally different ways. (1) Character may itself be an element of a crime, claim, or defense. A situation of this kind is commonly referred to as "character in issue." Illustrations are: the chastity of the victim under a statute specifying her chastity as an element of the crime of seduction, or the competency of the driver in an action for negligently entrusting a motor vehicle to an incompetent driver. No problem of the general relevancy of character evidence is involved, and the present rule therefore has no provision on the subject. The only question relates to allowable methods of proof, as to which see Rule 405, immediately following. (2) Character evidence is susceptible of being used for the purpose of suggesting an inference that the person acted on the occasion in question consistently with his character. This use of character is often described as "circumstantial." Illustrations are: evidence of a violent disposition to prove that the person was the aggressor in an affray, or evidence of honesty in disproof of a charge of theft. This circumstantial use of character evidence raises questions of relevancy as well as questions of allowable methods of proof.

In most jurisdictions today, the circumstantial use of character is rejected but with important exceptions: (1) an accused may introduce pertinent evidence of good character (often misleadingly described as "putting his character in issue"), in which event the prosecution may rebut with evidence of bad character; (2) an accused may introduce pertinent evidence of the character of the victim, as in support of a claim of self-defense to a charge of homicide or consent in a case of rape, and the prosecution may introduce similar evidence in rebuttal of the character evidence, or, in a homicide case, to rebut a claim that deceased was the first aggressor, however proved; and (3) the character of a witness may be gone into as bearing on his credibility. McCormick §§ 155–161. This pattern is incorporated in the rule. While its basis lies more in history and experience than in logic an underlying justification can fairly be found in terms of the relative presence and absence of prejudice in the various situations. Falknor, Extrinsic Policies Affecting Admissibility, 10 Rutgers L.Rev. 574, 584 (1956); McCormick § 157. In any event, the criminal rule is so deeply imbedded in our jurisprudence as to assume almost constitutional proportions and to override doubts of the basic relevancy of the evidence.

The limitation to pertinent traits of character, rather than character generally, in paragraphs (1) and (2) is in accordance with the prevailing view. McCormick § 158, p. 334. A similar provision in Rule 608, to which reference is made in paragraph (3), limits character evidence respecting witnesses to the trait of truthfulness or untruthfulness.

The argument is made that circumstantial use of character ought to be allowed in civil cases to the same extent as in criminal cases, i.e. evidence of good (nonprejudicial) character would be admissible in the first instance, subject to rebuttal by evidence of bad character. Falknor, Extrinsic Policies Affecting

Admissibility, 10 Rutgers L.Rev. 574, 581–583 (1956); Tentative Recommendation and a Study Relating to the Uniform Rules of Evidence (Art. VI. Extrinsic Policies Affecting Admissibility), Cal.Law Revision Comm'n, Rep., Rec. & Studies, 657–658 (1964). Uniform Rule 47 goes farther, in that it assumes that character evidence in general satisfies the conditions of relevancy, except as provided in Uniform Rule 48. The difficulty with expanding the use of character evidence in civil cases is set forth by the California Law Revision Commission in its ultimate rejection of Uniform Rule 47, id., 615:

> "Character evidence is of slight probative value and may be very prejudicial. It tends to distract the trier of fact from the main question of what actually happened on the particular occasion. It subtly permits the trier of fact to reward the good man and to punish the bad man because of their respective characters despite what the evidence in the case shows actually happened."

Much of the force of the position of those favoring greater use of character evidence in civil cases is dissipated by their support of Uniform Rule 48 which excludes the evidence in negligence cases, where it could be expected to achieve its maximum usefulness. Moreover, expanding concepts of "character," which seem of necessity to extend into such areas as psychiatric evaluation and psychological testing, coupled with expanded admissibility, would open up such vistas of mental examinations as caused the Court concern in Schlagenhauf v. Holder, 379 U.S. 104, 85 S.Ct. 234, 13 L.Ed.2d 152 (1964). It is believed that those espousing change have not met the burden of persuasion.

Subdivision (b) deals with a specialized but important application of the general rule excluding circumstantial use of character evidence. Consistently with that rule, evidence of other crimes, wrongs, or acts is not admissible to prove character as a basis for suggesting the inference that conduct on a particular occasion was in conformity with it. However, the evidence may be offered for another purpose, such as proof of motive, opportunity, and so on, which does not fall within the prohibition. In this situation the rule does not require that the evidence be excluded. No mechanical solution is offered. The determination must be made whether the danger of undue prejudice outweighs the probative value of the evidence in view of the availability of other means of proof and other factors appropriate for making decisions of this kind under Rule 403. Slough and Knightly, Other Vices, Other Crimes, 41 Iowa L.Rev. 325 (1956).

Report of House Committee on the Judiciary

The second sentence of Rule 404(b) as submitted to the Congress began with the words "This subdivision does not exclude the evidence when offered". The Committee amended this language to read "It may, however, be admissible", the words used in the 1971 Advisory Committee draft, on the ground that this formulation properly placed greater emphasis on admissibility than did the final Court version.

Report of Senate Committee on the Judiciary

This rule provides that evidence of other crimes, wrongs, or acts is not admissible to prove character but may be admissible for other specified purposes such as proof of motive.

Although your committee sees no necessity in amending the rule itself, it anticipates that the use of the discretionary word "may" with respect to the admissibility of evidence of crimes, wrongs, or acts is not intended to confer any arbitrary discretion on the trial judge. Rather, it is anticipated that with respect to permissible uses for such evidence, the trial judge may exclude it only on the basis of those considerations set forth in Rule 403, i.e. prejudice, confusion or waste of time.

Rule 405.

METHODS OF PROVING CHARACTER

(a) Reputation or opinion. In all cases in which evidence of character or a trait of character of a person is admissible, proof may be made by testimony as to reputation or by testimony in the form of an opinion. On cross-examination, inquiry is allowable into relevant specific instances of conduct.

(b) Specific instances of conduct. In cases in which character or a trait of character of a person is an essential element of a charge, claim, or defense, proof may also be made of specific instances of that person's conduct.

Note by Federal Judicial Center

The rule enacted by the Congress is the rule prescribed by the Supreme Court without change. The bill reported by the House Committee on the Judiciary deleted the provision in subdivision (a) for making proof by testimony in the form of an opinion, but the provision was reinstated on the floor of the House. See Congressional Record, February 6, 1974 (daily ed. pp. H546–H549).

Advisory Committee's Note

The rule deals only with allowable methods of proving character, not with the admissibility of character evidence, which is covered in Rule 404.

Of the three methods of proving character provided by the rule, evidence of specific instances of conduct is the most convincing. At the same time it possesses the greatest capacity to arouse prejudice, to confuse, to surprise, and to consume time. Consequently the rule confines the use of evidence of this kind to cases in which character is, in the strict sense, in issue and hence deserving of a searching inquiry. When character is used, circumstantially and hence occupies a lesser status in the case, proof may be only by reputation and opinion. These latter methods are also available when character is in issue. This treatment is, with respect to specific instances of conduct and reputation, conventional contemporary common law doctrine. McCormick § 153.

In recognizing opinion as a means of proving character, the rule departs from usual contemporary practice in favor of that of an earlier day. See 7 Wigmore § 1986, pointing out that the earlier practice permitted opinion and arguing strongly for evidence based on personal knowledge and belief as contrasted with "the secondhand, irresponsible product of multiplied guesses and gossip which we term 'reputation'." It seems likely that the persistence of reputation evidence is due to its largely being opinion in disguise. Traditionally character has been regarded primarily in moral overtones of good and bad: chaste, peaceable, truthful, honest. Nevertheless, on occasion nonmoral considerations crop up, as in the case of the incompetent driver, and this seems bound to happen increasingly. If character is defined as the kind of person one is, then account must be taken of varying ways of arriving at the estimate. These may range from the opinion of the employer who has found the man honest to the opinion of the psychiatrist based upon examination and testing. No effective dividing line exists between character and mental capacity, and the latter traditionally has been provable by opinion.

According to the great majority of cases, on cross-examination inquiry is allowable as to whether the reputation witness has heard of particular instances of conduct pertinent to the trait in question. Michelson v. United States, 335 U.S. 469, 69 S.Ct. 213, 93 L.Ed. 168 (1948); Annot., 47 A.L.R.2d 1258. The theory is that, since the reputation witness relates what he has heard, the inquiry tends to shed light on the accuracy of his hearing and reporting. Accordingly, the opinion witness would be asked whether he knew, as well as whether he had heard. The fact is, of course, that these distinctions are of slight if any practical significance, and the second sentence of subdivision (a) eliminates them as a factor in formulating questions. This recognition of the propriety of inquiring into specific instances of conduct does not circumscribe inquiry otherwise into the bases of opinion and reputation testimony.

The express allowance of inquiry into specific instances of conduct on cross-examination in subdivision (a) and the express allowance of it as part of a case in chief when character is actually in issue in subdivision (b) contemplate that testimony of specific instances is not generally permissible on the direct examination of an ordinary opinion witness to character. Similarly as to witnesses to the character of witnesses under Rule 608(b). Opinion testimony on direct in these situations ought in general to correspond to reputation testimony as now given, i.e., be confined to the nature and extent of observation and acquaintance upon which the opinion is based. See Rule 701.

Rule 406.

HABIT; ROUTINE PRACTICE

Evidence of the habit of a person or of the routine practice of an organization, whether corroborated or not and regardless of the presence of eyewitnesses, is relevant to prove that the conduct of the person or organization on a particular occasion was in conformity with the habit or routine practice.

Note by Federal Judicial Center

The rule enacted by the Congress is subdivision (a) of the rule prescribed by the Supreme Court. Subdivision (b)[4] of the Court's rule was deleted for reasons stated in the Report of the House Committee on the Judiciary set forth below.

Advisory Committee's Note

Subdivision (a). An oft-quoted paragraph, McCormick § 162, p. 340, describes habit in terms effectively contrasting it with character:

---

4. See Appendix of Deleted Materials, infra.

"Character and habit are close akin. Character is a generalized description of one's disposition, or of one's disposition in respect to a general trait, such as honesty, temperance, or peacefulness. 'Habit,' in modern usage, both lay and psychological, is more specific. It describes one's regular response to a repeated specific situation. If we speak of character for care, we think of the person's tendency to act prudently in all the varying situations of life, in business, family life, in handling automobiles and in walking across the street. A habit, on the other hand, is the person's regular practice of meeting a particular kind of situation with a specific type of conduct, such as the habit of going down a particular stairway two stairs at a time, or of giving the hand-signal for a left turn, or of alighting from railway cars while they are moving.

The doing of the habitual acts may become semi-automatic."

Equivalent behavior on the part of a group is designated "routine practice of an organization" in the rule.

Agreement is general that habit evidence is highly persuasive as proof of conduct on a particular occasion. Again quoting McCormick § 162, p. 341:

"Character may be thought of as the sum of one's habits though doubtless it is more than this. But unquestionably the uniformity of one's response to habit is far greater than the consistency with which one's conduct conforms to character or disposition. Even though character comes in only exceptionally as evidence of an act, surely any sensible man in investigating whether X did a particular act would be greatly helped in his inquiry by evidence as to whether he was in the habit of doing it."

When disagreement has appeared, its focus has been upon the question what constitutes habit, and the reason for this is readily apparent. The extent to which instances must be multiplied and consistency of behavior maintained in order to rise to the status of habit inevitably gives rise to differences of opinion. Lewan, Rationale of Habit Evidence, 16 Syracuse L.Rev. 39, 49 (1964). While adequacy of sampling and uniformity of response are key factors, precise standards for measuring their sufficiency for evidence purposes cannot be formulated.

The rule is consistent with prevailing views. Much evidence is excluded simply because of failure to achieve the status of habit. Thus, evidence of intemperate "habits" is generally excluded when offered as proof of drunkenness in accident cases, Annot., 46 A.L.R.2d 103, and evidence of other assaults is inadmissible to prove the instant one in a civil assault action, Annot., 66 A.L.R.2d 806. In Levin v. United States, 119 U.S.App.D.C. 156, 338 F.2d 265 (1964), testimony as to the religious "habits" of the accused, offered as tending to prove that he was at home observing the Sabbath rather than out obtaining money through larceny by trick, was held properly excluded:

"It seems apparent to us that an individual's religious practices would not be the type of activities which would lend themselves to the characterization of 'invariable regularity.' [1 Wigmore 520.] Certainly the very volitional basis of the activity raises serious questions as to its invariable nature, and hence its probative value." Id. at 272.

These rulings are not inconsistent with the trend towards admitting evidence of business transactions between one of the parties and a third person as tending to prove that he made the same bargain or proposal in the litigated situation. Slough, Relevancy Unraveled, 6 Kan.L.Rev. 38–41 (1957). Nor are they inconsistent with such cases as Whittemore v. Lockheed Aircraft Corp., 65 Cal.App.2d 737, 151 P.2d 670 (1944), upholding the admission of evidence that plaintiff's intestate had on four other occasions flown planes from defendant's factory for delivery to his employer airline, offered to prove that he was piloting rather than a guest on a plane which crashed and killed all on board while en route for delivery.

A considerable body of authority has required that evidence of the routine practice of an organization be corroborated as a condition precedent to its admission in evidence. Slough, Relevancy Unraveled, 5 Kan.L.Rev. 404, 449 (1957). This requirement is specifically rejected by the rule on the ground that it relates to the sufficiency of the evidence rather than admissibility. A similar position is taken in New Jersey Rule 49. The rule also rejects the requirement of the absence of eyewitnesses, sometimes encountered with respect to admitting habit evidence to prove freedom from contributory negligence in wrongful death cases. For comment critical of the requirements see Frank, J., in Cereste v. New York, N.H. & H.R. Co., 231 F.2d 50 (2d Cir.1956), cert. denied 351 U.S. 951, 76 S.Ct. 848, 100 L.Ed. 1475, 10 Vand.L.Rev. 447 (1956); McCormick § 162, p. 342. The omission of the requirement from the California Evidence Code is said to have effected its elimination. Comment, Cal.Ev.Code § 1105.

Report of House Committee on the Judiciary

Rule 406 as submitted to Congress contained a subdivision (b) providing that the method of proof of habit or routine practice could be "in the form of an opinion or by specific instances of conduct sufficient in number to warrant a finding that the habit existed or that the practice was routine." The Committee deleted this subdivision believing that the method of proof of habit and routine practice should be left to the courts to deal with on a case-by-case basis. At the same time, the Committee does not intend that its action be construed as sanctioning a general authorization of opinion evidence in this area.

Rule 407.

SUBSEQUENT REMEDIAL MEASURES

When, after an injury or harm allegedly caused by an event, measures are taken that, if taken previously, would have made the injury or harm less likely to occur, evidence of the subsequent measures is not admissible to prove negligence, culpable conduct, a defect in a product, a defect in a product's design, or a need for a warning or instruction. This rule does not require the exclusion of evidence of subsequent measures when offered for another purpose, such as proving ownership, control, or feasibility of precautionary measures, if controverted, or impeachment.

Committee Note to 1997 Amendment

The amendment to Rule 407 makes two changes in the rule. First, the words "an injury or harm allegedly caused by" were added to clarify that the rule applies only to changes made after the occurrence that produced the damages giving rise to the action. Evidence of measures taken by the defendant prior to the "event" do not fall within the exclusionary scope of Rule 407 even if they occurred after the manufacture or design of the product. See Chase v. General Motors Corp., 856 F.2d 17, 21–22 (4th Cir.1988).

Second, Rule 407 has been amended to provide that evidence of subsequent remedial measures may not be used to prove "a defect in a product, a defect in a product's design, or a need for a warning or instruction." This amendment adopts the view of a majority of the circuits that have interpreted Rule 407 to apply to products liability actions. See Raymond v. Raymond Corp., 938 F.2d 1518, 1522 (1st Cir.1991); In re Joint Eastern District and Southern District Asbestos Litigation v. Armstrong World Industries, Inc., 995 F.2d 343, 345 (2d Cir.1993); Cann v. Ford Motor Co., 658 F.2d 54, 60 (2d Cir.1981), cert. denied, 456 U.S. 960 (1982); Kelly v. Crown Equipment Co., 970 F.2d 1273, 1275 (3d Cir.1992); Werner v. Upjohn Co., Inc., 628 F.2d 848, 856 (4th Cir.1980), cert. denied, 449 U.S. 1080 (1981); Grenada Steel Industries, Inc. v. Alabama Oxygen Co., Inc., 695 F.2d 883, 887 (5th Cir.1983); Bauman v. Volkswagenwerk Aktiengesellschaft, 621 F.2d 230, 232 (6th Cir.1980); Flaminio v. Honda Motor Company, Ltd., 733 F.2d 463, 469 (7th Cir.1984); Gauthier v. AMF, Inc., 788 F.2d 634, 636–37 (9th Cir.1986).

Although this amendment adopts a uniform federal rule, it should be noted that evidence of subsequent remedial measures may be admissible pursuant to the second sentence of Rule 407. Evidence of subsequent measures that is not barred by Rule 407 may still be subject to exclusion on Rule 403 grounds when the dangers of prejudice or confusion substantially outweigh the probative value of the evidence.

Note by Federal Judicial Center

The rule enacted by the Congress is the rule prescribed by the Supreme Court without change.

Advisory Committee's Note

The rule incorporates conventional doctrine which excludes evidence of subsequent remedial measures as proof of an admission of fault. The rule rests on two grounds. (1) The conduct is not in fact an admission, since the conduct is equally consistent with injury by mere accident or through contributory negligence. Or, as Baron Bramwell put it, the rule rejects the notion that "because the world gets wiser as it gets older, therefore it was foolish before." Hart v. Lancashire & Yorkshire Ry. Co., 21 L.T.R. N.S. 261, 263 (1869). Under a liberal theory of relevancy this ground alone would not support exclusion as the inference is still a possible one. (2) The other, and more impressive, ground for exclusion rests on a social policy of encouraging people to take, or at least not discouraging them from taking, steps in furtherance of added safety. The courts have applied this principle to exclude evidence of subsequent repairs, installation of safety devices, changes in company rules, and discharge of employees, and the language of the present rule is broad enough to encompass all of them. See Falknor, Extrinsic Policies Affecting Admissibility, 10 Rutgers L.Rev. 574, 590 (1956).

The second sentence of the rule directs attention to the limitations of the rule. Exclusion is called for only when the evidence of subsequent remedial measures is offered as proof of negligence or culpable conduct. In effect it rejects the suggested inference that fault is admitted. Other purposes are, however, allowable, including ownership or control, existence of duty, and feasibility of precautionary measures, if controverted, and impeachment. 2 Wigmore § 283; Annot., 64 A.L.R.2d 1296. Two recent federal cases are illustrative. Boeing Airplane Co. v. Brown, 291 F.2d 310 (9th Cir.1961), an action against an airplane manufacturer for using an allegedly defectively designed alternator shaft which caused a plane crash, upheld the admission of evidence of subsequent design modification for the purpose of showing that design changes and safeguards were feasible. And Powers v. J.B. Michael & Co., 329 F.2d 674 (6th Cir.1964), an action against a road contractor for negligent failure to put out warning signs, sustained the admission of evidence that defendant subsequently put out signs to show that the portion of the road in question was under defendant's control. The requirement that the other purpose be controverted calls for automatic exclusion unless a genuine issue be present and allows the opposing party to lay the groundwork for exclusion by making an admission. Otherwise the factors of undue prejudice, confusion of issues, misleading the jury, and waste of time remain for consideration under Rule 403.

For comparable rules, see Uniform Rule 51; California Evidence Code § 1151; Kansas Code of Civil Procedure § 60–451; New Jersey Evidence Rule 51.

Rule 408.

COMPROMISE AND OFFERS TO COMPROMISE

(a) Prohibited uses. Evidence of the following is not admissible on behalf of any party, when offered to prove liability for, invalidity of, or amount of a claim that was disputed as to validity or amount, or to impeach through a prior inconsistent statement or contradiction:

(1) furnishing or offering or promising to furnish or accepting or offering or promising to accept a valuable consideration in compromising or attempting to compromise the claim; and

(2) conduct or statements made in compromise negotiations regarding the claim, except when offered in a criminal case and the negotiations related to a claim by a public office or agency in the exercise of regulatory, investigative, or enforcement authority.

(b) Permitted uses.—This rule does not require exclusion if the evidence is offered for purposes not prohibited by subdivision (a). Examples of permissible purposes include proving a witness's bias or prejudice; negating a contention of undue delay; and proving an effort to obstruct a criminal investigation or prosecution.

Advisory Committee Note to 2006 Amendment

Rule 408 has been amended to settle some questions in the courts about the scope of the Rule, and to make it easier to read. First, the amendment provides that Rule 408 does not prohibit the introduction in a criminal case of statements or conduct during compromise negotiations regarding a civil dispute by a government regulatory, investigative, or enforcement agency. *See, e.g., United States v. Prewitt,* 34 F.3d 436, 439 (7th Cir. 1994) (admissions of fault made in compromise of a civil securities enforcement action were admissible against the accused in a subsequent criminal action for mail fraud). Where an individual makes a statement in the presence of government agents, its subsequent admission in a criminal case should not be unexpected. The individual can seek to protect against subsequent disclosure through negotiation and agreement with the civil regulator or an attorney for the government.

Statements made in compromise negotiations of a claim by a government agency may be excluded in criminal cases where the circumstances so warrant under Rule 403. For example, if an individual was unrepresented at the time the statement was made in a civil enforcement proceeding, its probative value in a subsequent criminal case may be minimal. But there is no absolute exclusion imposed by Rule 408.

In contrast, statements made during compromise negotiations of other disputed claims are not admissible in subsequent criminal litigation, when offered to prove liability for, invalidity of, or amount of those claims. When private parties enter into compromise negotiations they cannot protect against the subsequent use of statements in criminal cases by way of private ordering. The inability to guarantee protection against subsequent use could lead to parties refusing to admit fault, even if by doing so they could favorably settle the private matter. Such a chill on settlement negotiations would be contrary to the policy of Rule 408.

The amendment distinguishes statements and conduct (such as direct admission of fault) made in compromise negotiations of a civil claim by a government agency from an offer or acceptance of a compromise of such a claim. An offer or acceptance of a compromise of any civil claim is excluded under the Rule if offered against the defendant as an admission of fault. In that case, the predicate for the evidence would be that the defendant, by compromising with the government agency, has admitted the validity and amount of the civil claim, and that this admission has sufficient probative value to be considered as evidence of guilt. But unlike a direct statement of fault, an offer or acceptance of a compromise is not very probative of the defendant's guilt. Moreover, admitting such an offer or acceptance could deter a defendant from settling a civil regulatory action, for fear of evidentiary use in a subsequent criminal action. *See, e.g.,* Fishman, *Jones on Evidence, Civil and Criminal,* § 22:16 at 199, n.83 (7th ed. 2000) ("A target of a potential criminal investigation may be unwilling to settle civil claims against him if by doing so he increases the risk of prosecution and conviction.").

The amendment retains the language of the original rule that bars compromise evidence only when offered as evidence of the "validity," "invalidity," or "amount" of the disputed claim. The intent is to retain the extensive case law finding Rule 408 inapplicable when compromise evidence is offered for a purpose other than to prove the validity, invalidity, or amount of a disputed claim. *See, e.g., Athey v. Farmers Ins. Exchange,* 234 F.3d 357 (8th Cir. 2000) (evidence of settlement offer by insurer was properly admitted to prove insurer's bad faith); *Coakley & Williams v. Structural Concrete Equip.,* 973 F.2d 349 (4th Cir. 1992) (evidence of settlement is not precluded by Rule 408 where offered to proved a party's intent with respect to the scope of a release); *Cates v. Morgan Portable Bldg. Corp.,* 780 F.2d 683 (7th Cir. 1985) (Rule 408 does not bar evidence of a settlement when offered to prove a breach of the settlement agreement, as the purpose of the evidence is to prove the fact of settlement as opposed to the validity or amount of the underlying claim); *Uforma/Shelby Bus. Forms, Inc. v. NLRB*, 111 F.3d 1284 (6th Cir. 1997) (threats made in settlement negotiations were admissible; Rule 408 is inapplicable when the claim is based upon a wrong that is committed during the course of settlement negotiations). So for example, Rule 408 is inapplicable if offered to show that a party made fraudulent statements in order to settle a litigation.

The amendment does not affect the case law providing that Rule 408 is inapplicable when evidence of the compromise is offered to prove notice. *See, e.g., United States v. Austin*, 54 F.3d 394 (7th Cir. 1995) (no error to admit evidence of the defendant's settlement with the FTC, because it was offered to prove that the defendant was on notice that subsequent similar conduct was wrongful); *Spell v. McDaniel*, 824 F.2d 1380 (4th Cir. 1987) (in a civil rights action alleging that an officer used excessive force, a prior settlement by the City of another brutality claim was properly admitted to prove that the City was on notice of aggressive behavior by police officers).

The amendment prohibits the use of statements made in settlement negotiations when offered to impeach by prior inconsistent statement or through contradiction. Such broad impeachment would tend to swallow the exclusionary rule and would impair the public policy of promoting settlements. *See McCormick on Evidence* at 186 (5th ed. 1999) ("Use of statements made in compromise negotiations to impeach the testimony of a party, which is not specifically treated in Rule 408, is fraught with danger of misuse of the statements to prove liability, threatens frank interchange of information during negotiations, and generally should not be permitted."). *See also EEOC v. Gear Petroleum, Inc.*, 948 F.2d 1542 (10th Cir. 1991) (letter sent as part of settlement negotiation cannot be used to impeach defense witnesses by way of contradiction or prior inconsistent statement; such broad impeachment would undermine the policy of encouraging uninhibited settlement negotiations).

The amendment makes clear that Rule 408 excludes compromise evidence even when a party seeks to admit its own settlement offer or statements made in settlement negotiations. If a party were to reveal its own statement or offer, this could itself reveal the fact that the adversary entered into settlement negotiations. The protections of Rule 408 cannot be waived unilaterally because the Rule, by definition, protects both parties from having the fact of negotiation disclosed to the jury. Moreover, proof of statement and offers made in settlement would often have to be made through the testimony of attorneys, leading to the risks and costs of disqualification. *See generally Pierce v. F.R. Tripler & Co.*, 955 F.2d 820, 828 (2d Cir. 1992) (settlement offers are excluded under Rule 408 even if it is the offeror who seeks to admit them; noting that the "widespread admissibility of the substance of settlement offers could bring with it a rash of motions for disqualification of a party's chosen counsel who would likely become a witness at trial").

The sentence of the Rule referring to evidence "otherwise discoverable" has been deleted as superfluous. *See, e.g.*, Advisory Committee Note to Maine Rule of Evidence 408 (refusing to include the sentence in the Maine version of Rule 408 and noting that the sentence "seems to state what the law would be if it were omitted"); Advisory Committee Note to Wyoming Rule of Evidence 408 (refusing to include the sentence in Wyoming Rule 408 on the ground that it was "superfluous"). The intent of the sentence was to prevent a party from trying to immunize admissible information, such as a pre-existing document, through the

Rule 408   *FEDERAL RULES OF EVIDENCE*

pretense of disclosing it during compromise negotiations. *See Ramada Development Co. v. Rauch*, 644 F.2d 1097 (5th Cir. 1981). But even without the sentence, the Rule cannot be read to protect pre-existing information simply because it was presented to the adversary in compromise negotiations.

Note by Federal Judicial Center

The rule enacted by the Congress is the rule prescribed by the Supreme Court, amended by the insertion of the third sentence. Other amendments, proposed by the House bill, were not enacted . . .

Advisory Committee's Note

As a matter of general agreement, evidence of an offer to compromise a claim is not receivable in evidence as an admission of, as the case may be, the validity or invalidity of the claim. As with evidence of subsequent remedial measures, dealt with in Rule 407, exclusion may be based on two grounds. (1) The evidence is irrelevant, since the offer may be motivated by a desire for peace rather than from any concession of weakness of position. The validity of this position will vary as the amount of the offer varies in relation to the size of the claim and may also be influenced by other circumstances. (2) A more consistently impressive ground is promotion of the public policy favoring the compromise and settlement of disputes. McCormick §§ 76, 251. While the rule is ordinarily phrased in terms of offers of compromise, it is apparent that a similar attitude must be taken with respect to completed compromises when offered against a party thereto. This latter situation will not, of course, ordinarily occur except when a party to the present litigation has compromised with a third person.

The same policy underlies the provision of Rule 68 of the Federal Rules of Civil Procedure that evidence of an unaccepted offer of judgment is not admissible except in a proceeding to determine costs.

The practical value of the common law rule has been greatly diminished by its inapplicability to admissions of fact, even though made in the course of compromise negotiations, unless hypothetical, stated to be "without prejudice," or so connected with the offer as to be inseparable from it. McCormick § 251, pp. 540–541. An inevitable effect is to inhibit freedom of communication with respect to compromise, even among lawyers. Another effect is the generation of controversy over whether a given statement falls within or without the protected area. These considerations account for the expansion of the rule herewith to include evidence of conduct or statements made in compromise negotiations, as well as the offer or completed compromise itself. For similar provisions see California Evidence Code §§ 1152, 1154.

The policy considerations which underlie the rule do not come into play when the effort is to induce a creditor to settle an admittedly due amount for a lesser sum. McCormick § 251, p. 540. Hence the rule requires that the claim be disputed as to either validity or amount.

The final sentence of the rule serves to point out some limitations upon its applicability. Since the rule excludes only when the purpose is proving the validity or invalidity of the claim or its amount, an offer for another purpose is not within the rule. The illustrative situations mentioned in the rule are supported by the authorities. As to proving bias or prejudice of a witness, see Annot., 161 A.L.R. 395, contra, *Fenberg v. Rosenthal*, 348 Ill.App. 510, 109

N.E.2d 402 (1952), and negativing a contention of lack of due diligence in presenting a claim, 4 Wigmore § 1061. An effort to "buy off" the prosecution or a prosecuting witness in a criminal case is not within the policy of the rule of exclusion. McCormick § 251, p. 542.

For other rules of similar import, see Uniform Rules 52 and 53; California Evidence Code §§ 1152, 1154; Kansas Code of Civil Procedure §§ 60–452, 60–453; New Jersey Evidence Rules 52 and 53.

Rule 409.

PAYMENT OF MEDICAL AND SIMILAR EXPENSES

Evidence of furnishing or offering or promising to pay medical, hospital, or similar expenses occasioned by an injury is not admissible to prove liability for the injury.

Note by Federal Judicial Center

The rule enacted by the Congress is the rule prescribed by the Supreme Court without change.

Advisory Committee's Note

The considerations underlying this rule parallel those underlying Rules 407 and 408, which deal respectively with subsequent remedial measures and offers of compromise. As stated in Annot., 20 A.L.R.2d 291, 293:

> "[G]enerally, evidence of payment of medical, hospital, or similar expenses of an injured party by the opposing party, is not admissible, the reason often given being that such payment or offer is usually made from humane impulses and not from an admission of liability, and that to hold otherwise would tend to discourage assistance to the injured person."

Contrary to Rule 408, dealing with offers of compromise, the present rule does not extend to conduct or statements not a part of the act of furnishing or offering or promising to pay. This difference in treatment arises from fundamental differences in nature. Communication is essential if compromises are to be effected, and consequently broad protection of statements is needed. This is not so in cases of payments or offers or promises to pay medical expenses, where factual statements may be expected to be incidental in nature.

For rules on the same subject, but phrased in terms of "humanitarian motives," see Uniform Rule 52; California Evidence Code § 1152; Kansas Code of Civil Procedure § 60–452; New Jersey Evidence Rule 52.

Rule 410.

INADMISSIBILITY OF PLEAS, OFFERS OF PLEAS, PLEA DISCUSSIONS, AND RELATED STATEMENTS

Except as otherwise provided in this rule, evidence of the following is not, in any civil or criminal proceeding, admissible against the defendant who made the plea or was a participant in the plea discussions:

(1) a plea of guilty which was later withdrawn;

(2) a plea of nolo contendere;

(3) any statement made in the course of any proceedings under Rule 11 of the Federal Rules of Criminal Procedure or comparable state procedure regarding either of the foregoing pleas; or

(4) any statement made in the course of plea discussions with an attorney for the prosecuting authority which do not result in a plea of guilty or which result in a plea of guilty later withdrawn.

However, such a statement is admissible (i) in any proceeding wherein another statement made in the course of the same plea or plea discussions has been introduced and the statement ought in fairness be considered contemporaneously with it, or (ii) in a criminal proceeding for perjury or false statement if the statement was made by the defendant under oath, on the record and in the presence of counsel.

(As amended, effective date December 1, 1980.)

Advisory Committee's Note to 1980 Amendment

[The Amendment to Rule 11(e)(6) of the Rules of Criminal Procedure corresponds to the Amendment to Rule 410].

The major objective of the amendment to rule 11(e)(6) is to describe more precisely, consistent with the original purpose of the provision, what evidence relating to pleas or plea discussions is inadmissible. The present language is susceptible to interpretation which would make it applicable to a wide variety of statements made under various circumstances other than within the context of those plea discussions authorized by rule 11(e) and intended to be protected by subdivision (e)(6) of the rule. See United States v. Herman, 544 F.2d 791 (5th Cir.1977), discussed herein.

Fed.R.Ev. 410, as originally adopted by Pub.L. 93–595, provided in part that "evidence of a plea of guilty, later withdrawn, or a plea of nolo contendere, or of an offer to plead guilty or nolo contendere to the crime charged or any other crime, or of statements made in connection with any of the foregoing pleas or offers, is not admissible in any civil or criminal action, case, or proceeding against the person who made the plea or offer." (This rule was adopted with the proviso that it "shall be superseded by any amendment to the Federal Rules of Criminal Procedure which is inconsistent with this rule.") As the Advisory Committee Note explained: "Exclusion of offers to plead guilty or nolo has as its purpose the promotion of disposition of criminal cases by compromise." The amendment of Fed.R.Crim.P. 11, transmitted to Congress by the Supreme Court in April 1974, contained a subdivision (e)(6) essentially identical to the rule 410 language quoted above, as a part of a substantial revision of rule 11. The most significant feature of this revision was the express recognition given to the fact that the "attorney for the government and the attorney for the defendant or the defendant when acting pro se may engage in discussions with a view toward reaching" a plea agreement. Subdivision (e)(6) was intended to encourage such discussions. As noted in H.R.Rep. No. 94–247, 94th Cong., 1st Sess. 7 (1975), the purpose of subdivision (e)(6) is to not "discourage defendants from being completely candid and open during plea negotiations." Similarly, H.R.Rep. No. 94–414, 94th Cong., 1st Sess. 10 (1975), states that "Rule 11(e)(6) deals with the use of statements made in connection with plea agreements." (Rule 11(e)(6) was thereafter enacted, with the addition of the proviso allowing use of statements for purposes of impeachment and in a prosecution for perjury, and with the qualification that the inadmissible statements must also be "relevant to" the inadmissible pleas or offers. Pub.L. 94–64; Fed.R.Ev. 410 was then amended to conform. Pub.L. 94–149.)

While this history shows that the purpose of Fed.R.Ev. 410 and Fed. R.Crim.P. 11(e)(6) is to permit the unrestrained candor which produces effective plea discussions between the "attorney for the government and the attorney for the defendant or the defendant when acting pro se," given visibility and sanction in rule 11(e), a literal reading of the language of these two rules could reasonably lead to the conclusion that a broader rule of inadmissibility obtains. That is, because "statements" are generally inadmissible if "made in connection with, and relevant to" an "offer to plead guilty," it might be thought that an otherwise voluntary admission to law enforcement officials is rendered inadmissible merely because it was made in the hope of obtaining leniency by a plea. Some decisions interpreting rule 11(e)(6) point in this direction. See United States v. Herman, 544 F.2d 791 (5th Cir.1977)(defendant in custody of two postal inspectors during continuance of removal hearing instigated conversation with them and at some point said he would plead guilty to armed robbery if the murder charge was dropped; one inspector stated they were not "in position" to make any deals in this regard; held, defendant's statement inadmissible under rule 11(e)(6) because the defendant "made the statements during the course of a conversation in which he sought concessions from the government in return for a guilty plea"); United States v. Brooks, 536 F.2d 1137 (6th Cir.1976)(defendant telephoned postal inspector and offered to plead guilty if he got 2–year maximum; statement inadmissible).

The amendment makes inadmissible statements made "in the course of any proceedings under this rule regarding" either a plea of guilty later withdrawn or a plea of nolo contendere, and also statements "made in the course of plea discussions with an attorney for the government which do not result in a plea of guilty or which result in a plea of guilty later withdrawn." It is not limited to statements by the defendant himself, and thus would cover statements by defense counsel regarding defendant's incriminating admissions to him. It thus fully protects the plea discussion process authorized by rule 11 without attempting to deal with confrontations between suspects and law enforcement agents, which involve problems of quite different dimensions. See, e.g., ALI Model Code of Pre–Arraignment Procedure art. 140 and § 150.2(8) (Proposed Official Draft, 1975) (latter section requires exclusion if "a law enforcement officer induces any person to make a statement by promising leniency"). This change, it must be emphasized, does not compel the conclusion that statements made to law enforcement agents, especially when the agents purport to have authority to bargain, are inevitably admissible. Rather, the point is that such cases are not covered by the per se rule of 11(e)(6) and thus must be resolved by that body of law dealing with police interrogations.

If there has been a plea of guilty later withdrawn or a plea of nolo contendere, subdivision (e)(6)(C) makes inadmissible statements made "in the course of any proceedings under this rule" regarding such pleas. This includes, for example, admissions by the defendant when he makes his plea in court pursuant to rule 11 and also admissions made to provide the factual basis pursuant to subdivision (f). However, subdivision (e)(6)(C) is not limited to statements made in court. If the court were to defer its decision on a plea agreement pending examination of the presentence report, as authorized by subdivision (e)(2), statements made to the probation officer in connection with the preparation of that report would come within this provision.

This amendment is fully consistent with all recent and major law reform efforts on this subject. ALI Model Code of Pre-Arraignment Procedure § 350.7 (Proposed Official Draft, 1975), and ABA Standards Relating to Pleas of Guilty § 3.4 (Approved Draft, 1968) both provide:

> Unless the defendant subsequently enters a plea of guilty or nolo contendere which is not withdrawn, the fact that the defendant or his counsel and the prosecuting attorney engaged in plea discussions or made a plea agreement should not be received in evidence against or in favor of the defendant in any criminal or civil action or administrative proceedings.

The Commentary to the latter states:

> The above standard is limited to discussions and agreements with the prosecuting attorney. Sometimes defendants will indicate to the police their willingness to bargain, and in such instances these statements are sometimes admitted in court against the defendant. State v. Christian, 245 S.W.2d 895 (Mo.1952). If the police initiate this kind of discussion, this may have some bearing on the admissibility of the defendant's statement. However, the policy considerations relevant to this issue are better dealt with in the context of standards governing in-custody interrogation by the police.

Similarly, Unif.R.Crim.P. 441(d) (Approved Draft, 1974) provides that except under limited circumstances "no discussion between the parties or statement by the defendant or his lawyer under this Rule," i.e., the rule providing "the parties may meet to discuss the possibility of pretrial diversion * * * or of a plea agreement," are admissible. The amendment is likewise consistent with the typical state provision on this subject; see, e.g., Ill.S.Ct. Rule 402(f).

The "in the course of or as a consequence of such pleas or plea discussions" language of the amendment identifies with more precision than the present language the necessary relationship between the statements and the plea or discussion. See the dispute between the majority and concurring opinion in United States v. Herman, 544 F.2d 791 (5th Cir.1977), concerning the meanings and effect of the phrases "connection to" and "relevant to" in the present rule. Moreover, by relating the statements to "plea discussions" rather than "an offer to plead," the amendment ensures "that even an attempt to open plea bargaining [is] covered under the same rule of inadmissibility." United States v. Brooks, 536 F.2d 1137 (6th Cir.1976).

The last sentence of Rule 11(e)(6) is amended to provide a second exception to the general rule of nonadmissibility of the described statements. Under the amendment, such a statement is also admissible "in any proceeding wherein another statement made in the course of the same plea or plea discussions has been introduced and the statement ought in fairness be considered contemporaneously with it." This change is necessary so that, when evidence of statements made in the course of or as a consequence of a certain plea or plea discussions are introduced under circumstances not prohibited by this rule (e.g., not "against" the person who made the plea), other statements relating to the same plea or plea discussions may also be admitted when relevant to the matter at issue. For example, if a defendant upon a motion to dismiss a prosecution on some ground were able to admit certain statements made in aborted plea discussions in his favor, then other irrelevant statements made in the same plea discussions should be admissible against the defendant in the interest of determining the truth of the matter at issue. The language of the amendment follows closely that in Fed.R.Evid. 106, as the considerations involved are very similar.

The phrase "in any civil or criminal proceeding" has been moved from its present position, following the word "against," for purposes of clarity. An ambiguity presently exists because the word "against" may be read as referring either to the kind of proceeding in which the evidence is offered or the purpose for which it is offered. The change makes it clear that the latter construction is correct. No change is intended with respect to provisions making evidence rules inapplicable in certain situations. See, e.g., Fed.R.Evid. 104(a) and 1101(d).

Unlike ABA Standards Relating to Pleas of Guilty § 3.4 (Approved Draft, 1968), and ALI Model Code of Pre-Arraignment Procedure § 350.7 (Proposed Official Draft, 1975), rule 11(e)(6) does not also provide that the described evidence is inadmissible "in favor of" the defendant. This is not intended to suggest, however, that such evidence will inevitably be admissible in the defendant's favor. Specifically, no disapproval is intended of such decisions as United States v. Verdoorn, 528 F.2d 103 (8th Cir.1976), holding that the trial judge properly refused to permit the defendants to put into evidence at their trial the fact the prosecution had attempted to plea bargain with them, as "meaningful dialogue between the parties would, as a practical matter, be impossible if either party had to assume the risk that plea offers would be admissible in evidence."

Rule 411.

LIABILITY INSURANCE

Evidence that a person was or was not insured against liability is not admissible upon the issue whether the person acted negligently or otherwise wrongfully. This rule does not require the exclusion of evidence of insurance against liability when offered for another purpose, such as proof of agency, ownership, or control, or bias or prejudice of a witness.

Note by Federal Judicial Center

The rule enacted by the Congress is the rule prescribed by the Supreme Court without change.

Advisory Committee's Note

The courts have with substantial unanimity rejected evidence of liability insurance for the purpose of proving fault, and absence of liability insurance as proof of lack of fault. At best the inference of fault from the fact of insurance coverage is a tenuous one, as is its converse. More important, no doubt, has been the feeling that knowledge of the presence or absence of liability insurance would induce juries to decide cases on improper grounds. McCormick § 168; Annot., 4 A.L.R.2d 761. The rule is drafted in broad terms so as to include contributory negligence or other fault of a plaintiff as well as fault of a defendant.

The second sentence points out the limits of the rule, using well established illustrations. Id.

For similar rules see Uniform Rule 54; California Evidence Code § 1155; Kansas Code of Civil Procedure § 60–454; New Jersey Evidence Rule 54.

Rule 412.

SEX OFFENSE CASES; RELEVANCE OF ALLEGED VICTIM'S PAST SEXUAL BEHAVIOR OR ALLEGED SEXUAL PREDISPOSITION

(a) Evidence generally inadmissible. The following evidence is not admissible in any civil or criminal proceeding involving alleged sexual misconduct except as provided in subdivisions (b) and (c):

(1) Evidence offered to prove that any alleged victim engaged in other sexual behavior.

(2) Evidence offered to prove any alleged victim's sexual predisposition.

(b) Exceptions.

(1) In a criminal case, the following evidence is admissible, if otherwise admissible under these rules:

(A) evidence of specific instances of sexual behavior by the alleged victim offered to prove that a person other than the accused was the source of semen, injury or other physical evidence;

(B) evidence of specific instances of sexual behavior by the alleged victim with respect to the person accused of the sexual misconduct offered by the accused to prove consent or by the prosecution; and

(C) evidence the exclusion of which would violate the constitutional rights of the defendant.

(2) In a civil case, evidence offered to prove the sexual behavior or sexual predisposition of any alleged victim is admissible if it is otherwise admissible under these rules and its probative value substantially outweighs the danger of harm to any victim and of unfair prejudice to any party. Evidence of an alleged victim's reputation is admissible only if it has been placed in controversy by the alleged victim.

(c) Procedure to determine admissibility.

(1) A party intending to offer evidence under subdivision (b) must—

(A) file a written motion at least 14 days before trial specifically describing the evidence and stating the purpose for which it is offered unless the court, for good cause requires a different time for filing or permits filing during trial; and

(B) serve the motion on all parties and notify the alleged victim or, when appropriate, the alleged victim's guardian or representative.

(2) Before admitting evidence under this rule the court must conduct a hearing in camera and afford the victim and parties a right to attend and be heard. The motion, related papers, and the record of the hearing must be sealed and remain under seal unless the court orders otherwise.

Advisory Committee's Note to 1994 Amendment

Rule 412 has been revised to diminish some of the confusion engendered by the original rule and to expand the protection afforded alleged victims of sexual misconduct. Rule 412 applies to both civil and criminal proceedings. The rule aims to safeguard the alleged victim against the invasion of privacy, potential embarrassment and sexual stereotyping that is associated with public disclosure of intimate sexual details and the infusion of sexual innuendo into the factfinding process. By affording victims protection in most instances, the rule also encourages victims of sexual misconduct to institute and to participate in legal proceedings against alleged offenders.

Rule 412 seeks to achieve these objectives by barring evidence relating to the alleged victim's sexual behavior or alleged sexual predisposition, whether offered as substantive evidence of for impeachment, except in designated circumstance in which the probative value of the evidence significantly outweighs possible harm to the victim.

The revised rule applies in all cases involving sexual misconduct without regard to whether the alleged victim or person accused is a party to the litigation. Rule 412 extends to "pattern" witnesses in both criminal and civil cases whose testimony about other instances of sexual misconduct by the person accused is otherwise admissible. When the case does not involve alleged sexual misconduct, evidence relating to a third-party witness' alleged sexual activities is not within the ambit of Rule 412. The witness will, however, be protected by other rules such as Rules 404 and 608, as well as Rule 403.

The terminology "alleged victim" is used because there will frequently be a factual dispute as to whether sexual misconduct occurred. It does not connote any requirement that the misconduct be alleged in the pleadings. Rule 412 does not, however, apply unless the person against whom the evidence is offered can reasonably be characterized as a "victim of alleged sexual misconduct." When this is not the case, as for instance in a defamation action involving statements concerning sexual misconduct in which the evidence is offered to show that the alleged defamatory statements were true or did not damage the plaintiff's reputation, neither Rule 404 nor this rule will operate to bar the evidence; Rule 401 and 403 will continue to control. Rule 412 will, however, apply in a Title VII action in which the plaintiff has alleged sexual harassment.

The reference to a person "accused" is also used in a non-technical sense. There is no requirement that there be a criminal charge pending against the person or even that the misconduct would constitute a criminal offense. Evidence offered to prove allegedly false prior claims by the victim is not barred by Rule 412. However, the evidence is subject to the requirements of Rule 404.

Subdivision (a). As amended, Rule 412 bars evidence offered to prove the victim's sexual behavior and alleged sexual predisposition. Evidence, which might otherwise be admissible under Rules 402, 404(b), 405, 607, 608, 609 or some other evidence rule, must be excluded if Rule 412 so requires. The word "other" is used to suggest some flexibility in admitting evidence "intrinsic" to the alleged sexual misconduct. Cf. Committee Note to 1991 amendment to Rule 404(b).

Past sexual behavior connotes all activities that involve actual physical conduct, i.e. sexual intercourse or sexual contact. See, e.g., United States v. Galloway, 937 F.2d 542 (10th Cir.1991), cert. denied, 506 U.S. 957, 113 S.Ct. 418, 121 L.Ed.2d 341 (1992)(use of contraceptives inadmissible since use implies sexual activity); United States v. One Feather, 702 F.2d 736 (8th Cir.1983) (birth of an illegitimate child inadmissible); State v. Carmichael, 240 Kan. 149, 727 P.2d 918, 925 (1986)(evidence of venereal disease inadmissible). In addition, the word "behavior" should be construed to include activities of the mind, such as fantasies of dreams. See 23 C. Wright and K. Graham, Jr., Federal Practice and Procedure, § 5384 at p. 548 (1980) ("While there may be some doubt under statutes that require 'conduct,' it would seem that the language of Rule 412 is broad enough to encompass the behavior of the mind.").

The rule has been amended to also exclude all other evidence relating to an alleged victim of sexual misconduct that is offered to prove a sexual predisposition. This amendment is designed to exclude evidence that does not directly refer to sexual activities or thoughts but that the proponent believes may have a sexual connotation for the factfinder. Admission of such evidence would contravene Rule 412's objectives of shielding the alleged victim from potential embarrassment and safeguarding the victim against stereotypical thinking. Consequently, unless the (b)(2) exception is satisfied, evidence such as that relating to the alleged victim's mode of dress, speech, or life-style will not be admissible.

The introductory phrase in subdivision (a) was deleted because it lacked clarity and contained no explicit reference to the other provisions of the law that were intended to be overridden. The conditional clause, "except as provided in subdivisions (b) and (c)" is intended to make clear that evidence of the types described in subdivision (a) is admissible only under the strictures of those sections.

The reason for extending the rule to all criminal cases is obvious. The strong social policy of protecting a victim's privacy and encouraging victims to come forward to report criminal acts is not confined to cases that involve a charge of sexual assault. The need to protect the victim is equally great when a defendant is charged with kidnapping, and evidence is offered, either to prove motive or as background, that the defendant sexually assaulted the victim.

The reason for extending Rule 412 to civil cases is equally obvious. The need to protect alleged victims against invasions of privacy, potential embarrassment, and unwarranted sexual stereotyping, and the wish to encourage victims to come forward when they have been sexually molested do not disappear because the context has shifted from a criminal prosecution to a claim for damages or injunctive relief. There is a strong social policy in not only punishing those who engage in sexual misconduct, but in also providing relief to the victim. Thus, Rule 412 applies in any civil case in which a person claims to be the victim of sexual misconduct, such as actions for sexual battery or sexual harassment.

Subdivision (b). Subdivision (b) spells out the specific circumstances in which some evidence may be admissible that would otherwise be barred by the general rule expressed in subdivision (a). As amended, Rule 412 will be virtually unchanged in criminal cases, but will provide protection to any person alleged to be a victim of sexual misconduct regardless of the charge actually brought against an accused. A new exception has been added for civil cases.

In a criminal case, evidence may be admitted under subdivision (b)(1) pursuant to three possible exceptions, provided the evidence also satisfies other requirements for admissibility specified in the Federal Rules of Evidence, including Rule 403. Subdivisions (b)(1)(A) and (b)(1)(B) require proof in the form of specific instances of sexual behavior in recognition of the limited probative value and dubious reliability of evidence of reputation or evidence in the form of an opinion.

Under subdivision (b)(1)(A), evidence of specific instances of sexual behavior with persons other than the person whose sexual misconduct is alleged may be admissible if it is offered to prove that another person was the source of semen, injury or other physical evidence. Where the prosecution has directly or indirectly asserted that the physical evidence originated with the accused, the defendant must be afforded an opportunity to prove that another person was responsible. See United States v. Begay, 937 F.2d 515, 523 n. 10 (10th Cir.1991). Evidence offered for the specific purpose identified in this subdivision may still be excluded if it does not satisfy Rules 401 or 403. See, e.g., United States v. Azure, 845 F.2d 1503, 1505–06 (8th Cir.1988)(10 year old victim's injuries indicated recent use of force; court excluded evidence of consensual sexual activities with witness who testified at in camera hearing that he had never hurt victim and failed to establish recent activities).

Under the exception in subdivision (b)(1)(B), evidence of specific instances of sexual behavior with respect to the person whose sexual misconduct is alleged is admissible if offered to prove consent or offered by the prosecution. Admissible pursuant to this exception might be evidence of prior instances of sexual activities between the alleged victim and the accused, as well as statements in which the alleged victim expresses an intent to engage in sexual intercourse with the accused, or voiced sexual fantasies involving that specific accused. In a prosecution for child sexual abuse, for example, evidence of uncharged sexual activity between the accused and the alleged victim offered by the prosecution may be admissible pursuant to Rule 404(b) to show a pattern of behavior. Evidence relating to the victim's alleged sexual predisposition is not admissible pursuant to this exception.

Under subdivision (b)(1)(C), evidence of specific instances of conduct may not be excluded if the result would be to deny a criminal defendant the protections afforded by the Constitution. For example, statements in which the victim has expressed an intent to have sex with the first person encountered on a particular occasion might not be excluded without violating the due process right of a rape defendant seeking to prove consent. Recognition of this basic principle was expressed in subdivision (b)(1) of the original rule. The United States Supreme Court has recognized that in various circumstances a defendant may have a right to introduce evidence otherwise precluded by an evidence rule under the Confrontation Clause. See, e.g., Olden v. Kentucky, 488 U.S. 227, 109 S.Ct. 480, 102 L.Ed.2d 513 (1988) (defendant in rape cases had right to inquire into alleged victim's cohabitation with another man to show bias).

Subdivision (b)(2) governs the admissibility of otherwise proscribed evidence in civil cases. It employs a balancing test rather than the specific exceptions stated in subdivision (b)(1) in recognition of the difficulty of foreseeing future developments in the law. Greater flexibility is needed to accommodate evolving causes of action such as claims for sexual harassment.

The balancing test requires the proponent of the evidence, whether plaintiff or defendant, to convince the court that the probative value of the proffered evidence "substantially outweighs the danger of harm to any victim and of unfair prejudice to any party." This test for admitting evidence offered to prove sexual behavior or sexual propensity in civil cases differs in three respects from the general rule governing admissibility set forth in Rule 403. First, it reverses the usual procedure spelled out in Rule 403 by shifting the burden to the proponent to demonstrate admissibility rather than making the opponent justify exclusion of the evidence. Second, the standard expressed in subdivision (b)(2) is more stringent than in the original rule; it raises the threshold for admission by requiring that the probative value of the evidence substantially outweigh the specified dangers. Finally, the Rule 412 test puts "harm to the victim" on the scale in addition to prejudice to the parties.

Evidence of reputation may be received in a civil case only if the alleged victim has put his or her reputation into controversy. The victim may do so without making a specific allegation in a pleading. Cf. Fed.R.Civ.P. 35(a).

Subdivision (c). Amended subdivision (c) is more concise and understandable than the subdivision it replaces. The requirement of a motion before trial is continued in the amended rule, as is the provision that a late motion may be permitted for good cause shown. In deciding whether to permit late filing, the court may take into account the conditions previously included in the rule: namely whether the evidence is newly discovered and could not have been obtained earlier through the existence of due diligence, and whether the issue to which such evidence relates has newly arisen in the case. The rule recognizes that in some instances the circumstances that justify an application to introduce evidence otherwise barred by Rule 412 will not become apparent until trial.

The amended rule provides that before admitting evidence that falls within the prohibition of Rule 412(a), the court must hold a hearing in camera at which the alleged victim and any party must be afforded the right to be present and an opportunity to be heard. All papers connected with the motion must be kept and remain under seal during the course of trial and appellate proceedings unless otherwise ordered. This is to assure that the privacy of the alleged victim is preserved in all cases in which the court rules that proffered evidence is not admissible, and in which the hearing refers to matters that are not received, or are received in another form.

The procedures set forth in subdivision (c) do not apply to discovery of a victim's past sexual conduct or predisposition in civil cases, which will be continued to be governed by Fed. R. Civ. P. 26. In order not to undermine the rationale of Rule 412, however, courts should enter appropriate orders pursuant to Fed. R. Civ. P. 26 (c) to protect the victim against unwarranted inquiries and to ensure confidentiality. Courts should presumptively issue protective orders barring discovery unless the party seeking discovery makes a showing that the evidence sought to be discovered would be relevant under the facts and theories of the particular case, and cannot be obtained except through discovery. In an action for sexual harassment, for instance, while some evidence of the alleged victim's sexual behavior and/or predisposition in the workplace may perhaps be relevant, non-work place conduct will usually be irrelevant. Cf. Burns v. McGregor Electronic Industries, Inc., 989 F.2d 959, 962–63 (8th Cir.1993) (posing for a nude magazine outside work hours is irrelevant to issue of unwelcomeness of sexual advances at work). Confidentiality orders should be presumptively granted as well.

One substantive change made in subdivision (c) is the elimination of the following sentence: "Notwithstanding subdivision (b) of Rule 104, if the relevancy of the evidence which the accused seeks to offer in the trial depends upon the fulfillment of a condition of fact, the court, at the hearing in chambers or at a subsequent hearing in chambers scheduled for such purpose, shall accept evidence on the issue of whether such condition of fact is fulfilled and shall determine such issue." On its face, this language would appear to authorize a trial judge to exclude evidence of past sexual conduct between alleged victim and an accused or a defendant in a civil case based upon the judge's belief that such past acts did not occur. Such an authorization raises questions of invasion of the right to a jury trial under the Sixth and Seventh Amendments. See 1 S. Saltzburg & M. Martin, Federal Rules of Evidence Manual, 396–97 (5th ed. 1990).

The Advisory Committee concluded that the amended rule provided adequate protection for all persons claiming to be the victims of sexual misconduct, and that it was inadvisable to continue to include a provision in the rule that has been confusing and that raises substantial constitutional issues.

Editorial Note

The 1994 amendment to Rule 412 was drafted by the Advisory Committee on the Federal Rules of Evidence, and proposed to the Supreme Court by the Judicial Conference. The Supreme Court promulgated the rule except for subdivision (b)(2) dealing with civil cases. It expressed concern that the civil provision might infringe the Rules Enabling Act, and be unfair to defendants. Congress, however, enacted the entire text of the rule proposed by the Judicial Conference pursuant to Pub.L. 103–322, Title IV, § 40141(b), September 13, 1994, 108 Stat. 1919, effective December 1, 1994. The congressional Conference Report stated: "the Conferees intend that the Advisory Committee Note on Rule 412, as transmitted by the Judicial Conference of the United States to the Supreme Court on October 25, 1993, applies to Rule 412 as enacted by this section." H.R. Conf. Rep. No. 103–711, 103d Cong., 2d Sess. 383, reprinted in 1994 U.S. Code Cong. & Ad. News 1801, 1851.

Rule 412 originally applied only to criminal cases. It was added to the Federal Rules of Evidence by P.L. 95–540, § 2(a), Oct. 28, 1978, (and amended by Sections 7046 and 7075 of the Anti–Drug Abuse Act of 1988, Pub.L. 100–690, 102 Stat. 4181, Nov. 18, 1988, which made the rule applicable to sex offenses as defined in chapter 109A of title 18, United States Code).

In the House of Representatives, Representatives Mann, Wiggins and Holtzman discussed the bill at length. The following excerpts from their remarks suggests the tenor of the discussion:

> Mr. MANN. Mr. Speaker, for many years in this country, evidentiary rules have permitted the introduction of evidence about a rape victim's prior sexual conduct. Defense lawyers were permitted great latitude in bringing out intimate details about a rape victim's life. Such evidence quite often

serves no real purpose and only results in embarrassment to the rape victim and unwarranted public intrusion into her private life.

The evidentiary rules that permit such inquiry have in recent years come under question: and the States have taken the lead to change and modernize their evidentiary rules about evidence of a rape victim's prior sexual behavior. The bill before us similarly seeks to modernize the Federal evidentiary rules.

The present Federal Rules of Evidence reflect the traditional approach. If a defendant in a rape case raises the defense of consent, that defendant may then offer evidence about the victim's prior sexual behavior. Such evidence may be in the form of opinion evidence, evidence of reputation, or evidence of specific instances of behavior. Rule 404(a)(2) of the Federal Rules of Evidence permits the introduction of evidence of a "pertinent character trait." The advisory committee note to that rule cites, as an example of what the rule covers, the character of a rape victim when the issue is consent. Rule 405 of the Federal Rules of Evidence permits the use of opinion or reputation evidence or the use of evidence of specific behavior to show a character trait.

Thus, Federal evidentiary rules permit a wide ranging inquiry into the private conduct of a rape victim, even though that conduct may have at best a tenuous connection to the offense for which the defendant is being tried. H.R. 4727 amends the Federal Rules of Evidence to add a new rule, applicable only in criminal cases, to spell out when, and under what conditions, evidence of a rape victim's prior sexual behavior can be admitted. The new rule provides that reputation or opinion evidence about a rape victim's prior sexual behavior is not admissible. The new rule also provides that a court cannot admit evidence of specific instances of a rape victim's prior sexual conduct except in three circumstances.

The first circumstance is where the Constitution requires that the evidence be admitted. This exception is intended to cover those infrequent instances where, because of an unusual chain of circumstances, the general rule of inadmissibility, if followed, would result in denying the defendant a constitutional right.

The second circumstance in which the defendant can offer evidence of specific instances of a rape victim's prior sexual behavior is where the defendant raises the issue of consent and the evidence is of sexual behavior with the defendant. To admit such evidence, however, the court must find that the evidence is relevant and that its probative value outweighs the danger of unfair prejudice.

The third circumstance in which a court can admit evidence of specific instances of a rape victim's prior sexual behavior is where the evidence is of behavior with someone other than the defendant and is offered by the defendant on the issue of whether or not he was the source of semen or injury. Again, such evidence will be admitted only if the court finds that the evidence is relevant and that its probative value outweighs the danger of unfair prejudice.

The new rule further provides that before evidence is admitted under any of these exceptions, there must be an in camera hearing—that is, a proceeding that takes place in the judge's chambers out of the presence of the jury and the general public. At this hearing, the defendant will present the evidence he intends to offer and be able to argue why it should be admitted. The prosecution, of course, will be able to argue against that evidence being admitted.

The purpose of the in camera hearing is twofold. It gives the defendant an opportunity to demonstrate to the court why certain evidence is admissible and ought to be presented to the jury. At the same time, it protects the privacy of the rape victim in those instances when the court finds that evidence is inadmissible. Of course, if the court finds the evidence to be admissible, the evidence will be presented to the jury in open court.

The effect of this legislation, therefore, is to preclude the routine use of evidence of specific instances of a rape victim's prior sexual behavior. Such evidence will be admitted only in clearly and narrowly defined circumstances and only after an in camera hearing. In determining the admissibility of such evidence, the court will consider all of the facts and circumstances surrounding the evidence, such as the amount of time that lapsed between the alleged prior act and the rape charged in the prosecution. The greater the lapse of time, of course, the less likely it is that such evidence will be admitted.

Mr. Speaker, the principal purpose of this legislation is to protect rape victims from the degrading and embarrassing disclosure of intimate details about their private lives. It does so by narrowly circumscribing when such evidence may be admitted. It does not do so, however, by sacrificing any constitutional right possessed by the defendant. The bill before us fairly balances the interests involved—the rape victim's interest in protecting her private life from unwarranted public exposure; the defendant's interest in being able adequately to present a defense by offering relevant and probative evidence; and society's interest in a fair trial, one where unduly prejudicial evidence is not permitted to becloud the issues before the jury.

. . .

Mr. WIGGINS. Mr. Speaker, this legislation addresses itself to a subject that is certainly a proper one for our consideration. Many of us have been troubled for years about the indiscriminate and prejudicial use of testimony with respect to a victim's prior sexual behavior in rape and similar cases. This bill deals with that problem. It is not, in my opinion, Mr. Speaker, a perfect bill in the manner in which it deals with the problem, but my objections are not so fundamental as would lead me to oppose the bill.

I think, Mr. Speaker, that it is unwise to adopt a per se rule absolutely excluding evidence of reputation and opinion with respect to the victim—and this bill does that—but it is difficult for me to foresee the specific case in which such evidence might be admissible. The trouble is this, Mr. Speaker: None of us can foresee perfectly all of the various circumstances under which the propriety of evidence might be before the court. If this bill has a defect, in my view it is because it adopts a per se rule with respect to opinion and reputation evidence. Alternatively we might have permitted that evidence to be considered in camera as we do other evidence under the bill.

I should note, however, in fairness, having expressed minor reservations, that the bill before the House at this time does improve significantly upon the bill which was presented to our committee.

I will not detail all of those improvements but simply observe that the bill upon which we shall soon vote is a superior product to that which was initially considered by our subcommittee.

. . .

Ms. HOLTZMAN. Too often in this country victims of rape are humiliated and harassed when they report and prosecute the rape. Bullied and cross-examined about their prior sexual experiences, many find the trial almost as degrading as the rape itself. Since rape trials become inquisitions into the victim's morality, not trials of the defendant's innocence or guilt, it is not surprising that it is the least reported crime. It is estimated that as few as one in ten rapes is ever reported.

Mr. Speaker, over 30 States have taken some action to limit the vulnerability of rape victims to such humiliating cross-examination of their past sexual experiences and intimate personal histories. In federal courts, however, it is permissible still to subject rape victims to brutal cross-examination about their past sexual histories. H.R. 4727 would rectify this problem in Federal courts and I hope, also serve as a model to suggest to the remaining states that reform of existing rape laws is important to the equity of our criminal justice system.

H.R. 4727 applies only to criminal rape cases in Federal courts. The bill provides that neither the prosecution nor the defense can introduce any reputation or opinion evidence about the victim's past sexual conduct. It does permit, however, the introduction of specific evidence about the victim's past sexual conduct in three very limited circumstances.

First, this evidence can be introduced if it deals with the victim's past sexual relations with the defendant and is relevant to the issue of whether she consented. Second, when the defendant claims he had no relations with the victim, he can use evidence of the victim's past sexual relations with others if the evidence rebuts the victim's claim that the rape caused certain physical consequences, such as semen or injury. Finally, the evidence can be introduced if it is constitutionally required. This last exception, added in subcommittee, will insure that the defendant's constitutional rights are protected.

Before any such evidence can be introduced, however, the court must determine at a hearing in chambers that the evidence falls within one of the exceptions.

Furthermore, unless constitutionally required, the evidence of specific instances of prior sexual conduct cannot be introduced at all if it would be more prejudicial and inflammatory than probative.

Congressional Record, October 10, 1978, H11944–11945.

In the Senate, further explanatory remarks were offered by Senators Thurmond, Bayh and Biden.

Mr. THURMOND....

H.R. 4727, as passed by the House, essentially does the following:

First. Prohibits any use of reputation or opinion evidence of the past sexual behavior of the victim in a criminal prosecution for rape or assault with intent to commit rape.

Second. Restricts the use of direct evidence of the past sexual behavior of the victim of rape and assault with intent to commit rape to three situations:

(a) Where the judge finds after a hearing that admission of the evidence is required under the Constitution;

(b) The judge finds after a hearing that the past sexual behavior was with a person other than the accused and is being offered to show that someone other than the accused was the source of semen or injury; and

(c) The judge finds after a hearing that the past sexual behavior was with the accused and is offered by the accused solely on the issue of consent.

Third. Creates notice and hearing procedures on the evidentiary issues delineated by the bill.

. . .

Mr. BAYH....

.... Under the provisions of H.R. 4727, a new rule of evidence applicable only in criminal cases would make evidence of prior sexual history inadmissible except under three circumstances.

First, in order to make sure that we are [not] infringing upon a defendant's civil liberties, such evidence may be admissible where it is required under the constitution. This exception is intended to cover those instances where, because of an unusual set of circumstances, if the general rule of inadmissibility were to be followed, it might deprive a defendant of his constitutional rights.

The second circumstance in which the defendant can offer evidence of a rape victim's prior sexual history is where the defendant raises the issue of consent and the evidence is of sexual behavior with the defendant.

The third circumstance in which a court can admit evidence of prior sexual history is where the evidence may show that sexual relations occurred between the victim and someone other than the defendant.

Evidence which might fall under these exceptions is not automatically admissible however. If the defendant proposed to offer evidence in either category, he must first make a written offer of proof which is submitted to the presiding judge. If the judge then decides after an in camera hearing that such evidence is admissible, he must make a written order specifically identifying the evidence to be admitted and describing exactly the areas of cross-examination to be permitted. This procedure is designed to afford the victim maximum notice of the questioning that may occur.

Mr. BIDEN....

... [It] is important that we keep in mind the constitutional rights of the defendant to a fair trial. Therefore this bill has been carefully drafted to keep the reform within constitutional limits.

The bill clearly permits the defendant to offer evidence where it is constitutionally required. Indeed, the bill specifically recognizes two circumstances where the evidence may be admitted. However, the bill also would establish a special in camera procedure whereby the question of admissibility could be litigated without harm to the privacy rights of the victim or the constitutional rights of the defendant.

Congressional Record, October 12, 1978, S18579–S18581.

Rule 413.

EVIDENCE OF SIMILAR CRIMES IN SEXUAL ASSAULT CASES

(a) In a criminal case in which the defendant is accused of an offense of sexual assault, evidence of the defendant's commission of another offense or offenses of sexual assault is admissible, and may be considered for its bearing on any matter to which it is relevant.

(b) In a case in which the Government intends to offer evidence under this rule, the attorney for the Government shall disclose the evidence to the defendant, including statements of witnesses or a summary of the substance of any testimony that is expected to be offered, at least fifteen days before the scheduled date of trial or at such later time as the court may allow for good cause.

(c) This rule shall not be construed to limit the admission or consideration of evidence under any other rule.

(d) For purposes of this rule and Rule 415, "offense of sexual assault" means a crime under Federal law or the law of a State (as defined in section 513 of title 18, United States Code) that involved—

(1) any conduct proscribed by chapter 109A of title 18, United States Code;

(2) contact, without consent, between any part of the defendant's body or an object and the genitals or anus of another person;

(3) contact, without consent, between the genitals or anus of the defendant and any part of another person's body;

(4) deriving sexual pleasure or gratification from the infliction of death, bodily injury, or physical pain on another person; or

(5) an attempt or conspiracy to engage in conduct described in paragraphs (1)–(4).

Editorial Note

See Editorial Note to Rule 415.

Rule 414.

EVIDENCE OF SIMILAR CRIMES IN CHILD MOLESTATION CASES

(a) In a criminal case in which the defendant is accused of an offense of child molestation, evidence of the defendant's commission of another offense or offenses of child molestation is admissible, and may be considered for its bearing on any matter to which it is relevant.

(b) In a case in which the Government intends to offer evidence under this rule, the attorney for the Government shall disclose the evidence to the defendant, including statements of witnesses or a summary of the substance of any testimony that is expected to be offered, at least fifteen days before the scheduled date of trial or at such later time as the court may allow for good cause.

(c) This rule shall not be construed to limit the admission or consideration of evidence under any other rule.

(d) For purposes of this rule and Rule 415, "child" means a person below the age of fourteen, and "offense of child molestation" means a crime under Federal law or the law of a State (as defined in section 513 of title 18, United States Code) that involved—

(1) any conduct proscribed by chapter 109A of title 18, United States Code, that was committed in relation to a child;

(2) any conduct proscribed by chapter 110 of title 18, United States Code;

(3) contact between any part of the defendant's body or an object and the genitals or anus of a child;

(4) contact between the genitals or anus of the defendant and any part of the body of a child;

(5) deriving sexual pleasure or gratification from the infliction of death, bodily injury, or physical pain on a child; or

(6) an attempt or conspiracy to engage in conduct described in paragraphs (1)–(5).

Editorial Note

See Editorial Note to Rule 415.

Rule 415.

EVIDENCE OF SIMILAR ACTS IN CIVIL CASES CONCERNING SEXUAL ASSAULT OR CHILD MOLESTATION

(a) In a civil case in which a claim for damages or other relief is predicated on a party's alleged commission of conduct constituting an offense of sexual assault or child molestation, evidence of that party's commission of another offense or offenses of sexual assault or child molestation is admissible and may be considered as provided in Rule 413 and Rule 414 of these rules.

(b) A party who intends to offer evidence under this Rule shall disclose the evidence to the party against whom it will be offered, including statements of witnesses or a summary of the substance of any testimony that is expected to be offered, at least fifteen days before the scheduled date of trial or at such later time as the court may allow for good cause.

(c) This rule shall not be construed to limit the admission or consideration of evidence under any other rule.

Editorial Note

Congress enacted Rules 413–415 pursuant to Pub.L. 103–322, Title XXXII, § 320935, September 13, 1994, 108 Stat. 2135 with a contingent effective date. The legislation required the Judicial Conference to make recommendations regarding the legislation within 150 days after enactment. The Judicial Conference disapproved of the policies expressed in Rules 413–415 and recommended that Congress should reconsider its decision, or that it should adopt an amendment to Rule 404 that embodies the policies of Rules 413–415. As provided in the 1994 legislation, Rules 413–415 took effect on July 10, 1995—150 days after the Judicial Conference's recommendation—because Congress failed to act.

ARTICLE V. PRIVILEGES

Rule 501.

GENERAL RULE

Except as otherwise required by the Constitution of the United States or provided by Act of Congress or in rules prescribed by the Supreme Court pursuant to statutory authority, the privilege of a witness, person, government, State, or political subdivision thereof shall be governed by the principles of the common law as they may be interpreted by the courts of the United States in the light of reason and experience. However, in civil actions and proceedings, with respect to an element of a claim or defense as to which State law supplies the rule of decision, the privilege of a witness, person, government, State, or political subdivision thereof shall be determined in accordance with State law.

Note by Federal Judicial Center

The rules enacted by the Congress substituted the single Rule 501 in place of the 13 rules dealing with privilege prescribed by the Supreme Court as Article V. The 13 superseded rules, with Advisory Committee's Notes, are included in the Appendix. The reasons given in support of the congressional action are stated in the Report of the House Committee on the Judiciary, the Report of the Senate Committee on the Judiciary, and Conference Report, set forth below.

Report of House Committee on the Judiciary

... The Committee also included in its amendment a proviso modeled after Rule 302 and similar to language added by the Committee to Rule 601 relating to the competency of witnesses. The proviso is designed to require the application of State privilege law in civil actions and proceedings governed by Erie R. Co. v. Tompkins, 304 U.S. 64, 58 S.Ct. 817, 82 L.Ed. 1188 (1938), a result in accord with current federal court decisions. See Republic Gear Co. v. Borg–Warner Corp., 381 F.2d 551, 555–556 n. 2 (2d Cir.1967). The Committee deemed the proviso to be necessary in the light of the Advisory Committee's view (see its note to Court Rule 501) that this result is not mandated under *Erie*.

The rationale underlying the proviso is that federal law should not supersede that of the States in substantive areas such as privilege absent a compelling reason. The Committee believes that in civil cases in the federal courts where an element of a claim or defense is not grounded upon a federal question, there is no federal interest strong enough to justify departure from State policy. In addition, the Committee considered that the Court's proposed Article V would have promoted forum shopping in some civil actions, depending upon differences in the privilege law applied as among the State and federal courts. The Committee's proviso, on the other hand, under which the federal courts are bound to apply the State's privilege law in actions founded upon a State-created right or defense, removes the incentive to "shop".

Report of Senate Committee on the Judiciary

Two other comments on the privilege rule should be made. The committee has received a considerable volume of correspondence from psychiatric organizations and psychiatrists concerning the deletion of rule 504 of the rule submitted by the Supreme Court. It should be clearly understood that, in approving this general rule as to privileges, the action of Congress should not be understood as disapproving any recognition of a psychiatrist-patient, or husband-wife, or any other of the enumerated privileges contained in the Supreme Court rules. Rather, our action should be understood as reflecting the view that the recognition of a privilege based on a confidential relationship and other privileges should be determined on a case-by-case basis.

Further, we would understand that the prohibition against spouses testifying against each other is considered a rule of privilege and covered by this rule and not by rule 601 of the competency of witnesses.

Conference Report

Rule 501 deals with the privilege of a witness not to testify. Both the House and Senate bills provide that federal privilege law applies in criminal cases. In civil actions and proceedings, the House bill provides that state privilege law applies "to an element of a claim or defense as to which State law supplies the rule of decision." The Senate bill provides that "in civil actions and proceedings arising under 28 U.S.C. § 1332 or 28 U.S.C. § 1335, or between citizens of different States and removed under 28 U.S.C. § 1441(b) the privilege of a witness, person, government, State or political subdivision thereof is determined in accordance with State law, unless with respect to the particular claim or defense, Federal law supplies the rule of decision."

The wording of the House and Senate bills differ in the treatment of civil actions and proceedings. The rule in the House bill applies to evidence that relates to "an element of a claim or defense." If an item of proof tends to support or defeat a claim or defense, or an element of a claim or defense, and if state law supplies the rule of decision for that claim or defense, then state privilege law applies to that item of proof.

Under the provision in the House bill, therefore, state privilege law will usually apply in diversity cases. There may be diversity cases, however, where a claim or defense is based upon federal law. In such instances, federal privilege law will apply to evidence relevant to the federal claim or defense. See Sola Electric Co. v. Jefferson Electric Co., 317 U.S. 173, 63 S.Ct. 172, 87 L.Ed. 165 (1942).

In nondiversity jurisdiction civil cases, federal privilege law will generally apply. In those situations where a federal court adopts or incorporates state law to fill interstices or gaps in federal statutory phrases, the court generally will apply federal privilege law. As Justice Jackson has said:

> A federal court sitting in a non-diversity case such as this does not sit as a local tribunal. In some cases it may see fit for special reasons to give the law of a particular state highly persuasive or even controlling effect, but in the last analysis its decision turns upon the law of the United States, not that of any state.

D'Oench, Duhme & Co. v. Federal Deposit Insurance Corp., 315 U.S. 447, 471, 62 S.Ct. 676, 685, 86 L.Ed. 956 (1942)(Jackson, J., concurring). When a federal court chooses to absorb state law, it is applying the state law as a matter of federal common law. Thus, state law does not supply the rule of decision (even though the federal court may apply a rule derived from state decisions), and state privilege law would not apply. See C.A. Wright, Federal Courts 251–252 (2d ed. 1970); Holmberg v. Armbrecht, 327 U.S. 392, 66 S.Ct. 582, 90 L.Ed. 743 (1946); DeSylva v. Ballentine, 351 U.S. 570, 581, 76 S.Ct. 974, 980, 100 L.Ed. 1415 (1956); 9 Wright & Miller, Federal Rules and Procedure § 2408.

In civil actions and proceedings, where the rule of decision as to a claim or defense or as to an element of a claim or defense is supplied by state law, the House provision requires that state privilege law apply.

The Conference adopts the House provision.

Rule 502.

ATTORNEY–CLIENT PRIVILEGE AND WORK PRODUCT; LIMITATIONS ON WAIVER

The following provisions apply, in the circumstances set out, to disclosure of a communication or information covered by the attorney-client privilege or work-product protection.

(a) DISCLOSURE MADE IN A FEDERAL PROCEEDING OR TO A FEDERAL OFFICE OR AGENCY; SCOPE OF A WAIVER.—When the disclosure is made in a Federal proceeding or to a Federal office or agency and waives the attorney-client privilege or work-product protection, the waiver extends to an undisclosed communication or information in a Federal or State proceeding only if:

(1) the waiver is intentional;

(2) the disclosed and undisclosed communications or information concern the same subject matter; and

(3) they ought in fairness to be considered together.

(b) INADVERTENT DISCLOSURE.—When made in a Federal proceeding or to a Federal office or agency, the disclosure does not operate as a waiver in a Federal or State proceeding if:

(1) the disclosure is inadvertent;

(2) the holder of the privilege or protection took reasonable steps to prevent disclosure; and

(3) the holder promptly took reasonable steps to rectify the error, including (if applicable) following Federal Rule of Civil Procedure 26(b)(5)(B).

(c) DISCLOSURE MADE IN A STATE PROCEEDING.—When the disclosure is made in a State proceeding and is not the subject of a State-court order concerning waiver, the disclosure does not operate as a waiver in a Federal proceeding if the disclosure:

(1) would not be a waiver under this rule if it had been made in a Federal proceeding; or

(2) is not a waiver under the law of the State where the disclosure occurred.

(d) CONTROLLING EFFECT OF A COURT ORDER.—A Federal court may order that the privilege or protection is not waived by disclosure connected with the litigation pending before the court—in which event the disclosure is also not a waiver in any other Federal or State proceeding.

(e) CONTROLLING EFFECT OF A PARTY AGREEMENT.—An agreement on the effect of disclosure in a Federal proceeding is binding only on the parties to the agreement, unless it is incorporated into a court order.

(f) CONTROLLING EFFECT OF THIS RULE.—Notwithstanding Rules 101 and 1101, this rule applies to State proceedings and to Federal court-annexed and Federal court-mandated arbitration proceedings, in the circumstances set out in the rule. And notwithstanding Rule 501, this rule applies even if State law provides the rule of decision.

(g) DEFINITIONS.—In this rule:

(1) "attorney-client privilege" means the protection that applicable law provides for confidential attorney-client communications; and

(2) "work-product protection" means the protection that applicable law provides for tangible material (or its intangible equivalent) prepared in anticipation of litigation or for trial.

. . .

(c) EFFECTIVE DATE.—The amendments made by this Act shall apply in all proceedings commenced after the date of enactment of this Act and, insofar as is just and practicable, in all proceedings pending on such date of enactment.

ADVISORY COMMITTEE NOTES

This new rule has two major purposes:

(1) It resolves some longstanding disputes in the courts about the effect of certain disclosures of communications or information protected by the attorney-client privilege or as work product—specifically those disputes involving inadvertent disclosure and subject matter waiver.

(2) It responds to the widespread complaint that litigation costs necessary to protect against waiver of attorney-client privilege or work product have become prohibitive due to the concern that any disclosure (however innocent or minimal) will operate as a subject matter waiver of all protected communications or information. This concern is especially troubling in cases involving electronic discovery. *See, e.g., Hopson v. City of Baltimore*, 232 F.R.D. 228, 244 (D.Md. 2005) (electronic discovery may encompass "millions of documents" and to insist upon "record-by-record pre-production privilege review, on pain of subject matter waiver, would impose upon parties costs of production that bear no proportionality to what is at stake in the litigation").

The rule seeks to provide a predictable, uniform set of standards under which parties can determine the consequences of a disclosure of a communication or information covered by the attorney-client privilege or work-product protection. Parties to litigation need to know, for example, that if they exchange privileged information pursuant to a confidentiality order, the court's order will be enforceable. Moreover, if a federal court's confidentiality order is not enforceable in a state court then the burdensome costs of privilege review and retention are unlikely to be reduced.

The rule makes no attempt to alter federal or state law on whether a communication or information is protected under the attorney-client privilege or work-product immunity as an initial matter. Moreover, while establishing some exceptions to waiver, the rule does not purport to supplant applicable waiver doctrine generally.

The rule governs only certain waivers by disclosure. Other common-law waiver doctrines may result in a finding of waiver even where there is no disclosure of privileged information or work product. *See, e.g., Nguyen v. Excel Corp.*, 197 F.3d 200 (5th Cir. 1999) (reliance on an advice of counsel defense waives the privilege with respect to attorney-client communications pertinent to that defense); *Byers v. Burleson*, 100 F.R.D. 436 (D.D.C. 1983) (allegation of lawyer malpractice constituted a waiver of confidential communications under the circumstances). The rule is not intended to displace or modify federal common law concerning waiver of privilege or work product where no disclosure has been made.

Subdivision (a). The rule provides that a voluntary disclosure in a federal proceeding or to a federal office or agency, if a waiver, generally results in a waiver only of the communication or information disclosed; a subject matter waiver (of either privilege or work product) is reserved for those unusual situations in which fairness requires a further disclosure of related, protected information, in order to prevent a selective and misleading presentation of evidence to the disadvantage of the adversary. *See, e.g., In re United Mine Workers of America Employee Benefit Plans Litig.*, 159 F.R.D. 307, 312 (D.D.C. 1994) (waiver of work product limited to materials actually disclosed, because the party did not deliberately disclose documents in an attempt to gain a tactical advantage). Thus, subject matter waiver is limited to situations in which a party intentionally puts protected information into the litigation in a selective, misleading and unfair manner. It follows that an inadvertent disclosure of protected information can never result in a subject matter waiver. *See* Rule 502(b). The rule rejects the result in *In re Sealed Case*, 877 F.2d 976 (D.C.Cir. 1989), which held that inadvertent disclosure of documents during discovery automatically constituted a subject matter waiver.

The language concerning subject matter waiver—"ought in fairness"—is taken from Rule 106, because the animating principle is the same. Under both Rules, a party that makes a selective, misleading presentation that is unfair to the adversary opens itself to a more complete and accurate presentation.

To assure protection and predictability, the rule provides that if a disclosure is made at the federal level, the federal rule on subject matter waiver governs subsequent state court determinations on the scope of the waiver by that disclosure.

Subdivision (b). Courts are in conflict over whether an inadvertent disclosure of a communication or information protected as privileged or work product constitutes a waiver. A few courts find that a disclosure must be intentional to be a waiver. Most courts find a waiver only if the disclosing party acted carelessly in disclosing the communication or information and failed to request its return in a timely manner. And a few courts hold that any inadvertent disclosure of a communication or information protected under the attorney-client privilege or as work product constitutes a waiver without regard to the protections taken to avoid such a disclosure. *See generally Hopson v. City of Baltimore*, 232 F.R.D. 228 (D.Md. 2005), for a discussion of this case law.

The rule opts for the middle ground: inadvertent disclosure of protected communications or information in connection with a federal proceeding or to a federal office or agency does not constitute a waiver if the holder took reasonable steps to prevent disclosure and also promptly took reasonable steps to rectify the error. This position is in accord with the majority view on whether inadvertent disclosure is a waiver.

Cases such as *Lois Sportswear, U.S.A., Inc. v. Levi Strauss & Co.*, 104 F.R.D. 103, 105 (S.D.N.Y. 1985) and *Hartford Fire Ins. Co. v. Garvey*, 109 F.R.D. 323, 332 (N.D.Cal. 1985), set out a multi-factor test for determining whether inadvertent disclosure is a waiver. The stated factors (none of which is dispositive) are the reasonableness of precautions taken, the time taken to rectify the error, the scope of discovery, the extent of disclosure and the overriding issue of fairness.

The rule does not explicitly codify that test, because it is really a set of non-determinative guidelines that vary from case to case. The rule is flexible enough to accommodate any of those listed factors. Other considerations bearing on the reasonableness of a producing party's efforts include the number of documents to be reviewed and the time constraints for production. Depending on the circumstances, a party that uses advanced analytical software applications and linguistic tools in screening for privilege and work product may be found to have taken "reasonable steps" to prevent inadvertent disclosure. The implementation of an efficient system of records management before litigation may also be relevant.

The rule does not require the producing party to engage in a post-production review to determine whether any protected communication or information has been produced by mistake. But the rule does require the producing party to follow up on any obvious indications that a protected communication or information has been produced inadvertently.

The rule applies to inadvertent disclosures made to a federal office or agency, including but not limited to an office or agency that is acting in the course of its regulatory, investigative or enforcement authority. The consequences of waiver, and the concomitant costs of pre-production privilege review, can be as great with respect to disclosures to offices and agencies as they are in litigation.

Subdivision (c). Difficult questions can arise when 1) a disclosure of a communication or information protected by the attorney-client privilege or as work product is made in a state proceeding, 2) the communication or information is offered in a subsequent federal proceeding on the ground that the disclosure waived the privilege or protection, and 3) the state and federal laws are in conflict on the question of waiver. The Committee determined that the proper solution for the federal court is to apply the law that is most protective of privilege and work product. If the state law is more protective (such as where the state law is that an inadvertent disclosure can never be a waiver), the holder of the privilege or protection may well have relied on that law when making the disclosure in the state proceeding. Moreover, applying a more restrictive federal law of waiver could impair the state objective of preserving the privilege or work-product protection for disclosures made in state proceedings. On the other hand, if the federal law is more protective, applying the state law of waiver to determine admissibility in federal court is likely to undermine the federal objective of limiting the costs of production.

The rule does not address the enforceability of a state court confidentiality order in a federal proceeding, as that question is covered both by statutory law and principles of federalism and comity. *See* 28 U.S.C. § 1738 (providing that state judicial proceedings "shall have the same full faith and credit in every court within the United States ... as they have by law or usage in the courts of such State ... from which they are taken").*See also Tucker v. Ohtsu Tire & Rubber Co.*, 191 F.R.D. 495, 499 (D.Md. 2000) (noting that a federal court considering the enforceability of a state confidentiality order is "constrained by principles of comity, courtesy, and ... federalism"). Thus, a state court order finding no waiver in connection with a disclosure made in a state court proceeding is enforceable under existing law in subsequent federal proceedings.

Subdivision (d). Confidentiality orders are becoming increasingly important in limiting the costs of privilege review and retention, especially in cases involving electronic discovery. But the utility of a confidentiality order in reducing discovery costs is substantially diminished if it provides no protection outside the particular litigation in which the order is entered. Parties are unlikely to be able to reduce the costs of pre-production review for privilege and work product if the consequence of disclosure is that the communications or information could be used by non-parties to the litigation.

There is some dispute on whether a confidentiality order entered in one case is enforceable in other proceedings. *See generally Hopson v. City of Baltimore*, 232 F.R.D. 228 (D.Md. 2005), for a discussion of this case law. The rule provides that when a confidentiality order governing the consequences of disclosure in that case is entered in a federal proceeding, its terms are enforceable against non-parties in any federal or state proceeding. For example, the court order may provide for return of documents without waiver irrespective of the care taken by the disclosing party; the rule contemplates enforcement of "claw-back" and "quick peek" arrangements as a way to avoid the excessive costs of pre-production review for privilege and work product. *See Zubulake v. UBS Warburg LLC*, 216 F.R.D. 280, 290 (S.D.N.Y. 2003) (noting that parties may enter into "so-called 'claw-back' agreements that allow the parties to forego privilege review altogether in favor of an agreement to return inadvertently produced privilege documents"). The rule provides a party with a predictable protection from a court order—predictability that is needed to allow the party to plan in advance to limit the prohibitive costs of privilege and work product review and retention.

Under the rule, a confidentiality order is enforceable whether or not it memorializes an agreement among the parties to the litigation. Party agreement should not be a condition of enforceability of a federal court's order....

Subdivision (e). Subdivision (e) codifies the well-established proposition that parties can enter an agreement to limit the effect of waiver by disclosure between or among them. Of course such an agreement can bind only the parties to the agreement. The rule makes clear that if parties want protection against non-parties from a finding of waiver by disclosure, the agreement must be made part of a court order.

Subdivision (f). The protections against waiver provided by Rule 502 must be applicable when protected communications or information disclosed in federal proceedings are subsequently offered in state proceedings. Otherwise the holders of protected communications and information, and their lawyers, could not rely on the protections provided by the Rule, and the goal of limiting costs in discovery would be substantially undermined. Rule 502(f) is intended to resolve any potential tension between the provisions of Rule 502 that apply to state proceedings and the possible limitations on the applicability of the Federal Rules of Evidence otherwise provided by Rules 101 and 1101.

The rule is intended to apply in all federal court proceedings, including court-annexed and court-ordered arbitrations, without regard to any possible limitations of Rules 101 and 1101. This provision is not intended to raise an inference about the applicability of any other rule of evidence in arbitration proceedings more generally.

The costs of discovery can be equally high for state and federal causes of action, and the rule seeks to limit those costs in all federal proceedings, regardless of whether the claim arises under state or federal law. Accordingly, the rule applies to state law causes of action brought in federal court.

Subdivision (g). The rule's coverage is limited to attorney-client privilege and work product. The operation of waiver by disclosure, as applied to other evidentiary privileges, remains a question of federal common law. Nor does the rule purport to apply to the Fifth Amendment privilege against compelled self-incrimination.

The definition of work product "materials" is intended to include both tangible and intangible information. *See In re Cendant Corp. Sec. Litig.*, 343 F.3d 658, 662 (3d Cir. 2003) ("work product protection extends to both tangible and intangible work product").

CONGRESSIONAL RECORD—HOUSE—SEPT. 8, 2008—H7818-19

During consideration of this rule in Congress, a number of questions were raised about the scope and contours of the effect of the proposed rule on current law regarding attorney-client privilege and work-product protection. These questions were ultimately answered satisfactorily, without need to revise the text of the rule as submitted to Congress by the Judicial Conference.

In general, these questions are answered by keeping in mind the limited though important purpose and focus of the rule. The rule addresses only the effect of disclosure, under specified circumstances, of a communication that is otherwise protected by attorney-client privilege, or of information that is protected by work-product protection, on whether the disclosure itself operates as a waiver of the privilege (or protection) to prove that the particular information (or communication) qualifies for it. And it is not intended to alter the rules and practices governing use of information outside this evidentiary context.

Some of these questions are addressed more specifically below, in order to help further avoid uncertainty in the interpretation and application of the rule.

Subdivision (a)—Disclosure vs. Use

This subdivision does not alter the substantive law regarding when a party's strategic use in litigation of otherwise privileged information obliges that party to waive the privilege regarding other information concerning the same subject matter, so that the information being used can be fairly considered in context. One situation in which this issue arises, the assertion as a defense in patent-infringement litigation that a party was relying on advice of counsel, is discussed elsewhere in this Note. In this and similar situations, under subdivision (a)(1) the party using an attorney-client communication to its advantage in the litigation has, in so doing, intentionally waived the privilege as to other communications concerning the same subject matter, regardless of the circumstances in which the communication being so used was initially disclosed.

Subdivision (b)—Fairness Considerations

The standard set forth in this subdivision for determining whether a disclosure operates as a waiver of the privilege or protection is, as explained elsewhere in this Note, the majority rule in the federal courts. The majority rule has simply been distilled here into a standard designed to be predictable in its application. This distillation is not intended to foreclose notions of fairness from continuing to inform application of the standard in all aspects as appropriate in particular cases—for example, as to whether steps taken to rectify an erroneous inadvertent disclosure were sufficiently prompt under subdivision (b)(3) where the receiving party has relied on the information disclosed.

Subdivisions (a) and (b)—Disclosures to Federal Office or Agency

This rule, as a Federal Rule of Evidence, applies to admissibility of evidence. While subdivisions (a) and (b) are written broadly to apply as appropriate to disclosures of information to a federal office or agency, they do not apply to uses of information—such as routine use in government publications—that fall outside the evidentiary context. Nor do these subdivisions relieve the party seeking to protect the information as privileged from the burden of proving that the privilege applies in the first place.

Subdivision (d)—Court Orders

This subdivision authorizes a court to enter orders only in the context of litigation pending before the court. And it does not alter the law regarding waiver of privilege resulting from having acquiesced in the use of otherwise privileged information. Therefore, this subdivision does not provide a basis for a court to enable parties to agree to a selective waiver of the privilege, such as to a federal agency conducting an investigation, while preserving the privilege as against other parties seeking the information. This subdivision is designed to enable a court to enter an order, whether on motion of one or more parties or on its own motion, that will allow the parties to conduct and respond to discovery expeditiously, without the need for exhaustive pre-production privilege reviews, while still preserving each party's right to assert the privilege to preclude use in litigation of information disclosed in such discovery.

While the benefits of a court order under this subdivision would be equally available in government enforcement actions as in private actions, acquiescence by the disclosing party in use by the federal agency of information disclosed pursuant to such an order would still be treated as under current law for the purposes of determining whether the acquiescence in use of the information, as opposed to its mere disclosure, effects a waiver of the privilege. The same applies to acquiescence in use by another private party.

Moreover, whether the order is entered on motion of one or more parties, or on the court's own motion, the court retains its authority to include the conditions it deems appropriate in the circumstances.

Subdivision (e)—Party Agreements

This subdivision simply makes clear that while parties to a case may agree among themselves regarding the effect of disclosures between each other in a federal proceeding, it is not binding on others unless it is incorporated into a court order. This subdivision does not confer any authority on a court to enter any order regarding the effect of disclosures. That authority must be found in subdivision (d), or elsewhere.

ARTICLE VI. WITNESSES

Rule 601.

GENERAL RULE OF COMPETENCY

Every person is competent to be a witness except as otherwise provided in these rules. However, in civil actions and proceedings, with respect to an element of a claim or defense as to which State law supplies the rule of decision, the competency of a witness shall be determined in accordance with State law.

Note by Federal Judicial Center

The first sentence of the rule enacted by the Congress is the entire rule prescribed by the Supreme Court, without change. The second sentence was added by congressional action.

Advisory Committee's Note

This general ground-clearing eliminates all grounds of incompetency not specifically recognized in the succeeding rules of this Article. Included among the grounds thus abolished are religious belief, conviction of crime, and connection with the litigation as a party or interested person or spouse of a party or interested person. With the exception of the so-called Dead Man's Acts, American jurisdictions generally have ceased to recognize these grounds.

The Dead Man's Acts are surviving traces of the common law disqualification of parties and interested persons. They exist in variety too great to convey conviction of their wisdom and effectiveness. These rules contain no provision of this kind. . . .

No mental or moral qualifications for testifying as a witness are specified. Standards of mental capacity have proved elusive in actual application. A leading commentator observes that few witnesses are disqualified on that ground. Weihofen, Testimonial Competence and Credibility, 34 Geo. Wash.L.Rev. 53 (1965). Discretion is regularly exercised in favor of allowing the testimony. A witness wholly without capacity is difficult to imagine. The question is one particularly suited to the jury as one of weight and credibility, subject to judicial authority to review the sufficiency of the evidence. 2 Wigmore §§ 501, 509. Standards of moral qualification in practice consist essentially of evaluating a person's truthfulness in terms of his own answers about it. Their principal utility is in affording an opportunity on voir dire examination to impress upon the witness his moral duty. This result may, however, be accomplished more directly, and without haggling in terms of legal standards, by the manner of administering the oath or affirmation under Rule 603.

Admissibility of religious belief as a ground of impeachment is treated in Rule 610. Conviction of crime as a ground of impeachment is the subject of Rule 609. Marital relationship is the basis for privilege under Rule 505. Interest in the outcome of litigation and mental capacity are, of course, highly relevant to credibility and require no special treatment to render them admissible along with other matters bearing upon the perception, memory, and narration of witnesses.

Rule 602.

LACK OF PERSONAL KNOWLEDGE

A witness may not testify to a matter unless evidence is introduced sufficient to support a finding that the witness has personal knowledge of the matter. Evidence to prove personal knowledge may, but need not, consist of the witness' own testimony. This rule is subject to the provisions of rule 703, relating to opinion testimony by expert witnesses.

Note by Federal Judicial Center

The rule enacted by the Congress is the rule prescribed by the Supreme Court without change.

Advisory Committee's Note

"... [T]he rule requiring that a witness who testifies to a fact which can be perceived by the senses must have had an opportunity to observe, and must have actually observed the fact" is a "most pervasive manifestation" of the common law insistence upon "the most reliable sources of information." McCormick § 10, p. 19. These foundation requirements may, of course, be furnished by the testimony of the witness himself; hence personal knowledge is not an absolute but may consist of what the witness thinks he knows from personal perception. 2 Wigmore § 650. It will be observed that the rule is in fact a specialized application of the provisions of Rule 104(b) on conditional relevancy.

This rule does not govern the situation of a witness who testifies to a hearsay statement as such, if he has personal knowledge of the making of the statement. Rules 801 and 805 would be applicable. This rule would, however, prevent him from testifying to the subject matter of the hearsay statement, as he has no personal knowledge of it.

The reference to Rule 703 is designed to avoid any question of conflict between the present rule and the provisions of that rule allowing an expert to express opinions based on facts of which he does not have personal knowledge.

Rule 603.

OATH OR AFFIRMATION

Before testifying, every witness shall be required to declare that the witness will testify truthfully, by oath or affirmation administered in a form calculated to awaken the witness' conscience and impress the witness' mind with the duty to do so.

Note by Federal Judicial Center

The rule enacted by the Congress is the rule prescribed by the Supreme Court without change.

Advisory Committee's Note

The rule is designed to afford the flexibility required in dealing with religious adults, atheists, conscientious objectors, mental defectives, and children. Affirmation is simply a solemn undertaking to tell the truth; no special verbal formula is required. As is true generally, affirmation is recognized by federal law. "Oath" includes affirmation, 1 U.S.C. § 1; judges and clerks may administer oaths and affirmations, 28 U.S.C. §§ 459, 953; and affirmations are acceptable in lieu of oaths under Rule 43(d) of the Federal Rules of Civil Procedure. Perjury by a witness is a crime, 18 U.S.C. § 1621.

Rule 604.

INTERPRETERS

An interpreter is subject to the provisions of these rules relating to qualification as an expert and the administration of an oath or affirmation to make a true translation.

Note by Federal Judicial Center

The rule enacted by the Congress is the rule prescribed by the Supreme Court without change.

Advisory Committee's Note

The rule implements Rule 43(f) of the Federal Rules of Civil Procedure and Rule 28(b) of the Federal Rules of Criminal Procedure, both of which contain provisions for the appointment and compensation of interpreters.

Rule 605.

COMPETENCY OF JUDGE AS WITNESS

The judge presiding at the trial may not testify in that trial as a witness. No objection need be made in order to preserve the point.

Note by Federal Judicial Center

The rule enacted by the Congress is the rule prescribed by the Supreme Court without change.

Advisory Committee's Note

In view of the mandate of 28 U.S.C. § 455 that a judge disqualify himself in "any case in which he ... is or has been a material witness," the likelihood that the presiding judge in a federal court might be called to testify in the trial over which he is presiding is slight. Nevertheless the possibility is not totally eliminated.

The solution here presented is a broad rule of incompetency, rather than such alternatives as incompetency only as to material matters, leaving the matter to the discretion of the judge, or recognizing no incompetency. The choice is the result of inability to evolve satisfactory answers to questions which arise when the judge abandons the bench for the witness stand. Who rules on objections? Who compels him to answer? Can he rule impartially on the weight and admissibility of his own testimony? Can he be impeached or cross-examined effectively? Can he, in a jury trial, avoid conferring his seal of approval on one side in the eyes of the jury? Can he, in a bench trial, avoid an involvement destructive of impartiality? The rule of general incompetency has substantial support. See Report of the Special Committee on the Propriety of Judges Appearing as Witnesses, 36 A.B.A.J. 630 (1950); cases collected in Annot. 157 A.L.R. 311; McCormick § 68, p. 147; Uniform Rule 42; California Evidence Code § 703; Kansas Code of Civil Procedure § 60–442; New Jersey Evidence Rule 42. Cf. 6 Wigmore § 1909, which advocates leaving the matter to the discretion of the judge, and statutes to that effect collected in Annot. 157 A.L.R. 311.

The rule provides an "automatic" objection. To require an actual objection would confront the opponent with a choice between not objecting, with the result of allowing the testimony, and objecting, with the probable result of excluding the testimony but at the price of continuing the trial before a judge likely to feel that his integrity had been attacked by the objector.

Rule 606.

COMPETENCY OF JUROR AS WITNESS

(a) At the trial. A member of the jury may not testify as a witness before that jury in the trial of the case in which the juror is sitting. If the juror is called so to testify, the opposing party shall be afforded an opportunity to object out of the presence of the jury.

(b) Inquiry into validity of verdict or indictment. Upon an inquiry into the validity of a verdict or indictment, a juror may not testify as to any matter or statement occurring during the course of the jury's deliberations or to the effect of anything upon that or any other juror's mind or emotions as influencing the juror to assent to or dissent from the verdict or indictment or concerning the juror's mental processes in connection therewith. But a juror may testify about (1) whether extraneous prejudicial information was improperly brought to the jury's attention, (2) whether any outside influence was improperly brought to bear upon any juror, or (3) whether there was a mistake in entering the verdict onto the verdict form. A juror's affidavit or evidence of any statement by the juror may not be received on a matter about which the juror would be precluded from testifying.

Advisory Committee Note to 2006 Amendment

Rule 606(b) has been amended to provide that juror testimony may be used to prove that the verdict reported was the result of a mistake in entering the verdict on the verdict form. The amendment responds to a divergence between the text of the Rule and the case law that has established an exception for proof of clerical errors. *See, e.g., Plummer v. Springfield Term. Ry.*, 5 F.3d 1, 3 (1st Cir. 1993) ("A number of circuit hold, and we agree, that juror testimony regarding an alleged clerical error, such as announcing a verdict different than agreed upon, does not challenge the validity of the verdict or the deliberation of mental processes, and therefore is not subject to Rule 606(b)."); *TeeVee Toons, Inc. v. MP3.Com, Inc.*, 148 F.Supp.2d 276, 278 (S.D.N.Y. 2001) (noting that Rule 606(b) has been silent regarding inquiries designed to confirm the accuracy of a verdict).

In adopting the exception for proof of mistakes in entering the verdict on the verdict form, the amendment specifically rejects the broader exception, adopted by some courts, permitting the use of juror testimony to prove that the jurors were operating under a misunderstanding about the consequences of the result that they agreed upon. *See, e.g., Attridge v. Cencorp Div. of Dover Techs. Int'l, Inc.*, 836 F.2d 113, 116 (2d Cir. 1987); *Eastridge Development Co. v. Halpert Associates, Inc.*, 853 F.2d 772 (10th Cir. 1988). The broader exception is rejected because an inquiry into whether the jury misunderstood or misapplied an instruction goes to the jurors' mental processes underlying the verdict, rather than the verdict's accuracy in capturing what the jurors had agreed upon. *See, e.g., Karl v. Burlington Northern R.R.*, 880 F.2d 68, 74 (8th Cir. 1989) (error to receive juror testimony on whether verdict was the result of jurors' misunderstanding of instructions: "The jurors did not state that the figure written by the foreman was different from that which they agreed upon, but indicated that the figure the foreman wrote down was intended to be a net figure, not a gross figure. Receiving such statements violates Rules 606(b) because the testimony relates to how the jury interpreted the court's instructions, and concerns the jurors' 'mental processes,' which is forbidden by the rule."); *Robles v. Exxon Corp.*, 862 F.2d 1201, 1208 (5th Cir. 1989) ("the alleged error here goes to the substance of what the jury was asked to decide, necessarily implicating the jury's mental processes insofar as it questions the jury's understanding of the court's instructions and application of those instructions to the facts of the case"). Thus, the exception established by the amendment is limited to cases such as "where the jury foreperson wrote down, in response to an interrogatory, a number different from that agreed upon by the jury, or mistakenly stated that the defendant was 'guilty' when the jury had actually agreed that the defendant was not guilty." *Id.*

It should be noted that the possibility of errors in the verdict form will be reduced substantially by polling the jury. Rule 606(b) does not, of course, prevent this precaution. *See* 8 C. Wigmore, *Evidence*, § 2350 at 691 (McNaughten ed. 1961) (noting that the reasons for the rule barring juror testimony, "namely, the dangers of uncertainty and of tampering with the jurors to procure testimony, disappear in large part if such investigation as may be desired is *made by the judge* and takes place *before the jurors' discharge* and separation") (emphasis in original). Errors that come to light after polling the jury "may be corrected on the spot, or the jury may be sent out to continue deliberations, or, if necessary, a new trial may be ordered." C. Mueller & L. Kirkpatrick, *Evidence Under the Rules* at 671 (2d ed. 1999) (citing *Sincox v. United States*, 571 F.2d 876, 878–79 (5th Cir. 1978)).

Note by Federal Judicial Center

The rule enacted by the Congress is the rule prescribed by the Supreme Court, amended only by the addition of the concluding phrase "for these purposes." The bill originally passed by the House did not contain in the first sentence the prohibition as to matters or statements during the deliberations or the clause beginning "except."

Advisory Committee's Note

Subdivision (a). The considerations which bear upon the permissibility of testimony by a juror in the trial in which he is sitting as juror bear an obvious similarity to those evoked when the judge is called as a witness. See Advisory Committee's Note to Rule 605. The judge is not, however, in this instance so involved as to call for departure from usual principles requiring objection to be made; hence the only provision on objection is that opportunity be afforded for its making out of the presence of the jury. Compare Rule 605.

Subdivision (b). Whether testimony, affidavits, or statements of jurors should be received for the purpose of invalidating or supporting a verdict or indictment, and if so, under what circumstances, has given rise to substantial differences of opinion. The familiar rubric that a juror may not impeach his own verdict, dating from Lord Mansfield's time, is a gross oversimplification. The values sought to be promoted by excluding the evidence include freedom of deliberation, stability and finality of verdicts, and protection of jurors against annoyance and embarrassment. McDonald v. Pless, 238 U.S. 264, 35 S.Ct. 783, 59 L.Ed. 1300 (1915). On the other hand, simply putting verdicts beyond effective reach can only promote irregularity and injustice. The rule offers an accommodation between these competing considerations.

The mental operations and emotional reactions of jurors in arriving at a given result would, if allowed as a subject of inquiry, place every verdict at the mercy of jurors and invite tampering and harassment. See Grenz v. Werre, 129 N.W.2d 681 (N.D.1964). The authorities are in virtually complete accord in excluding the evidence. Fryer, Note on Disqualification of Witnesses, Selected Writings on Evidence and Trial 345, 347 (Fryer ed.1957); Maguire, Weinstein, et al., Cases on Evidence 887 (5th ed. 1965); 8 Wigmore § 2349 (McNaughton Rev.1961). As to matters other than mental operations and emotional reactions of jurors, substantial authority refuses to allow a juror to disclose irregularities which occur in the jury room, but allows his testimony as to irregularities occurring outside and allows outsiders to testify as to occurrences both inside and out. 8 Wigmore § 2354 (McNaughton Rev.1961). However, the door of the jury room is not necessarily a satisfactory dividing point, and the Supreme Court has refused to accept it for every situation. Mattox v. United States, 146 U.S. 140, 13 S.Ct. 50, 36 L.Ed. 917 (1892).

Under the federal decisions the central focus has been upon insulation of the manner in which the jury reached its verdict, and this protection extends to each of the components of deliberation, including arguments, statements, discussions, mental and emotional reactions, votes, and any other feature of the process. Thus testimony or affidavits of jurors have been held incompetent to show a compromise verdict, Hyde v. United States, 225 U.S. 347, 382, 32 S.Ct. 793, 807, 56 L.Ed. 1114 (1912); a quotient verdict, McDonald v. Pless, 238 U.S. 264, 35 S.Ct. 783, 59 L.Ed. 1300 (1915); speculation as to insurance coverage, Holden v. Porter, 405 F.2d 878 (10th Cir.1969), Farmers Co–op. Elev. Ass'n v. Strand, 382 F.2d 224, 230 (8th Cir.1967), cert. denied 389 U.S. 1014, 88 S.Ct. 589, 19 L.Ed.2d 659; misinterpretation of instructions, Farmers Coop. Elev. Ass'n v. Strand, supra; mistake in returning verdict, United States v. Chereton, 309 F.2d 197 (6th Cir.1962); interpretation of guilty plea by one defendant as implicating others, United States v. Crosby, 294 F.2d 928, 949 (2d Cir.1961). The policy does not, however, foreclose testimony by jurors as to prejudicial extraneous information or influences injected into or brought to bear upon the deliberative process. Thus a juror is recognized as competent to testify to statements by the bailiff or the introduction of a prejudicial newspaper account into the jury room, Mattox v. United States, 146 U.S. 140, 13 S.Ct. 50, 36 L.Ed. 917 (1892). See also Parker v. Gladden, 385 U.S. 363, 87 S.Ct. 468, 17 L.Ed.2d 420 (1966).

This rule does not purport to specify the substantive grounds for setting aside verdicts for irregularity; it deals only with the competency of jurors to testify concerning those grounds.

See also Rule 6(e) of the Federal Rules of Criminal Procedure and 18 U.S.C. § 3500, governing the secrecy of grand jury proceedings. The present rule does not relate to secrecy and disclosure but to the competency of certain witnesses and evidence.

Report of Senate Judiciary Committee

The rule passed by the House embodies a suggestion by the Advisory Committee of the Judicial Conference that is considerably broader than the final version adopted by the Supreme Court, which embodied long-accepted Federal law. Although forbidding the impeachment of verdicts by inquiry into the jurors' mental processes, it deletes from the Supreme Court version the proscription against testimony "as to any matter or statement occurring during the course of the jury's deliberations." This deletion would have the effect of opening verdicts up to challenge on the basis of what happened during the jury's internal deliberations, for example, where a juror alleged that the jury refused to follow the trial judge's instructions or that some of the jurors did not take part in deliberations.

Public policy requires a finality to litigation. And common fairness requires that absolute privacy be preserved for jurors to engage in the full and free debate necessary to the attainment of just verdicts. Jurors will not be able to function effectively if their deliberations are to be scrutinized in post-trial litigation. In the interest of protecting the jury system and the citizens who make it work, rule 606 should not permit any inquiry into the internal deliberations of the jurors.

Conference Report

Rule 606(b) deals with juror testimony in an inquiry into the validity of a verdict or indictment. The House bill provides that a juror cannot testify about his mental processes or about the effect of anything upon his or another juror's mind as influencing him to assent to or dissent from a verdict or indictment. Thus, the House bill allows a juror to testify about objective matters occurring during the jury's deliberation, such as the misconduct of another juror or the reaching of a quotient verdict. The Senate bill does not permit juror testimony about any matter or statement occurring during the course of the jury's deliberations. The Senate bill does provide, however, that a juror may testify on the question whether extraneous prejudicial information was improperly brought to the jury's attention and on the question whether any outside influence was improperly brought to bear on any juror.

The Conference adopts the Senate amendment. The Conferees believe that jurors should be encouraged to be conscientious in promptly reporting to the court misconduct that occurs during jury deliberations.

Rule 607.

WHO MAY IMPEACH

The credibility of a witness may be attacked by any party, including the party calling the witness.

Note by Federal Judicial Center

The rule enacted by the Congress is the rule prescribed by the Supreme Court without change.

Advisory Committee's Note

The traditional rule against impeaching one's own witness is abandoned as based on false premises. A party does not hold out his witnesses as worthy of belief, since he rarely has a free choice in selecting them. Denial of the right leaves the party at the mercy of the witness and the adversary. If the impeachment is by a prior statement, it is free from hearsay dangers and is excluded from the category of hearsay under Rule 801(d)(1). Ladd, Impeachment of One's Own Witness—New Developments, 4 U.Chi.L.Rev. 69 (1936); McCormick § 38; 3 Wigmore §§ 896–918. The substantial inroads into the old rule made over the years by decisions, rules, and statutes are evidence of doubts as to its basic soundness and workability. Cases are collected in 3 Wigmore § 905. Revised Rule 32(a)(1) of the Federal Rules of Civil Procedure allows any party to impeach a witness by means of his deposition, and Rule 43(b) has allowed the calling and impeachment of an adverse party or person identified with him. Illustrative statutes allowing a party to impeach his own witness under varying circumstances are Ill.Rev.Stats.1967, c. 110, § 60; Mass.Laws Annot.1959, c. 233 § 23; 20 N.M.Stats.Annot.1953, § 20-2-4; N.Y.CPLR § 4514 (McKinney 1963); 12 Vt.Stats.Annot.1959, §§ 1641a, 1642. Complete judicial rejection of the old rule is found in United States v. Freeman, 302 F.2d 347 (2d Cir.1962). The same result is reached in Uniform Rule 20; California Evidence Code § 785; Kansas Code of Civil Procedure § 60–420. See also New Jersey Evidence Rule 20.

Rule 608.

EVIDENCE OF CHARACTER AND CONDUCT OF WITNESS

(a) Opinion and reputation evidence of character. The credibility of a witness may be attacked or supported by evidence in the form of opinion or reputation, but subject to these limitations: (1) the evidence may refer only to character for truthfulness or untruthfulness, and (2) evidence of truthful character is admissible only after the character of the witness for truthfulness has been attacked by opinion or reputation evidence or otherwise.

(b) Specific instances of conduct. Specific instances of the conduct of a witness, for the purpose of attacking or supporting the witness' character for truthfulness, other than conviction of crime as provided in rule 609, may not be proved by extrinsic evidence. They may, however, in the discretion of the court, if probative of truthfulness or untruthfulness, be inquired into on cross-examination of the witness (1) concerning the witness' character for truthfulness or untruthfulness, or (2) concerning the character for truthfulness or untruthfulness of another witness as to which character the witness being cross-examined has testified.

The giving of testimony, whether by an accused or by any other witness, does not operate as a waiver of the accused's or the witness' privilege against self-incrimination when examined with respect to matters that relate only to character for truthfulness.

Advisory Committee's Note to 2003 Amendment to Rule 608

The Rule has been amended to clarify that the absolute prohibition on extrinsic evidence applies only when the sole reason for proffering that evidence is to attack or support the witness' character for truthfulness. *See United States v. Abel,* 469 U.S. 45 (1984); *United States v. Fusco,* 748 F.2d 996 (5th Cir.1984) (Rule 608(b) limits the use of evidence "designed to show that the witness has done things, unrelated to the suit being tried, that make him more or less believable per se"); Ohio R.Evid. 608(b). On occasion the Rule's use of the overbroad term "credibility" has been read "to bar extrinsic evidence for bias, competency and contradiction impeachment since they too deal with credibility." American Bar Association Section of Litigation, *Emerging Problems Under the Federal Rules of Evidence* at 161 (3d ed. 1998). The amendment conforms the language of the Rule to its original intent, which was to impose an absolute bar on extrinsic evidence only if the sole purpose for offering the evidence was to prove the witness' character for veracity. *See* Advisory Committee Note to Rule 608(b) (stating that the Rule is "[i]n conformity with Rule 405, which forecloses use of evidence of specific incidents as proof in chief of character unless character is in issue in the case ...").

By limiting the application of the Rule to proof of a witness' character for truthfulness, the amendment leaves the admissibility of extrinsic evidence offered for other grounds of impeachment (such as contradiction, prior inconsistent statement, bias and mental capacity) to Rules 402 and 403. *See, e.g., United States v. Winchenbach,* 197 F.3d 548 (1st Cir.1999) (admissibility of a prior inconsistent statement offered for impeachment is governed by Rules 402 and 403, not Rule 608(b)); *United States v. Tarantino,* 846 F.2d 1384 (D.C.Cir.1988) (admissibility of extrinsic evidence offered to contradict a witness is governed by Rules 402 and 403); *United States v. Lindemann,* 85 F.3d 1232 (7th Cir.1996) (admissibility of extrinsic evidence of bias is governed by Rules 402 and 403).

It should be noted that the extrinsic evidence prohibition of Rule 608(b) bars any reference to the consequences that a witness might have suffered as a result of an alleged bad act. For example, Rule 608(b) prohibits counsel from mentioning that a witness was suspended or disciplined for the conduct that is the subject of impeachment, when that conduct is offered only to prove the character of the witness. *See United States v. Davis,* 183 F.3d 231, 257 n.12 (3d Cir.1999) (emphasizing that in attacking the defendant's character for truthfulness "the government cannot make reference to Davis's forty-four day suspension or that Internal Affairs found that he lied about" an incident because "[s]uch evidence would not only be hearsay to the extent it contains assertion of fact, it would be inadmissible extrinsic evidence under Rule 608(b)"). *See also* Stephen A. Saltzburg, *Impeaching the Witness: Prior Bad Acts and Extrinsic Evidence,* 7 Crim. Just. 28, 31 (Winter 1993) ("counsel should not be permitted to circumvent the no-extrinsic-evidence provision by tucking a third person's opinion about prior acts into a question asked of the witness who has denied the act").

For purposes of consistency the term "credibility" has been replaced by the term "character for truthfulness" in the last sentence of subdivision (b). The term "credibility" is also used in subdivision (a). But the Committee found it unnecessary to substitute "character for truthfulness" for "credibil-

WITNESSES — Rule 608

ity" in Rule 608(a), because subdivision (a)(1) already serves to limit impeachment to proof of such character.

Rules 609(a) and 610 also use the term "credibility" when the intent of those Rules is to regulate impeachment of a witness' character for truthfulness. No inference should be derived from the fact that the Committee proposed an amendment to Rule 608(b) but not to Rules 609 and 610.

Note by Federal Judicial Center

The rule enacted by the Congress is the rule prescribed by the Supreme Court, changed only by amending the second sentence of subdivision (b). The sentence as prescribed by the Court read: "They may, however, if probative of truthfulness or untruthfulness and not remote in time, be inquired into on cross-examination of the witness himself or on cross-examination of a witness who testifies to his character for truthfulness or untruthfulness." The effect of the amendments was to delete the phrase "and not remote in time," to add the phrase "in the discretion of the court," and otherwise only to clarify the meaning of the sentence. The reasons for the amendments are stated in the Report of the House Committee on the Judiciary, set forth below. See also Note to Rule 405(a) by Federal Judicial Center, supra.

Advisory Committee's Note

Subdivision (a). In Rule 404(a) the general position is taken that character evidence is not admissible for the purpose of proving that the person acted in conformity therewith, subject, however, to several exceptions, one of which is character evidence of a witness as bearing upon his credibility. The present rule develops that exception.

In accordance with the bulk of judicial authority, the inquiry is strictly limited to character for veracity, rather than allowing evidence as to character generally. The result is to sharpen relevancy, to reduce surprise, waste of time, and confusion, and to make the lot of the witness somewhat less unattractive. McCormick § 44.

The use of opinion and reputation evidence as means of proving the character of witnesses is consistent with Rule 405(a). While the modern practice has purported to exclude opinion, witnesses who testify to reputation seem in fact often to be giving their opinions, disguised somewhat misleadingly as reputation. See McCormick § 44. And even under the modern practice, a common relaxation has allowed inquiry as to whether the witnesses would believe the principal witness under oath. United States v. Walker, 313 F.2d 236 (6th Cir.1963), and cases cited therein; McCormick § 44, pp. 94–95, n. 3.

Character evidence in support of credibility is admissible under the rule only after the witness' character has first been attacked, as has been the case at common law. Maguire, Weinstein, et al., Cases on Evidence 295 (5th ed. 1965); McCormick § 49, p. 105; 4 Wigmore § 1104. The enormous needless consumption of time which a contrary practice would entail justifies the limitation. Opinion or reputation that the witness is untruthful specifically qualifies as an attack under the rule, and evidence of misconduct, including conviction of crime, and of corruption also fall within this category. Evidence of bias or interest does not. McCormick § 49; 4 Wigmore §§ 1106, 1107. Whether evidence in the form of contradiction is an attack upon the character of the witness must depend upon the circumstances. McCormick § 49. Cf. 4 Wigmore §§ 1108, 1109.

As to the use of specific instances on direct by an opinion witness, see the Advisory Committee's Note to Rule 405, supra.

Subdivision (b). In conformity with Rule 405, which forecloses use of evidence of specific incidents as proof in chief of character unless character is an issue in the case, the present rule generally bars evidence of specific instances of conduct of a witness for the purpose of attacking or supporting his credibility. There are, however, two exceptions: (1) specific instances are provable when they have been the subject of criminal conviction, and (2) specific instances may be inquired into on cross-examination of the principal witness or of a witness giving an opinion of his character for truthfulness.

(1) Conviction of crime as a technique of impeachment is treated in detail in Rule 609, and here is merely recognized as an exception to the general rule excluding evidence of specific incidents for impeachment purposes.

(2) Particular instances of conduct, though not the subject of criminal conviction, may be inquired into on cross-examination of the principal witness himself or of a witness who testifies concerning his character for truthfulness. Effective cross-examination demands that some allowance be made for going into matters of this kind, but the possibilities of abuse are substantial. Consequently safeguards are erected in the form of specific requirements that the instances inquired into be probative of truthfulness or its opposite.... Also, the overriding protection of Rule 403 requires that probative value not be outweighed by danger of unfair prejudice, confusion of issues, or misleading the jury, and that of Rule 611 bars harassment and undue embarrassment.

The final sentence constitutes a rejection of the doctrine of such cases as People v. Sorge, 301 N.Y. 198, 93 N.E.2d 637 (1950), that any past criminal act relevant to credibility may be inquired into on cross-examination, in apparent disregard of the privilege against self-incrimination. While it is clear that an ordinary witness cannot make a partial disclosure of incriminating matter and then invoke the privilege on cross-examination, no tenable contention can be made that merely by testifying he waives his right to foreclose inquiry on cross-examination into criminal activities for the purpose of attacking his credibility. So to hold would reduce the privilege to a nullity. While it is true that an accused, unlike an ordinary witness, has an option whether to testify, if the option can be exercised only at the price of opening up inquiry as to any and all criminal acts committed during his lifetime, the right to testify could scarcely be said to possess much vitality. In Griffin v. California, 380 U.S. 609, 85 S.Ct. 1229, 14 L.Ed.2d 106 (1965), the Court held that allowing comment on the election of an accused not to testify exacted a constitutionally impermissible price, and so here. While no specific provision in terms confers constitutional status on the right of an accused to take the stand in his own defense, the existence of the right is so completely recognized that a denial of it or substantial infringement upon it would surely be of due process dimensions. See Ferguson v. Georgia, 365 U.S. 570, 81 S.Ct. 756, 5 L.Ed.2d 783 (1961); McCormick § 131; 8 Wigmore § 2276 (McNaughton Rev.1961). In any event, wholly aside from constitutional considerations, the provision represents a sound policy.

Report of House Committee on the Judiciary

The Committee amended the Rule to emphasize the discretionary power of the court in permitting such testimony and deleted the reference to remoteness in time as being unnecessary and confusing (remoteness from time of trial or remoteness from the incident involved?). As recast, the Committee amendment also makes clear the antecedent of "his" in the original Court proposal.

Rule 609.

IMPEACHMENT BY EVIDENCE OF CONVICTION OF CRIME

(a) General rule. For the purpose of attacking the character for truthfulness of a witness,

> **(1)** evidence that a witness other than an accused has been convicted of a crime shall be admitted, subject to Rule 403, if the crime was punishable by death or imprisonment in excess of one year under the law under which the witness was convicted, and evidence that an accused has been convicted of such a crime shall be admitted if the court determines that the probative value of admitting this evidence outweighs its prejudicial effect to the accused; and

> **(2)** evidence that any witness has been convicted of a crime shall be admitted, regardless of the punishment, if it readily can be determined that establishing the elements of the crime required proof or admission of an act of dishonesty or false statement by the witness.

(b) Time limit. Evidence of a conviction under this rule is not admissible if a period of more than ten years has elapsed since the date of the conviction or of the release of the witness from the confinement imposed for that conviction, whichever is the later date, unless the court determines, in the interests of justice, that the probative value of the conviction supported by specific facts and circumstances substantially outweighs its prejudicial effect. However, evidence of a conviction more than 10 years old as calculated herein, is not admissible unless the proponent gives to the adverse party sufficient advance written notice of intent to use such evidence to provide the adverse party with a fair opportunity to contest the use of such evidence.

(c) Effect of pardon, annulment, or certificate of rehabilitation. Evidence of a conviction is not admissible under this rule if (1) the conviction has been the subject of a pardon, annulment, certificate of rehabilitation, or other equivalent procedure based on a finding of the rehabilitation of the person convicted, and that person has not been convicted of a subsequent crime that was punishable by death or imprisonment in excess of one year, or (2) the conviction has been the subject of a pardon, annulment, or other equivalent procedure based on a finding of innocence.

(d) Juvenile adjudications. Evidence of juvenile adjudications is generally not admissible under this rule. The court may, however, in a criminal case allow evidence of a juvenile adjudication of a witness other than the accused if conviction of the offense would be admissible to attack the credibility of an adult and the court is satisfied that admission in evidence is necessary for a fair determination of the issue of guilt or innocence.

(e) Pendency of appeal. The pendency of an appeal therefrom does not render evidence of a conviction inadmissible. Evidence of the pendency of an appeal is admissible.

Advisory Committee Note to 2006 Amendment

The amendment provides that Rule 609(a)(2) mandates the admission of evidence of a conviction only when the conviction required the proof of (or in the case of a guilty plea, the admission of) an act of dishonesty or false statement. Evidence of all other convictions is inadmissible under this subsection, irrespective of whether the witness exhibited dishonesty or made a false statement in the process of the commission of the crime of conviction. Thus, evidence that a witness was convicted for a crime of violence, such as murder, is not admissible under Rule 609(a)(2), even if the witness acted deceitfully in the course of committing the crime.

The amendment is meant to give effect to the legislative intent to limit the convictions that are to be automatically admitted under subdivision (a)(2). The Conference Committee provided that by "dishonesty and false statement" it meant "crimes such as perjury, subornation of perjury, false statement, criminal fraud, embezzlement, or false pretense, or any other offense in the nature of *crimen falsi*, the commission of which involves some element of deceit, untruthfulness, or falsification bearing on the [witness's] propensity to testify truthfully." Historically, offenses classified as *crimina falsi* have included only those crimes in which the ultimate criminal act was itself an act of deceit. See Green, *Deceit and the Classification of Crimes: Federal Rules of Evidence* 609(a)(2) *and the Origins of* Crimen Falsi, 90 J. Crim. L. & Criminology 1087 (2000).

Evidence of crimes in the nature of *crimina falsi* must be admitted under Rule 609(a)(2), regardless of how such crimes are specifically charged. For example, evidence that a witness was convicted of making a false claim to a federal agent is admissible under this subdivision regardless of whether the crime was charged under a section that expressly references deceit (e.g., 18 U.S.C. § 1001, Material Misrepresentation to the Federal Government) or a section that does not (e.g., 18 U.S.C. § 1503, Obstruction of Justice).

The amendment requires that the proponent have ready proof that the conviction required the factfinder to find, or the defendant to admit, an act of dishonesty or false statement. Ordinarily, the statutory elements of the crime will indicate whether it is one of dishonesty or false statement. Where the deceitful nature of the crime is not apparent from the statute and the face of the judgment—as, for example, where the conviction simply records a finding of guilt for a statutory offense that does not reference deceit expressly—a proponent may offer information such as an indictment, a statement of admitted facts, or jury instructions to show that the factfinder had to find, or the defendant had to admit, an act of dishonesty or false statement in order for the witness to have been convicted. *Cf. Taylor v. United States*, 495 U.S. 575, 602 (1990) (providing that a trial court may look to a charging instrument or jury instruction to ascertain the nature of a prior offense where the statute is insufficiently clear on its face); *Shepard v. United States*, 125 S.Ct. 1254 (2005) (the inquiry to determine whether a guilty plea to a crime defined by a nongeneric statute necessarily admitted elements of the generic offense was limited to the charging document's terms, the terms of a plea agreement or transcript of colloquy between judge and defendant in which the factual basis for the plea was confirmed by the defendant or a comparable judicial record). But the amendment does not contemplate a "mini-trial" in which the court plumbs the record of the previous proceeding to determine whether the crime was in the nature of *crimen falsi*.

The amendment also substitutes the term "character for truthfulness" for the term "credibility" in the first sentence of the Rule. The limitations of Rule 609 are not applicable if a conviction is admitted for a purpose other than to prove the witness's character for untruthfulness. *See, e.g., United States v. Lopez*, 979 F.2d 1024 (5th Cir. 1992) (Rule 609 was not applicable where the conviction was offered for purposes of contradiction). The use of the term "credibility" in subdivision (d) is retained, however, as that subdivision is intended to govern the use of a juvenile adjudication for any type of impeachment.

Committee Note to 1990 Amendment

The amendment to Rule 609(a) makes two changes in the rule. The first change removes from the rule the limitation that the conviction may only be elicited during cross-examination, a limitation that virtually every circuit has found to be inapplicable. It is common for witnesses to reveal on direct examination their convictions to "remove the sting" of the impeachment. See e.g., United States v. Bad Cob, 560 F.2d 877 (8th Cir.1977). The amendment does not contemplate that a court will necessarily permit proof of prior convictions through testimony, which might be time-consuming and more prejudicial than proof through a written record. Rules 403 and 611(a) provide sufficient authority for the court to protect against unfair or disruptive methods of proof.

The second change effected by the amendment resolves an ambiguity as to the relationship of Rules 609 and 403 with respect to impeachment of witnesses other than the criminal defendant. See, Green v. Bock Laundry Machine Co., 490 U.S. 504, 109 S.Ct. 1981, 104 L.Ed.2d 557 (1989). The amendment does not disturb the special balancing test for the criminal defendant who chooses to testify. Thus, the rule recognizes that, in virtually every case in which prior convictions are used to impeach the testifying defendant, the defendant faces a unique risk of prejudice—i.e., the danger that convictions that would be excluded under Fed.R.Evid. 404 will be misused by a jury as propensity evidence despite their introduction solely for impeachment purposes. Although the rule does not forbid all use of convictions to impeach a defendant, it requires that the government show that the probative value of convictions as impeachment evidence outweighs their prejudicial effect.

Prior to the amendment, the rule appeared to give the defendant the benefit of the special balancing test when defense witnesses other than the defendant were called to testify. In practice, however, the concern about unfairness to the defendant is most acute when the defendant's own convictions are offered as evidence. Almost all of the decided cases concern this type of impeachment, and the amendment does not deprive the defendant of any meaningful protection, since Rule 403 now clearly protects against unfair impeachment of any defense witness other than the defendant. There are cases in which a defendant might be prejudiced when a defense witness is impeached. Such cases may arise, for example, when the witness bears a special relationship to the defendant such that the defendant is likely to suffer some spill-over effect from impeachment of the witness.

The amendment also protects other litigants from unfair impeachment of their witnesses. The danger of prejudice from the use of prior convictions is not confined to criminal defendants. Although the danger that prior convictions will be misused as character evidence is particularly acute when the defendant is impeached, the danger exists in other situations as well. The amendment reflects the view that it is desirable to protect all litigants from the unfair use of prior convictions, and that the ordinary balancing test of Rule 403, which provides that evidence shall not be excluded unless its prejudicial effect substantially outweighs its probative value, is appropriate for assessing the admissibility of prior convictions for impeachment of any witness other than a criminal defendant.

The amendment reflects a judgment that decisions interpreting Rule 609(a) as requiring a trial court to admit convictions in civil cases that have little, if anything, to do with credibility reach undesirable results. See, e.g., Diggs v. Lyons, 741 F.2d 577 (3d Cir.1984), cert. denied, 471 U.S. 1078, 105 S.Ct. 2157, 85 L.Ed.2d 513 (1985). The amendment provides the same protection against unfair prejudice arising from prior convictions used for impeachment purposes as the rules provide for other evidence. The amendment finds support in decided cases. See, e.g., Petty v. Ideco, 761 F.2d 1146 (5th Cir.1985); Czajka v. Hickman, 703 F.2d 317 (8th Cir.1983).

Fewer decided cases address the question whether Rule 609(a) provides any protection against unduly prejudicial prior convictions used to impeach government witnesses. Some courts have read Rule 609(a) as giving the government no protection for its witnesses. See, e.g., United States v. Thorne, 547 F.2d 56 (8th Cir.1976); United States v. Nevitt, 563 F.2d 406 (9th Cir.1977), cert. denied, 444 U.S. 847, 100 S.Ct. 95, 62 L.Ed.2d 61 (1979). This approach also is rejected by the amendment. There are cases in which impeachment of government witnesses with prior convictions that have little, if anything, to do with credibility may result in unfair prejudice to the government's interest in a fair trial and unnecessary embarrassment to a witness. Fed.R.Evid. 412 already recognizes this and excluded certain evidence of past sexual behavior in the context of prosecutions for sexual assaults.

The amendment applies the general balancing test of Rule 403 to protect all litigants against unfair impeachment of witnesses. The balancing test protects civil litigants, the government in criminal cases, and the defendant in a criminal case who calls other witnesses. The amendment addresses prior convictions offered under Rule 609, not for other purposes, and does not run afoul, therefore, of Davis v. Alaska, 415 U.S. 308, 94 S.Ct. 1105, 39 L.Ed.2d 347 (1974). Davis involved the use of a prior juvenile adjudication not to prove a past law violation, but to prove bias. The defendant in a criminal case has the right to demonstrate the bias of a witness and to be assured a fair trial, but not to unduly prejudice a trier of fact. See generally Rule 412. In any case in which the trial court believes that confrontation rights require admission of impeachment evidence, obviously the Constitution would take precedence over the rule.

The probability that prior convictions of an ordinary government witness will be unduly prejudicial is low in most criminal cases. Since the behavior of the witness is not the issue in dispute in most cases, there is little chance that the trier of fact will misuse the convictions offered as impeachment evidence as propensity evidence. Thus, trial courts will be skeptical when the government objects to impeachment of its witnesses with prior convictions. Only when the government is able to point to a real danger of prejudice that is sufficient to outweigh substantially the probative value of the conviction for impeachment purposes will the conviction be excluded.

The amendment continues to divide subdivision (a) into subsections (1) and (2) thus facilitating retrieval under current computerized research programs which distinguish the two provisions. The Committee recommended no substantive change in subdivision (a)(2), even though some cases raise a concern about the proper interpretation of the words "dishonesty or false statement." These words were used but not explained in the original Advisory Committee Note accompanying Rule 609. Congress extensively debated the rule, and the Report of the House and Senate Conference Committee states that "[b]y the phrase 'dishonesty and false statement,' the Conference means crimes such as perjury, subordination of perjury, false statement, criminal fraud, embezzlement, or false pretense, or any other offense in the nature of crimen falsi, commission of which involves some element of deceit, untruthfulness, or falsification bearing on the accused's propensity to testify truthfully." The Advisory Committee concluded that the Conference Report provides sufficient guidance to trial courts and that no amendment is necessary, notwithstanding some decisions that take an unduly broad view of "dishonesty," admitting convictions such as for bank robbery or bank larceny. Subsection (a)(2) continues to apply to any witness, including a criminal defendant.

Finally, the Committee determined that it was unnecessary to add to the rule language stating that, when a prior conviction is offered under Rule 609, the trial court is to consider the probative value of the prior conviction for impeachment, not for other purposes. The Committee concluded that the title of the rule, its first sentence, and its placement among the impeachment rules clearly establish that evidence offered under Rule 609 is offered only for purposes of impeachment.

Note by Federal Judicial Center

Subdivision (a) of the rule prescribed by the Supreme Court was revised successively in the House, in the Senate, and in the Conference ...

Subdivision (b) of the rule prescribed by the Supreme Court was also revised successively in the House, in the Senate, and in the Conference ...

Subdivision (c) enacted by the Congress is the subdivision prescribed by the Supreme Court, with amendments and reasons therefor stated in the Report of the House Committee on the Judiciary, set forth below.

Subdivision (d) enacted by the Congress is the subdivision prescribed by the Supreme Court, amended in the second sentence by substituting "court" in place of "judge" and by adding the phrase "in a criminal case."

Subdivision (e) enacted by the Congress is the subdivision prescribed by the Supreme Court without change.

Advisory Committee's Note

As a means of impeachment, evidence of conviction of crime is significant only because it stands as proof of the commission of the underlying criminal act. There is little dissent from the general proposition that at least some crimes are relevant to credibility but much disagreement among the cases and commentators about which crimes are usable for this purpose. See McCormick § 43; 2 Wright, Federal Practice and Procedure: Criminal § 416 (1969). The weight of traditional authority has been to allow use of felonies generally, without regard to the nature of the particular offense, and of *crimen falsi* without regard to the grade of the offense. This is the view accepted by Congress in the 1970 amendment of § 14–305 of the District of Columbia Code, P.L. 91–358, 84 Stat. 473. Uniform Rule 21 and Model Code Rule 106 permit only crimes involving "dishonesty or false statement." Others have thought that the trial judge should have discretion to exclude convictions if the probative value of the evidence of the crime is substantially outweighed by the danger of unfair prejudice. Luck v. United States, 121 U.S.App.D.C. 151, 348 F.2d 763 (1965); McGowan, Impeachment of Criminal Defendants by Prior Convictions, 1970 Law & Soc. Order 1. . . .

The proposed rule incorporates certain basic safeguards, in terms applicable to all witnesses but of particular significance to an accused who elects to testify. These protections include the imposition of definite time limitations, giving effect to demonstrated rehabilitation, and generally excluding juvenile adjudications.

Subdivision (a). For purposes of impeachment, crimes are divided into two categories by the rule: (1) those of what is generally regarded as felony grade, without particular regard to the nature of the offense, and (2) those involving dishonesty or false statement, without regard to the grade of the offense. Provable convictions are not limited to violations of federal law. By reason of our constitutional structure, the federal catalog of crimes is far from being a complete one, and resort must be had to the laws of the states for the specification of many crimes. For example, simple theft as compared with theft from interstate commerce. Other instances of borrowing are the Assimilative Crimes Act, making the state law of crimes applicable to the special territorial and maritime jurisdiction of the United States, 18 U.S.C. § 13, and the provision of the Judicial Code disqualifying persons as jurors on the grounds of state as well as federal convictions, 28 U.S.C. § 1865. For evaluation of the crime in terms of seriousness, reference is made to the congressional measurement of felony (subject to imprisonment in excess of one year) rather than adopting state definitions which vary considerably. See 28 U.S.C. § 1865, supra, disqualifying jurors for conviction in state or federal court of crime punishable by imprisonment for more than one year.

Report of the House Committee on the Judiciary

. . .

Report of the Senate Committee on the Judiciary

. . .

. . . In your committee's view, the danger of unfair prejudice is far greater when the accused, as opposed to other witnesses, testifies, because the jury may be prejudiced not merely on the question of credibility but also on the ultimate question of guilt or innocence. Therefore, with respect to defendants, the committee agreed with the House limitation that only offenses involving false statement or dishonesty may be used. By that phrase, the committee means crimes such as perjury or subornation of perjury, false statement, criminal fraud, embezzlement or false pretense, or any other offense, in the nature of crimen falsi the commission of which involves some element of untruthfulness, deceit or falsification bearing on the accused's propensity to testify truthfully.

With respect to other witnesses, in addition to any prior conviction involving false statement or dishonesty, any other felony may be used to impeach if, and only if, the court finds that the probative value of such evidence outweighs its prejudicial effect against the party offering that witness.

Notwithstanding this provision, proof of any prior offense otherwise admissible under rule 404 could still be offered for the purposes sanctioned by that rule. Furthermore, the committee intends that notwithstanding this rule, a defendant's misrepresentation regarding the existence or nature of prior convictions may be met by rebuttal evidence, including the record of such prior convictions. Similarly, such records may be offered to rebut representations made by the defendant regarding his attitude toward or willingness to commit a general category of offense, although denials or other representations by the defendant regarding the specific conduct which forms the basis of the charge against him shall not make prior convictions admissible to rebut such statement.

In regard to either type of representation, of course, prior convictions may be offered in rebuttal only if the defendant's statement is made in response to defense counsel's questions or is made gratuitously in the course of cross-examination. Prior convictions may not be offered as rebuttal evidence if the prosecution has sought to circumvent the purpose of this rule by asking questions which elicit such representations from the defendant.

One other clarifying amendment has been added to this subsection, that is, to provide that the admissibility of evidence of a prior conviction is permitted only upon cross-examination of a witness. It is not admissible if a person does not testify. It is to be understood, however, that a court record of a prior conviction is admissible to prove that conviction if the witness has forgotten or denies its existence.

Conference Report

The House bill provides that the credibility of a witness can be attacked by proof of prior conviction of a crime only if the crime involves dishonesty or false statement. The Senate amendment provides that a witness' credibility may be attacked if the crime (1) was punishable by death or imprisonment in excess of one year under the law under which he was convicted or (2) involves dishonesty or false statement, regardless of the punishment.

The Conference adopts the Senate amendment with an amendment. The Conference amendment provides that the credibility of a witness, whether a defendant or someone else, may be attacked by proof of a prior conviction but only if the crime: (1) was punishable by death or imprisonment in excess of one year under the law under which he was convicted and the court determines that the probative value of the conviction outweighs its prejudicial effect to the defendant; or (2) involved dishonesty or false statement regardless of the punishment.

By the phrase "dishonesty and false statement" the Conference means crimes such as perjury or subornation of perjury, false statement, criminal fraud, embezzlement, or false pretense, or any other offense in the nature of crimen falsi, the commission of which involves some element of deceit, untruthfulness, or falsification bearing on the accused's propensity to testify truthfully.

The admission of prior convictions involving dishonesty and false statement is not within the discretion of the Court. Such convictions are peculiarly probative of credibility and, under this rule, are always to be admitted. Thus, judicial discretion granted with respect to the admissibility of other prior convictions is not applicable to those involving dishonesty or false statement.

With regard to the discretionary standard established by paragraph (1) of rule 609(a), the Conference determined that the prejudicial effect to be weighed against the probative value of the conviction is specifically the prejudicial effect *to the defendant*. The danger of prejudice to a witness other than the defendant (such as injury to the witness' reputation in his community) was considered and rejected by the Conference as an element to be weighed in determining admissibility. It was the judgment of the Conference that the danger of prejudice to a nondefendant witness is outweighed by the need for the trier of fact to have as much relevant evidence on the issue of credibility as possible. Such evidence should only be excluded where it presents a danger of improperly influencing the outcome of the trial by persuading the trier of fact to convict the defendant on the basis of his prior criminal record.

Advisory Committee's Note

Subdivision (b). Few statutes recognize a time limit on impeachment by evidence of conviction. However, practical considerations of fairness and relevancy demand that some boundary be recognized. See Ladd, Credibility Tests—Current Trends, 89 U.Pa.L.Rev. 166, 176–177 (1940). This portion of the rule is derived from the proposal advanced in Recommendation Proposing an Evidence Code, § 788(5), p. 142, Cal.Law Rev.Comm'n (1965), though not adopted. See California Evidence Code § 788.

Conference Report

The House bill provides in subsection (b) that evidence of conviction of a crime may not be used for impeachment purposes under subsection (a) if more than ten years have elapsed since the date of the conviction or the date the witness was released from confinement imposed for the conviction, whichever is later. The Senate amendment permits the use of convictions older than ten years, if the court determines, in the interests of justice, that the probative value of the conviction, supported by specific facts and circumstances, substantially outweighs its prejudicial effect.

The Conference adopts the Senate amendment with an amendment requiring notice by a party that he intends to request that the court allow him to use a conviction older than ten years. The Conferees anticipate that a written notice, in order to give the adversary a fair opportunity to contest the use of the evidence, will ordinarily include such information as the date of the conviction, the jurisdiction, and the offense or statute involved. In order to eliminate the possibility that the flexibility of this provision may impair the ability of a party-opponent to prepare for trial, the Conferees intend that the notice provision operate to avoid surprise.

Advisory Committee's Note

Subdivision (c). A pardon or its equivalent granted solely for the purpose of restoring civil rights lost by virtue of a conviction has no relevance to an inquiry into character. If, however, the pardon or other proceeding is hinged upon a showing of rehabilitation the situation is otherwise. The result under the rule is to render the conviction inadmissible. The alternative of allowing in evidence both the conviction and the rehabilitation has not been adopted for reasons of policy, economy of time, and difficulties of evaluation.

A similar provision is contained in California Evidence Code § 788. Cf. A.L.I. Model Penal Code, Proposed Official Draft § 306.6(3)(e) (1962), and discussion in A.L.I. Proceedings 310 (1961).

Pardons based on innocence have the effect, of course, of nullifying the conviction *ab initio*.

Report of House Committee on the Judiciary

... The Committee amended the Rule to provide that the "subsequent crime" must have been "punishable by death or imprisonment in excess of one year", on the ground that a subsequent conviction of an offense not a felony is insufficient to rebut the finding that the witness has been rehabilitated. The Committee also intends that the words "based on a finding of the rehabilitation of the person convicted" apply not only to "certificate of rehabilitation, or other equivalent procedure", but also to "pardon" and "annulment."

Subdivision (d). The prevailing view has been that a juvenile adjudication is not usable for impeachment. Thomas v. United States, 74 App.D.C. 167, 121 F.2d 905 (1941); Cotton v. United States, 355 F.2d 480 (10th Cir.1966). This conclusion was based upon a variety of circumstances. By virtue of its informality, frequently diminished quantum of required proof, and other departures from accepted standards for criminal trials under the theory of *parens patriae,* the juvenile adjudication was considered to lack the precision and general probative value of the criminal conviction. While In re Gault, 387 U.S. 1, 87 S.Ct. 1428, 18 L.Ed.2d 527 (1967), no doubt eliminates these characteristics insofar as objectionable, other obstacles remain. Practical problems of administration are raised by the common provisions in juvenile legislation that records be kept confidential and that they be destroyed after a short time. While *Gault* was skeptical as to the realities of confidentiality of juvenile records, it also saw no constitutional obstacles to improvement. 387 U.S. at 25, 87 S.Ct. 1428. See also Note, Rights and Rehabilitation in the Juvenile Courts, 67 Colum.L.Rev. 281, 289 (1967). In addition, policy considerations much akin to those which dictate exclusion of adult convictions after rehabilitation has been established strongly suggest a rule of excluding juvenile adjudications. Admittedly, however, the rehabilitative process may in a given case be a demonstrated failure, or the strategic importance of a given witness may be so great as to require the overriding of general policy in the interests of particular justice. See Giles v. Maryland, 386 U.S. 66, 87 S.Ct. 793, 17 L.Ed.2d 737 (1967). Wigmore was outspoken in his condemnation of the disallowance of juvenile adjudications to impeach, especially when the witness is the complainant in a case of molesting a minor. 1 Wigmore § 196; 3 id. §§ 924a, 980. The rule recognizes discretion in the judge to effect an accommodation among these various factors by departing from the general principle of exclusion. In deference to the general pattern and policy of juvenile statutes, however, no discretion is accorded when the witness is the accused in a criminal case.

Subdivision (e). The presumption of correctness which ought to attend judicial proceedings supports the position that pendency of an appeal does not preclude use of a conviction for impeachment. United States v. Empire Packing Co., 174 F.2d 16 (7th Cir.1949), cert. denied 337 U.S. 959, 69 S.Ct. 1534, 93 L.Ed. 1758; Bloch v. United States, 226 F.2d 185 (9th Cir.1955), cert. denied 350 U.S. 948, 76 S.Ct. 323, 100 L.Ed. 826 and 353 U.S. 959, 77 S.Ct. 868, 1 L.Ed.2d 910; and see Newman v. United States, 331 F.2d 968 (8th Cir.1964). Contra, Campbell v. United States, 85 U.S.App.D.C. 133, 176 F.2d 45 (1949). The pendency of an appeal is, however, a qualifying circumstance properly considerable.

Rule 610.

RELIGIOUS BELIEFS OR OPINIONS

Evidence of the beliefs or opinions of a witness on matters of religion is not admissible for the purpose of showing that by reason of their nature the witness' credibility is impaired or enhanced.

Note by Federal Judicial Center

The rule enacted by the Congress is the rule prescribed by the Supreme Court without change.

Advisory Committee's Note

While the rule forecloses inquiry into the religious beliefs or opinions of a witness for the purpose of showing that his character for truthfulness is affected by their nature, an inquiry for the purpose of showing interest or bias because of them is not within the prohibition. Thus disclosure of affiliation with a church which is a party to the litigation would be allowable under the rule. Cf. Tucker v. Reil, 51 Ariz. 357, 77 P.2d 203 (1938). To the same effect, though less specifically worded, is California Evidence Code § 789. See 3 Wigmore § 936.

Rule 611.

MODE AND ORDER OF INTERROGATION AND PRESENTATION

(a) Control by court. The court shall exercise reasonable control over the mode and order of interrogating witnesses and presenting evidence so as to (1) make the interrogation and presentation effective for the ascertainment of the truth, (2) avoid needless consumption of time, and (3) protect witnesses from harassment or undue embarrassment.

(b) Scope of cross-examination. Cross-examination should be limited to the subject matter of the direct examination and matters

195, 63 S.Ct. 549, 552, 87 L.Ed. 704 (1943). See also Brown v. United States, 356 U.S. 148, 78 S.Ct. 622, 2 L.Ed.2d 589 (1958). The situation of an accused who desires to testify on some but not all counts of a multiple-count indictment is one to be approached, in the first instance at least, as a problem of severance under Rule 14 of the Federal Rules of Criminal Procedure. Cross v. United States, 335 F.2d 987 (D.C.Cir.1964). Cf. United States v. Baker, 262 F.Supp. 657, 686 (D.D.C.1966). In all events, the extent of the waiver of the privilege against self-incrimination ought not to be determined as a by-product of a rule on scope of cross-examination.

Report of House Committee on the Judiciary

The Committee amended this provision to return to the rule which prevails in the federal courts and thirty-nine State jurisdictions. As amended, the Rule is in the text of the 1969 Advisory Committee draft. It limits cross-examination to credibility and to matters testified to on direct examination, unless the judge permits more, in which event the cross-examiner must proceed as if on direct examination. This traditional rule facilitates orderly presentation by each party at trial. Further, in light of existing discovery procedures, there appears to be no need to abandon the traditional rule.

Advisory Committee's Note

Subdivision (c). The rule continues the traditional view that the suggestive powers of the leading question are as a general proposition undesirable. Within this tradition, however, numerous exceptions have achieved recognition: The witness who is hostile, unwilling, or biased; the child witness or the adult with communication problems; the witness whose recollection is exhausted; and undisputed preliminary matters. 3 Wigmore §§ 774–778. An almost total unwillingness to reverse for infractions has been manifested by appellate courts. See cases cited in 3 Wigmore § 770. The matter clearly falls within the area of control by the judge over the mode and order of interrogation and presentation and accordingly is phrased in words of suggestion rather than command.

The rule also conforms to tradition in making the use of leading questions on cross-examination a matter of right. The purpose of the qualification "ordinarily" is to furnish a basis for denying the use of leading questions when the cross-examination is cross-examination in form only and not in fact, as for example the "cross-examination" of a party by his own counsel after being called by the opponent (savoring more of re-direct) or of an insured defendant who proves to be friendly to the plaintiff.

The final sentence deals with categories of witnesses automatically regarded and treated as hostile. Rule 43(b) of the Federal Rules of Civil Procedure has included only "an adverse party or an officer, director, or managing agent of a public or private corporation or of a partnership or association which is an adverse party." This limitation virtually to persons whose statements would stand as admissions is believed to be an unduly narrow concept of those who may safely be regarded as hostile without further demonstration. See, for example, Maryland Casualty Co. v. Kador, 225 F.2d 120 (5th Cir.1955), and Degelos v. Fidelity and Casualty Co., 313 F.2d 809 (5th Cir.1963), holding despite the language of Rule 43(b) that an insured fell within it, though not a party in an action under the Louisiana direct action statute. The phrase of the rule, "witness identified with" an adverse party, is designed to enlarge the category of persons thus callable.

Report of House Committee on the Judiciary

. . .

The Committee amended this Rule to permit leading questions to be used with respect to any hostile witness, not only an adverse party or person identified with such adverse party. The Committee also substituted the word "When" for the phrase "In civil cases" to reflect the possibility that in criminal cases a defendant may be entitled to call witnesses identified with the government, in which event the Committee believed the defendant should be permitted to inquire with leading questions.

Rule 612.

WRITING USED TO REFRESH MEMORY

Except as otherwise provided in criminal proceedings by section 3500 of title 18, United States Code, if a witness uses a writing to refresh memory for the purpose of testifying, either—

(1) while testifying, or

(2) before testifying, if the court in its discretion determines it is necessary in the interests of justice,

an adverse party is entitled to have the writing produced at the hearing, to inspect it, to cross-examine the witness thereon, and to introduce in evidence those portions which relate to the testimony of the witness. If it is claimed that the writing contains matters not related to the subject matter of the testimony the court shall examine the writing in camera, excise any portions not so related, and order delivery of the remainder to the party entitled thereto. Any portion withheld over objections shall be preserved and made available to the appellate court in the event of an appeal. If a writing is not produced or delivered pursuant to order under this rule, the court shall make any order justice requires, except that in criminal cases when the prosecution elects not to comply, the order shall be one striking the testimony or, if the court in its discretion determines that the interests of justice so require, declaring a mistrial.

Note by Federal Judicial Center

The rule enacted by the Congress is the rule prescribed by the Supreme Court, amended by substituting "court" in place of "judge," with appropriate pronominal change, and in the first sentence, by substituting "the writing" in place of "it" before "produced," and by substituting the phrase "(1) while testifying, or (2) before testifying if the court in its discretion determines it is necessary in the interests of justice" in place of "before or while testifying." The reasons for the latter amendment are stated in the Report of the House Committee on the Judiciary, set forth below.

Advisory Committee's Note

The treatment of writings used to refresh recollection while on the stand is in accord with settled doctrine. McCormick § 9, p. 15. The bulk of the case law has, however, denied the existence of any right to access by the opponent when the writing is used prior to taking the stand, though the judge may have discretion in the matter. Goldman v. United States, 316 U.S. 129, 62 S.Ct. 993, 86 L.Ed. 1322 (1942); Needelman v. United States, 261 F.2d 802 (5th Cir.1958), cert. dismissed 362 U.S. 600, 80 S.Ct. 960, 4 L.Ed.2d 980, rehearing denied 363 U.S. 858, 80 S.Ct. 1606, 4 L.Ed.2d 1739, Annot., 82 A.L.R.2d 473, 562 and 7 A.L.R.3d 181, 247. An increasing group of cases has repudiated the distinction, People v. Scott, 29 Ill.2d 97, 193 N.E.2d 814 (1963); State v. Mucci, 25 N.J. 423, 136 A.2d 761 (1957); State v. Hunt, 25 N.J. 514, 138 A.2d 1 (1958); State v. Deslovers, 40 R.I. 89, 100 A. 64 (1917), and this position is believed to be correct. As Wigmore put it, "the risk of imposition and the need of safeguard is just as great" in both situations. 3 Wigmore § 762, p. 111. To the same effect is McCormick § 9, p. 17.

The purpose of the phrase "for the purpose of testifying" is to safeguard against using the rule as a pretext for wholesale exploration of an opposing party's files and to insure that access is limited only to those writings which may fairly be said in fact to have an impact upon the testimony of the witness.

The purpose of the rule is the same as that of the *Jencks* statute, 18 U.S.C. § 3500: to promote the search of credibility and memory. The same sensitivity to disclosure of government files may be involved; hence the rule is expressly made subject to the statute, subdivision (a) of which provides: "In any criminal prosecution brought by the United States, no statement or report in the possession of the United States which was made by a Government witness or prospective Government witness (other than the defendant) shall be the subject of subpena, discovery, or inspection until said witness has testified on direct examination in the trial of the case." Items falling within the purview of the statute are producible only as provided by its terms, Palermo v. United States, 360 U.S. 343, 351, 79 S.Ct. 1217, 1224, 3 L.Ed.2d 1287 (1959), and disclosure under the rule is limited similarly by the statutory conditions. With this limitation in mind, some differences of application may be noted. The *Jencks* statute applies only to statements of witnesses; the rule is not so limited. The statute applies only to criminal cases; the rule applies to all cases. The statute applies only to government witnesses; the rule applies to all witnesses. The statute contains no requirement that the statement be consulted for purposes of refreshment before or while testifying; the rule so requires. Since many writings would qualify under either statute or rule, a substantial overlap exists, but the identity of procedures makes this of no importance.

The consequences of nonproduction by the government in a criminal case are those of the *Jencks* statute, striking the testimony or in exceptional cases a mistrial. 18 U.S.C. § 3500(d). In other cases these alternatives are unduly limited, and such possibilities as contempt, dismissal, finding issues against the offender, and the like are available. See Rule 16(g) of the Federal Rules of Criminal Procedure and Rule 37(b) of the Federal Rules of Civil Procedure for appropriate sanctions.

Report of House Committee on the Judiciary

... The Committee amended the Rule so as still to require the production of writings used by a witness while testifying, but to render the production of writings used by a witness to refresh his memory before testifying discretionary with the court in the interests of justice, as is the case under existing federal law. See Goldman v. United States, 316 U.S. 129, 62 S.Ct. 993, 86 L.Ed. 1322 (1942). The Committee considered that permitting an adverse party to require the production of writings used before testifying could result in fishing expeditions among a multitude of papers which a witness may have used in preparing for trial.

The Committee intends that nothing in the Rule be construed as barring the assertion of a privilege with respect to writings used by a witness to refresh his memory.

Editorial Note

Rule 26.2 of the Federal Rules of Criminal Procedure provides as follows:

Rule 26.2. Producing a Witness's Statement

(a) Motion to Produce. After a witness other than the defendant has testified on direct examination, the court, on motion of a party who did not call the witness, must order an attorney for the government or the defendant and the defendant's attorney to produce, for the examination and use of the moving party, any statement of the witness that is in their possession and that relates to the subject matter of the witness's testimony.

(b) Producing the Entire Statement. If the entire statement relates to the subject matter of the witness's testimony, the court must order that the statement be delivered to the moving party.

(c) Producing a Redacted Statement. If the party who called the witness claims that the statement contains information that is privileged or does not relate to the subject matter of the witness's testimony, the court must inspect the statement in camera. After excising any privileged or unrelated portions, the court must order delivery of the redacted statement to the moving party. If the defendant objects to an excision, the court must preserve the entire statement with the excised portion indicated, under seal, as part of the record.

(d) Recess to Examine a Statement. The court may recess the proceedings to allow time for a party to examine the statement and prepare for its use.

(e) Sanction for Failure to Produce or Deliver a Statement. If the party who called the witness disobeys an order to produce or deliver a statement, the court must strike the witness's testimony from the record. If an attorney for the government disobeys the order, the court must declare a mistrial if justice so requires.

(f) "Statement" Defined. As used in this rule, a witness's "statement" means:

(1) a written statement that the witness makes and signs, or otherwise adopts or approves;

(2) a substantially verbatim, contemporaneously recorded recital of the witness's oral statement that is contained in any recording or any transcription of a recording; or

(3) the witness's statement to a grand jury, however taken or recorded, or a transcription of such a statement.

(g) Scope. This rule applies at trial, at a suppression hearing under Rule 12, and to the extent specified in the following rules:

(1) Rule 5.1(h) (preliminary hearing);

(2) Rule 32(i)(2) (sentencing);

(3) Rule 32.1(e) (hearing to revoke or modify probation or supervised release);

(4) Rule 46(j) (detention hearing); and

(5) Rule 8 of the Rules Governing Proceedings under 28 U.S.C. § 2255.

Rule 613.

PRIOR STATEMENTS OF WITNESSES

(a) Examining witness concerning prior statement. In examining a witness concerning a prior statement made by the witness, whether written or not, the statement need not be shown nor its contents disclosed to the witness at that time, but on request the same shall be shown or disclosed to opposing counsel.

(b) Extrinsic evidence of prior inconsistent statement of witness. Extrinsic evidence of a prior inconsistent statement by a witness is not admissible unless the witness is afforded an opportunity to explain or deny the same and the opposite party is afforded an opportunity to interrogate the witness thereon, or the interests of justice otherwise require. This provision does not apply to admissions of a party-opponent as defined in rule 801(d)(2).

Note by Federal Judicial Center

The rule enacted by the Congress is the rule prescribed by the Supreme Court, amended only by substituting "nor" in place of "or" in subdivision (a).

Advisory Committee's Note

Subdivision (a). The Queen's Case, 2 Br. & B. 284, 129 Eng.Rep. 976 (1820), laid down the requirement that a cross-examiner, prior to questioning the witness about his own prior statement in writing, must first show it to the witness. Abolished by statute in the country of its origin, the requirement nevertheless gained currency in the United States. The rule abolishes this useless impediment, to cross-examination. Ladd, Some Observations on Credibility: Impeachment of Witnesses, 52 Cornell L.Q. 239, 246–247 (1967); McCormick § 28; 4 Wigmore §§ 1259–1260. Both oral and written statements are included.

The provision for disclosure to counsel is designed to protect against unwarranted insinuations that a statement has been made when the fact is to the contrary.

The rule does not defeat the application of Rule 1002 relating to production of the original when the contents of a writing are sought to be proved. Nor does it defeat the application of Rule 26(b)(3) of the Rules of Civil Procedure, as revised, entitling a person on request to a copy of his own statement, though the operation of the latter may be suspended temporarily.

Subdivision (b). The familiar foundation requirement that an impeaching statement first be shown to the witness before it can be proved by extrinsic evidence is preserved but with some modifications. See Ladd, Some Observations on Credibility: Impeachment of Witnesses, 52 Cornell L.Q. 239, 247 (1967). The traditional insistence that the attention of the witness be directed to the statement on cross-examination is relaxed in favor of simply providing the witness an opportunity to explain and the opposite party an opportunity to examine on the statement, with no specification of any particular time or sequence. Under this procedure, several collusive witnesses can be examined before disclosure of a joint prior inconsistent statement. See Comment to California Evidence Code § 770. Also, dangers of oversight are reduced. See McCormick § 37, p. 68.

In order to allow for such eventualities as the witness becoming unavailable by the time the statement is discovered, a measure of discretion is conferred upon the judge. Similar provisions are found in California Evidence Code § 770 and New Jersey Evidence Rule 22(b).

Under principles of *expressio unius* the rule does not apply to impeachment by evidence of prior inconsistent conduct. The use of inconsistent statements to impeach a hearsay declaration is treated in Rule 806.

Rule 614.

CALLING AND INTERROGATION OF WITNESSES BY COURT

(a) Calling by court. The court may, on its own motion or at the suggestion of a party, call witnesses, and all parties are entitled to cross-examine witnesses thus called.

(b) Interrogation by court. The court may interrogate witnesses, whether called by itself or by a party.

(c) Objections. Objections to the calling of witnesses by the court or to interrogation by it may be made at the time or at the next available opportunity when the jury is not present.

Note by Federal Judicial Center

The rule enacted by the Congress is the rule prescribed by the Supreme Court, amended only by substituting "court" in place of "judge," with conforming pronominal changes.

Advisory Committee's Note

Subdivision (a). While exercised more frequently in criminal than in civil cases, the authority of the judge to call witnesses is well established. McCormick § 8, p. 14; Maguire, Weinstein, et al., Cases on Evidence 303–304 (5th ed.1965); 9 Wigmore § 2484. One reason for the practice, the old rule against impeaching one's own witness, no longer exists by virtue of Rule 607, supra. Other reasons remain, however, to justify the continuation of the practice of calling court's witnesses. The right to cross-examine, with all it implies, is assured. The tendency of juries to associate a witness with the party calling him, regardless of technical aspects of vouching, is avoided. And the judge is not imprisoned within the case as made by the parties.

Subdivision (b). The authority of the judge to question witnesses is also well established. McCormick § 8, pp. 12–13; Maguire, Weinstein, et al., Cases on Evidence 737–739 (5th ed.1965); 3 Wigmore § 784. The authority is, of course, abused when the judge abandons his proper role and assumes that of advocate, but the manner in which interrogation should be conducted and the proper extent of its exercise are not susceptible of formulation in a rule. The omission in no sense precludes courts of review from continuing to reverse for abuse.

Subdivision (c). The provision relating to objections is designed to relieve counsel of the embarrassment attendant upon objecting to questions by the judge in the presence of the jury, while at the same time assuring that objections are made in apt time to afford the opportunity to take possible corrective measures. Compare the "automatic" objection feature of Rule 605 when the judge is called as a witness.

Rule 615.

EXCLUSION OF WITNESSES

At the request of a party the court shall order witnesses excluded so that they cannot hear the testimony of other witnesses, and it may make the order of its own motion. This rule does not authorize exclusion of (1) a party who is a natural person, or (2) an officer or employee of a party which is not a natural person designated as its representative by its attorney, or (3) a person whose presence is shown by a party to be essential to the presentation of the party's cause, or (4) a person authorized by statute to be present.

1998 Amendment

A fourth category was added to the second sentence of Rule 615 in order to conform Rule 615 with the Victim's Rights and Restitution Act of 1990, 42 U.S.C.A. § 10606, and with the Victim Rights Clarification Act of 1997, 18 U.S.C.A. § 3510.

The Victim's Rights and Restitution Act provides in 42 U.S.C.A.§ 10606(b):

A crime victim has the following rights:

. . .

(4) The right to be present at all public court proceedings related to the offense, unless the court determines that testimony by the victim would be materially affected if the victim heard other testimony at trial.

The Victim Rights Clarification Act of 1997 provides in 18 U.S.C.A. § 3510:

(a) Non-capital cases. Notwithstanding any statute, rule, or other provision of law, a United States district court shall not order any victim of an offense excluded from the trial of a defendant accused of that offense because such victim may, during the sentencing hearing, make a statement or present any information in relation to the sentence.

(b) Capital cases. Notwithstanding any statute, rule, or other provision of law, a United States district court shall not order any victim of an offense excluded from the trial of a defendant accused of that offense because such victim may, during the sentencing hearing, testify as to the effect of the offense on the victim and the victim's family or as to any other factor for which notice is required under section 3593(a).

Note by Federal Judicial Center

The rule enacted by the Congress is the rule prescribed by the Supreme Court, amended only by substituting "court," in place of "judge," with conforming pronominal changes.

Advisory Committee's Note

The efficacy of excluding or sequestering witnesses has long been recognized as a means of discouraging and exposing fabrication, inaccuracy, and collusion. 6 Wigmore §§ 1837–1838. The authority of the judge is admitted, the only question being whether the matter is committed to his discretion or one of right. The rule takes the latter position. No time is specified for making the request.

Several categories of persons are excepted. (1) Exclusion of persons who are parties would raise serious problems of confrontation and due process. Under accepted practice they are not subject to exclusion. 6 Wigmore § 1841. (2) As the equivalent of the right of a natural-person party to be present, a party which is not a natural person is entitled to have a representative present. Most of the cases have involved allowing a police officer who has been in charge of an investigation to remain in court despite the fact that he will be a witness. United States v. Infanzon, 235 F.2d 318 (2d Cir.1956); Portomene v. United States, 221 F.2d 582 (5th Cir.1955); Powell v. United States, 208 F.2d 618 (6th Cir.1953); Jones v. United States, 252 F.Supp. 781 (W.D.Okl.1966). Designation of the representative by the attorney rather than by the client may at first glance appear to be an inversion of the attorney-client relationship, but it may be assumed that the attorney will follow the wishes of the client, and the solution is simple and workable. See California Evidence Code § 777. (3) The category contemplates such persons as an agent who handled the transaction being litigated or an expert needed to advise counsel in the management of the litigation. See 6 Wigmore § 1841, n. 4.

Report of Senate Committee on the Judiciary

Many district courts permit government counsel to have an investigative agent at counsel table throughout the trial although the agent is or may be a witness. The practice is permitted as an exception to the rule of exclusion and compares with the situation defense counsel finds himself in—he always has the client with him to consult during the trial. The investigative agent's presence may be extremely important to government counsel, especially when the case is complex or involves some specialized subject matter. The agent, too, having lived with the case for a long time, may be able to assist in meeting trial surprises where the best-prepared counsel would otherwise have difficulty. Yet, it would not seem the Government could often meet the burden under rule 615 of showing that the agent's presence is essential. Furthermore, it could be dangerous to use the agent as a witness as early in the case as possible, so that he might then help counsel as a nonwitness, since the agent's testimony could be needed in rebuttal. Using another, nonwitness agent from the same investigative agency would not generally meet government counsel's needs.

This problem is solved if it is clear that investigative agents are within the group specified under the second exception made in the rule, for "an officer or employee of a party which is not a natural person designated as its representative by its attorney." It is our understanding that this was the intention of the House committee. It is certainly this committee's construction of the rule.

ARTICLE VII. OPINIONS AND EXPERT TESTIMONY

Rule 701.

OPINION TESTIMONY BY LAY WITNESSES

If the witness is not testifying as an expert, the witness' testimony in the form of opinions or inferences is limited to those opinions or inferences which are (a) rationally based on the perception of the witness, and (b) helpful to a clear understanding of the witness' testimony or the determination of a fact in issue, and (c) not based on scientific, technical or other specialized knowledge within the scope of Rule 702.

Advisory Committee's Note to 2000 Amendment to Rule 701

Rule 701 has been amended to eliminate the risk that the liability requirements set forth in Rule 702 will be evaded through the simple expedient of proffering an expert in lay witness clothing. Under the amendment, a witness' testimony must be scrutinized under the rules regulating expert opinion to the extent that the witness is providing testimony based on scientific, technical, or other specialized knowledge within the scope of Rule 702. *See generally Asplundh Mfg. Div. v. Benton Harbor Eng'g*, 57 F.3d 1190 (3d Cir.1995). By channeling testimony that is actually expert testimony to Rule 702, the amendment also ensures that a party will not evade the expert witness disclosure requirements set forth in Fed.R.Civ.P. 26 and Fed.R.Crim.P.16 by simply calling an expert witness in the guise of a layperson. *See* Joseph, *Emerging Expert Issues Under the 1993 Disclosure Amendments to the Federal Rules of Civil Procedure*, 164 F.R.D. 97, 108 (1996) (noting that "there is no good reason to allow what is essentially surprise expert testimony," and that "the Court should be vigilant to preclude manipulative conduct designed to thwart the expert disclosure and discovery process"). *See also United States v. Figueroa–Lopez*, 125 F.3d 1241, 1246 (9th Cir.1997) (law enforcement agents testifying that the defendant's conduct was consistent with that of a drug trafficker could not testify as lay witnesses; to permit such testimony under Rule 701 "subverts the requirements of Federal Rule of Criminal Procedure 16(a)(1)(E)").

The amendment does not distinguish between expert and lay *witnesses*, but rather between expert and lay *testimony*. Certainly it is possible for the same witness to provide both lay and expert testimony in a single case. *See, e.g, United States v. Figueroa–Lopez*, 125 F.3d 1241, 1246 (9th Cir.1997) (law enforcement agents could testify that the defendant was acting suspiciously, without being qualified as experts; however, the rules on experts were applicable where the agents testified on the basis of extensive experience that the defendant was using code words to refer to drug quantities and prices). The amendment makes clear that any part of a witness' testimony that is based upon scientific, technical, or other specialized knowledge within the scope of Rule 702 is governed by the standards of Rule 702 and the corresponding disclosure requirements of the Civil and Criminal Rules.

The amendment is not intended to affect the "prototypical example[s] of the type of evidence contemplated by the adoption of Rule 701 relat[ing] to the appearance of persons or things, identity, the manner of conduct, competency of a person, degrees of light or darkness, sound, size, weight, distance, and an endless number of items that cannot be described factually in words apart from inferences." *Asplundh Mfg. Div. v. Benton Harbor Eng'g,* 57 F.3d 1190, 1196 (3d Cir.1995).

For example, most courts have permitted the owner or officer of a business to testify to the value or projected profits of the business, without the necessity of qualifying the witness as an accountant, appraiser, or similar expert. *See, e.g., Lightning Lube, Inc. v. Witco Corp.* 4 F.3d 1153 (3d Cir.1993) (no abuse of discretion in permitting the plaintiff's owner to give lay opinion testimony as to damages, as it was based on his knowledge and participation in the day-to-day affairs of the business). Such opinion testimony is admitted not because of experience, training or specialized knowledge within the realm of an expert, but because of the particularized knowledge that the witness has by virtue of his or her position in the business. The amendment does not purport to change this analysis. Similarly, courts have permitted lay witnesses to testify that a substance appeared to be a narcotic, so long as a foundation of familiarity with the substance is established. *See, e.g., United States v. Westbrook,* 896 F.2d 330 (8th Cir.1990) (two lay witnesses who were heavy amphetamine users were properly permitted to testify that a substance was amphetamine; but it was error to permit another witness to make such an identification where she had no experience with amphetamines). Such testimony is not based on specialized knowledge within the scope of Rule 702, but rather is based upon a layperson's personal knowledge. If, however, that witness were to describe how a narcotic was manufactured, or to describe the intricate workings of a narcotic distribution network, then the witness would have to qualify as an expert under Rule 702. *United States v. Figueroa–Lopez, supra.*

The amendment incorporates the distinctions set forth in *State v. Brown,* 836 S.W.2d 530, 549 (1992), a case involving former Tennessee Rule of Evidence 701, a rule that precluded lay witness testimony based on "special knowledge." In *Brown,* the court declared that the distinction between lay and expert witness testimony is that lay testimony "results from a process of reasoning familiar in everyday life", while expert testimony "results from a process of reasoning which can be mastered only by specialists in the field." The court in *Brown* noted that a lay witness with experience could testify that a substance appeared to be blood, but that a witness would have to qualify as an expert before he could testify that bruising around the eyes is indicative of skull trauma. That is the kind of distinction made by the amendment to this Rule.

Note by Federal Judicial Center

The rule enacted by the Congress is the rule prescribed by the Supreme Court without change.

Advisory Committee's Note

The rule retains the traditional objective of putting the trier of fact in possession of an accurate reproduction of the event.

Limitation (a) is the familiar requirement of first-hand knowledge or observation.

Limitation (b) is phrased in terms of requiring testimony to be helpful in resolving issues. Witnesses often find difficulty in expressing themselves in language which is not that of an opinion or conclusion. While the courts have made concessions in certain recurring situations, necessity as a standard for permitting opinions and conclusions has proved too elusive and too unadaptable to particular situations for purposes of satisfactory judicial administration. McCormick § 11. Moreover, the practical impossibility of determining by rule what is a "fact," demonstrated by a century of litigation of the question of what is a fact for purposes of pleading under the Field Code, extends into evidence also. 7 Wigmore § 1919. The rule assumes that the natural characteristics of the adversary system will generally lead to an acceptable result, since the detailed account carries more conviction than the broad assertion, and a lawyer can be expected to display his witness to the best advantage. If he fails to do so, cross-examination and argument will point up the weakness. See Ladd, Expert Testimony, 5 Vand.L.Rev. 414, 415–417 (1952). If, despite these considerations, attempts are made to introduce meaningless assertions which amount to little more than choosing up sides, exclusion for lack of helpfulness is called for by the rule.

The language of the rule is substantially that of Uniform Rule 56(1). Similar provisions are California Evidence Code § 800; Kansas Code of Civil Procedure § 60–456(a); New Jersey Evidence Rule 56(1).

Rule 702.

TESTIMONY BY EXPERTS

If scientific, technical, or other specialized knowledge will assist the trier of fact to understand the evidence or to determine a fact in issue, a witness qualified as an expert by knowledge, skill, experience, training, or education, may testify thereto in the form of an opinion or otherwise, if (1) the testimony is based upon sufficient facts or data, (2) the testimony is the product of reliable principles and methods, and (3) the witness has applied the principles and methods reliably to the facts of the case.

Advisory Committee's Note to 2000 Amendment to Rule 702

Rule 702 has been amended in response to *Daubert v. Merrell Dow Pharmaceuticals, Inc.,* 509 U.S. 579 (1993), and to the many cases applying *Daubert,* including *Kumho Tire Co. v. Carmichael,* 119 S.Ct. 1167 (1999). In *Daubert* the Court charged trial judges with the responsibility of acting as gatekeepers to exclude unreliable expert testimony, and the Court in *Kumho* clarified that this gatekeeper function applies to all expert testimony, not just testimony based in science. *See also Kumho,* 119 S.Ct. at 1178 (citing the Committee Note to the proposed amendment to Rule 702, which had been released for public comment before the date of the Kumho decision). The amendment affirms the trial court's role as gatekeeper and provides some general standards that the trial court must use to assess the reliability and helpfulness of proffered expert testimony. Consistently with *Kumho,* the Rule as amended provides that all types of expert testimony present questions of admissibility for the trial court in deciding whether the evidence is reliable and helpful. Consequently, the admissibility of all expert testimony is governed by the principles of Rule 104(a). Under that Rule, the proponent has the burden of establishing that the pertinent admissibility requirements are met by a preponderance of the evidence. *See Bourjaily v. United States,* 483 U.S. 171 (1987).

Daubert set forth a non-exclusive checklist for trial courts to use in assessing the reliability of scientific expert testimony. The specific factors explicated by the *Daubert* Court are (1) whether the expert's technique or theory can be or has been tested—that is, whether the expert's theory can be challenged in some objective sense, or whether it is instead simply a subjective, conclusory approach that cannot reasonably be assessed for reliability; (2) whether the technique or theory has been subject to peer review and publication; (3) the known or potential rate of error of the technique or theory when applied; (4) the existence and maintenance of standards and controls; and (5) whether the technique or theory has been generally accepted in the scientific community. The Court in *Kumho* held that these factors might also be applicable in assessing the reliability of non-scientific expert testimony, depending upon "the particular circumstances of the particular case at issue." 119 S.Ct. at 1175.

No attempt has been made to "codify" these specific factors. *Daubert* itself emphasized that the factors were neither exclusive nor dispositive. Other cases have recognized that not all of the specific *Daubert* factors can apply to every type of expert testimony. In addition to *Kumho,* 119 S.Ct. at 1175, *see Tyus v. Urban Search Management,* 102 F.3d 256 (7th Cir.1996) (noting that the factors mentioned by the Court in *Daubert* do not neatly apply to expert testimony from a sociologist). *See also Kannankeril v. Terminix Int'l, Inc.,* 128 F.3d 802, 809 (3d Cir.1997) (holding that lack of peer review or publication was not dispositive where the expert's opinion was supported by "widely accepted scientific knowledge"). The standards set forth in the amendment are broad enough to require consideration of any or all of the specific *Daubert* factors where appropriate.

Courts both before and after *Daubert* have found other factors relevant in determining whether expert testimony is sufficiently reliable to be considered by the trier of fact. These factors include:

(1) Whether experts are "proposing to testify about matters growing naturally and directly out of research they have conducted independent of the litigation, or whether they have developed their opinions expressly for purposes of testifying." *Daubert v. Merrell Dow Pharmaceuticals, Inc.,* 43 F.3d 1311, 1317 (9th Cir.1995).

(2) Whether the expert has unjustifiably extrapolated from an accepted premise to an unfounded conclusion. *See General Elec. Co. v. Joiner,* 522 U.S. 136, 146 (1997) (noting that in some cases a trial court "may conclude that there is simply too great an analytical gap between the data and the opinion proffered").

(3) Whether the expert has adequately accounted for obvious alternative explanations. *See Claar v. Burlington N.R.R.,* 29 F.3d 499 (9th Cir.1994)

(testimony excluded where the expert failed to consider other obvious causes for the plaintiff's condition). Compare *Ambrosini v. Labarraque*, 101 F.3d 129 (D.C.Cir.1996) (the possibility of some uneliminated causes presents a question of weight, so long as the most obvious causes have been considered and reasonably ruled out by the expert).

(4) Whether the expert "is being as careful as he would be in his regular professional work outside his paid litigation consulting." *Sheehan v. Daily Racing Form, Inc.*, 104 F.3d 940, 942 (7th Cir.1997). See *Kumho Tire Co. v. Carmichael*, 119 S.Ct. 1167, 1176 (1999) (*Daubert* requires the trial court to assure itself that the expert "employs in the courtroom the same level of intellectual rigor that characterizes the practice of an expert in the relevant field").

(5) Whether the field of expertise claimed by the expert is known to reach reliable results for the type of opinion the expert would give. See *Kumho Tire Co. v. Carmichael*, 119 S.Ct. 1167, 1175 (1999) (*Daubert's* general acceptance factor does not "help show that an expert's testimony is reliable where the discipline itself lacks reliability, as, for example, do theories grounded in any so-called generally accepted principles of astrology or necromancy."); *Moore v. Ashland Chemical, Inc.*, 151 F.3d 269 (5th Cir. 1998) (en banc) (clinical doctor was properly precluded from testifying to the toxicological cause of the plaintiff's respiratory problem, where the opinion was not sufficiently grounded in scientific methodology); *Sterling v. Velsicol Chem. Corp.*, 855 F.2d 1188 (6th Cir.1988) (rejecting testimony based on "clinical ecology" as unfounded and unreliable).

All of these factors remain relevant to the determination of the reliability of expert testimony under the Rule as amended. Other factors may also be relevant. See *Kumho*, 119 S.Ct. 1167, 1176 ("[W]e conclude that the trial judge must have considerable leeway in deciding in a particular case how to go about determining whether particular expert testimony is reliable."). Yet no single factor is necessarily dispositive of the reliability of a particular expert's testimony. See, e.g., *Heller v. Shaw Industries, Inc.*, 167 F.3d 146, 155 (3d Cir.1999) ("not only must each stage of the expert's testimony be reliable, but each stage must be evaluated practically and flexibly without bright-line exclusionary (or inclusionary) rules."); *Daubert v. Merrell Dow Pharmaceuticals, Inc.*, 43 F.3d 1311, 1317, n. 5 (9th Cir.1995) (noting that some expert disciplines "have the courtroom as a principal theatre of operations" and as to these disciplines "the fact that the expert has developed an expertise principally for purposes of litigation will obviously not be a substantial consideration.").

A review of the caselaw after *Daubert* shows that the rejection of expert testimony is the exception rather than the rule. *Daubert* did not work a "seachange over federal evidence law," and "the trial court's role as gatekeeper is not intended to serve as a replacement for the adversary system." *United States v. 14.38 Acres of Land Situated in Leflore County, Mississippi*, 80 F.3d 1074, 1078 (5th Cir.1996). As the Court in *Daubert* stated: "Vigorous cross-examination, presentation of contrary evidence, and careful instruction on the burden of proof are the traditional and appropriate means of attacking shaky but admissible evidence." 509 U.S. at 595. Likewise, this amendment is not intended to provide an excuse for an automatic challenge to the testimony of every expert. See *Kumho Tire Co. v. Carmichael*, 119 S.Ct.1167, 1176 (1999) (noting that the trial judge has the discretion "both to avoid unnecessary 'reliability' proceedings n ordinary cases where the reliability of an expert's methods is properly taken for granted, and to require appropriate proceedings in the less usual or more complex cases where cause for questioning the expert's reliability arises.").

When a trial court, applying this amendment, rules that an expert's testimony is reliable, this does not necessarily mean that contradictory expert testimony is unreliable. The amendment is broad enough to permit testimony that is the product of competing principles or methods in the same field of expertise. *See, e.g., Heller v. Shaw Industries, Inc.*, 167 F.3d 146, 160 (3d Cir.1999) (expert testimony cannot be excluded simply because the expert uses one test rather than another, when both tests are accepted in the field and both reach reliable results). As the court stated in *In re Paoli R.R. Yard PCB Litigation*, 35 F.3d 717, 744 (3d Cir.1994), proponents "do not have to demonstrate to the judge by a preponderance of the evidence that the assessments of their experts are correct, they only have to demonstrate by a preponderance of evidence that their opinions are reliable.... The evidentiary requirement of reliability is lower than the merits standard of correctness." See also *Daubert v. Merrell Dow Pharmaceuticals, Inc.*, 43 F.3d 1311, 1318 (9th Cir.1995) (scientific experts might be permitted to testify if they could show that the methods they used were also employed by "a recognized minority of scientists in their field."); *Ruiz–Troche v. Pepsi Cola*, 161 F.3d 77, 85 (1st Cir.1998) (*"Daubert* neither requires nor empowers trial courts to determine which of several competing scientific theories has the best provenance.").

The Court in *Daubert* declared that the "focus, of course, must be solely on principles and methodology, not on the conclusions they generate." 509 U.S. at 595. Yet as the Court later recognized, "conclusions and methodology are not entirely distinct from one another." *General Elec. Co. v. Joiner*, 522 U.S. 136, 146 (1997). Under the amendment, as under *Daubert*, when an expert purports to apply principles and methods in accordance with professional standards, and yet reaches a conclusion that other experts in the field would not reach, the trial court may fairly suspect that the principles and methods have not been faithfully applied. *See Lust v. Merrell Dow Pharmaceuticals, Inc.*, 89 F.3d 594, 598 (9th Cir.1996). The amendment specifically provides that the trial court must scrutinize not only the principles and methods used by the expert, but also whether those principles and methods have been properly applied to the facts of the case. As the court noted in *In re Paoli R.R. Yard PCB Litig.*, 35 F.3d 717, 745 (3d Cir.1994), "*any* step that renders the analysis unreliable ... renders the expert's testimony inadmissible. *This is true whether the step completely changes a reliable methodology or merely misapplies that methodology.*"

If the expert purports to apply principles and methods to the facts of the case, it is important that this application be conducted reliably. Yet it might also be important in some cases for an expert to educate the factfinder about general principles, without ever attempting to apply these principles to the specific facts of the case. For example, experts might instruct the factfinder on the principles of thermodynamics, or bloodclotting, or on how financial markets respond to corporate reports, without ever knowing about or trying to tie their testimony into the facts of the case. The amendment does not alter the venerable practice of using expert testimony to educate the factfinder on general principles. For this kind of generalized testimony, Rule 702 simply requires that: (1) the expert be qualified; (2) the testimony address a subject matter on which the factfinder can be assisted by an expert; (3) the testimony be reliable; and (4) the testimony "fit" the facts of the case.

As stated earlier, the amendment does not distinguish between scientific and other forms of expert testimony. The trial court's gatekeeping function applies to testimony by any expert. See *Kumho Tire Co. v. Carmichael,* 119 S.Ct. 1167, 1171 (1999) ("We conclude that *Daubert's* general holding—setting forth the trial judge's general 'gatekeeping' obligation—applies not only to testimony based on 'scientific' knowledge, but also to testimony based on 'technical' and 'other specialized' knowledge."). While the relevant factors for determining reliability will vary from expertise to expertise, the amendment rejects the premise that an expert's testimony should be treated more permissively simply because it is outside the realm of science. An opinion from an expert who is not a scientist should receive the same degree of scrutiny for reliability as an opinion from an expert who purports to be a scientist. See Watkins *v. Telsmith, Inc.*, 121 F.3d 984, 991 (5th Cir.1997) ("[I]t seems exactly backwards that experts who purport to rely on general engineering principles and practical experience might escape screening by the district court simply by stating that their conclusions were not reached by any particular method or technique."). Some types of expert testimony will be more objectively verifiable, and subject to the expectations of falsifiability, peer review, and publication, than others. Some types of expert testimony will not rely on anything like a scientific method, and so will have to be evaluated by reference to other standard principles attendant to the particular area of expertise. The trial judge in all cases of proffered expert testimony must find that it is properly grounded, well-reasoned, and not speculative before it can be admitted. The expert's testimony must be grounded in an accepted body of learning or experience in the expert's field, and the expert must explain how the conclusion is so grounded. *See, e.g.,* American College of Trial Lawyers, *Standards and Procedures for Determining the Admissibility of Expert Testimony after Daubert,* 157 F.R.D. 571, 579 (1994) ("[W]hether the testimony concerns economic principles, accounting standards, property valuation or other non-scientific subjects, it should be evaluated by reference to the 'knowledge and experience' of that particular field.").

The amendment requires that the testimony must be the product of reliable principles and methods that are reliably applied to the facts of the case. While the terms "principles" and "methods" may convey a certain impression when applied to scientific knowledge, they remain relevant when applied to testimony based on technical or other specialized knowledge. For example, when a law enforcement agent testifies regarding the use of code words in a drug transaction, the principle used by the agent is that participants in such transactions regularly use code words to conceal the nature of their activities. The method used by the agent is the application of extensive experience to analyze the meaning of the conversations. So long as the principles and methods are reliable and applied reliably to the facts of the case, this type of testimony should be admitted.

Nothing in this amendment is intended to suggest that experience alone—or experience in conjunction with other knowledge, skill, training or education—may not provide a sufficient foundation for expert testimony. To the contrary, the text of Rule 702 expressly contemplates that an expert may be qualified on the basis of experience. In certain fields, experience is the predominant, if not sole, basis for a great deal of reliable expert testimony. *See, e.g., United States v.*

Jones, 107 F.3d 1147 (6th Cir.1997) (no abuse of discretion in admitting the testimony of a handwriting examiner who had years of practical experience and extensive training, and who explained his methodology in detail); *Tassin v. Sears Roebuck*, 946 F.Supp. 1241, 1248 (M.D.La.1996) (design engineer's testimony can be admissible when the expert's opinions "are based on facts, a reasonable investigation, and traditional technical/mechanical expertise, and he provides a reasonable link between the information and procedures he uses and the conclusions he reaches"). See also *Kumho Tire Co. v. Carmichael*, 119 S.Ct.1167, 1178 (1999) (stating that "no one denies that an expert might draw a conclusion from a set of observations based on extensive and specialized experience.").

If the witness is relying solely or primarily on experience, then the witness must explain how that experience leads to the conclusion reached, why that experience is a sufficient basis for the opinion, and how that experience is reliably applied to the facts. The trial court's gatekeeping function requires more than simply "taking the expert's word for it." *See Daubert v. Merrell Dow Pharmaceuticals, Inc.*, 43 F.3d 1311, 1319 (9th Cir.1995) ("We've been presented with only the experts' qualifications, their conclusions and their assurances of reliability. Under *Daubert*, that's not enough."). The more subjective and controversial the expert's inquiry, the more likely the testimony should be excluded as unreliable. *See O'Conner v. Commonwealth Edison Co.*, 13 F.3d 1090 (7th Cir.1994) (expert testimony based on a completely subjective methodology held properly excluded). See also *Kumho Tire Co. v. Carmichael*, 119 S.Ct. 1167, 1176 (1999) ("[I]t will at times be useful to ask even of a witness whose expertise is based purely on experience, say, a perfume tester able to distinguish among 140 odors at a sniff, whether his preparation is of a kind that others in the field would recognize as acceptable.").

Subpart (1) of Rule 702 calls for a quantitative rather than qualitative analysis. The amendment requires that expert testimony be based on sufficient underlying "facts or data." The term "data" is intended to encompass the reliable opinions of other experts. See the original Advisory Committee Note to Rule 703. The language "facts or data" is broad enough to allow an expert to rely on hypothetical facts that are supported by the evidence. *Id.*

When facts are in dispute, experts sometimes reach different conclusions based on competing versions of the facts. The emphasis in the amendment on "sufficient facts or data" is not intended to authorize a trial court to exclude an expert's testimony on the ground that the court believes one version of the facts and not the other.

There has been some confusion over the relationship between Rules 702 and 703. The amendment makes clear that the sufficiency of the basis of an expert's testimony is to be decided under Rule 702. Rule 702 sets forth the overarching requirement of reliability, and an analysis of the sufficiency of the expert's basis cannot be divorced from the ultimate reliability of the expert's opinion. In contrast, the "reasonable reliance" requirement of Rule 703 is a relatively narrow inquiry. When an expert relies on inadmissible information, Rule 703 requires the trial court to determine whether that information is of a type reasonably relied on by other experts in the field. If so, the expert can rely on the information in reaching an opinion. However, the question whether the expert is relying on a *sufficient* basis of information—whether admissible information or not—is governed by the requirements of Rule 702.

The amendment makes no attempt to set forth procedural requirements for exercising the trial court's gatekeeping function over expert testimony. *See* Daniel J. Capra, *The Daubert Puzzle*, 38 Ga.L.Rev. 699, 766 (1998) ("Trial courts should be allowed substantial discretion in dealing with *Daubert* questions; any attempt to codify procedures will likely give rise to unnecessary changes in practice and create difficult questions for appellate review."). Courts have shown considerable ingenuity and flexibility in considering challenges to expert testimony under *Daubert*, and it is contemplated that this will continue under the amended Rule. *See, e.g., Cortes–Irizarry v. Corporacion Insular*, 111 F.3d 184 (1st Cir.1997) (discussing the application of *Daubert* in ruling on a motion for summary judgment); *In re Paoli R.R. Yard PCB Litig.*, 35 F.3d 717, 736, 739 (3d Cir.1994) (discussing the use of *in limine* hearings); *Claar v. Burlington N.R.R.*, 29 F.3d 499, 502–05 (9th Cir.1994) (discussing the trial court's technique of ordering experts to submit serial affidavits explaining the reasoning and methods underlying their conclusions).

The amendment continues the practice of the original Rule in referring to a qualified witness as an "expert." This was done to provide continuity and to minimize change. The use of the term "expert" in the Rule does not, however, mean that a jury should actually be informed that a qualified witness is testifying as an "expert." Indeed, there is much to be said for a practice that prohibits the use of the term "expert" by both the parties and the court at trial. Such a practice "ensures that trial courts do not inadvertently put their stamp of authority" on a witness's opinion, and protects against the jury's being "overwhelmed by the so-called 'experts'." Hon. Charles Richey, *Proposals to Eliminate the Prejudicial Effect of the Use of the Word "Expert" Under the Federal Rules of Evidence in Criminal and Civil Jury Trials*, 154 F.R.D. 537, 559 (1994) (setting forth limiting instructions and a standing order employed to prohibit the use of the term "expert" in jury trials).

Note by Federal Judicial Center

The rule enacted by the Congress is the rule prescribed by the Supreme Court without change.

Advisory Committee's Note

An intelligent evaluation of facts is often difficult or impossible without the application of some scientific, technical, or other specialized knowledge. The most common source of this knowledge is the expert witness, although there are other techniques for supplying it.

Most of the literature assumes that experts testify only in the form of opinions. The assumption is logically unfounded. The rule accordingly recognizes that an expert on the stand may give a dissertation or exposition of scientific or other principles relevant to the case, leaving the trier of fact to apply them to the facts. Since much of the criticism of expert testimony has centered upon the hypothetical question, it seems wise to recognize that opinions are not indispensable and to encourage the use of expert testimony in nonopinion form when counsel believes the trier can itself draw the requisite inference. The use of opinions is not abolished by the rule, however. It will continue to be permissible for the expert to take the further step of suggesting the inference which should be drawn from applying the specialized knowledge to the facts. See Rules 703 to 705.

Whether the situation is a proper one for the use of expert testimony is to be determined on the basis of assisting the trier. "There is no more certain test for determining when experts may be used than the common sense inquiry whether the untrained layman would be qualified to determine intelligently and to the best possible degree the particular issue without enlightenment from those having a specialized understanding of the subject involved in the dispute." Ladd, Expert Testimony, 5 Vand.L.Rev. 414, 418 (1952). When opinions are excluded, it is because they are unhelpful and therefore superfluous and a waste of time. 7 Wigmore § 1918.

The rule is broadly phrased. The fields of knowledge which may be drawn upon are not limited merely to the "scientific" and "technical" but extend to all "specialized" knowledge. Similarly, the expert is viewed, not in a narrow sense, but as a person qualified by "knowledge, skill, experience, training or education." Thus within the scope of the rule are not only experts in the strictest sense of the word, e.g. physicians, physicists, and architects, but also the large group sometimes called "skilled" witnesses, such as bankers or landowners testifying to land values.

Rule 703.

BASES OF OPINION TESTIMONY BY EXPERTS

The facts or data in the particular case upon which an expert bases an opinion or inference may be those perceived by or made known to the expert at or before the hearing. If of a type reasonably relied upon by experts in the particular field in forming opinions or inferences upon the subject, the facts or data need not be admissible in evidence in order for the opinion or inference to be admitted. Facts or data that are otherwise inadmissible shall not be disclosed to the jury by the proponent of the opinion or inference unless the court determines that their probative value in assisting the jury to evaluate the expert's opinion substantially outweighs their prejudicial effect.

Advisory Committee's Note to 2000 Amendment to Rule 703

Rule 703 has been amended to emphasize that when an expert reasonably relies on inadmissible information to form an opinion or inference, the underlying information is not admissible simply because the opinion or inference is admitted. Courts have reached different results on how to treat inadmissible information when it is reasonably relied upon by an expert in forming an opinion or drawing an inference. *Compare United States v. Rollins,* 862 F.2d 1282 (7th Cir.1988) (admitting, as part of the basis of an FBI agent's expert opinion on the meaning of code language, the hearsay statements of an informant), *with United States v. 0.59 Acres of Land,* 109 F.3d 1493 (9th Cir.1997) (error to admit hearsay offered as the basis of an expert opinion, without a limiting instruction). Commentators have also taken differing views. See, e.g., Ronald Carlson, *Policing the Bases of Modern Expert Testimony,* 39 Vand.L.Rev. 577 (1986) (advocating limits on the jury's consideration of otherwise inadmissible evidence used as the basis for an expert opinion); Paul Rice, *Inadmissible Evidence as a Basis for Expert Testimony: A Response to Professor Carlson,* 40 Vand.L.Rev. 583 (1987) (advocating unrestricted use of information reasonably relied upon by an expert).

When information is reasonably relied upon by an expert and yet is admissible only for the purpose of assisting the jury in evaluating an expert's opinion, a trial court applying this Rule must consider the information's probative value in assisting the jury to weigh the expert's opinion on the one hand, and the risk of prejudice resulting from the jury's potential misuse of the information for substantive purposes on the other. The information may be disclosed to the jury, upon objection, only if the trial court finds that the probative value of the information in assisting the jury to evaluate the expert's opinion substantially outweighs its prejudicial effect. If the otherwise inadmissible information is admitted under this balancing test, the trial judge must give a limiting instruction upon request, informing the jury that the underlying information must not be used for substantive purposes. See Rule 105. In determining the appropriate course, the trial court should consider the probable effectiveness or lack of effectiveness of a limiting instruction under the particular circumstances.

The amendment governs only the disclosure to the jury of information that is reasonably relied on by an expert, when that information is not admissible for substantive purposes. It is not intended to affect the admissibility of an expert's testimony. Nor does the amendment prevent an expert from relying on information that is inadmissible for substantive purposes.

Nothing in this Rule restricts the presentation of underlying expert facts or data when offered by an adverse party. See Rule 705. Of course, an adversary's attack on an expert's basis will often open the door to a proponent's rebuttal with information that was reasonably relied upon by the expert, even if that information would not have been discloseable initially under the balancing test provided by this amendment. Moreover, in some circumstances the proponent might wish to disclose information that is relied upon by the expert in order to "remove the sting" from the opponent's anticipated attack, and thereby prevent the jury from drawing an unfair negative inference. The trial court should take this consideration into account in applying the balancing test provided by this amendment.

This amendment covers facts or data that cannot be admitted for any purpose other than to assist the jury to evaluate the expert's opinion. The balancing test provided in this amendment is not applicable to facts or data that are admissible for any other purpose but have not yet been offered for such a purpose at the time the expert testifies.

The amendment provides a presumption against disclosure to the jury of information used as the basis of an expert's opinion and not admissible for any substantive purpose, when that information is offered by the proponent of the expert. In a multi-party case, where one party proffers an expert whose testimony is also beneficial to other parties, each such party should be deemed a "proponent" within the meaning of the amendment.

Note by Federal Judicial Center

The rule enacted by the Congress is the rule prescribed by the Supreme Court without change.

Advisory Committee's Note

Facts or data upon which expert opinions are based may, under the rule, be derived from three possible sources. The first is the firsthand observation of the witness, with opinions based thereon traditionally allowed. A treating physician affords an example. Rheingold, The Basis of Medical Testimony, 15 Vand.L.Rev. 473, 489 (1962). Whether he must first relate his observations is treated in Rule 705. The second source, presentation at the trial, also reflects existing practice. The technique may be the familiar hypothetical question or having the expert attend the trial and hear the testimony establishing the facts. Problems of determining what testimony the expert relied upon, when the latter technique is employed and the testimony is in conflict, may be resolved by resort to Rule 705. The third source contemplated by the rule consists of presentation of data to the expert outside of court and other than by his own perception. In this respect the rule is designed to broaden the basis for expert opinions beyond that current in many jurisdictions and to bring the judicial practice into line with the practice of the experts themselves when not in court. Thus a physician in his own practice bases his diagnosis on information from numerous sources and of considerable variety, including statements by patients and relatives, reports and opinions from nurses, technicians and other doctors, hospital records, and X rays. Most of them are admissible in evidence, but only with the expenditure of substantial time in producing and examining various authenticating witnesses. The physician makes life-and-death decisions in reliance upon them. His validation, expertly performed and subject to cross-examination, ought to suffice for judicial purposes. Rheingold, supra, at 531; McCormick § 15. A similar provision is California Evidence Code § 801(b).

The rule also offers a more satisfactory basis for ruling upon the admissibility of public opinion poll evidence. Attention is directed to the validity of the techniques employed rather than to relatively fruitless inquiries whether hearsay is involved. See Judge Feinberg's careful analysis in Zippo Mfg. Co. v. Rogers Imports, Inc., 216 F.Supp. 670 (S.D.N.Y.1963). See also Blum et al., The Art of Opinion Research: A Lawyer's Appraisal of an Emerging Service, 24 U.Chi. L.Rev. 1 (1956); Bonynge, Trademark Surveys and Techniques and Their Use in Litigation, 48 A.B.A.J. 329 (1962); Zeisel, The Uniqueness of Survey Evidence, 45 Cornell L.Q. 322 (1960); Annot., 76 A.L.R.2d 919.

If it be feared that enlargement of permissible data may tend to break down the rules of exclusion unduly, notice should be taken that the rule requires that the facts or data "be of a type reasonably relied upon by experts in the particular field." The language would not warrant admitting in evidence the opinion of an "accidentologist" as to the point of impact in an automobile collision based on statements of bystanders, since this requirement is not satisfied. See Comment, Cal.Law Rev.Comm'n, Recommendation Proposing an Evidence Code 148–150 (1965).

Rule 704.

OPINION ON ULTIMATE ISSUE

(a) Except as provided in subdivision (b), testimony in the form of an opinion or inference otherwise admissible is not objectionable because it embraces an ultimate issue to be decided by the trier of fact.

(b) No expert witness testifying with respect to the mental state or condition of a defendant in a criminal case may state an opinion or inference as to whether the defendant did or did not have the mental state or condition constituting an element of the crime charged or of a defense thereto. Such ultimate issues are matters for the trier of fact alone. (Subdivision b was added by P.L. 98–473, Oct. 12, 1984).

Senate Judiciary Committee Report, 1984 Amendment

The purpose of this amendment is to eliminate the confusing spectacle of competing expert witnesses testifying to directly contradictory conclusions as to the ultimate legal issue to be found by the trier of fact. Under this proposal, expert psychiatric testimony would be limited to presenting and explaining their diagnoses, such as whether the defendant had a severe mental disease or defect and what the characteristics of such a disease or defect, if any, may have been. The basis for this limitation on expert testimony in insanity cases is ably stated by the American Psychiatric Association:

> [I]t is clear that psychiatrists are experts in medicine, not the law. As such, it is clear that the psychiatrist's first obligation and expertise in the courtroom is to "do psychiatry," i.e., to present medical information and opinion about the defendant's mental state and motivation and to explain in detail the reason for his medical-psychiatric conclusions. When, however, "ultimate issue" questions are formulated by the law and put to the expert witness who must then say "yea" and "nay," then the expert witness is required to make a leap in logic. He no longer addresses himself to medical concepts but instead must infer or intuit what is in fact unspeakable, namely, the probable relationship between medical concepts and legal or moral constructs such as free will. These impermissible leaps in logic made by expert witnesses confuse the jury. [Footnote omitted.] Juries thus find themselves listening to conclusory and seemingly contradictory psychiatric testimony that defendants are either "sane" or "insane" or that they do or do not meet the relevant legal test for insanity. This state of affairs does considerable injustice to psychiatry and, we believe, possibly to criminal defendants. In fact, in many criminal insanity trials both prosecution and defense psychiatrists do agree about the nature and even the extent of mental disorder exhibited by the defendant at the time of the act.
>
> Psychiatrists, of course, must be permitted to testify fully about the defendant's diagnosis, mental state and motivation (in clinical and common-sense terms) at the time of the alleged act so as to permit the jury or judge to reach the ultimate conclusion about which they and only they are expert. Determining whether a criminal defendant was legally insane is a matter for legal fact-finders, not for experts.

Moreover, the rationale for precluding ultimate opinion psychiatric testimony extends beyond the insanity defense to any ultimate mental state of the defendant that is relevant to the legal conclusion sought to be proven. The Committee has fashioned its Rule 704 provision to reach all such "ultimate" issues, *e.g.*, premeditation in a homicide case or lack of predisposition in entrapment.

Note by Federal Judicial Center

The rule enacted by the Congress is the rule prescribed by the Supreme Court without change.

Advisory Committee's Note

The basic approach to opinions, lay and expert, in these rules is to admit them when helpful to the trier of fact. In order to render this approach fully effective and to allay any doubt on the subject, the so-called "ultimate issue" rule is specifically abolished by the instant rule.

The older cases often contained strictures against allowing witnesses to express opinions upon ultimate issues, as a particular aspect of the rule against opinions. The rule was unduly restrictive, difficult of application, and generally served only to deprive the trier of fact of useful information. 7 Wigmore §§ 1920, 1921; McCormick § 12. The basis usually assigned for the rule, to prevent the witness from "usurping the province of the jury," is aptly characterized as "empty rhetoric." 7 Wigmore § 1920, p. 17. Efforts to meet the felt needs of particular situations led to odd verbal circumlocutions which were said not to violate the rule. Thus a witness could express his estimate of the criminal responsibility of an accused in terms of sanity or insanity, but not in terms of ability to tell right from wrong or other more modern standard. And in cases of medical causation, witnesses were sometimes required to couch their opinions in cautious phrases of "might or could," rather than "did," though the result was to deprive many opinions of the positiveness to which they were entitled, accompanied by the hazard of a ruling of insufficiency to support a verdict. In other instances the rule was simply disregarded, and, as concessions to need, opinions were allowed upon such matters as intoxication, speed, handwriting, and value, although more precise coincidence with an ultimate issue would scarcely be possible.

Many modern decisions illustrate the trend to abandon the rule completely. People v. Wilson, 25 Cal.2d 341, 153 P.2d 720 (1944), whether abortion necessary to save life of patient; Clifford–Jacobs Forging Co. v. Industrial Comm., 19 Ill.2d 236, 166 N.E.2d 582 (1960), medical causation; Dowling v. L.H. Shattuck, Inc., 91 N.H. 234, 17 A.2d 529 (1941), proper method of shoring ditch; Schweiger v. Solbeck, 191 Or. 454, 230 P.2d 195 (1951), cause of landslide. In each instance the opinion was allowed.

The abolition of the ultimate issue rule does not lower the bars so as to admit all opinions. Under Rules 701 and 702, opinions must be helpful to the trier of fact, and Rule 403 provides for exclusion of evidence which wastes time. These provisions afford ample assurances against the admission of opinions which would merely tell the jury what result to reach, somewhat in the manner of the oath-helpers of an earlier day. They also stand ready to exclude opinions phrased in terms of inadequately explored legal criteria. Thus the question, "Did T have capacity to make a will?" would be excluded, while the question, "Did T have sufficient mental capacity to know the nature and extent of his property and the natural objects of his bounty and to formulate a rational scheme of distribution?" would be allowed. McCormick § 12.

For similar provisions see Uniform Rule 56(4); California Evidence Code § 805; Kansas Code of Civil Procedure § 60–456(d); New Jersey Evidence Rule 56(3).

Rule 705.

DISCLOSURE OF FACTS OR DATA UNDERLYING EXPERT OPINION

The expert may testify in terms of opinion or inference and give reasons therefor without first testifying to the underlying facts or data, unless the court requires otherwise. The expert may in any event be required to disclose the underlying facts or data on cross-examination.

Committee Notes to 1993 Amendment

This rule, which relates to the manner of presenting testimony at trial, is revised to avoid an arguable conflict with revised Rules 26(a)(2)(B) and 26(e)(1) of the Federal Rules of Civil Procedure or with revised Rule 16 of the Federal Rules of Criminal Procedure, which require disclosure in advance of trial of the basis and reasons for an expert's opinions.

If a serious question is raised under Rule 702 or 703 as to the admissibility of expert testimony, disclosure of the underlying facts or data on which opinions are based may, of course, be needed by the court before deciding whether, and to what extent, the person should be allowed to testify. This rule does not preclude such an inquiry.

Note by Federal Judicial Center

The rule enacted by the Congress is the rule prescribed by the Supreme Court, amended only by substituting "court" in place of "judge."

Advisory Committee's Note

The hypothetical question has been the target of a great deal of criticism as encouraging partisan bias, affording an opportunity for summing up in the middle of the case, and as complex and time consuming. Ladd, Expert Testimony, 5 Vand.L.Rev. 414, 426–427 (1952). While the rule allows counsel to make disclosure of the underlying facts or data as a preliminary to the giving of an expert opinion, if he chooses, the instances in which he is required to do so are reduced. This is true whether the expert bases his opinion on data furnished him at secondhand or observed by him at firsthand.

The elimination of the requirement of preliminary disclosure at the trial of underlying facts or data has a long background of support. In 1937 the Commissioners on Uniform State Laws incorporated a provision to this effect in their Model Expert Testimony Act, which furnished the basis for Uniform Rules 57 and 58. Rule 4515, N.Y. CPLR (McKinney 1963), provides:

> "Unless the court orders otherwise, questions calling for the opinion of an expert witness need not be hypothetical in form, and the witness may state his opinion and reasons without first specifying the data upon which it is based. Upon cross-examination, he may be required to specify the data...."

See also California Evidence Code § 802; Kansas Code of Civil Procedure §§ 60–456, 60–457; New Jersey Evidence Rules 57, 58.

If the objection is made that leaving it to the cross-examiner to bring out the supporting data is essentially unfair, the answer is that he is under no compulsion to bring out any facts or data except those unfavorable to the opinion. The answer assumes that the cross-examiner has the advance knowledge which is essential for effective cross-examination. This advance knowledge has been afforded, though imperfectly, by the traditional foundation requirement. Rule 26(b)(4) of the Rules of Civil Procedure, as revised, provides for substantial discovery in this area, obviating in large measure the obstacles which have been raised in some instances to discovery of findings, underlying data, and even the identity of the experts. Friedenthal, Discovery and Use of an Adverse Party's Expert Information, 14 Stan.L.Rev. 455 (1962).

These safeguards are reinforced by the discretionary power of the judge to require preliminary disclosure in any event.

Rule 706.

COURT APPOINTED EXPERTS

(a) Appointment. The court may on its own motion or on the motion of any party enter an order to show cause why expert witnesses should not be appointed, and may request the parties to submit nominations. The court may appoint any expert witnesses agreed upon by the parties, and may appoint expert witnesses of its own selection. An expert witness shall not be appointed by the court unless the witness consents to act. A witness so appointed shall be informed of the witness' duties by the court in writing, a copy of which shall be filed with the clerk, or at a conference in which the parties shall have opportunity to participate. A witness so appointed shall advise the parties of the witness' findings, if any; the witness' deposition may be taken by any party; and the witness may be called to testify by the court or any party. The witness shall be subject to cross-examination by each party, including a party calling the witness.

(b) Compensation. Expert witnesses so appointed are entitled to reasonable compensation in whatever sum the court may allow. The compensation thus fixed is payable from funds which may be provided by law in criminal cases and civil actions and proceedings involving just compensation under the fifth amendment. In other civil actions and proceedings the compensation shall be paid by the parties in such proportion and at such time as the court directs, and thereafter charged in like manner as other costs.

(c) Disclosure of appointment. In the exercise of its discretion, the court may authorize disclosure to the jury of the fact that the court appointed the expert witness.

(d) Parties' experts of own selection. Nothing in this rule limits the parties in calling expert witnesses of their own selection.

Note by Federal Judicial Center

The rule enacted by the Congress is the rule prescribed by the Supreme Court, amended by substituting "court" in place of "judge," with conforming pronominal changes, and, in subdivision (b), by substituting the phrase "and civil actions and proceedings" in place of "and cases" before "involving" in the second sentence.

Advisory Committee's Note

The practice of shopping for experts, the venality of some experts, and the reluctance of many reputable experts to involve themselves in litigation, have been matters of deep concern. Though the contention is made that court appointed experts acquire an aura of infallibility to which they are not entitled, Levy, Impartial Medical Testimony—Revisited, 34 Temple L.Q. 416 (1961), the trend is increasingly to provide for their use. While experience indicates that actual appointment is a relatively infrequent occurrence, the assumption may be made that the availability of the procedure in itself decreases the need for resorting to it. The ever-present possibility that the judge *may* appoint an expert in a given case must inevitably exert a sobering effect on the expert witness of a party and upon the person utilizing his services.

The inherent power of a trial judge to appoint an expert of his own choosing is virtually unquestioned. Scott v. Spanjer Bros., Inc., 298 F.2d 928 (2d Cir. 1962); Danville Tobacco Assn. v. Bryant–Buckner Associates, Inc., 333 F.2d 202 (4th Cir.1964); Sink, The Unused Power of a Federal Judge to Call His Own Expert Witnesses, 29 S.Cal.L.Rev. 195 (1956); 2 Wigmore § 563, 9 *id.* § 2484; Annot., 95 A.L.R.2d 383. Hence the problem becomes largely one of detail.

The New York plan is well known and is described in Report by Special Committee of the Association of the Bar of the City of New York: Impartial Medical Testimony (1956). On recommendation of the Section of Judicial Administration, local adoption of an impartial medical plan was endorsed by the American Bar Association. 82 A.B.A.Rep. 184–185 (1957). Descriptions and analyses of plans in effect in various parts of the country are found in Van Dusen, A United States District Judge's View of the Impartial Medical Expert System, 32 F.R.D. 498 (1963); Wick and Kightlinger, Impartial Medical Testimony Under the Federal Civil Rules: A Tale of Three Doctors, 34 Ins.Counsel J. 115 (1967); and numerous articles collected in Klein, Judicial Administration and the Legal Profession 393 (1963). Statutes and rules include California Evidence Code §§ 730–733; Illinois Supreme Court Rule 215(d), Ill.Rev.Stat. 1969, c. 110A, § 215(d); Burns Indiana Stats. 1956, § 9–1702; Wisconsin Stats.Annot. 1958, § 957.27.

In the federal practice, a comprehensive scheme for court appointed experts was initiated with the adoption of Rule 28 of the Federal Rules of Criminal Procedure in 1946. The Judicial Conference of the United States in 1953 considered court appointed experts in civil cases, but only with respect to whether they should be compensated from public funds, a proposal which was rejected. Report of the Judicial Conference of the United States 23 (1953). The present rule expands the practice to include civil cases.

Subdivision (a) is based on Rule 28 of the Federal Rules of Criminal Procedure, with a few changes, mainly in the interest of clarity. Language has been added to provide specifically for the appointment either on motion of a party or on the judge's own motion. A provision subjecting the court appointed expert to deposition procedures has been incorporated. The rule has been revised to make definite the right of any party, including the party calling him, to cross-examine.

Subdivision (b) combines the present provision for compensation in criminal cases with what seems to be a fair and feasible handling of civil cases, originally found in the Model Act and carried from there into Uniform Rule 60. See also California Evidence Code §§ 730–731. The special provision for Fifth Amendment compensation cases is designed to guard against reducing constitutionally guaranteed just compensation by requiring the recipient to pay costs. See Rule 71A(*l*) of the Rules of Civil Procedure.

Subdivision (c) seems to be essential if the use of court appointed experts is to be fully effective. Uniform Rule 61 so provides.

Subdivision (d) is in essence the last sentence of Rule 28(a) of the Federal Rules of Criminal Procedure.

ARTICLE VIII. HEARSAY
Advisory Committee's Note

Introductory Note: The Hearsay Problem

The factors to be considered in evaluating the testimony of a witness are perception, memory, and narration. Morgan, Hearsay Dangers and the Application of the Hearsay Concept, 62 Harv.L.Rev. 177 (1948), Selected Writings on Evidence and Trial 764, 765 (Fryer ed. 1957); Shientag, Cross–Examination—A Judge's Viewpoint, 3 Record 12 (1948); Strahorn, A Reconsideration of the Hearsay Rule and Admissions, 85 U.Pa.L.Rev. 484, 485 (1937), Selected Writings, supra, 756, 757; Weinstein, Probative Force of Hearsay, 46 Iowa L.Rev. 331 (1961). Sometimes a fourth is added, sincerity, but in fact it seems merely to be an aspect of the three already mentioned.

In order to encourage the witness to do his best with respect to each of these factors, and to expose any inaccuracies which may enter in, the Anglo–American tradition has evolved three conditions under which witnesses will ideally be required to testify: (1) under oath, (2) in the personal presence of the trier of fact, (3) subject to cross-examination.

(1) Standard procedure calls for the swearing of witnesses. While the practice is perhaps less effective than in an earlier time, no disposition to relax the requirement is apparent, other than to allow affirmation by persons with scruples against taking oaths.

(2) The demeanor of the witness traditionally has been believed to furnish trier and opponent with valuable clues. Universal Camera Corp. v. N.L.R.B., 340 U.S. 474, 495–496, 71 S.Ct. 456, 468–469, 95 L.Ed. 456 (1951); Sahm, Demeanor Evidence: Elusive and Intangible Imponderables, 47 A.B.A.J. 580 (1961), quoting numerous authorities. The witness himself will probably be impressed with the solemnity of the occasion and the possibility of public disgrace. Willingness to falsify may reasonably become more difficult in the presence of the person against whom directed. Rules 26 and 43(a) of the Federal Rules of Criminal and Civil Procedure, respectively, include the general requirement that testimony be taken orally in open court. The Sixth Amendment right of confrontation is a manifestation of these beliefs and attitudes.

(3) Emphasis on the basis of the hearsay rule today tends to center upon the condition of cross-examination. All may not agree with Wigmore that cross-examination is "beyond doubt the greatest legal engine ever invented for the discovery of truth," but all will agree with his statement that it has become a "vital feature" of the Anglo–American system. 5 Wigmore § 1367, p. 29. The belief, or perhaps hope, that cross-examination is effective in exposing imperfections of perception, memory, and narration is fundamental. Morgan, Foreword to Model Code of Evidence 37 (1942).

The logic of the preceding discussion might suggest that no testimony be received unless in full compliance with the three ideal conditions. No one advocates this position. Common sense tells that much evidence which is not given under the three conditions may be inherently superior to much that is. Moreover, when the choice is between evidence which is less than best and no evidence at all, only clear folly would dictate an across-the-board policy of doing without. The problem thus resolves itself into effecting a sensible accommodation between these considerations and the desirability of giving testimony under the ideal conditions.

The solution evolved by the common law has been a general rule excluding hearsay but subject to numerous exceptions under circumstances supposed to furnish guarantees of trustworthiness. Criticisms of this scheme are that it is bulky and complex, fails to screen good from bad hearsay realistically, and inhibits the growth of the law of evidence.

Since no one advocates excluding all hearsay, three possible solutions may be considered: (1) abolish the rule against hearsay and admit all hearsay; (2) admit hearsay possessing sufficient probative force, but with procedural safeguards; (3) revise the present system of class exceptions.

(1) Abolition of the hearsay rule would be the simplest solution. The effect would not be automatically to abolish the giving of testimony under ideal conditions. If the declarant were available, compliance with the ideal conditions would be optional with either party. Thus the proponent could call the declarant as a witness as a form of presentation more impressive than his hearsay statement. Or the opponent could call the declarant to be cross-examined upon his statement. This is the tenor of Uniform Rule 63(1), admitting the hearsay declaration of a person "who is present at the hearing and available for cross-examination." Compare the treatment of declarations of available declarants in Rule 801(d)(1) of the instant rules. If the declarant were unavailable, a rule of free admissibility would make no distinctions in terms of degrees of noncompliance with the ideal conditions and would exact no quid pro quo in the form of assurances of trustworthiness. Rule 503 of the Model Code did exactly that, providing for the admissibility of any hearsay declaration by an unavailable declarant, finding support in the Massachusetts act of 1898, enacted at the instance of Thayer, Mass.Gen.L. 1932, c. 233, § 65, and in the English act of 1938, St.1938, c. 28, Evidence. Both are limited to civil cases. The draftsmen of the Uniform Rules chose a less advanced and more conventional position. Comment, Uniform Rule 63. The present Advisory Committee has been unconvinced of the wisdom of abandoning the traditional requirement of some particular assurance of credibility as a condition precedent to admitting the hearsay declaration of an unavailable declarant.

In criminal cases, the Sixth Amendment requirement of confrontation would no doubt move into a large part of the area presently occupied by the hearsay rule in the event of the abolition of the latter. The resultant split between civil and criminal evidence is regarded as an undesirable development.

(2) Abandonment of the system of class exceptions in favor of individual treatment in the setting of the particular case, accompanied by procedural safeguards, has been impressively advocated. Weinstein, The Probative Force of Hearsay, 46 Iowa L.Rev. 331 (1961). Admissibility would be determined by weighing the probative force of the evidence against the possibility of prejudice, waste of time, and the availability of more satisfactory evidence. The bases of the traditional hearsay exceptions would be helpful in assessing probative force. Ladd, The Relationship of the Principles of Exclusionary Rules of Evidence to the Problem of Proof, 18 Minn.L.Rev. 506 (1934). Procedural safeguards would consist of notice of intention to use hearsay, free comment by the judge on the weight of the evidence, and a greater measure of authority in both trial and appellate judges to deal with evidence on the basis of weight. The Advisory Committee has rejected this approach to hearsay as involving too great a measure of judicial discretion, minimizing the predictability of rulings, enhancing the difficulties of preparation for trial, adding a further element to the already over-complicated congeries of pretrial procedures, and requiring substantially different rules for civil and criminal cases. The only way in which the probative force of hearsay differs from the probative force of other testimony is in the absence of oath, demeanor, and cross-examination as aids in determining credibility. For a judge to exclude evidence because he does not believe it has been described as "altogether atypical, extraordinary...." Chadbourn, Bentham and the Hearsay Rule—A Benthamic View of Rule 63(4)(c) of the Uniform Rules of Evidence, 75 Harv.L.Rev. 932, 947 (1962).

(3) The approach to hearsay in these rules is that of the common law, i.e., a general rule excluding hearsay, with exceptions under which evidence is not required to be excluded even though hearsay. The traditional hearsay exceptions are drawn upon for the exceptions, collected under two rules, one dealing with situations where availability of the declarant is regarded as immaterial and the other with those where unavailability is made a condition to the admission of the hearsay statement. Each of the two rules concludes with a provision for hearsay statements not within one of the specified exceptions "but having comparable [equivalent] circumstantial guarantees of trustworthiness." Rules 803(24) and 804(b)(6)[5]. This plan is submitted as calculated to encourage growth and development in this area of the law, while conserving the values and experience of the past as a guide to the future.

Confrontation and Due Process

Until very recently, decisions invoking the confrontation clause of the Sixth Amendment were surprisingly few, a fact probably explainable by the former inapplicability of the clause to the states and by the hearsay rule's occupancy of much the same ground. The pattern which emerges from the earlier cases invoking the clause is substantially that of the hearsay rule, applied to criminal cases: an accused is entitled to have the witnesses against him testify under oath, in the presence of himself and trier, subject to cross-examination; yet considerations of public policy and necessity require the recognition of such exceptions as dying declarations and former testimony of unavailable witnesses.

Mattox v. United States, 156 U.S. 237, 15 S.Ct. 337, 39 L.Ed. 409 (1895); Motes v. United States, 178 U.S. 458, 20 S.Ct. 993, 44 L.Ed. 1150 (1900); Delaney v. United States, 263 U.S. 586, 44 S.Ct. 206, 68 L.Ed. 462 (1924). Beginning with Snyder v. Massachusetts, 291 U.S. 97, 54 S.Ct. 330, 78 L.Ed. 674 (1934), the Court began to speak of confrontation as an aspect of procedural due process, thus extending its applicability to state cases and to federal cases other than criminal. The language of *Snyder* was that of an elastic concept of hearsay. The deportation case of Bridges v. Wixon, 326 U.S. 135, 65 S.Ct. 1443, 89 L.Ed. 2103 (1945), may be read broadly as imposing a strictly construed right of confrontation in all kinds of cases or narrowly as the product of a failure of the Immigration and Naturalization Service to follow its own rules. In re Oliver, 333 U.S. 257, 68 S.Ct. 499, 92 L.Ed. 682 (1948), ruled that cross-examination was essential to due process in a state contempt proceeding, but in United States v. Nugent, 346 U.S. 1, 73 S.Ct. 991, 97 L.Ed. 1417 (1953), the court held that it was not an essential aspect of a "hearing" for a conscientious objector under the Selective Service Act. Stein v. New York, 346 U.S. 156, 196, 73 S.Ct. 1077, 1098, 97 L.Ed. 1522 (1953), disclaimed any purpose to read the hearsay rule into the Fourteenth Amendment, but in Greene v. McElroy, 360 U.S. 474, 79 S.Ct. 1400, 3 L.Ed.2d 1377 (1959), revocation of security clearance without confrontation and cross-examination was held unauthorized, and a similar result was reached in Willner v. Committee on Character, 373 U.S. 96, 83 S.Ct. 1175, 10 L.Ed.2d 224 (1963). Ascertaining the constitutional dimensions of the confrontation-hearsay aggregate against the background of these cases is a matter of some difficulty, yet the general pattern is at least not inconsistent with that of the hearsay rule.

In 1965 the confrontation clause was held applicable to the states. Pointer v. Texas, 380 U.S. 400, 85 S.Ct. 1065, 13 L.Ed.2d 923 (1965). Prosecution use of former testimony given at a preliminary hearing where petitioner was not represented by counsel was a violation of the clause. The same result would have followed under conventional hearsay doctrine read in the light of a constitutional right to counsel, and nothing in the opinion suggests any difference in essential outline between the hearsay rule and the right of confrontation. In the companion case of Douglas v. Alabama, 380 U.S. 415, 85 S.Ct. 1074, 13 L.Ed.2d 934 (1965), however, the result reached by applying the confrontation clause is one reached less readily via the hearsay rule. A confession implicating petitioner was put before the jury by reading it to the witness in portions and asking if he made that statement. The witness refused to answer on grounds of self-incrimination. The result, said the Court, was to deny cross-examination, and hence confrontation. True, it could broadly be said that the confession was a hearsay statement which for all practical purposes was put in evidence. Yet a more easily accepted explanation of the opinion is that its real thrust was in the direction of curbing undesirable prosecutorial behavior, rather than merely applying rules of exclusion, and that the confrontation clause was the means selected to achieve this end. Comparable facts and a like result appeared in Brookhart v. Janis, 384 U.S. 1, 86 S.Ct. 1245, 16 L.Ed.2d 314 (1966).

The pattern suggested in *Douglas* was developed further and more distinctly in a pair of cases at the end of the 1966 term. United States v. Wade, 388 U.S. 218, 87 S.Ct. 1926, 18 L.Ed.2d 1149 (1967), and Gilbert v. California, 388 U.S. 263, 87 S.Ct. 1951, 18 L.Ed.2d 1178 (1967), hinged upon practices followed in identifying accused persons before trial. This pretrial identification was said to be so decisive an aspect of the case that accused was entitled to have counsel present; a pretrial identification made in the absence of counsel was not itself receivable in evidence and, in addition, might fatally infect a courtroom identification. The presence of counsel at the earlier identification was described as a necessary prerequisite for "a meaningful confrontation at trial." United States v. Wade, supra, 388 U.S. at p. 236, 87 S.Ct. at p. 1937. *Wade* involved no evidence of the fact of a prior identification and hence was not susceptible of being decided on hearsay grounds. In *Gilbert,* witnesses did testify to an earlier identification, readily classifiable as hearsay under a fairly strict view of what constitutes hearsay. The Court, however, carefully avoided basing the decision on the hearsay ground, choosing confrontation instead. 388 U.S. 263, 272, n. 3, 87 S.Ct. 1951. See also Parker v. Gladden, 385 U.S. 363, 87 S.Ct. 468, 17 L.Ed.2d 420 (1966), holding that the right of confrontation was violated when the bailiff made prejudicial statements to jurors, and Note, 75 Yale L.J. 1434 (1966).

Under the earlier cases, the confrontation clause may have been little more than a constitutional embodiment of the hearsay rule, even including traditional exceptions but with some room for expanding them along similar lines. But under the recent cases the impact of the clause clearly extends beyond the confines of the hearsay rule. These considerations have led the Advisory Committee to conclude that a hearsay rule can function usefully as an adjunct to the confrontation right in constitutional areas and independently in nonconstitutional areas. In recognition of the separateness of the confrontation clause and the hearsay rule, and to avoid inviting collisions between them or between the hearsay rule and other exclusionary principles, the exceptions set forth in Rules 803 and 804 are stated in terms of exemption from the general exclusionary mandate of the hearsay rule, rather than in positive terms of admissibility. See Uniform Rule 63(1) to (31) and California Evidence Code §§ 1200–1340.

Rule 801.

DEFINITIONS

The following definitions apply under this article:

(a) Statement. A "statement" is (1) an oral or written assertion or (2) nonverbal conduct of a person, if it is intended by the person as an assertion.

(b) Declarant. A "declarant" is a person who makes a statement.

(c) Hearsay. "Hearsay" is a statement, other than one made by the declarant while testifying at the trial or hearing, offered in evidence to prove the truth of the matter asserted.

(d) Statements which are not hearsay. A statement is not hearsay if—

(1) Prior statement by witness. The declarant testifies at the trial or hearing and is subject to cross-examination concerning the statement, and the statement is (A) inconsistent with the declarant's testimony, and was given under oath subject to the penalty of perjury at a trial, hearing, or other proceeding, or in a deposition, or (B) consistent with the declarant's testimony and is offered to rebut an express or implied charge against the declarant of recent fabrication or improper influence or motive, or (C) one of identification of a person made after perceiving the person; or

(2) Admission by party-opponent. The statement is offered against a party and is (A) the party's own statement in either an individual or a representative capacity or (B) a statement of which the party has manifested an adoption or belief in its truth, or (C) a statement by a person authorized by the party to make a statement concerning the subject, or (D) a statement by the party's agent or servant concerning a matter within the scope of the agency or employment, made during the existence of the relationship, or (E) a statement by a coconspirator of a party during the course and in furtherance of the conspiracy. The contents of the statement shall be considered but are not alone sufficient to establish the declarant's authority under subdivision (C), the agency or employment relationship and scope thereof under subdivision (D), or the existence of the conspiracy and the participation therein of the declarant and the party against whom the statement is offered under subdivision (E).

Committee Note to 1997 Amendment

Rule 801(d)(2) has been amended in order to respond to three issues raised by Bourjaily v. United States, 483 U.S. 171 (1987). First, the amendment codifies the holding in Bourjaily by stating expressly that a court shall consider the contents of a coconspirator's statement in determining "the existence of the conspiracy and the participation therein of the declarant and the party against whom the statement is offered." According to Bourjaily, Rule 104(a) requires these preliminary questions to be established by a preponderance of the evidence.

Second, the amendment resolves an issue on which the Court had reserved decision. It provides that the contents of the declarant's statement do not alone suffice to establish a conspiracy in which the declarant and the defendant participated. The court must consider in addition the circumstances surrounding the statement, such as the identity of the speaker, the context in which the statement was made, or evidence corroborating the contents of the statement in making its determination as to each preliminary question. This amendment is in accordance with existing practice. Every court of appeals that has resolved this issue requires some evidence in addition to the contents of the statement. See, e.g., United States v. Beckham, 968 F.2d 47, 51 (D.C.Cir.1992); United States v. Sepulveda, 15 F.3d 1161, 1181–82 (1st Cir.1993), cert. denied, 114 S.Ct. 2714 (1994); United States v. Daly, 842 F.2d 1380, 1386 (2d Cir.), cert. denied, 488 U.S. 821 (1988); United States v. Clark, 18 F.3d 1337, 1341–42 (6th Cir.), cert. denied, 115 S.Ct. 152 (1994); United States v. Zambrana, 841 F.2d 1320, 1344–45 (7th Cir.1988); United States v. Silverman, 861 F.2d 571, 577 (9th Cir.1988); United States v. Gordon, 844 F.2d 1397, 1402 (9th Cir.1988); United States v. Hernandez, 829 F.2d 988, 993 (10th Cir.1987), cert. denied, 485 U.S. 1013 (1988); United States v. Byrom, 910 F.2d 725, 736 (11th Cir.1990).

Third, the amendment extends the reasoning of Bourjaily to statements offered under subparagraphs (C) and (D) of Rule 801(d)(2). In Bourjaily, the Court rejected treating foundational facts pursuant to the law of agency in favor

Rule 801 FEDERAL RULES OF EVIDENCE

of an evidentiary approach governed by Rule 104(a). The Advisory Committee believes it appropriate to treat analogously preliminary questions relating to the declarant's authority under subparagraph (C), and the agency or employment relationship and scope thereof under subparagraph (D).

Note by Federal Judicial Center

The rule enacted by the Congress is the rule prescribed by the Supreme Court, with two amendments to subdivision (d)(1). The first of these amendments inserted in item (A), after "testimony," the phrase "and was given under oath subject to the penalty of perjury at a trial, hearing, or other proceeding, or in a deposition." The other amendment consisted of the deletion of item (C), which dealt with prior statements of identification.* The reasons for these amendments are stated in the Report of the House Committee on the Judiciary, the Report of the Senate Committee on the Judiciary, and the Conference Report, set forth below.

Advisory Committee's Note

Subdivision (a). The definition of "statement" assumes importance because the term is used in the definition of hearsay in subdivision (c). The effect of the definition of "statement" is to exclude from the operation of the hearsay rule all evidence of conduct, verbal or nonverbal, not intended as an assertion. The key to the definition is that nothing is an assertion unless intended to be one.

It can scarcely be doubted that an assertion made in words is intended by the declarant to be an assertion. Hence verbal assertions readily fall into the category of "statement." Whether nonverbal conduct should be regarded as a statement for purposes of defining hearsay requires further consideration. Some nonverbal conduct, such as the act of pointing to identify a suspect in a lineup, is clearly the equivalent of words, assertive in nature, and to be regarded as a statement. Other nonverbal conduct, however, may be offered as evidence that the person acted as he did because of his belief in the existence of the condition sought to be proved, from which belief the existence of the condition may be inferred. This sequence is, arguably, in effect an assertion of the existence of the condition and hence properly includable within the hearsay concept. See Morgan, Hearsay Dangers and the Application of the Hearsay Concept, 62 Harv. L.Rev. 177, 214, 217 (1948), and the elaboration in Finman, Implied Assertions as Hearsay: Some Criticisms of the Uniform Rules of Evidence, 14 Stan.L.Rev. 682 (1962). Admittedly evidence of this character is untested with respect to the perception, memory, and narration (or their equivalents) of the actor, but the Advisory Committee is of the view that these dangers are minimal in the absence of an intent to assert and do not justify the loss of the evidence on hearsay grounds. No class of evidence is free of the possibility of fabrication, but the likelihood is less with nonverbal than with assertive verbal conduct. The situations giving rise to the nonverbal conduct are such as virtually to eliminate questions of sincerity. Motivation, the nature of the conduct, and the presence or absence of reliance will bear heavily upon the weight to be given the evidence. Falknor, The "Hear–Say" Rule as a "See–Do" Rule: Evidence of Conduct, 33 Rocky Mt.L.Rev. 133 (1961). Similar considerations govern nonassertive verbal

---

* The provision dealing with prior statements of identification was subsequently reinstated by Act of Congress. See Editorial Note, infra.

conduct and verbal conduct which is assertive but offered as a basis for inferring something other than the matter asserted, also excluded from the definition of hearsay by the language of subdivision (c).

When evidence of conduct is offered on the theory that it is not a statement, and hence not hearsay, a preliminary determination will be required to determine whether an assertion is intended. The rule is so worded as to place the burden upon the party claiming that the intention existed; ambiguous and doubtful cases will be resolved against him and in favor of admissibility. The determination involves no greater difficulty than many other preliminary questions of fact. Maguire, The Hearsay System: Around and Through the Thicket, 14 Vand.L.Rev. 741, 765–767 (1961).

For similar approaches, see Uniform Rule 62(1); California Evidence Code §§ 225, 1200; Kansas Code of Civil Procedure § 60–459(a); New Jersey Evidence Rule 62(1).

Subdivision (c). The definition follows along familiar lines in including only statements offered to prove the truth of the matter asserted. McCormick § 225; 5 Wigmore § 1361, 6 id. § 1766. If the significance of an offered statement lies solely in the fact that it was made, no issue is raised as to the truth of anything asserted, and the statement is not hearsay. Emich Motors Corp. v. General Motors Corp., 181 F.2d 70 (7th Cir.1950), rev'd on other grounds 340 U.S. 558, 71 S.Ct. 408, 95 L.Ed. 534, letters of complaint from customers offered as a reason for cancellation of dealer's franchise, to rebut contention that franchise was revoked for refusal to finance sales through affiliated finance company. The effect is to exclude from hearsay the entire category of "verbal acts" and "verbal parts of an act," in which the statement itself affects the legal rights of the parties or is a circumstance bearing on conduct affecting their rights.

The definition of hearsay must, of course, be read with reference to the definition of statement set forth in subdivision (a).

Testimony given by a witness in the course of court proceedings is excluded since there is compliance with all the ideal conditions for testifying.

Subdivision (d). Several types of statements which would otherwise literally fall within the definition are expressly excluded from it:

(1) *Prior statement by witness.* Considerable controversy has attended the question whether a prior out-of-court statement by a person now available for cross-examination concerning it, under oath and in the presence of the trier of fact, should be classed as hearsay. If the witness admits on the stand that he made the statement and that it was true, he adopts the statement and there is no hearsay problem. The hearsay problem arises when the witness on the stand denies having made the statement or admits having made it but denies its truth. The argument in favor of treating these latter statements as hearsay is based upon the ground that the conditions of oath, cross-examination, and demeanor observation did not prevail at the time the statement was made and cannot adequately be supplied by the later examination. The logic of the situation is troublesome. So far as concerns the oath, its mere presence has never been regarded as sufficient to remove a statement from the hearsay category, and it receives much less emphasis than cross-examination as a truth-compelling device. While strong expressions are found to the effect that no conviction can be had or important right taken away on the basis of statements not made under

fear of prosecution for perjury, Bridges v. Wixon, 326 U.S. 135, 65 S.Ct. 1443, 89 L.Ed. 2103 (1945), the fact is that, of the many common law exceptions to the hearsay rule, only that for reported testimony has required the statement to have been made under oath. [It should be noted, however, that rule 801(d)(1)(A), as enacted by the Congress, requires that a prior inconsistent statement have been made under oath.] Nor is it satisfactorily explained why cross-examination cannot be conducted subsequently with success. The decisions contending most vigorously for its inadequacy in fact demonstrate quite thorough exploration of the weaknesses and doubts attending the earlier statement. State v. Saporen, 205 Minn. 358, 285 N.W. 898 (1939); Ruhala v. Roby, 379 Mich. 102, 150 N.W.2d 146 (1967); People v. Johnson, 68 Cal.2d 646, 68 Cal.Rptr. 599, 441 P.2d 111 (1968). In respect to demeanor, as Judge Learned Hand observed in Di Carlo v. United States, 6 F.2d 364 (2d Cir.1925), when the jury decides that the truth is not what the witness says now, but what he said before, they are still deciding from what they see and hear in court. The bulk of the case law nevertheless has been against allowing prior statements of witnesses to be used generally as substantive evidence. Most of the writers and Uniform Rule 63(1) have taken the opposite position.

The position taken by the Advisory Committee in formulating this part of the rule is founded upon an unwillingness to countenance the general use of prior prepared statements as substantive evidence, but with a recognition that particular circumstances call for a contrary result. The judgment is one more of experience than of logic. The rule requires in each instance, as a general safeguard, that the declarant actually testify as a witness, and it then enumerates three situations in which the statement is excepted from the category of hearsay. Compare Uniform Rule 63(1) which allows any out-of-court statement of a declarant who is present at the trial and available for cross-examination.

(A) Prior inconsistent statements traditionally have been admissible to impeach but not as substantive evidence. Under the rule they are substantive evidence. As has been said by the California Law Revision Commission with respect to a similar provision:

> "Section 1235 admits inconsistent statements of witnesses because the dangers against which the hearsay rule is designed to protect are largely nonexistent. The declarant is in court and may be examined and cross-examined in regard to his statements and their subject matter. In many cases, the inconsistent statement is more likely to be true than the testimony of the witness at the trial because it was made nearer in time to the matter to which it relates and is less likely to be influenced by the controversy that gave rise to the litigation. The trier of fact has the declarant before it and can observe his demeanor and the nature of his testimony as he denies or tries to explain away the inconsistency. Hence, it is in as good a position to determine the truth or falsity of the prior statement as it is to determine the truth or falsity of the inconsistent testimony given in court. Moreover, Section 1235 will provide a party with desirable protection against the 'turncoat' witness who changes his story on the stand and deprives the party calling him of evidence essential to his case." Comment, California Evidence Code § 1235. See also McCormick § 39. The Advisory Committee finds these views more convincing than those expressed in People v. Johnson, 68 Cal.2d 646, 68 Cal.Rptr. 599, 441 P.2d 111 (1968). The constitutionality of the Advisory Committee's view

was upheld in California v. Green, 399 U.S. 149, 90 S.Ct. 1930, 26 L.Ed.2d 489 (1970). Moreover, the requirement that the statement be inconsistent with the testimony given assures a thorough exploration of both versions while the witness is on the stand and bars any general and indiscriminate use of previously prepared statements.

[It should be noted that the rule as enacted by the Congress also requires that the prior inconsistent statement have been made under oath at a trial, hearing, or other proceeding, or in a deposition.]

Report of House Committee on the Judiciary

Present federal law, except in the Second Circuit, permits the use of prior inconsistent statements of a witness for impeachment only. Rule 801(d)(1) as proposed by the Court would have permitted all such statements to be admissible as substantive evidence, an approach followed by a small but growing number of State jurisdictions and recently held constitutional in California v. Green, 399 U.S. 149, 90 S.Ct. 1930, 26 L.Ed.2d 489 (1970). Although there was some support expressed for the Court Rule, based largely on the need to counteract the effect of witness intimidation in criminal cases, the Committee decided to adopt a compromise version of the Rule similar to the position of the Second Circuit. The Rule as amended draws a distinction between types of prior inconsistent statements (other than statements of identification of a person made after perceiving him which are currently admissible, see United States v. Anderson, 406 F.2d 719, 720 (4th Cir.), cert. denied, 395 U.S. 967, 89 S.Ct. 2114, 23 L.Ed.2d 753 (1969)) and allows only those made while the declarant was subject to cross-examination at a trail [sic] or hearing or in a deposition, to be admissible for their truth. Compare United States v. DeSisto, 329 F.2d 929 (2d Cir.), cert. denied, 377 U.S. 979, 84 S.Ct. 1885, 12 L.Ed.2d 747 (1964); United States v. Cunningham, 446 F.2d 194 (2d Cir.1971) (restricting the admissibility of prior inconsistent statements as substantive evidence to those made under oath in a formal proceeding, but not requiring that there have been an opportunity for cross-examination). The rationale for the Committee's decision is that (1) unlike in most other situations involving unsworn or oral statements, there can be no dispute as to whether the prior statement was made; and (2) the context of a formal proceeding, an oath, and the opportunity for cross-examination provide firm additional assurances of the reliability of the prior statement.

Report of Senate Committee on the Judiciary

Rule 801 defines what is and what is not hearsay for the purpose of admitting a prior statement as substantive evidence. A prior statement of a witness at a trial or hearing which is inconsistent with his testimony is, of course, always admissible for the purpose of impeaching the witness' credibility.

As submitted by the Supreme Court, subdivision (d)(1)(A) made admissible as substantive evidence the prior statement of a witness inconsistent with his present testimony.

The House severely limited the admissibility of prior inconsistent statements by adding a requirement that the prior statement must have been subject to cross-examination, thus precluding even the use of grand jury statements. The requirement that the prior statement must have been subject to cross-examination appears unnecessary since this rule comes into play only when the witness testifies in the present trial. At that time, he is on the stand and can explain an earlier position and be cross-examined as to both.

The requirement that the statement be under oath also appears unnecessary. Notwithstanding the absence of an oath contemporaneous with the statement, the witness, when on the stand, qualifying or denying the prior statement, is under oath. In any event, of all the many recognized exceptions to the hearsay rule, only one (former testimony) requires that the out-of-court statement have been made under oath. With respect to the lack of evidence of the demeanor of the witness at the time of the prior statement, it would be difficult to improve upon Judge Learned Hand's observation that when the jury decides that the truth is not what the witness says now but what he said before, they are still deciding from what they see and hear in court.[1]

The rule as submitted by the Court has positive advantages. The prior statement was made nearer in time to the events, when memory was fresher and intervening influences had not been brought into play. A realistic method is provided for dealing with the turncoat witness who changes his story on the stand.[2]

New Jersey, California, and Utah have adopted a rule similar to this one; and Nevada, New Mexico, and Wisconsin have adopted the identical Federal rule.

For all of these reasons, we think the House amendment should be rejected and the rule as submitted by the Supreme Court reinstated.[3]

Conference Report

The Conference adopts the Senate amendment with an amendment, so that the rule now requires that the prior inconsistent statement be given under oath subject to the penalty of perjury at a trial, hearing, or other proceeding, or in a deposition. The rule as adopted covers statements before a grand jury. Prior inconsistent statements may, of course, be used for impeaching the credibility of a witness. When the prior inconsistent statement is one made by a defendant in a criminal case, it is covered by Rule 801(d)(2).

Advisory Committee's Note

(B) Prior consistent statements traditionally have been admissible to rebut charges of recent fabrication or improper influence or motive but not as substantive evidence. Under the rule they are substantive evidence. The prior statement is consistent with the testimony given on the stand, and, if the opposite party wishes to open the door for its admission in evidence, no sound reason is apparent why it should not be received generally.

1. Di Carlo v. United States, 6 F.2d 364 (2d Cir.1925).
2. See Comment, California Evidence Code § 1235; McCormick, Evidence, § 38 (2nd ed. 1972).
3. It would appear that some of the opposition to this Rule is based on a concern that a person could be convicted solely upon evidence admissible under this Rule. The Rule, however, is not addressed to the question of the sufficiency of evidence to send a case to the jury, but merely as to its admissibility. Factual circumstances could well arise where, if this were the sole evidence, dismissal would be appropriate.

Editorial Note

Subdivision (d)(1)(C) was included in the rule as prescribed by the Supreme Court but was deleted by the Congress in enacting the rules, as indicated in the Conference Report above. However, the subdivision was restored by Act effective Oct. 31, 1975. Therefore the Advisory Committee's Note to the subdivision is now reprinted below.

Advisory Committee's Note

(C) The admission of evidence of identification finds substantial support, although it falls beyond a doubt in the category of prior out-of-court statements. Illustrative are People v. Gould, 54 Cal.2d 621, 7 Cal.Rptr. 273, 354 P.2d 865 (1960); Judy v. State, 218 Md. 168, 146 A.2d 29 (1958); State v. Simmons, 63 Wash.2d 17, 385 P.2d 389 (1963); California Evidence Code § 1238; New Jersey Evidence Rule 63(1)(c); N.Y.Code of Criminal Procedure § 393–b. Further cases are found in 4 Wigmore § 1130. The basis is the generally unsatisfactory and inconclusive nature of courtroom identifications as compared with those made at an earlier time under less suggestive conditions. The Supreme Court considered the admissibility of evidence of prior identification in Gilbert v. California, 388 U.S. 263, 87 S.Ct. 1951, 18 L.Ed.2d 1178 (1967). Exclusion of lineup identification was held to be required because the accused did not then have the assistance of counsel. Significantly, the Court carefully refrained from placing its decision on the ground that testimony as to the making of a prior out-of-court identification ("That's the man") violated either the hearsay rule or the right of confrontation because not made under oath, subject to immediate cross-examination, in the presence of the trier. Instead the Court observed:

"There is a split among the States concerning the admissibility of prior extra-judicial identifications, as independent evidence of identity, both by the witness and third parties present at the prior identification. See 71 A.L.R.2d 449. It has been held that the prior identification is hearsay, and, when admitted through the testimony of the identifier, is merely a prior consistent statement. The recent trend, however, is to admit the prior identification under the exception that admits as substantive evidence a prior communication by a witness who is available for cross-examination at the trial. See 5 A.L.R.2d Later Case Service 1225–1228...." 388 U.S. at 272, n. 3, 87 S.Ct. at 1956.

Editorial Note

Rule 801(d)(1) of the Uniform Rules of Evidence (1974) omits prior statements of identification.

Advisory Committee's Note

(2) *Admissions.* Admissions by a party-opponent are excluded from the category of hearsay on the theory that their admissibility in evidence is the result of the adversary system rather than satisfaction of the conditions of the hearsay rule. Strahorn, A Reconsideration of the Hearsay Rule and Admissions, 85 U.Pa.L.Rev. 484, 564 (1937); Morgan, Basic Problems of Evidence 265 (1962); 4 Wigmore § 1048. No guarantee of trustworthiness is required in the case of an admission. The freedom which admissions have enjoyed from technical demands of searching for an assurance of trustworthiness in some against-interest circumstance, and from the restrictive influences of the opinion rule and the rule requiring firsthand knowledge, when taken with the apparently preva-

lent satisfaction with the results, calls for generous treatment of this avenue to admissibility.

The rule specifies five categories of statements for which the responsibility of a party is considered sufficient to justify reception in evidence against him:

(A) A party's own statement is the classic example of an admission. If he has a representative capacity and the statement is offered against him in that capacity, no inquiry whether he was acting in the representative capacity in making the statement is required; the statement need only be relevant to representative affairs. To the same effect is California Evidence Code § 1220. Compare Uniform Rule 63(7), requiring a statement to be made in a representative capacity to be admissible against a party in a representative capacity.

(B) Under established principles an admission may be made by adopting or acquiescing in the statement of another. While knowledge of contents would ordinarily be essential, this is not inevitably so: "X is a reliable person and knows what he is talking about." See McCormick § 246, p. 527, n. 15. Adoption or acquiescence may be manifested in any appropriate manner. When silence is relied upon, the theory is that the person would, under the circumstances, protest the statement made in his presence, if untrue. The decision in each case calls for an evaluation in terms of probable human behavior. In civil cases, the results have generally been satisfactory. In criminal cases, however, troublesome questions have been raised by decisions holding that failure to deny is an admission: the inference is a fairly weak one, to begin with; silence may be motivated by advice of counsel or realization that "anything you say may be used against you"; unusual opportunity is afforded to manufacture evidence; and encroachment upon the privilege against self-incrimination seems inescapably to be involved. However, recent decisions of the Supreme Court relating to custodial interrogation and the right to counsel appear to resolve these difficulties. Hence the rule contains no special provisions concerning failure to deny in criminal cases.

(C) No authority is required for the general proposition that a statement authorized by a party to be made should have the status of an admission by the party. However, the question arises whether only statements to third persons should be so regarded, to the exclusion of statements by the agent to the principal. The rule is phrased broadly so as to encompass both. While it may be argued that the agent authorized to make statements to his principal does not speak for him, Morgan, Basic Problems of Evidence 273 (1962), communication to an outsider has not generally been thought to be an essential characteristic of an admission. Thus a party's books or records are usable against him, without regard to any intent to disclose to third persons. 5 Wigmore § 1557. See also McCormick § 78, pp. 159–161. In accord is New Jersey Evidence Rule 63(8)(a). Cf. Uniform Rule 63(8)(a) and California Evidence Code § 1222 which limit status as an admission in this regard to statements authorized by the party to be made "for" him, which is perhaps an ambiguous limitation to statements to third persons. Falknor, Vicarious Admissions and the Uniform Rules, 14 Vand. L.Rev. 855, 860–861 (1961).

(D) The tradition has been to test the admissibility of statements by agents, as admissions, by applying the usual test of agency. Was the admission made by the agent acting in the scope of his employment? Since few principals employ agents for the purpose of making damaging statements, the usual result was exclusion of the statement. Dissatisfaction with this loss of valuable and helpful evidence has been increasing. A substantial trend favors admitting statements related to a matter within the scope of the agency or employment. Grayson v. Williams, 256 F.2d 61 (10th Cir. 1958); Koninklijke Luchtvaart Maatschappij N. V. KLM Royal Dutch Airlines v. Tuller, 110 U.S.App.D.C. 282, 292 F.2d 775, 784 (1961); Martin v. Savage Truck Line, 121 F.Supp. 417 (D.D.C.1954), and numerous state court decisions collected in 4 Wigmore, 1964 Supp., pp. 66–73, with comments by the editor that the statements should have been excluded as not within scope of agency. For the traditional view see Northern Oil Co. v. Socony Mobil Oil Co., 347 F.2d 81, 85 (2d Cir.1965) and cases cited therein. Similar provisions are found in Uniform Rule 63(9)(a), Kansas Code of Civil Procedure § 60–460(i)(1), and New Jersey Evidence Rule 63(9)(a).

(E) The limitation upon the admissibility of statements of co-conspirators to those made "during the course and in furtherance of the conspiracy" is in the accepted pattern. While the broadened view of agency taken in item (iv) might suggest wider admissibility of statements of co-conspirators, the agency of conspiracy is at best a fiction and ought not to serve as a basis for admissibility beyond that already established. See Levie, Hearsay and Conspiracy, 52 Mich.L.Rev. 1159 (1954); Comment, 25 U.Chi.L.Rev. 530 (1958). The rule is consistent with the position of the Supreme Court in denying admissibility to statements made after the objectives of the conspiracy have either failed or been achieved. Krulewitch v. United States, 336 U.S. 440, 69 S.Ct. 716, 93 L.Ed. 790 (1949); Wong Sun v. United States, 371 U.S. 471, 490, 83 S.Ct. 407, 418, 9 L.Ed.2d 441 (1963). For similarly limited provisions see California Evidence Code § 1223 and New Jersey Rule 63(9)(b). Cf. Uniform Rule 63(9)(b).

Report of Senate Committee on the Judiciary

The House approved the long-accepted rule that "a statement by a coconspirator of a party during the course and in furtherance of the conspiracy" is not hearsay as it was submitted by the Supreme Court. While the rule refers to a coconspirator, it is this committee's understanding that the rule is meant to carry forward the universally accepted doctrine that a joint venturer is considered as a coconspirator for the purposes of this rule even though no conspiracy has been charged. United States v. Rinaldi, 393 F.2d 97, 99 (2d Cir.), cert. denied 393 U.S. 913, 89 S.Ct. 233, 21 L.Ed.2d 198 (1968); United States v. Spencer, 415 F.2d 1301, 1304 (7th Cir.1969).

Rule 802.

HEARSAY RULE

Hearsay is not admissible except as provided by these rules or by other rules prescribed by the Supreme Court pursuant to statutory authority or by Act of Congress.

Rule 802 FEDERAL RULES OF EVIDENCE

Note by Federal Judicial Center

The rule enacted by the Congress is the rule prescribed by the Supreme Court, amended by substituting "prescribed" in place of "adopted" and by inserting the phrase "pursuant to statutory authority."

Advisory Committee's Note

The provision excepting from the operation of the rule hearsay which is made admissible by other rules adopted by the Supreme Court or by Act of Congress continues the admissibility thereunder of hearsay which would not qualify under these Evidence Rules. The following examples illustrate the working of the exception:

Federal Rules of Civil Procedure

Rule 4(g): proof of service by affidavit.

Rule 32: admissibility of depositions.

Rule 43(e): affidavits when motion based on facts not appearing of record.

Rule 56: affidavits in summary judgment proceedings.

Rule 65(b): showing by affidavit for temporary restraining order.

Federal Rules of Criminal Procedure

Rule 4(a): affidavits to show grounds for issuing warrants.

Rule 12(b)(4): affidavits to determine issues of fact in connection with motions.

Acts of Congress

10 U.S.C. § 7730: affidavits of unavailable witnesses in actions for damages caused by vessel in naval service, or towage or salvage of same, when taking of testimony or bringing of action delayed or stayed on security grounds.

29 U.S.C. § 161(4): affidavit as proof of service in NLRB proceedings.

38 U.S.C. § 5206: affidavit as proof of posting notice of sale of unclaimed property by Veterans Administration.

Rule 803.

HEARSAY EXCEPTIONS; AVAILABILITY OF DECLARANT IMMATERIAL

The following are not excluded by the hearsay rule, even though the declarant is available as a witness:

(1) Present sense impression. A statement describing or explaining an event or condition made while the declarant was perceiving the event or condition, or immediately thereafter.

(2) Excited utterance. A statement relating to a startling event or condition made while the declarant was under the stress of excitement caused by the event or condition.

(3) Then existing mental, emotional, or physical condition. A statement of the declarant's then existing state of mind, emotion, sensation, or physical condition (such as intent, plan, motive, design, mental feeling, pain, and bodily health), but not including a statement of memory or belief to prove the fact remembered or believed unless it relates to the execution, revocation, identification, or terms of declarant's will.

(4) Statements for purposes of medical diagnosis or treatment. Statements made for purposes of medical diagnosis or treatment and describing medical history, or past or present symptoms, pain, or sensations, or the inception or general character of the cause or external source thereof insofar as reasonably pertinent to diagnosis or treatment.

(5) Recorded recollection. A memorandum or record concerning a matter about which a witness once had knowledge but now has insufficient recollection to enable the witness to testify fully and accurately, shown to have been made or adopted by the witness when the matter was fresh in the witness' memory and to reflect that knowledge correctly. If admitted, the memorandum or record may be read into evidence but may not itself be received as an exhibit unless offered by an adverse party.

(6) Records of regularly conducted activity. A memorandum, report, record, or data compilation, in any form, of acts, events, conditions, opinions, or diagnoses, made at or near the time by, or from information transmitted by, a person with knowledge, if kept in the course of regularly conducted business activity, and if it was the regular practice of that business activity to make the memorandum, report, record, or data compilation, all as shown by the testimony of the custodian or other qualified witness, or by certification that complies with Rule 902(11), Rule 902(12), or a statute permitting certification, unless the source of information or the method or circumstances of preparation indicate lack of trustworthiness. The term "business" as used in this paragraph includes business, institution, association, profession, occupation, and calling of every kind, whether or not conducted for profit.

(7) Absence of entry in records kept in accordance with the provisions of paragraph (6). Evidence that a matter is not included in the memoranda, reports, records, or data compilations, in any form, kept in accordance with the provisions of paragraph (6), to prove the nonoccurrence or nonexistence of the matter, if the matter was of a kind of which a memorandum, report, record, or data compilation was regularly made and preserved, unless the sources of information or other circumstances indicate lack of trustworthiness.

(8) Public records and reports. Records, reports, statements, or data compilations, in any form, of public offices or agencies, setting forth (A) the activities of the office or agency, or (B) matters observed pursuant to duty imposed by law as to which matters there was a duty to report, excluding, however, in criminal cases matters observed by police officers and other law enforcement personnel, or (C) in civil actions and proceedings and against the Government in criminal cases, factual findings resulting from an investigation made pursuant to authority granted by law, unless the sources of information or other circumstances indicate lack of trustworthiness.

(9) Records of vital statistics. Records or data compilations, in any form, of births, fetal deaths, deaths, or marriages, if the report thereof was made to a public office pursuant to requirements of law.

(10) Absence of public record or entry. To prove the absence of a record, report, statement, or data compilation, in any form, or the nonoccurrence or nonexistence of a matter of which a record, report, statement, or data compilation, in any form, was regularly made and preserved by a public office or agency, evidence in the form of a certification in accordance with rule 902, or testimony, that diligent search failed to disclose the record, report, statement, or data compilation, or entry.

(11) Records of religious organizations. Statements of births, marriages, divorces, deaths, legitimacy, ancestry, relationship by blood or marriage, or other similar facts of personal or family history, contained in a regularly kept record of a religious organization.

(12) Marriage, baptismal, and similar certificates. Statements of fact contained in a certificate that the maker performed a marriage or other ceremony or administered a sacrament, made by a clergyman, public official, or other person authorized by the rules or practices of a religious organization or by law to perform the act certified, and purporting to have been issued at the time of the act or within a reasonable time thereafter.

(13) Family records. Statements of fact concerning personal or family history contained in family Bibles, genealogies, charts, engravings on rings, inscriptions on family portraits, engravings on urns, crypts, or tombstones or the like.

(14) Records of documents affecting an interest in property. The record of a document purporting to establish or affect an interest in property, as proof of the content of the original recorded document and its execution and delivery by each person by whom it purports to have been executed, if the record is a record of a public office and an applicable statute authorizes the recording of documents of that kind in that office.

(15) Statements in documents affecting an interest in property. A statement contained in a document purporting to establish or affect an interest in property if the matter stated was relevant to the purpose of the document, unless dealings with the property since the document was made have been inconsistent with the truth of the statement or the purport of the document.

(16) Statements in ancient documents. Statements in a document in existence twenty years or more the authenticity of which is established.

(17) Market reports, commercial publications. Market quotations, tabulations, lists, directories, or other published compilations, generally used and relied upon by the public or by persons in particular occupations.

(18) Learned treatises. To the extent called to the attention of an expert witness upon cross-examination or relied upon by the expert witness in direct examination, statements contained in published treatises, periodicals, or pamphlets on a subject of history, medicine, or other science or art, established as a reliable authority by the testimony or admission of the witness or by other expert testimony or by judicial notice. If admitted, the statements may be read into evidence but may not be received as exhibits.

(19) Reputation concerning personal or family history. Reputation among members of a person's family by blood, adoption, or marriage, or among a person's associates, or in the community, concerning a person's birth, adoption, marriage, divorce, death, legitimacy, relationship by blood, adoption, or marriage, ancestry, or other similar fact of personal or family history.

(20) Reputation concerning boundaries or general history. Reputation in a community, arising before the controversy, as to boundaries of or customs affecting lands in the community, and reputation as to events of general history important to the community or State or nation in which located.

(21) Reputation as to character. Reputation of a person's character among associates or in the community.

(22) Judgment of previous conviction. Evidence of a final judgment, entered after a trial or upon a plea of guilty (but not upon a plea of nolo contendere), adjudging a person guilty of a crime punishable by death or imprisonment in excess of one year, to prove any fact essential to sustain the judgment, but not including, when offered by the Government in a criminal prosecution for purposes other than impeachment, judgments against persons other than the accused. The pendency of an appeal may be shown but does not affect admissibility.

(23) Judgment as to personal, family, or general history, or boundaries. Judgments as proof of matters of personal, family or general history, or boundaries, essential to the judgment, if the same would be provable by evidence of reputation.

(24) [Transferred to Rule 807]

Advisory Committee's Note to 2000 Amendment to Rule 803

The amendment provides that the foundation requirements of Rule 803(6) can be satisfied under certain circumstances without the expense and inconvenience of producing time-consuming foundation witnesses. Under current law, courts have generally required foundation witnesses to testify. *See, e.g., Tongil Co., Ltd. v. Hyundai Merchant Marine Corp.*, 968 F.2d 999 (9th Cir.1992) (reversing a judgment based on business records where a qualified person filed an affidavit but did not testify). Protections are provided by the authentication requirements of Rule 902(11) for domestic records, Rule 902(12) for foreign records in civil cases, and 18 U.S.C. §§ 3505 for foreign records in criminal cases.

Committee Note to 1997 Amendment

The contents of Rule 803(24) and Rule 804(b)(5) have been combined and transferred to a new Rule 807. This was done to facilitate additions to Rules 803 and 804. No change in meaning is intended.

Note by Federal Judicial Center

The rule enacted by the Congress retains the 24 exceptions set forth in the rule prescribed by the Supreme Court. Three of the exceptions, numbered (6), (8), and (24) have been amended in respects that may fairly be described as substantial. Others, numbered (5), (7), (14), and (16), have been amended in lesser ways. The remaining 17 are unchanged. The amendments are, in numerical order, as follows.

Exception (5) as prescribed by the Supreme Court was amended by inserting after "made" the phrase "or adopted by the witness."

Exception (6) as prescribed by the Supreme Court was amended by substituting the phrase, "if kept in the course of a regularly conducted business activity, and if it was the regular practice of that business activity to make the memorandum, report, record, or data compilation, all," in place of "all in the course of a regularly conducted activity"; by substituting "source" in place of "sources"; by substituting the phrase, "the method or circumstances of preparation," in place of "other circumstances"; and by adding the second sentence.

Exception (7) as prescribed by the Supreme Court was amended by substituting the phrase, "kept in accordance with the provisions of paragraph (6)," in place of "of a regularly conducted activity." The exception prescribed by the Supreme Court included a comma after "memoranda," while the congressional enactment does not.

Exception (8) as prescribed by the Supreme Court was amended by inserting in item (B) after "law" the phrase, "as to which matters there was a duty to report, excluding, however, in criminal cases matters observed by police officers and other law enforcement personnel," and by substituting in item (C) the phrase "civil actions and proceedings," in place of "civil cases."

Exception (14) as prescribed by the Supreme Court was amended by substituting "authorizes" in place of "authorized."

Exception (16) as prescribed by the Supreme Court was amended by substituting the phrase, "the authenticity of which," in place of "whose authenticity."

Exception (24) as prescribed by the Supreme Court was amended by substituting "equivalent" in place of "comparable," and adding all that appears after "trustworthiness" in the exception as enacted by the Congress.

Advisory Committee's Note

The exceptions are phrased in terms of nonapplication of the hearsay rule, rather than in positive terms of admissibility, in order to repel any implication that other possible grounds for exclusion are eliminated from consideration.

The present rule proceeds upon the theory that under appropriate circumstances a hearsay statement may possess circumstantial guarantees of trustworthiness sufficient to justify nonproduction of the declarant in person at the trial even though he may be available. The theory finds vast support in the many exceptions to the hearsay rule developed by the common law in which unavailability of the declarant is not a relevant factor. The present rule is a synthesis of them, with revision where modern developments and conditions are believed to make that course appropriate.

In a hearsay situation, the declarant is, of course, a witness, and neither this rule nor Rule 804 dispenses with the requirement of first-hand knowledge. It may appear from his statement or be inferable from circumstances. See Rule 602.

Exceptions (1) and (2). In considerable measure these two examples overlap, though based on somewhat different theories. The most significant practical difference will lie in the time lapse allowable between event and statement.

The underlying theory of Exception (1) is that substantial contemporaneity of event and statement negative the likelihood of deliberate or conscious misrepresentation. Moreover, if the witness is the declarant, he may be examined on the statement. If the witness is not the declarant, he may be examined as to the circumstances as an aid in evaluating the statement. Morgan, Basic Problems of Evidence 340–341 (1962).

The theory of Exception (2) is simply that circumstances may produce a condition of excitement which temporarily stills the capacity of reflection and produces utterances free of conscious fabrication. 6 Wigmore § 1747, p. 135. Spontaneity is the key factor in each instance, though arrived at by somewhat different routes. Both are needed in order to avoid needless niggling.

While the theory of Exception (2) has been criticized on the ground that excitement impairs accuracy of observation as well as eliminating conscious fabrication, Hutchins and Slesinger, Some Observations on the Law of Evidence: Spontaneous Exclamations, 28 Colum.L.Rev. 432 (1928), it finds support in cases without number. See cases in 6 Wigmore § 1750; Annot., 53 A.L.R.2d 1245 (statements as to cause of or responsibility for motor vehicle accident); Annot., 4 A.L.R.3d 149 (accusatory statements by homicide victims). Since unexciting events are less likely to evoke comment, decisions involving Exception (1) are far less numerous. Illustrative are Tampa Elec. Co. v. Getrost, 151 Fla. 558, 10 So.2d 83 (1942); Houston Oxygen Co. v. Davis, 139 Tex. 1, 161 S.W.2d 474 (1942); and cases cited in McCormick § 273, p. 585, n. 4.

With respect to the *time element,* Exception (1) recognizes that in many, if not most, instances precise contemporaneity is not possible, and hence a slight lapse is allowable. Under Exception (2) the standard of measurement is the duration of the state of excitement. "How long can excitement prevail? Obviously there are no pat answers and the character of the transaction or event will largely determine the significance of the time factor." Slough, Spontaneous Statements and State of Mind, 46 Iowa L.Rev. 224, 243 (1961); McCormick § 272, p. 580.

Participation by the declarant is not required: a non-participant may be moved to describe what he perceives, and one may be startled by an event in which he is not an actor. Slough, supra; McCormick, supra; 6 Wigmore § 1755; Annot., 78 A.L.R.2d 300.

Whether *proof of the startling event* may be made by the statement itself is largely an academic question, since in most cases there is present at least circumstantial evidence that something of a startling nature must have occurred. For cases in which the evidence consists of the condition of the declarant (injuries, state of shock), see Travellers' Insurance Co. v. Mosley, 75 U.S. (8 Wall.) 397, 19 L.Ed. 437 (1869); Wheeler v. United States, 93 U.S.App.D.C. 159, 211 F.2d 19 (1953), cert. denied 347 U.S. 1019, 74 S.Ct. 876, 98 L.Ed. 1140; Wetherbee v. Safety Casualty Co., 219 F.2d 274 (5th Cir.1955); Lampe v. United States, 97 U.S.App.D.C. 160, 229 F.2d 43 (1956). Nevertheless, on occasion the only evidence may be the content of the statement itself, and rulings that it may be sufficient are described as "increasing," Slough, supra at 246, and as the "prevailing practice," McCormick § 272, p. 579. Illustrative are Armour & Co. v. Industrial Commission, 78 Colo. 569, 243 P. 546 (1926); Young v. Stewart, 191 N.C. 297, 131 S.E. 735 (1926). Moreover, under Rule 104(a) the judge is not limited by the hearsay rule in passing upon preliminary questions of fact.

Proof of declarant's perception by his statement presents similar considerations when declarant is identified. People v. Poland, 22 Ill.2d 175, 174 N.E.2d 804 (1961). However, when declarant is an unidentified bystander, the cases indicate hesitancy in upholding the statement alone as sufficient, Garrett v. Howden, 73 N.M. 307, 387 P.2d 874 (1963); Beck v. Dye, 200 Wash. 1, 92 P.2d 1113 (1939), a result which would under appropriate circumstances be consistent with the rule.

Permissible *subject matter* of the statement is limited under Exception (1) to description or explanation of the event or condition, the assumption being that spontaneity, in the absence of a startling event, may extend no farther. In Exception (2), however, the statement need only "relate" to the startling event or condition, thus affording a broader scope of subject matter coverage. 6 Wigmore §§ 1750, 1754. See Sanitary Grocery Co. v. Snead, 67 App.D.C. 129, 90 F.2d 374 (1937), slip-and-fall case sustaining admissibility of clerk's statement, "That has been on the floor for a couple of hours," and Murphy Auto Parts Co. v. Ball, 101 U.S.App.D.C. 416, 249 F.2d 508 (1957), upholding admission, on issue of driver's agency, of his statement that he had to call on a customer and was in a hurry to get home. Quick, Hearsay, Excitement, Necessity and the Uniform Rules: A Reappraisal of Rule 63(4), 6 Wayne L.Rev. 204, 206–209 (1960).

Similar provisions are found in Uniform Rule 63(4)(a) and (b); California Evidence Code § 1240 (as to Exception (2) only); Kansas Code of Civil Procedure § 60–460(d)(1) and (2); New Jersey Evidence Rule 63(4).

Exception (3) is essentially a specialized application of Exception (1), presented separately to enhance its usefulness and accessibility. See McCormick §§ 265, 268.

The exclusion of "statements of memory or belief to prove the fact remembered or believed" is necessary to avoid the virtual destruction of the hearsay rule which would otherwise result from allowing state of mind, provable by a hearsay statement, to serve as the basis for an inference of the happening of the event which produced the state of mind. Shepard v. United States, 290 U.S. 96, 54 S.Ct. 22, 78 L.Ed. 196 (1933); Maguire, The Hillmon Case—Thirty-three Years After, 38 Harv.L.Rev. 709, 719–731 (1925); Hinton, States of Mind and the Hearsay Rule, 1 U.Chi.L.Rev. 394, 421–423 (1934). The rule of Mutual Life Ins. Co. v. Hillmon, 145 U.S. 285, 12 S.Ct. 909, 36 L.Ed. 706 (1892), allowing evidence of intention as tending to prove the doing of the act intended, is, of course, left undisturbed.

The carving out, from the exclusion mentioned in the preceding paragraph, of declarations relating to the execution, revocation, identification, or terms of declarant's will represents an ad hoc judgment which finds ample reinforcement in the decisions, resting on practical grounds of necessity and expediency rather than logic. McCormick § 271, pp. 577–578; Annot., 34 A.L.R.2d 588, 62 A.L.R.2d 855. A similar recognition of the need for and practical value of this kind of evidence is found in California Evidence Code § 1260.

Report of House Committee on the Judiciary

Rule 803(3) was approved in the form submitted by the Court to Congress. However, the Committee intends that the Rule be construed to limit the doctrine of Mutual Life Insurance Co. v. Hillmon, 145 U.S. 285, 295–300, 12 S.Ct. 909, 912–914, 36 L.Ed. 706 (1892), so as to render statements of intent by a declarant admissible only to prove his future conduct, not the future conduct of another person.

Advisory Committee's Note

Exception (4). Even those few jurisdictions which have shied away from generally admitting statements of present condition have allowed them if made to a physician for purposes of diagnosis and treatment in view of the patient's strong motivation to be truthful. McCormick § 266, p. 563. The same guarantee of trustworthiness extends to statements of past conditions and medical history, made for purposes of diagnosis or treatment. It also extends to statements as to causation, reasonably pertinent to the same purposes, in accord with the current trend, Shell Oil Co. v. Industrial Commission, 2 Ill.2d 590, 119 N.E.2d 224 (1954); McCormick § 266, p. 564; New Jersey Evidence Rule 63(12)(c). Statements as to fault would not ordinarily qualify under this latter language. Thus a patient's statement that he was struck by an automobile would qualify but not his statement that the car was driven through a red light. Under the exception the statement need not have been made to a physician. Statements to hospital attendants, ambulance drivers, or even members of the family might be included.

Conventional doctrine has excluded from the hearsay exception, as not within its guarantee of truthfulness, statements to a physician consulted only for the purpose of enabling him to testify. While these statements were not admissible as substantive evidence, the expert was allowed to state the basis of his opinion, including statements of this kind. The distinction thus called for was one most unlikely to be made by juries. The rule accordingly rejects the limitation. This position is consistent with the provision of Rule 703 that the facts on which expert testimony is based need not be admissible in evidence if of a kind ordinarily relied upon by experts in the field.

Report of House Committee on the Judiciary

After giving particular attention to the question of physical examination made solely to enable a physician to testify, the Committee approved Rule 803(4) as submitted to Congress, with the understanding that it is not intended in any way to adversely affect present privilege rules or those subsequently adopted.

Report of Senate Committee on the Judiciary

The House approved this rule as it was submitted by the Supreme Court "with the understanding that it is not intended in any way to adversely affect present privilege rules." We also approve this rule, and we would point out with respect to the question of its relation to privileges, it must be read in conjunction with rule 35 of the Federal Rules of Civil Procedure which provides that whenever the physical or mental condition of a party (plaintiff or defendant) is in controversy, the court may require him to submit to an examination by a physician. It is these examinations which will normally be admitted under this exception.

Advisory Committee's Note

Exception (5). A hearsay exception for recorded recollection is generally recognized and has been described as having "long been favored by the federal and practically all the state courts that have had occasion to decide the question." United States v. Kelly, 349 F.2d 720, 770 (2d Cir.1965), citing numerous cases and sustaining the exception against a claimed denial of the right of confrontation. Many additional cases are cited in Annot., 82 A.L.R.2d 473, 520. The guarantee of trustworthiness is found in the reliability inherent in a record made while events were still fresh in mind and accurately reflecting them. Owens v. State, 67 Md. 307, 316, 10 A. 210, 212 (1887).

The principal controversy attending the exception has centered, not upon the propriety of the exception itself, but upon the question whether a preliminary requirement of impaired memory on the part of the witness should be imposed. The authorities are divided. If regard be had only to the accuracy of the evidence, admittedly impairment of the memory of the witness adds nothing to it and should not be required. McCormick § 277, p. 593; 3 Wigmore § 738, p. 76; Jordan v. People, 151 Colo. 133, 376 P.2d 699 (1962), cert. denied 373 U.S. 944, 83 S.Ct. 1553, 10 L.Ed.2d 699; Hall v. State, 223 Md. 158, 162 A.2d 751 (1960); State v. Bindhammer, 44 N.J. 372, 209 A.2d 124 (1965). Nevertheless, the absence of the requirement, it is believed, would encourage the use of statements carefully prepared for purposes of litigation under the supervision of attorneys, investigators, or claim adjusters. Hence the example includes a requirement that the witness not have "sufficient recollection to enable him to testify fully and accurately." To the same effect are California Evidence Code § 1237 and New Jersey Rule 63(1)(b), and this has been the position of the federal courts. Vicksburg & Meridian R.R. v. O'Brien, 119 U.S. 99, 7 S.Ct. 118, 30 L.Ed. 299 (1886); Ahern v. Webb, 268 F.2d 45 (10th Cir.1959); and see

N.L.R.B. v. Hudson Pulp and Paper Corp., 273 F.2d 660, 665 (5th Cir.1960); N.L.R.B. v. Federal Dairy Co., 297 F.2d 487 (1st Cir.1962). But cf. United States v. Adams, 385 F.2d 548 (2d Cir.1967).

No attempt is made in the exception to spell out the method of establishing the initial knowledge or the contemporaneity and accuracy of the record, leaving them to be dealt with as the circumstances of the particular case might indicate. Multiple person involvement in the process of observing and recording, as in Rathbun v. Brancatella, 93 N.J.L. 222, 107 A. 279 (1919), is entirely consistent with the exception.

Locating the exception at this place in the scheme of the rules is a matter of choice. There were two other possibilities. The first was to regard the statement as one of the group of prior statements of a testifying witness which are excluded entirely from the category of hearsay by Rule 801(d)(1). That category, however, requires that declarant be "subject to cross-examination," as to which the impaired memory aspect of the exception raises doubts. The other possibility was to include the exception among those covered by Rule 804. Since unavailability is required by that rule and lack of memory is listed as a species of unavailability by the definition of the term in Rule 804(a)(3), that treatment at first impression would seem appropriate. The fact is, however, that the unavailability requirement of the exception is of a limited and peculiar nature. Accordingly, the exception is located at this point rather than in the context of a rule where unavailability is conceived of more broadly.

Report of House Committee on the Judiciary

Rule 803(5) as submitted by the Court permitted the reading into evidence of a memorandum or record concerning a matter about which a witness once had knowledge but now has insufficient recollection to enable him to testify accurately and fully, "shown to have been made when the matter was fresh in his memory and to reflect that knowledge correctly." The Committee amended this Rule to add the words "or adopted by the witness" after the phrase "shown to have been made", a treatment consistent with the definition of "statement" in the Jencks Act, 18 U.S.C. 3500. Moreover, it is the Committee's understanding that a memorandum or report, although barred under this Rule, would nonetheless be admissible if it came within another hearsay exception. This last stated principle is deemed applicable to all the hearsay rules.

Report of Senate Committee on the Judiciary

The committee accepts the House amendment with the understanding and belief that it was not intended to narrow the scope of applicability of the rule. In fact, we understand it to clarify the rule's applicability to a memorandum adopted by the witness as well as one made by him. While the rule as submitted by the Court was silent on the question of who made the memorandum, we view the House amendment as a helpful clarification, noting, however, that the Advisory Committee's note to this rule suggests that the important thing is the accuracy of the memorandum rather than who made it.

The committee does not view the House amendment as precluding admissibility in situations in which multiple participants were involved.

When the verifying witness has not prepared the report, but merely examined it and found it accurate, he has adopted the report, and it is therefore admissible. The rule should also be interpreted to cover other situations involving multiple participants, e.g., employer dictating to secretary, secretary making memorandum at direction of employer, or information being passed along a chain of persons, as in Curtis v. Bradley.[1]

The committee also accepts the understanding of the House that a memorandum or report, although barred under this rule, would nonetheless be admissible if it came within another hearsay exception. We consider this principle to be applicable to all the hearsay rules.

Advisory Committee's Note

Exception (6) represents an area which has received much attention from those seeking to improve the law of evidence. The Commonwealth Fund Act was the result of a study completed in 1927 by a distinguished committee under the chairmanship of Professor Morgan. Morgan et al., The Law of Evidence: Some Proposals for its Reform 63 (1927). With changes too minor to mention, it was adopted by Congress in 1936 as the rule for federal courts. 28 U.S.C. § 1732. A number of states took similar action. The Commissioners on Uniform State Laws in 1936 promulgated the Uniform Business Records as Evidence Act, 9A U.L.A. 506, which has acquired a substantial following in the states. Model Code Rule 514 and Uniform Rule 63(13) also deal with the subject. Difference of varying degrees of importance exist among these various treatments.

These reform efforts were largely within the context of business and commercial records, as the kind usually encountered, and concentrated considerable attention upon relaxing the requirement of producing as witnesses, or accounting for the nonproduction of, all participants in the process of gathering, transmitting, and recording information which the common law had evolved as a burdensome and crippling aspect of using records of this type. In their areas of primary emphasis on witnesses to be called and the general admissibility of ordinary business and commercial records, the Commonwealth Fund Act and the Uniform Act appear to have worked well. The exception seeks to preserve their advantages.

On the subject of what witnesses must be called, the Commonwealth Fund Act eliminated the common law requirement of calling or accounting for all participants by failing to mention it. United States v. Mortimer, 118 F.2d 266 (2d Cir.1941); La Porte v. United States, 300 F.2d 878 (9th Cir.1962); McCormick § 290, p. 608. Model Code Rule 514 and Uniform Rule 63(13) did likewise. The Uniform Act, however, abolished the common law requirement in express terms, providing that the requisite foundation testimony might be furnished by "the custodian or other qualified witness." Uniform Business Records as Evidence Act, § 2; 9A U.L.A. 506. The exception follows the Uniform Act in this respect.

The element of unusual reliability of business records is said variously to be supplied by systematic checking, by regularity and continuity which produce habits of precision, by actual experience of business in relying upon them, or by a duty to make an accurate record as part of a continuing job or occupation. McCormick §§ 281, 286, 287; Laughlin, Business Entries and the Like, 46 Iowa

---

1. 65 Conn. 99, 31 A. 591 (1894). See also, Rathbun v. Brancatella, 93 N.J.L. 222, 107 A. 279 (1919); see also McCormick on Evidence, § 303 (2d ed. 1972) (footnote renumbered).

L.Rev. 276 (1961). The model statutes and rules have sought to capture these factors and to extend their impact by employing the phrase "regular course of business," in conjunction with a definition of "business" far broader than its ordinarily accepted meaning. The result is a tendency unduly to emphasize a requirement of routineness and repetitiveness and an insistence that other types of records be squeezed into the fact patterns which give rise to traditional business records....

Amplification of the kinds of activities producing admissible records has given rise to problems which conventional business records by their nature avoid. They are problems of the source of the recorded information, of entries in opinion form, of motivation, and of involvement as participant in the matters recorded.

Sources of information presented no substantial problem with ordinary business records. All participants, including the observer or participant furnishing the information to be recorded, were acting routinely, under a duty of accuracy, with employer reliance on the result, or in short "in the regular course of business." If, however, the supplier of the information does not act in the regular course, an essential link is broken; the assurance of accuracy does not extend to the information itself, and the fact that it may be recorded with scrupulous accuracy is of no avail. An illustration is the police report incorporating information obtained from a bystander: the officer qualifies as acting in the regular course but the informant does not. The leading case, Johnson v. Lutz, 253 N.Y. 124, 170 N.E. 517 (1930), held that a report thus prepared was inadmissible. Most of the authorities have agreed with the decision. Gencarella v. Fyfe, 171 F.2d 419 (1st Cir.1948); Gordon v. Robinson, 210 F.2d 192 (3d Cir.1954); Standard Oil Co. of California v. Moore, 251 F.2d 188, 214 (9th Cir.1957), cert. denied 356 U.S. 975, 78 S.Ct. 1139, 2 L.Ed.2d 1148; Yates v. Bair Transport, Inc., 249 F.Supp. 681 (S.D.N.Y.1965); Annot., 69 A.L.R.2d 1148. Cf. Hawkins v. Gorea Motor Express, Inc., 360 F.2d 933 (2d Cir.1966). Contra, 5 Wigmore § 1530a, n. 1, pp. 391–392. The point is not dealt with specifically in the Commonwealth Fund Act, the Uniform Act, or Uniform Rule 63(13). However, Model Code Rule 514 contains the requirement "that it was the regular course of that business for one with personal knowledge ... to make such a memorandum or record or to transmit information thereof to be included in such a memorandum or record...." The rule follows this lead in requiring an informant with knowledge acting in the course of the regularly conducted activity.

Entries in the form of opinions were not encountered in traditional business records in view of the purely factual nature of the items recorded, but they are now commonly encountered with respect to medical diagnoses, prognoses, and test results, as well as occasionally in other areas. The Commonwealth Fund Act provided only for records of an "act, transaction, occurrence, or event," while the Uniform Act, Model Code Rule 514, and Uniform Rule 63(13) merely added the ambiguous term "condition." The limited phrasing of the Commonwealth Fund Act, 28 U.S.C. § 1732, may account for the reluctance of some federal decisions to admit diagnostic entries. New York Life Ins. Co. v. Taylor, 79 U.S.App.D.C. 66, 147 F.2d 297 (1944); Lyles v. United States, 103 U.S.App.D.C. 22, 254 F.2d 725 (1957), cert. denied 356 U.S. 961, 78 S.Ct. 997, 2 L.Ed.2d 1067; England v. United States, 174 F.2d 466 (5th Cir.1949); Skogen v. Dow Chemical Co., 375 F.2d 692 (8th Cir.1967). Other federal decisions, however, experienced no difficulty in freely admitting diagnostic entries. Reed v. Order of United Commercial Travelers, 123 F.2d 252 (2d Cir.1941); Buckminster's Estate v. Commissioner of Internal Revenue, 147 F.2d 331 (2d Cir.1944); Medina v. Erickson, 226 F.2d 475 (9th Cir.1955); Thomas v. Hogan, 308 F.2d 355 (4th Cir.1962); Glawe v. Rulon, 284 F.2d 495 (8th Cir.1960). In the state courts, the trend favors admissibility. Borucki v. MacKenzie Bros. Co., 125 Conn. 92, 3 A.2d 224 (1938); Allen v. St. Louis Public Service Co., 365 Mo. 677, 285 S.W.2d 663, 55 A.L.R.2d 1022 (1956); People v. Kohlmeyer, 284 N.Y. 366, 31 N.E.2d 490 (1940); Weis v. Weis, 147 Ohio St. 416, 72 N.E.2d 245 (1947). In order to make clear its adherence to the latter position, the rule specifically includes both diagnoses and opinions, in addition to acts, events, and conditions, as proper subjects of admissible entries.

Problems of the motivation of the informant have been a source of difficulty and disagreement. In Palmer v. Hoffman, 318 U.S. 109, 63 S.Ct. 477, 87 L.Ed. 645 (1943), exclusion of an accident report made by the since deceased engineer, offered by defendant railroad trustees in a grade crossing collision case, was upheld. The report was not "in the regular course of business," not a record of the systematic conduct of the business as a business, said the Court. The report was prepared for use in litigating, not railroading. While the opinion mentions the motivation of the engineer only obliquely, the emphasis on records of routine operations is significant only by virtue of impact on motivation to be accurate. Absence of routineness raises lack of motivation to be accurate. The opinion of the Court of Appeals had gone beyond mere lack of motive to be accurate: the engineer's statement was "dripping with motivations to misrepresent." Hoffman v. Palmer, 129 F.2d 976, 991 (2d Cir.1942). The direct introduction of motivation is a disturbing factor, since absence of motive to misrepresent has not traditionally been a requirement of the rule; that records might be self-serving has not been a ground for exclusion. Laughlin, Business Records and the Like, 46 Iowa L.Rev. 276, 285 (1961). As Judge Clark said in his dissent, "I submit that there is hardly a grocer's account book which could not be excluded on that basis." 129 F.2d at 1002. A physician's evaluation report of a personal injury litigant would appear to be in the routine of his business. If the report is offered by the party at whose instance it was made, however, it has been held inadmissible, Yates v. Bair Transport, Inc., 249 F.Supp. 681 (S.D.N.Y.1965), otherwise if offered by the opposite party, Korte v. New York, N.H. & H.R. Co., 191 F.2d 86 (2d Cir.1951), cert. denied 342 U.S. 868, 72 S.Ct. 108, 96 L.Ed. 652.

The decisions hinge on motivation and which party is entitled to be concerned about it. Professor McCormick believed that the doctor's report or the accident report were sufficiently routine to justify admissibility. McCormick § 287, p. 604. Yet hesitation must be experienced in admitting everything which is observed and recorded in the course of a regularly conducted activity. Efforts to set a limit are illustrated by Hartzog v. United States, 217 F.2d 706 (4th Cir.1954), error to admit worksheets made by since deceased deputy collector in preparation for the instant income tax evasion prosecution, and United States v. Ware, 247 F.2d 698 (7th Cir.1957), error to admit narcotics agents' records of purchases. See also Exception (8), infra, as to the public record aspects of records of this nature. Some decisions have been satisfied as to motivation of an accident report if made pursuant to statutory duty, United States v. New York Foreign Trade Zone Operators, 304 F.2d 792 (2d Cir.1962); Taylor v. Baltimore & O.R. Co., 344 F.2d 281 (2d Cir.1965), since the report was oriented in a direction other than the litigation which ensued. Cf. Matthews v. United States, 217 F.2d 409 (5th Cir.1954). The formulation of specific terms which would assure satisfactory results in all cases is not possible. Consequently the rule proceeds from the base that records made in the course of a regularly conducted activity will be taken as admissible but subject to authority to exclude if "the sources of information or other circumstances indicate lack of trustworthiness."

Occasional decisions have reached for enhanced accuracy by requiring involvement as a participant in matters reported. Clainos v. United States, 82 U.S.App.D.C. 278, 163 F.2d 593 (1947), error to admit police records of convictions; Standard Oil Co. of California v. Moore, 251 F.2d 188 (9th Cir.1957), cert. denied 356 U.S. 975, 78 S.Ct. 1139, 2 L.Ed.2d 1148, error to admit employees' records of observed business practices of others. The rule includes no requirement of this nature. Wholly acceptable records may involve matters merely observed, e.g. the weather.

The form which the "record" may assume under the rule is described broadly as a "memorandum, report, record, or data compilation, in any form." The expression "data compilation" is used as broadly descriptive of any means of storing information other than the conventional words and figures in written or documentary form. It includes, but is by no means limited to, electronic computer storage. The term is borrowed from revised Rule 34(a) of the Rules of Civil Procedure.

Report of Senate Committee on the Judiciary

It is the understanding of the committee that the use of the phrase "person with knowledge" is not intended to imply that the party seeking to introduce the memorandum, report, record, or data compilation must be able to produce, or even identify, the specific individual upon whose first-hand knowledge the memorandum, report, record or data compilation was based. A sufficient foundation for the introduction of such evidence will be laid if the party seeking to introduce the evidence is able to show that it was the regular practice of the activity to base such memorandums, reports, records, or data compilations upon a transmission from a person with knowledge, e.g., in the case of the content of a shipment of goods, upon a report from the company's receiving agent or in the case of a computer printout, upon a report from the company's computer programmer or one who has knowledge of the particular record system. In short, the scope of the phrase "person with knowledge" is meant to be coterminous with the custodian of the evidence or other qualified witness. The committee believes this represents the desired rule in light of the complex nature of modern business organizations.

Conference Report

The House bill provides in subsection (6) that records of a regularly conducted "business" activity qualify for admission into evidence as an exception to the hearsay rule. "Business" is defined as including "business, profession, occupation and calling of every kind." The Senate amendment drops the requirement that the records be those of a "business" activity and eliminates the definition of "business." The Senate amendment provides that records are admissible if they are records of a regularly conducted "activity."

The Conference adopts the House provision that the records must be those of a regularly conducted "business" activity. The Conferees changed the definition of "business" contained in the House provision in order to make it clear that the records of institutions and associations like schools, churches and hospitals are admissible under this provision. The records of public schools and hospitals are also covered by Rule 803(8), which deals with public records and reports.

Advisory Committee's Note

Exception (7). Failure of a record to mention a matter which would ordinarily be mentioned is satisfactory evidence of its nonexistence. Uniform Rule 63(14), Comment. While probably not hearsay as defined in Rule 801, supra, decisions may be found which class the evidence not only as hearsay but also as not within any exception. In order to set the question at rest in favor of admissibility, it is specifically treated here. McCormick, § 289, p. 609; Morgan, Basic Problems of Evidence 314 (1962); 5 Wigmore § 1531; Uniform Rule 63(14); California Evidence Code § 1272; Kansas Code of Civil Procedure § 60-460(n); New Jersey Evidence Rule 63(14).

Exception (8). Public records are a recognized hearsay exception at common law and have been the subject of statutes without number. McCormick § 291. See, for example, 28 U.S.C. § 1733, the relative narrowness of which is illustrated by its nonapplicability to nonfederal public agencies, thus necessitating resort to the less appropriate business record exception to the hearsay rule. Kay v. United States, 255 F.2d 476 (4th Cir.1958). The rule makes no distinction between federal and nonfederal offices and agencies.

Justification for the exception is the assumption that a public official will perform his duty properly and the unlikelihood that he will remember details independently of the record. Wong Wing Foo v. McGrath, 196 F.2d 120 (9th Cir.1952), and see Chesapeake & Delaware Canal Co. v. United States, 250 U.S. 123, 39 S.Ct. 407, 63 L.Ed. 889 (1919). As to items (A) and (B), further support is found in the reliability factors underlying records of regularly conducted activities generally. See Exception (6), supra.

(A) Cases illustrating the admissibility of records of the office's or agency's own activities are numerous. Chesapeake & Delaware Canal Co. v. United States, 250 U.S. 123, 39 S.Ct. 407, 63 L.Ed. 889 (1919), Treasury records of miscellaneous receipts and disbursements; Howard v. Perrin, 200 U.S. 71, 26 S.Ct. 195, 50 L.Ed. 374 (1906), General Land Office records; Ballew v. United States, 160 U.S. 187, 16 S.Ct. 263, 40 L.Ed. 388 (1895), Pension Office records.

(B) Cases sustaining admissibility of records of matters observed are also numerous. United States v. Van Hook, 284 F.2d 489 (7th Cir.1960), remanded for resentencing 365 U.S. 609, 81 S.Ct. 823, 5 L.Ed.2d 821, letter from induction officer to District Attorney, pursuant to army regulations, stating fact and circumstances of refusal to be inducted; T'Kach v. United States, 242 F.2d 937 (5th Cir.1957), affidavit of White House personnel officer that search of records showed no employment of accused, charged with fraudulently representing himself as an envoy of the President; Minnehaha County v. Kelley, 150 F.2d 356 (8th Cir.1945); Weather Bureau records of rainfall; United States v. Meyer, 113 F.2d 387 (7th Cir.1940), cert. denied 311 U.S. 706, 61 S.Ct. 174, 85 L.Ed. 459, map prepared by government engineer from information furnished by men working under his supervision.

(C) The more controversial area of public records is that of the so-called "evaluative" report. The disagreement among the decisions has been due in part, no doubt, to the variety of situations encountered, as well as to differences in principle. Sustaining admissibility are such cases as United States v. Dumas, 149 U.S. 278, 13 S.Ct. 872, 37 L.Ed. 734 (1893), statement of account certified by Postmaster General in action against postmaster; McCarty v. United States, 185 F.2d 520 (5th Cir.1950), reh. denied 187 F.2d 234, Certificate of Settlement of General Accounting Office showing indebtedness and letter from Army official stating Government had performed, in action on contract to purchase and remove waste food from Army camp; Moran v. Pittsburgh–Des Moines Steel Co., 183 F.2d 467 (3d Cir.1950), report of Bureau of Mines as to cause of gas tank explosion; Petition of W___, 164 F.Supp. 659 (E.D.Pa.1958), report by Immigration and Naturalization Service investigator that petitioner was known in community as wife of man to whom she was not married. To the opposite effect and denying admissibility are Franklin v. Skelly Oil Co., 141 F.2d 568 (10th Cir.1944), State Fire Marshal's report of cause of gas explosion; Lomax Transp. Co. v. United States, 183 F.2d 331 (9th Cir.1950), Certificate of Settlement from General Accounting Office in action for naval supplies lost in warehouse fire; Yung Jin Teung v. Dulles, 229 F.2d 244 (2d Cir.1956), "Status Reports" offered to justify delay in processing passport applications.... Various kinds of evaluative reports are admissible under federal statutes: 7 U.S.C. § 78, findings of Secretary of Agriculture prima facie evidence of true grade of grain; 7 U.S.C. § 210(f), findings of Secretary of Agriculture prima facie evidence in action for damages against stockyard owner; 7 U.S.C. § 292, order by Secretary of Agriculture prima facie evidence in judicial enforcement proceedings against producers association monopoly; 7 U.S.C. § 1622(h), Department of Agriculture inspection certificates of products shipped in interstate commerce prima facie evidence; 8 U.S.C. § 1440(c), separation of alien from military service on conditions other than honorable provable by certificate from department in proceedings to revoke citizenship; 18 U.S.C. § 4245, certificate of Director of Prisons that convicted person has been examined and found probably incompetent at time of trial prima facie evidence in court hearing on competency; 42 U.S.C. § 269(b), bill of health by appropriate official prima facie evidence of vessel's sanitary history and condition and compliance with regulations; 46 U.S.C. § 679, certificate of consul presumptive evidence of refusal of master to transport destitute seamen to United States. While these statutory exceptions to the hearsay rule are left undisturbed, Rule 802, the willingness of Congress to recognize a substantial measure of admissibility for evaluative reports is a helpful guide.

Factors which may be of assistance in passing upon the admissibility of evaluative reports include: (1) the timeliness of the investigation, McCormick, Can the Courts Make Wider Use of Reports of Official Investigations? 42 Iowa L.Rev. 363 (1957); (2) the special skill or experience of the official, id., (3) whether a hearing was held and the level at which conducted, Franklin v. Skelly Oil Co., 141 F.2d 568 (10th Cir.1944); (4) possible motivation problems suggested by Palmer v. Hoffman, 318 U.S. 109, 63 S.Ct. 477, 87 L.Ed. 645 (1943). Others no doubt could be added.

The formulation of an approach which would give appropriate weight to all possible factors in every situation is an obvious impossibility. Hence the rule, as in Exception (6), assumes admissibility in the first instance but with ample provision for escape if sufficient negative factors are present. In one respect, however, the rule with respect to evaluative reports under item (C) is very specific: they are admissible only in civil cases and against the government in criminal cases in view of the almost certain collision with confrontation rights which would result from their use against the accused in a criminal case.

Report of Senate Committee on the Judiciary

The House approved Rule 803(8), as submitted by the Supreme Court, with one substantive change. It excluded from the hearsay exception reports containing matters observed by police officers and other law enforcement personnel in criminal cases. Ostensibly, the reason for this exclusion is that observations by police officers at the scene of the crime or the apprehension of the defendant are not as reliable as observations by public officials in other cases because of the adversarial nature of the confrontation between the police and the defendant in criminal cases.

Advisory Committee's Note

Exception (9). Records of vital statistics are commonly the subject of particular statutes making them admissible in evidence, Uniform Vital Statistics Act, 9C U.L.A. 350 (1957). The rule is in principle narrower than Uniform Rule 63(16) which includes reports required of persons performing functions authorized by statute, yet in practical effect the two are substantially the same. Comment Uniform Rule 63(16). The exception as drafted is in the pattern of California Evidence Code § 1281.

Exception (10). The principle of proving nonoccurrence of an event by evidence of the absence of a record which would regularly be made of its occurrence, developed in Exception (7) with respect to regularly conducted [business] activities, is here extended to public records of the kind mentioned in Exceptions (8) and (9). 5 Wigmore § 1633(6), p. 519. Some harmless duplication no doubt exists with Exception (7). For instances of federal statutes recognizing this method of proof, see 8 U.S.C. § 1284(b), proof of absence of alien crewman's name from outgoing manifest prima facie evidence of failure to detain or deport, and 42 U.S.C. § 405(c)(3), (4)(B), (4)(C), absence of HEW record prima facie evidence of no wages or self-employment income.

The rule includes situations in which absence of a record may itself be the ultimate focal point of inquiry, e.g. People v. Love, 310 Ill. 558, 142 N.E. 204 (1923), certificate of Secretary of State admitted to show failure to file documents required by Securities Law, as well as cases where the absence of a record is offered as proof of the nonoccurrence of an event ordinarily recorded.

The refusal of the common law to allow proof by certificate of the lack of a record or entry has no apparent justification, 5 Wigmore § 1678(7), p. 752. The rule takes the opposite position, as do Uniform Rule 63(17); California Evidence Code § 1284; Kansas Code of Civil Procedure § 60–460(c); New Jersey Evidence Rule 63(17). Congress has recognized certification as evidence of the lack of a record. 8 U.S.C. § 1360(d), certificate of Attorney General or other designated officer that no record of Immigration and Naturalization Service of specified nature or entry therein is found, admissible in alien cases.

Exception (11). Records of activities of religious organizations are currently recognized as admissible at least to the extent of the business records exception to the hearsay rule, 5 Wigmore § 1523, p. 371, and Exception (6) would be applicable. However, both the business record doctrine and Exception (6) require that the person furnishing the information be one in the business or activity. The result is such decisions as Dailey v. Grand Lodge, 311 Ill. 184, 142 N.E. 478 (1924), holding a church record admissible to prove fact, date, and place of baptism, but not age of child except that he had at least been born at the time. In view of the unlikelihood that false information would be furnished on occasions of this kind, the rule contains no requirement that the informant be in the course of the activity. See California Evidence Code § 1315 and Comment.

Exception (12). The principle of proof by certification is recognized as to public officials in Exceptions (8) and (10), and with respect to authentication in Rule 902. The present exception is a duplication to the extent that it deals with a certificate by a public official, as in the case of a judge who performs a marriage ceremony. The area covered by the rule is, however, substantially larger and extends the certification procedure to clergymen and the like who perform marriages and other ceremonies or administer sacraments. Thus certificates of such matters as baptism or confirmation, as well as marriage, are included. In principle they are as acceptable evidence as certificates of public officers. See 5 Wigmore § 1645, as to marriage certificates. When the person executing the certificate is not a public official, the self-authenticating character of documents purporting to emanate from public officials, see Rule 902, is lacking and proof is required that the person was authorized and did make the certificate. The time element, however, may safely be taken as supplied by the certificate, once authority and authenticity are established, particularly in view of the presumption that a document was executed on the date it bears.

For similar rules, some limited to certificates of marriage, with variations in foundation requirements, see Uniform Rule 63(18); California Evidence Code § 1316; Kansas Code of Civil Procedure § 60–460(p); New Jersey Evidence Rule 63(18).

Exception (13). Records of family history kept in family Bibles have by long tradition been received in evidence. 5 Wigmore §§ 1495, 1496, citing numerous statutes and decisions. See also Regulations, Social Security Administration, 20 C.F.R. § 404.703(c), recognizing family Bible entries as proof of age in the absence of public or church records. Opinions in the area also include inscriptions on tombstones, publicly displayed pedigrees, and engravings on rings. Wigmore, supra. The rule is substantially identical in coverage with California Evidence Code § 1312.

Exception (14). The recording of title documents is a purely statutory development. Under any theory of the admissibility of public records, the records would be receivable as evidence of the contents of the recorded document, else the recording process would be reduced to a nullity. When, however, the record is offered for the further purpose of proving execution and delivery, a problem of lack of first-hand knowledge by the recorder, not present as to contents, is presented. This problem is solved, seemingly in all jurisdictions, by qualifying for recording only those documents shown by a specified procedure, either acknowledgement or a form of probate, to have been executed and delivered. 5 Wigmore §§ 1647–1651. Thus what may appear in the rule, at first glance, as endowing the record with an effect independently of local law and inviting difficulties of an Erie nature under Cities Service Oil Co. v. Dunlap, 308 U.S. 208, 60 S.Ct. 201, 84 L.Ed. 196 (1939), is not present, since the local law in fact governs under the example.

Rule 803   FEDERAL RULES OF EVIDENCE

Exception (15). Dispositive documents often contain recitals of fact. Thus a deed purporting to have been executed by an attorney in fact may recite the existence of the power of attorney, or a deed may recite that the grantors are all the heirs of the last record owner. Under the rule, these recitals are exempted from the hearsay rule. The circumstances under which dispositive documents are executed and the requirement that the recital be germane to the purpose of the document are believed to be adequate guarantees of trustworthiness, particularly in view of the nonapplicability of the rule if dealings with the property have been inconsistent with the document. The age of the document is of no significance, though in practical application the document will most often be an ancient one. See Uniform Rule 63(29), Comment.

Similar provisions are contained in Uniform Rule 63(29); California Evidence Code § 1330; Kansas Code of Civil Procedure § 60–460(aa); New Jersey Evidence Rule 63(29).

Exception (16). Authenticating a document as ancient, essentially in the pattern of the common law, as provided in Rule 901(b)(8), leaves open as a separate question the admissibility of assertive statements contained therein as against a hearsay objection. 7 Wigmore § 2145a. Wigmore further states that the ancient document technique of authentication is universally conceded to apply to all sorts of documents, including letters, records, contracts, maps, and certificates, in addition to title documents, citing numerous decisions. Id. § 2145. Since most of these items are significant evidentially only insofar as they are assertive, their admission in evidence must be as a hearsay exception. But see 5 id. § 1573, p. 429, referring to recitals in ancient deeds as a "limited" hearsay exception. The former position is believed to be the correct one in reason and authority. As pointed out in McCormick § 298, danger of mistake is minimized by authentication requirements, and age affords assurance that the writing antedates the present controversy. See Dallas County v. Commercial Union Assurance Co., 286 F.2d 388 (5th Cir.1961), upholding admissibility of 58–year–old newspaper story. Cf. Morgan, Basic Problems of Evidence 364 (1962), but see id. 254.

For a similar provision, but with the added requirement that "the statement has since generally been acted upon as true by persons having an interest in the matter," see California Evidence Code § 1331.

Exception (17). Ample authority at common law supported the admission in evidence of items falling in this category. While Wigmore's text is narrowly oriented to lists, etc., prepared for the use of a trade or profession, 6 Wigmore § 1702, authorities are cited which include other kinds of publications, for example, newspaper market reports, telephone directories, and city directories. Id. §§ 1702–1706. The basis of trustworthiness is general reliance by the public or by a particular segment of it, and the motivation of the compiler to foster reliance by being accurate.

For similar provisions, see Uniform Rule 63(30); California Evidence Code § 1340; Kansas Code of Civil Procedure § 60–460(bb); New Jersey Evidence Rule 63(30). Uniform Commercial Code § 2–724 provides for admissibility in evidence of "reports in official publications or trade journals or in newspapers or periodicals of general circulation published as the reports of such [established commodity] market."

Exception (18). The writers have generally favored the admissibility of learned treatises, McCormick § 296, p. 621; Morgan, Basic Problems of Evidence 366 (1962); 6 Wigmore § 1692, with the support of occasional decisions and rules, City of Dothan v. Hardy, 237 Ala. 603, 188 So. 264 (1939); Lewandowski v. Preferred Risk Mut. Ins. Co., 33 Wis.2d 69, 146 N.W.2d 505 (1966), 66 Mich. L.Rev. 183 (1967); Uniform Rule 63(31); Kansas Code of Civil Procedure § 60–460(cc), but the great weight of authority has been that learned treatises are not admissible as substantive evidence though usable in the cross-examination of experts. The foundation of the minority view is that the hearsay objection must be regarded as unimpressive when directed against treatises since a high standard of accuracy is engendered by various factors: the treatise is written primarily and impartially for professionals, subject to scrutiny and exposure for inaccuracy, with the reputation of the writer at stake. 6 Wigmore § 1692. Sound as this position may be with respect to trustworthiness, there is, nevertheless, an additional difficulty in the likelihood that the treatise will be misunderstood and misapplied without expert assistance and supervision. This difficulty is recognized in the cases demonstrating unwillingness to sustain findings relative to disability on the basis of judicially noticed medical texts. Ross v. Gardner, 365 F.2d 554 (6th Cir.1966); Sayers v. Gardner, 380 F.2d 940 (6th Cir.1967); Colwell v. Gardner, 386 F.2d 56 (6th Cir.1967); Glendenning v. Ribicoff, 213 F.Supp. 301 (W.D.Mo.1962); Cook v. Celebrezze, 217 F.Supp. 366 (W.D.Mo.1963); Sosna v. Celebrezze, 234 F.Supp. 289 (E.D.Pa.1964); and see McDaniel v. Celebrezze, 331 F.2d 426 (4th Cir.1964). The rule avoids the danger of misunderstanding and misapplication by limiting the use of treatises as substantive evidence to situations in which an expert is on the stand and available to explain and assist in the application of the treatise if desired. The limitation upon receiving the publication itself physically in evidence, contained in the last sentence, is designed to further this policy.

The relevance of the use of treatises on cross-examination is evident. This use of treatises has been the subject of varied views. The most restrictive position is that the witness must have stated expressly on direct his reliance upon the treatise. A slightly more liberal approach still insists upon reliance but allows it to be developed on cross-examination. Further relaxation dispenses with reliance but requires recognition as an authority by the witness, developable on cross-examination. The greatest liberality is found in decisions allowing use of the treatise on cross-examination when its status as an authority is established by any means. Annot., 60 A.L.R.2d 77. The exception is hinged upon this last position, which is that of the Supreme Court, Reilly v. Pinkus, 338 U.S. 269, 70 S.Ct. 110, 94 L.Ed. 63 (1949), and of recent well considered state court decisions, City of St. Petersburg v. Ferguson, 193 So.2d 648 (Fla.App.1966), cert. denied Fla., 201 So.2d 556; Darling v. Charleston Community Memorial Hospital, 33 Ill.2d 326, 211 N.E.2d 253 (1965); Dabroe v. Rhodes Co., 64 Wash.2d 431, 392 P.2d 317 (1964).

In Reilly v. Pinkus, supra, the Court pointed out that testing of professional knowledge was incomplete without exploration of the witness' knowledge of and attitude toward established treatises in the field. The process works equally well in reverse and furnishes the basis of the rule.

The rule does not require that the witness rely upon or recognize the treatise as authoritative, thus avoiding the possibility that the expert may at the outset block cross-examination by refusing to concede reliance or authoritativeness. Dabroe v. Rhodes Co., supra. Moreover, the rule avoids the unreality of admitting evidence for the purpose of impeachment only, with an instruction to the jury not to consider it otherwise. The parallel to the treatment of prior inconsistent statements will be apparent. See Rules 613(b) and 801(d)(1).

Exceptions (19), (20), and (21). Trustworthiness in reputation evidence is found "when the topic is such that the facts are likely to have been inquired about and that persons having personal knowledge have disclosed facts which have thus been discussed in the community; and thus the community's conclusion, if any has been formed, is likely to be a trustworthy one." 5 Wigmore § 1580, p. 444, and see also § 1583. On this common foundation, reputation as to land boundaries, customs, general history, character, and marriage have come to be regarded as admissible. The breadth of the underlying principle suggests the formulation of an equally broad exception, but tradition has in fact been much narrower and more particularized, and this is the pattern of these exceptions in the rule.

Exception (19) is concerned with matters of personal and family history. Marriage is universally conceded to be a proper subject of proof by evidence of reputation in the community. 5 Wigmore § 1602. As to such items as legitimacy, relationship, adoption, birth, and death, the decisions are divided. Id. § 1605. All seem to be susceptible to being the subject of well founded repute. The "world" in which the reputation may exist may be family, associates, or community. This world has proved capable of expanding with changing times from the single uncomplicated neighborhood, in which all activities take place, to the multiple and unrelated worlds of work, religious affiliation, and social activity, in each of which a reputation may be generated. People v. Reeves, 360 Ill. 55, 195 N.E. 443 (1935); State v. Axilrod, 248 Minn. 204, 79 N.W.2d 677 (1956); Mass.Stat.1947, c. 410, M.G.L.A. c. 233 § 21A; 5 Wigmore § 1616. The family has often served as the point of beginning for allowing community reputation. 5 Wigmore § 1488. For comparable provisions see Uniform Rule 63(26), (27)(c); California Evidence Code §§ 1313, 1314; Kansas Code of Civil Procedure § 60–460(x), (y)(3); New Jersey Evidence Rule 63(26), (27)(c).

The first portion of Exception (20) is based upon the general admissibility of evidence of reputation as to land boundaries and land customs, expanded in this country to include private as well as public boundaries. McCormick § 299, p. 625. The reputation is required to antedate the controversy, though not to be ancient. The second portion is likewise supported by authority, id., and is designed to facilitate proof of events when judicial notice is not available. The historical character of the subject matter dispenses with any need that the reputation antedate the controversy with respect to which it is offered. For similar provisions see Uniform Rule 63(27)(a), (b); California Evidence Code §§ 1320–1322; Kansas Code of Civil Procedure § 60–460(y), (1), (2); New Jersey Evidence Rule 63(27)(a), (b).

Exception (21) recognizes the traditional acceptance of reputation evidence as a means of proving human character. McCormick §§ 44, 158. The exception deals only with the hearsay aspect of this kind of evidence. Limitations upon admissibility based on other grounds will be found in Rules 404, relevancy of character evidence generally, and 608, character of witness. The exception is in effect a reiteration, in the context of hearsay, of Rule 405(a). Similar provisions are contained in Uniform Rule 63(28); California Evidence Code § 1324; Kansas Code of Civil Procedure § 60–460(z); New Jersey Evidence Rule 63(28).

Exception (22). When the status of a former judgment is under consideration in subsequent litigation, three possibilities must be noted: (1) the former judgment is conclusive under the doctrine of res judicata, either as a bar or a collateral estoppel; or (2) it is admissible in evidence for what it is worth; or (3) it may be of no effect at all. The first situation does not involve any problem of evidence except in the way that principles of substantive law generally bear upon the relevancy and materiality of evidence. The rule does not deal with the substantive effect of the judgment as a bar or collateral estoppel. When, however, the doctrine of res judicata does not apply to make the judgment either a bar or a collateral estoppel, a choice is presented between the second and third alternatives. The rule adopts the second for judgments of criminal conviction of felony grade. This is the direction of the decisions, Annot., 18 A.L.R.2d 1287, 1299, which manifest an increasing reluctance to reject *in toto* the validity of the law's factfinding processes outside the confines of res judicata and collateral estoppel. While this may leave a jury with the evidence of conviction but without means to evaluate it, as suggested by Judge Hinton, Note 27 Ill.L.Rev. 195 (1932), it seems safe to assume that the jury will give it substantial effect unless defendant offers a satisfactory explanation, a possibility not foreclosed by the provision. But see North River Ins. Co. v. Militello, 104 Colo. 28, 88 P.2d 567 (1939), in which the jury found for plaintiff on a fire policy despite the introduction of his conviction for arson. For supporting federal decisions see Clark, J., in New York & Cuba Mail S.S. Co. v. Continental Ins. Co., 117 F.2d 404, 411 (2d Cir.1941); Connecticut Fire Ins. Co. v. Ferrara, 277 F.2d 388 (8th Cir.1960).

Practical considerations require exclusion of convictions of minor offenses, not because the administration of justice in its lower echelons must be inferior, but because motivation to defend at this level is often minimal or nonexistent. Cope v. Goble, 39 Cal.App.2d 448, 103 P.2d 598 (1940); Jones v. Talbot, 87 Idaho 498, 394 P.2d 316 (1964); Warren v. Marsh, 215 Minn. 615, 11 N.W.2d 528 (1943); Annot., 18 A.L.R.2d 1287, 1295–1297; 16 Brooklyn L.Rev. 286 (1950); 50 Colum.L.Rev. 529 (1950); 35 Cornell L.Q. 872 (1950). Hence the rule includes only convictions of felony grade, measured by federal standards.

Judgments of conviction based upon pleas of *nolo contendere* are not included. This position is consistent with the treatment of *nolo* pleas in Rule 410 and the authorities cited in the Advisory Committee's Note in support thereof.

While these rules do not in general purport to resolve constitutional issues, they have in general been drafted with a view to avoiding collision with constitutional principles. Consequently the exception does not include evidence of the conviction of a third person, offered against the accused in a criminal prosecution to prove any fact essential to sustain the judgment of conviction. A contrary position would seem clearly to violate the right of confrontation. Kirby v. United States, 174 U.S. 47, 19 S.Ct. 574, 43 L.Ed. 890 (1899), error to convict of possessing stolen postage stamps with the only evidence of theft being the record of conviction of the thieves. The situation is to be distinguished from cases in which conviction of another person is an element of the crime, e.g. 15 U.S.C. § 902(d), interstate shipment of firearms to a known convicted felon, and, as specifically provided, from impeachment.

For comparable provisions see Uniform Rule 63(20); California Evidence Code § 1300; Kansas Code of Civil Procedure § 60–460(r); New Jersey Evidence Rule 63(20).

Exception (23). A hearsay exception in this area was originally justified on the ground that verdicts were evidence of reputation. As trial by jury graduated from the category of neighborhood inquests, this theory lost its validity. It was never valid as to chancery decrees. Nevertheless the rule persisted, though the judges and writers shifted ground and began saying that the judgment or decree was as good evidence as reputation. See City of London v. Clerke, Carth. 181, 90 Eng.Rep. 710 (K.B.1691); Neill v. Duke of Devonshire, 8 App.Cas. 135 (1882). The shift appears to be correct, since the process of inquiry, sifting, and scrutiny which is relied upon to render reputation reliable is present in perhaps greater measure in the process of litigation. While this might suggest a broader area of application, the affinity to reputation is strong, and paragraph (23) goes no further, not even including character.

The leading case in the United States, Patterson v. Gaines, 47 U.S. (6 How.) 550, 599, 12 L.Ed. 553 (1847), follows in the pattern of the English decisions, mentioning as illustrative matters thus provable: manorial rights, public rights of way, immemorial custom, disputed boundary, and pedigree. More recent recognition of the principle is found in Grant Bros. Construction Co. v. United States, 232 U.S. 647, 34 S.Ct. 452, 58 L.Ed. 776 (1914), in action for penalties under Alien Contract Labor Law, decision of board of inquiry of Immigration Service admissible to prove alienage of laborers, as a matter of pedigree; United States v. Mid–Continent Petroleum Corp., 67 F.2d 37 (10th Cir.1933), records of commission enrolling Indians admissible on pedigree; Jung Yen Loy v. Cahill, 81 F.2d 809 (9th Cir.1936), board decisions as to citizenship of plaintiff's father admissible in proceeding for declaration of citizenship. Contra, In re Estate of Cunha, 49 Haw. 273, 414 P.2d 925 (1966).

Exception (24). The preceding 23 exceptions of Rule 803 and the first five [four] exceptions of Rule 804(b), infra, are designed to take full advantage of the accumulated wisdom and experience of the past in dealing with hearsay. It would, however, be presumptuous to assume that all possible desirable exceptions to the hearsay rule have been catalogued and to pass the hearsay rule to oncoming generations as a closed system. Exception (24) and its companion provision in Rule 804(b)(6)[5] are accordingly included. They do not contemplate an unfettered exercise of judicial discretion, but they do provide for treating new and presently unanticipated situations which demonstrate a trustworthiness within the spirit of the specifically stated exceptions. Within this framework, room is left for growth and development of the law of evidence in the hearsay area, consistently with the broad purposes expressed in Rule 102. See Dallas County v. Commercial Union Assur. Co., 286 F.2d 388 (5th Cir.1961).

Report of Senate Committee on the Judiciary

We disagree with the total rejection of a residual hearsay exception. While we view rule 102 as being intended to provide for a broader construction and interpretation of these rules, we feel that, without a separate residual provision, the specifically enumerated exceptions could become tortured beyond any reasonable circumstances which they were intended to include (even if broadly construed). Moreover, these exceptions, while they reflect the most typical and well recognized exceptions to the hearsay rule, may not encompass every situation in which the reliability and appropriateness of a particular piece of hearsay evidence make clear that it should be heard and considered by the trier of fact.

The committee believes that there are certain exceptional circumstances where evidence which is found by a court to have guarantees of trustworthiness equivalent to or exceeding the guarantees reflected by the presently listed exceptions, and to have a high degree of probativeness and necessity could properly be admissible.

The case of Dallas County v. Commercial Union Assur. Co., 286 F.2d 388 (5th Cir.1961) illustrates the point. The issue in that case was whether the tower of the county courthouse collapsed because it was struck by lightning (covered by insurance) or because of structural weakness and deterioration of the structure (not covered). Investigation of the structure revealed the presence of charcoal and charred timbers. In order to show that lightning may not have been the cause of the charring, the insurer offered a copy of a local newspaper published over 50 years earlier containing an unsigned article describing a fire in the courthouse while it was under construction. The Court found that the newspaper did not qualify for admission as a business record or an ancient document and did not fit within any other recognized hearsay exception. The court concluded, however, that the article was trustworthy because it was inconceivable that a newspaper reporter in a small town would report a fire in the courthouse if none had occurred. See also United States v. Barbati, 284 F.Supp. 409 (E.D.N.Y.1968).

Because exceptional cases like the *Dallas County* case may arise in the future, the committee has decided to reinstate a residual exception for rules 803 and 804(b).

The committee, however, also agrees with those supporters of the House version who felt that an overly broad residual hearsay exception could emasculate the hearsay rule and the recognized exceptions or vitiate the rationale behind codification of the rules.

Therefore, the committee has adopted a residual exception for rules 803 and 804(b) of much narrower scope and applicability than the Supreme Court version. In order to qualify for admission, a hearsay statement not falling within one of the recognized exceptions would have to satisfy at least four conditions. First, it must have "equivalent circumstantial guarantees of trustworthiness." Second, it must be offered as evidence of a material fact. Third, the court must determine that the statement "is more probative on the point for which it is offered than any other evidence which the proponent can procure through reasonable efforts." This requirement is intended to insure that only statements which have high probative value and necessity may qualify for admission under the residual exceptions. Fourth, the court must determine that "the general purposes of these rules and the interests of justice will best be served by admission of the statement into evidence."

It is intended that the residual hearsay exceptions will be used very rarely, and only in exceptional circumstances. The committee does not intend to establish a broad license for trial judges to admit hearsay statements that do not fall within one of the other exceptions contained in rules 803 and 804(b). The residual exceptions are not meant to authorize major judicial revisions of the hearsay rule, including its present exceptions. Such major revisions are best accomplished by legislative action. It is intended that in any case in which evidence is sought to be admitted under these subsections, the trial judge will exercise no less care, reflection and caution than the courts did under the common law in establishing the now-recognized exceptions to the hearsay rule.

In order to establish a well-defined jurisprudence, the special facts and circumstances which, in the court's judgment, indicates that the statement has a sufficiently high degree of trustworthiness and necessity to justify its admission should be stated on the record. It is expected that the court will give the opposing party a full and adequate opportunity to contest the admission of any statement sought to be introduced under these subsections.

Conference Report

The Senate amendment adds a new subsection, (24), which makes admissible a hearsay statement not specifically covered by any of the previous twenty-three subsections, if the statement has equivalent circumstantial guarantees of trustworthiness and if the court determines that (A) the statement is offered as evidence of a material fact; (B) the statement is more probative on the point for which it is offered than any other evidence the proponent can procure through reasonable efforts; and (C) the general purposes of these rules and the interests of justice will best be served by admission of the statement into evidence.

The House bill eliminated a similar, but broader, provision because of the conviction that such a provision injected too much uncertainty into the law of evidence regarding hearsay and impaired the ability of a litigant to prepare adequately for trial.

The Conference adopts the Senate amendment with an amendment that provides that a party intending to request the court to use a statement under this provision must notify any adverse party of this intention as well as of the particulars of the statement, including the name and address of the declarant. This notice must be given sufficiently in advance of the trial or hearing to provide any adverse party with a fair opportunity to prepare to contest the use of the statement.

Rule 804.

HEARSAY EXCEPTIONS; DECLARANT UNAVAILABLE

(a) Definition of unavailability. "Unavailability as a witness" includes situations in which the declarant—

(1) is exempted by ruling of the court on the ground of privilege from testifying concerning the subject matter of the declarant's statement; or

(2) persists in refusing to testify concerning the subject matter of the declarant's statement despite an order of the court to do so; or

(3) testifies to a lack of memory of the subject matter of the declarant's statement; or

(4) is unable to be present or to testify at the hearing because of death or then existing physical or mental illness or infirmity; or

(5) is absent from the hearing and the proponent of a statement has been unable to procure the declarant's attendance (or in the

case of a hearsay exception under subdivision (b)(2), (3), or (4), the declarant's attendance or testimony) by process or other reasonable means.

A declarant is not unavailable as a witness if exemption, refusal, claim of lack of memory, inability, or absence is due to the procurement or wrongdoing of the proponent of a statement for the purpose of preventing the witness from attending or testifying.

(b) Hearsay exceptions. The following are not excluded by the hearsay rule if the declarant is unavailable as a witness:

(1) Former testimony. Testimony given as a witness at another hearing of the same or a different proceeding, or in a deposition taken in compliance with law in the course of the same or another proceeding, if the party against whom the testimony is now offered, or, in a civil action or proceeding, a predecessor in interest, had an opportunity and similar motive to develop the testimony by direct, cross, or redirect examination.

(2) Statement under belief of impending death. In a prosecution for homicide or in a civil action or proceeding, a statement made by a declarant while believing that the declarant's death was imminent, concerning the cause or circumstances of what the declarant believed to be impending death.

(3) Statement against interest. A statement that: (A) a reasonable person in the declarant's position would have made only if the person believed it to be true because, when made, it was so contrary to the declarant's proprietary or pecuniary interest or had so great a tendency to invalidate the declarant's claim against someone else or to expose the declarant to civil or criminal liability; (B) is supported by corroborating circumstances that clearly indicate its trustworthiness, if it is offered in a criminal case as one that tends to expose the declarant to criminal liability.

(4) Statement of personal or family history. (A) A statement concerning the declarant's own birth, adoption, marriage, divorce, legitimacy, relationship by blood, adoption, or marriage, ancestry, or other similar fact of personal or family history, even though declarant had no means of acquiring personal knowledge of the matter stated; or (B) a statement concerning the foregoing matters, and death also, of another person, if the declarant was related to the other by blood, adoption, or marriage or was so intimately associated with the other's family as to be likely to have accurate information concerning the matter declared.

(5) [Transferred to Rule 807]

(6) **Forfeiture by wrongdoing.** A statement offered against a party that has engaged or acquiesced in wrongdoing that was intended to, and did, procure the unavailability of the declarant as a witness.

Committee Note to 1997 Amendment

Rule 804(b)(6) has been added to provide that a party forfeits the right to object on hearsay grounds to the admission of a declarant's prior statement when the party's deliberate wrongdoing or acquiescence therein procured the unavailability of the declarant as a witness. This recognizes the need for a prophylactic rule to deal with abhorrent behavior "which strikes at the heart of the system of justice itself." United States v. Mastrangelo, 693 F.2d 269, 273 (2d Cir.1982), on remand, 561 F. Supp. 1114 (E.D.N.Y.), aff'd, 722 F.2d 13 (2d Cir.1983), cert. denied, 467 U.S. 1204 (1984).

Every circuit that has resolved the question has recognized the principle of waiver by misconduct, although the tests for determining whether there is a waiver have varied. See, e.g., United States v. Aguiar, 975 F.2d 45, 47 (2d Cir.1992); United States v. Potamitis, 739 F.2d 784, 789 (2d Cir.), cert. denied, 469 U.S. 918 (1984); Steele v. Taylor, 684 F.2d 1193, 1199 (6th Cir.1982), cert. denied, 460 U.S. 1053 (1983); United States v. Balano, 618 F.2d 624, 629 (10th Cir.1979), cert. denied, 449 U.S. 840 (1980); United States v. Carlson, 547 F.2d 1346, 1358–59 (8th Cir.1976), cert. denied, 431 U.S. 914 (1977). The foregoing cases apply a preponderance of the evidence standard. Contra United States v. Thevis, 665 F.2d 616, 631 (5th Cir.) (clear and convincing standard), cert. denied, 459 U.S. 825 (1982). The usual Rule 104(a) preponderance of the evidence standard has been adopted in light of the behavior the new Rule 804(b)(6) seeks to discourage.

Note by Federal Judicial Center

The rule prescribed by the Supreme Court was amended by the Congress in a number of respects as follows:

Subdivision (a). Paragraphs (1) and (2) were amended by substituting "court" in place of "judge," and paragraph (5) was amended by inserting "(or in the case of a hearsay exception under subdivision (b)(2), (3), or (4), his attendance or testimony)".

Subdivision (b). Exception (1) was amended by inserting "the same or" after "course of," and by substituting the phrase "if the party against whom the testimony is now offered, or, in a civil action or proceeding, a predecessor in interest, had an opportunity and similar motive to develop the testimony by

HEARSAY Rule 804

direct, cross, or redirect examination" in place of "at the instance of or against a party with an opportunity to develop the testimony by direct, cross, or redirect examination, with motive and interest similar to those of the party against whom now offered."

Exception (2) as prescribed by the Supreme Court, dealing with statements of recent perception, was deleted by the Congress.* ... Exception (2) as enacted by the Congress is Exception (3) prescribed by the Supreme Court, amended by inserting at the beginning, "In a prosecution for homicide or in a civil action or proceeding".

Exception (3) as enacted by the Congress is Exception (4) prescribed by the Supreme Court, amended in the first sentence by deleting, after "another," the phrase "or to make him an object of hatred, ridicule, or disgrace," and amended in the second sentence by substituting, after "unless," the phrase, "corroborating circumstances clearly indicate the trustworthiness of the statement," in place of "corroborated."

Exception (4) as enacted by the Congress is Exception (5) prescribed by the Supreme Court without change.

Exception (5) as enacted by the Congress is Exception (6) prescribed by the Supreme Court, amended by substituting "equivalent" in place of "comparable" and by adding all after "trustworthiness."

Advisory Committee's Note

As to firsthand knowledge on the part of hearsay declarants, see the introductory portion of the Advisory Committee's Note to Rule 803.

Subdivision (a). The definition of unavailability implements the division of hearsay exceptions into two categories by Rules 803 and 804(b).

At common law the unavailability requirement was evolved in connection with particular hearsay exceptions rather than along general lines. For example, see the separate explications of unavailability in relation to former testimony, declarations against interest, and statements of pedigree, separately developed in McCormick §§ 234, 257, and 297. However, no reason is apparent for making distinctions as to what satisfies unavailability for the different exceptions. The treatment in the rule is therefore uniform although differences in the range of process for witnesses between civil and criminal cases will lead to a less exacting requirement under item (5). See Rule 45(e) of the Federal Rules of Civil Procedure and Rule 17(e) of the Federal Rules of Criminal Procedure.

Five instances of unavailability are specified:

(1) Substantial authority supports the position that exercise of a claim of privilege by the declarant satisfies the requirement of unavailability (usually in connection with former testimony). Wyatt v. State, 35 Ala.App. 147, 46 So.2d 837 (1950); State v. Stewart, 85 Kan. 404, 116 P. 489 (1911); Annot., 45 A.L.R.2d 1354; Uniform Rule 62(7)(a); California Evidence Code § 240(a)(1); Kansas Code of Civil Procedure § 60–459(g)(1). A ruling by the judge is required, which clearly implies that an actual claim of privilege must be made.

(2) A witness is rendered unavailable if he simply refuses to testify concerning the subject matter of his statement despite judicial pressures to do so, a

---

* See Uniform Rule 804(b)(5) set forth in the Editorial Note, infra.

position supported by similar considerations of practicality. Johnson v. People, 152 Colo. 586, 384 P.2d 454 (1963); People v. Pickett, 339 Mich. 294, 63 N.W.2d 681, 45 A.L.R.2d 1341 (1954). Contra, Pleau v. State, 255 Wis. 362, 38 N.W.2d 496 (1949).

(3) The position that a claimed lack of memory by the witness of the subject matter of his statement constitutes unavailability likewise finds support in the cases, though not without dissent. McCormick § 234, p. 494. If the claim is successful, the practical effect is to put the testimony beyond reach, as in the other instances. In this instance, however, it will be noted that the lack of memory must be established by the testimony of the witness himself, which clearly contemplates his production and subjection to cross-examination.

Report of House Committee on the Judiciary

Rule 804(a)(3) was approved in the form submitted by the Court. However, the Committee intends no change in existing federal law under which the court may choose to disbelieve the declarant's testimony as to his lack of memory. See United States v. Insana, 423 F.2d 1165, 1169–1170 (2d Cir.), cert. denied, 400 U.S. 841, 91 S.Ct. 83, 27 L.Ed.2d 76 (1970).

Advisory Committee's Note

(4) Death and infirmity find general recognition as grounds. McCormick §§ 234, 257, 297; Uniform Rule 62(7)(c); California Evidence Code § 240(a)(3); Kansas Code of Civil Procedure § 60–459(g)(3); New Jersey Evidence Rule 62(6)(c). See also the provisions on use of depositions in Rule 32(a)(3) of the Federal Rules of Civil Procedure and Rule 15(e) of the Federal Rules of Criminal Procedure.

(5) Absence from the hearing coupled with inability to compel attendance by process or other reasonable means also satisfies the requirement. McCormick § 234; Uniform Rule 62(7)(d) and (e); California Evidence Code § 240(a)(4) and (5); Kansas Code of Civil Procedure § 60–459(g)(4) and (5); New Jersey Rule 62(6)(b) and (d). See the discussion of procuring attendance of witnesses who are nonresidents or in custody in Barber v. Page, 390 U.S. 719, 88 S.Ct. 1318, 20 L.Ed.2d 255 (1968).

If the conditions otherwise constituting unavailability result from the procurement or wrongdoing of the proponent of the statement, the requirement is not satisfied....

Conference Report

Subsection (a) defines the term "unavailability as a witness". The House bill provides in subsection (a)(5) that the party who desires to use the statement must be unable to procure the declarant's attendance by process or other reasonable means. In the case of dying declarations, statements against interest and statements of personal or family history, the House bill requires that the proponent must also be unable to procure the declarant's *testimony* (such as by deposition or interrogatories) by process or other reasonable means. The Senate amendment eliminates this latter provision.

The Conference adopts the provision contained in the House bill.

HEARSAY Rule 804

Advisory Committee's Note

Subdivision (b). Rule 803, supra, is based upon the assumption that a hearsay statement falling within one of its exceptions possesses qualities which justify the conclusion that whether the declarant is available or unavailable is not a relevant factor in determining admissibility. The instant rule proceeds upon a different theory: hearsay which admittedly is not equal in quality to testimony of the declarant on the stand may nevertheless be admitted if the declarant is unavailable and if his statement meets a specified standard. The rule expresses preferences: testimony given on the stand in person is preferred over hearsay, and hearsay, if of the specified quality, is preferred over complete loss of the evidence of the declarant. The exceptions evolved at common law with respect to declarations of unavailable declarants furnish the basis for the exceptions enumerated in the proposal. The term "unavailable" is defined in subdivision (a).

Exception (1). Former testimony does not rely upon some set of circumstances to substitute for oath and cross-examination, since both oath and opportunity to cross-examine were present in fact. The only missing one of the ideal conditions for the giving of testimony is the presence of trier and opponent ("demeanor evidence"). This is lacking with all hearsay exceptions. Hence it may be argued that former testimony is the strongest hearsay and should be included under Rule 803, supra. However, opportunity to observe demeanor is what in a large measure confers depth and meaning upon oath and cross-examination. Thus in cases under Rule 803 demeanor lacks the significance which it possesses with respect to testimony. In any event, the tradition, founded in experience, uniformly favors production of the witness if he is available. The exception indicates continuation of the policy. This preference for the presence of the witness is apparent also in rules and statutes on the use of depositions, which deal with substantially the same problem.

Under the exception, the testimony may be offered (1) against the party *against* whom it was previously offered or (2) against the party *by* whom it was previously offered. In each instance the question resolves itself into whether fairness allows imposing, upon the party against whom now offered, the handling of the witness on the earlier occasion. (1) If the party against whom now offered is the one against whom the testimony was offered previously, no unfairness is apparent in requiring him to accept his own prior conduct of cross-examination or decision not to cross-examine. Only demeanor has been lost, and that is inherent in the situation. (2) If the party against whom now offered is the one *by* whom the testimony was offered previously, a satisfactory answer becomes somewhat more difficult. One possibility is to proceed somewhat along the line of an adoptive admission, i.e. by offering the testimony proponent in effect adopts it. However, this theory savors of discarded concepts of witnesses' belonging to a party, of litigants' ability to pick and choose witnesses, and of vouching for one's own witnesses. Cf. McCormick § 246, pp. 526–527; 4 Wigmore § 1075. A more direct and acceptable approach is simply to recognize direct and redirect examination of one's own witness as the equivalent of cross-examining an opponent's witness. Falknor, Former Testimony and the Uniform Rules: A Comment, 38 N.Y.U.L.Rev. 651, n. 1 (1963); McCormick § 231, p. 483. See also 5 Wigmore § 1389. Allowable techniques for dealing with hostile, double-crossing, forgetful, and mentally deficient witnesses leave no substance to a claim that one could not adequately develop his own witness at the former hearing. An even less appealing argument is presented when failure to develop fully was the result of a deliberate choice.

The common law did not limit the admissibility of former testimony to that given in an earlier trial of the same case, although it did require identity of issues as a means of insuring that the former handling of the witness was the equivalent of what would now be done if the opportunity were presented. Modern decisions reduce the requirement to "substantial" identity. McCormick § 233. Since identity of issues is significant only in that it bears on motive and interest in developing fully the testimony of the witness, expressing the matter in the latter terms is preferable. Id. Testimony given at a preliminary hearing was held in California v. Green, 399 U.S. 149, 90 S.Ct. 1930, 26 L.Ed.2d 489 (1970), to satisfy confrontation requirements in this respect.

As a further assurance of fairness in thrusting upon a party the prior handling of the witness, the common law also insisted upon identity of parties, deviating only to the extent of allowing substitution of successors in a narrowly construed privity. Mutuality as an aspect of identity is now generally discredited, and the requirement of identity of the offering party disappears except as it might affect motive to develop the testimony. Falknor, supra, at 652; McCormick § 232, pp. 487–488. The question remains whether strict identity, or privity, should continue as a requirement with respect to the party against whom offered. . . .

Report of House Committee on the Judiciary

Rule 804(b)(1) as submitted by the Court allowed prior testimony of an unavailable witness to be admissible if the party against whom it is offered or a person "with motive and interest similar" to his had an opportunity to examine the witness. The Committee considered that it is generally unfair to impose upon the party against whom the hearsay evidence is being offered responsibility for the manner in which the witness was previously handled by another party. The sole exception to this, in the Committee's view, is when a party's predecessor in interest in a civil action or proceeding had an opportunity and similar motive to examine the witness. The Committee amended the Rule to reflect these policy determinations.

Advisory Committee's Note

Exception (2). The exception is the familiar dying declaration of the common law, expanded somewhat beyond its traditionally narrow limits. While the original religious justification for the exception may have lost its conviction for some persons over the years, it can scarcely be doubted that powerful psychological pressures are present. See 5 Wigmore § 1443 and the classic statement of Chief Baron Eyre in Rex v. Woodcock, 1 Leach 500, 502, 168 Eng.Rep. 352, 353 (K.B.1789).

The common law required that the statement be that of the victim, offered in a prosecution for criminal homicide. Thus declarations by victims in prosecutions for other crimes, e.g. a declaration by a rape victim who dies in childbirth, and all declarations in civil cases were outside the scope of the exception. An occasional statute has removed these restrictions, as in Colo.R.S. § 52–1–20, or has expanded the area of offenses to include abortions, 5 Wigmore § 1432, p. 224, n. 4. Kansas by decision extended the exception to civil cases. Thurston v. Fritz, 91 Kan. 468, 138 P. 625 (1914). While the common law exception no doubt originated as a result of the exceptional need for the evidence in homicide cases, the theory of admissibility applies equally in civil cases.... The same considerations suggest abandonment of the limitation to circumstances attending the event in question, yet when the statement deals with matters other than the supposed death, its influence is believed to be sufficiently attenuated to justify the limitation. Unavailability is not limited to death. See subdivision (a) of this rule. Any problem as to declarations phrased in terms of opinion is laid at rest by Rule 701, and continuation of a requirement of first-hand knowledge is assured by Rule 602.

Comparable provisions are found in Uniform Rule 63(5); California Evidence Code § 1242; Kansas Code of Civil Procedure § 60–460(e); New Jersey Evidence Rule 63(5).

Exception (3). The circumstantial guaranty of reliability for declarations against interest is the assumption that persons do not make statements which are damaging to themselves unless satisfied for good reason that they are true. Hileman v. Northwest Engineering Co., 346 F.2d 668 (6th Cir.1965). If the statement is that of a party offered by his opponent, it comes in as an admission, Rule 803(d)(2) [sic], and there is no occasion to inquire whether it is against interest, this not being a condition precedent to admissibility of admissions by opponents.

The common law required that the interest declared against be pecuniary or proprietary but within this limitation demonstrated striking ingenuity in discovering an against-interest aspect. Higham v. Ridgway, 10 East 109, 103 Eng.Rep. 717 (K.B.1808); Reg. v. Overseers of Birmingham, 1 B. & S. 763, 121 Eng.Rep. 897 (Q.B.1861); McCormick, § 256, p. 551, nn. 2 and 3.

The exception discards the common law limitation and expands to the full logical limit. One result is to remove doubt as to the admissibility of declarations tending to establish a tort liability against the declarant or to extinguish one which might be asserted by him, in accordance with the trend of the decisions in this country. McCormick, § 254, pp. 548–549.... And finally exposure to criminal liability satisfies the against-interest requirement. The refusal of the common law to concede the adequacy of a penal interest was no doubt indefensible in logic, see the dissent of Mr. Justice Holmes in Donnelly v. United States, 228 U.S. 243, 33 S.Ct. 449, 57 L.Ed. 820 (1913), but one senses in the decisions a distrust of evidence of confessions by third persons offered to exculpate the accused arising from suspicions of fabrication either of the fact of the making of the confession or in its contents, enhanced in either instance by the required unavailability of the declarant. Nevertheless, an increasing amount of decisional law recognizes exposure to punishment for crime as a sufficient stake. People v. Spriggs, 60 Cal.2d 868, 36 Cal.Rptr. 841, 389 P.2d 377 (1964); Sutter v. Easterly, 354 Mo. 282, 189 S.W.2d 284 (1945); Band's Refuse Removal, Inc. v. Fair Lawn Borough, 62 N.J.Super. 522, 163 A.2d 465 (1960); Newberry v. Commonwealth, 191 Va. 445, 61 S.E.2d 318 (1950); Annot., 162 A.L.R. 446. The requirement of corroboration is included in the rule in order to effect an accommodation between these competing considerations. When the statement is offered by the accused by way of exculpation, the resulting situation is not adapted to control by rulings as to the weight of the evidence, and hence the provision is cast in terms of a requirement preliminary to admissibility. Cf. Rule 406(a). The requirement of corroboration should be construed in such a manner as to effectuate its purpose of circumventing fabrication.

Ordinarily the third-party confession is thought of in terms of exculpating the accused, but this is by no means always or necessarily the case: it may include statements implicating him, and under the general theory of declarations against interest they would be admissible as related statements. Douglas v. Alabama, 380 U.S. 415, 85 S.Ct. 1074, 13 L.Ed.2d 934 (1965), and Bruton v. United States, 389 U.S. 818, 88 S.Ct. 126, 19 L.Ed.2d 70 (1967), both involved confessions by codefendants which implicated the accused. While the confession was not actually offered in evidence in *Douglas,* the procedure followed effectively put it before the jury, which the Court ruled to be error. Whether the confession might have been admissible as a declaration against penal interest was not considered or discussed. *Bruton* assumed the inadmissibility, as against the accused, of the implicating confession of his codefendant, and centered upon the question of the effectiveness of a limiting instruction. These decisions, however, by no means require that all statements implicating another person be excluded from the category of declarations against interest. Whether a statement is in fact against interest must be determined from the circumstances of each case. Thus a statement admitting guilt and implicating another person, made while in custody, may well be motivated by a desire to curry favor with the authorities and hence fail to qualify as against interest. See the dissenting opinion of Mr. Justice White in *Bruton*. On the other hand, the same words spoken under different circumstances, e.g., to an acquaintance, would have no difficulty in qualifying. The rule does not purport to deal with questions of the right of confrontation.

The balancing of self-serving against disserving aspects of a declaration is discussed in McCormick § 256.

For comparable provisions, see Uniform Rule 63(10); California Evidence Code § 1230; Kansas Code of Civil Procedure § 60–460(j); New Jersey Evidence Rule 63(10).

Conference Report

The Senate amendment to subsection (b)(3) provides that a statement is against interest and not excluded by the hearsay rule when the declarant is unavailable as a witness, if the statement tends to subject a person to civil or criminal liability or renders invalid a claim by him against another. The House bill did not refer specifically to civil liability and to rendering invalid a claim against another. The Senate amendment also deletes from the House bill the provision that subsection (b)(3) does not apply to a statement or confession, made by a codefendant or another, which implicates the accused and the person who made the statement, when that statement or confession is offered against the accused in a criminal case.

The Conference adopts the Senate amendment. The Conferees intend to include within the purview of this rule, statements subjecting a person to civil liability and statements rendering claims invalid. The Conferees agree to delete the provision regarding statements by a codefendant, thereby reflecting the general approach in the Rules of Evidence to avoid attempting to codify constitutional evidentiary principles.

Advisory Committee's Note

Exception (4). The general common law requirement that a declaration in this area must have been made *ante litem motam* has been dropped, as bearing more appropriately on weight than admissibility. See 5 Wigmore § 1483. Item (i) specifically disclaims any need of firsthand knowledge respecting declarant's own personal history. In some instances it is self-evident (marriage) and in others impossible and traditionally not required (date of birth). Item (ii) deals with declarations concerning the history of another person. As at common law, declarant is qualified if related by blood or marriage. 5 Wigmore § 1489. In addition, and contrary to the common law, declarant qualifies by virtue of intimate association with the family. Id., § 1487. The requirement sometimes encountered that when the subject of the statement is the relationship between two other persons the declarant must qualify as to both is omitted. Relationship is reciprocal. Id., § 1491.

For comparable provisions, see Uniform Rule 63(23), (24), (25); California Evidence Code §§ 1310, 1311; Kansas Code of Civil Procedure § 60–460(u), (v), (w); New Jersey Evidence Rules 63(23), 63(24), 63(25).

Exception (5). In language and purpose, this exception is identical with Rule 803(24). See the Advisory Committee's Note to that provision.

Reports of House and Senate Committees on the Judiciary

[This exception and its companion exception in rule 803(24) are discussed together in the congressional committee reports. The reports are set forth under rule 803(24), supra.]

Conference Report

The Senate amendment adds a new subsection, (b)(6)[5], which makes admissible a hearsay statement not specifically covered by any of the five previous subsections, if the statement has equivalent circumstantial guarantees of trustworthiness and if the court determines that (A) the statement is offered as evidence of a material fact; (B) the statement is more probative on the point for which it is offered than any other evidence the proponent can procure through reasonable efforts; and (C) the general purposes of these rules and the interests of justice will best be served by admission of the statement into evidence.

The House bill eliminated a similar, but broader, provision because of the conviction that such a provision injected too much uncertainty into the law of evidence regarding hearsay and impaired the ability of a litigant to prepare adequately for trial.

The Conference adopts the Senate amendment with an amendment that renumbers this subsection and provides that a party intending to request the court to use a statement under this provision must notify any adverse party of this intention as well as of the particulars of the statement, including the name and address of the declarant. This notice must be given sufficiently in advance of the trial or hearing to provide any adverse party with a fair opportunity to prepare to contest the use of the statement.

Proposed Committee Note to Proposed Amendment to Rule 804(b)(3)

Subdivision (b)(3). The second sentence of Rule 804(b)(3) has been amended to provide that the corroborating circumstances requirement applies to all declarations against penal interest offered in criminal cases. A number of courts have applied the corroborating circumstances requirement to declarations against penal interest offered by the prosecution, even though the text of the Rule did not so provide. *See, e.g., United States v. Alvarez*, 584 F.2d 694, 701 (5th Cir. 1978) ("by transplanting the language governing exculpatory statements onto the analysis for admitting inculpatory hearsay, a unitary standard is derived which offers the most workable basis for applying Rule 804(b)(3)"); *United States v. Shukri*, 207 F.3d 412 (7th Cir. 2000) (requiring corroborating circumstances for against-penal-interest statements offered by the government). A unitary approach to declarations against penal interest assures both the prosecution and the accused that the Rule will not be abused and that only reliable hearsay statements will be admitted under the exception.

The Committee found no need to address the relationship between Rule 804(b)(3) and the Confrontation Clause. The Supreme Court in *Crawford v. Washington*, 541 U.S. 36, 53–54 (2004), held that the Confrontation Clause bars "admission of testimonial statements of a witness who did not appear at trial unless he was unavailable to testify, and the defendant had had a prior opportunity for cross-examination." Courts after *Crawford* have held that for a statement to be admissible under Rule 804(b)(3), it must be made in informal circumstances and not knowingly to a law enforcement officer—and those very requirements of admissibility assure that the statement is not testimonial under *Crawford* [.] *See, e g., United States v. Johnson*, 495 F.3d 951 (8th Cir. 2007) (accomplice's statements implicating himself and the defendant in a crime were not testimonial as they were made under informal circumstances to another prisoner, with no involvement of law enforcement; for the same reasons, the statements were admissible under Rule 804(b)(3)); *United States v. Franklin*, 415 F.3d 537 (6th Cir. 2005) (admissions of crime made informally to a friend were not testimonial, and for the same reason they were admissible under Rule 804(b)(3)).

The amendment does not address the use of the corroborating circumstances for declarations against penal interest offered in civil cases.

Rule 805.

HEARSAY WITHIN HEARSAY

Hearsay included within hearsay is not excluded under the hearsay rule if each part of the combined statements conforms with an exception to the hearsay rule provided in these rules.

Note by Federal Judicial Center

The rule enacted by the Congress is the rule prescribed by the Supreme Court without change.

Advisory Committee's Note

On principle it scarcely seems open to doubt that the hearsay rule should not call for exclusion of a hearsay statement which includes a further hearsay statement when both conform to the requirements of a hearsay exception. Thus a hospital record might contain an entry of the patient's age based on information furnished by his wife. The hospital record would qualify as a regular entry except that the person who furnished the information was not acting in the routine of the business. However, her statement independently qualifies as a statement of pedigree (if she is unavailable) or as a statement made for purposes of diagnosis or treatment, and hence each link in the chain falls under sufficient assurances. Or, further to illustrate, a dying declaration may incorporate a declaration against interest by another declarant. See McCormick § 290, p. 611.

Rule 806.

ATTACKING AND SUPPORTING CREDIBILITY OF DECLARANT

When a hearsay statement, or a statement defined in Rule 801(d)(2), (C), (D), or (E), has been admitted in evidence, the credibility of the declarant may be attacked, and if attacked may be supported, by any evidence which would be admissible for those purposes if declarant had testified as a witness. Evidence of a statement or conduct by the declarant at any time, inconsistent with the declarant's hearsay statement, is not subject to any requirement that the declarant may have been afforded an opportunity to deny or explain. If the party against whom a hearsay statement has been admitted calls the declarant as a witness, the party is entitled to examine the declarant on the statement as if under cross-examination.

Note by Federal Judicial Center

The rule enacted by the Congress is the rule prescribed by the Supreme Court, amended by inserting the phrase "or a statement defined in Rule 801(d)(2), (C), (D), or (E)."

Advisory Committee's Note

The declarant of a hearsay statement which is admitted in evidence is in effect a witness. His credibility should in fairness be subject to impeachment and support as though he had in fact testified. See Rules 608 and 609. There are however, some special aspects of the impeaching of a hearsay declarant which require consideration. These special aspects center upon impeachment by inconsistent statement, arise from factual differences which exist between the use of hearsay and an actual witness and also between various kinds of hearsay, and involve the question of applying to declarants the general rule disallowing evidence of an inconsistent statement to impeach a witness unless he is afforded an opportunity to deny or explain. See Rule 613(b).

The principal difference between using hearsay and an actual witness is that the inconsistent statement will in the case of the witness almost inevitably of necessity in the nature of things be a *prior* statement, which it is entirely possible and feasible to call to his attention, while in the case of hearsay the inconsistent statement may well be a *subsequent* one, which practically precludes calling it to the attention of the declarant. The result of insisting upon observation of this impossible requirement in the hearsay situation is to deny the opponent, already barred from cross-examination, any benefit of this important technique of impeachment. The writers favor allowing the subsequent statement. McCormick § 37, p. 69; 3 Wigmore § 1033. The cases, however, are divided. Cases allowing the impeachment include People v. Collup, 27 Cal.2d

829, 167 P.2d 714 (1946); People v. Rosoto, 58 Cal.2d 304, 23 Cal.Rptr. 779, 373 P.2d 867 (1962); Carver v. United States, 164 U.S. 694, 17 S.Ct. 228, 41 L.Ed. 602 (1897). Contra, Mattox v. United States, 156 U.S. 237, 15 S.Ct. 337, 39 L.Ed. 409 (1895); People v. Hines, 284 N.Y. 93, 29 N.E.2d 483 (1940). The force of *Mattox,* where the hearsay was the former testimony of a deceased witness and the denial of use of a subsequent inconsistent statement was upheld, is much diminished by *Carver,* where the hearsay was a dying declaration and denial of use of a subsequent inconsistent statement resulted in reversal. The difference in the particular brand of hearsay seems unimportant when the inconsistent statement is a *subsequent* one. True, the opponent is not totally deprived of cross-examination when the hearsay is former testimony or a deposition but he is deprived of cross-examining on the statement or a deposition but he is deprived of cross-examining on the statement or along lines suggested by it. Mr. Justice Shiras, with two justices joining him, dissented vigorously in *Mattox.*

When the impeaching statement was made *prior* to the hearsay statement, differences in the kinds of hearsay appear which arguably may justify differences in treatment. If the hearsay consisted of a simple statement by the witness, e.g. a dying declaration or a declaration against interest, the feasibility of affording him an opportunity to deny or explain encounters the same practical impossibility as where the statement is a subsequent one, just discussed, although here the impossibility arises from the total absence of anything resembling a hearing at which the matter could be put to him. The courts by a large majority have ruled in favor of allowing the statement to be used under these circumstances. McCormick § 37, p. 69; 3 Wigmore § 1033. If, however, the hearsay consists of former testimony or a deposition, the possibility of calling the prior statement to the attention of the witness or deponent is not ruled out, since the opportunity to cross-examine was available. It might thus be concluded that with former testimony or depositions the conventional foundation should be insisted upon. Most of the cases involve depositions, and Wigmore describes them as divided. 3 Wigmore § 1031. Deposition procedures at best are cumbersome and expensive, and to require the laying of the foundation may impose an undue burden. Under the federal practice, there is no way of knowing with certainty at the time of taking a deposition whether it is merely for discovery or will ultimately end up in evidence. With respect to both former testimony and depositions the possibility exists that knowledge of the statement might not be acquired until after the time of the cross-examination. Moreover, the expanded admissibility of former testimony and depositions under Rule 804(b)(1) calls for a correspondingly expanded approach to impeachment. The rule dispenses with the requirement in all hearsay situations, which is readily administered and best calculated to lead to fair results.

Notice should be taken that Rule 26(f) of the Federal Rules of Civil Procedure, as originally submitted by the Advisory Committee, ended with the following:

"... and, without having first called them to the deponent's attention, may show statements contradictory thereto made at any time by the deponent."

This language did not appear in the rule as promulgated in December, 1937. See 4 Moore's Federal Practice ¶¶ 26.01[9], 26.35 (2d ed. 1967). In 1951,

Nebraska adopted a provision strongly resembling the one stricken from the federal rule:

"Any party may impeach any adverse deponent by self-contradiction without having laid foundation for such impeachment at the time such deposition was taken." R.S.Neb. § 25-1267.07.

For similar provisions, see Uniform Rule 65; California Evidence Code § 1202; Kansas Code of Civil Procedure § 60-462; New Jersey Evidence Rule 65.

The provision for cross-examination of a declarant upon his hearsay statement is a corollary of general principles of cross-examination. A similar provision is found in California Evidence Code § 1203.

Conference Report

The Senate amendment permits an attack upon the credibility of the declarant of a statement if the statement is one by a person authorized by a party-opponent to make a statement concerning the subject, one by an agent of a party-opponent, or one by a coconspirator of the party-opponent, as these statements are defined in Rules 801(d)(2)(C), (D) and (E). The House bill has no such provision.

The Conference adopts the Senate amendment. The Senate amendment conforms the rule to present practice.

Rule 807.

RESIDUAL EXCEPTION

A statement not specifically covered by Rule 803 or 804, but having equivalent circumstantial guarantees of trustworthiness, is not excluded by the hearsay rule if the court determines that (A) the statement is offered as evidence of a material fact; (B) the statement is more probative on the point for which it is offered than any other evidence which the proponent can procure through reasonable efforts; and (C) the general purposes of these rules and the interests of justice will best be served by admission of the statement into evidence. However, a statement may not be admitted under this exception unless the proponent of it makes known to the adverse party sufficiently in advance of the trial or hearing to provide the adverse party with a fair opportunity to prepare to meet it, the proponent's intention to offer the statement and the particulars of it, including the name and address of the declarant.

Committee Note to 1997 Amendment

The contents of Rule 803(24) and Rule 804(b)(5) have been combined and transferred to a new Rule 807. This was done to facilitate additions to Rules 803 and 804. No change in meaning is intended.

ARTICLE IX. AUTHENTICATION AND IDENTIFICATION

Rule 901.

REQUIREMENT OF AUTHENTICATION OR IDENTIFICATION

(a) General provision. The requirement of authentication or identification as a condition precedent to admissibility is satisfied by evidence sufficient to support a finding that the matter in question is what its proponent claims.

(b) Illustrations. By way of illustration only, and not by way of limitation, the following are examples of authentication or identification conforming with the requirements of this rule:

(1) Testimony of witness with knowledge. Testimony that a matter is what it is claimed to be.

(2) Nonexpert opinion on handwriting. Nonexpert opinion as to the genuineness of handwriting, based upon familiarity not acquired for purposes of the litigation.

(3) Comparison by trier or expert witness. Comparison by the trier of fact or by expert witnesses with specimens which have been authenticated.

(4) Distinctive characteristics and the like. Appearance, contents, substance, internal patterns, or other distinctive characteristics, taken in conjunction with circumstances.

(5) Voice identification. Identification of a voice, whether heard firsthand or through mechanical or electronic transmission or recording, by opinion based upon hearing the voice at any time under circumstances connecting it with the alleged speaker.

(6) Telephone conversations. Telephone conversations, by evidence that a call was made to the number assigned at the time by the telephone company to a particular person or business, if (A) in the case of a person, circumstances, including self-identification, show the person answering to be the one called, or (B) in the case of a business, the call was made to a place of business and the conversation related to business reasonably transacted over the telephone.

(7) Public records or reports. Evidence that a writing authorized by law to be recorded or filed and in fact recorded or filed in a public office, or a purported public record, report, statement, or data compilation, in any form, is from the public office where items of this nature are kept.

(8) Ancient documents or data compilation. Evidence that a document or data compilation, in any form, (A) is in such condition as to create no suspicion concerning its authenticity, (B) was in a place where it, if authentic, would likely be, and (C) has been in existence 20 years or more at the time it is offered.

(9) Process or system. Evidence describing a process or system used to produce a result and showing that the process or system produces an accurate result.

(10) Methods provided by statute or rule. Any method of authentication or identification provided by Act of Congress or by other rules prescribed by the Supreme Court pursuant to statutory authority.

Note by Federal Judicial Center

The rule enacted by the Congress is the rule prescribed by the Supreme Court, amended in subdivision (b)(10) by substituting "prescribed" in place of "adopted," and by adding "pursuant to statutory authority."

Advisory Committee's Note

Subdivision (a). Authentication and identification represent a special aspect of relevancy. Michael and Adler, Real Proof, 5 Vand.L.Rev. 344, 362 (1952); McCormick §§ 179, 185; Morgan, Basic Problems of Evidence 378 (1962). Thus a telephone conversation may be irrelevant because on an unrelated topic or because the speaker is not identified. The latter aspect is the one here involved. Wigmore describes the need for authentication as "an inherent logical necessity." 7 Wigmore § 2129, p. 564.

This requirement of showing authenticity or identity falls in the category of relevancy dependent upon fulfillment of a condition of fact and is governed by the procedure set forth in Rule 104(b).

The common law approach to authentication of documents has been criticized as an "attitude of agnosticism," McCormick, Cases on Evidence 388, n. 4 (3rd ed. 1956), as one which "departs sharply from men's customs in ordinary affairs," and as presenting only a slight obstacle to the introduction of forgeries in comparison to the time and expense devoted to proving genuine writings which correctly show their origin on their face, McCormick § 185, pp. 395, 396. Today, such available procedures as requests to admit and pretrial conference afford the means of eliminating much of the need for authentication or identification. Also, significant inroads upon the traditional insistence on authentication and identification have been made by accepting as at least prima facie genuine items of the kind treated in Rule 902, infra. However, the need for suitable methods of proof still remains, since criminal cases pose their own obstacles to the use of preliminary procedures, unforeseen contingencies may arise, and cases of genuine controversy will still occur.

Subdivision (b). The treatment of authentication and identification draws largely upon the experience embodied in the common law and in statutes to furnish illustrative applications of the general principle set forth in subdivision (a). The examples are not intended as an exclusive enumeration of allowable methods but are meant to guide and suggest, leaving room for growth and development in this area of the law.

The examples relate for the most part to documents, with some attention given to voice communications and computer print-outs. As Wigmore noted, no special rules have been developed for authenticating chattels. Wigmore, Code of Evidence § 2086 (3rd ed. 1942).

It should be observed that compliance with requirements of authentication or identification by no means assures admission of an item into evidence, as other bars, hearsay for example, may remain.

Example (1) contemplates a broad spectrum ranging from testimony of a witness who was present at the signing of a document to testimony establishing narcotics as taken from an accused and accounting for custody through the period until trial, including laboratory analysis. See California Evidence Code § 1413, eyewitness to signing.

Example (2) states conventional doctrine as to lay identification of handwriting, which recognizes that a sufficient familiarity with the handwriting of another person may be acquired by seeing him write, by exchanging correspondence, or by other means, to afford a basis for identifying it on subsequent occasions. McCormick § 189. See also California Evidence Code § 1416. Testimony based upon familiarity acquired for purposes of the litigation is reserved to the expert under the example which follows.

Example (3). The history of common law restrictions upon the technique of proving or disproving the genuineness of a disputed specimen of handwriting through comparison with a genuine specimen, by either the testimony of expert witnesses or direct viewing by the triers themselves, is detailed in 7 Wigmore §§ 1991–1994. In breaking away, the English Common Law Procedure Act of 1854, 17 and 18 Vict., c. 125, § 27, cautiously allowed expert or trier to use exemplars "proved to the satisfaction of the judge to be genuine" for purposes of comparison. The language found its way into numerous statutes in this country, e.g., California Evidence Code §§ 1417, 1418. While explainable as a measure of prudence in the process of breaking with precedent in the handwriting situation, the reservation to the judge of the question of the genuineness of exemplars and the imposition of an unusually high standard of persuasion are at variance with the general treatment of relevancy which depends upon fulfillment of a condition of fact. Rule 104(b). No similar attitude is found in other comparison situations, e.g., ballistics comparison by jury, as in Evans v. Commonwealth, 230 Ky. 411, 19 S.W.2d 1091 (1929), or by experts, Annot., 26 A.L.R.2d 892, and no reason appears for its continued existence in handwriting cases. Consequently Example (3) sets no higher standard for handwriting specimens and treats all comparison situations alike, to be governed by Rule 104(b). This approach is consistent with 28 U.S.C. § 1731: "The admitted or proved handwriting of any person shall be admissible, for purposes of comparison, to determine genuineness of other handwriting attributed to such person."

Precedent supports the acceptance of visual comparison as sufficiently satisfying preliminary authentication requirements for admission in evidence. Brandon v. Collins, 267 F.2d 731 (2d Cir.1959); Wausau Sulphate Fibre Co. v. Commissioner of Internal Revenue, 61 F.2d 879 (7th Cir.1932); Desimone v. United States, 227 F.2d 864 (9th Cir.1955).

Example (4). The characteristics of the offered item itself, considered in the light of circumstances, afford authentication techniques in great variety. Thus a document or telephone conversation may be shown to have emanated from a particular person by virtue of its disclosing knowledge of facts known peculiarly to him; Globe Automatic Sprinkler Co. v. Braniff, 89 Okl. 105, 214 P. 127 (1923); California Evidence Code § 1421; similarly, a letter may be authenticated by content and circumstances indicating it was in reply to a duly authenticated one. McCormick § 192; California Evidence Code § 1420. Language patterns may indicate authenticity or its opposite. Magnuson v. State, 187 Wis. 122, 203 N.W. 749 (1925); Arens and Meadow, Psycholinguistics and the Confession Dilemma, 56 Colum.L.Rev. 19 (1956).

Example (5). Since aural voice identification is not a subject of expert testimony, the requisite familiarity may be acquired either before or after the particular speaking which is the subject of the identification, in this respect resembling visual identification of a person rather than identification of handwriting. Cf. Example (2), *supra,* People v. Nichols, 378 Ill. 487, 38 N.E.2d 766 (1941); McGuire v. State, 200 Md. 601, 92 A.2d 582 (1952); State v. McGee, 336 Mo. 1082, 83 S.W.2d 98 (1935).

Example (6). The cases are in agreement that a mere assertion of his identity by a person talking on the telephone is not sufficient evidence of the authenticity of the conversation and that additional evidence of his identity is required. The additional evidence need not fall in any set pattern. Thus the content of his statements or the reply technique, under Example (4), supra, or voice identification under Example (5), may furnish the necessary foundation. Outgoing calls made by the witness involve additional factors bearing upon authenticity. The calling of a number assigned by the telephone company reasonably supports the assumption that the listing is correct and that the number is the one reached. If the number is that of a place of business, the mass of authority allows an ensuing conversation if it relates to business reasonably transacted over the telephone, on the theory that the maintenance of the telephone connection is an invitation to do business without further identification. Mattan v. Hoover Co., 350 Mo. 506, 166 S.W.2d 557 (1942); City of Pawhuska v. Crutchfield, 147 Okl. 4, 293 P. 1095 (1930); Zurich General Acc. & Liability Ins. Co. v. Baum, 159 Va. 404, 165 S.E. 518 (1932). Otherwise, some additional circumstance of identification of the speaker is required. The authorities divide on the question whether the self-identifying statement of the person answering suffices. Example (6) answers in the affirmative on the assumption that usual conduct respecting telephone calls furnish adequate assurances of regularity, bearing in mind that the entire matter is open to exploration before the trier of fact. In general, see McCormick § 193; 7 Wigmore § 2155; Annot., 71 A.L.R. 5, 105 id. 326.

Example (7). Public records are regularly authenticated by proof of custody, without more. McCormick § 191; 7 Wigmore §§ 2158, 2159. The example extends the principle to include data stored in computers and similar methods, of which increasing use in the public records area may be expected. See California Evidence Code §§ 1532, 1600.

Example (8). The familiar ancient document rule of the common law is extended to include data stored electronically or by other similar means. Since the importance of appearance diminishes in this situation, the importance of custody or place where found increases correspondingly. This expansion is necessary in view of the widespread use of methods of storing data in forms other than conventional written records.

Any time period selected is bound to be arbitrary. The common law period of 30 years is here reduced to 20 years, with some shift of emphasis from the probable unavailability of witnesses to the unlikeliness of a still viable fraud after the lapse of time. The shorter period is specified in the English Evidence Act of 1938, 1 & 2 Geo. 6, c. 28, and in Oregon R.S.1963, § 41.360(34). See also the numerous statutes prescribing periods of less than 30 years in the case of recorded documents. 7 Wigmore § 2143.

The application of Example (8) is not subject to any limitation to title documents or to any requirement that possession, in the case of a title document, has been consistent with the document. See McCormick § 190.

Example (9) is designed for situations in which the accuracy of a result is dependent upon a process or system which produces it. X rays afford a familiar instance. Among more recent developments is the computer, as to which see Transport Indemnity Co. v. Seib, 178 Neb. 253, 132 N.W.2d 871 (1965); State v. Veres, 7 Ariz.App. 117, 436 P.2d 629 (1968); Merrick v. United States Rubber Co., 7 Ariz.App. 433, 440 P.2d 314 (1968); Freed, Computer Print-Outs as Evidence, 16 Am.Jur. Proof of Facts 273; Symposium, Law and Computers in the Mid–Sixties, ALI–ABA (1966); 37 Albany L.Rev. 61 (1967). Example (9) does not, of course, foreclose taking judicial notice of the accuracy of the process or system.

Example (10). The example makes clear that methods of authentication provided by Act of Congress and by the Rules of Civil and Criminal Procedure or by Bankruptcy Rules are not intended to be superseded. Illustrative are the provisions for authentication of official records in Civil Procedure Rule 44 and Criminal Procedure Rule 27, for authentication of records of proceedings by court reporters in 28 U.S.C. § 753(b) and Civil Procedure Rule 80(c), and for authentication of depositions in Civil Procedure Rule 30(f).

Rule 902.

SELF-AUTHENTICATION

Extrinsic evidence of authenticity as a condition precedent to admissibility is not required with respect to the following:

(1) Domestic public documents under seal. A document bearing a seal purporting to be that of the United States, or of any State, district, Commonwealth, territory, or insular possession thereof, or the Panama Canal Zone, or the Trust Territory of the Pacific Islands, or of a political subdivision, department, officer, or agency thereof, and a signature purporting to be an attestation or execution.

(2) Domestic public documents not under seal. A document purporting to bear the signature in the official capacity of an officer or employee of any entity included in paragraph (1) hereof, having no seal, if a public officer having a seal and having official duties in the district or political subdivision of the officer or employee certifies under seal that the signer has the official capacity and that the signature is genuine.

(3) Foreign public documents. A document purporting to be executed or attested in an official capacity by a person authorized by the laws of a foreign country to make the execution or attestation, and accompanied by a final certification as to the genuineness of the signature and official position (A) of the executing or attesting person, or (B) of any foreign official whose certificate of genuineness of signature and official position relates to the execution or attestation or is in a chain of certificates of genuineness of signature and official position relating to the execution or attestation. A final certification may be made by a secretary of an embassy or legation, consul general, consul, vice consul, or consular agent of the United States, or a diplomatic or consular official of the foreign country assigned or accredited to the United States. If reasonable opportunity has been given to all parties to investigate the authenticity and accuracy of official documents, the court may, for good cause shown, order that they be treated as presumptively authentic without final certification or permit them to be evidenced by an attested summary with or without final certification.

(4) **Certified copies of public records.** A copy of an official record or report or entry therein, or of a document authorized by law to be recorded or filed and actually recorded or filed in a public office, including data compilations in any form, certified as correct by the custodian or other person authorized to make the certification, by certificate complying with paragraph (1), (2), or (3) of this rule or complying with any Act of Congress or rule prescribed by the Supreme Court pursuant to statutory authority. *[must have the document sealed]*

(5) **Official publications.** Books, pamphlets, or other publications purporting to be issued by public authority. *(by government authorities)*

(6) **Newspapers and periodicals.** Printed materials purporting to be newspapers or periodicals.

(7) **Trade inscriptions and the like.** Inscriptions, signs, tags, or labels purporting to have been affixed in the course of business and indicating ownership, control, or origin.

(8) **Acknowledged documents.** Documents accompanied by a certificate of acknowledgment executed in the manner provided by law by a notary public or other officer authorized by law to take acknowledgments.

(9) **Commercial paper and related documents.** Commercial paper, signatures thereon, and documents relating thereto to the extent provided by general commercial law.

(10) **Presumptions under Acts of Congress.** Any signature, document, or other matter declared by Act of Congress to be presumptively or prima facie genuine or authentic.

(11) **Certified domestic records of regularly conducted activity.** The original or a duplicate of a domestic record of regularly conducted activity that would be admissible under Rule 803(6) if accompanied by a written declaration of its custodian or other qualified person,

in a manner complying with any Act of Congress or rule prescribed by the Supreme Court pursuant to statutory authority, certifying that the record—

>(A) was made at or near the time of the occurrence of the matters set forth by, or from information transmitted by, a person with knowledge of those matters;
>
>(B) was kept in the course of the regularly conducted activity; and
>
>(C) was made by the regularly conducted activity as a regular practice.

A party intending to offer a record into evidence under this paragraph must provide written notice of that intention to all adverse parties, and must make the record and declaration available for inspection sufficiently in advance of their offer into evidence to provide an adverse party with a fair opportunity to challenge them.

(12) Certified foreign records of regularly conducted activity. In a civil case, the original or a duplicate of a foreign record of regularly conducted activity that would be admissible under Rule 803(6) if accompanied by a written declaration by its custodian or other qualified person certifying that the record—

>(A) was made at or near the time of the occurrence of the matters set forth by, or from information transmitted by, a person with knowledge of those matters;
>
>(B) was kept in the course of the regularly conducted activity; and
>
>(C) was made by the regularly conducted activity as a regular practice.

The declaration must be signed in a manner that, if falsely made, would subject the maker to criminal penalty under the laws of the country where the declaration is signed. A party intending to offer a record into evidence under this paragraph must provide written notice of that intention to all adverse parties, and must make the record and declaration available for inspection sufficiently in advance of their offer into evidence to provide an adverse party with a fair opportunity to challenge them.

Advisory Committee's Note to 2000 Amendment to Rule 902

The amendment adds two new paragraphs to the rule on self-authentication. It sets forth a procedure by which parties can authenticate certain records of regularly conducted activity, other than through the testimony of a foundation witness. See the amendment to Rule 803(6). 18 U.S.C. §§ 3505 currently provides a means for certifying foreign records of regularly conducted activity in criminal cases, and this amendment is intended to establish a similar procedure for domestic records, and for foreign records offered in civil cases.

A declaration that satisfies 28 U.S.C. §§ 1746 would satisfy the declaration requirement of Rule 902(11), as would any comparable certification under oath.

The notice requirement in Rules 902(11) and (12) is intended to give the opponent of the evidence a full opportunity to test the adequacy of the foundation set forth in the declaration.

Note by Federal Judicial Center

The rule enacted by the Congress is the rule prescribed by the Supreme Court, amended as follows:

Paragraph (4) was amended by substituting "prescribed" in place of "adopted," and by adding "pursuant to statutory authority."

Paragraph (8) was amended by substituting "in the manner provided by law by" in place of "under the hand and seal of."

Advisory Committee's Note

Case law and statutes have, over the years, developed a substantial body of instances in which authenticity is taken as sufficiently established for purposes of admissibility without extrinsic evidence to that effect, sometimes for reasons of policy but perhaps more often because practical considerations reduce the possibility of unauthenticity to a very small dimension. The present rule collects and incorporates these situations, in some instances expanding them to occupy a larger area which their underlying considerations justify. In no instance is the opposite party foreclosed from disputing authenticity.

Paragraph (1). The acceptance of documents bearing a public seal and signature, most often encountered in practice in the form of acknowledgments or certificates authenticating copies of public records, is actually of broad application. Whether theoretically based in whole or in part upon judicial notice, the practical underlying considerations are that forgery is a crime and detection is fairly easy and certain. 7 Wigmore § 2161, p. 638; California Evidence Code § 1452. More than 50 provisions for judicial notice of official seals are contained in the United States Code.

Paragraph (2). While statutes are found which raise a presumption of genuineness of purported official signatures in the absence of an official seal, 7 Wigmore § 2167; California Evidence Code § 1453, the greater ease of effecting a forgery under these circumstances is apparent. Hence this paragraph of the rule calls for authentication by an officer who has a seal. Notarial acts by members of the armed forces and other special situations are covered in paragraph (10).

Paragraph (3). Provides a method for extending the presumption of authenticity to foreign official documents by a procedure of certification. It is derived from Rule 44(a)(2) of the Rules of Civil Procedure but is broader in applying to public documents rather than being limited to public records.

Paragraph (4). The common law and innumerable statutes have recognized the procedure of authenticating copies of public records by certificate. The certificate qualifies as a public document, receivable as authentic when in conformity with paragraph (1), (2), or (3). Rule 44(a) of the Rules of Civil Procedure and Rule 27 of the Rules of Criminal Procedure have provided authentication procedures of this nature for both domestic and foreign public records. It will be observed that the certification procedure here provided extends only to public records, reports, and recorded documents, all including data compilations, and does not apply to public documents generally. Hence documents provable when presented in original form under paragraphs (1), (2), or (3) may not be provable by certified copy under paragraph (4).

Paragraph (5). Dispensing with preliminary proof of the genuineness of purportedly official publications, most commonly encountered in connection with statutes, court reports, rules, and regulations, has been greatly enlarged by statutes and decisions. 5 Wigmore § 1684. Paragraph (5), it will be noted, does not confer admissibility upon all official publications; it merely provides a means whereby their authenticity may be taken as established for purposes of admissibility. Rule 44(a) of the Rules of Civil Procedure has been to the same effect.

Paragraph (6). The likelihood of forgery of newspapers or periodicals is slight indeed. Hence no danger is apparent in receiving them. Establishing the authenticity of the publication may, of course, leave still open questions of authority and responsibility for items therein contained. See 7 Wigmore § 2150. Cf. 39 U.S.C. § 4005(b), public advertisement prima facie evidence of agency of person named, in postal fraud order proceeding; Canadian Uniform Evidence Act, Draft of 1936, printed copy of newspaper prima facie evidence that notices or advertisements were authorized.

Paragraph (7). Several factors justify dispensing with preliminary proof of genuineness of commercial and mercantile labels and the like. The risk of forgery is minimal. Trademark infringement involves serious penalties. Great efforts are devoted to inducing the public to buy in reliance on brand names, and substantial protection is given them. Hence the fairness of this treatment finds recognition in the cases. Curtiss Candy Co. v. Johnson, 163 Miss. 426, 141 So. 762 (1932), Baby Ruth candy bar; Doyle v. Continental Baking Co., 262 Mass. 516, 160 N.E. 325 (1928), loaf of bread; Weiner v. Mager & Throne, 167 Misc. 338, 3 N.Y.S.2d 918 (1938), same. And see W.Va.Code 1966, § 47-3-5, trademark on bottle prima facie evidence of ownership. Contra, Keegan v. Green Giant Co., 150 Me. 283, 110 A.2d 599 (1954); Murphy v. Campbell Soup Co., 62 F.2d 564 (1st Cir.1933). Cattle brands have received similar acceptance in the western states. Rev.Code Mont.1947, § 46-606; State v. Wolfley, 75 Kan. 406, 89 P. 1046 (1907); Annot., 11 L.R.A. (N.S.) 87. Inscriptions on trains and vehicles are held to be prima facie evidence of ownership or control. Pittsburgh, Ft. W. & C. Ry. v. Callaghan, 157 Ill. 406, 41 N.E. 909 (1895); 9 Wigmore § 2510a. See also the provision of 19 U.S.C. § 1615(2) that marks, labels, brands, or stamps indicating foreign origin are prima facie evidence of foreign origin of merchandise.

Paragraph (8). In virtually every state, acknowledged title documents are receivable in evidence without further proof. Statutes are collected in 5 Wigmore § 1676. If this authentication suffices for documents of the importance of those affecting titles, logic scarcely permits denying this method when other kinds of documents are involved. Instances of broadly inclusive statutes are California Evidence Code § 1451 and N.Y. CPLR 4538, McKinney's Consol.Laws 1963.

Paragraph (9). Issues of the authenticity of commercial paper in federal courts will usually arise in diversity cases, will involve an element of a cause of action or defense, and with respect to presumptions and burden of proof will be controlled by Erie Railroad Co. v. Tompkins, 304 U.S. 64, 58 S.Ct. 817, 82 L.Ed. 1188 (1938). Rule 302, supra. There may, however, be questions of authenticity involving lesser segments of a case or the case may be one governed by federal common law. Clearfield Trust Co. v. United States, 318 U.S. 363, 63 S.Ct. 573, 87 L.Ed. 838 (1943). Cf. United States v. Yazell, 382 U.S. 341, 86 S.Ct. 500, 15 L.Ed.2d 404 (1966). In these situations, resort to the useful authentication provisions of the Uniform Commercial Code is provided for. While the phrasing is in terms of "general commercial law," in order to avoid the potential complications inherent in borrowing local statutes, today one would have difficulty in determining the general commercial law without referring to the Code. See Williams v. Walker–Thomas Furniture Co., 121 U.S.App.D.C. 315, 350 F.2d 445 (1965). Pertinent Code provisions are sections 1–202, 3–307, and 3–510, dealing with third-party documents, signatures on negotiable instruments, protests, and statements of dishonor.

Report of House Committee on the Judiciary

The Committee approved Rule 902(9) as submitted by the Court. With respect to the meaning of the phrase "general commercial law", the Committee intends that the Uniform Commercial Code, which has been adopted in virtually every State, will be followed generally, but that federal commercial law will apply where federal commercial paper is involved. See Clearfield Trust Co. v. United States, 318 U.S. 363, 63 S.Ct. 573, 87 L.Ed. 838 (1943). Further, in those instances in which the issues are governed by Erie R. Co. v. Tompkins, 304 U.S. 64, 58 S.Ct. 817, 82 L.Ed. 1188 (1938), State law will apply irrespective of whether it is the Uniform Commercial Code.

Advisory Committee's Note

Paragraph (10). The paragraph continues in effect dispensations with preliminary proof of genuineness provided in various Acts of Congress. See, for example, 10 U.S.C. § 936, signature, without seal, together with title, prima facie evidence of authenticity of acts of certain military personnel who are given notarial powers; 15 U.S.C. § 77f(a), signature on SEC registration presumed genuine; 26 U.S.C. § 6064, signature to tax return prima facie genuine.

Rule 903.

SUBSCRIBING WITNESS' TESTIMONY UNNECESSARY

The testimony of a subscribing witness is not necessary to authenticate a writing unless required by the laws of the jurisdiction whose laws govern the validity of the writing.

Note by Federal Judicial Center

The rule enacted by the Congress is the rule prescribed by the Supreme Court without change.

Advisory Committee's Note

The common law required that attesting witnesses be produced or accounted for. Today the requirement has generally been abolished except with respect to documents which must be attested to be valid, e.g. wills in some states.

McCormick § 188. Uniform Rule 71; California Evidence Code § 1411; Kansas Code of Civil Procedure § 60–468; New Jersey Evidence Rule 71; New York CPLR Rule 4537.

ARTICLE X. CONTENTS OF WRITINGS, RECORDINGS, AND PHOTOGRAPHS

Rule 1001.

DEFINITIONS

For purposes of this article the following definitions are applicable:

(1) Writings and recordings. "Writings" and "recordings" consist of letters, words, or numbers, or their equivalent, set down by handwriting, typewriting, printing, photostating, photographing, magnetic impulse, mechanical or electronic recording, or other form of data compilation.

(2) Photographs. "Photographs" include still photographs, X-ray films, video tapes, and motion pictures.

(3) Original. An "original" of a writing or recording is the writing or recording itself or any counterpart intended to have the same effect by a person executing or issuing it. An "original" of a photograph includes the negative or any print therefrom. If data are stored in a computer or similar device, any printout or other output readable by sight, shown to reflect the data accurately, is an "original".

(4) Duplicate. A "duplicate" is a counterpart produced by the same impression as the original, or from the same matrix, or by means of photography, including enlargements and miniatures, or by mechanical or electronic re-recording, or by chemical reproduction, or by other equivalent techniques which accurately reproduces the original.

Note by Federal Judicial Center

The rule enacted by the Congress is the rule prescribed by the Supreme Court, amended in paragraph (2) by inserting "video tapes."

Advisory Committee's Note

In an earlier day, when discovery and other related procedures were strictly limited, the misleading named "best evidence rule" afforded substantial guarantees against inaccuracies and fraud by its insistence upon production of original documents. The great enlargement of the scope of discovery and related procedures in recent times has measurably reduced the need for the rule. Nevertheless important areas of usefulness persist: discovery of documents outside the jurisdiction may require substantial outlay of time and money; the unanticipated document may not practically be discoverable; criminal cases have built-in limitations on discovery. Clearly and Strong, The Best Evidence Rule: An Evaluation in Context, 51 Iowa L.Rev. 825 (1966).

Paragraph (1). Traditionally the rule requiring the original centered upon accumulations of data and expressions affecting legal relations set forth in words and figures. This meant that the rule was one essentially related to writings. Present day techniques have expanded methods of storing data, yet the essential form which the information ultimately assumes for usable purposes is words and figures. Hence the considerations underlying the rule dictate its expansion to include computers, photographic systems, and other modern developments.

Paragraph (3). In most instances, what is an original will be self-evident and further refinement will be unnecessary. However, in some instances particularized definition is required. A carbon copy of a contract executed in duplicate becomes an original, as does a sales ticket carbon copy given to a customer. While strictly speaking the original of a photograph might be thought to be only the negative, practicality and common usage require that any print from the negative be regarded as an original. Similarly, practicality and usage confer the status of original upon any computer printout. Transport Indemnity Co. v. Seib, 178 Neb. 253, 132 N.W.2d 871 (1965).

Paragraph (4). The definition describes "copies" produced by methods possessing an accuracy which virtually eliminates the possibility of error. Copies thus produced are given the status of originals in large measure by Rule 1003, infra. Copies subsequently produced manually, whether handwritten or typed, are not within the definition. It should be noted that what is an original for some purposes may be a duplicate for others. Thus a bank's microfilm record of checks cleared is the original as a record. However, a print offered as a copy of a check whose contents are in controversy is a duplicate. This result is substantially consistent with 28 U.S.C. § 1732(b). Compare 26 U.S.C. § 7513(c), giving full status as originals to photographic reproductions of tax returns and other documents, made by authority of the Secretary of the Treasury, and 44 U.S.C. § 399(a), giving original status to photographic copies in the National Archives.

Rule 1002.

REQUIREMENT OF ORIGINAL

To prove the content of a writing, recording, or photograph, the original writing, recording, or photograph is required, except as otherwise provided in these rules or by Act of Congress.

Note by Federal Judicial Center

The rule enacted by the Congress is the rule prescribed by the Supreme Court without change.

Advisory Committee's Note

The rule is the familiar one requiring production of the original of a document to prove its contents, expanded to include writings, recordings, and photographs, as defined in Rule 1001(1) and (2), supra.

Application of the rule requires a resolution of the question whether contents are sought to be proved. Thus an event may be proved by nondocumentary evidence, even though a written record of it was made. If, however, the event is sought to be proved by the written record, the rule applies. For example, payment may be proved without producing the written receipt which was given.

Earnings may be proved without producing books of account in which they are entered. McCormick § 198; 4 Wigmore § 1245. Nor does the rule apply to testimony that books or records have been examined and found not to contain any reference to a designated matter.

The assumption should not be made that the rule will come into operation on every occasion when use is made of a photograph in evidence. On the contrary, the rule will seldom apply to ordinary photographs. In most instances a party *wishes* to introduce the item and the question raised is the propriety of receiving it in evidence. Cases in which an offer is made of the testimony of a witness as to what he saw in a photograph or motion picture, without producing the same, are most unusual. The usual course is for a witness on the stand to identify the photograph or motion picture as a correct representation of events which he saw or of a scene with which he is familiar. In fact he adopts the picture as his testimony, or, in common parlance, uses the picture to illustrate his testimony. Under these circumstances, no effort is made to prove the contents of the picture, and the rule is inapplicable. Paradis, The Celluloid Witness, 37 U.Colo.L.Rev. 235, 249–251 (1965).

On occasion, however, situations arise in which contents are sought to be proved. Copyright, defamation and invasion of privacy by photograph or motion picture falls in this category. Similarly as to situations in which the picture is offered as having independent probative value, e.g. automatic photograph of bank robber. See People v. Doggett, 83 Cal.App.2d 405, 188 P.2d 792 (1948), photograph of defendants engaged in indecent act; Mouser and Philbin, Photographic Evidence—Is There a Recognized Basis for Admissibility? 8 Hastings L.J. 310 (1957). The most commonly encountered of this latter group is of course, the X ray, with substantial authority calling for production of the original. Daniels v. Iowa City, 191 Iowa 811, 183 N.W. 415 (1921); Cellamare v. Third Ave. Transit Corp., 273 App.Div. 260, 77 N.Y.S.2d 91 (1948); Patrick & Tillman v. Matkin, 154 Okl. 232, 7 P.2d 414 (1932); Mendoza v. Rivera, 78 D.P.R. 599 (1955).

It should be noted, however, that Rule 703, supra, allows an expert to give an opinion based on matters not in evidence, and the present rule must be read as being limited accordingly in its application. Hospital records which may be admitted as business records under Rule 803(6) commonly contain reports interpreting X rays by the staff radiologist, who qualifies as an expert, and these reports need not be excluded from the records by the instant rule.

The reference to Acts of Congress is made in view of such statutory provisions as 26 U.S.C. § 7513, photographic reproductions of tax returns and documents, made by authority of the Secretary of the Treasury, treated as originals, and 44 U.S.C. § 399(a), photographic copies in National Archives treated as originals.

Rule 1003.

ADMISSIBILITY OF DUPLICATES

A duplicate is admissible to the same extent as an original unless (1) a genuine question is raised as to the authenticity of the original or (2) in the circumstances it would be unfair to admit the duplicate in lieu of the original.

Note by Federal Judicial Center

The rule enacted by the Congress is the rule prescribed by the Supreme Court without change.

Advisory Committee's Note

When the only concern is with getting the words or other contents before the court with accuracy and precision, then a counterpart serves equally as well as the original, if the counterpart is the product of a method which insures accuracy and genuineness. By definition in Rule 1001(4), supra, a "duplicate" possesses this character.

Therefore, if no genuine issue exists as to authenticity and no other reason exists for requiring the original, a duplicate is admissible under the rule. This position finds support in the decisions, Myrick v. United States, 332 F.2d 279 (5th Cir.1963), no error in admitting photostatic copies of checks instead of original microfilm in absence of suggestion to trial judge that photostats were incorrect; Johns v. United States, 323 F.2d 421 (5th Cir.1963), not error to admit concededly accurate tape recording made from original wire recording; Sauget v. Johnston, 315 F.2d 816 (9th Cir.1963), not error to admit copy of agreement when opponent had original and did not on appeal claim any discrepancy. Other reasons for requiring the original may be present when only a part of the original is reproduced and the remainder is needed for cross-examination or may disclose matters qualifying the part offered or otherwise useful to the opposing party. United States v. Alexander, 326 F.2d 736 (4th Cir.1964). And see Toho Bussan Kaisha, Ltd. v. American President Lines, Ltd., 265 F.2d 418, 76 A.L.R.2d 1344 (2d Cir.1959).

Report of House Committee on the Judiciary

The Committee approved this Rule in the form submitted by the Court, with the expectation that the courts would be liberal in deciding that a "genuine question is raised as to the authenticity of the original."

Rule 1004.

ADMISSIBILITY OF OTHER EVIDENCE OF CONTENTS

The original is not required, and other evidence of the contents of a writing, recording or photograph is admissible if—

(1) Originals lost or destroyed. All originals are lost or have been destroyed, unless the proponent lost or destroyed them in bad faith; or

(2) Original not obtainable. No original can be obtained by any available judicial process or procedure; or

(3) Original in possession of opponent. At a time when an original was under the control of the party against whom offered, that party was put on notice, by the pleadings or otherwise, that the contents would be a subject of proof at the hearing, and that party does not produce the original at the hearing; or

(4) Collateral matters. The writing, recording, or photograph is not closely related to a controlling issue.

Note by Federal Judicial Center

The rule enacted by the Congress is the rule prescribed by the Supreme Court without change.

Advisory Committee's Note

Basically the rule requiring the production of the original as proof of contents has developed as a rule of preference: if failure to produce the original is satisfactorily explained, secondary evidence is admissible. The instant rule specifies the circumstances under which production of the original is excused.

The rule recognizes no "degrees" of secondary evidence. While strict logic might call for extending the principle of preference beyond simply preferring the original, the formulation of a hierarchy of preferences and a procedure for making it effective is believed to involve unwarranted complexities. Most, if not all, that would be accomplished by an extended scheme of preferences will, in any event, be achieved through the normal motivation of a party to present the most convincing evidence possible and the arguments and procedures available to his opponent if he does not. Compare McCormick § 207.

Paragraph (1). Loss or destruction of the original, unless due to bad faith of the proponent, is a satisfactory explanation of nonproduction. McCormick § 201.

Report of House Committee on the Judiciary

The Committee approved Rule 1004(1) in the form submitted to Congress. However, the Committee intends that loss or destruction of an original by another person at the instigation of the proponent should be considered as tantamount to loss or destruction in bad faith by the proponent himself.

Advisory Committee's Note

Paragraph (2). When the original is in the possession of a third person, inability to procure it from him by resort to process or other judicial procedure is a sufficient explanation of nonproduction. Judicial procedure includes subpoena duces tecum as an incident to the taking of a deposition in another jurisdiction. No further showing is required. See McCormick § 202.

Paragraph (3). A party who has an original in his control has no need for the protection of the rule if put on notice that proof of contents will be made. He can ward off secondary evidence by offering the original. The notice procedure here provided is not to be confused with orders to produce or other discovery procedures, as the purpose of the procedure under this rule is to afford the opposite party an opportunity to produce the original, not to compel him to do so. McCormick § 203.

Paragraph (4). While difficult to define with precision, situations arise in which no good purpose is served by production of the original. Examples are the newspaper in an action for the price of publishing defendant's advertisement, Foster–Holcomb Investment Co. v. Little Rock Publishing Co., 151 Ark. 449, 236 S.W. 597 (1922), and the streetcar transfer of plaintiff claiming status as a passenger, Chicago City Ry. Co. v. Carroll, 206 Ill. 318, 68 N.E. 1087 (1903). Numerous cases are collected in McCormick § 200, p. 412, n. 1.

Rule 1005.

PUBLIC RECORDS

The contents of an official record, or of a document authorized to be recorded or filed and actually recorded or filed, including data compilations in any form, if otherwise admissible, may be proved by copy, certified as correct in accordance with rule 902 or testified to be correct by a witness who has compared it with the original. If a copy which complies with the foregoing cannot be obtained by the exercise of reasonable diligence, then other evidence of the contents may be given.

Note by Federal Judicial Center

The rule enacted by the Congress is the rule prescribed by the Supreme Court without change.

Advisory Committee's Note

Public records call for somewhat different treatment. Removing them from their usual place of keeping would be attended by serious inconvenience to the public and to the custodian. As a consequence judicial decisions and statutes commonly hold that no explanation need be given for failure to produce the original of a public record. McCormick § 204; 4 Wigmore §§ 1215–1228. This blanket dispensation from producing or accounting for the original would open the door to the introduction of every kind of secondary evidence of contents of public records were it not for the preference given certified or compared copies. Recognition of degrees of secondary evidence in this situation is an appropriate *quid pro quo* for not applying the requirement of producing the original.

The provisions of 28 U.S.C. § 1733(b) apply only to departments or agencies of the United States. The rule, however, applies to public records generally and is comparable in scope in this respect to Rule 44(a) of the Rules of Civil Procedure.

Rule 1006.

SUMMARIES

The contents of voluminous writings, recordings, or photographs which cannot conveniently be examined in court may be presented in the form of a chart, summary, or calculation. The originals, or duplicates, shall be made available for examination or copying, or both, by other parties at reasonable time and place. The court may order that they be produced in court.

Note by Federal Judicial Center

The rule enacted by the Congress is the rule prescribed by the Supreme Court without change.

Advisory Committee's Note

The admission of summaries of voluminous books, records, or documents offers the only practicable means of making their contents available to judge and jury. The rule recognizes this practice, with appropriate safeguards. 4 Wigmore § 1230.

Rule 1007.

TESTIMONY OR WRITTEN ADMISSION OF PARTY

Contents of writings, recordings, or photographs may be proved by the testimony or deposition of the party against whom offered or by that party's written admission, without accounting for the nonproduction of the original.

Note by Federal Judicial Center

The rule enacted by the Congress is the rule prescribed by the Supreme Court without change.

Advisory Committee's Note

While the parent case, Slatterie v. Pooley, 6 M. & W. 664, 151 Eng.Rep. 579 (Exch.1840), allows proof of contents by evidence of an oral admission by the party against whom offered, without accounting for nonproduction of the original, the risk of inaccuracy is substantial and the decision is at odds with the purpose of the rule giving preference to the original. See 4 Wigmore § 1255. The instant rule follows Professor McCormick's suggestion of limiting this use of admissions to those made in the course of giving testimony or in writing. McCormick § 208, p. 424. The limitation, of course, does not call for excluding evidence of an oral admission when nonproduction of the original has been accounted for and secondary evidence generally has become admissible. Rule 1004, supra.

A similar provision is contained in New Jersey Evidence Rule 70(1)(h).

Rule 1008.

FUNCTIONS OF COURT AND JURY

When the admissibility of other evidence of contents of writings, recordings, or photographs under these rules depends upon the fulfillment of a condition of fact, the question whether the condition has been fulfilled is ordinarily for the court to determine in accordance with the provisions of rule 104. However, when an issue is raised (a) whether the asserted writing ever existed, or (b) whether another writing, recording, or photograph produced at the trial is the original, or (c) whether other evidence of contents correctly reflects the contents, the issue is for the trier of fact to determine as in the case of other issues of fact.

Note by Federal Judicial Center

The rule enacted by the Congress is the rule prescribed by the Supreme Court, amended by substituting "court" in place of "judge," and by adding at the end of the first sentence the phrase "in accordance with the provisions of rule 104."

Advisory Committee's Note

Most preliminary questions of fact in connection with applying the rule preferring the original as evidence of contents are for the judge, under the general principles announced in Rule 104, supra. Thus, the question whether the loss of the originals has been established, or of the fulfillment of other conditions specified in Rule 1004, supra, is for the judge. However, questions may arise which go beyond the mere administration of the rule preferring the original and into the merits of the controversy. For example, plaintiff offers secondary evidence of the contents of an alleged contract, after first introducing evidence of loss of the original, and defendant counters with evidence that no such contract was ever executed. If the judge decides that the contract was never executed and excludes the secondary evidence, the case is at an end without ever going to the jury on a central issue. Levin, Authentication and Content of Writings, 10 Rutgers L.Rev. 632, 644 (1956). The latter portion of the instant rule is designed to insure treatment of these situations as raising jury questions. The decision is not one for uncontrolled discretion of the jury but is subject to the control exercised generally by the judge over jury determinations. See Rule 104(b), supra.

For similar provisions, see Uniform Rule 70(2); Kansas Code of Civil Procedure § 60–467(b); New Jersey Evidence Rule 70(2), (3).

ARTICLE XI. MISCELLANEOUS RULES

Rule 1101.

APPLICABILITY OF RULES

(a) Courts and judges. These rules apply to the United States district courts, the District Court of Guam, the District Court of the Virgin Islands, the District Court for the Northern Mariana Islands, the United States courts of appeals, the United States Claims Court, and to United States bankruptcy judges and United States magistrate judges, in the actions, cases, and proceedings and to the extent hereinafter set forth. The terms "judge" and "court" in these rules include United States bankruptcy judges and United States magistrate judges.

(b) Proceedings generally. These rules apply generally to civil actions and proceedings, including admiralty and maritime cases, to criminal cases and proceedings, to contempt proceedings except those in which the court may act summarily, and to proceedings and cases under title 11, United States Code.

(c) Rule of privilege. The rule with respect to privileges applies at all stages of all actions, cases, and proceedings.

(d) Rules inapplicable. The rules (other than with respect to privileges) do not apply in the following situations:

(1) Preliminary questions of fact. The determination of questions of fact preliminary to admissibility of evidence when the issue is to be determined by the court under rule 104.

(2) Grand jury. Proceedings before grand juries.

(3) Miscellaneous proceedings. Proceedings for extradition or rendition; preliminary examinations in criminal cases; sentencing, or granting or revoking probation; issuance of warrants for arrest, criminal summonses, and search warrants; and proceedings with respect to release on bail or otherwise.

(e) Rules applicable in part. In the following proceedings these rules apply to the extent that matters of evidence are not provided for in the statutes which govern procedure therein or in other rules prescribed by the Supreme Court pursuant to statutory authority: the trial of misdemeanors and other petty offenses before United States magistrate judges; review of agency actions when the facts are subject to trial de novo under section 706(2)(F) of title 5, United States Code; review of orders of the Secretary of Agriculture under section 2 of the Act entitled "An Act to authorize association of producers of agricultural products" approved February 18, 1922 (7 U.S.C. 292), and under sections 6 and 7(c) of the Perishable Agricultural Commodities Act, 1930 (7 U.S.C. 499f, 499g(c)); naturalization and revocation of naturalization under sections 310–318 of the Immigration and Nationality Act (8 U.S.C. 1421–1429); prize proceedings in admiralty under sections 7651–7681 of title 10, United States Code; review of orders of the Secretary of the Interior under section 2 of the Act entitled "An Act authorizing associations of producers of aquatic products" approved June 25, 1934 (15 U.S.C. 522); review of orders of petroleum control boards under section 5 of the Act entitled "An Act to regulate interstate and foreign commerce in petroleum and its products by prohibiting the shipment in such commerce of petroleum and its products produced in violation of State law, and for other purposes", approved February 22, 1935 (15 U.S.C. 715d); actions for fines, penalties, or forfeitures under part V of title IV of the Tariff Act of 1930 (19 U.S.C. 1581–1624), or under the Anti–Smuggling Act (19 U.S.C. 1701–1711); criminal libel for condemnation, exclusion of imports, or other proceedings under the Federal Food, Drug, and Cosmetic Act (21 U.S.C. 301–392); disputes between seamen under sections 4079, 4080, and 4081 of the Revised Statutes (22 U.S.C. 256–258); habeas corpus under sections 2241–2254 of title 28, United States Code; motions to vacate, set aside or correct sentence under section 2255 of title 28, United States Code; actions for penalties for refusal to transport destitute seamen under section 4578 of the Revised Statutes (46 U.S.C. 679); actions against the United States under the Act entitled "An Act authorizing suits against the United States in admiralty for damage caused by and salvage service rendered to public vessels belonging to the United States, and for other purposes", approved March 3, 1925 (46

U.S.C. 781–790), as implemented by section 7730 of title 10, United States Code.

Advisory Committee Notes to 1993 Amendment

This revision is made to conform the rule to changes in terminology made by Rule 58 of the Federal Rules of Criminal Procedure and to the changes in the title of United States magistrates made by the Judicial Improvements Act of 1990.

Advisory Committee's Note to 1987 Amendment

Subdivision (a) is amended to delete the reference to the District Court for the District of the Canal Zone, which no longer exists, and to add the District Court for the Northern Mariana Islands. The United States bankruptcy judges are added to conform the subdivision with Rule 1101(b) and Bankruptcy Rule 9017.

Note by Federal Judicial Center

The rule enacted by the Congress is the rule prescribed by the Supreme Court, amended as follows:

Subdivision (a) was amended in the first sentence by inserting "the Court of Claims" and by inserting "actions, cases, and." It was amended in the second sentence by substituting "terms" in place of "word," by inserting the phrase "and 'court'," and by adding "commissioners of the Court of Claims."

Subdivision (b) was amended by substituting "civil actions and proceedings" in place of "civil actions," and by substituting "criminal cases and proceedings" in place of "criminal proceedings."

Subdivision (c) was amended by substituting "rule" in place of "rules" and by changing the verb to the singular.

Subdivision (d) was amended by deleting "those" after "other than" and by substituting "Rule 104" in place of "Rule 104(a)."

Subdivision (e) was amended by substituting "prescribed" in place of "adopted" and by adding "pursuant to statutory authority." The form of the statutory citations was also changed.

Report of House Committee on the Judiciary

Subdivision (a) as submitted to the Congress, in stating the courts and judges to which the Rules of Evidence apply, omitted the Court of Claims and commissioners of that Court. At the request of the Court of Claims, the Committee amended the Rule to include the Court and its commissioners within the purview of the Rules.

Advisory Committee's Note

Subdivision (b) is a combination of the language of the enabling acts, supra, with respect to the kinds of proceedings in which the making of rules is authorized. It is subject to the qualifications expressed in the subdivisions which follow.

Subdivision (c) singling out the rules of privilege for special treatment, is made necessary by the limited applicability of the remaining rules.

Subdivision (d). The rule is not intended as an expression as to when due process or other constitutional provisions may require an evidentiary hearing. Paragraph (1) restates, for convenience, the provisions of the second sentence of Rule 104(a), supra. See Advisory Committee's Note to that rule.

(2) While some states have statutory requirements that indictments be based on "legal evidence," and there is some case law to the effect that the rules of evidence apply to grand jury proceedings, 1 Wigmore § 4(5), the Supreme Court has not accepted this view. In Costello v. United States, 350 U.S. 359, 76 S.Ct. 406, 100 L.Ed. 397 (1956), the Court refused to allow an indictment to be attacked, for either constitutional or policy reasons, on the ground that only hearsay evidence was presented.

> "It would run counter to the whole history of the grand jury institution, in which laymen conduct their inquiries unfettered by technical rules. Neither justice nor the concept of a fair trial requires such a change." Id. at 364.

The rule as drafted does not deal with the evidence required to support an indictment.

(3) The rule exempts preliminary examinations in criminal cases. Authority as to the applicability of the rules of evidence to preliminary examinations has been meagre and conflicting. Goldstein, The State and the Accused: Balance of Advantage in Criminal Procedure, 69 Yale L.J. 1149, 1168, n. 53 (1960); Comment, Preliminary Hearings on Indictable Offenses in Philadelphia, 106 U. of Pa.L.Rev. 589, 592–593 (1958). Hearsay testimony is, however, customarily received in such examinations. Thus in a Dyer Act case, for example, an affidavit may properly be used in a preliminary examination to prove ownership of the stolen vehicle, thus saving the victim of the crime the hardship of having to travel twice to a distant district for the sole purpose of testifying as to ownership. It is believed that the extent of the applicability of the Rules of Evidence to preliminary examinations should be appropriately dealt with by the Federal Rules of Criminal Procedure which regulate those proceedings.

Extradition and rendition proceedings are governed in detail by statute. 18 U.S.C. §§ 3181–3195. They are essentially administrative in character. Traditionally the rules of evidence have not applied. 1 Wigmore § 4(6). Extradition proceedings are accepted from the operation of the Rules of Criminal Procedure. Rule 54(b)(5) of Federal Rules of Criminal Procedure.

The rules of evidence have not been regarded as applicable to sentencing or probation proceedings, where great reliance is placed upon the presentence investigation and report. Rule 32(c) of the Federal Rules of Criminal Procedure requires a presentence investigation and report in every case unless the court otherwise directs. In Williams v. New York, 337 U.S. 241, 69 S.Ct. 1079, 93 L.Ed. 1337 (1949), in which the judge overruled a jury recommendation of life imprisonment and imposed a death sentence, the Court said that due process does not require confrontation or cross-examination in sentencing or passing on probation, and that the judge has broad discretion as to the sources and types of information relied upon. Compare the recommendation that the substance of all derogatory information be disclosed to the defendant, in A.B.A. Project on Minimum Standards for Criminal Justice, Sentencing Alternatives and Procedures § 4.4, Tentative Draft (1967, Sobeloff, Chm.). Williams was adhered to in Specht v. Patterson, 386 U.S. 605, 87 S.Ct. 1209, 18 L.Ed.2d 326 (1967), but not extended to a proceeding under the Colorado Sex Offenders Act, which was said to be a new charge leading in effect to punishment, more like the recidivist statutes where opportunity must be given to be heard on the habitual criminal issue.

Warrants for arrest, criminal summonses, and search warrants are issued upon complaint or affidavit showing probable cause. Rules 4(a) and 41(c) of the Federal Rules of Criminal Procedure. The nature of the proceedings makes application of the formal rules of evidence inappropriate and impracticable.

Criminal contempts are punishable summarily if the judge certifies that he saw or heard the contempt and that it was committed in the presence of the court. Rule 42(a) of the Federal Rules of Criminal Procedure. The circumstances which preclude application of the rules of evidence in this situation are not present, however, in other cases of criminal contempt.

Proceedings with respect to release on bail or otherwise do not call for application of the rules of evidence. The governing statute specifically provides:

> "Information stated in, or offered in connection with, any order entered pursuant to this section need not conform to the rules pertaining to the admissibility of evidence in a court of law." 18 U.S.C.A. § 3146(f).

This provision is consistent with the type of inquiry contemplated in A.B.A. Project on Minimum Standards for Criminal Justice, Standards Relating to Pretrial Release, § 4.5(b), (c), p. 16 (1968). The references to the weight of the evidence against the accused, in Rule 46(a)(1), (c) of the Federal Rules of Criminal Procedure and in 18 U.S.C.A. § 3146(b), as a factor to be considered, clearly do not have in view evidence introduced at a hearing under the rules of evidence.

The rule does not exempt habeas corpus proceedings. The Supreme Court held in Walker v. Johnston, 312 U.S. 275, 61 S.Ct. 574, 85 L.Ed. 830 (1941), that the practice of disposing of matters of fact on affidavit, which prevailed in some circuits, did not "satisfy the command of the statute that the judge shall proceed 'to determine the facts of the case, by hearing the testimony and arguments.'" This view accords with the emphasis in Townsend v. Sain, 372 U.S. 293, 83 S.Ct. 745, 9 L.Ed.2d 770 (1963), upon trial-type proceedings, id. 311, 83 S.Ct. 745, with demeanor evidence as a significant factor, id. 322, 83 S.Ct. 745, in applications by state prisoners aggrieved by unconstitutional detentions. Hence subdivision (e) applies the rules to habeas corpus proceedings to the extent not inconsistent with the statute.

Subdivision (e). In a substantial number of special proceedings, ad hoc evaluation has resulted in the promulgation of particularized evidentiary provisions, by Act of Congress or by rule adopted by the Supreme Court. Well adapted to the particular proceedings, though not apt candidates for inclusion in a set of general rules, they are left undisturbed. Otherwise, however, the rules of evidence are applicable to the proceedings enumerated in the subdivision.

Rule 1102.

AMENDMENTS

Amendments to the Federal Rules of Evidence may be made as provided in section 2072 of title 28 of the United States Code.

Note by Federal Judicial Center

This rule was not included among those prescribed by the Supreme Court. The rule prescribed by the Court as 1102 now appears as 1103.

Rule 1103.

TITLE

These rules may be known and cited as the Federal Rules of Evidence.

Note by Federal Judicial Center

The rule enacted by the Congress is the rule prescribed by the Supreme Court as Rule 1102 without change.

AMENDMENTS TO THE UNITED STATES CODE

SEC. 2. (a) Title 28 of the United States Code is amended—

(1) by inserting immediately after section 2075 the following new section:

"§ 2076. Rules of evidence

"The Supreme Court of the United States shall have the power to prescribe amendments to the Federal Rules of Evidence. Such amendments shall not take effect until they have been reported to Congress by the Chief Justice at or after the beginning of a regular session of Congress but not later than the first day of May, and until the expiration of one hundred and eighty days after they have been so reported; but if either House of Congress within that time shall by resolution disapprove any amendment so reported it shall not take effect. The effective date of any amendment so reported may be deferred by either House of Congress to a later date or until approved by Act of Congress. Any rule whether proposed or in force may be amended by Act of Congress. Any provision of law in force at the expiration of such time and in conflict with any such amendment not disapproved shall be of no further force or effect after such amendment has taken effect. Any such amendment creating, abolishing, or modifying a privilege shall have no force or effect unless it shall be approved by act of Congress"; and

(2) by adding at the end of the table of sections of chapter 131 the following new item:

"2076. Rules of evidence."

(b) Section 1732 of title 28 of the United States Code is amended by striking out subsection (a), and by striking out "(b)".

(c) Section 1733 of title 28 of the United States Code is amended by adding at the end thereof the following new subsection:

"(c) This section does not apply to cases, actions, and proceedings to which the Federal Rules of Evidence apply."

SEC. 3. The Congress expressly approves the amendments to the Federal Rules of Civil Procedure, and the amendments to the Federal Rules of Criminal Procedure, which are embraced by the orders entered by the Supreme Court of the United States on November 20, 1972, and December 18, 1972, and such amendments shall take effect on the one hundred and eightieth day beginning after the date of the enactment of this Act.

Approved Jan. 2, 1975.

APPENDIX OF DELETED MATERIALS

Rule 105.

SUMMING UP AND COMMENT BY JUDGE

[Not enacted.]

After the close of the evidence and arguments of counsel, the judge may fairly and impartially sum up the evidence and comment to the jury upon the weight of the evidence and the credibility of the witnesses, if he also instructs the jury that they are to determine for themselves the weight of the evidence and the credit to be given to the witnesses and that they are not bound by the judge's summation or comment.

REPORT OF THE HOUSE COMMITTEE ON THE JUDICIARY

... The Committee recognized that the Rule as submitted is consistent with long standing and current federal practice. However, the aspect of the Rule dealing with the authority of a judge to comment on the weight of the evidence and the credibility of witnesses—an authority not granted to judges in most State courts—was highly controversial. After much debate the Committee determined to delete the entire Rule, intending that its action be understood as reflecting no conclusion as to the merits of the proposed Rule and that the subject should be left for separate consideration at another time.

Rule 303.

PRESUMPTIONS IN CRIMINAL CASES

[Not enacted.]

(a) Scope. Except as otherwise provided by Act of Congress, in criminal cases, presumptions against an accused, recognized at common law or created by statute, including statutory provisions that certain facts are prima facie evidence of other facts or of guilt, are governed by this rule.

(b) Submission to jury. The judge is not authorized to direct the jury to find a presumed fact against the accused. When the presumed fact establishes guilt or is an element of the offense or negatives a defense, the judge may submit the question of guilt or of the existence of the presumed fact to the jury, if, but only if, a reasonable juror on the evidence as a whole, including the evidence of the basic facts, could find guilt or the presumed fact beyond a reasonable doubt. When the presumed fact has a lesser effect, its existence may be submitted to the jury if the basic facts are supported by substantial evidence, or are otherwise established, unless the evidence as a whole negatives the existence of the presumed fact.

(c) Instructing the jury. Whenever the existence of a presumed fact against the accused is submitted to the jury, the judge shall give an instruction that the law declares that the jury may regard the basic facts as sufficient evidence of the presumed fact but does not require it to do so. In addition, if the presumed fact establishes guilt or is an element of the offense or negatives a defense, the judge shall instruct the jury that its existence must, on all the evidence, be proved beyond a reasonable doubt.

Note by Federal Judicial Center

The foregoing rule prescribed by the Supreme Court was deleted from the rules enacted by the Congress.

Advisory Committee's Note

Subdivision (a). This rule is based largely upon A.L.I. Model Penal Code § 1.12(5) P.O.D. (1962) and United States v. Gainey, 380 U.S. 63, 85 S.Ct. 754, 13 L.Ed.2d 658 (1965). While the rule, unlike the Model Penal Code provision, spells out the effect of common law presumptions as well as those created by statute, cases involving the latter are no doubt of more frequent occurrence. Congress has enacted numerous provisions to lessen the burden of the prosecution, principally though not exclusively in the fields of narcotics control and taxation of liquor. Occasionally, in the pattern of the usual common law treatment of such matters as insanity, they take the form of assigning to the defense the responsibility of raising specified matters as affirmative defenses which are not within the scope of these rules. See Comment, A.L.I. Model Penal Code § 1.13, T.D. No. 4 (1955). In other instances they assume a variety of forms which are the concern of this rule. The provision may be that proof of a specified fact (possession or presence) is sufficient to authorize conviction. 26 U.S.C. § 4704(a), unlawful to buy or sell opium except from original stamped package—absence of stamps from package prima facie evidence of violation by person in possession; 26 U.S.C. § 4724(c), unlawful for person who has not registered and paid special tax to possess narcotics—possession presumptive evidence of violation. Sometimes the qualification is added, "unless the defendant explains the possession [presence] to the satisfaction of the jury." 18 U.S.C. § 545, possession of unlawfully imported goods sufficient for conviction of smuggling, unless explained; 21 U.S.C. § 174, possession sufficient for conviction of buying or selling narcotics known to have been imported unlawfully, unless explained. See also 26 U.S.C. § 5601(a)(1), (a)(4), (a)(8), (b)(1), (b)(2), (b)(4), relating to distilling operations. Another somewhat different pattern makes possession evidence of a particular element of the crime. 21 U.S.C. § 176b, crime to furnish unlawfully imported heroin to juveniles—possession sufficient proof of unlawful importation, unless explained; 50 U.S.C.A. App. § 462(b), unlawful to possess draft card not lawfully issued to holder, with intent to use for purposes of false identification—possession sufficient evidence of intent, unless explained. See also 15 U.S.C. § 902(f), (i).

Differences between the permissible operation of presumptions against the accused in criminal cases and in other situations prevent the formulation of a comprehensive definition of the term "presumption," and none is attempted. Nor do these rules purport to deal with problems of the validity of presumptions except insofar as they may be found reflected in the formulation of permissible procedures.

The presumption of innocence is outside the scope of the rule and unaffected by it.

Subdivisions (b) and (c). It is axiomatic that a verdict cannot be directed against the accused in a criminal case, 9 Wigmore § 2495, p. 312, with the corollary that the judge is without authority to direct the jury to find against the accused as to any element of the crime, A.L.I. Model Penal Code § 1.12(1) P.O.D. (1962). Although arguably the judge could direct the jury to find against the accused as to a lesser fact, the tradition is against it, and this rule makes no use of presumptions to remove any matters from final determination by the jury.

The only distinction made among presumptions under this rule is with respect to the measure of proof required in order to justify submission to the jury. If the effect of the presumption is to establish guilt or an element of the crime or to negative a defense, the measure of proof is the one widely accepted by the Courts of Appeals as the standard for measuring the sufficiency of the evidence in passing on motions for directed verdict (now judgment of acquittal): an acquittal should be directed when reasonable jurymen must have a reasonable doubt. Curley v. United States, 81 U.S.App.D.C. 389, 160 F.2d 229 (1947), cert. denied 331 U.S. 837, 67 S.Ct. 1511, 91 L.Ed. 1850; United States v. Honeycutt, 311 F.2d 660 (4th Cir.1962); Stephens v. United States, 354 F.2d 999 (5th Cir.1965); Lambert v. United States, 261 F.2d 799 (5th Cir.1958); United States v. Leggett, 292 F.2d 423 (6th Cir.1961); Cape v. United States, 283 F.2d 430 (9th Cir.1960); Cartwright v. United States, 335 F.2d 919 (10th Cir.1964). Cf. United States v. Gonzales Castro, 228 F.2d 807 (2d Cir.1956); United States v. Masiello, 235 F.2d 279 (2d Cir.1956), cert. denied Stickel v. United States, 352 U.S. 882, 77 S.Ct. 100, 1 L.Ed.2d 79; United States v. Feinberg, 140 F.2d 592 (2d Cir.1944). But cf. United States v. Arcuri, 282 F.Supp. 347 (E.D.N.Y.1968), aff'd. 405 F.2d 691, cert. denied 395 U.S. 913, 89 S.Ct. 1760, 23 L.Ed.2d 227; United States v. Melillo, 275 F.Supp. 314 (E.D.N.Y.1967). If the presumption operates upon a lesser aspect of the case than the issue of guilt itself or an element of the crime or negativing a defense, the required measure of proof is the less stringent one of substantial evidence, consistently with the attitude usually taken with respect to particular items of evidence. 9 Wigmore § 2497, p. 324.

The treatment of presumptions in the rule is consistent with United States v. Gainey, 380 U.S. 63, 85 S.Ct. 754, 13 L.Ed.2d 658 (1965), where the matter was considered in depth. After sustaining the validity of the provision of 26 U.S.C. § 5601(b)(2) that presence at the site is sufficient to convict of the offense of carrying on the business of distiller without giving bond, unless the presence is explained to the satisfaction of the jury, the Court turned to procedural considerations and reached several conclusions. The power of the judge to withdraw a case from the jury for insufficiency of evidence is left unimpaired; he may submit the case on the basis of presence alone, but he is not required to do so. Nor is he precluded from rendering judgment notwithstanding the verdict. It is proper to tell the jury about the "statutory inference," if they are told it is not conclusive. The jury may still acquit, even if it finds defendant present and his presence is unexplained. [Compare the mandatory character of the instruction condemned in Bollenbach v. United States, 326 U.S. 607, 66 S.Ct. 402, 90 L.Ed. 350 (1946).] To avoid any implication that the statutory language relative to explanation be taken as directing attention to failure of the accused to testify, the better practice, said the Court, would be to instruct the jury that they may draw the inference unless the evidence provides a satisfactory explanation of defendant's presence, omitting any explicit reference to the statute.

The Final Report of the National Commission on Reform of Federal Criminal Laws § 103(4) and (5)(1971) contains a careful formulation of the consequences of a statutory presumption with an alternative formulation set forth in the Comment thereto, and also of the effect of a prima facie case. In the criminal code there proposed, the terms "presumption" and "prima facie case" are used with precision and with reference to these meanings. In the federal criminal law as it stands today, these terms are not used with precision. Moreover, common law presumptions continue. Hence it is believed that the rule here proposed is better adapted to the present situation until such time as the Congress enacts legislation covering the subject, which the rule takes into account. If the subject of common law presumptions is not covered by legislation, the need for the rule in that regard will continue.

Report of House Committee on the Judiciary

Rule 303, as submitted by the Supreme Court was directed to the issues of when, in criminal cases, a court may submit a presumption to a jury and the type of instruction it should give. The Committee deleted this Rule since the subject of presumptions in criminal cases is addressed in detail in bills now pending before the Committee to revise the federal criminal code. The Committee determined to consider this question in the course of its study of these proposals.

Rule 406.

HABIT; ROUTINE PRACTICE

[Subdivision (b) not enacted.]

(b) Method of proof. Habit or routine practice may be proved by testimony in the form of an opinion or by specific instances of conduct sufficient in number to warrant a finding that the habit existed or that the practice was routine.

Advisory Committee's Note

Subdivision (b). Permissible methods of proving habit or routine conduct include opinion and specific instances sufficient in number to warrant a finding that the habit or routine practice in fact existed. Opinion evidence must be "rationally based on the perception of the witness" and helpful, under the provisions of Rule 701. Proof by specific instances may be controlled by the overriding provisions of Rule 403 for exclusion on grounds of prejudice, confusion, misleading the jury, or waste of time. Thus the illustrations following A.L.I. Model Code of Evidence Rule 307 suggests the possibility of admitting testimony by W that on numerous occasions he had been with X when X crossed a railroad track and that on each occasion X had first stopped and looked in both directions, but discretion to exclude offers of 10 witnesses, each testifying to a different occasion.

Rule 406   *DELETED MATERIALS*

Similar provisions for proof by opinion or specific instances are found in Uniform Rule 50 and Kansas Code of Civil Procedure § 60–450. New Jersey Rule 50 provides for proof by specific instances but is silent as to opinion. The California Evidence Code is silent as to methods of proving habit, presumably proceeding on the theory that any method is relevant and all relevant evidence is admissible unless otherwise provided. Tentative Recommendation and a Study Relating to the Uniform Rules of Evidence (Art. VI. Extrinsic Policies Affecting Admissibility), Rep., Rec. & Study, Cal. Law Rev. Comm'n, 620 (1964).

Report of House Committee on the Judiciary

[Reasons for deleting subdivision (b) are stated in the report, which is set forth in the main text under rule 406, supra.]

Rule 501.

PRIVILEGES RECOGNIZED ONLY AS PROVIDED

[Not enacted.]

Except as otherwise required by the Constitution of the United States or provided by Act of Congress, and except as provided in these rules or in other rules adopted by the Supreme Court, no person has a privilege to:

(1) Refuse to be a witness; or

(2) Refuse to disclose any matter; or

(3) Refuse to produce any object or writing; or

(4) Prevent another from being a witness or disclosing any matter or producing any object or writing.

Advisory Committee's Note

No attempt is made in these rules to incorporate the constitutional provisions which relate to the admission and exclusion of evidence, whether denominated as privileges or not. The grand design of these provisions does not readily lend itself to codification. The final reference must be the provisions themselves and the decisions construing them. Nor is formulating a rule an appropriate means of settling unresolved constitutional questions.

Similarly, privileges created by act of Congress are not within the scope of these rules. These privileges do not assume the form of broad principles; they are the product of resolving particular problems in particular terms. Among them are included such provisions as 13 U.S.C. § 9, generally prohibiting official disclosure of census information and conferring a privileged status on retained copies of census reports; 42 U.S.C. § 2000e–5(a), making inadmissible in evidence anything said or done during Equal Employment Opportunity conciliation proceeding; 42 U.S.C. § 2240, making required reports of incidents by nuclear facility licensees inadmissible in actions for damages; 45 U.S.C. §§ 33, 41, similarly as to reports of accidents by railroads; 49 U.S.C. § 1441(e), declaring C.A.B. accident investigation reports inadmissible in actions for damages. The rule leaves them undisturbed.

The reference to other rules adopted by the Supreme Court makes clear that provisions relating to privilege in those rules will continue in operation. See, for example, the "work product" immunity against discovery spelled out under the Rules of Civil Procedure in Hickman v. Taylor, 329 U.S. 495, 67 S.Ct. 385, 91 L.Ed. 451 (1947), now formalized in revised Rule 26(b)(3) of the Rules of Civil Procedure, and the secrecy of grand jury proceedings provided by Criminal Rule 6.

With respect to privileges created by state law, these rules in some instances grant them greater status than has heretofore been the case by according them recognition in federal criminal proceedings, bankruptcy, and federal question litigation. See Rules 502 and 510. There is, however, no provision generally adopting state-created privileges.

In federal criminal prosecutions the primacy of federal law as to both substance and procedure has been undoubted. See, for example, United States v. Krol, 374 F.2d 776 (7th Cir.1967), sustaining the admission in a federal prosecution of evidence obtained by electronic eavesdropping, despite a state statute declaring the use of these devices unlawful and evidence obtained therefrom inadmissible. This primacy includes matters of privilege. As stated in 4 Barron, Federal Practice and Procedure § 2151, p. 175 (1951):

> "The determination of the question whether a matter is privileged is governed by federal decisions and the state statutes or rules of evidence have no application."

In Funk v. United States, 290 U.S. 371, 54 S.Ct. 212, 78 L.Ed. 369 (1933), the Court had considered the competency of a wife to testify for her husband and concluded that, absent congressional action or direction, the federal courts were to follow the common law as they saw it "in accordance with present day standards of wisdom and justice." And in Wolfle v. United States, 291 U.S. 7, 54 S.Ct. 279, 78 L.Ed. 617 (1934), the Court said with respect to the standard appropriate in determining a claim of privilege for an alleged confidential communication between spouses in a federal criminal prosecution:

> "So our decision here, in the absence of Congressional legislation on the subject, is to be controlled by common law principles, not by local statute." Id., 13, 54 S.Ct. at 280.

On the basis of Funk and Wolfle, the Advisory Committee on Rules of Criminal Procedure formulated Rule 26, which was adopted by the Court. The pertinent part of the rule provided:

> "The ... privileges of witnesses shall be governed, except when an act of Congress or these rules otherwise provide, by the principles of the common law as they may be interpreted ... in the light of reason and experience."

As regards bankruptcy, section 21(a) of the Bankruptcy Act provides for examination of the bankrupt and his spouse concerning the acts, conduct, or property of the bankrupt. The Act limits examination of the spouse to business transacted by her or to which she is a party but provides "That the spouse may be so examined, any law of the United States or of any State to the contrary notwithstanding." 11 U.S.C. § 44(a). The effect of the quoted language is clearly to override any conflicting state rule of incompetency or privilege against spousal testimony. A fair reading would also indicate an overriding of any contrary state rule of privileged confidential spousal communications. Its validity has never been questioned and seems most unlikely to be. As to other privileges, the suggestion has been made that state law applies, though with little citation of authority. 2 Moore's Collier on Bankruptcy ¶ 21.13, p. 297 (14th ed. 1961). This position seems to be contrary to the expression of the Court in McCarthy v. Arndstein, 266 U.S. 34, 39, 45 S.Ct. 16, 16, 69 L.Ed. 158 (1924), which speaks in the pattern of Rule 26 of the Federal Rules of Criminal Procedure:

> "There is no provision [in the Bankruptcy Act] prescribing the rules by which the examination is to be governed. These are, impliedly, the general rules governing the admissibility of evidence and the competency and compellability of witnesses."

With respect to federal question litigation, the supremacy of federal law may be less clear, yet indications that state privileges are inapplicable preponderate in the circuits. In re Albert Lindley Lee Memorial Hospital, 209 F.2d 122 (2d Cir.1953), cert. denied Cincotta v. United States, 347 U.S. 960, 74 S.Ct. 709, 98 L.Ed. 1104; Colton v. United States, 306 F.2d 633 (2d Cir.1962); Falsone v. United States, 205 F.2d 734 (5th Cir.1953); Fraser v. United States, 145 F.2d 139 (6th Cir.1944), cert. denied 324 U.S. 849, 65 S.Ct. 684, 89 L.Ed. 1409; United States v. Brunner, 200 F.2d 276 (6th Cir.1952). Contra, Baird v. Koerner, 279 F.2d 623 (9th Cir.1960). Additional decisions of district courts are collected in Annot., 95 A.L.R.2d 320, 336. While a number of the cases arise from administrative income tax investigations, they nevertheless support the broad proposition of the inapplicability of state privileges in federal proceedings.

In view of these considerations, it is apparent that, to the extent that they accord state privileges standing in federal criminal cases, bankruptcy, and federal question cases, the rules go beyond what previously has been thought necessary or proper.

On the other hand, in diversity cases, or perhaps more accurately cases in which state law furnishes the rule of decision, the rules avoid giving state privileges the effect which substantial authority has thought necessary and proper. Regardless of what might once have been thought to be the command of Erie R. Co. v. Tompkins, 304 U.S. 64, 58 S.Ct. 817, 82 L.Ed. 1188 (1938), as to observance of state created privileges in diversity cases, Hanna v. Plumer, 380 U.S. 460, 85 S.Ct. 1136, 14 L.Ed.2d 8 (1965), is believed to locate the problem in the area of choice rather than necessity. Wright, Procedural Reform: Its Limitations and Its Future, 1 Ga.L.Rev. 563, 572–573 (1967). Contra, Republic Gear Co. v. Borg–Warner Corp., 381 F.2d 551, 555, n. 2 (2d Cir.1967), and see authorities there cited. Hence all significant policy factors need to be considered in order that the choice may be a wise one.

The arguments advanced in favor of recognizing state privileges are: a state privilege is an essential characteristic of a relationship or status created by state law and thus is substantive in the Erie sense; state policy ought not to be frustrated by the accident of diversity; the allowance or denial of a privilege is so likely to affect the outcome of litigation as to encourage forum selection on that basis, not a proper function of diversity jurisdiction. There are persuasive answers to these arguments.

(1) As to the question of "substance," it is true that a privilege commonly represents an aspect of a relationship created and defined by a State. For

example, a confidential communications privilege is often an incident of marriage. However, in litigation involving the relationship itself, the privilege is not ordinarily one of the issues. In fact, statutes frequently make the communication privilege inapplicable in cases of divorce. McCormick § 88, p. 177. The same is true with respect to the attorney-client privilege when the parties to the relationship have a falling out. The reality of the matter is that privilege is called into operation, not when the relation giving rise to the privilege is being litigated, but when the litigation involves something substantively devoid of relation to the privilege. The appearance of privilege in the case is quite by accident, and its effect is to block off the tribunal from a source of information. Thus its real impact is on the method of proof in the case, and in comparison any substantive aspect appears tenuous.

(2) By most standards, criminal prosecutions are attended by more serious consequences than civil litigation, and it must be evident that the criminal area has the greatest sensitivity where privilege is concerned. Nevertheless, as previously noted, state privileges traditionally have given way in federal criminal prosecutions. If a privilege is denied in the area of greatest sensitivity, it tends to become illusory as a significant aspect of the relationship out of which it arises. For example, in a state having by statute an accountant's privilege, only the most imperceptible added force would be given the privilege by putting the accountant in a position to assure his client that, while he could not block disclosure in a federal criminal prosecution, he could do so in diversity cases as well as in state court proceedings. Thus viewed, state interest in privilege appears less substantial than at first glance might seem to be the case.

Moreover, federal interest is not lacking. It can scarcely be contended that once diversity is invoked the federal government no longer has a legitimate concern in the quality of judicial administration conducted under its aegis. The demise of conformity and the adoption of the Federal Rules of Civil Procedure stand as witness to the contrary.

(3) A large measure of forum shopping is recognized as legitimate in the American judicial system. Subject to the limitations of jurisdiction and the relatively modest controls imposed by venue provisions and the doctrine of forum non conveniens, plaintiffs are allowed in general a free choice of forum. Diversity jurisdiction has as its basic purpose the giving of a choice, not only to plaintiffs but, in removal situations, also to defendants. In principle, the basis of the choice is the supposed need to escape from local prejudice. If the choice were tightly confined to that basis, then complete conformity to local procedure as well as substantive law would be required. This, of course, is not the case, and the choice may in fact be influenced by a wide range of factors. As Dean Ladd has pointed out, a litigant may select the federal court "because of the federal procedural rules, the liberal discovery provisions, the quality of jurors expected in the federal court, the respect held for federal judges, the control of federal judges over a trial, the summation and comment upon the weight of evidence by the judge, or the authority to grant a new trial if the judge regards the verdict against the weight of the evidence." Ladd, Privileges, 1969 Ariz.St.L.J. 555, 564. Present Rule 43(a) of the Civil Rules specifies a broader range of admissibility in federal than in state courts and makes no exception for diversity cases. Note should also be taken that Rule 26(b)(2) of the Rules of Civil Procedure, as revised, allows discovery to be had of liability insurance, without regard to local state law upon the subject.

When attention is directed to the practical dimensions of the problem, they are found not to be great. The privileges affected are few in number. Most states provide a physician-patient privilege; the proposed rules limit the privilege to a psychotherapist-patient relationship. See Advisory Committee's Note to Rule 504. The area of marital privilege under the proposed rules is narrower than in most states. See Rule 505. Some states recognize privileges for journalists and accountants; the proposed rules do not.

Physician-patient is the most widely recognized privilege not found in the proposed rules. As a practical matter it was largely eliminated in diversity cases when Rule 35 of the Rules of Civil Procedure became effective in 1938. Under that rule, a party physically examined pursuant to court order, by requesting and obtaining a copy of the report or by taking the deposition of the examiner, waives any privilege regarding the testimony of every other person who has examined him in respect of the same condition. While waiver may be avoided by neither requesting the report nor taking the examiner's deposition, the price is one which most litigant-patients are probably not prepared to pay.

Rule 502.

REQUIRED REPORTS PRIVILEGED BY STATUTE

[Not enacted.]

A person, corporation, association, or other organization or entity, either public or private, making a return or report required by law to be made has a privilege to refuse to disclose and to prevent any other person from disclosing the return or report, if the law requiring it to be made so provides. A public officer or agency to whom a return or report is required by law to be made has a privilege to refuse to disclose the return or report if the law requiring it to be made so provides. No privilege exists under this rule in actions involving perjury, false statements, fraud in the return or report, or other failure to comply with the law in question.

Advisory Committee's Note

Statutes which require the making of returns or reports sometimes confer on the reporting party a privilege against disclosure, commonly coupled with a prohibition against disclosure by the officer to whom the report is made. Some of the federal statutes of this kind are mentioned in the Advisory Committee's Note to Rule 501, supra. See also the Note to Rule 402, supra. A provision against disclosure may be included in a statute for a variety of reasons, the chief of which are probably assuring the validity of the statute against claims of self-incrimination, honoring the privilege against self-incrimination, and encouraging the furnishing of the required information by assuring privacy.

These statutes, both state and federal, may generally be assumed to embody policies of significant dimension. Rule 501 insulates the federal provisions against disturbance by these rules; the present rule reiterates a result commonly specified in federal statutes and extends its application to state statutes of similar character. Illustrations of the kinds of returns and reports contemplated by the rule appear in the cases, in which a reluctance to compel disclosure is manifested. In re Reid, 155 F. 933 (E.D.Mich.1906), assessor not compelled to produce bankrupt's property tax return in view of statute forbidding disclosure; In re Valecia Condensed Milk Co., 240 F. 310 (7th Cir.1917), secretary of state tax commission not compelled to produce bankrupt's income tax returns in violation of statute; Herman Bros. Pet Supply, Inc. v. N.L.R.B., 360 F.2d 176 (6th Cir.1966), subpoena denied for production of reports to state employment security commission prohibited by statute, in proceeding for back wages. And see the discussion of motor vehicle accident reports in Krizak v. W.C. Brooks & Sons, Inc., 320 F.2d 37, 42–43 (4th Cir.1963). Cf. In re Hines, 69 F.2d 52 (2d Cir.1934).

Rule 503.

LAWYER–CLIENT PRIVILEGE

[Not enacted.]

(a) Definitions. As used in this rule:

(1) A "client" is a person, public officer, or corporation, association, or other organization or entity, either public or private, who is rendered professional legal services by a lawyer, or who consults a lawyer with a view to obtaining professional legal services from him.

(2) A "lawyer" is a person authorized, or reasonably believed by the client to be authorized, to practice law in any state or nation.

(3) A "representative of the lawyer" is one employed to assist the lawyer in the rendition of professional legal services.

(4) A communication is "confidential" if not intended to be disclosed to third persons other than those to whom disclosure is in furtherance of the rendition of professional legal services to the client or those reasonably necessary for the transmission of the communication.

(b) General rule of privilege. A client has a privilege to refuse to disclose and to prevent any other person from disclosing confidential communications made for the purpose of facilitating the rendition of professional legal services to the client, (1) between himself or his representative and his lawyer or his lawyer's representative, or (2) between his lawyer and the lawyer's representative, or (3) by him or his lawyer to a lawyer representing another in a matter of common interest, or (4) between representatives of the client or between the client and a representative of the client, or (5) between lawyers representing the client.

(c) Who may claim the privilege. The privilege may be claimed by the client, his guardian or conservator, the personal representative of a deceased client, or the successor, trustee, or similar representative of a corporation, association, or other organization, whether or not in existence. The person who was the lawyer at the time of the communication may claim the privilege but only on behalf of the client. His authority to do so is presumed in the absence of evidence to the contrary.

(d) Exceptions. There is no privilege under this rule:

(1) Furtherance of crime or fraud. If the services of the lawyer were sought or obtained to enable or aid anyone to commit or plan to commit what the client knew or reasonably should have known to be a crime or fraud; or

(2) Claimants through same deceased client. As to a communication relevant to an issue between parties who claim through the same deceased client, regardless of whether the claims are by testate or intestate succession or by *inter vivos* transaction; or

(3) Breach of duty by lawyer or client. As to a communication relevant to an issue of breach of duty by the lawyer to his client or by the client to his lawyer; or

(4) Document attested by lawyer. As to a communication relevant to an issue concerning an attested document to which the lawyer is an attesting witness: or

(5) Joint clients. As to a communication relevant to a matter of common interest between two or more clients if the communication was made by any of them to a lawyer retained or consulted in common, when offered in an action between any of the clients.

Advisory Committee's Note

Subdivision (a). (1) The definition of "client" includes governmental bodies, Connecticut Mutual Life Ins. Co. v. Shields, 18 F.R.D. 448 (S.D.N.Y. 1955); People ex rel. Department of Public Works v. Glen Arms Estate, Inc., 230 Cal.App.2d 841, 41 Cal.Rptr. 303 (1964); Rowley v. Ferguson, 48 N.E.2d 243 (Ohio App.1942); and corporations, Radiant Burners, Inc. v. American Gas Assn., 320 F.2d 314 (7th Cir.1963). Contra, Gardner, A Personal Privilege for Communications of Corporate Clients—Paradox or Public Policy, 40 U.Det.L.J. 299, 323, 376 (1963). The definition also extends the status of client to one consulting a lawyer preliminarily with a view to retaining him, even though actual employment does not result. McCormick, § 92, p. 184. The client need not be involved in litigation; the rendition of legal service or advice under any circumstances suffices. 8 Wigmore § 2294 (McNaughton Rev.1961). The services must be professional legal services; purely business or personal matters do not qualify. McCormick § 92, p. 184.

The rule contains no definition of "representative of the client." In the opinion of the Advisory Committee, the matter is better left to resolution by decision on a case-by-case basis. The most restricted position is the "control group" test, limiting the category to persons with authority to seek and act upon legal advice for the client. See, e.g., City of Philadelphia v. Westinghouse Electric Corp., 210 F.Supp. 483 (E.D.Pa.1962), mandamus and prohibition denied sub nom. General Electric Co. v. Kirkpatrick, 312 F.2d 742 (3d Cir.), cert. denied 372 U.S. 943, 83 S.Ct. 937, 9 L.Ed.2d 969; Garrison v. General Motors Corp., 213 F.Supp. 515 (S.D.Cal.1963); Hogan v. Zletz, 43 F.R.D. 308 (N.D.Okla.1967), aff'd sub nom. Natta v. Hogan, 392 F.2d 686 (10th Cir.1968); Day v. Illinois Power Co., 50 Ill.App.2d 52, 199 N.E.2d 802 (1964). Broader formulations are found in other decisions. See, e.g., United States v. United Shoe Machinery Corp., 89 F.Supp. 357 (D.Mass.1950); Zenith Radio Corp. v. Radio Corp. of America, 121 F.Supp. 792 (D.Del.1954); Harper & Row Publishers, Inc. v. Decker, 423 F.2d 487 (7th Cir.1970), aff'd without opinion by equally divided court 400 U.S. 348, 91 S.Ct. 479, 27 L.Ed.2d 433 (1971), reh. denied 401 U.S. 950, 91 S.Ct. 917, 28 L.Ed.2d 234; D.I. Chadbourne, Inc. v. Superior Court, 60 Cal.2d 723, 36 Cal.Rptr. 468, 388 P.2d 700 (1964). Cf. Rucker v. Wabash R. Co., 418 F.2d 146 (7th Cir.1969). See, generally, Simon, The Attorney–Client Privilege as Applied to Corporations, 65 Yale L.J. 953, 956–966 (1956); Note, Attorney–Client Privilege for Corporate Clients: The Control Group Test, 84 Harv.L.Rev. 424 (1970).

Editorial Note

In Upjohn Co. v. United States, 449 U.S. 383, 101 S.Ct. 677, 66 L.Ed.2d 584 (1981), the Supreme Court rejected the narrow "control group test" applied by the court below.

Advisory Committee's Note

The status of employees who are used in the process of communicating, as distinguished from those who are parties to the communication, is treated in paragraph (4) of subdivision (a) of the rule.

(2) A "lawyer" is a person licensed to practice law in any state or nation. There is no requirement that the licensing state or nation recognize the attorney-client privilege, thus avoiding excursions into conflict of laws questions. "Lawyer" also includes a person reasonably believed to be a lawyer. For similar provisions, see California Evidence Code § 950.

(3) The definition of "representative of the lawyer" recognizes that the lawyer may, in rendering legal services, utilize the services of assistants in addition to those employed in the process of communicating. Thus the definition includes an expert employed to assist in rendering legal advice. United States v. Kovel, 296 F.2d 918 (2d Cir.1961) (accountant). Cf. Himmelfarb v. United States, 175 F.2d 924 (9th Cir.1949). It also includes an expert employed to assist in the planning and conduct of litigation, though not one employed to testify as a witness. Lalance & Grosjean Mfg. Co. v. Haberman Mfg. Co., 87 Fed. 563 (S.D.N.Y.1898), and see revised Civil Rule 26(b)(4). The definition does not, however, limit "representative of the lawyer" to experts. Whether his compensation is derived immediately from the lawyer or the client is not material.

(4) The requisite confidentiality of communication is defined in terms of intent. A communication made in public or meant to be relayed to outsiders or which is divulged by the client to third persons can scarcely be considered confidential. McCormick § 95. The intent is inferable from the circumstances. Unless intent to disclose is apparent, the attorney-client communication is confidential. Taking or failing to take precautions may be considered as bearing on intent.

Practicality requires that some disclosure be allowed beyond the immediate circle of lawyer-client and their representatives without impairing confidentiality. Hence the definition allows disclosure to persons "to whom disclosure is in furtherance of the rendition of professional legal services to the client," contemplating those in such relation to the client as "spouse, parent, business associate, or joint client." Comment, California Evidence Code § 952.

Disclosure may also be made to persons "reasonably necessary for the transmission of the communication," without loss of confidentiality.

Subdivision (b). Sets forth the privilege, using the previously defined terms: client, lawyer, representative of the lawyer, and confidential communication.

Substantial authority has in the past allowed the eavesdropper to testify to overheard privileged conversations and has admitted intercepted privileged letters. Today, the evolution of more sophisticated techniques of eavesdropping and interception calls for abandonment of this position. The rule accordingly adopts a policy of protection against these kinds of invasion of the privilege.

The privilege extends to communications (1) between client or his representative and lawyer or his representative, (2) between lawyer and lawyer's representative, (3) by client or his lawyer to a lawyer representing another in a matter of common interest, (4) between representatives of the client or the client and a representative of the client, and (5) between lawyers representing the client. All these communications must be specifically for the purpose of obtaining legal services for the client; otherwise the privilege does not attach.

The third type of communication occurs in the "joint defense" or "pooled information" situation, where different lawyers represent clients who have some interests in common. In Chahoon v. Commonwealth, 62 Va. 822 (1871), the court said that the various clients might have retained one attorney to represent all; hence everything said at a joint conference was privileged, and one of the clients could prevent another from disclosing what the other had himself said. The result seems to be incorrect in overlooking a frequent reason for retaining different attorneys by the various clients, namely actually or potentially conflicting interests in addition to the common interest which brings them together. The needs of these cases seem better to be met by allowing each client a privilege as to his own statements. Thus if all resist disclosure, none will occur. Continental Oil Co. v. United States, 330 F.2d 347 (9th Cir.1964). But, if for reasons of his own, a client wishes to disclose his own statements made at the joint conference, he should be permitted to do so, and the rule is to that effect. The rule does not apply to situations where there is no common interest to be promoted by a joint consultation, and the parties meet on a purely adversary basis. Vance v. State, 190 Tenn. 521, 230 S.W.2d 987 (1950), cert. denied 339 U.S. 988, 70 S.Ct. 1010, 94 L.Ed. 1389. Cf. Hunydee v. United States, 355 F.2d 183 (9th Cir.1965).

Subdivision (c). The privilege is, of course, that of the client, to be claimed by him or by his personal representative. The successor of a dissolved corporate client may claim the privilege. California Evidence Code § 953; New Jersey Evidence Rule 26(1). Contra, Uniform Rule 26(1).

The lawyer may not claim the privilege on his own behalf. However, he may claim it on behalf of the client. It is assumed that the ethics of the profession will require him to do so except under most unusual circumstances. American Bar Association, Canons of Professional Ethics, Canon 37. His authority to make the claim is presumed unless there is evidence to the contrary, as would be the case if the client were now a party to litigation in which the question arose and were represented by other counsel. Ex parte Lipscomb, 111 Tex. 409, 239 S.W. 1101 (1922).

Subdivision (d). In general incorporates well established exceptions.

(1) The privilege does not extend to advice in aid of future wrongdoing. 8 Wigmore § 2298 (McNaughton Rev.1961). The wrongdoing need not be that of the client. The provision that the client knew or reasonably should have known of the criminal or fraudulent nature of the act is designed to protect the client who is erroneously advised that a proposed action is within the law. No preliminary finding that sufficient evidence aside from the communication has been introduced to warrant a finding that the services were sought to enable the commission of a wrong is required. Cf. Clark v. United States, 289 U.S. 1, 15–16, 53 S.Ct. 465, 469–470, 77 L.Ed. 993 (1933); Uniform Rule 26(2)(a). While any general exploration of what transpired between attorney and client would, of course, be inappropriate it is wholly feasible, either at the discovery stage or during trial to focus the inquiry by specific questions as to avoid any broad inquiry into attorney-client communications. Numerous cases reflect this approach.

(2) Normally the privilege survives the death of the client and may be asserted by his representative. Subdivision (c), supra. When, however, the identity of the person who steps into the client's shoes is in issue, as in a will contest, the identity of the person entitled to claim the privilege remains undetermined until the conclusion of litigation. The choice is thus between allowing both sides or neither to assert the privilege, with authority and reason favoring the latter view. McCormick § 98; Uniform Rule 26(2)(b); California Evidence Code § 957; Kansas Code of Civil Procedure § 60–426(b)(2); New Jersey Evidence Rule 26(2)(b).

(3) The exception is required by considerations of fairness and policy when questions arise out of dealings between attorney and client as in cases of controversy over attorney's fees, claims of inadequacy, of representation, or charges of professional misconduct. McCormick § 95; Uniform Rule 26(2)(c); California Evidence Code § 958; Kansas Code of Civil Procedure § 60–426(b)(3); New Jersey Evidence Rule 26(2)(c).

(4) When the lawyer acts as attesting witness, the approval of the client to his so doing may safely be assumed, and waiver of the privilege as to any relevant lawyer-client communications is a proper result. McCormick § 92, p. 184; Uniform Rule 26(2)(d); California Evidence Code § 959; Kansas Code of Civil Procedure § 60–426(b)(d) [sic].

(5) The subdivision states existing law. McCormick § 95, pp. 192–193. For similar provisions, see Uniform Rule 26(2)(e); California Evidence Code § 962; Kansas Code of Civil Procedure § 60–426(b)(4); New Jersey Evidence Rule 26(2). The situation with which this provision deals is to be distinguished from the case of clients with a common interest who retain different lawyers. See subdivision (b)(3) of this rule, supra.

Rule 504.

PSYCHOTHERAPIST–PATIENT PRIVILEGE

[Not enacted.]

(a) Definitions.

(1) A "patient" is a person who consults or is examined or interviewed by a psychotherapist.

(2) A "psychotherapist" is (A) a person authorized to practice medicine in any state or nation, or reasonably believed by the patient so to be, while engaged in the diagnosis or treatment of a mental or emotional condition, including drug addiction, or (B) a person licensed or certified as a psychologist under the laws of any state or nation, while similarly engaged.

(3) A communication is "confidential" if not intended to be disclosed to third persons other than those present to further the interest of the patient in the consultation, examination, or interview, or persons reasonably necessary for the transmission of the communication, or persons who are participating in the diagnosis and treatment under the direction of the psychotherapist, including members of the patient's family.

(b) General rule of privilege. A patient has a privilege to refuse to disclose and to prevent any other person from disclosing confidential communications, made for the purposes of diagnosis or treatment of his mental or emotional condition, including drug addiction, among himself, his psychotherapist, or persons who are participating in the diagnosis or treatment under the direction of the psychotherapist, including members of the patient's family.

(c) Who may claim the privilege. The privilege may be claimed by the patient, by his guardian or conservator, or by the personal representative of a deceased patient. The person who was the psychotherapist may claim the privilege but only on behalf of the patient. His authority so to do is presumed in the absence of evidence to the contrary.

(d) Exceptions.

(1) Proceedings for hospitalization. There is no privilege under this rule for communications relevant to an issue in proceedings to hospitalize the patient for mental illness, if the psychotherapist in the course of diagnosis or treatment has determined that the patient is in need of hospitalization.

(2) Examination by order of judge. If the judge orders an examination of the mental or emotional condition of the patient, communications made in the course thereof are not privileged under this rule with respect to the particular purpose for which the examination is ordered unless the judge orders otherwise.

(3) Condition an element of claim or defense. There is no privilege under this rule as to communications relevant to an issue of the mental or emotional condition of the patient in any proceeding in which he relies upon the condition as an element of his claim or defense, or, after the patient's death, in any proceeding in which any party relies upon the condition as an element of his claim or defense.

Advisory Committee's Note

The rules contain no provision for a general physician-patient privilege. While many states have by statute created the privilege, the exceptions which have been found necessary in order to obtain information required by the public interest or to avoid fraud are so numerous as to leave little if any basis for the privilege. Among the exclusions from the statutory privilege, the following may be enumerated; communications not made for purposes of diagnosis and treatment; commitment and restoration proceedings; issues as to wills or otherwise between parties claiming by succession from the patient; actions on insurance policies; required reports (venereal diseases, gunshot wounds, child abuse); communications in furtherance of crime or fraud; mental or physical condition put in issue by patient (personal injury cases); malpractice actions; and some or all criminal prosecutions. California, for example, excepts cases in which the patient puts his condition in issue, all criminal proceedings, will and similar contests, malpractice cases, and disciplinary proceedings, as well as certain other situations, thus leaving virtually nothing covered by the privilege. California Evidence Code §§ 990–1007. For other illustrative statutes see Ill.Rev.Stat. 1967, c. 51, § 5.1; N.Y.C.P.L.R. § 4504; N.C.Gen.Stat.1953, § 8–53. Moreover, the possibility of compelling gratuitous disclosure by the physician is foreclosed by his standing to raise the question of relevancy. See Note on "Official Information" Privilege following Rule 509, infra.

The doubts attendant upon the general physician-patient privilege are not present when the relationship is that of psychotherapist and patient. While the common law recognized no general physician-patient privilege, it had indicated a disposition to recognize a psychotherapist-patient privilege, Note, Confidential Communications to a Psychotherapist: A New Testimonial Privilege, 47 Nw. U.L.Rev. 384 (1952), when legislatures began moving into the field.

The case for the privilege is convincingly stated in Report No. 45, Group for the Advancement of Psychiatry 92 (1960):

"Among physicians, the psychiatrist has a special need to maintain confidentiality. His capacity to help his patients is completely dependent upon their willingness and ability to talk freely. This makes it difficult if not impossible for him to function without being able to assure his patients of confidentiality and, indeed, privileged communication. Where there may be exceptions to this general rule . . ., there is wide agreement that confidentiality is a *sine qua non* for successful psychiatric treatment. The relationship may well be likened to that of the priest-penitent or the lawyer-client. Psychiatrists not only explore the very depths of their patients' conscious, but their unconscious feelings and attitudes as well. Therapeutic effectiveness necessitates going beyond a patient's awareness and, in order to do this, it must be possible to communicate freely. A threat to secrecy blocks successful treatment."

A much more extended exposition of the case for the privilege is made in Slovenko, Psychiatry and a Second Look at the Medical Privilege, 6 Wayne L.Rev. 175, 184 (1960), quoted extensively in the careful Tentative Recommendation and Study Relating to the Uniform Rules of Evidence (Article V. Privileges), Cal.Law Rev.Comm'n, 417 (1964). The conclusion is reached that Wigmore's four conditions needed to justify the existence of a privilege are amply satisfied.

Illustrative statutes are Cal.Evidence Code §§ 1010–1026; Ga.Code § 38–418 (1961 Supp.); Conn.Gen.Stat., § 52–146a (1966 Supp.); Ill.Rev.Stat.1967, c. 51, § 5.2.

While many of the statutes simply place the communications on the same basis as those between attorney and client, 8 Wigmore § 2286, n. 23 (McNaughton Rev.1961), basis differences between the two relationships forbid resorting to attorney-client save as a helpful point of departure. Goldstein and Katz, Psychiatrist–Patient Privilege: The GAP Proposal and the Connecticut Statute, 36 Conn.B.J. 175, 182 (1962).

Subdivision (a). (1) The definition of patient does not include a person submitting to examination for scientific purposes. Cf. Cal.Evidence Code § 1101. Attention is directed to 42 U.S.C. 242(a)(2), as amended by the Drug Abuse and Control Act of 1970, P.L. 91–513, authorizing the Secretary of Health, Education, and Welfare to withhold the identity of persons who are the subjects of research on the use and effect of drugs. The rule would leave this provision in full force. See Rule 501.

(2) The definition of psychotherapist embraces a medical doctor while engaged in the diagnosis or treatment of mental or emotional conditions, including drug addiction, in order not to exclude the general practitioner and to avoid the making of needless refined distinctions concerning what is and what is not the practice of psychiatry. The requirement that the psychologist be in fact licensed, and not merely be believed to be so, is believed to be justified by the number of persons, other than psychiatrists, purporting to render psychotherapeutic aid and the variety of their theories. Cal.Law Rev.Comm'n, supra, at pp. 434–437.

The clarification of mental or emotional condition as including drug addiction is consistent with current approaches to drug abuse problems. See, e.g., the definition of "drug dependent person" in 42 U.S.C. 201(q), added by the Drug Abuse Prevention and Control Act of 1970, P.L. 91–513.

(3) Confidential communication is defined in terms conformable with those of the lawyer-client privilege, Rule 503(a)(4), supra, with changes appropriate to the difference in circumstance.

Subdivisions (b) and (c). The lawyer-client rule is drawn upon for the phrasing of the general rule of privilege and the determination of those who may claim it. See Rule 503(b) and (c).

The specific inclusion of communications made for the diagnosis and treatment of drug addiction recognizes the continuing contemporary concern with rehabilitation of drug dependent persons and is designed to implement that policy by encouraging persons in need thereof to seek assistance. The provision is in harmony with Congressional actions in this area. See 42 U.S.C. § 260, providing for voluntary hospitalization of addicts or persons with drug dependence problems and prohibiting use of evidence of admission or treatment in any proceeding against him, and 42 U.S.C. § 3419 providing that in voluntary or involuntary commitment of addicts the results of any hearing, examination, test, or procedure used to determine addiction shall not be used against the patient in any criminal proceeding.

Subdivision (d). The exceptions differ substantially from those of the attorney-client privilege, as a result of the basic differences in the relationships. While it has been argued convincingly that the nature of the psychotherapist-patient relationship demands complete security against legally coerced disclosure in all circumstances, Louisell, The Psychologist in Today's Legal World: Part II, 41 Minn.L.Rev. 731, 746 (1957), the committee of psychiatrists and lawyers who drafted the Connecticut statute concluded that in three instances the need for disclosure was sufficiently great to justify the risk of possible impairment of the relationship. Goldstein and Katz, Psychiatrist–Patient Privilege: The GAP Proposal and the Connecticut Statute, 36 Conn.B.J. 175 (1962). These three exceptions are incorporated in the present rule.

(1) The interests of both patient and public call for a departure from confidentiality in commitment proceedings. Since disclosure is authorized only when the psychotherapist determines that hospitalization is needed, control over disclosure is placed largely in the hands of a person in whom the patient has already manifested confidence. Hence damage to the relationship is unlikely.

(2) In a court ordered examination, the relationship is likely to be an arm's length one, though not necessarily so. In any event, an exception is necessary for the effective utilization of this important and growing procedure. The exception, it will be observed, deals with a court ordered examination rather than with a court appointed psychotherapist. Also, the exception is effective only with respect to the particular purpose for which the examination is ordered. The rule thus conforms with the provisions of 18 U.S.C. § 4244 that no statement made by the accused in the course of an examination into competency to stand trial is admissible on the issue of guilt and of 42 U.S.C. § 3420 that a physician conducting an examination in a drug addiction commitment proceeding is a competent and compellable witness.

(3) By injecting his condition into litigation, the patient must be said to waive the privilege, in fairness and to avoid abuses. Similar considerations prevail after the patient's death.

Rule 505.

HUSBAND–WIFE PRIVILEGE

[Not enacted.]

(a) General rule of privilege. An accused in a criminal proceeding has a privilege to prevent his spouse from testifying against him.

(b) Who may claim the privilege. The privilege may be claimed by the accused or by the spouse on his behalf. The authority of the spouse to do so is presumed in the absence of evidence to the contrary.

(c) Exceptions. There is no privilege under this rule (1) in proceedings in which one spouse is charged with a crime against the person or property of the other or of a child of either, or with a crime against the person or property of a third person committed in the course of committing a crime against the other, or (2) as to matters occurring prior to the marriage, or (3) in proceedings in which a spouse is charged with importing an alien for prostitution or other immoral purpose in violation of 8 U.S.C. § 1328, with transporting a female in interstate commerce for immoral purposes or other offense in violation of 18 U.S.C. §§ 2421–2424, or with violation of other similar statutes.

Advisory Committee's Note

Subdivision (a). Rules of evidence have evolved around the marriage relationship in four respects: (1) incompetency of one spouse to testify for the other; (2) privilege of one spouse not to testify against the other; (3) privilege of one spouse not to have the other testify against him; and (4) privilege against disclosure of confidential communications between spouses, sometimes extended to information learned by virtue of the existence of the relationship. Today these matters are largely governed by statutes.

With the disappearance of the disqualification of parties and interested persons, the basis for spousal incompetency no longer existed, and it, too, virtually disappeared in both civil and criminal actions. Usually reached by statute, this result was reached for federal courts by the process of decision. Funk v. United States, 290 U.S. 371, 54 S.Ct. 212, 78 L.Ed. 369 (1933). These rules contain no recognition of incompetency of one spouse to testify for the other.

While some 10 jurisdictions recognize a privilege not to testify against one's spouse in a criminal case, and a much smaller number do so in civil cases, the great majority recognizes no privilege on the part of the testifying spouse, and this is the position taken by the rule. Compare Wyatt v. United States, 362 U.S. 525, 80 S.Ct. 901, 4 L.Ed.2d 931 (1960), a Mann Act prosecution in which the wife was the victim. The majority opinion held that she could not claim privilege and was compellable to testify. The holding was narrowly based: The Mann Act presupposed that the women with whom it dealt had no independent wills of their own, and this legislative judgment precluded allowing a victim-wife an option whether to testify, lest the policy of the statute be defeated. A vigorous dissent took the view that nothing in the Mann Act required departure from usual doctrine, which was conceived to be one of allowing the injured party to claim or waive privilege.

About 30 jurisdictions recognize a privilege of an accused in a criminal case to prevent his or her spouse from testifying. It is believed to represent the one aspect of marital privilege the continuation of which is warranted. In Hawkins v. United States, 358 U.S. 74, 79 S.Ct. 136, 3 L.Ed.2d 125 (1958) it was sustained. Cf. McCormick § 66; 8 Wigmore § 2228 (McNaughton Rev.1961): Comment, Uniform Rule 23(2).

The rule recognizes no privilege for confidential communications. The traditional justifications for privileges not to testify against a spouse and not to be testified against by one's spouse have been the prevention of marital dissension and the repugnancy of requiring a person to condemn or be condemned by his spouse. 8 Wigmore §§ 2228, 2241 (McNaughton Rev.1961). These considerations bear no relevancy to marital communications. Nor can it be assumed that marital conduct will be affected by a privilege for confidential communications of whose existence the parties in all likelihood are unaware. The other communication privileges, by way of contrast, have as one party a professional person who can be expected to inform the other of the existence of the privilege. Moreover, the relationships from which those privileges arise are essentially and almost exclusively verbal in nature, quite unlike marriage. See Hutchins and Slesinger, Some Observations on the Law of Evidence: Family Relations, 13 Minn.L.Rev. 675 (1929). Cf. McCormick § 90; 8 Wigmore § 2337 (McNaughton Rev.1961).

The parties are not spouses if the marriage was a sham, Lutwak v. United States, 344 U.S. 604, 73 S.Ct. 481, 97 L.Ed. 593 (1953), or they have been divorced, Barsky v. United States, 339 F.2d 180 (9th Cir.1964), and therefore the privilege is not applicable.

Editorial Note

In Trammel v. United States, 445 U.S. 40, 100 S.Ct. 906, 63 L.Ed.2d 186, (1980), the Supreme Court held that the witness spouse, and not the accused, is the holder of the privilege.

Advisory Committee's Note

Subdivision (b). This provision is a counterpart of Rules 503(c), 504(c), and 506(c). Its purpose is to provide a procedure for preventing the taking of the spouse's testimony notably in grand jury proceedings, when the accused is absent and does not know that a situation appropriate for a claim of privilege is presented. If the privilege is not claimed by the spouse, the protection of Rule 512 is available.

Subdivision (c) contains three exceptions to the privilege against spousal testimony in criminal cases.

(1) The need of limitation upon the privilege in order to avoid grave injustice in cases of offenses against the other spouse or a child of either can scarcely be denied. 8 Wigmore § 2239 (McNaughton Rev.1961). The rule therefore disallows any privilege against spousal testimony in these cases and in this respect is in accord with the result reached in Wyatt v. United States, 362 U.S. 525, 80 S.Ct. 901, 4 L.Ed.2d 931 (1960), a Mann Act prosecution, denying the accused the privilege of excluding his wife's testimony, since she was the woman who was transported for immoral purposes.

(2) The second exception renders the privilege inapplicable as to matters occurring prior to the marriage. This provision eliminates the possibility of suppressing testimony by marrying the witness.

(3) The third exception continues and expands established Congressional policy. In prosecutions for importing aliens for immoral purposes, Congress has specifically denied the accused any privilege not to have his spouse testify against him. 8 U.S.C. § 1328. No provision of this nature is included in the Mann Act, and in Hawkins v. United States, 358 U.S. 74, 79 S.Ct. 136, 3 L.Ed.2d 125 (1958), the conclusion was reached that the common law privilege continued. Consistency requires similar results in the two situations. The rule adopts the Congressional approach, as based upon a more realistic appraisal of the marriage relationship in cases of this kind, in preference to the specific result in *Hawkins*. Note the common law treatment of pimping and sexual offenses with third

persons as exceptions to marital privilege. 8 Wigmore § 2239 (McNaughton Rev.1961).

With respect to bankruptcy proceedings, the smallness of the area of spousal privilege under the rule and the general inapplicability of privileges created by state law render unnecessary any special provision for examination of the spouse of the bankrupt, such as that now contained in section 21(a) of the Bankruptcy Act. 11 U.S.C. § 44(a).

For recent statutes and rules dealing with husband-wife privileges, see California Evidence Code §§ 970–973, 980–987; Kansas Code of Civil Procedure §§ 60–423(b), 60–428; New Jersey Evidence Rules 23(2), 28.

Editorial Note

Uniform Rule 504, so numbered because the Uniform Rules (1974) did not adopt a rule comparable to Proposed Federal Rule 502, provides:

(a) Definition. A communication is confidential if it is made privately by any person to his or her spouse and is not intended for disclosure to any other person.

(b) General rule of privilege. An accused in a criminal proceeding has a privilege to prevent his spouse from testifying as to any confidential communication between the accused and the spouse.

(c) Who may claim the privilege. The privilege may be claimed by the accused or by the spouse on behalf of the accused. The authority of the spouse to do so is presumed.

(d) Exceptions. There is no privilege under this rule in a proceeding in which one spouse is charged with a crime against the person or property of (1) the other, (2) a child of either, (3) a person residing in the household of either, or (4) a third person committed in the course of committing a crime against any of them.

Rule 506.

COMMUNICATIONS TO CLERGYMEN

[Not enacted.]

(a) Definitions. As used in this rule:

(1) A "clergyman" is a minister, priest, rabbi, or other similar functionary of a religious organization, or an individual reasonably believed so to be by the person consulting him.

(2) A communication is "confidential" if made privately and not intended for further disclosure except to other persons present in furtherance of the purpose of the communication.

(b) General rule of privilege. A person has a privilege to refuse to disclose and to prevent another from disclosing a confidential communication by the person to a clergyman in his professional character as spiritual adviser.

(c) Who may claim the privilege. The privilege may be claimed by the person, by his guardian or conservator, or by his personal representative if he is deceased. The clergyman may claim the privilege on behalf of the person. His authority so to do is presumed in the absence of evidence to the contrary.

Advisory Committee's Note

The considerations which dictate the recognition of privileges generally seem strongly to favor a privilege for confidential communications to clergymen. During the period when most of the common law privileges were taking shape, no clear-cut privilege for communications between priest and penitent emerged. 8 Wigmore § 2394 (McNaughton Rev.1961). The English political climate of the time may well furnish the explanation. In this country, however, the privilege has been recognized by statute in about two-thirds of the states and occasionally by the common law process of decision. Id., § 2395 Mullen v. United States, 105 U.S.App.D.C. 25, 263 F.2d 275 (1958).

Subdivision (a). Paragraph (1) defines a clergyman as a "minister, priest, rabbi, or other similar functionary of a religious organization." The concept is necessarily broader than that inherent in the ministerial exemption for purposes of Selective Service. See United States v. Jackson, 369 F.2d 936 (4th Cir.1966). However, it is not so broad as to include all self-denominated "ministers." A fair construction of the language requires that the person to whom the status is sought to be attached be regularly engaged in activities conforming at least in a general way with those of a Catholic priest, Jewish rabbi, or minister of an established Protestant denomination, though not necessarily on a full-time basis. No further specification seems possible in view of the lack of licensing and certification procedures for clergymen. However, this lack seems to have occasioned no particular difficulties in connection with the solemnization of marriages, which suggests that none may be anticipated here. For similar definitions of "clergyman" see California Evidence Code § 1030; New Jersey Evidence Rule 29.

The "reasonable belief" provision finds support in similar provisions for lawyer-client in Rule 503 and for psychotherapist-patient in Rule 504. A parallel is also found in the recognition of the validity of marriages performed by unauthorized persons if the parties reasonably believed them legally qualified. Harper and Skolnick, Problems of the Family 153 (Rev.Ed.1962).

(2) The definition of "confidential" communication is consistent with the use of the term in Rule 503(a)(5) for lawyer-client and in Rule 504(a)(3) for psychotherapist-patient, suitably adapted to communications to clergymen.

Subdivision (b). The choice between a privilege narrowly restricted to doctrinally required confessions and a privilege broadly applicable to all confidential communications with a clergyman in his professional character as spiritual adviser has been exercised in favor of the latter. Many clergymen now receive training in marriage counseling and the handling of personality problems. Matters of this kind fall readily into the realm of the spirit. The same considerations which underlie the psychotherapist-patient privilege of Rule 504 suggest a broad application of the privilege for communications to clergymen.

State statutes and rules fall in both the narrow and the broad categories. A typical narrow statute proscribes disclosure of "a confession ... made ... in the course of discipline enjoined by the church to which he belongs." Ariz.Rev.Stats. Ann.1956, § 12–2233. See also California Evidence Code § 1032; Uniform Rule 29. Illustrative of the broader privilege are statutes applying to "information communicated to him in a confidential manner, properly entrusted to him in his professional capacity, and necessary to enable him to discharge the functions of his office according to the usual course of his practice or discipline, wherein such person so communicating ... is seeking spiritual counsel and advice," Fla.Stats. Ann.1960, § 90.241, or to any "confidential communication properly entrusted to him in his professional capacity, and necessary and proper to enable him to discharge the functions of his office according to the usual course of practice or discipline," Iowa Code Ann.1950, § 622.10. See also Ill.Rev.Stats.1967, c. 51, § 48.1; Minn.Stats.Ann.1945, § 595.02(3); New Jersey Evidence Rule 29.

Under the privilege as phrased, the communicating person is entitled to prevent disclosure not only by himself but also by the clergyman and by eavesdroppers. For discussion see Advisory Committee's Note under lawyer-client privilege, Rule 503(b).

The nature of what may reasonably be considered spiritual advice makes it unnecessary to include in the rule a specific exception for communications in furtherance of crime or fraud, as in Rule 503(d)(1).

Subdivision (c) makes clear that the privilege belongs to the communicating person. However, a prima facie authority on the part of the clergyman to claim the privilege on behalf of the person is recognized. The discipline of the particular church and the discreetness of the clergyman are believed to constitute sufficient safeguards for the absent communicating person. See Advisory Committee's Note to the similar provision with respect to attorney-client in Rule 503(c).

Rule 507.

POLITICAL VOTE

[Not enacted.]

Every person has a privilege to refuse to disclose the tenor of his vote at a political election conducted by secret ballot unless the vote was cast illegally.

Advisory Committee's Note

Secrecy in voting is an essential aspect of effective democratic government, insuring free exercise of the franchise and fairness in elections. Secrecy after the ballot has been cast is as essential as secrecy in the act of voting. Nutting, Freedom of Silence: Constitutional Protection Against Governmental Intrusion in Political Affairs, 47 Mich.L.Rev. 181, 191 (1948). Consequently a privilege has long been recognized on the part of a voter to decline to disclose how he voted. Required disclosure would be the exercise of "a kind of inquisitorial power unknown to the principles of our government and constitution, and might be highly injurious to the suffrages of a free people, as well as tending to create cabals and disturbances between contending parties in popular elections." Johnston v. Charleston, 1 Bay 441, 442 (S.C.1795).

The exception for illegally cast votes is a common one under both statutes and case law, Nutting, supra, at p. 192; 8 Wigmore § 2214, p. 163 (McNaughton Rev.1961). The policy considerations which underlie the privilege are not applicable to the illegal voter. However, nothing in the exception purports to foreclose an illegal voter from invoking the privilege against self-incrimination under appropriate circumstances.

For similar provisions, see Uniform Rule 31; California Evidence Code § 1050; Kansas Code of Civil Procedure § 60-431; New Jersey Evidence Rule 31.

Rule 508.

TRADE SECRETS

[Not enacted.]

A person has a privilege, which may be claimed by him or his agent or employee, to refuse to disclose and to prevent other persons from disclosing a trade secret owned by him, if the allowance of the privilege will not tend to conceal fraud or otherwise work injustice. When disclosure is directed, the judge shall take such protective measure as the interests of the holder of the privilege and of the parties and the furtherance of justice may require.

Advisory Committee's Note

While sometimes said not to be a true privilege, a qualified right to protection against disclosure of trade secrets has found ample recognition, and, indeed, a denial of it would be difficult to defend. 8 Wigmore § 2212(3)(McNaughton Rev.1961). And see 4 Moore's Federal Practice ¶¶ 30.12 and 34.15 (2nd ed. 1963 and Supp.1965) and 2A Barron and Holtzoff, Federal Practice and Procedure § 715.1 (Wright ed. 1961). Congressional policy is reflected in the Securities Exchange Act of 1934, 15 U.S.C. § 78x, and the Public Utility Holding Company Act of 1933, id. § 79v, which deny the Securities and Exchange Commission authority to require disclosure of trade secrets or processes in applications and reports. See also Rule 26(c)(7) of the Rules of Civil Procedure, as revised, mentioned further hereinafter.

Illustrative cases raising trade-secret problems are: E.I. Du Pont De Nemours Powder Co. v. Masland, 244 U.S. 100, 37 S.Ct. 575, 61 L.Ed. 1016 (1917), suit to enjoin former employee from using plaintiff's secret processes, countered by defense that many of the processes were well known to the trade; Segal Lock & Hardware Co. v. FTC, 143 F.2d 935 (2d Cir.1944), question whether expert locksmiths employed by FTC should be required to disclose methods used by them in picking petitioner's "pick-proof" locks; Dobson v. Graham, 49 Fed. 17 (E.D.Pa.1889), patent infringement suit in which plaintiff sought to elicit from former employees now in the hire of defendant the respects in which defendant's machinery differed from plaintiff's patented machinery; Putney v. Du Bois Co., 240 Mo.App. 1075, 226 S.W.2d 737 (1950), action for injuries allegedly sustained from using defendant's secret formula dishwashing compound. See 8 Wigmore § 2212(3)(McNaughton Rev.1961); Annot., 17 A.L.R.2d 383; 49 Mich.L.Rev. 133 (1950). The need for accommodation between protecting trade secrcts, on the one hand, and eliciting facts required for full and fair presentation of a case, on the other hand, is apparent. Whether disclosure should be required depends upon a weighing of the competing interests involved against the background of the total situation, including consideration of such factors as the dangers of abuse, good faith, adequacy of protective measures, and the availability of other means of proof.

The cases furnish examples of the bringing of judicial ingenuity to bear upon the problem of evolving protective measures which achieve a degree of control over disclosure. Perhaps the most common is simply to take testimony in camera. Annot., 62 A.L.R.2d 509. Other possibilities include making disclosure to opposing counsel but not to his client, E.I. Du Pont De Nemours Powder Co. v. Masland, 244 U.S. 100, 37 S.Ct. 575, 61 L.Ed. 1016 (1917); making disclosure only to the judge (hearing examiner), Segal Lock & Hardware Co. v. FTC, 143 F.2d 935 (2d Cir.1944); and placing those present under oath not to make disclosure, Paul v. Sinnott, 217 F.Supp. 84 (W.D.Pa.1963).

Rule 26(c) of the Rules of Civil Procedure, as revised, provides that the judge may make "any order which justice requires to protect a party or person from annoyance, embarrassment, oppression, or undue burden or expense, including one or more of the following: ... (7) that a trade secret or other confidential research, development, or commercial information not be disclosed or be disclosed only in a designated way...." While the instant evidence rule extends this underlying policy into the trial, the difference in circumstances between discovery stage and trial may well be such as to require a different ruling at the trial.

For other rules recognizing privilege for trade secrets, see Uniform Rule 32; California Evidence Code § 1060; Kansas Code of Civil Procedure § 60–432; New Jersey Evidence Rule 32.

Rule 509.

SECRETS OF STATE AND OTHER OFFICIAL INFORMATION

[Not enacted.]

(a) Definitions.

(1) Secret of state. A "secret of state" is a governmental secret relating to the national defense or the international relations of the United States.

(2) Official information. "Official information" is information within the custody or control of a department or agency of the government the disclosure of which is shown to be contrary to the public interest and which consists of: (A) intra-governmental opinions or recommendations submitted for consideration in the performance of decisional or policymaking functions, or (B) subject to the provisions of 18 U.S.C. § 3500, investigatory files compiled for law enforcement purposes and not otherwise available, or (C) information within the custody or control of a governmental department or agency whether initiated within the department or agency or acquired by it in its exercise of its official responsibilities and not otherwise available to the public pursuant to 5 U.S.C. § 552.

(b) General rule of privilege. The government has a privilege to refuse to give evidence and to prevent any person from giving evidence upon a showing of reasonable likelihood of danger that the evidence will disclose a secret of state or official information as defined in this rule.

(c) Procedures. The privilege for secrets of state may be claimed only by the chief officer of the government agency or department administering the subject matter which the secret information sought concerns, but the privilege for official information may be asserted by any attorney representing the government. The required showing may be made in whole or in part in the form of a written statement. The judge may hear the matter in chambers, but all counsel are entitled to inspect the claim and showing and to be heard thereon, except that, in the case of secrets of state, the judge upon motion of the government, may permit the government to make the required showing in the above form *in camera*. If the judge sustains the privilege upon a showing *in camera*, the entire text of the government's statements shall be sealed and preserved in the court's records in the event of appeal. In the case of privilege claimed for official information the court may require examination *in camera* of the information itself. The judge may take any protective measure which the interests of the government and the furtherance of justice may require.

(d) Notice to government. If the circumstances of the case indicate a substantial possibility that a claim of privilege would be appropriate but has not been made because of oversight or lack of knowledge, the judge shall give or cause notice to be given to the officer entitled to claim the privilege and shall stay further proceedings a reasonable time to afford opportunity to assert a claim of privilege.

(e) Effect of sustaining claim. If a claim of privilege is sustained in a proceeding to which the government is a party and it appears that another party is thereby deprived of material evidence, the judge shall make any further orders which the interests of justice require, including striking the testimony of a witness, declaring a mistrial, finding against the government upon an issue as to which the evidence is relevant, or dismissing the action.

Advisory Committee's Note

Subdivision (a). (1) The rule embodies the privilege protecting military and state secrets described as "well established in the law of evidence," United States v. Reynolds, 345 U.S. 1, 6, 73 S.Ct. 528, 531, 97 L.Ed. 727 (1953), and as one "the existence of which has never been doubted," 8 Wigmore § 2378, p. 794 (McNaughton Rev.1961).

The use of the term "national defense," without attempt at further elucidation, finds support in the similar usage in statutory provisions relating to the crimes of gathering, transmitting, or losing defense information, and gathering or delivering defense information to aid a foreign government. 18 U.S.C. §§ 793, 794. See also 5 U.S.C. § 1002; 50 U.S.C.App. § 2152(d). In determining whether military or state secrets are involved, due regard will, of course, be given to classification pursuant to executive order.

(2) The rule also recognizes a privilege for specified types of official information and in this respect is designed primarily to resolve questions of the availability to litigants of data in the files of governmental departments and agencies. In view of the lesser danger to the public interest than in cases of military and state secrets, the official information privilege is subject to a generally overriding requirement that disclosure would be contrary to the public interest. It is applicable to three categories of information.

(A) Intergovernmental opinions or recommendations submitted for consideration in the performance of decisional or policy making functions. The policy basis of this aspect of the privilege is found in the desirability of encouraging candor in the exchange of views within the government. Kaiser Aluminum & Chemical Corp. v. United States, 141 Ct.Cl. 38, 157 F.Supp. 939 (1958); Davis v. Braswell Motor Freight Lines, Inc., 363 F.2d 600 (5th Cir.1966); Ackerly v. Ley, 420 F.2d 1336 (D.C.Cir.1969). A privilege of this character is consistent with the Freedom of Information Act, 5 U.S.C. § 552(b)(5), and with the standing of the agency to raise questions of relevancy, though not a party, recognized in such decisions as Boeing Airplane Co. v. Coggeshall, 108 U.S.App.D.C. 106, 280 F.2d 654, 659 (1960)(Renegotiation Board) and Freeman v. Seligson, 132 U.S.App.D.C. 56, 405 F.2d 1326, 1334 (1968)(Secretary of Agriculture).

(B) Investigatory files compiled for law enforcement purposes. This category is expressly made subject to the provisions of the Jencks Act, 18 U.S.C. § 3500, which insulates prior statements or reports of government witnesses in criminal cases against subpoena, discovery, or inspection until the witness has testified on direct examination at the trial but then entitles the defense to its production. Rarely will documents of this nature be relevant until the author has testified and thus placed his credibility in issue. Further protection against discovery of government files in criminal cases is found in Criminal Procedure Rule 16(a) and (b). The breadth of discovery in civil cases, however, goes beyond ordinary bounds of relevancy and raises problems calling for the exercise of judicial control, and in making provision for it the rule implements the Freedom of Information Act, 18 U.S.C. § 552(b)(7).

(C) Information exempted from disclosure under the Freedom of Information Act, 5 U.S.C. § 552. In 1958 the old "housekeeping" statute which had been relied upon as a foundation for departmental regulations curtailing disclosure was amended by adding a provision that it did not authorize withholding information from the public. In 1966 the Congress enacted the Freedom of Information Act for the purpose of making information in the files of departments and agencies, subject to certain specified exceptions, available to the mass media and to the public generally. 5 U.S.C. § 552. These enactments are significant expressions of Congressional policy. The exceptions in the Act are not framed in terms of evidentiary privilege, thus recognizing by clear implication that the needs of litigants may stand on somewhat different footing from those of the public generally. Nevertheless, the exceptions are based on values obviously entitled to weighty consideration in formulating rules of evidentiary privilege. In some instances in these rules, exceptions in the Act have been made the subject of specific privileges, e.g., military and state secrets in the present rule and trade secrets in Rule 508. The purpose of the present provision is to incorporate the remaining exceptions of the Act into the qualified privilege here created, thus subjecting disclosure of the information to judicial determination with respect to the effect of disclosure on the public interest. This approach appears to afford a satisfactory resolution of the problems which may arise.

Subdivision (b). The rule vests the privileges in the government where they properly belong rather than a party or witness. See United States v. Reynolds, supra, p. 7, 345 U.S. 1, 73 S.Ct. 528, 97 L.Ed. 727. The showing required as a condition precedent to claiming the privilege represents a compromise between complete judicial control and accepting as final the decision of a departmental officer. See Machin v. Zuckert, 114 U.S.App.D.C. 335, 316 F.2d 336 (1963), rejecting in part a claim of privilege by the Secretary of the Air Force and ordering the furnishing of information for use in private litigation. This approach is consistent with *Reynolds*.

Subdivision (c). In requiring the claim of privilege for state secrets to be made by the chief departmental officer, the rule again follows *Reynolds,* insuring consideration by a high-level officer. This provision is justified by the lesser participation by the judge in cases of state secrets. The full participation by the judge in official information cases, on the contrary, warrants allowing the claim of privilege to be made by a government attorney.

Subdivision (d) spells out and emphasizes a power and responsibility on the part of the trial judge. An analogous provision is found in the requirement that the court certify to the Attorney General when the constitutionality of an act of Congress is in question in an action to which the government is not a party. 28 U.S.C. § 2403.

Subdivision (e). If privilege is successfully claimed by the government in litigation to which it is not a party, the effect is simply to make the evidence unavailable, as though a witness had died or claimed the privilege against self-incrimination, and no specification of the consequences is necessary. The rule therefore deals only with the effect of a successful claim of privilege by the government in proceedings to which it is a party. Reference to other types of cases serves to illustrate the variety of situations which may arise and the impossibility of evolving a single formula to be applied automatically to all of them. The privileged materials may be the statement of government witness, as under the *Jencks* statute, which provides that, if the government elects not to produce the statement, the judge is to strike the testimony of the witness, or that he may declare a mistrial if the interests of justice so require. 18 U.S.C. § 3500(d). Or the privileged materials may disclose a possible basis for applying pressure upon witnesses. United States v. Beekman, 155 F.2d 580 (2d Cir.1946). Or they may bear directly upon a substantive element of a criminal case, requiring dismissal in the event of a successful claim of privilege. United States v. Andolschek, 142 F.2d 503 (2d Cir.1944); and see United States v. Reynolds, 345 U.S. 1, 73 S.Ct. 528, 97 L.Ed. 727 (1953). Or they may relate to an element of a plaintiff's claim against the government, with the decisions indicating unwillingness to allow the government's claim of privilege for secrets of state to be used as an offensive weapon against it. United States v. Reynolds, supra; Republic of China v. National Union Fire Ins. Co., 142 F.Supp. 551 (D.Md.1956).

Rule 510.

IDENTITY OF INFORMER

[Not enacted.]

(a) Rule of privilege. The government or a state or subdivision thereof has a privilege to refuse to disclose the identity of a person who has furnished information relating to or assisting in an investigation of a possible violation of law to a law enforcement officer or member of a legislative committee or its staff conducting an investigation.

(b) Who may claim. The privilege may be claimed by an appropriate representative of the government, regardless of whether the information was furnished to an officer of the government or of a state or subdivision thereof. The privilege may be claimed by an appropriate representative of a state or subdivision if the information was furnished to an officer thereof, except that in criminal cases the privilege shall not be allowed if the government objects.

(c) Exceptions.

(1) *Voluntary disclosure; informer a witness.* No privilege exists under this rule if the identity of the informer or his interest in the subject matter of his communication has been disclosed to those who would have cause to resent the communication by a holder of the privilege or by the informer's own action, or if the informer appears as a witness for the government.

(2) *Testimony on merits.* If it appears from the evidence in the case or from other showing by a party that an informer may be able to give testimony necessary to a fair determination of the issue of guilt or innocence in a criminal case or of a material issue on the merits in a civil case to which the government is a party, and the government invokes the privilege, the judge shall give the government an opportunity to show *in camera* facts relevant to determining whether the informer can, in fact, supply that testimony. The showing will ordinarily be in the form of affidavits, but the judge may direct that testimony be taken if he finds that the matter cannot be resolved satisfactorily upon affidavit. If the judge finds that there is a reasonable probability that the informer can give the testimony, and the government elects not to disclose his identity, the judge on motion of the defendant in a criminal case shall dismiss the charges to which the testimony would relate, and the judge may do so on his own motion. In civil cases, he may make any order that justice requires. Evidence submitted to the judge shall be sealed and preserved to be made available to the appellate court in the event of an appeal, and the contents shall not otherwise be revealed without consent of the government. All counsel and parties shall be permitted to be present at every stage of proceedings under this

subdivision except a showing *in camera,* at which no counsel or party shall be permitted to be present.

(3) *Legality of obtaining evidence.* If information from an informer is relied upon to establish the legality of the means by which evidence was obtained and the judge is not satisfied that the information was received from an informer reasonably believed to be reliable or credible, he may require the identity of the informer to be disclosed. The judge shall, on request of the government, direct that the disclosure be made *in camera.* All counsel and parties concerned with the issue of legality shall be permitted to be present at every stage of proceedings under this subdivision except a disclosure *in camera,* at which no counsel or party shall be permitted to be present. If disclosure of the identity of the informer is made *in camera,* the record thereof shall be sealed and preserved to be made available to the appellate court in the event of an appeal, and the contents shall not otherwise be revealed without consent of the government.

Advisory Committee's Note

The rule recognizes the use of informers as an important aspect of law enforcement, whether the informer is a citizen who steps forward with information or a paid undercover agent. In either event, the basic importance of anonymity in the effective use of informers is apparent, Bocchicchio v. Curtis Publishing Co., 203 F.Supp. 403 (E.D.Pa.1962), and the privilege of withholding their identity was well established at common law. Roviaro v. United States, 353 U.S. 53, 59, 77 S.Ct. 623, 627, 1 L.Ed.2d 639 (1957); McCormick § 148; 8 Wigmore § 2374 (McNaughton Rev.1961).

Subdivision (a). The public interest in law enforcement requires that the privilege be that of the government, state, or political subdivision, rather than that of the witness. The rule blankets in as an informer anyone who tells a law enforcement officer about a violation of law without regard to whether the officer is one charged with enforcing the particular law. The rule also applies to disclosures to legislative investigating committees and their staffs, and is sufficiently broad to include continuing investigations.

Although the tradition of protecting the identity of informers has evolved in an essentially criminal setting, noncriminal law enforcement situations involving possibilities of reprisal against informers fall within the purview of the considerations out of which the privilege originated. In Mitchell v. Roma, 265 F.2d 633 (3d Cir.1959), the privilege was given effect with respect to persons informing as to violations of the Fair Labor Standards Act, and in Wirtz v. Continental Finance & Loan Co., 326 F.2d 561 (5th Cir.1964), a similar case, the privilege was recognized, although the basis of decision was lack of relevancy to the issues in the case.

Only identity is privileged; communications are not included except to the extent that disclosure would operate also to disclose the informer's identity. The common law was to the same effect. 8 Wigmore § 2374, at p. 765 (McNaughton Rev.1961). See also Roviaro v. United States, supra, 353 U.S. at 60, 77 S.Ct. at

627; Bowman Dairy Co. v. United States, 341 U.S. 214, 221, 71 S.Ct. 675, 679, 95 L.Ed. 879 (1951).

The rule does not deal with the question whether presentence reports made under Criminal Procedure Rule 32(c) should be made available to an accused.

Subdivision (b). Normally the "appropriate representative" to make the claim will be counsel. However, it is possible that disclosure of the informer's identity will be sought in proceedings to which the government, state, or subdivision, as the case may be, is not a party. Under these circumstances effective implementation of the privilege requires that other representatives be considered "appropriate." See, for example, Bocchicchio v. Curtis Publishing Co., 203 F.Supp. 403 (E.D.Pa.1962), a civil action for libel, in which a local police officer not represented by counsel successfully claimed the informer privilege.

The privilege may be claimed by a state or subdivision of a state if the information was given to its officer, except that in criminal cases it may not be allowed if the government objects.

Subdivision (c) deals with situations in which the informer privilege either does not apply or is curtailed.

(1) If the identity of the informer is disclosed, nothing further is to be gained from efforts to suppress it. Disclosure may be direct, or the same practical effect may result from action revealing the informer's interest in the subject matter. See, for example, Westinghouse Electric Corp. v. City of Burlington, 122 U.S.App.D.C. 65, 351 F.2d 762 (1965), on remand City of Burlington v. Westinghouse Electric Corp., 246 F.Supp. 839 (D.D.C.1965), which held that the filing of civil antitrust actions destroyed as to plaintiffs the informer privilege claimed by the Attorney General with respect to complaints of criminal antitrust violations. While allowing the privilege in effect to be waived by one not its holder, i.e. the informer himself, is something of a novelty in the law of privilege, if the informer chooses to reveal his identity, further efforts to suppress it are scarcely feasible.

The exception is limited to disclosure to "those who would have cause to resent the communication," in the language of Roviaro v. United States, 353 U.S. 53, 60, 77 S.Ct. 623, 627, 1 L.Ed.2d 639 (1957), since disclosure otherwise, e.g. to another law enforcing agency, is not calculated to undercut the objects of the privilege.

If the informer becomes a witness for the government, the interests of justice in disclosing his status as a source of bias or possible support are believed to outweigh any remnant of interest in nondisclosure which then remains. See Harris v. United States, 371 F.2d 365 (9th Cir.1967), in which the trial judge permitted detailed inquiry into the relationship between the witness and the government. Cf. Attorney General v. Briant, 15 M. & W. 169, 153 Eng.Rep. 808 (Exch.1846). The purpose of the limitation to witnesses for the government is to avoid the possibility of calling persons as witnesses as a means of discovery whether they are informers.

(2) The informer privilege, it was held by the leading case, may not be used in a criminal prosecution to suppress the identity of a witness when the public interest in protecting the flow of information is outweighed by the individual's right to prepare his defense. Roviaro v. United States, supra. The rule extends this balancing to include civil as well as criminal cases and phrases it in terms of

"a reasonable probability that the informer may be able to give testimony necessary to a fair determination of the issue of guilt or innocence in a criminal case or of a material issue on the merits in a civil case." Once the privilege is invoked a procedure is provided for determining whether the informer can in fact supply testimony of such nature as to require disclosure of his identity, thus avoiding a "judicial guessing game" on the question. United States v. Day, 384 F.2d 464, 470 (3d Cir.1967). An investigation *in camera* is calculated to accommodate the conflicting interests involved. The rule also spells out specifically the consequences of a successful claim of the privilege in a criminal case; the wider range of possibilities in civil cases demands more flexibility in treatment. See Advisory Committee's Note to Rule 509(e), supra.

(3) One of the acute conflicts between the interest of the public in nondisclosure and the avoidance of unfairness to the accused as a result of nondisclosure arises when information from an informer is relied upon to legitimate a search and seizure by furnishing probable cause for an arrest without a warrant or for the issuance of a warrant for arrest or search. McCray v. Illinois, 386 U.S. 300, 87 S.Ct. 1056, 18 L.Ed.2d 62 (1967), rehearing denied 386 U.S. 1042, 87 S.Ct. 1474, 18 L.Ed.2d 616. A hearing *in camera* provides an accommodation of these conflicting interests. United States v. Jackson, 384 F.2d 825 (3d Cir.1967). The limited disclosure to the judge avoids any significant impairment of secrecy, while affording the accused a substantial measure of protection against arbitrary police action. The procedure is consistent with McCray and the decisions there discussed.

Rule 511.

WAIVER OF PRIVILEGE BY VOLUNTARY DISCLOSURE

[Not enacted.]

A person upon whom these rules confer a privilege against disclosure of the confidential matter or communication waives the privilege if he or his predecessor while holder of the privilege voluntarily discloses or consents to disclosure of any significant part of the matter or communication. This rule does not apply if the disclosure is itself a privileged communication.

Advisory Committee's Note

The central purpose of most privileges is the promotion of some interest or relationship by endowing it with a supporting secrecy or confidentiality. It is evident that the privilege should terminate when the holder by his own act destroys this confidentiality. McCormick §§ 87, 97, 106; 8 Wigmore §§ 2242, 2327–2329, 2374, 2389–2390 (McNaughton Rev.1961).

The rule is designed to be read with a view to what it is that the particular privilege protects. For example, the lawyer-client privilege covers only communications, and the fact that a client has discussed a matter with his lawyer does not insulate the client against disclosure of the subject matter discussed, although he is privileged not to disclose the discussion itself. See McCormick § 93. The waiver here provided for is similarly restricted. Therefore a client, merely by disclosing a subject which he had discussed with his attorney, would not waive the applicable privilege; he would have to make disclosure of the communication itself in order to effect a waiver.

By traditional doctrine, waiver is the intentional relinquishment of a known right. Johnson v. Zerbst, 304 U.S. 458, 464, 58 S.Ct. 1019, 1023, 82 L.Ed. 1461 (1938). However, in the confidential privilege situations, once confidentiality is destroyed through voluntary disclosure, no subsequent claim of privilege can restore it, and knowledge or lack of knowledge of the existence of the privilege appears to be irrelevant. California Evidence Code § 912; 8 Wigmore § 2327 (McNaughton Rev.1961).

Rule 512.

PRIVILEGED MATTER DISCLOSED UNDER COMPULSION OR WITHOUT OPPORTUNITY TO CLAIM PRIVILEGE

[Not enacted.]

Evidence of a statement or other disclosure of privileged matter is not admissible against the holder of the privilege if the disclosure was (a) compelled erroneously or (b) made without opportunity to claim the privilege.

Advisory Committee's Note

Ordinarily a privilege is invoked in order to forestall disclosure. However, under some circumstances consideration must be given to the status and effect of a disclosure already made. Rule 511, immediately preceding, gives voluntary disclosure the effect of a waiver, while the present rule covers the effect of disclosure made under compulsion or without opportunity to claim the privilege.

Confidentiality, once destroyed, is not susceptible of restoration, yet some measure of repair may be accomplished by preventing use of the evidence against the holder of the privilege. The remedy of exclusion is therefore made available when the earlier disclosure was compelled erroneously or without opportunity to claim the privilege.

With respect to erroneously compelled disclosure, the argument may be made that the holder should be required in the first instance to assert the privilege, stand his ground, refuse to answer, perhaps incur a judgment of contempt, and exhaust all legal recourse, in order to sustain his privilege. See Fraser v. United States, 145 F.2d 139 (6th Cir.1944), cert. denied 324 U.S. 849, 65 S.Ct. 684, 89 L.Ed. 1409; United States v. Johnson, 76 F.Supp. 538 (M.D.Pa. 1947), aff'd 165 F.2d 42 (3d Cir.1947), cert. denied 332 U.S. 852, 68 S.Ct. 355, 92 L.Ed. 422, reh. denied 333 U.S. 834, 68 S.Ct. 457, 92 L.Ed. 1118. However, this exacts of the holder greater fortitude in the face of authority than ordinary individuals are likely to possess, and assumes unrealistically that a judicial remedy is always available. In self-incrimination cases, the writers agree that erroneously compelled disclosures are inadmissible in a subsequent criminal prosecution of the holder, Maguire, Evidence of Guilt 66 (1959); McCormick § 127; 8 Wigmore § 2270 (McNaughton Rev.1961), and the principle is equally sound when applied to other privileges. The modest departure from usual principles of res judicata which occurs when the compulsion is judicial is justified by the advantage of having one simple rule, assuring at least one opportunity for judicial supervision in every case.

The second circumstance stated as a basis for exclusion is disclosure made without opportunity to the holder to assert his privilege. Illustrative possibilities are disclosure by an eavesdropper, by a person used in the transmission of a privileged communication, by a family member participating in psychotherapy, or privileged data improperly made available from a computer bank.

Rule 513.

COMMENT UPON OR INFERENCE FROM CLAIM OF PRIVILEGE; INSTRUCTION

[Not enacted.]

(a) Comment or inference not permitted. The claim of a privilege, whether in the present proceeding or upon a prior occasion, is not a proper subject of comment by judge or counsel. No inference may be drawn therefrom.

(b) Claiming privilege without knowledge of jury. In jury cases, proceedings shall be conducted, to the extent practicable, so as to facilitate the making of claims of privilege without the knowledge of the jury.

(c) Jury instruction. Upon request, any party against whom the jury might draw an adverse inference from a claim of privilege is entitled to an instruction that no inference may be drawn therefrom.

Advisory Committee's Note

Subdivision (a). In Griffin v. California, 380 U.S. 609, 614, 5 Ohio Misc. 127, 85 S.Ct. 1229, 1232, 14 L.Ed.2d 106 (1965), the Court pointed out that allowing comment upon the claim of a privilege "cuts down on the privilege by making its assertion costly." Consequently it was held that comment upon the election of the accused not to take the stand infringed upon his privilege against self-incrimination so substantially as to constitute a constitutional violation. While the privileges governed by these rules are not constitutionally based, they are nevertheless founded upon important policies and are entitled to maximum effect. Hence the present subdivision forbids comment upon the exercise of a privilege, in accord with the weight of authority. Courtney v. United States, 390 F.2d 521 (9th Cir.1968); 8 Wigmore §§ 2243, 2322, 2386; Barnhart, Privilege in the Uniform Rules of Evidence, 24 Ohio St.L.J. 131, 137–138 (1963). Cf. McCormick § 80.

Subdivision (b). The value of a privilege may be greatly depreciated by means other than expressly commenting to a jury upon the fact that it was exercised. Thus, the calling of a witness in the presence of the jury and subsequently excusing him after a side-bar conference may effectively convey to the jury the fact that a privilege has been claimed, even though the actual claim has not been made in their hearing. Whether a privilege will be claimed is usually ascertainable in advance and the handling of the entire matter outside the presence of the jury is feasible. Destruction of the privilege by innuendo can and should be avoided. Tallo v. United States, 344 F.2d 467 (1st Cir.1965); United States v. Tomaiolo, 249 F.2d 683 (2d Cir.1957); San Fratello v. United States, 343 F.2d 711 (5th Cir.1965); Courtney v. United States, 390 F.2d 521 (9th Cir.1968); 6 Wigmore § 1808, pp. 275–276; 6 U.C.L.A.L.Rev. 455 (1959). This position is in accord with the general agreement of the authorities that an accused cannot be forced to make his election not to testify in the presence of the jury. 8 Wigmore § 2268, p. 407 (McNaughton Rev.1961).

Unanticipated situations are, of course, bound to arise, and much must be left to the discretion of the judge and the professional responsibility of counsel.

Subdivision (c). Opinions will differ as to the effectiveness of a jury instruction not to draw an adverse inference from the making of a claim of privilege. See Bruton v. United States, 389 U.S. 818, 88 S.Ct. 126, 19 L.Ed.2d 70 (1967). Whether an instruction shall be given is left to the sound judgment of counsel for the party against whom the adverse inference may be drawn. The instruction is a matter of right, if requested. This is the result reached in Bruno v. United States, 308 U.S. 287, 60 S.Ct. 198, 84 L.Ed. 257 (1939), holding that an accused is entitled to an instruction under the statute (now 18 U.S.C. § 3481) providing that his failure to testify creates no presumption against him.

The right to the instruction is not impaired by the fact that the claim of privilege is by a witness, rather than by a party, provided an adverse inference against the party may result.

Rule 804(b)(2).

STATEMENT OF RECENT PERCEPTION

[Not enacted.]

A statement, not in response to the instigation of a person engaged in investigating, litigating, or settling a claim, which narrates, describes, or explains an event or condition recently perceived by the declarant, made in good faith, not in contemplation of pending or anticipated litigation in which he was interested, and while his recollection was clear.

Advisory Committee's Note

The rule finds support in several directions. The well known Massachusetts Act of 1898 allows in evidence the declaration of any deceased person made in good faith before the commencement of the action and upon personal knowledge. Mass.G.L., c. 233, § 65. To the same effect is R.I.G.L. § 9–19–11. Under other statutes, a decedent's statement is admissible on behalf of his estate in actions against it, to offset the presumed inequality resulting from allowing a surviving opponent to testify. California Evidence Code § 1261; Conn.G.S., § 52–172; and statutes collected in 5 Wigmore § 1576. See also Va.Code § 8–286, allowing statements made when capable by a party now incapable of testifying.

In 1938 the Committee on Improvements in the Law of Evidence of the American Bar Association recommended adoption of a statute similar to that of Massachusetts but with the concept of unavailability expanded to include, in addition to death, cases of insanity or inability to produce a witness or take his deposition. 63 A.B.A.Reports 570, 584, 600 (1938). The same year saw enactment of the English Evidence Act of 1938, allowing written statements made on personal knowledge, if declarant is deceased or otherwise unavailable or if the court is satisfied that undue delay or expense would otherwise be caused, unless declarant was an interested person in pending or anticipated relevant proceedings. Evidence Act of 1938, 1 & 2 Geo. 6, c. 28; Cross on Evidence 482 (3rd ed. 1967).

Model Code Rule 503(a) provided broadly for admission of any hearsay declaration of an unavailable declarant. No circumstantial guarantees of trustworthiness were required. Debate upon the floor of the American Law Institute did not seriously question the propriety of the rule but centered upon what should constitute unavailability. 18 A.L.I. Proceedings 90–134 (1941).

The Uniform Rules draftsman took a less advanced position, more in the pattern of the Massachusetts statute, and invoked several assurances of accuracy: recency of perception, clarity of recollection, good faith, and antecedence to the commencement of the action. Uniform Rule 63(4)(c).

Opposition developed to the Uniform Rule because of its countenancing of the use of statements carefully prepared under the tutelage of lawyers, claim adjusters, or investigators with a view to pending or prospective litigation. Tentative Recommendation and a Study Relating to the Uniform Rules of Evidence (Art. VIII. Hearsay Evidence), Cal.Law Rev.Comm'n, 318 (1962); Quick, Excitement, Necessity and the Uniform Rules: A Reappraisal of Rule 63(4), 6 Wayne L.Rev. 204, 219–224 (1960). To meet this objection, the rule excludes statements made at the instigation of a person engaged in investigating, litigating, or setting a claim. It also incorporates as safeguards the good faith and clarity of recollection required by the Uniform Rule and the exclusion of a statement by a person interested in the litigation provided by the English act.

With respect to the question whether the introduction of a statement under this exception against the accused in a criminal case would violate his right of confrontation, reference is made to the last paragraph of the Advisory Committee's Note under Exception (1), supra.

CALIFORNIA EVIDENCE CODE

Introductory Note

The California Evidence Code and selected excerpts from the Comments to the Code are reproduced below. The Code was enacted after a nine-year period of study and drafting by the California Law Revision Commission. The Commission's mandate pursuant to a legislative resolution was to determine whether and to what extent the Uniform Rules of Evidence were to be adopted in California. The Commission engaged Professor James H. Chadbourn (then on the faculty at UCLA Law School, later of the Harvard Law School) to prepare a series of studies of the adaptability of the Uniform Rules to California Law.

The Chadbourn studies along with the Commission's tentative recommendations for legislation were published by the Commission between 1962 and 1964 in a series of nine pamphlets, each dealing with a major subject matter area of the law of evidence (reprinted in Volume 6 of the Commission's Reports, Recommendations and Studies (1964)). The Commission itself has indicated that these pamphlets "contain a statement of previous California law and may provide valuable assistance to persons using the Evidence Code." References to relevant materials in the pamphlets are made in the Comments to specific provisions of the Code.

The Law Revision Commission prepared most of the Comments to the Code. In a number of instances, however, as designated in the headings, the Comments were prepared by one of the two state legislative committees that reported out the bill that became the Code. The reports of those two committees indicated that each viewed the Law Revision Commission Comments that accompanied the final version of the Code, as well as the new or revised Comments prepared by the committee itself, as reflecting the intent of the committee.

CALIFORNIA EVIDENCE CODE*

Table of Code Sections

DIVISION 1. PRELIMINARY PROVISIONS AND CONSTRUCTION

Section		Page
1.	Short title	248
2.	Common law rule construing code abrogated	248
3.	Constitutionality	248
4.	Construction of code	248
5.	Effect of headings	248
6.	References to statutes	248
7.	"Division," "chapter," "article," "section," "subdivision," and "paragraph"	248
8.	Construction of tenses	249
9.	Construction of genders	249
10.	Construction of singular and plural	249
11.	"Shall" and "may"	249
12.	Code becomes operative January 1, 1967; effect on pending proceedings	249

DIVISION 2. WORDS AND PHRASES DEFINED

100.	Application of definitions	250
105.	"Action"	250
110.	"Burden of producing evidence"	250
115.	"Burden of proof"	250
120.	"Civil action"	250
125.	"Conduct"	250
130.	"Criminal action"	250
135.	"Declarant"	250
140.	"Evidence"	251
145.	"The hearing"	251
150.	"Hearsay evidence"	251
160.	"Law"	251
165.	"Oath"	251
170.	"Perceive"	251
175.	"Person"	251
177.	"Dependent person"	251
180.	"Personal property"	251
185.	"Property"	252
190.	"Proof"	252
195.	"Public employee"	252
200.	"Public entity"	252
205.	"Real property"	252
210.	"Relevant evidence"	252
220.	"State"	252
225.	"Statement"	252
230.	"Statute"	252
235.	"Trier of fact"	253

* Approved May 18, 1965, effective January 1, 1967. Amendments approved through June 1, 2007 included.

CALIFORNIA EVIDENCE CODE

Section		Page
240.	"Unavailable as a witness"	253
250.	"Writing"	254
255.	"Original"	254
260.	"Duplicate"	254

DIVISION 3. GENERAL PROVISIONS

CHAPTER 1. APPLICABILITY OF CODE

300.	Applicability of code	255

CHAPTER 2. PROVINCE OF COURT AND JURY

310.	Questions of law for court	255
311.	Procedure when foreign or sister-state law cannot be determined	255
312.	Jury as trier of fact	256

CHAPTER 3. ORDER OF PROOF

320.	Power of court to regulate order of proof	256

CHAPTER 4. ADMITTING AND EXCLUDING EVIDENCE

Article 1. General Provisions

350.	Only relevant evidence admissible	256
351.	Admissibility of relevant evidence	256
351.1	Polygraph examinations; results, opinion of examiner or reference; exclusion	257
352.	Discretion of court to exclude evidence	257
352.1	Criminal sex acts; victim's address and telephone number	257
353.	Effect of erroneous admission of evidence	257
354.	Effect of erroneous exclusion of evidence	258
355.	Limited admissibility	258
356.	Entire act, declaration, conversation, or writing may be brought out to elucidate part offered	258

Article 2. Preliminary Determinations on Admissibility of Evidence

400.	"Preliminary fact"	259
401.	"Proffered evidence"	259
402.	Procedure for determining foundational and other preliminary facts	259
403.	Determination of foundational and other preliminary facts where relevancy, personal knowledge, or authenticity is disputed	259
404.	Determination of whether proffered evidence is incriminatory	264
405.	Determination of foundational and other preliminary facts in other cases	264
406.	Evidence affecting weight or credibility	268

CHAPTER 5. WEIGHT OF EVIDENCE GENERALLY

410.	"Direct evidence"	268
411.	Direct evidence of one witness sufficient	269
412.	Party having power to produce better evidence	269
413.	Party's failure to explain or deny evidence	269

CALIFORNIA EVIDENCE CODE

DIVISION 4. JUDICIAL NOTICE

Section		Page
450.	Judicial notice may be taken only as authorized by law	270
451.	Matters which must be judicially noticed	270
452.	Matters which may be judicially noticed	272
452.5	Criminal conviction records; computer-generated records; admissibility	273
453.	Compulsory judicial notice upon request	273
454.	Information that may be used in taking judicial notice	275
455.	Opportunity to present information to court	275
456.	Noting for record denial of request to take judicial notice	276
457.	Instructing jury on matter judicially noticed	276
458.	Judicial notice by trial court in subsequent proceedings	276
459.	Judicial notice by reviewing court	276
460.	Appointment of expert by court	277

DIVISION 5. BURDEN OF PROOF; BURDEN OF PRODUCING EVIDENCE; PRESUMPTIONS AND INFERENCES

CHAPTER 1. BURDEN OF PROOF

Article 1. General

500.	Party who has the burden of proof	278
501.	Burden of proof in criminal action generally	279
502.	Instructions on burden of proof	279

Article 2. Burden of Proof on Specific Issues

520.	Claim that person guilty of crime or wrongdoing	279
521.	Claim that person did not exercise care	279
522.	Claim that person is or was insane	279
524.	Burden of proof on State Board of Equalization; Standard	280

CHAPTER 2. BURDEN OF PRODUCING EVIDENCE

550.	Party who has the burden of producing evidence	280

CHAPTER 3. PRESUMPTIONS AND INFERENCES

Article 1. General

600.	Presumption and inference defined	280
601.	Classification of presumptions	281
602.	Statute making one fact prima facie evidence of another fact	282
603.	Presumption affecting the burden of producing evidence defined	282
604.	Effect of presumption affecting burden of producing evidence	283
605.	Presumption affecting the burden of proof defined	284
606.	Effect of presumption affecting burden of proof	284
607.	Effect of certain presumptions in a criminal action	285

Article 2. Conclusive Presumptions

620.	Conclusive presumptions	286
621.	Child of marriage; notice of motion for blood tests	286
622.	Facts recited in written instrument	286
623.	Estoppel by own statement or conduct	287
624.	Estoppel of tenant to deny title of landlord	287

CALIFORNIA EVIDENCE CODE

Section		Page

Article 3. Presumptions Affecting the Burden of Producing Evidence

630.	Presumptions affecting the burden of producing evidence	287
631.	Money delivered by one to another	287
632.	Thing delivered by one to another	287
633.	Obligation delivered up to the debtor	287
634.	Person in possession of order on himself	287
635.	Obligation possessed by creditor	287
636.	Payment of earlier rent or installments	287
637.	Ownership of things possessed	287
638.	Ownership of property by person who exercises acts of ownership	287
639.	Judgment correctly determines rights of parties	287
640.	Writing truly dated	288
641.	Letter received in ordinary course of mail	288
642.	Conveyance by person having duty to convey real property	288
643.	Authenticity of ancient document	288
644.	Book purporting to be published by public authority	289
645.	Book purporting to contain reports of cases	289
645.1	Printed materials purporting to be particular newspaper or periodical	288
646.	Res ipsa loquitur; instruction	289
647.	Return of process served by registered process server	290

Article 4. Presumptions Affecting the Burden of Proof

660.	Presumptions affecting the burden of proof	290
662.	Owner of legal title to property is owner of beneficial title	290
663.	Ceremonial marriage	290
664.	Official duty regularly performed	290
665.	Ordinary consequences of voluntary act	290
666.	Judicial action lawful exercise of jurisdiction	290
667.	Death of person not heard from in five years	291
668.	Unlawful intent	291
669.	Failure to exercise due care	291
669.1	Standards of conduct for public employees; presumption of failure to exercise due care	292
669.5	Ordinances limiting building permits or development of buildable lots for residential purposes; impact on supply of residential units; actions challenging validity	293

DIVISION 6. WITNESSES

CHAPTER 1. COMPETENCY

700.	General rule as to competency	295
701.	Disqualification of witness	295
702.	Personal knowledge of witness	296
703.	Judge as witness	296
703.5	Judge as witness; subsequent civil proceeding; exceptions	297
704.	Juror as witness	297

CHAPTER 2. OATH AND CONFRONTATION

710.	Oath required	298
711.	Confrontation	298
712.	Blood samples; technique in taking; affidavits in criminal actions; service; objections	298

CALIFORNIA EVIDENCE CODE

Section		Page
	CHAPTER 3. EXPERT WITNESSES	
	Article 1. Expert Witnesses Generally	
720.	Qualification as an expert witness	298
721.	Cross-examination of expert witness	299
722.	Credibility of expert witness	300
723.	Limit on number of expert witnesses	300
	Article 2. Appointment of Expert Witness by Court	
730.	Appointment of expert by court	300
731.	Payment of court-appointed expert	300
732.	Calling and examining court-appointed expert	301
733.	Right to produce other expert evidence	301
	CHAPTER 4. INTERPRETERS AND TRANSLATORS	
750.	Rules relating to witnesses apply to interpreters and translators	301
751.	Oath required of interpreters and translators	301
752.	Interpreters for witnesses	301
753.	Translators of writings	302
754.	Deaf persons; interpreters; civil or criminal actions; infractions; juvenile court proceedings; mental competency proceedings; administrative hearings	302
	CHAPTER 5. METHOD AND SCOPE OF EXAMINATION	
	Article 1. Definitions	
760.	"Direct examination"	306
761.	"Cross-examination"	306
762.	"Redirect examination"	307
763.	"Recross-examination"	307
764.	"Leading question"	307
	Article 2. Examination of Witnesses	
765.	Court to control mode of interrogation	307
766.	Responsive answers	307
767.	Leading questions	307
768.	Writings	308
769.	Inconsistent statement or conduct	308
770.	Evidence of inconsistent statement of witness	308
771.	Production of writing used to refresh memory	309
772.	Order of examination	310
773.	Cross-examination	310
774.	Re-examination	310
775.	Court may call witnesses	311
776.	Examination of adverse party or witness	311
777.	Exclusion of witness	312
778.	Recall of witness	312
	CHAPTER 6. CREDIBILITY OF WITNESSES	
	Article 1. Credibility Generally	
780.	General rule as to credibility	313
782.	Sexual offenses; evidence of sexual conduct of complaining witness; procedure for admissibility	314

Section		Page
783.	Sexual harassment, sexual assault, or sexual battery cases; admissibility of evidence of plaintiff's sexual conduct; procedure ...	315

Article 2. Attacking or Supporting Credibility

785.	Parties may attack or support credibility	316
786.	Character evidence generally	316
787.	Specific instances of conduct	316
788.	Prior felony conviction	317
789.	Religious belief	318
790.	Good character of witness	318
791.	Prior consistent statement of witness	318

CHAPTER 7. HYPNOSIS OF WITNESSES

795.	Testimony of hypnosis subject; admissibility; conditions	319

DIVISION 7. OPINION TESTIMONY AND SCIENTIFIC EVIDENCE

CHAPTER 1. EXPERT AND OTHER OPINION TESTIMONY

Article 1. Expert and Other Opinion Testimony Generally

800.	Opinion testimony by lay witness	320
801.	Opinion testimony by expert witness	320
802.	Statement of basis of opinion	321
803.	Opinion based on improper matter	322
804.	Opinion based on opinion or statement of another	322
805.	Opinion on ultimate issue	323

Article 2. Value, Damages, and Benefits in Eminent Domain and Inverse Condemnation Cases

810.	Application of article	323
811.	Value of property	323
812.	Market value; interpretation of meaning	323
813.	Value of property; authorized opinions; view of property; admissible evidence	323
814.	Matter upon which opinion must be based	324
815.	Sales of subject property	324
816.	Comparable sales	324
817.	Leases of subject property	325
818.	Comparable leases	325
819.	Capitalization of income	325
820.	Reproduction cost	325
821.	Conditions in general vicinity of subject property	326
822.	Matter upon which opinion may not be based	326
823.	No relevant market for property	327
824.	No relevant market; nonprofit special use property	327

Article 3. Opinion Testimony on Particular Subjects

870.	Opinion as to sanity	327

CHAPTER 2. BLOOD TESTS TO DETERMINE PATERNITY

890.	Short title	328
891.	Interpretation	328
892.	Order for blood tests in civil actions involving paternity	328
893.	Tests made by experts	328
894.	Compensation of experts	328

CALIFORNIA EVIDENCE CODE

Section		Page
895.	Determination of paternity	328
896.	Limitation on application in criminal matters	329
897.	Right to produce other expert evidence	329

DIVISION 8. PRIVILEGES

CHAPTER 1. DEFINITIONS

900.	Application of definitions	330
901.	"Proceeding"	330
902.	"Civil proceeding"	330
903.	"Criminal proceeding"	330
905.	"Presiding officer"	330

CHAPTER 2. APPLICABILITY OF DIVISION

910.	Applicability of division	331

CHAPTER 3. GENERAL PROVISIONS RELATING TO PRIVILEGES

911.	General rule as to privileges	332
912.	Waiver of privilege	332
913.	Comment on, and inferences from, exercise of privilege	333
914.	Determination of claim of privilege; limitation on punishment for contempt	334
915.	Disclosure of information in ruling on claim of privilege	335
916.	Exclusion of privileged information where persons authorized to claim privilege are not present	336
917.	Presumption that certain communications are confidential; privileged character of electronic communications	336
918.	Effect of error in overruling claim of privilege	337
919.	Admissibility where disclosure erroneously compelled; claim of privilege; coercion	337
920.	No implied repeal	337

CHAPTER 4. PARTICULAR PRIVILEGES

Article 1. Privilege of Defendant in Criminal Case

930.	Privilege not to be called as a witness and not to testify	337

Article 2. Privilege Against Self–Incrimination

940.	Privilege against self-incrimination	337

Article 3. Lawyer–Client Privilege

950.	"Lawyer"	338
951.	"Client"	338
952.	"Confidential communication between client and lawyer"	338
953.	"Holder of the privilege"	339
954.	Lawyer-client privilege	339
955.	When lawyer required to claim privilege	340
956.	Exception: Crime or fraud	340
956.5	Exception: Criminal act likely to result in death or substantial bodily harm	340
957.	Exception: Parties claiming through deceased client	342
958.	Exception: Breach of duty arising out of lawyer-client relationship	342
959.	Exception: Lawyer as attesting witness	342

CALIFORNIA EVIDENCE CODE

Section		Page
960.	Exception: Intention of deceased client concerning writing affecting property interest	342
961.	Exception: Validity of writing affecting property interest	343
962.	Exception: Joint clients	343

Article 4. Privilege Not to Testify Against Spouse

970.	Privilege not to testify against spouse	343
971.	Privilege not to be called as a witness against spouse	343
972.	When privilege not applicable	344
973.	Waiver of privilege	345

Article 5. Privilege for Confidential Marital Communications

980.	Privilege for confidential marital communications	346
981.	Exception: Crime or fraud	346
982.	Exception: Commitment or similar proceeding	347
983.	Exception: Proceeding to establish competence	347
984.	Exception: Proceeding between spouses	347
985.	Exception: Certain criminal proceedings	347
986.	Exception: Juvenile court proceeding	347
987.	Exception: Communication offered by spouse who is criminal defendant	348

Article 6. Physician–Patient Privilege

990.	"Physician"	348
991.	"Patient"	348
992.	"Confidential communication between patient and physician"	348
993.	"Holder of the privilege"	349
994.	Physician-patient privilege	349
995.	When physician required to claim privilege	350
996.	Exception: Patient-litigant exception	350
997.	Exception: Crime or tort	350
998.	Exception: Criminal proceeding	350
999.	Exception: Communication relating to patient condition in proceeding to recover damages; good cause	350
1000.	Exception: Parties claiming through deceased patient	351
1001.	Exception: Breach of duty arising out of physician-patient relationship	351
1002.	Exception: Intention of deceased patient concerning writing affecting property interest	351
1003.	Exception: Validity of writing affecting property interest	351
1004.	Exception: Commitment or similar proceeding	352
1005.	Exception: Proceeding to establish competence	352
1006.	Exception: Required report	352
1007.	Exception: Proceeding to terminate rights, license or privilege	352

Article 7. Psychotherapist–Patient Privilege

1010.	"Psychotherapist"	352
1010.5	Privileged communication between patient and educational psychologist	353
1011.	"Patient"	353
1012.	"Confidential communication between patient and psychotherapist"	354
1013.	"Holder of the privilege"	354

CALIFORNIA EVIDENCE CODE

Section		Page
1014.	Psychotherapist-patient privilege; application to individuals and entities	354
1015.	When psychotherapist required to claim privilege	356
1016.	Exception: Patient-litigant exception	356
1017.	Exception: Psychotherapist appointed by court or board of prison terms	356
1018.	Exception: Crime or tort	356
1019.	Exception: Parties claiming through deceased patient	357
1020.	Exception: Breach of duty arising out of psychotherapist-patient relationship	357
1021.	Exception: Intention of deceased patient concerning writing affecting property interest	357
1022.	Exception: Validity of writing affecting property interest	357
1023.	Exception: Proceeding to determine sanity of criminal defendant	357
1024.	Exception: Patient dangerous to himself or others	357
1025.	Exception: Proceeding to establish competence	357
1026.	Exception: Required report	357
1027.	Exception: Child under 16 victim of crime	357

Article 8. Clergyman–Penitent Privileges

1030.	"Member of the clergy"	358
1031.	"Penitent"	358
1032.	"Penitential communication"	358
1033.	Privilege of penitent	358
1034.	Privilege of clergy member	358

Article 8.5 Sexual Assault Counselor–Victim Privilege

1035.	Victim	359
1035.2	Sexual assault counselor	359
1035.4	Confidential communication between the sexual assault counselor and the victim; disclosure	360
1035.6	Holder of the privilege	361
1035.8	Sexual assault counselor privilege	361
1036.	Claim of privilege by sexual assault counselor	362
1036.2	Sexual assault	362

Article 8.7 Domestic Violence Counselor–Victim Privilege

1037.	Victim	362
1037.1	Domestic violence counselor; qualifications	362
1037.2	Confidential communication; compulsion of disclosure by court; claim of privilege	363
1037.3	Child abuse; reporting	364
1037.4	Holder of the privilege	364
1037.5	Privilege of refusal to disclose communication; claimants	364
1037.6	Claiming of privilege by counselor	365
1037.7	Domestic violence; abuse; family or household member; other persons	365
1037.8	Notice; limitations on confidential communications	365

Article 8.8 Human Trafficking Caseworker–Victim Privilege

1038.	Claimant of the privilege	365
1038.1	Disclosure of information	366
1038.2	Definitions	366

CALIFORNIA EVIDENCE CODE

Section		Page
	Article 9. Official Information and Identity of Informer	
1040.	Privilege for official information	367
1041.	Privilege for identity of informer	368
1042.	Adverse order or finding in certain cases	369
1043.	Peace or custodial officer personnel records; discovery or disclosure; procedure	370
1044.	Medical or psychological history records; right of access	371
1045.	Peace or custodial officers; access to records of complaints or discipline imposed; relevancy; protective orders	371
1046.	Allegation of excessive force by peace or custodial officer; copy of police or crime report	372
1047.	Records of peace or custodial officers; exemption from disclosure	372

Article 10. Political Vote

1050.	Privilege to protect secrecy of vote	372

Article 11. Trade Secret

1060.	Privilege to protect trade secret	373
1061.	Procedure for assertion of trade secret privilege	373

CHAPTER 5. IMMUNITY OF NEWSMAN FROM CITATION FOR CONTEMPT

Article I, Section 2(b), California Constitution *

DIVISION 9. EVIDENCE AFFECTED OR EXCLUDED BY EXTRINSIC POLICIES

CHAPTER 1. EVIDENCE OF CHARACTER, HABIT, OR CUSTOM

1100.	Manner of proof of character	377
1101.	Evidence of character to prove conduct	377
1102.	Opinion and reputation evidence of character of criminal defendant to prove conduct	378
1103.	Evidence of character of victim of crime to prove conduct; evidence of complaining witness' sexual conduct in rape prosecution	380
1104.	Character trait for care or skill	381
1105.	Habit or custom to prove specific behavior	381
1106.	Sexual harassment, sexual assault, or sexual battery cases; opinion or reputation evidence of plaintiff's sexual conduct; inadmissibility; exception; cross-examination	382
1107.	Intimate partner battering and its effects; expert testimony in criminal actions; sufficiency of foundation; abuse and domestic violence; applicability to Penal Code; impact on decisional law	382
1108.	Evidence of another sexual offense	383
1109.	Evidence of defendant's other acts of domestic violence	384

CHAPTER 2. MEDIATION

1115.	Definitions	385
1116.	Limits on effects of chapter	385

* This constitutional provision dealing with newsmen's refusal to disclose news sources effectively replaced Section 1070 of the Evidence Code which deals with the same subject.

CALIFORNIA EVIDENCE CODE

Section		Page
1117.	Application of chapter	385
1118.	Oral agreement	386
1119.	Admissibility of evidence; subject to being compelled; confidentiality	386
1120.	Evidence used in mediation; effect on admissibility	386
1121.	Consideration of mediator's report in other proceedings	387
1122.	Conditions under which communication made in mediation proceeding becomes admissible in other proceedings	387
1123.	Conditions governing admissibility of written settlement agreement in mediation	387
1124.	Conditions governing admissibility of oral agreement in mediation	388
1125.	Confidentiality; end of mediation	388
1126.	Admissibility and confidentiality of mediation statements after mediation ends	389
1127.	Attorney's fees; person who unsuccessfully seeks to compel mediation statements	389
1128.	Reference to mediation in subsequent trial	389

CHAPTER 3. OTHER EVIDENCE AFFECTED OR EXCLUDED BY EXTRINSIC POLICIES

1150.	Evidence to test a verdict	389
1151.	Subsequent remedial conduct	390
1152.	Offer to compromise and the like	390
1153.	Offer to plead guilty or withdraw plea of guilty by criminal defendant	391
1153.5	Offer for civil resolution of crimes against property	391
1154.	Offer to discount a claim	391
1155.	Liability insurance	391
1156.	Records of medical study of in-hospital staff committee	391
1156.1	Records of medical or psychiatric studies of quality assurance committees	392
1157.	Proceedings and records of medical, medical-dental, podiatric, registered dietitian, psychological, marriage and family therapist, licensed clinical social worker, or veterinary staffs, hospital review committees; local medical, dental, dental hygienist, podiatric, dietetic, veterinary, chiropractic society, or state or local psychological review committees	393
1157.5	Organized committee of nonprofit medical care foundation or professional standards review organization; proceedings and records	394
1157.6	Proceedings and records of quality assurance committees for county health facilities	394
1157.7	Application of Section 1157 discovery or testimony prohibitions; application of public records and meetings provisions	394
1158.	Presentation of authorization for inspection and copying of patient's records; failure to comply; costs	394
1159.	Live animal experimentation evidence	395
1160.	Evidence of expressions of sympathy; statements of fault	396

DIVISION 10. HEARSAY EVIDENCE

CHAPTER 1. GENERAL PROVISIONS

1200.	The hearsay rule	397
1201.	Multiple hearsay	398
1202.	Credibility of hearsay declarant	398

CALIFORNIA EVIDENCE CODE

Section		Page
1203.	Cross-examination of hearsay declarant	399
1204.	Hearsay statement offered against criminal defendant	399
1205.	No implied repeal	400

CHAPTER 2. EXCEPTIONS TO THE HEARSAY RULE

Article 1. Confessions and Admissions

1220.	Admission of party	400
1221.	Adoptive admission	400
1222.	Authorized admission	400
1223.	Admission of co-conspirator	401
1224.	Statement of declarant whose liability or breach of duty is in issue	401
1225.	Statement of declarant whose right or title is in issue	402
1226.	Statement of minor child in parent's action for child's injury	402
1227.	Statement of declarant in action for his wrongful death	402
1228.	Admissibility of certain out-of-court statements of minors under the age of 12; establishing elements of certain sexually oriented crimes	403
1228.1	No use of parent's acceptance of child welfare services case plan as evidence against parent; use of parent's failure to cooperate as evidence against parent	403

Article 2. Declarations Against Interest

1230.	Declarations against interest	404

Article 2.5 Sworn Statements Regarding Gang–Related Crimes

1231.	General requirements	404
1231.1	Advance notice of intention to offer	405
1231.2	Administration of oath by peace officer	405
1231.3	Experience or training of law enforcement officer witness	405
1231.4	Information provided to jury relating to cause of declarant's death	405

Article 3. Prior Statements of Witnesses

1235.	Inconsistent statement	406
1236.	Prior consistent statement	406
1237.	Past recollection recorded	407
1238.	Prior identification	407

Article 4. Spontaneous, Contemporaneous, and Dying Declarations

1240.	Spontaneous statement	408
1241.	Contemporaneous statement	408
1242.	Dying declaration	409

Article 5. Statements of Mental or Physical State

1250.	Statement of declarant's then existing mental or physical state	409
1251.	Statement of declarant's previously existing mental or physical state	411
1252.	Limitation on admissibility of statement of mental or physical state	411

CALIFORNIA EVIDENCE CODE

Section		Page

Article 6. Statements Relating to Wills and to Claims Against Estates

1260. Statement concerning declarant's will or revocable trust; Trustworthiness of statement 412
1261. Statement of decedent offered in action against his estate 412

Article 7. Business Records

1270. "A business" 413
1271. Business record 413
1272. Absence of entry in business records 414

Article 8. Official Records and Other Official Writings

1280. Record by public employee 414
1281. Record of vital statistic 414
1282. Finding of presumed death by authorized federal employee 414
1283. Record by federal employee that person is missing, captured, or the like 415
1284. Statement of absence of public record 415

Article 9. Former Testimony

1290. "Former testimony" 415
1291. Former testimony offered against party to former proceeding ... 415
1292. Former testimony offered against person not a party to former proceeding 416
1293. Former testimony made at a preliminary examination by a minor child as a complaining witness; admissibility 417
1294. Prior inconsistent statements in preliminary hearing or trial of same matter. Former testimony of same witness admitted 418

Article 10. Judgments

1300. Judgment of conviction of crime punishable as felony 418
1301. Judgment against person entitled to indemnity 419
1302. Judgment determining liability of third person 419

Article 11. Family History

1310. Statement concerning declarant's own family history 419
1311. Statement concerning family history of another 420
1312. Entries in family records and the like 420
1313. Reputation in family concerning family history 420
1314. Reputation in community concerning family history 421
1315. Church records concerning family history 421
1316. Marriage, baptismal, and similar certificates 421

Article 12. Reputation and Statements Concerning Community History, Property Interests, and Character

1320. Reputation concerning community history 422
1321. Reputation concerning public interest in property 422
1322. Reputation concerning boundary or custom affecting land 422
1323. Statement concerning boundary 422
1324. Reputation concerning character 422

Article 13. Dispositive Instruments and Ancient Writings

1330. Recitals in writings affecting property 422
1331. Recitals in ancient writings 423

CALIFORNIA EVIDENCE CODE

Section		Page

Article 14. Commercial, Scientific, and Similar Publications

1340.	Commercial lists and the like	423
1341.	Publications concerning facts of general notoriety and interest	423

Article 15. Declarant Unavailable as Witness

1350.	Unavailable declarant; hearsay rule	423
1360.	Minor victim's statement describing child abuse or neglect	424
1370.	Victim's statement describing physical injury or threat thereof	425
1380.	Statement of elder or dependent adult victim of abuse	426
1390.	Evidence of statement; elements; conduct of foundational hearing; considerations; applicability; effect of repeal	427

DIVISION 11. WRITINGS

CHAPTER 1. AUTHENTICATION AND PROOF OF WRITINGS

Article 1. Requirement of Authentication

1400.	Authentication defined	429
1401.	Authentication required	430
1402.	Authentication of altered writing	430

Article 2. Means of Authenticating and Proving Writings

1410.	Article not exclusive	431
1410.5	Graffiti constitutes a writing; admissibility	431
1411.	Subscribing witness' testimony unnecessary	431
1412.	Use of other evidence when subscribing witness' testimony required	431
1413.	Witness to the execution of a writing	431
1414.	Authentication by admission	431
1415.	Authentication by handwriting evidence	432
1416.	Proof of handwriting by person familiar therewith	432
1417.	Comparison of handwriting by trier of fact	432
1418.	Comparison of writing by expert witness	432
1419.	Exemplars when writing is 30 years old	432
1420.	Authentication by evidence of reply	433
1421.	Authentication by content	433

Article 3. Presumptions Affecting Acknowledged Writings and Official Writings

1450.	Classification of presumptions in article	433
1451.	Acknowledged writings	433
1452.	Official seals	433
1453.	Domestic official signatures	434
1454.	Foreign official signatures	434

CHAPTER 2. SECONDARY EVIDENCE OF WRITINGS

Article 1. Proof of the Content of a Writing

1520.	Proof of the Content of a Writing	435
1521.	Secondary Evidence	435
1522.	Original in Proponent's Possession	435
1523.	Oral Testimony of Content of a Writing	435

CALIFORNIA EVIDENCE CODE

Section		Page
	Article 2. Official Writings and Recorded Writings	
1530.	Copy of writing in official custody	436
1531.	Certification of copy for evidence	437
1532.	Official record of recorded writing	437

Article 3. Photographic Copies and Printed Representations of Writings

1550.	Types of evidence as writing admissible as the writing itself	437
1550.1	Microphotographed reproductions: admissibility	438
1551.	Photographic copies where original destroyed or lost	438
1552.	Printed Representation of Computer Information or Computer Program	438
1553.	Printed Representation of Images Stored on Video or Digital Medium	438

Article 4. Hospital Records

1560.	Compliance with subpoena duces tecum for business records	439
1561.	Affidavit accompanying records	440
1562.	Admissibility of affidavit and copy of records	441
1563.	One witness and mileage fee	441
1564.	Personal attendance of custodian and production of original records	443
1565.	Service of more than one subpoena duces tecum	443
1566.	Applicability of article	443
1567.	Income and benefit information form	443

CHAPTER 3. OFFICIAL WRITINGS AFFECTING PROPERTY

1600.	Record of document affecting property interest	444
1601.	Proof of content of lost official record affecting property	444
1603.	Deed by officer in pursuance of court process	445
1604.	Certificate of purchase or of location of lands	445
1605.	Authenticated Spanish title records	445

Division 1

PRELIMINARY PROVISIONS AND CONSTRUCTION

§ 1. Short title. This code shall be known as the Evidence Code.

§ 2. Common law rule construing code abrogated. The rule of the common law, that statutes in derogation thereof are to be strictly construed, has no application to this code. This code establishes the law of this state respecting the subject to which it relates, and its provisions are to be liberally construed with a view to effecting its objects and promoting justice.

§ 3. Constitutionality. If any provision or clause of this code or application thereof to any person or circumstances is held invalid, such invalidity shall not affect other provisions or applications of the code which can be given effect without the invalid provision or application, and to this end the provisions of this code are declared to be severable.

§ 4. Construction of code. Unless the provision or context otherwise requires, these preliminary provisions and rules of construction shall govern the construction of this code.

§ 5. Effect of headings. Division, chapter, article, and section headings do not in any manner affect the scope, meaning, or intent of the provisions of this code.

§ 6. References to statutes. Whenever any reference is made to any portion of this code or of any other statute, such reference shall apply to all amendments and additions heretofore or hereafter made.

§ 7. "Division," "chapter," "article," "section," "subdivision," and "paragraph". Unless otherwise expressly stated:

(a) "Division" means a division of this code.

(b) "Chapter" means a chapter of the division in which that term occurs.

(c) "Article" means an article of the chapter in which that term occurs.

(d) "Section" means a section of this code.

(e) "Subdivision" means a subdivision of the section in which that term occurs.

(f) "Paragraph" means a paragraph of the subdivision in which that term occurs.

§ 8. Construction of tenses. The present tense includes the past and future tenses; and the future, the present.

§ 9. Construction of genders. The masculine gender includes the feminine and neuter.

§ 10. Construction of singular and plural. The singular number includes the plural; and the plural, the singular.

§ 11. "Shall" and "may". "Shall" is mandatory and "may" is permissive.

§ 12. Code becomes operative January 1, 1967; effect on pending proceedings. (a) This code shall become operative on January 1, 1967, and shall govern proceedings in actions brought on or after that date and, except as provided in subdivision (b), further proceedings in actions pending on that date.

(b) Subject to subdivision (c), a trial commenced before January 1, 1967, shall not be governed by this code. For the purpose of this subdivision:

(1) A trial is commenced when the first witness is sworn or the first exhibit is admitted into evidence and is terminated when the issue upon which such evidence is received is submitted to the trier of fact. A new trial, or a separate trial of a different issue, commenced on or after January 1, 1967, shall be governed by this code.

(2) If an appeal is taken from a ruling made at a trial commenced before January 1, 1967, the appellate court shall apply the law applicable at the time of the commencement of the trial.

(c) The provisions of Division 8 (commencing with Section 900) relating to privileges shall govern any claim of privilege made after December 31, 1966.

Division 2

WORDS AND PHRASES DEFINED

§ 100. Application of definitions. Unless the provision or context otherwise requires, these definitions govern the construction of this code.

§ 105. "Action". "Action" includes a civil action and a criminal action.

§ 110. "Burden of producing evidence". "Burden of producing evidence" means the obligation of a party to introduce evidence sufficient to avoid a ruling against him on the issue.

Comment—Assembly Committee on Judiciary

The phrases defined in Sections 110 and 115 provide a convenient means for distinguishing between the burden of *proving a fact* and the burden of *going forward* with the evidence. They recognize a distinction that is well established in California.

§ 115. "Burden of proof". "Burden of proof" means the obligation of a party to establish by evidence a requisite degree of belief concerning a fact in the mind of the trier of fact or the court. The burden of proof may require a party to raise a reasonable doubt concerning the existence or nonexistence of a fact or that he establish the existence or nonexistence of a fact by a preponderance of the evidence, by clear and convincing proof, or by proof beyond a reasonable doubt.

Except as otherwise provided by law, the burden of proof requires proof by a preponderance of the evidence.

§ 120. "Civil action". "Civil action" includes civil proceedings.

§ 125. "Conduct". "Conduct" includes all active and passive behavior, both verbal and nonverbal.

§ 130. "Criminal action". "Criminal action" includes criminal proceedings.

§ 135. "Declarant". "Declarant" is a person who makes a statement.

Comment—Law Revision Commission

Ordinarily, the word "declarant" is used in the Evidence Code to refer to a person who makes a hearsay statement as distinguished from the witness who testifies to the content of the statement.

§ 140. "Evidence". "Evidence" means testimony, writings, material objects, or other things presented to the senses that are offered to prove the existence or nonexistence of a fact.

Comment—Law Revision Commission

"Evidence" is defined broadly to include the testimony of witnesses, tangible objects, sights (such as a jury view or the appearance of a person exhibited to a jury), sounds (such as the sound of a voice demonstrated for a jury), and any other thing that may be presented as a basis of proof. The definition includes anything offered in evidence whether or not it is technically inadmissible and whether or not it is received.

Under this definition, a presumption is not evidence. See also Evidence Code § 600 and the Comment thereto.

§ 145. "The hearing". "The hearing" means the hearing at which a question under this code arises, and not some earlier or later hearing.

Comment—Law Revision Commission

This definition is much broader than would be a reference to the trial itself; the definition includes, for example, preliminary hearings and post-trial proceedings.

§ 150. "Hearsay evidence". "Hearsay evidence" is defined in Section 1200.

§ 160. "Law". "Law" includes constitutional, statutory, and decisional law.

§ 165. "Oath". "Oath" includes affirmation or declaration under penalty of perjury.

§ 170. "Perceive". "Perceive" means to acquire knowledge through one's senses.

§ 175. "Person". "Person" includes a natural person, firm, association, organization, partnership, business trust, corporation, limited liability company, or public entity.

§ 177. "Dependent person". "Dependent person" means any person who has a physical or mental impairment that substantially restricts his or her ability to carry out normal activities or to protect his or her rights, including, but not limited to, persons who have physical or developmental disabilities or whose physical or mental abilities have significantly diminished because of age. "Dependent person" includes any person who is admitted as an inpatient to a 24-hour health facility, as defined in Sections 1250, 1250.2, and 1250.3 of the Health and Safety Code.

§ 180. "Personal property". "Personal property" includes money, goods, chattels, things in action, and evidences of debt.

§ 185. "Property". "Property" includes both real and personal property.

§ 190. "Proof". "Proof" is the establishment by evidence of a requisite degree of belief concerning a fact in the mind of the trier of fact or the court.

Comment—Law Revision Commission

The disjunctive reference to "the trier of fact or the court" is needed because, even when the jury is the trier of fact, the court is required to determine preliminary questions of fact on the basis of proof.

§ 195. "Public employee". "Public employee" means an officer, agent, or employee of a public entity.

§ 200. "Public entity". "Public entity" includes a nation, state, county, city and county, city, district, public authority, public agency, or any other political subdivision or public corporation, whether foreign or domestic.

§ 205. "Real property". "Real property" includes lands, tenements, and hereditaments.

§ 210. "Relevant evidence". "Relevant evidence" means evidence, including evidence relevant to the credibility of a witness or hearsay declarant, having any tendency in reason to prove or disprove any disputed fact that is of consequence to the determination of the action.

Comment—Law Revision Commission

[U]nder Section 210, "relevant evidence" includes not only evidence of the ultimate facts actually in dispute but also evidence of other facts from which such ultimate facts may be presumed or inferred. In addition, Section 210 makes it clear that evidence relating to the credibility of witnesses and hearsay declarants is "relevant evidence." This restates existing law. See Tentative Recommendation and a Study Relating to the Uniform Rules of Evidence (Article VIII. Hearsay Evidence), 6 Cal.Law Revision Comm'n, Rep., Rec. & Studies Appendix at 339–340, 569–575 (1964) (credibility of hearsay declarants).

§ 220. "State". "State" means the State of California, unless applied to the different parts of the United States. In the latter case, it includes any state, district, commonwealth, territory, or insular possession of the United States.

§ 225. "Statement". "Statement" means (a) oral or written verbal expression or (b) nonverbal conduct of a person intended by him as a substitute for oral or written verbal expression.

§ 230. "Statute". "Statute" includes a treaty and a constitutional provision.

§ 235. "Trier of fact".

"Trier of fact" includes (a) the jury and (b) the court when the court is trying an issue of fact other than one relating to the admissibility of evidence.

§ 240. "Unavailable as a witness".

(a) Except as otherwise provided in subdivision (b), "unavailable as a witness" means that the declarant is any of the following:

(1) Exempted or precluded on the ground of privilege from testifying concerning the matter to which his or her statement is relevant.

(2) Disqualified from testifying to the matter.

(3) Dead or unable to attend or to testify at the hearing because of then-existing physical or mental illness or infirmity.

(4) Absent from the hearing and the court is unable to compel his or her attendance by its process.

(5) Absent from the hearing and the proponent of his or her statement has exercised reasonable diligence but has been unable to procure his or her attendance by the court's process.

(6) Persistent in refusing to testify concerning the subject matter of the declarant's statement despite having been found in contempt for refusal to testify.

(b) A declarant is not unavailable as a witness if the exemption, preclusion, disqualification, death, inability, or absence of the declarant was brought about by the procurement or wrongdoing of the proponent of his or her statement for the purpose of preventing the declarant from attending or testifying.

(c) Expert testimony which establishes that physical or mental trauma resulting from an alleged crime has caused harm to a witness of sufficient severity that the witness is physically unable to testify or is unable to testify without suffering substantial trauma may constitute a sufficient showing of unavailability pursuant to paragraph (3) of subdivision (a). As used in this section, the term "expert" means a physician and surgeon, including a psychiatrist, or any person described by subdivision (b), (c), or (e) of Section 1010.

The introduction of evidence to establish the unavailability of a witness under this subdivision shall not be deemed procurement of unavailability, in absence of proof to the contrary.

Comment—Assembly Committee on Judiciary

"Unavailable as a witness" includes, in addition to cases where the declarant is physically unavailable (i.e., dead, insane, or beyond the reach of the court's process), situations in which the declarant is legally unavailable (i.e., prevented from testifying by a claim of privilege or disqualified from testifying). Of course, if the declaration made out of court is itself privileged, the fact that the declarant is unavailable to testify at the hearing on the ground of privilege does not make the declaration admissible. The exceptions to the hearsay rule that are set forth

§ 240

in Division 10 (commencing with Section 1200) of the Evidence Code do not declare that the evidence described is necessarily admissible. They merely declare that such evidence is not inadmissible under the hearsay rule. If there is some other rule of law—such as privilege—which makes the evidence inadmissible, the court is not authorized to admit the evidence merely because it falls within an exception to the hearsay rule. Accordingly, the hearsay exceptions permit the introduction of evidence where the declarant is unavailable because of privilege only if the declaration itself is not privileged or is not inadmissible for some other reason.

Subdivision (b) is designed to establish safeguards against sharp practices and, in the words of the Commissioners on Uniform State Laws, to assure "that unavailability is honest and not planned in order to gain an advantage." Uniform Rules of Evidence, Rule 62 Comment. Under this subdivision, a party may not arrange a declarant's disappearance in order to use the declarant's out-of-court statement. Moreover, if the out-of-court statement is that of the party himself, he may not create "unavailability" under this section by invoking a privilege not to testify.

Section 240 substitutes a uniform standard for the varying standards of unavailability provided by the superseded Code of Civil Procedure sections providing hearsay exceptions. See the cases cited in Tentative Recommendation and a Study Relating to the Uniform Rules of Evidence (Article VIII. Hearsay Evidence), 6 Cal.Law Revision Comm'n, Rep., Rec. & Studies Appendix at 411 note 7 (1964).

§ 250. "Writing". "Writing" means handwriting, typewriting, printing, photostating, photographing, photocopying, transmitting by electronic mail or facsimile, and every other means of recording upon any tangible thing, any form of communication or representation, including letters, words, pictures, sounds, or symbols, or combinations thereof, and any record thereby created, regardless of the manner in which the record has been stored.

Comment—Law Revision Commission

"Writing" is defined very broadly to include all forms of tangible expression, including pictures and sound recordings.

§ 255. "Original". "Original" means the writing itself or any counterpart intended to have the same effect by a person executing or issuing it. An "original" of a photograph includes the negative or any print therefrom. If data are stored in a computer or similar device, any printout or other output readable by sight, shown to reflect the data accurately, is an "original."

§ 260. "Duplicate". A "duplicate" is a counterpart produced by the same impression as the original, or from the same matrix, or by means of photography, including enlargements and miniatures, or by mechanical or electronic rerecording, or by chemical reproduction, or by other equivalent technique which accurately reproduces the original.

Division 3

GENERAL PROVISIONS

Chapter 1

APPLICABILITY OF CODE

§ 300. Applicability of code. Except as otherwise provided by statute, this code applies in every action before the Supreme Court or a court of appeal or superior court, including proceedings in such actions conducted by a referee, court commissioner, or similar officer, but does not apply in grand jury proceedings.

Comment—Law Revision Commission

Section 300 makes the Evidence Code applicable to all proceedings conducted by California courts except those court proceedings to which it is made inapplicable by statute. The provisions of the code do not apply in administrative proceedings, legislative hearings, or any other proceedings unless some statute so provides or the agency concerned chooses to apply them.

Chapter 2

PROVINCE OF COURT AND JURY

§ 310. Questions of law for court. (a) All questions of law (including but not limited to questions concerning the construction of statutes and other writings, the admissibility of evidence, and other rules of evidence) are to be decided by the court. Determination of issues of fact preliminary to the admission of evidence are to be decided by the court as provided in Article 2 (commencing with Section 400) of Chapter 4.

(b) Determination of the law of an organization of nations or of the law of a foreign nation or a public entity in a foreign nation is a question of law to be determined in the manner provided in Division 4 (commencing with Section 450).

§ 311. Procedure when foreign or sister-state law cannot be determined. If the law of an organization of nations, a foreign nation or a state other than this state, or a public entity in a foreign nation or a state other than this state, is applicable and such law cannot be determined, the court may, as the ends of justice require, either:

(a) Apply the law of this state if the court can do so consistently with the Constitution of the United States and the Constitution of this state; or

(b) Dismiss the action without prejudice or, in the case of a reviewing court, remand the case to the trial court with directions to dismiss the action without prejudice.

§ 312. Jury as trier of fact. Except as otherwise provided by law, where the trial is by jury:

(a) All questions of fact are to be decided by the jury.

(b) Subject to the control of the court, the jury is to determine the effect and value of the evidence addressed to it, including the credibility of witnesses and hearsay declarants.

Chapter 3

ORDER OF PROOF

§ 320. Power of court to regulate order of proof. Except as otherwise provided by law, the court in its discretion shall regulate the order of proof.

Chapter 4

ADMITTING AND EXCLUDING EVIDENCE

Article 1. General Provisions

§ 350. Only relevant evidence admissible. No evidence is admissible except relevant evidence.

§ 351. Admissibility of relevant evidence. Except as otherwise provided by statute, all relevant evidence is admissible.

Comment—Law Revision Commission

The Evidence Code contains a number of provisions that exclude relevant evidence either for reasons of public policy or because the evidence is too unreliable to be presented to the trier of fact. See, e.g., Evidence Code § 352 (cumulative, unduly prejudicial, etc. evidence), §§ 900–1070 (privileges), §§ 1100–1156 (extrinsic policies), § 1200 (hearsay). Other codes also contain provisions that may in some cases result in the exclusion of relevant evidence.

Editorial Note

In June 1982, section 28 was added to Article I of the California Constitution through approval by the electorate of an initiative titled, Proposition 8—"The Victims' Bill of Rights." Section 28(d) of that constitutional amendment provides:

> 28. (d) **Right to Truth-in-Evidence.** Except as provided by statute hereafter enacted by a two-thirds vote of the membership in each house of the Legislature, relevant evidence shall not be excluded in any criminal proceeding, including pretrial and post conviction motions and hearings, or in any trial or hearing of a juvenile for a criminal offense, whether heard in

juvenile or adult court. Nothing in this section shall affect any existing statutory rule of evidence relating to privilege or hearsay, or Evidence Code, Sections 352, 782 or 1103. Nothing in this section shall affect any existing statutory or constitutional right of the press.

§ 351.1. Polygraph examinations; results, opinion of examiner or reference; exclusion.
(a) Notwithstanding any other provision of law, the results of a polygraph examination, the opinion of a polygraph examiner, or any reference to an offer to take, failure to take, or taking of a polygraph examination, shall not be admitted into evidence in any criminal proceeding, including pretrial and post conviction motions and hearings, or in any trial or hearing of a juvenile for a criminal offense, whether heard in juvenile or adult court, unless all parties stipulate to the admission of such results.

(b) Nothing in this section is intended to exclude from evidence statements made during a polygraph examination which are otherwise admissible.

§ 352. Discretion of court to exclude evidence.
The court in its discretion may exclude evidence if its probative value is substantially outweighed by the probability that its admission will (a) necessitate undue consumption of time or (b) create substantial danger of undue prejudice, of confusing the issues, or of misleading the jury.

§ 352.1. Criminal sex acts; victim's address and telephone number.
In any criminal proceeding under Section 261, 262, or 264.1, subdivision (d) of Section 286, or subdivision (d) of Section 288a of the Penal Code, or in any criminal proceeding under subdivision (c) of Section 286 or subdivision (c) of Section 288a of the Penal Code in which the defendant is alleged to have compelled the participation of the victim by force, violence, duress, menace, or threat of great bodily harm, the district attorney may, upon written motion with notice to the defendant or the defendant's attorney, if he or she is represented by an attorney, within a reasonable time prior to any hearing, move to exclude from evidence the current address and telephone number of any victim at the hearing.

The court may order that evidence of the victim's current address and telephone number be excluded from any hearings conducted pursuant to the criminal proceeding if the court finds that the probative value of the evidence is outweighed by the creation of substantial danger to the victim.

Nothing in this section shall abridge or limit the defendant's right to discover or investigate the information.

§ 353. Effect of erroneous admission of evidence.
A verdict or finding shall not be set aside, nor shall the judgment or decision based

thereon be reversed, by reason of the erroneous admission of evidence unless:

(a) There appears of record an objection to or a motion to exclude or to strike the evidence that was timely made and so stated as to make clear the specific ground of the objection or motion; and

(b) The court which passes upon the effect of the error or errors is of the opinion that the admitted evidence should have been excluded on the ground stated and that the error or errors complained of resulted in a miscarriage of justice.

§ 354. Effect of erroneous exclusion of evidence. A verdict or finding shall not be set aside, nor shall the judgment or decision based thereon be reversed, by reason of the erroneous exclusion of evidence unless the court which passes upon the effect of the error or errors is of the opinion that the error or errors complained of resulted in a miscarriage of justice and it appears of record that:

(a) The substance, purpose, and relevance of the excluded evidence was made known to the court by the questions asked, an offer of proof, or by any other means;

(b) The rulings of the court made compliance with subdivision (a) futile; or

(c) The evidence was sought by questions asked during cross-examination or recross-examination.

§ 355. Limited admissibility. When evidence is admissible as to one party or for one purpose and is inadmissible as to another party or for another purpose, the court upon request shall restrict the evidence to its proper scope and instruct the jury accordingly.

Comment—Law Revision Commission

Under Section 352, as under existing law, the judge is permitted to exclude such evidence if he deems it so prejudicial that a limiting instruction would not protect a party adequately and the matter in question can be proved sufficiently by other evidence. See Tentative Recommendation and a Study Relating to the Uniform Rules of Evidence (Article VI. Extrinsic Policies Affecting Admissibility), 6 Cal.Law Revision Comm'n, Rep., Rec. & Studies 601, 612, 639–640 (1964).

§ 356. Entire act, declaration, conversation, or writing may be brought out to elucidate part offered. Where part of an act, declaration, conversation, or writing is given in evidence by one party, the whole on the same subject may be inquired into by an adverse party; when a letter is read, the answer may be given; and when a detached act, declaration, conversation, or writing is given in evidence, any other act, declaration, conversation, or writing which is necessary to make it understood may also be given in evidence.

Article 2. Preliminary Determinations on Admissibility of Evidence

§ 400. "Preliminary fact". As used in this article, "preliminary fact" means a fact upon the existence or nonexistence of which depends the admissibility or inadmissibility of evidence. The phrase "the admissibility or inadmissibility of evidence" includes the qualification or disqualification of a person to be a witness and the existence or nonexistence of a privilege.

Comment—Law Revision Commission

"Preliminary fact" is defined to distinguish those facts upon which the admissibility of evidence depends from those facts sought to be proved by that evidence.

§ 401. "Proffered evidence". As used in this article, "proffered evidence" means evidence, the admissibility or inadmissibility of which is dependent upon the existence or nonexistence of a preliminary fact.

Comment—Law Revision Commission

"Proffered evidence" is defined to avoid confusion between evidence whose admissibility is in question and evidence offered on the preliminary fact issue. "Proffered evidence" includes such matters as the testimony to be elicited from a witness who is claimed to be disqualified, testimony or tangible evidence claimed to be privileged, and any other evidence to which objection is made.

§ 402. Procedure for determining foundational and other preliminary facts. (a) When the existence of a preliminary fact is disputed, its existence or nonexistence shall be determined as provided in this article.

(b) The court may hear and determine the question of the admissibility of evidence out of the presence or hearing of the jury; but in a criminal action, the court shall hear and determine the question of the admissibility of a confession or admission of the defendant out of the presence and hearing of the jury if any party so requests.

(c) A ruling on the admissibility of evidence implies whatever finding of fact is prerequisite thereto; a separate or formal finding is unnecessary unless required by statute.

§ 403. Determination of foundational and other preliminary facts where relevancy, personal knowledge, or authenticity is disputed. (a) The proponent of the proffered evidence has the burden of producing evidence as to the existence of the preliminary fact, and the proffered evidence is inadmissible unless the court finds that there is evidence sufficient to sustain a finding of the existence of the preliminary fact, when:

(1) The relevance of the proffered evidence depends on the existence of the preliminary fact;

(2) The preliminary fact is the personal knowledge of a witness concerning the subject matter of his testimony;

(3) The preliminary fact is the authenticity of a writing; or

(4) The proffered evidence is of a statement or other conduct of a particular person and the preliminary fact is whether that person made the statement or so conducted himself.

(b) Subject to Section 702, the court may admit conditionally the proffered evidence under this section, subject to evidence of the preliminary fact being supplied later in the course of the trial.

(c) If the court admits the proffered evidence under this section, the court:

(1) May, and on request shall, instruct the jury to determine whether the preliminary fact exists and to disregard the proffered evidence unless the jury finds that the preliminary fact does exist.

(2) Shall instruct the jury to disregard the proffered evidence if the court subsequently determines that a jury could not reasonably find that the preliminary fact exists.

Comment—Assembly Committee on Judiciary

[T]he judge does not determine in all instances whether a preliminary fact exists or does not exist. At times, the judge must admit the proffered evidence if there is evidence sufficient to sustain a finding of the preliminary fact, and the jury must finally decide whether the preliminary fact exists. Section 403 covers those situations in which the judge is required to admit the proffered evidence upon the introduction of evidence sufficient to sustain a finding of the preliminary fact.

Subdivision (a)

Some writers have attempted to distinguish the kinds of questions to be decided under the standard prescribed in Section 403 from the kinds of questions to be decided under the standard described in Section 405 on the ground that the former questions involve the *relevancy* of the proffered evidence while the latter questions involve the *competency* of evidence that is relevant. Maguire & Epstein, Preliminary Questions of Fact in Determining the Admissibility of Evidence, 40 Harv.L.Rev. 392 (1927); Morgan, Functions of Judge and Jury in the Determination of Preliminary Questions of Fact, 43 Harv.L.Rev. 165 (1929). It is difficult, however, to distinguish all preliminary fact questions upon this principle. And eminent legal authorities sometimes differ over whether a particular preliminary fact question is one of relevancy or competency. For example, Wigmore classifies admissions with questions of relevancy (4 Wigmore, Evidence 1 (3d ed. 1940)) while Morgan classifies admissions with questions of competency to be decided under the standard prescribed in Section 405 (Morgan, Basic Problems of Evidence 244 (1957)).

To eliminate uncertainties of classification, subdivision (a) lists the kinds of preliminary fact questions that are to be determined under the standard prescribed in Section 403. And to eliminate any uncertainties that are not resolved by this listing, various Evidence Code sections state specifically that admissibility depends on "evidence sufficient to sustain a finding" of certain facts. See, e.g., Evidence Code §§ 1222, 1223, 1400.

The preliminary fact questions listed in subdivision (a), or identified elsewhere as matters to be determined under the Section 403 standard, are not finally decided by the judge because they have been traditionally regarded as jury questions. The questions involve the credibility of testimony or the probative value of evidence that is admitted on the ultimate issues. It is the jury's function to determine the effect and value of the evidence addressed to it. Evidence Code § 312. Hence, the judge's function on questions of this sort is merely to determine whether there is evidence sufficient to permit a jury to decide the question.

For example, if the question of A's title to land is in issue, A may seek to prove his title by a deed from former owner O. Section 1401 requires that the deed be authenticated, and the judge, under Section 403, must rule on the question of authentication. If A introduces evidence sufficient to sustain a finding of the genuineness of the deed, the judge is required to admit it. If the rule were otherwise and the judge, on the basis of the adverse party's evidence, were permitted to decide that the deed was spurious and not admissible, the judge would be resolving the basic factual issue in the case and A would be deprived of a jury finding on the issue, even though he is entitled to a jury decision and even though he has introduced evidence sufficient to warrant a jury finding in his favor.

Illustrative of the preliminary fact questions that should be decided under Section 403 are the following:

Section 350—Relevancy. Under existing law, as under Section 403, if the relevancy of proffered evidence depends on the existence of some preliminary fact, the evidence is admissible if there is evidence sufficient to warrant a jury finding of the preliminary fact. Thus, for example, if P sues D upon an alleged agreement, evidence of negotiations with A is inadmissible because irrelevant unless A is shown to be D's agent; but the evidence of the negotiations with A is admissible if there is evidence sufficient to sustain a finding of the agency.

The same rule is applicable when a person is charged with criminal responsibility for the acts of another because they are conspirators.

Section 702—Requirement of personal knowledge. Evidence sufficient to sustain a finding of a witness' personal knowledge seems to be sufficient under the existing California practice. See also Tentative Recommendation and a Study Relating to the Uniform Rules of Evidence (Article IV. Witnesses), 6 Cal.Law Revision Comm'n, Rep., Rec. & Studies 701, 711–713 (1964).

Section 788—Conviction of a crime when offered to attack credibility. In this situation, the preliminary fact issue to be decided under Section 403 is whether the witness is actually the person who was convicted. This involves the relevancy of the evidence (since, obviously, the conviction of another does not affect the witness' credibility) and should be a question to be resolved by the jury. The judge should not be able to decide finally that it was the witness who was convicted and, thus, to prevent a contest on that issue before the jury. The existing law is uncertain in this regard; however, it seems likely that any evidence sufficient to identify the witness as the person convicted is sufficient to warrant admission of the conviction.

Section 800—Requirement that lay opinion be based on personal perception. The requirement specified in Section 800 is merely a specific application of the personal knowledge requirement in Section 702. See the discussion of Section 702 in this Comment, supra.

Sections 1200–1341—Identity of hearsay declarant. For most hearsay evidence, admissibility depends upon two preliminary determinations: (1) Did the declarant actually make the statement as claimed by the proponent of the evidence? (2) Does the statement meet certain standards of trustworthiness required by some exception to the hearsay rule?

The first determination involves the relevancy of the evidence. For example, if the issue is the state of mind of X, a person's statement as to his state of mind has no tendency to prove X's state of mind unless the declarant was X. Relevancy depends on the fact that X made the statement. Accordingly, if otherwise competent, a hearsay statement is admitted upon evidence sufficient to sustain a finding that the claimed declarant made the statement.

The second determination involves the competency of the evidence. Unless the evidence meets the requisite standards of an exception to the hearsay rule, it must be kept from the trier of fact despite its relevancy either because it is too unreliable or because public policy requires its suppression. For example, if an admission was in fact made by a defendant to a criminal action, the admission is relevant. But public policy requires that the admission be held inadmissible if it was not given voluntarily.

The admissibility of some hearsay declarations is dependent solely upon the determination that a particular declarant made the statement. Some of these exceptions to the hearsay rule—such as inconsistent statements of trial witnesses and admissions—are mentioned specifically below. Since the only preliminary fact to be determined in regard to these declarations involves the relevancy of the evidence, they should be admitted upon the introduction of evidence sufficient to sustain a finding of the preliminary fact.

When the admissibility of hearsay depends both upon a determination that a particular declarant made the statement and upon a determination that the requisite standards of a hearsay exception have been met, the former determination is to be made upon evidence sufficient to sustain a finding of the preliminary fact. Paragraph (4) is included in subdivision (a) to make this clear.

Section 1220—Admissions of a party. The only preliminary fact that is subject to dispute is the identity of the declarant. Under Section 403(a)(4), an admission is admissible upon the introduction of evidence sufficient to sustain a finding that the party made the statement.

An admission is not admissible in a criminal case unless it was given voluntarily. The voluntariness of an admission by a criminal defendant is determined under Section 405, not Section 403.

Sections 1221, 1222—Authorized and adoptive admissions. Under existing law, both authorized admissions (by an agent of a party) and adoptive admissions are admitted upon the introduction of evidence sufficient to sustain a finding of the foundational fact.

Section 1223—Admission of coconspirator. The admission of a coconspirator is another form of an authorized admission. Hence, the proffered evidence is admissible upon the introduction of evidence sufficient to sustain a finding of the conspiracy.

Sections 1224–1227—Admission of third person whose liability, breach of duty, or right is in issue. The only preliminary fact subject to dispute is the identity of the declarant; and the preliminary showing required in regard to this class of admissions is the same as if the declarant were being sued directly. Any evidence of the making of the statement by the claimed declarant is sufficient to warrant its admission.

Sections 1225, 1236—Previous statements of witnesses. Prior inconsistent statements and prior consistent statements made before bias or other improper motive arose are dealt with in Sections 1235 and 1236. In each case, the evidence is relevant and probative if the witnesses to the statements are credible. The credibility of the witnesses testifying to these statements should be decided finally by the jury. Moreover, the only preliminary fact subject to dispute insofar as alleged inconsistent statements are concerned is the identity of the declarant. Hence, evidence is admitted under these sections upon the introduction of evidence sufficient to sustain a finding of the preliminary fact.

Sections 1400–1402—Authentication of writings. Under existing law, an otherwise competent writing is admissible upon the introduction of evidence sufficient to sustain a finding of the authenticity of the writing.

Sections 1410–1421—Means of authenticating writings. Sections 1410 through 1421 merely state several ways in which the requirements of Sections 1400 through 1402 may be met. Hence, to the extent that Sections 1410 through 1421 specify facts that may be shown to authenticate writings, the same principles apply: In each case, the judge must decide whether the evidence offered is sufficient to sustain a finding of the authenticity of the proffered writing and admit the writing if there is such evidence. Care should be exercised, however, to distinguish those cases where the disputed preliminary fact is the authenticity of an exemplar with which the proffered writing is to be compared (Evidence Code §§ 1417–1419) or the qualification of a witness to give an opinion concerning the authenticity of a writing (Evidence Code §§ 1416, 1418); the judge is required to determine such questions under the provisions of Section 405.

Subdivision (b)

Under this subdivision, the judge may receive evidence that is conditionally admissible under Section 403, subject to the presentation of evidence of the preliminary fact later in the course of the trial.

Subdivision (c)

Subdivision (c) relates to the instructions to be given the jury when evidence is admitted whose admissibility depends on the existence of a preliminary fact determined under Section 403. When such evidence is admitted, the jury is required to make the ultimate determination of the existence of the preliminary fact. Unless the jury is persuaded that the preliminary fact exists, it is not permitted to consider the evidence.

For example, if P offers evidence of his negotiations with A in his contract action against D, the judge must admit the evidence if there is other evidence sufficient to sustain a finding that A was D's agent. If the jury is not persuaded that A was in fact D's agent, then it is not permitted to consider the evidence of the negotiations with A in determining D's liability.

Frequently, the jury's duty to disregard conditionally admissible evidence when it is not persuaded of the existence of the preliminary fact on which relevancy is conditioned is so clear that an instruction to this effect is unnecessary. For example, if the disputed preliminary fact is the authenticity of a deed, it hardly seems necessary to instruct the jury to disregard the deed if it should find that the deed is not genuine. No rational jury could find the deed to be spurious and, yet, to be still effective to transfer title from the purported grantor.

At times, however, it is not quite so clear that conditionally admissible evidence should be disregarded unless the preliminary fact is found to exist. In such cases, the jury should be appropriately instructed. For example, the theory upon which agent's and co-conspirator's statements are admissible is that the party is vicariously responsible for the acts and statements of agents and co-conspirators within the scope of the agency or conspiracy. Yet, it is not always clear that statements made by a purported agent or co-conspirator should be disregarded if not made in furtherance of the agency or conspiracy. Hence, the jury should be instructed to disregard such statements unless it is persuaded that the statements were made within the scope of the agency or conspiracy.

§ 404. Determination of whether proffered evidence is incriminatory.

Whenever the proffered evidence is claimed to be privileged under Section 940, the person claiming the privilege has the burden of showing that the proffered evidence might tend to incriminate him; and the proffered evidence is inadmissible unless it clearly appears to the court that the proffered evidence cannot possibly have a tendency to incriminate the person claiming the privilege.

Comment—Law Revision Commission

Section 404 provides a special procedure to be followed by the judge when an objection is made in reliance upon the privilege against self-incrimination. Under Section 404, the objecting party has the burden of showing that the testimony sought might incriminate him. However, the party is not required to produce evidence as such. In addition to considering evidence, the judge must consider the matters disclosed in argument, the implications of the question, the setting in which it is asked, the applicable statute of limitations, and all other relevant factors. Nonetheless, the burden is on the objector to present to the judge information of this sort sufficient to indicate that the proffered evidence might incriminate him. If he presents information of this sort, Section 404 requires the judge to sustain the claim of privilege unless it clearly appears that the proffered evidence cannot possibly have a tendency to incriminate the person claiming the privilege.

§ 405. Determination of foundational and other preliminary facts in other cases.

With respect to preliminary fact determinations not governed by Section 403 or 404:

(a) When the existence of a preliminary fact is disputed, the court shall indicate which party has the burden of producing evidence and the burden of proof on the issue as implied by the rule of law under which the question arises. The court shall determine the existence or nonexistence of the preliminary fact and shall admit or exclude the proffered evidence as required by the rule of law under which the question arises.

(b) If a preliminary fact is also a fact in issue in the action:

(1) The jury shall not be informed of the court's determination as to the existence or nonexistence of the preliminary fact.

(2) If the proffered evidence is admitted, the jury shall not be instructed to disregard the evidence if its determination of the fact differs from the court's determination of the preliminary fact.

Comment—Assembly Committee on Judiciary

Section 405 requires the judge to determine the existence or nonexistence of disputed preliminary facts except in certain situations covered by Sections 403 and 404. Section 405 deals with evidentiary rules designed to withhold evidence from the jury because it is too unreliable to be evaluated properly or because public policy requires its exclusion.

Under Section 405, the judge first indicates to the parties who has the burden of proof and the burden of producing evidence on the disputed issue as implied by the rule of law under which the question arises. For example, Section 1200 indicates that the burden of proof is usually on the proponent of the evidence to show that the proffered evidence is within a hearsay exception. Thus, if the disputed preliminary fact is whether the proffered statement was spontaneous, as required by Section 1240, the proponent would have the burden of persuading the judge as to the spontaneity of the statement. On the other hand, the privilege rules usually place the burden of proof on the objecting party to show that a privilege is applicable. Thus, if the disputed preliminary fact is whether a person is married to a party and, hence, whether their confidential communications are privileged under Section 980, the burden of proof is on the party asserting the privilege to persuade the judge of the existence of the marriage.

After the judge has indicated to the parties who has the burden of proof and the burden of producing evidence, the parties submit their evidence on the preliminary issue to the judge. If the judge is persuaded by the party with the burden of proof, he finds in favor of that party in regard to the preliminary fact and either admits or excludes the proffered evidence as required by the rule of law under which the question arises. Otherwise, he finds against that party on the preliminary fact and either admits or excludes the proffered evidence as required by such finding.

Examples of preliminary fact issues to be decided under Section 405

Illustrative of the preliminary fact questions that should be decided under Section 405 are the following:

§ 405   CALIFORNIA EVIDENCE CODE

Section 701—Disqualification of a witness for lack of mental capacity. Under existing law, as under this code, the party objecting to a proffered witness has the burden of proving the witness' lack of capacity.

Section 720—Qualifications of an expert witness. Under Section 720, as under existing law, the proponent must persuade the judge that his expert is qualified, and it is error for the judge to submit the qualifications of the expert to the jury.

Section 788—Conviction of a crime when offered to attack credibility. If the disputed preliminary fact is whether a pardon or some similar relief has been granted to a witness convicted of a crime, the judge's determination is made under Section 405. Cf. Comment to Section 403.

Section 870—Opinion evidence on sanity. Whether a witness is sufficiently acquainted with a person whose sanity is in question to be qualified to express an opinion on the matter involves, in effect, the expertise of the witness on that limited subject. The witness' qualifications to express such an opinion, therefore, are to be determined by the judge under Section 405 just as the qualifications of other experts are decided by the judge.

Sections 900-1070—Privileges. Under this code, as under existing law, the party claiming a privilege has the burden of proof on the preliminary facts. The proponent of the proffered evidence, however, has the burden of proof upon any preliminary fact necessary to show that an exception to the privilege is applicable.

Sections 1152, 1154—Admissions made during compromise negotiations. With respect to admissions made during compromise negotiations, the disputed preliminary fact to be decided by the judge is whether the admission occurred during compromise negotiations or at some other time. This code places the burden on the objecting party to satisfy the judge that the admission occurred during such negotiations.

Sections 1200-1341—Hearsay evidence. When hearsay evidence is offered, two preliminary fact questions may be raised. The first question relates to the authenticity of the proffered declaration—was the statement actually made by the person alleged to have made it? The second question relates to the existence of those circumstances that make the hearsay sufficiently trustworthy to be received in evidence—e.g., was the declaration spontaneous, the confession voluntary, the business record trustworthy? Under this code, questions relating to the authenticity of the proffered declaration are decided under Section 403. See the Comment to Section 403. But other preliminary fact questions are decided under Section 405.

For example, the court must decide whether a statement offered as a dying declaration was made under a sense of impending death, and the proponent of the evidence has the burden of proof on this issue. Under this code, the proponent of a hearsay declaration has the burden of proof on the unavailability of the declarant as a witness under Section 1291 or 1310; but the party objecting to the evidence has the burden of proving that the unavailability of the declarant was procured by the proponent in order to prevent the declarant from testifying. See Evidence Code § 240.

Section 1416—Opinion evidence on handwriting. Whether a witness is sufficiently acquainted with the handwriting of a person to give an opinion on whether a questioned writing is in that person's handwriting involves, in effect, the expertise of the witness on the limited subject of the supposed writer's handwriting. The witness' qualifications to express such an opinion, therefore, are to be determined by the judge under Section 405 just as the qualifications of other experts are decided by the judge. See the discussion of Section 720 in this Comment, supra.

Sections 1417–1419—Comparison of writing with exemplar. Under Sections 1417 through 1419, as under existing law, the judge must be satisfied that a writing is genuine before he may admit it for comparison with other writings whose authenticity is in dispute.

Sections 1500–1510—Best evidence rule. Under Section 405, as under existing law, the trial judge is required to determine the preliminary fact necessary to warrant reception of secondary evidence of a writing, and the burden of proof on the issue is on the proponent of the secondary evidence.

Sections 1550, 1551—Photographic copy of writing. Sections 1550 and 1551 are special exceptions to the best evidence rule; hence, Section 405 governs the determination of any disputed preliminary fact under these sections just as it governs the determination of disputed preliminary facts under Sections 1500 through 1510.

Function of court and jury under Section 405

When preliminary fact question is also an issue involved in merits of case. In some cases, a factual issue to be decided by the judge under Section 405 will coincide with an issue involved in the merits of the case. For example, in People v. MacDonald, 24 Cal.App.2d 702, 76 P.2d 121 (1938), the defendant in an incest prosecution objected to the testimony of the prosecutrix on the ground that she was his wife. The judge, in ruling on the objection, had to determine whether the prosecutrix was also the defendant's daughter and, hence, whether their marriage was incestuous and void. In such a case, it would be prejudicial to the parties for the judge to inform the jury how he had decided the same factual question that it must decide in determining the merits of the case. Subdivision (b), therefore, prohibits a judge from informing the jury how he decided a question under Section 405 that the jury must ultimately resolve on the merits.

The judge is also prohibited from instructing the jury to disregard evidence that has been admitted if the jury's determination of a fact in deciding the merits differs from the judge's determination of the same fact under Section 405. The rules of admissibility being applied by the judge under Section 405 are designed to withhold evidence from the jury because it is too unreliable to be evaluated properly or because public policy requires its exclusion. The policies underlying these rules are served only by the exclusion of the evidence. No valid public or evidentiary purpose is served by submitting the admissibility question again to the jury.

Confessions, dying declarations, and spontaneous statements. Although Section 405 is generally consistent with existing law, it will, however, substantially change the law relating to confessions, dying declarations, and spontaneous statements. Under existing law, the judge considers all of the evidence and decides whether evidence of this sort is admissible, as indicated in Section 405. But if he decides the proffered evidence is admissible, he submits the preliminary question to the jury for a final determination whether the confession was voluntary, whether the dying declaration was made in realization of impending doom, or whether the spontaneous statement was in fact spontaneous; and the jury is instructed to disregard the statement if it does not believe that the condition of admissibility has been satisfied.

Under Section 405, the judge's rulings on these questions are final; the jury does not have an opportunity to redetermine the issue.

Section 405 will have no effect on the admissibility of confessions where the uncontradicted evidence shows that the confession was not voluntary. Under existing law, as under the Evidence Code, such a confession may not be admitted for consideration by the jury. Section 405 will also have no effect on the admissibility of confessions in those instances where, despite a conflict in the evidence, the court is persuaded that the confession was not voluntary.

Hence, Section 405 changes the law relating to confessions only where there is a substantial conflict in the evidence over voluntariness and the court is not persuaded that the confession was involuntary. Under existing law, a court that is in doubt may "pass the buck" concerning such a confession to the jury when there is a difficult factual question to resolve. Under the Evidence Code, however, the court is required to withhold a confession from the jury unless the court is persuaded that the confession was made freely and voluntarily. The court has no "discretion" to avoid difficult decisions by shifting the responsibility to the jury. If the court is in doubt, if the prosecution has not persuaded it of the voluntary nature of the confession, Section 405 requires the court to exclude the confession.

The existing law is based on the belief that a jury, in determining the defendant's guilt or innocence, can and will refuse to consider a confession that it has determined was involuntary even though it believes that the confession is true. Section 405, on the other hand, proceeds upon the belief that it is unrealistic to expect a jury to perform such a feat.

The foregoing discussion has focused on confessions because the case law is well developed there. But the "second crack" doctrine is equally unsatisfactory when applied to dying declarations and spontaneous statements. Hence, Section 405 requires the court to rule finally on the admissibility of these statements as well.

Of course, Section 405 does not prevent the presentation of any evidence to the jury that is relevant to the reliability of the hearsay statement.

§ 406. Evidence affecting weight or credibility. This article does not limit the right of a party to introduce before the trier of fact evidence relevant to weight or credibility.

Chapter 5

WEIGHT OF EVIDENCE GENERALLY

§ 410. "Direct evidence". As used in this chapter, "direct evidence" means evidence that directly proves a fact, without an inference or presumption, and which in itself if true, conclusively establishes that fact.

§ 411. Direct evidence of one witness sufficient. Except where additional evidence is required by statute, the direct evidence of one witness who is entitled to full credit is sufficient for proof of any fact.

§ 412. Party having power to produce better evidence. If weaker and less satisfactory evidence is offered when it was within the power of the party to produce stronger and more satisfactory evidence, the evidence offered should be viewed with distrust.

§ 413. Party's failure to explain or deny evidence. In determining what inferences to draw from the evidence or facts in the case against a party, the trier of fact may consider, among other things, the party's failure to explain or to deny by his testimony such evidence or facts in the case against him, or his willful suppression of evidence relating thereto, if such be the case.

Division 4

JUDICIAL NOTICE

Comment—Law Revision Commission

The statutory scheme in Division 4 is based on Article 2 (Rules 9–12) of the Uniform Rules of Evidence. The court is required to take judicial notice of the matters listed in Section 451. It may take judicial notice of the matters listed in Section 452 even when not requested to do so; it is required to notice them, however, if a party requests it and satisfies the requirements of Section 453.

There is some overlap between the matters listed in the mandatory notice provisions of Section 451 and the matters listed in the permissive-unless-a-request-is-made provisions of Section 452. Thus, when a matter falls within Section 451, judicial notice is mandatory even though the matter would otherwise fall within Section 452. The introductory clause of Section 452 makes this clear. For example, public statutory law is required to be noticed under subdivision (a) of Section 451 even though it would also be included under official acts of the legislative department under subdivision (c) of Section 452. Certain regulations are required to be noticed under subdivision (b) of Section 451 even though they might also be included under subdivisions (b) and (c) of Section 452. And indisputable matters of universal knowledge are required to be noticed under subdivision (f) of Section 451 even though such matters might be included under subdivisions (g) and (h) of Section 452.

§ 450. Judicial notice may be taken only as authorized by law.

Judicial notice may not be taken of any matter unless authorized or required by law.

Comment—Law Revision Commission

Section 450 provides that judicial notice may not be taken of any matter unless authorized or required by law. See Evidence Code § 160, defining "law." Sections 451 and 452 state a number of matters which must or may be judicially noticed. Judicial notice of other matters is authorized or required by other statutes or by decisional law. E.g., Civil Code § 53; Corp.Code § 6602.

Under the Evidence Code, as under existing law, courts may consider whatever materials are appropriate in construing statutes, determining constitutional issues, and formulating rules of law. That a court may consider legislative history, discussions by learned writers in treatises and law reviews, materials that contain controversial economic and social facts or findings or that indicate contemporary opinion, and similar materials is inherent in the requirement that it take judicial notice of the law. In many cases, the meaning and validity of statutes, the precise nature of a common law rule, or the correct interpretation of a constitutional provision can be determined only with the help of such extrinsic aids.

§ 451. Matters which must be judicially noticed

Judicial notice shall be taken of the following:

(a) The decisional, constitutional, and public statutory law of this state and of the United States and the provisions of any charter described in Section 3, 4, or 5 of Article XI of the California Constitution.

(b) Any matter made a subject of judicial notice by Section 11343.6, 11344.6, or 18576 of the Government Code or by Section 1507 of Title 44 of the United States Code.

(c) Rules of professional conduct for members of the bar adopted pursuant to Section 6076 of the Business and Professions Code and rules of practice and procedure for the courts of this state adopted by the Judicial Council.

(d) Rules of pleading, practice, and procedure prescribed by the United States Supreme Court, such as the Rules of the United States Supreme Court, the Federal Rules of Civil Procedure, the Federal Rules of Criminal Procedure, the Admiralty Rules, the Rules of the Court of Claims, the Rules of the Customs Court, and the General Orders and Forms in Bankruptcy.

(e) The true signification of all English words and phrases and of all legal expressions.

(f) Facts and propositions of generalized knowledge that are so universally known that they cannot reasonably be the subject of dispute.

Comment—Assembly Committee on Judiciary

Judicial notice of the matters specified in Section 451 is *mandatory,* whether or not the court is requested to notice them. Although the court errs if it fails to take judicial notice of the matters specified in this section, such error is not necessarily reversible error. Depending upon the circumstances, the appellate court may hold that the error was "invited" (and, hence, is not reversible error) or that points not urged in the trial court may not be advanced on appeal.

Listed below are the matters that must be judicially noticed under Section 451.

California and federal law. The decisional, constitutional, and public statutory law of California and of the United States must be judicially noticed under subdivision (a).

Charter provisions of California cities and counties. Judicial notice must be taken under subdivision (a) of the provisions of charters adopted pursuant to Section 7½ or 8 of Article XI of the California Constitution.

Regulations of California and federal agencies. Judicial notice must be taken under subdivision (b) of the rules, regulations, orders, and standards of general application adopted by California state agencies and filed with the Secretary of State or printed in the California Administrative Code or the California Administrative Register.

Subdivision (b) also requires California courts to judicially notice documents published in the Federal Register (such as (1) presidential proclamations and executive orders having general applicability and legal effect and (2) orders, regulations, rules, certificates, codes of fair competition, licenses, notices, and similar instruments, having general applicability and legal effect, that are issued, prescribed, or promulgated by federal agencies).

"Universally known" facts. Subdivision (f) requires the court to take judicial notice of indisputable facts and propositions universally known. "Universally known" does not mean that every man on the street has knowledge of such facts. A fact known among persons of reasonable and average intelligence and knowledge will satisfy the "universally known" requirement.

Subdivision (f) should be contrasted with subdivisions (g) and (h) of Section 452, which provide for judicial notice of indisputable facts and propositions that are matters of common knowledge or are capable of immediate and accurate determination by resort to sources of reasonably indisputable accuracy. Subdivisions (g) and (h) permit notice of facts and propositions that are indisputable but are not "universally" known.

Judicial notice does not apply to facts merely because they are known to the judge to be indisputable. The facts must fulfill the requirements of subdivision (f) of Section 451 or subdivision (g) or (h) of Section 452. If a judge happens to know a fact that is not widely enough known to be subject to judicial notice under this division, he may not "notice" it.

§ 452. Matters which may be judicially noticed.

Judicial notice may be taken of the following matters to the extent that they are not embraced within Section 451:

(a) The decisional, constitutional, and statutory law of any state of the United States and the resolutions and private acts of the Congress of the United States and of the Legislature of this state.

(b) Regulations and legislative enactments issued by or under the authority of the United States or any public entity in the United States.

(c) Official acts of the legislative, executive, and judicial departments of the United States and of any state of the United States.

(d) Records of (1) any court of this state or (2) any court of record of the United States or of any state of the United States.

(e) Rules of court of (1) any court of this state or (2) any court of record of the United States or of any state of the United States.

(f) The law of an organization of nations and of foreign nations and public entities in foreign nations.

(g) Facts and propositions that are of such common knowledge within the territorial jurisdiction of the court that they cannot reasonably be the subject of dispute.

(h) Facts and propositions that are not reasonably subject to dispute and are capable of immediate and accurate determination by resort to sources of reasonably indisputable accuracy.

Comment—Assembly Committee on Judiciary

Section 452 includes matters both of law and of fact. The court *may* take judicial notice of these matters, even when not requested to do so; it is *required* to notice them if a party requests it and satisfies the requirements of Section 453.

The matters of law included under Section 452 may be neither known to the court nor easily discoverable by it because the sources of information are not readily available. However, if a party requests it and furnishes the court with "sufficient information" for it to take judicial notice, the court must do so if proper notice has been given to each adverse party. See Evidence Code § 453.

Matters of "common knowledge" and verifiable facts. Subdivision (g) provides for judicial notice of matters of common knowledge within the court's territorial jurisdiction that are not subject to dispute. "Territorial jurisdiction," in this context, refers to the county in which a superior court is located or the judicial district in which a municipal or justice court is located. The fact of which notice is taken need not be something physically located within the court's territorial jurisdiction, but common knowledge of the fact must exist within the court's territorial jurisdiction.

Subdivision (h) provides for judicial notice of indisputable facts immediately ascertainable by reference to sources of reasonably indisputable accuracy. In other words, the facts need not be actually known if they are readily ascertainable and indisputable. Sources of "reasonably indisputable accuracy" include not only treatises, encyclopedias, almanacs, and the like, but also persons learned in the subject matter.

Subdivisions (g) and (h) include, for example, facts which are accepted as established by experts and specialists in the natural, physical, and social sciences, if those facts are of such wide acceptance that to submit them to the jury would be to risk irrational findings.

§ 452.5. Criminal conviction records; computer-generated records; admissibility.

(a) The official acts and records specified in subdivisions (c) and (d) of Section 452 include any computer-generated official court records, as specified by the Judicial Council which relate to criminal convictions, when the record is certified by a clerk of the superior court pursuant to Section 69844.5 of the Government Code at the time of computer entry.

(b) An official record of conviction certified in accordance with subdivision (a) of Section 1530 is admissible pursuant to Section 1280 to prove the commission, attempted commission, or solicitation of a criminal offense, prior conviction, service of a prison term, or other act, condition, or event recorded by the record.

§ 453. Compulsory judicial notice upon request.

The trial court shall take judicial notice of any matter specified in Section 452 if a party requests it and:

(a) Gives each adverse party sufficient notice of the request, through the pleadings or otherwise, to enable such adverse party to prepare to meet the request; and

(b) Furnishes the court with sufficient information to enable it to take judicial notice of the matter.

§ 453   CALIFORNIA EVIDENCE CODE

Comment—Law Revision Commission

Section 453 is intended as a safeguard and not as a rigid limitation on the court's power to take judicial notice. The section does not affect the discretionary power of the court to take judicial notice under Section 452 where the party requesting that judicial notice be taken fails to give the requisite notice to each adverse party or fails to furnish sufficient information as to the propriety of taking judicial notice or as to the tenor of the matter to be noticed. Hence, when he considers it appropriate, the judge may take judicial notice under Section 452 and may consult and use any source of pertinent information, whether or not furnished by the parties. However, where the matter noticed under Section 452 is one that is of substantial consequence to the action—even though the court may take judicial notice under Section 452 when the requirements of Section 453 have not been satisfied—the party adversely affected must be given a reasonable opportunity to present information as to the propriety of taking judicial notice and as to the tenor of the matter to be noticed. See Evidence Code § 455 and the Comment thereto.

The "notice" requirement.

The notice requirement is an important one since judicial notice is binding on the jury under Section 457. Accordingly, the adverse parties should be given ample notice so that they will have an opportunity to prepare to oppose the taking of judicial notice and to obtain information relevant to the tenor of the matter to be noticed.

Since Section 452 relates to a wide variety of facts and law, the notice requirement should be administered with flexibility in order to insure that the policy behind the judicial notice rules is properly implemented. In many cases, it will be reasonable to expect the notice to be given at or before the time of the pretrial conference. In other cases, matters of fact or law of which the court should take judicial notice may come up at the trial. Section 453 merely requires reasonable notice, and the reasonableness of the notice given will depend upon the circumstances of the particular case.

The "sufficient information" requirement. Under Section 453, the court is not required to resort to any sources of information not provided by the parties. If the party requesting that judicial notice be taken under Section 453 fails to provide the court with "sufficient information," the judge may decline to take judicial notice. For example, if the party requests the court to take judicial notice of the specific gravity of gold, the party requesting that notice be taken must furnish the judge with definitive information as to the specific gravity of gold. The judge is not required to undertake the necessary research to determine the fact, though, of course, he is not precluded from doing such research if he so desires.

Section 453 does not define "sufficient information"; this will necessarily vary from case to case.

Burden on party requesting that judicial notice be taken. Where a request is made to take judicial notice under Section 453, the court may decline to take judicial notice unless the party requesting that notice be taken persuades the judge that the matter is one that properly may be noticed under Section 452 and also persuades the judge as to the tenor of the matter to be noticed. The degree of the judge's persuasion regarding a particular matter is determined by the subdivision of Section 452 which authorizes judicial notice of the matter. For example, if the matter is claimed to be a fact of common knowledge under paragraph (g) of Section 452, the party must persuade the judge that the fact is of such common knowledge within the territorial jurisdiction of the court that it cannot reasonably be subject to dispute.

§ 454. Information that may be used in taking judicial notice.

(a) In determining the propriety of taking judicial notice of a matter, or the tenor thereof:

(1) Any source of pertinent information, including the advice of persons learned in the subject matter, may be consulted or used, whether or not furnished by a party.

(2) Exclusionary rules of evidence do not apply except for Section 352 and the rules of privilege.

(b) Where the subject of judicial notice is the law of an organization of nations, a foreign nation, or a public entity in a foreign nation and the court resorts to the advice of persons learned in the subject matter, such advice, if not received in open court, shall be in writing.

§ 455. Opportunity to present information to court.

With respect to any matter specified in Section 452 or in subdivision (f) of Section 451 that is of substantial consequence to the determination of the action:

(a) If the trial court has been requested to take or has taken or proposes to take judicial notice of such matter, the court shall afford each party reasonable opportunity, before the jury is instructed or before the cause is submitted for decision by the court, to present to the court information relevant to (1) the propriety of taking judicial notice of the matter and (2) the tenor of the matter to be noticed.

(b) If the trial court resorts to any source of information not received in open court, including the advice of persons learned in the subject matter, such information and its source shall be made a part of the record in the action and the court shall afford each party reasonable opportunity to meet such information before judicial notice of the matter may be taken.

Comment—Law Revision Commission

Section 455 provides procedural safeguards designed to afford the parties reasonable opportunity to be heard both as to the propriety of taking judicial notice of a matter and as to the tenor of the matter to be noticed.

Subdivision (a). This subdivision guarantees to the parties a reasonable opportunity to present information to the court as to the propriety of taking judicial notice and as to the tenor of the matter to be noticed. In a jury case, the subdivision provides the parties with an opportunity to present their information to the judge before a jury instruction based on a matter judicially noticed is given. Where the matter subject to judicial notice relates to a cause tried by the court, the subdivision guarantees the parties an opportunity to dispute the taking of judicial notice of the matter before the cause is submitted for decision.

§ 456. Noting for record denial of request to take judicial notice. If the trial court denies a request to take judicial notice of any matter, the court shall at the earliest practicable time so advise the parties and indicate for the record that it has denied the request.

§ 457. Instructing jury on matter judicially noticed. If a matter judicially noticed is a matter which would otherwise have been for determination by the jury, the trial court may, and upon request shall, instruct the jury to accept as a fact the matter so noticed.

§ 458. Judicial notice by trial court in subsequent proceedings. The failure or refusal of the trial court to take judicial notice of a matter, or to instruct the jury with respect to the matter, does not preclude the trial court in subsequent proceedings in the action from taking judicial notice of the matter in accordance with the procedure specified in this division.

§ 459. Judicial notice by reviewing court. (a) The reviewing court shall take judicial notice of (1) each matter properly noticed by the trial court and (2) each matter that the trial court was required to notice under Section 451 or 453. The reviewing court may take judicial notice of any matter specified in Section 452. The reviewing court may take judicial notice of a matter in a tenor different from that noticed by the trial court.

(b) In determining the propriety of taking judicial notice of a matter, or the tenor thereof, the reviewing court has the same power as the trial court under Section 454.

(c) When taking judicial notice under this section of a matter specified in Section 452 or in subdivision (f) of Section 451 that is of substantial consequence to the determination of the action, the reviewing court shall comply with the provisions of subdivision (a) of Section 455 if the matter was not theretofore judicially noticed in the action.

(d) In determining the propriety of taking judicial notice of a matter specified in Section 452 or in subdivision (f) of Section 451 that is of substantial consequence to the determination of the action, or the tenor thereof, if the reviewing court resorts to any source of information not received in open court or not included in the record of the action, including the advice of persons learned in the subject matter, the reviewing court shall afford each party reasonable opportunity to meet such information before judicial notice of the matter may be taken.

Comment—Law Revision Commission

Section 459 sets forth a separate set of rules for the taking of judicial notice by a reviewing court.

Subdivision (a). Subdivision (a) requires that a reviewing court take judicial notice of any matter that the trial court properly noticed or was obliged to notice. This means that the matters specified in Section 451 must be judicially noticed by the reviewing court even though the trial court failed to take judicial notice of such matters. A matter specified in Section 452 also must be judicially noticed by the reviewing court if such matter was properly noticed by the trial court in the exercise of its discretion or an appropriate request was made at the trial level and the party making the request satisfied the conditions specified in Section 453. However, if the trial court erred, the reviewing court is not bound by the tenor of the notice taken by the trial court.

Having taken judicial notice of such a matter, the reviewing court may or may not apply it in the particular case on appeal. The effect to be given to matters judicially noticed on appeal, where the question has not been raised below, depends on factors that are not evidentiary in character and are not mentioned in this code. For example, the appellate court is required to notice the matters of law mentioned in Section 451, but it may hold that an error which the appellant has "invited" is not reversible error or that points not urged in the trial court may not be advanced on appeal, and refuse, therefore, to apply the law to the pending case. These principles do not mean that the appellate court does not take judicial notice of the applicable law; they merely mean that, for reasons of policy governing appellate review, the appellate court may refuse to apply the law to the case before it.

In addition to requiring the reviewing court to judicially notice those matters which the trial court properly noticed or was required to notice, the subdivision also provides authority for the reviewing court to exercise the same discretionary power to take judicial notice as is possessed by the trial court.

Subdivision (b). The reviewing court may consult any source of pertinent information for the purpose of determining the propriety of taking judicial notice or the tenor of the matter to be noticed.

§ 460. Appointment of expert by court.

Where the advice of persons learned in the subject matter is required in order to enable the court to take judicial notice of a matter, the court on its own motion or on motion of any party may appoint one or more such persons to provide such advice. If the court determines to appoint such a person, he shall be appointed and compensated in the manner provided in Article 2 (commencing with Section 730) of Chapter 3 of Division 6.

Division 5

BURDEN OF PROOF; BURDEN OF PRODUCING EVIDENCE; PRESUMPTIONS AND INFERENCES

Chapter 1

BURDEN OF PROOF

Article 1. General

§ 500. Party who has the burden of proof. Except as otherwise provided by law, a party has the burden of proof as to each fact the existence or nonexistence of which is essential to the claim for relief or defense that he is asserting.

Comment—Law Revision Commission

As used in Section 500, the burden of proof means the obligation of a party to produce a particular state of conviction in the mind of the trier of fact as to the existence or nonexistence of a fact. See Evidence Code §§ 115, 190. If this requisite degree of conviction is not achieved as to the existence of a particular fact, the trier of fact must assume that the fact does not exist. Usually, the burden of proof requires a party to convince the trier of fact that the existence of a particular fact is more probable than its nonexistence—a degree of proof usually described as proof by a preponderance of the evidence. However, in some instances, the burden of proof requires a party to produce a substantially greater degree of belief in the mind of the trier of fact concerning the existence of the fact—a burden usually described by stating that the party must introduce clear and convincing proof or, with respect to the prosecution in a criminal case, proof beyond a reasonable doubt.

The defendant in a criminal case sometimes has the burden of proof in regard to a fact essential to negate his guilt. However, in such cases, he usually is not required to persuade the trier of fact as to the existence of such fact; he is merely required to raise a reasonable doubt in the mind of the trier of fact as to his guilt.

Section 500 does not attempt to indicate what facts may be essential to a particular party's claim for relief or defense. The facts that must be shown to establish a cause of action or a defense are determined by the substantive law, not the law of evidence.

The general rule allocating the burden of proof applies "except as otherwise provided by law." The exception is included in recognition of the fact that the burden of proof is sometimes allocated in a manner that is at variance with the general rule. In determining whether the normal allocation of the burden of proof should be altered, the courts consider a number of factors: the knowledge of the parties concerning the particular fact, the availability of the evidence to the parties, the most desirable result in terms of public policy in the absence of proof of the particular fact, and the probability of the existence or nonexistence of the fact.

§ 501. Burden of proof in criminal action generally. Insofar as any statute, except Section 522, assigns the burden of proof in a criminal action, such statute is subject to Penal Code Section 1096.

Comment—Law Revision Commission

Section 501 is intended to make it clear that the statutory allocations of the burden of proof appearing in this chapter and elsewhere in the codes are subject to Penal Code Section 1096, which requires that a criminal defendant be proved guilty beyond a reasonable doubt, i.e., that the statutory allocations do not (except on the issue of insanity) require the defendant to persuade the trier of fact of his innocence. Under Evidence Code Section 522, as under existing law, the defendant must prove his insanity by a preponderance of the evidence.

§ 502. Instructions on burden of proof. The court on all proper occasions shall instruct the jury as to which party bears the burden of proof on each issue and as to whether that burden requires that a party raise a reasonable doubt concerning the existence or nonexistence of a fact by a preponderance of the evidence, by clear and convincing proof, or by proof beyond a reasonable doubt.

Article 2. Burden of Proof on Specific Issues

§ 520. Claim that person guilty of crime or wrongdoing. The party claiming that a person is guilty of crime or wrongdoing has the burden of proof on that issue.

§ 521. Claim that person did not exercise care. The party claiming that a person did not exercise a requisite degree of care has the burden of proof on that issue.

§ 522. Claim that person is or was insane. The party claiming that any person, including himself, is or was insane has the burden of proof on that issue.

§ 523. In any action where the state is a party, regardless of who is the moving party, where (a) the boundary of land patented or otherwise granted by the state is in dispute, or (b) the validity of any state patent or grant dated prior to 1950 is in dispute, the state shall have the burden of proof on all issues relating to the historic locations of rivers, streams, and other water bodies and the authority of the state in issuing the patent or grant.

This section is not intended to nor shall it be construed to supersede existing statutes governing disputes where the state is a party and regarding title to real property.

§ 524. Burden of proof on State Board of Equalization; Standard

(a) Notwithstanding any other provision of law, in a civil proceeding to which the State Board of Equalization is a party, that board shall have the burden of proof by clear and convincing evidence in sustaining its assertion of a penalty for intent to evade or fraud against a taxpayer, with respect to any factual issue relevant to ascertaining the liability of a taxpayer.

(b) Nothing in this section shall be construed to override any requirement for a taxpayer to substantiate any item on a return or claim filed with the State Board of Equalization.

(c) Nothing in this section shall subject a taxpayer to unreasonable search or access to records in violation of the United States Constitution, the California Constitution, or any other law.

(d) For purposes of this section, "taxpayer" includes a person on whom fees administered by the State Board of Equalization are imposed.

Chapter 2

BURDEN OF PRODUCING EVIDENCE

§ 550. Party who has the burden of producing evidence.
(a) The burden of producing evidence as to a particular fact is on the party against whom a finding on that fact would be required in the absence of further evidence.

(b) The burden of producing evidence as to a particular fact is initially on the party with the burden of proof as to that fact.

Comment—Law Revision Commission

Section 550 deals with the allocation of the burden of producing evidence. At the outset of the case, this burden will coincide with the burden of proof. However, during the course of the trial, the burden may shift from one party to another, irrespective of the incidence of the burden of proof. For example, if the party with the initial burden of producing evidence establishes a fact giving rise to a presumption, the burden of producing evidence will shift to the other party, whether or not the presumption is one that affects the burden of proof. In addition, a party may introduce evidence of such overwhelming probative force that no person could reasonably disbelieve it in the absence of countervailing evidence, in which case the burden of producing evidence would shift to the opposing party to produce some evidence.

Chapter 3

PRESUMPTIONS AND INFERENCES

Article 1. General

§ 600. Presumption and inference defined.
(a) A presumption is an assumption of fact that the law requires to be made from another fact

or group of facts found or otherwise established in the action. A presumption is not evidence.

(b) An inference is a deduction of fact that may logically and reasonably be drawn from another fact or group of facts found or otherwise established in the action.

§ **601. Classification of presumptions.** A presumption is either conclusive or rebuttable. Every rebuttable presumption is either (a) a presumption affecting the burden of producing evidence or (b) a presumption affecting the burden of proof.

Comment—Law Revision Commission

Some presumptions are conclusive. The court or jury is required to find the existence of the presumed fact regardless of the strength of the opposing evidence. All presumptions that are not conclusive are rebuttable presumptions.

For several decades, courts and legal scholars have wrangled over the purpose and function of presumptions. The view espoused by Professors Thayer, Preliminary Treatise on Evidence 313–352 (1898) and Wigmore (9 Wigmore, Evidence §§ 2485–2491 (3d ed. 1940)), accepted by most courts (see Morgan, Presumptions, 10 Rutgers L.Rev. 512, 516 (1956)), and adopted by the American Law Institute's Model Code of Evidence, is that a presumption is a preliminary assumption of fact that disappears from the case upon the introduction of evidence sufficient to sustain a finding of the nonexistence of the presumed fact. In Professor Thayer's view, a presumption merely reflects the judicial determination that the same conclusionary fact exists so frequently when the preliminary fact exists that, once the preliminary fact is established, proof of the conclusionary fact may be dispensed with unless there is actually some contrary evidence:

> Many facts and groups of facts often recur, and when a body of men with a continuous tradition has carried on for some length of time this process of reasoning upon facts that often repeat themselves, they cut short the process and lay down a rule. To such facts they affix, by a general declaration, the character and operation which common experience has assigned to them. [Thayer, Preliminary Treatise on Evidence 326 (1898).]

Professors Morgan and McCormick argue that a presumption should shift the burden of proof to the adverse party. Morgan, Some Problems of Proof 81 (1956); McCormick, Evidence § 317 at 671–672 (1954). They believe that presumptions are created for reasons of policy and argue that, if the policy underlying a presumption is of sufficient weight to require a finding of the presumed fact when there is no contrary evidence, it should be of sufficient weight to require a finding when the mind of the trier of fact is in equilibrium, and, *a fortiori*, it should be of sufficient weight to require a finding if the trier of fact does not believe the contrary evidence.

The classification of presumptions in the Evidence Code is based on a third view suggested by Professor Bohlen in 1920. Bohlen, The Effect of Rebuttable Presumptions of Law Upon the Burden of Proof, 68 U.Pa.L.Rev. 307 (1920). Underlying the presumptions provisions of the Evidence Code is the conclusion that the Thayer view is correct as to some presumptions, but that the Morgan view is right as to others. The fact is that presumptions are created for a variety of reasons, and no single theory or rationale of presumptions can deal adequately with all of them. Hence, the Evidence Code classifies all rebuttable presumptions as either (1) presumptions affecting the burden of producing evidence (essentially Thayer presumptions), or (2) presumptions affecting the burden of proof (essentially Morgan presumptions).

Sections 603 and 605 set forth the criteria by which the two classes of rebuttable presumptions may be distinguished, and Sections 604, 606, and 607 prescribe their effect. Articles 3 and 4 (Sections 630–668) classify many presumptions found in California law; but many other presumptions, both statutory and common law, must await classification by the courts in accordance with the criteria contained in Sections 603 and 605.

§ 602. Statute making one fact prima facie evidence of another fact.
A statute providing that a fact or group of facts is prima facie evidence of another fact establishes a rebuttable presumption.

Comment—Law Revision Commission

Section 602 indicates the construction to be given to the large number of statutes scattered through the codes that state that one fact or group of facts is prima facie evidence of another fact. Section 602 provides that these statutes are to be regarded as rebuttable presumptions. Hence, unless some specific language applicable to the particular statute in question indicates whether it affects the burden of proof or only the burden of producing evidence, the courts will be required to classify these statutes as presumptions affecting the burden of proof or the burden of producing evidence in accordance with the criteria set forth in Sections 603 and 605.

§ 603. Presumption affecting the burden of producing evidence defined.
A presumption affecting the burden of producing evidence is a presumption established to implement no public policy other than to facilitate the determination of the particular action in which the presumption is applied.

Comment—Law Revision Commission

Sections 603 and 605 set forth the criteria for determining whether a particular presumption is a presumption affecting the burden of producing evidence or a presumption affecting the burden of proof. Many presumptions are classified in Articles 3 and 4 (Sections 630–668) of this chapter. In the absence of specific statutory classification, the courts may determine whether a presumption is a presumption affecting the burden of producing evidence or a presumption affecting the burden of proof by applying the standards contained in Sections 603 and 605.

Section 603 describes those presumptions that are not based on any public policy extrinsic to the action in which they are invoked. These presumptions are designed to dispense with unnecessary proof of facts that are likely to be true if not disputed. Typically, such presumptions are based on an underlying logical inference. In some cases, the presumed fact is so likely to be true and so little likely to be disputed that the law requires it to be assumed in the absence of contrary evidence. In other cases, evidence of the nonexistence of the presumed fact, if there is any, is so much more readily available to the party against whom the presumption operates that he is not permitted to argue that the presumed fact does not exist unless he is willing to produce such evidence. In still other cases, there may be no direct evidence of the existence or nonexistence of the presumed fact; but, because the case must be decided, the law requires a determination that the presumed fact exists in light of common experience indicating that it usually exists in such cases. Cf. Bohlen, Studies in the Law of Torts 644 (1926). Typical of such presumptions are the presumption that a mailed letter was received (Section 641) and presumptions relating to the authenticity of documents (Sections 643–645).

The presumptions described in Section 603 are not expressions of policy; they are expressions of experience. They are intended solely to eliminate the need for the trier of fact to reason from the proven or established fact to the presumed fact and to forestall argument over the existence of the presumed fact when there is no evidence tending to prove the nonexistence of the presumed fact.

§ 604. Effect of presumption affecting burden of producing evidence.

The effect of a presumption affecting the burden of producing evidence is to require the trier of fact to assume the existence of the presumed fact unless and until evidence is introduced which would support a finding of its nonexistence, in which case the trier of fact shall determine the existence or nonexistence of the presumed fact from the evidence and without regard to the presumption. Nothing in this section shall be construed to prevent the drawing of any inference that may be appropriate.

Comment—Assembly Committee on Judiciary

Section 604 describes the manner in which a presumption affecting the burden of producing evidence operates. Such a presumption is merely a preliminary assumption in the absence of contrary evidence, i.e., evidence sufficient to sustain a finding of the nonexistence of the presumed fact. If contrary evidence is introduced, the trier of fact must weigh the inferences arising from the facts that gave rise to the presumption against the contrary evidence and resolve the conflict. For example, if a party proves that a letter was mailed, the trier of fact is required to find that the letter was received in the absence of any believable contrary evidence. However, if the adverse party denies receipt, the presumption is gone from the case. The trier of fact must then weigh the denial of receipt against the inference of receipt arising from proof of mailing and decide whether or not the letter was received.

If a presumption affecting the burden of producing evidence is relied on, the judge must determine whether there is evidence sufficient to sustain a finding of the nonexistence of the presumed fact. If there is such evidence, the presumption disappears and the judge need say nothing about it in his instructions. If there is not evidence sufficient to sustain a finding of the nonexistence of the presumed fact, the judge should instruct the jury concerning the presumption. If the basic fact from which the presumption arises is established (by the pleadings, by stipulation, by judicial notice, etc.) so that the existence of the basic fact is not a question of fact for the jury, the jury should be instructed that the presumed fact is also established. If the basic fact is a question of fact for the jury, the judge should charge the jury that, if it finds the basic fact, the jury must also find the presumed fact. Morgan, Basic Problems of Evidence 36–38 (1957).

Of course, in a criminal case, the jury has the *power* to disregard the judge's instructions and find a defendant guilty of a lesser crime than that shown by the evidence or acquit a defendant despite the facts established by the undisputed evidence. Nonetheless, the jury should be instructed on the rules of law applicable, including those rules of law called presumptions. The fact that the jury may choose to disregard the applicable rules of law should not affect the nature of the instructions given.

§ 605. Presumption affecting the burden of proof defined.

A presumption affecting the burden of proof is a presumption established to implement some public policy other than to facilitate the determination of the particular action in which the presumption is applied, such as the policy in favor of establishment of a parent and child relationship, the validity of marriage, the stability of titles to property, or the security of those who entrust themselves or their property to the administration of others.

Comment—Law Revision Commission

Section 605 describes a presumption affecting the burden of proof. Such presumptions are established in order to carry out or to effectuate some public policy other than or in addition to the policy of facilitating the trial of actions. It is the existence of this further basis in policy that distinguishes a presumption affecting the burden of proof from a presumption affecting the burden of producing evidence. For example, the presumption of death from seven years' absence (Section 667) exists in part to facilitate the disposition of actions by supplying a rule of thumb to govern certain cases in which there is likely to be no direct evidence of the presumed fact. But the policy in favor of distributing estates, of settling titles, and of permitting life to proceed normally at some time prior to the expiration of the absentee's normal life expectancy (perhaps 30 or 40 years) that underlies the presumption indicates that it should be a presumption affecting the burden of proof.

Frequently, too, a presumption affecting the burden of proof will have an underlying basis in probability and logical inference. For example, the presumption of the validity of a ceremonial marriage may be based in part on the probability that most marriages are valid. However, an underlying logical inference is not essential. In fact, the lack of an underlying inference is a strong indication that the presumption affects the burden of proof. Only the needs of public policy can justify the direction of a particular assumption that is not warranted by the application of probability and common experience to the known facts.

§ 606. Effect of presumption affecting burden of proof.

The effect of a presumption affecting the burden of proof is to impose upon the party against whom it operates the burden of proof as to the nonexistence of the presumed fact.

Comment—Assembly Committee on Judiciary

Section 606 describes the manner in which a presumption affecting the burden of proof operates. In the ordinary case, the party against whom it is invoked will have the burden of proving the nonexistence of the presumed fact by a preponderance of the evidence. Certain presumptions affecting the burden of proof may be overcome only by clear and convincing proof.

If the party against whom the presumption operates already has the same burden of proof as to the nonexistence of the presumed fact that is assigned by the presumption, the presumption can have no effect on the case and no instruction in regard to the presumption should be given. If the evidence is not sufficient to sustain a finding of the nonexistence of the presumed fact, the judge's instructions will be the same as if the presumption were merely a presumption affecting the burden of producing evidence. See the Comment to Section 604. If there is evidence of the nonexistence of the presumed fact, the judge should instruct the jury on the manner in which the presumption affects the factfinding process. If the basic fact from which the presumption arises is so established that the existence of the basic fact is not a question of fact for the jury (as, for example, by the pleadings, by judicial notice, or by stipulation of the parties), the judge should instruct the jury that the existence of the presumed fact is to be assumed until the jury is persuaded to the contrary by the requisite degree of proof (proof by a preponderance of the evidence, clear and convincing proof, etc.). See McCormick, Evidence § 317 at 672 (1954). If the basic fact is a question of fact for the jury, the judge should instruct the jury that, if it finds the basic fact, it must also find the presumed fact unless persuaded of the nonexistence of the presumed fact by the requisite degree of proof. Morgan, Basic Problems of Evidence 38 (1957).

In a criminal case, a presumption affecting the burden of proof may be relied upon by the prosecution *to establish an element of the crime* with which the defendant is charged. The effect of the presumption on the factfinding process and the nature of the instructions in such a case are described in Section 607 and the Comment thereto.

§ 607. Effect of certain presumptions in a criminal action.
When a presumption affecting the burden of proof operates in a criminal action to establish presumptively any fact that is essential to the defendant's guilt, the presumption operates only if the facts that give rise to the presumption have been found or otherwise established beyond a reasonable doubt and, in such case, the defendant need only raise a reasonable doubt as to the existence of the presumed fact.

Comment—Assembly Committee on Judiciary

Section 607 does not apply to the "presumption" of sanity. Under the Evidence Code, the burden of proof on the issue of sanity is allocated by Section 522, and there is no "presumption" of sanity. Hence, notwithstanding the provisions of Section 607, a defendant who pleads insanity has the burden of proving by a preponderance of the evidence that he was insane.

Article 2. Conclusive Presumptions

§ 620. Conclusive presumptions. The presumptions established by this article, and all other presumptions declared by law to be conclusive, are conclusive presumptions.

Comment—Law Revision Commission

Conclusive presumptions are not evidentiary rules so much as they are rules of substantive law. Hence, the Commission has not recommended any substantive revision of the conclusive presumptions contained in this article.

§ 621. Child of marriage; notice of motion for blood tests

(a) Except as provided in subdivision (b), the issue of a wife cohabiting with her husband, who is not impotent or sterile, is conclusively presumed to be a child of the marriage.

(b) Notwithstanding the provisions of subdivision (a), if the court finds that the conclusions of all the experts, as disclosed by the evidence based upon blood tests performed pursuant to Chapter 2 (commencing with Section 890) of Division 7 are that the husband is not the father of the child, the question of paternity of the husband shall be resolved accordingly.

(c) The notice of motion for blood tests under subdivision (b) may be raised by the husband not later than two years from the child's date of birth.

(d) The notice of motion for blood tests under subdivision (b) may be raised by the mother of the child not later than two years from the child's date of birth if the child's biological father has filed an affidavit with the court acknowledging paternity of the child.

(e) The provisions of subdivision (b) shall not apply to any case coming within the provisions of Section 7005 of the Civil Code or to any case in which the wife, with the consent of the husband, conceived by means of a surgical procedure.

(f) The notice of motion for the blood tests pursuant to subdivision (b) shall be supported by a declaration under oath submitted by the moving party stating the factual basis for placing the issue of paternity before the court. This requirement shall not apply to any case pending before the court on September 30, 1980.

(g) The provisions of subdivision (b) shall not apply to any case which has reached final judgment of paternity on September 30, 1980.

§ 622. Facts recited in written instrument. The facts recited in a written instrument are conclusively presumed to be true as between the parties thereto, or their successors in interest; but this rule does not apply to the recital of a consideration.

§ 623. Estoppel by own statement or conduct. Whenever a party has, by his own statement or conduct, intentionally and deliberately led another to believe a particular thing true and to act upon such belief, he is not, in any litigation arising out of such statement or conduct, permitted to contradict it.

§ 624. Estoppel of tenant to deny title of landlord. A tenant is not permitted to deny the title of his landlord at the time of the commencement of the relation.

Article 3. Presumptions Affecting the Burden of Producing Evidence

§ 630. Presumptions affecting the burden of producing evidence. The presumptions established by this article, and all other rebuttable presumptions established by law that fall within the criteria of Section 603, are presumptions affecting the burden of producing evidence.

Comment—Law Revision Commission

Article 3 sets forth a list of presumptions, recognized in existing law, that are classified here as presumptions affecting the burden of producing evidence. The list is not exhaustive. Other presumptions affecting the burden of producing evidence may be found in other codes. Others will be found in the common law.

§ 631. Money delivered by one to another. Money delivered by one to another is presumed to have been due to the latter.

§ 632. Thing delivered by one to another. A thing delivered by one to another is presumed to have belonged to the latter.

§ 633. Obligation delivered up to the debtor. An obligation delivered up to the debtor is presumed to have been paid.

§ 634. Person in possession of order on himself. A person in possession of an order on himself for the payment of money, or delivery of a thing, is presumed to have paid the money or delivered the thing accordingly.

§ 635. Obligation possessed by creditor. An obligation possessed by the creditor is presumed not to have been paid.

§ 636. Payment of earlier rent or installments. The payment of earlier rent or installments is presumed from a receipt for later rent or installments.

§ 637. Ownership of things possessed. The things which a person possesses are presumed to be owned by him.

§ 638. Ownership of property by person who exercises acts of ownership. A person who exercises acts of ownership over property is presumed to be the owner of it.

§ 639. Judgment correctly determines rights of parties. A judgment, when not conclusive, is presumed to correctly determine or set forth the rights of the parties, but there is no presumption that the facts essential to the judgment have been correctly determined.

Comment—Law Revision Commission

The presumption involved here is that the judgment correctly determines that one party owes another money, or that the parties are divorced, or their marriage has been annulled, or any similar rights of the parties. The presumption does not apply to the facts underlying the judgment. For example, a judgment of annulment is presumed to determine correctly that the marriage is void. However, the judgment may not be used to establish presumptively that one of the parties was guilty of fraud as against some third party who is not bound by the judgment.

§ 640. Writing truly dated. A writing is presumed to have been truly dated.

§ 641. Letter received in ordinary course of mail. A letter correctly addressed and properly mailed is presumed to have been received in the ordinary course of mail.

§ 642. Conveyance by person having duty to convey real property. A trustee or other person, whose duty it was to convey real property to a particular person, is presumed to have actually conveyed to him when such presumption is necessary to perfect title of such person or his successor in interest.

§ 643. Authenticity of ancient document. A deed or will or other writing purporting to create, terminate, or affect an interest in real or personal property is presumed to be authentic if it:

(a) Is at least 30 years old;

(b) Is in such condition as to create no suspicion concerning its authenticity;

(c) Was kept, or if found was found, in a place where such writing, if authentic, would be likely to be kept or found; and

(d) Has been generally acted upon as authentic by persons having an interest in the matter.

Comment—Law Revision Commission

The requirement that the document be acted upon as genuine is, in substance, a requirement of the possession of property by those persons who would be entitled to such possession under the document if it were genuine. See 7 Wigmore, Evidence §§ 2141, 2146 (3d ed. 1940); Tentative Recommendation and a Study Relating to the Uniform Rules of Evidence (Article IX. Authentication and Content of Writings), 6 Cal.Law Revision Comm'n, Rep., Rec. & Studies 101, 135–137 (1964). Giving the ancient documents rule a presumptive effect—i.e., requiring a finding of the authenticity of an ancient document—seems justified when it is a dispositive instrument and the persons interested in the matter have acted upon the instrument for a period of at least 30 years as if it were genuine. Evidence which is not of this strength may be sufficient in particular cases to warrant an inference of genuineness and thus justify the admission of the document into evidence, but the presumption should be confined to those cases where the evidence of genuineness is not likely to be disputed. See 7 Wigmore, Evidence § 2146 (3d ed. 1940). Accordingly, Section 643 limits the presumptive application of the ancient documents rule to dispositive instruments.

§ 644. Book purporting to be published by public authority. A book, purporting to be printed or published by public authority, is presumed to have been so printed or published.

§ 645. Book purporting to contain reports of cases. A book, purporting to contain reports of cases adjudged in the tribunals of the state or nation where the book is published, is presumed to contain correct reports of such cases.

§ 645.1. Printed materials purporting to be particular newspaper or periodical. Printed materials, purporting to be a particular newspaper or periodical, are presumed to be that newspaper or periodical if regularly issued at average intervals not exceeding three months.

§ 646. Res ipsa loquitur; instruction

(a) As used in this section, "defendant" includes any party against whom the res ipsa loquitur presumption operates.

(b) The judicial doctrine of res ipsa loquitur is a presumption affecting the burden of producing evidence.

(c) If the evidence, or facts otherwise established, would support a res ipsa loquitur presumption and the defendant has introduced evidence which would support a finding that he was not negligent or that any negligence on his part was not a proximate cause of the occurrence, the court may, and upon request shall, instruct the jury to the effect that:

(1) If the facts which would give rise to a res ipsa loquitur presumption are found or otherwise established, the jury may draw the inference from such facts that a proximate cause of the occurrence was some negligent conduct on the part of the defendant; and

(2) The jury shall not find that a proximate cause of the occurrence was some negligent conduct on the part of the defendant unless the jury believes, after weighing all the evidence in the case and drawing such inferences therefrom as the jury believes are warranted, that it is more probable than not that the occurrence was caused by some negligent conduct on the part of the defendant.

§ 647. Return of process served by registered process server. The return of a process server registered pursuant to Chapter 16 (commencing with Section 22350) of Division 8 of the Business and Professions Code upon process or notice establishes a presumption, affecting the burden of producing evidence, of the facts stated in the return.

Article 4. Presumptions Affecting the Burden of Proof

§ 660. Presumptions affecting the burden of proof. The presumptions established by this article, and all other rebuttable presumptions established by law that fall within the criteria of Section 605, are presumptions affecting the burden of proof.

Comment—Law Revision Commission

In some cases it may be difficult to determine whether a particular presumption is a presumption affecting the burden of proof or a presumption affecting the burden of producing evidence. To avoid uncertainty, it is desirable to classify as many presumptions as possible. Article 4 (§§ 660–668), therefore, lists several presumptions that are to be regarded as presumptions affecting the burden of proof. The list is not exclusive. Other statutory and common law presumptions that affect the burden of proof must await classification by the courts.

§ 662. Owner of legal title to property is owner of beneficial title. The owner of the legal title to property is presumed to be the owner of the full beneficial title. This presumption may be rebutted only by clear and convincing proof.

§ 663. Ceremonial marriage. A ceremonial marriage is presumed to be valid.

§ 664. Official duty regularly performed. It is presumed that official duty has been regularly performed. This presumption does not apply on an issue as to the lawfulness of an arrest if it is found or otherwise established that the arrest was made without a warrant.

§ 665. Ordinary consequences of voluntary act. A person is presumed to intend the ordinary consequences of his voluntary act. This presumption is inapplicable in a criminal action to establish the specific intent of the defendant where specific intent is an element of the crime charged.

§ 666. Judicial action lawful exercise of jurisdiction. Any court of this state or the United States, or any court of general jurisdiction in any other state or nation, or any judge of such a court, acting as such, is presumed to have acted in the lawful exercise of its jurisdiction. This presumption applies only when the act of the court or judge is under collateral attack.

§ 667. Death of person not heard from in five years. A person not heard from in five years is presumed to be dead.

§ 668. Unlawful intent. An unlawful intent is presumed from the doing of an unlawful act. This presumption is inapplicable in a criminal action to establish the specific intent of the defendant where specific intent is an element of the crime charged.

§ 669. Failure to exercise due care. (a) The failure of a person to exercise due care is presumed if:

(1) He violated a statute, ordinance, or regulation of a public entity;

(2) The violation proximately caused death or injury to person or property;

(3) The death or injury resulted from an occurrence of the nature which the statute, ordinance, or regulation was designed to prevent; and

(4) The person suffering the death or the injury to his person or property was one of the class of persons for whose protection the statute, ordinance, or regulation was adopted.

(b) This presumption may be rebutted by proof that:

(1) The person violating the statute, ordinance, or regulation did what might reasonably be expected of a person of ordinary prudence, acting under similar circumstances, who desired to comply with the law; or

(2) The person violating the statute, ordinance, or regulation was a child and exercised the degree of care ordinarily exercised by persons of his maturity, intelligence, and capacity under similar circumstances, but the presumption may not be rebutted by such proof if the violation occurred in the course of an activity normally engaged in only by adults and requiring adult qualifications.

Comment—Law Revision Commission

Effect of Presumption

If the conditions listed in subdivision (a) are established, a presumption of negligence arises which may be rebutted by proof of the facts specified in subdivision (b). The presumption is one of simple negligence only, not gross negligence.

Section 669 is a presumption affecting the burden of proof. Thus, if it is established that a person violated a statute under the conditions specified in subdivision (a), the opponent of the presumption is required to prove to the trier of fact that it is more probable than not that the violation of the statute was reasonable and justifiable under the circumstances. Since the ultimate question is whether the opponent of the presumption was negligent rather than whether he violated the statute, proof of justification or excuse under subdivision (b) negates the existence of negligence instead of merely establishing an excuse for negligent conduct. Therefore, if the presumption is rebutted by proof of justification or excuse under subdivision (b), the trier of fact is required to find that the violation of the statute was not negligent.

Failure to establish conditions of presumption. Even though a party fails to establish that a violation occurred or that a proven violation meets all the requirements of subdivision (a), it is still possible for the party to recover by proving negligence apart from any statutory violation.

Functions of Judge and Jury

If a case is tried without a jury, the judge is responsible for deciding both questions of law and questions of fact arising under Section 669. However, in a case tried by a jury, there is an allocation between the judge and jury of the responsibility for determining the existence or nonexistence of the elements underlying the presumption and the existence of excuse or justification.

Subdivision (a), paragraphs (3) and (4). Whether the death or injury involved in an action resulted from an occurrence of the nature which the statute, ordinance, or regulation was designed to prevent (paragraph (3) of subdivision (a)) and whether the plaintiff was one of the class of persons for whose protection the statute, ordinance, or regulation was adopted (paragraph (4) of subdivision (a)) are questions of law.

Subdivision (a), paragraphs (1) and (2). Whether or not a party to an action has violated a statute, ordinance, or regulation (paragraph (1) of subdivision (a)) is generally a question of fact. However, if a party admits the violation or if the evidence of the violation is undisputed, it is appropriate for the judge to instruct the jury that a violation of the statute, ordinance, or regulation has been established as a matter of law.

The question of whether the violation has proximately caused or contributed to the plaintiff's death or injury (paragraph (2) of subdivision (a)) is normally a question for the jury. However, the existence or nonexistence of proximate cause becomes a question of law to be decided by the judge if reasonable men can draw but one inference from the facts.

Subdivision (b). Normally, the question of justification or excuse is a jury question. The jury should be instructed on the issue of justification or excuse whether the excuse or justification appears from the circumstances surrounding the violation itself or appears from evidence offered specifically to show justification. However, an instruction on the issue of excuse or justification should not be given if there is no evidence that would sustain a finding by the jury that the violation was excused.

§ 669.1. Standards of conduct for public employees; presumption of failure to exercise due care. A rule, policy, manual, or guideline of state or local government setting forth standards of conduct or guidelines for its employees in the conduct of their public employment shall not be considered a statute, ordinance, or regulation of that public entity within the meaning of Section 669, unless the rule, manual, policy, or guideline has been formally adopted as a statute, as an ordinance of a local governmental entity in this state empowered to adopt ordinances, or as a regulation by an agency of the state pursuant to the Administrative Procedure Act (Chapter 3.5 (commencing with

Section 11340) of Division 3 of Title 2 of the Government Code), or by an agency of the United States government pursuant to the federal Administrative Procedure Act (Chapter 5 (commencing with Section 5001) of Title 5 of the United States Code). This section affects only the presumption set forth in Section 669, and is not otherwise intended to affect the admissibility or inadmissibility of the rule, policy, manual, or guideline under other provisions of law.

§ 669.5. Ordinances limiting building permits or development of buildable lots for residential purposes; impact on supply of residential units; actions challenging validity

(a) Any ordinance enacted by the governing body of a city, county, or city and county which (1) directly limits, by number, the building permits that may be issued for residential construction or the buildable lots which may be developed for residential purposes, or (2) changes the standards of residential development on vacant land so that the governing body's zoning is rendered in violation of Section 65913.1 of the Government Code is presumed to have an impact on the supply of residential units available in an area which includes territory outside the jurisdiction of the city, county, or city and county.

(b) With respect to any action which challenges the validity of an ordinance specified in subdivision (a) the city, county, or city and county enacting the ordinance shall bear the burden of proof that the ordinance is necessary for the protection of the public health, safety, or welfare of the population of the city, county, or city and county.

(c) This section does not apply to state and federal building code requirements or local ordinances which (1) impose a moratorium, to protect the public health and safety, on residential construction for a specified period of time, if, under the terms of the ordinance, the moratorium will cease when the public health or safety is no longer jeopardized by the construction, (2) create agricultural preserves under Chapter 7 (commencing with Section 51200) of Part 1 of Division 1 of Title 5 of the Government Code, or (3) restrict the number of buildable parcels or designate lands within a zone for nonresidential uses in order to protect agricultural uses as defined in subdivision (b) of Section 51201 of the Government Code or open-space land as defined in subdivision (b) of Section 65560 of the Government Code.

(d) This section shall not apply to a voter approved ordinance adopted by referendum or initiative prior to the effective date of this section which (1) requires the city, county, or city and county to establish a population growth limit which represents its fair share of each year's statewide population growth, or (2) which sets a growth rate of no more than the average population growth rate experienced by the state as a whole. Paragraph (2) of subdivision (a) does not apply to a voter-approved ordinance adopted by referendum or initiative which exempts housing affordable to persons and families of low or moderate income, as defined in Section 50093 of the Health and Safety Code, or which otherwise provides low- and moderate-income housing sites equivalent to such an exemption.

§ 670. (a) In any dispute concerning payment by means of a check, a copy of the check produced in accordance with Section 1550 of the Evidence Code, together with the original bank statement that reflects payment of the check by the bank on which it was drawn or a copy thereof produced in the same manner, creates a presumption that the check has been paid.

(b) As used in this section:

(1) "Bank" means any person engaged in the business of banking and includes, in addition to a commercial bank, a savings and loan association, savings bank, or credit union.

(2) "Check" means a draft, other than a documentary draft, payable on demand and drawn on a bank, even though it is described by another term, such as "share draft" or "negotiable order of withdrawal."

Division 6

WITNESSES

Chapter 1

COMPETENCY

§ 700. General rule as to competency. Except as otherwise provided by statute, every person, irrespective of age, is qualified to be a witness and no person is disqualified to testify to any matter.

Comment—Law Revision Commission

The broad rule stated in Section 700 is substantially qualified by statutory restrictions appearing in the Evidence Code and in other California codes. See, e.g., Evidence Code § 701 (mental or physical capacity to be a witness), § 702 (requirement of personal knowledge), § 703 (judge as a witness), § 704 (juror as a witness), §§ 900–1070 (privileges), § 1150 (continuing existing law limiting use of juror's evidence concerning jury misconduct).

§ 701. Disqualification of witness

(a) A person is disqualified to be a witness if he or she is:

(1) Incapable of expressing himself or herself concerning the matter so as to be understood, either directly or through interpretation by one who can understand him; or

(2) Incapable of understanding the duty of a witness to tell the truth.

(b) In any proceeding held outside the presence of a jury, the court may reserve challenges to the competency of a witness until the conclusion of the direct examination of that witness.

Comment—Law Revision Commission

Under existing law, the competency of a person to be a witness is a question to be determined by the court and depends upon his capacity to understand the oath and to perceive, recollect, and communicate that which he is offered to relate.

Under the Evidence Code, too, the competency of a person to be a witness is a question to be determined by the court. See Evidence Code § 405 and the Comment thereto. However, Section 701 requires the court to determine only the prospective witness' capacity to communicate and his understanding of the duty to tell the truth. The missing qualifications—the capacity to perceive and to recollect—are determined in a different manner. Because a witness, qualified under Section 701, must have personal knowledge of the facts to which he

§ 701   CALIFORNIA EVIDENCE CODE

testifies (Section 702), he must, of course, have the capacity to perceive and to recollect those facts. But the court may exclude the testimony of a witness for lack of personal knowledge only if no jury could reasonably find that he has such knowledge. See Evidence Code § 403 and the Comment thereto. Thus, the Evidence Code has made a person's capacity to perceive and to recollect a condition for the admission of his testimony concerning a particular matter instead of a condition for his competency to be a witness. And, under the Evidence Code, if there is evidence that the witness has those capacities, the determination whether he in fact perceived and does recollect is left to the trier of fact. See Evidence Code §§ 403 and 702 and the Comments thereto.

Although Section 701 modifies the existing law with respect to determining competency of witnesses, it seems unlikely that the change will have much practical significance. Theoretically, Section 701 may permit children and persons suffering from mental impairment to testify in some instances where they are now disqualified from testifying; in practice, however, the California courts have permitted children of very tender years and persons with mental impairment to testify.

For further discussion, see Tentative Recommendation and a Study Relating to the Uniform Rules of Evidence (Article IV, Witnesses), 6 Cal.Law Revision Comm'n, Rep., Rec. & Studies 701, 709–710 (1964).

§ 702. Personal knowledge of witness. (a) Subject to Section 801, the testimony of a witness concerning a particular matter is inadmissible unless he has personal knowledge of the matter. Against the objection of a party, such personal knowledge must be shown before the witness may testify concerning the matter.

(b) A witness' personal knowledge of a matter may be shown by any otherwise admissible evidence, including his own testimony.

Comment—Law Revision Commission

Section 702 states the general requirement that a witness must have personal knowledge of the facts to which he testifies. "Personal knowledge" means a present recollection of an impression derived from the exercise of the witness' own senses.

Except to the extent that experts may give opinion testimony not based on personal knowledge (see Evidence Code § 801), the requirement of Section 702 is applicable to all witnesses, whether expert or not.

Under existing law, as under Section 702, an objection must be made to the testimony of a witness who does not have personal knowledge; but, if there is no reasonable opportunity to object before the testimony is given, a motion to strike is appropriate after lack of knowledge has been shown.

If a timely objection is made that a witness lacks personal knowledge, the court may not receive his testimony subject to the condition that evidence of personal knowledge be supplied later in the trial. Section 702 thus limits the ordinary power of the court with respect to the order of proof.

§ 703. Judge as witness. (a) Before the judge presiding at the trial of an action may be called to testify in that trial as a witness, he shall, in proceedings held out of the presence and hearing of the jury, inform the parties of the information he has concerning any fact or matter about which he will be called to testify.

(b) Against the objection of a party, the judge presiding at the trial of an action may not testify in that trial as a witness. Upon such objection, the judge shall declare a mistrial and order the action assigned for trial before another judge.

(c) The calling of the judge presiding at a trial to testify in that trial as a witness shall be deemed a consent to the granting of a motion for mistrial, and an objection to such calling of a judge shall be deemed a motion for mistrial.

(d) In the absence of objection by a party, the judge presiding at the trial of an action may testify in that trial as a witness.

§ 703.5 Judge as witness; subsequent civil proceeding; exceptions. No person presiding at any judicial or quasi-judicial proceeding, and no arbitrator or mediator, shall be competent to testify in any subsequent civil proceeding as to any statement, conduct, decision, or ruling occurring at or in conjunction with the prior proceeding, except as to a statement or conduct that could (a) give rise to civil or criminal contempt, (b) constitute a crime, (c) be the subject of investigation by the State Bar or Commission on Judicial Performance, or (d) give rise to disqualification proceedings under paragraph (1) or (6) of subdivision (a) of Section 170.1 of the Code of Civil Procedure. However, this section does not apply to a mediator with regard to any mediation under Chapter 11 (commencing with Section 3160) of Part 2 of Division 8 of the Family Code.

§ 704. Juror as witness. (a) Before a juror sworn and impaneled in the trial of an action may be called to testify before the jury in that trial as a witness, he shall, in proceedings conducted by the court out of the presence and hearing of the remaining jurors, inform the parties of the information he has concerning any fact or matter about which he will be called to testify.

(b) Against the objection of a party, a juror sworn and impaneled in the trial of an action may not testify before the jury in that trial as a witness. Upon such objection, the court shall declare a mistrial and order the action assigned for trial before another jury.

(c) The calling of a juror to testify before the jury as a witness shall be deemed a consent to the granting of a motion for mistrial, and an objection to such calling of a juror shall be deemed a motion for mistrial.

(d) In the absence of objection by a party, a juror sworn and impaneled in the trial of an action may be compelled to testify in that trial as a witness.

Chapter 2

OATH AND CONFRONTATION

§ 710. Oath required. Every witness before testifying shall take an oath or make an affirmation or declaration in the form provided by law, except that a child under the age of 10 or a dependent person with a substantial cognitive impairment, in the court's discretion, may be required only to promise to tell the truth.

§ 711. Confrontation. At the trial of an action, a witness can be heard only in the presence and subject to the examination of all the parties to the action, if they choose to attend and examine.

§ 712. Blood samples; technique in taking; affidavits in criminal actions; service; objections. Notwithstanding Sections 711 and 1200, at the trial of a criminal action, evidence of the technique used in taking blood samples may be given by a registered nurse, licensed vocational nurse, or licensed clinical laboratory technologist or clinical laboratory bioanalyst, by means of an affidavit. The affidavit shall be admissible, provided the party offering the affidavit as evidence has served all other parties to the action, or their counsel, with a copy of the affidavit no less than 10 days prior to trial. Nothing in this section shall preclude any party or his counsel from objecting to the introduction of the affidavit at any time, and requiring the attendance of the affiant, or compelling attendance by subpoena.

Chapter 3

EXPERT WITNESSES

Article 1. Expert Witnesses Generally

§ 720. Qualification as an expert witness. (a) A person is qualified to testify as an expert if he has special knowledge, skill, experience, training, or education sufficient to qualify him as an expert on the subject to which his testimony relates. Against the objection of a party, such special knowledge, skill, experience, training, or education must be shown before the witness may testify as an expert.

(b) A witness' special knowledge, skill, experience, training, or education may be shown by any otherwise admissible evidence, including his own testimony.

Comment—Law Revision Commission

Against the objection of a party, the special qualifications of the proposed witness must be shown as a prerequisite to his testimony as an expert. With the consent of the parties, the judge may receive a witness' testimony conditionally, subject to the necessary foundation being supplied later in the trial.

The judge's determination that a witness qualifies as an expert witness is binding on the trier of fact, but the trier of fact may consider the witness' qualifications as an expert in determining the weight to be given his testimony.

§ 721. Cross-examination of expert witness. (a) Subject to subdivision (b), a witness testifying as an expert may be cross-examined to the same extent as any other witness and, in addition, may be fully cross-examined as to (1) his or her qualifications, (2) the subject to which his or her expert testimony relates, and (3) the matter upon which his or her opinion is based and the reasons for his or her opinion.

(b) If a witness testifying as an expert testifies in the form of an opinion, he or she may not be cross-examined in regard to the content or tenor of any scientific, technical, or professional text, treatise, journal, or similar publication unless any of the following occurs:

(1) The witness referred to, considered, or relied upon such publication in arriving at or forming his or her opinion.

(2) The publication has been admitted in evidence.

(3) The publication has been established as a reliable authority by the testimony or admission of the witness or by other expert testimony or by judicial notice.

If admitted, relevant portions of the publication may be read into evidence but may not be received as exhibits.

Comment—Law Revision Commission

Subdivision (b) clarifies a matter concerning which there is considerable confusion in the California decisions.

If an expert witness has relied on a particular publication in forming his opinion, it is necessary to permit cross-examination in regard to that publication in order to show whether the expert correctly read, interpreted, and applied the portions he relied on. Similarly, it is important to permit an expert witness to be cross-examined concerning those publications referred to or considered by him even though not specifically relied on by him in forming his opinion. However, a rule permitting cross-examination on technical treatises not considered by the expert witness would permit the cross-examiner to utilize this opportunity not for its ostensible purpose—to test the expert's opinion—but to bring before the trier of fact the opinions of absentee authors without the safeguard of cross-examination. Although the court would be required upon request to caution the jury that the statements read are not to be considered evidence of the truth of the propositions stated, there is a danger that at least some jurors might rely on the author's statements for this purpose. Yet, the statements in the text might be based on inadequate background research, might be subject to unexpressed qualifications that would be applicable to the case before the court, or might be unreliable for some other reason that could be revealed if the author were subject to cross-examination. Therefore, subdivision (b) does not permit cross-examination of an expert witness on scientific, technical, or professional works not referred to, considered, or relied on by him.

If a particular publication has already been admitted in evidence, however, the reason for subdivision (b)—to prevent inadmissible evidence from being brought before the jury—is inapplicable. Hence, the subdivision permits an expert witness to be examined concerning such a publication without regard to whether he referred to, considered, or relied on it in forming his opinion.

§ 722. Credibility of expert witness. (a) The fact of the appointment of an expert witness by the court may be revealed to the trier of fact.

(b) The compensation and expenses paid or to be paid to an expert witness by the party calling him is a proper subject of inquiry by any adverse party as relevant to the credibility of the witness and the weight of his testimony.

§ 723. Limit on number of expert witnesses. The court may, at any time before or during the trial of an action, limit the number of expert witnesses to be called by any party.

Article 2. Appointment of Expert Witness by Court

§ 730. Appointment of expert by court

When it appears to the court, at any time before or during the trial of an action, that expert evidence is or may be required by the court or by any party to the action, the court on its own motion or on motion of any party may appoint one or more experts to investigate, to render a report as may be ordered by the court, and to testify as an expert at the trial of the action relative to the fact or matter as to which such expert evidence is or may be required. The court may fix the compensation for such services, if any, rendered by any person appointed under this section, in addition to any service as a witness, at such amount as seems reasonable to the court.

§ 731. Payment of court-appointed expert

(a) In all criminal actions and juvenile court proceedings, the compensation fixed under Section 730 shall be a charge against the county in which such action or proceeding is pending and shall be paid out of the treasury of such county on order of the court.

(b) In any county in which the board of supervisors so provides, the compensation fixed under Section 730 for medical experts in civil actions in such county shall be a charge against and paid out of the treasury of such county on order of the court.

(c) Except as otherwise provided in this section, in all civil actions, the compensation fixed under Section 730 shall, in the first instance, be apportioned and charged to the several parties in such proportion as the court may determine and may thereafter be taxed and allowed in like manner as other costs.

§ 732. **Calling and examining court-appointed expert.** Any expert appointed by the court under Section 730 may be called and examined by the court or by any party to the action. When such witness is called and examined by the court, the parties have the same right as is expressed in Section 775 to cross-examine the witness and to object to the questions asked and the evidence adduced.

§ 733. **Right to produce other expert evidence.** Nothing contained in this article shall be deemed or construed to prevent any party to any action from producing other expert evidence on the same fact or matter mentioned in Section 730; but, where other expert witnesses are called by a party to the action, their fees shall be paid by the party calling them and only ordinary witness fees shall be taxed as costs in the action.

Chapter 4

INTERPRETERS AND TRANSLATORS

§ 750. **Rules relating to witnesses apply to interpreters and translators.** A person who serves as an interpreter or translator in any action is subject to all the rules of law relating to witnesses.

§ 751. **Oath required of interpreters and translators.** (a) An interpreter shall take an oath that he or she will make a true interpretation to the witness in a language that the witness understands and that he or she will make a true interpretation of the witness' answers to questions to counsel, court, or jury, in the English language, with his or her best skill and judgment.

(b) In any proceeding in which a deaf or hard-of-hearing person is testifying under oath, the interpreter certified pursuant to subdivision (f) of Section 754 shall advise the court whenever he or she is unable to comply with his or her oath taken pursuant to subdivision (a).

(c) A translator shall take an oath that he or she will make a true translation in the English language of any writing he or she is to decipher or translate.

(d) An interpreter regularly employed by the court and certified or registered in accordance with Article 4 (commencing with Section 68560) of Chapter 2 of Title 8 of the Government Code, or a translator regularly employed by the court, may file an oath as prescribed by this section with the clerk of the court. The filed oath shall serve for all subsequent court proceedings until the appointment is revoked by the court.

§ 752. **Interpreters for witnesses.** (a) When a witness is incapable of understanding the English language or is incapable of expressing himself or herself in the English language so as to be understood directly by counsel, court, and jury, an interpreter whom he or she can under-

§ 752   CALIFORNIA EVIDENCE CODE

stand and who can understand him or her shall be sworn to interpret for him or her.

(b) The record shall identify the interpreter who may be appointed and compensated as provided in Article 2 (commencing with Section 730) of Chapter 3.

§ 753. Translators of writings. (a) When the written characters in a writing offered in evidence are incapable of being deciphered or understood directly, a translator who can decipher the characters or understand the language shall be sworn to decipher or translate the writing.

(b) The record shall identify the translator who may be appointed and compensated as provided in Article 2 (commencing with Section 730) of Chapter 3.

§ 754. Deaf persons; interpreters; civil or criminal actions; infractions; juvenile court proceedings; mental competency proceedings; administrative hearings. (a) As used in this section, "individual who is deaf or hearing impaired" means an individual with a hearing loss so great as to prevent his or her understanding language spoken in a normal tone, but does not include an individual who is hearing impaired provided with, and able to fully participate in the proceedings through the use of, an assistive listening system or computer-aided transcription equipment provided pursuant to Section 54.8 of the Civil Code.

(b) In any civil or criminal action, including, but not limited to, any action involving a traffic or other infraction, any small claims court proceeding, any juvenile court proceeding, any family court proceeding or service, or any proceeding to determine the mental competency of a person, in any court-ordered or court-provided alternative dispute resolution, including mediation and arbitration, or any administrative hearing, where a party or witness is an individual who is deaf or hearing impaired and the individual who is deaf or hearing impaired is present and participating, the proceedings shall be interpreted in a language that the individual who is deaf or hearing impaired understands by a qualified interpreter appointed by the court or other appointing authority, or as agreed upon.

(c) For purposes of this section, "appointing authority" means a court, department, board, commission, agency, licensing or legislative body, or other body for proceedings requiring a qualified interpreter.

(d) For the purposes of this section, "interpreter" includes, but is not limited to, an oral interpreter, a sign language interpreter, or a deaf-blind interpreter, depending upon the needs of the individual who is deaf or hearing impaired.

(e) For purposes of this section, "intermediary interpreter" means an individual who is deaf or hearing impaired, or a hearing individual who is able to assist in providing an accurate interpretation between spoken English and sign language or between variants of sign language or between American Sign Language and other foreign languages by acting as an intermediary between the individual who is deaf or hearing impaired and the qualified interpreter.

(f) For purposes of this section, "qualified interpreter" means an interpreter who has been certified as competent to interpret court proceedings by a testing organization, agency, or educational institution approved by the Judicial Council as qualified to administer tests to court interpreters for individuals who are deaf or hearing impaired.

(g) In the event that the appointed interpreter is not familiar with the use of particular signs by the individual who is deaf or hearing impaired or his or her particular variant of sign language, the court or other appointing authority shall, in consultation with the individual who is deaf or hearing impaired or his or her representative, appoint an intermediary interpreter.

(h) Prior to July 1, 1992, the Judicial Council shall conduct a study to establish the guidelines pursuant to which it shall determine which testing organizations, agencies, or educational institutions will be approved to administer tests for certification of court interpreters for individuals who are deaf or hearing impaired. It is the intent of the Legislature that the study obtain the widest possible input from the public, including, but not limited to, educational institutions, the judiciary, linguists, members of the State Bar, court interpreters, members of professional interpreting organizations, and members of the deaf and hearing-impaired communities. After obtaining public comment and completing its study, the Judicial Council shall publish these guidelines. By January 1, 1997, the Judicial Council shall approve one or more entities to administer testing for court interpreters for individuals who are deaf or hearing impaired. Testing entities may include educational institutions, testing organizations, joint powers agencies, or public agencies.

Commencing July 1, 1997, court interpreters for individuals who are deaf or hearing impaired shall meet the qualifications specified in subdivision (f).

(i) Persons appointed to serve as interpreters under this section shall be paid, in addition to actual travel costs, the prevailing rate paid to persons employed by the court to provide other interpreter services unless such service is considered to be a part of the person's regular duties as an employee of the state, county, or other political subdivision of the state. Payment of the interpreter's fee shall be a charge against the county, or other political subdivision of the state, in which that action is pending. Payment of the interpreter's fee in administrative proceedings shall be a charge against the appointing board or authority.

(j) Whenever a peace officer or any other person having a law enforcement or prosecutorial function in any criminal or quasi-criminal investigation or proceeding questions or otherwise interviews an alleged victim or witness who demonstrates or alleges deafness or hearing impairment, a good faith effort to secure the services of an interpreter shall be made, without any unnecessary delay unless either the individual who is deaf or hearing impaired affirmatively indicates that he or she does not need or cannot use an interpreter, or an interpreter is not otherwise required by Title II of the Americans with Disabilities Act of 1990 (Public Law 101–336) and federal regulations adopted thereunder.

(k) No statement, written or oral, made by an individual who the court finds is deaf or hearing impaired in reply to a question of a peace officer, or any other person having a law enforcement or prosecutorial function in any criminal or quasi-criminal investigation or proceeding, may be used against that individual who is deaf or hearing impaired unless the question was accurately interpreted and the statement was made knowingly, voluntarily, and intelligently and was accurately interpreted, or the court makes special findings that either the individual could not have used an interpreter or an interpreter was not otherwise required by Title II of the Americans with Disabilities Act of 1990 (Public Law 101–336) and federal regulations adopted thereunder and that the statement was made knowingly, voluntarily, and intelligently.

(*l*) In obtaining services of an interpreter for purposes of subdivision (j) or (k), priority shall be given to first obtaining a qualified interpreter.

(m) Nothing in subdivision (j) or (k) shall be deemed to supersede the requirement of subdivision (b) for use of a qualified interpreter for individuals who are deaf or hearing impaired participating as parties or witnesses in a trial or hearing.

(n) In any action or proceeding in which an individual who is deaf or hearing impaired is a participant, the appointing authority shall not commence proceedings until the appointed interpreter is in full view of and spatially situated to assure proper communication with the participating individual who is deaf or hearing impaired.

(*o*) Each superior court shall maintain a current roster of qualified interpreters certified pursuant to subdivision (f).

§ 754.5. Whenever an otherwise valid privilege exists between an individual who is deaf or hearing impaired and another person, that privilege is not waived merely because an interpreter was used to facilitate their communication.

§ 755. (a) In any action or proceeding under Division 10 (commencing with Section 6200) of the Family Code, and in any action or proceeding under the Uniform Parentage Act (Part 3 (commencing with Section 7600) of Division 12 of the Family Code) or for dissolution or nullity of marriage or legal separation of the parties in which a protective order has been granted or is being sought pursuant to Section 6221 of the Family Code, in which a party does not proficiently speak or understand the English language, and that party is present, an interpreter, as provided in this section, shall be present to interpret the proceedings in a language that the party understands, and to assist communication between the party and his or her attorney. Notwithstanding this requirement, a court may issue an ex parte order pursuant to Sections 2045 and 7710 of, and Article 1 (commencing with Section 6320) of Chapter 2 of Part 4 of Division 10 of the Family Code, without the presence of an interpreter. The interpreter selected shall be certified pursuant to Article 4 (commencing with Section 68560) of Chapter 2 of Title 8 of the Government Code, unless the court in its discretion appoints an interpreter who is not certified.

(b) The fees of interpreters utilized under this section shall be paid as provided in subdivision (b) of Section 68092 of the Government Code. However, the fees of an interpreter shall be waived for a party who needs an interpreter and appears in forma pauperis pursuant to Section 68511.3 of the Government Code. The Judicial Council shall amend subdivision (i) of California Rule of Court 985 and revise its forms accordingly by July 1, 1996.

(c) In any civil action in which an interpreter is required under this section, the court shall not commence proceedings until the appointed interpreter is present and situated near the party and his or her attorney. However, this section shall not prohibit the court from doing any of the following:

(1) Issuing an order when the necessity for the order outweighs the necessity for an interpreter.

(2) Extending the duration of a previously issued temporary order if an interpreter is not readily available.

(3) Issuing a permanent order where a party who requires an interpreter fails to make appropriate arrangements for an interpreter after receiving proper notice of the hearing with information about obtaining an interpreter.

(d) This section does not prohibit the presence of any other person to assist a party.

(e) A local public entity may, and the Judicial Council shall, apply to the appropriate state agency that receives federal funds authorized pursuant to the federal Violence Against Women Act (P.L. 103–322) for these federal funds or for funds from sources other than the state to implement this section. A local public entity and the Judicial Council

§ 755   CALIFORNIA EVIDENCE CODE

shall comply with the requirements of this section only to the extent that any of these funds are made available.

(f) The Judicial Council shall draft rules and modify forms necessary to implement this section, including those for the petition for a temporary restraining order and related forms, to inform both parties of their right to an interpreter pursuant to this section.

§ 755.5. (a) During any medical examination, requested by an insurer or by the defendant, of a person who is a party to a civil action and who does not proficiently speak or understand the English language, conducted for the purpose of determining damages in a civil action, an interpreter shall be present to interpret the examination in a language that the person understands. The interpreter shall be certified pursuant to Article 8 (commencing with Section 11435.05) of Chapter 4.5 of Part 1 of Division 3 of Title 2 of the Government Code.

(b) The fees of interpreters used under subdivision (a) shall be paid by the insurer or defendant requesting the medical examination.

(c) The record of, or testimony concerning, any medical examination conducted in violation of subdivision (a) shall be inadmissible in the civil action for which it was conducted or any other civil action.

(d) This section does not prohibit the presence of any other person to assist a party.

(e) In the event that interpreters certified pursuant to Article 8 (commencing with Section 11435.05) of Chapter 4.5 of Part 1 of Division 3 of Title 2 of the Government Code cannot be present at the medical examination, upon stipulation of the parties the requester specified in subdivision (a) shall have the discretionary authority to provisionally qualify and use other interpreters.

Chapter 5

METHOD AND SCOPE OF EXAMINATION

Article 1. Definitions

§ 760. "Direct examination". "Direct examination" is the first examination of a witness upon a matter that is not within the scope of a previous examination of the witness.

§ 761. "Cross-examination". "Cross-examination" is the examination of a witness by a party other than the direct examiner upon a matter that is within the scope of the direct examination of the witness.

Comment—Law Revision Commission

Section 761 limits cross-examination of a witness to the scope of the witness' direct examination.

§ 762. "Redirect examination". "Redirect examination" is an examination of a witness by the direct examiner subsequent to the cross-examination of the witness.

§ 763. "Recross-examination". "Recross-examination" is an examination of a witness by a cross-examiner subsequent to a redirect examination of the witness.

§ 764. "Leading question". A "leading question" is a question that suggests to the witness the answer that the examining party desires.

Article 2. Examination of Witnesses

§ 765. Court to control mode of interrogation. (a) The court shall exercise reasonable control over the mode of interrogation of a witness so as to make interrogation as rapid, as distinct, and as effective for the ascertainment of the truth, as may be, and to protect the witness from undue harassment or embarrassment.

(b) With a witness under the age of 14 or a dependent person with a substantial cognitive impairment, the court shall take special care to protect him or her from undue harassment or embarrassment, and to restrict the unnecessary repetition of questions. The court shall also take special care to ensure that questions are stated in a form which is appropriate to the age or cognitive level of the witness. The court may, in the interests of justice, on objection by a party, forbid the asking of a question which is in a form that is not reasonably likely to be understood by a person of the age or cognitive level of the witness.

Editorial Note

In recent years, the California legislature has enacted a series of amendments of existing provisions and new statutory sections aimed at protecting a child witness and also a witness who is a dependent person with a cognitive impairment. In addition to section 765, see sections 700 and 767 of this Code. A number of relevant provisions have also been added to the California Penal Code. See, e.g., Penal Code sections 861.5, 868.5, 868.6, 868.7, 868.8, 1346, and 1347.

§ 766. Responsive answers. A witness must give responsive answers to questions, and answers that are not responsive shall be stricken on motion of any party.

§ 767. Leading questions. (a) Except under special circumstances where the interests of justice otherwise require:

(1) A leading question may not be asked of a witness on direct or redirect examination.

(2) A leading question may be asked of a witness on cross-examination or recross-examination.

(b) The court may, in the interests of justice permit a leading question to be asked of a child under 10 years of age or a dependent

§ 767   CALIFORNIA EVIDENCE CODE

person with a substantial cognitive impairment in a case involving a prosecution under Section 273a, 273d, 288.5, 368, or any of the acts described in Section 11165.1 or 11165.2 of the Penal Code.

Comment—Assembly Committee on Judiciary

The exception stated at the beginning of the section continues the present law that permits leading questions on direct examination where there is little danger of improper suggestion or where such questions are necessary to obtain relevant evidence. This would permit leading questions on direct examination for preliminary matters, refreshing recollection, and examining handicapped witnesses, expert witnesses, and hostile witnesses. The court may also forbid the asking of leading questions on cross-examination where the witness is biased in favor of the cross-examiner and would be unduly susceptible to the influence of questions that suggested the desired answer. See 3 Wigmore, Evidence § 773 (3d ed. 1940).

§ 768. Writings. (a) In examining a witness concerning a writing, it is not necessary to show, read, or disclose to him any part of the writing.

(b) If a writing is shown to a witness, all parties to the action must be given an opportunity to inspect it before any question concerning it may be asked of the witness.

§ 769. Inconsistent statement or conduct. In examining a witness concerning a statement or other conduct by him that is inconsistent with any part of his testimony at the hearing, it is not necessary to disclose to him any information concerning the statement or other conduct.

Comment—Assembly Committee on Judiciary

Section 769 permits a witness to be asked questions concerning a prior inconsistent statement, whether written or oral, even though no disclosure is made to him concerning the prior statement. (Whether a foundational showing is required before other evidence of the prior statement may be admitted is not covered in Section 769; the prerequisites for the admission of such evidence are set forth in Section 770.) The disclosure of inconsistent written statements that is required under existing law limits the effectiveness of cross-examination by removing the element of surprise. The forewarning gives the dishonest witness the opportunity to reshape his testimony in conformity with the prior statement. The existing rule is based on an English common law rule that has been abandoned in England for 100 years. See McCormick, Evidence § 28 at 53 (1954).

§ 770. Evidence of inconsistent statement of witness. Unless the interests of justice otherwise require, extrinsic evidence of a statement made by a witness that is inconsistent with any part of his testimony at the hearing shall be excluded unless:

(a) The witness was so examined while testifying as to give him an opportunity to explain or to deny the statement; or

(b) The witness has not been excused from giving further testimony in the action.

Comment—Law Revision Commission

Unless the interests of justice otherwise require, Section 770 permits the judge to exclude evidence of an inconsistent statement only if the witness during his examination was not given an opportunity to explain or deny the statement *and* he has been unconditionally excused and is not subject to being recalled as a witness. Among other things, Section 770 will permit more effective cross-examination and impeachment of several collusive witnesses, since there need be no disclosure of prior inconsistency before all such witnesses have been examined.

Where the interests of justice require it, the court may permit extrinsic evidence of an inconsistent statement to be admitted even though the witness has been excused and has had no opportunity to explain or deny the statement. An absolute rule forbidding introduction of such evidence where the specified conditions are not met may cause hardship in some cases. For example, the party seeking to introduce the statement may not have learned of its existence until after the witness has left the court and is no longer available to testify. For the foundational requirements for the admission of a hearsay declarant's inconsistent statement, see Evidence Code § 1202 and the Comment thereto.

§ 771. Production of writing used to refresh memory.

(a) Subject to subdivision (c), if a witness, either while testifying or prior thereto, uses a writing to refresh his memory with respect to any matter about which he testifies, such writing must be produced at the hearing at the request of an adverse party and, unless the writing is so produced, the testimony of the witness concerning such matter shall be stricken.

(b) If the writing is produced at the hearing, the adverse party may, if he chooses, inspect the writing, cross-examine the witness concerning it, and introduce in evidence such portion of it as may be pertinent to the testimony of the witness.

(c) Production of the writing is excused, and the testimony of the witness shall not be stricken, if the writing:

(1) Is not in the possession or control of the witness or the party who produced his testimony concerning the matter; and

(2) Was not reasonably procurable by such party through the use of the court's process or other available means.

Comment—Assembly Committee on Judiciary

Section 771 grants a right of inspection without regard to when the writing is used to refresh recollection. If a witness' testimony depends upon the use of a writing to refresh his recollection, the adverse party's right to inspect the writing should not be made to depend upon the happenstance of when the writing is used.

Subdivision (c) excuses the nonproduction of the memory-refreshing writing where the writing cannot be produced through no fault of the witness or the party eliciting his testimony concerning the matter.

It should be noted that there is no restriction in the Evidence Code on the means that may be used to refresh recollection. Thus, the limitations on the types of writings that may be used as recorded memory under Section 1237 do not limit the types of writings that may be used to refresh recollection under Section 771.

§ 772. Order of examination. (a) The examination of a witness shall proceed in the following phases: direct examination, cross-examination, redirect examination, recross-examination, and continuing thereafter by redirect and recross-examination.

(b) Unless for good cause the court otherwise directs, each phase of the examination of a witness must be concluded before the succeeding phase begins.

(c) Subject to subdivision (d), a party may, in the discretion of the court, interrupt his cross-examination, redirect examination, or recross-examination of a witness, in order to examine the witness upon a matter not within the scope of a previous examination of the witness.

(d) If the witness is the defendant in a criminal action, the witness may not, without his consent, be examined under direct examination by another party.

Comment—Assembly Committee on Judiciary

Under subdivision (c), as under existing law, a party examining a witness under cross-examination, redirect examination, or recross-examination may go beyond the scope of the initial direct examination if the court permits. Under the definition in Section 760, such an extended examination is direct examination. Such direct examination may, however, be subject to the rules applicable to a cross-examination by virtue of the provisions of Section 776, 804, or 1203.

Subdivision (d) states an exception for the defendant-witness in a criminal action that reflects existing law.

§ 773. Cross-examination. (a) A witness examined by one party may be cross-examined upon any matter within the scope of the direct examination by each other party to the action in such order as the court directs.

(b) The cross-examination of a witness by any party whose interest is not adverse to the party calling him is subject to the same rules that are applicable to the direct examination.

§ 774. Re-examination. A witness once examined cannot be reexamined as to the same matter without leave of the court, but he may be reexamined as to any new matter upon which he has been examined by another party to the action. Leave may be granted or withheld in the court's discretion.

§ 775. Court may call witnesses. The court, on its own motion or on the motion of any party, may call witnesses and interrogate them the same as if they had been produced by a party to the action, and the parties may object to the questions asked and the evidence adduced the same as if such witnesses were called and examined by an adverse party. Such witnesses may be cross-examined by all parties to the action in such order as the court directs.

§ 776. Examination of adverse party or witness. (a) A party to the record of any civil action, or a person identified with such a party, may be called and examined as if under cross-examination by any adverse party at any time during the presentation of evidence by the party calling the witness.

(b) A witness examined by a party under this section may be cross-examined by all other parties to the action in such order as the court directs; but, subject to subdivision (e), the witness may be examined only as if under redirect examination by:

(1) In the case of a witness who is a party, his own counsel and counsel for a party who is not adverse to the witness.

(2) In the case of a witness who is not a party, counsel for the party with whom the witness is identified and counsel for a party who is not adverse to the party with whom the witness is identified.

(c) For the purpose of this section, parties represented by the same counsel are deemed to be a single party.

(d) For the purpose of this section, a person is identified with a party if he is:

(1) A person for whose immediate benefit the action is prosecuted or defended by the party.

(2) A director, officer, superintendent, member, agent, employee, or managing agent of the party or of a person specified in paragraph (1), or any public employee of a public entity when such public entity is the party.

(3) A person who was in any of the relationships specified in paragraph (2) at the time of the act or omission giving rise to the cause of action.

(4) A person who was in any of the relationships specified in paragraph (2) at the time he obtained knowledge of the matter concerning which he is sought to be examined under this section.

(e) Paragraph (2) of subdivision (b) does not require counsel for the party with whom the witness is identified and counsel for a party who is not adverse to the party with whom the witness is identified to examine the witness as if under redirect examination if the party who called the witness for examination under this section:

(1) Is also a person identified with the same party with whom the witness is identified.

(2) Is the personal representative, heir, successor, or assignee of a person identified with the same party with whom the witness is identified.

Comment—Law Revision Commission

Subdivision (b) is based in part on similar provisions contained in Code of Civil Procedure Section 2055. Unlike Section 2055, however, this subdivision is drafted in recognition of the problems involved in multiple party litigation. Thus, the introductory portion of subdivision (b) states the general rule that a witness examined under this section may be cross-examined by all other parties to the action in such order as the court directs. For example, a party whose interest in the action is identical with that of the party who called the witness for examination under this section has a right to cross-examine the witness fully because he, too, has the right to call the witness for examination under this section. Similarly, a party whose interest in the action is adverse to the party who calls the witness for examination under this section has the right to cross-examine the witness fully unless he is identified with the witness as described in paragraphs (1) and (2) of this subdivision. Paragraphs (1) and (2) restrict the nature of the cross-examination permitted of a witness by a party with whom the witness is identified and by parties whose interest in the action is not adverse to the party with whom the witness is identified. These parties are limited to examination of the witness as if under redirect examination. In essence, this means that leading questions cannot be asked of the witness by these parties. See Evidence Code § 767. Although the examination must proceed as if it were a redirect examination, under Section 761 it is in fact a cross-examination and limited to the scope of the direct. See also Evidence Code §§ 760, 773.

[T]he premise upon which Section 776 is based does not necessarily apply when the party calling the witness is also closely identified with the adverse party; hence, the adverse party should be entitled to the usual rights of a cross-examiner when he examines the witness. For example, when an employee sues his employer and calls a co-employee as a witness, there is no reason to assume that the witness will be adverse to the employee-party and in sympathy with the employer-party. The reverse may be the case.

§ 777. Exclusion of witness. (a) Subject to subdivisions (b) and (c), the court may exclude from the courtroom any witness not at the time under examination so that such witness cannot hear the testimony of other witnesses.

(b) A party to the action cannot be excluded under this section.

(c) If a person other than a natural person is a party to the action, an officer or employee designated by its attorney is entitled to be present.

§ 778. Recall of witness. After a witness has been excused from giving further testimony in the action, he cannot be recalled without leave of the court. Leave may be granted or withheld in the court's discretion.

Chapter 6

CREDIBILITY OF WITNESSES

Article 1. Credibility Generally

§ 780. General rule as to credibility. Except as otherwise provided by statute, the court or jury may consider in determining the credibility of a witness any matter that has any tendency in reason to prove or disprove the truthfulness of his testimony at the hearing, including but not limited to any of the following:

(a) His demeanor while testifying and the manner in which he testifies.

(b) The character of his testimony.

(c) The extent of his capacity to perceive, to recollect, or to communicate any matter about which he testifies.

(d) The extent of his opportunity to perceive any matter about which he testifies.

(e) His character for honesty or veracity or their opposites.

(f) The existence or nonexistence of a bias, interest, or other motive.

(g) A statement previously made by him that is consistent with his testimony at the hearing.

(h) A statement made by him that is inconsistent with any part of his testimony at the hearing.

(i) The existence or nonexistence of any fact testified to by him.

(j) His attitude toward the action in which he testifies or toward the giving of testimony.

(k) His admission of untruthfulness.

Comment—Law Revision Commission

Section 780 is a general catalog of those matters that have any tendency in reason to affect the credibility of a witness. So far as the admissibility of evidence relating to credibility is concerned, Section 780 is technically unnecessary because Section 351 declares that "all relevant evidence is admissible." However, this section makes it clear that matters that may not be "evidence" in a technical sense can affect the credibility of a witness, and it provides a convenient list of the most common factors that bear on the question of credibility. Limitations on the admissibility of evidence offered to attack or support the credibility of a witness are stated in Article 2 (commencing with Section 785).

There is no specific limitation in the Evidence Code on the use of impeaching evidence on the ground that it is "collateral". The so-called "collateral matter" limitation on attacking the credibility of a witness excludes evidence relevant to credibility unless such evidence is independently relevant to the issue being tried. It is based on the sensible notion that trials should be confined to settling those disputes between the parties upon which their rights in the litigation depend. Under existing law, this "collateral matter" doctrine has been treated as an inflexible rule excluding evidence relevant to the credibility of the witness.

The effect of Section 780 (together with Section 351) is to eliminate this inflexible rule of exclusion. This is not to say that all evidence of a collateral nature offered to attack the credibility of a witness would be admissible. Under Section 352, the court has substantial discretion to exclude collateral evidence. The effect of Section 780, therefore, is to change the present somewhat inflexible rule of exclusion to a rule of discretion to be exercised by the trial judge.

There is no limitation in the Evidence Code on the use of opinion evidence to prove the character of a witness for honesty, veracity, or the lack thereof. Hence, under Sections 780 and 1100, such evidence is admissible. This represents a change in the present law.

§ 782. Sexual offenses; evidence of sexual conduct of complaining witness; procedure for admissibility; treatment of resealed affidavits.

(a) In any of the circumstances described in subdivision (c), if evidence of sexual conduct of the complaining witness is offered to attack the credibility of the complaining witness under Section 780, the following procedure shall be followed:

> (1) A written motion shall be made by the defendant to the court and prosecutor stating that the defense has an offer of proof of the relevancy of evidence of the sexual conduct of the complaining witness proposed to be presented and its relevancy in attacking the credibility of the complaining witness.
>
> (2) The written motion shall be accompanied by an affidavit in which the offer of proof shall be stated. The affidavit shall be filed under seal and only unsealed by the court to determine if the offer of proof is sufficient to order a hearing pursuant to paragraph (3). After that determination, the affidavit shall be resealed by the court.
>
> (3) If the court finds that the offer of proof is sufficient, the court shall order a hearing out of the presence of the jury, if any, and at the hearing allow the questioning of the complaining witness regarding the offer of proof made by the defendant.
>
> (4) At the conclusion of the hearing, if the court finds that evidence proposed to be offered by the defendant regarding the sexual conduct of the complaining witness is relevant pursuant to Section 780, and is not inadmissible pursuant to Section 352, the court may make an order stating what evidence may be introduced by the defendant, and the nature of the questions to be permitted. The defendant may then offer evidence pursuant to the order of the court.

(5) An affidavit resealed by the court pursuant to paragraph (2) shall remain sealed, unless the defendant raises an issue on appeal or collateral review relating to the offer of proof contained in the sealed document. If the defendant raises that issue on appeal, the court shall allow the Attorney General and appellate counsel for the defendant access to the sealed affidavit. If the issue is raised on collateral review, the court shall allow the district attorney and defendant's counsel access to the sealed affidavit. The use of the information contained in the affidavit shall be limited solely to the pending proceeding.

(b) As used in this section, "complaining witness" means:

(1) The alleged victim of the crime charged, the prosecution of which is subject to this section, pursuant to paragraph (1) of subdivision (c).

(2) An alleged victim offering testimony pursuant to paragraph (2) or (3) of subdivision (c).

(c) The procedure provided by subdivision (a) shall apply in any of the following circumstances:

(1) In a prosecution under Section 261, 262, 264.1, 286, 288, 288a, 288.5, or 289 of the Penal Code, or for assault with intent to commit, attempt to commit, or conspiracy to commit any crime defined in any of those sections, except if the crime is alleged to have occurred in a local detention facility, as defined in Section 6031.4 of the Penal Code, or in the state prison, as defined in Section 4504.

(2) When an alleged victim testifies pursuant to subdivision (b) of Section 1101 as a victim of a crime listed in Section 243.4, 261, 261.5, 269, 285, 286, 288, 288a, 288.5, 289, 314, or 647.6 of the Penal Code, except if the crime is alleged to have occurred in a local detention facility, as defined in Section 6031.4 of the Penal Code, or in the state prison, as defined in Section 4504 of the Penal Code.

(3) When an alleged victim of a sexual offense testifies pursuant to Section 1108, except if the crime is alleged to have occurred in a local detention facility, as defined in Section 6031.4 of the Penal Code, or in the state prison, as defined in Section 4504 of the Penal Code.

Cross References

Sexual conduct of complaining witness, inadmissible to prove consent; effect on admissibility under this section, see § 1103.

§ 783. Sexual harassment, sexual assault, or sexual battery cases; admissibility of evidence of plaintiff's sexual conduct; procedure.

In any civil action alleging conduct which constitutes sexual harassment, sexual assault, or sexual battery, if evidence of sexual conduct of the plaintiff is offered to attack credibility of the plaintiff under Section 780, the following procedures shall be followed:

(a) A written motion shall be made by the defendant to the court and the plaintiff's attorney stating that the defense has an offer of proof of the relevancy of evidence of the sexual conduct of the plaintiff proposed to be presented.

(b) The written motion shall be accompanied by an affidavit in which the offer of proof shall be stated.

(c) If the court finds that the offer of proof is sufficient, the court shall order a hearing out of the presence of the jury, if any, and at the hearing allow the questioning of the plaintiff regarding the offer of proof made by the defendant.

(d) At the conclusion of the hearing, if the court finds that evidence proposed to be offered by the defendant regarding the sexual conduct of the plaintiff is relevant pursuant to Section 780, and is not inadmissible pursuant to Section 352, the court may make an order stating what evidence may be introduced by the defendant, and the nature of the questions to be permitted. The defendant may then offer evidence pursuant to the order of the court.

Article 2. Attacking or Supporting Credibility

§ 785. Parties may attack or support credibility. The credibility of a witness may be attacked or supported by any party, including the party calling him.

Comment—Law Revision Commission

Section 785 eliminates the present restriction on attacking the credibility of one's own witness. Under the existing law, a party is precluded from attacking the credibility of his own witness unless he has been surprised and damaged by the witness' testimony. In large part, the present law rests upon the theory that a party producing a witness is bound by his testimony. This theory has long been abandoned in several jurisdictions where the practical exigencies of litigation have been recognized.

§ 786. Character evidence generally. Evidence of traits of his character other than honesty or veracity, or their opposites, is inadmissible to attack or support the credibility of a witness.

Comment—Law Revision Commission

Section 786 limits evidence relating to the character of a witness to the character traits necessarily involved in a proper determination of credibility. Other character traits are not sufficiently probative of a witness' honesty or veracity to warrant their consideration on the issue of credibility.

§ 787. Specific instances of conduct. Subject to Section 788, evidence of specific instances of his conduct relevant only as tending to prove a trait of his character is inadmissible to attack or support the credibility of a witness.

§ 788. Prior felony conviction.

For the purpose of attacking the credibility of a witness, it may be shown by the examination of the witness or by the record of the judgment that he has been convicted of a felony unless:

(a) A pardon based on his innocence has been granted to the witness by the jurisdiction in which he was convicted.

(b) A certificate of rehabilitation and pardon has been granted to the witness under the provisions of Chapter 3.5 (commencing with Section 4852.01) of Title 6 of Part 3 of the Penal Code.

(c) The accusatory pleading against the witness has been dismissed under the provisions of Penal Code Section 1203.4, but this exception does not apply to any criminal trial where the witness is being prosecuted for a subsequent offense.

(d) The conviction was under the laws of another jurisdiction and the witness has been relieved of the penalties and disabilities arising from the conviction pursuant to a procedure substantially equivalent to that referred to in subdivision (b) or (c).

Comment—Senate Committee on Judiciary

Under Section 787, evidence of specific instances of a witness' conduct is inadmissible for the purpose of attacking or supporting his credibility. Section 788 states an exception to this general rule where the evidence of the witness' misconduct consists of his conviction of a felony. A judgment of conviction that is offered to prove that the person adjudged guilty committed the crime is hearsay. See Evidence Code §§ 1200 and 1300 and the Comments thereto. But the hearsay objection to the evidence specified in Section 788 is overcome by the declaration in the section that such evidence "may be shown" for the purpose of attacking a witness' credibility.

Editorial Note

In June 1982, section 28 was added to Article I of the California Constitution through approval by the electorate of an initiative titled, Proposition 8—"The Victims' Bill of Rights." Section 28(f) of that constitutional amendment provides:

> 28. (f) **Use of Prior Convictions.** Any prior felony conviction of any person in any criminal proceeding, whether adult or juvenile, shall subsequently be used without limitation for purposes of impeachment or enhancement of sentence in any criminal proceeding. When a prior felony conviction is an element of any felony offense, it shall be proven to the trier of fact in open court.

See People v. Castro, 38 Cal.3d 301, 211 Cal.Rptr. 719, 696 P.2d 111 (1985). Also see section 28(d) of Proposition 8—"The Victims' Bill of Rights," quoted supra, following § 351.

§ 789. Religious belief. Evidence of his religious belief or lack thereof is inadmissible to attack or support the credibility of a witness.

§ 790. Good character of witness. Evidence of the good character of a witness is inadmissible to support his credibility unless evidence of his bad character has been admitted for the purpose of attacking his credibility.

Comment—Law Revision Commission

Unless the credibility of a witness is put in issue by an attack impugning his character for honesty or veracity (see Section 786), evidence of the witness' good character admitted merely to support his credibility introduces collateral material that is unnecessary to a proper determination of any legitimate issue in the action.

§ 791. Prior consistent statement of witness. Evidence of a statement previously made by a witness that is consistent with his testimony at the hearing is inadmissible to support his credibility unless it is offered after:

(a) Evidence of a statement made by him that is inconsistent with any part of his testimony at the hearing has been admitted for the purpose of attacking his credibility, and the statement was made before the alleged inconsistent statement; or

(b) An express or implied charge has been made that his testimony at the hearing is recently fabricated or is influenced by bias or other improper motive, and the statement was made before the bias, motive for fabrication, or other improper motive is alleged to have arisen.

Comment—Law Revision Commission

Section 791 sets forth the conditions for admitting a witness' prior consistent statements for the purpose of supporting his credibility as a witness.

Subdivision (a). Subdivision (a) permits the introduction of a witness' prior consistent statement if evidence of an inconsistent statement of the witness has been admitted for the purpose of attacking his credibility and if the consistent statement was made *before* the alleged inconsistent statement.

Under existing California law, evidence of a prior consistent statement is admissible to rebut a charge of bias, interest, recent fabrication, or other improper motive. See the Comment to subdivision (b), infra. Existing law may preclude admission of a prior consistent statement to rehabilitate a witness where only a prior inconsistent statement has been admitted for the purpose of attacking his credibility. However, recent cases indicate that the offering of a prior inconsistent statement necessarily is an implied charge that the witness has fabricated his testimony since the time the inconsistent statement was made and justifies the admission of a consistent statement made prior to the alleged inconsistent statement. People v. Bias, 170 Cal.App.2d 502, 511–512, 339 P.2d 204, 210–211 (1959). Subdivision (a) makes it clear that evidence of a previous consistent statement is admissible under these circumstances to show that no such fabrication took place. Subdivision (a), thus, is no more than a logical extension of the general rule that evidence of a prior consistent statement is admissible to rehabilitate a witness following an express or implied charge of recent fabrication.

Subdivision (b). This subdivision codifies existing law. Of course, if the consistent statement was made *after* the time the improper motive is alleged to have arisen, the logical thrust of the evidence is lost and the statement is inadmissible.

Chapter 7

HYPNOSIS OF WITNESSES

§ 795. Testimony of hypnosis subject; admissibility; conditions.

(a) The testimony of a witness is not inadmissible in a criminal proceeding by reason of the fact that the witness has previously undergone hypnosis for the purpose of recalling events that are the subject of the witness's testimony, if all of the following conditions are met:

(1) The testimony is limited to those matters that the witness recalled and related prior to the hypnosis.

(2) The substance of the prehypnotic memory was preserved in a writing, audio recording, or video recording prior to the hypnosis.

(3) The hypnosis was conducted in accordance with all of the following procedures:

(A) A written record was made prior to hypnosis documenting the subject's description of the event, and information that was provided to the hypnotist concerning the subject matter of the hypnosis.

(B) The subject gave informed consent to the hypnosis.

(C) The hypnosis session, including the pre-and post-hypnosis interviews, was video recorded for subsequent review.

(D) The hypnosis was performed by a licensed medical doctor, psychologist, licensed clinical social worker, or a licensed marriage and family therapist experienced in the use of hypnosis and independent of and not in the presence of law enforcement, the prosecution, or the defense.

(4) Prior to admission of the testimony, the court holds a hearing pursuant to Section 402 at which the proponent of the evidence proves by clear and convincing evidence that the hypnosis did not so affect the witness as to render the witness's prehypnosis recollection unreliable or to substantially impair the ability to cross-examine the witness concerning the witness's prehypnosis recollection. At the hearing, each side shall have the right to present expert testimony and to cross-examine witnesses.

(b) Nothing in this section shall be construed to limit the ability of a party to attack the credibility of a witness who has undergone hypnosis, or to limit other legal grounds to admit or exclude the testimony of that witness.

Division 7

OPINION TESTIMONY AND SCIENTIFIC EVIDENCE

Comment—Law Revision Commission

Two matters concerning the terminology used in this division should be noted: (1) The word "opinion" is used to include all opinions, inferences, conclusions, and other subjective statements made by a witness. (2) The word "matter" is used to encompass facts, data, and such matters as a witness' knowledge, experience, and other intangibles upon which an opinion may be based. Thus, every conceivable basis for an opinion is included within this term.

Chapter 1

EXPERT AND OTHER OPINION TESTIMONY

Article 1. Expert and Other Opinion Testimony Generally

§ 800. Opinion testimony by lay witness. If a witness is not testifying as an expert, his testimony in the form of an opinion is limited to such an opinion as is permitted by law, including but not limited to an opinion that is:

(a) Rationally based on the perception of the witness; and

(b) Helpful to a clear understanding of his testimony.

§ 801. Opinion testimony by expert witness. If a witness is testifying as an expert, his testimony in the form of an opinion is limited to such an opinion as is:

(a) Related to a subject that is sufficiently beyond common experience that the opinion of an expert would assist the trier of fact; and

(b) Based on matter (including his special knowledge, skill, experience, training, and education) perceived by or personally known to the witness or made known to him at or before the hearing, whether or not admissible, that is of a type that reasonably may be relied upon by an expert in forming an opinion upon the subject to which his testimony relates, unless an expert is precluded by law from using such matter as a basis for his opinion.

Comment—Law Revision Commission

Subdivision (a), which states *when* an expert may give his opinion upon a subject that is within the scope of his expertise, codifies the existing rule that expert opinion is limited to those subjects that are beyond the competence of persons of common experience, training, and education.

Subdivision (b) states a general rule in regard to the permissible bases upon which the opinion of an expert may be founded. The California courts have made it clear that the nature of the matter upon which an expert may base his opinion varies from case to case. In some fields of expert knowledge, an expert may rely on statements made by and information received from other persons; in some other fields of expert knowledge, an expert may not do so. For example, a physician may rely on statements made to him by the patient concerning the history of his condition. A physician may also rely on reports and opinions of other physicians. An expert on the valuation of real or personal property, too, may rely on inquiries made of others, commercial reports, market quotations, and relevant sales known to the witness. On the other hand, an expert on automobile accidents may not rely on extrajudicial statements of others as a partial basis for an opinion as to the point of impact, whether or not the statements would be admissible evidence.

Likewise, under existing law, irrelevant or speculative matters are not a proper basis for an expert's opinion.

The variation in the permissible bases of expert opinion is unavoidable in light of the wide variety of subjects upon which such opinion can be offered. In regard to some matters of expert opinion, an expert must, if he is going to give an opinion that will be helpful to the jury, rely on reports, statements, and other information that might not be admissible evidence. A physician in many instances cannot make a diagnosis without relying on the case history recited by the patient or on reports from various technicians or other physicians. Similarly, an appraiser must rely on reports of sales and other market data if he is to give an opinion that will be of value to the jury. In the usual case where a physician's or an appraiser's opinion is required, the adverse party also will have its expert who will be able to check the data relied upon by the adverse expert. On the other hand, a police officer can analyze skid marks, debris, and the condition of vehicles that have been involved in an accident without relying on the statements of bystanders; and it seems likely that the jury would be as able to evaluate the statements of others in the light of the physical facts, as interpreted by the officer, as would the officer himself.

§ 802. Statement of basis of opinion.

A witness testifying in the form of an opinion may state on direct examination the reasons for his opinion and the matter (including, in the case of an expert, his special knowledge, skill, experience, training, and education) upon which it is based, unless he is precluded by law from using such reasons or matter as a basis for his opinion. The court in its discretion may require that a witness before testifying in the form of an opinion be first examined concerning the matter upon which his opinion is based.

Comment—Law Revision Commission

Although Section 802 provides that a witness may state the basis for his opinion on direct examination, it is clear that, in some cases, a witness is *required* to do so in order to show that his opinion is applicable to the action before the court. Under existing law, where a witness testifies in the form of opinion not based upon his personal observation, the assumed facts upon which his opinion is based must be stated in order to show that the witness has some basis for forming an intelligent opinion and to permit the trier of fact to

§ 802 CALIFORNIA EVIDENCE CODE

determine the applicability of the opinion in light of the existence or nonexistence of such facts. Evidence Code Section 802 will not affect the rule set forth in these cases, for it is based essentially on the requirement that all evidence must be shown to be applicable—or relevant—to the action. Evidence Code §§ 350, 403. But under Section 802, as under existing law, a witness testifying from his personal observation of the facts upon which his opinion is based need not be examined concerning such facts before testifying in the form of opinion; his personal observation is a sufficient basis upon which to found his opinion. However, the court may require a witness to state the facts observed before stating his opinion. In this respect Section 802 codifies the existing rule concerning lay witnesses and, although the existing law is unclear, probably states the existing rule as to expert witnesses. See Tentative Recommendation and a Study Relating to the Uniform Rules of Evidence, (Article VII. Expert and Other Opinion Testimony), 6 Cal.Law Revision Comm'n, Rep., Rec. & Studies 901, 934 (lay witness), 939 (expert witness)(1964).

§ 803. Opinion based on improper matter. The court may, and upon objection shall, exclude testimony in the form of an opinion that is based in whole or in significant part on matter that is not a proper basis for such an opinion. In such case, the witness may, if there remains a proper basis for his opinion, then state his opinion after excluding from consideration the matter determined to be improper.

§ 804. Opinion based on opinion or statement of another. (a) If a witness testifying as an expert testifies that his opinion is based in whole or in part upon the opinion or statement of another person, such other person may be called and examined by any adverse party as if under cross-examination concerning the opinion or statement.

(b) This section is not applicable if the person upon whose opinion or statement the expert witness has relied is (1) a party, (2) a person identified with a party within the meaning of subdivision (d) of Section 776, or (3) a witness who has testified in the action concerning the subject matter of the opinion or statement upon which the expert witness has relied.

(c) Nothing in this section makes admissible an expert opinion that is inadmissible because it is based in whole or in part on the opinion or statement of another person.

(d) An expert opinion otherwise admissible is not made inadmissible by this section because it is based on the opinion or statement of a person who is unavailable for examination pursuant to this section.

Comment—Law Revision Commission

Section 804 is designed to provide protection to a party who is confronted with an expert witness who relies on the opinion or statement of some other person. In such a situation, a party may find that cross-examination of the witness will not reveal the weakness in his opinion, for the crucial parts are based on the observations or opinions of someone else. Under existing law, if that other person is called as a witness, he is the witness of the party calling him and, therefore, that party may not subject him to cross-examination.

The existing law operates unfairly, for it unnecessarily restricts meaningful cross-examination. Hence, Section 804 permits a party to extend his cross-examination into the underlying bases of the opinion testimony introduced against him by calling the authors of opinions and statements relied on by adverse witnesses and examining them as if under cross-examination concerning the subject matter of their opinions and statements.

§ 805. Opinion on ultimate issue. Testimony in the form of an opinion that is otherwise admissible is not objectionable because it embraces the ultimate issue to be decided by the trier of fact.

Article 2. Value, Damages, and Benefits in Eminent Domain and Inverse Condemnation Cases

§ 810. Application of article. (a) Except where another rule is provided by statute, this article provides special rules of evidence applicable to any action in which the value of property is to be ascertained.

(b) This article does not govern ad valorem property tax assessment or equalization proceedings.

§ 811. Value of property. As used in this article, "value of property" means market value of any of the following:

(a) Real property or any interest therein

(b) Real property or any interest therein and tangible personal property valued as a unit.

§ 812. Market value; interpretation of meaning. This article is not intended to alter or change the existing substantive law, whether statutory or decisional, interpreting the meaning of "market value," whether denominated "fair market value" or otherwise.

§ 813. Value of property; authorized opinions; view of property; admissible evidence. (a) The value of property may be shown only by the opinions of any of the following:

(1) Witnesses qualified to express such opinions;

(2) The owner or the spouse of the owner of the property or property interest being valued.

(3) An officer, regular employee, or partner designated by a corporation, partnership, or unincorporated association that is the owner of the property or property interest being valued, if the designee is knowledgeable as to the value of the property or property interest.

(b) Nothing in this section prohibits a view of the property being valued or the admission of any other admissible evidence (including but not limited to evidence as to the nature and condition of the property and, in an eminent domain proceeding, the character of the improvement proposed to be constructed by the plaintiff) for the limited purpose of enabling the court, jury, or referee to understand and weigh the testimony given under subdivision (a); and such evidence, except evidence of the character of the improvement proposed to be constructed by the plaintiff in an eminent domain proceeding, is subject to impeachment and rebuttal.

(c) For the purposes of subdivision (a), "owner of the property or property interest being valued" includes, but is not limited to, the following persons:

(1) A person entitled to possession of the property.

(2) Either party in an action or proceeding to determine the ownership of the property between the parties if the court determines that it would not be in the interest of efficient administration of justice to determine the issue of ownership prior to the admission of the opinion of the party.

§ 814. Matter upon which opinion must be based. The opinion of a witness as to the value of property is limited to such an opinion as is based on matter perceived by or personally known to the witness or made known to the witness at or before the hearing, whether or not admissible, that is of a type that reasonably may be relied upon by an expert in forming an opinion as to the value of property, including but not limited to the matters listed in Sections 815 to 821, inclusive, unless a witness is precluded by law from using such matter as a basis for an opinion.

§ 815. Sales of subject property. When relevant to the determination of the value of property, a witness may take into account as a basis for an opinion the price and other terms and circumstances of any sale or contract to sell and purchase which included the property or property interest being valued or any part thereof if the sale or contract was freely made in good faith within a reasonable time before or after the date of valuation, except that in an eminent domain proceeding where the sale or contract to sell and purchase includes only the property or property interest being taken or a part thereof, such sale or contract to sell and purchase may not be taken into account if it occurs after the filing of the lis pendens.

§ 816. Comparable sales. When relevant to the determination of the value of property, a witness may take into account as a basis for his opinion the price and other terms and circumstances of any sale or contract to sell and purchase comparable property if the sale or contract was freely made in good faith within a reasonable time before or after the date of valuation. In order to be considered comparable, the sale or contract must have been made sufficiently near in time to the date of valuation, and the property sold must be located sufficiently near the property being valued, and must be sufficiently alike in respect to character, size, situation, usability, and improvements, to make it clear that the property sold and the property being valued are comparable in value and that the price realized for the property sold may fairly be considered as shedding light on the value of the property being valued.

§ 817. Leases of subject property. (a) Subject to subdivision (b), when relevant to the determination of the value of property, a witness may take into account as a basis for an opinion the rent reserved and other terms and circumstances of any lease which included the property or property interest being valued or any part thereof which was in effect within a reasonable time before or after the date of valuation, except that in an eminent domain proceeding where the lease includes only the property or property interest being taken or a part thereof, such lease may not be taken into account in the determination of the value of property if it is entered into after the filing of the lis pendens.

(b) A witness may take into account a lease providing for a rental fixed by a percentage or other measurable portion of gross sales or gross income from a business conducted on the leased property only for the purpose of arriving at an opinion as to the reasonable net rental value attributable to the property or property interest being valued as provided in Section 819 or determining the value of a leasehold interest.

§ 818. Comparable leases. For the purpose of determining the capitalized value of the reasonable net rental value attributable to the property or property interest being valued as provided in Section 819 or determining the value of a leasehold interest, a witness may take into account as a basis for his opinion the rent reserved and other terms and circumstances of any lease of comparable property if the lease was freely made in good faith within a reasonable time before or after the date of valuation.

§ 819. Capitalization of income. When relevant to the determination of the value of property, a witness may take into account as a basis for his opinion the capitalized value of the reasonable net rental value attributable to the land and existing improvements thereon (as distinguished from the capitalized value of the income or profits attributable to the business conducted thereon).

§ 820. Reproduction cost. When relevant to the determination of the value of property, a witness may take into account as a basis for his opinion the value of the property or property interest being valued as indicated by the value of the land together with the cost of replacing or reproducing the existing improvements thereon, if the improvements enhance the value of the property or property interest for its highest and best use, less whatever depreciation or obsolescence the improvements have suffered.

§ 821. Conditions in general vicinity of subject property. When relevant to the determination of the value of property, a witness may take into account as a basis for his opinion the nature of the improvements on properties in the general vicinity of the property or property interest being valued and the character of the existing uses being made of such properties.

§ 822. Matter upon which opinion may not be based. (a) In an eminent domain or inverse condemnation proceeding, notwithstanding the provisions of Sections 814 to 821, inclusive, the following matter is inadmissible as evidence and shall not be taken into account as a basis for an opinion as to the value of property:

(1) The price or other terms and circumstances of an acquisition of property or a property interest if the acquisition was for a public use for which the property could have been taken by eminent domain. The price or other terms and circumstances shall not be excluded pursuant to this paragraph if the proceeding relates to the valuation of all or part of a water system as defined in Section 240 of the Public Utilities Code.

(2) The price at which an offer or option to purchase or lease the property or property interest being valued or any other property was made, or the price at which the property or interest was optioned, offered, or listed for sale or lease, except that an option, offer, or listing may be introduced by a party as an admission of another party to the proceeding; but nothing in this subdivision permits an admission to be used as direct evidence upon any matter that may be shown only by opinion evidence under Section 813.

(3) The value of any property or property interest as assessed for taxation purposes or the amount of taxes which may be due on the property, but nothing in this subdivision prohibits the consideration of actual or estimated taxes for the purpose of determining the reasonable net rental value attributable to the property or property interest being valued.

(4) An opinion as to the value of any property or property interest other than that being valued.

(5) The influence upon the value of the property or property interest being valued of any noncompensable items of value, damage, or injury.

(6) The capitalized value of the income or rental from any property or property interest other than that being valued.

(b) In an action other than an eminent domain or inverse condemnation proceeding, the matters listed in subdivision (a) are not admissible as evidence, and may not be taken into account as a basis for an opinion as to the value of property, except to the extent permitted under the rules of law otherwise applicable.

(c) The amendments made to this section during the 1987 portion of the 1987–88 Regular Session of the Legislature shall not apply to or affect any petition filed pursuant to this section before January 1, 1988.

§ 823. No relevant market for property. Notwithstanding any other provision of this article, the value of property for which there is no relevant, comparable market may be determined by any method of valuation that is just and equitable.

§ 824. No relevant market; nonprofit special use property. (a) Notwithstanding any other provision of this article, a just and equitable method of determining the value of nonprofit, special use property, as defined by Section 1235.155 of the Code of Civil Procedure, for which there is no relevant, comparable market, is the cost of purchasing land and the reasonable cost of making it suitable for the conduct of the same nonprofit, special use, together with the cost of constructing similar improvements. The method for determining compensation for improvements shall be as set forth in subdivision (b).

(b) Notwithstanding any other provision of this article, a witness providing opinion testimony on the value of nonprofit, special use property, as defined by Section 1235.155 of the Code of Civil Procedure, for which there is no relevant, comparable market, shall base his or her opinion on the value of reproducing the improvements without taking into consideration any depreciation or obsolescence of the improvements.

(c) This section does not apply to actions or proceedings commenced by a public entity or public utility to acquire real property or any interest in real property for the use of water, sewer, electricity, telephone, natural gas, or flood control facilities or rights-of-way where those acquisitions neither require removal or destruction of existing improvements, nor render the property unfit for the owner's present or proposed use.

Article 3. Opinion Testimony on Particular Subjects

§ 870. Opinion as to sanity. A witness may state his opinion as to the sanity of a person when:

(a) The witness is an intimate acquaintance of the person whose sanity is in question;

(b) The witness was a subscribing witness to a writing, the validity of which is in dispute, signed by the person whose sanity is in question and the opinion relates to the sanity of such person at the time the writing was signed; or

(c) The witness is qualified under Section 800 or 801 to testify in the form of an opinion.

Comment—Law Revision Commission

Subdivision (c) merely makes it clear that a witness who meets the requirements of Section 800 or Section 801 is qualified to testify in the form of an opinion as to the sanity of a person. Section 870 does not disturb the present rule that permits a witness to testify to a person's rational or irrational appearance or conduct, even though the witness is not qualified under Section 870 to express an opinion on the person's sanity.

Chapter 2

BLOOD TESTS TO DETERMINE PATERNITY

§ 890. Short title. This chapter may be cited as the Uniform Act on Blood Tests to Determine Paternity.

§ 891. Interpretation. This act shall be so interpreted and construed as to effectuate its general purpose to make uniform the law of those states which enact it.

§ 892. Order for blood tests in civil actions involving paternity. In a civil action in which paternity is a relevant fact, the court may upon its own initiative or upon suggestion made by or on behalf of any person whose blood is involved, and shall upon motion of any party to the action made at a time so as not to delay the proceedings unduly, order the mother, child, and alleged father to submit to blood tests. If any party refuses to submit to such tests, the court may resolve the question of paternity against such party or enforce its order if the rights of others and the interests of justice so require. Any party's refusal to submit to such tests shall be admissible in evidence in any proceeding to determine paternity.

§ 893. Tests made by experts. The tests shall be made by experts qualified as examiners of blood types who shall be appointed by the court. The experts shall be called by the court as witnesses to testify to their findings and shall be subject to cross-examination by the parties. Any party or person at whose suggestion the tests have been ordered may demand that other experts, qualified as examiners of blood types, perform independent tests under order of the court, the results of which may be offered in evidence. The number and qualifications of such experts shall be determined by the court.

§ 894. Compensation of experts. The compensation of each expert witness appointed by the court shall be fixed at a reasonable amount. It shall be paid as the court shall order. The court may order that it be paid by the parties in such proportions and at such times as it shall prescribe, or that the proportion of any party be paid by the county, and that, after payment by the parties or the county or both, all or part or none of it be taxed as costs in the action.

§ 895. Determination of paternity. If the court finds that the conclusions of all the experts, as disclosed by the evidence based upon the tests, are that the alleged father is not the father of the child, the question of paternity shall be resolved accordingly. If the experts disagree in their findings or conclusions, or if the tests show the probability of the alleged father's paternity, the question, subject to the provisions of Section 352, shall be submitted upon all the evidence, including evidence based upon the tests.

§ 896. Limitation on application in criminal matters. This chapter applies to criminal actions subject to the following limitations and provisions:

(a) An order for the tests shall be made only upon application of a party or on the court's initiative.

(b) The compensation of the experts shall be paid by the county under order of court.

(c) The court may direct a verdict of acquittal upon the conclusions of all the experts under the provisions of Section 895; otherwise, the case shall be submitted for determination upon all the evidence.

§ 897. Right to produce other expert evidence. Nothing contained in this chapter shall be deemed or construed to prevent any party to any action from producing other expert evidence on the matter covered by this chapter; but, where other expert witnesses are called by a party to the action, their fees shall be paid by the party calling them and only ordinary witness fees shall be taxed as costs in the action.

Division 8

PRIVILEGES

Chapter 1

DEFINITIONS

§ 900. Application of definitions. Unless the provision or context otherwise requires, the definitions in this chapter govern the construction of this division. They do not govern the construction of any other division.

§ 901. "Proceeding". "Proceeding" means any action, hearing, investigation, inquest, or inquiry (whether conducted by a court, administrative agency, hearing officer, arbitrator, legislative body, or any other person authorized by law) in which, pursuant to law, testimony can be compelled to be given.

§ 902. "Civil proceeding". "Civil proceeding" means any proceeding except a criminal proceeding.

§ 903. "Criminal proceeding". "Criminal proceeding" means:

(a) A criminal action; and

(b) A proceeding pursuant to Article 3 (commencing with Section 3060) of Chapter 7 of Division 4 of Title 1 of the Government Code to determine whether a public officer should be removed from office for willful or corrupt misconduct in office.

§ 905. "Presiding officer". "Presiding officer" means the person authorized to rule on a claim of privilege in the proceeding in which the claim is made.

Comment—Law Revision Commission

"Presiding officer" is defined so that reference may be made in Division 8 to the person who makes rulings on questions of privilege in nonjudicial proceedings. The term includes arbitrators, hearing officers, referees, and any other person who is authorized to make rulings on claims of privilege. It, of course, includes the judge or other person presiding in a judicial proceeding.

Chapter 2

APPLICABILITY OF DIVISION

§ 910. Applicability of division. Except as otherwise provided by statute, the provisions of this division apply in all proceedings. The provisions of any statute making rules of evidence inapplicable in particular proceedings, or limiting the applicability of rules of evidence in particular proceedings, do not make this division inapplicable to such proceedings.

Comment—Law Revision Commission

Most rules of evidence are designed for use in courts. Generally, their purpose is to keep unreliable or prejudicial evidence from being presented to the trier of fact. Privileges are granted, however, for reasons of policy unrelated to the reliability of the information involved. A privilege is granted because it is considered more important to keep certain information confidential than it is to require disclosure of all the information relevant to the issues in a pending proceeding. Thus, for example, to protect the attorney-client relationship, it is necessary to prevent disclosure of confidential communications made in the course of that relationship.

If confidentiality is to be protected effectively by a privilege, the privilege must be recognized in proceedings other than judicial proceedings. The protection afforded by a privilege would be insufficient if a court were the only place where the privilege could be invoked. Every officer with power to issue subpoenas for investigative purposes, every administrative agency, every local governing board, and many more persons could pry into the protected information if the privilege rules were applicable only in judicial proceedings.

Therefore, the policy underlying the privilege rules requires their recognition in all proceedings of any nature in which testimony can be compelled by law to be given. Section 910 makes the privilege rules applicable to all such proceedings. In this respect, it follows the precedent set in New Jersey when privilege rules, based in part on the Uniform Rules of Evidence, were enacted. See N.J.Laws 1960, Ch. 52, p. 452 (N.J.Rev.Stat. §§ 2A:84A-1 to 2A:84A-49).

Statutes that relax the rules of evidence in particular proceedings do not have the effect of making privileges inapplicable in such proceedings. For example, Labor Code Section 5708, which provides that the officer conducting an Industrial Accident Commission proceeding "shall not be bound by the common law or statutory rules of evidence," does not make privileges inapplicable in such proceedings. Thus, the lawyer-client privilege must be recognized in an Industrial Accident Commission proceeding. On the other hand, Division 8 and other statutes provide exceptions to particular privileges for particular types of proceedings. E.g., Evidence Code § 998 (physician-patient privilege inapplicable in criminal proceeding); Labor Code §§ 4055, 6407, 6408 (testimony by physician and certain reports of physicians admissible as evidence in Industrial Accident Commission proceedings).

See generally Tentative Recommendation and a Study Relating to the Uniform Rules of Evidence (Article V. Privileges), 6 Cal.Law Revision Comm'n, Rep., Rec. & Studies 201, 309–327 (1964).

Chapter 3

GENERAL PROVISIONS RELATING TO PRIVILEGES

§ 911. General rule as to privileges. Except as otherwise provided by statute:

(a) No person has a privilege to refuse to be a witness.

(b) No person has a privilege to refuse to disclose any matter or to refuse to produce any writing, object, or other thing.

(c) No person has a privilege that another shall not be a witness or shall not disclose any matter or shall not produce any writing, object, or other thing.

Comment—Law Revision Commission

This section codifies the existing law that privileges are not recognized in the absence of statute. This is one of the few instances where the Evidence Code precludes the courts from elaborating upon the statutory scheme. Even with respect to privileges, however, the courts to a limited extent are permitted to develop the details of declared principles. See, e.g., Section 1060 (trade secret).

§ 912. Waiver of privilege. (a) Except as otherwise provided in this section, the right of any person to claim a privilege provided by Section 954 (lawyer-client privilege), 980 (privilege for confidential marital communications), 994 (physician-patient privilege), 1014 (psychotherapist-patient privilege), 1033 (privilege of penitent), 1034 (privilege of clergyman), 1035.8 (sexual assault counselor-victim privilege), or 1037.5 (domestic violence counselor-victim privilege) is waived with respect to a communication protected by the privilege if any holder of the privilege, without coercion, has disclosed a significant part of the communication or has consented to disclosure made by anyone. Consent to disclosure is manifested by any statement or other conduct of the holder of the privilege indicating consent to the disclosure, including failure to claim the privilege in any proceeding in which the holder has the legal standing and opportunity to claim the privilege.

(b) Where two or more persons are joint holders of a privilege provided by Section 954 (lawyer-client privilege), 994 (physician-patient privilege), 1014 (psychotherapist-patient privilege), 1035.8 (sexual assault counselor-victim privilege), or 1037.5 (domestic violence counselor-victim privilege), a waiver of the right of a particular joint holder of the privilege to claim the privilege does not affect the right of another joint holder to claim the privilege. In the case of the privilege provided by Section 980 (privilege for confidential marital communications), a waiver of the right of one spouse to claim the privilege does not affect the right of the other spouse to claim the privilege.

(c) A disclosure that is itself privileged is not a waiver of any privilege.

(d) A disclosure in confidence of a communication that is protected by a privilege provided by Section 954 (lawyer-client privilege), 994 (physician-patient privilege), 1014 (psychotherapist-patient privilege), 1035.8 (sexual assault counselor-victim privilege), or 1037.5 (domestic violence counsel or-victim privilege), when disclosure is reasonably necessary for the accomplishment of the purpose for which the lawyer, physician, psychotherapist, sexual assault counselor, or domestic violence counselor was consulted, is not a waiver of the privilege.

Comment—Senate Committee on Judiciary

Subdivision (a). Subdivision (a) states the general rule with respect to the manner in which a privilege is waived. Failure to claim the privilege where the holder of the privilege has the legal standing and the opportunity to claim the privilege constitutes a waiver.

Subdivision (c). A privilege is not waived when a revelation of the privileged matter takes place in another privileged communication. Thus, for example, a person does not waive his lawyer-client privilege by telling his wife in confidence what it was that he told his attorney. A privileged communication should not cease to be privileged merely because it has been related in the course of another privileged communication. The theory underlying the concept of waiver is that the holder of the privilege has abandoned the secrecy to which he is entitled under the privilege. Where the revelation of the privileged matter takes place in another privileged communication, there has not been such an abandonment. Of course, this rule does not apply unless the revelation was within the scope of the relationship in which it was made; a client consulting his lawyer on a contract matter who blurts out that he told his doctor that he had a venereal disease has waived the privilege, even though he intended the revelation to be confidential, because the revelation was not necessary to the contract business at hand.

Subdivision (d). Subdivision (d) is designed to maintain the confidentiality of communications in certain situations where the communications are disclosed to others in the course of accomplishing the purpose for which the lawyer, physician, or psychotherapist was consulted. For example, where a confidential communication from a client is related by his attorney to a physician, appraiser, or other expert in order to obtain that person's assistance so that the attorney will better be able to advise his client, the disclosure is not a waiver of the privilege, even though the disclosure is made with the client's knowledge and consent. Nor would a physician's or psychotherapist's keeping of confidential records necessary to diagnose or treat a patient, such as confidential hospital records, be a waiver of the privilege, even though other authorized persons have access to the records. Here, again, the privilege holder has not evidenced any abandonment of secrecy. Hence, he should be entitled to maintain the confidential nature of his communications to his attorney or physician despite the necessary further disclosure.

§ 913. Comment on, and inferences from, exercise of privilege.

(a) If in the instant proceeding or on a prior occasion a privilege is or was exercised not to testify with respect to any matter, or to refuse to disclose or to prevent another from disclosing any matter, neither the presiding officer nor counsel may comment thereon, no presumption shall arise because of the exercise of the privilege, and the trier of fact may not draw any inference therefrom as to the credibility of the witness or as to any matter at issue in the proceeding.

(b) The court, at the request of a party who may be adversely affected because an unfavorable inference may be drawn by the jury because a privilege has been exercised, shall instruct the jury that no presumption arises because of the exercise of the privilege and that the jury may not draw any inference therefrom as to the credibility of the witness or as to any matter at issue in the proceeding.

§ 914. Determination of claim of privilege; limitation on punishment for contempt. (a) The presiding officer shall determine a claim of privilege in any proceeding in the same manner as a court determines such a claim under Article 2 (commencing with Section 400) of Chapter 4 of Division 3.

(b) No person may be held in contempt for failure to disclose information claimed to be privileged unless he has failed to comply with an order of a court that he disclose such information. This subdivision does not apply to any governmental agency that has constitutional contempt power, nor does it apply to hearings and investigations of the Industrial Accident Commission, nor does it impliedly repeal Chapter 4 (commencing with Section 9400) of Part 1 of Division 2 of Title 2 of the Government Code. If no other statutory procedure is applicable, the procedure prescribed by Section 1991 of the Code of Civil Procedure shall be followed in seeking an order of a court that the person disclose the information claimed to be privileged.

Comment—Assembly Committee on Judiciary

Subdivision (a) makes the general provisions concerning preliminary determinations on admissibility of evidence (Sections 400–406) applicable when a presiding officer who is not a judge is called upon to determine whether or not a privilege exists. Subdivision (a) is necessary because Sections 400–406, by their terms, apply only to determinations by a court.

Subdivision (b) is needed to protect persons claiming privileges in nonjudicial proceedings. Because such proceedings are often conducted by persons untrained in law, it is desirable to have a judicial determination of whether a person is required to disclose information claimed to be privileged before he can be held in contempt for failing to disclose such information. What is contemplated is that, if a claim of privilege is made in a nonjudicial proceeding and is overruled, application must be made to a court for an order compelling the witness to answer. Only if such order is made and is disobeyed may a witness be held in contempt.

§ 915. Disclosure of information in ruling on claim of privilege.
(a) Subject to subdivision (b), the presiding officer may not require disclosure of information claimed to be privileged under this division or attorney work product under subdivision (a) of Section 2018.030 of the Code of Civil Procedure in order to rule on the claim of privilege; provided, however, that in any hearing conducted pursuant to subdivision (c) of Section 1524 of the Penal Code in which a claim of privilege is made and the court determines that there is no other feasible means to rule on the validity of the claim other than to require disclosure, the court shall proceed in accordance with subdivision (b).

(b) When a court is ruling on a claim of privilege under Article 9 (commencing with Section 1040) of Chapter 4 (official information and identity of informer) or under Section 1060 (trade secret) or under subdivision (b) of Section 2018.030 of the Code of Civil Procedure (attorney work product) and is unable to do so without requiring disclosure of the information claimed to be privileged, the court may require the person from whom disclosure is sought or the person authorized to claim the privilege, or both, to disclose the information in chambers out of the presence and hearing of all persons except the person authorized to claim the privilege and any other persons as the person authorized to claim the privilege is willing to have present. If the judge determines that the information is privileged, neither the judge nor any other person may ever disclose, without the consent of a person authorized to permit disclosure, what was disclosed in the course of the proceedings in chambers.

Comment—Law Revision Commission

Subdivision (a) states the general rule that revelation of the information asserted to be privileged may not be compelled in order to determine whether or not it is privileged.

Subdivision (b) provides an exception to this general rule for information claimed to be privileged under Section 1040 (official information), Section 1041 (identity of an informer), or Section 1060 (trade secret). [ed. An amendment in 2001 added attorney work product rulings to the list of matters covered by this section.] These privileges exist only if the interest in maintaining the secrecy of the information outweighs the interest in seeing that justice is done in the particular case. In at least some cases, it will be necessary for the judge to examine the information claimed to be privileged in order to balance these competing considerations intelligently. Even in these cases, Section 915 undertakes to give adequate protection to the person claiming the privilege by providing that the information be disclosed in confidence to the judge and requiring that it be kept in confidence if it is found to be privileged.

The exception in subdivision (b) applies only when a court is ruling on the claim of privilege. Thus, in view of subdivision (a), disclosure of the information cannot be required, for example, in an administrative proceeding.

§ 916. Exclusion of privileged information where persons authorized to claim privilege are not present.
(a) The presiding officer, on his own motion or on the motion of any party, shall exclude information that is subject to a claim of privilege under this division if:

(1) The person from whom the information is sought is not a person authorized to claim the privilege; and

(2) There is no party to the proceeding who is a person authorized to claim the privilege.

(b) The presiding officer may not exclude information under this section if:

(1) He is otherwise instructed by a person authorized to permit disclosure; or

(2) The proponent of the evidence establishes that there is no person authorized to claim the privilege in existence.

Comment—Assembly Committee on Judiciary
Section 916 is needed to protect the holder of a privilege when he is not available to protect his own interest. For example, a third party—perhaps the lawyer's secretary—may have been present when a confidential communication to a lawyer was made. In the absence of both the holder himself and the lawyer, the secretary could be compelled to testify concerning the communication if there were no provision such as Section 916 which requires the presiding officer to recognize the privilege.

§ 917. Presumption that certain communications are confidential; privileged character of electronic communications.
(a) If a privilege is claimed on the ground that the matter sought to be disclosed is a communication made in confidence in the course of the lawyer-client, physician-patient, psychotherapist-patient, clergy-penitent, husband-wife, sexual assault counselor-victim, or domestic violence counselor-victim relationship, the communication is presumed to have been made in confidence and the opponent of the claim of privilege has the burden of proof to establish that the communication was not confidential.

(b) A communication between persons in a relationship listed in subdivision (a) does not lose its privileged character for the sole reason that it is communicated by electronic means or because persons involved in the delivery, facilitation, or storage of electronic communication may have access to the content of the communication.

(c) For purposes of this section, "electronic" has the same meaning provided in Section 1633.2 of the Civil Code.

Comment—Assembly Committee on Judiciary
If the privilege claimant were required to show that the communication was made in confidence, he would be compelled, in many cases, to reveal the subject matter of the communication in order to establish his right to the privilege. Hence, Section 917 is included to establish a presumption of confidentiality.

To overcome the presumption, the proponent of the evidence must persuade the presiding officer that the communication was not made in confidence. Of course, if the facts show that the communication was not intended to be kept in confidence, the communication is not privileged. And the fact that the communication was made under circumstances where others could easily overhear is a strong indication that the communication was not intended to be confidential and is, therefore, unprivileged.

§ 918. Effect of error in overruling claim of privilege. A party may predicate error on a ruling disallowing a claim of privilege only if he is the holder of the privilege, except that a party may predicate error on a ruling disallowing a claim of privilege by his spouse under Section 970 or 971.

§ 919. Admissibility where disclosure erroneously compelled; claim of privilege; coercion. (a) Evidence of a statement or other disclosure of privileged information is inadmissible against a holder of the privilege if:

(1) A person authorized to claim the privilege claimed it but nevertheless disclosure erroneously was required to be made; or

(2) The presiding officer did not exclude the privileged information as required by Section 916.

(b) If a person authorized to claim the privilege claimed it, whether in the same or a prior proceeding, but nevertheless disclosure erroneously was required by the presiding officer to be made, neither the failure to refuse to disclose nor the failure to seek review of the order of the presiding officer requiring disclosure indicates consent to the disclosure or constitutes a waiver and, under these circumstances, the disclosure is one made under coercion.

§ 920. No implied repeal. Nothing in this division shall be construed to repeal by implication any other statute relating to privileges.

Chapter 4
PARTICULAR PRIVILEGES

Article 1. Privilege of Defendant in Criminal Case

§ 930. Privilege not to be called as a witness and not to testify. To the extent that such privilege exists under the Constitution of the United States or the State of California, a defendant in a criminal case has a privilege not to be called as a witness and not to testify.

Article 2. Privilege Against Self-Incrimination

§ 940. Privilege against self-incrimination. To the extent that such privilege exists under the Constitution of the United States or the State of California, a person has a privilege to refuse to disclose any matter that may tend to incriminate him.

Article 3. Lawyer–Client Privilege

§ 950. "Lawyer". As used in this article, "lawyer" means a person authorized, or reasonably believed by the client to be authorized, to practice law in any state or nation.

Comment—Law Revision Commission

There is no requirement that the lawyer be licensed to practice in a jurisdiction that recognizes the lawyer-client privilege. Legal transactions frequently cross state and national boundaries and require consultation with attorneys from many different jurisdictions. When a California resident travels outside the State and has occasion to consult a lawyer during such travel, or when a lawyer from another state or nation participates in a transaction involving a California client, the client should be entitled to assume that his communications will be given as much protection as they would be if he consulted a California lawyer in California. A client should not be forced to inquire about the jurisdictions where the lawyer is authorized to practice and whether such jurisdictions recognize the lawyer-client privilege before he may safely communicate with the lawyer.

§ 951. "Client". As used in this article, "client" means a person who, directly or through an authorized representative, consults a lawyer for the purpose of retaining the lawyer or securing legal service or advice from him in his professional capacity, and includes an incompetent (a) who himself so consults the lawyer or (b) whose guardian or conservator so consults the lawyer in behalf of the incompetent.

Comment—Law Revision Commission

Under Section 951, public entities have a privilege insofar as communications made in the course of the lawyer-client relationship are concerned. Likewise, such unincorporated organizations as labor unions, social clubs, and fraternal societies have a lawyer-client privilege when the organization (rather than its individual members) is the client. See Evidence Code § 175 (defining "person") and § 200 (defining "public entity").

§ 952. Confidential communication between client and lawyer. As used in this article, "confidential communication between client and lawyer" means information transmitted between a client and his or her lawyer in the course of that relationship and in confidence by a means which, so far as the client is aware, discloses the information to no third persons other than those who are present to further the interest of the client in the consultation or those to whom disclosure is reasonably necessary for the transmission of the information or the accomplishment of the purpose for which the lawyer is consulted, and includes a legal opinion formed and the advice given by the lawyer in the course of that relationship.

Comment—Law Revision Commission

Confidential communications also include those made to third parties—such as the lawyer's secretary, a physician, or similar expert—for the purpose of transmitting such information to the lawyer because they are "reasonably necessary for the transmission of the information."

A lawyer at times may desire to have a client reveal information to an expert consultant in order that the lawyer may adequately advise his client. The inclusion of the words "or the accomplishment of the purpose for which the lawyer is consulted" assures that these communications, too, are within the scope of the privilege.

The words "other than those who are present to further the interest of the client in the consultation" indicate that a communication to a lawyer is nonetheless confidential even though it is made in the presence of another person—such as a spouse, parent, business associate, or joint client—who is present to further the interest of the client in the consultation. These words refer, too, to another person and his attorney who may meet with the client and his attorney in regard to a matter of joint concern.

The express inclusion of "a legal opinion" in the last clause will preclude a possible construction of this section that would leave the attorney's uncommunicated legal opinion—which includes his impressions and conclusions—unprotected by the privilege. Such a construction would virtually destroy the privilege.

§ 953. "Holder of the privilege". As used in this article, "holder of the privilege" means:

(a) The client, if the client has no guardian or conservator.

(b) A guardian or conservator of the client, if the client has a guardian or conservator.

(c) The personal representative of the client if the client is dead, including a personal representative appointed pursuant to Section 12252 of the Probate Code.

(d) A successor, assign, trustee in dissolution, or any similar representative of a firm, association, organization, partnership, business trust, corporation, or public entity that is no longer in existence.

§ 954. Lawyer-client privilege. Subject to Section 912 and except as otherwise provided in this article, the client, whether or not a party, has a privilege to refuse to disclose, and to prevent another from disclosing, a confidential communication between client and lawyer if the privilege is claimed by:

(a) The holder of the privilege;

(b) A person who is authorized to claim the privilege by the holder of the privilege; or

(c) The person who was the lawyer at the time of the confidential communication, but the person may not claim the privilege if there is no holder of the privilege in existence or if he is otherwise instructed by a person authorized to permit disclosure.

§ 954　　　　CALIFORNIA EVIDENCE CODE

The relationship of attorney and client shall exist between a law corporation as defined in Article 10 (commencing with Section 6160) of Chapter 4 of Division 3 of the Business and Professions Code and the persons to whom it renders professional services, as well as between such persons and members of the State Bar employed by such corporation to render services to such persons. The word "persons" as used in this subdivision includes partnerships, corporations, limited liability companies, associations and other groups and entities.

Comment—Law Revision Commission

Eavesdroppers. Under Section 954, the lawyer-client privilege can be asserted to prevent *anyone* from testifying to a confidential communication. Thus, clients are protected against the risk of disclosure by eavesdroppers and other wrongful interceptors of confidential communications between lawyer and client. The use of the privilege to prevent testimony by eavesdroppers and those to whom the communication was wrongfully disclosed does not, however, affect the rule that the making of the communication under circumstances where others could easily overhear it is evidence that the client did not intend the communication to be confidential.

Termination of privilege. The privilege may be claimed by a person listed in Section 954, or the privileged information excluded by the presiding officer under Section 916, only if there is a holder of the privilege in existence. Hence, the privilege ceases to exist when the client's estate is finally distributed and his personal representative is discharged. This is apparently a change in California law. Under the existing law, it seems likely that the privilege continues to exist indefinitely after the client's death and that no one has authority to waive the privilege. See discussion of the analogous situation in connection with the physician-patient privilege in Tentative Recommendation and a Study Relating to the Uniform Rules of Evidence (Article V. Privileges), 6 Cal.Law Revision Comm'n, Rep., Rec. & Studies 201, 408–410 (1964). Although there is good reason for maintaining the privilege while the estate is being administered—particularly if the estate is involved in litigation—there is little reason to preserve secrecy at the expense of excluding relevant evidence after the estate is wound up and the representative is discharged.

§ 955. When lawyer required to claim privilege. The lawyer who received or made a communication subject to the privilege under this article shall claim the privilege whenever he is present when the communication is sought to be disclosed and is authorized to claim the privilege under subdivision (c) of Section 954.

§ 956. Exception: Crime or fraud. There is no privilege under this article if the services of the lawyer were sought or obtained to enable or aid anyone to commit or plan to commit a crime or a fraud.

§ 956.5. Exception: Criminal act likely to result in death or substantial bodily harm. There is no privilege under this article if the lawyer reasonably believes that disclosure of any confidential communication relating to representation of a client is necessary to prevent a criminal act that the lawyer reasonably believes is likely to result in the death of, or substantial bodily harm to, an individual.

Editorial Note

The Act that amended section 956.5 of the Evidence Code to its present form also amended section 6068 of the California Business and Professions Code to read as follows:

§ 6068. It is the duty of an attorney to do all of the following:

* * *

(e)(1) To maintain inviolate the confidence, and at every peril to himself or herself to preserve the secrets, of his or her client.

(2) Notwithstanding paragraph (1), an attorney may, but is not required to, reveal confidential information relating to the representation of a client to the extent that the attorney reasonably believes the disclosure is necessary to prevent a criminal act that the attorney reasonably believes is likely to result in death of, or substantial bodily harm to, an individual.

Additionally, Sections 3 and 4 of the same Act provide as follows:

. . . Sec. 3. (a) It is the intent of the Legislature that the President of the State Bar shall, upon consultation with the Supreme Court, appoint an advisory task force to study and make recommendations for a rule of professional conduct regarding professional responsibility issues related to the implementation of this act.

(b) The task force should consider the following issues:

(1) Whether an attorney must inform a client or a prospective client about the attorney's discretion to reveal the client's or prospective client's confidential information to the extent that the attorney reasonably believes that the disclosure is necessary to prevent a criminal act that the attorney reasonably believes is likely to result in the death of, or substantial bodily harm to, an individual.

(2) Whether an attorney must attempt to dissuade the client from committing the perceived criminal conduct prior to revealing the client's confidential information, and how those conflicts might be avoided or minimized.

(3) Whether conflict-of-interest issues between the attorney and client arise once the attorney elects to disclose the client's confidential information, and how those conflicts might be avoided or minimized.

(4) Other similar issues that are directly related to the disclosure of confidential information permitted by this act.

(c) Members of the task force shall include the following:

(1) Civil and criminal law practitioners, including criminal defense practitioners.

(2) Representatives from the judicial, executive, and legislative branches.

(3) Representatives from the State Bar Commission for the Revision of the Rules of Professional Conduct and from the State Bar Committee on Professional Responsibility and Conduct.

(4) Public members.

Sec. 4. The provisions of this act shall become operative on July 1, 2004.

§ 957. Exception: Parties claiming through deceased client. There is no privilege under this article as to a communication relevant to an issue between parties all of whom claim through a deceased client, regardless of whether the claims are by testate or intestate succession, nonprobate transfer, or inter vivos transaction.

Comment—Law Revision Commission

The traditional exception for litigation between claimants by testate or intestate succession is based on the theory that claimants in privity with the estate claim *through* the client not adversely, and the deceased client presumably would want his communications disclosed in litigation between such claimants so that his desires in regard to the disposition of his estate might be correctly ascertained and carried out. This rationale is equally applicable where one or more of the parties is claiming by inter vivos transaction as, for example, in an action between a party who claims under a deed (executed by a client in full possession of his faculties) and a party who claims under a will executed while the client's mental stability was dubious. See the discussion in Tentative Recommendation and a Study Relating to the Uniform Rules of Evidence (Article V. Privileges), 6 Cal.Law Revision Comm'n, Rep., Rec. & Studies 201, 392–396 (1964).

§ 958. Exception: Breach of duty arising out of lawyer-client relationship. There is no privilege under this article as to a communication relevant to an issue of breach, by the lawyer or by the client, of a duty arising out of the lawyer-client relationship.

Comment—Law Revision Commission

It would be unjust to permit a client either to accuse his attorney of a breach of duty and to invoke the privilege to prevent the attorney from bringing forth evidence in defense of the charge or to refuse to pay his attorney's fee and invoke the privilege to defeat the attorney's claim. Thus, for example, if the defendant in a criminal action claims that his lawyer did not provide him with an adequate defense, communications between the lawyer and client relevant to that issue are not privileged.

§ 959. Exception: Lawyer as attesting witness. There is no privilege under this article as to a communication relevant to an issue concerning the intention or competence of a client executing an attested document of which the lawyer is an attesting witness, or concerning the execution or attestation of such a document.

§ 960. Exception: Intention of deceased client concerning writing affecting property interest. There is no privilege under this article as to a communication relevant to an issue concerning the intention of a client, now deceased, with respect to a deed of conveyance, will, or other writing, executed by the client, purporting to affect an interest in property.

§ 961. **Exception: Validity of writing affecting property interest.** There is no privilege under this article as to a communication relevant to an issue concerning the validity of a deed of conveyance, will, or other writing, executed by a client, now deceased, purporting to affect an interest in property.

§ 962. **Exception: Joint clients.** Where two or more clients have retained or consulted a lawyer upon a matter of common interest, none of them, nor the successor in interest of any of them, may claim a privilege under this article as to a communication made in the course of that relationship when such communication is offered in a civil proceeding between one of such clients (or his successor in interest) and another of such clients (or his successor in interest).

Article 4. Privilege Not to Testify Against Spouse

§ 970. **Privilege not to testify against spouse.** Except as otherwise provided by statute, a married person has a privilege not to testify against his spouse in any proceeding.

Comment—Law Revision Commission

Under this article, a married person has two privileges: (1) a privilege not to testify against his spouse in any proceeding (Section 970) and (2) a privilege not to be called as a witness in any proceeding to which his spouse is a party (Section 971).

The privileges under this article are not as broad as the privilege provided by existing law. Under existing law, a married person has a privilege to prevent his spouse from testifying against him, but only the witness spouse has a privilege under this article. Under the existing law, a married person may refuse to testify *for* the other spouse, but no such privilege exists under this article.

The rationale of the privilege provided by Section 970 not to testify against one's spouse is that such testimony would seriously disturb or disrupt the marital relationship. Society stands to lose more from such disruption than it stands to gain from the testimony which would be available if the privilege did not exist. The privilege is based in part on a previous recommendation and study of the California Law Revision Commission. See 1 Cal.Law Revision Comm'n, Rep., Rec. & Studies, Recommendation and Study Relating to the Marital "For and Against" Testimonial Privilege at F–1 (1957).

§ 971. **Privilege not to be called as a witness against spouse.** Except as otherwise provided by statute, a married person whose spouse is a party to a proceeding has a privilege not to be called as a witness by an adverse party to that proceeding without the prior express consent of the spouse having the privilege under this section unless the party calling the spouse does so in good faith without knowledge of the marital relationship.

Comment—Law Revision Commission

The privilege of a married person not to be called as a witness against his spouse is somewhat similar to the privilege given the defendant in a criminal case not to be called as a witness (Section 930). This privilege is necessary to avoid the prejudicial effect, for example, of the prosecution's calling the defendant's wife as a witness, thus forcing her to object before the jury. The privilege not to be called as a witness does not apply, however, in a proceeding where the other spouse is not a party. Thus, a married person may be called as a witness in a grand jury proceeding because his spouse is not a party to that proceeding, but the witness in the grand jury proceeding may claim the privilege under Section 970 to refuse to answer a question that would compel him to testify *against* his spouse.

§ 972. When privilege not applicable. A married person does not have a privilege under this article in:

(a) A proceeding brought by or on behalf of one spouse against the other spouse.

(b) A proceeding to commit or otherwise place his or her spouse or his or her spouse's property, or both, under the control of another because of the spouse's alleged mental or physical condition.

(c) A proceeding brought by or on behalf of a spouse to establish his or her competence.

(d) A proceeding under the Juvenile Court Law, Chapter 2 (commencing with Section 200) of Part 1 of Division 2 of the Welfare and Institutions Code.

(e) A criminal proceeding in which one spouse is charged with:

(1) A crime against the person or property of the other spouse or of a child, parent, relative, or cohabitant of either, whether committed before or during marriage.

(2) A crime against the person or property of a third person committed in the course of committing a crime against the person or property of the other spouse, whether committed before or during marriage.

(3) Bigamy.

(4) A crime defined by Section 270 or 270a of the Penal Code.

(f) A proceeding resulting from a criminal act which occurred prior to legal marriage of the spouses to each other regarding knowledge acquired prior to that marriage if prior to the legal marriage the witness spouse was aware that his or her spouse had been arrested for or had been formally charged with the crime or crimes about which the spouse is called to testify.

(g) A proceeding brought against the spouse by a former spouse so long as the property and debts of the marriage have not been adjudicated, or in order to establish, modify, or enforce a child, family or spousal support obligation arising from the marriage to the former spouse; in a proceeding brought against a spouse by the other parent in order to establish, modify, or enforce a child support obligation for a child of a nonmarital relationship of the spouse; or in a proceeding brought against a spouse by the guardian of a child of that spouse in order to establish, modify, or enforce a child support obligation of the spouse. The married person does not have a privilege under this subdivision to refuse to provide information relating to the issues of income, expenses, assets, debts, and employment of either spouse, but may assert the privilege as otherwise provided in this article if other information is requested by the former spouse, guardian, or other parent of the child.

Any person demanding the otherwise privileged information made available by this subdivision, who also has an obligation to support the child for whom an order to establish, modify, or enforce child support is sought, waives his or her marital privilege to the same extent as the spouse as provided in this subdivision.

§ 973. Waiver of privilege. (a) Unless erroneously compelled to do so, a married person who testifies in a proceeding to which his spouse is a party, or who testifies against his spouse in any proceeding, does not have a privilege under this article in the proceeding in which such testimony is given.

(b) There is no privilege under this article in a civil proceeding brought or defended by a married person for the immediate benefit of his spouse or of himself and his spouse.

Comment—Assembly Committee on Judiciary

Subdivision (a). Under subdivision (a), a married person who testifies in a proceeding to which his spouse is *a party* waives both privileges provided for in this article. Thus, for example, a married person cannot call his spouse as a witness to give favorable testimony and have that spouse invoke the privilege provided in Section 970 to keep from testifying on cross-examination to unfavorable matters; nor can a married person testify for an adverse party as to particular matters and then invoke the privilege not to testify against his spouse as to other matters.

In any proceeding where a married person's spouse is *not a party*, the privilege not to be called as a witness is not available, and a married person may testify like any other witness without waiving the privilege provided under Section 970 so long as he does not *testify against* his spouse. However, under subdivision (a), the privilege not to testify against his spouse in that proceeding is waived as to all matters if he *testifies against* his spouse as to any matter.

The word "proceeding" is defined in Section 901 to include any action, civil or criminal. Hence, the privilege is waived for all purposes in an action if the spouse entitled to claim the privilege testifies at any time during the action. For example, if a civil action involves issues being separately tried, a wife whose husband is a party to the litigation may not testify for her husband at one trial and invoke the privilege in order to avoid testifying against him at a separate trial of a different issue. Nor may a wife testify against her husband at a preliminary hearing of a criminal action and refuse to testify against him at the trial.

Subdivision (b). This subdivision precludes married persons from taking unfair advantage of their marital status to escape their duty to give testimony under Section 776, which supersedes Code of Civil Procedure Section 2055. It recognizes a doctrine of waiver that has been developed in the California cases. Thus, for example, when suit is brought to set aside a conveyance from husband to wife allegedly in fraud of the husband's creditors, both spouses being named as defendants, it has been held that setting up the conveyance in the answer as a defense waives the privilege.

Article 5. Privilege for Confidential Marital Communications

§ 980. Privilege for confidential marital communications. Subject to Section 912 and except as otherwise provided in this article, a spouse (or his guardian or conservator when he has a guardian or conservator), whether or not a party, has a privilege during the marital relationship and afterwards to refuse to disclose, and to prevent another from disclosing, a communication if he claims the privilege and the communication was made in confidence between him and the other spouse while they were husband and wife.

Comment—Law Revision Commission

Who can claim the privilege. Under Section 980, both spouses are the holders of the privilege and either spouse may claim it.

A guardian of an incompetent spouse may claim the privilege on behalf of that spouse. However, when a spouse is dead, no one can claim the privilege for him; the privilege, if it is to be claimed at all, can be claimed only by or on behalf of the surviving spouse.

Termination of marriage. The privilege may be claimed as to confidential communications made during a marriage even though the marriage has been terminated at the time the privilege is claimed. Free and open communication between spouses would be unduly inhibited if one of the spouses could be compelled to testify as to the nature of such communications after the termination of the marriage.

Eavesdroppers. The privilege may be asserted to prevent testimony by anyone, including eavesdroppers. Section 980 also changes the existing law which permits a third party, to whom one of the spouses had revealed a confidential communication, to testify concerning it. Under Section 912, such conduct would constitute a waiver of the privilege only as to the spouse who makes the disclosure.

§ 981. Exception: Crime or fraud. There is no privilege under this article if the communication was made, in whole or in part, to enable or aid anyone to commit or plan to commit a crime or a fraud.

Comment—Law Revision Commission

It is important to note that the exception provided by Section 981 is quite limited. It does not permit disclosure of communications that merely reveal a plan to commit a crime or fraud; it permits disclosure only of communications made to *enable* or *aid* anyone to commit or plan to commit a crime or fraud.

Thus, unless the communication is for the purpose of obtaining assistance in the commission of the crime or fraud or in furtherance thereof, it is not made admissible by the exception provided in this section.

§ 982. Exception: Commitment or similar proceeding. There is no privilege under this article in a proceeding to commit either spouse or otherwise place him or his property, or both, under the control of another because of his alleged mental or physical condition.

Comment—Law Revision Commission

Commitment and competency proceedings are undertaken for the benefit of the subject person. Frequently, much or all of the evidence bearing on a spouse's competency or lack of competency will consist of communications to the other spouse. It would be undesirable to permit either spouse to invoke a privilege to prevent the presentation of this vital information inasmuch as these proceedings are of such vital importance both to society and to the spouse who is the subject of the proceedings.

§ 983. Exception: Proceeding to establish competence. There is no privilege under this article in a proceeding brought by or on behalf of either spouse to establish his competence.

§ 984. Exception: Proceeding between spouses. There is no privilege under this article in:

(a) A proceeding brought by or on behalf of one spouse against the other spouse.

(b) A proceeding between a surviving spouse and a person who claims through the deceased spouse, regardless of whether such claim is by testate or intestate succession or by inter vivos transaction.

§ 985. Exception: Certain criminal proceedings. There is no privilege under this article in a criminal proceeding in which one spouse is charged with:

(a) A crime committed at any time against the person or property of the other spouse or of a child of either.

(b) A crime committed at any time against the person or property of a third person committed in the course of committing a crime against the person or property of the other spouse.

(c) Bigamy.

(d) A crime defined by Section 270 or 270a of the Penal Code.

§ 986. Exception: Juvenile court proceeding. There is no privilege under this article in a proceeding under the Juvenile Court Law, Chapter 2 (commencing with Section 200) of Part 1 of Division 2 of the Welfare and Institutions Code.

§ 987. Exception: Communication offered by spouse who is criminal defendant. There is no privilege under this article in a criminal proceeding in which the communication is offered in evidence by a defendant who is one of the spouses between whom the communication was made.

Comment—Law Revision Commission

When a married person is the defendant in a criminal proceeding and seeks to introduce evidence which is material to his defense, his spouse (or his former spouse) should not be privileged to withhold the information.

Article 6. Physician–Patient Privilege

§ 990. "Physician". As used in this article, "physician" means a person authorized, or reasonably believed by the patient to be authorized, to practice medicine in any state or nation.

§ 991. "Patient". As used in this article, "patient" means a person who consults a physician or submits to an examination by a physician for the purpose of securing a diagnosis or preventive, palliative, or curative treatment of his physical or mental or emotional condition.

Comment—Senate Committee on Judiciary

"Patient" means a person who consults a physician for the purpose of diagnosis or treatment.

There seems to be little reason to perpetuate the distinction made between consultations for the purpose of diagnosis and consultations for the purpose of treatment. Persons do not ordinarily consult physicians from idle curiosity. They may be sent by their attorney to obtain a diagnosis in contemplation of some legal proceeding—in which case the attorney-client privilege will afford protection. They may submit to an examination for insurance purposes—in which case the insurance contract will contain appropriate waiver provisions. They may seek diagnosis from one physician to check the diagnosis made by another. They may seek diagnosis from one physician in contemplation of seeking treatment from another. Communications made under such circumstances are as deserving of protection as are communications made to a treating physician.

§ 992. "Confidential communication between patient and physician". As used in this article, "confidential communication between patient and physician" means information, including information obtained by an examination of the patient, transmitted between a patient and his physician in the course of that relationship and in confidence by a means which, so far as the patient is aware, discloses the information to no third persons other than those who are present to further the interest of the patient in the consultation or those to whom disclosure is reasonably necessary for the transmission of the information or the accomplishment of the purpose for which the physician is consulted, and includes a diagnosis made and the advice given by the physician in the course of that relationship.

§ 993. "Holder of the privilege". As used in this article, "holder of the privilege" means:

(a) The patient when he has no guardian or conservator.

(b) A guardian or conservator of the patient when the patient has a guardian or conservator.

(c) The personal representative of the patient if the patient is dead.

Comment—Law Revision Commission

A guardian of the patient is the holder of the privilege if the patient has a guardian. If the patient has separate guardians of his estate and of his person, either guardian may claim the privilege. The provision making the personal representative of the patient the holder of the privilege when the patient is dead may change California law. The existing law may be that the privilege survives the death of the patient in some cases and that no one can waive it on behalf of the patient. See the discussion in Tentative Recommendation and a Study Relating to the Uniform Rules of Evidence (Article V. Privileges), 6 Cal.Law Revision Comm'n, Rep., Rec. & Studies 201, 408–410 (1964). Sections 993 and 994 enable the personal representative to protect the interest of the patient's estate in the confidentiality of these statements and to waive the privilege when the estate would benefit by waiver. When the patient's estate has no interest in preserving confidentiality, or when the estate has been distributed and the representative discharged, the importance of providing complete access to information relevant to a particular proceeding should prevail over whatever remaining interest the decedent may have had in secrecy.

§ 994. Physician-patient privilege. Subject to Section 912 and except as otherwise provided in this article, the patient, whether or not a party, has a privilege to refuse to disclose, and to prevent another from disclosing, a confidential communication between patient and physician if the privilege is claimed by:

(a) The holder of the privilege;

(b) A person who is authorized to claim the privilege by the holder of the privilege; or

(c) The person who was the physician at the time of the confidential communication, but such person may not claim the privilege if there is no holder of the privilege in existence or if he or she is otherwise instructed by a person authorized to permit disclosure.

The relationship of a physician and patient shall exist between a medical or podiatry corporation as defined in the Medical Practice Act and the patient to whom it renders professional services, as well as between such patients and licensed physicians and surgeons employed by such corporation to render services to such patients. The word "persons" as used in this subdivision includes partnerships, corporations, limited liability companies, associations, and other groups and entities.

§ 995. When physician required to claim privilege. The physician who received or made a communication subject to the privilege under this article shall claim the privilege whenever he is present when the communication is sought to be disclosed and is authorized to claim the privilege under subdivision (c) of Section 994.

§ 996. Exception: Patient-litigant exception. There is no privilege under this article as to a communication relevant to an issue concerning the condition of the patient if such issue has been tendered by:

(a) The patient;

(b) Any party claiming through or under the patient;

(c) Any party claiming as a beneficiary of the patient through a contract to which the patient is or was a party; or

(d) The plaintiff in an action brought under Section 376 or 377 of the Code of Civil Procedure for damages for the injury or death of the patient.

§ 997. Exception: Crime or tort. There is no privilege under this article if the services of the physician were sought or obtained to enable or aid anyone to commit or plan to commit a crime or a tort or to escape detection or apprehension after the commission of a crime or a tort.

Comment—Law Revision Commission

This section is considerably broader in scope than Section 956 which provides that the lawyer-client privilege does not apply when the communication was made to enable anyone to commit or plan to commit a crime or a *fraud*. Section 997 creates an exception to the physician-patient privilege where the services of the physician were sought or obtained to enable or aid anyone to commit or plan to commit a crime or a *tort,* or to escape detection or apprehension after commission of a crime or a *tort*. People seldom, if ever, consult their physicians in regard to matters which might subsequently be determined to be a tort, and there is no desirable end to be served by encouraging such communications. On the other hand, people often consult lawyers about matters which may later turn out to be torts and it is desirable to encourage discussion of such matters with lawyers.

§ 998. Exception: Criminal proceeding. There is no privilege under this article in a criminal proceeding.

§ 999. Exception: Communication relating to patient condition in proceeding to recover damages; good cause. There is no privilege under this article as to a communication relevant to an issue concerning the condition of the patient in a proceeding to recover damages on account of the conduct of the patient if good cause for disclosure of the communication is shown.

Assembly Committee on Judiciary Comment

Section 999 permits disclosure not only in a case where the patient is a party to the action but also in a case where a party's liability is based on the conduct of the patient. An example of the latter situation is a personal injury action brought against an employer based on the negligent conduct of his employee who was killed in the accident. On the other hand, the section does not affect the privilege of nonparty patients in malpractice actions.

The requirement that good cause be shown for the disclosure permits the court to protect the defendant against a "fishing expedition" into his medical records. Compare Evid.Code § 996 (patient-litigant exception). It should be noted that the exception provided by Section 999, like the other exceptions in this article, does not apply to the psychotherapist-patient privilege. That privilege is a separate and distinct privilege, and the exceptions to that privilege are much more narrowly drawn. See Evid.Code §§ 1010–1028.

Formerly, Section 999 provided an exception only in a proceeding to recover damages arising out of the criminal conduct of the patient. This "criminal conduct" exception has been eliminated as unnecessary in view of the "good cause" exception now provided by Section 999. Moreover, the "criminal conduct" exception was burdensome, difficult to administer, and ill designed to achieve the purpose of making needed evidence available.

§ 1000. Exception: Parties claiming through deceased patient. There is no privilege under this article as to a communication relevant to an issue between parties all of whom claim through a deceased patient, regardless of whether the claims are by testate or intestate succession or by inter vivos transaction.

§ 1001. Exception: Breach of duty arising out of physician-patient relationship. There is no privilege under this article as to a communication relevant to an issue of breach, by the physician or by the patient, of a duty arising out of the physician-patient relationship.

§ 1002. Exception: Intention of deceased patient concerning writing affecting property interest. There is no privilege under this article as to a communication relevant to an issue concerning the intention of a patient, now deceased, with respect to a deed of conveyance, will, or other writing, executed by the patient, purporting to affect an interest in property.

§ 1003. Exception: Validity of writing affecting property interest. There is no privilege under this article as to a communication relevant to an issue concerning the validity of a deed of conveyance, will, or other writing, executed by a patient, now deceased, purporting to affect an interest in property.

§ 1004. Exception: Commitment or similar proceeding. There is no privilege under this article in a proceeding to commit the patient or otherwise place him or his property, or both, under the control of another because of his alleged mental or physical condition.

§ 1005. Exception: Proceeding to establish competence. There is no privilege under this article in a proceeding brought by or on behalf of the patient to establish his competence.

§ 1006. Exception: Required report. There is no privilege under this article as to information that the physician or the patient is required to report to a public employee, or as to information required to be recorded in a public office, if such report or record is open to public inspection.

§ 1007. Exception: Proceeding to terminate rights, license or privilege. There is no privilege under this article in a proceeding brought by a public entity to determine whether a right, authority, license, or privilege (including the right or privilege to be employed by the public entity or to hold a public office) should be revoked, suspended, terminated, limited, or conditioned.

Article 7. Psychotherapist–Patient Privilege

§ 1010. "Psychotherapist". As used in this article, "psychotherapist" means a person who is, or is reasonably believed by the patient to be:

(a) A person authorized to practice medicine in any state or nation who devotes, or is reasonably believed by the patient to devote, a substantial portion of his or her time to the practice of psychiatry.

(b) A person licensed as a psychologist under Chapter 6.6 (commencing with Section 2900) of Division 2 of the Business and Professions Code.

(c) A person licensed as a clinical social worker under Article 4 (commencing with Section 4996) of Chapter 14 of Division 2 of the Business and Professions Code, when he or she is engaged in applied psychotherapy of a nonmedical nature.

(d) A person who is serving as a school psychologist and holds a credential authorizing that service issued by the state.

(e) A person licensed as a marriage and family therapist under Chapter 13 (commencing with Section 4980) of Division 2 of the Business and Professions Code.

(f) A person registered as a psychological assistant who is under the supervision of a licensed psychologist or board certified psychiatrist as required by Section 2913 of the Business and Professions Code, or a person registered as a marriage and family therapist intern who is under the supervision of a licensed marriage and family therapist, a licensed clinical social worker, a licensed psychologist, or a licensed physician certified in psychiatry, as specified in Section 4980.44 of the Business and Professions Code.

(g) A person registered as an associate clinical social worker who is under the supervision of a licensed clinical social worker, a licensed psychologist, or a board certified psychiatrist as required by Section 4996.20 or 4996.21 of the Business and Professions Code.

(h) A person exempt from the Psychology Licensing Law pursuant to subdivision (d) of Section 2909 of the Business and Professions Code who is under the supervision of a licensed psychologist or board certified psychiatrist.

(i) A psychological intern as defined in Section 2911 of the Business and Professions Code who is under the supervision of a licensed psychologist or board certified psychiatrist.

(j) A trainee, as defined in subdivision (c) of Section 4980.03 of the Business and Professions Code, who is fulfilling his or her supervised practicum required by subparagraph (B) of paragraph (1) of subdivision (d) of Section 4980.36 of, or subdivision (c) of Section 4980.37 of, the Business and Professions Code and is supervised by a licensed psychologist, board certified psychiatrist, a licensed clinical social worker, or a licensed marriage and family therapist.

(k) A person licensed as a registered nurse pursuant to Chapter 6 (commencing with Section 2700) of Division 2 of the Business and Professions Code, who possesses a master's degree in psychiatric-mental health nursing and is listed as a psychiatric-mental health nurse by the Board of Registered Nursing.

(*l*) An advanced practice registered nurse who is certified as a clinical nurse specialist pursuant to Article 9 (commencing with Section 2838) of Chapter 6 of Division 2 of the Business and Professions Code and who participates in expert clinical practice in the specialty of psychiatric-mental health nursing.

(m) A person rendering mental health treatment or counseling services as authorized pursuant to Section 6924 of the Family Code.

§ 1010.5. Privileged communication between patient and educational psychologist. A communication between a patient and an educational psychologist, licensed under Article 5 (commencing with Section 4986) of Chapter 13 of Division 2 of the Business and Professions Code, shall be privileged to the same extent, and subject to the same limitations, as a communication between a patient and a psychotherapist described in subdivisions (c), (d), and (e) of Section 1010.

§ 1011. "Patient". As used in this article, "patient" means a person who consults a psychotherapist or submits to an examination by a psychotherapist for the purpose of securing a diagnosis or preventive, palliative, or curative treatment of his mental or emotional condition or who submits to an examination of his mental or emotional condition for the purpose of scientific research on mental or emotional problems.

§ 1012. "Confidential communication between patient and psychotherapist". As used in this article, "confidential communication between patient and psychotherapist" means information, including information obtained by an examination of the patient, transmitted between a patient and his psychotherapist in the course of that relationship and in confidence by a means which, so far as the patient is aware, discloses the information to no third persons other than those who are present to further the interest of the patient in the consultation, or those to whom disclosure is reasonably necessary for the transmission of the information or the accomplishment of the purpose for which the psychotherapist is consulted, and includes a diagnosis made and the advice given by the psychotherapist in the course of that relationship.

§ 1013. "Holder of the privilege". As used in this article, "holder of the privilege" means:

(a) The patient when he has no guardian or conservator.

(b) A guardian or conservator of the patient when the patient has a guardian or conservator.

(c) The personal representative of the patient if the patient is dead.

§ 1014. Psychotherapist-patient privilege; application to individuals and entities. Subject to Section 912 and except as otherwise provided in this article, the patient, whether or not a party, has a privilege to refuse to disclose, and to prevent another from disclosing, a confidential communication between patient and psychotherapist if the privilege is claimed by:

(a) The holder of the privilege.

(b) A person who is authorized to claim the privilege by the holder of the privilege.

(c) The person who was the psychotherapist at the time of the confidential communication, but the person may not claim the privilege if there is no holder of the privilege in existence or if he or she is otherwise instructed by a person authorized to permit disclosure.

The relationship of a psychotherapist and patient shall exist between a psychological corporation as defined in Article 9 (commencing with Section 2995) of Chapter 6.6 of Division 2 of the Business and Professions Code, a marriage and family therapy corporation as defined in Article 6 (commencing with Section 4987.5) of Chapter 13 of Division 2 of the Business and Professions Code, or a licensed clinical social workers corporation as defined in Article 5 (commencing with Section

4998) of Chapter 14 of Division 2 of the Business and Professions Code, and the patient to whom it renders professional services, as well as between those patients and psychotherapists employed by those corporations to render services to those patients. The word "persons" as used in this subdivision includes partnerships, corporations, limited liability companies, associations and other groups and entities.

Comment—Senate Committee on Judiciary

A broad privilege should apply to both psychiatrists and certified psychologists. Psychoanalysis and psychotherapy are dependent upon the fullest revelation of the most intimate and embarrassing details of the patient's life. Research on mental or emotional problems requires similar disclosure. Unless a patient or research subject is assured that such information can and will be held in utmost confidence, he will be reluctant to make the full disclosure upon which diagnosis and treatment or complete and accurate research depends.

The Law Revision Commission has received several reliable reports that persons in need of treatment sometimes refuse such treatment from psychiatrists because the confidentiality of their communications cannot be assured under existing law. Many of these persons are seriously disturbed and constitute threats to other persons in the community. Accordingly, this article establishes a new privilege that grants to patients of psychiatrists a privilege much broader in scope than the ordinary physician-patient privilege.

Generally, the privilege provided by this article follows the physician-patient privilege, and the Comments to Sections 990 through 1007 are pertinent. The following differences, however, should be noted:

(1) The psychotherapist-patient privilege applies in all proceedings. The physician-patient privilege does not apply in criminal proceedings. This difference in the scope of the two privileges is based on the fact that the Law Revision Commission has been advised that proper psychotherapy often is denied a patient solely because he will not talk freely to a psychotherapist for fear that the latter may be compelled in a criminal proceeding to reveal what he has been told. The Commission has also been advised that research in this field will be unduly hampered unless the privilege is available in criminal proceedings.

Although the psychotherapist-patient privilege applies in a criminal proceeding, the privilege is not available to a defendant who puts his mental or emotional condition in issue, as, for example, by a plea of insanity or a claim of diminished responsibility. See Evidence Code §§ 1016 and 1023. In such a proceeding, the trier of fact should have available to it all information that can be obtained in regard to the defendant's mental or emotional condition. That evidence can often be furnished by the psychotherapist who examined or treated the patient-defendant.

(2) There is an exception in the physician-patient privilege for commitment or guardianship proceedings for the patient. Evidence Code § 1004. Section 1024 provides a considerably narrower exception in the psychotherapist-patient privilege.

(3) The physician-patient privilege does not apply in civil actions for damages arising out of the patient's criminal conduct. Evidence Code § 999. Nor does it apply in certain administrative proceedings. Evidence Code § 1007. No

§ 1014

similar exceptions are provided in the psychotherapist-patient privilege. These exceptions appear in the physician-patient privilege because that privilege does not apply in criminal proceedings. See Evidence Code § 998. Therefore, an exception is also created for comparable civil and administrative cases. The psychotherapist-patient privilege, however, does apply in criminal cases; hence, there is no similar exception in administrative proceedings or civil actions involving the patient's criminal conduct.

§ 1015. When psychotherapist required to claim privilege. The psychotherapist who received or made a communication subject to the privilege under this article shall claim the privilege whenever he is present when the communication is sought to be disclosed and is authorized to claim the privilege under subdivision (c) of Section 1014.

§ 1016. Exception: Patient-litigant exception. There is no privilege under this article as to a communication relevant to an issue concerning the mental or emotional condition of the patient if such issue had been tendered by:

(a) The patient;

(b) Any party claiming through or under the patient;

(c) Any party claiming as a beneficiary of the patient through a contract to which the patient is or was a party; or

(d) The plaintiff in an action brought under Section 376 or 377 of the Code of Civil Procedure for damages for the injury or death of the patient.

§ 1017. Exception: Psychotherapist appointed by court or board of prison terms. (a) There is no privilege under this article if the psychotherapist is appointed by order of a court to examine the patient, but this exception does not apply where the psychotherapist is appointed by order of the court upon the request of the lawyer for the defendant in a criminal proceeding in order to provide the lawyer with information needed so that he or she may advise the defendant whether to enter or withdraw a plea based on insanity or to present a defense based on his or her mental or emotional condition.

(b) There is no privilege under this article if the psychotherapist is appointed by the Board of Prison Terms to examine a patient pursuant to the provisions of Article 4 (commencing with Section 2960) of Chapter 7 of Title 1 of Part 3 of the Penal Code.

§ 1018. Exception: Crime or tort. There is no privilege under this article if the services of the psychotherapist were sought or obtained to enable or aid anyone to commit or plan to commit a crime or a tort or to escape detection or apprehension after the commission of a crime or a tort.

§ 1019. Exception: Parties claiming through deceased patient. There is no privilege under this article as to a communication relevant to an issue between parties all of whom claim through a deceased patient, regardless of whether the claims are by testate or intestate succession or by inter vivos transaction.

§ 1020. Exception: Breach of duty arising out of psychotherapist-patient relationship. There is no privilege under this article as to a communication relevant to an issue of breach, by the psychotherapist or by the patient, of a duty arising out of the psychotherapist-patient relationship.

§ 1021. Exception: Intention of deceased patient concerning writing affecting property interest. There is no privilege under this article as to a communication relevant to an issue concerning the intention of a patient, now deceased, with respect to a deed of conveyance, will, or other writing, executed by the patient, purporting to affect an interest in property.

§ 1022. Exception: Validity of writing affecting property interest. There is no privilege under this article as to a communication relevant to an issue concerning the validity of a deed of conveyance, will, or other writing, executed by a patient, now deceased, purporting to affect an interest in property.

§ 1023. Exception: Proceeding to determine sanity of criminal defendant. There is no privilege under this article in a proceeding under Chapter 6 (commencing with Section 1367) of Title 10 of Part 2 of the Penal Code initiated at the request of the defendant in a criminal action to determine his sanity.

§ 1024. Exception: Patient dangerous to himself or others. There is no privilege under this article if the psychotherapist has reasonable cause to believe that the patient is in such mental or emotional condition as to be dangerous to himself or to the person or property of another and that disclosure of the communication is necessary to prevent the threatened danger.

§ 1025. Exception: Proceeding to establish competence. There is no privilege under this article in a proceeding brought by or on behalf of the patient to establish his competence.

§ 1026. Exception: Required report. There is no privilege under this article as to information that the psychotherapist or the patient is required to report to a public employee or as to information required to be recorded in a public office, if such report or record is open to public inspection.

§ 1027. Exception: Child under 16 victim of crime. There is no privilege under this article if all of the following circumstances exist:

(a) The patient is a child under the age of 16.

(b) The psychotherapist has reasonable cause to believe that the patient has been the victim of a crime and that disclosure of the communication is in the best interest of the child.

Law Revision Commission Comment

Section 1027 provides an exception to the psychotherapist-patient privilege that is analogous to the exception provided by Section 1024 (patient dangerous to himself or others). The exception provided by Section 1027 is necessary to permit court disclosure of communications to a psychotherapist by a child who has been the victim of a crime (such as child abuse) in a proceeding in which the commission of such crime is a subject of inquiry.

Article 8. Clergy–Penitent Privileges

§ 1030. Member of the Clergy. As used in this article, a "member of the clergy" means a priest, minister, religious practitioner, or similar functionary of a church or of a religious denomination or religious organization.

§ 1031. "Penitent". As used in this article, "penitent" means a person who has made a penitential communication to a member of the clergy.

§ 1032. "Penitential communication". As used in this article, "penitential communication" means a communication made in confidence, in the presence of no third person so far as the penitent is aware, to a member of the clergy who, in the course of the discipline or practice of the clergy member's church, denomination, or organization, is authorized or accustomed to hear those communications and, under the discipline or tenets of his or her church, denomination, or organization, has a duty to keep those communications secret.

§ 1033. Privilege of penitent. Subject to Section 912, a penitent, whether or not a party, has a privilege to refuse to disclose, and to prevent another from disclosing, a penitential communication if he or she claims the privilege.

§ 1034. Privilege of clergy member. Subject to Section 912, a member of the clergy, whether or not a party, has a privilege to refuse to disclose a penitential communication if he or she claims the privilege.

Comment—Law Revision Commission

This section provides the clergyman with a privilege in his own right. Moreover, he may claim this privilege even if the penitent has waived the privilege granted him by Section 1033.

There may be several reasons for granting [a] clergyman the traditional priest-penitent privilege. At least one underlying reason seems to be that the law will not compel a clergyman to violate—nor punish him for refusing to violate—the tenets of his church which require him to maintain secrecy as to confidential statements made to him in the course of his religious duties. See generally 8 Wigmore, Evidence §§ 2394–2396 (McNaughton rev. 1961).

The clergyman is under no legal compulsion to claim the privilege. Hence, a penitential communication will be admitted if the clergyman fails to claim the privilege and the penitent is deceased, incompetent, absent, or fails to claim the privilege. This probably changes existing law; but, if so, the change is desirable. For example, if a murderer had confessed the crime to a clergyman, the clergyman might under some circumstances (e.g., if the murderer has died) decline to claim the privilege and instead, give the evidence on behalf of an innocent third party who had been indicted for the crime. The extent to which a clergyman should keep secret or reveal penitential communications is not an appropriate subject for legislation; the matter is better left to the discretion of the individual clergyman involved and the discipline of the religious body of which he is a member.

Article 8.5 Sexual Assault Counselor–Victim Privilege

§ 1035. Victim. As used in this article, "victim" means a person who consults a sexual assault counselor for the purpose of securing advice or assistance concerning a mental, physical, or emotional condition caused by a sexual assault.

§ 1035.2. Sexual assault counselor. As used in this article, "sexual assault counselor" means any of the following:

(a) A person who is engaged in any office, hospital, institution, or center commonly known as a rape crisis center, whose primary purpose is the rendering of advice or assistance to victims of sexual assault and who has received a certificate evidencing completion of a training program in the counseling of sexual assault victims issued by a counseling center that meets the criteria for the award of a grant established pursuant to Section 13837 of the Penal Code and who meets one of the following requirements:

(1) Is a psychotherapist as defined in Section 1010; has a master's degree in counseling or a related field; or has one year of counseling experience, at least six months of which is in rape crisis counseling.

(2) Has 40 hours of training as described below and is supervised by an individual who qualifies as a counselor under paragraph (1). The training, supervised by a person qualified under paragraph (1), shall include, but not be limited to, the following areas:

(A) Law.

(B) Medicine.

(C) Societal attitudes.

(D) Crisis intervention and counseling techniques.

(E) Role playing.

§ 1035.2

(F) Referral services.

(G) Sexuality.

(b) A person who is employed by any organization providing the programs specified in Section 13835.2 of the Penal Code, whether financially compensated or not, for the purpose of counseling and assisting sexual assault victims, and who meets one of the following requirements:

(1) Is a psychotherapist as defined in Section 1010; has a master's degree in counseling or a related field; or has one year of counseling experience, at least six months of which is in rape assault counseling.

(2) Has the minimum training for sexual assault counseling required by guidelines established by the employing agency pursuant to subdivision (c) of Section 13835.10 of the Penal Code, and is supervised by an individual who qualifies as a counselor under paragraph (1). The training, supervised by a person qualified under paragraph (1), shall include, but not be limited to, the following areas:

(A) Law.

(B) Victimology.

(C) Counseling.

(D) Client and system advocacy.

(E) Referral services.

§ 1035.4. Confidential communication between the sexual assault counselor and the victim; disclosure. As used in this article, "confidential communication between the sexual assault counselor and the victim" means information transmitted between the victim and the sexual assault counselor in the course of their relationship and in confidence by a means which, so far as the victim is aware, discloses the information to no third persons other than those who are present to further the interests of the victim in the consultation or those to whom disclosures are reasonably necessary for the transmission of the information or an accomplishment of the purposes for which the sexual assault counselor is consulted. The term includes all information regarding the facts and circumstances involving the alleged sexual assault and also includes all information regarding the victim's prior or subsequent sexual conduct, and opinions regarding the victim's sexual conduct or reputation in sexual matters.

The court may compel disclosure of information received by the sexual assault counselor which constitutes relevant evidence of the facts and circumstances involving an alleged sexual assault about which the victim is complaining and which is the subject of a criminal proceeding if the court determines that the probative value outweighs the effect on the victim, the treatment relationship, and the treatment services if disclosure is compelled. The court may also compel disclosure in proceedings related to child abuse if the court determines the probative value outweighs the effect on the victim, the treatment relationship, and the treatment services if disclosure is compelled.

When a court is ruling on a claim of privilege under this article, the court may require the person from whom disclosure is sought or the person authorized to claim the privilege, or both, to disclose the information in chambers out of the presence and hearing of all persons except the person authorized to claim the privilege and such other persons as the person authorized to claim the privilege is willing to have present. If the judge determines that the information is privileged and must not be disclosed, neither he or she nor any other person may ever disclose, without the consent of a person authorized to permit disclosure, what was disclosed in the course of the proceedings in chambers.

If the court determines certain information shall be disclosed, the court shall so order and inform the defendant. If the court finds there is a reasonable likelihood that particular information is subject to disclosure pursuant to the balancing test provided in this section, the following procedure shall be followed:

(1) The court shall inform the defendant of the nature of the information which may be subject to disclosure.

(2) The court shall order a hearing out of the presence of the jury, if any, and at the hearing allow the questioning of the sexual assault counselor regarding the information which the court has determined may be subject to disclosure.

(3) At the conclusion of the hearing, the court shall rule which items of information, if any, shall be disclosed. The court may make an order stating what evidence may be introduced by the defendant and the nature of questions to be permitted. The defendant may then offer evidence pursuant to the order of the court. Admission of evidence concerning the sexual conduct of the complaining witness is subject to Sections 352, 782, and 1103.

§ 1035.6. **Holder of the privilege.** As used in this article, "holder of the privilege" means:

(a) The victim when such person has no guardian or conservator.

(b) A guardian or conservator of the victim when the victim has a guardian or conservator.

(c) The personal representative of the victim if the victim is dead.

§ 1035.8. **Sexual assault counselor privilege**. A victim of a sexual assault, whether or not a party, has a privilege to refuse to disclose, and to prevent another from disclosing, a confidential communication be-

§ 1035.8

tween the victim and a sexual assault counselor if the privilege is claimed by any of the following:

(a) The holder of the privilege;

(b) A person who is authorized to claim the privilege by the holder of the privilege; or

(c) The person who was the sexual assault counselor at the time of the confidential communication, but that person may not claim the privilege if there is no holder of the privilege in existence or if he or she is otherwise instructed by a person authorized to permit disclosure.

§ 1036. Claim of privilege by sexual assault counselor. The sexual assault counselor who received or made a communication subject to the privilege under this article shall claim the privilege if he or she is present when the communication is sought to be disclosed and is authorized to claim the privilege under subdivision (c) of Section 1035.8.

§ 1036.2. Sexual assault. As used in this article, "sexual assault" includes all of the following:

(a) Rape, as defined in Section 261 of the Penal Code.

(b) Unlawful sexual intercourse, as defined in Section 261.5 of the Penal Code.

(c) Rape in concert with force and violence, as defined in Section 264.1 of the Penal Code.

(d) Rape of a spouse, as defined in Section 262 of the Penal Code.

(e) Sodomy, as defined in Section 286 of the Penal Code, except a violation of subdivision (e) of that section.

(f) A violation of Section 288 of the Penal Code.

(g) Oral copulation, as defined in Section 288a of the Penal Code, except a violation of subdivision (e) of that section.

(h) Sexual penetration, as defined in Section 289 of the Penal Code.

(i) Annoying or molesting a child under 18, as defined in Section 647a of the Penal Code.

(j) Any attempt to commit any of the above acts.

Article 8.7 Domestic Violence Counselor–Victim Privilege

§ 1037. Victim. As used in this article, "victim" means any person who suffers domestic violence, as defined in Section 1037.7.

§ 1037.1. Domestic violence counselor; qualifications; domestic violence victim service organization. (a)(1) As used in this article, "domestic violence counselor" means a person who is employed by a domestic violence victim service organization, as defined in this article, whether financially compensated or not, for the purpose of rendering advice or assistance to victims of domestic violence and who has at least 40 hours of training as specified in paragraph (2).

(2) The 40 hours of training shall be supervised by an individual who qualifies as a counselor under paragraph (1), and who has at least one year of experience counseling domestic violence victims for the domestic violence victim service organization. The training shall include, but need not be limited to, the following areas: history of domestic violence, civil and criminal law as it relates to domestic violence, the domestic violence victim-counselor privilege and other laws that protect the confidentiality of victim records and information, societal attitudes towards domestic violence, peer counseling techniques, housing, public assistance and other financial resources available to meet the financial needs of domestic violence victims, and referral services available to domestic violence victims.

(3) A domestic violence counselor who has been employed by the domestic violence victim service organization for a period of less than six months shall be supervised by a domestic violence counselor who has at least one year of experience counseling domestic violence victims for the domestic violence victim service organization.

(b) As used in this article, "domestic violence victim service organization" means a nongovernmental organization or entity that provides shelter, programs, or services to victims of domestic violence and their children, including, but not limited to, either of the following:

(1) Domestic violence shelter-based programs, as described in Section 18294 of the Welfare and Institutions Code.

(2) Other programs with the primary mission to provide services to victims of domestic violence whether or not that program exists in an agency that provides additional services.

§ 1037.2. Confidential communication; compulsion of disclosure by court; claim of privilege.

(a) As used in this article, "confidential communication" means any information, including, but not limited to, written or oral communication, transmitted between the victim and the counselor in the course of their relationship and in confidence by a means which, so far as the victim is aware, discloses the information to no third persons other than those who are present to further the interests of the victim in the consultation or those to whom disclosures are reasonably necessary for the transmission of the information or an accomplishment of the purposes for which the domestic violence counselor is consulted. The term includes all information regarding the facts and circumstances involving all incidences of domestic violence, as well as all information about the children of the victim or abuser and the relationship of the victim with the abuser.

(b) The court may compel disclosure of information received by a domestic violence counselor which constitutes relevant evidence of the

§ 1037.2   CALIFORNIA EVIDENCE CODE

facts and circumstances involving a crime allegedly perpetrated against the victim or another household member and which is the subject of a criminal proceeding, if the court determines that the probative value of the information outweighs the effect of disclosure of the information on the victim, the counseling relationship, and the counseling services. The court may compel disclosure if the victim is either dead or not the complaining witness in a criminal action against the perpetrator. The court may also compel disclosure in proceedings related to child abuse if the court determines that the probative value of the evidence outweighs the effect of the disclosure on the victim, the counseling relationship, and the counseling services.

(c) When a court rules on a claim of privilege under this article, it may require the person from whom disclosure is sought or the person authorized to claim the privilege, or both, to disclose the information in chambers out of the presence and hearing of all persons except the person authorized to claim the privilege and such other persons as the person authorized to claim the privilege consents to have present. If the judge determines that the information is privileged and shall not be disclosed, neither he nor she nor any other person may disclose, without the consent of a person authorized to permit disclosure, any information disclosed in the course of the proceedings in chambers.

(d) If the court determines that information shall be disclosed, the court shall so order and inform the defendant in the criminal action. If the court finds there is a reasonable likelihood that any information is subject to disclosure pursuant to the balancing test provided in this section, the procedure specified in subdivisions (1), (2), and (3) of Section 1035.4 shall be followed.

§ 1037.3. Child abuse; reporting. Nothing in this article shall be construed to limit any obligation to report instances of child abuse as required by Section 11166 of the Penal Code.

§ 1037.4. Holder of the privilege. As used in this article, "holder of the privilege" means:

(a) The victim when he or she has no guardian or conservator.

(b) A guardian or conservator of the victim when the victim has a guardian or conservator, unless the guardian or conservator is accused of perpetrating domestic violence against the victim.

§ 1037.5. Privilege of refusal to disclose communication; claimants. A victim of domestic violence, whether or not a party to the action, has a privilege to refuse to disclose, and to prevent another from disclosing, a confidential communication between the victim and a domestic violence counselor in any proceeding specified in Section 901 if the privilege is claimed by any of the following persons:

(a) The holder of the privilege.

(b) A person who is authorized to claim the privilege by the holder of the privilege.

(c) The person who was the domestic violence counselor at the time of the confidential communication. However, that person may not claim the privilege if there is no holder of the privilege in existence or if he or she is otherwise instructed by a person authorized to permit disclosure.

§ 1037.6. Claiming of privilege by counselor. The domestic violence counselor who received or made a communication subject to the privilege granted by this article shall claim the privilege whenever he or she is present when the communication is sought to be disclosed and he or she is authorized to claim the privilege under subdivision (c) of Section 1037.5.

§ 1037.7. As used in this article, "domestic violence" means "domestic violence" as defined in Section 6211 of the Family Code.

§ 1037.8. Notice; limitations on confidential communications. A domestic violence counselor shall inform a domestic violence victim of any applicable limitations on confidentiality of communications between the victim and the domestic violence counselor. This information may be given orally.

Article 8.8 Human Trafficking Caseworker–Victim Privilege

§ 1038. Claimant of the privilege. (a) A trafficking victim, whether or not a party to the action, has a privilege to refuse to disclose, and to prevent another from disclosing, a confidential communication between the victim and a human trafficking caseworker if the privilege is claimed by any of the following persons:

(1) The holder of the privilege.

(2) A person who is authorized to claim the privilege by the holder of the privilege.

(3) The person who was the human trafficking caseworker at the time of the confidential communication. However, that person may not claim the privilege if there is no holder of the privilege in existence or if he or she is otherwise instructed by a person authorized to permit disclosure. The human trafficking caseworker who received or made a communication subject to the privilege granted by this article shall claim the privilege whenever he or she is present when the communication is sought to be disclosed and he or she is authorized to claim the privilege under this section.

(b) A human trafficking caseworker shall inform a trafficking victim of any applicable limitations on confidentiality of communications between the victim and the caseworker. This information may be given orally.

§ 1038.1. Disclosure of information. (a) The court may compel disclosure of information received by a human trafficking caseworker that constitutes relevant evidence of the facts and circumstances involving a crime allegedly perpetrated against the victim and that is the subject of a criminal proceeding, if the court determines that the probative value of the information outweighs the effect of disclosure of the information on the victim, the counseling relationship, and the counseling services. The court may compel disclosure if the victim is either dead or not the complaining witness in a criminal action against the perpetrator.

(b) When a court rules on a claim of privilege under this article, it may require the person from whom disclosure is sought or the person authorized to claim the privilege, or both, to disclose the information in chambers out of the presence and hearing of all persons except the person authorized to claim the privilege and those other persons that the person authorized to claim the privilege consents to have present.

(c) If the judge determines that the information is privileged and shall not be disclosed, neither he nor she nor any other person may disclose, without the consent of a person authorized to permit disclosure, any information disclosed in the course of the proceedings in chambers. If the court determines that information shall be disclosed, the court shall so order and inform the defendant in the criminal action. If the court finds there is a reasonable likelihood that any information is subject to disclosure pursuant to the balancing test provided in this section, the procedure specified in paragraphs (1), (2), and (3) of Section 1035.4 shall be followed.

§ 1038.2. Definitions. (a) As used in this article, "victim" means any person who is a "trafficking victim" as defined in Section 236.1.

(b) As used in this article, "human trafficking caseworker" means any of the following:

(1) A person who is employed by any organization providing the programs specified in Section 18294 of the Welfare and Institutions Code, whether financially compensated or not, for the purpose of rendering advice or assistance to victims of human trafficking, who has received specialized training in the counseling of human trafficking victims, and who meets one of the following requirements:

(A) Has a master's degree in counseling or a related field; or has one year of counseling experience, at least six months of which is in the counseling of human trafficking victims.

(B) Has at least 40 hours of training as specified in this paragraph and is supervised by an individual who qualifies as a counselor under subparagraph (A), or is a psychotherapist, as defined in Section 1010. The training, supervised by a person qualified under subparagraph (A), shall include, but need not be limited to, the following areas: history of human trafficking, civil and criminal law as it relates to human trafficking, societal attitudes towards human trafficking, peer counseling techniques, housing, public assistance and other financial resources available to meet the financial needs of human trafficking victims, and referral services available to human trafficking victims. A portion of this training must include an explanation of privileged communication.

(2) A person who is employed by any organization providing the programs specified in Section 13835.2 of the Penal Code, whether financially compensated or not, for the purpose of counseling and assisting human trafficking victims, and who meets one of the following requirements:

(A) Is a psychotherapist as defined in Section 1010, has a master's degree in counseling or a related field, or has one year of counseling experience, at least six months of which is in rape assault counseling.

(B) Has the minimum training for human trafficking counseling required by guidelines established by the employing agency pursuant to subdivision (c) of Section 13835.10 of the Penal Code, and is supervised by an individual who qualifies as a counselor under subparagraph (A). The training, supervised by a person qualified under subparagraph (A), shall include, but not be limited to, law, victimology, counseling techniques, client and system advocacy, and referral services. A portion of this training must include an explanation of privileged communication.

(c) As used in this article, "confidential communication" means information transmitted between the victim and the caseworker in the course of their relationship and in confidence by a means which, so far as the victim is aware, discloses the information to no third persons other than those who are present to further the interests of the victim in the consultation or those to whom disclosures are reasonably necessary for the transmission of the information or an accomplishment of the purposes for which the human trafficking counselor is consulted. It includes all information regarding the facts and circumstances involving all incidences of human trafficking.

(d) As used in this article, "holder of the privilege" means the victim when he or she has no guardian or conservator, or a guardian or conservator of the victim when the victim has a guardian or conservator.

Article 9. Official Information and Identity of Informer

§ 1040. Privilege for official information. (a) As used in this section, "official information" means information acquired in confidence by a public employee in the course of his or her duty and not open, or officially disclosed, to the public prior to the time the claim of privilege is made.

(b) A public entity has a privilege to refuse to disclose official information, and to prevent another from disclosing official information, if the privilege is claimed by a person authorized by the public entity to do so and:

(1) Disclosure is forbidden by an act of the Congress of the United States or a statute of this state; or

(2) Disclosure of the information is against the public interest because there is a necessity for preserving the confidentiality of the information that outweighs the necessity for disclosure in the interest of justice; but no privilege may be claimed under this paragraph if any person authorized to do so has consented that the information be disclosed in the proceeding. In determining whether disclosure of the information is against the public interest, the interest of the public entity as a party in the outcome of the proceeding may not be considered.

(c) Notwithstanding any other provision of law, the Employment Development Department shall disclose to law enforcement agencies, in accordance with the provisions of subdivision (k) of Section 1095 and subdivision (b) of Section 2714 of the Unemployment Insurance Code, information in its possession relating to any person if an arrest warrant has been issued for the person for commission of a felony.

Comment—Assembly Committee on Judiciary

Section 1040 permits the official information privilege to be invoked by the public entity or its authorized representative. Since the privilege is granted to enable the government to protect its secrets, no reason exists for permitting the privilege to be exercised by persons who are not concerned with the public interest. It should be noted, however, that another statute may provide a person with a privilege not to disclose a report he made to the government; the Evidence Code has no effect on that privilege. See the Comment to Evidence Code § 920. Where the government has received a report from an informant, the official information privilege may apply to that report. It does not apply, however, to the knowledge of the informant. The government does not acquire a privilege to prevent an informant from revealing his knowledge merely because that knowledge has been communicated to the government.

The official information privilege provided in Section 1040 does not extend to the identity of an informer. Section 1041 provides special rules for determining when the government has a privilege to keep secret the identity of an informer.

Official information is absolutely privileged if its disclosure is forbidden by either a federal or state statute. Other official information is subject to a conditional privilege: The judge must determine in each instance the consequences to the public of disclosure and the consequences to the litigant of nondisclosure and then decide which outweighs the other. He should, of course, be aware that the public has an interest in seeing that justice is done in the particular cause as well as an interest in the secrecy of the information.

§ 1041. Privilege for identity of informer. (a) Except as provided in this section, a public entity has a privilege to refuse to disclose the identity of a person who has furnished information as provided in subdivision (b) purporting to disclose a violation of a law of the United States or of this state or of a public entity in this state, and to prevent another from disclosing such identity, if the privilege is claimed by a person authorized by the public entity to do so and:

(1) Disclosure is forbidden by an act of the Congress of the United States or a statute of this state; or

(2) Disclosure of the identity of the informer is against the public interest because there is a necessity for preserving the confidentiality of his identity that outweighs the necessity for disclosure in the interest of justice; but no privilege may be claimed under this paragraph if any person authorized to do so has consented that the identity of the informer be disclosed in the proceeding. In determining whether disclosure of the identity of the informer is against the public interest, the interest of the public entity as a party in the outcome of the proceeding may not be considered.

(b) This section applies only if the information is furnished in confidence by the informer to:

(1) A law enforcement officer;

(2) A representative of an administrative agency charged with the administration or enforcement of the law alleged to be violated; or

(3) Any person for the purpose of transmittal to a person listed in paragraph (1) or (2).

(c) There is no privilege under this section to prevent the informer from disclosing his identity.

Comment—Law Revision Commission

This privilege may be claimed under the same conditions as the official information privilege may be claimed, except that it does not apply if a person is called as a witness and asked if he is the informer.

§ 1042. Adverse order or finding in certain cases. (a) Except where disclosure is forbidden by an act of the Congress of the United States, if a claim of privilege under this article by the state or a public entity in this state is sustained in a criminal proceeding, the presiding officer shall make such order or finding of fact adverse to the public entity bringing the proceeding as is required by law upon any issue in the proceeding to which the privileged information is material.

(b) Notwithstanding subdivision (a), where a search is made pursuant to a warrant valid on its face, the public entity bringing a criminal proceeding is not required to reveal to the defendant official information or the identity of an informer in order to establish the legality of the search or the admissibility of any evidence obtained as a result of it.

(c) Notwithstanding subdivision (a), in any preliminary hearing, criminal trial, or other criminal proceeding, any otherwise admissible evidence of information communicated to a peace officer by a confidential informant, who is not a material witness to the guilt or innocence of the accused of the offense charged, is admissible on the issue of reasonable cause to make an arrest or search without requiring that the name or identity of the informant be disclosed if the judge or magistrate is satisfied, based upon evidence produced in open court, out of the presence of the jury, that such information was received from a reliable informant and in his discretion does not require such disclosure.

(d) When, in any such criminal proceeding, a party demands disclosure of the identity of the informant on the ground the informant is a material witness on the issue of guilt, the court shall conduct a hearing at which all parties may present evidence on the issue of disclosure. Such hearing shall be conducted outside the presence of the jury, if any. During the hearing, if the privilege provided for in Section 1041 is claimed by a person authorized to do so or if a person who is authorized to claim such privilege refuses to answer any question on the ground that the answer would tend to disclose the identity of the informant, the prosecuting attorney may request that the court hold an in camera hearing. If such a request is made, the court shall hold such a hearing outside the presence of the defendant and his counsel. At the in camera hearing, the prosecution may offer evidence which would tend to disclose or which discloses the identity of the informant to aid the court in its determination whether there is a reasonable possibility that nondisclosure might deprive the defendant of a fair trial. A reporter shall be present at the in camera hearing. Any transcription of the proceedings at the in camera hearing, as well as any physical evidence presented at the hearing, shall be ordered sealed by the court, and only a court may have access to its contents. The court shall not order disclosure, nor strike the testimony of the witness who invokes the privilege, nor dismiss the criminal proceeding, if the party offering the witness refuses to disclose the identity of the informant, unless, based upon the evidence presented at the hearing held in the presence of the defendant and his counsel and the evidence presented at the in camera hearing, the court concludes that there is a reasonable possibility that nondisclosure might deprive the defendant of a fair trial.

§ 1043. Peace or custodial officer personnel records; discovery or disclosure; procedure. (a) In any case in which discovery or disclosure is sought of peace or custodial officer personnel records or records maintained pursuant to Section 832.5 of the Penal Code or information from those records, the party seeking the discovery or disclosure shall file a written motion with the appropriate court or administrative body upon written notice to the governmental agency which has custody and control of the records. The written notice shall be given at the times prescribed by subdivision (b) of Section 1005 of the

Code of Civil Procedure. Upon receipt of the notice the governmental agency served shall immediately notify the individual whose records are sought.

(b) The motion shall include all of the following:

(1) Identification of the proceeding in which discovery or disclosure is sought, the party seeking discovery or disclosure, the peace or custodial officer whose records are sought, the governmental agency which has custody and control of the records, and the time and place at which the motion for discovery or disclosure shall be heard.

(2) A description of the type of records or information sought.

(3) Affidavits showing good cause for the discovery or disclosure sought, setting forth the materiality thereof to the subject matter involved in the pending litigation and stating upon reasonable belief that the governmental agency identified has the records or information from the records.

(c) No hearing upon a motion for discovery or disclosure shall be held without full compliance with the notice provisions of this section except upon a showing by the moving party of good cause for noncompliance, or upon a waiver of the hearing by the governmental agency identified as having the records.

§ 1044. **Medical or psychological history records; right of access.** Nothing in this article shall be construed to affect the right of access to records of medical or psychological history where such access would otherwise be available under Section 996 or 1016.

§ 1045. **Peace or custodial officers; access to records of complaints or discipline imposed; relevancy; protective orders.** (a) Nothing in this article shall be construed to affect the right of access to records of complaints, or investigations of complaints, or discipline imposed as a result of such investigations, concerning an event or transaction in which the peace officer or custodial officer, as defined in Section 831.5 of the Penal Code, participated, or which he or she perceived, and pertaining to the manner in which he or she performed his or her duties, provided that information is relevant to the subject matter involved in the pending litigation.

(b) In determining relevance the court shall examine the information in chambers in conformity with Section 915, and shall exclude from disclosure:

(1) Information consisting of complaints concerning conduct occurring more than five years before the event or transaction that is the subject of the litigation in aid of which discovery or disclosure is sought.

(2) In any criminal proceeding the conclusions of any officer investigating a complaint filed pursuant to Section 832.5 of the Penal Code.

(3) Facts sought to be disclosed that are so remote as to make disclosure of little or no practical benefit.

(c) In determining relevance where the issue in litigation concerns the policies or pattern of conduct of the employing agency, the court shall consider whether the information sought may be obtained from other records maintained by the employing agency in the regular course of agency business which would not necessitate the disclosure of individual personnel records.

(d) Upon motion seasonably made by the governmental agency which has custody or control of the records to be examined or by the officer whose records are sought, and upon good cause showing the necessity thereof, the court may make any order which justice requires to protect the officer or agency from unnecessary annoyance, embarrassment or oppression.

(e) The court shall, in any case or proceeding permitting the disclosure or discovery of any peace or custodial officer records requested pursuant to Section 1043, order that the records disclosed or discovered may not be used for any purpose other than a court proceeding pursuant to applicable law.

§ 1046. Allegation of excessive force by peace or custodial officer; copy of police or crime report. In any case, otherwise authorized by law, in which the party seeking disclosure is alleging excessive force by a peace or custodial officer, as defined in Section 831.5 of the Penal Code, in connection with the arrest of that party, or for conduct alleged to have occurred within a jail facility, the motion shall include a copy of the police report setting forth the circumstances under which the party was stopped and arrested or a copy of the crime report setting forth the circumstances under which the conduct is alleged to have occurred within a jail facility.

§ 1047. Records of peace or custodial officers; exemption from disclosure. Records of peace officers or custodial officers, as defined in Section 831.5 of the Penal Code, including supervisorial officers, who either were not present during the arrest or had no contact with the party seeking disclosure from the time of the arrest until the time of booking, or who were not present at the time the conduct is alleged to have occurred within a jail facility, shall not be subject to disclosure.

Article 10. Political Vote

§ 1050. Privilege to protect secrecy of vote. If he claims the privilege, a person has a privilege to refuse to disclose the tenor of his vote at a public election where the voting is by secret ballot unless he voted illegally or he previously made an unprivileged disclosure of the tenor of his vote.

Article 11. Trade Secret

§ 1060. Privilege to protect trade secret. If he or his agent or employee claims the privilege, the owner of a trade secret has a privilege to refuse to disclose the secret, and to prevent another from disclosing it, if the allowance of the privilege will not tend to conceal fraud or otherwise work injustice.

Comment—Law Revision Commission

This privilege is granted so that secret information essential to the continued operation of a business or industry may be afforded some measure of protection against unnecessary disclosure. Thus, the privilege prevents the use of the witness' duty to testify as the means for injuring an otherwise profitable business where more important interests will not be jeopardized. See generally 8 Wigmore, Evidence § 2212 (3)(McNaughton rev.1961). Nevertheless, there are dangers in the recognition of such a privilege. Copyright and patent laws provide adequate protection for many of the matters that might otherwise be classified as trade secrets. Recognizing the privilege as to such information would serve only to hinder the courts in determining the truth without providing the owner of the secret any needed protection. Again, disclosure of the matters protected by the privilege may be essential to disclose unfair competition or fraud or to reveal the improper use of dangerous materials by the party asserting the privilege. Recognizing the privilege in such cases would amount to a legally sanctioned license to commit the wrongs complained of, for the wrongdoer would be privileged to withhold his wrongful conduct from legal scrutiny.

Therefore, the privilege exists under this section only if its application will not tend to conceal fraud or otherwise work injustice. The limits of the privilege are necessarily uncertain and will have to be worked out through judicial decisions.

§ 1061. Procedure for assertion of trade secret privilege. (a) For purposes of this section, and Sections 1062 and 1063:

(1) "Trade secret" means "trade secret," as defined in subdivision (d) of Section 3426.1 of the Civil Code, or paragraph (9) of subdivision (a) of Section 499c of the Penal Code.

(2) "Article" means "article," as defined in paragraph (2) of subdivision (a) of Section 499c of the Penal Code.

(b) In addition to Section 1062, the following procedure shall apply whenever the owner of a trade secret wishes to assert his or her trade secret privilege, as provided in Section 1060, during a criminal proceeding:

(1) The owner of the trade secret shall file a motion for a protective order, or the people may file the motion on the owner's behalf and with the owner's permission. The motion shall include an affidavit based upon personal knowledge listing the affiant's qualifications to give an opinion concerning the trade secret at issue, identifying, without revealing, the alleged trade secret and articles which disclose the secret, and presenting

evidence that the secret qualifies as a trade secret under either subdivision (d) of Section 3426.1 of the Civil Code or paragraph (9) of subdivision (a) of Section 499c of the Penal Code. The motion and affidavit shall be served on all parties in the proceeding.

(2) Any party in the proceeding may oppose the request for the protective order by submitting affidavits based upon the affiant's personal knowledge. The affidavits shall be filed under seal, but shall be provided to the owner of the trade secret and to all parties in the proceeding. Neither the owner of the trade secret nor any party in the proceeding may disclose the affidavit to persons other than to counsel of record without prior court approval.

(3) The movant shall, by a preponderance of the evidence, show that the issuance of a protective order is proper. The court may rule on the request without holding an evidentiary hearing. However, in its discretion, the court may choose to hold an in camera evidentiary hearing concerning disputed articles with only the owner of the trade secret, the people's representative, the defendant, and defendant's counsel present. If the court holds such a hearing, the parties' right to examine witnesses shall not be used to obtain discovery, but shall be directed solely toward the question of whether the alleged trade secret qualifies for protection.

(4) If the court finds that a trade secret may be disclosed during any criminal proceeding unless a protective order is issued and that the issuance of a protective order would not conceal a fraud or work an injustice, the court shall issue a protective order limiting the use and dissemination of the trade secret, including, but not limited to, articles disclosing that secret. The protective order may, in the court's discretion, include the following provisions:

(A) That the trade secret may be disseminated only to counsel for the parties, including their associate attorneys, paralegals, and investigators, and to law enforcement officials or clerical officials.

(B) That the defendant may view the secret only in the presence of his or her counsel, or if not in the presence of his or her counsel, at counsel's offices.

(C) That any party seeking to show the trade secret, or articles containing the trade secret, to any person not designated by the protective order shall first obtain court approval to do so:

(i) The court may require that the person receiving the trade secret do so only in the presence of counsel for the party requesting approval.

(ii) The court may require the person receiving the trade secret to sign a copy of the protective order and to agree to be bound by its terms. The order may include a provision recognizing the owner of the trade secret to be a third-party beneficiary of that agreement.

(iii) The court may require a party seeking disclosure to an expert to provide that expert's name, employment history, and any other relevant information to the court for examination. The court shall accept that information under seal, and the information shall not be disclosed by any court except upon termination of the action and upon a showing of good cause to believe the secret has been disseminated by a court-approved expert. The court shall evaluate the expert and determine whether the expert poses a discernible risk of disclosure. The court shall withhold approval if the expert's economic interests place the expert in a competitive position with the victim, unless no other experts are available. The court may interview the expert in camera in aid of its ruling. If the court rejects the expert, it shall state its reasons for doing so on the record and a transcript of those reasons shall be prepared and sealed.

(D) That no articles disclosing the trade secret shall be filed or otherwise made a part of the court record available to the public without approval of the court and prior notice to the owner of the secret. The owner of the secret may give either party permission to accept the notice on the owner's behalf.

(E) Other orders as the court deems necessary to protect the integrity of the trade secret.

(c) A ruling granting or denying a motion for a protective order filed pursuant to subdivision (b) shall not be construed as a determination that the alleged trade secret is or is not a trade secret as defined by subdivision (d) of Section 3426.1 of the Civil Code or paragraph (9) of subdivision (a) of Section 499c of the Penal Code. Such a ruling shall not have any effect on any civil litigation.

(d) This section shall have prospective effect only and shall not operate to invalidate previously entered protective orders.

Chapter 5

IMMUNITY OF NEWSMAN FROM CITATION FOR CONTEMPT

Article I, Section 2(b), California Constitution

[**Note:** Section 1070 of the Evidence Code which deals with the immunity of newsmen from contempt citations was effectively replaced by the addition of subsection (b) to Section 2, Article I, of the California Constitution.

This constitutional amendment was submitted to the electorate through the initiative process (Proposition 5) and was approved in an election held on June 3, 1980. The language of the constitutional amendment is substantially identical to that of Section 1070. Consequently, an excerpt from the Comment to Section 1070 is also reproduced here.]

SEC. 2

(b) A publisher, editor, reporter, or other person connected with or employed upon a newspaper, magazine, or other periodical publication, or by a press association or wire service, or any person who has been so connected or employed, shall not be adjudged in contempt by a judicial, legislative, or administrative body, or any other body having the power to issue subpoenas, for refusing to disclose the source of any information procured while so connected or employed for publication in a newspaper, magazine or other periodical publication, or for refusing to disclose any unpublished information obtained or prepared in gathering, receiving or processing of information for communication to the public.

Nor shall a radio or television news reporter or other person connected with or employed by a radio or television station, or any person who has been so connected or employed, be so adjudged in contempt for refusing to disclose the source of any information procured while so connected or employed for news or news commentary purposes on radio or television, or for refusing to disclose any unpublished information obtained or prepared in gathering, receiving or processing of information for communication to the public.

As used in this subdivision, "unpublished information" includes information not disseminated to the public by the person from whom disclosure is sought, whether or not related information has been disseminated and includes, but is not limited to, all notes, outtakes, photographs, tapes or other data of whatever sort not itself disseminated to the public through a medium of communication, whether or not published information based upon or related to such material has been disseminated.

Comment—Assembly Committee on Judiciary

It should be noted that Section 1070, like the existing law, provides an immunity from being adjudged in contempt; it does not create a privilege. Thus, the section will not prevent the use of other sanctions for refusal of a newsman to make discovery when he is a party to a civil proceeding.

Division 9

EVIDENCE AFFECTED OR EXCLUDED BY EXTRINSIC POLICIES

Chapter 1

EVIDENCE OF CHARACTER, HABIT, OR CUSTOM

§ 1100. Manner of proof of character. Except as otherwise provided by statute, any otherwise admissible evidence (including evidence in the form of an opinion, evidence of reputation, and evidence of specific instances of such person's conduct) is admissible to prove a person's character or a trait of his character.

Comment—Law Revision Commission

Subject to certain statutory restrictions, the character evidence described in Section 1100 is admissible under Section 351 whenever it is relevant. Evidence of a person's character or a trait of his character is relevant in three situations: (1) when offered on the issue of his credibility as a witness, (2) when offered as circumstantial evidence of his conduct in conformity with such character or trait of character, and (3) when his character or a trait of his character is an ultimate fact in dispute in the action.

Sections 786–790 establish restrictions that are applicable when character evidence is offered to attack or to support the credibility of a witness. See the Comments to Sections 787 and 788 for a discussion of the restrictions on the kinds of evidence admissible for this purpose.

Sections 1101–1104 substantially restrict the extent to which character evidence is offered to attack or to support the *credibility of a witness*. See the Comments to Sections 787 and 788 for a discussion of the restrictions on the kinds of evidence admissible for this purpose.

Section 1100 applies without restriction only when character or a trait of character is an *ultimate fact in dispute* in the action.

§ 1101. Evidence of character to prove conduct. (a) Except as provided in this section and in Sections 1102 and 1103, 1108, and 1109, evidence of a person's character or a trait of his or her character (whether in the form of an opinion, evidence of reputation, or evidence of specific instances of his or her conduct) is inadmissible when offered to prove his or her conduct on a specified occasion.

(b) Nothing in this section prohibits the admission of evidence that a person committed a crime, civil wrong, or other act when relevant to prove some fact (such as motive, opportunity, intent, preparation, plan, knowledge, identity, absence of mistake or accident, or whether a defen-

§ 1101   CALIFORNIA EVIDENCE CODE

dant in a prosecution for an unlawful sexual act or attempted unlawful sexual act did not reasonably and in good faith believe that the victim consented) other than his or her disposition to commit such an act.

(c) Nothing in this section affects the admissibility of evidence offered to support or attack the credibility of a witness.

Comment—Law Revision Commission

Section 1101 is concerned with evidence of a person's character (i.e., his propensity or disposition to engage in a certain type of conduct) that is offered as a basis for an inference that he behaved in conformity with that character on a particular occasion.

Civil cases. Section 1101 excludes evidence of character to prove conduct in a civil case for the following reasons. *First,* character evidence is of slight probative value and may be very prejudicial. *Second,* character evidence tends to distract the trier of fact from the main question of what actually happened on the particular occasion and permits the trier of fact to reward the good man and to punish the bad man because of their respective characters. *Third,* introduction of character evidence may result in confusion of issues and require extended collateral inquiry.

Criminal cases. Section 1101 states the general rule that evidence of character to prove conduct is inadmissible in a criminal case. Sections 1102 and 1103 state exceptions to this general principle. See the Comment to Section 1102.

§ 1102. Opinion and reputation evidence of character of criminal defendant to prove conduct.

In a criminal action, evidence of the defendant's character or a trait of his character in the form of an opinion or evidence of his reputation is not made inadmissible by Section 1101 if such evidence is:

(a) Offered by the defendant to prove his conduct in conformity with such character or trait of character.

(b) Offered by the prosecution to rebut evidence adduced by the defendant under subdivision (a).

Comment—Law Revision Commission

Sections 1102 and 1103 state exceptions (applicable only in criminal cases) to the general rule of Section 1101 that character evidence is not admissible to prove conduct in conformity with that character.

Sections 1102 and 1103 generally

Under Section 1102, the accused in a criminal case may introduce evidence of his good character to show his innocence of the alleged crime—provided that the character or trait of character to be shown is relevant to the charge made against him. Sections 1101 and 1102 make it clear that the prosecution may not, on its own initiative, use character evidence to prove that the defendant had the disposition to commit the crime charged; but, if the defendant first introduces evidence of his good character to show the likelihood of innocence, the prosecution may meet his evidence by introducing evidence of the defendant's bad character to show the likelihood of guilt.

Likewise, under Section 1103, the defendant may introduce evidence of the character of the victim of the crime where the conduct of the victim in conformity with his character would tend to exculpate the defendant; and, if the defendant introduces evidence of the bad character of the victim, the prosecution may introduce evidence of the victim's good character.

Thus, under Sections 1102 and 1103, the defendant in a criminal case is given the right to introduce character evidence that would be inadmissible in a civil case. However, evidence of the character of the defendant or the victim—though weak—may be enough to raise a reasonable doubt in the mind of the trier of fact concerning the defendant's guilt. And, since his life or liberty is at stake, the defendant should not be deprived of the right to introduce evidence even of such slight probative value.

Kinds of character evidence admissible to prove conduct under Sections 1102 and 1103.

The three kinds of evidence that might be offered to prove character as circumstantial evidence of conduct are: (1) evidence as to reputation, (2) opinion evidence as to character, and (3) evidence of specific acts indicating character. The admissibility of each of these kinds of evidence when character is sought to be proved as circumstantial evidence of conduct under Sections 1102 and 1103 is discussed below.

Reputation evidence. Reputation evidence is the ordinary means sanctioned by the cases for proving character as circumstantial evidence of conduct. Both Sections 1102 and 1103 codify the existing law permitting character to be proved by reputation.

Opinion evidence. The general rule under existing law excludes the most reliable form of character evidence and admits the least reliable. The opinions of those whose personal intimacy with a person gives them firsthand knowledge of that person's character are a far more reliable indication of that character than is reputation, which is little more than accumulated hearsay. See 7 Wigmore, Evidence § 1986 (3d ed. 1940). The danger of collateral issues seems no greater than that inherent in reputation evidence. Accordingly, both Section 1102 and Section 1103 permit character to be proved by opinion evidence.

Evidence of specific acts. Under existing law, the admissibility of evidence of specific acts to prove character as circumstantial evidence of conduct depends upon the nature of the conduct sought to be proved. Evidence of specific acts of the accused is excluded as a general rule in order to avoid the possibility of prejudice, undue confusion of the issues with collateral matters, unfair surprise, and the like. Thus, it is usually held that evidence of specific acts by the defendant is inadmissible to prove his guilt even though the defendant has opened the question by introducing evidence of his good character. On the other hand, it is well settled that in a rape case the defendant may show the unchaste character of the prosecutrix by evidence of prior voluntary intercourse in order to indicate the unlikelihood of resistance on the occasion in question. However, in a homicide or assault case where the defense is self-defense, evidence of specific acts of violence by the victim is inadmissible to prove his violent nature (and, hence, that the victim was the aggressor) unless the prior acts were directed against the defendant himself.

Section 1102 codifies the general rule under existing law which precludes evidence of specific acts of the defendant to prove character as circumstantial evidence of his innocence or of his disposition to commit the crime with which he is charged.

Section 1103 permits both the defendant and the prosecution to use evidence of specific acts of the victim of the crime to prove the victim's character as circumstantial evidence of his conduct. In this respect, the section harmonizes conflicting rules found in existing law.

§ 1103. Evidence of character of victim of crime to prove conduct; evidence of complaining witness' sexual conduct in rape prosecution.

(a) In a criminal action, evidence of the character or a trait of character (in the form of an opinion, evidence of reputation, or evidence of specific instances of conduct) of the victim of the crime for which the defendant is being prosecuted is not made inadmissible by Section 1101 if the evidence is:

(1) Offered by the defendant to prove conduct of the victim in conformity with the character or trait of character.

(2) Offered by the prosecution to rebut evidence adduced by the defendant under paragraph (1).

(b) In a criminal action, evidence of the defendant's character for violence or trait of character for violence (in the form of an opinion, evidence of reputation, or evidence of specific instances of conduct) is not made inadmissible by Section 1101 if the evidence is offered by the prosecution to prove conduct of the defendant in conformity with the character or trait of character and is offered after evidence that the victim had a character for violence or a trait of character tending to show violence has been adduced by the defendant under paragraph (1) of subdivision (a).

(c)(1) Notwithstanding any other provision of this code to the contrary, and except as provided in this subdivision, in any prosecution under Section 261, 262 or 264.1 of the Penal Code, or under Section 286, 288a, or 289 of the Penal Code, or for assault with intent to commit, attempt to commit, or conspiracy to commit a crime defined in any of those sections, except where the crime is alleged to have occurred in a local detention facility, as defined in Section 6031.4, or in a state prison, as defined in Section 4504, opinion evidence, reputation evidence, and evidence of specific instances of the complaining witness' sexual conduct, or any of that evidence, is not admissible by the defendant in order to prove consent by the complaining witness.

(2) Notwithstanding paragraph (3), evidence of the manner in which the victim was dressed at the time of the commission of the offense shall

not be admissible when offered by either party on the issue of consent in any prosecution for an offense specified in paragraph (1), unless the evidence is determined by the court to be relevant and admissible in the interests of justice. The proponent of the evidence shall make an offer of proof outside the hearing of the jury. The court shall then make its determination and at that time, state the reasons for its ruling on the record. For the purposes of this paragraph, "manner of dress" does not include the condition of the victim's clothing before, during, or after the commission of the offense.

(3) Paragraph (1) shall not be applicable to evidence of the complaining witness' sexual conduct with the defendant.

(4) If the prosecutor introduces evidence, including testimony of a witness, or the complaining witness as a witness gives testimony, and that evidence or testimony relates to the complaining witness' sexual conduct, the defendant may cross-examine the witness who gives the testimony and offer relevant evidence limited specifically to the rebuttal of the evidence introduced by the prosecutor or given by the complaining witness.

(5) Nothing in this subdivision shall be construed to make inadmissible any evidence offered to attack the credibility of the complaining witness as provided in Section 782.

(6) As used in this section, "complaining witness" means the alleged victim of the crime charged, the prosecution of which is subject to this subdivision.

Comment—Law Revision Commission

See the Comment to Section 1102.*

§ 1104. Character trait for care or skill. Except as provided in Sections 1102 and 1103, evidence of a trait of a person's character with respect to care or skill is inadmissible to prove the quality of his conduct on a specified occasion.

Comment—Law Revision Commission

Under Section 1104, character evidence with respect to care or skill is inadmissible to prove that conduct on a specific occasion was either careless or careful, skilled or unskilled, except to the extent permitted by Sections 1102 and 1103.

§ 1105. Habit or custom to prove specific behavior. Any otherwise admissible evidence of habit or custom is admissible to prove conduct on a specified occasion in conformity with the habit or custom.

---

* Those parts of the Comment to § 1102 that refer to § 1103 relate to § 1103 as it stood before it was amended by the addition of subsection (b) [ed.]

§ 1105   CALIFORNIA EVIDENCE CODE

Comment—Law Revision Commission

Section 1105, like Section 1100, declares that certain evidence is admissible. Hence, Section 1105 is technically unnecessary because Section 351 declares that all relevant evidence is admissible. Nonetheless, Section 1105 is desirable to assure that evidence of custom or habit (a regular response to a repeated specific situation) is admissible even where evidence of a person's character (his general disposition or propensity to engage in a certain type of conduct) is inadmissible.

§ 1106. Sexual harassment, sexual assault, or sexual battery cases; opinion or reputation evidence of plaintiff's sexual conduct; inadmissibility; exception; cross-examination. (a) In any civil action alleging conduct which constitutes sexual harassment, sexual assault, or sexual battery, opinion evidence, reputation evidence, and evidence of specific instances of plaintiff's sexual conduct, or any of such evidence, is not admissible by the defendant in order to prove consent by the plaintiff or the absence of injury to the plaintiff, unless the injury alleged by the plaintiff is in the nature of loss of consortium.

(b) Subdivision (a) shall not be applicable to evidence of the plaintiff's sexual conduct with the alleged perpetrator.

(c) If the plaintiff introduces evidence, including testimony of a witness, or the plaintiff as a witness gives testimony, and the evidence or testimony relates to the plaintiff's sexual conduct, the defendant may cross-examine the witness who gives the testimony and offer relevant evidence limited specifically to the rebuttal of the evidence introduced by the plaintiff or given by the plaintiff.

(d) Nothing in this section shall be construed to make inadmissible any evidence offered to attack the credibility of the plaintiff as provided in Section 783.

§ 1107. Intimate partner battering and its effects; expert testimony in criminal actions; sufficiency of foundation; abuse and domestic violence; applicability to Penal Code; impact on decisional law.

(a) In a criminal action, expert testimony is admissible by either the prosecution or the defense regarding intimate partner battering and its effects, including the nature and effect of physical, emotional, or mental abuse on the beliefs, perceptions, or behavior of victims of domestic violence, except when offered against a criminal defendant to prove the occurrence of the act or acts of abuse which form the basis of the criminal charge.

(b) The foundation shall be sufficient for admission of this expert testimony if the proponent of the evidence establishes its relevancy and the proper qualifications of the expert witness. Expert opinion testimony on intimate partner battering and its effects shall not be considered a new scientific technique whose reliability is unproven.

(c) For purposes of this section, "abuse" is defined in Section 6203 of the Family Code, and "domestic violence" is defined in Section 6211 of the Family Code and may include acts defined in Section 242, subdivision (e) of Section 243, Section 262, 273.5, 273.6, 422, or 653m of the Penal Code.

(d) This section is intended as a rule of evidence only and no substantive change affecting the Penal Code is intended.

(e) This section shall be known, and may be cited, as the Expert Witness Testimony on Intimate Partner Battering and Its Effects Section of the Evidence Code.

(f) The changes in this section that become effective on January 1, 2005, are not intended to impact any existing decisional law regarding this section, and that decisional law should apply equally to this section as it refers to "intimate partner battering and its effects" in place of "battered women's syndrome."

§ 1108. Evidence of another sexual offense.

(a) In a criminal action in which the defendant is accused of a sexual offense, evidence of the defendant's commission of another sexual offense or offenses is not made inadmissible by Section 1101, if the evidence is not inadmissible pursuant to Section 352.

(b) In an action in which evidence is to be offered under this section, the people shall disclose the evidence to the defendant, including statements of witnesses or a summary of the substance of any testimony that is expected to be offered, in compliance with the provisions of Section 1054.7 of the Penal Code.

(c) This section shall not be construed to limit the admission or consideration of evidence under any other section of this code.

(d) As used in this section, the following definitions shall apply:

(1) "Sexual offense" means a crime under the law of a state or of the United States that involved any of the following:

(A) Any conduct proscribed by Section 243.4, 261, 261.5, 262, 264.1, 266c, 269, 286, 288, 288a, 288.2, 288.5, or 289, or subdivision (b), (c), or (d) of Section 311.2 or Section 311.3, 311.4, 311.10, 311.11, 314, or 647.6, of the Penal Code.

(B) Any conduct proscribed by Section 220 of the Penal Code, except assault with intent to commit mayhem.

(C) Contact, without consent, between any part of the defendant's body or an object and the genitals or anus of another person.

(D) Contact, without consent, between the genitals or anus of the defendant and any part of another person's body.

(E) Deriving sexual pleasure or gratification from the infliction of death, bodily injury, or physical pain on another person.

(F) An attempt or conspiracy to engage in conduct described in this paragraph.

(2) "Consent" shall have the same meaning as provided in Section 261.6 of the Penal Code, except that it does not include consent which is legally ineffective because of the age, mental disorder, or developmental or physical disability of the victim.

§ 1109. Evidence of defendant's other acts of domestic violence.

(a)(1) Except as provided in subdivision (e) or (f), in a criminal action in which the defendant is accused of an offense involving domestic violence, evidence of the defendant's commission of other domestic violence is not made inadmissible by Section 1101 if the evidence is not inadmissible pursuant to Section 352.

(2) Except as provided in subdivision (e) or (f), in a criminal action in which the defendant is accused of an offense involving abuse of an elder or dependent person, evidence of the defendant's commission of other abuse of an elder or dependent person is not made inadmissible by Section 1101 if the evidence is not inadmissible pursuant to Section 352.

(3) Except as provided in subdivision (e) or (f) and subject to a hearing conducted pursuant to Section 352, which shall include consideration of any corroboration and remoteness in time, in a criminal action in which the defendant is accused of an offense involving child abuse, evidence of the defendant's commission of child abuse is not made inadmissible by Section 1101 if the evidence is not inadmissible pursuant to Section 352. Nothing in this paragraph prohibits or limits the admission of evidence pursuant to subdivision (b) of Section 1101.

(b) In an action in which evidence is to be offered under this section, the people shall disclose the evidence to the defendant, including statements of witnesses or a summary of the substance of any testimony that is expected to be offered, in compliance with the provisions of Section 1054.7 of the Penal Code.

(c) This section shall not be construed to limit or preclude the admission or consideration of evidence under any other statute or case law.

(d) As used in this section:

(1) "Abuse of an elder or dependent person" means physical or sexual abuse, neglect, financial abuse, abandonment, isolation, abduction, or other treatment that results in physical harm, pain, or mental suffering, the deprivation of care by a caregiver, or other deprivation by a custodian or provider of goods or services that are necessary to avoid physical harm or mental suffering.

(2) "Child abuse" means an act proscribed by Section 273d of the Penal Code.

(3) "Domestic violence" has the meaning set forth in Section 13700 of the Penal Code. Subject to a hearing conducted pursuant to Section 352, which shall include consideration of any corroboration and remoteness in time, "domestic violence" has the further meaning as set forth in Section 6211 of the Family Code, if the act occurred no more than five years before the charged offense.

(e) Evidence of acts occurring more than 10 years before the charged offense is inadmissible under this section, unless the court determines that the admission of this evidence is in the interest of justice.

(f) Evidence of the findings and determinations of administrative agencies regulating the conduct of health facilities licensed under Section 1250 of the Health and Safety Code is inadmissible under this section.

Chapter 2

MEDIATION

§ 1115. Definitions. For purposes of this chapter:

(a) "Mediation" means a process in which a neutral person or persons facilitate communication between the disputants to assist them in reaching a mutually acceptable agreement.

(b) "Mediator" means a neutral person who conducts a mediation. "Mediator" includes any person designated by a mediator either to assist in the mediation or to communicate with the participants in preparation for a mediation.

(c) "Mediation consultation" means a communication between a person and a mediator for the purpose of initiating, considering, or reconvening a mediation or retaining the mediator.

§ 1116. Limits on effects of chapter. (a) Nothing in this chapter expands or limits a court's authority to order participation in a dispute resolution proceeding. Nothing in this chapter authorizes or affects the enforceability of a contract clause in which parties agree to the use of mediation.

(b) Nothing in this chapter makes admissible evidence that is inadmissible under Section 1152 or any other statute.

§ 1117. Application of chapter. (a) Except as provided in subdivision (b), this chapter applies to a mediation as defined in Section 1115.

(b) This chapter does not apply to either of the following:

(1) A proceeding under Part 1 (commencing with Section 1800) of Division 5 of the Family Code or Chapter 11 (commencing with Section 3160) of Part 2 of Division 8 of the Family Code.

(2) A settlement conference pursuant to Rule 3.1380 of the California Rules of Court.

§ 1118. Oral agreement. An oral agreement "in accordance with Section 1118" means an oral agreement that satisfies all of the following conditions:

(a) The oral agreement is recorded by a court reporter or reliable means of audio recording.

(b) The terms of the oral agreement are recited on the record in the presence of the parties and the mediator, and the parties express on the record that they agree to the terms recited.

(c) The parties to the oral agreement expressly state on the record that the agreement is enforceable or binding, or words to that effect.

(d) The recording is reduced to writing and the writing is signed by the parties within 72 hours after it is recorded.

§ 1119. Admissibility of evidence; subject to being compelled; confidentiality. Except as otherwise provided in this chapter:

(a) No evidence of anything said or any admission made for the purpose of, in the course of, or pursuant to, a mediation or a mediation consultation is admissible or subject to discovery, and disclosure of the evidence shall not be compelled, in any arbitration, administrative adjudication, civil action, or other noncriminal proceeding in which, pursuant to law, testimony can be compelled to be given.

(b) No writing, as defined in Section 250, that is prepared for the purpose of, in the course of, or pursuant to, a mediation or a mediation consultation, is admissible or subject to discovery, and disclosure of the writing shall not be compelled, in any arbitration, administrative adjudication, civil action, or other noncriminal proceeding in which, pursuant to law, testimony can be compelled to be given.

(c) All communications, negotiations, or settlement discussions by and between participants in the course of a mediation or a mediation consultation shall remain confidential.

§ 1120. Evidence used in mediation; effect on admissibility. (a) Evidence otherwise admissible or subject to discovery outside of a mediation or a mediation consultation shall not be or become inadmissible or protected from disclosure solely by reason of its introduction or use in a mediation or a mediation consultation.

(b) This chapter does not limit any of the following:

(1) The admissibility of an agreement to mediate a dispute.

(2) The effect of an agreement not to take a default or an agreement to extend the time within which to act or refrain from acting in a pending civil action.

(3) Disclosure of the mere fact that a mediator has served, is serving, will serve, or was contacted about serving as a mediator in a dispute.

§ 1121. Consideration of mediator's report in other proceedings. Neither a mediator nor anyone else may submit to a court or other adjudicative body, and a court or other adjudicative body may not consider, any report, assessment, evaluation, recommendation, or finding of any kind by the mediator concerning a mediation conducted by the mediator, other than a report that is mandated by court rule or other law and that states only whether an agreement was reached, unless all parties to the mediation expressly agree otherwise in writing, or orally in accordance with Section 1118.

§ 1122. Conditions under which communication made in mediation proceeding becomes admissible in other proceedings. (a) A communication or a writing, as defined in Section 250, that is made or prepared for the purpose of, or in the course of, or pursuant to, a mediation or a mediation consultation, is not made inadmissible, or protected from disclosure, by provisions of this chapter if either of the following conditions is satisfied:

(1) All persons who conduct or otherwise participate in the mediation expressly agree in writing, or orally in accordance with Section 1118, to disclosure of the communication, document, or writing.

(2) The communication, document, or writing was prepared by or on behalf of fewer than all of the mediation participants, those participants expressly agree in writing, or orally in accordance with Section 1118, to its disclosure, and the communication, document, or writing does not disclose anything said or done or any admission made in the course of the mediation.

(b) For purposes of subdivision (a), if the neutral person who conducts a mediation expressly agrees to disclosure, that agreement also binds any other person described in subdivision (b) of Section 1115.

§ 1123. Conditions governing admissibility of written settlement agreement in mediation. A written settlement agreement prepared in the course of, or pursuant to, a mediation, is not made inadmissible, or protected from disclosure, by provisions of this chapter if the agreement is signed by the settling parties and any of the following conditions are satisfied:

(a) The agreement provides that it is admissible or subject to disclosure, or words to that effect.

(b) The agreement provides that it is enforceable or binding or words to that effect.

(c) All parties to the agreement expressly agree in writing, or orally in accordance with Section 1118, to its disclosure.

(d) The agreement is used to show fraud, duress, or illegality that is relevant to an issue in dispute.

§ 1124. Conditions governing admissibility of oral agreement in mediation. An oral agreement made in the course of, or pursuant to, a mediation is not made inadmissible, or protected from disclosure, by the provisions of this chapter if any of the following conditions are satisfied:

(a) The agreement is in accordance with Section 1118.

(b) The agreement is in accordance with subdivision (a), (b), and (d) of Section 1118, and all parties to the agreement expressly agree, in writing or orally in accordance with Section 1118, to disclosure of the agreement.

(c) The agreement is in accordance with subdivisions (a), (b), and (d) of Section 1118, and the agreement is used to show fraud, duress, or illegality that is relevant to an issue in dispute.

§ 1125. Confidentiality; end of mediation. (a) For purposes of confidentiality under this chapter, a mediation ends when any one of the following conditions is satisfied:

(1) The parties execute a written settlement agreement that fully resolves the dispute.

(2) An oral agreement that fully resolves the dispute is reached in accordance with Section 1118.

(3) The mediator provides the mediation participants with a writing signed by the mediator that states the mediation is terminated, or words to that effect, which shall be consistent with Section 1121.

(4) A party provides the mediator and the other mediation participants with a writing stating that the mediation is terminated, or words to that effect, which shall be consistent with Section 1121. In a mediation involving more than two parties, the mediation may continue as to the remaining parties or be terminated in accordance with this section.

(5) For 10 calendar days, there is no communication between the mediator and any of the parties to the mediation relating to the dispute. The mediator and the parties may shorten or extend this time by agreement.

(6) For purposes of confidentiality under this chapter, if a mediation partially resolves a dispute, mediation ends when either of the following conditions is satisfied:

(1) The parties execute a written settlement agreement that partially resolves the dispute.

(2) An oral agreement that partially resolves the dispute is reached in accordance with Section 1118.

(c) This section does not preclude a party from ending a mediation without reaching an agreement. This section does not otherwise affect the extent to which a party may terminate a mediation.

§ 1126. Admissibility and confidentiality of mediation statements after mediation ends. Anything said, any admission made, or any writing that is inadmissible, protected from disclosure, and confidential under this chapter before a mediation ends, shall remain inadmissible protected from disclosure, and confidential to the same extent after the mediation ends.

§ 1127. Attorney's fees; person who unsuccessfully seeks to compel mediation statements. If a person subpoenas or otherwise seeks to compel a mediator to testify or produce a writing, as defined in Section 250, and the court or other adjudicative body determines that the testimony or writing is inadmissible under this chapter, or protected from disclosure under this chapter, the court or adjudicative body making the determination shall award reasonable attorney's fees and costs to the mediator against the person seeking the testimony or writing.

§ 1128. Reference to mediation in subsequent trial. Any reference to a mediation during any subsequent trial is an irregularity in the proceedings of the trial for the purposes of Section 657 of the Code of Civil Procedure. Any reference to a mediation during any other subsequent noncriminal proceeding is grounds for vacating or modifying the decision in that proceeding, in whole or in part, and granting a new or further hearing on all or part of the issues, if the reference materially affected the substantial rights of the party requesting relief.

Chapter 3

OTHER EVIDENCE AFFECTED OR EXCLUDED BY EXTRINSIC POLICIES

§ 1150. Evidence to test a verdict. (a) Upon an inquiry as to the validity of a verdict, any otherwise admissible evidence may be received as to statements made, or conduct, conditions, or events occurring, either within or without the jury room, of such a character as is likely to have influenced the verdict improperly. No evidence is admissible to show the effect of such statement, conduct, condition, or event upon a juror either in influencing him to assent to or dissent from the verdict or concerning the mental processes by which it was determined.

(b) Nothing in this code affects the law relating to the competence of a juror to give evidence to impeach or support a verdict.

§ 1151. Subsequent remedial conduct. When, after the occurrence of an event, remedial or precautionary measures are taken, which, if taken previously, would have tended to make the event less likely to occur, evidence of such subsequent measures is inadmissible to prove negligence or culpable conduct in connection with the event.

Comment—Law Revision Commission

The admission of evidence of subsequent repairs to prove negligence would substantially discourage persons from making repairs after the occurrence of an accident.

Section 1151 does not prevent the use of evidence of subsequent remedial conduct for the purpose of impeachment in appropriate cases.

§ 1152. Offer to compromise and the like. (a) Evidence that a person has, in compromise or from humanitarian motives, furnished or offered or promised to furnish money or any other thing, act, or service to another who has sustained or will sustain or claims that he has sustained or will sustain loss or damage, as well as any conduct or statements made in negotiation thereof, is inadmissible to prove his or her liability for the loss or damage or any part of it.

(b) In the event that evidence of an offer to compromise is admitted in an action for breach of the covenant of good faith and fair dealing or violation of subdivision (h) of Section 790.03 of the Insurance Code, then at the request of the party against whom the evidence is admitted, or at the request of the party who made the offer to compromise that was admitted, evidence relating to any other offer or counteroffer to compromise the same or substantially the same claimed loss or damage shall also be admissible for the same purpose as the initial evidence regarding settlement. Other than as may be admitted in an action for breach of the covenant of good faith and fair dealing or violation of subdivision (h) of Section 790.03 of the Insurance Code, evidence of settlement offers shall not be admitted in a motion for a new trial, in any proceeding involving an additur or remittitur, or on appeal.

(c) This section does not affect the admissibility of evidence of any of the following:

(1) Partial satisfaction of an asserted claim or demand without questioning its validity when such evidence is offered to prove the validity of the claim.

(2) A debtor's payment or promise to pay all or a part of his or her preexisting debt when such evidence is offered to prove the creation of a new duty on his or her part or a revival of his or her preexisting duty.

Comment—Law Revision Commission

Section 1152, like Section 2078 of the Code of Civil Procedure which it supersedes, declares that compromise offers are inadmissible to prove liability. Because of the particular wording of Section 2078, an offer of compromise probably may not be considered as an admission even though admitted without objection. See Tentative Recommendation and a Study Relating to the Uniform Rules of Evidence (Article VI. Extrinsic Policies Affecting Admissibility), 6 Cal.Law Revision Comm'n, Rep., Rec. & Studies 601, 675–676 (1964). Under Section 1152, however, nothing prohibits the consideration of an offer of settlement on the issue of liability if the evidence is received without objection. This modest change in the law is desirable. An offer of compromise, like other incompetent evidence, should be considered to the extent that it is relevant when it is presented to the trier of fact without objection.

The words "as well as any conduct or statements made in negotiation thereof" make it clear that statements made by parties during negotiations for the settlement of a claim may not be used as admissions in later litigation. This language will change the existing law under which certain statements made during settlement negotiations may be used as admissions.

§ 1153. Offer to plead guilty or withdraw plea of guilty by criminal defendant.
Evidence of a plea of guilty, later withdrawn, or of an offer to plead guilty to the crime charged or to any other crime, made by the defendant in a criminal action is inadmissible in any action or in any proceeding of any nature, including proceedings before agencies, commissions, boards, and tribunals.

§ 1153.5. Offer for civil resolution of crimes against property.
Evidence of an offer for civil resolution of a criminal matter pursuant to the provisions of Section 33 of the Code of Civil Procedure, or admissions made in the course of or negotiations for the offer shall not be admissible in any action.

§ 1154. Offer to discount a claim.
Evidence that a person has accepted or offered or promised to accept a sum of money or any other thing, act, or service in satisfaction of a claim, as well as any conduct or statements made in negotiation thereof, is inadmissible to prove the invalidity of the claim or any part of it.

§ 1155. Liability insurance.
Evidence that a person was, at the time a harm was suffered by another, insured wholly or partially against loss arising from liability for that harm is inadmissible to prove negligence or other wrongdoing.

§ 1156. Records of medical study of in-hospital staff committee.
(a) In-hospital medical or medical-dental staff committees of a licensed hospital may engage in research and medical or dental study for the purpose of reducing morbidity or mortality, and may make findings and recommendations relating to such purpose. Except as provided in subdivision (b), the written records of interviews, reports, statements, or

§ 1156   CALIFORNIA EVIDENCE CODE

memoranda of such in-hospital medical or medical-dental staff committees relating to such medical or dental studies are subject to Title 4 (commencing with Section 2016.010) of Part 4 of the Code of Civil Procedure (relating to discovery proceedings) but, subject to subdivisions (c) and (d), shall not be admitted as evidence in any action or before any administrative body, agency, or person.

(b) The disclosure, with or without the consent of the patient, of information concerning him to such in-hospital medical or medical-dental staff committee does not make unprivileged any information that would otherwise be privileged under Section 994 or 1014; but, notwithstanding Sections 994 and 1014, such information is subject to discovery under subdivision (a) except that the identity of any patient may not be discovered under subdivision (a) unless the patient consents to such disclosure.

(c) This section does not affect the admissibility in evidence of the original medical or dental records of any patient.

(d) This section does not exclude evidence which is relevant evidence in a criminal action.

§ 1156.1. Records of medical or psychiatric studies of quality assurance committees. (a) A committee established in compliance with Sections 4070 and 5624 of the Welfare and Institutions Code may engage in research and medical or psychiatric study for the purpose of reducing morbidity or mortality, and may make findings and recommendations to the county and state relating to such purpose. Except as provided in subdivision (b), the written records of interviews, reports, statements, or memoranda of such committees relating to such medical or psychiatric studies are subject to Title 4 (commencing with Section 2016.010) of Part 4 of the Code of Civil Procedure but, subject to subdivisions (c) and (d), shall not be admitted as evidence in any action or before any administrative body, agency, or person.

(b) The disclosure, with or without the consent of the patient, of information concerning him or her to such committee does not make unprivileged any information that would otherwise be privileged under Section 994 or 1014. However, notwithstanding Sections 994 and 1014, such information is subject to discovery under subdivision (a) except that the identity of any patient may not be discovered under subdivision (a) unless the patient consents to such disclosure.

(c) This section does not affect the admissibility in evidence of the original medical or psychiatric records of any patient.

(d) This section does not exclude evidence which is relevant evidence in a criminal action.

§ 1157. Proceedings and records of medical, medical-dental, podiatric, registered dietitian, psychological, marriage and family therapist, licensed clinical social worker, or veterinary staffs, hospital review committees; local medical, dental, dental hygienist, podiatric, dietetic, veterinary, chiropractic society, or state or local psychological review committees. (a) Neither the proceedings nor the records of organized committees of medical, medical-dental, podiatric, registered dietitian, psychological, marriage and family therapist, licensed clinical social worker, or veterinary staffs in hospitals, or of a peer review body, as defined in Section 805 of the Business and Professions Code, having the responsibility of evaluation and improvement of the quality of care rendered in the hospital, or for that peer review body, or medical or dental review or dental hygienist review or chiropractic review or podiatric review or registered dietitian review or veterinary review or acupuncturist review committees of local medical, dental, dental hygienist, podiatric, dietetic, veterinary, acupuncture, or chiropractic societies, marriage and family therapist, licensed clinical social worker, or psychological review committees of state or local marriage and family therapist, state or local licensed clinical social worker, or state or local psychological associations or societies having the responsibility of evaluation and improvement of the quality of care, shall be subject to discovery.

(b) Except as hereinafter provided, no person in attendance at a meeting of any of those committees shall be required to testify as to what transpired at that meeting.

(c) The prohibition relating to discovery or testimony does not apply to the statements made by any person in attendance at a meeting of any of those committees who is a party to an action or proceeding the subject matter of which was reviewed at that meeting, or to any person requesting hospital staff privileges, or in any action against an insurance carrier alleging bad faith by the carrier in refusing to accept a settlement offer within the policy limits.

(d) The prohibitions in this section do not apply to medical, dental, dental hygienist, podiatric, dietetic, psychological, marriage and family therapist, licensed clinical social worker, veterinary, acupuncture, or chiropractic society committees that exceed 10 percent of the membership of the society, nor to any of those committees if any person serves upon the committee when his or her own conduct or practice is being reviewed.

(e) The amendments made to this section by Chapter 1081 of the Statutes of 1983, or at the 1985 portion of the 1985–86 Regular Session of the Legislature, or at the 1990 portion of the 1989–90 Regular Session of the Legislature, or at the 2000 portion of the 1999–2000 Regular Session of the Legislature, do not exclude the discovery or use of relevant evidence in a criminal action.

§ 1157.5. **Organized committee of nonprofit medical care foundation or professional standards review organization; proceedings and records.** Except in actions involving a claim of a provider of health care services for payment for such services, the prohibition relating to discovery or testimony provided by Section 1157 shall be applicable to the proceedings or records of an organized committee of any nonprofit medical care foundation or professional standards review organization which is organized in a manner which makes available professional competence to review health care services with respect to medical necessity, quality of care, or economic justification of charges or level of care.

§ 1157.6. **Proceedings and records of quality assurance committees for county health facilities.** Neither the proceedings nor the records of a committee established in compliance with Sections 4070 and 5624 of the Welfare and Institutions Code having the responsibility of evaluation and improvement of the quality of mental health care rendered in county operated and contracted mental health facilities shall be subject to discovery. Except as provided in this section, no person in attendance at a meeting of any such committee shall be required to testify as to what transpired thereat. The prohibition relating to discovery or testimony shall not apply to the statements made by any person in attendance at such a meeting who is a party to an action or proceeding the subject matter of which was reviewed at such meeting, or to any person requesting facility staff privileges.

§ 1157.7. **Application of Section 1157 discovery or testimony prohibitions; application of public records and meetings provisions.** The prohibition relating to discovery or testimony provided in Section 1157 shall be applicable to proceedings and records of any committee established by a local governmental agency to monitor, evaluate, and report on the necessity, quality, and level of specialty health services, including, but not limited to, trauma care services, provided by a general acute care hospital which has been designated or recognized by that governmental agency as qualified to render specialty health care services. The provisions of Chapter 3.5 (commencing with Section 6250) of Division 7 of Title 1 of the Government Code and Chapter 9 (commencing with Section 54950) of Division 2 of Title 5 of the Government Code shall not be applicable to the committee records and proceedings.

§ 1158. **Presentation of authorization for inspection and copying of patient's records; failure to comply; costs.** Whenever, prior to the filing of any action or the appearance of a defendant in an action, an attorney at law or his or her representative presents a written authorization therefor signed by an adult patient, by the guardian or conservator of his or her person or estate, or, in the case of a minor, by a parent or guardian of the minor, or by the personal representative or an heir of a deceased patient, or a copy thereof, a physician and surgeon, dentist, registered nurse, dispensing optician, registered physical therapist, podiatrist, licensed psychologist, osteopathic physician and surgeon, chiropractor, clinical laboratory bioanalyst, clinical laboratory technologist, or pharmacist or pharmacy, duly licensed as such under the laws of the state, or a licensed hospital, shall make all of the patient's records under his, hers or its custody or control available for inspection and copying by the attorney at law or his, or her, representative, promptly upon the presentation of the written authorization.

No copying may be performed by any medical provider or employer enumerated above, or by an agent thereof, when the requesting attorney has employed a professional photocopier or anyone identified in Section 22451 of the Business and Professions Code as his or her representative to obtain or review the records on his or her behalf. The presentation of the authorization by the agent on behalf of the attorney shall be sufficient proof that the agent is the attorney's representative.

Failure to make the records available, during business hours, within five days after the presentation of the written authorization, may subject the person or entity having custody or control of the records to liability for all reasonable expenses, including attorney's fees, incurred in any proceeding to enforce this section.

All reasonable costs incurred by any person or entity enumerated above in making patient records available pursuant to this section may be charged against the person whose written authorization required the availability of the records.

"Reasonable cost," as used in this section, shall include, but not be limited to, the following specific costs: ten cents ($0.10) per page for standard reproduction of documents of a size 8½ by 14 inches or less; twenty cents ($0.20) per page for copying of documents from microfilm; actual costs for the reproduction of oversize documents or the reproduction of documents requiring special processing which are made in response to an authorization; reasonable clerical costs incurred in locating and making the records available to be billed at the maximum rate of sixteen dollars ($16) per hour per person, computed on the basis of four dollars ($4) per quarter hour or fraction thereof; actual postage charges; and actual costs, if any, charged to the witness by a third person for the retrieval and return of records held by that third person.

Where the records are delivered to the attorney or the attorney's representative for inspection or photocopying at the record custodian's place of business, the only fee for complying with the authorization shall not exceed fifteen dollars ($15), plus actual costs, if any, charged to the record custodian by a third person for retrieval and return of records held offsite by the third person.

§ 1159. Live animal experimentation evidence. (a) No evidence pertaining to live animal experimentation, including, but not limited to, injury, impact, or crash experimentation, shall be admissible in any product liability action involving a motor vehicle or vehicles.

(b) This section shall apply to cases for which a trial has not actually commenced, as described in paragraph (6) of subdivision (a) of Section 581 of the Code of Civil Procedure, on January 1, 1993.

§ 1160. Evidence of expressions of sympathy; statements of fault. (a) The portion of statements, writings, or benevolent gestures expressing sympathy or a general sense of benevolence relating to the pain, suffering, or death of a person involved in an accident and made to that person or to the family of that person shall be inadmissible as evidence of an admission of liability in a civil action. A statement of fault, however, which is part of, or in addition to, any of the above shall not be inadmissible pursuant to this section.

(b) For purposes of this section:

(1) "Accident" means an occurrence resulting in injury or death to one or more persons which is not the result of willful action by a party.

(2) "Benevolent gestures" means actions which convey a sense of compassion or commiseration emanating from humane impulses.

(3) "Family" means the spouse, parent, grandparent, stepmother, stepfather, child, grandchild, brother, sister, half brother, half sister, adopted children of parent, or spouse's parents of an injured party.

Division 10

HEARSAY EVIDENCE

Comment—Law Revision Commission

Division 10 contains the hearsay rule and the most commonly used exceptions to the rule. Other exceptions may be found in other statutes scattered throughout the codes. Under the Evidence Code, the hearsay objection is met if the evidence offered falls within any of the exceptions to the hearsay rule. But the fact that the hearsay objection is overcome does not necessarily make the evidence admissible. All other exclusionary rules apply and may require exclusion of the evidence.

Chapter 1

GENERAL PROVISIONS

§ 1200. The hearsay rule. (a) "Hearsay evidence" is evidence of a statement that was made other than by a witness while testifying at the hearing and that is offered to prove the truth of the matter stated.

(b) Except as provided by law, hearsay evidence is inadmissible.

(c) This section shall be known and may be cited as the hearsay rule.

Comment—Senate Committee on Judiciary

Section 1200 states the hearsay rule. It defines hearsay evidence and provides that such evidence is inadmissible unless it meets the conditions of an exception established by law. Chapter 2 (commencing with Section 1220) of this division contains a series of exceptions to the hearsay rule. Other exceptions may be found in other statutes or in decisional law. But the fact that certain evidence meets the requirements of an exception to the hearsay rule does not necessarily make such evidence admissible. The exception merely provides that such evidence is not inadmissible under the hearsay rule. If there is some other rule of law—such as privilege or the best evidence rule—that makes the evidence inadmissible, the court is not authorized to admit the evidence merely because it falls within an exception to the hearsay rule.

"Hearsay evidence" is defined in Section 1200 as "evidence of a statement that was made other than by a witness while testifying at the hearing and that is offered to prove the truth of the matter stated." Under this definition, as under existing case law, a statement that is offered for some purpose other than to prove the fact stated therein is not hearsay.

The word "statement" used in the definition of "hearsay evidence" is defined in Section 225 as "oral or written verbal expression" or "non-verbal conduct ... intended ... as a substitute for oral or written verbal expression." Hence, evidence of a person's conduct out of court is not inadmissible under the hearsay rule expressed in Section 1200 unless that conduct is clearly assertive in character. Nonassertive conduct is not hearsay.

Under the Evidence Code, nonassertive conduct is not regarded as hearsay for two reasons. *First,* one of the principal reasons for the hearsay rule—to exclude declarations where the veracity of the declarant cannot be tested by cross-examination—does not apply because such conduct, being nonassertive, does not involve the veracity of the declarant. *Second,* there is frequently a guarantee of the trustworthiness of the inference to be drawn from such nonassertive conduct because the actor has based his actions on the correctness of his belief, i.e., his actions speak louder than words.

Of course, if the probative value of evidence of nonassertive conduct is outweighed by the probability that such evidence will be unduly prejudicial, confuse the issues, mislead the jury, or consume too much time, the judge may exclude the evidence under Section 352.

Under Section 1200, exceptions to the hearsay rule may be found either in statutes or in decisional law. Under existing law, too, the courts have recognized exceptions to the exclusionary rule in addition to those exceptions expressed in the statutes.

§ 1201. Multiple hearsay. A statement within the scope of an exception to the hearsay rule is not inadmissible on the ground that the evidence of such statement is hearsay evidence if such hearsay evidence consists of one or more statements each of which meets the requirements of an exception to the hearsay rule.

Comment—Law Revision Commission

Section 1201 makes it possible to use admissible hearsay to prove another statement that is also admissible hearsay. For example, under Section 1201, an official reporter's transcript of the testimony at a previous trial may be used to prove the testimony previously given (Evidence Code § 1280); the former testimony may be used as evidence (Evidence Code § 1291) to prove that a party made a statement; and the party's statement is admissible against him as an admission (Evidence Code § 1220). Thus, under Section 1201, the evidence of the admission contained in the transcript is admissible because each of the hearsay statements involved is within an exception to the hearsay rule.

§ 1202. Credibility of hearsay declarant. Evidence of a statement or other conduct by a declarant that is inconsistent with a statement by such declarant received in evidence as hearsay evidence is not inadmissible for the purpose of attacking the credibility of the declarant though he is not given and has not had an opportunity to explain or to deny such inconsistent statement or other conduct. Any other evidence offered to attack or support the credibility of the declarant is admissible if it would have been admissible had the declarant been a witness at the hearing. For the purposes of this section, the deponent of a deposition taken in the action in which it is offered shall be deemed to be a hearsay declarant.

Comment—Law Revision Commission

Section 1202 deals with the impeachment of a declarant whose hearsay statement is in evidence as distinguished from the impeachment of a witness who has testified. It clarifies two points. *First,* evidence to impeach a hearsay declarant is not to be excluded on the ground that it is collateral. *Second,* the rule applying to the impeachment of a witness—that a witness may be impeached by an inconsistent statement only if he is provided with an opportunity to explain or deny it—does not apply to a hearsay declarant.

Of course, the trial judge may curb efforts to impeach hearsay declarants if he determines that the inquiry is becoming too remote from the issues that are actually at stake in the litigation. Evidence Code § 352.

Section 1235 provides that evidence of inconsistent statements made by a trial witness may be admitted to prove the truth of the matter stated. No similar exception to the hearsay rule is applicable to a hearsay declarant's inconsistent statements that are admitted under Section 1202. Hence, the hearsay rule prohibits any such statement from being used to prove the truth of the matter stated.

§ 1203. Cross-examination of hearsay declarant.
(a) The declarant of a statement that is admitted as hearsay evidence may be called and examined by any adverse party as if under cross-examination concerning the statement.

(b) This section is not applicable if the declarant is (1) a party, (2) a person identified with a party within the meaning of subdivision (d) of Section 776, or (3) a witness who has testified in the action concerning the subject matter of the statement.

(c) This section is not applicable if the statement is one described in Article 1 (commencing with Section 1220), Article 3 (commencing with Section 1235), or Article 10 (commencing with Section 1300) of Chapter 2 of this division.

(d) A statement that is otherwise admissible as hearsay evidence is not made inadmissible by this section because the declarant who made the statement is unavailable for examination pursuant to this section.

§ 1204. Hearsay statement offered against criminal defendant.
A statement that is otherwise admissible as hearsay evidence is inadmissible against the defendant in a criminal action if the statement was made, either by the defendant or by another, under such circumstances that it is inadmissible against the defendant under the Constitution of the United States or the State of California.

Comment—Assembly Committee on Judiciary

Section 1204 is a statutory recognition that hearsay evidence that fits within an exception to the hearsay rule may nonetheless be inadmissible under the Constitution of the United States or the Constitution of California. Thus, Section 1220, which creates an exception for the statements of a party, is subject to the constitutional rule excluding evidence of involuntary confessions against a criminal defendant.

Insofar as the Constitution of the United States is concerned, Section 1204 refers only to those rules required to be observed in state proceedings. It is not intended to make applicable in proceedings in California courts those rules the United States Constitution requires to be observed only in federal proceedings.

§ 1205. No implied repeal. Nothing in this division shall be construed to repeal by implication any other statute relating to hearsay evidence.

Chapter 2

EXCEPTIONS TO THE HEARSAY RULE

Article 1. Confessions and Admissions

§ 1220. Admission of party. Evidence of a statement is not made inadmissible by the hearsay rule when offered against the declarant in an action to which he is a party in either his individual or representative capacity, regardless of whether the statement was made in his individual or representative capacity.

Comment—Law Revision Commission

The rationale underlying this exception is that the party cannot object to the lack of the right to cross-examine the declarant since the party himself made the statement. Moreover, the party can cross-examine the witness who testifies to the party's statement and can explain or deny the purported admission. The statement need not be one which would be admissible if made at the hearing.

In a criminal action, a defendant's statement is not admissible under this section unless it was made voluntarily. Evidence Code § 1204.

§ 1221. Adoptive admission. Evidence of a statement offered against a party is not made inadmissible by the hearsay rule if the statement is one of which the party, with knowledge of the content thereof, has by words or other conduct manifested his adoption or his belief in its truth.

§ 1222. Authorized admission. Evidence of a statement offered against a party is not made inadmissible by the hearsay rule if:

(a) The statement was made by a person authorized by the party to make a statement or statements for him concerning the subject matter of the statement; and

(b) The evidence is offered either after admission of evidence sufficient to sustain a finding of such authority or, in the court's discretion as to the order of proof, subject to the admission of such evidence.

Comment—Law Revision Commission

Section 1222 provides a hearsay exception for authorized admissions. Under this exception, if a party authorized an agent to make statements on his behalf, such statements may be introduced against the party under the same conditions as if they had been made by the party himself. The authority of the declarant to make the statement need not be express; it may be implied. It is to be determined in each case under the substantive law of agency. See Tentative Recommendation and a Study Relating to the Uniform Rules of Evidence (Article VIII. Hearsay Evidence), 6 Cal.Law Revision Comm'n, Rep., Rec. & Studies Appendix at 484–490 (1964).

§ 1223. Admission of co-conspirator. Evidence of a statement offered against a party is not made inadmissible by the hearsay rule if:

(a) The statement was made by the declarant while participating in a conspiracy to commit a crime or civil wrong and in furtherance of the objective of that conspiracy;

(b) The statement was made prior to or during the time that the party was participating in that conspiracy; and

(c) The evidence is offered either after admission of evidence sufficient to sustain a finding of the facts specified in subdivisions (a) and (b) or, in the court's discretion as to the order of proof, subject to the admission of such evidence.

Comment—Law Revision Commission

Section 1223 is a specific example of a kind of authorized admission that is admissible under Section 1222. The statement is admitted because it is an act of the conspiracy for which the party, as a co-conspirator, is legally responsible.

§ 1224. Statement of declarant whose liability or breach of duty is in issue. When the liability, obligation, or duty of a party to a civil action is based in whole or in part upon the liability, obligation, or duty of the declarant, or when the claim or right asserted by a party to a civil action is barred or diminished by a breach of duty by the declarant, evidence of a statement made by the declarant is as admissible against the party as it would be if offered against the declarant in an action involving that liability, obligation, duty, or breach of duty.

Comment—Law Revision Commission

Section 1224 limits this hearsay exception to civil actions. Much of the evidence within this exception is also covered by Section 1230, which makes declarations against interest admissible. However, to be admissible under Section 1230, the statement must have been against the declarant's interest when made; this requirement is not stated in Section 1224.

See Tentative Recommendation and a Study Relating to the Uniform Rules of Evidence (Article VIII. Hearsay Evidence), 6 Cal.Law Revision Comm'n, Rep., Rec. & Studies Appendix at 491–496 (1964).

§ 1225. Statement of declarant whose right or title is in issue.

When a right, title, or interest in any property or claim asserted by a party to a civil action requires a determination that a right, title, or interest exists or existed in the declarant, evidence of a statement made by the declarant during the time the party now claims the declarant was the holder of the right, title, or interest is as admissible against the party as it would be if offered against the declarant in an action involving that right, title, or interest.

Comment—Law Revision Commission

It should be noted that "statements made *before title accrued in the declarant* will not be receivable. On the other hand, the time of divestiture, *after* which no statements could be treated as admissions, is the time when the party against whom they are offered has by his own hypothesis acquired the title; thus, in a suit, for example, between A's heir and A's grantee, A's statements at any time before his death are receivable against the heir; but only his statements before the grant are receivable against the grantee." 4 Wigmore, Evidence § 1082 at 153 (3d ed.1940).

Despite the limitations of Section 1225, some statements of a grantor made after divestiture of title will be admissible; but another theory of admissibility must be found. For example, later statements of his state of mind may be admissible on the issue of his intent. Evidence Code §§ 1250 and 1251. Where it is claimed that a conveyance was in fraud of creditors, the later statements of the grantor may be admissible not as hearsay but as evidence of the fraud itself or as declarations of a co-conspirator in the fraud.

§ 1226. Statement of minor child in parent's action for child's injury.

Evidence of a statement by a minor child is not made inadmissible by the hearsay rule if offered against the plaintiff in an action brought under Section 376 of the Code of Civil Procedure for injury to such minor child.

§ 1227. Statement of declarant in action for his wrongful death.

Evidence of a statement by the deceased is not made inadmissible by the hearsay rule if offered against the plaintiff in an action for wrongful death brought under Section 377 of the Code of Civil Procedure.

Comment—Law Revision Commission

Under Section 1224, the admissions of a decedent are admissible to establish the liability of his executor. Similarly, when the executor brings an action for the decedent's death under Code of Civil Procedure Section 377, the defendant should be permitted to introduce the admissions of the decedent. Without Section 1227, in an action between two executors arising out of an accident which was fatal to both participants, the plaintiff executor would be able to introduce admissions of the defendant's decedent, but the defending executor would be unable to introduce admissions of the plaintiff's decedent.

§ 1228. **Admissibility of certain out-of-court statements of minors under the age of 12; establishing elements of certain sexually oriented crimes.** Notwithstanding any other provision of law, for the purpose of establishing the elements of the crime in order to admit as evidence the confession of a person accused of violating Section 261, 264.1, 285, 286, 288, 288a, 289, or 647a of the Penal Code, a court, in its discretion, may determine that a statement of the complaining witness is not made inadmissible by the hearsay rule if it finds all of the following:

(a) The statement was made by a minor child under the age of 12, and the contents of the statement were included in a written report of a law enforcement official or an employee of a county welfare department.

(b) The statement describes the minor child as a victim of sexual abuse.

(c) The statement was made prior to the defendant's confession. The court shall view with caution the testimony of a person recounting hearsay where there is evidence of personal bias or prejudice.

(d) There are no circumstances, such as significant inconsistencies between the confession and the statement concerning material facts establishing any element of the crime or the identification of the defendant, that would render the statement unreliable.

(e) The minor child is found to be unavailable pursuant to paragraph (2) or (3) of subdivision (a) of Section 240 or refuses to testify.

(f) The confession was memorialized in a trustworthy fashion by a law enforcement official.

If the prosecution intends to offer a statement of the complaining witness pursuant to this section, the prosecution shall serve a written notice upon the defendant at least 10 days prior to the hearing or trial at which the prosecution intends to offer the statement.

If the statement is offered during trial, the court's determination shall be made out of the presence of the jury. If the statement is found to be admissible pursuant to this section, it shall be admitted out of the presence of the jury and solely for the purpose of determining the admissibility of the confession of the defendant.

§ 1228.1. **No use of parent's acceptance of child welfare services case plan as evidence against parent; use of parent's failure to cooperate as evidence against parent.** (a) Except as provided in subdivision (b), neither the signature of any parent or legal guardian on a child welfare services case plan nor the acceptance of any services prescribed in the child welfare services case plan by any parent or legal guardian shall constitute an admission of guilt or be used as evidence against the parent or legal guardian in a court of law.

(b) A parent's or guardian's failure to cooperate, except for good cause, in the provision of services specified in the child welfare services

§ 1228.1   CALIFORNIA EVIDENCE CODE

case plan may be used as evidence, if relevant, in any hearing held pursuant to Section 366.21, 366.22, or 388 of the Welfare and Institutions Code and at any jurisdictional or dispositional hearing held on a petition filed pursuant to Section 300, 342, or 387 of the Welfare and Institutions Code.

Article 2.   Declarations Against Interest

§ 1230.   Declarations against interest. Evidence of a statement by a declarant having sufficient knowledge of the subject is not made inadmissible by the hearsay rule if the declarant is unavailable as a witness and the statement, when made, was so far contrary to the declarant's pecuniary or proprietary interest, or so far subjected him to the risk of civil or criminal liability, or so far tended to render invalid a claim by him against another, or created such a risk of making him an object of hatred, ridicule, or social disgrace in the community, that a reasonable man in his position would not have made the statement unless he believed it to be true.

Comment—Assembly Committee on Judiciary

Under existing law, a declaration against interest is admissible regardless of the availability of the declarant to testify as a witness. Section 1230, however, conditions admissibility upon the unavailability of the declarant in order to require the proponent of the evidence to use the in-court testimony of the declarant if it is possible to do so. If the declarant disappoints the proponent and testifies inconsistently, the proponent may then show the prior inconsistent statement as substantive evidence of the facts stated. See Evidence Code § 1235 and the Comment thereto. The requirement that the declarant have "sufficient knowledge of the subject" continues the similar common law requirement that the declarant must have had some peculiar means—such as personal observation—for obtaining accurate knowledge of the matter stated.

Article 2.5   Sworn Statements Regarding Gang-Related Crimes

§ 1231.   General requirements. Evidence of a prior statement made by a declarant is not made inadmissible by the hearsay rule if the declarant is deceased and the proponent of introducing the statement establishes each of the following:

(a) The statement relates to acts or events relevant to a criminal prosecution under provisions of the California Street Terrorism Enforcement and Prevention Act (Chapter 11 (commencing with Section 186.20) of Title 7 of Part 1 of the Penal Code).

(b) A verbatim transcript, copy, or record of the statement exists. A record may include a statement preserved by means of an audio or video recording or equivalent technology.

(c) The statement relates to acts or events within the personal knowledge of the declarant.

(d) The statement was made under oath or affirmation in an affidavit; or was made at a deposition, preliminary hearing, grand jury hearing, or other proceeding in compliance with law, and was made under penalty of perjury.

(e) The declarant died from other than natural causes.

(f) The statement was made under circumstances that would indicate its trustworthiness and render the declarant's statement particularly worthy of belief. For purposes of this subdivision, circumstances relevant to the issue of trustworthiness include, but are not limited to, all of the following:

(1) Whether the statement was made in contemplation of a pending or anticipated criminal or civil matter, in which the declarant had an interest, other than as a witness.

(2) Whether the declarant had a bias or motive for fabricating the statement, and the extent of any bias or motive.

(3) Whether the statement is corroborated by evidence other than statements that are admissible only pursuant to this section.

(4) Whether the statement was a statement against the declarant's interest.

§ 1231.1 Advance notice of intention to offer. A statement is admissible pursuant to Section 1231 only if the proponent of the statement makes known to the adverse party the intention to offer the statement and the particulars of the statement sufficiently in advance of the proceedings to provide the adverse party with a fair opportunity to prepare to meet the statement.

§ 1231.2 Administration of oath by peace officer. A peace officer may administer and certify oaths for purposes of this article.

§ 1231.3 Experience or training of law enforcement officer witness. Any law enforcement officer testifying as to any hearsay statement pursuant to this article shall either have five years of law enforcement experience or have completed a training course certified by the Commission on Peace Officer Standards and Training which includes training in the investigation and reporting of cases and testifying at preliminary hearings and trials.

§ 1231.4 Information provided to jury relating to cause of declarant's death. If evidence of a prior statement is introduced pursuant to this article, the jury may not be told that the declarant died from other than natural causes, but shall merely be told that the declarant is unavailable.

[Note: Section 2 of the act legislating the foregoing Article provided as follows:

SEC.2 This act shall not affect other evidentiary requirements, including, but not limited to, Sections 351 and 352 of the Evidence Code, shall not impair a party's right to attack the credibility of the declarant pursuant to Section 1202 of the Evidence Code, shall not affect the defendant's right to discovery for purposes of producing rebuttal evidence attacking the declarant's credibility, and shall not be used in a manner inconsistent with the defendant's right to due process and to confront witnesses under the United States or California Constitution.]

Article 3. Prior Statements of Witnesses

§ 1235. Inconsistent statement. Evidence of a statement made by a witness is not made inadmissible by the hearsay rule if the statement is inconsistent with his testimony at the hearing and is offered in compliance with Section 770.

Comment—Law Revision Commission

Under existing law, when a prior statement of a witness that is inconsistent with his testimony at the trial is admitted in evidence, it may not be used as evidence of the truth of the matters stated. Because of the hearsay rule, a witness' prior inconsistent statement may be used only to discredit his testimony given at the trial.

Because a witness' inconsistent statement is not substantive evidence, the courts do not permit a party—even when surprised by the testimony—to impeach his own witness with inconsistent statements if the witness' testimony at the trial has not damaged the party's case in any way. Evidence tending only to discredit the witness is irrelevant and immaterial when the witness has not given damaging testimony.

Section 1235 permits an inconsistent statement of a witness to be used as substantive evidence if the statement is otherwise admissible under the conditions specified in Section 770—which do not include surprise on the part of the party calling the witness if he is the party offering the inconsistent statement. Because Section 1235 permits a witness' inconsistent statements to be considered as evidence of the matters stated and not merely as evidence casting discredit on the witness, it follows that a party may introduce evidence of inconsistent statements of his own witness whether or not the witness gave damaging testimony and whether or not the party was surprised by the testimony, for such evidence is no longer irrelevant (and, hence, inadmissible).

Section 1235 admits inconsistent statements of witnesses because the dangers against which the hearsay rule is designed to protect are largely nonexistent. The declarant is in court and may be examined and cross-examined in regard to his statements and their subject matter.

§ 1236. Prior consistent statement. Evidence of a statement previously made by a witness is not made inadmissible by the hearsay rule if the statement is consistent with his testimony at the hearing and is offered in compliance with Section 791.

Comment—Law Revision Commission

Section 1236 permits a prior consistent statement of a witness to be used as substantive evidence if the statement is otherwise admissible under the rules relating to the rehabilitation of impeached witnesses. See Evidence Code § 791.

There is no reason to perpetuate the subtle distinction made in the cases. It is not realistic to expect a jury to understand that it cannot believe that a witness was telling the truth on a former occasion even though it believes that the same story given at the hearing is true.

§ 1237. Past recollection recorded.

(a) Evidence of a statement previously made by a witness is not made inadmissible by the hearsay rule if the statement would have been admissible if made by him while testifying, the statement concerns a matter as to which the witness has insufficient present recollection to enable him to testify fully and accurately, and the statement is contained in a writing which:

(1) Was made at a time when the fact recorded in the writing actually occurred or was fresh in the witness' memory;

(2) Was made (i) by the witness himself or under his direction or (ii) by some other person for the purpose of recording the witness' statement at the time it was made;

(3) Is offered after the witness testifies that the statement he made was a true statement of such fact; and

(4) Is offered after the writing is authenticated as an accurate record of the statement.

(b) The writing may be read into evidence, but the writing itself may not be received in evidence unless offered by an adverse party.

Comment—Assembly Committee on Judiciary

Under Section 1237, the writing may be made not only by the witness himself or under his direction but also by some other person for the purpose of recording the witness' statement at the time it was made. In addition, Section 1237 permits testimony of the person who recorded the statement to be used to establish that the writing is a correct record of the statement. Sufficient assurance of the trustworthiness of the statement is provided if the declarant is available to testify that he made a true statement and if the person who recorded the statement is available to testify that he accurately recorded the statement.

§ 1238. Prior identification.

Evidence of a statement previously made by a witness is not made inadmissible by the hearsay rule if the statement would have been admissible if made by him while testifying and:

(a) The statement is an identification of a party or another as a person who participated in a crime or other occurrence;

(b) The statement was made at a time when the crime or other occurrence was fresh in the witness' memory; and

§ 1238   CALIFORNIA EVIDENCE CODE

(c) The evidence of the statement is offered after the witness testifies that he made the identification and that it was a true reflection of his opinion at that time.

Comment—Law Revision Commission

Under Section 1235, evidence of a prior identification is admissible if the witness denies having made the prior identification or in any other way testifies inconsistently with the prior statement. Under Section 1238, evidence of a prior identification is admissible if the witness admits the prior identification and vouches for its accuracy.

The failure of the witness to repeat the extrajudicial identification in court does not destroy its probative value, for such failure may be explained by loss of memory or other circumstances.

Sections 1235 and 1238 deal only with the admissibility of evidence; they do not determine what constitutes evidence sufficient to sustain a verdict or finding.

Article 4. Spontaneous, Contemporaneous, and Dying Declarations

§ 1240. Spontaneous statement. Evidence of a statement is not made inadmissible by the hearsay rule if the statement:

(a) Purports to narrate, describe, or explain an act, condition, or event perceived by the declarant; and

(b) Was made spontaneously while the declarant was under the stress of excitement caused by such perception.

Comment—Law Revision Commission

Section 1240 is a codification of the existing exception to the hearsay rule for statements made spontaneously under the stress of excitement engendered by the event to which they relate. See Tentative Recommendation and a Study relating to the Uniform Rules of Evidence, (Article VIII. Hearsay Evidence), 6 Cal.Law Revision Comm'n, Rep., Rec. & Studies Appendix at 465–466 (1964). The rationale of this exception is that the spontaneity of such statements and the consequent lack of opportunity for reflection and deliberate fabrication provide an adequate guarantee of their trustworthiness.

§ 1241. Contemporaneous statement. Evidence of a statement is not made inadmissible by the hearsay rule if the statement:

(a) Is offered to explain, qualify, or make understandable conduct of the declarant; and

(b) Was made while the declarant was engaged in such conduct.

Comment—Assembly Committee on Judiciary

Under existing law, where a person's conduct or act is relevant but is equivocal or ambiguous, the statements accompanying it may be admitted to explain and make the conduct or act understandable. Some writers do not regard evidence of this sort as hearsay evidence, but the definition in Section

1200 seems applicable to many of the statements received under this exception. *Cf.* 6 Wigmore, Evidence § 1772 et seq. (1940). Section 1241 removes any doubt that might otherwise exist concerning the admissibility of such evidence under the hearsay rule.

§ 1242. Dying declaration. Evidence of a statement made by a dying person respecting the cause and circumstances of his death is not made inadmissible by the hearsay rule if the statement was made upon his personal knowledge and under a sense of immediately impending death.

Comment—Law Revision Commission

For the purpose of the *admissibility* of dying declarations, there is no rational basis for differentiating between civil and criminal actions or among various types of criminal actions. Hence, Section 1242 makes the exception applicable in all actions.

Under Section 1242, as under existing law, the dying declaration is admissible only if the declarant made the statement on personal knowledge.

Article 5. Statements of Mental or Physical State

§ 1250. Statement of declarant's then existing mental or physical state. (a) Subject to Section 1252, evidence of a statement of the declarant's then existing state of mind, emotion, or physical sensation (including a statement of intent, plan, motive, design, mental feeling, pain, or bodily health) is not made inadmissible by the hearsay rule when:

(1) The evidence is offered to prove the declarant's state of mind, emotion, or physical sensation at that time or at any other time when it is itself an issue in the action; or

(2) The evidence is offered to prove or explain acts or conduct of the declarant.

(b) This section does not make admissible evidence of a statement of memory or belief to prove the fact remembered or believed.

Comment—Assembly Committee on Judiciary

Section 1250 provides an exception to the hearsay rule for statements of the declarant's *then* existing mental or physical state. Under Section 1250, as under existing law, a statement of the declarant's state of mind at the time of the statement is admissible when the then existing state of mind is itself an issue in the case. A statement of the declarant's then existing state of mind is also admissible when relevant to show the declarant's state of mind at a time prior or subsequent to the statement. Section 1250 also makes a statement of then existing state of mind admissible to "prove or explain acts or conduct of the declarant." Thus, a statement of the declarant's intent to do certain acts is admissible to prove that he did those acts. People v. Alcalde, 24 Cal.2d 177, 148 P.2d 627 (1944). Statements of then existing pain or other bodily condition also are admissible to prove the existence of such condition.

A statement is not admissible under Section 1250 if the statement was made under circumstances indicating that the statement is not trustworthy. See Evidence Code § 1252 and the Comment thereto.

In light of the definition of "hearsay evidence" in Section 1200, a distinction should be noted between the use of a declarant's statements of his then existing mental state to prove such mental state and the use of a declarant's statements of other facts as circumstantial evidence of his mental state. Under the Evidence Code, no hearsay problem is involved if the declarant's statements are not being used to prove the truth of their contents but are being used as circumstantial evidence of the declarant's mental state. See the Comment to Section 1200.

Section 1250(b) does not permit a statement of memory or belief to be used to prove the fact remembered or believed. This limitation is necessary to preserve the hearsay rule. Any statement of a past event is, of course, a statement of the declarant's then existing state of mind—his memory or belief—concerning the past event. If the evidence of that state of mind—the statement of memory—were admissible to show that the fact remembered or believed actually occurred, any statement narrating a past event would be, by a process of circuitous reasoning, admissible to prove that the event occurred.

A major exception to the principle expressed in Section 1250(b) was created in People v. Merkouris, 52 Cal.2d 672, 344 P.2d 1 (1959). That case held that certain murder victims' statements relating threats by the defendant were admissible to show the victims' mental state—their fear of the defendant. Their fear was not itself an issue in the case, but the court held that the fear was relevant to show that the defendant had engaged in conduct engendering the fear, *i.e.*, that the defendant had in fact threatened them. That the defendant had threatened them was, of course, relevant to show that the threats were carried out in the homicide. Thus, in effect, the court permitted the statements to be used to prove the truth of the matters stated in them. In People v. Purvis, 56 Cal.2d 93, 13 Cal.Rptr. 801, 362 P.2d 713 (1961), the doctrine of the Merkouris case was limited to cases where identity is an issue; however, at least one subsequent decision has applied the doctrine where identity was not in issue. See People v. Cooley, 211 Cal.App.2d 173, 27 Cal.Rptr. 543 (1962).

The doctrine of the Merkouris case is repudiated in Section 1250(b) because that doctrine undermines the hearsay rule itself. Statements of a decedent's then existing fear—i.e., his state of mind—may be offered under Section 1250, as under existing law, either to prove that fear when it is itself in issue or to prove or explain the decedent's subsequent conduct. Statements of a decedent narrating threats or brutal conduct by some other person may also be used as circumstantial evidence of the decedent's fear—his state of mind—when that fear is itself in issue or when it is relevant to prove or explain the decedent's subsequent conduct; and, for that purpose, the evidence is not subject to a hearsay objection because it is not offered to prove the truth of the matter stated. See the Comment to Section 1200. See also the Comment to Section 1252. But when such evidence is used as a basis for inferring that the alleged threatener must have made threats, the evidence falls within the language of Section 1250(b) and is inadmissible hearsay evidence.

§ 1251. Statement of declarant's previously existing mental or physical state. Subject to Section 1252, evidence of a statement of the declarant's state of mind, emotion, or physical sensation (including a statement of intent, plan, motive, design, mental feeling, pain, or bodily health) at a time prior to the statement is not made inadmissible by the hearsay rule if:

(a) The declarant is unavailable as a witness; and

(b) The evidence is offered to prove such prior state of mind, emotion, or physical sensation when it is itself an issue in the action and the evidence is not offered to prove any fact other than such state of mind, emotion, or physical sensation.

Comment—Law Revision Commission

Section 1250 forbids the use of a statement of memory or belief to prove the fact remembered or believed. Section 1251, however, permits a statement of memory or belief of a past mental or physical state to be used to prove the previous mental or physical state when the previous mental or physical state is itself an issue in the case. If the past mental or physical state is to be used merely as circumstantial evidence of some other fact, the limitation in Section 1250 still applies and the statement of the past mental state is inadmissible hearsay.

Section 1251 requires a showing of the declarant's unavailability because the statements involved are narrations of past conditions. There is, therefore, a greater opportunity for the declarant to remember inaccurately or even to fabricate. Hence, Section 1251 permits such statements to be admitted only when the declarant's unavailability necessitates reliance upon his out-of-court statements.

A statement is not admissible under Section 1251 if the statement was made under circumstances indicating that the statement is not trustworthy. See Evidence Code 1252 and the Comment thereto.

§ 1252. Limitation on admissibility of statement of mental or physical state. Evidence of a statement is inadmissible under this article if the statement was made under circumstances such as to indicate its lack of trustworthiness.

§ 1253. Subject to Section 1252, evidence of a statement is not made inadmissible by the hearsay rule if the statement was made for purposes of medical diagnosis or treatment and describes medical history, or past or present symptoms, pain, or sensations, or the inception or general character of the cause or external source thereof insofar as reasonably pertinent to diagnosis or treatment. This section applies only to a statement made by a victim who is a minor at the time of the proceedings, provided the statement was made when the victim was under the age of 12 describing any act, or attempted act, of child abuse or neglect. "Child abuse" and "child neglect," for purposes of this section, have the meanings provided in subdivision (c) of Section 1360. In addition, "child abuse" means any act proscribed by Chapter 5 (commencing with

Section 281) of Title 9 of Part 1 of the Penal Code committed against a minor.

Article 6. Statements Relating to Wills and to Claims Against Estates

§ 1260. Statement concerning declarant's will or revocable trust; trustworthiness of statement

(a) Except as provided in subdivision (b), evidence of any of the following statements made by a declarant who is unavailable as a witness is not made inadmissible by the hearsay rule:

(1) That the declarant has or has not made a will or established or amended a revocable trust.

(2) That the declarant has or has not revoked his or her will, revocable trust, or an amendment to a revocable trust.

(3) That identifies the declarant's will, revocable trust, or an amendment to a revocable trust.

(b) Evidence of a statement is inadmissible under this section if the statement was made under circumstances that indicate its lack of trustworthiness.

§ 1261. Statement of decedent offered in action against his estate.
(a) Evidence of a statement is not made inadmissible by the hearsay rule when offered in an action upon a claim or demand against the estate of the declarant if the statement was made upon the personal knowledge of the declarant at a time when the matter had been recently perceived by him and while his recollection was clear.

(b) Evidence of a statement is inadmissible under this section if the statement was made under circumstances such as to indicate its lack of trustworthiness.

Comment—Law Revision Commission

The dead man statute (subdivision 3 of Section 1880 of the Code of Civil Procedure) prohibits a party who sues on a claim against a decedent's estate from testifying to any fact occurring prior to the decedent's death. The theory apparently underlying the statute is that it would be unfair to permit the surviving claimant to testify to such facts when the decedent is precluded by his death from doing so. To balance the positions of the parties, the living may not speak because the dead cannot.

The dead man statute operates unsatisfactorily. It prohibits testimony concerning matters of which the decedent had no knowledge and, hence, to which he could not have testified even if he had survived. It operates unevenly since it does not prohibit testimony relating to claims *under,* as distinguished from claims *against,* the decedent's estate even though the effect of such a claim may be to frustrate the decedent's plan for the disposition of his property. See the Law Revision Commission's Comment to Code of Civil Procedure Section

1880 and 1 Cal.Law Revision Comm'n, Rep., Rec. & Studies, Recommendation and Study Relating to the Dead Man Statute at D-1 (1957). The dead man statute excludes otherwise relevant and competent evidence—even if it is the only available evidence—and frequently this forces the courts to decide cases with a minimum of information concerning the actual facts.

Under the Evidence Code, the positions of the parties are balanced by throwing more light, not less, on the actual facts. Repeal of the dead man statute permits the claimant to testify without restriction. To balance this advantage, Section 1261 permits hearsay evidence of the decedent's statements to be admitted. Certain safeguards—i.e., personal knowledge, recent perception, and circumstantial evidence of trustworthiness—are included in the section to provide some protection for the party against whom the statements are offered, for he has no opportunity to test the hearsay by cross-examination.

Article 7. Business Records

§ 1270. "A business". As used in this article, "a business" includes every kind of business, governmental activity, profession, occupation, calling, or operation of institutions, whether carried on for profit or not.

Comment—Law Revision Commission

The definition is sufficiently broad to encompass institutions not customarily thought of as businesses. For example, the baptismal and wedding records of a church would be admissible under the section to prove the events recorded.

§ 1271. Business record. Evidence of a writing made as a record of an act, condition, or event is not made inadmissible by the hearsay rule when offered to prove the act, condition, or event if:

(a) The writing was made in the regular course of a business;

(b) The writing was made at or near the time of the act, condition, or event;

(c) The custodian or other qualified witness testifies to its identity and the mode of its preparation; and

(d) The sources of information and method and time of preparation were such as to indicate its trustworthiness.

Comment—Law Revision Commission

[T]he cases have rejected a variety of business records on the ground that they were not based on the personal knowledge of the recorder or of someone with a business duty to report to the recorder. Police accident and arrest reports are usually held inadmissible because they are based on the narrations of persons who have no business duty to report to the police. Similar investigative reports on the origin of fires have been held inadmissible because they were not based on personal knowledge.

Section 1271 will continue the law developed in these cases that a business report is admissible only if the sources of information and the time and method of preparation are such as to indicate its trustworthiness.

§ 1272. Absence of entry in business records. Evidence of the absence from the records of a business of a record of an asserted act, condition, or event is not made inadmissible by the hearsay rule when offered to prove the nonoccurrence of the act or event, or the nonexistence of the condition, if:

(a) It was the regular course of that business to make records of all such acts, conditions, or events at or near the time of the act, condition, or event and to preserve them; and

(b) The sources of information and method and time of preparation of the records of that business were such that the absence of a record of an act, condition, or event is a trustworthy indication that the act or event did not occur or the condition did not exist.

Article 8. Official Records and Other Official Writings

§ 1280. Record by public employee. Evidence of a writing made as a record of an act, condition, or event is not made inadmissible by the hearsay rule when offered in any civil or criminal proceeding to prove the act, condition, or event if all of the following applies:

(a) The writing was made by and within the scope of duty of a public employee.

(b) The writing was made at or near the time of the act, condition, or event.

(c) The sources of information and method and time of preparation were such as to indicate its trustworthiness.

Comment—Law Revision Commission

The evidence that is admissible under this section is also admissible under Section 1271, the business records exception. However, Section 1271 requires a witness to testify as to the identity of the record and its mode of preparation in every instance. In contrast, Section 1280, as does existing law, permits the court to admit an official record or report without necessarily requiring a witness to testify as to its identity and mode of preparation if the court takes judicial notice or if sufficient independent evidence shows that the record or report was prepared in such a manner as to assure its trustworthiness.

§ 1281. Record of vital statistic. Evidence of a writing made as a record of a birth, fetal death, death, or marriage is not made inadmissible by the hearsay rule if the maker was required by law to file the writing in a designated public office and the writing was made and filed as required by law.

§ 1282. Finding of presumed death by authorized federal employee. A written finding of presumed death made by an employee of the United States authorized to make such finding pursuant to the Federal Missing Persons Act (56 Stats. 143, 1092, and P.L. 408, Ch. 371, 2d Sess. 78th Cong.; 50 U.S.C.App. 1001–1016), as enacted or as heretofore or hereafter amended, shall be received in any court, office, or other place in this state as evidence of the death of the person therein found to be dead and of the date, circumstances, and place of his disappearance.

§ 1283. Record by federal employee that person is missing, captured, or the like. An official written report or record that a person is missing, missing in action, interned in a foreign country, captured by a hostile force, beleaguered by a hostile force, besieged by a hostile force, or detained in a foreign country against his will, or is dead or is alive, made by an employee of the United States authorized by any law of the United States to make such report or record shall be received in any court, office, or other place in this state as evidence that such person is missing, missing in action, interned in a foreign country, captured by a hostile force, beleaguered by a hostile force, besieged by a hostile force, or detained in a foreign country against his will, or is dead or is alive.

§ 1284. Statement of absence of public record. Evidence of a writing made by the public employee who is the official custodian of the records in a public office, reciting diligent search and failure to find a record, is not made inadmissible by the hearsay rule when offered to prove the absence of a record in that office.

Article 9. Former Testimony

§ 1290. "Former testimony". As used in this article, "former testimony" means testimony given under oath in:

(a) Another action or in a former hearing or trial of the same action;

(b) A proceeding to determine a controversy conducted by or under the supervision of an agency that has the power to determine such a controversy and is an agency of the United States or a public entity in the United States;

(c) A deposition taken in compliance with law in another action; or

(d) An arbitration proceeding if the evidence of such former testimony is a verbatim transcript thereof.

§ 1291. Former testimony offered against party to former proceeding. (a) Evidence of former testimony is not made inadmissible by the hearsay rule if the declarant is unavailable as a witness and:

(1) The former testimony is offered against a person who offered it in evidence in his own behalf on the former occasion or against the successor in interest of such person; or

(2) The party against whom the former testimony is offered was a party to the action or proceeding in which the testimony was given and

§ 1291

had the right and opportunity to cross-examine the declarant with an interest and motive similar to that which he has at the hearing.

(b) The admissibility of former testimony under this section is subject to the same limitations and objections as though the declarant were testifying at the hearing, except that former testimony offered under this section is not subject to:

(1) Objections to the form of the question which were not made at the time the former testimony was given.

(2) Objections based on competency or privilege which did not exist at the time the former testimony was given.

Comment—Assembly Committee on Judiciary

Section 1291 provides a hearsay exception for former testimony offered against a person who was a party to the proceeding in which the former testimony was given. For example, if a series of cases arises involving several plaintiffs and but one defendant, Section 1291 permits testimony given in the first trial to be used against the defendant in a later trial if the conditions of admissibility stated in the section are met.

Former testimony is admissible under Section 1291 only if the declarant is unavailable as a witness.

Paragraph (1) of subdivision (a) of Section 1291 provides for the admission of former testimony if it is offered against the party who offered it in the previous proceeding. Since the witness is no longer available to testify, the party's previous direct and redirect examination should be considered an adequate substitute for his present right to cross-examine the declarant.

Paragraph (2) of subdivision (a) of Section 1291 provides for the admissibility of former testimony where the party against whom it is now offered had the right and opportunity in the former proceeding to cross-examine the declarant with an interest and motive similar to that which he now has. The determination of similarity of interest and motive in cross-examination should be based on practical considerations and not merely on the similarity of the party's position in the two cases. For example, testimony contained in a deposition that was taken, but not offered in evidence at the trial, in a different action should be excluded if the judge determines that the deposition was taken for discovery purposes and that the party did not subject the witness to a thorough cross-examination because he sought to avoid a premature revelation of the weakness in the testimony of the witness or in the adverse party's case. In such a situation, the party's interest and motive for cross-examination on the previous occasion would have been substantially different from his present interest and motive.

§ 1292. Former testimony offered against person not a party to former proceeding.
(a) Evidence of former testimony is not made inadmissible by the hearsay rule if:

(1) The declarant is unavailable as a witness;

(2) The former testimony is offered in a civil action; and

(3) The issue is such that the party to the action or proceeding in which the former testimony was given had the right and opportunity to cross-examine the declarant with an interest and motive similar to that which the party against whom the testimony is offered has at the hearing.

(b) The admissibility of former testimony under this section is subject to the same limitations and objections as though the declarant were testifying at the hearing, except that former testimony offered under this section is not subject to objections based on competency or privilege which did not exist at the time the former testimony was given.

Comment—Assembly Committee on Judiciary

Section 1292 provides a hearsay exception for former testimony given at the former proceeding by a person who is now unavailable as a witness when such former testimony is offered against a person who was not a party to the former proceeding but whose motive for cross-examination is similar to that of a person who had the right and opportunity to cross-examine the declarant when the former testimony was given. For example, if one occurrence gives rise to a series of cases involving one defendant and several plaintiffs, Section 1292 permits testimony given against the plaintiff in the first action to be used against a different plaintiff in a subsequent action if the conditions of admissibility stated in the section are met. The trustworthiness of the former testimony is sufficiently guaranteed because the former adverse party had the right and opportunity to cross-examine the declarant with an interest and motive similar to that of the present adverse party. Although the party against whom the former testimony is offered did not himself have an opportunity to cross-examine the witness on the former occasion, it can be generally assumed that most prior cross-examination is adequate if the same stakes are involved. If the same stakes are not involved, the difference in interest or motivation would justify exclusion. Even where the prior cross-examination was inadequate, there is better reason here for providing a hearsay exception than there is for many of the presently recognized exceptions to the hearsay rule.

Section 1292 does not make former testimony admissible in a criminal case. This limitation preserves the right of a person accused of crime to confront and cross-examine the witnesses against him.

§ 1293. Former testimony made at a preliminary examination by a minor child as a complaining witness; admissibility.

(a) Evidence of former testimony made at a preliminary examination by a minor child who was the complaining witness is not made inadmissible by the hearsay rule if:

(1) The former testimony is offered in a proceeding to declare the minor a dependent child of the court pursuant to Section 300 of the Welfare and Institutions Code.

(2) The issues are such that a defendant in the preliminary examination in which the former testimony was given had the right and opportunity to cross-examine the minor child with an interest and motive similar to that which the parent or guardian against whom the

§ 1293

testimony is offered has at the proceeding to declare the minor a dependent child of the court.

(b) The admissibility of former testimony under this section is subject to the same limitations and objections as though the minor child were testifying at the proceeding to declare him or her a dependent child of the court.

(c) The attorney for the parent or guardian against whom the former testimony is offered or, if none, the parent or guardian may make a motion to challenge the admissibility of the former testimony upon a showing that new substantially different issues are present in the proceeding to declare the minor a dependent child than were present in the preliminary examination.

(d) As used in this section, "complaining witness" means the alleged victim of the crime for which a preliminary examination was held.

(e) This section shall apply only to testimony made at a preliminary examination on and after January 1, 1990.

§ 1294. Admissibility of video recording or transcript of prior inconsistent statement admitted in preliminary hearing or criminal trial.
(a) The following evidence of prior inconsistent statements of a witness properly admitted in a preliminary hearing or trial of the same criminal matter pursuant to Section 1235 is not made inadmissible by the hearsay rule if the witness is unavailable and former testimony of the witness is admitted pursuant to Section 1291:

(1) A video recorded statement introduced at a preliminary hearing or prior proceeding concerning the same criminal matter.

(2) A transcript, containing the statements, of the preliminary hearing or prior proceeding concerning the same criminal matter.

(b) The party against whom the prior inconsistent statements are offered, at his or her option, may examine or cross-examine any person who testified at the preliminary hearing or prior proceeding as to the prior inconsistent statements of the witness.

Article 10. Judgments

§ 1300. Judgment of conviction of crime punishable as felony.
Evidence of a final judgment adjudging a person guilty of a crime punishable as a felony is not made inadmissible by the hearsay rule when offered in a civil action to prove any fact essential to the judgment whether or not the judgment was based on a plea of nolo contendere.

Comment—Law Revision Commission

Analytically, a judgment that is offered to prove the matters determined by the judgment is hearsay evidence. Uniform Rules of Evidence, Rule 63(20) Comment (1953); Tentative Recommendation and a Study Relating to the

Uniform Rules of Evidence (Article VIII. Hearsay Evidence), 6 Cal.Law Revision Comm'n, Rep., Rec. & Studies Appendix at 539–541 (1964). It is in substance a statement of the court that determined the previous action ("a statement that was made other than by a witness while testifying at the hearing") that is offered "to prove the truth of the matter stated." Evidence Code § 1200. Therefore, unless an exception to the hearsay rule is provided, a judgment would be inadmissible if offered in a subsequent action to prove the matters determined. The sections of this article do not purport to deal with the doctrines of res judicata and estoppel by judgment. These sections deal only with the

evidentiary use of judgments in those cases where the substantive law does not require that the judgments be given conclusive effect.

Section 1300 provides an exception to the hearsay rule for a final judgment adjudging a person guilty of a crime punishable as a felony. Hence, if a plaintiff sues to recover a reward offered by the defendant for the arrest and conviction of a person who committed a particular crime, Section 1300 permits the plaintiff to use a judgment of conviction as evidence that the person convicted committed the crime. The exception does not, however, apply in criminal actions. Thus, Section 1300 does not permit the judgment to be used in a criminal action as evidence of the identity of the person who committed the crime or as evidence that the crime was committed.

[T]he evidence involved is peculiarly reliable. The seriousness of the charge assures that the facts will be thoroughly litigated, and the fact that the judgment must be based upon a determination that there was no reasonable doubt concerning the defendant's guilt assures that the question of guilt will be thoroughly considered.

§ 1301. Judgment against person entitled to indemnity.

Evidence of a final judgment is not made inadmissible by the hearsay rule when offered by the judgment debtor to prove any fact which was essential to the judgment in an action in which he seeks to:

(a) Recover partial or total indemnity or exoneration for money paid or liability incurred because of the judgment;

(b) Enforce a warranty to protect the judgment debtor against the liability determined by the judgment; or

(c) Recover damages for breach of warranty substantially the same as the warranty determined by the judgment to have been breached.

§ 1302. Judgment determining liability of third person.

When the liability, obligation, or duty of a third person is in issue in a civil action, evidence of a final judgment against that person is not made inadmissible by the hearsay rule when offered to prove such liability, obligation, or duty.

Article 11. Family History

§ 1310. Statement concerning declarant's own family history.

(a) Subject to subdivision (b), evidence of a statement by a declarant who is unavailable as a witness concerning his own birth, marriage, divorce, a parent and child relationship, relationship by blood or marriage, race, ancestry, or other similar fact of his family history is not made inadmissible by the hearsay rule, even though the declarant had no means of acquiring personal knowledge of the matter declared.

(b) Evidence of a statement is inadmissible under this section if the statement was made under circumstances such as to indicate its lack of trustworthiness.

§ 1311. Statement concerning family history of another. (a) Subject to subdivision (b), evidence of a statement concerning the birth, marriage, divorce, death, parent and child relationship, race, ancestry, relationship by blood or marriage, or other similar fact of the family history of a person other than the declarant is not made inadmissible by the hearsay rule if the declarant is unavailable as a witness and:

(1) The declarant was related to the other by blood or marriage; or

(2) The declarant was otherwise so intimately associated with the other's family as to be likely to have had accurate information concerning the matter declared and made the statement (i) upon information received from the other or from a person related by blood or marriage to the other or (ii) upon repute in the other's family.

(b) Evidence of a statement is inadmissible under this section if the statement was made under circumstances such as to indicate its lack of trustworthiness.

§ 1312. Entries in family records and the like. Evidence of entries in family Bibles or other family books or charts, engravings on rings, family portraits, engravings on urns, crypts, or tombstones, and the like, is not made inadmissible by the hearsay rule when offered to prove the birth, marriage, divorce, death, parent and child relationship, race, ancestry, relationship by blood or marriage, or other similar fact of the family history of a member of the family by blood or marriage.

§ 1313. Reputation in family concerning family history. Evidence of reputation among members of a family is not made inadmissible by the hearsay rule if the reputation concerns the birth, marriage, divorce, death, parent and child relationship, race, ancestry, relationship by blood or marriage, or other similar fact of the family history of a member of the family by blood or marriage.

Comment—Law Revision Commission

The family reputation admitted under Section 1313 is necessarily multiple hearsay. If, however, such reputation were inadmissible because of the hearsay rule, and if direct statements of pedigree were inadmissible because they are based on such reputation (as most of them are), the courts would be virtually helpless in determining matters of pedigree. See Tentative Recommendation and a Study Relating to the Uniform Rules of Evidence (Article VIII. Hearsay

Evidence), 6 Cal. Law Revision Comm'n, Rep., Rec. & Studies Appendix at 548 (1964).

§ 1314. Reputation in community concerning family history.
Evidence of reputation in a community concerning the date or fact of birth, marriage, divorce, or death of a person resident in the community at the time of the reputation is not made inadmissible by the hearsay rule.

§ 1315. Church records concerning family history.
Evidence of a statement concerning a person's birth, marriage, divorce, death, parent and child relationship, race, ancestry, relationship by blood or marriage, or other similar fact of family history which is contained in a writing made as a record of a church, religious denomination, or religious society is not made inadmissible by the hearsay rule if:

(a) The statement is contained in a writing made as a record of an act, condition, or event that would be admissible as evidence of such act, condition, or event under Section 1271; and

(b) The statement is of a kind customarily recorded in connection with the act, condition, or event recorded in the writing.

Comment—Law Revision Commission

Church records generally are admissible as business records under the provisions of Section 1271. Under Section 1271, such records would be admissible to prove the occurrence of the church activity—the baptism, confirmation, or marriage—recorded in the writing. However, it is unlikely that Section 1271 would permit such records to be used as evidence of the age or relationship of the participants, for the business records act has been held to authorize business records to be used to prove only facts known personally to the recorder of the information or to other employees of the business.

Section 1315 permits church records to be used to prove certain additional information. Facts of family history, such as birth dates, relationships, marital histories, etc., that are ordinarily reported to church authorities and recorded in connection with the church's baptismal, confirmation, marriage, and funeral records may be proved by such records under Section 1315.

§ 1316. Marriage, baptismal, and similar certificates.
Evidence of a statement concerning a person's birth, marriage, divorce, death, parent and child relationship, race, ancestry, relationship by blood or marriage, or other similar fact of family history is not made inadmissible by the hearsay rule if the statement is contained in a certificate that the maker thereof performed a marriage or other ceremony or administered a sacrament and:

(a) The maker was a clergyman, civil officer, or other person authorized to perform the acts reported in the certificate by law or by the rules, regulations, or requirements of a church, religious denomination, or religious society; and

(b) The certificate was issued by the maker at the time and place of the ceremony or sacrament or within a reasonable time thereafter.

Article 12. Reputation and Statements Concerning Community History, Property Interests, and Character

§ 1320. Reputation concerning community history. Evidence of reputation in a community is not made inadmissible by the hearsay rule if the reputation concerns an event of general history of the community or of the state or nation of which the community is a part and the event was of importance to the community.

§ 1321. Reputation concerning public interest in property. Evidence of reputation in a community is not made inadmissible by the hearsay rule if the reputation concerns the interest of the public in property in the community and the reputation arose before controversy.

§ 1322. Reputation concerning boundary or custom affecting land. Evidence of reputation in a community is not made inadmissible by the hearsay rule if the reputation concerns boundaries of, or customs affecting, land in the community and the reputation arose before controversy.

§ 1323. Statement concerning boundary. Evidence of a statement concerning the boundary of land is not made inadmissible by the hearsay rule if the declarant is unavailable as a witness and had sufficient knowledge of the subject, but evidence of a statement is not admissible under this section if the statement was made under circumstances such as to indicate its lack of trustworthiness.

§ 1324. Reputation concerning character. Evidence of a person's general reputation with reference to his character or a trait of his character at a relevant time in the community in which he then resided or in a group with which he then habitually associated is not made inadmissible by the hearsay rule.

Article 13. Dispositive Instruments and Ancient Writings

§ 1330. Recitals in writings affecting property. Evidence of a statement contained in a deed of conveyance or a will or other writing purporting to affect an interest in real or personal property is not made inadmissible by the hearsay rule if:

(a) The matter stated was relevant to the purpose of the writing;

(b) The matter stated would be relevant to an issue as to an interest in the property; and

(c) The dealings with the property since the statement was made have not been inconsistent with the truth of the statement.

§ 1331. Recitals in ancient writings. Evidence of a statement is not made inadmissible by the hearsay rule if the statement is contained in a writing more than 30 years old and the statement has been since generally acted upon as true by persons having an interest in the matter.

Article 14. Commercial, Scientific, and Similar Publications

§ 1340. Commercial lists and the like. Evidence of a statement, other than an opinion, contained in a tabulation, list, directory, register, or other published compilation is not made inadmissible by the hearsay rule if the compilation is generally used and relied upon as accurate in the course of a business as defined in Section 1270.

§ 1341. Publications concerning facts of general notoriety and interest. Historical works, books of science or art, and published maps or charts, made by persons indifferent between the parties, are not made inadmissible by the hearsay rule when offered to prove facts of general notoriety and interest.

Article 15. Declarant Unavailable as Witness

§ 1350. Unavailable declarant; hearsay rule. (a) In a criminal proceeding charging a serious felony, evidence of a statement made by a declarant is not made inadmissible by the hearsay rule if the declarant is unavailable as a witness, and all of the following are true:

(1) There is clear and convincing evidence that the declarant's unavailability was knowingly caused by, aided by, or solicited by the party against whom the statement is offered for the purpose of preventing the arrest or prosecution of the party and is the result of the death by homicide or the kidnapping of the declarant.

(2) There is no evidence that the unavailability of the declarant was caused by, aided by, solicited by, or procured on behalf of, the party who is offering the statement.

(3) The statement has been memorialized in a tape recording made by a law enforcement official, or in a written statement prepared by a law enforcement official and signed by the declarant and notarized in the presence of the law enforcement official, prior to the death or kidnapping of the declarant.

(4) The statement was made under circumstances which indicate its trustworthiness and was not the result of promise, inducement, threat, or coercion.

(5) The statement is relevant to the issues to be tried.

(6) The statement is corroborated by other evidence which tends to connect the party against whom the statement is offered with the commission of the serious felony with which the party is charged. The

corroboration is not sufficient if it merely shows the commission of the offense or the circumstances thereof.

(b) If the prosecution intends to offer a statement pursuant to this section, the prosecution shall serve a written notice upon the defendant at least 10 days prior to the hearing or trial at which the prosecution intends to offer the statement, unless the prosecution shows good cause for the failure to provide that notice. In the event that good cause is shown, the defendant shall be entitled to a reasonable continuance of the hearing or trial.

(c) If the statement is offered during trial, the court's determination shall be made out of the presence of the jury. If the defendant elects to testify at the hearing on a motion brought pursuant to this section, the court shall exclude from the examination every person except the clerk, the court reporter, the bailiff, the prosecutor, the investigating officer, the defendant and his or her counsel, an investigator for the defendant, and the officer having custody of the defendant. Notwithstanding any other provision of law, the defendant's testimony at the hearing shall not be admissible in any other proceeding except the hearing brought on the motion pursuant to this section. If a transcript is made of the defendant's testimony, it shall be sealed and transmitted to the clerk of the court in which the action is pending.

(d) As used in this section, "serious felony" means any of the felonies listed in subdivision (c) of Section 1192.7 of the Penal Code or any violation of Section 11351, 11352, 11378, or 11379 of the Health and Safety Code.

(e) If a statement to be admitted pursuant to this section includes hearsay statements made by anyone other than the declarant who is unavailable pursuant to subdivision (a), those hearsay statements are inadmissible unless they meet the requirements of an exception to the hearsay rule.

§ 1360. Minor victim's statement describing child abuse or neglect. (a) In a criminal prosecution where the victim is a minor, a statement made by the victim when under the age of 12 describing any act of child abuse or neglect performed with or on the child by another, or describing any attempted act of child abuse or neglect with or on the child by another, is not made inadmissible by the hearsay rule if all of the following apply:

(1) The statement is not otherwise admissible by statute or court rule.

(2) The court finds, in a hearing conducted outside the presence of the jury, that the time, content, and circumstances of the statement provide sufficient indicia of reliability.

(3) The child either:

(A) Testifies at the proceedings.

(B) Is unavailable as a witness, in which case the statement may be admitted only if there is evidence of the child abuse or neglect that corroborates the statement made by the child.

(b) A statement may not be admitted under this section unless the proponent of the statement makes known to the adverse party the intention to offer the statement and the particulars of the statement sufficiently in advance of the proceedings in order to provide the adverse party with a fair opportunity to prepare to meet the statement.

(c) For purposes of this section, "child abuse" means an act proscribed by Section 273a, 273d, or 288.5 of the Penal Code, or nay of the acts described in Section 11165.1 of the Penal Code, and "child neglect" means any of the acts described in Section 11165.2 of the Penal Code.

§ **1370. Victim's statement describing physical injury or threat thereof.** (a) Evidence of a statement by a declarant is not made inadmissible by the hearsay rule if all of the following conditions are met:

(1) The statement purports to narrate, describe, or explain the infliction or threat of physical injury upon the declarant.

(2) The declarant is unavailable as a witness pursuant to Section 240.

(3) The statement was made at or near the time of the infliction or threat of physical injury. Evidence of statements made more than five years before the filing of the current action or proceeding shall be inadmissible under this section.

(4) The statement was made under circumstances that would indicate its trustworthiness.

(5) The statement was made in writing, was electronically recorded, or made to a physician, nurse, paramedic, or to a law enforcement official.

(b) For purposes of paragraph (4) of subdivision (a), circumstances relevant to the issue of trustworthiness include, but are not limited to, the following:

(1) Whether the statement was made in contemplation of pending or anticipated litigation in which the declarant was interested.

(2) Whether the declarant has a bias or motive for fabricating the statement, and the extent of any bias or motive.

(3) Whether the statement is corroborated by evidence other than statements that are admissible only pursuant to this section.

(c) A statement is admissible pursuant to this section only if the proponent of the statement makes known to the adverse party the intention to offer the statement and the particulars of the statement

§ 1370   CALIFORNIA EVIDENCE CODE

sufficiently in advance of the proceedings in order to provide the adverse party with a fair opportunity to prepare to meet the statement.

Note: Section 1370 was enacted as section 2 of AB 2068. Section 1. of the same bill provided:

> SECTION 1. It is the intent of the Legislature that enactment of this statute shall not affect other evidentiary requirements, including, but not limited to, Sections 351 and 352, shall not impair a party's right to attack the credibility of the declarant pursuant to Section 1202, shall not affect the defendant's right to discovery for purposes of producing rebuttal evidence attacking the declarant's credibility, and shall not be used in a manner inconsistent with the defendant's right to due process and to confront witnesses under the United States or California Constitution.

§ 1380. Statement of elder or dependent adult victim of abuse. (a) In a criminal proceeding charging a violation, or attempted violation, of Section 368 of the Penal Code, evidence of a statement made by a declarant is not made inadmissible by the hearsay rule if the declarant is unavailable as a witness, as defined in subdivisions (a) and (b) of Section 240, and all of the following are true:

(1) The party offering the statement has made a showing of particularized guarantees of trustworthiness regarding the statement, the statement was made under circumstances which indicate its trustworthiness, and the statement was not the result of promise, inducement, threat, or coercion. In making its determination, the court may consider only the circumstances that surround the making of the statement and that render the declarant particularly worthy of belief.

(2) There is no evidence that the unavailability of the declarant was caused by, aided by, solicited by, or procured on behalf of, the party who is offering the statement.

(3) The entire statement has been memorialized in a videotape recording made by a law enforcement official, prior to the death or disabling of the declarant.

(4) The statement was made by the victim of the alleged violation.

(5) The statement is supported by corroborative evidence.

(6) The victim of the alleged violation is an individual who meets both of the following requirements:

(A) Was 65 years of age or older or was a dependent adult when the alleged violation or attempted violation occurred.

(B) At the time of any criminal proceeding, including, but not limited to, a preliminary hearing or trial, regarding the alleged violation or attempted violation, is either deceased or suffers from the infirmities of aging as manifested by advanced age or organic brain damage, or other physical, mental, or emotional dysfunction, to the extent that the ability of the person to provide adequately for the person's own care or protection is impaired.

(b) If the prosecution intends to offer a statement pursuant to this section, the prosecution shall serve a written notice upon the defendant at least 10 days prior to the hearing or trial at which the prosecution intends to offer the statement, unless the prosecution shows good cause for the failure to provide that notice. In the event that good cause is shown, the defendant shall be entitled to a reasonable continuance of the hearing or trial.

(c) If the statement is offered during trial, the court's determination as to the availability of the victim as a witness shall be made out of the presence of the jury. If the defendant elects to testify at the hearing on a motion brought pursuant to this section, the court shall exclude from the examination every person except the clerk, the court reporter, the bailiff, the prosecutor, the investigating officer, the defendant and his or her counsel, an investigator for the defendant, and the officer having custody of the defendant. Notwithstanding any other provision of law, the defendant's testimony at the hearing shall not be admissible in any other proceeding except the hearing brought on the motion pursuant to this section. If a transcript is made of the defendant's testimony, it shall be sealed and transmitted to the clerk of the court in which the action is pending.

§ 1390. (Repealed January 1, 2016) Evidence of statement; elements; conduct of foundational hearing; considerations; applicability; effect of repeal

(a) Evidence of a statement is not made inadmissible by the hearsay rule if the statement is offered against a party that has engaged or aided and abetted in the wrongdoing that was intended to, and did, procure the unavailability of the declarant as a witness.

(b)

(1) The party seeking to introduce a statement pursuant to subdivision (a) shall establish, by a preponderance of the evidence, that the elements of subdivision (a) have been met at a foundational hearing.

(2) The hearsay evidence that is the subject of the foundational hearing is admissible at the foundational hearing. However, a finding that the elements of subdivision (a) have been met shall not be based solely on the unconfronted hearsay statement of the unavailable declarant, and shall be supported by independent corroborative evidence.

(3) The foundational hearing shall be conducted outside the presence of the jury. However, if the hearing is conducted after a jury trial has begun, the judge presiding at the hearing may consider evidence already presented to the jury in deciding whether the elements of subdivision (a) have been met.

(4) In deciding whether or not to admit the statement, the judge may take into account whether it is trustworthy and reliable.

(c) This section shall apply to any civil, criminal, or juvenile case or proceeding initiated or pending as of January 1, 2011.

(d) This section shall remain in effect only until January 1, 2016, and as of that date is repealed, unless a later enacted statute, that is enacted before January 1, 2016, deletes or extends that date. If this section is repealed, the fact that it is repealed should it occur, shall not be deemed to give rise to any ground for an appeal or a postverdict challenge based on its use in a criminal or juvenile case or proceeding before January 1, 2016.

Division 11

WRITINGS

Chapter 1

AUTHENTICATION AND PROOF OF WRITINGS

Article 1. Requirement of Authentication

§ 1400. Authentication defined. Authentication of a writing means (a) the introduction of evidence sufficient to sustain a finding that it is the writing that the proponent of the evidence claims it is or (b) the establishment of such facts by any other means provided by law.

Comment—Law Revision Commission

Before any tangible object may be admitted into evidence, the party seeking to introduce the object must make a preliminary showing that the object is in some way relevant to the issues to be decided in the action. When the object sought to be introduced is a writing, this preliminary showing of relevancy usually entails some proof that the writing is authentic—i.e., that the writing was made or signed by its purported maker. Hence, this showing is normally referred to as "authentication" of the writing. But authentication, correctly understood, may involve a preliminary showing that the writing is a forgery or is a writing found in particular files regardless of its authorship. When the requisite preliminary showing has been made, the judge admits the writing into evidence for consideration by the trier of fact. However, the fact that the judge permits the writing to be admitted in evidence does not necessarily establish the authenticity of the writing; all that the judge has determined is that there has been a sufficient showing of the authenticity of the writing to permit the trier of fact to find that it is authentic. The trier of fact independently determines the question of authenticity, and, if the trier of fact does not believe the evidence of authenticity, it may find that the writing is not authentic despite the fact that the judge has determined that it was "authenticated." See 7 Wigmore, Evidence §§ 2129–2135 (3d ed. 1940).

This chapter sets forth the rules governing this process of authentication. Sections 1400–1402 (Article 1) define and state the general requirement of authentication—either by evidence sufficient to sustain a finding of authenticity or by other means sanctioned by law. Sections 1410–1454 (Articles 2 and 3) set forth some of the means that may be used to authenticate certain kinds of writings. The operation and effect of these sections is explained in separate Comments relating to them.

Under Section 1400, as under existing law, a writing may be authenticated by the presentation of evidence sufficient to sustain a finding of its authenticity. Under Section 1400, as under existing law, the authenticity of a particular writing also may be established by some means other than the introduction of evidence of authenticity. Thus, the authenticity of a writing may be established by stipulation or by the pleadings.

The requisite preliminary showing may also be supplied by a presumption. See, e.g., Evidence Code §§ 1450–1454, 1530. In some instances, a presumption of authenticity may also attach to a writing authenticated in a particular manner. See, e.g., Evidence Code § 643 (the ancient documents rule).

§ 1401. Authentication required. (a) Authentication of a writing is required before it may be received in evidence.

(b) Authentication of a writing is required before secondary evidence of its content may be received in evidence.

Comment—Assembly Committee on Judiciary

The "writing" referred to in subdivision (a) is any writing offered in evidence; although it may be either an original or a copy, it must be authenticated before it may be received in evidence.

Subdivision (b) of Section 1401 requires that a writing be authenticated even when it is not offered in evidence but is sought to be proved by a copy or by testimony as to its content under the circumstances permitted by Sections 1500–1510 (the best evidence rule). Under Section 1401, therefore, if a person offers in evidence a copy of a writing, he must make a sufficient preliminary showing of the authenticity of both the copy and the original.

In some instances, however, authentication of a copy will provide the necessary evidence to authenticate the original writing at the same time. For example: If a copy of a recorded deed is offered in evidence, Section 1401 requires that the copy be authenticated—proved to be a copy of the official record. It also requires that the official record be authenticated—proved to be the official record—because the official record is a writing of which secondary evidence of its content is being offered. Finally, Section 1401 requires the original deed itself to be authenticated—proved to have been executed by its purported maker—for it, too, is a writing of which secondary evidence of its content is being offered. The copy offered in evidence may be authenticated by the attestation or certification of the official custodian of the record as provided by Section 1530. Under Section 1530, the authenticated copy is prima facie evidence of the existence and content of the official record itself. Thus, the authenticated copy supplies the necessary authenticating evidence for the official record. Under Section 1600, the official record is prima facie evidence of the existence and content of the original deed and of its execution by its purported maker; hence, the official record is the requisite authenticating evidence for the original deed. Thus, the duly attested or certified copy of the record meets the requirement of authentication for the copy itself, for the official record, and for the original deed.

§ 1402. Authentication of altered writing. The party producing a writing as genuine which has been altered, or appears to have been altered, after its execution, in a part material to the question in dispute, must account for the alteration or appearance thereof. He may show that the alteration was made by another, without his concurrence, or was made with the consent of the parties affected by it, or otherwise properly or innocently made, or that the alteration did not change the meaning or language of the instrument. If he does that, he may give the writing in evidence, but not otherwise.

Article 2. Means of Authenticating and Proving Writings

§ 1410. Article not exclusive. Nothing in this article shall be construed to limit the means by which a writing may be authenticated or proved.

Comment—Law Revision Commission

This article (Sections 1410–1421) lists many of the evidentiary means for authenticating writings and supersedes the existing statutory expressions of such means.

Section 1410 ensures that the means of authentication listed in this article or stated elsewhere in the codes will not be considered the exclusive means of authenticating writings.

§ 1410.5 Graffiti constitutes a writing; admissibility. (a) For purposes of this chapter, a writing shall include any graffiti consisting of written words, insignia, symbols, or any other markings which convey a particular meaning.

(b) Any writing described in subdivision (a), or any photograph thereof, may be admitted into evidence in an action for vandalism, for the purpose of proving that the writing was made by the defendant.

(c) The admissibility of any fact offered to prove that the writing was made by the defendant shall, upon motion of the defendant, be ruled upon outside the presence of the jury, and is subject to the requirements of Sections 1416, 1417, and 1418.

§ 1411. Subscribing witness' testimony unnecessary. Except as provided by statute, the testimony of a subscribing witness is not required to authenticate a writing.

§ 1412. Use of other evidence when subscribing witness' testimony required. If the testimony of a subscribing witness is required by statute to authenticate a writing and the subscribing witness denies or does not recollect the execution of the writing, the writing may be authenticated by other evidence.

§ 1413. Witness to the execution of a writing. A writing may be authenticated by anyone who saw the writing made or executed, including a subscribing witness.

§ 1414. Authentication by admission. A writing may be authenticated by evidence that:

(a) The party against whom it is offered has at any time admitted its authenticity; or

(b) The writing has been acted upon as authentic by the party against whom it is offered.

§ 1415. Authentication by handwriting evidence. A writing may be authenticated by evidence of the genuineness of the handwriting of the maker.

§ 1416. Proof of handwriting by person familiar therewith. A witness who is not otherwise qualified to testify as an expert may state his opinion whether a writing is in the handwriting of a supposed writer if the court finds that he has personal knowledge of the handwriting of the supposed writer. Such personal knowledge may be acquired from:

(a) Having seen the supposed writer write;

(b) Having seen a writing purporting to be in the handwriting of the supposed writer and upon which the supposed writer has acted or been charged;

(c) Having received letters in the due course of mail purporting to be from the supposed writer in response to letters duly addressed and mailed by him to the supposed writer; or

(d) Any other means of obtaining personal knowledge of the handwriting of the supposed writer.

§ 1417. Comparison of handwriting by trier of fact. The genuineness of handwriting, or the lack thereof, may be proved by a comparison made by the trier of fact with handwriting (a) which the court finds was admitted or treated as genuine by the party against whom the evidence is offered or (b) otherwise proved to be genuine to the satisfaction of the court.

§ 1418. Comparison of writing by expert witness. The genuineness of writing, or the lack thereof, may be proved by a comparison made by an expert witness with writing (a) which the court finds was admitted or treated as genuine by the party against whom the evidence is offered or (b) otherwise proved to be genuine to the satisfaction of the court.

Comment—Law Revision Commission

Section 1418 applies to any form of writing, not just handwriting. This is in recognition of the fact that experts can now compare typewriting specimens and other forms of writing.

§ 1419. Exemplars when writing is 30 years old. Where a writing whose genuineness is sought to be proved is more than 30 years old, the comparison under Section 1417 or 1418 may be made with writing purporting to be genuine, and generally respected and acted upon as such, by persons having an interest in knowing whether it is genuine.

§ 1420. Authentication by evidence of reply. A writing may be authenticated by evidence that the writing was received in response to a communication sent to the person who is claimed by the proponent of the evidence to be the author of the writing.

§ 1421. Authentication by content. A writing may be authenticated by evidence that the writing refers to or states matters that are unlikely to be known to anyone other than the person who is claimed by the proponent of the evidence to be the author of the writing.

Article 3. Presumptions Affecting Acknowledged Writings and Official Writings

§ 1450. Classification of presumptions in article. The presumptions established by this article are presumptions affecting the burden of producing evidence.

Comment—Law Revision Commission

This article (Sections 1450–1454) lists several presumptions that may be used to authenticate particular kinds of writings. Section 1450 prescribes the effect of these presumptions. They require a finding of authenticity unless the adverse party produces evidence sufficient to sustain a finding that the writing in question is not authentic. See Evidence Code § 604 and the Comment thereto.

§ 1451. Acknowledged writings. A certificate of the acknowledgment of a writing other than a will, or a certificate of the proof of such a writing, is prima facie evidence of the facts recited in the certificate and the genuineness of the signature of each person by whom the writing purports to have been signed if the certificate meets the requirements of Article 3 (commencing with Section 1180) of Chapter 4, Title 4, Part 4, Division 2 of the Civil Code.

§ 1452. Official seals. A seal is presumed to be genuine and its use authorized if it purports to be the seal of:

(a) The United States or a department, agency, or public employee of the United States.

(b) A public entity in the United States or a department, agency, or public employee of such public entity.

(c) A nation recognized by the executive power of the United States or a department, agency, or officer of such nation.

(d) A public entity in a nation recognized by the executive power of the United States or a department, agency, or officer of such public entity.

(e) A court of admiralty or maritime jurisdiction.

(f) A notary public within any state of the United States.

Comment—Law Revision Commission

Under existing law, formal proof of many of the signatures and seals mentioned in Sections 1452 and 1453 is not required because such signatures and seals are the subject of judicial notice. The parties may not dispute a matter that has been judicially noticed. Code Civ.Proc. § 2102 (superseded by Evidence Code § 457). Hence, judicial notice of facts should be confined to matters concerning which there can be no reasonable dispute. The authenticity of writings purporting to be official writings should not be determined conclusively by the judge when there is serious dispute as to such authenticity. Therefore, Sections 1452 and 1453 provide that the official seals and signatures mentioned shall be presumed genuine and authorized until evidence is introduced sufficient to sustain a finding that they are not genuine or authorized. When there is such evidence disputing the authenticity of an official seal or signature, the trier of fact is required to determine the question of authenticity without regard to any presumption created by this section. See Evidence Code § 604 and the Comment thereto.

§ 1453. Domestic official signatures. A signature is presumed to be genuine and authorized if it purports to be the signature, affixed in his official capacity, of:

(a) A public employee of the United States.

(b) A public employee of any public entity in the United States.

(c) A notary public within any state of the United States.

§ 1454. Foreign official signatures. A signature is presumed to be genuine and authorized if it purports to be the signature, affixed in his official capacity, of an officer, or deputy of an officer, of a nation or public entity in a nation recognized by the executive power of the United States and the writing to which the signature is affixed is accompanied by a final statement certifying the genuineness of the signature and the official position of (a) the person who executed the writing or (b) any foreign official who has certified either the genuineness of the signature and official position of the person executing the writing or the genuineness of the signature and official position of another foreign official who has executed a similar certificate in a chain of such certificates beginning with a certificate of the genuineness of the signature and official position of the person executing the writing. The final statement may be made only by a secretary of an embassy or legation, consul general, consul, vice consul, consular agent, or other officer in the foreign service of the United States stationed in the nation, authenticated by the seal of his office.

Chapter 2

SECONDARY EVIDENCE OF WRITINGS

Article 1. Proof of the Content of a Writing

§ 1520. Proof of Content of a Writing. The content of a writing may be proved by an otherwise admissible original.

§ 1521. Secondary Evidence. (a) The content of a writing may be proved by otherwise admissible secondary evidence. The court shall exclude secondary evidence of the content of writing if the court determines either of the following:

(1) A genuine dispute exists concerning material terms of the writing and justice requires the exclusion.

(2) Admission of the secondary evidence would be unfair.

(b) Nothing in this section makes admissible oral testimony to prove the content of a writing if the testimony is inadmissible under Section 1523 (oral testimony of the content of a writing).

(c) Nothing in this section excuses compliance with Section 1401 (authentication).

(d) This section shall be known as the "Secondary Evidence Rule."

§ 1522. Original in Proponent's Possession. (a) In addition to the grounds for exclusion authorized by Section 1521, in a criminal action the court shall exclude secondary evidence of the content of a writing if the court determines that the original is in the proponent's possession, custody, or control, and the proponent has not made the original reasonably available for inspection at or before trial. This section does not apply to any of the following:

(1) A duplicate as defined in Section 260.

(2) A writing that is not closely related to the controlling issues in the action.

(3) A copy of a writing in the custody of a public entity.

(4) A copy of a writing that is recorded in the public records, if the record or a certified copy of it is made evidence of the writing by statute.

(b) In a criminal action, a request to exclude secondary evidence of the content of a writing, under this section or any other law, shall not be made in the presence of the jury.

§ 1523. Oral Testimony of Content of a Writing. (a) Except as otherwise provided by statute, oral testimony is not admissible to prove the content of a writing.

(b) Oral testimony of the content of a writing is not made inadmissible by subdivision (a) if the proponent does not have possession or control of a copy of the writing and the original is lost or has been destroyed without fraudulent intent on the part of the proponent of the evidence.

(c) Oral testimony of the content of a writing is not made inadmissible by subdivision (a) if the proponent does not have possession or control of the original or a copy of the writing and either of the following conditions is satisfied:

(1) Neither the writing nor a copy of the writing was reasonably procurable by the proponent by use of the court's process or by other available means.

(2) The writing is not closely related to the controlling issues and it would be inexpedient to require its production.

(d) Oral testimony of the content of a writing is not made inadmissible by subdivision (a) if the writing consists of numerous accounts or other writings that cannot be examined in court without great loss of time, and the evidence sought from them is only the general result of the whole.

Article 2. Official Writings and Recorded Writings

§ 1530. Copy of writing in official custody. (a) A purported copy of a writing in the custody of a public entity, or of an entry in such a writing, is prima facie evidence of the existence and content of such writing or entry if:

(1) The copy purports to be published by the authority of the nation or state, or public entity therein in which the writing is kept;

(2) The office in which the writing is kept is within the United States or within the Panama Canal Zone, the Trust Territory of the Pacific Islands, or the Ryukyu Islands, and the copy is attested or certified as a correct copy of the writing or entry by a public employee, or a deputy of a public employee, having the legal custody of the writing; or

(3) The office in which the writing is kept is not within the United States or any other place described in paragraph (2) and the copy is attested as a correct copy of the writing or entry by a person having authority to make attestation. The attestation must be accompanied by a final statement certifying the genuineness of the signature and the official position of (i) the person who attested the copy as a correct copy or (ii) any foreign official who has certified either the genuineness of the signature and official position of the person attesting the copy or the genuineness of the signature and official position of another foreign official who has executed a similar certificate in a chain of such certificates beginning with a certificate of the genuineness of the signature and official position of the person attesting the copy. Except as provided in

the next sentence, the final statement may be made only by a secretary of an embassy or legation, consul general, consul, vice consul, or consular agent of the United States, or a diplomatic or consular official of the foreign country assigned or accredited to the United States. Prior to January 1, 1971, the final statement may also be made by a secretary of an embassy or legation, consul general, consul, vice consul, consular agent, or other officer in the foreign service of the United States stationed in the nation in which the writing is kept, authenticated by the seal of his office. If reasonable opportunity has been given to all parties to investigate the authenticity and accuracy of the documents, the court may, for good cause shown, (i) admit an attested copy without the final statement or (ii) permit the writing or entry in foreign custody to be evidenced by an attested summary with or without a final statement.

(b) The presumptions established by this section are presumptions affecting the burden of producing evidence.

§ 1531. Certification of copy for evidence. For the purpose of evidence, whenever a copy of a writing is attested or certified, the attestation or certificate must state in substance that the copy is a correct copy of the original, or of a specified part thereof, as the case may be.

§ 1532. Official record of recorded writing. (a) The official record of a writing is prima facie evidence of the existence and content of the original recorded writing if:

(1) The record is in fact a record of an office of a public entity; and

(2) A statute authorized such a writing to be recorded in that office.

(b) The presumption established by this section is a presumption affecting the burden of producing evidence.

Article 3. Photographic Copies and Printed Representations of Writings

§ 1550. Types of evidence as writing admissible as the writing itself. (a) If made and preserved as a part of the records of a business, as defined in Section 1270, in the regular course of that business, the following types of evidence of a writing are as admissible as the writing itself:

(1) A nonerasable optical image reproduction or any other reproduction of a public record by a trusted system, as defined in Section 12168.7 of the Government Code, if additions, deletions, or changes to the original document are not permitted by the technology.

(2) A photostatic copy or reproduction.

(3) A microfilm, microcard, or miniature photographic copy, reprint, or enlargement.

(4) Any other photographic copy or reproduction, or an enlargement thereof.

(b) The introduction of evidence of a writing pursuant to subdivision (a) does not preclude admission of the original writing if it is still in existence. A court may require the introduction of a hard copy printout of the document.

§ 1550.1 Microphotographed reproductions: admissibility. Reproductions of files, records, writings, photographs, fingerprints or other instruments in the official custody of a criminal justice agency that were microphotographed or otherwise reproduced in a manner that conforms with the provisions of Section 11106.1, 11106.2, or 11106.3 of the Penal Code shall be admissible to the same extent and under the same circumstances as the original file, record, writing or other instrument would be admissible.

§ 1551. Photographic copies where original destroyed or lost. A print, whether enlarged or not, from a photographic film (including a photographic plate, microphotographic film, photostatic negative, or similar reproduction) of an original writing destroyed or lost after such film was taken or a reproduction from an electronic recording of video images on magnetic surfaces is admissible as the original writing itself if, at the time of the taking of such film or electronic recording, the person under whose direction and control it was taken attached thereto, or to the sealed container in which it was placed and has been kept, or incorporated in the film or electronic recording, a certification complying with the provisions of Section 1531 and stating the date on which, and the fact that, it was so taken under his direction and control.

§ 1552. Printed Representation of Computer Information or Computer Program. (a) A printed representation of computer information or a computer program is presumed to be an accurate representation of the computer information or computer program that it purports to represent. This presumption is a presumption affecting the burden of producing evidence. If a party to an action introduces evidence that a printed representation of computer information or computer program is inaccurate or unreliable, the party introducing the printed representation into evidence has the burden of proving, by a preponderance of evidence, that the printed representation is an accurate representation of the existence and content of the computer information or computer program that it purports to represent.

(b) Subdivision (a) shall not apply to computer-generated official records certified in accordance with Section 452.5 or 1530.

§ 1553. Printed Representation of Images Stored on Video or Digital Medium. A printed representation of images stored on a video or digital medium is presumed to be an accurate representation of the images it purports to represent. This presumption is a presumption affecting the burden of producing evidence. If a party to an action introduces evidence that a printed representation of images stored on a video or digital medium is inaccurate or unreliable, the party introducing the printed representation into evidence has the burden of proving, by a preponderance of evidence, that the printed representation is an accurate representation of the existence and content of the images that it purports to represent.

Article 4. Hospital Records

§ 1560. Compliance with subpoena duces tecum for business records. (a) As used in this article:

(1) "Business" includes every kind of business described in Section 1270.

(2) "Record" includes every kind of record maintained by a business.

(b) Except as provided in Section 1564, when a subpoena duces tecum is served upon the custodian of records or other qualified witness of a business in an action in which the business is neither a party nor the place where any cause of action is alleged to have arisen, and the subpoena requires the production of all or any part of the records of the business, it is sufficient compliance therewith if the custodian or other qualified witness delivers by mail or otherwise a true, legible, and durable copy of all of the records described in the subpoena to the clerk of the court or to another person described in subdivision (d) of Section 2026.010 of the Code of Civil Procedure, together with the affidavit described in Section 1561, within one of the following time periods:

(1) In any criminal action, five days after the receipt of the subpoena.

(2) In any civil action, within 15 days after the receipt of the subpoena.

(3) Within the time agreed upon by the party who served the subpoena and the custodian or other qualified witness.

(c) The copy of the records shall be separately enclosed in an inner envelope or wrapper, sealed, with the title and number of the action, name of witness, and date of subpoena clearly inscribed thereon; the sealed envelope or wrapper shall then be enclosed in an outer envelope or wrapper, sealed, and directed as follows:

(1) If the subpoena directs attendance in court, to the clerk of the court.

(2) If the subpoena directs attendance at a deposition, to the officer before whom the deposition is to be taken, at the place

designated in the subpoena for the taking of the deposition or at the officer's place of business.

(3) In other cases, to the officer, body, or tribunal conducting the hearing, at a like address.

(d) Unless the parties to the proceeding otherwise agree, or unless the sealed envelope or wrapper is returned to a witness who is to appear personally, the copy of the records shall remain sealed and shall be opened only at the time of trial, deposition, or other hearing, upon the direction of the judge, officer, body, or tribunal conducting the proceeding, in the presence of all parties who have appeared in person or by counsel at the trial, deposition, or hearing. Records that are original documents and that are not introduced in evidence or required as part of the record shall be returned to the person or entity from whom received. Records that are copies may be destroyed.

(e) As an alternative to the procedures described in subdivisions (b), (c), and (d), the subpoenaing party in a civil action may direct the witness to make the records available for inspection or copying by the party's attorney, the attorney's representative, or deposition officer as described in Section 2020.420 of the Code of Civil Procedure, at the witness' business address under reasonable conditions during normal business hours. Normal business hours, as used in this subdivision, means those hours that the business of the witness is normally open for business to the public. When provided with at least five business days' advance notice by the party's attorney, attorney's representative, or deposition officer, the witness shall designate a time period of not less than six continuous hours on a date certain for copying of records subject to the subpoena by the party's attorney, attorney's representative, or deposition officer. It shall be the responsibility of the attorney's representative to deliver any copy of the records as directed in the subpoena. Disobedience to the deposition subpoena issued pursuant to this subdivision is punishable as provided in Section 2020.240 of the Code of Civil Procedure.

§ 1561. Affidavit accompanying records. (a) The records shall be accompanied by the affidavit of the custodian or other qualified witness, stating in substance each of the following:

(1) The affiant is the duly authorized custodian of the records or other qualified witness and has authority to certify the records.

(2) The copy is a true copy of all the records described in the subpoena duces tecum, or pursuant to subdivision (e) of Section 1560 the records were delivered to the attorney, the attorney's representative, or deposition officer, for copying at the custodian's or witness' place of business, as the case may be.

(3) The records were prepared by the personnel of the business in the ordinary course of business at or near the time of the act, condition, or event.

(4) The identity of the records.

(5) A description of the mode of preparation of the records.

(b) If the business has none of the records described, or only part thereof, the custodian or other qualified witness shall so state in the affidavit, and deliver the affidavit and those records that are available in one of the manners provided in Section 1560.

(c) Where the records described in the subpoena were delivered to the attorney or his or her representative or deposition officer for copying at the custodian's or witness' place of business, in addition to the affidavit required by subdivision (a), the records shall be accompanied by an affidavit by the attorney or his or her representative or deposition officer stating that the copy is a true copy of all the records delivered to the attorney or his or her representative or deposition officer for copying.

§ 1562. Admissibility of affidavit and copy of records. If the original records would be admissible in evidence if the custodian or other qualified witness had been present and testified to the matters stated in the affidavit, and if the requirements of Section 1271 have been met, the copy of the records is admissible in evidence. The affidavit is admissible as evidence of the matters stated therein pursuant to Section 1561 and the matters so stated are presumed true. When more than one person has knowledge of the facts, more than one affidavit may be made. The presumption established by this section is a presumption affecting the burden of producing evidence.

§ 1563. One witness and mileage fee

(a) This article shall not be interpreted to require tender or payment of more than one witness fee and one mileage fee or other charge, to a witness or witness' business, unless there is an agreement to the contrary between the witness and the requesting party.

(b) All reasonable costs incurred in a civil proceeding by any witness which is not a party with respect to the production of all or any part of business records the production of which is requested pursuant to a subpoena duces tecum may be charged against the party serving the subpoena duces tecum.

(1) "Reasonable cost," as used in this section, shall include, but not be limited to, the following specific costs: ten cents ($0.10) per page for standard reproduction of documents of a size 8½ by 14 inches or less; twenty cents ($0.20) per page for copying of documents from microfilm; actual costs for the reproduction of oversize documents or the reproduction of documents requiring special processing which are made in re-

§ 1563   CALIFORNIA EVIDENCE CODE

sponse to a subpoena; reasonable clerical costs incurred in locating and making the records available to be billed at the maximum rate of twenty-four dollars ($24) per hour per person, computed on the basis of six dollars ($6) per quarter hour or fraction thereof; actual postage charges; and actual costs, if any, charged to the witness by a third person for the retrieval and return of records held offsite by that third person.

(2) The requesting party, or the requesting party's deposition officer, shall not be required to pay those costs or any estimate thereof prior to the time the records are available for delivery pursuant to the subpoena, but the witness may demand payment of costs pursuant to this section simultaneous with actual delivery of the subpoenaed records, and until payment is made, is under no obligation to deliver the records.

(3) The witness shall submit an itemized statement for the costs to the requesting party, or the requesting party's deposition officer, setting forth the reproduction and clerical costs incurred by the witness. Should the costs exceed those authorized in paragraph (1), or the witness refuses to produce an itemized statement of costs as required by paragraph (3), upon demand by the requesting party, or the requesting party's deposition officer, the witness shall furnish a statement setting forth the actions taken by the witness in justification of the costs.

(4) The requesting party may petition the court in which the action is pending to recover from the witness all or a part of the costs paid to the witness, or to reduce all or a part of the costs charged by the witness, pursuant to this subdivision, on the grounds that those costs were excessive. Upon the filing of the petition the court shall issue an order to show cause and from the time the order is served on the witness the court has jurisdiction over the witness. The court may hear testimony on the order to show cause and if it finds that the costs demanded and collected, or charged but not collected, exceed the amount authorized by this subdivision, it shall order the witness to remit to the requesting party, or reduce its charge to the requesting party by an amount equal to, the amount of the excess. In the event that the court finds the costs excessive and charged in bad faith by the witness, the court shall order the witness to remit the full amount of the costs demanded and collected, or excuse the requesting party from any payment of costs charged but not collected, and the court shall also order the witness to pay the requesting party the amount of the reasonable expenses incurred in obtaining the order including attorney's fees. If the court finds the costs were not excessive, the court shall order the requesting party to pay the witness the amount of the reasonable expenses incurred in defending the petition, including attorney's fees.

(5) If a subpoena is served to compel the production of business records and is subsequently withdrawn, or is quashed, modified or limited on a motion made other than by the witness, the witness shall be entitled to reimbursement pursuant to paragraph (1) for all costs incurred in compliance with the subpoena to the time that the requesting

party has notified the witness that the subpoena has been withdrawn or quashed, modified or limited. In the event the subpoena is withdrawn or quashed, if those costs are not paid within 30 days after demand therefor, the witness may file a motion in the court in which the action is pending for an order requiring payment, and the court shall award the payment of expenses and attorney's fees in the manner set forth in paragraph (4).

(6) Where the records are delivered to the attorney, the attorney's representative, or the deposition officer for inspection or photocopying at the witness' place of business, the only fee for complying with the subpoena shall not exceed fifteen dollars ($15) plus actual costs, if any, charged to the witness by a third person for retrieval and return of records held offsite by the third person. If the records are retrieved from microfilm, the reasonable cost, as defined in paragraph (1), shall also apply.

(c) When the personal attendance of the custodian of a record or other qualified witness is required pursuant to Section 1564, in a civil proceeding, he or she shall be entitled to the same witness fees and mileage permitted in a case where the subpoena requires the witness to attend and testify before a court in which the action or proceeding is pending and to any additional costs incurred as provided by subdivision (b).

§ 1564. Personal attendance of custodian and production of original records. The personal attendance of the custodian or other qualified witness and the production of the original records is not required unless, at the discretion of the requesting party, the subpoena duces tecum contains a clause which reads:

"The personal attendance of the custodian or other qualified witness and the production of the original records are required by this subpoena. The procedure authorized pursuant to subdivision (b) of Section 1560, and Sections 1561 and 1562, of the Evidence Code will not be deemed sufficient compliance with this subpoena."

§ 1565. Service of more than one subpoena duces tecum. If more than one subpoena duces tecum is served upon the custodian of records or other qualified witness and the personal attendance of the custodian or other qualified witness is required pursuant to Section 1564, the witness shall be deemed to be the witness of the party serving the first such subpoena duces tecum.

§ 1566. Applicability of article. This article applies in any proceeding in which testimony can be compelled.

§ 1567. Income and benefit information form. A completed form described in Section 3664 of the Family Code for income and benefit information provided by the employer may be admissible in a proceeding for modification or termination of an order for child, family, or spousal support if both of the following requirements are met:

(a) The completed form complies with Sections 1561 and 1562.

(b) A copy of the completed form and notice was served on the employee named therein pursuant to Section 3664 of the Family Code.

Chapter 3

OFFICIAL WRITINGS AFFECTING PROPERTY

§ 1600. Record of document affecting property interest. (a) The record of an instrument or other document purporting to establish or affect an interest in property is prima facie evidence of the existence and content of the original recorded document and its execution and delivery by each person by whom it purports to have been executed if:

(1) The record is in fact a record of an office of a public entity; and

(2) A statute authorized such a document to be recorded in that office.

(b) The presumption established by this section is a presumption affecting the burden of proof.

Comment—Law Revision Commission

Under Section 1600, as under existing law, if an instrument purporting to affect an interest in property is recorded, a presumption of execution and delivery of the instrument arises.

One effect of making the official record "prima facie evidence" is to create a rebuttable presumption. See Evidence Code § 602 ("A statute providing that a fact or group of facts is prima facie evidence of another fact establishes a rebuttable presumption."). The classification of this presumption as one affecting the burden of proof is consistent with the prior case law. Such a classification tends to support the record title to property by requiring that the record title be sustained unless the party attacking it can actually prove its validity. See Evidence Code § 606 and Comment thereto.

§ 1601. Proof of content of lost official record affecting property. (a) Subject to subdivisions (b) and (c), when in any action it is desired to prove the contents of the official record of any writing lost or destroyed by conflagration or other public calamity, after proof of such loss or destruction, the following may, without further proof, be admitted in evidence to prove the contents of such record:

(1) Any abstract of title made and issued and certified as correct prior to such loss or destruction, and purporting to have been prepared and made in the ordinary course of business by any person engaged in the business of preparing and making abstracts of title prior to such loss or destruction; or

(2) Any abstract of title, or of any instrument affecting title, made, issued, and certified as correct by any person engaged in the business of insuring titles or issuing abstracts of title to real estate, whether the same was made, issued, or certified before or after such loss or destruction and whether the same was made from the original records or from abstract and notes, or either, taken from such records in the preparation and upkeeping of its plant in the ordinary course of its business.

(b) No proof of the loss of the original writing is required other than the fact that the original is not known to the party desiring to prove its contents to be in existence.

(c) Any party desiring to use evidence admissible under this section shall give reasonable notice in writing to all other parties to the action who have appeared therein, of his intention to use such evidence at the trial of the action, and shall give all such other parties a reasonable opportunity to inspect the evidence, and also the abstracts, memoranda, or notes from which it was compiled, and to take copies thereof.

§ 1603. Deed by officer in pursuance of court process. A deed of conveyance of real property, purporting to have been executed by a proper officer in pursuance of legal process of any of the courts of record of this state, acknowledged and recorded in the office of the recorder of the county wherein the real property therein described is situated, or the record of such deed, or a certified copy of such record, is prima facie evidence that the property or interest therein described was thereby conveyed to the grantee named in such deed. The presumption established by this section is a presumption affecting the burden of proof.

§ 1604. Certificate of purchase or of location of lands. A certificate of purchase, or of location, of any lands in this state, issued or made in pursuance of any law of the United States or of this state, is prima facie evidence that the holder or assignee of such certificate is the owner of the land described therein; but this evidence may be overcome by proof that, at the time of the location, or time of filing a preemption claim on which the certificate may have been issued, the land was in the adverse possession of the adverse party, or those under whom he claims, or that the adverse party is holding the land for mining purposes.

§ 1605. Authenticated Spanish title records. Duplicate copies and authenticated translations of original Spanish title papers relating to land claims in this state, derived from the Spanish or Mexican governments, prepared under the supervision of the Keeper of Archives, authenticated by the Surveyor–General or his successor and by the Keeper of Archives, and filed with a county recorder, in accordance with Chapter 281 of the Statutes of 1865–66, are admissible as evidence with like force and effect as the originals and without proving the execution of such originals.

UNIFORM RULES OF EVIDENCE (1999) WITH PREFATORY NOTE AND COMMENTS*

Table of Rules

Article I. General Provisions

Rule		Page
101.	Definitions	452
102.	Scope, purpose, and construction	453
103.	Rulings on evidence	454
104.	Preliminary questions	455
105.	Limited admissibility	456
106.	Remainder of, or related, record	457

Article II. Judicial Notice

201.	Judicial notice of adjudicative facts	457

Article III. Presumptions

301.	Definitions	458
302.	Effect of presumptions in civil cases	458
303.	Scope and effect of presumptions in criminal cases	459

Article IV. Relevancy and its Limits

401.	Definition of "relevant evidence."	460
402.	Relevant evidence generally admissible; irrelevant evidence inadmissible	460
403.	Exclusion of relevant evidence on grounds of prejudice, confusion, or waste of time	460
404.	Character evidence not admissible to prove conduct, exceptions; other crimes	460
405.	Methods of proving character	462
406.	Habit; routine practice	462
407.	Subsequent remedial measures	463
408.	Compromise and offers to compromise	463
409.	Payment of medical and similar expenses	464
410.	Inadmissibility of pleas, plea discussions, and related statements	464
411.	Liability insurance	465
412.	Sexual behavior	465

Article V. Privileges

501.	Privileges recognized only as provided	468
502.	Lawyer–client privilege	468
503.	[Psychotherapist] [physician and psychotherapist] [physician and mental-health provider] [mental-health provider]-patient privilege	470
504.	Spousal privilege	473

* Reprinted by permission of the National Conference of Commissioners on Uniform State Laws, 211 E. Ontario Street, Suite 1300 Chicago, Illinois 60611.

UNIFORM RULES OF EVIDENCE

Rule		Page
505.	Religious privilege	474
506.	Political vote	474
507.	Trade secrets	474
508.	Secrets of state and other official information; governmental privileges	475
509.	Identity of informer	475
510.	Waiver of privilege	476
511.	Comment upon or inference from claim of privilege; instruction	476

Article VI. Witnesses

601.	General rule of competency	477
602.	Lack of personal knowledge	477
603.	Oath or affirmation	477
604.	Interpreters	477
605.	Competency of judge as witness	478
606.	Competency of juror as witness	478
607.	Who may impeach	478
608.	Evidence of character and conduct of witness	479
609.	Impeachment by evidence of conviction of crime	479
610.	Religious beliefs and opinions	481
611.	Mode and order of interrogation and presentation	481
612.	Record or object used to refresh memory	482
613.	Prior statement of witness	483
614.	Calling and interrogation of witness by court	483
615.	Exclusion of witnesses	483
616.	Bias of witness	484

Article VII. Opinions and Expert Testimony

701.	Opinion testimony by lay witnesses	484
702.	Testimony by experts	484
703.	Basis of opinion testimony by expert	486
704.	Opinion on ultimate issue	487
705.	Disclosure of facts or data underlying expert opinion	487
706.	Court appointed expert witness	487

Article VIII. Hearsay

801.	Definitions; exclusions	488
802.	Hearsay rule	489
803.	Hearsay exceptions: availability of declarant immaterial	490
804.	Hearsay exceptions: declarant unavailable	495
805.	Hearsay within hearsay	497
806.	Attacking and supporting credibility of declarant	497
807.	Statement of child victim	497
808.	Residual exception	499

Article IX. Authentication and Identification

901.	Requirement of authentication or identification	500
902.	Self-authentication	502
903.	Subscribing witness' testimony unnecessary	505

Article X. Content of Record, Writing, Recording, Photograph, Image, and Other Record

1001.	Definitions	505
1002.	Requirement of original	506
1003.	Admissibility of duplicates	506

UNIFORM RULES OF EVIDENCE

Rule		Page
1004.	Admissibility of other evidence of contents	506
1005.	Public records	507
1006.	Summaries	507
1007.	Testimony, or admission in record of party	507
1008.	Functions of court and jury	508

Article XI. Miscellaneous Rules

1101.	Title	508

PREFATORY NOTE

Codification of rules of evidence has proven to be more of a "work in progress" enterprise than was originally anticipated by the various drafting bodies at work in the 1970's. Societal changes, advances in both the hard and soft science and improvements in information technology have exposed many problematic evidentiary situations routinely faced by lawyers and judges. With increasing frequency, the rules fail to fit into a new environment, or alternatively, if they fit, they produce measurable inequity. It is within this context that the Drafting Committee to revise the Uniform Rules of Evidence of 1974, as amended, presented its final work product to the National Conference of Commissioners on Uniform State Laws at its 1999 Annual Meeting in Denver, Colorado.

The assignment from the Conference's Scope and Program and Executive Committees authorized a comprehensive analysis of significant problems, with directions to keep in mind that the law of evidence, being applicable to an almost unlimited range of subject matter, does not reasonably respond to micro-management by the rule maker.

It may be prudent to anticipate one area of inquiry arising from an earlier mandate directed to the Drafting Committee that concluded its work with the 1986 amendments adopted at the Boston Conference. Responding to the expanding interstate and intercourt nature of the practice of law, the Drafting Committee was charged with bringing the language of the Uniform Rules of Evidence into line with comparable provisions in the Federal Rules of Evidence, where reasonably possible. The underlying theory was, apparently, that a trial practitioner need master only one set of rules to comfortably practice in both federal and state forums located in various States, Districts, and Circuits. However, in practice, this theory does not seem to work as well as expected. In operation, the same words are often construed differently by different courts, even by sister federal circuits and state jurisdictions. Thus, the careful lawyer must continue to research certain rules of evidence on a case-by-case basis.

As a result, the current Drafting Committee has endeavored to draft the amended rules in clear and reasonably understandable terms without slavish regard for other existing work product. In this context, you will note, for the first time, that we have created a definitions rule, as amended Rule 101, containing terms that are used in several different Uniform Rules. The Drafting Committee is also proposing a unique approach to accommodate the admissibility of electronic evidence through the use of the term "record" throughout the rules in lieu of the terminology "writings," "recordings," and "photographs" and appropriately defining "record" in Rule 101(3). Numerous stylistic changes have also been made throughout the Uniform Rules as recommended by the Committee on Style.

The Drafting Committee also met on October 30–November 1, 1998 and February 26–28, 1999 to consider the comments, criticisms and suggestions of the Committee of the Whole of the Conference at the First Reading in 1988 of proposed amendments to the Uniform Rules. Hopefully, the Committee gave due consideration to all of the views expressed by Commissioners at the First Reading even though for various reasons all of them were not recommended or adopted. Among the Uniform Rules in which substantive revisions have been made based upon recommendations of the Committee of the Whole are: Rule 404(c) narrowing the scope of the procedural rules to apply in criminal cases when evidence of other crimes, wrongs or acts is offered against an accused; Rule 407 clarifying the meaning of an event in determining the applicability of the rule excluding evidence of subsequent remedial measures; Rules 803(6) and 803(8) to provide that public records inadmissible under Rule 803(8) are inadmissible as business records under Rule 803(6); and Rule 807 which tightens up the criteria for determining the admissibility of statements of children relating to neglect, or physical or sexual abuse.

It should also again be noted that Congress added Rules 413 through 415 of the Federal Rules of Evidence on September 13, 1994, Pub. L. 103–222, § 320935(a), 108 Stat. 2135, effective July 9, 1995. Rules 413 through 415 permit respectively, (1) the admissibility of evidence of prior offenses of sexual assault when, in a criminal proceeding, a person is accused of such an offense; (2) the admissibility of evidence of prior offenses of child molestation when, in a criminal proceeding, a person is accused of child molestation, and (3) the admissibility of evidence of prior offenses of sexual assault, or of child molestation when, in a civil proceeding, a claim for damages or other relief is sought against a party who is alleged to have committed an act of sexual assault or child molestation.

The overwhelming majority of judges, lawyers, law professors and legal organizations who responded to the Federal Advisory Committee's call for public response opposed the enactment of Rules 413 through 415 without equivocation. The principal objections expressed were twofold. First, the rules would permit the admission of unfairly prejudicial evidence by focusing on convicting a criminal defendant for what the defendant **is** rather than what the defendant **has done**.

Second, the rules contained numerous drafting problems apparently not intended by their authors. For example, mandating the admissibility of the evidence without regard to the other rules of evidence such as the

Rule 403 balancing test and the hearsay rule. In turn, it was believed that serious constitutional questions would arise in criminal proceedings in which the rules were invoked. For these and related reasons, the Advisory Committee on the Federal Rules of Evidence, the Standing Committee on Rules of Practice and Procedure and the Judicial Conference of the United States opposed the enactment of Rules 413 through 415.

Alternatively, the Standing Committee and the Judicial Conference recommended the adoption of an amendment to Rules 404 and 405 of the Federal Rules of Evidence proposed by the Advisory Committee which would provide for the admission of such evidence under limited conditions. However, Congress elected not to accept the recommendation.

In spite of the expressed concerns for the constitutionality of Rules 413 through 415, they are being given surprising vitality among the federal circuit courts that have considered the issue. These courts have held that the rules do not violate the Due Process Clause subject to the balancing of relevancy against unfair prejudice as provided in Rule 403 of the Federal Rules of Evidence. *See United States v. Mound*, 149 F.3d 799 (8th Cir.1998); *United States v. Sumner*, 119 F.3d 658 (8th Cir. 1997); *United States v. Castillo*, 140 F.3d 874 (10th Cir.1998); *United States v. Guardia*, 135 F.3d 1326 (10th Cir.1998); *United States v. Enjady*, 134 F.3d 1427 (10th Cir.1998); and *United States v. Larson*, 112 F.3d 600 (2d Cir.1997).

However, there is still some lingering for the constitutionality of these rules. *See* the dissenting opinion from an order denying a petition for rehearing *en banc* in *United States v. Mound*, 157 F.3d 1153 (8th Cir.1998), in which it is argued that an *en banc* court ought to consider the constitutionality of Rule 413 because the rule "presents [so] great a risk that the jury will convict a defendant for his past conduct or unsavory character" that it violates due process. *Id.* at 157 F.3d 1153. *See further*, M.A. Sheft, *Federal Rules of Evidence 413: A Dangerous New Frontier*, 33 Am. Crim. L. Rev. 57, 77–82 (1995).

In any event, the propriety of including Rules 413 through 415 in the Uniform Rules of Evidence was considered questionable at best. There is no state which has adopted these rules to date. In Arizona, their adoption was considered by the Supreme Court of Arizona, but was rejected largely for the same reasons they were rejected by the Judicial Conference of the United States. *See* Robert L. Gottsfield, *We Just Don't Get It: Improper Admission of Other Acts Under Evidence Rule 404(B) as Needless Cause of Reversal in Civil and Criminal Cases*, Ariz. Att'y, Apr. 1997 at 24. Connecticut has reprinted Federal Rules 413 through 415 in its Trial Lawyers Guide to Evidence, but they are inapplicable in state court proceedings. Indiana has a rule similar to Federal Rule 414, but it is more carefully drawn with procedural safeguards. *See* Ind. Code Ann. § 35-37-4-15 (West 1997). California also has statutes authorizing the introduction of prior sexual offenses or acts of domestic violence subject to balancing relevancy against unfair prejudice. *See* Cal. Evid. Code §§ 1108, 1109 (West 1997). Section 1108 has been held constitutional by the California Court of Appeal in *People v. Fitch* (App. 3 Dist. 1997), 63 Cal. Rptr. 753, 55 Cal. App. 4th 172. Missouri also had a blanket statutory rule, since held unconstitutional, admitting evidence of prior acts of child molestation similar to Federal Rule 414. *See* Mo. Ann. Stat. § 566.025 (West 1978).

For the foregoing reasons and apparent lack of support to date among the several states for the enactment of rules similar to Rules 413 through 415, the Drafting Committee, at its meeting in Cleveland, Ohio, on October 46, 1996, voted unanimously not to include or recommend the adoption of Rules 413 through 415 by the Conference.

Similarly, the Drafting Committee did not recommend the adoption of the Advisory Committee's earlier carefully drawn proposed amendment to Rule 404 of the Federal Rules of Evidence to deal with the issue.

These decisions of the Drafting Committee have now been reinforced by the decision of the Supreme Court of Missouri in *State v. Burns*, 978 S.W.2d 759 (Mo.1998), holding that Section 566.025, *supra*, contravened the Missouri Constitution. In Burns, a prosecution for statutory sodomy, the trial court admitted the testimony of two witnesses relating to prior uncharged acts of sexual abuse committed by the defendant pursuant to Section 566.025, RSMo 1994, providing that evidence of other charged and uncharged crimes "shall be admissible for the purpose of showing the propensity of the defendant to commit the crime or crimes with which he is charged."

The Missouri Supreme Court reasoned that Section 566.025 violated Article I, Section 17 providing "[t]hat no person shall be prosecuted criminally for felony or misdemeanor otherwise than by indictment or information" and Article I, Section 18(a) providing "[t]hat in criminal prosecutions the accused shall have the right ... to demand the nature and cause of the accusation;...." In doing so it rejected the state's argument that Section 566.062 did not violate Sections 17 and 18(a) of Article I since the defendant was not "on trial" for the uncharged conduct because he could be convicted only for the formally charged crime. This interpretation, the Court reasoned, would enable the jury to "improperly convict the defendant because of his propensity to commit such crimes without regard to whether he is actually guilty of the charged crime. * * * As a result, the defendant is forced to defend against the uncharged conduct in addition to the charged crime."

The Court also rejected the State's argument that in determining the admissibility of propensity evidence under Section 566.025 the trial court can balance the value and effect of evidence of other crimes. This interpretation, the Court also reasoned, would require ignoring the Legislature's use of the mandatory term "shall," an approach which has largely been ignored by the federal circuit courts in dealing with this issue. Finally, the defendant also contended that Section 566.025 violated the Fifth, Sixth, and Fourteenth Amendments to the United States Constitution. However, the Court did not reach these issues by concluding that the challenge under the Missouri Constitution was dispositive.

Within the foregoing approach the proposed amendments of the Uniform Rules of Evidence (1999) were approved and recommended for enactment in all states at the Conference's Annual Meeting, meeting in its One-Hundred-and-Eighth Year in Denver, Colorado, July 23-30, 1999.

ARTICLE I. GENERAL PROVISIONS

Rule 101.

DEFINITIONS

In these rules:

(1) "Person" means an individual, corporation, business trust, estate, trust, partnership, limited liability company, association, joint venture, government; governmental subdivision, agency, or instrumentality; public corporation; or any other legal or commercial entity.

(2) "Public record" means a record of a public office or agency in which the record is prepared, filed, or recorded pursuant to law.

(3) "Record" means information that is inscribed on a tangible medium or that is stored in an electronic or other medium and is retrievable in perceivable form.

(4) "State" means a State of the United States, the District of Columbia, Puerto Rico, the United States Virgin Islands, or any territory or insular possession subject to the jurisdiction of the United States.

Comment

Rules 101 and 102 have been reorganized to include a definitions rule as Rule 101. The definitions in Rule 101 are of terms that have a generic application in their use throughout the Uniform Rules of Evidence. In contrast, terms that have application only in specific Articles or Rules are separately defined in those particular Articles or Rules. With the exception of the definition of "record" in Rule 101(3), the definitions in Rule 101 are self-evident and do not need further comment.

"Record" is separately defined in Rule 101(3) to support the use of the term in Rules 106, 612, 801(a), 803(5) through 803(17), 901 through 903 and 1001 through 1007. Although the Uniform Rules prior to their amendment in 1999 included specific reference to "data compilations" to accommodate the admissibility of records stored electronically, many business and governmental records do not now consist solely of "data compilations." Rather, in today's technological environment, or as it may develop in the future, records are, or may be, kept in a variety of mediums other than in just "data compilations." Presently, "records" may include items created, or originated, on a computer, such as through word processing or spreadsheet programs; records sent and received, such as electronic mail; data stored through scanning or image processing of paper originals; and information compiled into data bases. One, or all, of these processes may be involved in ordinary and customary business and governmental record-keeping. Modern technology thus dictates that any of the foregoing types of records should be admissible when they are relevant if reasonable evidentiary thresholds of evidentiary reliability are satisfied. The Rule 101(3) definition of "record" and the substitution of the word "record" for the terms "writing," "memorandum," "report," "document," "recorded statement," and "data compilation," when appropriate, are intended to accommodate the foregoing modern innovations in record keeping. At the same time, the approach accommodates the use of these more traditional forms of record keeping as evidence.

The definition of "record" in Rule 101(3) is derived from § 5–102(a)(14) of the Uniform Commercial Code and carries forward consistently the established policy of the Conference to accommodate the use of electronic evidence in business and governmental transactions. It should be made clear that the definition includes all writings, recordings, photographs and images for the purpose of interpreting the amendments to the Uniform Rules where the term "record" is used. "Writings," "recordings," "photographs," and "images" are separately defined in Rule 1001 of Article X as these terms are used in the interpretation of the original writing rule. See further, the Comment to Uniform Rule 1001.

Rule 102.

SCOPE, PURPOSE, AND CONSTRUCTION

(a) Rules applicable. Except as otherwise provided in subdivision (b), these rules apply to all actions and proceedings in the courts of this State.

(b) Rules inapplicable. These rules, other than those applicable to privileges, do not apply in:

(1) the determination of questions of fact preliminary to admissibility of evidence if the issue is to be determined by the court under Rule 104(a);

(2) proceedings before grand juries;

(3) proceedings for contempt in which the court may act summarily; and

(4) miscellaneous proceedings, such as proceedings involving extradition or rendition; [preliminary] [probable cause] hearings in criminal cases; [sentencing]; granting or revoking probation; issuance of warrants for arrest, criminal summonses, and search warrants; and release on bail or otherwise.

(c) Purpose and construction. These rules must be construed to secure fairness, eliminate unjustifiable expense and delay, and promote the growth and development of the law of evidence, to the end that truth may be ascertained and issues justly determined.

Comment

Rule 102 combines in three subdivisions the black letter of former Rule 101 dealing with the scope of the Uniform Rules with the black letter of revisions in Rule 102 dealing with the purpose and construction of the Uniform Rules. This was done to facilitate the drafting of definitions Rule 101.

Subdivisions (a) and (b) incorporate the black letter of Uniform Rule 1101 with one technical change in subdivisions (a) and (b), style changes and one substantive change. In subdivision (b)(4) "probable cause hearing" is substituted for "detention hearing" to conform the rule to Rule 345 of the Uniform Rules of Criminal Procedure.

The phrase "miscellaneous proceedings, such as" is included in Rule 102(b)(4) to accommodate the expansion of the types of proceedings in which the rules of evidence should not apply, such as juvenile disposition hearings, to avoid attempting to catalogue the myriad types of proceedings in which the rules of evidence may not apply in the several state jurisdictions.

The word "sentencing" is bracketed in Rule 102(b)(4) to give the states flexibility in determining the extent to which rules of evidence are to apply in sentencing proceedings. This accommodates the diversity that currently exists among the several states with respect to the applicability of the rules of evidence in sentencing proceedings.

Rule 103.

RULINGS ON EVIDENCE.

(a) Effect of erroneous ruling. Error may not be predicated upon a ruling that admits or excludes evidence unless a substantial right of the party is affected, and:

> (1) if the ruling is one admitting evidence, a timely objection or motion to strike appears of record, stating the specific ground of objection, if the specific ground was not apparent from the context; or
>
> (2) if the ruling is one excluding evidence, the substance of the evidence was made known to the court by offer or was apparent from the context within which questions were asked.

(b) Record of offer and ruling. The court may add any other or further statement that shows the character of the evidence, the form in which it was offered, the objection made, and the ruling thereon. It may direct the making of an offer in question and answer form.

(c) Effect of pretrial ruling. If the court makes a definitive pretrial ruling on the record admitting or excluding evidence, a party need not renew an objection or offer of proof at trial to preserve a claim of error for appeal.

(d) Hearing of jury. In jury cases, proceedings must be conducted, to the extent practicable, so as to prevent inadmissible evidence from being suggested to the jury by any means, such as making statements or offers of proof or asking questions within the hearing of the jury.

(e) Errors affecting substantial rights. This rule does not preclude a court from taking notice of an error affecting a substantial right even if it was not brought to the attention of the trial court.

Comment

Rule 103 is amended to add a subdivision (c) to promote a uniform rule among the several states that if the court makes a definitive pretrial ruling on the record on the admission or exclusion of evidence a party need not renew the objection at trial.

RULE 104.

PRELIMINARY QUESTIONS

(a) Questions of admissibility generally. Preliminary questions concerning the qualification of an individual to be a witness, the existence of a privilege, or the admissibility of evidence must be determined by the court, subject to subdivision (b). In making its determination, the court is not bound by the rules of evidence except the rules with respect to privileges.

(b) Determination of privilege. A person claiming a privilege must prove that the conditions prerequisite to the existence of the privilege are more probably true than not. A person claiming an exception to a privilege must prove that the conditions prerequisite to the applicability of the exception are more probably true than not. If there is a factual basis to support a good faith belief that a review of the allegedly privileged material is necessary, the court, in making its determination, may review the material outside the presence of any other person.

(c) Relevancy conditioned on fact. If the relevancy of evidence depends upon the fulfillment of a condition of fact, the court shall admit it upon, in the court's discretion, subject to the introduction of evidence sufficient to support a finding of the fulfillment of the condition.

(d) Hearing of jury. A hearing on the admissibility of a confession in a criminal case must be conducted out of the hearing of the jury. A hearing on any other preliminary matter must be so conducted if the interests of justice require or, in a criminal case, an accused is a witness and so requests.

(e) Testimony by accused. An accused, by testifying upon a preliminary matter, does not become subject to cross-examination as to other issues in the case.

(f) Weight and credibility. This rule does not limit the right of a party to introduce before the jury evidence relevant to weight or credibility.

Comment

The amendment of Uniform Rule 104 to include a subdivision (b) is a condensed version of procedural rules originally proposed by the ABA Criminal Justice Section's Committee on Rules of Criminal Procedure and Evidence. Rule 104(b) is intended to accomplish two purposes.

First, it carries forward the ABA proposal by placing upon the proponent or contestant of a privilege the ultimate burden of persuasion "more probably true than not" rather than simply the production of evidence because of the importance which the existence of a privilege has in the trial of an issue of fact. It is true, at least at the federal level, that codification of an evidentiary burden is an issue which is open to dispute with one commentator taking the position that "[t]he absence of any test ... has the advantage of leaving the question for the good sense of the trial judge." *See* 2 Weinstein's Evidence, ¶ 503–121 (1992). *See further*, the opinion of the Supreme Court of the United States in *United States v. Zolin*, 491 U.S. 554, 109 S.Ct. 2619, 105 L.Ed. 2d 469, n. 7 (1989), in which the Court deferred a decision on the issue. At the same time, if determining the existence of a privilege is a critical decision in the trial, requiring this minimal degree of persuasion provides both guidance to the court and emphasizes the importance of the admissibility issue when the existence of a privilege is involved.

Second, the proposed amendment also deals with the anomaly in Rule 104(a) that arguably forecloses the disclosure of privileged matter in determining the existence of a privilege by providing that "[i]n making its determination ... [the court] is not bound by the rules of evidence except those with respect to privileges." The amendment addresses this problem by providing for disclosure of the privileged matter "outside the presence of any other person." This language in the black letter is employed in lieu of the language "in camera" sometimes employed to describe a judge's private review of evidentiary material. The terminology "in camera" is sometimes used to describe a court's private review of files without the presence of the parties, their attorneys, or spectators. *See State v. Warren*, 304 Or. 428. 746 P.2d 711 (1987). However, this is not invariably the case. The term "in camera" is sometimes used to describe a hearing outside the presence of the jury or unnecessary spectators. *See Wofford v. State*, 903 S.W.2d 796 (Tex.App.1995). Accordingly, the rule contains the more specific language to describe the type of review authorized under Rule 104(b). However, the discretion accorded to the trial court in reviewing the material outside the presence of any other person is not unfettered. The rule requires that the court find that "there is a factual basis to support a good faith belief that a review of the allegedly privilege material is necessary ..." *See United States v. Zolin*, 491 U.S. 554, 109 S.Ct. 2619, 105 L.Ed.2d 469 (1989) to the same effect

Rule 105.

LIMITED ADMISSIBILITY

If evidence that is admissible as to one party or for one purpose but not admissible as to another party or for another purpose is admitted, the court, upon request, shall restrict the evidence to its proper scope and instruct the jury accordingly.

Comment

This rule is not intended to affect a power of a court to order a severance or separate trial of issues in a multi-party case.

Rule 106.

REMAINDER OF, OR RELATED, RECORD

If a record or part thereof is introduced by a party, an adverse party may require the introduction at that time of any other part or any other record that in fairness ought to be considered contemporaneously with it.

Comment

A determination of what constitutes "fairness" includes consideration of completeness and relevancy as well as possible unfair prejudice.

ARTICLE II. JUDICIAL NOTICE

RULE 201.

JUDICIAL NOTICE OF ADJUDICATIVE FACTS

(a) Scope of rule. This rule governs only judicial notice of adjudicative facts.

(b) Kinds of facts. A judicially noticed fact must be one that is not subject to reasonable dispute because it is:

(1) generally known within the territorial jurisdiction of the trial court; or

(2) capable of accurate and ready determination by resort to sources whose accuracy cannot reasonably be questioned.

(c) When discretionary. A court may take judicial notice, whether requested or not.

(d) When mandatory. A court shall take judicial notice if requested by a party and supplied with the necessary information.

(e) Opportunity to be heard. A party is entitled upon timely request to an opportunity to be heard as to the propriety of taking judicial notice and the tenor of the matter noticed. In the absence of earlier notification, the request may be made after judicial notice has been taken.

(f) Time of taking notice. Judicial notice may be taken at any stage of the proceeding.

(g) Instructing jury. The court shall instruct the jury to accept as conclusive a fact judicially noticed.

ARTICLE III. PRESUMPTIONS

Rule 301.

DEFINITIONS

In this article:

(1) "Basic fact" means a fact or group of facts that give rise to a presumption.

(2) "Inconsistent presumption" means that the presumed fact of one presumption is inconsistent with the presumed fact of another presumption.

(3) "Presumed fact" means a fact that is assumed upon the finding of a basic fact.

(4) "Presumption" means that when a basic fact is found to exist, the presumed fact is assumed to exist until the nonexistence of the presumed fact is determined as provided in Rules 302 and 303.

Comment

This definitions rule is intended to circumvent the various confusing uses of the word "presumption" and clarify its meaning by confining its use to what has been known and applied traditionally as a "rebuttable presumption." In addition to defining the terms "basic fact" and "presumed fact," a "presumption" is given a rebuttable effect by defining the word in Rule 301(4) to mean that the presumed fact of the presumption is assumed to exist until it is determined not to exist as provided in Rule 302 governing the effect of presumptions in civil cases or Rule 303 governing the effect of presumptions in criminal cases.

Rule 302.

EFFECT OF PRESUMPTIONS IN CIVIL CASES

(a) General rule. In a civil action or proceeding, unless otherwise provided by statute, judicial decision, or these rules, a presumption imposes on the party against whom it is directed the burden of proving that the nonexistence of the presumed fact is more probable than its existence.

(b) Inconsistent presumptions. If presumptions are inconsistent, the presumption applies that is founded upon weightier considerations of policy. If considerations of policy are of equal weight, neither presumption applies.

(c) Effect if federal law provides the rule of decision. The effect of presumption respecting a fact that is an element of a claim or defense as to which federal law provides the rule of decision is determined in accordance with federal law.

Comment

Rule 302(a) in its amended form governs the effect of presumptions in civil cases by retaining former Uniform Rule 301 providing that a presumption, unless otherwise provided by statute, judicial decision, or these rules, imposes upon the party against whom it is directed the burden of proving that the nonexistence of the presumed fact is more probable than its existence. The reasons for giving this effect to rebuttable presumptions are set forth in the United States Supreme Court Advisory Committee's Note, 56 F.R.D. 183 (1972).

Rule 302(b) deals with the effect of inconsistent presumptions and retains the effect of former Rule 301(b) by providing that the presumption applies that is founded on weightier policy considerations. Neither presumption applies if the presumptions are based upon policy considerations of equal weight.

Rule 302(c) incorporates former Uniform Rule 302 providing for the effect of presumptions when federal law supplies the rule of decision. Parallel jurisdiction in state and federal courts exists in many instances. The modification of Rule 302(c) is made in recognition of this situation. The rule prescribes that when a federally created right is litigated in a state court, any prescribed federal presumption shall be applied.

Rule 303.

SCOPE AND EFFECT OF PRESUMPTIONS IN CRIMINAL CASES

(a) Scope. Except as otherwise provided by statute or judicial decision, this rule governs presumptions against an accused in criminal cases, recognized at common law or created by statute, including statutory provisions that certain facts are prima facie evidence of other facts or of guilt.

(b) Submission to jury. The court may not direct the jury to find a presumed fact against an accused. If a presumed fact establishes guilt, is an element of the offense, or negates a defense, the court may submit the question of guilt or of the existence of the presumed fact to the jury, but only if a reasonable juror on the evidence as a whole, including the evidence of the basic fact, could find guilt or the presumed fact beyond a reasonable doubt. If the presumed fact has a lesser effect, the question of its existence may be submitted to the jury if the basic fact is supported by substantial evidence or is otherwise established, unless the court determines that a reasonable juror could not find on the evidence as a whole the existence of the presumed fact.

(c) Instructing the jury. At the time the existence of a presumed fact against the accused is submitted to the jury, the court shall instruct the jury that it may regard the basic fact as sufficient evidence of the presumed fact but is not required to do so. In addition, if a presumed fact establishes guilt, is an element of the offense, or negates a defense, the court shall instruct the jury that its existence, on all the evidence, must be proved beyond a reasonable doubt.

Comment

Rule 303 retains the substance of former Uniform Rule 303 which is the same in substance as Proposed Rule 303 of the Federal Rules of Evidence. The rule provides that the effect of a presumption in a criminal case is permissive only by providing that the court may not direct the jury to find a presumed fact against an accused. If the court submits the question of the existence of a presumed fact to the jury, it shall instruct the jury that it may regard the basic fact as sufficient evidence of the presumed fact but is not required to do so. The permissive effect given to a presumption in criminal cases under Rule 303 is constitutionally in accord with this lesser effect to be given presumptions in criminal cases without incorporating the complexities associated with the allocation of the burden of producing evidence or of persuasion where a presumption is found to be mandatory. *See County Court of Ulster County v. Allen*, 442 U.S. 140, 99 S.Ct. 2213, 60 L.Ed.2d 777 (1979), *Sandstrom v. Montana*, 442 U.S. 510, 99 S.Ct. 2450, 61 L.Ed.2d 39 (1979) and *Francis v. Franklin*, 471 U.S. 307, 105 S.Ct. 1965, 85 L.Ed.2d 344 (1985).

ARTICLE IV. RELEVANCY AND ITS LIMITS

Rule 401.

DEFINITION OF "RELEVANT EVIDENCE"

In this article, "relevant evidence" means evidence having any tendency to make the existence of any fact that is of consequence to the determination of the action more probable or less probable than it would be without the evidence.

Rule 402.

RELEVANT EVIDENCE GENERALLY ADMISSIBLE; IRRELEVANT EVIDENCE INADMISSIBLE

All relevant evidence is admissible, except as otherwise provided by statute, these rules, or other rules applicable in the courts of this State. Evidence that is not relevant is not admissible.

Rule 403.

EXCLUSION OF RELEVANT EVIDENCE ON GROUNDS OF PREJUDICE, CONFUSION, OR WASTE OF TIME

Although relevant, evidence may be excluded if its probative value is substantially outweighed by the danger of unfair prejudice, confusion of the issues, or misleading the jury, or by considerations of undue delay, waste of time, or needless presentation of cumulative evidence.

Rule 404.

CHARACTER EVIDENCE NOT ADMISSIBLE TO PROVE CONDUCT, EXCEPTIONS; OTHER CRIMES

(a) Character evidence generally. Evidence of a person's character or a trait of character is not admissible for the purpose of proving the person acted in conformity therewith on a particular occasion, except:

(1) evidence of a pertinent trait of the accused's character offered by an accused, or by the prosecution to rebut that evidence;

(2) evidence of a pertinent trait of character of the alleged victim of the crime offered by an accused, or by the prosecution to rebut that evidence, or evidence of a character trait of peacefulness of the alleged victim offered by the prosecution in a homicide case to rebut evidence that the alleged victim was the first aggressor; and

(3) evidence of the character of a witness, as provided in Rules 607, 608, and 609.

(b) Other crimes, wrongs, or acts. Evidence of other crimes, wrongs, or acts is not admissible to prove the character of a person in order to show the person acted in conformity therewith. However, it may be admissible for another purpose, such as proof of motive, opportunity, intent, preparation, plan, knowledge, identity, or absence of mistake or accident.

(c) Determination of admissibility. Evidence is not admissible under subdivision (b) unless:

(1) the proponent gives to all adverse parties reasonable notice in advance of trial, or during trial if the court excuses pretrial notice for good cause shown, of the nature of the evidence the proponent intends to introduce at trial;

(2) if offered against an accused in a criminal case, the court conducts a hearing to determine the admissibility of the evidence and finds:

(A) by clear and convincing evidence, that the other crime, wrong, or act was committed;

(B) that the evidence is relevant to a purpose for which the evidence is admissible under subdivision (b); and

(C) that the probative value of the evidence outweighs the danger of unfair prejudice; and

(3) upon the request of a party, the court gives an instruction on the limited admissibility of the evidence pursuant to Rule 105.

Comment

Rule 404 has been amended to add a subdivision (c) to incorporate procedural guidelines to govern the admissibility of other crimes wrongs, or acts evidence when it is offered for one of the permissible purposes authorized by Rule 404(b) and reflect in black letter a substantial body of decisional law existing among the several states The notice provision in Rule 404(c)(1) applies to any party seeking to offer the evidence in any case, civil or criminal, without requiring a request by the accused, or any other party.

Rules 404 (c)(2) through (c)(3) apply in criminal cases only when offered against an accused. The procedural provisions would then have to be satisfied before evidence could be admitted for one of the exceptional purposes authorized in Rule 404(b). Subdivision (c)(2) requires the trial court to conduct a hearing to determine the admissibility of the evidence and determine as a preliminary question for the court that the other crime, wrong, or act was committed. Subdivisions (c)(2)(A) through (C) also require that the court find by the clear and convincing evidence standard of persuasion that the other crime, wrong, or act was committed, is relevant to a purpose for which the evidence is admissible under Rule 404(b) other than conduct conforming with a character trait and that the probative value of the evidence outweighs the danger of unfair prejudice.

Subdivision (c)(3) provides that upon the request of a party the court shall give an instruction on the limited admissibility of the evidence pursuant to Uniform Rule 105. This approach is preferable for three reasons. First, it gives the party against whom the evidence is being admitted the discretion of deciding whether a limiting instruction ought to be given against the risk of unnecessarily emphasizing the limited purpose for which the evidence is being admitted. Second, at the same time, it requires the trial court to give the instruction when requested by a party. Third, it emphasizes the importance of a party considering, and the court giving, a limiting instruction because of the risks associated with the admission of other crimes, wrongs, or acts evidence.

Rule 405.

METHODS OF PROVING CHARACTER

(a) Reputation or opinion. If evidence of character or a trait of character of a person is admissible, proof may be by testimony as to reputation or in the form of opinion. On cross-examination, inquiry is allowable into relevant specific instances of conduct.

(b) Specific instances of conduct. If character or a trait of character of a person is an essential element of a charge, claim, or defense, proof may also be made of specific instances of the person's conduct.

Rule 406.

HABIT; ROUTINE PRACTICE

(a) Admissibility. Evidence of the habit of an individual or of the routine practice of a person other than an individual, whether corroborated or not and regardless of the presence of eyewitnesses, is relevant to prove that the conduct of the individual or other person on a particular occasion was in conformity with the habit or routine practice.

(b) Method of proof. Habit or routine practice may be proved by testimony in the form of an opinion or by specific instances of conduct sufficient in number to warrant a finding that the habit existed or that the practice was routine.

Rule 407.

SUBSEQUENT REMEDIAL MEASURES

If, after an event, measures are taken that, if taken previously, would have made injury or harm less likely to occur, evidence of the subsequent measures is not admissible to prove negligence, culpable conduct, a defect in a product, a defect in a product's design, or a need for a warning or instruction. Evidence of subsequent measures may be admissible if offered for another purpose, such as impeachment or, if controverted, proof of ownership, control, or feasibility of precautionary measures. An event includes the sale of a product to a user or consumer.

Comment

Rule 407 has been amended to make the rule applicable to products liability cases even though the states are almost evenly divided on the issue. Nevertheless, the rule as amended reflects the judgment of the Conference that the policy supporting the exclusion of evidence of subsequent remedial measures ought to apply to products liability cases as well as to negligence actions unless the evidence is offered for one or the other of the purposes set forth in the second sentence of the rule. An "event," as used in the rule, is defined in the last sentence to include "the sale of a product to a user or consumer" and also reflects the judgment of the Conference that the rule ought to apply to pre-accident, post-manufacturing remedial measures as well as to post-accident remedial measures. The rule thereby provides an incentive to take remedial measures before the injury, or harm, giving rise to the cause of action has occurred.

Rule 408.

COMPROMISE AND OFFERS TO COMPROMISE

Evidence of furnishing, offering, promising to furnish, or accepting, offering, or promising to accept, a valuable consideration in compromising or attempting to compromise a claim that was disputed as to either validity or amount is not admissible to prove liability for, invalidity of, or amount of the claim, or any other claim. Evidence of conduct or statements made in compromise negotiations is likewise not admissible. This rule does not require the exclusion of evidence otherwise discoverable merely because it is presented in the course of compromise negotiations. This rule also does not require exclusion if the evidence is offered for another purpose, such as proving bias or prejudice of a witness, negating a contention of undue delay, or proving an effort to obstruct a criminal investigation or prosecution.

Comment

Rule 408 has been adopted as amended in 1988 with the exception of the last sentence "[c]ompromise negotiations encompass mediation." As amended the rule is silent with respect to the forms of voluntary dispute resolution in which compromise negotiations falling within the rule can be conducted. The rule thus avoids any attempt at uniformity with respect to what constitutes inadmissible compromise negotiations in voluntary dispute resolution mechanisms, an area with respect to which there is considerable disagreement from state to state. This is left to state statutory or decisional law on a case-by-case basis.

Rule 409.

PAYMENT OF MEDICAL AND SIMILAR EXPENSES

Evidence of furnishing, offering, or promising to pay medical, hospital, or similar expenses occasioned by an injury is not admissible to prove liability for the injury.

Rule 410.

INADMISSIBILITY OF PLEAS, PLEA DISCUSSIONS, AND RELATED STATEMENTS

(a) General. Except as otherwise provided in subdivision (b), evidence of the following is not admissible in a civil or criminal proceeding against the defendant who made the plea or was a participant in the plea discussions:

(1) a plea of guilty that was later withdrawn;

(2) a plea of nolo contendere;

(3) a statement made in the course of any proceedings under Rule 11 of the Federal Rules of Criminal Procedure, [Rules 443 and 444 of the Uniform Rules of Criminal Procedure, or comparable state procedure of this or any other State] regarding either of the foregoing pleas; and

(4) a statement made in the course of plea discussions with an attorney for the prosecuting authority which do not result in a plea of guilty or which result in a plea of guilty later withdrawn.

(b) Exceptions. A statement described in subdivision (a) is admissible:

(1) in a proceeding in which another statement made in the course of the same plea or plea discussions has been introduced and, in fairness, the statement should be considered contemporaneously with the other statement; and

(2) in a criminal proceeding for perjury or false statement if the statement was made by the defendant under oath, on the record, and in the presence of counsel.

Comment

Rule 410, with changes in format, has been amended by substituting the substance of revised Rule 410 of the Federal Rules of Evidence which became effective December 1, 1980 for the former Rule 410 excluding evidence of withdrawn pleas, offers to plead and statements made in connection with any such pleas or offers to plead. Most of the litigation throughout the several states has centered on the statements that are made during the plea negotiation process and the persons to whom such statements must be made to determine whether the statutory ban on the admission of evidence of such negotiations is applicable. In the latter case, interpretive difficulties have been encountered in determining whether statements made to persons other than attorneys for the prosecuting authorities fall within the exclusionary rule. This problem is avoided in Rule 410 by providing only for the exclusion of "any statement made in the course of plea discussions with an attorney for the prosecuting authority which do not result in a plea of guilty or which result in a plea of guilty later withdrawn."

Rule 411.

LIABILITY INSURANCE

Evidence that a person was or was not insured against liability is not admissible upon the issue as to whether the person acted negligently or otherwise wrongfully. This rule does not require the exclusion of evidence of insurance against liability when offered for another purpose, such as proof of agency, ownership, or control, or bias or prejudice of a witness.

Rule 412.

SEXUAL BEHAVIOR

(a) Definition. In this rule, "sexual behavior" means behavior relating to the sexual activities of an individual, including the individual's experience or observation of sexual intercourse or sexual contact, use of contraceptives, history of marriage or divorce, sexual predisposition, expressions of sexual ideas or emotions, and activities of the mind such as fantasies or dreams.

(b) Evidence of sexual behavior generally inadmissible. Except as otherwise provided in subdivisions (c) and (d), in a criminal proceeding involving the alleged sexual misconduct of an accused, evidence may not be admitted to prove that the alleged victim engaged in other sexual behavior.

(c) Exceptions. Evidence of specific instances of an alleged victim's sexual behavior, if otherwise admissible under these rules, is admissible to prove:

(1) that a person other than the accused was the source of the semen, injury, disease, other physical evidence, or pregnancy;

(2) that a person other than the accused was the source of the alleged victim's knowledge of sexual behavior;

(3) consent, if the alleged victim's sexual behavior involved the accused or constituted conduct so distinctive and which so closely

resembles the accused's version of the sexual behavior of the alleged victim at the time of the alleged sexual misconduct that it corroborates the accused's claim of reasonable belief that the alleged victim consented to the alleged misconduct; or

(4) a fact of consequence whose exclusion would violate the constitutional rights of the accused.

(d) Procedure to determine admissibility. Evidence is not admissible under subdivision (c) unless:

(1) the proponent gives to all parties and to the alleged victim, or the alleged victim's guardian or representative, reasonable notice in advance of trial, or during trial if the court excuses pretrial notice for good cause shown, of the nature of such evidence the proponent intends to introduce at trial;

(2) the court conducts a hearing in chambers, affords the alleged victim and the parties a right to attend the hearing and be heard, and finds:

(A) that the evidence is relevant to a fact of consequence for which the evidence is admissible under subdivision (c); and

(B) that the probative value of the evidence is not substantially outweighed by the danger of harm to the alleged victim or of unfair prejudice to any party; and

(3) upon request, the court gives an instruction on the limited admissibility of the evidence, pursuant to Rule 105.

Comment

Rule 412 constitutes a new rule providing for the exclusion in a criminal proceeding involving the alleged sexual misconduct of an accused of evidence of the past sexual behavior of the alleged victim. There are six features of Rule 412 that deserve comment. First, the applicability of the rule is limited to criminal cases and is consistent in this respect with the overwhelming majority rule among the several states. Applying Rule 412 in all criminal cases seems obvious in view of the strong social policy of protecting the privacy of victims of sexual misconduct, as well as encouraging victims to report criminal acts of sexual misconduct. It is less clear whether the rule should apply in the civil context in view of the few state jurisdictions which inconsistently apply the exclusionary rule in such proceedings. For these reasons a rule has been adopted which applies only to criminal proceedings.

Second, consistently with state jurisdictions, Rule 412 employs and broadly defines the term "sexual behavior" for the broadest type of protection to alleged victims of sexual misconduct of an accused.

Third, Rule 412 applies only to the "alleged victims" of sexual misconduct. This terminology is used because there will frequently be a dispute as to whether the alleged sexual misconduct occurred. However, the rule does not apply unless the person against whom the evidence is offered can reasonably be characterized as a victim of the alleged sexual misconduct. In addition, and consistently with the statutory rules in force in most of the states, Rule 412 applies only where the accused is a party to the proceeding on the complaint of the victim of the alleged sexual misconduct.

Fourth, Rule 412 seeks to achieve its objectives by affording the broadest possible protection to alleged victims of sexual misconduct, whether offered as substantive evidence or for impeachment, unless permitted under one of the designated exceptions set forth in subdivision (c).

Fifth, generally speaking, the exceptions to the general rule excluding evidence of the sexual behavior of an alleged victim are narrower than in former Rule 412. Subdivision (c)(1) admitting specific instances of the alleged victim's sexual behavior to prove that a person other than the accused was the source of the semen, injury, disease, other physical evidence, or pregnancy is consistent with former Uniform Rule 412 and is a commonly recognized exception throughout the several states.

The exception in subdivision (c)(2) admitting specific instances of an alleged victim's sexual behavior to prove that a person other than the accused was the source of the alleged victim's knowledge of sexual behavior applies where that victim's knowledge of sexual behavior is unusual, given the age, intelligence, or level of experience of the victim. At the same time, this exception should not be read so broadly as to permit the introduction of evidence of other sexual behavior that has not been raised as an issue in the case. Balancing the relevancy of the evidence against the danger of unfair prejudice under Uniform Rules 401 and 403 is also required in determining the admissibility of the evidence under subdivision (c)(2).

Subdivision (c)(3) is intended to facilitate proof of consent to the sexual behavior where it has been made an issue in the case. *See* Model Penal Code § 2.11(1) providing that consent is a defense to a crime "if such consent negatives an element of the offense" or if it "precludes the infliction of the harm or evil sought to be prevented by the law defining the offense." The defense is based upon the general rule that mistake of fact will disprove a crime if the mistaken belief is honestly entertained, based upon reasonable grounds and is of such a nature that the conduct would have been lawful and proper if the facts had been as they reasonably seemed to be. *See* Perkins and Boyce, Criminal Law 1045 (3d ed. 1982). However, even if the sexual behavior involved the accused it is not automatically admissible. The factors of remoteness and similarity should be considered in determining the relevancy of the alleged victim's sexual behavior with the accused, as well as determining whether the relevancy of the evidence is substantially outweighed by the danger of unfair prejudice within the meaning of Uniform Rules 401 and 403.

If the sexual behavior involved the alleged victim's sexual behavior with a person other than the accused it must be so distinctive and so closely resemble the accused's version of the sexual behavior of the alleged victim with the accused that it corroborates the accused's claim of reasonable belief that the alleged victim had consented to the alleged sexual misconduct. As in the case of consent based upon the past sexual behavior of the accused, the rule also requires a Uniform Rule 401 and 403 balancing process in the determining the admissibility of the evidence of sexual behavior of the alleged victim with a person other than the accused.

The exception in subdivision (c)(4) provides that specific instances of the alleged victim's sexual behavior is admissible to prove "a fact of consequence the exclusion of which would violate the constitutional rights of the accused." This exception is based upon the recognition of the Supreme Court of the United States that an accused may have a right to introduce evidence pursuant to the Confrontation Clause which would otherwise be precluded by an evidence rule. *See Olden v. Kentucky*, 488 U.S. 227, 109 S.Ct. 480, 102 L.Ed.2d 513 (1988), in which the Court held that a defendant in his prosecution for rape had a right to inquire into the alleged victim's cohabitation with another man to prove bias. If the evidence is constitutionally required it is admissible without regard to the balancing process provided for in the procedural rules of subdivision (d).

The procedural rules set forth in subdivision (d) requiring the giving of notice, holding a hearing in chambers to determine the admissibility of the evidence, a finding that the evidence is relevant to a fact of consequence for which it is offered, a finding that the relevancy of the evidence is not substantially outweighed by the danger of unfair prejudice and the giving of a limiting instruction are consistent with, though not necessarily identical to, varying procedural rules in force in the several states.

ARTICLE V. PRIVILEGES

Rule 501.

PRIVILEGES RECOGNIZED ONLY AS PROVIDED

Except as otherwise provided by constitution or statute or by these or other rules promulgated by [the Supreme Court of this State], no person has a privilege to:

(1) refuse to be a witness;

(2) refuse to disclose any matter;

(3) refuse to produce any object or record; or

(4) prevent another from being a witness or disclosing any matter or producing any object or record.

Comment

The word "record" has been substituted for the word "writing." See the Comment to Rule 101.

Rule 502.

LAWYER–CLIENT PRIVILEGE

(a) Definitions. In this rule:

(1) "Client" means a person for whom a lawyer renders professional legal services or who consults a lawyer with a view to obtaining professional legal services from the lawyer.

(2) A communication is "confidential" if it is not intended to be disclosed to third persons other than those to whom disclosure is made in furtherance of the rendition of professional legal services to

the client or those reasonably necessary for the transmission of the communication.

(3) "Lawyer" means a person authorized, or reasonably believed by the client to be authorized, to engage in the practice of law in any State or country.

(4) "Representative of the client" means a person having authority to obtain professional legal services, or to act on legal advice rendered, on behalf of the client or a person who, for the purpose of effectuating legal representation for the client, makes or receives a confidential communication while acting in the scope of employment for the client.

(5) "Representative of the lawyer" means a person employed, or reasonably believed by the client to be employed, by the lawyer to assist the lawyer in rendering professional legal services.

(b) General rule of privilege. A client has a privilege to refuse to disclose and to prevent any other person from disclosing a confidential communication made for the purpose of facilitating the rendition of professional legal services to the client:

(1) between the client or a representative of the client and the client's lawyer or a representative of the lawyer;

(2) between the lawyer and a representative of the lawyer;

(3) by the client or a representative of the client or the client's lawyer or a representative of the lawyer to a lawyer or a representative of a lawyer representing another party in a pending action and concerning a matter of common interest therein;

(4) between representatives of the client or between the client and a representative of the client; or

(5) among lawyers and their representatives representing the same client.

(c) Who may claim privilege. The privilege under this rule may be claimed by the client, the client's guardian or conservator, the personal representative of a deceased client, or the successor, trustee, or similar representative of a corporation, association, or other organization, whether or not in existence. A person who was the lawyer or the lawyer's representative at the time of the communication is presumed to have authority to claim the privilege, but only on behalf of the client.

(d) Exceptions. There is no privilege under this rule:

(1) if the services of the lawyer were sought or obtained to enable or aid anyone to commit or plan to commit what the client knew or reasonably should have known was a crime or fraud;

(2) as to a communication relevant to an issue between parties who claim through the same deceased client, regardless of whether

the claims are by testate or intestate succession or by transaction inter vivos;

(3) as to a communication relevant to an issue of breach of duty by a lawyer to the client or by a client to the lawyer;

(4) as to a communication necessary for a lawyer to defend in a legal proceeding an accusation that the lawyer assisted the client in criminal or fraudulent conduct;

(5) as to a communication relevant to an issue concerning an attested document to which the lawyer is an attesting witness;

(6) as to a communication relevant to a matter of common interest between or among two or more clients if the communication was made by any of them to a lawyer retained or consulted in common, when offered in an action between or among any of the clients; or

(7) as to a communication between a public officer or agency and its lawyers unless the communication concerns a pending investigation, claim, or action and the court determines that disclosure will seriously impair the ability of the public officer or agency to act upon the claim or conduct a pending investigation, litigation, or proceeding in the public interest.

Comment

The language, "or reasonably believed by the client to be employed," is added in subdivision (a)(5) to assure that the client does not lose the benefit of the privilege in situations where a representative of a lawyer is not in the employment of the lawyer, but is nevertheless reasonably believed by the client to be employed by the lawyer at the time of the communication intended by the client to be confidential. While the test in this subdivision, as in subdivision (a)(3), is partially subjective, it is not totally subjective since there must be some reasonable basis for the belief.

Rule 502 has also been amended to include a subdivision (d)(4) providing that there is no privilege under the rule "as to a communication necessary for a lawyer to defend in a legal proceeding a charge that the lawyer assisted the client in criminal or fraudulent conduct." Access to otherwise privileged communications seems essential if the lawyer is defending a charge of assisting a client in criminal or fraudulent conduct.

Rule 503.

[PSYCHOTHERAPIST] [PHYSICIAN AND PSYCHOTHERAPIST] [PHYSICIAN AND MENTAL-HEALTH PROVIDER] [MENTAL-HEALTH PROVIDER]-PATIENT PRIVILEGE

(a) Definitions. In this rule:

(1) A communication is "confidential" if it is not intended to be disclosed to third persons, except those present to further the

interest of the patient in the consultation, examination, or interview, those reasonably necessary for the transmission of the communication, and persons who are participating in the diagnosis and treatment of the patient under the direction of a [psychotherapist] [physician or psychotherapist] [physician or mental-health provider] [mental-health provider], including members of the patient's family.

[(2) "Mental-health provider" means a person authorized, in any State or country, or reasonably believed by the patient to be authorized, to engage in the diagnosis or treatment of a mental or emotional condition, including addiction to alcohol or drugs.]

[(3) "Patient" means an individual who consults or is examined or interviewed by a [psychotherapist] [physician or psychotherapist] [physician or mental-health provider] [mental-health provider].]

[(4) "Physician" means a person authorized in any State or country, or reasonably believed by the patient to be authorized to practice medicine.]

[(5) "Psychotherapist" means a person authorized in any State or country, or reasonably believed by the patient to be authorized, to practice medicine, while engaged in the diagnosis or treatment of a mental or emotional condition, including addiction to alcohol or drugs, or a person licensed or certified under the laws of any State or country, or reasonably believed by the patient to be licensed or certified, as a psychologist, while similarly engaged.]

(b) General rule of privilege. A patient has a privilege to refuse to disclose and to prevent any other person from disclosing confidential communications made for the purpose of diagnosis or treatment of the patient's [physical,] mental[,] or emotional condition, including addiction to alcohol or drugs, among the patient, the patient's [psychotherapist] [physician or psychotherapist] [physician or mental-health provider] [mental-health provider] and persons, including members of the patient's family, who are participating in the diagnosis or treatment under the direction of the [psychotherapist] [physician or psychotherapist] [physician or mental-health provider] [mental-health provider].

(c) Who may claim the privilege. The privilege under this rule may be claimed by the patient, the patient's guardian or conservator, or the personal representative of a deceased patient. The person who was the [psychotherapist] [physician or psychotherapist] [physician or mental-health provider] [mental-health provider] at the time of the communication is presumed to have authority to claim the privilege, but only on behalf of the patient.

(d) Exceptions. There is no privilege under this rule for a communication:

(1) relevant to an issue in proceedings to hospitalize the patient for mental illness, if the [psychotherapist] [physician or psychothera-

pist] [physician or mental-health provider] [mental-health provider], in the course of diagnosis or treatment, has determined that the patient is in need of hospitalization;

(2) made in the course of a court-ordered investigation or examination of the [physical,] mental[,] or emotional condition of the patient, whether a party or a witness, with respect to the particular purpose for which the examination is ordered, unless the court orders otherwise;

(3) relevant to an issue of the [physical,] mental[,] or emotional condition of the patient in any proceeding in which the patient relies upon the condition as an element of the patient's claim or defense or, after the patient's death, in any proceeding in which any party relies upon the condition as an element of the party's claim or defense;

(4) if the services of the [psychotherapist] [physician or psychotherapist] [physician or mental-health provider] [mental-health provider] were sought or obtained to enable or aid anyone to commit or plan to commit what the patient knew, or reasonably should have known, was a crime or fraud or mental or physical injury to the patient or another individual;

(5) in which the patient has expressed an intent to engage in conduct likely to result in imminent death or serious bodily injury to the patient or another individual;

(6) relevant to an issue in a proceeding challenging the competency of the [psychotherapist] [physician or psychotherapist] [physician or mental-health provider] [mental-health provider];

(7) relevant to a breach of duty by the [psychotherapist] [physician or psychotherapist] [physician or mental-health provider] [mental-health provider]; or

(8) that is subject to a duty to disclose under [statutory law].

Comment

The amendment of Rule 503 to incorporate a "mental health provider" privilege is an outgrowth of a belief that some form of a "licensed social worker" privilege should be incorporated in the Uniform Rules of Evidence to comport, at least in part, with the decision of the Supreme Court of the United States in *Jaffee v. Redmond*, 518 U.S. 1, 116 S.Ct. 1923, 135 L.Ed.2d 337 (1996), recognizing what may be generally described as a "social worker privilege" privilege. However, the amendment represents a narrower concept of the privilege than a broadly defined "social worker privilege" which would be fraught with interpretive difficulties and unnecessarily interfere with litigation in an evidentiary system based largely upon the fundamental principle that "the public ... has a right to every ... [person's] evidence" and that testimonial privileges "are not lightly created nor expansively construed, for they are in derogation of the search for truth." See *Trammel v. United States*, 445 U.S. 40, 50, 100 S.Ct. 906, 912, 63 L.Ed.2d 186 (1980), together with *United States v. Nixon*, 418 U.S. 683, 710, 94

S.Ct. 3090, 3108, 41 L.Ed.2d 1039 (1974). This policy led the Conference to adopt a narrower form of the privilege denominated a "mental health provider" privilege protecting only communications relating to the "treatment of a mental or emotional condition, including alcohol or drug addiction" and incorporating the privilege in the physician and psychotherapist-patient privilege of Rule 503.

The exceptions to the privilege established by Rule 503 have also been broadened in subdivision (d). The exceptions have a generic application, not only to the mental health provider privilege, but also to the physician-patient or psychotherapist-patient privilege embraced within the rule as well. The exceptions to the "social worker privilege" recognized in the several states are numerous and varied. However, it is believed that most of the exceptions recognized in the several states will be subsumed under one or the other of the exceptions set forth in amended Rule 503(d), in particular, under subdivision (d)(8) providing that there is no privilege under the rule for a communication "that is subject to a duty to disclose under [statutory law]."

Finally, flexibility for the several states in the adoption of the rule is preserved through bracketing the provisions relating to the physician-patient, psychotherapist-patient and mental health provider privileges.

Rule 504.

SPOUSAL PRIVILEGE

(a) Confidential communication. A communication is confidential if it is made privately by an individual to the individual's spouse and is not intended for disclosure to any other person.

(b) Marital communications. An individual has a privilege to refuse to testify and to prevent the individual's spouse or former spouse from testifying as to any confidential communication made by the individual to the spouse during their marriage. The privilege may be waived only by the individual holding the privilege or by the holder's guardian or conservator, or the individual's personal representative if the individual is deceased.

(c) Spousal testimony in criminal proceeding. The spouse of an accused in a criminal proceeding has a privilege to refuse to testify against the accused spouse.

(d) Exceptions. There is no privilege under this rule:

(1) in any civil proceeding in which the spouses are adverse parties;

(2) in any criminal proceeding in which an unrefuted showing is made that the spouses acted jointly in the commission of the crime charged,;

(3) in any proceeding in which one spouse is charged with a crime or tort against the person or property of the other, a minor child of either, an individual residing in the household of either, or a third person if the crime or tort is committed in the course of committing a crime or tort against the other spouse, a minor child of

either spouse, or an individual residing in the household of either spouse; or

(4) in any other proceeding, in the discretion of the court, if the interests of a minor child of either spouse may be adversely affected by invocation of the privilege.

Rule 505.

RELIGIOUS PRIVILEGE

(a) Definitions. In this rule:

(1) "Cleric" means a minister, priest, rabbi, accredited Christian Science Practitioner, or other similar functionary of a religious organization, or an individual reasonably believed so to be by the individual consulting the cleric.

(2) A communication is "confidential" if it is made privately and not intended for further disclosure except to other persons present in furtherance of the purpose of the communication.

(b) General rule of privilege. An individual has a privilege to refuse to disclose and to prevent another from disclosing a confidential communication by the individual to a cleric in the cleric's professional capacity as spiritual adviser.

(c) Who may claim the privilege. The privilege under this rule may be claimed by an individual or the individual's guardian or conservator, or the individual's personal representative if the individual is deceased. The individual who was the cleric at the time of the communication is presumed to have authority to claim the privilege but only on behalf of the communicant.

Rule 506.

POLITICAL VOTE

(a) General rule of privilege. An individual has a privilege to refuse to disclose the tenor of the individual's vote at a political election conducted by secret ballot.

(b) Exceptions. The privilege under subdivision (a) does not apply if the court finds that the vote was cast illegally or determines that disclosure should be compelled pursuant to [the election laws of the State].

Rule 507.

TRADE SECRETS

A person has a privilege, which may be claimed by the person or the person's agent or employee, to refuse to disclose and to prevent other persons from disclosing a trade secret owned by the person, if the allowance of the privilege will not tend to conceal fraud or otherwise work injustice. If disclosure is directed, the court shall take such protective measures as the interest of the holder of the privilege and of the parties and the interests of justice require.

Rule 508.

SECRETS OF STATE AND OTHER OFFICIAL INFORMATION; GOVERNMENTAL PRIVILEGES

(a) Claim of privilege under law of United States. If the law of the United States creates a governmental privilege that the courts of this State must recognize under the Constitution of the United States, the privilege may be claimed as provided by the law of the United States.

(b) Privileges created by laws of State. No governmental privilege is recognized except as provided in subdivision (a) or created by the constitution, statutes, or rules of this State.

(c) Effect of sustaining claim. If a claim of governmental privilege is sustained and it appears that a party is thereby deprived of material evidence, the court shall make any further orders the interests of justice require, including striking the testimony of a witness, declaring a mistrial, finding upon an issue as to which the evidence is relevant, or dismissing the action.

Rule 509.

IDENTITY OF INFORMER

(a) Rule of privilege. The United States or a State has a privilege to refuse to disclose the identity of an individual who has furnished information relating to or assisted in an investigation of a possible violation of a law to a law enforcement officer or member of a legislative committee or its staff conducting an investigation.

(b) Who may claim. The privilege under this rule may be claimed by an appropriate representative of the government to which the information was furnished.

(c) Exceptions. There is no privilege under this rule if the identity of the informer or the informer's interest in the subject matter of the informer's communication has been disclosed by a holder of the privilege or by the informer's own action to persons who would have cause to resent the communication or if the informer appears as a witness for the government.

(d) Procedures. If it appears that an informer may be able to give testimony relevant to an issue in a criminal case, or to a fair determination of a material issue on the merits in a civil case to which the government is a party, and the informed government invokes the privilege, the court shall give the government an opportunity to show in chambers facts relevant to whether the informer can, in fact, supply the testimony. The showing ordinarily will be by affidavit, but the court may direct that testimony be taken if it finds that the matter cannot be resolved satisfactorily upon affidavit. If the court finds there is a reasonable probability that the informer can give the testimony, and the government elects not to disclose the informer's identity, in criminal cases the court on motion of the defendant or on its own motion shall grant appropriate relief, which may include one or more of the following: requiring the prosecuting attorney to comply, granting the defendant additional time or a continuance, relieving the defendant from making disclosures otherwise required of the defendant, prohibiting the prosecuting attorney from introducing specified evidence, and dismissing charges. In civil cases, the court may issue any order the interests of justice require. Evidence submitted to the court must be sealed and preserved to be made available to the appellate court in the event of an appeal, and the contents may not otherwise be revealed without consent of the informed government. All counsel and parties may be present at every stage of a proceeding under this subdivision except a showing in chambers, if the court has determined that no counsel or party may be present.

Rule 510.

WAIVER OF PRIVILEGE

(a) Voluntary disclosure. A person upon whom these rules confer a privilege against disclosure waives the privilege if the person or the person's predecessor, while holder of the privilege, voluntarily discloses or consents to disclosure of any significant part of the privileged matter. This rule does not apply if the disclosure itself is privileged.

(b) Involuntary disclosure. A claim of privilege is not waived by a disclosure that was compelled erroneously or made without an opportunity to claim the privilege.

Comment

Uniform Rule 510 has been amended to deal with both the voluntary and involuntary waiver of a privilege in one comprehensive rule. Existing Rule 511 has been deleted and Rule 512 has been renumbered as Rule 511. There is no change in the substance of either of the rules.

Rule 511.

COMMENT UPON OR INFERENCE FROM CLAIM OF PRIVILEGE; INSTRUCTION

(a) Comment or inference not permitted. A claim of privilege, whether in the present proceeding or upon a previous occasion, is not a proper subject of comment by judge or counsel. No inference may be drawn from the claim.

(b) Claiming privilege without knowledge of jury. In jury cases, proceedings must be conducted, to the extent practicable, so as to facilitate the making of claims of privilege without the knowledge of the jury.

(c) Jury instruction. Upon request, any party against whom the jury might draw an adverse inference from a claim of privilege is entitled to an instruction that no inference may be drawn therefrom.

ARTICLE VI. WITNESSES

Rule 601.

GENERAL RULE OF COMPETENCY

Every individual is competent to be a witness except as otherwise provided in these rules.

Rule 602.

LACK OF PERSONAL KNOWLEDGE

A witness may not testify to a matter unless evidence is introduced sufficient to support a finding that the witness has personal knowledge of the matter. Evidence to prove personal knowledge may, but need not, consist of the witness's own testimony. This rule is subject to Rule 703, relating to opinion testimony by expert witnesses.

Rule 603.

OATH OR AFFIRMATION

Before testifying, each witness must declare under oath or affirmation that the witness will testify truthfully. The oath or affirmation must be administered in a form calculated to awaken the witness's conscience and impress the witness's mind with the duty to testify truthfully.

Rule 604.

INTERPRETERS

An interpreter is subject to the provisions of these rules relating to qualification as an expert and the administration of an oath or affirmation to make a true and complete rendition of all communications made during the interpretive process to the best of the interpreter's knowledge and belief.

Comment

Rule 604 has been amended to reflect the interpretive process involved in the translation of languages. The Rule avoids requiring a conscientious interpreter to swear or affirm that the translation to be rendered will be a one-hundred percent true rendition of the statements in the original language. As explained elsewhere "[t]ranslation [or interpretation] is not a matter of substituting words in one language for words in another. It is a matter of understanding the thought expressed in one language and then explaining it using the resources of another language." See Russian Interpreters Co-op, Cambridge, Mass. (1997)

Rule 605.

COMPETENCY OF JUDGE AS WITNESS

The judge presiding at a trial may not testify in that trial as a witness. An objection need not be made to preserve the point.

Rule 606.

COMPETENCY OF JUROR AS WITNESS

(a) At the trial. A member of a jury may not testify as a witness before the jury in the trial of the case in which the juror is sitting. If the juror is called so to testify, the parties must be afforded an opportunity to object out of the presence of the jury.

(b) Inquiry into validity of verdict or indictment. Upon an inquiry into the validity of a verdict or indictment the following rules apply:

(1) A juror may not testify to a matter or statement occurring during the course of the jury's deliberations or to the effect of anything upon that or any other juror's mind or emotions as influencing the juror to assent to or dissent from the verdict or indictment or concerning the juror's mental processes in connection therewith.

(2) A juror's affidavit or evidence of any statement by the juror concerning a matter about which the juror would be precluded from testifying may not be received.

(3) A juror may testify as to whether extraneous prejudicial information was improperly brought to the jury's attention or whether any outside influence was improperly brought to bear upon a juror.

Rule 607.

WHO MAY IMPEACH

The credibility of a witness may be attacked by any party, including the party calling the witness.

Rule 608.

EVIDENCE OF CHARACTER AND CONDUCT OF WITNESS

(a) Opinion and reputation evidence of character. The credibility of a witness may be attacked or supported by evidence in the form of opinion or reputation, subject to the following:

(1) The evidence may refer only to character for truthfulness or untruthfulness, and

(2) Evidence of truthful character is admissible only after the character of the witness for truthfulness has been attacked by opinion or reputation evidence or otherwise.

(b) Specific instances of conduct. Specific instances of the conduct of a witness, for the purpose of attacking or supporting the witness's credibility, other than conviction of crime as provided in Rule 609, may not be proved by extrinsic evidence. However, in the discretion of the court, if probative of truthfulness or untruthfulness, they may be inquired into on cross-examination of the witness (i) concerning the witness's character for truthfulness or untruthfulness, or (ii) concerning the character for truthfulness or untruthfulness of another witness as to which character the witness being cross-examined has testified.

(c) Privilege against self-incrimination. The giving of testimony, whether by an accused or by any other witness, does not operate as a waiver of the accused's or the witness's privilege against self-incrimination when examined with respect to matters that relate only to credibility.

Rule 609.

IMPEACHMENT BY EVIDENCE OF CONVICTION OF CRIME

(a) General rule. For the purpose of attacking the credibility of a witness:

(1) Evidence that a witness other than an accused has been convicted of a crime is admissible, subject to Rule 403, if the crime was punishable by death or imprisonment in excess of one year under the law under which the witness was convicted, and evidence that an accused has been convicted of such a crime is admissible if the court determines that the probative value of the evidence substantially outweighs the danger of unfair prejudice the accused.

(2) Evidence that a witness has been convicted of a crime of untruthfulness or falsification is admissible, regardless of punishment, if the statutory elements of the crime necessarily involve untruthfulness or falsification.

(b) Time limit. Evidence of a conviction is not admissible under this rule if a period of more than 10 years has elapsed since the date of the conviction or of the release of the witness from the confinement imposed for the conviction, whichever is the later date, unless the court determines, in the interests of justice, that the probative value of evidence of the conviction supported by specific facts and circumstances substantially outweighs its unfair prejudicial effect.

(c) Effect of pardon, annulment, or certificate of rehabilitation. Evidence of a conviction is not admissible under this rule if the conviction has been:

(1) the subject of a pardon, annulment, certificate of rehabilitation, or other equivalent procedure based on a finding of the rehabilitation of the individual convicted, and that individual has not been convicted of a subsequent crime punishable by death or imprisonment in excess of one year; or

(2) the subject of a pardon, annulment, or other equivalent procedure based on a finding of innocence.

(d) Juvenile adjudications. Evidence of a juvenile adjudication is generally not admissible under this rule. Except as otherwise provided by statute, however, in a criminal case the court may allow evidence of a juvenile adjudication of a witness other than the accused if conviction of the offense would be admissible to attack the credibility of an adult and the court is satisfied that admission of the evidence is necessary for a fair determination of the issue of guilt or innocence.

(e) Pendency of appeal. The pendency of an appeal from a conviction does not render evidence of the conviction inadmissible. Evidence of the pendency of an appeal is admissible.

(f) Notice. Evidence is not admissible under this rule unless the proponent of the evidence gives to all adverse parties reasonable notice in advance of trial, or during trial if the court excuses pretrial notice for good cause shown, of the nature of the conviction.

(g) Record. If objection is made to evidence offered pursuant to subdivision (a)(1) or (2), the court shall state on the record the factors it considered in determining admissibility.

(h) Evidence. If admissible, evidence of a conviction may be by testimony of the witness during direct or cross-examination, by the introduction of a public record, or by other extrinsic evidence if the public record is not available and good cause is shown.

Comment

Rule 609 has been amended substantively in five respects. First, subdivision (a)(1) has been amended to make the admissibility of a conviction for the impeachment of a witness other than the accused subject to the balancing process of Rule 403 of the Uniform Rules. As amended the rule is in accord with the parallel rule in the Federal Rules of Evidence.

Second, in the case of a witness who is the accused the word "substantially" is incorporated in the applicable balancing test by providing "that the probative value of the evidence substantially outweighs the danger of unfair prejudice to the accused."

Third, to clarify the types of convictions admissible for impeachment purposes without regard to punishment, Rule 609(a)(2) has been amended to provide that only those crimes that contain the statutory elements of untruthfulness or falsification are admissible. The amendment is derived from the 1987 recommendation of the American Bar Association Criminal Justice Section's Committee on Rules of Criminal Procedure and Evidence to clarify the meaning of the language "dishonesty or false statement" in the former rule and avoid the endless dispute and divergent results reached in the several states as to what crimes are embraced within the language "dishonesty or false statement."

Fourth, Rule 609(b) has been amended to require that convictions more than ten years old are not admissible unless it is determined "that the probative value of the evidence of the conviction supported by specific facts and circumstances substantially outweighs its unfair prejudicial effect." The rule as amended in this respect is now in accord with the comparable balancing test applicable under Rule 609(b) of the Federal Rules of Evidence.

Finally, subdivisions (f), (g) and (h) set forth procedures to be followed in determining the admissibility of convictions for impeachment purposes. These include, respectively, the giving of notice, the making of a record of the factors considered by the court in ruling on the admissibility of the evidence and the methods of proof of the conviction.

Rule 610.

RELIGIOUS BELIEFS AND OPINIONS

Evidence of the beliefs or opinions of a witness on matters of religion is not admissible for the purpose of showing that by reason of their nature the witness's credibility is impaired or enhanced.

Rule 611.

MODE AND ORDER OF INTERROGATION AND PRESENTATION

(a) Control by court. The court shall exercise reasonable control over the mode and order of interrogating witnesses and presenting evidence so as to make the interrogation and presentation effective for the ascertainment of the truth, avoid needless consumption of time, and protect witnesses from harassment or undue embarrassment.

(b) Scope of cross-examination. Cross-examination should be limited to the subject matter of the direct examination and matters affecting the credibility of the witness. The court, in the exercise of discretion, may permit inquiry into additional matters as if on direct examination.

(c) Leading questions. Leading questions should not be used on the direct examination of a witness except as is necessary to develop the

Rule 611 *UNIFORM RULES OF EVIDENCE*

witness's testimony. Ordinarily leading questions should be permitted on cross-examination. A party may interrogate a hostile witness, an adverse party, or a witness identified with an adverse party, by leading questions.

Comment

In applying subdivision (a) of Rule 611 to protect witnesses from harassment or undue embarrassment the court should be particularly sensitive to protecting the sensibilities of children while testifying in court.

Rule 612.

RECORD OR OBJECT USED TO REFRESH MEMORY

(a) While testifying. If, while testifying, a witness uses a record or object to refresh the witness's memory, an adverse party is entitled to have the record or object produced at the trial, hearing, or deposition in which the witness is testifying.

(b) Before testifying. If, before testifying, a witness uses a record or object to refresh memory for the purpose of testifying and the court in its discretion determines that the interests of justice so require, an adverse party is entitled to have the record or object produced, if practicable, at the trial, hearing, or deposition in which the witness is testifying.

(c) Terms and conditions of production and use. A party entitled to have a record or object produced under this rule is entitled to inspect it, cross-examine the witness thereon, and introduce in evidence portions of the record which relate to the testimony of the witness. If production of the record or object at the trial, hearing, or deposition is impracticable, the court may order it made available for inspection. If it is claimed that the record or object contains matter not related to the subject matter of the testimony, the court shall examine the record or object in chambers, excise any portions not so related, and order delivery of the remainder to the party entitled thereto. Any portion withheld over objections must be preserved and made available to the appellate court in the event of an appeal. If a record or object is not produced, made available for inspection, or delivered pursuant to order under this rule, the court shall make any order justice requires, but in criminal cases if the prosecution elects not to comply, the order must be one striking the testimony or, if the court in its discretion determines that the interests of justice so require, declaring a mistrial.

Comment

Rule 612 has been amended to substitute the word "record" for the language "writing" in the rule. See the Comment to Rule 101.

Rule 613.

PRIOR STATEMENT OF WITNESS

(a) Examining witness concerning prior statement. In examining a witness concerning a prior statement made by the witness, whether in a record or not, the statement need not be shown nor its contents disclosed to the witness at that time, but on request it must be shown or disclosed to opposing counsel.

(b) Extrinsic evidence of prior inconsistent statement of witness. Extrinsic evidence of a prior inconsistent statement by a witness is not admissible unless the witness is afforded an opportunity to explain or deny the statement and the opposing party is afforded an opportunity to interrogate the witness thereon, or the interests of justice otherwise require. This subdivision does not apply to admissions of a party-opponent as defined in Rule 801(d)(2).

Rule 614.

CALLING AND INTERROGATION OF WITNESS BY COURT

(a) Calling by court. The court, at the suggestion of a party or on its own motion, may call a witness, and all parties may cross-examine the witness thus called.

(b) Interrogation by court. The court may interrogate a witness, whether called by the court or a party.

(c) Objection. An objection to the calling or interrogation of a witness by the court may be made at the time or at the next available opportunity when the jury is not present.

Rule 615.

EXCLUSION OF WITNESSES

At the request of a party the court shall order witnesses excluded so that they cannot hear the testimony of other witnesses, and it may make the order on its own motion. This Rule does not authorize exclusion of a party who is an individual, an officer or employee of a party that is not an individual designated as its representative by its attorney, or an individual whose presence is shown by a party to be essential to the presentation of the party's cause or is otherwise authorized by statute, judicial decision, or court rule.

Comment

The phrase "or is otherwise authorized by statute, judicial decision, or court rule" has been added at the end of Rule 615 to accommodate state law permitting other individuals, such as victims, to be present in the hearing room.

Rule 616.

BIAS OF WITNESS

For the purpose of attacking the credibility of a witness, evidence of bias, prejudice, or interest of the witness for or against a party to the case is admissible.

ARTICLE VII. OPINIONS AND EXPERT TESTIMONY

Rule 701.

OPINION TESTIMONY BY LAY WITNESSES

If a witness's testimony is not based on scientific, technical, or other specialized knowledge within the scope of Rule 702, the witness's testimony in the form of opinions or inferences is limited to those opinions or inferences that are rationally based on the perception of the witness, and helpful to a clear understanding of the witness's testimony or the determination of a fact in issue.

Comment

Rule 701 has been amended by adding a new provision that scientific, technical or other specialized knowledge may not form the basis for opinions or inferences of lay witnesses under Rule 701. The amendment is intended to eliminate the risk that the reliability requirements for the admissibility of scientific, technical or specialized knowledge under Rule 702 will be evaded through the expedient of proffering an expert as a lay witness under Rule 701. The amendment distinguishes between expert and lay **testimony** and not between expert and lay **witnesses** since it is possible for the same witness to give both lay and expert testimony in the same case. However, the amendment makes clear that any of the testimony of the witness that is based on scientific, technical, or specialized knowledge must be governed by the standards of Rule 702.

Rule 702.

TESTIMONY BY EXPERTS

(a) General rule. If a witness's testimony is based on scientific, technical, or other specialized knowledge, the witness may testify in the form of opinion or otherwise if the court determines the following are satisfied:

(1) the testimony will assist the trier of fact to understand evidence or determine a fact in issue;

(2) the witness is qualified by knowledge, skill, experience, training, or education as an expert in the scientific, technical, or other specialized field;

(3) the testimony is based upon principles or methods that are reasonably reliable, as established under subdivision (b), (c), (d), or (e);

(4) the testimony is based upon sufficient and reliable facts or data; and

(5) the witness has applied the principles or methods reliably to the facts of the case.

(b) Reliability deemed to exist. A principle or method is reasonably reliable if its reliability has been established by controlling legislation or judicial decision.

(c) Presumption of reliability. A principle or method is presumed to be reasonably reliable if it has substantial acceptance within the relevant scientific, technical, or specialized community. A party may rebut the presumption by proving that it is more probable than not that the principle or method is not reasonably reliable.

(d) Presumption of unreliability. A principle or method is presumed not to be reasonably reliable if it does not have substantial acceptance within the relevant scientific, technical, or specialized community. A party may rebut the presumption by proving that it is more probable than not that the principle or method is reasonably reliable.

(e) Other reliability factors. In determining the reliability of a principle or method, the court shall consider all relevant additional factors, which may include:

(1) the extent to which the principle or method has been tested;

(2) the adequacy of research methods employed in testing the principle or method;

(3) the extent to which the principle or method has been published and subjected to peer review;

(4) the rate of error in the application of the principle or method;

(5) the experience of the witness in the application of the principle or method;

(6) the extent to which the principle or method has gained acceptance within the relevant scientific, technical, or specialized community; and

(7) the extent to which the witness's specialized field of knowledge has gained acceptance within the general scientific, technical, or specialized community.

Comment

Rule 702 combines the modified historic Frye standard governing the admissibility of expert testimony as a procedural rule with the reliability standards established in *Daubert v. Merrell Dow Pharmaceuticals, Inc.*, 509 U.S. 579, 113 S.Ct. 2786, 125 L.Ed.2d 469 (1993) and *Kumho Tire Company, L.T.D. v. Carmichael*, 526 U.S.137, 119 S.Ct. 1167, 143 L.Ed.2d 238 (1999). The presumption of reliability or of unreliability in subdivisions (c) and (d) can be rebutted by resort to, among others, the reliability criteria set forth in subdivision (e). Rule 702 meaningfully avoids the use of the terminology "scientific" and "nonscientific" principles or methods and does not mandate that the Daubert reliability criteria necessarily apply in determining the admissibility of scientific, technical, or specialized knowledge, an approach which is consistent with *Kumho Tire Company, Ltd. v. Carmichael, supra*. This facilitates the admissibility of expert testimony in social science areas where the falsifiability and potential rate of error factors enumerated in the Daubert case could rarely be met. Also, by eliminating the focus on "scientific knowledge" in Rule 702 the criteria set forth in subdivision (e) accommodates the admissibility of expert testimony involving only the application of a principle or method provided for in subdivision (a)(5) as opposed to the determination of the reliability of the principle or method in the first instance. Subdivision (e) further meets concerns that have been expressed with respect to whether the Daubert criteria, as reaffirmed in the Kumho case, apply when the expert is testifying solely on the basis of experience.

Reinstating a modified Frye standard as a procedural rule in subdivisions (c) and (d) is expected to promote greater reliability in the evidence offered, relieve the trial judge of the initial gate-keeping responsibility and avoid the criticism that the Daubert approach to admissibility "will result in a 'free-for-all' in which befuddled juries are confounded by absurd and irrational pseudoscientific assertions." *See Daubert v. Merrell Dow Pharmaceuticals, Inc.*, 509 U.S. 579, 595–596, 113 S.Ct. 2786, 2798, 125 L.Ed.2d 469 (1993).

Finally, Rule 702 accommodates the divergence that exists among the several states between applying the historic Frye standard, a pre-Daubert standard of reliability, a Daubert standard of reliability and varying other approaches to the admissibility of expert testimony and thereby promotes uniformity among the several states in determining the admissibility of expert testimony.

Rule 703.

BASIS OF OPINION TESTIMONY BY EXPERT

The facts or data in a particular case upon which an expert bases an opinion or inference may be those perceived by or made known to the expert at or before the hearing. If of a type reasonably relied upon by experts in the particular field in forming opinions or inferences upon the subject, the facts or data need not be admissible in evidence for the opinion or inference to be admissible.

Comment

The language "for the opinion or inference to be admissible" has been incorporated in Rule 703 to clarify that the admission of the opinion or inference does not thereby render the underlying facts or data admissible. See, in this connection, Rule 705 providing for the disclosure of the facts or data underlying expert opinion.

Rule 704.

OPINION ON ULTIMATE ISSUE

Testimony in the form of an opinion or inference otherwise admissible is not objectionable because it embraces an ultimate issue to be decided by the trier of fact.

Rule 705.

DISCLOSURE OF FACTS OR DATA UNDERLYING EXPERT OPINION

An expert may testify in terms of opinion or inference and give reasons therefore without previous disclosure of the underlying facts or data, unless the court requires otherwise. The expert may be required to disclose the underlying facts or data on cross-examination.

Rule 706.

COURT APPOINTED EXPERT WITNESS

(a) Appointment. The court, on motion of any party or its own motion, may issue an order to show cause why an expert witness should not be appointed, and may request the parties to submit nominations. The court may appoint an expert witness agreed upon by the parties, and may appoint an expert witness of its own selection. An expert witness may not be appointed by the court unless the witness consents to act. A witness so appointed must be informed of the witness's duties by the court in writing, a copy of which must be filed with the clerk, or at a conference in which the parties have an opportunity to participate. A witness so appointed shall advise the parties of the witness's findings, if any. The witness's deposition may be taken by any party. The witness may be called to testify by the court or any party. The witness is subject to cross-examination by each party, including a party calling the witness.

(b) Compensation. An expert witness appointed by the court is entitled to reasonable compensation as determined by the court. The compensation is payable from funds that are provided by law in criminal cases and in civil actions and proceedings involving just compensation for the taking of property. In other civil actions and proceedings the parties shall pay the compensation in such proportion and at such time as the court directs, and the compensation is to be charged as costs.

(c) Disclosure of appointment. The court may authorize disclosure to the jury of the fact that the court appointed the expert witness.

(d) Parties' experts of own selection. This rule does not limit the parties in calling expert witnesses of their own selection.

Comment

The caption to Rule 706 has been changed to "Court Appointed Witness" to more nearly reflect the testimonial functions performed by the expert pursuant to Rule 706. Rule 706 thus applies only to expert *witnesses* and not to expert *consultants* appointed by the trial judge in performing the gate-keeping function in admitting scientific, technical, or specialized knowledge under Rule 702. See the Comment to Rule 702.

ARTICLE VIII. HEARSAY

Rule 801.

DEFINITIONS; EXCLUSIONS

(a) General. In this article:

(1) "Declarant" means a person who makes a statement.

(2) "Hearsay" means a statement, other than one made by the declarant while testifying at the trial or hearing, offered in evidence to prove the truth of the matter asserted.

(3) "Statement" means an oral assertion, an assertion in a record, or nonverbal conduct of a person who intends it as an assertion.

(b) A statement is not hearsay if:

(1) the declarant testifies at the trial or hearing, is subject to cross-examination concerning the statement, and the statement is:

(A) inconsistent with the declarant's testimony and was given under oath and subject to the penalty of perjury at a trial, hearing, or other proceeding, or in a deposition;

(B) consistent with the declarant's testimony, is offered to rebut an express or implied charge against the declarant of recent fabrication or improper influence or motive and was made before the supposed fabrication, influence, or motive arose; or

(C) one of identification made shortly after perceiving the individual identified.

(2) the statement is offered against a party and is:

(A) the party's own statement, in either an individual or a representative capacity;

(B) a statement of which the party has manifested adoption or belief in its truth;

(C) a statement by an individual authorized by the party to make a statement concerning the subject;

(D) a statement by the party's agent or servant concerning a matter within the scope of the agency or employment, made during the existence of the relationship; or

(E) a statement by a coconspirator of a party during the course and in furtherance of the conspiracy.

Comment

Rule 801 has been amended in three respects. First, in subdivision (a)(3) the words "an assertion in a record" have been substituted for the words "or written." See the Comment to Rule 101.

Second, in subdivision (b)(1)(A) the phrase ", if offered in a criminal proceeding," has been stricken to require the oath as a foundational requirement in **both** civil and criminal proceedings for admitting a prior inconsistent statement of a witness. There is no significant difference between civil and criminal proceedings in requiring an oath as a condition to the admissibility of a prior inconsistent statement under Rule 801(b)(1)(A). The amendment also brings the rule into accord with both the federal rule and the rule followed in a majority of the states.

Third, in subdivision (b)(1)(B) the rule has been amended by adding the language "and was made before the supposed fabrication, influence, or motive arose" to codify the holding of the United States Supreme Court in *Tome v. United States*, 513 U.S. 150, 115 S.Ct. 696, 130 L.Ed.2d 574 (1995). The rule as amended is thereby in accord with at least half of the states adhering to a pre-motive requirement

An amendment to subdivision (b)(2)(E) to conform the Uniform Rule to Rule 801(d)(2)(E) of the Federal Rules of Evidence which took effect on December 1, 1997 to incorporate the holding in *Bourjaily v. United States*, 483 U.S. 171, 107 S.Ct. 2775, 97 L.Ed.2d 144 (1987), was considered and rejected. In *Bourjaily* the United States Supreme Court held that a court may consider the contents of a co-conspirator's statement in determining the existence of, and participation in, the conspiracy by the declarant and the defendant, but left unresolved the question of whether the declarant's statement alone was sufficient to establish a conspiracy in which the declarant and the defendant participated. The amendment to Federal Rule 801(a)(2)(E) resolved both issues by providing that the declarant's statement could be considered, but was not alone sufficient to establish the existence of, or participation in, the conspiracy. However, the division of authority that currently exists among the several states, including the majority rule that the existence of the conspiracy must be determined by evidence independent of the hearsay statements themselves, led the Conference to conclude that a uniform rule on the issue should not be promulgated at this time. *See*, in this connection, *Glasser v. United States*, 315 U.S. 60, 62 S.Ct. 457, 86 L.Ed. 680 (1942) and *United States v. Nixon*, 418 U.S. 683, 94 S.Ct. 3090, 41 L.Ed.2d 1039 (1974).

Rule 802.

HEARSAY RULE

Hearsay is not admissible except as provided by law or by these rules.

Rule 803.

HEARSAY EXCEPTIONS: AVAILABILITY OF DECLARANT IMMATERIAL

The following are not excluded by the hearsay rule, even if the declarant is available as a witness:

(1) Present sense impression. A statement describing or explaining an event or condition made while the declarant was perceiving the event or condition, or immediately thereafter.

(2) Excited utterance. A statement relating to a startling event or condition made while the declarant was under the stress of excitement caused by the event or condition.

(3) Then existing mental, emotional, or physical condition. A statement of the declarant's then existing state of mind, emotion, sensation, or physical condition, such as intent, plan, motive, design, mental feeling, pain, and bodily health, but not a statement of memory or belief to prove the fact remembered or believed unless it relates to the execution, revocation, identification, or terms of declarant's will.

(4) Statements for purposes of medical diagnosis or treatment. Statements made for purposes of medical diagnosis or treatment and describing medical history, or past or present symptoms, pain, or sensation, or the inception or general character of the cause or external source thereof insofar as reasonably pertinent to diagnosis or treatment.

(5) Recorded recollection. A record concerning a matter about which a witness once had knowledge but now has insufficient recollection to testify fully and accurately, shown to have been made or adopted by the witness when the matter was fresh in the witness's memory and to reflect that knowledge correctly, which record may be read into evidence but may not be received as an exhibit unless offered by an adverse party.

Comment

Rule 803(5) has been amended to substitute the word "record" for the words "memorandum or." See the Comment to Rule 101.

(6) Record of regularly conducted business activity. A record of acts, events, conditions, opinions, or diagnoses, made at or near the time by, or from information transmitted by, a person having knowledge, if kept in the course of a regularly conducted business activity, and if it was the regular practice of that business activity to make the record, all as shown by the testimony of the custodian or other qualified witness, or by certification that complies with Rule 902(11) or (12), or with a statute providing for certification, unless the sources of information or the method or circumstances of preparation indicate lack of trustworthiness. In this paragraph, business includes business, institution, association, profession, occupation, and calling of every kind, whether or not conducted for profit. A public record inadmissible under paragraph (8) is inadmissible under this exception.

Comment

First, Rule 803(6) has been amended to delete the words "memorandum," "report" ", or data compilation, in any form," "memorandum," "report," "or data compilation,". See the Comment to Rule 101.

Second, Rule 803(6) has been amended to provide for satisfying the foundational requirements for the admissibility of a business record through certification as an alternative to the expense and inconvenience of producing a time-consuming foundational witness. This amendment should also be interpreted with reference to Uniform Rules 901(11) and 902(12) providing for the self-authentication of domestic and foreign records under the certification procedure provided for in Rule 803(6).

Third, Rule 803(6) has been amended to add the provision at the end of the rule that "[a] public record inadmissible under paragraph (8) is inadmissible under this exception." This forecloses admitting under the business records exception a public record that is inadmissible under Uniform Rule 803(8). See the Comment to Rule 803(8).

(7) Absence of entry in records kept in accordance with paragraph (6). Evidence that a matter is not included in the records kept in accordance with paragraph (6), to prove the nonoccurrence or nonexistence of the matter, if the matter was of a kind of which a record was regularly made and preserved, all as shown by the testimony of the custodian or other qualified witness, or by certification that complies with Rule 902(11) or (12), or with a statute providing for certification, unless the sources of information or other circumstances indicate lack of trustworthiness.

Comment

First, Rule 803(7) has been amended to delete the words "memoranda," "reports," "or data compilations, in any form," "memorandum," "report," "or data compilation." See the Comment to Rule 101.

Second, as in the case of Rule 803(6), Rule 803(7) has been amended to provide for satisfying the foundational requirements for the admissibility of the absence of a business entry in a record through certification. See also Rules 901(11) and (12) providing for the authentication of domestic and foreign under the certification procedure of Rule 803(7).

(8) Record or report of public office. Unless the sources of information or other circumstances indicate lack of trustworthiness, a record of a public office or agency setting forth its regularly conducted and regularly recorded activities, or matters observed pursuant to duty imposed by law and as to which there was a duty to report, or factual findings resulting from an investigation made pursuant to authority granted by law. The following are not within this exception to the hearsay rule:

(A) an investigative report by police and other law enforcement personnel, except when offered by an accused in a criminal case;

(B) an investigative report prepared by or for a government, public office, or agency when offered by it in a case in which it is a party;

(C) factual findings offered by the government in criminal cases; and

(D) factual findings resulting from special investigation of a particular complaint, case, or incident, unless offered by an accused in a criminal case.

Comment

First, Rule 803(8) has been amended to delete the words "records, reports, statements, or data compilations in any form" and insert the words "a record". See the Comment to Rule 101.

Second, an issue addressed in the amendment of Rule 803(6) relates to the introductory clause of the exceptions to Rule 803(8) stating "[t]he following are not *within this exception* to the hearsay rule." (Emphasis Added) The rule as originally adopted created an interpretive problem with respect to whether the foregoing narrowing language "opened the back door" to the admissibility of a public record under another exception, such as the business record exception of Uniform Rule 803(6). The Drafting Committee recommended that a record inadmissible under Rule 803(8) ought not to be admissible under Uniform Rule 803(6) and its recommendation was accepted by amending Rule 803(6) to include the limiting language that "[a] public record inadmissible under paragraph (8) is inadmissible under this exception." See the Comment to Rule 803(6).

(9) Record of vital statistics. A record of birth, fetal death, death, or marriage, if the report thereof was made to a public office.

Comment

Rule 803(9) has been amended to delete the words "[r]ecords or data compilations, in any form". See Comment to Rule 101.

(10) Absence of record or entry. To prove the absence of a record, or the nonoccurrence or nonexistence of a matter of which a record was regularly made and preserved by a public office or agency, evidence in the form of a certification in accordance with Rule 902, or testimony, that diligent search failed to disclose the record, or entry.

Comment

Rule 803(10) has been amended to delete the words "report, statement, or data compilation, in any form" and "report, statement, or data compilation,". See the Comment to Rule 101.

(11) Record of religious organization. A statement of birth, marriage, divorce, death, legitimacy, ancestry, relationship by blood or marriage, or other similar fact of personal or family history, contained in a regularly kept record of a religious organization.

(12) Marriage, baptismal, and similar certified record. A statement of fact contained in a certified record that the maker performed a marriage or other ceremony or administered a sacrament, made by a cleric, public official, or other person authorized by the rules or practices of a religious organization or by law to perform the act certified, and purporting to have been issued at the time of the act or within a reasonable time thereafter.

Comment

Rule 803(12) has been amended to substitute the words "certified record" for "certificates." See the Comment to Rule 101.

(13) Family record. A statement of fact concerning personal or family history contained in a family Bible, genealogy, chart, engraving on a ring, an inscription on a family portrait, an engraving on an urn, crypt, or tombstone, or the like.

(14) Record of document affecting an interest in property. A public record purporting to establish or affect an interest in property, as proof of the content of the original recorded document and its execution and delivery by each person by whom it purports to have been executed and delivered.

Comment

Rule 803(14) has been amended to delete the words "of a document." See the Comment to Rule 101.

(15) Statement in record affecting an interest in property. A statement contained in a record purporting to establish or affect an interest in property if the matter stated was relevant to the purpose of the record, unless dealings with the property since the record was made have been inconsistent with the truth of the statement or the purport of the record.

Comment

Rule 803(15) has been amended to substitute the word "record" for the words "documents" and "document." See the Comment to Rule 101.

(16) Statement in ancient record. A statement in a record in existence 20 years or more, the authenticity of which is established.

Comment

Rule 803(16) has been amended to substitute the word "record" for the word "documents" and "document." See the Comment to Rule 101.

(17) Market report, commercial publication. Market quotation, tabulation, list, directory, or other published or publicly recorded compilations, generally used and relied upon by the public or by persons in particular occupations.

Comment

Rule 803(17) has been amended to add the words "or publicly recorded" to accommodate the admissibility of records kept in electronic form. See the Comment to Rule 101.

(18) Learned treatise. To the extent called to the attention of an expert witness upon cross-examination or relied upon by the witness in direct examination, a statement contained in a published treatise, periodical, or pamphlet on a subject of history, medicine, or other science or art, established as a reliable authority by testimony or admission of the witness, by other expert testimony, or by judicial notice. If admitted, the statement may be read into evidence but may not be received as an exhibit.

(19) Reputation concerning personal or family history. Reputation among members of an individual's family by blood, adoption, or marriage, or among the individual's associates, or in the community, concerning the individual's birth, adoption, marriage, divorce, death, legitimacy, relationship by blood, adoption, or marriage, ancestry, or other similar fact of the individual's personal or family history.

(20) Reputation concerning boundaries or general history. Reputation in a community, arising before the controversy, as to boundaries of or customs affecting land in the community, and reputation as to an event of general history important to the community, State, or country in which located.

(21) Reputation as to character. Reputation of a person's character among the person's associates or in the community.

(22) Judgment of previous conviction. Evidence of a final judgment adjudging a person guilty of a crime punishable by death or imprisonment in excess of one year, to prove any fact essential to sustain the judgment, but not including, when offered by the State in a criminal prosecution for purposes other than impeachment, a judgment against a person other than the accused. The pendency of an appeal may be shown but does not affect admissibility.

(23) Judgment as to personal, family, or general history, or boundaries. A judgment as proof of a matter of personal, family or general history, or boundaries, essential to the judgment, if the matter is provable by evidence of reputation.

Comment

Rule 803(24) is eliminated to combine the rule with the identical Uniform Rule 804(b)(5) in a single new Uniform Rule 808 governing the admissibility of evidence under the residual exception to the hearsay rule. See the Comment to Uniform Rule 808.

Rule 804.

HEARSAY EXCEPTIONS: DECLARANT UNAVAILABLE

(a) Unavailability as a witness. In this rule:

(1) Unavailability as a witness includes situations in which the declarant:

(A) is exempted by ruling of the court on the ground of privilege from testifying concerning the subject matter of the declarant's statement;

(B) persists in refusing to testify concerning the subject matter of the declarant's statement despite an order of the court to do so;

(C) testifies to a lack of memory of the subject matter of the declarant's statement;

(D) is unable to be present or to testify at the hearing because of death or then existing physical or mental illness or infirmity; or

(E) is absent from the hearing and the proponent of the declarant's statement has been unable to procure the declarant's attendance, or in the case of a hearsay exception under subdivision (b)(2), (3), or (4), the declarant's attendance or testimony, by process or other reasonable means.

(2) A declarant is not unavailable as a witness if the declarant's exemption, refusal, claim of lack of memory, inability, or absence is due to the procurement or wrongdoing of the proponent of the declarant's statement for the purpose of preventing the declarant from attending or testifying.

(b) Hearsay exceptions. The following are not excluded by the hearsay rule if the declarant is unavailable as a witness:

(1) *Former testimony.* Testimony given as a witness at another hearing of the same or a different proceeding, or in a deposition taken in compliance with law in the course of the same or another proceeding, if the party against whom the testimony is now offered, or, in a civil action or proceeding a predecessor in interest, had an opportunity and similar motive to develop the testimony by direct, cross, or redirect examination.

(2) *Statement under belief of impending death.* A statement made by a declarant while believing that the declarant's death was imminent, concerning the cause or circumstances of what the declarant believed to be the declarant's impending death.

(3) *Statement against interest.* A statement that at the time of its making was so far contrary to the declarant's pecuniary or

proprietary interest, or so far tended to subject the declarant to civil or criminal liability or to render invalid a claim by the declarant against another or to make the declarant an object of hatred, ridicule, or disgrace, that a reasonable individual in the declarant's position would not have made the statement unless the individual believed it to be true. A statement tending to expose the declarant to criminal liability and offered to exculpate an accused is not admissible unless corroborating circumstances clearly indicate the trustworthiness of the statement. A statement or confession offered against the accused in a criminal case, made by a codefendant or other individual implicating both the codefendant or other individual and the accused, is not within this exception.

(4) *Statement of personal or family history.* A statement concerning:

(A) the declarant's own birth, adoption, marriage, divorce, legitimacy, relationship by blood, adoption, marriage, ancestry, or other similar fact of personal or family history, even though declarant had no means of acquiring personal knowledge of the matter stated or

(B) the matters listed in subparagraph (A) or the death of another individual if the declarant was related to the other individual by blood, adoption, or marriage or was so intimately associated with the other individual's family as to be likely to have accurate information concerning the matter declared.

Comment

In jurisdictions that enact the Uniform Parentage Act, the word "parentage" should be substituted for the word "legitimacy" in Rule 804(b)(4)(A).

Rule 804(b)(5) is deleted from the Uniform Rules. This exception was promulgated by the United States Supreme Court as Rule 804(b)(2) of the proposed Federal Rules of Evidence. However, it was rejected by House Committee on the Judiciary and not reinstated on the ground it did not bear sufficient guarantees of trustworthiness, even though it was recommended by the Standing Committees on Rules of Practice and Procedure of the Judicial Conference of the United States and the Advisory Committee on the Federal Rules. See Report of Committee on the Judiciary, House of Representatives, 93rd Congress, 1st Session, Federal Rules of Evidence, No. 93–650, p. 6 (1973). The rule as recommended, or in a modified form, has only been adopted in five states. Moreover, statements of recent perception would be admissible in appropriate circumstances under the newly approved residual exception of Uniform Rule 808

Rule 80(b)(6) is eliminated to combine the rule with the identical Uniform Rule 803(24) in a single new Uniform Rule 808 governing the admissibility of evidence under the residual exception to the hearsay rule. See the Comment to Uniform Rule 808.

(5) *Forfeiture by wrongdoing.* A statement offered against a party that has engaged or acquiesced in wrongdoing that was

intended to and did cause the unavailability of the declarant as a witness.

Comment

Rule 804(b)(5) has been added to provide that a party forfeits the right to object to the admission of a declarant's statement when the unavailability of the declarant has been procured through a party's wrongdoing or the party's acquiescence in the wrongdoing of another. It is a preventative rule designed to deal with abhorrent behavior that is inconsistent with the system of justice. As adopted the rule is in accord with Rule 804(b)(6) of the Federal Rules of Evidence.

Rule 805.

HEARSAY WITHIN HEARSAY

Hearsay included within hearsay is not excluded under the hearsay rule if each part of the combined statements conforms with an exception to the hearsay rule provided in these rules.

Rule 806.

ATTACKING AND SUPPORTING CREDIBILITY OF DECLARANT

If a hearsay statement, or a statement described in Rule 801(b)(2)(C), (D), or (E), has been admitted in evidence, the credibility of the declarant may be attacked, and if attacked may be supported, by any evidence that would be admissible for those purposes if the declarant had testified as a witness. Evidence of a statement or conduct by the declarant inconsistent with the declarant's hearsay statement is not subject to a requirement that the declarant has been afforded an opportunity to deny or explain. If the party against whom a hearsay statement has been admitted calls the declarant as a witness, the party may examine the declarant on the statement as if under cross-examination.

Rule 807.

STATEMENT OF CHILD VICTIM

(a) Statement of child not excluded. A statement made by a child under [seven] years of age describing an alleged act of neglect, physical or sexual abuse, or sexual contact performed against, with, or on the child by another individual is not excluded by the hearsay rule if:

(1) subject to subdivision (b), the court conducts a hearing outside the presence of the jury and finds that the statement concerns an event within the child's personal knowledge and is inherently trustworthy; and

(2) the child testifies at the proceeding [or pursuant to an applicable state procedure for the giving of testimony by a child], or the child is unavailable to testify at the proceeding, as defined in Rule 804(a), and, in the latter case, there is evidence corroborative of the alleged act of neglect, physical or sexual abuse, or sexual contact.

(b) Determining trustworthiness. In determining the trustworthiness of a child's statement, the court shall consider the circumstances surrounding the making of the statement, including:

(1) the child's ability to observe, remember, and relate the details of the event;

(2) the child's age and mental and physical maturity;

(3) whether the child used terminology not reasonably expected of a child of similar age, mental and physical maturity, and socioeconomic circumstances;

(4) the child's relationship to the alleged offender;

(5) the nature and duration of the alleged neglect, physical or sexual abuse, or sexual contact;

(6) whether any other descriptions of the event by the child have been consistent with the statement;

(7) whether the child had a motive to fabricate the statement;

(8) the identity, knowledge and experience of the person taking the statement;

(9) whether there is a video or audio recording of the statement and, if so, the circumstances surrounding the taking of the statement; and

(10) whether the child made the statement spontaneously or in response to suggestive or leading questions.

(c) Making a record. The court shall state on the record the circumstances that support its determination of the admissibility of the statement offered pursuant to subdivision (a).

(d) Notice. Evidence is not admissible under this rule unless the proponent gives to all adverse parties reasonable notice in advance of trial, or during trial if the court excuses pretrial notice for good cause shown, of the nature of any such evidence the proponent intends to introduce at trial.

Comment

The substance of former Rule 807 was rejected and a new child victim witness exception was adopted to account for intervening developments in the law since Rule 807 was adopted by the Conference in 1986. There are seven aspects of the rule that deserve comment. First, the favored age at which the exception should apply is seven years of age. However, the age is bracketed to afford the states flexibility in determining at what age the exception should apply.

Second, the scope of the rule is broadened to include acts of neglect and sexual contact in addition to physical or sexual abuse.

Third, the rule applies in all proceedings, civil, juvenile and criminal as provided in Rule 102(a). See the Comment to Rule 102.

Fourth, the rule focuses on the requirement of trustworthiness and the criteria to be considered in making this determination. *See Idaho v. Wright*, 497 U.S. 805, 110 S.Ct. 3139, 111 L.Ed.2d 638 (1990).

Fifth, in lieu of providing within the exception for the admissibility of recorded statements or the methods of taking the testimony of children, Rule 807(a)(2) requires that the child either testify at the proceeding or pursuant to an applicable state procedure for the giving of testimony, such as closed circuit television, currently recognized in thirty states, or a videotape recording of the child's testimony, currently also recognized in thirty states. If the child is unavailable to testify either in person or through an applicable state procedure, the statement is admissible only if there is corroborating evidence of the statement.

Sixth, as provided in subdivision (c), the court must make a record of the circumstances supporting its determination of the admissibility of the statement.

Finally, notice is required in subdivision (d) by a rule consistent with the other notice provisions in the amended Uniform Rules.

Rule 808.

RESIDUAL EXCEPTION

(a) Exception. In exceptional circumstances a statement not covered by Rules 803, 804, or 807 but possessing equivalent, though not identical, circumstantial guarantees of trustworthiness, is not excluded by the hearsay rule if the court determines that

(1) the statement is offered as evidence of a fact of consequence;

(2) the statement is more probative on the point for which it is offered than any other evidence that the proponent can procure through reasonable efforts; and

(3) the general purposes of these rules and the interests of justice will best be served by admission of the statement into evidence.

(b) Making a record. The court shall state on the record the circumstances that support its determination of the admissibility of the statement offered pursuant to subdivision (a).

(c) Notice. A statement is not admissible under this exception unless the proponent gives to all parties reasonable notice in advance of trial, or during trial if the court excuses pretrial notice for good cause shown, of the substance of the statement and the identity of the declarant.

Comment

Uniform Rule 808 combines the abrogated Rules 803(24) and 804(b)(5) named "Other Exceptions" and renames the rule "Residual Exception." Substantive changes have been made in subdivision (1) to deal with two difficult and recurring issues that have arisen in the states under comparable black letter rules. The first of these is whether a statement which almost, but fails to meet the requisite foundational requirements of one of the specific exceptions can nevertheless be admitted under the residual exception. The black letter of the amended rule is intended to foreclose the admission of statements under the residual exception that fail to meet all of the specific exception's foundational requirements for admissibility. *See*, in this connection, *Shakespeare v. State*, 827 P.2d 454, 460 (Alaska App.1992) and *Shoch's Estate v. Kail*, 209 Neb. 812, 311 N.W.2d 903 (1981).

The second issue arises out of the language "having equivalent circumstantial guarantees of trustworthiness." *See Shakespeare v. State* and *Shoch's Estate v. Kail, supra*. Accordingly, the rule has been amended to provide that a statement may be admitted under Rule 808 in only "exceptional circumstances" and then only if the statement possesses "equivalent, though not identical, circumstantial guarantees of trustworthiness."

A determination of whether the statement possesses circumstantial guarantees of trustworthiness is a fact-intensive inquiry to be resolved on a case-by-case basis. *See People v. Bowers*, 773 P.2d 1093, 1096 (Colo.App.1988), *affirmed*, 801 P.2d 511 (1990). Among the factors that have been identified in determining trustworthiness are: (1) the age, education and experience of the declarant; (2) the personal knowledge of the declarant regarding the subject matter of the statement; (3) the oral or written nature of the statement; (4) the ambiguity of the statement; (5) the consistency with which the statement is repeated; (6) the time lapse between the event and the making of the statement; (7) the partiality of the declarant and the relationship between the declarant and the witness; (8) the declarant's motive to speak truthfully or untruthfully; (9) the spontaneity of the statement, as opposed to responding to leading questions; (10) the making of the statement under oath; (11) the declarant being subject to cross-examination at the time the statement was made; and (12) the recantation or repudiation of the statement after it was made. *See*, for example, *State v. Toney*, 243 Neb. 237, 498 N.W.2d 544, 550–551 (1993).

Subdivision (b) requires the court to state on the record the circumstances supporting its admission of a statement pursuant to subdivision (a).

Subdivision (c) requires the giving of notice to offer a statement under Rule 808 and is consistent with other notice requirements in the Uniform Rules.

ARTICLE IX. AUTHENTICATION AND IDENTIFICATION

Rule 901.

REQUIREMENT OF AUTHENTICATION OR IDENTIFICATION

(a) General provision. The requirement of authentication or identification as a condition precedent to admissibility is satisfied by evidence sufficient to support a finding that the matter in question is what its proponent claims.

(b) Illustrations. By way of illustration only, and not by way of limitation, the following are examples of authentication or identification conforming with the requirements of this rule:

(1) *Testimony of witness having knowledge.* Testimony of a witness with knowledge that a matter is what it is claimed to be.

(2) *Nonexpert opinion on handwriting.* Nonexpert opinion as to the genuineness of handwriting, based upon familiarity not acquired for purposes of the litigation.

(3) *Comparison by trier or expert witness.* Comparison by the trier of fact or by an expert witness with a specimen that has been authenticated.

(4) *Distinctive characteristics and the like.* Appearance, contents, substance, internal patterns, or other distinctive characteristics, taken in conjunction with circumstances.

(5) *Voice identification.* Identification of a voice, whether heard firsthand or through mechanical or electronic transmission or recording, by opinion based upon hearing the voice under circumstances connecting it with the alleged speaker.

(6) *Telephone conversations.* Telephone conversations, by evidence that a call was made to the number assigned at the time by the telephone company to a particular person, if:

(A) in the case of an individual, circumstances, including self-identification, which show that the individual who answered was the one called; or

(B) in the case of a person other than an individual, the call was made to a place of business and the conversation related to business reasonably transacted over the telephone.

(7) *Public records or reports.* Evidence that a public record or a purported public record is from the public office where items of this nature are kept.

Comment

The rule has been amended to delete the words "writing" and "report, statement, or data compilation, in any form" to accommodate the admissibility of records kept in electronic form. See the Comment to Rule 101.

(8) *Ancient records.* Evidence that a record is in such condition as to create no suspicion concerning its authenticity, was in a place where it, if authentic, would likely be, and has been in existence 20 years or more at the time it is offered.

Comment

Rule 901(b)(8) has been amended to add the word "record" and delete the words "document or data compilation, in any form" to accommodate the admissibility of records kept in electronic form. See the Comment to Rule 101.

(9) *Process or system.* Evidence describing a process or system used to produce a result and showing that the process or system produces an accurate result.

(10) *Method provided by statute or rule.* Any method of authentication or identification provided by [the Supreme Court of this State or by] a statute or as provided in the constitution of this State.

Rule 902.

SELF-AUTHENTICATION

Extrinsic evidence of authenticity as a condition precedent to admissibility is not required with respect to the following:

(1) Domestic public document under seal. A document bearing a seal purporting to be that of the United States, or of any State, or of a political subdivision, department, officer, or agency of one of them, and a signature purporting to be an attestation or execution.

(2) Domestic public document not under seal. A document purporting to bear a signature in the official capacity of an officer or employee of any entity designated in paragraph (1), having no seal, if a public officer having a seal and having official duties in the district or political subdivision of the officer or employee certifies under seal that the signer has the official capacity and that the signature is genuine.

(3) Foreign public document. A document purporting to be executed or attested in the official capacity of an individual authorized by the laws of a foreign country to make the execution or attestation, and accompanied by a final certification as to the genuineness of the signature and official position (i) of the executing or attesting individual, or (ii) of any foreign official whose certificate of genuineness of signature and official position relates to the execution or attestation or is in a chain of certificates of genuineness of signature and official position relating to the execution or attestation. A final certification may be made by a secretary of embassy or legation, consul general, consul, vice consul, or consular agent of the United States, or a diplomatic or consular official of the foreign country assigned or accredited to the United States. If all parties have been given a reasonable opportunity to investigate the authenticity and accuracy of an official document, the court may for good cause shown order that it be treated as presumptively authentic without final certification or permit it to be evidenced by an attested summary with or without final certification.

(4) Certified copy of public record. A copy of a public record or report or entry therein, or of a document authorized by law to be recorded or filed and actually recorded or filed in a public office, certified as correct by the custodian or other authorized person by certificate complying with paragraph (1), (2), or (3) or complying with any law of the United States or of this State.

(5) Official publication. A book, pamphlet, publication, or other publicly issued record issued by public authority, if in a form indicative of the genuineness of such a record.

Comment

Rule 902(5) has been amended to add the words "or other publicly issued record issued by public authority, if in a form indicative of the genuineness of such a record" to accommodate the admissibility of public records kept in electronic form. See the Comment to Rule 101.

(6) Newspaper or periodical. Publicly distributed material purporting to be a newspaper or periodical.

(7) Trade inscriptions and the like. Inscriptions, signs, tags, or labels purporting to have been affixed in the course of business and indicating ownership, control, or origin.

(8) Acknowledged record. A record accompanied by a certificate of acknowledgment executed in the manner provided by law by a notary public or other officer authorized by law to take acknowledgments.

Comment

Rule 902(8) has been amended to delete the word "Documents" and add the words "A record" to accommodate the admissibility of an acknowledged record kept in electronic form. See the Comment to Rule 101.

(9) Commercial paper and related record. Commercial paper, a signature thereon, and a record relating thereto or having the same legal effect as commercial paper, to the extent provided by general commercial law.

Comment

Rule 902(9) has been amended to substitute the word "record" for "documents" to accommodate the admissibility of records kept in electronic form. See the Comment to Rule 101.

(10) Presumption created by law. A signature, document, or other matter declared by any law of the United States or of this State to be presumptively or prima facie genuine or authentic.

(11) Certified domestic record of regularly conducted business activity. The original or a duplicate of a domestic record of regularly conducted activity, within the scope of Rule 803(6), which the custodian thereof acts, events, conditions, opinions, or diagnoses if:

(A) the document is accompanied by a written declaration under oath of the custodian of the record or other qualified individual that the record was made, at or near the time of the occurrence of the matters set forth, by, or from information transmitted by, a person having knowledge of those matters; was kept in the course of the regularly conducted business activity; and was made pursuant to the regularly conducted activity;

(B) the party intending to offer the record in evidence gives notice of that intention to all adverse parties and makes the record available for inspection sufficiently in advance of its offer to provide the adverse parties with a fair opportunity to challenge the record; and

(C) notice is not given to the proponent, sufficiently in advance of the offer to provide the proponent with a fair opportunity to meet the objection or obtain the testimony of a foundation witness, raising a genuine question as to the trustworthiness or authenticity of the record.

Comment

Rule 902(11) has been amended to provide for self-authentication through certification of domestic records of regularly conducted activity in both civil and criminal cases. The rule complements the amendment of Uniform Rule 803(6) providing for the admissibility of business records through certification as an alternative to the testimony of a foundation witness.

The notice provision of subdivision (1)(B) differs from the notice provisions incorporated generally in the amendments to the Uniform Rules by requiring that the record be made available for inspection by all adverse parties prior to its offer in evidence to provide them with a fair opportunity to challenge the record.

A separate, but comparable provision for the authentication of foreign records of a regularly conducted activity is contained in Rule 902(12).

(12) Certified foreign record of regularly conducted business activity. The original or a duplicate of a record from a foreign country of acts, events, conditions, opinions, or diagnoses if:

(A) the document is accompanied by a written declaration under oath of the custodian of the record or other qualified individual that the record was made, at or near the time of the occurrence of the matters set forth, by or from information transmitted by a person having knowledge of those matters, was kept in the course of a regularly conducted business activity, and was made pursuant to the regularly conducted activity;

(B) the party intending to offer the record in evidence gives notice of that intention to all adverse parties and makes the record available for inspection sufficiently in advance of its offer to provide the adverse parties with a fair opportunity to challenge the record; and

(C) notice is not given to the proponent, sufficiently in advance of the offer to provide the proponent with a fair opportunity to meet the objection or obtain the testimony of a foundation witness, raising a genuine question as to the trustworthiness or authenticity of the record.

Comment

See the Comment to Rule 902(11).

Rule 903.

SUBSCRIBING WITNESS' TESTIMONY UNNECESSARY

The testimony of a subscribing witness is not necessary to authenticate a record unless required by the laws of the jurisdiction whose laws govern the validity of the record.

Comment

The word "record" has been substituted for the word "writing" to accommodate the admissibility of records kept in electronic form. See the Comment to Rule 101.

ARTICLE X. CONTENT OF RECORD, WRITING, RECORDING, PHOTOGRAPH, IMAGE, AND OTHER RECORD

Rule 1001.

DEFINITIONS

In this article:

(1) "Duplicate" means a counterpart in the form of a record produced by the same impression as the original, from the same matrix, by means of photography, including enlargements and miniatures, by mechanical or electronic re-recording, by chemical reproduction, or by another equivalent technique that accurately reproduces the original.

(2) "Image" means a form of a record which consists of a digitized copy or image of information.

(3) An "original" of a writing, recording, or other record means the writing, recording, or other record itself or any counterpart intended to have the same effect by a person executing or issuing it. The term, when applied to a photograph, includes the negative or any print therefrom. The term includes a printout or other perceivable output of a record of data or images stored in a computer or similar device, if shown to reflect the data or images accurately.

(4) "Photograph" means a form of a record which consists of a still photograph, stored image, X-ray film, video tape, or motion picture.

(5) "Writing" and "recording" mean letters, words, sounds, or numbers, or their equivalent, inscribed on a tangible medium or stored in an electronic or other machine and retrievable in perceivable form by

handwriting, typewriting, printing, photostating, photographing, mechanical or electronic recording, or other technique.

Comment

The amendments to Article X consisting of Rules 1001 through 1008 elaborate on the meaning of the term "record" to facilitate the use of the term throughout Articles I through IX, as well as Article X governing various applications of the original writing ("best evidence") rule to provide guarantees against inaccuracies and fraud. However, it should be made clear that the term "record," when used in Rule 1002 through 1008, includes writings, recordings and photographs. Accordingly, when more traditional forms of record keeping are called in question within the original writing rule, the same governing rules are applicable as has been the case under Article X of the Uniform Rules prior to their amendment. This application of the original writing rule to writings, recordings and photographs is facilitated through the definition of these terms in the amendments to Rules 1001(4) and (5) as well as the definition of record in Rule 101(c). See the Comment to Rule 101.

Rule 1002.

REQUIREMENT OF ORIGINAL

To prove the content of a writing, recording, photograph, or other record, the original record, writing, recording, photograph, or other record is required, except as otherwise provided in these rules or by [rules adopted by the Supreme Court of this State or by] statute.

Comment

See the Comment to Rule 1001.

Rule 1003.

ADMISSIBILITY OF DUPLICATES

A duplicate is admissible to the same extent as an original unless a genuine question is raised as to the authenticity or continuing effectiveness of the original or in the circumstances it would be unfair to admit the duplicate in lieu of the original.

Comment

See the Comment to Rule 1001.

Rule 1004.

ADMISSIBILITY OF OTHER EVIDENCE OF CONTENTS

The original is not required, and other evidence of the contents of a record is admissible if:

(1) all originals are lost or have been destroyed, unless the proponent lost or destroyed them in bad faith;

(2) an original cannot be obtained by any available judicial process or procedure;

(3) at a time when an original was under the control of the party against whom offered, the party was put on notice, by the pleadings or otherwise, that the contents would be a subject of proof at the hearing, and the party does not produce the original at the hearing; or

(4) the record is not closely related to a controlling issue.

Comment

See the Comment to Rule 1001.

Rule 1005.

PUBLIC RECORDS

The contents of an official record, or of a private record authorized to be recorded or filed in the public records and actually recorded or filed, if otherwise admissible, may be proved by a copy in perceivable form, certified as correct in accordance with Rule 902 or testified to be correct by a witness who has compared it with the original. If a copy complying with the foregoing cannot be obtained by the exercise of reasonable diligence, other evidence of the contents may be admitted.

Comment

See the Comment to Rule 1001.

Rule 1006.

SUMMARIES

The contents of voluminous records which cannot conveniently be examined in court may be presented in the form of a chart, summary, calculation, or other perceivable presentation. The original, or a duplicate, must be made available for examination or copying, or both, by other parties at a reasonable time and place. The court may order that they be produced in court.

Comment

See the Comment to Rule 1001.

Rule 1007.

TESTIMONY, OR ADMISSION IN RECORD OF PARTY

The contents of a record may be proved by the testimony or deposition of the party against whom offered or by that party's written admission without accounting for the nonproduction of the original.

Comment

See the Comment to Rule 1001.

Rule 1008.

FUNCTIONS OF COURT AND JURY

If the admissibility under these rules of other evidence of the contents of a record depends upon the fulfillment of a condition of fact, the question whether the condition has been fulfilled is ordinarily for the court to determine in accordance with Rule 104. However, if an issue is raised as to whether the asserted record ever existed, another record produced at the trial is the original, or other evidence of contents correctly reflects the contents, the issue is for the trier of fact to determine.

Comment

See the Comment to Rule 1001.

ARTICLE XI. MISCELLANEOUS RULES

Rule 1101.

TITLE

These rules shall be known and may be cited as Uniform Rules of Evidence.

EXTRACTS FROM DELAWARE LAWYERS' RULES OF PROFESSIONAL CONDUCT[1]

Contents

Preamble: A lawyer's responsibilities

Rule		Page
1.2	Scope of Representation	511
1.3	Diligence	513
1.4	Communication	514
1.6	Confidentiality of Information	515
1.7	Conflict of Interest: Current Clients	518
1.10	Imputation of Conflicts of Interest: General Rule	520
1.13	Organization as Client	521
1.16	Declining or Terminating Representation	524
3.1	Meritorious Claims and Contentions	526
3.3	Candor Toward the Tribunal	526
3.4	Fairness to Opposing Party and Counsel	530
3.5	Impartiality and Decorum of the Tribunal	531
3.7	Lawyer as Witness	532
3.8	Special Responsibilities of a Prosecutor	534
4.1	Truthfulness in Statements to Others	536
8.3	Reporting Professional Misconduct	536
8.4	Misconduct	538

Preamble: A Lawyer's Responsibilities.

[1] A lawyer, as a member of the legal profession, is a representative of clients, an officer of the legal system and a public citizen having special responsibility for the quality of justice.

[2] As a representative of clients, a lawyer performs various functions. As advisor, a lawyer provides a client with an informed understanding of the client's legal rights and obligations and explains their practical implications. As advocate, a lawyer zealously asserts the client's position under the rules of the adversary system. As negotiator, a lawyer seeks a result advantageous to the client but consistent with requirements of honest dealings with others. As an evaluator, a lawyer acts by examining a client's legal affairs and reporting about them to the client or to others.

. . .

---

1. Effective July 1, 2003 and current through October 16, 2007. The excerpts printed here are nearly identical with the same provisions in the ABA Model Rules of Professional Conduct. The ABA rules themselves are not printed because of copyright restrictions.

[4] In all professional functions a lawyer should be competent, prompt and diligent. A lawyer should maintain communication with a client concerning the representation. A lawyer should keep in confidence information relating to representation of a client except so far as disclosure is required or permitted by the Rules of Professional Conduct or other law.

[5] A lawyer's conduct should conform to the requirements of the law, both in professional service to clients and in the lawyer's business and personal affairs. A lawyer should use the law's procedures only for legitimate purposes and not to harass or intimidate others. A lawyer should demonstrate respect for the legal system and for those who serve it, including judges, other lawyers and public officials. While it is a lawyer's duty, when necessary, to challenge the rectitude of official action, it is also a lawyer's duty to uphold legal process.

. . .

[9] In the nature of law practice, however, conflicting responsibilities are encountered. Virtually all difficult ethical problems arise from conflict between a lawyer's responsibilities to clients, to the legal system and to the lawyer's own interest in remaining an ethical person while earning a satisfactory living. The Rules of Professional Conduct often prescribe terms for resolving such conflicts. Within the framework of these Rules, however, many difficult issues of professional discretion can arise. Such issues must be resolved through the exercise of sensitive professional and moral judgment guided by the basic principles underlying the Rules. These principles include the lawyer's obligation zealously to protect and pursue a client's legitimate interests, within the bounds of the law, while maintaining a professional, courteous and civil attitude toward all persons involved in the legal system.

. . .

[19] Failure to comply with an obligation or prohibition imposed by a Rule is a basis for invoking the disciplinary process. The Rules presuppose that disciplinary assessment of a lawyer's conduct will be made on the basis of the facts and circumstances as they existed at the time of the conduct in question and in recognition of the fact that a lawyer often has to act upon uncertain or incomplete evidence of the situation. Moreover, the Rules presuppose that whether or not discipline should be imposed for a violation, and the severity of a sanction, depend on all the circumstances, such as the willfulness and seriousness of the violation, extenuating factors and whether there have been previous violations.

[20] Violation of a Rule should not itself give rise to a cause of action against a lawyer nor should it create any presumption in such a case that a legal duty has been breached. In addition, violation of a Rule does not necessarily warrant any other nondisciplinary remedy, such as

disqualification of a lawyer in pending litigation. The Rules are designed to provide guidance to lawyers and to provide a structure for regulating conduct through disciplinary agencies. They are not designed to be a basis for civil liability. Furthermore, the purpose of the Rules can be subverted when they are invoked by opposing parties as procedural weapons. The fact that a Rule is a just basis for a lawyer's self-assessment, or for sanctioning a lawyer under the administration of a disciplinary authority, does not imply that an antagonist in a collateral proceeding or transaction has standing to seek enforcement of the Rule.

. . .

RULE 1.2 SCOPE OF REPRESENTATION.

(a) Subject to paragraphs (c) and (d), a lawyer shall abide by a client's decisions concerning the objectives of representation and, as required by Rule 1.4, shall consult with the client as to the means by which they are to be pursued. A lawyer may take such action on behalf of the client as is impliedly authorized to carry out the representation. A lawyer shall abide by a client's decision whether to settle a matter. In a criminal case, the lawyer shall abide by the client's decision, after consultation with the lawyer, as to a plea to be entered, whether to waive jury trial and whether the client will testify.

(b) A lawyer's representation of a client, including representation by appointment, does not constitute an endorsement of the client's political, economic, social or moral views or activities.

(c) A lawyer may limit the scope of the representation if the limitation is reasonable under the circumstances and the client gives informed consent.

(d) A lawyer shall not counsel a client to engage, or assist a client, in conduct that the lawyer knows is criminal or fraudulent, but a lawyer may discuss the legal consequences of any proposed course of conduct with a client and may counsel or assist a client to make a good faith effort to determine the validity, scope, meaning or application of the law.

Comment

[1] *Allocation of Authority between Client and Lawyer.*—Paragraph (a) confers upon the client the ultimate authority to determine the purposes to be served by legal representation, within the limits imposed by law and the lawyer's professional obligations. The decisions specified in paragraph (a), such as whether to settle a civil matter, must also be made by the client. See Rule 1.4(a)(1) for the lawyer's duty to communicate with the client about such decisions. With respect to the means by which the client's objectives are to be pursued, the lawyer shall consult with the client as required by Rule 1.4(a)(2) and may take such action as is impliedly authorized to carry out the representation.

[2] On occasion, however, a lawyer and a client may disagree about the means to be used to accomplish the client's objectives. Clients normally defer to the special knowledge and skill of their lawyer with respect to the means to be

used to accomplish their objectives, particularly with respect to technical, legal and tactical matters. Conversely, lawyers usually defer to the client regarding such questions as the expense to be incurred and concern for third persons who might be adversely affected. Because of the varied nature of the matters about which a lawyer and client might disagree and because the actions in question may implicate the interests of a tribunal or other persons, this Rule does not prescribe how such disagreements are to be resolved. Other law, however, may be applicable and should be consulted by the lawyer. The lawyer should also consult with the client and seek a mutually acceptable resolution of the disagreement. If such efforts are unavailing and the lawyer has a fundamental disagreement with the client, the lawyer may withdraw from the representation. See Rule 1.16(b)(4). Conversely, the client may resolve the disagreement by discharging the lawyer. See Rule 1.16(a)(3).

[3] At the outset of a representation, the client may authorize the lawyer to take specific action on the client's behalf without further consultation. Absent a material change in circumstances and subject to Rule 1.4, a lawyer may rely on such an advance authorization. The client may, however, revoke such authority at any time.

[4] In a case in which the client appears to be suffering diminished capacity, the lawyer's duty to abide by the client's decisions is to be guided by reference to Rule 1.14.

[5] *Independence from Client's Views or Activities.*—Legal representation should not be denied to people who are unable to afford legal services, or whose cause is controversial or the subject of popular disapproval. By the same token, representing a client does not constitute approval of the client's views or activities.

[6] *Agreements Limiting Scope of Representation.*—The scope of services to be provided by a lawyer may be limited by agreement with the client or by the terms under which the lawyer's services are made available to the client. When a lawyer has been retained by an insurer to represent an insured, for example, the representation may be limited to matters related to the insurance coverage. A limited representation may be appropriate because the client has limited objectives for the representation. In addition, the terms upon which representation is undertaken may exclude specific means that might otherwise be used to accomplish the client's objectives. Such limitations may exclude actions that the client thinks are too costly or that the lawyer regards as repugnant or imprudent.

[7] Although this Rule affords the lawyer and client substantial latitude to limit the representation, the limitation must be reasonable under the circumstances. If, for example, a client's objective is limited to securing general information about the law the client needs in order to handle a common and typically uncomplicated legal problem, the lawyer and client may agree that the lawyer's services will be limited to a brief telephone consultation. Such a limitation, however, would not be reasonable if the time allotted was not sufficient to yield advice upon which the client could rely. Although an agreement for a limited representation does not exempt a lawyer from the duty to provide competent representation, the limitation is a factor to be considered when determining the legal knowledge, skill, thoroughness and preparation reasonably necessary for the representation. See Rule 1.1.

[8] All agreements concerning a lawyer's representation of a client must accord with the Rules of Professional Conduct and other law. See, e.g., Rules 1.1, 1.8 and 5.6.

[9] *Criminal, Fraudulent and Prohibited Transactions.*—Paragraph (d) prohibits a lawyer from knowingly counseling or assisting a client to commit a crime or fraud. This prohibition, however, does not preclude the lawyer from giving an honest opinion about the actual consequences that appear likely to result from a client's conduct. Nor does the fact that a client uses advice in a course of action that is criminal or fraudulent of itself make a lawyer a party to the course of action. There is a critical distinction between presenting an analysis of legal aspects of questionable conduct and recommending the means by which a crime or fraud might be committed with impunity.

[10] When the client's course of action has already begun and is continuing, the lawyer's responsibility is especially delicate. The lawyer is required to avoid assisting the client, for example, by drafting or delivering documents that the lawyer knows are fraudulent or by suggesting how the wrongdoing might be concealed. A lawyer may not continue assisting a client in conduct that the lawyer originally supposed was legally proper but then discovers is criminal or fraudulent. The lawyer must, therefore, withdraw from the representation of the client in the matter. See Rule 1.16(a). In some cases, withdrawal alone might be insufficient. It may be necessary for the lawyer to give notice of the fact of withdrawal and to disaffirm any opinion, document, affirmation or the like. See Rule 4.1.

[11] Where the client is a fiduciary, the lawyer may be charged with special obligations in dealings with a beneficiary.

[12] Paragraph (d) applies whether or not the defrauded party is a party to the transaction. Hence, a lawyer must not participate in a transaction to effectuate criminal or fraudulent avoidance of tax liability. Paragraph (d) does not preclude undertaking a criminal defense incident to a general retainer for legal services to a lawful enterprise. The last clause of paragraph (d) recognizes that determining the validity or interpretation of a statute or regulation may require a course of action involving disobedience of the statute or regulation or of the interpretation placed upon it by governmental authorities.

[13] If a lawyer comes to know or reasonably should know that a client expects assistance not permitted by the Rules of Professional Conduct or other law or if the lawyer intends to act contrary to the client's instructions, the lawyer must consult with the client regarding the limitations on the lawyer's conduct. See Rule 1.4(a)(5).

RULE 1.3 DILIGENCE.

A lawyer shall act with reasonable diligence and promptness in representing a client.

Comment

[1] A lawyer should pursue a matter on behalf of a client despite opposition, obstruction or personal inconvenience to the lawyer, and take whatever lawful and ethical measures are required to vindicate a client's cause or endeavor. A lawyer must also act with commitment and dedication to the interests of the client and with zeal in advocacy upon the client's behalf. A lawyer is not

bound, however, to press for every advantage that might be realized for a client. For example, a lawyer may have authority to exercise professional discretion in determining the means by which a matter should be pursued. See Rule 1.2. The lawyer's duty to act with reasonable diligence does not require the use of offensive tactics or preclude the treating of all persons involved in the legal process with courtesy and respect.

[2] A lawyer's workload must be controlled so that each matter can be handled competently.

[3] Perhaps no professional shortcoming is more widely resented than procrastination. A client's interests often can be adversely affected by the passage of time or the change of conditions; in extreme instances, as when a lawyer overlooks a statute of limitations, the client's legal position may be destroyed. Even when the client's interests are not affected in substance, however, unreasonable delay can cause a client needless anxiety and undermine confidence in the lawyer's trustworthiness. A lawyer's duty to act with reasonable promptness, however, does not preclude the lawyer from agreeing to a reasonable request for a postponement that will not prejudice the lawyer's client.

[4] Unless the relationship is terminated as provided in Rule 1.16, a lawyer should carry through to conclusion all matters undertaken for a client. If a lawyer's employment is limited to a specific matter, the relationship terminates when the matter has been resolved. If a lawyer has served a client over a substantial period in a variety of matters, the client sometimes may assume that the lawyer will continue to serve on a continuing basis unless the lawyer gives notice of withdrawal. Doubt about whether a client-lawyer relationship still exists should be clarified by the lawyer, preferably in writing, so that the client will not mistakenly suppose the lawyer is looking after the client's affairs when the lawyer has ceased to do so. For example, if a lawyer has handled a judicial or administrative proceeding that produced a result adverse to the client and the lawyer and the client have not agreed that the lawyer will handle the matter on appeal, the lawyer must consult with the client about the possibility of appeal before relinquishing responsibility for the matter. See Rule 1.4(a)(2). Whether the lawyer is obligated to prosecute the appeal for the client depends on the scope of the representation the lawyer has agreed to provide to the client. See Rule 1.2.

. . .

RULE 1.4 COMMUNICATION.

(a) A lawyer shall:

(1) promptly inform the client of any decision or circumstance with respect to which the client's informed consent, as defined in Rule 1.0(e), is required by these Rules;

(2) reasonably consult with the client about the means by which the client's objectives are to be accomplished;

(3) keep the client reasonably informed about the status of the matter;

(4) promptly comply with reasonable requests for information; and

(5) consult with the client about any relevant limitation on the lawyer's conduct when the lawyer knows that the client expects assistance not permitted by the Rules of Professional Conduct or other law.

(b) A lawyer shall explain a matter to the extent reasonably necessary to permit the client to make informed decisions regarding the representation.

. . .

RULE 1.6 CONFIDENTIALITY OF INFORMATION.

(a) A lawyer shall not reveal information relating to the representation of a client unless the client gives informed consent, the disclosures is impliedly authorized in order to carry out the representation, or the disclosure is permitted by paragraph (b).

(b) A lawyer may reveal information relating to the representation of a client to the extent the lawyer reasonably believes necessary:

(1) to prevent reasonably certain death or substantial bodily harm;

(2) to prevent the client from committing a crime or fraud that is reasonably certain to result in substantial injury to the financial interests or property of another and in furtherance of which the client has used or is using the lawyer's services;

(3) to prevent, mitigate, or rectify substantial injury to the financial interests or property of another that is reasonably certain to result or has resulted from the client's commission of a crime or fraud in furtherance of which the client has used the lawyer's services;

(4) to secure legal advice about the lawyer's compliance with these Rules;

(5) to establish a claim or defense on behalf of the lawyer in a controversy between the lawyer and the client, to establish a defense to a criminal charge or civil claim against the lawyer based upon conduct in which the client was involved, or to respond to allegations in any proceeding concerning the lawyer's representation of the client; or

(6) to comply with other law or a court order.

Comment

[1] This Rule governs the disclosure by a lawyer of information relating to the representation of a client during the lawyer's representation of the client. See Rule 1.18 for the lawyer's duties with respect to information provided to the lawyer by a prospective client, Rule 1.9(c)(2) for the lawyer's duty not to reveal information relating to the lawyer's prior representation of a former client and

Rule 1.6 DELAWARE LAWYERS' RULES

Rules 1.8(b) and 1.9(c)(1) for the lawyer's duties with respect to the use of such information to the disadvantage of clients and former clients.

[2] A fundamental principle in the client-lawyer relationship is that, in the absence of the client's informed consent, the lawyer must not reveal information relating to the representation. See Rule 1.0(e) for the definition of informed consent. This contributes to the trust that is the hallmark of the client-lawyer relationship. The client is thereby encouraged to seek legal assistance and to communicate fully and frankly with the lawyer even as to embarrassing or legally damaging subject matter. The lawyer needs this information to represent the client effectively and, if necessary, to advise the client to refrain from wrongful conduct. Almost without exception, clients come to lawyers in order to determine their rights and what is, in the complex of laws and regulations, deemed to be legal and correct. Based upon experience, lawyers know that almost all clients follow the advice given, and the law is upheld.

[3] The principle of client-lawyer confidentiality is given effect by related bodies of law: the attorney-client privilege, the work product doctrine and the rule of confidentiality established in professional ethics. The attorney-client privilege and work product doctrine apply in judicial and other proceedings in which a lawyer may be called as a witness or otherwise required to produce evidence concerning a client. The rule of client-lawyer confidentiality applies in situations other than those where evidence is sought from the lawyer through compulsion of law. The confidentiality rule, for example, applies not only to matters communicated in confidence by the client but also to all information relating to the representation, whatever its source. A lawyer may not disclose such information except as authorized or required by the Rules of Professional Conduct or other law. See also Scope.

[4] Paragraph (a) prohibits a lawyer from revealing information relating to the representation of a client. This prohibition also applies to disclosures by a lawyer that do not in themselves reveal protected information but could reasonably lead to the discovery of such information by a third person. A lawyer's use of a hypothetical to discuss issues relating to the representation is permissible so long as there is no reasonable likelihood that the listener will be able to ascertain the identity of the client or the situation involved.

[5] *Authorized Disclosure.*—Except to the extent that the client's instructions or special circumstances limit that authority, a lawyer is impliedly authorized to make disclosures about a client when appropriate in carrying out the representation. In some situations, for example, a lawyer may be impliedly authorized to admit a fact that cannot properly be disputed or to make a disclosure that facilitates a satisfactory conclusion to a matter. Lawyers in a firm may, in the course of the firm's practice, disclose to each other information relating to a client of the firm, unless the client has instructed that particular information be confined to specified lawyers.

[6] *Disclosure Adverse to Client.*—Although the public interest is usually best served by a strict rule requiring lawyers to preserve the confidentiality of information relating to the representation of their clients, the confidentiality rule is subject to limited exceptions. Paragraph (b)(1) recognizes the overriding value of life and physical integrity and permits disclosure reasonably necessary to prevent reasonably certain death or substantial bodily harm. Such harm is reasonably certain to occur if it will be suffered imminently or if there is a

present and substantial threat that a person will suffer such harm at a later date if the lawyer fails to take action necessary to eliminate the threat. Thus, a lawyer who knows that a client has accidentally discharged toxic waste into a town's water supply may reveal this information to the authorities if there is a present and substantial risk that a person who drinks the water will contract a life-threatening or debilitating disease and the lawyer's disclosure is necessary to eliminate the threat or reduce the number of victims.

[7] Paragraph (b)(2) is a limited exception to the rule of confidentiality that permits the lawyer to reveal information to the extent necessary to enable affected persons or appropriate authorities to prevent the client from committing a crime or a fraud, as defined in Rule 1.0(d), that is reasonably certain to result in substantial injury to the financial or property interests of another and in furtherance of which the client has used or is using the lawyer's services. Such a serious abuse of the client-lawyer relationship by the client forfeits the protection of this Rule. The client can, of course, prevent such disclosure by refraining from the wrongful conduct. Although paragraph (b)(2) does not require the lawyer to reveal the client's misconduct, the lawyer may not counsel or assist the client in conduct the lawyer knows is criminal or fraudulent. See Rule 1.2(d). See also Rule 1.16 with respect to the lawyer's obligation or right to withdraw from the representation of the client in such circumstances. Where the client is an organization, the lawyer may be in doubt whether contemplated conduct will actually be carried out by the organization. Where necessary to guide conduct in connection with this Rule, the lawyer may make inquiry within the organization as indicated in Rule 1.13(b).

[8] Paragraph (b)(3) addresses the situation in which the lawyer does not learn of the client's crime or fraud until after it has been consummated. Although the client no longer has the option of preventing disclosure by refraining from the wrongful conduct, there will be situations in which the loss suffered by the affected person can be prevented, rectified or mitigated. In such situations, the lawyer may disclose information relating to the representation to the extent necessary to enable the affected persons to prevent or mitigate reasonably certain losses or to attempt to recoup their losses. Disclosure is not permitted under paragraph (b)(3) when a person who has committed a crime or fraud thereafter employs a lawyer for representation concerning that offense if that lawyer's services were not used in the initial crime or fraud; disclosure would be permitted, however, if the lawyer's services are used to commit a further crime or fraud, such as the crime of obstructing justice. While applicable law may provide that a completed act is regarded for some purposes as a continuing offense, if commission of the initial act has already occurred without the use of the lawyer's services, the lawyer does not have discretion under this paragraph to use or disclose the client's information.

[9] A lawyer's confidentiality obligations do not preclude a lawyer from securing confidential legal advice about the lawyer's personal responsibility to comply with these Rules. In most situations, disclosing information to secure such advice will be impliedly authorized for the lawyer to carry out the representation. Even when the disclosure is not impliedly authorized, paragraph (b)(2) permits such disclosure because of the importance of a lawyer's compliance with the Rules of Professional Conduct.

[10] Where a legal claim or disciplinary charge alleges complicity of the lawyer in a client's conduct or other misconduct of the lawyer involving repre-

sentation of the client, the lawyer may respond to the extent the lawyer reasonably believes necessary to establish a defense. The same is true with respect to a claim involving the conduct or representation of a former client. Such a charge can arise in a civil, criminal, disciplinary or other proceeding and can be based on a wrong allegedly committed by the lawyer against the client or on a wrong alleged by a third person, for example, a person claiming to have been defrauded by the lawyer and client acting together. The lawyer's right to respond arises when an assertion of such complicity has been made. Paragraph (b)(5) does not require the lawyer to await the commencement of an action or proceeding that charges such complicity, so that the defense may be established by responding directly to a third party who has made such an assertion. The right to defend also applies, of course, where a proceeding has been commenced.

. . .

RULE 1.7 CONFLICT OF INTEREST: CURRENT CLIENTS.

(a) Except as provided in paragraph (b), a lawyer shall not represent a client if the representation involves a concurrent conflict of interest. A concurrent conflict of interest exists if:

(1) the representation of one client will be directly adverse to another client; or

(2) there is a significant risk that the representation of one or more clients will be materially limited by the lawyer's responsibilities to another client, a former client or a third person or by a personal interest of the lawyer.

(b) Notwithstanding the existence of a concurrent conflict of interest under paragraph (a), a lawyer may represent a client if:

(1) the lawyer reasonably believes that the lawyer will be able to provide competent and diligent representation to each affected client;

(2) the representation is not prohibited by law;

(3) the representation does not involve the assertion of a claim by one client against another client represented by the lawyer in the same litigation or other proceeding before a tribunal; and

(4) each affected client gives informed consent, confirmed in writing.

Comment

[1] *General Principles.*—Loyalty and independent judgment are essential elements in the lawyer's relationship to a client. Concurrent conflicts of interest can arise from the lawyer's responsibilities to another client, a former client or a third person or from the lawyer's own interests. For specific Rules regarding certain concurrent conflicts of interest, see Rule 1.8. For former client conflicts of interest, see Rule 1.9. For conflicts of interest involving prospective clients, see Rule 1.18. For definitions of "informed consent" and "confirmed in writing," see Rule 1.0(e) and (b).

[2] Resolution of a conflict of interest problem under this Rule requires the lawyer to: 1) clearly identify the client or clients; 2) determine whether a conflict of interest exists; 3) decide whether the representation may be undertaken despite the existence of a conflict, i.e., whether the conflict is consentable; and 4) if so, consult with the clients affected under paragraph (a) and obtain their informed consent, confirmed in writing. The clients affected under paragraph (a) include both of the clients referred to in paragraph (a)(1) and the one or more clients whose representation might be materially limited under paragraph (a)(2).

[3] A conflict of interest may exist before representation is undertaken, in which event the representation must be declined, unless the lawyer obtains the informed consent of each client under the conditions of paragraph (b). To determine whether a conflict of interest exists, a lawyer should adopt reasonable procedures, appropriate for the size and type of firm and practice, to determine in both litigation and non-litigation matters the persons and issues involved. See also Comment to Rule 5.1. Ignorance caused by a failure to institute such procedures will not excuse a lawyer's violation of this Rule. As to whether a client-lawyer relationship exists or, having once been established, is continuing, see Comment to Rule 1.3 and Scope.

[4] If a conflict arises after representation has been undertaken, the lawyer ordinarily must withdraw from the representation, unless the lawyer has obtained the informed consent of the client under the conditions of paragraph (b). See Rule 1.16. Where more than one client is involved, whether the lawyer may continue to represent any of the clients is determined both by the lawyer's ability to comply with duties owed to the former client and by the lawyer's ability to represent adequately the remaining client or clients, given the lawyer's duties to the former client. See Rule 1.9. See also Comments [5] and [29].

[5] Unforeseeable developments, such as changes in corporate and other organizational affiliations or the addition or realignment of parties in litigation, might create conflicts in the midst of a representation, as when a company sued by the lawyer on behalf of one client is bought by another client represented by the lawyer in an unrelated matter. Depending on the circumstances, the lawyer may have the option to withdraw from one of the representations in order to avoid the conflict. The lawyer must seek court approval where necessary and take steps to minimize harm to the clients. See Rule 1.16. The lawyer must continue to protect the confidences of the client from whose representation the lawyer has withdrawn. See Rule 1.9(c).

[6] *Identifying Conflicts of Interest: Directly Adverse.*—Loyalty to a current client prohibits undertaking representation directly adverse to that client without that client's informed consent. Thus, absent consent, a lawyer may not act as an advocate in one matter against a person the lawyer represents in some other matter, even when the matters are wholly unrelated. The client as to whom the representation is directly adverse is likely to feel betrayed, and the resulting damage to the client-lawyer relationship is likely to impair the lawyer's ability to represent the client effectively. In addition, the client on whose behalf the adverse representation is undertaken reasonably may fear that the lawyer will pursue that client's case less effectively out of deference to the other client, i.e., that the representation may be materially limited by the lawyer's interest in retaining the current client. Similarly, a directly adverse conflict may arise when a lawyer is required to cross-examine a client who appears as a witness in a lawsuit involving another client, as when the testimony will be damaging to the

client who is represented in the lawsuit. On the other hand, simultaneous representation in unrelated matters of clients whose interests are only economically adverse, such as representation of competing economic enterprises in unrelated litigation, does not ordinarily constitute a conflict of interest and thus may not require consent of the respective clients.

[7] Directly adverse conflicts can also arise in transactional matters. For example, if a lawyer is asked to represent the seller of a business in negotiations with a buyer represented by the lawyer, not in the same transaction but in another, unrelated matter, the lawyer could not undertake the representation without the informed consent of each client.

[8] *Identifying Conflicts of Interest: Material Limitation.*—Even where there is no direct adverseness, a conflict of interest exists if there is a significant risk that a lawyer's ability to consider, recommend or carry out an appropriate course of action for the client will be materially limited as a result of the lawyer's other responsibilities or interests. For example, a lawyer asked to represent several individuals seeking to form a joint venture is likely to be materially limited in the lawyer's ability to recommend or advocate all possible positions that each might take because of the lawyer's duty of loyalty to the others. The conflict in effect forecloses alternatives that would otherwise be available to the client. The mere possibility of subsequent harm does not itself require disclosure and consent. The critical questions are the likelihood that a difference in interests will eventuate and, if it does, whether it will materially interfere with the lawyer's independent professional judgment in considering alternatives or foreclose courses of action that reasonably should be pursued on behalf of the client.

. . .

RULE 1.10 IMPUTATION OF CONFLICTS OF INTEREST: GENERAL RULE.

(a) Except as otherwise provided in this rule, while lawyers are associated in a firm, none of them shall knowingly represent a client when any one of them practicing alone would be prohibited from doing so by Rules 1.7 or 1.9, unless the prohibition is based on a personal interest of the prohibited lawyer and does not present a significant risk of materially limiting the representation of the client by the remaining lawyers in the firm.

(b) When a lawyer has terminated an association with a firm, the firm is not prohibited from thereafter representing a person with interests materially adverse to those of a client represented by the formerly associated lawyer and not currently represented by the firm, unless:

(1) the matter is the same or substantially related to that in which the formerly associated lawyer represented the client; and

(2) any lawyer remaining in the firm has information protected by Rules 1.6 and 1.9(c) that is material to the matter.

(c) When a lawyer becomes associated with a firm, no lawyer associated in the firm shall knowingly represent a client in a matter in which that lawyer is disqualified under Rule 1.9 unless:

(1) the personally disqualified lawyer is timely screened from any participation in the matter and is apportioned no part of the fee therefrom; and

(2) written notice is promptly given to the affected former client.

(d) A disqualification prescribed by this rule may be waived by the affected client under the conditions stated in Rule 1.7.

(e) The disqualification of lawyers associated in a firm with former or current government lawyers is governed by Rule 1.11.

. . .

RULE 1.13 ORGANIZATION AS CLIENT.

(a) A lawyer employed or retained by an organization represents the organization acting through its duly authorized constituents.

(b) If a lawyer for an organization knows that an officer, employee or other person associated with the organization is engaged in action, intends to act or refuses to act in a matter related to the representation that is a violation of a legal obligation to the organization, or a violation of law which reasonably might be imputed to the organization, and is likely to result in substantial injury to the organization, the lawyer shall proceed as is reasonably necessary in the best interest of the organization. In determining how to proceed, the lawyer shall give due consideration to the seriousness of the violation and its consequences, the scope and nature of the lawyer's representation, the responsibility in the organization and the apparent motivation of the person involved, the policies of the organization concerning such matters and any other relevant considerations. Any measures taken shall be designed to minimize disruption of the organization and the risk of revealing information relating to the representation to persons outside the organization. Such measures may include among others:

(1) asking for reconsideration of the matter;

(2) advising that a separate legal opinion on the matter be sought for presentation to appropriate authority in the organization; and

(3) referring the matter to higher authority in the organization, including, if warranted by the seriousness of the matter, referral to the highest authority that can act on behalf of the organization as determined by applicable law.

(c) If, despite the lawyer's efforts in accordance with paragraph (b), the highest authority that can act on behalf of the organization insists upon action, or a refusal to act, that is clearly a violation of law and is likely to result in substantial injury to the organization, the lawyer may resign in accordance with Rule 1.16.

(d) In dealing with an organization's directors, officers, employees, members, shareholders or other constituents, a lawyer shall explain the identity of the client when the lawyer knows or reasonably should know that the organization's interests are adverse to those of the constituents with whom the lawyer is dealing.

(e) A lawyer representing an organization may also represent any of its directors, officers, employees, members, shareholders or other constituents, subject to the provisions of Rule 1.7. If the organization's consent to the dual representation is required by Rule 1.7, the consent shall be given by an appropriate official of the organization other than the individual who is to be represented, or by the shareholders.

Comment

[1] *The Entity as the Client.*—An organizational client is a legal entity, but it cannot act except through its officers, directors, employees, shareholders and other constituents. Officers, directors, employees and shareholders are the constituents of the corporate organizational client. The duties defined in this Comment apply equally to unincorporated associations. "Other constituents" as used in this Comment means the positions equivalent to officers, directors, employees and shareholders held by persons acting for organizational clients that are not corporations.

[2] When one of the constituents of an organizational client communicates with the organization's lawyer in that person's organizational capacity, the communication is protected by Rule 1.6. Thus, by way of example, if an organizational client requests its lawyer to investigate allegations of wrongdoing, interviews made in the course of that investigation between the lawyer and the client's employees or other constituents are covered by Rule 1.6. This does not mean, however, that constituents of an organizational client are the clients of the lawyer. The lawyer may not disclose to such constituents information relating to the representation except for disclosures explicitly or impliedly authorized by the organizational client in order to carry out the representation or as otherwise permitted by Rule 1.6.

[3] When constituents of the organization make decisions for it, the decisions ordinarily must be accepted by the lawyer even if their utility or prudence is doubtful. Decisions concerning policy and operations, including ones entailing serious risk, are not as such in the lawyer's province. However, different considerations arise when the lawyer knows that the organization may be substantially injured by action of a constituent that is in violation of law. In such a circumstance, it may be reasonably necessary for the lawyer to ask the constituent to reconsider the matter. If that fails, or if the matter is of sufficient seriousness and importance to the organization, it may be reasonably necessary for the lawyer to take steps to have the matter reviewed by a higher authority in the organization. Clear justification should exist for seeking review over the head of the constituent normally responsible for it. The stated policy of the organization may define circumstances and prescribe channels for such review, and a

lawyer should encourage the formulation of such a policy. Even in the absence of organization policy, however, the lawyer may have an obligation to refer a matter to higher authority, depending on the seriousness of the matter and whether the constituent in question has apparent motives to act at variance with the organization's interest. Review by the chief executive officer or by the board of directors may be required when the matter is of importance commensurate with their authority. At some point it may be useful or essential to obtain an independent legal opinion.

[4] The organization's highest authority to whom a matter may be referred ordinarily will be the board of directors or similar governing body. However, applicable law may prescribe that under certain conditions the highest authority reposes elsewhere, for example, in the independent directors of a corporation.

[5] *Relation to Other Rules.*—The authority and responsibility provided in this Rule are concurrent with the authority and responsibility provided in other Rules. In particular, this Rule does not limit or expand the lawyer's responsibility under Rule 1.6, 1.8, 1.16, 3.3 or 4.1. If the lawyer's services are being used by an organization to further a crime or fraud by the organization, Rule 1.2(d) can be applicable.

[6] *Government Agency.*—The duty defined in this Rule applies to governmental organizations. Defining precisely the identity of the client and prescribing the resulting obligations of such lawyers may be more difficult in the government context and is a matter beyond the scope of these Rules. See Scope [18]. Although in some circumstances the client may be a specific agency, it may also be a branch of government, such as the executive branch, or the government as a whole. For example, if the action or failure to act involves the head of a bureau, either the department of which the bureau is a part or the relevant branch of government may be the client for purposes of this Rule. Moreover, in a matter involving the conduct of government officials, a government lawyer may have authority under applicable law to question such conduct more extensively than that of a lawyer for a private organization in similar circumstances. Thus, when the client is a governmental organization, a different balance may be appropriate between maintaining confidentiality and assuring that the wrongful act is prevented or rectified, for public business is involved. In addition, duties of lawyers employed by the government or lawyers in military service may be defined by statutes and regulation. This Rule does not limit that authority. See Scope.

[7] *Clarifying the Lawyer's Role.*—There are times when the organization's interest may be or become adverse to those of one or more of its constituents. In such circumstances the lawyer should advise any constituent, whose interest the lawyer finds adverse to that of the organization of the conflict or potential conflict of interest, that the lawyer cannot represent such constituent, and that such person may wish to obtain independent representation. Care must be taken to assure that the individual understands that, when there is such adversity of interest, the lawyer for the organization cannot provide legal representation for that constituent individual, and that discussions between the lawyer for the organization and the individual may not be privileged.

[8] Whether such a warning should be given by the lawyer for the organization to any constituent individual may turn on the facts of each case.

[9] *Dual Representation.*—Paragraph (e) recognizes that a lawyer for an organization may also represent a principal officer or major shareholder.

[10] *Derivative Actions.*—Under generally prevailing law, the shareholders or members of a corporation may bring suit to compel the directors to perform their legal obligations in the supervision of the organization. Members of unincorporated associations have essentially the same right. Such an action may be brought nominally by the organization, but usually is, in fact, a legal controversy over management of the organization.

[11] The question can arise whether counsel for the organization may defend such an action. The proposition that the organization is the lawyer's client does not alone resolve the issue. Most derivative actions are a normal incident of an organization's affairs, to be defended by the organization's lawyer like any other suit. However, if the claim involves serious charges of wrongdoing by those in control of the organization, a conflict may arise between the lawyer's duty to the organization and the lawyer's relationship with the board. In those circumstances, Rule 1.7 governs who should represent the directors and the organization.

. . .

RULE 1.16 DECLINING OR TERMINATING REPRESENTATION.

(a) Except as stated in paragraph (c), a lawyer shall not represent a client or, where representation has commenced, shall withdraw from the representation of a client if:

(1) the representation will result in violation of the rules of professional conduct or other law;

(2) the lawyer's physical or mental condition materially impairs the lawyer's ability to represent the client; or

(3) the lawyer is discharged.

(b) Except as stated in paragraph (c), a lawyer may withdraw from representing a client if:

(1) withdrawal can be accomplished without material adverse effect on the interests of the client;

(2) the client persists in a course of action involving the lawyer's services that the lawyer reasonably believes is criminal or fraudulent;

(3) the client has used the lawyer's service to perpetrate a crime or fraud;

(4) a client insists upon taking action that the lawyer considers repugnant or with which the lawyer has a fundamental disagreement;

(5) the client fails substantially to fulfill an obligation to the lawyer regarding the lawyer's services and has been given reason-

able warning that the lawyer will withdraw unless the obligation is fulfilled;

(6) the representation will result in an unreasonable financial burden on the lawyer or has been rendered unreasonably difficult by the client; or

(7) other good cause for withdrawal exists.

(c) A lawyer must comply with applicable law requiring notice to or permission of a tribunal when terminating a representation. When ordered to do so by a tribunal, a lawyer shall continue representation notwithstanding good cause for terminating the representation.

(d) Upon termination of representation, a lawyer shall take steps to the extent reasonably practicable to protect a client's interests, such as giving reasonable notice to the client, allowing time for employment of other counsel, surrendering papers and property to which the client is entitled and refunding any advance payment of fee or expense that has not been earned or incurred. The lawyer may retain papers relating to the client to the extent permitted by other law.

Comment

[1] A lawyer should not accept representation in a matter unless it can be performed competently, promptly, without improper conflict of interest and to completion. Ordinarily, a representation in a matter is completed when the agreed-upon assistance has been concluded. See Rules 1.2(c) and 6.5. See also Rule 1.3, Comment [4].

[2] *Mandatory Withdrawal.*—A lawyer ordinarily must decline or withdraw from representation if the client demands that the lawyer engage in conduct that is illegal or violates the Rules of Professional Conduct or other law. The lawyer is not obliged to decline or withdraw simply because the client suggests such a course of conduct; a client may make such a suggestion in the hope that a lawyer will not be constrained by a professional obligation.

[3] When a lawyer has been appointed to represent a client, withdrawal ordinarily requires approval of the appointing authority. See also Rule 6.2. Similarly, court approval or notice to the court is often required by applicable law before a lawyer withdraws from pending litigation. Difficulty may be encountered if withdrawal is based on the client's demand that the lawyer engage in unprofessional conduct. The court may request an explanation for the withdrawal, while the lawyer may be bound to keep confidential the facts that would constitute such an explanation. The lawyer's statement that professional considerations require termination of the representation ordinarily should be accepted as sufficient. Lawyers should be mindful of their obligations to both clients and the court under Rules 1.6 and 3.3.

[4] *Discharge.*—A client has a right to discharge a lawyer at any time, with or without cause, subject to liability for payment for the lawyer's services. Where future dispute about the withdrawal may be anticipated, it may be advisable to prepare a written statement reciting the circumstances.

[5] Whether a client can discharge appointed counsel may depend on applicable law. A client seeking to do so should be given a full explanation of the consequences. These consequences may include a decision by the appointing authority that appointment of successor counsel is unjustified, thus requiring self-representation by the client.

[6] If the client has severely diminished capacity, the client may lack the legal capacity to discharge the lawyer, and in any event the discharge may be seriously adverse to the client's interests. The lawyer should make special effort to help the client consider the consequences and may take reasonably necessary protective action as provided in Rule 1.14.

[7] *Optional Withdrawal.*—A lawyer may withdraw from representation in some circumstances. The lawyer has the option to withdraw if it can be accomplished without material adverse effect on the client's interests. Withdrawal is also justified if the client persists in a course of action that the lawyer reasonably believes is criminal or fraudulent, for a lawyer is not required to be associated with such conduct even if the lawyer does not further it. Withdrawal is also permitted if the lawyer's services were misused in the past even if that would materially prejudice the client. The lawyer may also withdraw where the client insists on taking action that the lawyer considers repugnant or with which the lawyer has a fundamental disagreement.

[8] A lawyer may withdraw if the client refuses to abide by the terms of an agreement relating to the representation, such as an agreement concerning fees or court costs or an agreement limiting the objectives of the representation.

[9] *Assisting the Client upon Withdrawal.*—Even if the lawyer has been unfairly discharged by the client, a lawyer must take all reasonable steps to mitigate the consequences to the client. The lawyer may retain papers as security for a fee only to the extent permitted by law. See Rule 1.15.

. . .

RULE 3.1 MERITORIOUS CLAIMS AND CONTENTIONS.

A lawyer shall not bring or defend a proceeding, or assert or controvert an issue therein, unless there is a basis in law and fact for doing so that is not frivolous, which includes a good faith argument for an extension, modification or reversal of existing law. A lawyer for the defendant in a criminal proceeding, or the respondent in a proceeding that could result in incarceration, may nevertheless so defend the proceeding as to require that every element of the case be established.

. . .

RULE 3.3 CANDOR TOWARD THE TRIBUNAL.

(a) A lawyer shall not knowingly:

(1) make a false statement of fact or law to a tribunal or fail to correct a false statement of material fact or law previously made to the tribunal by the lawyer;

(2) fail to disclose to the tribunal legal authority in the controlling jurisdiction known to the lawyer to be directly adverse to the position of the client and not disclosed by opposing counsel; or

(3) offer evidence that the lawyer knows to be false. If a lawyer, the lawyer's client, or a witness called by the lawyer, has offered material evidence and the lawyer comes to know of its falsity, the lawyer shall take reasonable remedial measures, including, if necessary, disclosure to the tribunal. A lawyer may refuse to offer evidence, other than the testimony of a defendant in a criminal matter, that the lawyer reasonably believes is false.

(b) A lawyer who represents a client in an adjudicative proceeding and who knows that a person intends to engage, is engaging or has engaged in criminal or fraudulent conduct related to the proceeding shall take reasonable remedial measures, including, if necessary, disclosure to the tribunal.

(c) The duties stated in paragraph (a) and (b) continue to the conclusion of the proceeding, and apply even if compliance requires disclosure of information otherwise protected by Rule 1.6.

(d) In an ex parte proceeding, a lawyer shall inform the tribunal of all material facts known to the lawyer which will enable the tribunal to make an informed decision, whether or not the facts are adverse.

Comment

[1] This Rule governs the conduct of a lawyer who is representing a client in the proceedings of a tribunal. See Rule 1.0(m) for the definition of "tribunal." It also applies when the lawyer is representing a client in an ancillary proceeding conducted pursuant to the tribunal's adjudicative authority, such as a deposition. Thus, for example, paragraph (a)(3) requires a lawyer to take reasonable remedial measures if the lawyer comes to know that a client who is testifying in a deposition has offered evidence that is false.

[2] This Rule sets forth the special duties of lawyers as officers of the court to avoid conduct that undermines the integrity of the adjudicative process. A lawyer acting as an advocate in an adjudicative proceeding has an obligation to present the client's case with persuasive force. Performance of that duty while maintaining confidences of the client, however, is qualified by the advocate's duty of candor to the tribunal. Consequently, although a lawyer in an adversary proceeding is not required to present an impartial exposition of the law or to vouch for the evidence submitted in a cause, the lawyer must not allow the tribunal to be misled by false statements of law or fact or evidence that the lawyer knows to be false.

[3] *Representations by a Lawyer.*—An advocate is responsible for pleadings and other documents prepared for litigation, but is usually not required to have personal knowledge of matters asserted therein, for litigation documents ordinarily present assertions by the client, or by someone on the client's behalf, and not assertions by the lawyer. Compare Rule 3.1. However, an assertion purporting to be on the lawyer's own knowledge, as in an affidavit by the lawyer or in a statement in open court, may properly be made only when the lawyer knows the

Rule 3.3   DELAWARE LAWYERS' RULES

assertion is true or believes it to be true on the basis of a reasonably diligent inquiry. There are circumstances where failure to make a disclosure is the equivalent of an affirmative misrepresentation. The obligation prescribed in Rule 1.2(d) not to counsel a client to commit or assist the client in committing a fraud applies in litigation. Regarding compliance with Rule 1.2(d), see the Comment to that Rule. See also the Comment to Rule 8.4(b).

[4] *Legal Argument.*—Legal argument based on a knowingly false representation of law constitutes dishonesty toward the tribunal. A lawyer is not required to make a disinterested exposition of the law, but must recognize the existence of pertinent legal authorities. Furthermore, as stated in paragraph (a)(2), an advocate has a duty to disclose directly adverse authority in the controlling jurisdiction that has not been disclosed by the opposing party. The underlying concept is that legal argument is a discussion seeking to determine the legal premises properly applicable to the case.

[5] *Offering Evidence.*—Paragraph (a)(3) requires that the lawyer refuse to offer evidence that the lawyer knows to be false, regardless of the client's wishes. This duty is premised on the lawyer's obligation as an officer of the court to prevent the trier of fact from being misled by false evidence. A lawyer does not violate this Rule if the lawyer offers the evidence for the purpose of establishing its falsity.

[6] If a lawyer knows that the client intends to testify falsely or wants the lawyer to introduce false evidence, the lawyer should seek to persuade the client that the evidence should not be offered. If the persuasion is ineffective and the lawyer continues to represent the client, the lawyer must refuse to offer the false evidence. If only a portion of a witness's testimony will be false, the lawyer may call the witness to testify but may not elicit or otherwise permit the witness to present the testimony that the lawyer knows is false.

[7] The duties stated in paragraphs (a) and (b) apply to all lawyers, including defense counsel in criminal cases. In some jurisdictions, however, courts have required counsel to present the accused as a witness or to give a narrative statement if the accused so desires, even if counsel knows that the testimony or statement will be false. The obligation of the advocate under the Rules of Professional Conduct is subordinate to such requirements. See also Comment [9].

[8] The prohibition against offering false evidence only applies if the lawyer knows that the evidence is false. A lawyer's reasonable belief that evidence is false does not preclude its presentation to the trier of fact. A lawyer's knowledge that evidence is false, however, can be inferred from the circumstances. See Rule 1.0(f). Thus, although a lawyer should resolve doubts about the veracity of testimony or other evidence in favor of the client, the lawyer cannot ignore an obvious falsehood.

[9] Although paragraph (a)(3) only prohibits a lawyer from offering evidence the lawyer knows to be false, it permits the lawyer to refuse to offer testimony or other proof that the lawyer reasonably believes is false. Offering such proof may reflect adversely on the lawyer's ability to discriminate in the quality of evidence and thus impair the lawyer's effectiveness as an advocate. Because of the special protections historically provided criminal defendants, however, this Rule does not permit a lawyer to refuse to offer the testimony of such a client where the lawyer reasonably believes but does not know that the

testimony will be false. Unless the lawyer knows the testimony will be false, the lawyer must honor the client's decision to testify. See also Comment [7].

[10] *Remedial Measures.*—Having offered material evidence in the belief that it was true, a lawyer may subsequently come to know that the evidence is false. Or, a lawyer may be surprised when the lawyer's client, or another witness called by the lawyer, offers testimony the lawyer knows to be false, either during the lawyer's direct examination or in response to cross-examination by the opposing lawyer. In such situations or if the lawyer knows of the falsity of testimony elicited from the client during a deposition, the lawyer must take reasonable remedial measures. In such situations, the advocate's proper course is to remonstrate with the client confidentially, advise the client of the lawyer's duty of candor to the tribunal and seek the client's cooperation with respect to the withdrawal or correction of the false statements or evidence. If that fails, the advocate must take further remedial action. If withdrawal from the representation is not permitted or will not undo the effect of the false evidence, the advocate must make such disclosure to the tribunal as is reasonably necessary to remedy the situation, even if doing so requires the lawyer to reveal information that otherwise would be protected by Rule 1.6. It is for the tribunal then to determine what should be done—making a statement about the matter to the trier of fact, ordering a mistrial or perhaps nothing.

[11] The disclosure of a client's false testimony can result in grave consequences to the client, including not only a sense of betrayal but also loss of the case and perhaps a prosecution for perjury. But the alternative is that the lawyer cooperate in deceiving the court, thereby subverting the truth-finding process which the adversary system is designed to implement. See Rule 1.2(d). Furthermore, unless it is clearly understood that the lawyer will act upon the duty to disclose the existence of false evidence, the client can simply reject the lawyer's advice to reveal the false evidence and insist that the lawyer keep silent. Thus the client could in effect coerce the lawyer into being a party to fraud on the court.

[12] *Preserving Integrity of Adjudicative Process.*—Lawyers have a special obligation to protect a tribunal against criminal or fraudulent conduct that undermines the integrity of the adjudicative process, such as bribing, intimidating or otherwise unlawfully communicating with a witness, juror, court official or other participant in the proceeding, unlawfully destroying or concealing documents or other evidence or failing to disclose information to the tribunal when required by law to do so. Thus, paragraph (b) requires a lawyer to take reasonable remedial measures, including disclosure if necessary, whenever the lawyer knows that a person, including the lawyer's client, intends to engage, is engaging or has engaged in criminal or fraudulent conduct related to the proceeding.

[13] *Duration of Obligation.*—A practical time limit on the obligation to rectify false evidence or false statements of law and fact has to be established. The conclusion of the proceeding is a reasonably definite point for the termination of the obligation. A proceeding has concluded within the meaning of this Rule when a final judgment in the proceeding has been affirmed on appeal or the time for review has passed.

[14] *Ex Parte Proceedings.*—Ordinarily, an advocate has the limited responsibility of presenting one side of the matters that a tribunal should consider

in reaching a decision; the conflicting position is expected to be presented by the opposing party. However, in any ex parte proceeding, such as an application for a temporary restraining order, there is no balance of presentation by opposing advocates. The object of an ex parte proceeding is nevertheless to yield a substantially just result. The judge has an affirmative responsibility to accord the absent party just consideration. The lawyer for the represented party has the correlative duty to make disclosures of material facts known to the lawyer and that the lawyer reasonably believes are necessary to an informed decision.

[15] *Withdrawal.*—Normally, a lawyer's compliance with the duty of candor imposed by this Rule does not require that the lawyer withdraw from the representation of a client whose interests will be or have been adversely affected by the lawyer's disclosure. The lawyer may, however, be required by Rule 1.16(a) to seek permission of the tribunal to withdraw if the lawyer's compliance with this Rule's duty of candor results in such an extreme deterioration of the client-lawyer relationship that the lawyer can no longer competently represent the client. Also see Rule 1.16(b) for the circumstances in which a lawyer will be permitted to seek a tribunal's permission to withdraw. In connection with a request for permission to withdraw that is premised on a client's misconduct, a lawyer may reveal information relating to the representation only to the extent reasonably necessary to comply with this Rule or as otherwise permitted by Rule 1.6.

RULE 3.4 FAIRNESS TO OPPOSING PARTY AND COUNSEL.

A lawyer shall not:

(a) unlawfully obstruct another party's access to evidence or unlawfully alter, destroy or conceal a document or other material having potential evidentiary value. A lawyer shall not counsel or assist another person to do any such act;

(b) falsify evidence, counsel or assist a witness to testify falsely, or offer an inducement to a witness that is prohibited by law;

(c) knowingly disobey an obligation under the rules of a tribunal, except for an open refusal based on an assertion that no valid obligation exists;

(d) in pretrial procedure, make a frivolous discovery request or fail to make reasonably diligent efforts to comply with a legally proper discovery request by an opposing party;

(e) in trial, allude to any matter that the lawyer does not reasonably believe is relevant or that will not be supported by admissible evidence, assert personal knowledge of facts in issue except when testifying as a witness, or state a personal opinion as to the justness of a cause, the credibility of a witness, the culpability of a civil litigant or the guilt or innocence of an accused; or

(f) request a person other than a client to refrain from voluntarily giving relevant information to another party unless:

(1) the person is a relative or an employee or other agent of a client; and

(2) the lawyer reasonably believes that the person's interests will not be adversely affected by refraining from giving such information.

Comment

[1] The procedure of the adversary system contemplates that the evidence in a case is to be marshalled competitively by the contending parties. Fair competition in the adversary system is secured by prohibitions against destruction or concealment of evidence, improperly influencing witnesses, obstructive tactics in discovery procedure, and the like.

[2] Documents and other items of evidence are often essential to establish a claim or defense. Subject to evidentiary privileges, the right of an opposing party, including the government, to obtain evidence through discovery or subpoena is an important procedural right. The exercise of that right can be frustrated if relevant material is altered, concealed or destroyed. Applicable law in many jurisdictions makes it an offense to destroy material for purpose of impairing its availability in a pending proceeding or one whose commencement can be foreseen. Falsifying evidence is also generally a criminal offense. Paragraph (a) applies to evidentiary material generally, including computerized information. Applicable law may permit a lawyer to take temporary possession of physical evidence of client crimes for the purpose of conducting a limited examination that will not alter or destroy material characteristics of the evidence. In such a case, applicable law may require the lawyer to turn the evidence over to the police or other prosecuting authority, depending on the circumstances.

[3] With regard to paragraph (b), it is not improper to pay a witness's expenses or to compensate an expert witness on terms permitted by law. The common law rule in most jurisdictions is that it is improper to pay an occurrence witness any fee for testifying and that it is improper to pay an expert witness a contingent fee.

[4] Paragraph (f) permits a lawyer to advise employees of a client to refrain from giving information to another party, for the employees may identify their interests with those of the client. See also Rule 4.2.

RULE 3.5 IMPARTIALITY AND DECORUM OF THE TRIBUNAL.

A lawyer shall not:

(a) seek to influence a judge, juror, prospective juror or other official by means prohibited by law;

(b) communicate or cause another to communicate ex parte with such a person or members of such person's family during the proceeding unless authorized to do so by law or court order; or

(c) communicate with a juror or prospective juror after discharge of the jury unless the communication is permitted by court rule;

(d) engage in conduct intended to disrupt a tribunal or engage in undignified or discourteous conduct that is degrading to a tribunal.

Rule 3.5   DELAWARE LAWYERS' RULES

Comment

[1] Many forms of improper influence upon a tribunal are proscribed by criminal law. Others are specified in the ABA Model Code of Judicial Conduct, with which an advocate should be familiar. A lawyer is required to avoid contributing to a violation of such provisions.

[2] During a proceeding a lawyer may not communicate or cause another to communicate ex parte with persons serving in an official capacity in the proceeding, such as judges, masters or jurors, or with members of such person's family, unless authorized to do so by law or court order. Furthermore, a lawyer shall not conduct or cause another to conduct a vexatious or harassing investigation of such persons or their family members.

[3] A lawyer may not communicate with a juror or prospective juror after the jury has been discharged unless permitted by court rule. The lawyer may not engage in improper conduct during the communication.

[4] The advocate's function is to present evidence and argument so that the cause may be decided according to law. Refraining from abusive or obstreperous conduct is a corollary of the advocate's right to speak on behalf of litigants. A lawyer may stand firm against abuse by a judge but should avoid reciprocation; the judge's default is no justification for similar dereliction by an advocate. An advocate can present the cause, protect the record for subsequent review and preserve professional integrity by patient firmness no less effectively than by belligerence or theatrics.

[5] The duty to refrain from disruptive, undignified or discourteous conduct applies to any proceeding of a tribunal, including a deposition. See Rule 1.0(m).

. . .

RULE 3.7 LAWYER AS WITNESS.

(a) A lawyer shall not act as advocate at a trial in which the lawyer is likely to be a necessary witness unless:

    (1) the testimony relates to an uncontested issue;

    (2) the testimony relates to the nature and value of legal services rendered in the case; or

    (3) disqualification of the lawyer would work substantial hardship on the client.

(b) A lawyer may act as advocate in a trial in which another lawyer in the lawyer's firm is likely to be called as a witness unless precluded from doing so by Rule 1.7 or Rule 1.9.

Comment

[1] Combining the roles of advocate and witness can prejudice the tribunal and the opposing party and can also involve a conflict of interest between the lawyer and client.

[2] *Advocate–Witness Rule.*—The tribunal has proper objection when the trier of fact may be confused or misled by a lawyer serving as both advocate and

witness. The opposing party has proper objection where the combination of roles may prejudice that party's rights in the litigation. A witness is required to testify on the basis of personal knowledge, while an advocate is expected to explain and comment on evidence given by others. It may not be clear whether a statement by an advocate-witness should be taken as proof or as an analysis of the proof.

[3] To protect the tribunal, paragraph (a) prohibits a lawyer from simultaneously serving as advocate and necessary witness except in those circumstances specified in paragraphs (a)(1) through (a)(3). Paragraph (a)(1) recognizes that if the testimony will be uncontested, the ambiguities in the dual role are purely theoretical. Paragraph (a)(2) recognizes that where the testimony concerns the extent and value of legal services rendered in the action in which the testimony is offered, permitting the lawyers to testify avoids the need for a second trial with new counsel to resolve that issue. Moreover, in such a situation the judge has firsthand knowledge of the matter in issue; hence, there is less dependence on the adversary process to test the credibility of the testimony.

[4] Apart from these two exceptions, paragraph (a)(3) recognizes that a balancing is required between the interests of the client and those of the tribunal and the opposing party. Whether the tribunal is likely to be misled or the opposing party is likely to suffer prejudice depends on the nature of the case, the importance and probable tenor of the lawyer's testimony, and the probability that the lawyer's testimony will conflict with that of other witnesses. Even if there is risk of such prejudice, in determining whether the lawyer should be disqualified, due regard must be given to the effect of disqualification on the lawyer's client. It is relevant that one or both parties could reasonably foresee that the lawyer would probably be a witness. The conflict of interest principles stated in Rules 1.7, 1.9 and 1.10 have no application to this aspect of the problem.

[5] Because the tribunal is not likely to be misled when a lawyer acts as advocate in a trial in which another lawyer in the lawyer's firm will testify as a necessary witness, paragraph (b) permits the lawyer to do so except in situations involving a conflict of interest.

[6] *Conflict of Interest.*—In determining if it is permissible to act as advocate in a trial in which the lawyer will be a necessary witness, the lawyer must also consider that the dual role may give rise to a conflict of interest that will require compliance with Rules 1.7 or 1.9. For example, if there is likely to be substantial conflict between the testimony of the client and that of the lawyer, the representation involves a conflict of interest that requires compliance with Rule 1.7. This would be true even though the lawyer might not be prohibited by paragraph (a) from simultaneously serving as advocate and witness because the lawyer's disqualification would work a substantial hardship on the client. Similarly, a lawyer who might be permitted to simultaneously serve as an advocate and a witness by paragraph (a)(3) might be precluded from doing so by Rule 1.9. The problem can arise whether the lawyer is called as a witness on behalf of the client or is called by the opposing party. Determining whether or not such a conflict exists is primarily the responsibility of the lawyer involved. If there is a conflict of interest, the lawyer must secure the client's informed consent, confirmed in writing. In some cases, the lawyer will be precluded from seeking the client's consent. See Rule 1.7. See Rule 1.0(b) for the definition of "confirmed in writing" and Rule 1.0(e) for the definition of "informed consent."

[7] Paragraph (b) provides that a lawyer is not disqualified from serving as an advocate because a lawyer with whom the lawyer is associated in a firm is precluded from doing so by paragraph (a). If, however, the testifying lawyer would also be disqualified by Rule 1.7 or Rule 1.9 from representing the client in the matter, other lawyers in the firm will be precluded from representing the client by Rule 1.10 unless the client gives informed consent under the conditions stated in Rule 1.7.

RULE 3.8 SPECIAL RESPONSIBILITIES OF A PROSECUTOR.

The prosecutor in a criminal case shall:

(a) refrain from prosecuting a charge that the prosecutor knows is not supported by probable cause;

(b) make reasonable efforts to assure that the accused has been advised of the right to, and the procedure for obtaining, counsel and has been given reasonable opportunity to obtain counsel;

(c) not seek to obtain from an unrepresented accused a waiver of important pretrial rights, such as the right to a preliminary hearing;

(d)(1) make timely disclosure to the defense of all evidence or information known to the prosecutor that tends to negate the guilt of the accused or mitigates the offense, and, in connection with sentencing, disclose to the defense and to the tribunal all unprivileged mitigating information known to the prosecutor, except when the prosecutor is relieved of this responsibility by a protective order of the tribunal; . . .

(e) not subpoena a lawyer in a grand jury or other criminal proceeding to present evidence about a past or present client unless the prosecutor reasonably believes:

   (1) the information sought is not protected from disclosure by any applicable privilege;

   (2) the evidence sought is essential to the successful completion of an ongoing investigation or prosecution; and

   (3) there is no other feasible alternative to obtain the information;

(f) except for statements that are necessary to inform the public of the nature and extent of the prosecutor's action and that serve a legitimate law enforcement purpose, refrain from making extrajudicial comments that have a substantial likelihood of heightening public condemnation of the accused and exercise reasonable care to prevent investigators, law enforcement personnel, employees or other persons assisting or associated with the prosecutor in a criminal case from making an extrajudicial statement that the prosecutor would be prohibited from making under Rule 3.6 or this Rule.

Comment

[1] A prosecutor has the responsibility of a minister of justice and not simply that of an advocate. This responsibility carries with it specific obligations to see that the defendant is accorded procedural justice and that guilt is decided upon the basis of sufficient evidence. Precisely how far the prosecutor is required to go in this direction is a matter of debate and varies in different jurisdictions. Many jurisdictions have adopted the ABA Standards of Criminal Justice Relating to the Prosecution Function, which in turn are the product of prolonged and careful deliberation by lawyers experienced in both criminal prosecution and defense. Applicable law may require other measures by the prosecutor and knowing disregard of those obligations or a systematic abuse of prosecutorial discretion could constitute a violation of Rule 8.4.

[2] In some jurisdictions, a defendant may waive a preliminary hearing and thereby lose a valuable opportunity to challenge probable cause. Accordingly, prosecutors should not seek to obtain waivers of preliminary hearings or other important pretrial rights from unrepresented accused persons. Paragraph (c) does not apply, however, to an accused appearing pro se with the approval of the tribunal. Nor does it forbid the lawful questioning of an uncharged suspect who has knowingly waived the rights to counsel and silence.

[3] ... The exception in paragraph (d) recognizes that a prosecutor may seek an appropriate protective order from the tribunal if disclosure of information to the defense could result in substantial harm to an individual or to the public interest.

[4] Paragraph (e) is intended to limit the issuance of lawyer subpoenas in grand jury and other criminal proceedings to those situations in which there is a genuine need to intrude into the client-lawyer relationship.

[5] Paragraph (f) supplements Rule 3.6, which prohibits extra judicial statements that have a substantial likelihood of prejudicing an adjudicatory proceeding. In the context of a criminal prosecution, a prosecutor's extrajudicial statement can create the additional problem of increasing public condemnation of the accused. Although the announcement of an indictment, for example, will necessarily have severe consequences for the accused, a prosecutor can, and should, avoid comments that have no legitimate law enforcement purpose and have a substantial likelihood of increasing public opprobrium of the accused. Nothing in this Comment is intended to restrict the statements which a prosecutor may make which comply with Rule 3.6(b) or 3.6(c).

[6] Like other lawyers, prosecutors are subject to Rules 5.1 and 5.3, which relate to responsibilities regarding lawyers and nonlawyers who work for or are associated with the lawyer's office. Paragraph (f) reminds the prosecutor of the importance of these obligations in connection with the unique dangers of improper extrajudicial statements in a criminal case. In addition, paragraph (f) requires a prosecutor to exercise reasonable care to prevent persons assisting or associated with the prosecutor from making improper extrajudicial statements, even when such persons are not under the direct supervision of the prosecutor. Ordinarily, the reasonable care standard will be satisfied if the prosecutor issues the appropriate cautions to law-enforcement personnel and other relevant individuals.

. . .

RULE 4.1 TRUTHFULNESS IN STATEMENTS TO OTHERS.

In the course of representing a client a lawyer shall not knowingly:

(a) make a false statement of material fact or law to a third person; or

(b) fail to disclose a material fact when disclosure is necessary to avoid assisting a criminal or fraudulent act by a client, unless disclosure is prohibited by Rule 1.6.

Comment

[1] *Misrepresentation.*—A lawyer is required to be truthful when dealing with others on a client's behalf, but generally has no affirmative duty to inform an opposing party of relevant facts. A misrepresentation can occur if the lawyer incorporates or affirms a statement of another person that the lawyer knows is false. Misrepresentations can also occur by partially true but misleading statements or omissions that are the equivalent of affirmative false statements. For dishonest conduct that does not amount to a false statement or for misrepresentations by a lawyer other than in the course of representing a client, see Rule 8.4.

[2] *Statement of Fact.*—This Rule refers to statements of fact. Whether a particular statement should be regarded as one of fact can depend on the circumstances. Under generally accepted conventions in negotiation, certain types of statements ordinarily are not taken as statements of material fact. Estimates of price or value placed on the subject of a transaction and a party's intentions as to an acceptable settlement of a claim are ordinarily in this category, and so is the existence of an undisclosed principal except where nondisclosure of the principal would constitute fraud. Lawyers should be mindful of their obligations under applicable law to avoid criminal and tortious misrepresentation.

[3] *Crime or Fraud by Client.*—Under Rule 1.2(d), a lawyer is prohibited from counseling or assisting a client in conduct that the lawyer knows is criminal or fraudulent. Paragraph (b) states a specific application of the principle set forth in Rule 1.2(d) and addresses the situation where a client's crime or fraud takes the form of a lie or misrepresentation. Ordinarily, a lawyer can avoid assisting a client's crime or fraud by withdrawing from the representation. Sometimes it may be necessary for the lawyer to give notice of the fact of withdrawal and to disaffirm an opinion, document, affirmation or the like. In extreme cases, substantive law may require a lawyer to disclose information relating to the representation to avoid being deemed to have assisted the client's crime or fraud. If the lawyer can avoid assisting a client's crime or fraud only by disclosing this information, then under paragraph (b) the lawyer is to do so, unless the disclosure is prohibited by Rule 1.6.

. . .

RULE 8.3 REPORTING PROFESSIONAL MISCONDUCT.

(a) A lawyer who knows that another lawyer has committed a violation of the rules of Professional Conduct that raises a substantial question as to that lawyer's honesty, trustworthiness or fitness as a lawyer in other respects, shall inform the appropriate professional authority.

(b) A lawyer who knows that a judge has committed a violation of applicable rules of judicial conduct that raises a substantial question as to the judge's fitness for office shall inform the appropriate authority.

(c) This Rule does not require disclosure of information otherwise protected by Rule 1.6.

(d) Notwithstanding anything in this or other of the rules to the contrary, the relationship between members of either (i) the Lawyers Assistance Committee of the Delaware State Bar Association and counselors retained by the Bar Association, or (ii) the Professional Ethics Committee of the Delaware State Bar Association, or (iii) the Fee Dispute Conciliation and Mediation Committee of the Delaware State Bar Association, or (iv) the Professional Guidance Committee of the Delaware State Bar Association, and a lawyer or a judge shall be the same as that of attorney and client.

Comment

[1] Self-regulation of the legal profession requires that members of the profession initiate disciplinary investigation when they know of a violation of the Rules of Professional Conduct. Lawyers have a similar obligation with respect to judicial misconduct. An apparently isolated violation may indicate a pattern of misconduct that only a disciplinary investigation can uncover. Reporting a violation is especially important where the victim is unlikely to discover the offense.

[2] A report about misconduct is not required where it would involve violation of Rule 1.6. However, a lawyer should encourage a client to consent to disclosure where prosecution would not substantially prejudice the client's interests.

[3] If a lawyer were obliged to report every violation of the Rules, the failure to report any violation would itself be a professional offense. Such a requirement existed in many jurisdictions but proved to be unenforceable. This Rule limits the reporting obligation to those offenses that a self-regulating profession must vigorously endeavor to prevent. A measure of judgment is, therefore, required in complying with the provisions of this Rule. The term "substantial" refers to the seriousness of the possible offense and not the quantum of evidence of which the lawyer is aware. A report should be made to the bar disciplinary agency unless some other agency, such as a peer review agency, is more appropriate in the circumstances. Similar considerations apply to the reporting of judicial misconduct.

[4] The duty to report professional misconduct does not apply to a lawyer retained to represent a lawyer whose professional conduct is in question. Such a situation is governed by the Rules applicable to the client-lawyer relationship.

[5] Information about a lawyer's or judge's misconduct or fitness may be received by a lawyer in the course of that lawyer's participation in an approved lawyers or judges assistance program. In that circumstance, providing for an exception to the reporting requirements of paragraphs (a) and (b) of this Rule

encourages lawyers and judges to seek treatment through such a program. Conversely, without such an exception, lawyers and judges may hesitate to seek assistance from these programs, which may then result in additional harm to their professional careers and additional injury to the welfare of clients and the public. These Rules do not otherwise address the confidentiality of information received by a lawyer or judge participating in an approved lawyers assistance program; such an obligation, however, may be imposed by the rules of the program or other law.

RULE 8.4 MISCONDUCT.

It is professional misconduct for a lawyer to:

(a) violate or attempt to violate the Rules of Professional Conduct, knowingly assist or induce another to do so or do so through the acts of another;

(b) commit a criminal act that reflects adversely on the lawyer's honesty, trustworthiness or fitness as a lawyer in other respects;

(c) engage in conduct involving dishonesty, fraud, deceit or misrepresentation;

(d) engage in conduct that is prejudicial to the administration of justice;

(e) state or imply an ability to influence improperly a government agency or official or to achieve results by means that violate the Rules of Professional Conduct or other law; or

(f) knowingly assist a judge or judicial officer in conduct that is a violation of applicable rules of judicial conduct or other law.

Comment

[1] Lawyers are subject to discipline when they violate or attempt to violate the Rules of Professional Conduct, knowingly assist or induce another to do so or do so through the acts of another, as when they request or instruct an agent to do so on the lawyer's behalf. Paragraph (a), however, does not prohibit a lawyer from advising a client concerning action the client is legally entitled to take.

[2] Many kinds of illegal conduct reflect adversely on fitness to practice law, such as offenses involving fraud and the offense of willful failure to file an income tax return. However, some kinds of offenses carry no such implication. Traditionally, the distinction was drawn in terms of offenses involving "moral turpitude." That concept can be construed to include offenses concerning some matters of personal morality, such as adultery and comparable offenses, which have no specific connection to fitness for the practice of law. Although a lawyer is personally answerable to the entire criminal law, a lawyer should be professionally answerable only for offenses that indicate lack of those characteristics relevant to law practice. Offenses involving violence, dishonesty, breach of trust, or serious interference with the administration of justice are in that category. A pattern of repeated offenses, even ones of minor significance when considered separately, can indicate indifference to legal obligation.

[3] A lawyer who, in the course of representing a client, knowingly manifests by words or conduct, bias or prejudice based upon race, sex, religion, national origin, disability, age, sexual orientation or socioeconomic status, violates paragraph (d) when such actions are prejudicial to the administration of justice. Legitimate advocacy respecting the foregoing factors does not violate paragraph (d). A trial judge's finding that peremptory challenges were exercised on a discriminatory basis does not alone establish a violation of this rule.

[4] A lawyer may refuse to comply with an obligation imposed by law upon a good faith belief that no valid obligation exists. The provisions of Rule 1.2(d) concerning a good faith challenge to the validity, scope, meaning or application of the law apply to challenges of legal regulation of the practice of law.

[5] Lawyers holding public office assume legal responsibilities going beyond those of other citizens. A lawyer's abuse of public office can suggest an inability to fulfill the professional role of lawyers. The same is true of abuse of positions of private trust such as trustee, executor, administrator, guardian, agent and officer, director or manager of a corporation or other organization.

. . .

SELECTED CASES

Table of Contents

	Page
Chapter 1. Relevancy and Related Problems	544
A. Relevancy	544
Sprint v. Mendelsohn	544
Chapter 2. Real Proof	545
Section 5. Reproductions of the Event and of Evidence of the Event	545
United States v. Garcia	545
United States v. Holden	551
Section 7. Writings and Related Matters	553
A. Authentication	553
Lorraine v. Markel Am. Ins. Co.	553
B. Best Evidence Rule	553
United States v. Smith	553
United States v. Buchanan	556
State of Hawai'i v. Espiritu	559
United States v. McElroy	562
Chapter 3. Testimonial Proof	565
United States v. Recendiz	565
Section 1. Competency	567
A. Disqualifications Under the Common Law	567
2. Interest	567
United States v. Scheffer	567
Holmes v. South Carolina	579
Clark v. Arizona	585
Section 3. Form of Examination	588
C. Lay Options	588
United States v. Yannotti	588
D. Cross-Examination	591
State v. Vogelsberg	591
Section 4. Credibility	591
B. Discrediting	591
2. Opponent's Witness	591
United States v. Gilmore	591
United States v. Kincaid Chauncey	596
United States v. Reid	596
United States v. Osazuwa	596
Ohler v. United States	604
United States v. Jefferson	604
United States v. Hinkson	606
United States v. Neighbors	608
Robinson v. State of Delaware	610
Kansas v. Ventris	610
D. Mechanical and Chemical Means of Assessing Credibility	611
1. The Lie Detector	611
United States v. Hamilton	611

SELECTED CASES

	Page
Chapter 4. Hearsay	615
Section 2. Prior Statements of Witnesses	616
Section 8. Former Testimony	616
Section 9. Dying Declarations	616
Section 10. Forfeiture	616
Giles v. California	616
Section 12. Non–Class Exceptions	628
Section 13. Constitutional Restraints	628
Crawford v. Washington	628
Davis v. Washington	649
Michigan v. Bryant	661
Melendez–Diaz v. Massachusetts	677
Briscoe v. Virginia (excerpts from oral argument)	686
Bullcoming v. New Mexico	696
Chapter 5. Circumstantial Proof: Further Problems	714
Section 1. Evidence of Other Crimes	714
State of Iowa v. Nelson	714
United States v. Crane	723
United States v. Commanche	726
United States v. Mound	728
United States v. Hollow Horn	732
United States v. Batton	734
Garceau v. Woodford	734
Section 2. Evidence of a Criminal Defendant's Reputation and Opinion Evidence of His Character; Evidence of Victim's Character	734
Barbe v. McBride	734
Gagne v. Booker	739
United States of America v. Pablo	739
Zakrzewska v. New School	741
Rhodes v. Motion Industries, Inc.	743
Martinez v. Cui	744
Section 4. Similar Occurrences	744
Johnson v. Elk Lake School District	744
Section 6. Repairs, Liability Insurance	750
Pineda v. Ford Motor Co.	751
Section 7. Compromises	751
Hernandez v. State of Arizona	751
Lyondell Chemical Co. v. Occidental Chemical Corp.	751
United States v. Davis	752
Chapter 6. Expert Evidence	755
Section 1. The Nature and Function of Expert Evidence	755
Trademark Properties, Inc. v. A & E Television Networks	755
Hynix Semiconductor Inc. v. Rambus Inc.	756
United States v. Kaplan	760
United States v. Anchrum	764
United States v. Abu–Jihaad	766
United States v. Moore	770
United States v. Lee	774
General Electric Co. v. Joiner	776
Kumho Tire Co., Ltd. v. Carmichael	785
Primiano v. Yan Cook	797
Section 2. The Basis of Expert Testimony	801
United States v. Smith	801
United States v. Mejia	801

Selected Cases

	Page
Chapter 7. Procedural Considerations	818
Section 1. Burdens of Proof	818
C. Allocating Burdens	818
Dixon v. United States	818
Section 2. Presumptions and Related Subjects	818
Theriault v. Burnham	818
Chapter 8. Judicial Notice	819
Section 2. Facts	819
State of Vermont v. Gokey	819
Chapter 9. Privileges	820
Section 2. Privilege Belonging to the Individual: The Privilege Against Self–Incrimination	820
B. History and Rationale	820
Chavez v. Martinez	820
C. Basic Elements	833
1. The Test for Self-Incrimination	833
United States v. Balsys	834
Mitchell v. United States	845
United States v. Hubbell	852
E. Immunity	854
McKune v. Lile	854
Section 3. The Attorney–Client Privilege	855
B. Basic Elements	855
Swidler & Berlin and Hamilton v. United States	855
I. The Sixth Amendment Right to Counsel and the Attorney–Client Privilege	860
J. Interlocutory Appeals? Disclosure Order Adverse to Attorney–Client Privilege	862
Mohawk Industries, Inc. v. Carpenter	862
Section 6. Other Relationship Privileges	886
A. Clergy–Penitent	886
Section 7. Institutional and Institutional Process Privileges	874
B. Government Information—Executive Privilege	874
1. State Secrets	874
Cheney v. United States District Court for the District of Columbia	874

CHAPTER 1

RELEVANCY AND RELATED PROBLEMS

A. RELEVANCY

Page 5. After first full paragraph, add:

Sprint v. Mendelsohn

Supreme Court of the United States, 2008.
128 S.Ct. 1140.

. . .

We note that, had the District Court applied a *per se* rule excluding the evidence, the Court of Appeals would have been correct to conclude that it had abused its discretion. Relevance and prejudice under Rules 401 and 403 are determined in the context of the facts and arguments in a particular case, and thus are generally not amenable to broad *per se* rules. See Advisory Committee's Notes on Fed. Rule Evid. 401, 28 U.S.C.App., p. 864 ("Relevancy is not an inherent characteristic of any item of evidence but exists only as a relation between an item of evidence and a matter properly provable in the case"). But, as we have discussed, there is no basis in the record for concluding that the District Court applied a blanket rule.

. . .

The question whether evidence of discrimination by other supervisors is relevant in an individual ADEA case is fact based and depends on many factors, including how closely related the evidence is to the plaintiff's circumstances and theory of the case. Applying Rule 403 to determine if evidence is prejudicial also requires a fact-intensive, context-specific inquiry. Because Rules 401 and 403 do not make such evidence *per se* admissible or *per se* inadmissible, and because the inquiry required by those Rules is within the province of the District Court in the first instance, we vacate the judgment of the Court of Appeals and remand the case with instructions to have the District Court clarify the basis for its evidentiary ruling under the applicable Rules.

CHAPTER 2

REAL PROOF

SECTION 5. REPRODUCTIONS OF THE EVENT AND OF EVIDENCE OF THE EVENT

Page 175. Note 9. Add to Note:

United States v. Garcia

United States Court of Appeals for the Fifth Circuit.
530 F.3d 348 (5th Cir. 2008).

■ PRISCILLA R. OWEN, Circuit Judge:

. . .

At trial, Agent Ayoub testified from his "independent recollection" about statements Garcia made during the interview. The government never attempted to introduce an audiotape or transcript of the interview. On cross-examination, defense counsel asked Ayoub whether the interview was recorded. After Ayoub answered that the interview was audiotaped, defense counsel requested that Ayoub read aloud a portion of the transcript, which she provided. The government objected, arguing that the transcript was not in evidence. During a series of bench conferences, defense counsel argued the transcript was admissible under Fed.R.Evid. 106 and the common law rule of completeness. The district court ruled that both were inapplicable since the government did not place any portion of the transcript into evidence. After the jury found Garcia guilty, he moved for a new trial based, in part, on the district court's exclusion of the transcript.

Garcia now appeals his conviction and argues that the district court's exclusion of the transcript was error and requires a new trial. He cites five of his statements Ayoub relayed that Garcia argues were taken out of context and which he was unable to explain since the transcript was excluded. First, Ayoub testified that "Mr. Garcia also told us he was very suspicious that the vehicle was loaded." Garcia argues that he only answered affirmatively to an agent's question that "you had to have been pretty suspicious." Additionally, Garcia says he did not use the term "loaded," which implied he was familiar with drug smuggling terminology. Second, Ayoub testified that Garcia was unemployed and "further in his discussion with us after that question said 'As a matter of fact, I have a child at home . . . and I'm trying to do anything I can do right now to help support this child.'" Garcia argues that this implied a level of desperation that the transcript does not indicate because he also told the agents he was waiting to hear about a prospective job. Third, Ayoub testified that "Mr. Garcia claimed that Brenda Menchaca had no involvement in this," which Garcia argues implied he was guilty and was protecting her. Nonetheless, the interrogation transcript includes an agent's statement "if she has something to do with it, I need to know," and Garcia's reply "No sir." Fourth, Ayoub testified that Garcia said "How am I going to help myself when I'm going to jail already?" Garcia also argues this was prejudicial, because it implied he knew he had broken the law. Garcia argues he only said this in response to the agent's statement that Garcia was likely facing prison time and needed to answer honestly. Finally, Ayoub testified that Garcia changed his story three times regarding where he was to meet Roy Mendez and return the pick-up truck. Garcia argues that during the interrogation he mentioned the same location twice and once stated it was possible he would meet at Mendez's home.

. . .

We must first determine whether the district judge erred in concluding that Rule 106 was inapplicable and excluding the transcript....

The government contends that the district court correctly ruled that Rule 106 is inapplicable because the rule "is expressly limited to situations in which part of a writing or recorded statement is introduced into evidence." Since the government did not introduce or attempt to introduce the tape recording or transcript—relying solely on Agent Ayoub's memory—it argues the rule is facially inapplicable. The government further argues that the Advisory Committee's Note bolsters this argument because the note provides that "[f]or practical reasons, the rule is limited to writings and recorded statements and does not apply to conversations."[1]

We have encountered, but not decided, this issue in *United States v. Branch*.[2] In that case, the government argued that Rule 106 did not permit the defendant to introduce a Texas ranger's written postarrest report after the ranger testified from memory about the defendant's postarrest statements and the government had not introduced the written report. As here, the government argued Rule 106 applied only to writings or recorded statements. We observed that other circuits had declined to apply the rule to testimony regarding conversations.[3] Without deciding the issue, we noted that Rule 106 only allows the admission of portions that are "relevant and 'necessary to qualify, explain, or place into context the portion already introduced.'"[4] Since the *Branch* appel-

1. [Some footnotes omitted.]
2. 91 F.3d at 727.
3. *Id.* at 727–28.
4. *Id.* at 728 (quoting *United States v. Pendas-Martinez*, 845 F.2d 938, 944 (11th Cir.1988)).

lant failed to demonstrate the excluded portions' relevance or necessity, we held that even if the testimony was subject to Rule 106, the rule did not require the admission of the excluded portions.[5]

Citing an Eleventh Circuit opinion, *United States v. Pendas–Martinez*, Garcia argues Rule 106 applies both when a party introduces "a writing or recorded statement" or elicits testimony that is "tantamount to the introduction of" the writing or recorded statement.[6] Garcia contends Agent Ayoub's testimony regarding Garcia's statements was tantamount to introducing portions of the transcript.

In *Pendas–Martinez*, the government sought to introduce a Coast Guard officer's report of a boat chase and subsequent arrest of alleged drug smugglers.[7] The government asserted that defense counsel had read from and extensively used the report on cross-examination which was tantamount to introducing the report as evidence. The *Pendas–Martinez* court disagreed with the government's argument. While defense counsel had used the report, he did not "read from the report to suggest that [the Coast Guard officer's] testimony was inconsistent with the report"—notwithstanding one inadvertently read remark, which counsel struck—"or otherwise attack [his] credibility with the report."[8]

The *Pendas–Martinez* court compared these facts with *Rainey v. Beech Aircraft*,[9] the foundation of the Eleventh Circuit's "tantamount" standard. In Rainey, the plaintiff sued an aircraft manufacturer after his wife, a navy flight instructor, died in an airplane crash. Previously, a navy investigation concluded pilot error, not manufacturer's defect, caused the crash. In a letter to the navy investigator, the plaintiff, also a navy flight instructor, disputed that conclusion and argued that mechanical malfunction caused the crash.[10] Nonetheless, in two paragraphs, the plaintiff wrote that his wife was under "unnecessary" pressure, tried to cancel the practice flights on three occasions, and had violated "pattern integrity" when her plane "turned crosswind without proper interval."[11] Since these statements supported the defendant-manufacturer's theory of pilot error, the defendant called the plaintiff as an adverse witness and asked him whether he had written these statements in his letter. On cross-examination, the trial court sustained the defendant's objection to the question: "in the same letter to which [defense counsel] made reference ... did you also say that the ... primary cause of this mishap was [mechanical error]?"[12]

---

5. *Id.*

6. 845 F.2d at 943.

7. *Id.* at 940.

8. *Id.* at 944.

9. 784 F.2d 1523 (11th Cir.1986), *aff'd in part, rev'd in part*, 488 U.S. 153, 109 S.Ct. 439, 102 L.Ed.2d 445 (1988).

10. *Id.* at 1526 (noting plaintiff argued in a letter that the accident was "caused by some form of pneumatic sensing/fuel flow malfunction, probably in the fuel control unit").

11. *Id.* at 1528–29.

12. *Id.* at 1529.

The Eleventh Circuit disagreed with the trial court's ruling and reasoned that "the jury was given an incomplete and misleading impression of [plaintiff]'s position."[13] In affirming the holding of this portion of the *Rainey* opinion, but without explicitly adopting the "tantamount" standard,[14] the Supreme Court noted that plaintiff's letter explained at length his malfunction theory, including how the evidence supported that theory and not a pilot error theory.[15] Nonetheless, the jury was told that the plaintiff had written six months before and essentially admitted pilot error as the cause.[16] The jury could infer that the plaintiff "did not believe his theory of power failure and had developed it only later for purposes of litigation."[17] Thus, while defense counsel in *Rainey* did not enter the letter into evidence, the Eleventh Circuit noted in *Pendas–Martinez* that "isolated sentences were read out of context," creating a misleading impression of the entire document and making it "tantamount to the introduction of the letter into evidence" and within the ambit of Rule 106.[18]

Here, it is undisputed that the government did not introduce as evidence the transcript or tape recording of the interrogation. Rule 106 does not apply to a witness's testimony at trial. Nor did the government quote or read from the transcript during direct examination. Therefore, even were we to adopt the Eleventh Circuit's "tantamount" standard, it would not apply here. In *Rainey*, the defendants questioned the plaintiff about isolated statements read from the letter. In other words, the jury was relayed quotations from the disputed letter. The fact that the defense counsel spoke those statements, rather than having the jury read them, was inconsequential. In this case, Agent Ayoub testified from memory as to a conversation. The jury did not hear or read quotations allegedly out of context that were tape recorded or transcribed. They heard Agent Ayoub testify as to his memory of the conversation.

While this distinction at first seems minor, the government persuasively argues that it is quite meaningful. A recording played or a document read in isolation is not subject to cross-examination. But an adversary can attack a live witness's credibility, confront the witness with previous inconsistent statements, or demonstrate bias or poor memory....:

FED. R. EVID. 106 seeks to relieve this tactical disadvantage by permitting an opposing party to combat an unquestioned "cold transcript" at the moment of its introduction by entering into evidence the

---

13. *Id.* at 1530.

14. *Beech Aircraft Corp. v. Rainey*, 488 U.S. 153, 172, 109 S.Ct. 439, 102 L.Ed.2d 445 (1988) ("While much of the controversy in this suit has centered on whether Rule 106 applies, we find it unnecessary to address that issue. Clearly the concerns underlying Rule 106 are relevant here, but, as the general rules of relevancy permit a ready resolution to this litigation, we need go no further in exploring the scope and meaning of Rule 106.").

15. *Id.* at 171, 109 S.Ct. 439.

16. *Id.*

17. *Id.*

18. *United States v. Pendas–Martinez*, 845 F.2d 938, 943–44 (11th Cir.1988).

remainder. If courts were to ignore this distinction, then any time a party elicited testimony from a witness regarding events also described in writing, the opposing party could attempt, not merely to impeach the witness on cross-examination, but to introduce contemporaneously through Rule 106 that document if the witness's statements did not perfectly match the written out-of-court description. Such a result is particularly troubling since it remains unsettled whether Rule 106 trumps other evidentiary rules and makes the inadmissible admissible.[19] In a similar case, *United States v. Ramirez–Perez*, the Eleventh Circuit drew this distinction and declined to extend its "tantamount" standard. In that case, the defendant gave a statement during interrogation that was later reduced to writing. At trial, a Georgia Bureau of Investigation agent testified as to the oral statement. The defendant sought to introduce the written statement under Rule 106, arguing in part that the agent's testimony was "tantamount" to introducing the written statement and that the written statement contextualized the agent's testimony. The Eleventh Circuit distinguished Rainey as we have here and held that the district court did not err when it excluded the written statement. We agree with the Eleventh Circuit's holding.

In sum, we conclude the district court did not abuse its discretion in denying the introduction of the full transcript under Rule 106. Since Garcia's argument does not meet the Eleventh Circuit's "tantamount" standard, we leave to another day the decision to adopt or reject that standard.

. . .

Garcia next argues that even if Rule 106 did not allow the admission of the transcript, the common law rule of completeness does. The Supreme Court has acknowledged that Rule 106 only partially codifies this common law rule. Garcia cites *United States v. Paquet*,[20] in which we held that it was error for the district court to disallow a defendant from offering any proof of his version of a conversation with a government informant after a government agent testified to the conversation's contents.[21]

---

19. *Barrett v. United States*, 965 F.2d 1184, 1194 (1st Cir.1992) ("[T]here is considerable disagreement whether FED. R. EVID. 106 can ever serve as a basis for admitting evidence which is inadmissible on other grounds."). Compare *United States v. Costner*, 684 F.2d 370, 373 (6th Cir.1982) ("[Rule 106] covers an order of proof problem; it is not designed to make something admissible that should be excluded."); *United States v. Burreson*, 643 F.2d 1344, 1349 (9th Cir.1981) (same) with *United States v. Sutton*, 801 F.2d 1346, 1368 (D.C.Cir.1986) ("Rule 106 can adequately fulfill its function only by permitting the admission of some otherwise inadmissible evidence when the court finds in fairness that the proferred evidence should be considered contemporaneously.").

20. 484 F.2d 208, 212 (5th Cir.1973).

21. *Id.* (" 'If it were competent for one party to prove this conversation, it was equally competent for the other party to prove their version of it. It may not have differed essentially from the government's version, and it may be that defendant was not prejudiced by the conversation as actually proved; but where the whole or a part of a conversation has been put in evidence by one party, the other party is entitled to

CHAPTER 2 REAL PROOF

Reading the record, we do not see an abuse of discretion similar to that committed in *Paquet*. Without introducing the document or laying a foundation, defense counsel handed Ayoub a copy of the transcript and asked him to read aloud from it. The district court sustained the government's objection and told defense counsel that Agent Ayoub could not testify from a document that was not yet entered into evidence. Afterwards, defense counsel did not attempt to lay a foundation or introduce the transcript. The court then permitted Ayoub to read silently the document to refresh Ayoub's memory. The court stated that on cross-examination Ayoub could then testify, provided he remembered, about his specific questions and Garcia's answers during the interrogation. Thereafter, the record reflects several bench conferences, during which the court explained to defense counsel how she might refresh Ayoub's memory with the transcript. Defense counsel then gave Agent Ayoub a portion of the transcript and requested that he read silently a single line. Ayoub stated that it refreshed his memory, but he nonetheless believed his testimony regarding Garcia's statements pertained to another portion of the interrogation and remained correct and truthful. Defense counsel again conferred with the court, now requesting the court to play an audiotape of the interview under the rule of completeness. For the same reasons it gave regarding the transcript, the court declined. The court then instructed defense counsel on a proper method of cross-examination and suggested questions defense counsel might ask to elicit the testimony she sought. Defense counsel told the court she believed the line of questioning was ineffective. She then requested that the court require Agent Ayoub to re-read silently the entire transcript; the court took a recess and directed Ayoub to read the entire transcript. The Court again suggested to defense counsel four more times how she might cross-examine Agent Ayoub after he was finished reading. Defense counsel then asked a short series of questions based on the district court's suggestions and passed the witness.

The trial transcript reflects that the district judge was willing to entertain and suggest a variety of methods defense counsel could use to elicit testimony "explain[ing], vary[ing], or contradict[ing]" Ayoub's portrayal of the conversation. The Federal Rules of Evidence provide a district court control over the mode and order of interrogation and grounds to exclude relevant evidence. While *Garcia* argues that some portions of the transcript were not hearsay because they were not offered for the truth of the matter asserted, we see no error in a district court refusing to accept a "lengthy" transcript when the court was prepared to accommodate the defendant by numerous other means. While cases like *Paquet* allow parties to present evidence explaining, varying, or contradicting a witness's portrayal of the conversation, we do

explain, vary, or contradict it.'") (quoting S.Ct. 228, 41 L.Ed. 602 (1897)).
Carver v. United States, 164 U.S. 694, 17

550

not read those cases as providing carte blanche to do so by any means desired. Garcia was given ample opportunity to explain his side of the conversation; that defense counsel did not exercise the variety of means available is not an error we attribute to the district court.

For the foregoing reasons, we AFFIRM the district court's ruling and find no error in its exclusion of the transcript.

[Concurring opinion omitted.]

United States v. Holden

United States Court of Appeals for the Sixth Circuit.
557 F.3d 698, 706 (6th Cir. 2009).

■ BOYCE F. MARTIN, JR., CIRCUIT JUDGE.

. . .

3. The Rule of Completeness

The district court held that certain admissions Mike Holden made to Agent Stegall were admissible under Federal Rule of Evidence 801(d)(2), but sustained the government's hearsay objections to other statements from the same conversation when Holden sought to bring them out during cross-examination. Holden argues that the judge erred in holding that the defense waived its ability to invoke the "rule of completeness," and that these statements should have been admitted under that rule. . . .

The "rule of completeness" allows a party to correct a misleading impression created by the introduction of part of a writing or conversation by introducing additional parts of it necessary to put the admitted portions in proper context. The common law version of the rule was codified for written statements in Fed.R.Evid. 106,[1] and has since been extended to oral statements through interpretation of Fed.R.Evid. 611(a).[2] Courts treat the two as equivalent. *United States v. Shaver*, 89 Fed.Appx. 529, 532 (6th Cir.2004). Because admitting the curative evidence later in the trial may not be adequate to remedy the effect of the misleading impression, Rule 106 authorizes a party to interrupt the proceedings to have the curative evidence introduced immediately. However, "[t]he rule does not in any way circumscribe the right of the adversary to develop the matter on cross-examination or as part of his own case." Fed.R.Evid. 106 advisory committee's note.

Here, the judge held that Mike Holden waived his rights under the rule of completeness by failing to invoke the rule when the purportedly

---

1. [Some of the footnotes omitted.]
2. "The court shall exercise reasonable control over the mode and order of interrogating witnesses and presenting evidence so as to (1) make the interrogation and presentation effective for the ascertainment of the truth, (2) avoid needless consumption of time, and (3) protect witnesses from harassment or undue embarrassment." Fed. R.Evid. 611(a).

misleading evidence was introduced. Whether a party waives their right of completeness under these circumstances is an open question in this circuit, but we now reject the waiver rule adopted by the district court. As the advisory committee's note to Rule 106 makes clear, the rule does not restrict admission of completeness evidence to the time the misleading evidence is introduced: "The rule does not in any way circumscribe the right of the adversary to develop the matter on cross-examination or as part of his own case." Congress's decision to put the timing of the completeness evidence in the hands of the party offering it weighs against imposing an additional requirement that parties invoke the rule at the time evidence is introduced. Further, the purpose of the rule of completeness is to ensure fairness in the presentation of evidence at trial; in delaying completion or denying it altogether a strict waiver rule frustrates this purpose without serving any corresponding value. If a party fails to invoke the rule at the time the misleading evidence is introduced, the chance to do so is lost independent of the effect of a waiver rule, and allowing parties to invoke the rule of completeness after the misleading evidence is introduced does not limit the district judge's discretion to determine whether and when the curative evidence should be admitted. See 21A WRIGHT & MILLER, FEDERAL PRACTICE & PROCEDURE § 5076 ("[T]o put it in the language of the Rule, when the invocation comes late, the question is whether 'fairness' requires completion prior to the opponent's next opportunity to complete as part of her own case."). Thus, we hold that the district court erred by ruling that Mike Holden waived his rights under the rule of completeness by waiting to introduce the evidence. *See Phoenix Assoc. III v. Stone*, 60 F.3d 95, 103 (2d Cir.1995); see also 21A WRIGHT & MILLER, FEDERAL PRACTICE & PROCEDURE § 5076 (endorsing Phoenix Assoc. III, stating that "the better-reasoned cases hold that the opponent need not invoke Rule 106 at the time the truncated evidence is introduced").

That raises the question of whether this error was harmless. Because the statements Holden seeks to introduce are inadmissible hearsay, we hold that it was. The inculpatory statements against Holden were admissible under Fed.R.Evid. 801(d)(2), the hearsay exclusion for admissions of a party opponent. However, Mike Holden was unable to avail himself of this exception because he sought to introduce his own statement. Thus, his statements are inadmissible hearsay and were properly excluded. See Fed.R.Evid. 801(d)(2); *United States v. Costner*, 684 F.2d 370, 373 (6th Cir.1982) ("Rule 106 is intended to eliminate the misleading impression created by taking a statement out of context . . . it is not designed to make something admissible that should be excluded.").

. . .

For the foregoing reasons, we AFFIRM the convictions of Mike and Larry Holden.

SECTION 7 WRITINGS AND RELATED MATTERS

Page 175:

There is a conflict between the Federal Courts of Appeals regarding 106, which may ultimately have to be resolved by the Supreme Court. See United States of American v. Young, 2010 U.S. Dist. LEXIS 35494, and United States v. Henderson, 626 F.3d 326, 343 (6th Cir. 2010).

SECTION 7. WRITINGS AND RELATED MATTERS

A. AUTHENTICATION

Page 194. Note 3, after first full paragraph, add:

For an exhaustive discussion of the application of the authentication requirement (Fed. R. Evid. 901, 902) to e-mails, web sites and other electronically stored information, see Lorraine v. Markel Am. Ins. Co., 241 F.R.D. 534 (D. Md. 2007).

B. BEST EVIDENCE RULE

Page 217. Note 1. After first full paragraph, add:

United States v. Smith

United States Court of Appeals for the Fourth Circuit, 2009.
566 F.3d 410.

■ Before NIEMEYER and GREGORY, Circuit Judges, and EUGENE E. SILER, JR., Senior Circuit Judge of the United States Court of Appeals for the Sixth Circuit, sitting by designation.

■ NIEMEYER, Circuit Judge:

Cordell Smith was convicted of drug trafficking and firearms offenses, and the district court sentenced him to 197 months' imprisonment. On appeal, Smith contends (1) that the district court erroneously allowed a government witness to testify, in violation of the "best evidence rule," Federal Rule of Evidence 1002, about the place where the firearms were manufactured in order to demonstrate that they traveled in interstate commerce....

We find no violation of the "best evidence rule,"....

During a search of Smith's apartment in Charlotte, North Carolina, on November 9, 2005, police recovered, among other things, crack cocaine, marijuana, electronic scales, drug paraphernalia, two loaded handguns, two shotguns, ammunition, and cash. Smith was indicted on three counts charging him with (1) possessing with intent to distribute a quantity of crack cocaine, in violation of 21 U.S.C. § 841(a), (b); (2) using and carrying one or more firearms during and in relation to a drug-trafficking crime, in violation of 18 U.S.C. § 924(c)(1); and (3) possessing one or more firearms, having been previously convicted of a felony, in violation of 18 U.S.C. § 922(g).

To prove at trial the interstate nexus element of the felon-in-possession count, the government presented the testimony of Special Agent Andrew Cheramie of the Bureau of Alcohol, Tobacco, Firearms and Explosives ("ATF") that the firearms recovered from Smith's apartment had been manufactured in States other than North Carolina. Smith's attorney objected to the proposed testimony of Special Agent Cheramie on the ground that it would violate Federal Rule of Evidence 1002, which he referred to as the "best evidence rule." He argued that Cheramie's testimony based on written reference materials and ATF computer databases, none of which were offered into evidence, violated the rule. The district court overruled the objection and allowed Cheramie to testify without requiring him to introduce any reference materials into evidence.

The jury convicted Smith on all counts, and the district court sentenced him to 197 months' imprisonment, a sentence at the top of the Sentencing Guidelines range. This appeal followed.

. . .

Smith contends first that the district court erred in overruling his objection to the testimony of Special Agent Cheramie about where the firearms were manufactured to prove the interstate nexus of the four firearms seized from Smith's apartment—as necessary for a violation of 18 U.S.C. § 922(g). Smith contends that the district court's ruling violated Federal Rule of Evidence 1002, and therefore that his felon-in-possession conviction should be vacated.

At trial, the government sought to qualify Special Agent Cheramie "as an expert in the analysis of the location of where firearms are manufactured," and counsel for Smith conducted voir dire eliciting the fact that Special Agent Cheramie relied on reference materials, as well as an examination of the firearms themselves, to determine where the firearms were manufactured. Cheramie explained that he examined the firearms themselves, obtaining the manufacturers' names and, on three of the four firearms, the serial numbers. He then consulted published materials on the origins of firearms, a reference book, which he had with him in the courtroom, and an ATF computerized database that had been compiled "over many, many years as agents have done this practice and had communication with various firearms manufacturers from around the world." Counsel for Smith then objected to the proposed testimony, stating, "I think the testimony violates the best evidence rule, Rule 1002. The witness is essentially repeating things that he's read in documents, that he could bring and that the jury could look at them and make that judgment. And instead he's just repeating that information for us." The district court overruled Smith's objection and allowed Special Agent Cheramie to testify, stating, "the court will not designate the witness as an expert in interstate nexus, but the witness can testify from his training and experience at ATF where he specifically said he had specialized training in interstate nexus, where he can testify as to what conclusions he would draw from his training and experience as to whether these weapons traveled in interstate commerce."

Special Agent Cheramie then testified that "based on [his] training and experience," he was able to determine that Smith's Talon Industries Model T200 pistol was manufactured in Montana; the Ruger P85 Mark II pistol was manufactured in Prescott, Arizona; the Winchester Model 12 shotgun was manufactured in New Haven, Connecticut; and the High Standard Model K1200 shotgun was manufactured in Hamden, Connecticut. On cross examination, Special Agent Cheramie acknowledged that he had never been to any of the factories that manufactured the firearms, nor had he talked to any of the employees at those factories.

Smith argues that "the materials on which Cheramie relied were clearly 'writings' or 'recordings' under Rule 1001" and therefore "Cheramie's testimony plainly sought to prove the content of writings or recordings because Cheramie himself had no independent, first-hand knowledge of where the firearms were manufactured," in violation of Rule 1002. He states that "the district court's conclusion that Cheramie's testimony was the 'best evidence' of the information in books and files is unsustainable." Smith asserts that the district court, in allowing Special Agent Cheramie to testify without requiring production of the originals or copies, erred "as a matter of law."

Smith's argument, however, appears to rest on a misconception of the "best evidence rule" and Rule 1002. In asserting that Cheramie should not have been allowed to testify to the fact of a firearm's place of manufacture without introducing the writings and other materials from which he learned that fact, Smith suggests that the best evidence rule required the government to introduce the best evidence of that fact, *i.e.*, the writings and other materials from which Cheramie learned the fact, especially when Cheramie did not have personal first-hand knowledge of the fact. But Federal Rule of Evidence 1002 is not nearly so broad.

Federal Rule of Evidence 1002 provides in pertinent part: "To prove the content of a writing, recording, or photograph, the original writing, recording, or photograph is required." As the Rule's language states, the Rule applies to the circumstance where the proponent seeks *"to prove the content"* of a document. The Rule exists to afford guarantees against inaccuracies and fraud by requiring that *the original* of the document be offered, subject to exceptions in Rule 1003 (allowing the use of duplicates) and Rule 1004 (providing exceptions to the requirement of an original). See generally Fed.R.Evid. 1001 advisory committee's note. Thus it is more accurate to refer to Rule 1002 as the "original document rule," not the "best evidence rule." *See* 2 Kenneth S. Broun, *McCormick on Evidence* § 231 (6th ed.2006); *see also Seiler v. Lucasfilm, Ltd.*, 808 F.2d 1316, 1318 (9th Cir.1986) ("Dating back to 1700, the rule requires not, as its common name implies, the best evidence in every case but rather the production of an original document instead of a copy. Many commentators refer to the rule not as the best evidence rule but as the original document rule").

In this case, the government never sought to prove the content of any writing or recording relating to the firearms or their places of manufacture. It sought only to prove *the fact* that the firearms were manufactured in States other than North Carolina, where they were recovered during the search of Smith's apartment. The place of the firearms' manufacture was a fact existing independently of the content of any book, document, recording, or writing. Just because Special Agent Cheramie consulted books and computer databases in reaching his conclusion about the firearms' place of manufacture does not mean that his testimony was offered "to prove the content" of the books and computer files. Accordingly, Rule 1002 did not require submission of the books and computer files into evidence. See *United States v. Sliker*, 751 F.2d 477, 483 (2d Cir.1984) (no need to introduce original bank insurance policy just because witness testified to the fact the bank was insured); *cf. United States v. Alexander*, 326 F.2d 736, 740 (4th Cir.1964) (proving the contents of a check); see generally 2 *McCormick on Evidence* § 234 (entitled "What constitutes proving the content").

Thus the district court did not violate Rule 1002 in overruling Smith's objection to Special Agent Cheramie's testimony.

. . .

AFFIRMED IN PART; VACATED AND REMANDED IN PART

Page 217. Add Note 4:

United States of American v. Buchanan

United States Court of Appeals for Eighth Circuit, 2010.
604 F.3d 517, cert. denied, 131 S.Ct. 344 (2010).

■ SMITH, CIRCUIT JUDGE.

. . .

Buchanan next maintains that even if the writings inscribed on the safe's interior did not constitute hearsay, the government's witnesses could not testify as to the contents of the writing without the required foundation and authentication being laid and the writing being introduced into evidence. According to Buchanan, the assertion within the interior of the safe that it was a "2010" model and that the key with the inscription "2010" belonged to the safe is clearly a "writing" or "recording" under Federal Rule of Evidence 1002; therefore, the safe itself—which officers admittedly did not seize—should have been introduced into evidence.

In response, the government asserts that the best evidence rule is inapplicable because the safe was not a "writing" but instead a "chattel."

Federal Rule of Evidence 1002, known as the "best evidence rule," provides that "[t]o prove the content of a writing, recording, or photograph, the original writing, recording, or photograph is required, except as otherwise provided in these rules or by Act of Congress."

The "Rule" as it exists today, may be stated as follows:

> [I]n proving the terms of a *writing*, where such terms are material, the original writing must be produced, unless it is shown to be unavailable for some reason other than the serious fault of the proponent.

United States v. Duffy, 454 F.2d 809, 811 (5th Cir.1972) (quoting McCormick, Evidence 409 (1954)) (emphasis added in *Duffy*). The best evidence rule "is applicable only to the proof of the contents of a writing," even though it "is frequently used in general terms." *Id*. The policy-justifications for preferring the original writing include:

> (1) ... precision in presenting to the court the exact words of the writing is of more than average importance, particularly as respects operative or dispositive instruments, such as deeds, wills and contracts, since a slight variation in words may mean a great difference in rights, (2) ... there is a substantial hazard of inaccuracy in the human process of making a copy by handwriting or typewriting, and (3) as respects oral testimony purporting to give from memory the terms of a writing, there is a special risk of error, greater than in the case of attempts at describing other situations generally. In the light of these dangers of mistransmission, accompanying the use of written copies or of recollection, largely avoided through proving the terms by presenting the writing itself, the preference for the original writing is justified.

Id. at 812 (quoting McCormick, Evidence 410 (1954)).

In *Duffy*, law enforcement officials testified that the trunk of a stolen car contained two suitcases. *Id*. at 811. According to the witnesses, inside one of the suitcases was a white shirt imprinted with a laundry mark reading "D–U–F." *Id*. The defendant, charged with transporting a motor vehicle in interstate commerce knowing it to have been stolen, objected to the admission of the testimony about the shirt and requested that the government produce the shirt. *Id*. The district court overruled the objection and admitted the testimony. *Id*. On appeal, the defendant argued that such testimony violated the best evidence rule. *Id*. The Fifth Circuit rejected the defendant's argument, holding:

> The "Rule" is not, by its terms or because of the policies underlying it, applicable to the instant case. The shirt with a laundry mark would not, under ordinary understanding, be considered a writing and would not, therefore, be covered by the "Best Evidence Rule[."] *When the disputed evidence, such as the shirt in this case, is an object bearing a mark or inscription, and is, therefore, a chattel and a writing*, the trial judge has discretion to treat the evidence as a chattel or as a writing. See 4 Wigmore, Evidence § 1182 and cases cited therein; McCormick, Evidence 411–412 and cases cited therein.

In reaching his decision, the trial judge should consider the policy-consideration behind the "Rule[."] In the instant case, the trial judge was correct in allowing testimony about the shirt without requiring the production of the shirt. Because the writing involved in this case was simple, the inscription "D–U–F[,"] there was little danger that the witness would inaccurately remember the terms of the "writing[."] Also, the terms of the "writing" were by no means central or critical to the case against Duffy. The crime charged was not possession of a certain article, where the failure to produce the article might prejudice the defense. *The shirt was collateral evidence of the crime. Furthermore, it was only one piece of evidence in a substantial case against Duffy.*

Id. at 812 (emphasis added).

Following *Duffy*, a defendant convicted on various counts related to trafficking in counterfeit watches appealed his conviction, arguing that the district court plainly erred in not requiring the government to produce the actual watches sold as the best evidence that he had trafficked in counterfeit goods. *United States v. Yamin*, 868 F.2d 130, 132 (5th Cir.1989). The court rejected the defendant's argument, explaining:

This novel argument appears plausible because it is, at least in part, the writing on the watch that makes it a counterfeit. Thus it may be argued that it is the content of that writing that must be proved. The purpose of the best evidence rule, however, is to prevent inaccuracy and fraud when attempting to prove the contents of a writing. Neither of those purposes was violated here. The viewing of a simple and recognized trademark is not likely to be inaccurately remembered. While the mark is in writing, it is more like a picture or a symbol than a written document. In addition, an object bearing a mark is both a chattel and a writing, and the trial judge has discretion to treat it as a chattel, to which the best evidence rule does not apply.

Id. at 134 (internal footnotes omitted).

Here, the district court appropriately treated the safe as chattel. The policy considerations behind the best evidence rule, as in *Duffy* and *Yamin*, are not implicated. The writing—"2010"—was simple, meaning that little danger existed that the witness would inaccurately remember the terms of the "writing" on the safe. And, as the district court noted, the likelihood of fraud was small because the government also admitted into evidence the safe's instructional manual, which was found inside the safe and also bore the number "2010."

Moreover, as the district court explained, "the testimony regarding the inscription on the safe was only a small part of the substantial evidence presented against Buchanan." *See infra* Part II.C. The numeric inscription was not "critical" to the case against Buchanan; instead, the safe was merely collateral evidence of the crime.

. . .

Accordingly, we affirm the judgment of the district court.

Page 227. Add to Note 1:

State of Hawai'i v. Espiritu

Supreme Court of Hawai'i
117 Haw. 127, 176 P. 3d 885 (2008)

■ Opinion of the Court by Acoba, J.:

. . .

Petitioner also argues that the court committed error in allowing the Complainant to testify "because her testimony neither constituted the original nor a duplicate of the text message" as required by HRE Rule 1002 (1993). Petitioner contends that the original text messages for purposes of HRE Rule 1002 "would have consisted of the cell phone itself with the saved messages or a printout of the messages." Respondent counters that (1) HRE 1002 is inapplicable in this case because a text message does not qualify as a writing, recording, or photograph; (2) there was no evidence that it was possible to obtain a printout of the messages; (3) that no photographs were taken of the messages does not preclude the admission of the Complainant's testimony about the messages; (4) even if HRE Rule 1002 is applicable here, HRE Rule 1004 (1993) allows the admission of other evidence in place of the original where the original is lost or destroyed; and (5) Petitioner failed to raise an objection to the Complainant's testimony based on HRE Rule 1002 and, thus, waived the right to raise an argument based on HRE Rule 1002. HRE Rule 1002 provides that "[t]o prove the content of a writing, recording, or photograph, the original writing, recording, or photograph is required, except as otherwise provided in these rules or by statute."[1] A writing or recording is defined in HRE 1001 (1993) as "consist[ing] of letters, words, sounds, or numbers, or their equivalent, set down by handwriting, typewriting, printing, photostating, photographing, magnetic impulse, mechanical or electronic recording, or other form of data compilation." This definition is identical to FRE Rule 1001.

Contrary to Respondent's assertion, a text message is a writing because it consists of letters, words, or numbers set down by mechanical or electronic recording, or other form of data compilation. Although neither party makes this assertion, text messages received on cell phones appear akin to messages received on computers and email for purposes of HRE Rule 1002. *See Laughner v. State,* 769 N.E.2d 1147, 1159 (Ind.Ct.

---

1. HRE Rule 1002 is identical to Federal Rules of Evidence (FRE) Rule 1002 except that the word statute in HRE Rule 1002 is substituted for the phrase "Act of Congress" found in FRE Rule 1002. [Some footnotes are omitted.]

App.2002) (holding that text messages sent between computers through an internet chat room were subject to the original writing rule and a printout of the messages was an original for purposes of the rule), *cert. denied,* 538 U.S. 1013, 123 S.Ct. 1929, 155 L.Ed.2d 849 (2003), *abrogated on other grounds by Fajardo v. State,* 859 N.E.2d 1201 (Ind.2007). Thus, HRE Rule 1002 which requires an original in order to prove the content of a writing is applicable unless an exception under the HRE or a statute provides otherwise.

. . .

Although HRE Rule 1002 would ordinarily preclude the admission of testimony about the text messages because such testimony is not an original, the testimony here is admissible because HRE Rule 1004 applies to the text messages such that other evidence may be admitted to prove the content of the text messages. HRE Rule 1004 provides an exception to the original writings requirement of HRE Rule 1002 inasmuch as HRE Rule 1004 provides that:

> The original or a duplicate is not required, and other evidence of the contents of a writing, recording, or photograph is admissible if:
>
> (1) *Originals lost or destroyed.* All originals are lost or have been destroyed, unless the proponent lost or destroyed them in bad faith[.]

(Emphasis added.)

This Rule is identical to FRE Rule 1004 except that HRE Rule 1004 eliminates the need for a duplicate as well if the aforementioned condition is met.

The Complainant no longer had the actual text messages because the Complainant no longer had the cell phone or the cell phone service from Verizon through which she received the messages. No other original version of the text messages appear to have existed because there is no indication from the record that the text messages were ever printed out, nor is it clear that it was possible for the messages to be printed from the phone. Thus, for purposes of HRE Rule 1004, the original text messages were "lost or destroyed."

Petitioner argues that "the original writing was lost or destroyed due to the bad faith of the State of Hawai'i." However, there is no evidence that Respondent exercised bad faith that led to the loss of the cell phone, which Petitioner contends was the original for purposes of HRE Rule 1002. Bad faith cannot reasonably be inferred because the Complainant failed to preserve text messages for over two years on a cell phone for which she discontinued service. Similarly, bad faith cannot be inferred because the text messages were not printed out when there is no indication that such a printout was even possible.

Indeed, courts agree that HRE Rule 1004(1) is "particularly suited" to electronic evidence "[g]iven the myriad ways that electronic records may be deleted, lost as a result of system malfunctions, purged as a result of routine electronic records management software (such as the automatic deletion of e-mail after a set time period) or otherwise unavailable...." *Lorraine v. Markel Am. Ins. Co.*, 241 F.R.D. 534, 580 (D.Md.2007). *See also King v. Kirkland's Stores, Inc.*, No. 2:04–cv–1055–MEF, 2006 WL 2239203, at *5 (D.Ala. Aug. 4, 2006) (unpublished decision) (holding that plaintiff's testimony regarding the content of an e-mail from defendant was admissible although plaintiff argued only that a copy of the e-mail, as opposed to the original or sole copy, was in the possession of the defendant); *Bidbay.com, Inc. v. Spry*, No. B160126, 2003 WL 723297, at *7 (Cal.App. Mar. 4, 2003) (unpublished opinion) (stating that the exception to the original writing rule permitting the substitution of secondary evidence would apply in light of the "tenuous and ethereal nature of writings posted in Internet chat rooms and message boards").

Petitioner argues that Respondent "should not be excused from producing the original or a duplicate of the text messages, which are otherwise inadmissible under the best evidence rule," because Respondent "has not shown that it would have been impossible or even difficult to download, photograph, or print out the data from [the Complainant's] cell phone." In support of this argument, Petitioner cites *United States v. Bennett*, 363 F.3d 947, 953–54 (9th Cir.2004), wherein the Court of Appeals for the Ninth Circuit held that in accordance with the best evidence rule, the court could not admit secondary evidence pertaining to a global positioning system (GPS) reading as the government failed to show that it would have been difficult or impossible to download or print out the GPS data. That case is distinguishable in that there was no evidence that the GPS data had been lost or destroyed. *Id.* at 954. Rather, the witness testifying about the data stated that he was not the GPS custodian and it was not necessary to videotape or photograph the GPS contents. *Id.* In contrast, here, it appears that the cell phone containing the text messages is unavailable. The Complainant testified that she changed cell phone service providers since the time of the accident. Furthermore, Petitioner concedes that "the original cell phone is no longer available and there is no indication that any photographs exist of the text messages" therefore, "neither the original nor any duplicates exist."

In addition, this court is not bound by the holding in *Bennett*. The plain language of HRE Rule 1004 states that an original or duplicate is not required to prove the contents of a writing or recording so long as the originals are lost or destroyed and such loss or destruction was not due to the bad faith of the proponent of the evidence. There is no requirement that the proponent must show that it was impossible or difficult to download or print out the writing at the time that it existed.

. . .

CHAPTER 2 REAL PROOF

Page 235. Add to Note 8:

United States v. McElroy

United States Court of Appeals for the First Circuit.
587 F. 3d 73 (1st Cir. 2009)

■ RIPPLE, Circuit Judge:

. . .

We now turn to whether the district court committed reversible error by admitting into evidence summary testimony and charts. The defendants objected to admission of the evidence and we review the district court's decision to admit evidence for an abuse of discretion. *United States v. Stierhoff,* 549 F.3d 19, 27 (1st Cir.2008).

1.

Several individuals testified at trial about the amount of money that the defendants allegedly had failed to pay the IRS. IRS Special Agent Joseph Guidoboni testified as a summary witness. He related that he had computed the unreported payroll for the three companies and had concluded that the total amount of unpaid federal taxes was $9,982,690.51. His calculations were based on witness testimony, at least 1000 documents (including tax returns) and records of the defendants' check payroll system. Neil Johnson, an insurance fraud investigator, also testified as a summary witness. He stated that he had calculated insurance losses based on a review of the companies' workers' compensation insurance applications and related documents, tax returns filed with the IRS, tax returns provided to auditors and worksheets prepared by the insurers. He prepared summary charts estimating the total loss in insurance premiums to be $6,457,500. These charts were admitted into evidence over the defendants' objections.

2.

The defendants submit that the testimony of Agent Guidoboni and Mr. Johnson, as well as their exhibits, were not admissible under Federal Rule of Evidence 1006 because the rule only allows the introduction of summary evidence that summarizes documents, as opposed to evidence that summarizes testimony.[1] While not contesting the admissibility of the evidence under Rule 611(a) and Rules 702 and 703, they claim that the evidence should not have been admitted under Rule 403 because Agent Guidoboni and Mr. Johnson relied on the testimony of Wallace, whose credibility, they contend, was hotly contested at trial. In the defendants' view, the district court erred by failing to instruct the jury that it had to weigh the credibility of the testimony that formed the basis of Agent Guidoboni's and Mr. Johnson's testimony. They contend

---

1. [Some footnotes omitted.]

that the error was unfairly prejudicial because it allowed the Government to "bolster the credibility" of Wallace. Appellant's Br. 51.

The Government characterizes the testimony of Mr. Johnson and Agent Guidoboni and their charts as permissible pedagogical devices used to "clarify and simplify complex testimony or other information" and to help counsel present its argument to the jury. Appellee's Br. 46 (quoting *United States v. Milkiewicz*, 470 F.3d 390, 397 (1st Cir.2006)). The Government contends that the evidence was admissible under Rule 611(a). See *Milkiewicz*, 470 F.3d at 397. The Government also submits that Mr. Johnson's summary charts and testimony were permissible summaries of documents under Rule 1006. As to the testimony and charts introduced by Agent Guidoboni, the Government maintains that testimony of an IRS agent may be admissible under Rules 702 and 703, even if the district court does not qualify the agent as an expert. See *United States v. Hatch*, 514 F.3d 145, 164 (1st Cir.2008) (holding that the district court did not abuse its discretion in allowing an IRS agent to testify about tax issues despite not being admitted as an expert witness).

. . .

Our case law permits the use of summary tools to clarify complex testimony and evidence. *Milkiewicz*, 470 F.3d at 396–98. Although the defendants argue in their reply brief that this case can be distinguished from *Milkiewicz* because the summary evidence was admitted into evidence, that case does not rule out the possibility of such evidence being admitted. In *Milkiewicz* we said that "in most cases a Rule 1006 chart will be the *only* evidence the fact finder will examine concerning a voluminous set of documents." *Id.* at 396 (emphasis in original). In some instances, however, a Rule 1006 chart may itself be admitted into evidence or summary witness testimony may be permitted pursuant to Rule 611(a). *Id.* at 397–98; see also *Stierhoff*, 549 F.3d at 27–28. Rule 611(a) testimony and exhibits "typically are used as pedagogical devices to clarify and simplify complex testimony or other information and evidence or to assist counsel in the presentation of argument to the court or jury." *Milkiewicz*, 470 F.3d at 397 (internal quotation marks omitted). In some cases, "such pedagogical devices may be sufficiently accurate and reliable that they, too, are admissible in evidence, even though they do not meet the specific requirements of Rule 1006." *Id.* at 398.

With regard to summary witness testimony, we have urged caution, noting that such witnesses are allowed only in limited situations. *United States v. Flores–De–Jesus*, 569 F.3d 8, 18 (1st Cir.2009). We noted: "The reluctance of courts to allow the government an additional opportunity to present its case in a tidy package at the end of its presentation of evidence, even when the summary evidence is, by definition, completely consistent with the rest of the trial record, confirms that the imprimatur problem with such repetitive testimony is inescapable whether that testimony comes at the beginning or end of the government's case." *Id.*

at 19. Nevertheless, we have found summary witnesses to be appropriate within the context of tax cases: "We have recognized as a general proposition that testimony by an IRS agent that allows the witness to apply the basic assumptions and principles of tax accounting to particular facts is appropriate in a tax evasion case." *Stierhoff*, 549 F.3d at 27–28. We held that "in a tax evasion case, a summary witness may be permitted to summarize and analyze the facts of record as long as the witness does not directly address the ultimate question of whether the accused did in fact intend to evade federal income taxes." *Id.* at 28.

Applying these principles to the situation before us, we conclude that the testimony of Agent Guidoboni and Mr. Johnson, as well as their exhibits, were properly admitted. Agent Guidoboni's testimony and exhibits fell within the permissible uses of Rules 1006 and 611(a) evidence we described in *Milkiewicz* and *Stierhoff*. His testimony did "no more than analyze facts already introduced into evidence and spell out the tax consequences that necessarily flow from those facts." *Id.*; *see also United States v. DeSimone,* 488 F.3d 561, 577 (1st Cir.2007) ("The chart listed complicated transactions from many sources to summarize the government's calculations concerning taxable income, an essential part of the government's case."). Moreover, the same reasoning that would permit an IRS agent to give summary testimony in a tax evasion case applies to an insurance executive giving summary testimony about unpaid workers' compensation insurance premiums. Consequently, the summary testimony and exhibits of Mr. Johnson were proper as well.

. . .

For the foregoing reasons, we affirm the judgment of the district court.

CHAPTER 3

TESTIMONIAL PROOF

Page 248. Add to Note on "In–Court Identifications":

United States v. Recendiz

United States Court of Appeals for the Seventh Circuit.
557 F.3d 511 (7th Cir.), cert. denied, 130 S.Ct 340 (2009).

■ KANNE, CIRCUIT JUDGE.

. . .

During the trial, Ahmed Tmiri testified that he delivered drugs and collected money for Jesus Herrera. He stated that Herrera began obtaining drugs from someone known as "the Doctor," whose real name was "Navarro." Toward the beginning of his testimony, when asked whether he saw "the Doctor" in the courtroom, Tmiri replied that he did not. However, he testified that he had seen "the Doctor" more than twenty times and described his physical characteristics: "He's dark skin, he's got a mustache, black hair, kind of straight, and I think he's got a little scar on his face." Tmiri was also unable to identify Thomas, despite the fact that both defendants were seated at the defense table. Later in his testimony, however, Tmiri explained that he had broken his glasses prior to the trial and could not even make out the facial features of the prosecutor who was questioning him.

. . .

First, we must determine whether the in-court identification procedure was so suggestive that it likely produced an unreliable identification. In the courtroom, a defendant does not have a constitutional right to the same type of identification procedure used in a police line-up, and the manner of an in-court identification is typically left to the trial court's discretion. *United States v. Davies,* 768 F.2d 893, 903–04 (7th Cir.1985). Navar's argument boils down to two allegedly suggestive circumstances: first, that Navar was seated at the defense table; and second, that the prosecutor's request for Tmiri to move closer to the audience—after Tmiri had already stated that he could not identify Navar—suggested that "the Doctor" was in fact in the courtroom.

As to the first, we have indicated on multiple occasions that a defendant's mere presence at the defense table is not enough to establish a violation of due process. *United States v. Bush,* 749 F.2d 1227, 1232 (7th Cir.1984); *accord Johnson v. McCaughtry,* 92 F.3d 585, 597 (7th Cir.1996); *Rodriguez,* 63 F.3d at 556; *United States ex rel. Haywood v.*

O'Leary, 827 F.2d 52, 59 (7th Cir.1987). Nothing here requires us to deviate from that general rule. Similarly, simply increasing a witness's proximity to the individuals in the courtroom, without more, does not suggest to a witness whom he should identify. As we have stated, "[t]o satisfy the first prong of our analysis, the defendant must show both that the identification procedure was suggestive and that such suggestiveness was unnecessary." *Hawkins,* 499 F.3d at 707. Because Tmiri testified that he could not see, permitting him to move forward was a necessary step for him to make *any* identification. Even the sequence of the questioning itself was necessary, for no one in the courtroom was aware that Tmiri could not see without his glasses until after he was initially unable to identify Navar and Thomas. Nothing about the sequence of the questions suggested to Tmiri whom he should identify or that Navar was in fact present.

Even if we determined that the procedure at trial was unduly suggestive, it was sufficiently reliable to prevent "a very substantial likelihood of irreparable misidentification." *Neil v. Biggers,* 409 U.S. 188, 198, 93 S.Ct. 375, 34 L.Ed.2d 401 (1972) (quoting *Simmons,* 390 U.S. at 384, 88 S.Ct. 967). The Supreme Court has said that "reliability is the linchpin in determining the admissibility of identification testimony." *Manson v. Brathwaite,* 432 U.S. 98, 114, 97 S.Ct. 2243, 53 L.Ed.2d 140 (1977). In assessing whether an identification was reliable, a court should consider the following factors: (1) the opportunity of the witness to view the criminal at the time of the crime (or prior to the identification), (2) the witness's degree of attention during such an opportunity, (3) the accuracy of the witness's prior description of the criminal, if he made one, (4) the level of certainty demonstrated at the time of the identification, and (5) the time between the crime and the identification. *See id.* at 114, 97 S.Ct. 2243 (citing *Biggers,* 409 U.S. at 199–200, 93 S.Ct. 375).

After evaluating the totality of the circumstances and applying the *Biggers* factors, the circumstances in this case support the reliability of Tmiri's identification. Tmiri testified that he knew Navar and had seen him over twenty times, providing him ample opportunity to view Navar prior to trial. Tmiri did not testify regarding his degree of attention during the times he saw Navar, nor did he provide a description of Navar prior to trial, but Tmiri did provide a detailed description of Navar prior to his visual identification of him. Navar does not contest the accuracy of this description, nor does he suggest that the description itself was the result of any suggestive circumstance. Tmiri exhibited no uncertainty at trial that Navar was in fact "the Doctor." Regarding the last factor, the trial occurred approximately two years after Tmiri last interacted with Navar,[1] but any concern over that length of time is diminished by the strength of the other factors—particularly Tmiri's familiarity with Navar and his specific description of him.

1. [Footnote omitted.]

Furthermore, Tmiri's testimony and ultimate identification occurred in direct view of the jury, which observed and presumably weighed any arguably suggestive circumstances. As we noted, our role is not to judge the accuracy of the identification, *Kosik,* 814 F.2d at 1156, and such testimony should be kept from the jury *only* if it is so unreliable that it presents "a very substantial likelihood of irreparable misidentification," *Simmons,* 390 U.S. at 384, 88 S.Ct. 967. "Misidentification is 'irreparable' when the source of the error is so elusive that it cannot be demonstrated to a jury, which therefore will give excessive weight to the eyewitness testimony." *Williams,* 522 F.3d at 811. We have also noted that "[t]he deference shown the jury in weighing the reliability of potentially suggestive out-of-court identification would seem even more appropriate for in-court identifications where the jury is present and able to see first-hand the circumstances which may influence a witness." *Bush,* 749 F.2d at 1231. In circumstances such as these, where the in-court identification was not tainted by a previous out-of-court identification, the jury is in the unique position of observing the entire identification procedure, and it may weigh the accuracy of the identification accordingly. The jury's conclusions are not our concern, so long as the procedure used to identify Navar was not unduly suggestive and produced a sufficiently reliable identification. The procedure used here did not violate Navar's constitutional rights, and the district court did not err by permitting Tmiri's in-court identification.

. . .

SECTION 1. COMPETENCY

A. DISQUALIFICATIONS UNDER THE COMMON LAW

2. INTEREST

Page 270. Note 2(c). After the statement of the holding of the Court of Appeals for the Armed Forces in United States v. Scheffer, add:

United States v. Scheffer

Supreme Court of the United States, 1998.
523 U.S. 303, 118 S. Ct. 1261, 140 L. Ed. 2d 413.

■ JUSTICE THOMAS announced the judgment of the Court and delivered the opinion of the Court with respect to Parts I, II–A, and II–D, and an opinion with respect to Parts II–B and II–C, in which THE CHIEF JUSTICE, JUSTICE SCALIA, and JUSTICE SOUTER joined.

This case presents the question whether Military Rule of Evidence 707, which makes polygraph evidence inadmissible in court-martial proceedings, unconstitutionally abridges the right of accused members of the military to present a defense. We hold that it does not.

CHAPTER 3 TESTIMONIAL PROOF

I

In March 1992, respondent Edward Scheffer, an airman stationed at March Air Force Base in California, volunteered to work as an informant on drug investigations for the Air Force Office of Special Investigations (OSI). His OSI supervisors advised him that, from time to time during the course of his undercover work, they would ask him to submit to drug testing and polygraph examinations. In early April, one of the OSI agents supervising respondent requested that he submit to a urine test. Shortly after providing the urine sample, but before the results of the test were known, respondent agreed to take a polygraph test administered by an OSI examiner. In the opinion of the examiner, the test "indicated no deception" when respondent denied using drugs since joining the Air Force.

On April 30, respondent unaccountably failed to appear for work and could not be found on the base. He was absent without leave until May 13, when an Iowa state patrolman arrested him following a routine traffic stop and held him for return to the base. OSI agents later learned that respondent's urinalysis revealed the presence of methamphetamine.

Respondent was tried by general court-martial on charges of using methamphetamine, failing to go to his appointed place of duty, wrongfully absenting himself from the base for 13 days, and, with respect to an unrelated matter, uttering 17 insufficient funds checks. He testified at trial on his own behalf, relying upon an "innocent ingestion" theory and denying that he had knowingly used drugs while working for OSI. On cross-examination, the prosecution attempted to impeach respondent with inconsistencies between his trial testimony and earlier statements he had made to OSI.

Respondent sought to introduce the polygraph evidence in support of his testimony that he did not knowingly use drugs. The military judge denied the motion, relying on Military Rule of Evidence 707, which provides, in relevant part:

> "(a) Notwithstanding any other provision of law, the results of a polygraph examination, the opinion of a polygraph examiner, or any reference to an offer to take, failure to take, or taking of a polygraph examination, shall not be admitted into evidence."

The military judge determined that Rule 707 was constitutional because "the President may, through the Rules of Evidence, determine that credibility is not an area in which a fact finder needs help, and the polygraph is not a process that has sufficient scientific acceptability to be relevant." App. 28. He further reasoned that the factfinder might give undue weight to the polygraph examiner's testimony, and that collateral arguments about such evidence could consume "an inordinate amount of time and expense." Ibid.

Respondent was convicted on all counts and was sentenced to a bad-conduct discharge, confinement for 30 months, total forfeiture of all pay and allowances, and reduction to the lowest enlisted grade. The Air Force Court of Criminal Appeals affirmed in all material respects, explaining that Rule 707 "does not arbitrarily limit the accused's ability to present reliable evidence." 41 M.J. 683, 691 (1995) (en banc).

By a 3–to–2 vote, the United States Court of Appeals for the Armed Forces reversed. 44 M.J. 442 (1996). Without pointing to any particular language in the Sixth Amendment, the Court of Appeals held that "[a] *per se* exclusion of polygraph evidence offered by an accused to rebut an attack on his credibility, ... violates his Sixth Amendment right to present a defense." Id., at 445. Judge Crawford, dissenting, stressed that a defendant's right to present relevant evidence is not absolute, that relevant evidence can be excluded for valid reasons, and that Rule 707 was supported by a number of valid justifications. Id., at 449–451. We granted certiorari, 520 U.S. 1227, 117 S.Ct. 1817, 137 L.Ed. 2d 1026 (1997), and we now reverse.

II

A defendant's right to present relevant evidence is not unlimited, but rather is subject to reasonable restrictions.[1] See Taylor v. Illinois, 484 U.S. 400, 410, 108 S. Ct. 646, 653–54, 98 L. Ed. 2d 798 (1988); Rock v. Arkansas, 483 U.S. 44, 55, 107 S. Ct. 2704, 2711, 97 L. Ed. 2d 37 (1987); Chambers v. Mississippi, 410 U.S. 284, 295, 93 S. Ct. 1038, 1045–1046, 35 L. Ed. 2d 297 (1973). A defendant's interest in presenting such evidence may thus " 'bow to accommodate other legitimate interests in the criminal trial process.' " Rock, supra, at 55, 107 S.Ct., at 2711 (quoting Chambers, supra, at 295, 93 S.Ct. at 1046); accord Michigan v. Lucas, 500 U.S. 145, 149, 111 S. Ct. 1743, 1746, 114 L. Ed. 2d 205 (1991). As a result, state and federal rulemakers have broad latitude under the Constitution to establish rules excluding evidence from criminal trials. Such rules do not abridge an accused's right to present a defense so long as they are not "arbitrary" or "disproportionate to the purposes they are designed to serve." Rock, supra, at 56, 107 S.Ct., at 2711; accord Lucas, supra, at 151, 111 S.Ct., at 1747. Moreover, we have found the exclusion of evidence to be unconstitutionally arbitrary or disproportionate only where it has infringed upon a weighty interest of the accused. See Rock, supra, at 58, 107 S.Ct., at 2712–2713; Chambers, supra, at 302, 93 S.Ct., at 1049; Washington v. Texas, 388 U.S. 14, 22–23, 87 S. Ct. 1920, 1924–1925, 18 L. Ed. 2d 1019 (1967).

Rule 707 serves several legitimate interests in the criminal trial process. These interests include ensuring that only reliable evidence is introduced at trial, preserving the jury's role in determining credibility, and avoiding litigation that is collateral to the primary purpose of the

---

1. The words "defendant" and "jury" are used throughout in reference to general principles of law and in discussing nonmilitary precedents. In reference to this case or to the military specifically, the terms "court," "court members," or "court-martial" are used throughout, as is the military term, "accused," rather than the civilian term, "defendant." [Some footnotes omitted, others renumbered.]

trial. The rule is neither arbitrary nor disproportionate in promoting these ends. Nor does it implicate a sufficiently weighty interest of the defendant to raise a constitutional concern under our precedents.

A

State and federal governments unquestionably have a legitimate interest in ensuring that reliable evidence is presented to the trier of fact in a criminal trial. Indeed, the exclusion of unreliable evidence is a principal objective of many evidentiary rules. See, e.g., Fed. Rule Evid. 702; Fed. Rule Evid. 802; Fed. Rule Evid. 901; see also Daubert v. Merrell Dow Pharmaceuticals, Inc., 509 U.S. 579, 589, 113 S. Ct. 2786, 2794–2795, 125 L. Ed. 2d 469 (1993).

The contentions of respondent and the dissent notwithstanding, there is simply no consensus that polygraph evidence is reliable. To this day, the scientific community remains extremely polarized about the reliability of polygraph techniques....

The approach taken by the President in adopting Rule 707—excluding polygraph evidence in all military trials—is a rational and proportional means of advancing the legitimate interest in barring unreliable evidence. Although the degree of reliability of polygraph evidence may depend upon a variety of identifiable factors, there is simply no way to know in a particular case whether a polygraph examiner's conclusion is accurate, because certain doubts and uncertainties plague even the best polygraph exams. Individual jurisdictions therefore may reasonably reach differing conclusions as to whether polygraph evidence should be admitted. We cannot say, then, that presented with such widespread uncertainty, the President acted arbitrarily or disproportionately in promulgating a *per se* rule excluding all polygraph evidence.

B

It is equally clear that Rule 707 serves a second legitimate governmental interest: Preserving the jury's core function of making credibility determinations in criminal trials. A fundamental premise of our criminal trial system is that "the *jury* is the lie detector." United States v. Barnard, 490 F.2d 907, 912 (C.A.9 1973) (emphasis added), cert. denied, 416 U.S. 959, 94 S. Ct. 1976, 40 L. Ed. 2d 310 (1974). Determining the weight and credibility of witness testimony, therefore, has long been held to be the "part of every case [that] belongs to the jury, who are presumed to be fitted for it by their natural intelligence and their practical knowledge of men and the ways of men." Aetna Life Ins. Co. v. Ward, 140 U.S. 76, 88, 11 S.Ct. 720, 724–725, 35 L.Ed. 371 (1891).

By its very nature, polygraph evidence may diminish the jury's role in making credibility determinations. The common form of polygraph test measures a variety of physiological responses to a set of questions asked by the examiner, who then interprets these physiological correlates of anxiety and offers an opinion to the jury about whether the witness—often, as in this case, the accused—was deceptive in answering questions about the very matters at issue in the trial. See 1 McCormick § 206. Unlike other expert witnesses who testify about factual matters outside the jurors' knowledge, such as the analysis of fingerprints, ballistics, or DNA found at a crime scene, a polygraph expert can supply the jury only with another opinion, in addition to its own, about whether the witness was telling the truth. Jurisdictions, in promulgating rules of evidence, may legitimately be concerned about the risk that juries will give excessive weight to the opinions of a polygrapher, clothed as they are in scientific expertise and at times offering, as in respondent's case, a conclusion about the ultimate issue in the trial. Such jurisdictions may legitimately determine that the aura of infallibility attending polygraph evidence can lead jurors to abandon their duty to assess credibility and guilt. Those jurisdictions may also take into account the fact that a judge cannot determine, when ruling on a motion to admit polygraph evidence, whether a particular polygraph expert is likely to influence the jury unduly. For these reasons, the President is within his constitutional prerogative to promulgate a *per se* rule that simply excludes all such evidence.

C

A third legitimate interest served by Rule 707 is avoiding litigation over issues other than the guilt or innocence of the accused. Such collateral litigation prolongs criminal trials and threatens to distract the jury from its central function of determining guilt or innocence. Allowing proffers of polygraph evidence would inevitably entail assessments of such issues as whether the test and control questions were appropriate, whether a particular polygraph examiner was qualified and had properly interpreted the physiological responses, and whether other factors such as countermeasures employed by the examinee had distorted the exam results. Such assessments would be required in each and every case. It thus offends no constitutional principle for the President to conclude that a *per se* rule excluding all polygraph evidence is appropriate. Because litigation over the admissibility of polygraph evidence is by its very nature collateral, a *per se* rule prohibiting its admission is not an arbitrary or disproportionate means of avoiding it.[2]

D

The three of our precedents upon which the Court of Appeals principally relied, Rock v. Arkansas, Washington v. Texas, and Chambers

---

2. Although the Court of Appeals stated that it had "merely remove[d] the obstacle of the *per se* rule against admissibility" of polygraph evidence in cases where the accused wishes to proffer an exculpatory polygraph to rebut an attack on his credibility, 44 M.J. 442, 446 (1996), and respondent thus implicitly argues that the Constitution would require collateral litigation only in such cases, we cannot see a principled justification whereby a right derived from the Constitution could be so narrowly contained.

v. Mississippi, do not support a right to introduce polygraph evidence, even in very narrow circumstances. The exclusions of evidence that we declared unconstitutional in those cases significantly undermined fundamental elements of the accused's defense. Such is not the case here.

In Rock, the defendant, accused of a killing to which she was the only eyewitness, was allegedly able to remember the facts of the killing only after having her memory hypnotically refreshed. See Rock v. Arkansas, 483 U.S. at 46, 107 S.Ct., at 2706. Because Arkansas excluded all hypnotically refreshed testimony, the defendant was unable to testify about certain relevant facts, including whether the killing had been accidental. See id., at 47–49, 107 S.Ct., at 2706–2708. In holding that the exclusion of this evidence violated the defendant's "right to present a defense," we noted that the rule deprived the jury of the testimony of the only witness who was at the scene and had firsthand knowledge of the facts. See id., at 57, 107 S.Ct., at 2712. Moreover, the rule infringed upon the accused's interest in testifying in her own defense—an interest that we deemed particularly significant, as it is the defendant who is the target of any criminal prosecution. See id., at 52, 107 S.Ct., at 2709–2710. For this reason, we stated that an accused ought to be allowed "to present his own version of events in his own words." Ibid.

In Washington, the statutes involved prevented co-defendants or co-participants in a crime from testifying for one another and thus precluded the accused from introducing his accomplice's testimony that the accomplice had in fact committed the crime. See Washington v. Texas, 388 U.S. at 16–17, 87 S.Ct., at 1921–1922. In reversing Washington's conviction, we held that the Sixth Amendment was violated because "the State arbitrarily denied [the accused] the right to put on the stand a witness who was physically and mentally capable of testifying to events that he had personally observed." Id., at 23, 87 S.Ct., at 1925.[3]

In Chambers, we found a due process violation in the combined application of Mississippi's common law "voucher rule," which prevented a party from impeaching his own witness, and its hearsay rule that excluded the testimony of three persons to whom that witness had confessed. See Chambers v. Mississippi, 410 U.S. at 302, 93 S.Ct., at 1049. Chambers specifically confined its holding to the "facts and circumstances" presented in that case; we thus stressed that the ruling did not "signal any diminution in the respect traditionally accorded to the States in the establishment and implementation of their own criminal trial rules and procedures." Id., at 302–303, 93 S.Ct., at 1049. Chambers therefore does not stand for the proposition that the accused is denied a fair opportunity to defend himself whenever a state or federal rule excludes favorable evidence.

3. In addition, we noted that the State of Texas could advance no legitimate interests in support of the evidentiary rules at issue, and those rules burdened only the defense and not the prosecution. See 388 U.S., at 22–23, 87 S.Ct., at 1924–1925. Rule 707 suffers from neither of these defects.

SECTION 1 COMPETENCY

Rock, Washington, and Chambers do not require that Rule 707 be invalidated, because, unlike the evidentiary rules at issue in those cases, Rule 707 does not implicate any significant interest of the accused. Here, the court members heard all the relevant details of the charged offense from the perspective of the accused, and the Rule did not preclude him from introducing any factual evidence.[4] Rather, respondent was barred merely from introducing expert opinion testimony to bolster his own credibility. Moreover, in contrast to the rule at issue in Rock, Rule 707 did not prohibit respondent from testifying on his own behalf; he freely exercised his choice to convey his version of the facts to the court-martial members. We therefore cannot conclude that respondent's defense was significantly impaired by the exclusion of polygraph evidence. Rule 707 is thus constitutional under our precedents.

. . .

For the foregoing reasons, Military Rule of Evidence 707 does not unconstitutionally abridge the right to present a defense. The judgment of the Court of Appeals is reversed.

It is so ordered.

■ JUSTICE KENNEDY, with whom JUSTICE O'CONNOR, JUSTICE GINSBURG, and JUSTICE BREYER join, concurring in part and concurring in the judgment.

I join Parts I, II–A, and II–D of the opinion of the Court.

In my view it should have been sufficient to decide this case to observe, as the principal opinion does, that various courts and jurisdictions "may reasonably reach differing conclusions as to whether polygraph evidence should be admitted." Ante, at 1266. The continuing, good-faith disagreement among experts and courts on the subject of polygraph reliability counsels against our invalidating a *per se* exclusion of polygraph results or of the fact an accused has taken or refused to take a polygraph examination. If we were to accept respondent's position, of course, our holding would bind state courts, as well as military and federal courts. Given the ongoing debate about polygraphs, I agree

---

4. The dissent suggests, post, at 1275–1276, that polygraph results constitute "factual evidence." The raw results of a polygraph exam—the subject's pulse, respiration, and perspiration rates—may be factual data, but these are not introduced at trial, and even if they were, they would not be "facts" about the alleged crime at hand. Rather, the evidence introduced is the expert opinion testimony of the polygrapher about whether the subject was truthful or deceptive in answering questions about the alleged crime. A *per se* rule excluding polygraph results therefore does not prevent an accused—just as it did not prevent respondent here—from introducing factual evidence or testimony about the crime itself, such as alibi witness testimony, see post, at 1275. For the same reasons, an expert polygrapher's interpretation of polygraph results is not evidence of "'the accused's whole conduct,'" see post, at 1278, to which Dean Wigmore referred. It is not evidence of the "accused's ... conduct" at all, much less "conduct" concerning the actual crime at issue. It is merely the opinion of a witness with no knowledge about any of the facts surrounding the alleged crime, concerning whether the defendant spoke truthfully or deceptively on another occasion.

the rule of exclusion is not so arbitrary or disproportionate that it is unconstitutional.

I doubt, though, that the rule of *per se* exclusion is wise, and some later case might present a more compelling case for introduction of the testimony than this one does. Though the considerable discretion given to the trial court in admitting or excluding scientific evidence is not a constitutional mandate, see Daubert v. Merrell Dow Pharmaceuticals, Inc., 509 U.S. 579, 587, 113 S.Ct. 2786, 2793–2794, 125 L. Ed. 2d 469 (1993), there is some tension between that rule and our holding today. And, as Justice STEVENS points out, there is much inconsistency between the Government's extensive use of polygraphs to make vital security determinations and the argument it makes here, stressing the inaccuracy of these tests.

With all respect, moreover, it seems the principal opinion overreaches when it rests its holding on the additional ground that the jury's role in making credibility determinations is diminished when it hears polygraph evidence. I am in substantial agreement with Justice STEVENS' observation that the argument demeans and mistakes the role and competence of jurors in deciding the factual question of guilt or innocence. Post, at 1278....

. . .

Neither in the federal system nor in the military courts, then, is it convincing to say that polygraph test results should be excluded because of some lingering concern about usurping the jury's responsibility to decide ultimate issues.

■ JUSTICE STEVENS, dissenting.

... I ... agree with the Court of Appeals that the Rule is unconstitutional. This Court's contrary holding rests on a serious undervaluation of the importance of the citizen's constitutional right to present a defense to a criminal charge and an unrealistic appraisal of the importance of the governmental interests that undergird the Rule....

I

Rule 707 is a blanket rule of exclusion. No matter how reliable and how probative the results of a polygraph test may be, Rule 707 categorically denies the defendant any opportunity to persuade the court that the evidence should be received for any purpose. Indeed, even if the parties stipulate in advance that the results of a lie detector test may be admitted, the Rule requires exclusion.

The principal charge against the respondent in this case was that he had knowingly used methamphetamine. His principal defense was "innocent ingestion"; even if the urinalysis test conducted on April 7, 1992, correctly indicated that he did ingest the substance, he claims to have been unaware of that fact. The results of the lie detector test conducted three days later, if accurate, constitute factual evidence that his physical condition at that time was consistent with the theory of his defense and inconsistent with the theory of the prosecution. The results were also relevant because they tended to confirm the credibility of his testimony. Under Rule 707, even if the results of the polygraph test were more reliable than the results of the urinalysis, the weaker evidence is admissible and the stronger evidence is inadmissible.

Under the now discredited reasoning in a case decided 75 years ago, Frye v. United States, 54 App. D.C. 46, 293 F. 1013 (1923), that anomalous result would also have been reached in non-military cases tried in the federal courts. In recent years, however, we have not only repudiated Frye's general approach to scientific evidence, but the federal courts have also been engaged in the process of rejecting the once-popular view that all lie detector evidence should be categorically inadmissible. Well reasoned opinions are concluding, consistently with this Court's decisions in Daubert v. Merrell Dow Pharmaceuticals, Inc., 509 U.S. 579, 113 S. Ct. 2786, 125 L. Ed. 2d 469 (1993), and General Electric Co. v. Joiner, 522 U.S. 136, 118 S.Ct. 512, 139 L.Ed.2d 508 (1997), that the federal rules wisely allow district judges to exercise broad discretion when evaluating the admissibility of scientific evidence. Those opinions correctly observe that the rules of evidence generally recognized in the trial of civil and criminal cases in the federal courts do not contain any blanket prohibition against the admissibility of polygraph evidence.

. . .

II

The Court's opinion barely acknowledges that a person accused of a crime has a constitutional right to present a defense. It is not necessary to point to "any particular language in the Sixth Amendment," ante, at 1264, to support the conclusion that the right is firmly established. It is, however, appropriate to comment on the importance of that right before discussing the three interests that the Government relies upon to justify Rule 707.

. . .

Over the years, with respect to category after category, strict rules of exclusion have been replaced by rules that broaden the discretion of trial judges to admit potentially unreliable evidence and to allow properly instructed juries to evaluate its weight. While that trend has included both rulemaking and non-constitutional judicial decisions, the direction of the trend has been consistent and it has been manifested in constitutional holdings as well.

. . .

III

The constitutional requirement that a blanket exclusion of potentially unreliable evidence must be proportionate to the purposes served by the rule obviously makes it necessary to evaluate the interests on both sides of the balance. Today the Court all but ignores the strength of the defendant's interest in having polygraph evidence admitted in certain cases. As the facts of this case illustrate, the Court is quite wrong in assuming that the impact of Rule 707 on respondent's defense was not significant because it did not preclude the introduction of any "factual evidence" or prevent him from conveying "his version of the facts to the court-martial members." Ante, at 1268–1269. Under such reasoning, a rule that excluded the testimony of alibi witnesses would not be significant as long as the defendant is free to testify himself. But given the defendant's strong interest in the outcome—an interest that was sufficient to make his testimony presumptively untrustworthy and therefore inadmissible at common law—his uncorroborated testimony is certain to be less persuasive than that of a third-party witness. A rule that bars him "from introducing expert opinion testimony to bolster his own credibility," ibid., unquestionably impairs any "meaningful opportunity to present a complete defense"; indeed, it is sure to be outcome-determinative in many cases.

Moreover, in this case the results of the polygraph test, taken just three days after the urinalysis, constitute independent factual evidence that is not otherwise available and that strongly supports his defense of "innocent ingestion." Just as flight or other evidence of "consciousness of guilt" may sometimes be relevant, on some occasions evidence of "consciousness of innocence" may also be relevant to the central issue at trial. Both the answers to the questions propounded by the examiner, and the physical manifestations produced by those utterances, were probative of an innocent state of mind shortly after he ingested the drugs. In Dean Wigmore's view, both "conduct" and "utterances" may constitute factual evidence of a "consciousness of innocence."[1] As the Second Circuit has held, when there is a serious factual dispute over the "basic defense [that defendant] was unaware of any criminal wrongdoing," evidence of his innocent state of mind is "critical to a fair adjudication of criminal charges."[2] The exclusion of the test results in this case cannot be fairly equated with a ruling that merely prevented the defendant from encumbering the record with cumulative evidence. Because the Rule may well have affected the outcome of the trial, it

---

1. "Moreover, there are other principles by which a defendant may occasionally avail himself of conduct as evidence in his favor—in particular, of conduct indicating consciousness of innocence, ... of utterances asserting his innocence ..., and, in sedition charges, of conduct indicating a loyal state of mind...." 1A J. Wigmore, Evidence § 56.1, p. 1180 (Tillers rev. ed. 1983); see United States v. Reifsteck, 841 F.2d 701, 705 (C.A.6 1988).

2. ... United States v. Biaggi, 909 F.2d 662, 691–692 (C.A.2 1990)....

unquestionably "infringed upon a weighty interest of the accused." Ante, at 1264.

The question, then, is whether the three interests on which the Government relies are powerful enough to support a categorical rule excluding the results of all polygraph tests no matter how unfair such a rule may be in particular cases.

Reliability

There are a host of studies that place the reliability of polygraph tests at 85% to 90%. While critics of the polygraph argue that accuracy is much lower, even the studies cited by the critics place polygraph accuracy at 70%. Moreover, to the extent that the polygraph errs, studies have repeatedly shown that the polygraph is more likely to find innocent people guilty than vice versa. Thus, exculpatory polygraphs—like the one in this case—are likely to be more reliable than inculpatory ones.

Of course, within the broad category of lie detector evidence, there may be a wide variation in both the validity and the relevance of particular test results. Questions about the examiner's integrity, independence, choice of questions, or training in the detection of deliberate attempts to provoke misleading physiological responses may justify exclusion of specific evidence. But such questions are properly addressed in adversary proceedings; they fall far short of justifying a blanket exclusion of this type of expert testimony.

There is no legal requirement that expert testimony must satisfy a particular degree of reliability to be admissible. Expert testimony about a defendant's "future dangerousness" to determine his eligibility for the death penalty, even if wrong "most of the time," is routinely admitted. Barefoot v. Estelle, 463 U.S. 880, 898–901, 103 S. Ct. 3383, 3397–3399, 77 L. Ed. 2d 1090 (1983). Studies indicate that handwriting analysis, and even fingerprint identifications, may be less trustworthy than polygraph evidence in certain cases. And, of course, even highly dubious eyewitness testimony is, and should be, admitted and tested in the crucible of cross-examination. The Court's reliance on potential unreliability as a justification for a categorical rule of inadmissibility reveals that it is "overly pessimistic about the capabilities of the jury and of the adversary system generally. Vigorous cross-examination, presentation of contrary evidence, and careful instruction on the burden of proof are the traditional and appropriate means of attacking shaky but admissible evidence." Daubert, 509 U.S. at 596.

The Role of the Jury

It is the function of the jury to make credibility determinations. In my judgment evidence that tends to establish either a consciousness of guilt or a consciousness of innocence may be of assistance to the jury in making such determinations. That also was the opinion of Dean Wigmore:

"Let the accused's whole conduct come in; and whether it tells for consciousness of guilt or for consciousness of innocence, let us take it for what it is worth, remembering that in either case it is open to varying explanations and is not to be emphasized. Let us not deprive an innocent person, falsely accused, of the inference which common sense draws from a consciousness of innocence and its natural manifestations." 2 J. Wigmore, Evidence § 293, p. 232 (J. Chadbourn rev. ed. 1979).

There is, of course, some risk that some "juries will give excessive weight to the opinions of a polygrapher, clothed as they are in scientific expertise," ante, at 1267. In my judgment, however, it is much more likely that juries will be guided by the instructions of the trial judge concerning the credibility of expert as well as lay witnesses. The strong presumption that juries will follow the court's instructions, see, e.g., Richardson v. Marsh, 481 U.S. 200, 211, 107 S. Ct. 1702, 1709, 95 L. Ed. 2d 176 (1987), applies to exculpatory as well as inculpatory evidence. Common sense suggests that the testimony of disinterested third parties that is relevant to the jury's credibility determination will assist rather than impair the jury's deliberations. As with the reliance on the potential unreliability of this type of evidence, the reliance on a fear that the average jury is not able to assess the weight of this testimony reflects a distressing lack of confidence in the intelligence of the average American.[3]

Collateral Litigation

The potential burden of collateral proceedings to determine the examiner's qualifications is a manifestly insufficient justification for a categorical exclusion of expert testimony. Such proceedings are a routine predicate for the admission of any expert testimony, and may always give rise to searching cross-examination. If testimony that is critical to a fair determination of guilt or innocence could be excluded for that reason, the right to a meaningful opportunity to present a defense would be an illusion.

It is incongruous for the party that selected the examiner, the equipment, the testing procedures, and the questions asked of the defendant to complain about the examinee's burden of proving that the test was properly conducted. While there may well be a need for substantial collateral proceedings when the party objecting to admissibility has a basis for questioning some aspect of the examination, it seems quite obvious that the Government is in no position to challenge the

---

3. Indeed, research indicates that jurors do not "blindly" accept polygraph evidence, but that they instead weigh polygraph evidence along with other evidence. Cavoukian & Heslegrave, The Admissibility of Polygraph Evidence in Court: Some Empirical Findings, 4 Law and Human Behavior 117, 123, 127–128, 130 (1980) (hereinafter Cavoukian & Heslegrave); see also Honts & Perry 366–367. One study found that expert testimony about the limits of the polygraph "*completely eliminated* the effect of the polygraph evidence" on the jury. Cavoukian & Heslegrave 128–129 (emphasis added).

competence of the procedures that it has developed and relied upon in hundreds of thousands of cases.

In all events the concern about the burden of collateral debates about the integrity of a particular examination, or the competence of a particular examiner, provides no support for a categorical rule that requires exclusion even when the test is taken pursuant to a stipulation and even when there has been a stipulation resolving all potential collateral issues. Indeed, in this very case there would have been no need for any collateral proceedings because respondent did not question the qualifications of the expert who examined him, and surely the Government is in no position to argue that one who has successfully completed its carefully developed training program is unqualified. The interest in avoiding burdensome collateral proceedings might support a rule prescribing minimum standards that must be met before any test is admissible, but it surely does not support the blunderbuss at issue.[4]

IV

The Government's concerns would unquestionably support the exclusion of polygraph evidence in particular cases, and may well be sufficient to support a narrower rule designed to respond to specific concerns. In my judgment, however, those concerns are plainly insufficient to support a categorical rule that prohibits the admission of polygraph evidence in all cases, no matter how reliable or probative the evidence may be. Accordingly, I respectfully dissent.

See also Casebook, pp. 470, 962, 972.

Holmes v. South Carolina

Supreme Court of the United States, 2006.
547 U.S. 319, 126 S.Ct. 1727, 164 L.Ed.2d 503.

■ JUSTICE ALITO delivered the opinion of the Court.

This case presents the question whether a criminal defendant's federal constitutional rights are violated by an evidence rule under which the defendant may not introduce proof of third-party guilt if the prosecution has introduced forensic evidence that, if believed, strongly supports a guilty verdict.

---

4. It has been suggested that if exculpatory polygraph evidence may be adduced by the defendant, the prosecutor should also be allowed to introduce inculpatory test results. That conclusion would not be dictated by a holding that vindicates the defendant's Sixth Amendment right to summon witnesses. Moreover, as noted above, studies indicate that exculpatory polygraphs are more reliable than inculpatory ones.... In any event, a concern about possible future legal developments is surely not implicated by the narrow issue presented by the holding of the Court of Military Appeals in this case. Even if it were, I can see nothing fundamentally unfair about permitting the results of a test taken pursuant to stipulation being admitted into evidence to prove consciousness of guilt as well as consciousness of innocence.

CHAPTER 3   TESTIMONIAL PROOF

I

On the morning of December 31, 1989, 86–year–old Mary Stewart was beaten, raped, and robbed in her home. She later died of complications stemming from her injuries. Petitioner was convicted by a South Carolina jury of murder, first-degree criminal sexual conduct, first-degree burglary, and robbery, and he was sentenced to death. State v. Holmes, 320 S.C. 259, 262, 464 S.E.2d 334, 336 (1995). The South Carolina Supreme Court affirmed his convictions and sentence, and this Court denied certiorari. Ibid., cert. denied, 517 U.S. 1248, 116 S.Ct. 2507, 135 L.Ed.2d 197 (1996). Upon state postconviction review, however, petitioner was granted a new trial. 361 S.C. 333, 335, n. 1, 605 S.E.2d 19, 20, n. 1 (2004).

At the second trial, the prosecution relied heavily on the following forensic evidence:

> "(1) [Petitioner's] palm print was found just above the door knob on the interior side of the front door of the victim's house; (2) fibers consistent with a black sweatshirt owned by [petitioner] were found on the victim's bed sheets; (3) matching blue fibers were found on the victim's pink nightgown and on [petitioner's] blue jeans; (4) microscopically consistent fibers were found on the pink nightgown and on [petitioner's] underwear; (5) [petitioner's] underwear contained a mixture of DNA from two individuals, and 99.99% of the population other than [petitioner] and the victim were excluded as contributors to that mixture; and (6) [petitioner's] tank top was found to contain a mixture of [petitioner's] blood and the victim's blood." Id., at 343, 605 S.E.2d, at 24.

In addition, the prosecution introduced evidence that petitioner had been seen near Stewart's home within an hour of the time when, according to the prosecution's evidence, the attack took place. Id., at 337–338, 343, 605 S.E.2d, at 21, 24.

As a major part of his defense, petitioner attempted to undermine the State's forensic evidence by suggesting that it had been contaminated and that certain law enforcement officers had engaged in a plot to frame him. Id., at 339, 605 S.E.2d, at 22. Petitioner's expert witnesses criticized the procedures used by the police in handling the fiber and DNA evidence and in collecting the fingerprint evidence. App. 299–311, 313–323. Another defense expert provided testimony that petitioner cited as supporting his claim that the palm print had been planted by the police. Id., at 326–327, 605 S.E.2d 19.

Petitioner also sought to introduce proof that another man, Jimmy McCaw White, had attacked Stewart. 361 S.C., at 340, 605 S.E.2d, at 22. At a pretrial hearing, petitioner proffered several witnesses who placed White in the victim's neighborhood on the morning of the assault, as well as four other witnesses who testified that White had either acknowledged that petitioner was "'innocent'" or had actually admitted to committing the crimes. Id., at 340–342, 605 S.E.2d, at 22–23. One witness recounted that when he asked White about the "word ... on the street" that White was responsible for Stewart's murder, White "put his head down and he raised his head back up and he said, well, you know I like older women." App. 119. According to this witness, White added that "he did what they say he did" and that he had "no regrets about it at all." Id., at 120. Another witness, who had been incarcerated with White, testified that White had admitted to assaulting Stewart, that a police officer had asked the witness to testify falsely against petitioner, and that employees of the prosecutor's office, while soliciting the witness' cooperation, had spoken of manufacturing evidence against petitioner. Id., at 38–50. White testified at the pretrial hearing and denied making the incriminating statements. 361 S.C., at 341–342, 605 S.E.2d, at 23. He also provided an alibi for the time of the crime, but another witness refuted his alibi. Id., at 342, 605 S.E.2d, at 23.

The trial court excluded petitioner's third-party guilt evidence citing State v. Gregory, 198 S.C. 98, 16 S.E.2d 532 (1941), which held that such evidence is admissible if it " 'raise[s] a reasonable inference or presumption as to [the defendant's] own innocence' " but is not admissible if it merely " 'cast[s] a bare suspicion upon another' " or " 'raise[s] a conjectural inference as to the commission of the crime by another.' " App. 133–134 (quoting Gregory, supra, at 104, 16 S.E.2d, at 534). On appeal, the South Carolina Supreme Court found no error in the exclusion of petitioner's third-party guilt evidence. Citing both Gregory and its later decision in State v. Gay, 343 S.C. 543, 541 S.E.2d 541 (2001), the State Supreme Court held that "where there is strong evidence of an appellant's guilt, especially where there is strong forensic evidence, the proffered evidence about a third party's alleged guilt does not raise a reasonable inference as to the appellant's own innocence." 361 S.C., at 342–343, 605 S.E.2d, at 24. Applying this standard, the court held that petitioner could not "overcome the forensic evidence against him to raise a reasonable inference of his own innocence." Id., at 343, 605 S.E.2d, at 24. We granted certiorari. 545 U.S. 1164, 126 S.Ct. 34, 162 L.Ed.2d 932 (2005).

II

"[S]tate and federal rulemakers have broad latitude under the Constitution to establish rules excluding evidence from criminal trials." United States v. Scheffer, 523 U.S. 303, 308, 118 S.Ct. 1261, 140 L.Ed.2d 413 (1998); see also Crane v. Kentucky, 476 U.S. 683, 689–690, 106 S.Ct. 2142, 90 L.Ed.2d 636 (1986); Marshall v. Lonberger, 459 U.S. 422, 438, n. 6, 103 S.Ct. 843, 74 L.Ed.2d 646 (1983); Chambers v. Mississippi, 410 U.S. 284, 302–303, 93 S.Ct. 1038, 35 L.Ed.2d 297 (1973); Spencer v. Texas, 385 U.S. 554, 564, 87 S.Ct. 648, 17 L.Ed.2d 606 (1967). This latitude, however, has limits. "Whether rooted directly in the Due Process Clause of the Fourteenth Amendment or in the Compulsory

Process or Confrontation clauses of the Sixth Amendment, the Constitution guarantees criminal defendants 'a meaningful opportunity to present a complete defense.' " Crane, supra, at 690, 106 S.Ct. 2142 (quoting California v. Trombetta, 467 U.S. 479, 485, 104 S.Ct. 2528, 81 L.Ed.2d 413 (1984); citations omitted). This right is abridged by evidence rules that "infring[e] upon a weighty interest of the accused" and are " 'arbitrary' or 'disproportionate to the purposes they are designed to serve.' " Scheffer, supra, at 308, 118 S.Ct. 1261 (quoting Rock v. Arkansas, 483 U.S. 44, 56, 107 S.Ct. 2704, 97 L.Ed.2d 37 (1987)).

This Court's cases contain several illustrations of "arbitrary" rules, i.e., rules that excluded important defense evidence but that did not serve any legitimate interests. In Washington v. Texas, 388 U.S. 14, 87 S.Ct. 1920, 18 L.Ed.2d 1019 (1967), state statutes barred a person who had been charged as a participant in a crime from testifying in defense of another alleged participant unless the witness had been acquitted. As a result, when the defendant in Washington was tried for murder, he was precluded from calling as a witness a person who had been charged and previously convicted of committing the same murder. Holding that the defendant's right to put on a defense had been violated, we noted that the rule embodied in the statutes could not "even be defended on the ground that it rationally sets apart a group of persons who are particularly likely to commit perjury" since the rule allowed an alleged participant to testify if he or she had been acquitted or was called by the prosecution. Id., at 22–23, 87 S.Ct. 1920.

A similar constitutional violation occurred in Chambers v. Mississippi, supra. A murder defendant called as a witness a man named McDonald, who had previously confessed to the murder. When McDonald repudiated the confession on the stand, the defendant was denied permission to examine McDonald as an adverse witness based on the State's " 'voucher' rule," which barred parties from impeaching their own witnesses. Id., at 294, 93 S.Ct. 1038. In addition, because the state hearsay rule did not include an exception for statements against penal interest, the defendant was not permitted to introduce evidence that McDonald had made self-incriminating statements to three other persons. Noting that the State had not even attempted to "defend" or "explain [the] underlying rationale" of the "voucher rule," id., at 297, 93 S.Ct. 1038, this Court held that "the exclusion of [the evidence of McDonald's out-of-court statements], coupled with the State's refusal to permit [the defendant] to cross-examine McDonald, denied him a trial in accord with traditional and fundamental standards of due process," id., at 302, 93 S.Ct. 1038.

Another arbitrary rule was held unconstitutional in Crane v. Kentucky, supra. There, the defendant was prevented from attempting to show at trial that his confession was unreliable because of the circumstances under which it was obtained, and neither the State Supreme Court nor the prosecution "advanced any rational justification for the wholesale exclusion of this body of potentially exculpatory evidence." Id., at 691, 106 S.Ct. 2142.

In Rock v. Arkansas, supra, this Court held that a rule prohibiting hypnotically refreshed testimony was unconstitutional because "[w]holesale inadmissibility of a defendant's testimony is an arbitrary restriction on the right to testify in the absence of clear evidence by the State repudiating the validity of all post-hypnotic recollections." Id., at 61, 107 S.Ct. 2704. By contrast, in United States v. Scheffer, supra, we held that a rule excluding all polygraph evidence did not abridge the right to present a defense because the rule "serve[d] several legitimate interests in the criminal trial process," was "neither arbitrary nor disproportionate in promoting these ends," and did not "implicate a sufficiently weighty interest of the defendant." Id., at 309, 118 S.Ct. 1261.

While the Constitution thus prohibits the exclusion of defense evidence under rules that serve no legitimate purpose or that are disproportionate to the ends that they are asserted to promote, well-established rules of evidence permit trial judges to exclude evidence if its probative value is outweighed by certain other factors such as unfair prejudice, confusion of the issues, or potential to mislead the jury. See, e.g., Fed. Rule Evid. 403; Uniform Rule of Evid. 45 (1953); ALI, Model Code of Evidence Rule 303 (1942); 3 J. Wigmore, Evidence §§ 1863, 1904 (1904). Plainly referring to rules of this type, we have stated that the Constitution permits judges "to exclude evidence that is 'repetitive ..., only marginally relevant' or poses an undue risk of 'harassment, prejudice, [or] confusion of the issues.'" Crane, supra, at 689–690, 106 S.Ct. 2142 (quoting Delaware v. Van Arsdall, 475 U.S. 673, 679, 106 S.Ct. 1431, 89 L.Ed.2d 674 (1986); ellipsis and brackets in original). See also Montana v. Egelhoff, 518 U.S. 37, 42, 116 S.Ct. 2013, 135 L.Ed.2d 361 (1996) (plurality opinion) (terming such rules "familiar and unquestionably constitutional")....

In Gay and this case, however, the South Carolina Supreme Court radically changed and extended the rule. In Gay, after recognizing the standard applied in Gregory, the court stated that "[i]n view of the strong evidence of appellant's guilt—especially the forensic evidence—... the proffered evidence ... did not raise 'a reasonable inference' as to appellant's own innocence." Gay, 343 S.C., at 550, 541 S.E.2d, at 545 (quoting Gregory, supra, at 104, 16 S.E.2d, at 534, in turn quoting 16 C.J., § 1085, at 560). Similarly, in the present case, as noted, the State Supreme Court applied the rule that "where there is strong evidence of [a defendant's] guilt, especially where there is strong forensic evidence, the prufferod evidence about a third party's alleged guilt" may (or perhaps must) be excluded. 361 S.C., at 342, 605 S.E.2d, at 24.

Under this rule, the trial judge does not focus on the probative value or the potential adverse effects of admitting the defense evidence of third-party guilt. Instead, the critical inquiry concerns the strength of the prosecution's case: If the prosecution's case is strong enough, the evidence of third-party guilt is excluded even if that evidence, if viewed independently, would have great probative value and even if it would not pose an undue risk of harassment, prejudice, or confusion of the issues.

Furthermore, as applied in this case, the South Carolina Supreme Court's rule seems to call for little, if any, examination of the credibility of the prosecution's witnesses or the reliability of its evidence. Here, for example, the defense strenuously claimed that the prosecution's forensic evidence was so unreliable (due to mishandling and a deliberate plot to frame petitioner) that the evidence should not have even been admitted. The South Carolina Supreme Court responded that these challenges did not entirely "eviscerate" the forensic evidence and that the defense challenges went to the weight and not to the admissibility of that evidence. Id., at 343, n. 8, 605 S.E.2d, at 24, n. 8. Yet, in evaluating the prosecution's forensic evidence and deeming it to be "strong"—and thereby justifying exclusion of petitioner's third-party guilt evidence—the South Carolina Supreme Court made no mention of the defense challenges to the prosecution's evidence.

Interpreted in this way, the rule applied by the State Supreme Court does not rationally serve the end that the Gregory rule and its analogues in other jurisdictions were designed to promote, i.e., to focus the trial on the central issues by excluding evidence that has only a very weak logical connection to the central issues. The rule applied in this case appears to be based on the following logic: Where (1) it is clear that only one person was involved in the commission of a particular crime and (2) there is strong evidence that the defendant was the perpetrator, it follows that evidence of third-party guilt must be weak. But this logic depends on an accurate evaluation of the prosecution's proof, and the true strength of the prosecution's proof cannot be assessed without considering challenges to the reliability of the prosecution's evidence. Just because the prosecution's evidence, if credited, would provide strong support for a guilty verdict, it does not follow that evidence of third-party guilt has only a weak logical connection to the central issues in the case. And where the credibility of the prosecution's witnesses or the reliability of its evidence is not conceded, the strength of the prosecution's case cannot be assessed without making the sort of factual findings that have traditionally been reserved for the trier of fact and that the South Carolina courts did not purport to make in this case.

The rule applied in this case is no more logical than its converse would be, i.e., a rule barring the prosecution from introducing evidence of a defendant's guilt if the defendant is able to proffer, at a pretrial hearing, evidence that, if believed, strongly supports a verdict of not guilty. In the present case, for example, the petitioner proffered evidence that, if believed, squarely proved that White, not petitioner, was the perpetrator. It would make no sense, however, to hold that this proffer precluded the prosecution from introducing its evidence, including the forensic evidence that, if credited, provided strong proof of the petitioner's guilt.

The point is that, by evaluating the strength of only one party's evidence, no logical conclusion can be reached regarding the strength of contrary evidence offered by the other side to rebut or cast doubt. Because the rule applied by the State Supreme Court in this case did not heed this point, the rule is "arbitrary" in the sense that it does not rationally serve the end that the Gregory rule and other similar third-party guilt rules were designed to further. Nor has the State identified any other legitimate end that the rule serves. It follows that the rule applied in this case by the State Supreme Court violates a criminal defendant's right to have " 'a meaningful opportunity to present a complete defense.' " Crane, 476 U.S., at 690, 106 S.Ct. 2142 (quoting Trombetta, 467 U.S., at 485, 104 S.Ct. 2528).

III

For these reasons, we vacate the judgment of the South Carolina Supreme Court and remand the case for further proceedings not inconsistent with this opinion.

It is so ordered.

Page 270. Note 2(e). After United States v. Roberts, add:

In State v. Reiner, 93 Ohio St. 3d 601, 757 N.E.2d 1143 (2001), cert. denied, 536 U.S. 940 (2002), a father was prosecuted for manslaughter for shaking his baby so severely as to cause the baby's death. A babysitter who could have been the person who shook the baby was subpoenaed by both the prosecution and defense, but was granted immunity at the request of the prosecution. The babysitter testified, denying all culpability and stating to the jury that she had refused to answer questions without a grant of immunity on advice of counsel, although she had done nothing wrong.

> The jury should have been permitted to hear ... [the babysitter] take the Fifth Amendment and to evaluate her testimony on that basis. The defense would have been able to present its theory of the babysitter's culpability without the court's giving the jury the impression that ... [the babysitter] was immune from prosecution because she did not commit the crime. Therefore, it did not further the administration of justice when the trial court agreed to grant her immunity from future prosecution. Instead, it severely prejudiced the rights of the defendant.

Clark v. Arizona

Supreme Court of the United States, 2006.
548 U.S. 735, 126 S.Ct. 2709, 165 L.Ed.2d 842.

■ JUSTICE SOUTER delivered the opinion of the Court.[1]

[Does not violate Due Process for a state to limit use of evidence of capacity or mental disease to establishing the defense of insanity and to forbid its use to negate mens rea, an element of the offense.]

1. [Footnotes omitted.]

CHAPTER 3   TESTIMONIAL PROOF

* * *

The third principle implicated by Clark's argument is a defendant's right as a matter of simple due process to present evidence favorable to himself on an element that must be proven to convict him. As already noted, evidence tending to show that a defendant suffers from mental disease and lacks capacity to form *mens rea* is relevant to rebut evidence that he did in fact form the required *mens rea* at the time in question; this is the reason that Clark claims a right to require the factfinder in this case to consider testimony about his mental illness and his incapacity directly, when weighing the persuasiveness of other evidence tending to show *mens rea*, which the prosecution has the burden to prove.

As Clark recognizes, however, the right to introduce relevant evidence can be curtailed if there is a good reason for doing that. "While the Constitution ... prohibits the exclusion of defense evidence under rules that serve no legitimate purpose or that are disproportionate to the ends that they are asserted to promote, well-established rules of evidence permit trial judges to exclude evidence if its probative value is outweighed by certain other factors such as unfair prejudice, confusion of the issues, or potential to mislead the jury." *Holmes v. South Carolina*, 547 U.S. 319, ___ 126 S.Ct. 1727, 1732, 164 L.Ed.2d 503 (2006); see *Crane v. Kentucky*, 476 U.S. 683, 689–690 106 S.Ct. 2142, 90 L.Ed.2d 636 (1986) (permitting exclusion of evidence that "poses an undue risk of 'harassment, prejudice, [or] confusion of the issues'" (quoting *Delaware v. Van Arsdall*, 475 U.S. 673, 679 106 S.Ct. 1431, 9 L.Ed.2d 674 (1986))); see also *Egelhoff*, 518 U.S. 37, 116 S.Ct. 2013, 135 L.Ed.2d 361; *Chambers v. Mississippi*, 410 U.S. 284, 302 93 S.Ct. 1038, 35 L.Ed.2d 297 (1973). And if evidence may be kept out entirely, its consideration may be subject to limitation, which Arizona claims the power to impose here. State law says that evidence of mental disease and incapacity may be introduced and considered, and if sufficiently forceful to satisfy the defendant's burden of proof under the insanity rule it will displace the presumption of sanity and excuse from criminal responsibility. But mental-disease and capacity evidence may be considered only for its bearing on the insanity defense, and it will avail a defendant only if it is persuasive enough to satisfy the defendant's burden as defined by the terms of that defense. The mental-disease and capacity evidence is thus being channeled or restricted to one issue and given effect only if the defendant carries the burden to convince the factfinder of insanity; the evidence is not being excluded entirely, and the question is whether reasons for requiring it to be channeled and restricted are good enough to satisfy the standard of fundamental fairness that due process requires. We think they are.

* * *

And Clark presses no objection to Arizona's decision to require persuasion to a clear and convincing degree before the presumption of sanity and normal responsibility is overcome....

But if a State is to have this authority in practice as well as in theory, it must be able to deny a defendant the opportunity to displace the presumption of sanity more easily when addressing a different issue in the course of the criminal trial. Yet, as we have explained, just such an opportunity would be available if expert testimony of mental disease and incapacity could be considered for whatever a factfinder might think it was worth on the issue of *mens rea*. As we mentioned, the presumption of sanity would then be only as strong as the evidence a factfinder would accept as enough to raise a reasonable doubt about *mens rea* for the crime charged; once reasonable doubt was found, acquittal would be required, and the standards established for the defense of insanity would go by the boards.

* * *

What counts for due process, however, is simply that a State that wishes to avoid a second avenue for exploring capacity, less stringent for a defendant, has a good reason for confining the consideration of evidence of mental disease and incapacity to the insanity defense.

* * *

Are there, then, characteristics of mental-disease and capacity evidence giving rise to risks that may reasonably be hedged by channeling the consideration of such evidence to the insanity issue on which, in States like Arizona, a defendant has the burden of persuasion? We think there are: in the controversial character of some categories of mental disease, in the potential of mental-disease evidence to mislead, and in the danger of according greater certainty to capacity evidence than experts claim for it.

* * *

Next, there is the potential of mental-disease evidence to mislead jurors (when they are the factfinders) through the power of this kind of evidence to suggest that a defendant suffering from a recognized mental disease lacks cognitive, moral, volitional, or other capacity, when that may not be a sound conclusion at all. Even when a category of mental disease is broadly accepted and the assignment of a defendant's behavior to that category is uncontroversial, the classification may suggest something very significant about a defendant's capacity, when in fact the classification tells us little or nothing about the ability of the defendant to form *mens rea* or to exercise the cognitive, moral, or volitional capacities that define legal sanity.... Evidence of mental disease, then, can easily mislead; it is very easy to slide from evidence that an individual with a professionally recognized mental disease is very different, into doubting that he has the capacity to form *mens rea*, whereas that doubt may not be justified. And of course, in the cases mentioned before, in which the categorization is doubtful or the category of mental disease is itself subject to controversy, the risks are even greater that opinions about mental disease may confuse a jury into thinking the opinions show more than they do. Because allowing mental-disease evidence on *mens rea* can thus easily mislead, it is not unreasonable to address that tendency by confining consideration of this kind of evidence to insanity, on which a defendant may be assigned the burden of persuasion.

* * *

In sum, these empirical and conceptual problems add up to a real risk that an expert's judgment in giving capacity evidence will come with an apparent authority that psychologists and psychiatrists do not claim to have. We think that this risk, like the difficulty in assessing the significance of mental-disease evidence, supports the State's decision to channel such expert testimony to consideration on the insanity defense, on which the party seeking the benefit of this evidence has the burden of persuasion.

* * *

Arizona's rule serves to preserve the State's chosen standard for recognizing insanity as a defense and to avoid confusion and misunderstanding on the part of jurors. For these reasons, there is no violation of due process under *Chambers* and its progeny, and no cause to claim that channeling evidence on mental disease and capacity offends any " 'principle of justice so rooted in the traditions and conscience of our people as to be ranked as fundamental,' " *Patterson*, 432 U.S., at 202 97 S.Ct. 2319 (quoting *Speiser*, 357 U.S., at 523, 78 S.Ct. 1332).

■ [JUSTICES STEVENS and GINSBURG dissented.]

SECTION 3. FORM OF EXAMINATION

C. LAY OPTIONS

Page 359, Section 3, Note 6A. (See also p. 954):

United States v. Yannotti

United States Court of Appeals for the Second Circuit.
541 F.3d 112 (2d Cir. 2008), cert. denied, 129 S.Ct. 1648 (2009).

■ B.D. PARKER, JR., CIRCUIT JUDGE:

Michael Yannotti appeals from a judgment of conviction in the United States District Court for the Southern District of New York

SECTION 3 FORM OF EXAMINATION

(*Scheindlin, J.*). The jury convicted him of conspiring to engage in racketeering in violation of the Racketeer Influenced and Corrupt Organizations ("RICO") Act. *See* 18 U.S.C. § 1962(d). The district court sentenced Yannotti principally to 240 months' incarceration. Yannotti's appeal raises several issues. We consider whether one of the counts of conviction was time-barred, whether the district court properly admitted certain intercepted communications, and whether the evidence was sufficient to support his conviction for racketeering conspiracy. We also review the reasonableness of his sentence. We affirm.

. . .

Yannotti next asserts that Andrew DiDonato, a government witness, provided inadmissible opinion testimony which did not conform to the definition of lay testimony under Federal Rule of Evidence 701 because it was based on DiDonato's specialized knowledge as a member of the Gambino Crime Family. DiDonato was allowed to testify about comments made by Yannotti during the two intercepted phone conversations. Yannotti complains that the government did not seek to admit this testimony as expert opinion testimony under Rule 702 and that he was not afforded the protections provided by Federal Rule of Criminal Procedure 16(a)(1)(G). The government, on the other hand, claims that DiDonato was not an expert as contemplated by Rule 702 because he acquired his particular knowledge about loansharking through experience as a member of the conspiracy, rather than through specialized study or training.

Under Rule 701, a lay witness' testimony "in the form of opinions or inferences is limited to those opinions or inferences which are (a) rationally based on the perception of the witness, (b) helpful to a clear understanding of the witness' testimony or the determination of a fact in issue, and (c) not based on scientific, technical, or other specialized knowledge within the scope of Rule 702." Fed.R.Evid. 701. A rational perception is one involving first-hand knowledge or observation. *United States v. Rea*, 958 F.2d 1206, 1215 (2d Cir.1992). The advisory note to the 2000 Amendments to Rule 701 provides that "most courts have permitted the owner or officer of a business to testify to the value or projected profits of the business, without the necessity of qualifying the witness as an ... expert.... Such opinion testimony is admitted not because of experience, training or specialized knowledge within the realm of an expert, but because of the particularized knowledge that the witness has by virtue of his or her position in the business." Fed.R.Evid. 701, advisory committee's note. In contrast under Rule 702, a witness purporting to offer expert opinion testimony must be first qualified to offer this testimony on the basis of his knowledge, skill, or education. Fed.R.Evid. 702.

Although Yannotti challenges the admissibility of DiDonato's testimony under Rule 701 only on the ground that it derived from specialized knowledge in contravention of the third requirement under Rule 701, we conclude that DiDonato's testimony easily met both the first and second requirements under Rule 701, which are that the testimony be "rationally based on the perception of the witness" and "helpful to a clear understanding of the witness' testimony or the determination of a fact in issue." *Id.*

First, DiDonato's testimony was rationally based on his own perception because it derived from his direct participation in the loansharking activities of the charged enterprise, not on participation in the loansharking activities of some unrelated criminal scheme.[1] Second, there is little question that DiDonato's testimony was helpful to the jury. As we have explained in another context, individuals engaging in illicit activities rarely describe their transactions in an open or transparent manner and the government may call witnesses to provide insight into coded language through lay opinion testimony. *See United States v. Garcia,* 291 F.3d 127, 139 (2d Cir.2002). The conversation between Yannotti and the individual identified by the government as "Andy" was cryptic and required interpretation. As discussed earlier, DiDonato explained that the individual collecting the debts informed the loansharking victim about the amount of the weekly interest by referring to a single number or "points." DiDonato stated that in the phone call with "Andy," Yannotti was seeking exorbitant amounts of interest at regular intervals ranging from two hundred to six hundred dollars. Given its discretion in such matters, the district court did not err in allowing DiDonato to provide interpretative testimony because the "language on the tape [was] ... punctuated with ambiguous references to events that are clear only to the conversants." *United States v. Aiello,* 864 F.2d 257, 265 (2d Cir.1988) (internal quotation marks and alterations omitted). Accordingly, we find that DiDonato's testimony met the requirements of Rule 701 and was properly admitted as lay opinion testimony.

Mindful of making explicit the requirements for lay witness testimony in comparison to expert testimony, we now conclude that where a witness derives his opinion solely from insider perceptions of a conspiracy of which he was a member, he may share his perspective as to aspects of the scheme about which he has gained knowledge as a lay witness subject to Rule 701, not as an expert subject to Rule 702. *See United States v. Rigas,* 490 F.3d 208, 225 (2d Cir.2007) (concluding the district

---

1. This distinction applies equally to evaluating the admissibility of agent testimony. An undercover agent whose infiltration of a criminal scheme has afforded him particular perceptions of its methods of operation may offer helpful lay opinion testimony under Rule 701 even as to co-conspirators' actions that he did not witness directly. By contrast, an investigative agent who offers an opinion about the conduct or statements of conspirators based on his general knowledge of similar conduct learned through other investigations, review of intelligence reports, or other special training, does not meet the requirements of Rule 701 and must qualify as an expert pursuant to Rule 702. *See United States v. Garcia,* 413 F.3d 201, 216 (2d Cir.2005).

court did not abuse its discretion in allowing a lay witness to testify about an organization's fraudulent financial conduct where that witness made first-hand observations and was well aware of the organization's financial misstatements). No different conclusion is mandated by Rule 701's requirement that a lay opinion must be the product of "reasoning processes familiar to the average person in everyday life," and not "scientific, technical, or other specialized knowledge." *United States v. Garcia,* 413 F.3d 201, 216–17 (2d Cir.2005). While we do not profess that loansharking is an activity about which the average person has knowledge, we find that the opinion DiDonato reached from his own loansharking experience derived from a reasoning process familiar to average persons. In short, his opinion did not depend on the sort of specialized training that scientific witnesses or statisticians rely upon when interpreting the results of their own experiments or investigations.

. . .

D. Cross-Examination

Page 367. At end of Note 5, add:

In State v. Vogelsberg, 724 N.W.2d 649 (Wis. App. 2006), cert. denied, 2007 WL 811699, the court held that Crawford v. Washington, Supp. p. 615, did not overrule Maryland v. Craig, and that placing a screen so that a child witness would not see the defendant did not violate the defendant's Confrontation Clause right where the trial court had made a particularized inquiry into the risk of trauma to the child, even though it had not made a determination whether the trauma would have caused such distress as to impair the child's ability to communicate. It may be noted that Justice Scalia, the author of the Court's opinion in *Crawford*, dissented in *Craig*.

Section 4. Credibility

B. Discrediting

2. OPPONENT'S WITNESS

Page 405, following Note on "Impeachment Through Contradiction":

United States v. Gilmore

United States Court of Appeals for the Third Circuit.
553 F.3d 266 (3d Cir. 2009).

■ Smith, Circuit Judge.

This case presents us with a textbook example of how trial counsel may properly use past criminal conduct to impeach a witness' testimony by contradiction. . . .

On June 26, 2006, Appellant Walter Gilmore called Cesar Severino, a suspected drug dealer, and requested that they meet in person. After the meeting, Severino contacted Julio Lebron and asked him to deliver a kilogram of cocaine from Philadelphia, PA, to Camden, NJ. Lebron agreed. Upon arriving in Camden, Lebron went to Severino's house where Severino tested the cocaine in Lebron's presence.

That evening, Gilmore called Severino and told him to "bring 2 99 cent [ ] sodas and come to my house." (J.A. 32.) Severino then left his home carrying the cocaine in a black plastic grocery bag. After arriving at Gilmore's house, Severino walked in with a black plastic grocery bag, stayed for about five minutes, and left without it.

When Severino returned home, he paid Lebron $20,000 for the cocaine. Lebron took the money, put it in his wife's purse, and began to drive back to Philadelphia. Along the way, police stopped Lebron's car for speeding, and recovered $20,418 from Lebron's wife's purse.

. . .

During his direct examination, Gilmore and his attorney had the following exchange:

Q: After you were indicted in this case, you got a chance to go through the evidence?

A: Uh-huh.

Q: That they had against you to show that you were a drug dealer, correct?

A: Yes.

Q: And we went through that evidence, didn't we?

A: Yes, we did.

Q: And you see any evidence in this case that you're a drug dealer, sir?

A: No, I didn't sell no drugs. *I never did.* (J.A. 743–44) (emphasis added).

Before beginning its cross-examination, the Government advised the District Court that it intended to ask Gilmore about two prior felony drug distribution convictions[1] in order to contradict his sworn statement that he never sold drugs. Gilmore objected. The District Court overruled the objection, stating that it was going to permit the government to cross examine [Gilmore] on that conviction, to contradict his statement that he's never sold drugs. (J.A. 745.) The District Court, however, would not allow the Government to offer the certified judgments into evidence unless Gilmore denied the convictions. The District Court also informed the parties that it would issue a limiting instruction to the jury to use the convictions only for credibility purposes and not as evidence of guilt.

1. [Some footnotes omitted.]

SECTION 4 CREDIBILITY

Pursuant to the District Court's ruling, the Government cross-examined Gilmore about his prior drug convictions:

Q: Mr. Gilmore, you testified on direct that you never sold drugs, correct?

A: Yes, I did.

Q: Isn't it a fact, Mr. Gilmore, that you were convicted here in the Superior Court of Camden County on May 22nd, 1992 of possession with intent to distribute [controlled dangerous substances]? And possession of [controlled dangerous substances] with intent to distribute within a thousand feet of a school?

A: That was a long time ago.

Q: But you were convicted of selling drugs?

A: Yes, I was, a long time ago, and I changed my life around when I got out.

(J.A. 788.) The District Court provided a limiting instruction to the jury following this testimony, and repeated that instruction in its final charge. The Government did not offer any additional proof of the convictions into evidence.

. . .

At the outset, we reject Gilmore's assertion that the District Court admitted the evidence of his prior felony convictions for an improper purpose under Rule 404(b). Rule 404(b) prohibits the admission of evidence of past crimes "to prove the character of a person in order to show action in conformity therewith." Fed.R.Evid. 404(b). It does not, however, bar the use of such evidence for other purposes. *United States v. Boone*, 279 F.3d 163, 187 (3d Cir.2002). Here, the District Court permitted the Government to ask Gilmore about his prior convictions for another purpose, namely to contradict Gilmore's testimony that he never sold drugs.

Impeachment by contradiction is a means of "policing the 'defendant's obligation to speak the truth in response to proper questions.'" *United States v. Greenidge*, 495 F.3d 85, 99 (3d Cir.2007) (quoting *United States v. Havens*, 446 U.S. 620, 626, 100 S.Ct. 1912, 64 L.Ed.2d 559 (1980)). Accordingly, "[w]here a defendant testifies on direct examination regarding a specific fact, the prosecution may prove on cross-examination that the defendant lied as to that fact." *Id.* (quoting *United States v. Gambino*, 951 F.2d 498, 503 (2d Cir.1991)). Rule 607 of the Federal Rules of Evidence authorizes impeachment by contradiction, and Rule 403 governs its application. *Id.* Therefore, the Government may impeach a defendant's testimony with contradictory evidence unless the "probative value [of the evidence] is substantially outweighed by the danger of unfair prejudice, confusion of the issues, or misleading the jury, or by considerations of undue delay, waste of time, or needless presentation of cumulative evidence." Fed.R.Evid. 403.

Here, the District Court did not abuse its discretion in allowing the Government to ask Gilmore about his two prior felony drug convictions. Gilmore's denial concerning his involvement in drug sales was unqualified; he testified that he "never" sold drugs. His prior convictions indicate otherwise and are of undisputable probative value. Certainly, any similarities between the nature of Gilmore's prior drug convictions and his allegedly criminal conduct in this case have the potential to cause unfair prejudice; however, the District Court minimized that potential by not allowing the Government to enter the certified judgments into evidence unless Gilmore denied the convictions, and by twice issuing a limiting instruction to the jury.

Our conclusion is consistent with those reached by other courts of appeal. *See, e.g., United States v. Bender,* 265 F.3d 464, 470–71 (6th Cir.2001) (permitting the government to cross-examine the defendant about prior drug trafficking convictions because she testified on direct examination that she had never sold drugs and did not start using them until 1992); *United States v. Norton,* 26 F.3d 240, 243–45 (1st Cir.1994) (affirming the District Court's decision to allow the government to cross-examine the defendant about his prior conviction for unlawfully carrying a firearm after the defendant testified that "I never had a gun in my life in that car. Or on my possession or anywhere"); *United States v. Lopez,* 979 F.2d 1024, 1032–35 (5th Cir.1992) (allowing the government to produce a record of the defendant's prior conviction for possession of marijuana in order to impeach the defendant's testimony that he had never seen the drug in person). Like Gilmore, the defendants in each of those cases had prior convictions that belied their blanket denials on the witness stand of ever engaging in conduct similar to the charged conduct. Like the District Court here, the trial courts in each of those cases issued a limiting instruction to the jury. *Bender,* 265 F.3d at 471; *Norton,* 26 F.3d at 245; *Lopez,* 979 F.2d at 1032. Like the courts of appeal in those cases, we hold that the District Court did not abuse its discretion here.

Gilmore suggests that the ages of his convictions should weigh against their admissibility. Indeed, Rule 609(b) sets two conditions on the use of a prior felony conviction to attack the credibility of a witness if the conviction is over ten years old: 1) its probative value must substantially outweigh its prejudicial effect, and 2) the proponent must give advance written notice to the adverse party that is sufficient to give the adverse party a fair opportunity to contest its use. Fed.R.Evid. 609(b).

Rule 609, however, does not govern here. Rule 609 controls the use of prior felony convictions to impeach a witness' general character for truthfulness, but impeachment by contradiction concerns the use of evidence to impeach a witness' specific testimony. *See Norton,* 26 F.3d at

243–44 (noting that "Rule 609 evidence is admissible for the purpose of attacking credibility generally," but that "[p]rior convictions are admissible under Rules 402 and 403 to contradict specific testimony"); *Lopez,* 979 F.2d. at 1033 ("The fundamental problem with the application of either Rule 608 or 609 is that neither rule applies 'in determining the admissibility of relevant evidence introduced to contradict a witness's testimony as to a material issue.'" (citations omitted)). Accordingly, prior felony convictions more than ten years old may be used to impeach by contradiction even if they do not satisfy Rule 609's balancing and notice conditions. *See Norton,* 26 F.3d at 244 (affirming the use of a twenty-nine year-old conviction because it was admissible under Rules 402 and 403); *Lopez,* 979 F.2d at 1032–34 (upholding the use of a seventeen year-old conviction to impeach by contradiction because it passed Rule 403 balancing); *see also Bender,* 265 F.3d at 470–71 (allowing the use of two twelve year-old convictions to impeach the credibility of a witness who had made "misleading" statements).

Notwithstanding Rule 609's inapplicability, a prior conviction's age may still bear on the Rule 403 analysis required for impeachment by contradiction. For example, a conviction's age may affect its probative value. A witness' broad denial of ever selling drugs makes any drug sale conviction probative, regardless of its age. A more limited denial like "I don't sell drugs," however, may make the probative value of a prior drug sale conviction dependent on its age; the more recent the conviction, the more probative it will be. Additionally, the age of a conviction may influence its potential for unfair prejudice. Under certain circumstances, an older conviction might even be less prejudicial than a more recent one. *See Norton,* 26 F.3d at 244–45 (remarking that the fact that "[t]he conviction was 29 years old, and ... [defendant's] transgression had occurred many years ago, when he was a 'very young man'" helped minimize the prejudicial effect of the conviction). Accordingly, a district judge faced with the proffer of past criminal conduct to impeach a witness' testimony by contradiction may properly consider the age of that conviction using standard Rule 403 analysis, though without resort to Rule 609.

Here, the ages of Gilmore's prior convictions offer him no aid. Any prior drug sale conviction, regardless of age, is highly probative of whether Gilmore "never did" sell drugs. Any unfair prejudice resulting from the ages of the proffered convictions does not substantially outweigh this probative value.

. . .

Gilmore's complete denial of ever selling drugs opened the door to his prior felony drug convictions. The District Court did not abuse its discretion by giving the Government permission to step through that door. Accordingly, we will affirm the District Court's judgment.

Page 405, following Note on "Impeachment through Contradictions":

United States v. Kincaid–Chauncey, 556 F.3d 923, 929–34 (9th Cir.), cert. denied, 130 S.Ct. 795 (2009):

Because the testimony that was sought to be contradicted came out on cross-examination, the Third Circuit Court did not abuse its discretion by forbidding the contradiction.

a. Bias, Interest and Corruption

Page 412. Note 2. After 2d paragraph of Note, add:

United States v. Reid, 2008 WL 4876822 (2d Cir. 2008), cert. denied, 129 S.Ct. 2382 (2009). "Reid also claims that the District Court improperly curtailed his cross-examination of the government's cooperating witnesses. We review this decision for abuse of discretion and see none. Reid already had elicited testimony from the cooperating witnesses reflecting their motivation to lie and their extensive criminal histories. In addition, the District Court was understandably reluctant to expose the jury to potentially highly prejudicial information regarding both the potential sentences the witnesses would have faced had they been charged and convicted under 18 U.S.C. § 924(c), and the sentence Reid actually faced under that statute. For these reasons, we hold that the District Court's curtailment of Reid's cross-examination on this point was not an abuse of discretion."

b. Prior Convictions

Page 422. Note 5. After this Note, add:

United States v. Osazuwa

United States Court of Appeals for the Ninth Circuit, 2009.
564 F.3d 1169.

■ GRABER, Circuit Judge:

Defendant Daniel Osazuwa was convicted of assaulting a federal prison guard while he was incarcerated for failing to pay restitution associated with a bank fraud conviction. Defendant and the guard, who were the only two eyewitnesses, unsurprisingly offered different accounts of the events. The government cross-examined Defendant concerning his veracity. Defendant challenges the government's use, as impeachment evidence, of the facts underlying his bank fraud conviction. We hold that the district court abused its discretion in admitting that evidence and, accordingly, reverse and remand for a new trial.

FACTUAL AND PROCEDURAL HISTORY

Defendant was convicted of bank fraud in 2003. He was sentenced to one day in jail, restitution, and a period of supervised release. His supervised release was revoked in 2007 for failure to pay restitution and, consequently, he was sentenced to 90 days of incarceration at the Metropolitan Detention Center ("MDC") in Los Angeles.

SECTION 4 CREDIBILITY

The incident in question occurred three weeks before Defendant's scheduled release date. Defendant had been transferred to a transitional unit for inmates whose releases were imminent. Officer Oscar Medina testified at trial that, sometime in the morning, he saw Defendant wearing green prison clothing, rather than the khaki clothing that inmates in the transitional unit are required to wear. Medina asked Defendant to change into khaki clothes. The next time Medina saw Defendant, he was still wearing green clothing, so Medina again asked him to change. Shortly thereafter, Medina saw Defendant grab a loaf of bread from the kitchen, which was against MDC's rules. Medina shouted at Defendant to drop the bread, which Defendant did. Medina testified that Defendant cursed at him, but Defendant denied swearing at Medina. Medina called MDC's Activities Lieutenant, who instructed Medina to secure Defendant in his cell so that the Lieutenant could question him about the incident. Another lieutenant checked Defendant's disciplinary record and reported to Medina that Defendant was a "moderate inmate without any prior incidents." When the Activities Lieutenant did not arrive, the second lieutenant gave Medina permission to unlock Defendant's cell and explain to him that he would be placed in official lockdown status if he refused to change his clothing.

From this point on, Defendant's and Medina's versions of the events diverge considerably. Medina testified that when he entered the cell, Defendant stood up and clenched his fists in a fighting position, prompting Medina to activate his body alarm to call for assistance. Medina stated that Defendant "launched" forward and threw two punches, the second of which hit Medina in the back of the head when he turned his face to avoid being hit. Medina responded with a "bear hug" to stop the punches, but Defendant moved forward and Medina lost his footing, causing both men to fall. Medina hit his head on the cell floor and blacked out for a few seconds. When he came to, he testified, Defendant was spitting on him. Medina got up, pinned Defendant to the cell wall, and let the officer who arrived to assist Medina in removing Defendant from the cell. Medina suffered a bruised rib, a swollen hand, and a cut behind his ear.

By contrast, Defendant testified that Medina was frowning when he entered the cell, so Defendant walked toward him. Medina was talking fast, so Defendant patted him and told him to relax. Medina responded to the patting by hitting Defendant's hand back. In Defendant's version, Medina wobbled while pushing Defendant's hands away and grabbed Defendant's shirt for balance, causing both men to fall. Defendant denied ever punching Medina, "launching" forward at him, or spitting in his face.

On direct examination, Defendant was asked what sentence of incarceration he had received for his 2003 bank fraud conviction. Defendant truthfully answered that he was sentenced to, and served, one day in jail. On cross-examination, the government asked a series of questions related to the dishonest conduct that led to Defendant's bank fraud conviction:

Q: Mr. [Osazuwa,] you have been convicted of lying before, haven't you?

A: Lying?

Q: Yes. Lying.

A: I wouldn't—I don't understand. Could you—

Q: Lying means you don't tell the truth.

A: I can't—I pled—I plead [sic] to fraud, yes, but not lying.

Q: Well, weren't you lying as part of your bank fraud?

A: To whom?

Q: Well, you tell us.

A: Tell you?

Q: To anyone. Who were you lying to as part of your bank fraud, sir?

A: Oh, to the bank, yes.

Q: To the bank?

A: Yes.

Q: So you did lie to the bank?

A: Yes. To—

Q: To get some money; right?

A: Yes.

Q: In fact, you lied about who you were to the bank to get some money; right?

A: Yes.

Q: You presented a bank in Ohio with a Visa card in another person's name; correct?

[DEFENSE COUNSEL]: Your Honor, I am going to object to the extent of this. I think the prosecutor can ask the fact of the conviction, but nothing more.

THE COURT: Well, no. I will allow a few more questions.

Q: You presented a Visa card in someone else's name to a bank in Ohio; right?

A: Yes.

. . . .

Q: In fact, you had taken over that person's credit card account by lying—

[DEFENSE COUNSEL]: Your Honor, again, I am going to object to the particulars of the conviction.

THE COURT: Overruled.

Q: In fact, you had taken over that person's credit card account by lying to the credit card company that you were, in fact, that person; isn't that right?

A: Yes, sir.

Q: And that's how you got the money; right?

A: Yes, sir.

Q: You had that person's mail delivered to your address, pretending that that was the other person's address. That's a lie, too, isn't it, sir?

A: Yes. We are talking about 1997; right?

Q: That's correct.

. . . .

Q: In fact, you even admitted to your probation officer, didn't you, that you had a fake identification in another person's name; right?

. . . .

[DEFENSE COUNSEL]: Your Honor, again I am going to object.

THE COURT: Sustained. Why don't you move on, [Prosecutor].

Q: In fact, you also, as part of your bank fraud—you also lied to get office space in someone else's name; isn't that correct?

[DEFENSE COUNSEL]: Again, I am going to object to the prosecutor going into all the details of the conviction. [Defendant] has admitted that he was convicted, and I don't think the prosecutor can inquire further than what he has already. I don't believe that the purpose of cross is to go through everything that happened in 1997.

At this point, the district court called for a sidebar conference and acknowledged that it did not know the full contours of the law regarding whether the underlying facts of the conviction could properly be used for impeachment. The court asked the parties to submit briefing on this point and dismissed the jury for the day. The next morning, before the jury returned, the court decided that the government should be allowed to use specific instances of untruthfulness as impeachment because Defendant had "opened the door" to this line of questioning by attempting to minimize the seriousness of his conduct. This minimization occurred, in the court's view, when Defendant (truthfully) stated that he had served only one day in custody for the bank fraud conviction. Therefore, the court held that Defendant had opened the door to the evidence of prior acts that otherwise would have been inadmissible as beyond the limits of Federal Rule of Evidence 609.

The court also ruled that the evidence was admissible under Federal Rule of Evidence 608 as past specific instances probative of untruthfulness. The court stated that Rule 608 "clearly allows specific instances of untruthfulness to be introduced but not to be proved by extrinsic evidence." The court further held that the extent of the questioning was not improper because it had taken only a few minutes, but that the issue whether Defendant had lied to his probation officer was irrelevant and could not be mentioned again. After the jury returned, the court gave a limiting instruction about the proper use of the impeachment evidence. The prosecutor continued cross-examination, asking Defendant whether he had given a false name on two specific occasions, and then moved on to another topic. The government did not mention bank fraud in its closing argument.

The jury returned a guilty verdict. Defendant timely appeals, arguing that the court impermissibly allowed the government to elicit the facts underlying his bank fraud conviction.

. . .

A. *Rule 608*

Defendant first argues that the district court erred in holding that the admission of the facts underlying his bank fraud conviction was warranted under Rule 608....

The crux of Defendant's argument is that Rule 608 applies only to specific instances of conduct that were *not* the basis of a criminal conviction. Evidence relating to a conviction, he argues, is treated solely under Rule 609. For the following reasons, we agree.

We begin by noting, as one of our sister circuits has, that the interplay between Rules 608 and 609 is complex. *See United States v. Cudlitz*, 72 F.3d 992, 995 (1st Cir.1996) ("The rules governing this subject—cross-examining a criminal defendant about prior wrongs—are among the most complex and confusing in the entire law of evidence."). We attempt here to clarify the relationship between these two rules.

"We interpret the legislatively enacted Federal Rules of Evidence as we would any statute." *Daubert v. Merrell Dow Pharms., Inc.*, 509 U.S. 579, 587, 113 S.Ct. 2786, 125 L.Ed.2d 469 (1993). We begin with the text of Rule 608, which we recognize is ambiguous. Defendant argues that Rule 608 exempts from its coverage a witness' prior criminal convictions and instead delegates to Rule 609 any questions relating to such convictions. The government advances a different construction of Rule 608, arguing that the rule is concerned solely with the admissibility of extrinsic evidence. In the government's view, Rule 608 provides only that, while specific instances of the conduct of a witness may not be proved by extrinsic evidence, extrinsic evidence is admissible to prove criminal convictions. Both Defendant's and the government's constructions are plausible. *See* H. Richard Uviller, *Credence, Character, and the*

Rules of Evidence: Seeing Through the Liar's Tale, 42 Duke L.J. 776, 804–05, 822 (1993) (advocating for the "extrinsic evidence" reading of the rule but noting that, in a questionnaire sent to 300 federal district judges, the responding group was "almost evenly divided" between the two readings).

Because the plain meaning of the rule is not apparent from its text alone, we turn to legislative history. The 1972 advisory committee's notes to Rule 608(b) support Defendant's "delegation" construction of the rule. The notes provide that "[p]articular instances of conduct, *though not the subject of criminal conviction,* may be inquired into on cross-examination" and "[c]*onviction of crime* as a technique of impeachment *is treated in detail in Rule 609, and here is merely recognized as an exception to the general rule excluding evidence* of specific incidents for impeachment purposes." Fed.R.Evid. 608 advisory committee's notes (1972) (emphases added). Those comments suggest that evidence relating to convictions falls within the exclusive purview of Rule 609.

. . .

We further recognize the unfairness that would result if evidence relating to a conviction is prohibited by Rule 609 but admitted through the "back door" of Rule 608. *See* Donald H. Ziegler, *Harmonizing Rules 609 and 608(b) of the Federal Rules of Evidence,* 2003 Utah L.Rev. 635, 677 (2003) ("[I]t plainly seems unfair to forbid impeachment under Rule 609[ ] but allow the defendant to be questioned about the underlying acts under Rule 608(b).").

The government's citation to *United States v. Hurst,* 951 F.2d 1490, 1500–01 (6th Cir.1991), is unavailing. In *Hurst,* the court permitted brief questioning under Rule 608(b) about the conduct leading to the conviction because the name of the offense, subornation of perjury, did not convey enough information to the jury to assess how the conviction related to the witness' credibility. *Id.* at 1501. Bank fraud, the name of the offense at issue here, is more self-explanatory than subornation of perjury. Moreover, the dishonesty aspect of the crime was covered adequately by the initial questioning, to which Defendant did not object. Therefore, *Hurst* is not particularly persuasive.

The government also argues on policy grounds that it does not make sense to bar inquiry into dishonest acts just because a witness was eventually convicted for them. But that argument ignores that evidence of a prior conviction for dishonest acts can be far more prejudicial to a defendant than evidence of dishonest acts that have not been held to violate the law. Under the government's interpretation, a bad act resulting in a conviction would be, in a sense, counted twice—once by presenting the bad act itself and once by presenting the conviction that flowed from it. The risk of unfair prejudice or undue emphasis is the reason why Rule 609 and its related case law carefully guide the admission of prior convictions and their underlying facts.

Echoing the observations of the Fifth, Eighth, and Tenth Circuits, we hold that Rule 608(b) permits impeachment only by specific acts that have not resulted in a criminal conviction. Evidence relating to impeachment by way of criminal conviction is treated exclusively under Rule 609, to which we now turn.

B. *Rule 609*

The next question is whether the impeachment evidence was properly admitted under Rule 609, which provides in part: "[E]vidence that any witness has been convicted of a crime shall be admitted regardless of the punishment, if it readily can be determined that establishing the elements of the crime required proof or admission of an act of dishonesty or false statement by the witness." Fed.R.Evid. 609(a)(2).

It is undisputed that bank fraud is an act of dishonesty, so the offense falls under Rule 609(a)(2). But the scope of inquiry into prior convictions is limited. " '[A]bsent exceptional circumstances, evidence of a prior conviction admitted for impeachment purposes may not include collateral details and circumstances attendant upon the conviction.' " *United States v. Sine,* 493 F.3d 1021, 1036 n. 14 (9th Cir.2007) (quoting *United States v. Rubio,* 727 F.2d 786, 797 n. 5 (9th Cir.1983)). Generally, "only the prior conviction, its general nature, and punishment of felony range [are] fair game for testing the defendant's credibility." *United States v. Albers,* 93 F.3d 1469, 1480 (10th Cir.1996); *see also United States v. Gordon,* 780 F.2d 1165, 1176 (5th Cir.1986) (limiting cross-examination to "the number of convictions, the nature of the crimes and the dates and times of the convictions" and excluding "the particular facts of [the defendant's] previous offenses").

The scope of the inquiry is limited because of the unfair prejudice and confusion that could result from eliciting details of the prior crime. *See United States v. Robinson,* 8 F.3d 398, 410 (7th Cir.1993) (holding that the impeaching party is not "entitled to harp on the witness's crime, parade it lovingly before the jury in all its gruesome details, and thereby shift the focus of attention from the events at issue in the present case to the witness's conviction in a previous case") (internal quotations marks omitted); *United States v. Roenigk,* 810 F.2d 809, 815 (8th Cir.1987) ("The problem with excessive references to the details of prior criminal conduct is that the jury is likely to infer that the defendant is more likely to have committed the offense for which he is being tried than if he had previously led a blameless life.").

The government does not argue in this case that its cross-examination of Defendant stayed within the established bounds of inquiry under Rule 609. It instead asserts that Defendant "opened the door" to questions about his specific dishonest acts because his testimony about serving only one day in prison minimized the seriousness of his bank fraud offense. We disagree.

SECTION 4 CREDIBILITY

In a criminal prosecution, the government may introduce otherwise inadmissible evidence when the defendant "opens the door" by introducing potentially misleading testimony. *United States v. Beltran–Rios,* 878 F.2d 1208, 1212 (9th Cir.1989). A defendant may open the door by minimizing, or attempting to explain away, a prior conviction. *See, e.g., United States v. Baylor,* 97 F.3d 542, 545 (D.C.Cir.1996) (noting that "a witness may 'open the door' to more extensive cross-examination by attempting to minimize the conduct for which he was convicted"). If a defendant opens the door, the prosecution may "introduce evidence on the same issue to rebut any *false* impression that might have resulted from the earlier admission." *Sine,* 493 F.3d at 1037 (internal quotation marks omitted).

In *Sine,* we held that a defendant's accurate testimony did not open the door to the introduction of otherwise inadmissible evidence by the government. *Id.* The defendant had stated in his direct testimony that a judge " 'wrote up some bad things about [him]' " in an order from a prior criminal contempt proceeding that was inadmissible in his criminal fraud trial. *Id.* On cross-examination, the government questioned the defendant using specific phrases that appeared in the judge's order, such as "chicanery," "mendacity," and "rife with deceit." *Id.* at 1029. We held that the defendant's "limited" *accurate* testimony about the judge's order "was insufficient to open the door to the government's otherwise impermissible references to the order, as [the defendant] did not introduce an inaccurate portrait of the order itself." *Id.* at 1037. We rejected the government's argument that the defendant's testimony had painted a picture of " 'selflessness and hope,' " thereby opening the door to use of the inadmissible order. *Id.* "Presenting a theory of the case that can be effectively rebutted by otherwise-inadmissible evidence," we held, "does not by itself open the door to using such evidence; only partial, misleading use of the evidence can do so." *Id.* at 1038.

Sine controls here. Defendant was asked how much time he had spent in prison for bank fraud, and he accurately answered "one day." Defendant did not attempt to explain away or otherwise minimize his conviction, as did the defendants in the cases cited by the government. *See, e.g., United States v. Jackson,* 310 F.3d 1053, 1053–54 (8th Cir.2002) (per curiam) (holding that where a defendant testified that he was previously convicted for attempted capital murder because " '[t]here's no self-defense law in Arkansas,' " the prosecution could elicit, on cross-examination, several details of the crime that were inconsistent with the implication that the defendant had acted in self-defense (alteration in original)); *United States v. Perry,* 857 F.2d 1346, 1352 (9th Cir.1988) (holding that the defendant opened the door when he attempted to "explain away" his prior convictions "by offering his own version of the underlying facts" (internal quotation marks omitted)). Defendant did not testify about the underlying facts of, or create a false impression about, his conviction; he truthfully answered the question asked. Under

Sine, that answer was insufficient to open the door to questions about the details of his offense. If the government believed that Defendant's answer about incarceration risked minimizing his crime in the eyes of the jury, it could have questioned Defendant further about the sentence, such as by inquiring how much restitution he had to pay, rather than asking several collateral and prejudicial questions about the underlying dishonest acts.

. . .

For these reasons, we hold that the district court abused its discretion in admitting evidence of the acts underlying Defendant's conviction for bank fraud and that the error was not harmless.

Page 423. After Note 7, add:

In Ohler v. United States, 529 U.S. 753 (2000), the Supreme Court held that when a trial court has ruled in limine that a prior conviction is admissible to impeach a criminal defendant if he takes the stand, and the defendant does take the stand and during his direct testimony reveals the fact of the conviction, possibly to "remove the sting" from its being revealed by the prosecution, the defendant may not cite on appeal the in limine ruling as error. Four dissenters distinguished Luce v. United States on the ground that in that case an appellate court would have difficulty knowing whether the defendant had stayed off the stand because of the in limine ruling or for other reasons, and whether, if he had taken the stand and testified, the prior conviction, if introduced by the prosecution, would have damaged him. In the litigated case, on the other hand, the dissenters said, the defendant had testified, the content of his testimony was known, it was clear that he had mentioned the conviction on direct because of the in limine ruling, and there was a practical certainty that if he had not mentioned it, the prosecution would have brought it out on cross.

See also discussion of in limine rulings, p. 91; of impeaching own witness and "removing the sting," pp. 386, 400.

Page 427. Add to Note 1:

United States of America v. Jefferson

United States Court of Appeals for the Fifth Circuit.
623 F. 3d 227, 233 (5th Cir. 2010).

. . .

Federal Rule of Evidence 609 governs the admissibility of evidence of convictions for impeachment purposes. Relevant here, the rule provides that "[f]or the purpose of attacking the character for truthfulness of a witness ... evidence that any witness has been convicted of a crime shall be admitted regardless of the punishment, if it readily can be determined that establishing the elements of the crime required proof or admission of an act of dishonesty or false statement by the witness." FED R. EVID. 609(a)(2). "Crimes qualifying for admission under Rule 609(a)(2) are not subject to Rule 403 balancing and must be admitted." United States v. Harper, 527 F.3d 396, 408 (5th Cir.2008). Rule 609(a)(2) contains "mandatory language [and] requires that a trial court admit evidence of such crimes to allow a party to impeach an adversary witness's credibility." *Coursey v. Broadhurst*, 888 F.2d 338, 341–42 (5th Cir.1989) (emphasis added).

Jefferson's prior convictions for bribery are crimes involving dishonesty. "[B]ribery is a *crimen falsi* in that it involves dishonesty.... Hence, it is automatically admissible [under] FED.R.EVID. 609(a)(2)." *United States v. Williams*, 642 F.2d 136, 140 (5th Cir.1981).

Jefferson's prior convictions for obstruction of justice in violation of 18 U.S.C. § 1512(b)(3) are admissible under Rule 609(a)(2) "if it readily can be determined that establishing the elements of the crime required proof or admission of an act of dishonesty or false statement by the witness." FED R. EVID. 609(a)(2). Section 1512 provides:

> (b) Whoever knowingly uses intimidation, threatens or corruptly persuades another person, or attempts to do so, or engages in misleading conduct toward another person, with intent to—
>
> ...
>
> (3) hinder, delay, or prevent the communication to a law enforcement officer or judge of the United States of information relating to the commission or possible commission of a Federal offense or a violation of conditions of probation, supervised release, parole, or release pending judicial proceedings.

18 U.S.C. § 1512(b)(3). "Ordinarily, the statutory elements of the crime will indicate whether it is one of dishonesty or false statement." FED. R.EVID. 609, advisory committee's note to 2006 amendments. A defendant can be convicted of § 1512(b)(3) for intimidating or threatening another person—actions which do not involve acts of dishonesty or false statement. The statutory elements of § 1512(b)(3) therefore do not indicate whether Jefferson's convictions thereunder are crimes of dishonesty or false statement warranting automatic admission under Rule 609(a)(2). However, "[w]here the deceitful nature of the crime is not apparent from the statute and the face of the judgment ... a proponent may offer information such as an indictment ... or jury instructions to show that the factfinder had to find ... an act of dishonesty or false statement in order for the witness to have been convicted." *Id*.

We turn to the indictment in the earlier case and conclude that Jefferson's convictions for obstruction of justice involve dishonesty or false statement. The obstruction of justice charges contained therein, counts 6 and 7, read, in relevant part, as follows:

> Count 6: On or about May 21, 2007, in the Eastern District of Louisiana, defendant MOSE JEFFERSON did knowingly and corruptly attempt to persuade Ellenese Brooks-Simms to lie to federal law enforcement authorities....

Count 7: On or about May 25, 2007, in the Eastern District of Louisiana, defendant MOSE JEFFERSON did knowingly and corruptly attempt to persuade Ellenese Brooks-Simms to lie to federal law enforcement authorities....

Indictment at 9, *United States v. Mose Jefferson*, No. 08–CR–085 (E.D.La. Apr. 2, 2009). Because counts 6 and 7 each charge that Jefferson knowingly and corruptly attempted to persuade another to lie to the authorities, we hold that the indictment shows that "the factfinder had to find ... an act of dishonesty or false statement in order for [Jefferson] to have been convicted." FED.R.EVID. 609, advisory committee's note to 2006 amendments. Accordingly, we hold that evidence of Jefferson's obstruction of justice convictions must be admitted for impeachment purposes under Rule 609(a)(2) should he choose to testify.

. . .

"The admission of prior convictions involving dishonesty and false statement is not within the discretion of the Court." FED.R.EVID. 609, advisory committee's note to subsection (a). "Such convictions are peculiarly probative of credibility and, under this rule, are always to be admitted. Thus, judicial discretion granted with respect to the admissibility of other prior convictions is not applicable to those involving dishonesty or false statement." *Id.* Accordingly, we hold that the district court abused its discretion in excluding evidence of Jefferson's convictions for impeachment purposes. [one footnote omitted]

Page 435. Add to Note 5:

United States of America v. Hinkson

United States Court of Appeals for the Ninth Circuit.
611 F.3d 1098 (9th Cir. 2010), cert. denied, 2010 WL 2757419.

The district court deemed the documents bearing on Swisher's military experience "extrinsic evidence probative of a specific incident of untruthfulness" and therefore inadmissible under Rule 608(b).

The district court erred as a matter of law in holding that the Tolbert letter, the Dowling letter, and the other documents in Swisher's file could be excluded under Rule 608(b). The 2003 Advisory Committee Notes to Rule 608 make clear that "the absolute prohibition on extrinsic evidence applies only when the sole reason for proffering that evidence is to attack or support the witness' character for truthfulness." Fed.R.Evid. 608(b), advisory comm. notes (2003). Hinkson did not seek to introduce those documents for the sole "purpose of attacking ... the witness' character for truthfulness." Rather, Hinkson sought to introduce the documents for the specific purpose of contradicting in-court testimony by Swisher. Such evidence is governed by Rule 607, which "permits courts to admit extrinsic evidence that specific testimony is false, because contradicted by other evidence." *United States v. Castillo*, 181 F.3d 1129, 1132 (9th Cir.1999).

SECTION 4 CREDIBILITY

Swisher took the witness stand wearing a Purple Heart lapel pin, thereby affirmatively stating that he had been wounded in combat while serving in the United States armed forces. Rule 801(a) provides, "A 'statement' is ... nonverbal conduct of a person, if it is intended by the person as an assertion." Recall that in his opening statement to the jury three days before, the prosecutor had described Swisher as "a Combat Veteran from Korea during the Korean conflict[who] was not adverse to ... violent, dangerous activity." Particularly given the prosecutor's statement, the jury could hardly avoid understanding Swisher's wearing of the Purple Heart as "non-verbal conduct ... intended ... as an assertion" that he had been wounded in military combat. The documents Hinkson sought to introduce would have directly contradicted that statement, and would have shown Swisher to be a liar.

The district court also erred by refusing to allow Hinkson to introduce this extrinsic evidence to impeach Swisher based on Rule 403. Rule 403 provides:

> Although relevant, evidence may be excluded if its probative value is substantially outweighed by the danger of unfair prejudice, confusion of the issues, or misleading the jury, or by considerations of undue delay, waste of time, or needless presentation of cumulative evidence.

The district court abused its discretion by concluding that it would be unduly time-consuming and confusing to the jury to admit the official military documents showing that Swisher lied about receiving a Purple Heart, and that, when challenged, he lied about having a so-called "replacement DD–214." Although some parts of Swisher's military record may have been difficult for a lay jury to understand, other parts were easy to comprehend....

■ CHIEF JUDGE KOZINSKI, dissenting: [from denial of en banc hearing]

I continue to agree with, and join, that portion of the opinion explaining how we review for abuse of discretion, but now disagree with the application of this standard to the case before us. I had underestimated the trust some jurors would have placed in Swisher if they thought he was a decorated combat veteran, and the likely backlash if they had learned he was a fraud.....

■ W. FLETCHER, CIRCUIT JUDGE, dissenting, joined by KOZINSKI, CHIEF JUDGE, and PREGERSON, WARDLAW, and PAEZ, CIRCUIT JUDGES:

I dissent.

Following a two-week trial in federal district court in Boise, Idaho, a jury convicted David Roland Hinkson of soliciting the murder of three federal officials. The government's star witness supporting the conviction was Elven Joe Swisher. Wearing a Purple Heart lapel pin on the witness stand, Swisher testified that he had told Hinkson that he was a

Korean War combat veteran and that Hinkson, impressed by Swisher's military exploits, solicited him to kill the officials.

. . .

Page 438. Add Note 11:

United States v. Neighbors
United States Court of Appeals for the Seventh Circuit.
590 F.3d 485 (7th Cir. 2009).

■ FLAUM, CIRCUIT JUDGE.

. . .

In 2008, a grand jury indicted David Neighbors, LaFrederick Taylor, Kamal Sims and Trevor Perry for participating in a conspiracy to distribute crack cocaine and powder cocaine. After an eight-day trial, a jury convicted Neighbors, Taylor, Sims and Perry of conspiracy to possess and distribute crack cocaine, finding each responsible for various levels of drugs involved in the conspiracy. The jury also found Neighbors guilty of three additional drug charges and Taylor guilty of a gun charge. The jury acquitted Perry of a felon in possession of a weapon charge and acquitted one of their co-defendants completely. Neighbors, Taylor, Sims, and Perry now appeal various aspects of their consolidated trial and Perry appeals his sentence. For the reasons set forth below, we affirm on all counts.

. . .

Kareem Davidovic testified as a cooperating witness for the government. On direct examination, Davidovic provided the following pieces of incriminating testimony: Davidovic participated in drug transactions involving cocaine powder with Neighbors on at least three occasions; Davidovic was familiar with drug transactions at 619 Jackson and the transactions would occur in the front room closet; Davidovic observed Taylor cook cocaine on the stove in a Pyrex jar; and Davidovic observed Neighbors give Sims money at various times. Davidovic also admitted that he faced a mandatory life sentence and the government agreed to recommend a more lenient sentence if he cooperated.

On cross-examination, Neighbors's attorney asked Davidovic, "Have you ever told anyone that you either have lied in this particular case or intended to lie in this particular case?" (Trial Tr. 180). Davidovic denied ever telling anyone he lied in this case or intended to lie in this case. At that time, Neighbors's attorney attempted to introduce a number of letters Davidovic admitted to writing. One of the letters stated, "I did lie on that Haitian N*****. I said he used to serve me my blow. You know I never F*** with him." The government objected on the grounds that this letter was impermissible extrinsic evidence of a specific instance of untruthfulness. Appellants advanced two arguments to the district court for why the court should admit this evidence. First, appellants argued that this letter directly contradicted Davidovic's statement that he never told anyone that he lied in this case or intended to lie in this case because the Haitian referred to Selmo Cadet, another party arrested in this case. Appellants also argued, "[I]t goes straight to the issue of his truthfulness, veracity, or lack thereof." (Trial Tr. 187). Later in the argument regarding the admissibility of this evidence, appellants also said that the letters constitute an "admission by the witness that he is able to lie and use deceit to achieve his own goals." (Trial Tr. 189). The district court sustained the government's objection and prohibited the introduction of these letters. However, the district court acknowledged that it was willing to revisit its ruling depending on how the evidence developed.

Appellants argue that the district court erred by not allowing them to introduce the letters written by Kareem Davidovic. We review the district court's evidentiary rulings for abuse of discretion. *United States v. McGee*, 408 F.3d 966, 981 (7th Cir.2005). If we identify an error that amounts to an abuse of discretion and a timely objection to the error was raised at trial, we must determine if the error was harmless. *Id.*

As a preliminary matter we must determine if this evidence falls within the ambit of Federal Rule of Evidence 608(b) or Federal Rule of Evidence 613. Rule 608(b) explicitly states, "[s]pecific instances of the conduct of a witness for the purpose of attacking or supporting the witness' character for truthfulness, other than the conviction of crime as provided in rule 609, may not be proved by extrinsic evidence." It is uncontested that these letters are extrinsic evidence and should be excluded if they fall solely within Rule 608(b). However, if Rule 613 governs the admission of these letters, this becomes a much closer issue. Under Rule 613, extrinsic evidence of prior inconsistent statements of a "witness is admissible so long as the witness is afforded an opportunity to explain or deny the same and the opposite party is afforded an opportunity to interrogate the witness thereon."

We specifically addressed the tension between Rule 608(b) and Rule 613 in *United States v. McGee*, 408 F.3d 966, 981–82 (7th Cir.2005). In *McGee*, the government sought to introduce tape-recorded phone calls from the Metropolitan Correctional Center (MCC) in which the defendant, Smith, told his boss an elaborate lie regarding his whereabouts and then called his wife and laughed about the lie he told his boss. 408 F.3d at 980–81. The government prefaced the introduction of these tapes with the question, "Have you ever made up a story regarding your situation in this case to get out of a jam, Mr. Smith?" *Id.* Smith answered, "[N]o." *Id.* The district court allowed the introduction of these tapes based on the contradiction between Smith's answer to the question posed at trial and Smith's admission on the tape that he lied to his boss. *Id.* at 981. In finding that the district court erred in admitting the tapes, we reasoned,

> the force of the MCC phone call recording was not due to a comparison of Smith's statements and his equivocations at trial.

CHAPTER 3 TESTIMONIAL PROOF

Rather, Smith's elaborate lie to his supervisor, in and of itself, cast significant doubt on Smith's character for truthfulness. For this reason, the MCC tape falls squarely within the ambit of Rule 608(b), and it was error for the district court to allow the government to play the tape.

Id. at 982.

Based on our reasoning in *McGee* and the arguments of appellants on the record, Davidovic's letters fall within the ambit of Rule 608(b). Similar to the MCC tapes in *McGee*, the probative value of Davidovic's letters is his underlying lie, not the contradiction between his statement at trial and the content of the letter. This is clear from appellants' arguments that these letters "go[ ] straight to the issue of his truthfulness, veracity, or lack thereof," and that they are an "admission by the witness that he is able to lie and use deceit to achieve his own goals." This is precisely the type of evidence of character for truthfulness that Rule 608(b) controls and prohibits. By asking Davidovic whether he had lied in this case and then arguing that the letters were contradiction evidence admissible under Rule 613, appellants attempted to sneak the letters through the loophole between Rule 608(b) and Rule 613 that we closed in *McGee*.

Moreover, even if we found that Rule 613 governed, these letters still have admissibility problems. The record indicates that the district court found that these letters were not in direct contradiction with Davidovic's trial testimony. Selmo Cadet being the Haitian referred to in the letters is crucial to appellants' argument that these letters directly contradict Davidovic's testimony that he never told lies in this case. Davidovic testified that he was not sure that he knew Selmo Cadet, the only Haitian involved in this case. Therefore, it is unclear from the testimony that the individual mentioned in the letter is Selmo Cadet. The district court made it clear that it would reconsider its ruling depending on how the evidence developed. However, appellants made no further attempts to develop the evidence connecting the Haitian referred to in the letter to Selmo Cadet. Based on this record, the district court did not abuse its discretion in excluding this evidence, even under Rule 613.

. . .

e. Prior Inconsistent Statements

Page 461. Add to first full paragraph:

Robinson v. State of Delaware, 3 A. 3d 257, 264 (2010). A recent decision of the Supreme Court of Delaware held that the trial judge did not exceed his discretion by imposing Queen Caroline procedure; Delaware has adopted Fed. R. of Evid. 613.

Page 463. Note 9, after fourth full paragraph, add:

Kansas v. Ventris, 129 S.Ct. 1841 (2009): A conceded violation of the right to counsel, through the use of an informant who was under instruction to report any incriminating statements that defendant made, although the statements could not be used in the prosecutor's case in chief, they could be used to impeach the defendant when he took the stand. The Court attached significance to the fact that although there was a violation of the right to counsel at the time of the interrogation by the informant, "exclusion comes by way of deterrent sanction rather than to avoid violation of the substantive guarantee." Stevens and Ginsburg, JJ. dissented.

D. MECHANICAL AND CHEMICAL MEANS OF ASSESSING CREDIBILITY

1. THE LIE DETECTOR

Page 471, Section 1, before the last full paragraph in the section:

United States v. Hamilton

United States District Court for the District of New Jersey.
579 F.Supp.2d 637 (D.N.J. 2008).

■ LINARES, DISTRICT JUDGE.

. . .

[But the Court reserved judgment] as to the Government's motion to preclude testimony regarding Hamilton's two offers to take a polygraph test (Docket No. 90). Having reviewed the submissions and having heard oral argument, the Court grants in part and denies in part the Government's motion.

. . .

The Third Circuit has not adopted a *per se* exclusionary rule regarding admissibility of the results of polygraph examinations. *Nawrocki v. Twp. of Coolbaugh,* 34 Fed.Appx. 832, 838 (3d Cir.2002); *United States v. Lee,* 315 F.3d 206, 214 (3d Cir.2003). And while the Third Circuit has yet to opine on the admissibility into evidence of an *offer* to take a polygraph test, other circuit courts have placed the question squarely within the province of the district court's discretion. *See, e.g., United States v. Harris,* 9 F.3d 493, 501–02 (6th Cir.1993) (citing *Wolfel v. Holbrook,* 823 F.2d 970, 972) (6th Cir.1987) ("In limited circumstances, evidence of a party's willingness to submit to a polygraph may, within the discretion of a trial court, become admissible if it is relevant at trial"); *United States v. Elekwachi,* 111 F.3d 139, 1997 WL 174160 at *1 n. 1 (9th Cir.1997) ("the decision of whether to admit polygraph evidence remains discretionary with the trial court.") In the absence of Third Circuit guidance on the issue, this Court exercises its discretion with respect to the admissibility of an offer to take a polygraph test by following the two-step analysis enunciated by the Sixth Circuit—first, determine whether the evidence is relevant under Federal Rule of Evidence 401, and second, conduct the probative versus unfair prejudice balancing test mandated by Federal Rule of Evidence 403. *Murphy v. Cincinnati Ins. Co.,* 772 F.2d 273, 277 (6th Cir.1985).

A. Rule 401

Relevant evidence is "evidence having any tendency to make the existence of any fact that is of consequence to the determination of the action more probable or less probable than it would be without the evidence." Fed.R.Evid. 401. As the language indicates, the "threshold for relevance is low." *Thomas v. Dragovich,* 142 Fed.Appx. 33, 37 (3d Cir.2005); *see also United States v. Paz,* 124 Fed.Appx. 743, 746 (3d Cir.2005) ("[R]elevance is not a difficult condition to satisfy under the Federal Rules of Evidence.")

Count Five of the Superceding Indictment charges Hamilton with "knowingly and willfully mak[ing] a false, fictitious, and fraudulent statement and representation" to the F.B.I. on November 11, 2002, in violation of 18 U.S.C. § 1001. Superceding Indictment, Count Five at ¶ 3. Hamilton argues that the proffered evidence is directly probative of, and relevant to, his state of mind during that interview with Agent Kamerman. Thus, he argues that his offers to undergo a polygraph test—during both the 2002 and 2005 interviews—implicate his consciousness of innocence. They make the fact of whether he acted knowingly less probable that it would be otherwise.

The Government argues that any probative value as to Hamilton's state of mind is diminished significantly—if not altogether eliminated—by the self-serving nature of his offer to take a polygraph. For an offer to be self-serving, however, the offeror must be aware of the consequences of his actions. Thus, with regard to a polygraph, a defendant must know that polygraph results are generally inadmissible in federal court, *United States v. Zhang,* No. CR 98–425, 1999 WL 61416 at *10 n. 6 (D.N.J. Feb.8, 1999), and that offering to take one is inherently a no-lose proposition. Only then can the offer itself be self-serving. Thus,

> [A] guilty defendant could make such offer knowing (1) the government is unlikely to accept his offer and, if they decline, he can attempt to introduce evidence of his offer as consciousness of innocence, or (2) if the government agrees to his offer and he fails the polygraph test, the results are still inadmissible.

United States v. Graziano, 558 F.Supp.2d 304, 325–326 (E.D.N.Y.2008). In most of the cases cited by the Government, including Judge Bianco's recent decision in *Graziano,* a defendant offers to take a polygraph upon the advice of, or in the presence of, counsel. In each case, the presence of counsel immediately calls into question the authenticity of the defendant's offer, thereby undermining its probative value. *See, e.g., United States v. Harris,* 9 F.3d 493, 502 (6th Cir.1993) (defendant's "willingness to submit to polygraph testing, *in the presence of an attorney,* was marginally relevant at best ...")(emphasis added); *Graziano,* 558

F.Supp.2d at 325–26 (finding that defendant offered to take a polygraph during a proffer session with the government held little probative value because of the presence of counsel and the resulting lack of "adverse consequences"). Thus, the defendant's offer to take a polygraph is inherently self-serving because the defendant *knows* that no adverse consequences will result from making the offer. In that scenario, the offer itself clearly sheds no light at all upon the defendant's actual state of mind.

Not so here. Hamilton's November 11, 2002 interview occurred *before* he had obtained counsel. Without the presence of counsel, Hamilton had no way of knowing whether or not his offer would be accepted nor whether it would be admissible in a future court proceeding. Thus, Hamilton's offer was unencumbered by the usual attorney advice that hinders the admissibility of most such offers. As such, his offer to take a polygraph during the 2002 interview is highly probative of his consciousness of innocence—it directly implicates Count Five of the Superceding Indictment.

The same, however, does not hold true with regard to the 2005 interview. As an initial matter, Hamilton's state of mind on November 22, 2005 holds minimal probative value as to whether or not he lied to the FBI three years earlier, on November 11, 2002. Moreover, even that minimal probative value is substantially diminished by the surrounding facts—Hamilton had three years between interviews during which he knew that he was the target of an investigation and during which he likely spoke to an attorney to seek advice as to any potential charges that he might face. Thus, this second offer to take a polygraph is irrelevant to whether he lied in 2002 and it is more likely to have been the by-product of advice from counsel, thereby implicating the self-serving concerns enunciated in *Graziano*.

. . .

The potential for unfair prejudice associated with admission of the polygraph evidence is certainly high. A jury could reasonably infer that the FBI agent chose not to give Hamilton a polygraph test because he feared that the results of the test would help Hamilton's case. Speculating as to why the test was not given or as to what the results would have been had a test been given are exactly the types of imaginative leaps that could unfairly prejudice the Government's case. In *Graziano,* the court found that the "jury's inability to assess the weight to be given such testimony" because of its "lack of understanding about the numerous legal and practical variables that surround such an offer to take a polygraph" is enough to substantiate excluding the evidence. *Graziano,* 558 F.Supp.2d at 326.

Rather than precluding the evidence as per *Graziano,* however, this Court finds that a limiting instruction can cure any resulting unfair prejudice. . . . A limiting instruction warning the jury to consider the evidence only as to Hamilton's state of mind is therefore precisely the right tool to excise any unfair prejudice associated with its admission....

For the reasons set forth above, Hamilton's November 11, 2002 offer to take a polygraph is admissible pursuant to Federal Rules of Evidence 401 and 403. However, his identical November 22, 2005 offer is inadmissible under Rule 401. Thus, the Government's motion is DENIED IN PART AND GRANTED IN PART. An appropriate order accompanies this opinion.

Page 471. After the reference to United States v. Scheffer, add:

See p. 567 supra.

CHAPTER 4

HEARSAY

INTRODUCTION

Page 475. Substitute for last paragraph:

What role does the Confrontation Clause play in criminal cases? Hearsay statements offered against an accused that satisfy a hearsay exception must now be analyzed under the Supreme Court's new Confrontation Clause jurisprudence announced in Crawford v. Washington, 124 S.Ct. 1354 (2004). If the statement is "testimonial," then the statement is inadmissible unless the declarant appears as a witness, or if the accused previously had an adequate opportunity for cross-examination and the declarant is now unavailable. While the meaning of "testimonial" is as yet far from clear, the notes that follow in this supplement indicate

SECTION 2. PRIOR STATEMENTS OF WITNESSES

Page 561. Add to Note 1:

According to Crawford, the answer is "no." See footnote 9.

SECTION 8. FORMER TESTIMONY

Page 747. Add new Note 3 before DiNapoli case:

Statements admitted pursuant to Rule 804(b)(2) satisfy the Crawford test because the rule requires unavailability and an opportunity for cross-examination.

SECTION 9. DYING DECLARATIONS

Page 760. Add new Note 8:

The Court in Crawford suggested that dying declarations might require sui generis treatment.

SECTION 10. FORFEITURE

Consider the following case along with Crawford and the other cases in this section, and also in connection with Section 10, Forfeiture, pages 760–763 in the main volume:

Giles v. California

Supreme Court of the United States, 2008.
554 U.S. 353, 128 S.Ct. 2678, 171 L.Ed.2d 488.

■ JUSTICE SCALIA delivered the opinion of the Court, except as to Part II–D–2.

We consider whether a defendant forfeits his Sixth Amendment right to confront a witness against him when a judge determines that a wrongful act by the defendant made the witness unavailable to testify at trial.

I

On September 29, 2002, petitioner Dwayne Giles shot his ex-girlfriend, Brenda Avie, outside the garage of his grandmother's house. No witness saw the shooting, but Giles' niece heard what transpired from inside the house. She heard Giles and Avie speaking in conversational tones. Avie then yelled "Granny" several times and a series of gunshots sounded. Giles' niece and grandmother ran outside and saw Giles standing near Avie with a gun in his hand. Avie, who had not been carrying a weapon, had been shot six times.... Giles fled the scene after the shooting. He was apprehended by police about two weeks later and charged with murder.

At trial, Giles testified that he had acted in self-defense. Giles described Avie as jealous, and said he knew that she had once shot a man, that he had seen her threaten people with a knife, and that she had vandalized his home and car on prior occasions. He said that on the day of the shooting, Avie came to his grandmother's house and threatened to kill him and his new girlfriend, who had been at the house earlier. He said that Avie had also threatened to kill his new girlfriend when Giles and Avie spoke on the phone earlier that day. Giles testified that after Avie threatened him at the house, he went into the garage and retrieved a gun, took the safety off, and started walking toward the back door of the house. He said that Avie charged at him, and that he was afraid she had something in her hand. According to Giles, he closed his eyes and fired several shots, but did not intend to kill Avie.

Prosecutors sought to introduce statements that Avie had made to a police officer responding to a domestic-violence report about three weeks before the shooting. Avie, who was crying when she spoke, told the officer that Giles had accused her of having an affair, and that after the two began to argue, Giles grabbed her by the shirt, lifted her off the floor, and began to choke her. According to Avie, when she broke free and fell to the floor, Giles punched her in the face and head, and after she broke free again, he opened a folding knife, held it about three feet away from her, and threatened to kill her if he found her cheating on him. Over Giles' objection, the trial court admitted these statements into evidence under a provision of California law that permits admission of out-of-court statements describing the infliction or threat of physical injury on a declarant when the declarant is unavailable to testify at trial and the prior statements are deemed trustworthy. Cal. Evid.Code Ann. § 1370 (West Supp.2008).

A jury convicted Giles of first-degree murder. He appealed. While his appeal was pending, this Court decided in Crawford v. Washington, 541 U.S. 36, 53–54, 124 S.Ct. 1354, 158 L.Ed.2d 177 (2004), that the Confrontation Clause requires that a defendant have the opportunity to confront the witnesses who give testimony against him, except in cases where an exception to the confrontation right was recognized at the time of the founding. The California Court of Appeal held that the admission of Avie's unconfronted statements at Giles' trial did not violate the Confrontation Clause as construed by Crawford because Crawford recognized a doctrine of forfeiture by wrongdoing. 19 Cal.Rptr.3d 843, 847 (2004) (officially depublished). It concluded that Giles had forfeited his right to confront Avie because he had committed the murder for which he was on trial, and because his intentional criminal act made Avie unavailable to testify. The California Supreme Court affirmed on the same ground. 40 Cal.4th 833, 837, 55 Cal.Rptr.3d 133, 152 P.3d 433, 435 (2007). We granted certiorari. 552 U.S. 1136, 128 S.Ct. 976, 169 L.Ed.2d 800 (2008).

II

The Sixth Amendment provides that "[i]n all criminal prosecutions, the accused shall enjoy the right ... to be confronted with the witnesses against him." The Amendment contemplates that a witness who makes testimonial statements admitted against a defendant will ordinarily be present at trial for cross-examination, and that if the witness is unavailable, his prior testimony will be introduced only if the defendant had a prior opportunity to cross-examine him. Crawford, 541 U.S., at 68, 124 S.Ct. 1354. The State does not dispute here, and we accept without deciding, that Avie's statements accusing Giles of assault were testimonial. But it maintains (as did the California Supreme Court) that the Sixth Amendment did not prohibit prosecutors from introducing the statements because an exception to the confrontation guarantee permits the use of a witness's unconfronted testimony if a judge finds, as the judge did in this case, that the defendant committed a wrongful act that rendered the witness unavailable to testify at trial. We held in Crawford that the Confrontation Clause is "most naturally read as a reference to the right of confrontation at common law, admitting only those exceptions established at the time of the founding." We therefore ask whether the theory of forfeiture by wrongdoing accepted by the California Supreme Court is a founding-era exception to the confrontation right.

A

We have previously acknowledged that two forms of testimonial statements were admitted at common law even though they were unconfronted. See id., at 56, n. 6, 62, 124 S.Ct. 1354. The first of these were declarations made by a speaker who was both on the brink of death and aware that he was dying.... Avie did not make the unconfronted statements admitted at Giles' trial when she was dying, so her statements do not fall within this historic exception.

A second common-law doctrine, which we will refer to as forfeiture by wrongdoing, permitted the introduction of statements of a witness who was "detained" or "kept away" by the "means or procurement" of the defendant. See, e.g., Lord Morley's Case, 6 How. St. Tr. 769, 771 (H.L.1666) ("detained"); Harrison's Case, 12 How. St. Tr. 833, 851 (H.L.1692) ("made him keep away"); Queen v. Scaife, 117 Q.B. 238, 242, 117 Eng. Rep. 1271, 1273 (K.B.1851) ("kept away"); see also 2 W. Hawkins, Pleas of the Crown 425 (4th ed. 1762) (hereinafter Hawkins) (same); T. Peake, Compendium of the Law of Evidence 62 (2d ed. 1804) ("sent" away); 1 G. Gilbert, Law of Evidence 214 (1791) ("detained and kept back from appearing by the means and procurement of the prisoner"). The doctrine has roots in the 1666 decision in Lord Morley's Case, at which judges concluded that a witness's having been "detained by the means or procurement of the prisoner," provided a basis to read testimony previously given at a coroner's inquest. 6 How. St. Tr., at 770–771. Courts and commentators also concluded that wrongful procurement of a witness's absence was among the grounds for admission of statements made at bail and committal hearings conducted under the Marian statutes, which directed justices of the peace to take the statements of felony suspects and the persons bringing the suspects before the magistrate, and to certify those statements to the court, . . . This class of confronted statements was also admissible if the witness who made them was dead or unable to travel.

The terms used to define the scope of the forfeiture rule suggest that the exception applied only when the defendant engaged in conduct designed to prevent the witness from testifying. The rule required the witness to have been "kept back" or "detained" by "means or procurement" of the defendant. Although there are definitions of "procure" and "procurement" that would merely require that a defendant have caused the witness's absence, other definitions would limit the causality to one that was designed to bring about the result "procured." See 2 N. Webster, An American Dictionary of the English Language (1828) (defining "procure" as "to contrive and effect" (emphasis added)); ibid. (defining "procure" as "to get; to gain; to obtain; as by request, loan, effort, labor or purchase"); 12 Oxford English Dictionary 559 (2d ed.1989) (def.I(3)) (defining "procure" as "[t]o contrive or devise with care (an action or proceeding); to endeavour to cause or bring about (mostly something evil) to or for a person"). Similarly, while the term "means" could sweep in all cases in which a defendant caused a witness to fail to appear, it can also connote that a defendant forfeits confrontation rights when he uses an intermediary for the purpose of making a witness absent. ("[A] person who intercedes for another or uses influence in order to bring about a desired result"); N. Webster, An American Dictionary of the English Language 822 (1869) ("That through which, or by the help of which, an end is attained").

Cases and treatises of the time indicate that a purpose-based definition of these terms governed. . . .

B

The manner in which the rule was applied makes plain that unconfronted testimony would not be admitted without a showing that the defendant intended to prevent a witness from testifying. In cases where the evidence suggested that the defendant had caused a person to be absent, but had not done so to prevent the person from testifying—as in the typical murder case involving accusatorial statements by the victim—the testimony was excluded unless it was confronted or fell within the dying-declaration exception. Prosecutors do not appear to have even argued that the judge could admit the unconfronted statements because the defendant committed the murder for which he was on trial.

. . .

King v. Dingler, 2 Leach 561, 168 Eng. Rep. 383 (1791), applied the . . . test to exclude unconfronted statements by a murder victim. George Dingler was charged with killing his wife Jane, who suffered multiple stab wounds that left her in the hospital for 12 days before she died. The day after the stabbing, a Magistrate took Jane Dingler's deposition—. . . under oath—"of the facts and circumstances which had attended the outrage committed upon her." 2 Leach, at 561, 168 Eng. Rep., at 383. George Dingler's attorney argued that the statements did not qualify as dying declarations and were not admissible Marian examinations because they were not taken in the presence of the prisoner, with the result that the defendant did not "have, as he is entitled to have, the benefit of cross-examination." Id., at 562, 168 Eng. Rep., at 384. The prosecutor agreed, but argued the deposition should still be admitted because "it was the best evidence that the nature of the case would afford." Id., at 563, 168 Eng. Rep., at 384. . . .

Many other cases excluded victims' statements when there was insufficient evidence that the witness was aware he was about to die. See Thomas John's Case, 1 East 357, 358 (P.C. 1790); Welbourn's Case, 1 East 358, 360 (P.C. 1792); United States v. Woods, 28 F. Cas. 762, 763 (No. 16,760) (CC DC 1834); Lewis v. State, 17 Miss. 115, 120 (1847); Montgomery v. State, 11 Ohio 424, 425–426 (1842); Nelson v. State, 26 Tenn. 542, 543 (1847); Smith v. State, 28 Tenn. 9, 23 (1848). Courts in all these cases did not even consider admitting the statements on the ground that the defendant's crime was to blame for the witness's absence—even when the evidence establishing that was overwhelming. . . .

Similarly, in Smith v. State, supra, the evidence that the defendant had caused the victim's death included, but was not limited to, the defendant's having obtained arsenic from a local doctor a few days before his wife became violently ill; the defendant's paramour testifying at trial that the defendant admitted to poisoning his wife; the defendant's having asked a physician "whether the presence of arsenic could be discovered in the human stomach a month after death"; and, the answer to that inquiry apparently not having been satisfactory, the defendant's having tried to hire a person to burn down the building containing his wife's body. Id., at 10–11. If the State's reading of common law were correct, the dying declarations in these cases and others like them would have been admissible.

Judges and prosecutors also failed to invoke forfeiture as a sufficient basis to admit unconfronted statements in the cases that did apply the dying-declarations exception. This failure, too, is striking. At a murder trial, presenting evidence that the defendant was responsible for the victim's death would have been no more difficult than putting on the government's case in chief. Yet prosecutors did not attempt to obtain admission of dying declarations on wrongful-procurement-of-absence grounds before going to the often considerable trouble of putting on evidence to show that the crime victim had not believed he could recover. See, e.g., King v. Commonwealth, 4 Va., at 80–81 (three witnesses called to testify on the point); Gibson v. Commonwealth, 4 Va. 111, 116–117 (Gen.Ct.1817) (testimony elicited from doctor and witness); Anthony v. State, 19 Tenn. 265, 278–279 (1838) (doctor questioned about expected fatality of victim's wound and about victim's demeanor).

The State offers another explanation for the above cases. It argues that when a defendant committed some act of wrongdoing that rendered a witness unavailable, he forfeited his right to object to the witness's testimony on confrontation grounds, but not on hearsay grounds. See Brief for Respondent 23–24. No case or treatise that we have found, however, suggested that a defendant who committed wrongdoing forfeited his confrontation rights but not his hearsay rights. And the distinction would have been a surprising one, because courts prior to the founding excluded hearsay evidence in large part because it was unconfronted. See, e.g., 2 Hawkins 606 (6th ed. 1787); 2 M. Bacon, A New Abridgment of the Law 313 (1736). As the plurality said in Dutton v. Evans, 400 U.S. 74, 86, 91 S.Ct. 210, 27 L.Ed.2d 213 (1970), "[i]t seems apparent that the Sixth Amendment's Confrontation Clause and the evidentiary hearsay rule stem from the same roots."

The State and the dissent note that common-law authorities justified the wrongful-procurement rule by invoking the maxim that a defendant should not be permitted to benefit from his own wrong. See, e.g., G. Gilbert, Law of Evidence 140–141 (1756) (if a witness was "detained and kept back from appearing by the means and procurement" testimony would be read because a defendant "shall never be admitted to shelter himself by such evil Practices on the Witness, that being to give him Advantage of his own Wrong"). But as the evidence amply shows, the "wrong" and the "evil Practices" to which these statements referred was conduct designed to prevent a witness from testifying. The absence of a forfeiture rule covering this sort of conduct would create an intolerable incentive for defendants to bribe, intimidate, or even kill witnesses against them. There is nothing mysterious about courts' refusal to carry the rationale further. The notion that judges may strip the defendant of a right that the Constitution deems essential to a fair trial, on the basis of a prior judicial assessment that the defendant is guilty as charged, does not sit well with the right to trial by jury. It is akin, one might say, to "dispensing with jury trial because a defendant is obviously guilty." Crawford, 541 U.S., at 62, 124 S.Ct. 1354.

C

Not only was the State's proposed exception to the right of confrontation plainly not an "exceptio[n] established at the time of the founding," id., at 54, 124 S.Ct. 1354; it is not established in American jurisprudence since the founding. American courts never-prior to 1985—invoked forfeiture outside the context of deliberate witness tampering.

This Court first addressed forfeiture in Reynolds v. United States, 98 U.S. 145, 25 L.Ed. 244 (1879), where, after hearing testimony that suggested the defendant had kept his wife away from home so that she could not be subpoenaed to testify, the trial court permitted the government to introduce testimony of the defendant's wife from the defendant's prior trial. On appeal, the Court held that admission of the statements did not violate the right of the defendant to confront witnesses at trial, because when a witness is absent by the defendant's "wrongful procurement," the defendant "is in no condition to assert that his constitutional rights have been violated" if "their evidence is supplied in some lawful way." Reynolds invoked broad forfeiture principles to explain its holding. The decision stated, for example, that "[t]he Constitution does not guarantee an accused person against the legitimate consequences of his own wrongful acts," and that the wrongful-procurement rule "has its foundation" in the principle that no one should be permitted to take advantage of his wrong, and is "the outgrowth of a maxim based on the principles of common honesty.".

Reynolds relied on these maxims (as the common-law authorities had done) to be sure. But it relied on them (as the common-law authorities had done) to admit prior testimony in a case where the defendant had engaged in wrongful conduct designed to prevent a witness's testimony. The Court's opinion indicated that it was adopting the common-law rule. It cited leading common-law cases—Lord Morley's Case, Harrison's Case, and Scaife—described itself as "content with" the "long-established usage" of the forfeiture principle, and admitted prior confronted statements under circumstances where admissibility was open to no doubt under Lord Morley's Case.

If the State's rule had an historical pedigree in the common law or even in the 1879 decision in Reynolds, one would have expected it to be routinely invoked in murder prosecutions like the one here, in which the victim's prior statements inculpated the defendant. It was never invoked in this way. The earliest case identified by the litigants and amici curiae which admitted unconfronted statements on a forfeiture theory without evidence that the defendant had acted with the purpose of preventing the witness from testifying was decided in 1985. United States v. Rouco, 765 F.2d 983 (C.A.11).

In 1997, this Court approved a Federal Rule of Evidence, entitled "Forfeiture by wrongdoing," which applies only when the defendant "engaged or acquiesced in wrongdoing that was intended to, and did, procure the unavailability of the declarant as a witness." Fed. Rule of Evid. 804(b)(6). We have described this as a rule "which codifies the forfeiture doctrine." Davis v. Washington, 547 U.S. 813, 833, 126 S.Ct. 2266, 165 L.Ed.2d 224 (2006). Every commentator we are aware of has concluded the requirement of intent "means that the exception applies only if the defendant has in mind the particular purpose of making the witness unavailable." 5 C. Mueller & L. Kirkpatrick, Federal Evidence § 8:134, p. 235 (3d ed.2007); 5 J. Weinstein & M. Berger, Weinstein's Federal Evidence § 804.03[7][b], p. 804–32 (J. McLaughlin ed., 2d ed.2008); 2 S. Brown, McCormick on Evidence 176 (6th ed.2006).[2] The commentators come out this way because the dissent's claim that knowledge is sufficient to show intent is emphatically not the modern view. See 1 W. LaFave, Substantive Criminal Law § 5.2, p. 340 (2d ed.2003).

In sum, our interpretation of the common-law forfeiture rule is supported by (1) the most natural reading of the language used at common law; (2) the absence of common-law cases admitting prior statements on a forfeiture theory when the defendant had not engaged in conduct designed to prevent a witness from testifying; (3) the common law's uniform exclusion of unconfronted inculpatory testimony by murder victims (except testimony given with awareness of impending death) in the innumerable cases in which the defendant was on trial for killing the victim, but was not shown to have done so for the purpose of preventing testimony; (4) a subsequent history in which the dissent's broad forfeiture theory has not been applied. The first two and the last are highly persuasive; the third is in our view conclusive.

D

1

The dissent evades the force of that third point by claiming that no testimony would come in at common law based on a forfeiture theory unless it was confronted....

. . .

---

2. Only a single state evidentiary code appears to contain a forfeiture rule broader than our holding in this case (and in Crawford) allow. Seven of the 12 States that recognize wrongdoing as grounds for forfeiting objection to out-of-court statements duplicate the language of the federal forfeiture provision that requires purpose, see Del. Rule Evid. 804(b)(6) (2001); Ky. Rule Evid. 804(b)(5) (2004); N.D. Rule Evid. 804(b)(6) (2007); Pa. Rule Evid. 804(b)(6) (2005); Vt. Rule Evid. 804(b)(6) (2004); see also Tenn. Rule Evid. 804(b)(6) (2003) (identical except that it excludes mention of acquiescence); Mich. Rule Evid. 804(b)(6) (2008) (substitutes "engaged in or encouraged" for "engaged or acquiesced in"). Two others require "purpose" by their terms. Ohio Rule Evid. 804(B)(6) (2008); Cal. Evid. Code Ann. § 1350 (West Supp.2008). Two of the three remaining forfeiture provisions require the defendant to have "procured" the unavailability of a witness, Haw. Rule 804(b)(7) (2007); Md. Cts. & Jud. Proc.Code Ann. § 10–901 (Lexis 2006)—which, as we have discussed, is a term traditionally used in the forfeiture context to require intent. Maryland's rule has thus been described as "requir[ing] that the judge must find that [the] wrongdoing or misconduct was undertaken with the intent of making the witness unavailable to testify." 6A L. McLain, Maryland Evidence, State and Federal § 804(6):1, p. 230 (West Supp.2007–2008). These rules cast more than a little doubt on the dissent's assertion that the historic forfeiture rule creates intolerable problems of proof. The lone forfeiture exception whose text reaches more broadly than the rule we adopt is an Oregon rule adopted in 2005. See 2005 Ore. Laws p. 1232, Ch. 458 (S.B. 287).

Although the case law is sparse, in light of these decisions and the absence of even a single case declining to admit unconfronted statements of an absent witness on wrongful-procurement grounds when the defendant sought to prevent the witness from testifying, we are not persuaded to displace the understanding of our prior cases that wrongful procurement permits the admission of prior unconfronted testimony.

But the parsing of cases aside, the most obvious problem with the dissent's theory that the forfeiture rule applied only to confronted testimony is that it amounts to self-immolation. If it were true, it would destroy not only our case for a narrow forfeiture rule, but the dissent's case for a broader one as well. Prior confronted statements by witnesses who are unavailable are admissible whether or not the defendant was responsible for their unavailability. If the forfeiture doctrine did not admit unconfronted prior testimony at common law, the conclusion must be, not that the forfeiture doctrine requires no specific intent in order to render unconfronted testimony available, but that unconfronted testimony is subject to no forfeiture doctrine at all.

2

Having destroyed its own case, the dissent issues a thinly veiled invitation to overrule Crawford and adopt an approach not much different from the regime of Ohio v. Roberts, 448 U.S. 56, 100 S.Ct. 2531, 65 L.Ed.2d 597 (1980), under which the Court would create the exceptions that it thinks consistent with the policies underlying the confrontation guarantee, regardless of how that guarantee was historically understood. The "basic purposes and objectives" of forfeiture doctrine, it says, require that a defendant who wrongfully caused the absence of a witness be deprived of his confrontation rights, whether or not there was any such rule applicable at common law.

If we were to reason from the "basic purposes and objectives" of the forfeiture doctrine, we are not at all sure we would come to the dissent's favored result. The common-law forfeiture rule was aimed at removing the otherwise powerful incentive for defendants to intimidate, bribe, and kill the witnesses against them—in other words, it is grounded in "the ability of courts to protect the integrity of their proceedings." Davis, 547 U.S., at 834, 126 S.Ct. 2266. The boundaries of the doctrine seem to us intelligently fixed so as to avoid a principle repugnant to our constitutional system of trial by jury: that those murder defendants whom the judge considers guilty (after less than a full trial, mind you, and of course before the jury has pronounced guilt) should be deprived of fair-trial rights, lest they benefit from their judge-determined wrong.[6]

6. The dissent identifies one circumstance—and only one—in which a court may determine the outcome of a case before it goes to the jury: A judge may determine the existence of a conspiracy in order to make incriminating statements of co-conspirators admissible against the defendant under Federal Rule of Evidence 801(d)(2)(E). Bourjaily v. United States, 483 U.S. 171, 107 S.Ct. 2775, 97 L.Ed.2d 144

SECTION 10 FORFEITURE

Since it is most certainly not the norm that trial rights can be "forfeited" on the basis of a prior judicial determination of guilt, the dissent must go far afield to argue even by analogy for its forfeiture rule. See post, at—(discussing common-law doctrine that prohibits the murderer from collecting insurance on the life of his victim, or an inheritance from the victim's estate); post, at—(noting that many criminal statutes punish a defendant regardless of his purpose). These analogies support propositions of which we have no doubt: States may allocate property rights as they see fit, and a murderer can and should be punished, without regard to his purpose, after a fair trial. But a legislature may not "punish" a defendant for his evil acts by stripping him of the right to have his guilt in a criminal proceeding determined by a jury, and on the basis of evidence the Constitution deems reliable and admissible.

The larger problem with the dissent's argument, however, is that the guarantee of confrontation is no guarantee at all if it is subject to whatever exceptions courts from time to time consider "fair." It is not the role of courts to extrapolate from the words of the Sixth Amendment to the values behind it, and then to enforce its guarantees only to the extent they serve (in the courts' views) those underlying values. The Sixth Amendment seeks fairness indeed—but seeks it through very specific means (one of which is confrontation) that were the trial rights of Englishmen. It "does not suggest any open-ended exceptions from the confrontation requirement to be developed by the courts."

E

The dissent closes by pointing out that a forfeiture rule which ignores Crawford would be particularly helpful to women in abusive relationships—or at least particularly helpful in punishing their abusers. Not as helpful as the dissent suggests, since only testimonial statements are excluded by the Confrontation Clause. Statements to friends and neighbors about abuse and intimidation, and statements to physicians in the course of receiving treatment would be excluded, if at all, only by hearsay rules, which are free to adopt the dissent's version of forfeiture by wrongdoing. In any event, we are puzzled by the dissent's decision to

(1987), held that admission of the evidence did not violate the Confrontation Clause because it "falls within a firmly rooted hearsay exception"—the test under Ohio v. Roberts, 448 U.S. 56, 66, 100 S.Ct. 2531, 65 L.Ed.2d 597 (1980), the case that Crawford overruled. In fact it did not violate the Confrontation Clause for the quite different reason that it was not (as an incriminating statement in furtherance of the conspiracy would probably never be) testimonial. The co-conspirator hearsay rule does not pertain to a constitutional right and is in fact quite unusual. We do not say, of course, that a judge can never be allowed to inquire into guilt of the charged offense in order to make a preliminary evidentiary ruling. That must sometimes be done under the forfeiture rule that we adopt—when, for example, the defendant is on trial for murdering a witness in order to prevent his testimony. But the exception to ordinary practice that we support is (1) needed to protect the integrity of court proceedings, (2) based upon longstanding precedent, and (3) much less expansive than the exception proposed by the dissent.

devote its peroration to domestic abuse cases. Is the suggestion that we should have one Confrontation Clause (the one the Framers adopted and Crawford described) for all other crimes, but a special, improvised, Confrontation Clause for those crimes that are frequently directed against women? Domestic violence is an intolerable offense that legislatures may choose to combat through many means—from increasing criminal penalties to adding resources for investigation and prosecution to funding awareness and prevention campaigns. But for that serious crime, as for others, abridging the constitutional rights of criminal defendants is not in the State's arsenal.

The domestic-violence context is, however, relevant for a separate reason. Acts of domestic violence often are intended to dissuade a victim from resorting to outside help, and include conduct designed to prevent testimony to police officers or cooperation in criminal prosecutions. Where such an abusive relationship culminates in murder, the evidence may support a finding that the crime expressed the intent to isolate the victim and to stop her from reporting abuse to the authorities or cooperating with a criminal prosecution-rendering her prior statements admissible under the forfeiture doctrine. Earlier abuse, or threats of abuse, intended to dissuade the victim from resorting to outside help would be highly relevant to this inquiry, as would evidence of ongoing criminal proceedings at which the victim would have been expected to testify. This is not, as the dissent charges nothing more than "knowledge-based intent."

The state courts in this case did not consider the intent of the defendant because they found that irrelevant to application of the forfeiture doctrine. This view of the law was error, but the court is free to consider evidence of the defendant's intent on remand.

* * *

We decline to approve an exception to the Confrontation Clause unheard of at the time of the founding or for 200 years thereafter. The judgment of the California Supreme Court is vacated, and the case is remanded for further proceedings not inconsistent with this opinion.

It is so ordered.

. . .

■ JUSTICE SOUTER, with whom JUSTICE GINSBURG joins, concurring in part.

I am convinced that the Court's historical analysis is sound and I join all but Part II–D–2 of the opinion. As the Court demonstrates, the confrontation right as understood at the Framing and ratification of the Sixth Amendment was subject to exception on equitable grounds for an absent witness's prior relevant, testimonial statement, when the defendant brought about the absence with intent to prevent testimony. It was, and is, reasonable to place the risk of untruth in an unconfronted, out-of-court statement on a defendant who meant to preclude the testing that confrontation provides. The importance of that intent in assessing the fairness of placing the risk on the defendant is most obvious when a defendant is prosecuted for the very act that causes the witness's absence, homicide being the extreme example. If the victim's prior statement were admissible solely because the defendant kept the witness out of court by committing homicide, admissibility of the victim's statement to prove guilt would turn on finding the defendant guilty of the homicidal act causing the absence; evidence that the defendant killed would come in because the defendant probably killed. The only thing saving admissibility and liability determinations from question begging would be (in a jury case) the distinct functions of judge and jury: judges would find by a preponderance of evidence that the defendant killed (and so would admit the testimonial statement), while the jury could so find only on proof beyond a reasonable doubt. Equity demands something more than this near circularity before the right to confrontation is forfeited, and more is supplied by showing intent to prevent the witness from testifying. Cf. Davis v. Washington, 547 U.S. 813, 833, 126 S.Ct. 2266, 165 L.Ed.2d 224 (2006).

It is this rationale for the limit on the forfeiture exception rather than a dispositive example from the historical record that persuades me that the Court's conclusion is the right one in this case. The contrast between the Court's and Justice BREYER's careful examinations of the historical record tells me that the early cases on the exception were not calibrated finely enough to answer the narrow question here. The historical record as revealed by the exchange simply does not focus on what should be required for forfeiture when the crime charged occurred in an abusive relationship or was its culminating act; today's understanding of domestic abuse had no apparent significance at the time of the Framing, and there is no early example of the forfeiture rule operating in that circumstance.

Examining the early cases and commentary, however, reveals two things that count in favor of the Court's understanding of forfeiture when the evidence shows domestic abuse. The first is the substantial indication that the Sixth Amendment was meant to require some degree of intent to thwart the judicial process before thinking it reasonable to hold the confrontation right forfeited; otherwise the right would in practical terms boil down to a measure of reliable hearsay, a view rejected in Crawford v. Washington, 541 U.S. 36, 124 S.Ct. 1354, 158 L.Ed.2d 177 (2004). The second is the absence from the early material of any reason to doubt that the element of intention would normally be satisfied by the intent inferred on the part of the domestic abuser in the classic abusive relationship, which is meant to isolate the victim from outside help, including the aid of law enforcement and the judicial process. If the evidence for admissibility shows a continuing relationship of this sort, it would make no sense to suggest that the oppressing defendant miraculously abandoned the dynamics of abuse the instant before he killed his victim, say in a fit of anger. The Court's conclusion in Part II–E thus fits the rationale that equity requires and the historical record supports.

Page 762. Add new Note:

Confrontation. The Crawford Court recognizes than an accused may forfeit his right to confrontation.

SECTION 12. NON-CLASS EXCEPTIONS

Page 789. Substitute for Note 1:

Is the statement in Wright "testimonial" because an agent of the police elicited the statement, or is it non-testimonial because a child of Kathy's age would have no basis for understanding that "the statement would be available for use at a later trial?"

Page 792. Substitute for Note 5. Grand jury testimony:

Admission of grand jury testimony against an accused under any hearsay exception violates the accused's right to confrontation according to the Crawford opinion.

SECTION 13. CONSTITUTIONAL RESTRAINTS

Page 796, main volume. Omit White v. Illinois and Notes following White, pp. 805–807. Substitute Crawford v. Washington and the additional cases and Notes in this section:

Crawford v. Washington

Supreme Court of the United States, 2004.
541 U.S. 36 124 S.Ct. 1354, 158 L.Ed.2d 177.

■ JUSTICE SCALIA delivered the opinion of the Court.

Petitioner Michael Crawford stabbed a man who allegedly tried to rape his wife, Sylvia. At his trial, the state played for the jury Sylvia's tape-recorded statement to the police describing the stabbing, even though he had no opportunity for cross-examination. The Washington Supreme Court upheld petitioner's conviction after determining that Sylvia's statement was reliable. The question presented is whether this procedure complied with the Sixth Amendment's guarantee that, "[i]n all criminal prosecutions, the accused shall enjoy the right ... to be confronted with the witnesses against him."

I

On August 5, 1999, Kenneth Lee was stabbed at his apartment. Police arrested petitioner later that night. After giving petitioner and his wife *Miranda* warnings, detectives interrogated each of them twice.

Petitioner eventually confessed that he and Sylvia had gone in search of Lee because he was upset over an earlier incident in which Lee had tried to rape her.

Petitioner gave the following account of the fight:

"Q. Okay. Did you ever see anything in [Lee's] hands?"

"A. I think so, but I'm not positive.

"Q. Okay, when you think so, what do you mean by that?"

"A. I coulda swore I seen him goin' for somethin' before, right before everything happened. He was like reachin', fiddlin' around down here and stuff ... and I just ... I don't know, I think, this is just a possibility, but I think, I think that he pulled somethin' out and I grabbed for it and that's how I got cut ... but I'm not positive. I, I, my mind goes blank when things like this happen. I mean, I just, I remember things wrong, I remember things that just doesn't, don't make sense to me later." App. 155 (punctuation added).

Sylvia generally corroborated petitioner's story about the events leading up to the fight, but her account of the fight itself was arguably different—particularly with respect to whether Lee had drawn a weapon before petitioner assaulted him:

"Q. Did Kenny do anything to fight back from this assault?"

"A. (pausing) I know he reached into his pocket ... or somethin' ... I don't know what.

"Q. After he was stabbed?"

"A. He saw Michael coming up. He lifted his hand ... his chest open, he might [have] went to go strike his hand out or something and then (inaudible).

"Q. Okay, you, you gotta speak up.

"A. Okay, he lifted his hand over his head maybe to strike Michael's hand down or something and then he put his hands in his ... put his right hand in his right pocket ... took a step back ... Michael proceeded to stab him ... then his hands were like ... how do you explain this ... open arms ... with his hands open and he fell down ... and we ran (describing subject holding hands open, palms toward assailant).

"Q. Okay, when he's standing there with his open hands, you're talking about Kenny, correct?"

"A. Yeah, after, after the fact, yes.

"Q. Did you see anything in his hands at that point?"

"A. (pausing) um um (no)." *Id.,* at 137 (punctuation added).

The State charged petitioner with assault and attempted murder. At trial, he claimed self-defense. Sylvia did not testify because of the state marital privilege, which generally bars a spouse from testifying without the other spouse's consent.... In Washington, this privilege does not extend to a spouse's out-of-court statements admissible under a hearsay exception ... so the State sought to introduce Sylvia's tape-recorded statements to the police as evidence that the stabbing was not in self-defense. Noting that Sylvia had admitted she led petitioner to Lee's apartment and thus had facilitated the assault, the State invoked the hearsay exception for statements against penal interest, Wash. Rule Evid. 804(b)(3) (2003).

Petitioner countered that, state law notwithstanding, admitting the evidence would violate his federal constitutional right to be "confronted with the witnesses against him." Amdt. 6. According to our description of that right in *Ohio v. Roberts,* 448 U.S. 56 (1980), it does not bar admission of an unavailable witness's statement against a criminal defendant if the statement bears "adequate 'indicia of reliability.'" *Id.,* at 66. To meet that test, evidence must either fall within a "firmly rooted hearsay exception" or bear "particularized guarantees of trustworthiness." *Ibid.* The trial court here admitted the statement on the latter ground, offering several reasons why it was trustworthy: Sylvia was not shifting blame but rather corroborating her husband's story that he acted in self-defense or "justified reprisal"; she had direct knowledge as an eyewitness; she was describing recent events; and she was being questioned by a "neutral" law enforcement officer. The prosecution played the tape for the jury and relied on it in closing, arguing that it was "damning evidence" that "completely refutes [petitioner's] claim of self-defense." The jury convicted petitioner of assault.

The Washington Court of Appeals reversed. It applied a nine-factor test to determine whether Sylvia's statement bore particularized guarantees of trustworthiness, and noted several reasons why it did not: The statement contradicted one she had previously given; it was made in response to specific questions; and at one point she admitted she had shut her eyes during the stabbing. The court considered and rejected the State's argument that Sylvia's statement was reliable because it coincided with petitioner's to such a degree that the two "interlocked." The court determined that, although the two statements agreed about the events leading up to the stabbing, they differed on the issue crucial to petitioner's self-defense claim: "[Petitioner's] version asserts that Lee may have had something in his hand when he stabbed him; but Sylvia's version has Lee grabbing for something only after he has been stabbed."

The Washington Supreme Court reinstated the conviction, unanimously concluding that, although Sylvia's statement did not fall under a firmly rooted hearsay exception, it bore guarantees of trustworthiness: "'[W]hen a codefendant's confession is virtually identical [to, *i.e.,* interlocks with,] that of a defendant, it may be deemed reliable.' " The court explained:

> "Although the Court of Appeals concluded that the statements were contradictory, upon closer inspection they appear to overlap. . . .
>
> "[B]oth of the Crawfords' statements indicate that Lee was possibly grabbing for a weapon, but they are equally unsure when this event may have taken place. They are also equally unsure how Michael received the cut on his hand, leading the court to question when, if ever, Lee possessed a weapon. In this respect they overlap.
>
> "[N]either Michael nor Sylvia clearly stated that Lee had a weapon in hand from which Michael was simply defending himself. And it is this omission by both that interlocks the statements and makes Sylvia's statement reliable."[1]

We granted certiorari to determine whether the State's use of Sylvia's statement violated the Confrontation Clause. 539 U.S. 914, 123 S.Ct. 2275, 156 L.Ed.2d 129 (2003).

II

The Sixth Amendment's Confrontation Clause provides that, "[i]n all criminal prosecutions, the accused shall enjoy the right ... to be confronted with the witnesses against him." We have held that this bedrock procedural guarantee applies to both federal and state prosecutions. *Pointer v. Texas,* 380 U.S. 400, 406(1965). As noted above, *Roberts* says that an unavailable witness's out-of-court statement may be admitted so long as it has adequate indicia of reliability—*i.e.,* falls within a "firmly rooted hearsay exception" or bears "particularized guarantees of trustworthiness." 448 U.S., at 66. Petitioner argues that this test strays from the original meaning of the Confrontation Clause and urges us to reconsider it.

A

The Constitution's text does not alone resolve this case. One could plausibly read "witnesses against" a defendant to mean those who actually testify at trial, those whose statements are offered at trial, or something in-between. We must therefore turn to the historical background of the Clause to understand its meaning.

---

1. The court rejected the State's argument that guarantees of trustworthiness were unnecessary since petitioner waived his confrontation rights by invoking the marital privilege. It reasoned that "forcing the defendant to choose between the marital privilege and confronting his spouse presents an untenable Hobson's choice." The State has not challenged this holding here. The State also has not challenged the Court of Appeals' conclusion (not reached by the State Supreme Court) that the confrontation violation, if it occurred, was not harmless. We express no opinion on these matters. [Ed. Note: Some footnotes and citations have been omitted].

CHAPTER 4 HEARSAY

The right to confront one's accusers is a concept that dates back to Roman times. The founding generation's immediate source of the concept, however, was the common law. English common law has long differed from continental civil law in regard to the manner in which witnesses give testimony in criminal trials. The common-law tradition is one of live testimony in court subject to adversarial testing, while the civil law condones examination in private by judicial officers ...

Nonetheless, England at times adopted elements of the civil-law practice. Justices of the peace or other officials examined suspects and witnesses before trial. These examinations were sometimes read in court in lieu of live testimony, a practice that "occasioned frequent demands by the prisoner to have his 'accusers,' *i.e.* the witnesses against him, brought before him face to face." 1 J. Stephen, History of the Criminal Law of England 326 (1883). In some cases, these demands were refused. See 9 W. Holdsworth, History of English Law 216–217, 228 (3d ed.1944); *e.g., Raleigh's Case,* 2 How. St. Tr. 1, 15–16, 24 (1603); *Throckmorton's Case,* 1 How. St. Tr. 869, 875–876 (1554); cf. *Lilburn's Case,* 3 How. St. Tr. 1315, 1318–1322, 1329 (Star Chamber 1637).

Pretrial examinations became routine under two statutes passed during the reign of Queen Mary in the 16th century, 1 & 2 Phil. & M., c. 13 (1554), and 2 & 3 *id.,* c. 10 (1555). These Marian bail and committal statutes required justices of the peace to examine suspects and witnesses in felony cases and to certify the results to the court. It is doubtful that the original purpose of the examinations was to produce evidence admissible at trial. See J. Langbein, Prosecuting Crime in the Renaissance 21–34 (1974). Whatever the original purpose, however, they came to be used as evidence in some cases, resulting in an adoption of continental procedure.

The most notorious instances of civil-law examination occurred in the great political trials of the 16th and 17th centuries. One such was the 1603 trial of Sir Walter Raleigh for treason. Lord Cobham, Raleigh's alleged accomplice, had implicated him in an examination before the Privy Council and in a letter. At Raleigh's trial, these were read to the jury. Raleigh argued that Cobham had lied to save himself: "Cobham is absolutely in the King's mercy; to excuse me cannot avail him; by accusing me he may hope for favour." Suspecting that Cobham would recant, Raleigh demanded that the judges call him to appear, arguing that "[t]he Proof of the Common Law is by witness and jury: let Cobham be here, let him speak it. Call my accuser before my face...." The judges refused, and, despite Raleigh's protestations that he was being tried "by the Spanish Inquisition," the jury convicted, and Raleigh was sentenced to death.

One of Raleigh's trial judges later lamented that "the justice of England has never been so degraded and injured as by the condemnation of Sir Walter Raleigh." Through a series of statutory and judicial reforms, English law developed a right of confrontation that limited these abuses. For example, treason statutes required witnesses to confront the accused "face to face" at his arraignment. *E.g.,* 13 Car. 2, c. 1, § 5 (1661). Courts, meanwhile, developed relatively strict rules of unavailability, admitting examinations only if the witness was demonstrably unable to testify in person. Several authorities also stated that a suspect's confession could be admitted only against himself, and not against others he implicated.

One recurring question was whether the admissibility of an unavailable witness's pretrial examination depended on whether the defendant had had an opportunity to cross-examine him. In 1696, the Court of King's Bench answered this question in the affirmative, in the widely reported misdemeanor libel case of *King v. Paine,* 5 Mod. 163, 87 Eng. Rep. 584. The court ruled that, even though a witness was dead, his examination was not admissible where "the defendant not being present when [it was] taken before the mayor . . . had lost the benefit of a cross-examination." *Id.,* at 165, 87 Eng. Rep., at 585. The question was also debated at length during the infamous proceedings against Sir John Fenwick on a bill of attainder. Fenwick's counsel objected to admitting the examination of a witness who had been spirited away, on the ground that Fenwick had had no opportunity to cross-examine. See *Fenwick's Case,* 13 How. St. Tr. 537, 591–592 (H.C. 1696) (Powys) ("[T]hat which they would offer is something that Mr. Goodman hath sworn when he was examined . . .; sir J.F. not being present or privy, and no opportunity given to cross-examine the person; and I conceive that cannot be offered as evidence . . ."); *id.,* at 592 (Shower) ("[N]o deposition of a person can be read, though beyond sea, unless in cases where the party it is to be read against was privy to the examination, and might have cross-examined him. . . . [O]ur constitution is, that the person shall see his accuser"). The examination was nonetheless admitted on a closely divided vote after several of those present opined that the common-law rules of procedure did not apply to parliamentary attainder proceedings—one speaker even admitting that the evidence would normally be inadmissible. Fenwick was condemned, but the proceedings "must have burned into the general consciousness the vital importance of the rule securing the right of cross-examination."

. . .

B

Controversial examination practices were also used in the Colonies. Early in the 18th century, for example, the Virginia Council protested against the Governor for having "privately issued several commissions to examine witnesses against particular men *ex parte,*" complaining that "the person accused is not admitted to be confronted with, or defend himself against his defamers." A decade before the Revolution, England gave jurisdiction over Stamp Act offenses to the admiralty courts, which followed civil-law rather than common-law procedures and thus routinely took testimony by deposition or private judicial examination. Colonial representatives protested that the Act subverted their rights "by extending the jurisdiction of the courts of admiralty beyond its ancient limits." John Adams, defending a merchant in a high-profile admiralty case, argued: "Examinations of witnesses upon Interrogatories, are only by the Civil Law. Interrogatories are unknown at common Law, and Englishmen and common Lawyers have an aversion to them if not an Abhorrence of them."

Many declarations of rights adopted around the time of the Revolution guaranteed a right of confrontation. See Virginia Declaration of Rights § 8 (1776); Pennsylvania Declaration of Rights § IX (1776); Delaware Declaration of Rights § 14 (1776); Maryland Declaration of Rights § XIX (1776); North Carolina Declaration of Rights § VII (1776); Vermont Declaration of Rights Ch. I, § X (1777); Massachusetts Declaration of Rights § XII (1780); New Hampshire Bill of Rights § XV (1783). The proposed Federal Constitution, however, did not. At the Massachusetts ratifying convention, Abraham Holmes objected to this omission precisely on the ground that it would lead to civil-law practices: "The mode of trial is altogether indetermined; ... whether [the defendant] is to be allowed to confront the witnesses, and have the advantage of cross-examination, we are not yet told.... [W]e shall find Congress possessed of powers enabling them to institute judicatories little less inauspicious than a certain tribunal in Spain, ... the *Inquisition*." Similarly, a prominent Antifederalist writing under the pseudonym Federal Farmer criticized the use of "written evidence" while objecting to the omission of a vicinage right: "Nothing can be more essential than the cross examining [of] witnesses, and generally before the triers of the facts in question.... [W]ritten evidence ... [is] almost useless; it must be frequently taken ex parte, and but very seldom leads to the proper discovery of truth." R. Lee, Letter IV by the Federal Farmer (Oct. 15, 1787), reprinted in 1 Schwartz, *supra*, at 469, 473. The First Congress responded by including the Confrontation Clause in the proposal that became the Sixth Amendment.

Early state decisions shed light upon the original understanding of the common-law right. *State v. Webb*, 2 N.C. 103 (1794) *(per curiam)*, decided a mere three years after the adoption of the Sixth Amendment, held that depositions could be read against an accused only if they were taken in his presence. Rejecting a broader reading of the English authorities, the court held: "[I]t is a rule of the common law, founded on natural justice, that no man shall be prejudiced by evidence which he had not the liberty to cross examine." *Id.*, at 104.

Similarly, in *State v. Campbell*, 1 Rich. 124, 1844 WL 2558 (S.C. 1844), South Carolina's highest law court excluded a deposition taken by a coroner in the absence of the accused. It held: "[I]f we are to decide the question by the established rules of the common law, there could not be a dissenting voice. For, notwithstanding the death of the witness, and whatever the respectability of the court taking the depositions, the solemnity of the occasion and the weight of the testimony, such depositions are *ex parte,* and, therefore, utterly incompetent." *Id.,* at 125. The court said that one of the "indispensable conditions" implicitly guaranteed by the State Constitution was that "prosecutions be carried on to the conviction of the accused, by witnesses confronted by him, and subjected to his personal examination." *Ibid.*

Many other decisions are to the same effect....

III

This history supports two inferences about the meaning of the Sixth Amendment.

A

First, the principal evil at which the Confrontation Clause was directed was the civil-law mode of criminal procedure, and particularly its use of *ex parte* examinations as evidence against the accused. It was these practices that the Crown deployed in notorious treason cases like Raleigh's; that the Marian statutes invited; that English law's assertion of a right to confrontation was meant to prohibit; and that the founding-era rhetoric decried. The Sixth Amendment must be interpreted with this focus in mind.

Accordingly, we once again reject the view that the Confrontation Clause applies of its own force only to in-court testimony, and that its application to out-of-court statements introduced at trial depends upon "the law of Evidence for the time being." 3 Wigmore § 1397, at 101; accord, *Dutton v. Evans,* 400 U.S. 74, 94 (1970) (Harlan, J., concurring in result). Leaving the regulation of out-of-court statements to the law of evidence would render the Confrontation Clause powerless to prevent even the most flagrant inquisitorial practices. Raleigh was, after all, perfectly free to confront those who read Cobham's confession in court.

This focus also suggests that not all hearsay implicates the Sixth Amendment's core concerns. An off-hand, overheard remark might be unreliable evidence and thus a good candidate for exclusion under hearsay rules, but it bears little resemblance to the civil-law abuses the Confrontation Clause targeted. On the other hand, *ex parte* examinations might sometimes be admissible under modern hearsay rules, but the Framers certainly would not have condoned them.

The text of the Confrontation Clause reflects this focus. It applies to "witnesses" against the accused—in other words, those who "bear testimony." 1 N. Webster, An American Dictionary of the English Language (1828). "Testimony," in turn, is typically "[a] solemn declaration or affirmation made for the purpose of establishing or proving some fact." *Ibid.* An accuser who makes a formal statement to government officers bears testimony in a sense that a person who makes a casual remark to an acquaintance does not. The constitutional text, like the history underlying the common-law right of confrontation, thus reflects an especially acute concern with a specific type of out-of-court statement.

Various formulations of this core class of "testimonial" statements exist: "*ex parte* in-court testimony or its functional equivalent—that is, material such as affidavits, custodial examinations, prior testimony that the defendant was unable to cross-examine, or similar pretrial statements that declarants would reasonably expect to be used prosecutorially," Brief for Petitioner 23; "extrajudicial statements ... contained in formalized testimonial materials, such as affidavits, depositions, prior testimony, or confessions," *White v. Illinois,* 502 U.S. 346, 365, 112 S.Ct. 736, 116 L.Ed.2d 848 (1992) (THOMAS, J., joined by SCALIA, J., concurring in part and concurring in judgment); "statements that were made under circumstances which would lead an objective witness reasonably to believe that the statement would be available for use at a later trial," Brief for National Association of Criminal Defense Lawyers et al. as *Amici Curiae* 3. These formulations all share a common nucleus and then define the Clause's coverage at various levels of abstraction around it. Regardless of the precise articulation, some statements qualify under any definition—for example, *ex parte* testimony at a preliminary hearing.

Statements taken by police officers in the course of interrogations are also testimonial under even a narrow standard. Police interrogations bear a striking resemblance to examinations by justices of the peace in England. The statements are not *sworn* testimony, but the absence of oath was not dispositive. Cobham's examination was unsworn, yet Raleigh's trial has long been thought a paradigmatic confrontation violation. Under the Marian statutes, witnesses were typically put on oath, but suspects were not. Yet Hawkins and others went out of their way to caution that such unsworn confessions were not admissible against anyone but the confessor.

That interrogators are police officers rather than magistrates does not change the picture either. Justices of the peace conducting examinations under the Marian statutes were not magistrates as we understand that office today, but had an essentially investigative and prosecutorial function. England did not have a professional police force until the 19th century, so it is not surprising that other government officers performed the investigative functions now associated primarily with the police. The involvement of government officers in the production of testimonial evidence presents the same risk, whether the officers are police or justices of the peace.

In sum, even if the Sixth Amendment is not solely concerned with testimonial hearsay, that is its primary object, and interrogations by law enforcement officers fall squarely within that class.[4]

4. We use the term "interrogation" in its colloquial, rather than any technical legal, sense. Just as various definitions of "testimonial" exist, one can imagine vari-

B

The historical record also supports a second proposition: that the Framers would not have allowed admission of testimonial statements of a witness who did not appear at trial unless he was unavailable to testify, and the defendant had had a prior opportunity for cross-examination. The text of the Sixth Amendment does not suggest any open-ended exceptions from the confrontation requirement to be developed by the courts. Rather, the "right . . . to be confronted with the witnesses against him," Amdt. 6, is most naturally read as a reference to the right of confrontation at common law, admitting only those exceptions established at the time of the founding. See *Mattox v. United States*, 156 U.S. 237, 243 (1895); cf. *Houser*, 26 Mo., at 433–435. As the English authorities above reveal, the common law in 1791 conditioned admissibility of an absent witness's examination on unavailability and a prior opportunity to cross-examine. The Sixth Amendment therefore incorporates those limitations. The numerous early state decisions applying the same test confirm that these principles were received as part of the common law in this country.

We do not read the historical sources to say that a prior opportunity to cross-examine was merely a sufficient, rather than a necessary, condition for admissibility of testimonial statements. They suggest that this requirement was dispositive, and not merely one of several ways to establish reliability. This is not to deny, as THE CHIEF JUSTICE notes, that "[t]here were always exceptions to the general rule of exclusion" of hearsay evidence. Several had become well established by 1791. See 3 Wigmore § 1397, at 101. But there is scant evidence that exceptions were invoked to admit *testimonial* statements against the accused in a *criminal* case.[6] Most of the hearsay exceptions covered statements that by their nature were not testimonial—for example, business records or statements in furtherance of a conspiracy. We do not infer from these that the Framers thought exceptions would apply even to prior testimony. Cf. *Lilly v. Virginia*, 527 U.S. 116, 134 (1999) (plurality opinion) ("[A]ccomplices' confessions that inculpate a criminal defendant are not within a firmly rooted exception to the hearsay rule").[7]

---

ous definitions of "interrogation," and we need not select among them in this case. Sylvia's recorded statement, knowingly given in response to structured police questioning, qualifies under any conceivable definition.

6. The one deviation we have found involves dying declarations. The existence of that exception as a general rule of criminal hearsay law cannot be disputed. See, *e.g.*, *Mattox v. United States*, 156 U.S. 237, 243–244 (1895); *King v. Reason*, 16 How. St. Tr. 1, 24–38 (K.B.1722); 1 D. Jardine, Criminal Trials 435 (1832); Cooley, Constitutional Limitations, at *318; 1 G. Gilbert, Evidence 211 (C. Lofft ed. 1791); see also F. Heller, The Sixth Amendment 105 (1951) (asserting that this was the *only* recognized criminal hearsay exception at common law). Although many dying declarations may not be testimonial, there is authority for admitting even those that clearly are. We need not decide in this case whether the Sixth Amendment incorporates an exception for testimonial dying declarations. If this exception must be accepted on historical grounds, it is *sui generis*.

7. We cannot agree with THE CHIEF JUSTICE that the fact "[t]hat a statement might be testimonial does nothing to under-

IV

Our case law has been largely consistent with these two principles. Our leading early decision, for example, involved a deceased witness's prior trial testimony. *Mattox v. United States,* 156 U.S. 237 (1895). In allowing the statement to be admitted, we relied on the fact that the defendant had had, at the first trial, an adequate opportunity to confront the witness: "The substance of the constitutional protection is preserved to the prisoner in the advantage he has once had of seeing the witness face to face, and of subjecting him to the ordeal of a cross-examination. This, the law says, he shall under no circumstances be deprived of...." *Id.,* at 244.

Our later cases conform to *Mattox's* holding that prior trial or preliminary hearing testimony is admissible only if the defendant had an adequate opportunity to cross-examine. See *Mancusi v. Stubbs,* 408 U.S. 204 (1972); *California v. Green,* 399 U.S. 149, 165–168 (1970); *Pointer v. Texas,* 380 U.S., at 406–408; cf. *Kirby v. United States,* 174 U.S. 47, 55–61 (1899). Even where the defendant had such an opportunity, we excluded the testimony where the government had not established unavailability of the witness. See *Barber v. Page,* 390 U.S. 719, 722–725 (1968); cf. *Motes v. United States,* 178 U.S. 458 (1900). We similarly excluded accomplice confessions where the defendant had no opportunity to cross-examine. See *Roberts v. Russell,* 392 U.S. 293, 294–295 (1968) *(per curiam); Bruton v. United States,* 391 U.S. 123, 126–128 (1968); *Douglas v. Alabama,* 380 U.S. 415, 418–420 (1965). In contrast, we considered reliability factors beyond prior opportunity for cross-examination when the hearsay statement at issue was not testimonial. See *Dutton v. Evans,* 400 U.S., at 87–89 (plurality opinion).

Even our recent cases, in their outcomes, hew closely to the traditional line. *Ohio v. Roberts,* 448 U.S., at 67–70, admitted testimony from a preliminary hearing at which the defendant had examined the witness. *Lilly v. Virginia, supra,* excluded testimonial statements that the defendant had had no opportunity to test by cross-examination. And *Bourjaily v. United States,* 483 U.S. 171, 181–184 (1987), admitted statements made unwittingly to an FBI informant after applying a more general test that did *not* make prior cross-examination an indispensable requirement.[8]

---

mine the wisdom of one of these [hearsay] exceptions." Involvement of government officers in the production of testimony with an eye toward trial presents unique potential for prosecutorial abuse—a fact borne out time and again throughout a history with which the Framers were keenly familiar. This consideration does not evaporate when testimony happens to fall within some broad, modern hearsay exception, even if that exception might be justifiable in other circumstances.

8. One case arguably in tension with the rule requiring a prior opportunity for cross-examination when the proffered statement is testimonial is *White v. Illinois,* 502 U.S. 346 (1992), which involved, *inter alia,* statements of a child victim to an investigating police officer admitted as spontaneous declarations. It is questionable whether testimonial statements would ever have been admissible on that ground in 1791; to the extent the hearsay exception for spontane-

Lee v. Illinois, 476 U.S. 530 (1986), on which the State relies, is not to the contrary. There, we *rejected* the State's attempt to admit an accomplice confession. The State had argued that the confession was admissible because it "interlocked" with the defendant's. We dealt with the argument by rejecting its premise, holding that "when the discrepancies between the statements are not insignificant, the codefendant's confession may not be admitted." Respondent argues that "[t]he logical inference of this statement is that when the discrepancies between the statements *are* insignificant, then the codefendant's statement *may* be admitted." But this is merely a possible inference, not an inevitable one, and we do not draw it here. If *Lee* had meant authoritatively to announce an exception—previously unknown to this Court's jurisprudence—for interlocking confessions, it would not have done so in such an oblique manner. Our only precedent on interlocking confessions had addressed the entirely different question whether a limiting instruction cured prejudice to codefendants from admitting a defendant's *own* confession against him in a joint trial. See *Parker v. Randolph,* 442 U.S. 62, 69–76 (1979) (plurality opinion), abrogated by *Cruz v. New York,* 481 U.S. 186 (1987).

Our cases have thus remained faithful to the Framers' understanding: Testimonial statements of witnesses absent from trial have been admitted only where the declarant is unavailable, and only where the defendant has had a prior opportunity to cross-examine.[9]

V

Although the results of our decisions have generally been faithful to the original meaning of the Confrontation Clause, the same cannot be said of our rationales. *Roberts* conditions the admissibility of all hearsay evidence on whether it falls under a "firmly rooted hearsay exception"

---

ous declarations existed at all, it required that the statements be made "immediat[ely] upon the hurt received, and before [the declarant] had time to devise or contrive any thing for her own advantage." *Thompson v. Trevanion,* Skin. 402, 90 Eng. Rep. 179 (K.B.1694). In any case, the only question presented in *White* was whether the Confrontation Clause imposed an unavailability requirement on the types of hearsay at issue. See 502 U.S., at 348–349. The holding did not address the question whether certain of the statements, because they were testimonial, had to be excluded *even if* the witness was unavailable. We "[took] as a given ... that the testimony properly falls within the relevant hearsay exceptions." *Id.,* at 351, n. 4.

9. ... THE CHIEF JUSTICE fails to identify a single case (aside from one minor, arguable exception, see *supra,* n. 8), where we have admitted testimonial statements based on indicia of reliability other than a prior opportunity for cross-examination. If nothing else, the test we announce is an empirically accurate explanation of the results our cases have reached.

Finally, we reiterate that, when the declarant appears for cross-examination at trial, the Confrontation Clause places no constraints at all on the use of his prior testimonial statements. See *California v. Green,* 399 U.S. 149 (1970). It is therefore irrelevant that the reliability of some out-of-court statements " 'cannot be replicated, even if the declarant testifies to the same matters in court.' " The Clause does not bar admission of a statement so long as the declarant is present at trial to defend or explain it. (The Clause also does not bar the use of testimonial statements for purposes other than establishing the truth of the matter asserted. See *Tennessee v. Street,* 471 U.S. 409, 414 (1985).)

or bears "particularized guarantees of trustworthiness." This test departs from the historical principles identified above in two respects. First, it is too broad: It applies the same mode of analysis whether or not the hearsay consists of *ex parte* testimony. This often results in close constitutional scrutiny in cases that are far removed from the core concerns of the Clause. At the same time, however, the test is too narrow: It admits statements that *do* consist of *ex parte* testimony upon a mere finding of reliability. This malleable standard often fails to protect against paradigmatic confrontation violations.

Members of this Court and academics have suggested that we revise our doctrine to reflect more accurately the original understanding of the Clause. See, *e.g., Lilly,* 527 U.S., at 140–143 (BREYER, J., concurring); *White,* 502 U.S., at 366 (THOMAS, J., joined by SCALIA, J., concurring in part and concurring in judgment); A. Amar, The Constitution and Criminal Procedure 125–131 (1997); Friedman, Confrontation: The Search for Basic Principles, 86 Geo. L.J. 1011 (1998). They offer two proposals: First, that we apply the Confrontation Clause only to testimonial statements, leaving the remainder to regulation by hearsay law—thus eliminating the overbreadth referred to above. Second, that we impose an absolute bar to statements that are testimonial, absent a prior opportunity to cross-examine—thus eliminating the excessive narrowness referred to above.

In *White,* we considered the first proposal and rejected it. Although our analysis in this case casts doubt on that holding, we need not definitively resolve whether it survives our decision today, because Sylvia Crawford's statement is testimonial under any definition. This case does, however, squarely implicate the second proposal.

A

Where testimonial statements are involved, we do not think the Framers meant to leave the Sixth Amendment's protection to the vagaries of the rules of evidence, much less to amorphous notions of "reliability." Certainly none of the authorities discussed above acknowledges any general reliability exception to the common-law rule. Admitting statements deemed reliable by a judge is fundamentally at odds with the right of confrontation. To be sure, the Clause's ultimate goal is to ensure reliability of evidence, but it is a procedural rather than a substantive guarantee. It commands, not that evidence be reliable, but that reliability be assessed in a particular manner: by testing in the crucible of cross-examination. The Clause thus reflects a judgment, not only about the desirability of reliable evidence (a point on which there could be little dissent), but about how reliability can best be determined. Cf. 3 Blackstone, Commentaries, at 373 ("This open examination of witnesses ... is much more conducive to the clearing up of truth"); M. Hale, History and Analysis of the Common Law of England 258 (1713) (adversarial testing "beats and bolts out the Truth much better").

The *Roberts* test allows a jury to hear evidence, untested by the adversary process, based on a mere judicial determination of reliability. It thus replaces the constitutionally prescribed method of assessing reliability with a wholly foreign one. In this respect, it is very different from exceptions to the Confrontation Clause that make no claim to be a surrogate means of assessing reliability. For example, the rule of forfeiture by wrongdoing (which we accept) extinguishes confrontation claims on essentially equitable grounds; it does not purport to be an alternative means of determining reliability. See *Reynolds v. United States*, 98 U.S. 145, 158–159 (1879).

The Raleigh trial itself involved the very sorts of reliability determinations that *Roberts* authorizes. In the face of Raleigh's repeated demands for confrontation, the prosecution responded with many of the arguments a court applying *Roberts* might invoke today: that Cobham's statements were self-inculpatory, that they were not made in the heat of passion, and that they were not "extracted from [him] upon any hopes or promise of Pardon". It is not plausible that the Framers' only objection to the trial was that Raleigh's judges did not properly weigh these factors before sentencing him to death. Rather, the problem was that the judges refused to allow Raleigh to confront Cobham in court, where he could cross-examine him and try to expose his accusation as a lie.

Dispensing with confrontation because testimony is obviously reliable is akin to dispensing with jury trial because a defendant is obviously guilty. This is not what the Sixth Amendment prescribes.

B

The legacy of *Roberts* in other courts vindicates the Framers' wisdom in rejecting a general reliability exception. The framework is so unpredictable that it fails to provide meaningful protection from even core confrontation violations.

Reliability is an amorphous, if not entirely subjective, concept. There are countless factors bearing on whether a statement is reliable; the nine-factor balancing test applied by the Court of Appeals below is representative. See, *e.g., People v. Farrell*, 34 P.3d 401, 406–407 (Colo. 2001) (eight-factor test). Whether a statement is deemed reliable depends heavily on which factors the judge considers and how much weight he accords each of them. Some courts wind up attaching the same significance to opposite facts. For example, the Colorado Supreme Court held a statement more reliable because its inculpation of the defendant was "detailed," while the Fourth Circuit found a statement more reliable because the portion implicating another was "fleeting," *United States v. Photogrammetric Data Scrvs., Inc.*, 259 F.3d 229, 245 (C.A.4 2001). The Virginia Court of Appeals found a statement more reliable because the witness was in custody and charged with a crime (thus making the statement more obviously against her penal interest), see *Nowlin v. Commonwealth*, 40 Va.App. 327, 335–338 (2003), while the

Wisconsin Court of Appeals found a statement more reliable because the witness was *not* in custody and *not* a suspect, see *State v. Bintz,* 2002 WI App. 204, ¶ 13. Finally, the Colorado Supreme Court in one case found a statement more reliable because it was given "immediately after" the events at issue, *Farrell, supra,* at 407, while that same court, in another case, found a statement more reliable because two years had elapsed, *Stevens v. People,* 29 P.3d 305, 316 (Colo.2001).

The unpardonable vice of the *Roberts* test, however, is not its unpredictability, but its demonstrated capacity to admit core testimonial statements that the Confrontation Clause plainly meant to exclude. Despite the plurality's speculation in *Lilly,* 527 U.S., at 137, that it was "highly unlikely" that accomplice confessions implicating the accused could survive *Roberts,* courts continue routinely to admit them. One recent study found that, after *Lilly,* appellate courts admitted accomplice statements to the authorities in 25 out of 70 cases—more than one-third of the time. Kirst, Appellate Court Answers to the Confrontation Questions in *Lilly v. Virginia,* 53 Syracuse L.Rev. 87, 105 (2003). Courts have invoked *Roberts* to admit other sorts of plainly testimonial statements despite the absence of any opportunity to cross-examine. See *United States v. Aguilar,* 295 F.3d 1018, 1021–1023 (C.A.9 2002) (plea allocution showing existence of a conspiracy); *United States v. Centracchio,* 265 F.3d 518, 527–530 (C.A.7 2001) (same); *United States v. Dolah,* 245 F.3d 98, 104–105 (C.A.2 2001) (same); *United States v. Petrillo,* 237 F.3d 119, 122–123 (C.A.2 2000) (same); *United States v. Moskowitz,* 215 F.3d 265, 268–269 (C.A.2 2000) (same); *United States v. Gallego,* 191 F.3d 156, 166–168 (C.A.2 1999) (same); *United States v. Papajohn,* 212 F.3d 1112, 1118–1120 (C.A.8 2000) (grand jury testimony); *United States v. Thomas,* 30 Fed.Appx. 277, 279 (C.A.4 2002) (same); *Bintz, supra,* ¶ ¶ 15–22, 257 Wis.2d, at 188–191, 650 N.W.2d, at 918–920 (prior trial testimony); *State v. McNeill,* 140 N.C.App. 450, 457–460, 537 S.E.2d 518, 523–524 (2000) (same).

To add insult to injury, some of the courts that admit untested testimonial statements find reliability in the very factors that *make* the statements testimonial. As noted earlier, one court relied on the fact that the witness's statement was made to police while in custody on pending charges—the theory being that this made the statement more clearly against penal interest and thus more reliable. *Nowlin, supra,* at 335–338. Other courts routinely rely on the fact that a prior statement is given under oath in judicial proceedings. *E.g., Gallego, supra,* at 168 (plea allocution); *Papajohn, supra,* at 1120 (grand jury testimony). That inculpating statements are given in a testimonial setting is not an antidote to the confrontation problem, but rather the trigger that makes the Clause's demands most urgent. It is not enough to point out that most of the usual safeguards of the adversary process attend the statement, when the single safeguard missing is the one the Confrontation Clause demands.

C

Roberts' failings were on full display in the proceedings below. Sylvia Crawford made her statement while in police custody, herself a potential suspect in the case. Indeed, she had been told that whether she would be released "depend[ed] on how the investigation continues." In response to often leading questions from police detectives, she implicated her husband in Lee's stabbing and at least arguably undermined his self-defense claim. Despite all this, the trial court admitted her statement, listing several reasons why it was reliable. In its opinion reversing, the Court of Appeals listed several *other* reasons why the statement was *not* reliable. Finally, the State Supreme Court relied exclusively on the interlocking character of the statement and disregarded every other factor the lower courts had considered. The case is thus a self-contained demonstration of *Roberts'* unpredictable and inconsistent application.

Each of the courts also made assumptions that cross-examination might well have undermined. The trial court, for example, stated that Sylvia Crawford's statement was reliable because she was an eyewitness with direct knowledge of the events. But Sylvia at one point told the police that she had "shut [her] eyes and ... didn't really watch" part of the fight, and that she was "in shock." The trial court also buttressed its reliability finding by claiming that Sylvia was "being questioned by law enforcement, and, thus, the [questioner] is ... neutral to her and not someone who would be inclined to advance her interests and shade her version of the truth unfavorably toward the defendant." The Framers would be astounded to learn that *ex parte* testimony could be admitted against a criminal defendant because it was elicited by "neutral" government officers. But even if the court's assessment of the officer's motives was accurate, it says nothing about Sylvia's perception of her situation. Only cross-examination could reveal that.

The State Supreme Court gave dispositive weight to the interlocking nature of the two statements—that they were both ambiguous as to when and whether Lee had a weapon. The court's claim that the two statements were *equally* ambiguous is hard to accept. Petitioner's statement is ambiguous only in the sense that he had lingering doubts about his recollection: "A. I coulda swore I seen him goin' for somethin' before, right before everything happened.... [B]ut I'm not positive." Sylvia's statement, on the other hand, is truly inscrutable, since the key timing detail was simply assumed in the leading question she was asked: "Q. Did Kenny do anything to fight back from this assault?" Moreover, Sylvia specifically said Lee had nothing in his hands after he was stabbed, while petitioner was not asked about that.

The prosecutor obviously did not share the court's view that Sylvia's statement was ambiguous—he called it "damning evidence" that "completely refutes [petitioner's] claim of self-defense." We have no way of knowing whether the jury agreed with the prosecutor or the court. Far from obviating the need for cross-examination, the "interlocking" ambiguity of the two statements made it all the more imperative that they be tested to tease out the truth.

We readily concede that we could resolve this case by simply reweighing the "reliability factors" under *Roberts* and finding that Sylvia Crawford's statement falls short. But we view this as one of those rare cases in which the result below is so improbable that it reveals a fundamental failure on our part to interpret the Constitution in a way that secures its intended constraint on judicial discretion. Moreover, to reverse the Washington Supreme Court's decision after conducting our own reliability analysis would perpetuate, not avoid, what the Sixth Amendment condemns. The Constitution prescribes a procedure for determining the reliability of testimony in criminal trials, and we, no less than the state courts, lack authority to replace it with one of our own devising.

We have no doubt that the courts below were acting in utmost good faith when they found reliability. The Framers, however, would not have been content to indulge this assumption. They knew that judges, like other government officers, could not always be trusted to safeguard the rights of the people; the likes of the dread Lord Jeffreys were not yet too distant a memory. They were loath to leave too much discretion in judicial hands. By replacing categorical constitutional guarantees with open-ended balancing tests, we do violence to their design. Vague standards are manipulable, and, while that might be a small concern in run-of-the-mill assault prosecutions like this one, the Framers had an eye toward politically charged cases like Raleigh's—great state trials where the impartiality of even those at the highest levels of the judiciary might not be so clear. It is difficult to imagine *Roberts'* providing any meaningful protection in those circumstances.

* * *

Where nontestimonial hearsay is at issue, it is wholly consistent with the Framers' design to afford the States flexibility in their development of hearsay law—as does *Roberts,* and as would an approach that exempted such statements from Confrontation Clause scrutiny altogether. Where testimonial evidence is at issue, however, the Sixth Amendment demands what the common law required: unavailability and a prior opportunity for cross-examination. We leave for another day any effort to spell out a comprehensive definition of "testimonial."[10] Whatever else the term covers, it applies at a minimum to prior testimony at a preliminary hearing, before a grand jury, or at a former trial; and to police interrogations. These are the modern practices with closest kinship to the abuses at which the Confrontation Clause was directed.

---

10. We acknowledge THE CHIEF JUSTICE's objection, that our refusal to articulate a comprehensive definition in this case will cause interim uncertainty. But it can hardly be any worse than the status quo. The difference is that the *Roberts* test is *inherently,* and therefore *permanently,* unpredictable.

In this case, the State admitted Sylvia's testimonial statement against petitioner, despite the fact that he had no opportunity to cross-examine her. That alone is sufficient to make out a violation of the Sixth Amendment. *Roberts* notwithstanding, we decline to mine the record in search of indicia of reliability. Where testimonial statements are at issue, the only indicium of reliability sufficient to satisfy constitutional demands is the one the Constitution actually prescribes: confrontation.

The judgment of the Washington Supreme Court is reversed, and the case is remanded for further proceedings not inconsistent with this opinion.

It is so ordered.

■ CHIEF JUSTICE REHNQUIST, with whom JUSTICE O'CONNOR joins, concurring in the judgment.

I dissent from the Court's decision to overrule Ohio v. Roberts, 448 U.S. 56 (1980). I believe that the Court's adoption of a new interpretation of the Confrontation Clause is not backed by sufficiently persuasive reasoning to overrule long-established precedent. Its decision casts a mantle of uncertainty over future criminal trials in both federal and state courts, and is by no means necessary to decide the present case.

The Court's distinction between testimonial and nontestimonial statements, contrary to its claim, is no better rooted in history than our current doctrine. Under the common law, although the courts were far from consistent, out-of-court statements made by someone other than the accused and not taken under oath, unlike *ex parte* depositions or affidavits, were generally not considered substantive evidence upon which a conviction could be based. Testimonial statements such as accusatory statements to police officers likely would have been disapproved of in the 18th century, not necessarily because they resembled *ex parte* affidavits or depositions as the Court reasons, but more likely than not because they were not made under oath. Without an oath, one usually did not get to the second step of whether confrontation was required.

Thus, while I agree that the Framers were mainly concerned about sworn affidavits and depositions, it does not follow that they were similarly concerned about the Court's broader category of testimonial statements. See 1 N. Webster, An American Dictionary of the English Language (1828) (defining "Testimony" as "[a] solemn declaration or affirmation made for the purpose of establishing or proving some fact. *Such affirmation in judicial proceedings, may be verbal or written, but must be under oath*"(emphasis added)). As far as I can tell, unsworn testimonial statements were treated no differently at common law than were nontestimonial statements, and it seems to me any classification of statements as testimonial beyond that of sworn affidavits and depositions will be somewhat arbitrary, merely a proxy for what the Framers might have intended had such evidence been liberally admitted as substantive evidence like it is today.

I therefore see no reason why the distinction the Court draws is preferable to our precedent. Starting with Chief Justice Marshall's interpretation as a Circuit Justice in 1807, 16 years after the ratification of the Sixth Amendment, United States v. Burr, 25 F.Cas. 187, 193 (No. 14,694) (CC Va. 1807), continuing with our cases in the late 19th century, Mattox v. United States, 156 U.S. 237, 243–244 (1895); Kirby v. United States, 174 U.S. 47, 54–57 (1899), and through today, *e.g.,* White v. Illinois, 502 U.S. 346, 352–353 (1992), we have never drawn a distinction between testimonial and nontestimonial statements. And for that matter, neither has any other court of which I am aware. I see little value in trading our precedent for an imprecise approximation at this late date.

I am also not convinced that the Confrontation Clause categorically requires the exclusion of testimonial statements. Although many States had their own Confrontation Clauses, they were of recent vintage and were not interpreted with any regularity before 1791. State cases that recently followed the ratification of the Sixth Amendment were not uniform; the Court itself cites state cases from the early 19th century that took a more stringent view of the right to confrontation than does the Court, prohibiting former testimony even if the witness was subjected to cross-examination.

Nor was the English law at the time of the framing entirely consistent in its treatment of testimonial evidence. Generally *ex parte* affidavits and depositions were excluded as the Court notes, but even that proposition was not universal. See *King v. Eriswell,* 3 T.R. 707, 100 Eng. Rep. 815 (K.B.1790) (affirming by an equally divided court the admission of an *ex parte* examination because the declarant was unavailable to testify); *King v. Westbeer,* 1 Leach 12, 13, 168 Eng. Rep. 108, 109 (1739) (noting the admission of an *ex parte* affidavit); see also 1 M. Hale, Pleas of the Crown 585–586 (1736) (noting that statements of "accusers and witnesses" which were taken under oath could be admitted into evidence if the declarant was "dead or not able to travel"). Wigmore notes that sworn examinations of witnesses before justices of the peace in certain cases would not have been excluded until the end of the 1700's, 5 Wigmore § 1364, at 26–27, and sworn statements of witnesses before coroners became excluded only by statute in the 1800's, see *ibid.; id.,* § 1374, at 59. With respect to unsworn testimonial statements, there is no indication that once the hearsay rule was developed courts ever excluded these statements if they otherwise fell within a firmly rooted exception. See, *e.g., Eriswell, supra,* at 715–719 (Buller, J.), 720 (Ashhurst, J.), 100 Eng. Rep., at 819–822 (concluding that an *ex parte* examination was admissible as an exception to the hearsay rule because it was a declaration by a party of his state and condition). Dying declarations are one example. See, *e.g., Woodcock, supra,* at 502–504, 168

Eng. Rep., at 353–354; King v. Reason, 16 How. St. Tr. 1, 22–23 (K.B.1722).

Between 1700 and 1800 the rules regarding the admissibility of out-of-court statements were still being developed. There were always exceptions to the general rule of exclusion, and it is not clear to me that the Framers categorically wanted to eliminate further ones. It is one thing to trace the right of confrontation back to the Roman Empire; it is quite another to conclude that such a right absolutely excludes a large category of evidence. It is an odd conclusion indeed to think that the Framers created a cut-and-dried rule with respect to the admissibility of testimonial statements when the law during their own time was not fully settled.

To find exceptions to exclusion under the Clause is not to denigrate it as the Court suggests. Chief Justice Marshall stated of the Confrontation Clause: "I know of no principle in the preservation of which all are more concerned. I know none, by undermining which, life, liberty and property, might be more endangered. It is therefore incumbent on courts to be watchful of every inroad on a principle so truly important." *Burr*, 25 F.Cas., at 193. Yet, he recognized that such a right was not absolute, acknowledging that exceptions to the exclusionary component of the hearsay rule, which he considered as an "inroad" on the right to confrontation, had been introduced.

Exceptions to confrontation have always been derived from the experience that some out-of-court statements are just as reliable as cross-examined in-court testimony due to the circumstances under which they were made. We have recognized, for example, that co-conspirator statements simply "cannot be replicated, even if the declarant testifies to the same matters in court." United States v. Inadi, 475 U.S. 387, 395(1986). Because the statements are made while the declarant and the accused are partners in an illegal enterprise, the statements are unlikely to be false and their admission "actually furthers the 'Confrontation Clause's very mission' which is to 'advance the accuracy of the truth-determining process in criminal trials.'" Similar reasons justify the introduction of spontaneous declarations, see *White*, 502 U.S., at 356, statements made in the course of procuring medical services, see *ibid.*, dying declarations, see *Kirby, supra*, at 61, and countless other hearsay exceptions. That a statement might be testimonial does nothing to undermine the wisdom of one of these exceptions.

Indeed, cross-examination is a tool used to flesh out the truth, not an empty procedure. See Kentucky v. Stincer, 482 U.S. 730, 737 (1987) ("The right to cross-examination, protected by the Confrontation Clause, thus is essentially a 'functional' right designed to promote reliability in the truth-finding functions of a criminal trial"); see also Maryland v. Craig, 497 U.S. 836, 845 (1990) ("The central concern of the Confrontation Clause is to ensure the reliability of the evidence against a criminal defendant by subjecting it to rigorous testing in the context of an adversary proceeding before the trier of fact"). "[I]n a given instance [cross-examination may] be superfluous; it may be sufficiently clear, in that instance, that the statement offered is free enough from the risk of inaccuracy and untrustworthiness, so that the test of cross-examination would be a work of supererogation." 5 Wigmore § 1420, at 251. In such a case, as we noted over 100 years ago, "The law in its wisdom declares that the rights of the public shall not be wholly sacrificed in order that an incidental benefit may be preserved to the accused." *Mattox,* 156 U.S., at 243. By creating an immutable category of excluded evidence, the Court adds little to a trial's truth-finding function and ignores this longstanding guidance.

In choosing the path it does, the Court of course overrules Ohio v. Roberts, 448 U.S. 56, 100 S.Ct. 2531, 65 L.Ed.2d 597 (1980), a case decided nearly a quarter of a century ago. *Stare decisis* is not an inexorable command in the area of constitutional law, but by and large, it "is the preferred course because it promotes the evenhanded, predictable, and consistent development of legal principles, fosters reliance on judicial decisions, and contributes to the actual and perceived integrity of the judicial process." And in making this appraisal, doubt that the new rule is indeed the "right" one should surely be weighed in the balance. Though there are no vested interests involved, unresolved questions for the future of everyday criminal trials throughout the country surely counsel the same sort of caution. The Court grandly declares that "[w]e leave for another day any effort to spell out a comprehensive definition of 'testimonial,' " But the thousands of federal prosecutors and the tens of thousands of state prosecutors need answers as to what beyond the specific kinds of "testimony" the Court lists, is covered by the new rule. They need them now, not months or years from now. Rules of criminal evidence are applied every day in courts throughout the country, and parties should not be left in the dark in this manner.

To its credit, the Court's analysis of "testimony" excludes at least some hearsay exceptions, such as business records and official records. To hold otherwise would require numerous additional witnesses without any apparent gain in the truth-seeking process. Likewise to the Court's credit is its implicit recognition that the mistaken application of its new rule by courts which guess wrong as to the scope of the rule is subject to harmless-error analysis.

But these are palliatives to what I believe is a mistaken change of course. It is a change of course not in the least necessary to reverse the judgment of the Supreme Court of Washington in this case. The result the Court reaches follows inexorably from *Roberts* and its progeny without any need for overruling that line of cases. In Idaho v. Wright, 497 U.S. 805, 820–824, we held that an out-of-court statement was not admissible simply because the truthfulness of that statement was corroborated by other evidence at trial. As the Court notes, the Supreme Court of Washington gave decisive weight to the "interlocking nature of the two statements." No re-weighing of the "reliability factors," which is hypothesized by the Court, is required to reverse the judgment here. A citation to *Idaho v. Wright,* would suffice. For the reasons stated, I believe that this would be a far preferable course for the Court to take here.

Davis v. Washington

Supreme Court of the United States, 2006.
547 U.S. 813, 126 S.Ct. 2266, 165 L.Ed.2d 224.

■ JUSTICE SCALIA delivered the opinion of the Court.

These cases require us to determine when statements made to law enforcement personnel during a 911 call or at a crime scene are "testimonial" and thus subject to the requirements of the Sixth Amendment's Confrontation Clause.

I

A

The relevant statements in *Davis v. Washington,* No. 05–5224, were made to a 911 emergency operator on February 1, 2001. When the operator answered the initial call, the connection terminated before anyone spoke. She reversed the call, and Michelle McCottry answered. In the ensuing conversation, the operator ascertained that McCottry was involved in a domestic disturbance with her former boyfriend Adrian Davis, the petitioner in this case:

"911 Operator: Hello.

"Complainant: Hello.

"911 Operator: What's going on?

"Complainant: He's here jumpin' on me again.

"911 Operator: Okay. Listen to me carefully. Are you in a house or an apartment?

"Complainant: I'm in a house.

"911 Operator: Are there any weapons?

"Complainant: No. He's usin' his fists.

"911 Operator: Okay. Has he been drinking?

"Complainant: No.

"911 Operator: Okay, sweetie. I've got help started. Stay on the line with me, okay?

"Complainant: I'm on the line.

"911 Operator: Listen to me carefully. Do you know his last name?

"Complainant: It's Davis.

"911 Operator: Davis? Okay, what's his first name?

"Complainant: Adran

"911 Operator: What is it?

"Complainant: Adrian.

"911 Operator: Adrian?

"Complainant: Yeah.

"911 Operator: Okay. What's his middle initial?

"Complainant: Martell. He's runnin' now." App. in No. 05–5224, pp. 8–9.

As the conversation continued, the operator learned that Davis had "just r[un] out the door" after hitting McCottry, and that he was leaving in a car with someone else. *Id.*, at 9–10. McCottry started talking, but the operator cut her off, saying, "Stop talking and answer my questions." *Id.*, at 10. She then gathered more information about Davis (including his birthday), and learned that Davis had told McCottry that his purpose in coming to the house was "to get his stuff," since McCottry was moving. *Id.*, at 11–12. McCottry described the context of the assault, *id.*, at 12, after which the operator told her that the police were on their way. "They're gonna check the area for him first," the operator said, "and then they're gonna come talk to you." *Id.*, at 12–13.

The police arrived within four minutes of the 911 call and observed McCottry's shaken state, the "fresh injuries on her forearm and her face," and her "frantic efforts to gather her belongings and her children so that they could leave the residence." 154 Wash.2d 291, 296, 111 P.3d 844, 847 (2005) (en banc).

The State charged Davis with felony violation of a domestic no-contact order. "The State's only witnesses were the two police officers who responded to the 911 call. Both officers testified that McCottry exhibited injuries that appeared to be recent, but neither officer could testify as to the cause of the injuries." *Ibid.* McCottry presumably could have testified as to whether Davis was her assailant, but she did not appear. Over Davis's objection, based on the Confrontation Clause of the Sixth Amendment, the trial court admitted the recording of her exchange with the 911 operator, and the jury convicted him. The Washington Court of Appeals affirmed, 116 Wash.App. 81, 64 P.3d 661 (2003). The Supreme Court of Washington, with one dissenting justice, also affirmed, concluding that the portion of the 911 conversation in which McCottry identified Davis was not testimonial, and that if other portions of the conversation were testimonial, admitting them was harmless beyond a reasonable doubt. 154 Wash.2d, at 305, 111 P.3d, at 851. We granted certiorari. 546 U.S. 976 (2005).

SECTION 13 CONSTITUTIONAL RESTRAINTS

B

In *Hammon v. Indiana,* No. 05–5705, police responded late on the night of February 26, 2003, to a "reported domestic disturbance" at the home of Hershel and Amy Hammon. 829 N.E.2d 444, 446 (Ind.2005). They found Amy alone on the front porch, appearing " 'somewhat frightened,' " but she told them that " 'nothing was the matter,' " *id.,* at 446, 447. She gave them permission to enter the house, where an officer saw "a gas heating unit in the corner of the living room" that had "flames coming out of the . . . partial glass front. There were pieces of glass on the ground in front of it and there was flame emitting from the front of the heating unit." App. in No. 05–5705, p. 16.

Hershel, meanwhile, was in the kitchen. He told the police "that he and his wife had 'been in an argument' but 'everything was fine now' and the argument 'never became physical.' " 829 N.E.2d, at 447. By this point Amy had come back inside. One of the officers remained with Hershel; the other went to the living room to talk with Amy, and "again asked [her] what had occurred." *Ibid.;* App. in No. 05–5705, at 17, 32. Hershel made several attempts to participate in Amy's conversation with the police, see *id.,* at 32, but was rebuffed. The officer later testified that Hershel "became angry when I insisted that [he] stay separated from Mrs. Hammon so that we can investigate what had happened." *Id.,* at 34. After hearing Amy's account, the officer "had her fill out and sign a battery affidavit." *Id.,* at 18. Amy handwrote the following: "Broke our Furnace & shoved me down on the floor into the broken glass. Hit me in the chest and threw me down. Broke our lamps & phone. Tore up my van where I couldn't leave the house. Attacked my daughter." *Id.,* at 2.

The State charged Hershel with domestic battery and with violating his probation. Amy was subpoenaed, but she did not appear at his subsequent bench trial. The State called the officer who had questioned Amy, and asked him to recount what Amy told him and to authenticate the affidavit. Hershel's counsel repeatedly objected to the admission of this evidence. See *id.,* at 11, 12, 13, 17, 19, 20, 21. At one point, after hearing the prosecutor defend the affidavit because it was made "under oath," defense counsel said, "That doesn't give us the opportunity to cross examine [the] person who allegedly drafted it. Makes me mad." *Id.,* at 19. Nonetheless, the trial court admitted the affidavit as a "present sense impression," *id.,* at 20, and Amy's statements as "excited utterances" that "are expressly permitted in these kinds of cases even if the declarant is not available to testify." *Id.,* at 40. The officer thus testified that Amy

> "informed me that she and Hershel had been in an argument. That he became irrate [sic] over the fact of their daughter going to a boyfriend's house. The argument became . . . physical after being verbal and she informed me that Mr. Hammon, during the verbal part of the argument was breaking things in the living room and I believe she stated he broke the phone, broke the lamp, broke the

front of the heater. When it became physical he threw her down into the glass of the heater.

"She informed me Mr. Hammon had pushed her onto the ground, had shoved her head into the broken glass of the heater and that he had punched her in the chest twice I believe." *Id.*, at 17–18.

The trial judge found Hershel guilty on both charges, *id.*, at 40, and the Indiana Court of Appeals affirmed in relevant part, 809 N.E.2d 945 (2004). The Indiana Supreme Court also affirmed, concluding that Amy's statement was admissible for state-law purposes as an excited utterance, 829 N.E.2d, at 449; that "a 'testimonial' statement is one given or taken in significant part for purposes of preserving it for potential future use in legal proceedings," where "the motivations of the questioner and declarant are the central concerns," *id.*, at 456, 457; and that Amy's oral statement was not "testimonial" under these standards, *id.*, at 458. It also concluded that, although the affidavit was testimonial and thus wrongly admitted, it was harmless beyond a reasonable doubt, largely because the trial was to the bench. *Id.*, at 458–459. We granted certiorari. 546 U.S. 976 (2005).

II

The Confrontation Clause of the Sixth Amendment provides: "In all criminal prosecutions, the accused shall enjoy the right ... to be confronted with the witnesses against him." In *Crawford v. Washington*, 541 U.S. 36, 53–54, 124 S.Ct. 1354, 158 L.Ed.2d 177 (2004), we held that this provision bars "admission of testimonial statements of a witness who did not appear at trial unless he was unavailable to testify, and the defendant had had a prior opportunity for cross-examination." A critical portion of this holding, and the portion central to resolution of the two cases now before us, is the phrase "testimonial statements." Only statements of this sort cause the declarant to be a "witness" within the meaning of the Confrontation Clause. See *id.*, at 51. It is the testimonial character of the statement that separates it from other hearsay that, while subject to traditional limitations upon hearsay evidence, is not subject to the Confrontation Clause.

Our opinion in *Crawford* set forth "[v]arious formulations" of the core class of " 'testimonial' " statements, *ibid.*, but found it unnecessary to endorse any of them, because "some statements qualify under any definition," *id.*, at 52. Among those, we said, were "[s]tatements taken by police officers in the course of interrogations," *ibid.*; see also *id.*, at 53. The questioning that generated the deponent's statement in *Crawford*—which was made and recorded while she was in police custody, after having been given *Miranda* warnings as a possible suspect herself—"qualifies under any conceivable definition" of an " 'interrogation,' " 541 U.S., at 53, n. 4. We therefore did not define that term, except to say that "[w]e use [it] ... in its colloquial, rather than any technical legal, sense," and that "one can imagine various definitions

..., and we need not select among them in this case." *Ibid.* The character of the statements in the present cases is not as clear, and these cases require us to determine more precisely which police interrogations produce testimony.

Without attempting to produce an exhaustive classification of all conceivable statements—or even all conceivable statements in response to police interrogation—as either testimonial or nontestimonial, it suffices to decide the present cases to hold as follows: Statements are nontestimonial when made in the course of police interrogation under circumstances objectively indicating that the primary purpose of the interrogation is to enable police assistance to meet an ongoing emergency. They are testimonial when the circumstances objectively indicate that there is no such ongoing emergency, and that the primary purpose of the interrogation is to establish or prove past events potentially relevant to later criminal prosecution.[1]

III

A

In *Crawford*, it sufficed for resolution of the case before us to determine that "even if the Sixth Amendment is not solely concerned with testimonial hearsay, that is its primary object, and interrogations by law enforcement officers fall squarely within that class." *Id.*, at 53. Moreover, as we have just described, the facts of that case spared us the need to define what we meant by "interrogations." The *Davis* case today does not permit us this luxury of indecision. The inquiries of a police operator in the course of a 911 call[2] are an interrogation in one sense, but not in a sense that "qualifies under any conceivable definition." We must decide, therefore, whether the Confrontation Clause applies only to testimonial hearsay; and, if so, whether the recording of a 911 call qualifies.

1. Our holding refers to interrogations because, as explained below, the statements in the cases presently before us are the products of interrogations—which in some circumstances tend to generate testimonial responses. This is not to imply, however, that statements made in the absence of any interrogation are necessarily nontestimonial. The Framers were no more willing to exempt from cross-examination volunteered testimony or answers to open-ended questions than they were to exempt answers to detailed interrogation. (Part of the evidence against Sir Walter Raleigh was a letter from Lord Cobham that was plainly *not* the result of sustained questioning. *Raleigh's Case*, 2 How. St. Tr. 1, 27 (1603).) And of course even when interrogation exists, it is in the final analysis the declarant's statements, not the interrogator's questions, that the Confrontation Clause requires us to evaluate.

2. If 911 operators are not themselves law enforcement officers, they may at least be agents of law enforcement when they conduct interrogations of 911 callers. For purposes of this opinion (and without deciding the point), we consider their acts to be acts of the police. As in *Crawford v. Washington*, 541 U.S. 36, 124 S.Ct. 1354, 158 L.Ed.2d 177 (2004), therefore, our holding today makes it unnecessary to consider whether and when statements made to someone other than law enforcement personnel are "testimonial."

CHAPTER 4 HEARSAY

The answer to the first question was suggested in *Crawford*, even if not explicitly held:

"The text of the Confrontation Clause reflects this focus [on testimonial hearsay]. It applies to 'witnesses' against the accused—in other words, those who 'bear testimony.' 1 N. Webster, An American Dictionary of the English Language (1828). 'Testimony,' in turn, is typically 'a solemn declaration or affirmation made for the purpose of establishing or proving some fact.' *Ibid.* An accuser who makes a formal statement to government officers bears testimony in a sense that a person who makes a casual remark to an acquaintance does not." 541 U.S., at 51.

A limitation so clearly reflected in the text of the constitutional provision must fairly be said to mark out not merely its "core," but its perimeter.

We are not aware of any early American case invoking the Confrontation Clause or the common-law right to confrontation that did not clearly involve testimony as thus defined. Well into the 20th century, our own Confrontation Clause jurisprudence was carefully applied only in the testimonial context. See, *e.g., Reynolds v. United States,* 98 U.S. 145, 158, 25 L.Ed. 244 (1879) (testimony at prior trial was subject to the Confrontation Clause, but petitioner had forfeited that right by procuring witness's absence); *Mattox v. United States,* 156 U.S. 237, 240–244, 15 S.Ct. 337, 39 L.Ed. 409 (1895) (prior trial testimony of deceased witnesses admitted because subject to cross-examination); *Kirby v. United States,* 174 U.S. 47, 55–56, 19 S.Ct. 574, 43 L.Ed. 890 (1899) (guilty pleas and jury conviction of others could not be admitted to show that property defendant received from them was stolen); *Motes v. United States,* 178 U.S. 458, 467, 470–471, 20 S.Ct. 993, 44 L.Ed. 1150 (1900) (written deposition subject to cross-examination was not admissible because witness was available); *Dowdell v. United States,* 221 U.S. 325, 330–331, 31 S.Ct. 590, 55 L.Ed. 753 (1911) (facts regarding conduct of prior trial certified to by the judge, the clerk of court, and the official reporter did not relate to defendants' guilt or innocence and hence were not statements of "witnesses" under the Confrontation Clause).

Even our later cases, conforming to the reasoning of *Ohio v. Roberts,* 448 U.S. 56, 100 S.Ct. 2531, 65 L.Ed.2d 597 (1980), never in practice dispensed with the Confrontation Clause requirements of unavailability and prior cross-examination in cases that involved testimonial hearsay, see *Crawford,* 541 U.S., at 57–59 (citing cases), with one arguable exception, see *id.,* at 58, n. 8 (discussing *White v. Illinois,* 502 U.S. 346, 112 S.Ct. 736, 116 L.Ed.2d 848 (1992)). Where our cases did dispense with those requirements—even under the *Roberts* approach—the statements at issue were clearly nontestimonial. See, *e.g., Bourjaily v. United States,* 483 U.S. 171, 181–184, 107 S.Ct. 2775, 97 L.Ed.2d 144 (1987) (statements made unwittingly to a Government informant); *Dutton v.*

Evans, 400 U.S. 74, 87–89, 91 S.Ct. 210, 27 L.Ed.2d 213 (1970) (plurality opinion) (statements from one prisoner to another).

Most of the American cases applying the Confrontation Clause or its state constitutional or common-law counterparts involved testimonial statements of the most formal sort—sworn testimony in prior judicial proceedings or formal depositions under oath—which invites the argument that the scope of the Clause is limited to that very formal category. But the English cases that were the progenitors of the Confrontation Clause did not limit the exclusionary rule to prior court testimony and formal depositions, see *Crawford, supra,* at 52, and n. 3. In any event, we do not think it conceivable that the protections of the Confrontation Clause can readily be evaded by having a note-taking policeman *recite* the unsworn hearsay testimony of the declarant, instead of having the declarant sign a deposition. Indeed, if there is one point for which no case—English or early American, state or federal—can be cited, that is it.

The question before us in *Davis,* then, is whether, objectively considered, the interrogation that took place in the course of the 911 call produced testimonial statements. When we said in *Crawford, supra,* at 53, that "interrogations by law enforcement officers fall squarely within [the] class" of testimonial hearsay, we had immediately in mind (for that was the case before us) interrogations solely directed at establishing the facts of a past crime, in order to identify (or provide evidence to convict) the perpetrator. The product of such interrogation, whether reduced to a writing signed by the declarant or embedded in the memory (and perhaps notes) of the interrogating officer, is testimonial. It is, in the terms of the 1828 American dictionary quoted in *Crawford,* " '[a] solemn declaration or affirmation made for the purpose of establishing or proving some fact.' " 541 U.S., at 51. (The solemnity of even an oral declaration of relevant past fact to an investigating officer is well enough established by the severe consequences that can attend a deliberate falsehood. See, *e.g., United States v. Stewart,* 433 F.3d 273, 288 (C.A.2 2006) (false statements made to federal investigators violate 18 U.S.C. § 1001); *State v. Reed,* 2005 WI 53, ¶ 30, 280 Wis.2d 68, 695 N.W.2d 315, 323 (state criminal offense to "knowingly giv[e] false information to [an] officer with [the] intent to mislead the officer in the performance of his or her duty").) A 911 call, on the other hand, and at least the initial interrogation conducted in connection with a 911 call, is ordinarily not designed primarily to "establis[h] or prov[e]" some past fact, but to describe current circumstances requiring police assistance.

The difference between the interrogation in *Davis* and the one in *Crawford* is apparent on the face of things. In *Davis,* McCottry was speaking about events *as they were actually happening,* rather than "describ[ing] past events," *Lilly v. Virginia,* 527 U.S. 116, 137, 119 S.Ct. 1887, 144 L.Ed.2d 117 (1999) (plurality opinion). Sylvia Crawford's interrogation, on the other hand, took place hours after the events she described had occurred. Moreover, any reasonable listener would recognize that McCottry (unlike Sylvia Crawford) was facing an ongoing emergency. Although one *might* call 911 to provide a narrative report of a crime absent any imminent danger, McCottry's call was plainly a call for help against bona fide physical threat. Third, the nature of what was asked and answered in *Davis,* again viewed objectively, was such that the elicited statements were necessary to be able to *resolve* the present emergency, rather than simply to learn (as in *Crawford*) what had happened in the past. That is true even of the operator's effort to establish the identity of the assailant, so that the dispatched officers might know whether they would be encountering a violent felon. See, *e.g., Hiibel v. Sixth Judicial Dist. Court of Nev., Humboldt Cty.,* 542 U.S. 177, 186, 124 S.Ct. 2451, 159 L.Ed.2d 292 (2004). And finally, the difference in the level of formality between the two interviews is striking. Crawford was responding calmly, at the station house, to a series of questions, with the officer-interrogator taping and making notes of her answers; McCottry's frantic answers were provided over the phone, in an environment that was not tranquil, or even (as far as any reasonable 911 operator could make out) safe.

We conclude from all this that the circumstances of McCottry's interrogation objectively indicate its primary purpose was to enable police assistance to meet an ongoing emergency. She simply was not acting as a *witness;* she was not *testifying.* What she said was not "a weaker substitute for live testimony" at trial, *United States v. Inadi,* 475 U.S. 387, 394, 106 S.Ct. 1121, 89 L.Ed.2d 390 (1986), like Lord Cobham's statements in *Raleigh's Case,* 2 How. St. Tr. 1 (1603), or Jane Dingler's *ex parte* statements against her husband in *King v. Dingler,* 2 Leach 561, 168 Eng. Rep. 383 (1791), or Sylvia Crawford's statement in *Crawford.* In each of those cases, the *ex parte* actors and the evidentiary products of the *ex parte* communication aligned perfectly with their courtroom analogues. McCottry's emergency statement does not. No "witness" goes into court to proclaim an emergency and seek help.

Davis seeks to cast McCottry in the unlikely role of a witness by pointing to English cases. None of them involves statements made during an ongoing emergency. In *King v. Brasier,* 1 Leach 199, 168 Eng. Rep. 202 (1779), for example, a young rape victim, "immediately on her coming home, told all the circumstances of the injury" to her mother. *Id.,* at 200, 168 Eng. Rep., at 202. The case would be helpful to Davis if the relevant statement had been the girl's screams for aid as she was being chased by her assailant. But by the time the victim got home, her story was an account of past events.

This is not to say that a conversation which begins as an interrogation to determine the need for emergency assistance cannot, as the Indiana Supreme Court put it, "evolve into testimonial statements," 829 N.E.2d, at 457, once that purpose has been achieved. In this case, for example, after the operator gained the information needed to address the exigency of the moment, the emergency appears to have ended (when Davis drove away from the premises). The operator then told McCottry to be quiet, and proceeded to pose a battery of questions. It could readily be maintained that, from that point on, McCottry's statements were testimonial, not unlike the "structured police questioning" that occurred in *Crawford,* 541 U.S., at 53, n. 4. This presents no great problem. Just as, for Fifth Amendment purposes, "police officers can and will distinguish almost instinctively between questions necessary to secure their own safety or the safety of the public and questions designed solely to elicit testimonial evidence from a suspect," *New York v. Quarles,* 467 U.S. 649, 658–659, 104 S.Ct. 2626, 81 L.Ed.2d 550 (1984), trial courts will recognize the point at which, for Sixth Amendment purposes, statements in response to interrogations become testimonial. Through *in limine* procedure, they should redact or exclude the portions of any statement that have become testimonial, as they do, for example, with unduly prejudicial portions of otherwise admissible evidence. Davis's jury did not hear the *complete* 911 call, although it may well have heard some testimonial portions. We were asked to classify only McCottry's early statements identifying Davis as her assailant, and we agree with the Washington Supreme Court that they were not testimonial. That court also concluded that, even if later parts of the call were testimonial, their admission was harmless beyond a reasonable doubt. Davis does not challenge that holding, and we therefore assume it to be correct.

B

Determining the testimonial or nontestimonial character of the statements that were the product of the interrogation in *Hammon* is a much easier task, since they were not much different from the statements we found to be testimonial in *Crawford.* It is entirely clear from the circumstances that the interrogation was part of an investigation into possibly criminal past conduct—as, indeed, the testifying officer expressly acknowledged, App. in No. 05–5705, at 25, 32, 34. There was no emergency in progress; the interrogating officer testified that he had heard no arguments or crashing and saw no one throw or break anything, *id.,* at 25. When the officers first arrived, Amy told them that things were fine, *id.,* at 14, and there was no immediate threat to her person. When the officer questioned Amy for the second time, and elicited the challenged statements, he was not seeking to determine (as in *Davis*) "what is happening," but rather "what happened." Objectively viewed, the primary, if not indeed the sole, purpose of the interrogation was to investigate a possible crime—which is, of course, precisely what the officer *should* have done.

It is true that the *Crawford* interrogation was more formal. It followed a *Miranda* warning, was tape-recorded, and took place at the station house, see 541 U.S., at 53, n. 4. While these features certainly strengthened the statements' testimonial aspect—made it more objectively apparent, that is, that the purpose of the exercise was to nail down the truth about past criminal events—none was essential to the point. It was formal enough that Amy's interrogation was conducted in a separate room, away from her husband (who tried to intervene), with the officer receiving her replies for use in his "investigat[ion]." App. in No. 05–5705, at 34. What we called the "striking resemblance" of the *Crawford* statement to civil-law *ex parte* examinations, 541 U.S., at 52, is shared by Amy's statement here. Both declarants were actively separated from the defendant—officers forcibly prevented Hershel from participating in the interrogation. Both statements deliberately recounted, in response to police questioning, how potentially criminal past events began and progressed. And both took place some time after the events described were over. Such statements under official interrogation are an obvious substitute for live testimony, because they do precisely *what a witness does* on direct examination; they are inherently testimonial.[5]

Both Indiana and the United States as *amicus curiae* argue that this case should be resolved much like *Davis*. For the reasons we find the comparison to *Crawford* compelling, we find the comparison to *Davis* unpersuasive. The statements in *Davis* were taken when McCottry was alone, not only unprotected by police (as Amy Hammon was protected), but apparently in immediate danger from Davis. She was seeking aid, not telling a story about the past. McCottry's present-tense statements showed immediacy; Amy's narrative of past events was delivered at some remove in time from the danger she described. And after Amy answered the officer's questions, he had her execute an affidavit, in order, he testified, "[t]o establish events that have occurred previously." App. in No. 05–5705, at 18.

Although we necessarily reject the Indiana Supreme Court's implication that virtually any "initial inquiries" at the crime scene will not be testimonial, see 829 N.E.2d, at 453, 457, we do not hold the opposite— that *no* questions at the scene will yield nontestimonial answers. We have already observed of domestic disputes that "[o]fficers called to investigate ... need to know whom they are dealing with in order to assess the situation, the threat to their own safety, and possible danger to the potential victim." *Hiibel,* 542 U.S., at 186. Such exigencies may *often* mean that "initial inquiries" produce nontestimonial statements.

---

5. ... As for the charge that our holding is not a "targeted attempt to reach the abuses forbidden by the [Confrontation] Clause," which the dissent describes as the depositions taken by Marian magistrates, characterized by a high degree of formality. We do not dispute that formality is indeed essential to testimonial utterance. But we no longer have examining Marian magistrates; and we do have, as our 18th–century forebears did not, examining police officers, see L. Friedman, Crime and Punishment in American History 67–68 (1993)—who perform investigative and testimonial functions once performed by examining Marian magistrates, see J. Langbein, The Origins of Adversary Criminal Trial 41 (2003). It imports sufficient formality, in our view, that lies to such officers are criminal offenses. Restricting the Confrontation Clause to the precise forms against which it was originally directed is a recipe for its extinction. Cf. *Kyllo v. United States,* 533 U.S. 27, 121 S.Ct. 2038, 150 L.Ed.2d 94 (2001).

But in cases like this one, where Amy's statements were neither a cry for help nor the provision of information enabling officers immediately to end a threatening situation, the fact that they were given at an alleged crime scene and were "initial inquiries" is immaterial. Cf. *Crawford, supra,* at 52, n. 3.[6]

IV

Respondents in both cases, joined by a number of their *amici,* contend that the nature of the offenses charged in these two cases—domestic violence—requires greater flexibility in the use of testimonial evidence. This particular type of crime is notoriously susceptible to intimidation or coercion of the victim to ensure that she does not testify at trial. When this occurs, the Confrontation Clause gives the criminal a windfall. We may not, however, vitiate constitutional guarantees when they have the effect of allowing the guilty to go free. Cf. *Kyllo v. United States,* 533 U.S. 27, 121 S.Ct. 2038, 150 L.Ed.2d 94 (2001) (suppressing evidence from an illegal search). But when defendants seek to undermine the judicial process by procuring or coercing silence from witnesses and victims, the Sixth Amendment does not require courts to acquiesce. While defendants have no duty to assist the State in proving their guilt, they *do* have the duty to refrain from acting in ways that destroy the integrity of the criminal-trial system. We reiterate what we said in *Crawford:* that "the rule of forfeiture by wrongdoing ... extinguishes confrontation claims on essentially equitable grounds." 541 U.S., at 62 (citing *Reynolds,* 98 U.S., at 158–159). That is, one who obtains the absence of a witness by wrongdoing forfeits the constitutional right to confrontation.

We take no position on the standards necessary to demonstrate such forfeiture, but federal courts using Federal Rule of Evidence 804(b)(6), which codifies the forfeiture doctrine, have generally held the Government to the preponderance-of-the-evidence standard, see, *e.g., United States v. Scott,* 284 F.3d 758, 762 (C.A.7 2002). State courts tend to follow the same practice, see, *e.g., Commonwealth v. Edwards,* 444 Mass. 526, 542, 830 N.E.2d 158, 172 (2005). Moreover, if a hearing on forfeiture is required, *Edwards,* for instance, observed that "hearsay evidence, including the unavailable witness's out-of-court statements, may be considered." *Id.,* at 545, 830 N.E.2d, at 174. The *Roberts* approach to the Confrontation Clause undoubtedly made recourse to this doctrine less necessary, because prosecutors could show the "reliability" of *ex parte*

---

6. Police investigations themselves are, of course, in no way impugned by our characterization of their fruits as testimonial. Investigations of past crimes prevent future harms and lead to necessary arrests. While prosecutors may hope that inculpatory "nontestimonial" evidence is gathered, this is essentially beyond police control. Their saying that an emergency exists cannot make it be so. The Confrontation Clause in no way governs police conduct, because it is the trial *use* of, not the investigatory *collection* of, *ex parte* testimonial statements which offends that provision. But neither can police conduct govern the Confrontation Clause; testimonial statements are what they are.

statements more easily than they could show the defendant's procurement of the witness's absence. *Crawford,* in overruling *Roberts,* did not destroy the ability of courts to protect the integrity of their proceedings.

We have determined that, absent a finding of forfeiture by wrongdoing, the Sixth Amendment operates to exclude Amy Hammon's affidavit. The Indiana courts may (if they are asked) determine on remand whether such a claim of forfeiture is properly raised and, if so, whether it is meritorious.

* * *

We affirm the judgment of the Supreme Court of Washington in No. 05-5224. We reverse the judgment of the Supreme Court of Indiana in No. 05-5705, and remand the case to that Court for proceedings not inconsistent with this opinion.

It is so ordered.

■ JUSTICE THOMAS, concurring in the judgment in part and dissenting in part.

* * *

This requirement of solemnity supports my view that the statements regulated by the Confrontation Clause must include "extrajudicial statements ... contained in formalized testimonial materials, such as affidavits, depositions, prior testimony, or confessions." *White, supra,* at 365 (opinion of THOMAS, J.). Affidavits, depositions, and prior testimony are, by their very nature, taken through a formalized process. Likewise, confessions, when extracted by police in a formal manner, carry sufficient indicia of solemnity to constitute formalized statements and, accordingly, bear a "striking resemblance," *Crawford, supra,* at 52, to the examinations of the accused and accusers under the Marian statutes. See generally Langbein, *supra,* at 21-34.

Although the Court concedes that the early American cases invoking the right to confrontation or the Confrontation Clause itself all "clearly involve[d] testimony" as defined in *Crawford, ante,* at 9, it fails to acknowledge that all of the cases it cites fall within the narrower category of formalized testimonial materials I have proposed. See *ante,* at 9, n. 3. Interactions between the police and an accused (or witnesses) resemble Marian proceedings—and these early cases—only when the interactions are somehow rendered "formal." In *Crawford,* for example, the interrogation was custodial, taken after warnings given pursuant to *Miranda v. Arizona,* 384 U.S. 436, 86 S.Ct. 1602, 16 L.Ed.2d 694 (1966). 541 U.S., at 38. *Miranda* warnings, by their terms, inform a prospective defendant that " 'anything he says can be used against him in a court of law.' " *Dickerson v. United States,* 530 U.S. 428, 435, 120 S.Ct. 2326, 147 L.Ed.2d 405 (2000) (quoting *Miranda, supra,* at 479). This imports a solemnity to the process that is not present in a mere conversation between a witness or suspect and a police officer.

* * *

B

Neither the 911 call at issue in *Davis* nor the police questioning at issue in *Hammon* is testimonial under the appropriate framework. Neither the call nor the questioning is itself a formalized dialogue. Nor do any circumstances surrounding the taking of the statements render those statements sufficiently formal to resemble the Marian examinations; the statements were neither Mirandized nor custodial, nor accompanied by any similar indicia of formality.

* * *

Michigan v. Bryant

Supreme Court of the United States, 2011.
131 S.Ct. 1143

■ [SOTOMAYOR, J., delivered the opinion of the court, in which ROBERTS, C.J., and KENNEDY, BREYER, and ALITO, JJ., joined. THOMAS, J., filed an opinion concurring in the judgment. SCALIA, J., and GINSBURG, J., filed dissenting opinions. KAGAN, J., took no part in the consideration or decision of the case.]

■ JUSTICE SOTOMAYOR delivered the opinion of the Court.

At respondent Richard Bryant's trial, the court admitted statements that the victim, Anthony Covington, made to police officers who discovered him mortally wounded in a gas station parking lot. A jury convicted Bryant of, *inter alia,* second-degree murder. On appeal, the Supreme Court of Michigan held that the Sixth Amendment's Confrontation Clause, rendered Covington's statements inadmissible testimonial hearsay, and the court reversed Bryant's conviction. We granted the State's petition for a writ of certiorari to consider whether the Confrontation Clause barred the admission at trial of Covington's statements to the police. We hold that the circumstances of the interaction between Covington and the police objectively indicate that the "primary purpose of the interrogation" was "to enable police assistance to meet an ongoing emergency." Therefore, Covington's identification and description of the shooter and the location of the shooting were not testimonial statements, and their admission at Bryant's trial did not violate the Confrontation Clause. We vacate the judgment of the Supreme Court of Michigan and remand.

I

Around 3:25 a.m. on April 29, 2001, Detroit, Michigan police officers responded to a radio dispatch indicating that a man had been shot. At the scene, they found the victim, Anthony Covington, lying on the ground next to his car in a gas station parking lot. Covington had a gunshot wound to his abdomen, appeared to be in great pain, and spoke with difficulty.

The police asked him "what had happened, who had shot him, and where the shooting had occurred." Covington stated that "Rick" shot him at around 3 a.m. He also indicated that he had a conversation with Bryant, whom he recognized based on his voice, through the back door of Bryant's house. Covington explained that when he turned to leave, he was shot through the door and then drove to the gas station, where police found him.

Covington's conversation with the police ended within 5 to 10 minutes when emergency medical services arrived. Covington was transported to a hospital and died within hours. The police left the gas station after speaking with Covington, called for backup, and traveled to Bryant's house. They did not find Bryant there but did find blood and a bullet on the back porch and an apparent bullet hole in the back door. Police also found Covington's wallet and identification outside the house.

At trial, which occurred prior to our decisions in *Crawford,* and *Davis,* the police officers who spoke with Covington at the gas station testified about what Covington had told them...

...

Before the Supreme Court of Michigan, Bryant argued that Covington's statements to the police were testimonial under *Crawford* and *Davis* and were therefore inadmissible. The State, on the other hand, argued that the statements were admissible as "excited utterances" under the Michigan Rules of Evidence. There was no dispute that Covington was unavailable at trial and Bryant had no prior opportunity to cross-examine him. The court therefore assessed whether Covington's statements to the police identifying and describing the shooter and the time and location of the shooting were testimonial hearsay for purposes of the Confrontation Clause. The court concluded that the circumstances "clearly indicate that the 'primary purpose' of the questioning was to establish the facts of an event that had *already* occurred; the 'primary purpose' was not to enable police assistance to meet an ongoing emergency." The court explained that, in its view, Covington was describing past events and as such, his "primary purpose in making these statements to the police ... was ... to tell the police who had committed the crime against him, where the crime had been committed, and where the police could find the criminal." Noting that the officers' actions did not suggest that they perceived an ongoing emergency at the gas station, the court held that there was in fact no ongoing emergency. The court distinguished the facts of this case from those in *Davis,* where we held a declarant's statements in a 911 call to be nontestimonial. It instead analogized this case to *Hammon v. Indiana,* which we decided jointly with *Davis* and in which we found testimonial a declarant's statements to police just after an assault. Based on this analysis, the Supreme Court of Michigan held that the admission of Covington's statements constituted prejudicial plain error warranting reversal and ordered a new trial. The court did not address whether, absent a Confrontation Clause bar, the statements' admission would have been otherwise consistent with Michigan's hearsay rules or due process.[1]

We granted certiorari to determine whether the Confrontation Clause barred admission of Covington's statements.

II

. . .

In 2006, the Court in *Davis v. Washington* and *Hammon v. Indiana,* took a further step to "determine more precisely which police interrogations produce testimony" and therefore implicate a Confrontation Clause bar. We explained that when *Crawford* said that

> " 'interrogations by law enforcement officers fall squarely within [the] class' of testimonial hearsay, we had immediately in mind (for that was the case before us) interrogations solely directed at establishing the facts of a past crime, in order to identify (or provide evidence to convict) the perpetrator. The product of such interrogation, whether reduced to a writing signed by the declarant or embedded in the memory (and perhaps notes) of the interrogating officer, is testimonial." *Davis,* 547 U.S., at 826.

We thus made clear in *Davis* that not all those questioned by the police are witnesses and not all "interrogations by law enforcement officers," are subject to the Confrontation Clause.

Davis and *Hammon* were both domestic violence cases. In *Davis,* Michelle McCottry made the statements at issue to a 911 operator during a domestic disturbance with Adrian Davis, her former boyfriend. McCottry told the operator, " 'He's here jumpin' on me again,' " and, " 'He's usin' his fists.' " The operator then asked McCottry for Davis' first and last names and middle initial, and at that point in the conversation McCottry reported that Davis had fled in a car. McCottry

---

1. The Supreme Court of Michigan held that the question whether the victim's statements would have been admissible as "dying declarations" was not properly before it because at the preliminary examination, the prosecution, after first invoking both the dying declaration and excited utterance hearsay exceptions, established the factual foundation only for admission of the statements as excited utterances. The trial court ruled that the statements were admissible as excited utterances and did not address their admissibility as dying declarations. This occurred prior to our 2004 decision in *Crawford v. Washington,* where we first suggested that dying declarations, even if testimonial, might be admissible as a historical exception to the Confrontation Clause; see also *Giles v. California,* 554 U.S. 353 (2008). We noted in *Crawford* that we "need not decide in this case whether the Sixth Amendment incorporates an exception for testimonial dying declarations." Because of the State's failure to preserve its argument with regard to dying declarations, we similarly need not decide that question here. See also *post,* (GINSBURG, J., dissenting).

did not appear at Davis' trial, and the State introduced the recording of her conversation with the 911 operator.

In *Hammon,* decided along with *Davis,* police responded to a domestic disturbance call at the home of Amy and Hershel Hammon, where they found Amy alone on the front porch. She appeared " 'somewhat frightened,' " but told them " 'nothing was the matter.' " She gave the police permission to enter the house, where they saw a gas heating unit with the glass front shattered on the floor. One officer remained in the kitchen with Hershel, while another officer talked to Amy in the living room about what had happened. Hershel tried several times to participate in Amy's conversation with the police and became angry when the police required him to stay separated from Amy. The police asked Amy to fill out and sign a battery affidavit. She wrote: " 'Broke our Furnace & shoved me down on the floor into the broken glass. Hit me in the chest and threw me down. Broke our lamps & phone. Tore up my van where I couldn't leave the house. Attacked my daughter.' " Amy did not appear at Hershel's trial, so the police officers who spoke with her testified as to her statements and authenticated the affidavit. The trial court admitted the affidavit as a present sense impression and admitted the oral statements as excited utterances under state hearsay rules. The Indiana Supreme Court affirmed Hammon's conviction, holding that Amy's oral statements were not testimonial and that the admission of the affidavit, although erroneous because the affidavit was testimonial, was harmless.

To address the facts of both cases, we expanded upon the meaning of "testimonial" that we first employed in *Crawford* and discussed the concept of an ongoing emergency. We explained:

> "Statements are nontestimonial when made in the course of police interrogation under circumstances objectively indicating that the primary purpose of the interrogation is to enable police assistance to meet an ongoing emergency. They are testimonial when the circumstances objectively indicate that there is no such ongoing emergency, and that the primary purpose of the interrogation is to establish or prove past events potentially relevant to later criminal prosecution."

Examining the *Davis* and *Hammon* statements in light of those definitions, we held that the statements at issue in *Davis* were nontestimonial and the statements in *Hammon* were testimonial. We distinguished the statements in *Davis* from the testimonial statements in *Crawford* on several grounds, including that the victim in *Davis* was "speaking about events *as they were actually happening,* rather than 'describ[ing] past events,' " that there was an ongoing emergency, that the "elicited statements were necessary to be able to *resolve* the present emergency," and that the statements were not formal. In *Hammon,* on the other hand, we held that, "[i]t is entirely clear from the circumstances that the interrogation was part of an investigation into possibly criminal past conduct." There was "no emergency in progress." The officer questioning Amy "was not seeking to determine ... 'what is happening,' but rather 'what happened.'" It was "formal enough" that the police interrogated Amy in a room separate from her husband where, "some time after the events described were over," she "deliberately recounted, in response to police questioning, how potentially criminal past events began and progressed." Because her statements "were neither a cry for help nor the provision of information enabling officers immediately to end a threatening situation," we held that they were testimonial.

Davis did not "attemp[t] to produce an exhaustive classification of all conceivable statements—or even all conceivable statements in response to police interrogation—as either testimonial or nontestimonial."[2] The basic purpose of the Confrontation Clause was to "targe[t]" the sort of "abuses" exemplified at the notorious treason trial of Sir Walter Raleigh. Thus, the most important instances in which the Clause restricts the introduction of out-of-court statements are those in which state actors are involved in a formal, out-of-court interrogation of a witness to obtain evidence for trial. Even where such an interrogation is conducted with all good faith, introduction of the resulting statements at trial can be unfair to the accused if they are untested by cross-examination. Whether formal or informal, out-of-court statements can evade the basic objective of the Confrontation Clause, which is to prevent the accused from being deprived of the opportunity to cross-examine the declarant about statements taken for use at trial. When, as in *Davis*, the primary purpose of an interrogation is to respond to an "ongoing emergency," its purpose is not to create a record for trial and thus is not within the scope of the Clause. But there may be *other* circumstances, aside from ongoing emergencies, when a statement is not procured with a primary purpose of creating an out-of-court substitute for trial testimony. In making the primary purpose determination, standard rules of hearsay, designed to identify some statements as reliable, will be relevant. Where no such primary purpose exists, the admissibility of a statement is the concern of state and federal rules of evidence, not the Confrontation Clause.

Deciding this case also requires further explanation of the "ongoing emergency" circumstance addressed in *Davis*. Because *Davis* and *Hammon* arose in the domestic violence context, that was the situation "we had immediately in mind (for that was the case before us)." We now face a new context: a nondomestic dispute, involving a victim found in a public location, suffering from a fatal gunshot wound, and a perpetrator whose location was unknown at the time the police located the victim.

---

2. [Renumbered] *Davis* explained that 911 operators "may at least be agents of law enforcement when they conduct interrogations of 911 callers," and therefore "consider[ed] their acts to be acts of the police" for purposes of the opinion. *Davis* explicitly reserved the question of "whether and when statements made to someone other than law enforcement personnel are 'testimonial.'" *Ibid*. We have no need to decide that question in this case either because Covington's statements were made to police officers....

Thus, we confront for the first time circumstances in which the "ongoing emergency" discussed in *Davis* extends beyond an initial victim to a potential threat to the responding police and the public at large. This new context requires us to provide additional clarification with regard to what *Davis* meant by "the primary purpose of the interrogation is to enable police assistance to meet an ongoing emergency."

III

To determine whether the "primary purpose" of an interrogation is "to enable police assistance to meet an ongoing emergency," which would render the resulting statements nontestimonial, we objectively evaluate the circumstances in which the encounter occurs and the statements and actions of the parties.

A

The Michigan Supreme Court correctly understood that this inquiry is objective. *Davis* uses the word "objective" or "objectively" no fewer than eight times in describing the relevant inquiry. "Objectively" also appears in the definitions of both testimonial and nontestimonial statements that *Davis* established.

An objective analysis of the circumstances of an encounter and the statements and actions of the parties to it provides the most accurate assessment of the "primary purpose of the interrogation." The circumstances in which an encounter occurs—*e.g.,* at or near the scene of the crime versus at a police station, during an ongoing emergency or afterwards—are clearly matters of objective fact. The statements and actions of the parties must also be objectively evaluated. That is, the relevant inquiry is not the subjective or actual purpose of the individuals involved in a particular encounter, but rather the purpose that reasonable participants would have had, as ascertained from the individuals' statements and actions and the circumstances in which the encounter occurred.

B

As our recent Confrontation Clause cases have explained, the existence of an "ongoing emergency" at the time of an encounter between an individual and the police is among the most important circumstances informing the "primary purpose" of an interrogation. The existence of an ongoing emergency is relevant to determining the primary purpose of the interrogation because an emergency focuses the participants on something other than "prov[ing] past events potentially relevant to later criminal prosecution."[3] Rather, it focuses them on "end[ing] a threaten-

---

3. [Renumbered] The existence of an ongoing emergency must be objectively assessed from the perspective of the parties to the interrogation at the time, not with the benefit of hindsight. If the information the parties knew at the time of the encounter would lead a reasonable person to believe that there was an emergency, even if that

ing situation." Implicit in *Davis* is the idea that because the prospect of fabrication in statements given for the primary purpose of resolving that emergency is presumably significantly diminished, the Confrontation Clause does not require such statements to be subject to the crucible of cross-examination.

This logic is not unlike that justifying the excited utterance exception in hearsay law. Statements "relating to a startling event or condition made while the declarant was under the stress of excitement caused by the event or condition," Fed. Rule Evid. 803(2); see also Mich. Rule Evid. 803(2) (2010), are considered reliable because the declarant, in the excitement, presumably cannot form a falsehood. See ... 5 J. Weinstein & M. Berger, Weinstein's Federal Evidence § 803.04[1] (J. McLaughlin ed., 2d ed.2010) (same); Advisory Committee's Notes on Fed. Rule Evid. 803(2), 28 U.S.C.App., p. 371 (same). An ongoing emergency has a similar effect of focusing an individual's attention on responding to the emergency.[4]

Following our precedents, the court below correctly began its analysis with the circumstances in which Covington interacted with the police. But in doing so, the court construed *Davis* to have decided more than it did and thus employed an unduly narrow understanding of "ongoing emergency" that *Davis* does not require.

First, the Michigan Supreme Court repeatedly and incorrectly asserted that *Davis* "defined" " 'ongoing emergency.' " In fact, *Davis* did not even define the extent of the emergency in that case. The Michigan Supreme Court erroneously read *Davis* as deciding that "the statements made after the defendant stopped assaulting the victim and left the premises did *not* occur during an 'ongoing emergency.'" We explicitly explained in *Davis*, however, that we were asked to review only the

belief was later proved incorrect, that is sufficient for purposes of the Confrontation Clause. The emergency is relevant to the "primary purpose of the interrogation" because of the effect it has on the parties' purpose, not because of its actual existence.

4. [Renumbered] Many other exceptions to the hearsay rules similarly rest on the belief that certain statements are, by their nature, made for a purpose other than use in a prosecution and therefore should not be barred by hearsay prohibitions. See, *e.g.*, Fed. Rule Evid. 801(d)(2)(E) (statement by a co-conspirator during and in furtherance of the conspiracy); 803(4) (Statements for Purposes of Medical Diagnosis or Treatment); 803(6) (Records of Regularly Conducted Activity); 803(8) (Public Records and Reports); 803(9) (Records of Vital Statistics); 803(11) (Records of Religious Organizations); 803(12) (Marriage, Baptismal, and Similar Certificates); 803(13) (Family Records); 804(b)(3) (Statement Against Interest); see also *Melendez–Diaz v. Massachusetts,* 557 U.S. ___, ___ 129 S.Ct., at 2539–2540 ("Business and public records are generally admissible absent confrontation not because they qualify under an exception to the hearsay rules, but because—having been created for the administration of an entity's affairs and not for the purpose of establishing or proving some fact at trial—they are not testimonial"); *Giles v. California,* (noting in the context of domestic violence that "[s]tatements to friends and neighbors about abuse and intimidation and statements to physicians in the course of receiving treatment would be excluded, if at all, only by hearsay rules"); *Crawford,* ("Most of the hearsay exceptions covered statements that by their nature were not testimonial—for example, business records or statements in furtherance of a conspiracy").

testimonial nature of Michelle McCottry's initial statements during the 911 call; we therefore merely *assumed* the correctness of the Washington Supreme Court's holding that admission of her other statements was harmless, without deciding whether those subsequent statements were also made for the primary purpose of resolving an ongoing emergency.

Second, by assuming that *Davis* defined the outer bounds of "ongoing emergency," the Michigan Supreme Court failed to appreciate that whether an emergency exists and is ongoing is a highly context-dependent inquiry. *Davis* and *Hammon* involved domestic violence, a known and identified perpetrator, and, in *Hammon,* a neutralized threat. Because *Davis* and *Hammon* were domestic violence cases, we focused only on the threat to the victims and assessed the ongoing emergency from the perspective of whether there was a continuing threat *to them.*

Domestic violence cases like *Davis* and *Hammon* often have a narrower zone of potential victims than cases involving threats to public safety. An assessment of whether an emergency that threatens the police and public is ongoing cannot narrowly focus on whether the threat solely to the first victim has been neutralized because the threat to the first responders and public may continue. . . . The Michigan Supreme Court also did not appreciate that the duration and scope of an emergency may depend in part on the type of weapon employed. The court relied on *Davis* and *Hammon,* in which the assailants used their fists, as controlling the scope of the emergency here, which involved the use of a gun. The problem with that reasoning is clear when considered in light of the assault on Amy Hammon. Hershel Hammon was armed only with his fists when he attacked his wife, so removing Amy to a separate room was sufficient to end the emergency. If Hershel had been reported to be armed with a gun, however, separation by a single household wall might not have been sufficient to end the emergency.

The Michigan Supreme Court's failure to focus on the context-dependent nature of our *Davis* decision also led it to conclude that the medical condition of a declarant is irrelevant. . . . But *Davis* and *Hammon* did not present medical emergencies, despite some injuries to the victims Thus, we have not previously considered, much less ruled out, the relevance of a victim's severe injuries to the primary purpose inquiry.

Taking into account the victim's medical state does not, as the Michigan Supreme Court below thought, "rende[r] non-testimonial" "all statements made while the police are questioning a seriously injured complainant." The medical condition of the victim is important to the primary purpose inquiry to the extent that it sheds light on the ability of the victim to have any purpose at all in responding to police questions and on the likelihood that any purpose formed would necessarily be a testimonial one. The victim's medical state also provides important context for first responders to judge the existence and magnitude of a continuing threat to the victim, themselves, and the public.

As the Solicitor General's brief observes, Brief for United States as *Amicus Curiae* 20, and contrary to the Michigan Supreme Court's claims, none of this suggests that an emergency is ongoing in every place or even just surrounding the victim for the entire time that the perpetrator of a violent crime is on the loose. As we recognized in *Davis,* "a conversation which begins as an interrogation to determine the need for emergency assistance" can "evolve into testimonial statements." This evolution may occur if, for example, a declarant provides police with information that makes clear that what appeared to be an emergency is not or is no longer an emergency or that what appeared to be a public threat is actually a private dispute. It could also occur if a perpetrator is disarmed, surrenders, is apprehended, or, as in *Davis,* flees with little prospect of posing a threat to the public. Trial courts can determine in the first instance when any transition from nontestimonial to testimonial occurs, and exclude "the portions of any statement that have become testimonial, as they do, for example, with unduly prejudicial portions of otherwise admissible evidence."

Finally, our discussion of the Michigan Supreme Court's misunderstanding of what *Davis* meant by "ongoing emergency" should not be taken to imply that the existence *vel non* of an ongoing emergency is dispositive of the testimonial inquiry. As *Davis* made clear, whether an ongoing emergency exists is simply one factor—albeit an important factor—that informs the ultimate inquiry regarding the "primary purpose" of an interrogation. Another factor the Michigan Supreme Court did not sufficiently account for is the importance of *informality* in an encounter between a victim and police. Formality is not the sole touchstone of our primary purpose inquiry because, although formality suggests the absence of an emergency and therefore an increased likelihood that the purpose of the interrogation is to "establish or prove past events potentially relevant to later criminal prosecution," informality does not necessarily indicate the presence of an emergency or the lack of testimonial intent. . . . The court below, however, too readily dismissed the informality of the circumstances in this case in a single brief footnote and in fact seems to have suggested that the encounter in this case was formal. As we explain further below, the questioning in this case occurred in an exposed, public area, prior to the arrival of emergency medical services, and in a disorganized fashion. All of those facts make this case distinguishable from the formal station-house interrogation in *Crawford.*

C

In addition to the circumstances in which an encounter occurs, the statements and actions of both the declarant and interrogators provide objective evidence of the primary purpose of the interrogation. . . .

As the Michigan Supreme Court correctly recognized, *Davis* requires a combined inquiry that accounts for both the declarant and the interrogator. In many instances, the primary purpose of the interrogation will be most accurately ascertained by looking to the contents of both the questions and the answers. To give an extreme example, if the police say to a victim, "Tell us who did this to you so that we can arrest and prosecute them," the victim's response that "Rick did it," appears purely accusatory because by virtue of the phrasing of the question, the victim necessarily has prosecution in mind when she answers.

The combined approach also ameliorates problems that could arise from looking solely to one participant. Predominant among these is the problem of mixed motives on the part of both interrogators and declarants. Police officers in our society function as both first responders and criminal investigators. Their dual responsibilities may mean that they act with different motives simultaneously or in quick succession...

Victims are also likely to have mixed motives when they make statements to the police. During an ongoing emergency, a victim is most likely to want the threat to her and to other potential victims to end, but that does not necessarily mean that the victim wants or envisions prosecution of the assailant. A victim may want the attacker to be incapacitated temporarily or rehabilitated. Alternatively, a severely injured victim may have no purpose at all in answering questions posed; the answers may be simply reflexive. The victim's injuries could be so debilitating as to prevent her from thinking sufficiently clearly to understand whether her statements are for the purpose of addressing an ongoing emergency or for the purpose of future prosecution Taking into account a victim's injuries does not transform this objective inquiry into a subjective one. The inquiry is still objective because it focuses on the understanding and purpose of a reasonable victim in the circumstances of the actual victim—circumstances that prominently include the victim's physical state.

The dissent suggests, (opinion of SCALIA, J.), that we intend to give controlling weight to the "intentions of the police". That is a misreading of our opinion. At trial, the declarant's statements, not the interrogator's questions, will be introduced to "establis[h] the truth of the matter asserted," and must therefore pass the Sixth Amendment test. In determining whether a declarant's statements are testimonial, courts should look to all of the relevant circumstances. Even Justice SCALIA concedes that the interrogator is relevant to this evaluation, and we agree that "[t]he identity of an interrogator, and the content and tenor of his questions," can illuminate the "primary purpose of the interrogation." The dissent, (opinion of SCALIA, J.), criticizes the complexity of our approach, but we, at least, are unwilling to sacrifice accuracy for simplicity. Simpler is not always better, and courts making a "primary purpose" assessment should not be unjustifiably restrained from consulting all relevant information, including the statements and actions of interrogators.

. . .

IV

As we suggested in *Davis*, when a court must determine whether the Confrontation Clause bars the admission of a statement at trial, it should determine the "primary purpose of the interrogation" by objectively evaluating the statements and actions of the parties to the encounter, in light of the circumstances in which the interrogation occurs. The existence of an emergency or the parties' perception that an emergency is ongoing is among the most important circumstances that courts must take into account in determining whether an interrogation is testimonial because statements made to assist police in addressing an ongoing emergency presumably lack the testimonial purpose that would subject them to the requirement of confrontation.[5] As the context of this case brings into sharp relief, the existence and duration of an emergency depend on the type and scope of danger posed to the victim, the police, and the public.

Applying this analysis to the facts of this case is more difficult than in *Davis* because we do not have the luxury of reviewing a transcript of the conversation between the victim and the police officers. Further complicating our task is the fact that the trial in this case occurred before our decisions in *Crawford* and *Davis*. We therefore review a record that was not developed to ascertain the "primary purpose of the interrogation."

We first examine the circumstances in which the interrogation occurred. The parties disagree over whether there was an emergency when the police arrived at the gas station. Bryant argues, and the Michigan Supreme Court accepted, that there was no ongoing emergency because "there ... was no criminal conduct occurring. No shots were being fired, no one was seen in possession of a firearm, nor were any witnesses seen cowering in fear or running from the scene." Bryant, while conceding that "a serious or life-threatening injury creates a medical emergency for a victim," further argues that a declarant's medical emergency is not relevant to the ongoing emergency determination.

In contrast, Michigan and the Solicitor General explain that when the police responded to the call that a man had been shot and found Covington bleeding on the gas station parking lot, "they did not know who Covington was, whether the shooting had occurred at the gas station or at a different location, who the assailant was, or whether the assailant posed a continuing threat to Covington or others." ("[W]hen an officer arrives on the scene and does not know where the perpetrator is, whether he is armed, whether he might have other targets, and

---

5. [Renumbered] Of course the Confrontation Clause is not the only bar to admissibility of hearsay statements at trial. State and federal rules of evidence prohibit the introduction of hearsay, subject to exceptions. Consistent with those rules, the Due Process Clauses of the Fifth and Fourteenth Amendments may constitute a further bar to admission of, for example, unreliable evidence....

whether the violence might continue at the scene or elsewhere, interrogation that has the primary purpose of establishing those facts to assess the situation is designed to meet the ongoing emergency and is nontestimonial").

The Michigan Supreme Court stated that the police asked Covington, "what had happened, who had shot him, and where the shooting had occurred." The joint appendix contains the transcripts of the preliminary examination, suppression hearing, and trial testimony of five officers who responded to the scene and found Covington. The officers' testimony is essentially consistent but, at the same time, not specific. The officers basically agree on what information they learned from Covington, but not on the order in which they learned it or on whether Covington's statements were in response to general or detailed questions. They all agree that the first question was "what happened?" The answer was either "I was shot" or "Rick shot me."

As explained above, the scope of an emergency in terms of its threat to individuals other than the initial assailant and victim will often depend on the type of dispute involved. Nothing Covington said to the police indicated that the cause of the shooting was a purely private dispute or that the threat from the shooter had ended. The record reveals little about the motive for the shooting. The police officers who spoke with Covington at the gas station testified that Covington did not tell them what words Covington and Rick had exchanged prior to the shooting. What Covington did tell the officers was that he fled Bryant's back porch, indicating that he perceived an ongoing threat. The police did not know, and Covington did not tell them, whether the threat was limited to him. The potential scope of the dispute and therefore the emergency in this case thus stretches more broadly than those at issue in *Davis* and *Hammon* and encompasses a threat potentially to the police and the public.

This is also the first of our post-*Crawford* Confrontation Clause cases to involve a gun. The physical separation that was sufficient to end the emergency in *Hammon* was not necessarily sufficient to end the threat in this case; Covington was shot through the back door of Bryant's house. Bryant's argument that there was no ongoing emergency because "[n]o shots were being fired," surely construes ongoing emergency too narrowly. An emergency does not last only for the time between when the assailant pulls the trigger and the bullet hits the victim. If an out-of-sight sniper pauses between shots, no one would say that the emergency ceases during the pause. That is an extreme example and not the situation here, but it serves to highlight the implausibility, at least as to certain weapons, of construing the emergency to last only precisely as long as the violent act itself, as some have construed our opinion in *Davis*.

At no point during the questioning did either Covington or the police know the location of the shooter. In fact, Bryant was not at home by the time the police searched his house at approximately 5:30 a.m. At some point between 3 a.m. and 5:30 a.m., Bryant left his house. At bottom, there was an ongoing emergency here where an armed shooter, whose motive for and location after the shooting were unknown, had mortally wounded Covington within a few blocks and a few minutes of the location where the police found Covington.[6]

This is not to suggest that the emergency continued until Bryant was arrested in California a year after the shooting. We need not decide precisely when the emergency ended because Covington's encounter with the police and all of the statements he made during that interaction occurred within the first few minutes of the police officers' arrival and well before they secured the scene of the shooting—the shooter's last known location.

We reiterate, moreover, that the existence *vel non* of an ongoing emergency is not the touchstone of the testimonial inquiry; rather, the ultimate inquiry is whether the "primary purpose of the interrogation [was] to enable police assistance to meet [the] ongoing emergency." We turn now to that inquiry, as informed by the circumstances of the ongoing emergency just described. The circumstances of the encounter provide important context for understanding Covington's statements to the police. . . . When he made the statements, Covington was lying in a gas station parking lot bleeding from a mortal gunshot wound to his abdomen. His answers to the police officers' questions were punctuated with questions about when emergency medical services would arrive. He was obviously in considerable pain and had difficulty breathing and talking. From this description of his condition and report of his statements, we cannot say that a person in Covington's situation would have had a "primary purpose" "to establish or prove past events potentially relevant to later criminal prosecution."

For their part, the police responded to a call that a man had been shot. As discussed above, they did not know why, where, or when the shooting had occurred. Nor did they know the location of the shooter or anything else about the circumstances in which the crime occurred. The questions they asked—"what had happened, who had shot him, and where the shooting occurred,"—were the exact type of questions necessary to allow the police to " 'assess the situation, the threat to their own safety, and possible danger to the potential victim' " and to the public, ...

Nothing in Covington's responses indicated to the police that, contrary to their expectation upon responding to a call reporting a shooting, there was no emergency or that a prior emergency had ended. Covington did indicate that he had been shot at another location about 25 minutes

---

6. [Renumbered] It hardly bears mention that the emergency situation in this case is readily distinguishable from the "treasonous conspiracies of unknown scope, aimed at killing or overthrowing the king," about which Justice SCALIA's dissent is quite concerned.

earlier, but he did not know the location of the shooter at the time the police arrived and, as far as we can tell from the record, he gave no indication that the shooter, having shot at him twice, would be satisfied that Covington was only wounded. In fact, Covington did not indicate any possible motive for the shooting, and thereby gave no reason to think that the shooter would not shoot again if he arrived on the scene. As we noted in *Davis,* "initial inquiries" may "*often* . . . produce nontestimonial statements." The initial inquiries in this case resulted in the type of nontestimonial statements we contemplated in *Davis.*

Finally, we consider the informality of the situation and the interrogation. This situation is more similar, though not identical, to the informal, harried call in *Davis* than to the structured, station-house interview in *Crawford.* . . . The informality suggests that the interrogators' primary purpose was simply to address what they perceived to be an ongoing emergency, and the circumstances lacked any formality that would have alerted Covington to or focused him on the possible future prosecutorial use of his statements.

Because the circumstances of the encounter as well as the statements and actions of Covington and the police objectively indicate that the "primary purpose of the interrogation" was "to enable police assistance to meet an ongoing emergency," Covington's identification and description of the shooter and the location of the shooting were not testimonial hearsay. The Confrontation Clause did not bar their admission at Bryant's trial.

* * *

. . . We leave for the Michigan courts to decide on remand whether the statements' admission was otherwise permitted by state hearsay rules. The judgment of the Supreme Court of Michigan is vacated, and the case is remanded for further proceedings not inconsistent with this opinion.

Justice KAGAN took no part in the consideration or decision of this case.

■ [In a separate opinion, JUSTICE THOMAS, concurred in the judgment.]

■ JUSTICE SCALIA, dissenting.

Today's tale—a story of five officers conducting successive examinations of a dying man with the primary purpose, not of obtaining and preserving his testimony regarding his killer, but of protecting him, them, and others from a murderer somewhere on the loose—is so transparently false that professing to believe it demeans this institution. But reaching a patently incorrect conclusion on the facts is a relatively benign judicial mischief; it affects, after all, only the case at hand. In its vain attempt to make the incredible plausible, however—or perhaps as an intended second goal—today's opinion distorts our Confrontation Clause jurisprudence and leaves it in a shambles. Instead of clarifying the law, the Court makes itself the obfuscator of last resort. Because I continue to adhere to the Confrontation Clause that the People adopted, as described in *Crawford v. Washington,* I dissent.

. . .

A final word about the Court's active imagination. The Court invents a world where an ongoing emergency exists whenever "an armed shooter, whose motive for and location after the shooting [are] unknown, ... mortally wound[s]" one individual "within a few blocks and [25] minutes of the location where the police" ultimately find that victim. Breathlessly, it worries that a shooter could leave the scene armed and ready to pull the trigger again.. Nothing suggests the five officers in this case shared the Court's dystopian review of Detroit, where drug dealers hunt their shooting victim down and fire into a crowd of police officers to finish him off, or where spree killers shoot through a door and then roam the streets leaving a trail of bodies behind. Because almost 90 percent of murders involve a single victim, it is much more likely—indeed, I think it certain—that the officers viewed their encounter with Covington for what it was: an investigation into a past crime with no ongoing or immediate consequences.

. . .

But today's decision is not only a gross distortion of the facts. It is a gross distortion of the law—a revisionist narrative in which reliability continues to guide our Confrontation Clause jurisprudence, at least where emergencies and faux emergencies are concerned.

According to today's opinion, the *Davis* inquiry into whether a declarant spoke to end an ongoing emergency or rather to "prove past events potentially relevant to later criminal prosecution," is *not* aimed at answering whether the declarant acted as a witness. Instead, the *Davis* inquiry probes the *reliability* of a declarant's statements, "[i]mplicit[ly]" importing the excited-utterances hearsay exception into the Constitution. A statement during an ongoing emergency is sufficiently reliable, the Court says, "because the prospect of fabrication ... is presumably significantly diminished," so it "does not [need] to be subject to the crucible of cross-examination." *Id.*, at 1157.

Compare that with the holding of *Crawford:* "Where testimonial statements are at issue, the only indicium of reliability sufficient to satisfy constitutional demands is the one the Constitution actually prescribes: confrontation." ...

The Court announces that in future cases it will look to "standard rules of hearsay, designed to identify some statements as reliable," when deciding whether a statement is testimonial.

The Court attempts to fit its resurrected interest in reliability into the *Crawford* framework, but the result is incoherent. Reliability, the Court tells us, is a good indicator of whether "a statement is ... an out-of-court substitute for trial testimony." That is patently false. Reliability tells us *nothing* about whether a statement is testimonial. Testimonial and nontestimonial statements alike come in varying degrees of reliability. An eyewitness's statements to the police after a fender-bender, for example, are both reliable and testimonial. Statements to the police from one driver attempting to blame the other would be similarly testimonial but rarely reliable.

. . .

Is it possible that the Court does not recognize the contradiction between its focus on reliable statements and *Crawford*'s focus on testimonial ones? Does it not realize that the two cannot coexist? Or does it intend, by following today's illogical roadmap, to resurrect *Roberts* by a thousand unprincipled distinctions without ever explicitly overruling *Crawford?* After all, honestly overruling *Crawford* would destroy the illusion of judicial minimalism and restraint. And it would force the Court to explain how the Justices' preference comports with the meaning of the Confrontation Clause that the People adopted—or to confess that only the Justices' preference really matters.

The Court recedes from *Crawford* in a second significant way. It requires judges to conduct "open-ended balancing tests" and "amorphous, if not entirely subjective," inquiries into the totality of the circumstances bearing upon reliability. Where the prosecution cries "emergency," the admissibility of a statement now turns on "a highly context-dependent inquiry," into the type of weapon the defendant wielded, the type of crime the defendant committed, the medical condition of the declarant, if the declarant is injured, whether paramedics have arrived on the scene,; whether the encounter takes place in an "exposed public area," whether the encounter appears disorganized, whether the declarant is capable of forming a purpose, whether the police have secured the scene of the crime, the formality of the statement, and finally, whether the statement strikes us as reliable. This is no better than the nine-factor balancing test we rejected in <u>Crawford,</u> I do not look forward to resolving conflicts in the future over whether knives and poison are more like guns or fists for Confrontation Clause purposes, or whether rape and armed robbery are more like murder or domestic violence.

It can be said, of course, that under *Crawford* analysis of whether a statement is testimonial requires consideration of all the circumstances, and so is also something of a multifactor balancing test. But the "reliability" test does not replace that analysis; it supplements it. As I understand the Court's opinion, even when it is determined that no emergency exists (or perhaps before that determination is made) the statement would be found admissible as far as the Confrontation Clause is concerned if it is not testimonial.

. . .

Judicial decisions, like the Constitution itself, are nothing more than "parchment barriers," 5 Writings of James Madison 269, 272 (G. Hunt ed.1901). Both depend on a judicial culture that understands its constitutionally assigned role, has the courage to persist in that role when it means announcing unpopular decisions, and has the modesty to persist when it produces results that go against the judges' policy preferences. Today's opinion falls far short of living up to that obligation—short on the facts, and short on the law.

For all I know, Bryant has received his just deserts. But he surely has not received them pursuant to the procedures that our Constitution requires. And what has been taken away from him has been taken away from us all.

■ JUSTICE GINSBURG, dissenting.

I agree with Justice SCALIA that Covington's statements were testimonial and that "[t]he declarant's intent is what counts." ...

I would add, however, this observation. In *Crawford v. Washington,* this Court noted that, in the law we inherited from England, there was a well-established exception to the confrontation requirement: The cloak protecting the accused against admission of out-of-court testimonial statements was removed for dying declarations. This historic exception, we recalled, *Giles v. California,* applied to statements made by a person about to die and aware that death was imminent. Were the issue properly tendered here, I would take up the question whether the exception for dying declarations survives our recent Confrontation Clause decisions. The Michigan Supreme Court, however, held, as a matter of state law, that the prosecutor had abandoned the issue. The matter, therefore, is not one the Court can address in this case.

Melendez–Diaz v. Massachusetts

Supreme Court of the United States, 2009.
129 S.Ct. 2527.

■ JUSTICE SCALIA delivered the opinion of the Court.

The Massachusetts courts in this case admitted into evidence affidavits reporting the results of forensic analysis which showed that material seized by the police and connected to the defendant was cocaine. The question presented is whether those affidavits are "testimonial," rendering the affiants "witnesses" subject to the defendant's right of confrontation under the Sixth Amendment.

I

. . .

During the short drive to the police station, the officers observed their passengers fidgeting and making furtive movements in the back of the car. After depositing the men at the station, they searched the police cruiser and found a plastic bag containing 19 smaller plastic bags hidden in the partition between the front and back seats. They submitted the seized evidence to a state laboratory required by law to conduct chemical analysis upon police request.

Melendez–Diaz was charged with distributing cocaine and with trafficking in cocaine in an amount between 14 and 28 grams. At trial, the prosecution placed into evidence the bags seized from Wright and from the police cruiser. It also submitted three "certificates of analysis" showing the results of the forensic analysis performed on the seized substances. The certificates reported the weight of the seized bags and stated that the bags "[h]a[ve] been examined with the following results: The substance was found to contain: Cocaine." The certificates were sworn to before a notary public by analysts at the State Laboratory Institute of the Massachusetts Department of Public Health, as required under Massachusetts law.

Petitioner objected to the admission of the certificates, asserting that our Confrontation Clause decision in *Crawford v. Washington*, required the analysts to testify in person. The objection was overruled, and the certificates were admitted pursuant to state law as "prima facie evidence of the composition, quality, and the net weight of the narcotic ... analyzed."

The jury found Melendez–Diaz guilty. He appealed, contending, among other things, that admission of the certificates violated his Sixth Amendment right to be confronted with the witnesses against him. The Appeals Court of Massachusetts rejected the claim, ... The Supreme Judicial Court denied review. We granted certiorari. 552 U.S. 1256 (2008).

II

The Sixth Amendment to the United States Constitution, made applicable to the States via the Fourteenth Amendment, provides that "[i]n all criminal prosecutions, the accused shall enjoy the right ... to be confronted with the witnesses against him." In *Crawford,* after reviewing the Clause's historical underpinnings, we held that it guarantees a defendant's right to confront those "who 'bear testimony' " against him. A witness's testimony against a defendant is thus inadmissible unless the witness appears at trial or, if the witness is unavailable, the defendant had a prior opportunity for cross-examination.

Our opinion described the class of testimonial statements covered by the Confrontation Clause as follows:

"Various formulations of this core class of testimonial statements exist: *ex parte* in-court testimony or its functional equivalent—that is, material such as affidavits, custodial examinations, prior testimony that the defendant was unable to cross-examine, or similar pretrial statements that declarants would reasonably expect to be used prosecutorially; extrajudicial statements ... contained in formalized testimonial materials, such as affidavits, depositions, prior testimony, or confessions; statements that were made under circumstances which would lead an objective witness reasonably to believe that the statement would be available for use at a later trial."

There is little doubt that the documents at issue in this case fall within the "core class of testimonial statements" thus described. Our description of that category mentions affidavits twice.... The documents at issue here, while denominated by Massachusetts law "certificates," are quite plainly affidavits: "declaration[s] of facts written down and sworn to by the declarant before an officer authorized to administer oaths." Black's Law Dictionary 62 (8th ed.2004). They are incontrovertibly a " 'solemn declaration or affirmation made for the purpose of establishing or proving some fact.' " *Crawford, supra,* at 51 (quoting 2 N. Webster, An American Dictionary of the English Language (1828)). The fact in question is that the substance found in the possession of Melendez–Diaz and his codefendants was, as the prosecution claimed, cocaine—the precise testimony the analysts would be expected to provide if called at trial. The "certificates" are functionally identical to live, in-court testimony, doing "precisely what a witness does on direct examination."

Here, moreover, not only were the affidavits " 'made under circumstances which would lead an objective witness reasonably to believe that the statement would be available for use at a later trial,' " but under Massachusetts law the *sole purpose* of the affidavits was to provide "prima facie evidence of the composition, quality, and the net weight" of the analyzed substance. We can safely assume that the analysts were aware of the affidavits' evidentiary purpose, since that purpose—as stated in the relevant state-law provision—was reprinted on the affidavits themselves.

In short, under our decision in *Crawford* the analysts' affidavits were testimonial statements, and the analysts were "witnesses" for purposes of the Sixth Amendment. Absent a showing that the analysts were unavailable to testify at trial *and* that petitioner had a prior opportunity to cross-examine them, petitioner was entitled to " 'be confronted with' " the analysts at trial.[1]

---

1. Contrary to the dissent's suggestion, (opinion of KENNEDY, J.), we do not hold, and it is not the case, that anyone whose testimony may be relevant in establishing the chain of custody, authenticity of the sample, or accuracy of the testing device, must appear in person as part of the prosecution's case. While the dissent is correct that "[i]t is the obligation of the prosecution to establish the chain of custody," this does not mean that everyone who laid hands on the evidence must be called. As stated in the dissent's own quotation, *ibid.,* from *United States v. Lott,* 854 F.2d 244, 250 (C.A.7 1988), "gaps in the chain [of custody] normally go to the weight of the evidence rather than its admissibility." It is up to the prosecution to decide what steps in the chain of custody are so crucial as to require evidence; but what testimony *is* introduced must (if the defendant objects) be

III

Respondent and the dissent advance a potpourri of analytic arguments in an effort to avoid this rather straightforward application of our holding in *Crawford*. Before addressing them, however, we must assure the reader of the falsity of the dissent's opening alarum that we are "sweep[ing] away an accepted rule governing the admission of scientific evidence" that has been "established for at least 90 years" and "extends across at least 35 States and six Federal Courts of Appeals."

The vast majority of the state-court cases the dissent cites in support of this claim come not from the last 90 years, but from the last 30, and not surprisingly nearly all of them rely on our decision in *Ohio v. Roberts,* 448 U.S. 56, 100 S.Ct. 2531, 65 L.Ed.2d 597 (1980), or its since-rejected theory that unconfronted testimony was admissible as long as it bore indicia of reliability. As for the six Federal Courts of Appeals cases cited by the dissent, five of them postdated and expressly relied on *Roberts*. The sixth predated *Roberts* but relied entirely on the same erroneous theory.

. . .

We turn now to the various legal arguments raised by respondent and the dissent.

A

Respondent first argues that the analysts are not subject to confrontation because they are not "accusatory" witnesses, in that they do not directly accuse petitioner of wrongdoing; rather, their testimony is inculpatory only when taken together with other evidence linking petitioner to the contraband. This finds no support in the text of the Sixth Amendment or in our case law.

The Sixth Amendment guarantees a defendant the right "to be confronted with the witnesses *against him*." (Emphasis added.) To the extent the analysts were witnesses (a question resolved above), they certainly provided testimony *against* petitioner, proving one fact necessary for his conviction—that the substance he possessed was cocaine. . . .

It is often, indeed perhaps usually, the case that an adverse witness's testimony, taken alone, will not suffice to convict. Yet respondent fails to cite a single case in which such testimony was admitted absent a defendant's opportunity to cross-examine. Unsurprisingly, since such a holding would be contrary to longstanding case law. . . .

B

. . .

introduced live. Additionally, documents prepared in the regular course of equipment maintenance may well qualify as nontestimonial records.

Respondent and the dissent argue that the analysts should not be subject to confrontation because they are not "conventional" (or "typical" or "ordinary") witnesses of the sort whose *ex parte* testimony was most notoriously used at the trial of Sir Walter Raleigh. It is true, as the Court recognized in *Crawford*, that *ex parte* examinations of the sort used at Raleigh's trial have "long been thought a paradigmatic confrontation violation." But the paradigmatic case identifies the core of the right to confrontation, not its limits. The right to confrontation was not invented in response to the use of the *ex parte* examinations in *Raleigh's Case*, 2 How. St. Tr. 1 (1603). That use provoked such an outcry precisely because it flouted the deeply rooted common-law tradition "of live testimony in court subject to adversarial testing."

A second reason the dissent contends that the analysts are not "conventional witnesses" (and thus not subject to confrontation) is that they "observe[d] neither the crime nor any human action related to it." The dissent provides no authority for this particular limitation of the type of witnesses subject to confrontation. Nor is it conceivable that all witnesses who fit this description would be outside the scope of the Confrontation Clause. For example, is a police officer's investigative report describing the crime scene admissible absent an opportunity to examine the officer? The dissent's novel exception from coverage of the Confrontation Clause would exempt all expert witnesses—a hardly "unconventional" class of witnesses.

A third respect in which the dissent asserts that the analysts are not "conventional" witnesses and thus not subject to confrontation is that their statements were not provided in response to interrogation. As we have explained, "[t]he Framers were no more willing to exempt from cross-examination volunteered testimony or answers to open-ended questions than they were to exempt answers to detailed interrogation." Respondent and the dissent cite no authority, and we are aware of none, holding that a person who volunteers his testimony is any less a " 'witness against' the defendant,", than one who is responding to interrogation....

C

Respondent claims that there is a difference, for Confrontation Clause purposes, between testimony recounting historical events, which is "prone to distortion or manipulation," and the testimony at issue here, which is the "resul[t] of neutral, scientific testing." Relatedly, respondent and the dissent argue that confrontation of forensic analysts would be of little value because "one would not reasonably expect a laboratory professional ... to feel quite differently about the results of his scientific test by having to look at the defendant."

This argument is little more than an invitation to return to our overruled decision in *Roberts*, which held that evidence with "particularized guarantees of trustworthiness" was admissible notwithstanding the Confrontation Clause....

Respondent and the dissent may be right that there are other ways—and in some cases better ways—to challenge or verify the results of a forensic test. But the Constitution guarantees one way: confrontation. We do not have license to suspend the Confrontation Clause when a preferable trial strategy is available.

Nor is it evident that what respondent calls "neutral scientific testing" is as neutral or as reliable as respondent suggests. Forensic evidence is not uniquely immune from the risk of manipulation.... A forensic analyst responding to a request from a law enforcement official may feel pressure—or have an incentive—to alter the evidence in a manner favorable to the prosecution.

Confrontation is one means of assuring accurate forensic analysis. While it is true, as the dissent notes, that an honest analyst will not alter his testimony when forced to confront the defendant, the same cannot be said of the fraudulent analyst. See Brief for National Innocence Network as *Amicus Curiae* 15–17 (discussing cases of documented "drylabbing" where forensic analysts report results of tests that were never performed); National Academy Report 1–8 to 1–10 (discussing documented cases of fraud and error involving the use of forensic evidence). Like the eyewitness who has fabricated his account to the police, the analyst who provides false results may, under oath in open court, reconsider his false testimony. And, of course, the prospect of confrontation will deter fraudulent analysis in the first place.

Confrontation is designed to weed out not only the fraudulent analyst, but the incompetent one as well. Serious deficiencies have been found in the forensic evidence used in criminal trials. One commentator asserts that "[t]he legal community now concedes, with varying degrees of urgency, that our system produces erroneous convictions based on discredited forensics." Metzger, Cheating the Constitution, 59 Vand. L.Rev. 475, 491 (2006). One study of cases in which exonerating evidence resulted in the overturning of criminal convictions concluded that invalid forensic testimony contributed to the convictions in 60% of the cases. Garrett & Neufeld, Invalid Forensic Science Testimony and Wrongful Convictions, 95 Va. L.Rev. 1, 14 (2009).

Like expert witnesses generally, an analyst's lack of proper training or deficiency in judgment may be disclosed in cross-examination.

This case is illustrative. The affidavits submitted by the analysts contained only the bare-bones statement that "[t]he substance was found to contain: Cocaine." At the time of trial, petitioner did not know what tests the analysts performed, whether those tests were routine, and whether interpreting their results required the exercise of judgment or the use of skills that the analysts may not have possessed. While we still do not know the precise tests used by the analysts, we are told that the laboratories use "methodology recommended by the Scientific Working Group for the Analysis of Seized Drugs," At least some of that methodology requires the exercise of judgment and presents a risk of error that might be explored on cross-examination. See 2 P. Giannelli & E. Imwinkelried, Scientific Evidence § 23.03[c], pp. 532–533, ch. 23A, p. 607 (4th ed.2007) (identifying four "critical errors" that analysts may commit in interpreting the results of the commonly used gas chromatography/mass spectrometry analysis); Shellow, The Application of *Daubert* to the Identification of Drugs, 2 Shepard's Expert & Scientific Evidence Quarterly 593, 600 (1995) (noting that while spectrometers may be equipped with computerized matching systems, "forensic analysts in crime laboratories typically do not utilize this feature of the instrument, but rely exclusively on their subjective judgment").

The same is true of many of the other types of forensic evidence commonly used in criminal prosecutions. "[T]here is wide variability across forensic science disciplines with regard to techniques, methodologies, reliability, types and numbers of potential errors, research, general acceptability, and published material." National Academy Report S–5.... Contrary to respondent's and the dissent's suggestion, there is little reason to believe that confrontation will be useless in testing analysts' honesty, proficiency, and methodology—the features that are commonly the focus in the cross-examination of experts.

D

Respondent argues that the analysts' affidavits are admissible without confrontation because they are "akin to the types of official and business records admissible at common law." But the affidavits do not qualify as traditional official or business records, and even if they did, their authors would be subject to confrontation nonetheless.

Documents kept in the regular course of business may ordinarily be admitted at trial despite their hearsay status. See Fed. Rule Evid. 803(6). But that is not the case if the regularly conducted business activity is the production of evidence for use at trial. Our decision in *Palmer v. Hoffman*, 318 U.S. 109, 63 S.Ct. 477, 87 L.Ed. 645 (1943), made that distinction clear. There we held that an accident report provided by an employee of a railroad company did not qualify as a business record because, although kept in the regular course of the railroad's operations, it was "calculated for use essentially in the court, not in the business." The analysts' certificates—like police reports generated by law enforcement officials—do not qualify as business or public records for precisely the same reason. See Rule 803(8) (defining public records as "excluding, however, in criminal cases matters observed by police officers and other law enforcement personnel").

Respondent seeks to rebut this limitation by noting that at common law the results of a coroner's inquest were admissible without an opportunity for confrontation. But as we have previously noted, whatever the status of coroner's reports at common law in England, they were not accorded any special status in American practice. See *Crawford,* 541 U.S., at 47, n. 2; *Giles v. California,* 554 U.S. 353, ___ (2008) (slip op., at 20) (BREYER, J., dissenting)....

. . .

Respondent also misunderstands the relationship between the business-and-official-records hearsay exceptions and the Confrontation Clause. As we stated in *Crawford:* "Most of the hearsay exceptions covered statements that by their nature were not testimonial—for example, business records or statements in furtherance of a conspiracy." 541 U.S., at 56. Business and public records are generally admissible absent confrontation not because they qualify under an exception to the hearsay rules, but because—having been created for the administration of an entity's affairs and not for the purpose of establishing or proving some fact at trial—they are not testimonial. Whether or not they qualify as business or official records, the analysts' statements here—prepared specifically for use at petitioner's trial—were testimony against petitioner, and the analysts were subject to confrontation under the Sixth Amendment.

E

Respondent asserts that we should find no Confrontation Clause violation in this case because petitioner had the ability to subpoena the analysts. But that power—whether pursuant to state law or the Compulsory Process Clause—is no substitute for the right of confrontation. Unlike the Confrontation Clause, those provisions are of no use to the defendant when the witness is unavailable or simply refuses to appear.... Converting the prosecution's duty under the Confrontation Clause into the defendant's privilege under state law or the Compulsory Process Clause shifts the consequences of adverse-witness no-shows from the State to the accused. More fundamentally, the Confrontation Clause imposes a burden on the prosecution to present its witnesses, not on the defendant to bring those adverse witnesses into court. Its value to the defendant is not replaced by a system in which the prosecution presents its evidence via *ex parte* affidavits and waits for the defendant to subpoena the affiants if he chooses.

F

Finally, respondent asks us to relax the requirements of the Confrontation Clause to accommodate the "necessities of trial and the adversary process." It is not clear whence we would derive the authority to do so. The Confrontation Clause may make the prosecution of criminals more burdensome, but that is equally true of the right to trial by jury and the privilege against self-incrimination. The Confrontation Clause—like those other constitutional provisions—is binding, and we may not disregard it at our convenience.

We also doubt the accuracy of respondent's and the dissent's dire predictions. The dissent, respondent, and its *amici* highlight the substantial total number of controlled-substance analyses performed by state and federal laboratories in recent years. But only some of those tests are implicated in prosecutions, and only a small fraction of those cases actually proceed to trial....

Perhaps the best indication that the sky will not fall after today's decision is that it has not done so already. Many States have already adopted the constitutional rule we announce today, while many others permit the defendant to assert (or forfeit by silence) his Confrontation Clause right after receiving notice of the prosecution's intent to use a forensic analyst's report. Despite these widespread practices, there is no evidence that the criminal justice system has ground to a halt in the States that, one way or another, empower a defendant to insist upon the analyst's appearance at trial. Indeed, in Massachusetts itself, a defendant may subpoena the analyst to appear at trial, and yet there is no indication that obstructionist defendants are abusing the privilege.

The dissent finds this evidence "far less reassuring than promised." But its doubts rest on two flawed premises. First, the dissent believes that those state statutes "requiring the defendant to give early notice of his intent to confront the analyst," are "burden-shifting statutes [that] may be invalidated by the Court's reasoning." That is not so. In their simplest form, notice-and-demand statutes require the prosecution to provide notice to the defendant of its intent to use an analyst's report as evidence at trial, after which the defendant is given a period of time in which he may object to the admission of the evidence absent the analyst's appearance live at trial. Contrary to the dissent's perception, these statutes shift no burden whatever. The defendant *always* has the burden of raising his Confrontation Clause objection; notice-and-demand statutes simply govern the *time* within which he must do so. States are free to adopt procedural rules governing objections.... There is no conceivable reason why he cannot similarly be compelled to exercise his Confrontation Clause rights before trial. Today's decision will not disrupt criminal prosecutions in the many large States whose practice is already in accord with the Confrontation Clause.

... It is true that many of these decisions are recent, but if the dissent's dire predictions were accurate, and given the large number of drug prosecutions at the state level, one would have expected immediate and dramatic results. The absence of such evidence is telling.

But it is not surprising. Defense attorneys and their clients will often stipulate to the nature of the substance in the ordinary drug case. It is unlikely that defense counsel will insist on live testimony whose effect will be merely to highlight rather than cast doubt upon the forensic analysis. Nor will defense attorneys want to antagonize the judge or jury by wasting their time with the appearance of a witness whose testimony defense counsel does not intend to rebut in any fashion....

* * *

This case involves little more than the application of our holding in *Crawford v. Washington*. The Sixth Amendment does not permit the prosecution to prove its case via *ex parte* out-of-court affidavits, and the admission of such evidence against Melendez–Diaz was error. We therefore reverse the judgment of the Appeals Court of Massachusetts and remand the case for further proceedings not inconsistent with this opinion.

■ [THOMAS, J., filed a concurring opinion. KENNEDY, J., filed a dissenting opinion, in which ROBERTS, C.J., and BREYER and ALITO, JJ., joined.]

NOTE

At the end of the term in June, 2009, a few days after handling down the decision in Melendez–Diaz v. Massachusetts, the Supreme Court granted review in Briscoe v. Virginia, 129 S.Ct. 2858 (2009). The question upon which review was granted was the following:

> If a state allows a prosecutor to introduce a certificate of a forensic laboratory analysis, without presenting the testimony of the analyst who prepared the certificate, does the state avoid violating the Confrontation Clause of the Sixth Amendment by providing that the accused has a right to call the analyst as his own witness?

The Briscoe case was argued on January 11, 2010. Subsequently, on January 25, 2010, in Briscoe v. Virginia, 130 S.Ct. 1316 (2010) the Supreme Court vacated the judgment of the Supreme Court of Virginia and remanded the case "for further proceedings not inconsistent with the opinion in Melendez–Diaz v. Massachusetts...."

1. Why do you think the Court agreed to review Briscoe in the immediate aftermath of having decided Melendez–Diaz?
2. What are the substantive implications of the Court's subsequent decision to vacate the judgment and remand in Briscoe for further proceedings in light of the Melendez–Diaz opinion?
3. What should the Supreme Court of Virginia do on remand?

In addressing these questions, consider the implications of the following excerpts from the oral argument before the U.S. Supreme Court in the Briscoe case.

PROCEEDINGS

CHIEF JUSTICE ROBERTS: We will hear argument next in Case 07–11191, Briscoe v. Virginia.

ORAL ARGUMENT OF RICHARD D. FRIEDMAN[1]
ON BEHALF OF THE PETITIONERS

MR. FRIEDMAN: Mr. Chief Justice, and may it please the Court:

1. [Ed. Professor Friedman is a member of the faculty of the University of Michigan School of Law.]

SECTION 13 CONSTITUTIONAL RESTRAINTS

We ask the Court in this case to take no new ground beyond that established just last term in the Melendez–Diaz case, but the stakes of this case are high. If the Court were to reverse Melendez–Diaz and hold that a State may impose on the defendant the burden of calling a prosecution witness to the stand, it would severely impair the confrontation right and threaten a fundamental transformation in the way Anglo–American trials have been conducted for hundreds of years.

JUSTICE SOTOMAYOR: The State court has interpreted their provision to give the defendant the choice of subpoenaing the witness or asking the State to bring in the witness. Why is that overruling Melendez–Diaz?

. . .

JUSTICE SOTOMAYOR: So that's our first question: Does the Confrontation Clause require, not just the ability to cross-examine . . . but an affirmative obligation to place the witness on the stand?

MR. FRIEDMAN: That's correct. . . .

. . .

JUSTICE SOTOMAYOR: Would swearing the witness in and saying to the witness "Is this your report" and the witness saying "Yes," what would be unconstitutional about that, given our case law that says that any prior statements by a witness are admissible once the witness is on the stand or constitutionally admissible once they are on the stand?

. . .

MR. FRIEDMAN: No. I mean, I think the Constitution—I think constitutionally, . . . the prosecution would be compelled at least to ask, "What is your recollection? Do you endorse this statement?" But even if that's not true—

JUSTICE SOTOMAYOR: Do you have anything historically or in any case that would suggest that that is a constitutional requirement? I mean, I do accept that there is plenty that says you have a right to be—to confront the witness.

MR. FRIEDMAN: Right. . . .

JUSTICE SOTOMAYOR: But what would require the prosecutor to actually do more than I just suggested? "Is this your statement? Is this your lab report?"

. . .

JUSTICE SCALIA: Well, he says, "Is this your lab report and do you stand by it?"

MR. FRIEDMAN: The "Do you stand by it?," that's the critical point. That's going beyond the hypothetical, as I understood it from Justice Sotomayor.

. . .

JUSTICE ALITO: It's not clear to me what your answer to these questions is. If all the prosecution does is call the analyst on the stand and admit—have the analyst provide a foundation for the admission of the report, let's say, pursuant to the hearsay exception for recorded recollection, and does nothing more, would there be a Confrontation Clause problem?

CHAPTER 4 HEARSAY

MR. FRIEDMAN: And there is—there is the question, is this your report, do you stand by it? Then—then I don't think there is a Confrontation Clause problem, because—because the prosecution has put the witness on the stand, has asked those questions and then the witness—and—

JUSTICE ALITO: What's the difference between that situation and the situation in which the report is—is admitted, subject to—and the analyst is available, and the defense can question the analyst if the defense wishes to?

. . . .

JUSTICE SOTOMAYOR: You are asking us now to state something that you admit is in really no constitutional case or historical case, that says the right to confrontation means that the witness has to tell the story, and the form of telling that story has to be a verbal recitation; it can't be past recorded recollection because you just said they have to tell the story. It can't be based on official documents or anything else, because it has to be their story. Am I hearing you wrong?

MR. FRIEDMAN: No, I don't believe so. I'm saying that the—that the witness has to take the stand, has to—has to testify live, viva voce, face-to-face, in the time-honored phrases which have always governed testimony in an Anglo–American trial. Then the—I think the witness has to at least be asked what happened. If the witness says, I don't recall, then the prior statement may be introduced. I am not—I am not asking the Court to go beyond anything that has previously been said.

JUSTICE BREYER: What is the—what is the theory of this? I understand in hearsay, which as we have just seen demonstrated, is very complicated, filled with all kinds of rules. . . . Bring in the witnesses. Now, once you bring them in, the defendant can do what he wants. He has had his chance to cross-examine them. End of the matter, and leave the rest up to the hearsay law?

MR. FRIEDMAN: I want to emphasize that the Confrontation Clause is about a lot more—there were nearly 200 years of history between Walter Raleigh and the Confrontation Clause, and what was established is that in an Anglo–America trial witnesses give their testimony live, face-to-face, and Melendez–Diaz emphasized last term, you can't prove the case via an affidavit. So—so it's—it's the . . . fundamental principle that Crawford establishes, is this is the way witnesses testify in our trials: live, in front of the jury, subject to oath and then cross-exam.

. . .

JUSTICE SOTOMAYOR:—and the fact that it's much more effective when the witness tells their story and you get a chance to cross-examine than if you have to start from the platform of cross-examination. Once a defendant makes it known that a—he's going to cross-examine a lab technician, don't you think that in the vast majority of cases the prosecutor is going to put that witness on? . . . And if he does or doesn't, why shouldn't we leave it to the normal trial strategy and practice to leave to that prosecutor the burden of non-persuasion? I thought that was what confrontation was about.

MR. FRIEDMAN: Right. Yes. . . . If—if the prosecutor is certain that the defendant is going to put the witness on the stand, then—then the prosecutor has some reason to—to put the witness on first. The problem is that the—the defunct Virginia statute puts the burden on the defendant of bringing the witness in, and the defense—

SECTION 13 CONSTITUTIONAL RESTRAINTS

...

JUSTICE BREYER:—will defense attorneys, if they have the right under the Constitution to insist that a lab technician be present, in cases where they happen to know that lab technician's left the job and is married and is living in a different State, and say, okay, let's call her, and that way the prosecution really cannot present the case except at inordinate expense. And I'm concerned about that, but I don't see quite how to deal with it, how much of a problem it is, and the impact on this particular situation.

MR. FRIEDMAN: I don't think it's a significant problem,....

JUSTICE SCALIA: Mr. Friedman, aren't there states that have been proceeding this way even before we came down with our opinion?

MR. FRIEDMAN: Absolutely, absolutely,....

JUSTICE SCALIA: And which States are they?

MR. FRIEDMAN: They—well, they include my own State of Michigan, they include the State of New York—

JUSTICE SCALIA: And they are not under water, are they?

MR. FRIEDMAN: The problems of the State of Michigan are not attributable to the use of this procedure, no.

(Laughter.)

CHIEF JUSTICE ROBERTS: Your answer to Justice Breyer has to be, of course, you would insist that the person be called. It would be malpractice for you not to.

MR. FRIEDMAN: It—it is—yes, but it's not a significant problem, and one reason it is not a significant problem is that the possibility of a deposition is always—

JUSTICE BREYER: I don't know except anecdotally, but Massachusetts seems to be having huge problems, reported anecdotally, with the—

MR. FRIEDMAN: Not according to—not according to the chief of—chief trial counsel, Suffolk—the Suffolk district attorney's office—

...

JUSTICE BREYER: What happens if the lab is—is divided into four or five parts and there is several different machines and we have different people at different times using these different machines and performing different operations and each at the end, certifies that the red light was on or it was this or it was that. Now, do we have to call all those people?

MR. FRIEDMAN: No, I don't believe you have to call all those people. I do believe that—

JUSTICE BREYER: Why not? Each of them—each of them looked at a special part. Each of them said that it was this or that, and in respect to each of those statements, it was this or that. That is hearsay.

MR. FRIEDMAN: Right. The problem, of course, isn't hearsay. The problem is—the only question is—

JUSTICE BREYER: No, no, it's no confrontation because in this instance the hearsay prevents the confrontation.

MR. FRIEDMAN: Right. The—the prosecution has to present the testimony of witnesses. It has to present the testimony live. Depending on how the lab is organized—usually, labs can organize so that only one person needs to—needs to present.

In any event, of course, the State is acknowledging that, if the defendant brings—demands, they have to bring in the witnesses, and that is not—

JUSTICE BREYER: But your answer to my question is, if a laboratory is so organized so that six or seven people perform different steps of the operation, if it is organized in that way, all of them must be brought?

MR. FRIEDMAN: I—I don't believe so. I believe—

JUSTICE BREYER: You don't believe so, but you gave me an answer saying they did have to, but you said they could organize differently. So now explain to me why they don't.

MR. FRIEDMAN: But even if—even if they are organized in that way, for instance if one person observes all the—all the procedures, that is sufficient. Apart from that, as Melendez–Diaz indicates, it's up to the—it's up to the State to decide what the evidence they are going to present is.

JUSTICE KENNEDY: Suppose one person doesn't observe all the procedures. One person prepares the sample, another person puts it on the paper, another person reads the machine, another person calibrates the machine.

MR. FRIEDMAN: Yes. Right. Well, I think Melendez–Diaz indicates that it is up to the State to determine what the—the evidence that is going to be presented, and there may be gaps. I do want to emphasize that this is an issue—

JUSTICE KENNEDY: No, no, no. The evidence is presented, and the test comes out so—positive, so that the gun fires or that it's a drug or that it's a DNA sample. Can the conclusion be presented by one witness from the lab, when that witness did not observe all of the procedures?

MR. FRIEDMAN: I think—I think that there probably has to be a witness who has observed the procedures....

. . .

JUSTICE GINSBURG: But, in your view it wouldn't satisfy the Confrontation Clause if, say, the supervisor shows up and said, this is way—this is the way the analysts operate, and describes the procedures.

MR. FRIEDMAN: In my view it wouldn't, but if I'm wrong, it doesn't change this case whatsoever. It does not change this case whatsoever. It has nothing to do with the issue here. The issue here is—is the witnesses who are going to testify and how much they—they testify, and I want to—

JUSTICE BREYER: Well, the reason that I ask is because floating in the back of my mind is, A, does the Confrontation Clause apply?

MR. FRIEDMAN: Right.

JUSTICE BREYER: And if the answer to A is yes, then are there different kinds of implementation rules in different areas where there are other signs of security, where there are other reasons for thinking it's not bad testimony? That line is not something that is necessarily workable, and—but I brought it up to try to think about it.

SECTION 13 CONSTITUTIONAL RESTRAINTS

MR. FRIEDMAN: Yes. I think—I think it's an interesting question, ... But I think that an issue that the Court will have to resolve. And, as I say, my views are what they—what they are, but if you reject my views on that it doesn't change this case whatsoever. What I think is important to recognize is how fundamental a transformation in the Anglo–American trial is threatened if—if the Court were to hold that the prosecution can present an affidavit and leave it to the defendant, if he dares, to put the witness on the stand.

JUSTICE ALITO: Well, does that square with where we started out? We have situation A, where the prosecutor calls the lab analyst, and the lab analyst says, this is my report, and I stand by it, period. Now, it's up to the defense to cross-examine. That's situation A.

Situation B is the report is admitted without the analyst present, but the defense can then—without the analyst on the stand—

MR. FRIEDMAN: Right.

JUSTICE ALITO: But the defense can then cross-examine the analyst.

MR. FRIEDMAN: I wouldn't call that cross-exam—

JUSTICE ALITO: Such a slight difference between those two situations. Now, how is that a fundamental transformation of the way Anglo–American trials are conducted?

MR. FRIEDMAN: It's fundamental transformation because the prosecution can present a stack of affidavits, and they wouldn't even have to be affidavits. They could just be signed—they could just be statements. It could present videotapes. It could present audio tapes. It could craft those and rehearse those behind the scene. It could present those to the trial—

JUSTICE ALITO: No. Let's just not get beyond the facts of this case—we're all—all that we are dealing with is an analyst's report relating to the—the nature of the substance that was tested and, if it's a controlled substance, the amount. That's it. It doesn't extend to anything else, videotapes or anything more. There is such a slight difference between those two situations.

MR. FRIEDMAN: I think there is an enormous difference in—in impact. ... I don't believe it's cross-examination. In practice, it is as if the defendant said, "I don't want to cross-examine," but I still insist that the witness get up on the stand and let's see what the witness can do. And the Commonwealth makes no attempt to distinguish between these witnesses and other witnesses for what is—what is satisfactory confrontation. It says: This is good confrontation. He could do it with all witnesses. If the Court pleases, I will reserve the balance of my time.

CHIEF JUSTICE ROBERTS: Thank you, Mr. Friedman.

. . .

ORAL ARGUMENT OF STEPHEN R. McCULLOUGH[2] ON BEHALF OF THE RESPONDENT

MR. McCULLOUGH: Mr. Chief Justice, and may it please the Court:

. . .

---

2. [Ed. Solicitor General of the State of Virginia.]

JUSTICE SOTOMAYOR: Could I ask you: If we were to—how do we articulate a rule, or do we need to, that would take care of the fears of your adversary that trials would become trials by affidavit, that prosecutors will choose to put all witnesses on—by videotape, by affidavit, by deposition, whatever mode they choose except bringing them into court—and forcing defendants then to call the witnesses and do a what's—what I call a cold-cross?

What rule would we announce in this case that would avoid—what constitutional construction of the Confrontation Clause would we issue that would protect against that?

MR. McCULLOUGH: I think there are several constitutional, legal, and practical considerations that make this—

JUSTICE SOTOMAYOR: No, no. Forget the practical. Talk about the legal, constitutional.

MR. McCULLOUGH: Right. Constitutionally, there are two obstacles to a wholesale type of trial system where the prosecution would simply present a stack of affidavits.

The first of those is the Due Process Clause, which—if, for example, in these child witness cases—what a number of courts have held is that it's going to inflame the jury against the defendant if a videotape is introduced and then the defendant is . . . forced to call the witness to the stand. And that's simply not the case with these types of witness. So the Due Process Clause itself puts the brakes on the type of wholesale at-trial—

JUSTICE SCALIA: They're trial witnesses. Anything else?

MR. McCULLOUGH: Another is the fact that under the Confrontation Clause, the cross-examination has to be effective. And so if the prosecution on the day of trial dumps a series of affidavits on the defense, it's going to be pretty difficult for the defense to be in a position to effectively cross-examine.

JUSTICE SCALIA: So just one or two. Just one or two affidavits. Or it—the Court has a rule you have to provide those affidavits several weeks before trial. That would be okay? We'd have a whole European-type trial, right? . . . trial by affidavit.

MR. McCULLOUGH: Right. I don't think the Confrontation Clause, in terms of what it's historically intended to protect, blocks that scenario.

I think the key to the Confrontation Clause, what this Court has said for a long time, turning to the history of the clause, is that it's designed to protect the reliability of the government's evidence. And the way it does that is by subjecting that to the crucible of cross-examination, face-to-face, of live witnesses. And this statute protects exactly that; that is, the defendant says he wants the witness there—

JUSTICE SCALIA: It does more than that. It does more than that. It is the prosecution that has had to place the witness on the stand. It has not been up to the defense to say, "Oh, no, I object to this affidavit. I would like you to bring"—no. The prosecution has to bring in the witness. That has been what the Confrontation Clause has meant.

MR. McCULLOUGH: We agree that we have to produce the witness for court, but we see little—

JUSTICE SCALIA: No, you don't agree with that. You say you don't have to do it unless the defendant objects and issue—gets a subpoena issued.

MR. McCULLOUGH: Well, we agree that if the defendant does provide the notice, as with the notice on demand statute, that it's—that it is our burden to make sure that witness is there. And if—as the statute provides, the witness has to be summoned and appear.

. . .

ORAL ARGUMENT OF LEONDRA R. KRUGER[3] FOR UNITED STATES, AS AMICUS CURIAE, SUPPORTING RESPONDENT

MS. KRUGER: Mr. Chief Justice, and may it please the Court:

A state adequately safeguards the confrontation right recognized in Melendez–Diaz when it guarantees that it will, on the defendant's request, bring the analyst into court for face-to-face confrontation and cross-examination at trial.

JUSTICE SCALIA: That's not what we said in Melendez–Diaz, unfortunately.

MS. KRUGER: Well, Melendez–Diaz—

JUSTICE SCALIA: We said the following: More fundamentally, the Confrontation Clause imposes a burden on the prosecution to present its witnesses, not on the defendant to bring those adverse witnesses into court. Its value to the defendant is not replaced by a system in which the prosecution presents its evidence via ex parte affidavits and waits for the defendant to subpoena the affiants, if he chooses. So you are asking us to overrule that—that statement?

MS. KRUGER: No, Justice Scalia, not at all. We believe that the state complies with that very rule from Melendez–Diaz when it ensures that the analyst is present in Court to submit to cross-examination, which is the core of the confrontation right. This Court affirmed—

JUSTICE SCALIA: He's present only if the defendant asks for him, right?

MS. KRUGER: That's right, and that's because—

JUSTICE SCALIA: And that's exactly what this addressed. It's not—it's not replaced by a system in which the prosecution presents its evidence by—and waits for the defendant to subpoena the affiants if he chooses.

MS. KRUGER: This Court has recognized that the confrontation right is designed to achieve a particular purpose, and that is to ensure that the government's evidence is subject to adversarial testing at trial.

It is ultimately up to the defendant in every case to decide, no matter how the prosecution presents its evidence on direct, whether or not it wants to confront the witness and submit that witness' testimony to adversarial testing—

JUSTICE SCALIA: That may be. It's a perfectly reasonable argument. I just object to your saying that it doesn't contradict Melendez–Diaz.

MS. KRUGER: I think it would be surprising to discover that Melendez–Diaz went quite so far. This Court has never before recognized a dimension of the Confrontation Clause that would govern the manner in which the prosecution presents its evidence, except for the rules that it affirmed it in Crawford, which is that so long as the government ensures that the witness is available for cross-

3. [Ed. Assistant to the Solicitor General, U.S. Department of Justice.]

examination at trial, the Confrontation Clause places no constraints on the government's use of prior testimony or statements.

JUSTICE BREYER: All right. So the statement, the sentence in this opinion, that, in your opinion, would have the affect of limiting Melendez–Diaz without overruling it, what is that statement?

MS. KRUGER: I think the statement is it requires only that the court reaffirm what it already said in Crawford, in the context of the lab analyst testimony at issue in this case, which is, again, when the analyst is available for cross-examination at trial, the government has complied with what the Confrontation Clause demands.

It has provided a constitutionally sufficient opportunity for the defendants to submit that analysts's findings—

JUSTICE SCALIA: And it just doesn't—doesn't apply just to analysts, right? I mean, is there anything peculiar about analysts? Would it not exist for any other witness?

MS. KRUGER: Well, our principle submission is that the Confrontation Clause provides, in every case, an opportunity for effective cross-examination.

JUSTICE SCALIA: Okay.

MS. KRUGER: And there may be independent constraints on the manner in which the prosecution presents its evidence under the laws of evidence in the jurisdiction because of the government's need to satisfy its burden of proof and ensure a fundamentally fair trial under the Due Process Clause.

To the extent that the Court—

JUSTICE SCALIA: I don't understand what—is that a yes or a no?

MS. KRUGER: Well, it is to say that [the] Confrontation Clause is not what prohibits that practice. What prohibits that practice are other equally effective verses in the law—

JUSTICE SCALIA: Okay. So as far as the Confrontation Clause is concerned, this would apply to other witnesses as well?

MS. KRUGER: I think that that is right, ...

. . .

JUSTICE STEVENS: Ms. Kruger, can I just ask this question? I just want to be sure. Supposing you have an eyewitness. Can you follow the same procedure that you recommend for the scientific eyewitness—forensic eyewitness?

MS. KRUGER: We think that you could, so long as the defendant has an adequate opportunity to cross-examine that eye witness about the testimonial statement. But even if you disagreed with that, we think that the Court could take a due account of the fact that there is a significant difference between the kind of testimony that an eyewitness provides and the kind of testimony that a forensic analyst provides.

The forensic analyst's lab report is not merely a weaker substitute for live testimony. It is, in fact, I think, as we see, by the relative infrequency with which analysts are called into Court before Melendez–Diaz, something that has been seen to have equal value, regardless of the manner in which it is presented.

SECTION 13 CONSTITUTIONAL RESTRAINTS

And, for that reason, we think that, in order to decide this case, all this Court needs to decide is that, in the context of forensic lab analysts, what the Court said in Crawford still stands, so long as the government presents the analyst at trial for face-to-face confrontation and cross-examination.

JUSTICE SCALIA: Why—why do we have to say anything? Why is this case here except as an opportunity to upset Melendez–Diaz.

MS. KRUGER: I think that—

JUSTICE SCALIA: This Virginia statute no longer exists, does it? So we are pronouncing on the validity of a Virginia statute that is now gone, right? They have adopted a statute that complies completely with Melendez–Diaz.

MS. KRUGER: That's true, and I think that that's because Virginia was unwilling to stake the validity of however many convictions in the interim on the outcome—

JUSTICE SCALIA: I'm not criticizing Virginia; I'm criticizing us for taking the case.

(Laughter.)

MS. KRUGER: I think that this—this case presents, I think, an important opportunity for the Court to provide guidance to States that are currently grappling with how to respond to the practical problems that have been presented in the wake of Melendez–Diaz.

JUSTICE SOTOMAYOR: So we say to them contrary to what Melendez–Diaz says, that subpoena statutes—when you read the statute, it says the defendant has to subpoena the witness. On its—on the face of this statute, without the Commonwealth court's gloss on it.

MS. KRUGER: I don't mean to quibble, Justice Sotomayor, but the statute does not in fact on its face say defendant must subpoena. It says the witness shall be summoned. But I think to the extent that you had any questions about whether or not the Commonwealth's interpretation of that language were correct, the appropriate course would be to remand to the Virginia Supreme Court to allow them to address that question of State law in the first instance.

JUSTICE SCALIA: That question of prior State law, right?

MS. KRUGER: Thank you, Your Honor.

CHIEF JUSTICE ROBERTS: Thank you, counsel.

. . .

REBUTTAL ARGUMENT OF RICHARD D. FRIEDMAN, ON BEHALF OF THE PETITIONERS

. . .

MR. FRIEDMAN: I don't think this is a question of order of proof. This is a question of who puts the witness on the stand. Melendez addressed that very explicitly in part III–F, and said that an affidavit doesn't do, that the prosecution has to present prosecution witnesses.

JUSTICE GINSBURG: So is the proper to grant, vacate and remand in light of Melendez–Diaz?

MR. FRIEDMAN: May—may I respond to that?

CHIEF JUSTICE ROBERTS: Yes.

MR. FRIEDMAN: Thank you.

Your Honor, I think that the—the proper response here is the Court has taken the case; there is enough without any—resolving any ambiguities of the Virginia statute to say that the—this procedure is unconstitutional, because it imposes, even without worrying about the no-show point, it imposes upon the defendant the burden of putting the witness on the stand. Given that all of these States in the United States are contesting that this procedure is acceptable, I think is proper for the Court to say right now that it—that it is not.

CHIEF JUSTICE ROBERTS: Thank you, counsel, the case is submitted.

Bullcoming v. New Mexico

Supreme Court of the United States, 2011.
___ S.Ct. ___, 2011 WL 2472799 (U.S.).

■ [GINSBURG, J., delivered the opinion of the Court, except as to Part IV and footnote 6. SCALIA, J., joined that opinion in full, SOTOMAYOR and KAGAN, JJ., joined as to all but Part IV, and THOMAS, J., joined as to all but Part IV and footnote 6. SOTOMAYOR, J., filed an opinion concurring in part. KENNEDY, J., filed a dissenting opinion, in which ROBERTS, C. J., and BREYER and ALITO, JJ., joined.]

■ JUSTICE GINSBURG delivered the opinion of the Court, except as to Part IV and footnote 6.

In *Melendez-Diaz* v. *Massachusetts*, 557 U.S. ___ (2009), this Court held that a forensic laboratory report stating that a suspect substance was cocaine ranked as testimonial for purposes of the Sixth Amendment's Confrontation Clause. The report had been created specifically to serve as evidence in a criminal proceeding. Absent stipulation, the Court ruled, the prosecution may not introduce such a report without offering a live witness competent to testify to the truth of the statements made in the report.

In the case before us, petitioner Donald Bullcoming was arrested on charges of driving while intoxicated (DWI). Principal evidence against Bullcoming was a forensic laboratory report certifying that Bullcoming's blood-alcohol concentration was well above the threshold for aggravated DWI. At trial, the prosecution did not call as a witness the analyst who signed the certification. Instead, the State called another analyst who was familiar with the laboratory's testing procedures, but had neither participated in nor observed the test on Bullcoming's blood sample. The New Mexico Supreme Court determined that, although the blood-alcohol analysis was "testimonial," the Confrontation Clause did not require the certifying analyst's in-court testimony. Instead, New Mexico's high court held, live testimony of another analyst satisfied the constitutional requirements.

The question presented is whether the Confrontation Clause permits the prosecution to introduce a forensic laboratory report containing a testimonial certification—made for the purpose of proving a particular fact—through the in-court testimony of a scientist who did not sign the certification or perform or observe the test reported in the certification. We hold that surrogate testimony of that order does not meet the constitutional requirement. The accused's right is to be confronted with the analyst who made the certification, unless that analyst is unavailable at trial, and the accused had an opportunity, pretrial, to cross-examine that particular scientist.

I

A

In August 2005, a vehicle driven by petitioner Donald Bullcoming rear-ended a pick-up truck at an intersection in Farmington, New Mexico. When the truckdriver exited his vehicle and approached Bullcoming to exchange insurance information, he noticed that Bullcoming's eyes were bloodshot. Smelling alcohol on Bullcoming's breath, the truckdriver told his wife to call the police. Bullcoming left the scene before the police arrived, but was soon apprehended by an officer who observed his performance of field sobriety tests. Upon failing the tests, Bullcoming was arrested for driving a vehicle while "under the influence of intoxicating liquor" (DWI), in violation of N. M. Stat. Ann. § 66–8–102 (2004).

Because Bullcoming refused to take a breath test, the police obtained a warrant authorizing a blood-alcohol analy-sis. Pursuant to the warrant, a sample of Bullcoming's blood was drawn at a local hospital. To determine Bullcoming's blood-alcohol concentration (BAC), the police sent the sample to the New Mexico Department of Health, Scientific Laboratory Division (SLD). In a standard SLD form titled "Report of Blood Alcohol Analysis," participants in the testing were identified, and the forensic analyst certified his finding.

SLD's report contained in the top block "information ... filled in by [the] arresting officer." This information included the "reason [the] suspect [was] stopped" (the officer checked "Accident"), and the date ("8.14.05") and time ("18:25 PM") the blood sample was drawn. The arresting officer also affirmed that he had arrested Bullcoming and witnessed the blood draw. The next two blocks contained certifications by the nurse who drew Bullcoming's blood and the SLD intake employee who received the blood sample sent to the laboratory.

Following these segments, the report presented the "certificate of analyst," completed and signed by Curtis Caylor, the SLD forensic analyst assigned to test Bullcoming's blood sample. Caylor recorded that the BAC in Bullcoming's sample was 0.21 grams per hundred milliliters, an inordinately high level. Caylor also affirmed that "[t]he seal of th[e] sample was received intact and broken in the laboratory," that "the statements in [the analyst's block of the report] are correct," and that he had "followed the procedures set out on the reverse of th[e] report." Those "procedures" instructed analysts, *inter alia*, to "retai[n] the sample container and the raw data from the analysis," and to "not[e] any circumstance or condition which might affect the integrity of the sample or otherwise affect the validity of the analysis." Finally, in a block headed "certificate of reviewer," the SLD examiner who reviewed Caylor's analysis certified that Caylor was qualified to conduct the BAC test, and that the "established procedure" for handling and analyzing Bullcoming's sample "ha[d] been followed."

SLD analysts use gas chromatograph machines to determine BAC levels. Operation of the machines requires specialized knowledge and training. Several steps are involved in the gas chromatograph process, and human error can occur at each step.[1]

Caylor's report that Bullcoming's BAC was 0.21 supported a prosecution for aggravated DWI, the threshold for which is a BAC of 0.16 grams per hundred milliliters, § 66–8–102(D)(1). The State accordingly charged Bullcoming with this more serious crime.

B

The case was tried to a jury in November 2005, after our decision in *Crawford v. Washington*, 541 U. S. 36 (2004), but before *Melendez-Diaz*. On the day of trial, the State announced that it would not be calling SLD analyst Curtis Caylor as a witness because he had "very recently [been] put on unpaid leave" for a reason not revealed. A startled defense counsel objected. . . . The State, however, proposed to introduce Caylor's finding as a "business record" during the testimony of Gerasimos

---

[1]. Gas chromatography is a widely used scientific method of quantitatively analyzing the constituents of a mixture. See generally H. McNair & J. Miller, Basic Gas Chromatography (2d ed. 2009) (hereinafter McNair). Under SLD's standard testing protocol, the analyst extracts two blood samples and inserts them into vials containing an "internal standard"—a chemical additive. The analyst then "cap[s] the [two] sample[s]," "crimp[s] them with an aluminum top," and places the vials into the gas chromatograph machine . . . . Within a few hours, this device produces a printed graph—a chromatogram—along with calculations representing a software-generated interpretation of the data. . . . Although the State presented testimony that obtaining an accurate BAC measurement merely entails "look[ing] at the [gas chromatograph] machine and record[ing] the results," authoritative sources reveal that the matter is not so simple or certain. "In order to perform quantitative analyses satisfactorily and . . . support the results under rigorous examination in court, the analyst must be aware of, and adhere to, good analytical practices and understand what is being done and why." Stafford, Chromatography, in Principles of Forensic Toxicology 92, 114 (B. Levine 2d ed. 2006). See also McNair 137 ("Errors that occur in any step can invalidate the best chromatographic analysis, so attention must be paid to all steps."); D. Bartell, M. McMurray, & A. ImObersteg, Attacking and Defending Drunk Driving Tests § 16:80 (2d revision 2010) (stating that 93% of errors in laboratory tests for BAC levels are human errors that occur either before or after machines analyze samples). Even after the machine has produced its printed result, a review of the chromatogram may indicate that the test was not valid. . . . Nor is the risk of human error so remote as to be negligible. *Amici* inform us, for example, that in neighboring Colorado, a single forensic laboratory produced at least 206 flawed blood-alcohol readings over a three-year span, prompting the dismissal of several criminal prosecutions. . . . An analyst had used improper amounts of the internal standard, causing the chromatograph machine systematically to inflate BAC measurements. The analyst's error, a supervisor said, was "fairly complex."

Razatos, an SLD scientist who had neither observed nor reviewed Caylor's analysis.

Bullcoming's counsel opposed the State's proposal. Without Caylor's testimony, defense counsel maintained, introduction of the analyst's finding would violate Bullcoming's Sixth Amendment right "to be confronted with the witnesses against him." The trial court overruled the objection, and admitted the SLD report as a business record. The jury convicted Bullcoming of aggravated DWI, and the New Mexico Court of Appeals upheld the conviction, concluding that "the blood alcohol report in the present case was non-testimonial and prepared routinely with guarantees of trustworthiness."

C

While Bullcoming's appeal was pending before the New Mexico Supreme Court, this Court decided *Melendez-Diaz*. In that case, "[t]he Massachusetts courts [had] admitted into evidence affidavits reporting the results of forensic analysis which showed that material seized by the police and connected to the defendant was cocaine." Those affidavits, the Court held, were " 'testimonial,' rendering the affiants 'witnesses' subject to the defendant's right of confrontation under the Sixth Amendment."

In light of *Melendez-Diaz*, the New Mexico Supreme Court acknowledged that the blood-alcohol report introduced at Bullcoming's trial qualified as testimonial evidence. Like the affidavits in *Melendez-Diaz*, the court observed, the report was "functionally identical to live, in-court testimony, doing precisely what a witness does on direct examination." Nevertheless, for two reasons, the court held that admission of the report did not violate the Confrontation Clause.

First, the court said certifying analyst Caylor "was a mere scrivener," who "simply transcribed the results generated by the gas chromatograph machine." Second, SLD analyst Razatos, although he did not participate in testing Bullcoming's blood, "qualified as an expert witness with respect to the gas chromatograph machine." "Razatos provided live, in-court testimony," the court stated, "and, thus, was available for cross-examination regarding the operation of the ... machine, the results of [Bullcoming's] BAC test, and the SLD's established laboratory procedures." Razatos' testimony was crucial, the court explained, because Bullcoming could not cross-examine the machine or the written report. But "[Bullcoming's] right of confrontation was preserved," the court concluded, because Razatos was a qualified analyst, able to serve as a surrogate for Caylor.

We granted certiorari to address this question: Does the Confrontation Clause permit the prosecution to introduce a forensic laboratory report containing a testimonial certification, made in order to prove a fact at a criminal trial, through the in-court testimony of an analyst who did not sign the certification or personally perform or observe the performance of the test reported in the certification. Our answer is in line with controlling precedent: As a rule, if an out-of-court statement is testimonial in nature, it may not be introduced against the accused at trial unless the witness who made the statement is unavailable and the accused has had a prior opportunity to confront that witness. Because the New Mexico Supreme Court permitted the testimonial statement of one witness, *i.e.*, Caylor, to enter into evidence through the in-court testimony of a second person, *i.e.*, Razatos, we reverse that court's judgment.

II

The Sixth Amendment's Confrontation Clause confers upon the accused "[i]n all criminal prosecutions, ... the right ... to be confronted with the witnesses against him." In a pathmarking 2004 decision, *Crawford* v. *Washington*, we overruled which had interpreted the Confrontation Clause to allow admission of absent witnesses' testimonial statements based on a judicial determination of reliability. Rejecting *Roberts*' "amorphous notions of 'reliability,'" *Crawford* held that fidelity to the Confrontation Clause permitted admission of "[t]estimonial statements of witnesses absent from trial ... only where the declarant is unavailable, and only where the defendant has had a prior opportunity to cross-examine," ... *Melendez-Diaz*, relying on *Crawford*'s rationale, refused to create a "forensic evidence" exception to this rule. An analyst's certification prepared in connection with a criminal investigation or prosecution, the Court held, is "testimonial," and therefore within the compass of the Confrontation Clause.[2]

The State in the instant case never asserted that the analyst who signed the certification, Curtis Caylor, was unavailable. The record showed only that Caylor was placed on unpaid leave for an undisclosed reason. Nor did Bullcoming have an opportunity to cross-examine Caylor. *Crawford* and *Melendez-Diaz*, therefore, weigh heavily in Bullcoming's favor. The New Mexico Supreme Court, however, although recognizing that the SLD report was testimonial for purposes of the Confrontation Clause, considered SLD analyst Razatos an adequate substitute for Caylor. We explain first why Razatos' appearance did not meet the Confrontation Clause requirement. We next address the State's argument that the SLD report ranks as "nontestimonial," and therefore "[was] not subject to the Confrontation Clause" in the first place.

2. [Renumbered—footnote 6 in the Justice Ginsburg's opinion] To rank as "testimonial," a statement must have a "primary purpose" of "establish[ing] or prov[ing] past events potentially relevant to later criminal prosecution." Elaborating on the purpose for which a "testimonial report" is created, we observed in *Melendez-Diaz* that business and public records "are generally admissible absent confrontation ... because—having been created for the administration of an entity's affairs and not for the purpose of establishing or proving some fact at trial—they are not testimonial."

A

The New Mexico Supreme Court held surrogate testimony adequate to satisfy the Confrontation Clause in this case because analyst Caylor "simply transcribed the resul[t] generated by the gas chromatograph machine," presenting no interpretation and exercising no independent judgment.... Bullcoming's "true 'accuser,'" the court said, was the machine, while testing analyst Caylor's role was that of "mere scrivener." Caylor's certification, however, reported more than a machine-generated number.

Caylor certified that he received Bullcoming's blood sample intact with the seal unbroken, that he checked to make sure that the forensic report number and the sample number "correspond[ed]," and that he performed on Bullcoming's sample a particular test, adhering to a precise protocol. He further represented, by leaving the "[r]emarks" section of the report blank, that no "circumstance or condition ... affect[ed] the integrity of the sample or ... the validity of the analysis." These representations, relating to past events and human actions not revealed in raw, machine-produced data, are meet for cross-examination.

The potential ramifications of the New Mexico Supreme Court's reasoning, furthermore, raise red flags. Most witnesses, after all, testify to their observations of factual conditions or events, *e.g.*, "the light was green," "the hour was noon." Such witnesses may record, on the spot, what they observed. Suppose a police report recorded an objective fact—Bullcoming's counsel posited the address above the front door of a house or the read-out of a radar gun. Could an officer other than the one who saw the number on the house or gun present the information in court—so long as that officer was equipped to testify about any technology the observing officer deployed and the police department's standard operating procedures? As our precedent makes plain, the answer is emphatically "No." ...

The New Mexico Supreme Court stated that the number registered by the gas chromatograph machine called for no interpretation or exercise of independent judgment on Caylor's part. We have already explained that Caylor certified to more than a machine-generated number. In any event, the comparative reliability of an analyst's testimonial report drawn from machine-produced data does not overcome the Sixth Amendment bar. This Court settled in *Crawford* that the "obviou[s] reliab[ility]" of a testimonial statement does not dispense with the Confrontation Clause. (Clause "commands, not that evidence be reliable, but that reliability be assessed in a particular manner: by testing [the evidence] in the crucible of cross-examination"). Accordingly, the analysts who write reports that the prosecution introduces must be made available for confrontation even if they possess "the scientific acumen of Mme. Curie and the veracity of Mother Teresa."

B

Recognizing that admission of the blood-alcohol analysis depended on "live, in-court testimony [by] a qualified analyst," New Mexico Supreme Court believed that Razatos could substitute for Caylor because Razatos "qualified as an expert witness with respect to the gas chromatograph machine and the SLD's laboratory procedures," But surrogate testimony of the kind Razatos was equipped to give could not convey what Caylor knew or observed about the events his certification concerned, *i.e.*, the particular test and testing process he employed. Nor could such surrogate testimony expose any lapses or lies on the certifying analyst's part.

Significant here, Razatos had no knowledge of the reason why Caylor had been placed on unpaid leave. With Caylor on the stand, Bullcoming's counsel could have asked questions designed to reveal whether incompetence, evasiveness, or dishonesty accounted for Caylor's removal from his work station. Notable in this regard, the State never asserted that Caylor was "unavailable"; the prosecution conveyed only that Caylor was on uncompensated leave. Nor did the State assert that Razatos had any "independent opinion" concerning Bullcoming's BAC. In this light, Caylor's live testimony could hardly be typed "a hollow formality."

More fundamentally, as this Court stressed in *Crawford*, "[t]he text of the Sixth Amendment does not suggest any open-ended exceptions from the confrontation requirement to be developed by the courts." Nor is it "the role of courts to extrapolate from the words of the [Confrontation Clause] to the values behind it, and then to enforce its guarantees only to the extent they serve (in the courts' views) those underlying values." *Giles* v. *California*. Accordingly, the Clause does not tolerate dispensing with confrontation simply because the court believes that questioning one witness about another's testimonial statements provides a fair enough opportunity for cross-examination.

. . .

In short, when the State elected to introduce Caylor's certification, Caylor became a witness Bullcoming had the right to confront. Our precedent cannot sensibly be read any other way. See *Melendez-Diaz*.

III

We turn, finally, to the State's contention that the SLD's blood-alcohol analysis reports are nontestimonial in character, therefore no Confrontation Clause question even arises in this case. *Melendez-Diaz* left no room for that argument, the New Mexico Supreme Court concluded, a conclusion we find inescapable.

In *Melendez-Diaz*, a state forensic laboratory, on police request, analyzed seized evidence (plastic bags) and reported the laboratory's analysis to the police (the substance found in the bags contained cocaine). The "certificates of analysis" prepared by the analysts who tested the evidence in *Melendez-Diaz*, this Court held, were "incontrovertibly ... affirmation[s] made for the purpose of establishing or proving some fact" in a criminal proceeding. The same purpose was served by the certificate in question here.

The State maintains that the affirmations made by analyst Caylor were not "adversarial" or "inquisitorial"; instead, they were simply observations of an "independent scientis[t]" made "according to a nonadversarial public duty,". That argument fares no better here than it did in *Melendez-Diaz*. A document created solely for an "evidentiary purpose," *Melendez-Diaz* clarified, made in aid of a police investigation, ranks as testimonial.

. . .

In all material respects, the laboratory report in this case resembles those in *Melendez-Diaz*.

. . .

In sum, the formalities attending the "report of blood alcohol analysis" are more than adequate to qualify Caylor's assertions as testimonial. The absence of notarization does not remove his certification from Confrontation Clause governance. The New Mexico Supreme Court, guided by *Melendez-Diaz*, correctly recognized that Caylor's report "fell within the core class of testimonial statements" in this Court's leading Confrontation Clause decisions.

IV

The State and its *amici* urge that unbending application of the Confrontation Clause to forensic evidence would impose an undue burden on the prosecution. This argument, also advanced in the dissent, largely repeats a refrain rehearsed and rejected in *Melendez-Diaz*. The constitutional requirement, we reiterate, "may not [be] disregard[ed] ... at our convenience," and the predictions of dire consequences, we again observe, are dubious.

New Mexico law, it bears emphasis, requires the laboratory to preserve samples, which can be retested by other analysts, and neither party questions SLD's compliance with that requirement. Retesting "is almost always an option ... in [DWI] cases," Brief for Public Defender Service for District of Columbia et al. as *Amici Curiae* 25 (hereinafter PDS Brief), and the State had that option here: New Mexico could have avoided any Confrontation Clause problem by asking Razatos to retest the sample, and then testify to the results of his retest rather than to the results of a test he did not conduct or observe.

Notably, New Mexico advocates retesting as an effective means to preserve a defendant's confrontation right "when the [out-of-court] statement is raw data or a mere transcription of raw data onto a public record." (defense "remains free to.... call and examine the technician who performed a test"), ("free retesting" is available to defendants). The prosecution, however, bears the burden of proof. ("[T]he Confrontation Clause imposes a burden on the prosecution to present its witnesses, not on the defendant to bring those adverse witnesses into court."). Hence the obligation to propel retesting when the original analyst is unavailable is the State's, not the defendant's.

Furthermore, notice-and-demand procedures, long in effect in many jurisdictions, can reduce burdens on forensic laboratories. Statutes governing these procedures typically "render ... otherwise hearsay forensic reports admissible[,] while specifically preserving a defendant's right to demand that the prosecution call the author/ analyst of [the] report." PDS Brief 9; see *Melendez-Diaz* (observing that notice-and-demand statutes "permit the defendant to assert (or forfeit by silence) his Confrontation Clause right after receiving notice of the prosecution's intent to use a forensic analyst's report").

Even before this Court's decision in *Crawford*, moreover, it was common prosecutorial practice to call the forensic analyst to testify. Prosecutors did so "to bolster the persuasive power of [the State's] case[,] ... [even] when the defense would have preferred that the analyst did *not* testify." PDS Brief 8.

We note also the "small fraction of ... cases" that "actually proceed to trial." (*Melendez-Diaz*,) (citing estimate that "nearly 95% of convictions in state and federal courts are obtained via guilty plea"). And, "when cases in which forensic analysis has been conducted [do] go to trial," defendants "regularly ... [stipulate] to the admission of [the] analysis." PDS Brief 20. "[A]s a result, analysts testify in only a very small percentage of cases," for "[i]t is unlikely that defense counsel will insist on live testimony whose effect will be merely to highlight rather than cast doubt upon the forensic analysis.".

Tellingly, in jurisdictions in which "it is the [acknowledged] job of ... analysts to testify in court ... about their test results," the sky has not fallen. PDS Brief 23. State and municipal laboratories "make operational and staffing decisions" to facilitate analysts' appearance at trial. Prosecutors schedule trial dates to accommodate analysts' availability, and trial courts liberally grant continuances when unexpected conflicts arise. In rare cases in which the analyst is no longer employed by the laboratory at the time of trial, "the prosecution makes the effort to bring that analyst ... to court." And, as is the practice in New Mexico, laboratories ordinarily retain additional samples, enabling them to run tests again when necessary.

* * *

For the reasons stated, the judgment of the New Mexico Supreme Court is reversed, and the case is remanded for further proceedings not inconsistent with this opinion.[3]

■ JUSTICE SOTOMAYOR, concurring in part.

I agree with the Court that the trial court erred by admitting the blood alcohol concentration (BAC) report. I write separately first to highlight why I view the report at issue to be testimonial—specifically because its "primary purpose" is evidentiary—and second to emphasize the limited reach of the Court's opinion.

I

A

. . .

As we explained earlier this Term in *Michigan v. Bryant*, 562 U.S. ___ (2010), "[i]n making the primary purpose determination, standard rules of hearsay . . . will be relevant."[1] As applied to a scientific report, *Melendez-Diaz* explained that pursuant to Federal Rule of Evidence 803, "[d]ocuments kept in the regular course of business may ordinarily be admitted at trial despite their hearsay status," except "if the regularly conducted business activity is the production of evidence for use at trial." (citing Fed. Rule Evid. 803(6)). In that circumstance, the hearsay rules bar admission of even business records. Relatedly, in the Confrontation Clause context, business and public records "are generally admissible absent confrontation . . . because—having been created for the administration of an entity's affairs and not for the purpose of establishing or proving some fact at trial—they are not testimonial." *Melendez-Diaz*, We concluded, therefore, that because the purpose of the certificates of analysis was use at trial, they were not properly admissible as business or public records under the hearsay rules, nor were they admissible under the Confrontation Clause. The hearsay rule's recognition of the certificates' evidentiary purpose thus confirmed our decision that the certificates were testimonial under the primary purpose analysis required by the Confrontation Clause. (explaining that under Massachusetts law not just the purpose but the "*sole purpose* of the affidavits was to provide" evidence).

Similarly, in this case, for the reasons the Court sets forth the BAC report and Caylor's certification on it clearly have a "primary purpose of

---

3. [Renumbered] As in *Melendez-Diaz*, we express no view on whether the Confrontation Clause error in this case was harmless. The New Mexico Supreme Court did not reach that question, and nothing in this opinion impedes a harmless-error inquiry on remand.

1. Contrary to the dissent's characterization, *Bryant* deemed reliability, as reflected in the hearsay rules, to be "relevant," not "essential," (opinion of KENNEDY, J.). The rules of evidence, not the Confrontation Clause, are designed primarily to police reliability; the purpose of the Confrontation Clause is to determine whether statements are testimonial and therefore require confrontation.

creating an out-of-court substitute for trial testimony." The Court also explains why the BAC report is not materially distinguishable from the certificates we held testimonial in *Melendez-Diaz*.[2]

The formality inherent in the certification further suggests its evidentiary purpose. . . . The formality derives from the fact that the analyst is asked to sign his name and "certify" to both the result and the statements on the form. A "certification" requires one "[t]o attest" that the accompanying statements are true. Black's Law Dictionary 258 (9th ed. 2009) (definition of "certify"); . . .

In sum, I am compelled to conclude that the report has a "primary purpose of creating an out-of-court substitute for trial testimony," which renders it testimonial.

. . .

II

Although this case is materially indistinguishable from the facts we considered in *Melendez-Diaz*, I highlight some of the factual circumstances that this case does *not* present.

First, this is not a case in which the State suggested an alternate purpose, much less an alternate *primary* purpose, for the BAC report. For example, the State has not claimed that the report was necessary to provide Bullcoming with medical treatment. . . .

Second, this is not a case in which the person testifying is a supervisor, reviewer, or someone else with a personal, albeit limited, connection to the scientific test at issue. Razatos conceded on cross-examination that he played no role in producing the BAC report and did not observe any portion of Curtis Caylor's conduct of the testing. It would be a different case if, for example, a supervisor who observed an analyst conducting a test testified about the results or a report about such results. We need not address what degree of involvement is sufficient because here Razatos had no involvement whatsoever in the relevant test and report.

Third, this is not a case in which an expert witness was asked for his independent opinion about underlying testimonial reports that were not themselves admitted into evidence. See Fed. Rule Evid. 703 (explaining that facts or data of a type upon which experts in the field would reasonably rely in forming an opinion need not be admissible in order for the expert's opinion based on the facts and data to be admitted). As the Court notes, the State does not assert that Razatos offered an indepen-

---

2. This is not to say, however, that every person noted on the BAC report must testify. As we explained in *Melendez-Diaz*, it is not the case "that anyone whose testimony may be relevant in establishing the chain of custody, authenticity of the sample, or accuracy of the testing device, must appear in person as part of the prosecution's case. . . . It is up to the prosecution to decide what steps in the chain of custody are so crucial as to require evidence. . . ."

dent, expert opinion about Bullcoming's blood alcohol concentration. Rather, the State explains, "[a]side from reading a report that was introduced as an exhibit, Mr. Razatos offered no opinion about Petitioner's blood alcohol content...." Here the State offered the BAC report, including Caylor's testimonial statements, into evidence. We would face a different question if asked to determine the constitutionality of allowing an expert witness to discuss others' testimonial statements if the testimonial statements were not themselves admitted as evidence.

Finally, this is not a case in which the State introduced only machine-generated results, such as a printout from a gas chromatograph. The State here introduced Caylor's statements, which included his transcription of a blood alcohol concentration, apparently copied from a gas chromatograph printout, along with other statements about the procedures used in handling the blood sample.... Thus, we do not decide whether, as the New Mexico Supreme Court suggests, a State could introduce (assuming an adequate chain of custody foundation) raw data generated by a machine in conjunction with the testimony of an expert witness.

This case does not present, and thus the Court's opinion does not address, any of these factual scenarios.

* * *

As in *Melendez-Diaz*, the primary purpose of the BAC report is clearly to serve as evidence. It is therefore testimonial, and the trial court erred in allowing the State to introduce it into evidence via Razatos' testimony. I respectfully concur.

■ JUSTICE KENNEDY, with whom THE CHIEF JUSTICE, JUSTICE BREYER, and JUSTICE ALITO join, dissenting.

... Two Terms ago, in a case arising from a state criminal prosecution, the Court interpreted the Clause to mandate exclusion of a laboratory report sought to be introduced based on the authority of that report's own sworn statement that a test had been performed yielding the results as shown. *Melendez-Diaz* v. *Massachusetts*. The Court's opinion in that case held the report inadmissible because no one was present at trial to testify to its contents.

Whether or not one agrees with the reasoning and the result in *Melendez-Diaz*, the Court today takes the new and serious misstep of extending that holding to instances like this one. Here a knowledgeable representative of the laboratory was present to testify and to explain the lab's processes and the details of the report; but because he was not the analyst who filled out part of the form and transcribed onto it the test result from a machine printout, the Court finds a confrontation violation.

I

Before today, the Court had not held that the Confrontation Clause bars admission of scientific findings when an employee of the testing laboratory authenticates the findings, testifies to the laboratory's methods and practices, and is cross-examined at trial. Far from replacing live testimony with "systematic" and "extrajudicial" examinations, ... these procedures are fully consistent with the Confrontation Clause and with well-established principles for ensuring that criminal trials are conducted in full accord with requirements of fairness and reliability and with the confrontation guarantee. ...

The procedures followed here, but now invalidated by the Court, make live testimony rather than the "solemnity" of a document the primary reason to credit the laboratory's scientific results. Unlike *Melendez-Diaz*, where the jury was asked to credit a laboratory's findings based solely on documents that were "quite plainly affidavits," here the signature, heading, or legend on the document were routine authentication elements for a report that would be assessed and explained by in-court testimony subject to full cross-examination. The only sworn statement at issue was that of the witness who was present and who testified.

The record reveals that the certifying analyst's role here was no greater than that of anyone else in the chain of custody. ... The information contained in the report was the result of a scientific process comprising multiple participants' acts, each with its own evidentiary significance. These acts included receipt of the sample at the laboratory; recording its receipt; storing it; placing the sample into the testing device; transposing the printout of the results of the test onto the report; and review of the results.

In the New Mexico scientific laboratory where the blood sample was processed, analyses are run in batches involving 40–60 samples. Each sample is identified by a computer-generated number that is not linked back to the file containing the name of the person from whom the sample came until after all testing is completed. The analysis is mechanically performed by the gas chromatograph, which may operate—as in this case—after all the laboratory employees leave for the day. And whatever the result, it is reported to both law enforcement and the defense.

The representative of the testing laboratory whom the prosecution called was a scientific analyst named Mr. Razatos. He testified that he "help[ed] in overseeing the administration of these programs throughout the State," and he was qualified to answer questions concerning each of these steps. The Court has held that the government need not produce at trial "everyone who laid hands on the evidence,". Here, the defense used the opportunity in cross-examination to highlight the absence at trial of certain laboratory employees. Under questioning by Bullcoming's attorney, Razatos acknowledged that his name did not appear on the report; that he did not receive the sample, perform the analysis, or complete the review; and that he did not know the reason for some personnel decisions. After weighing arguments from defense counsel concerning these admissions, and after considering the testimony of Mr. Razatos, who knew the laboratory's protocols and processes, the jury found no reasonable doubt as to the defendant's guilt.

In these circumstances, requiring the State to call the technician who filled out a form and recorded the results of a test is a hollow formality. The defense remains free to challenge any and all forensic evidence. It may call and examine the technician who performed a test. And it may call other expert witnesses to explain that tests are not always reliable or that the technician might have made a mistake. The jury can then decide whether to credit the test, as it did here. The States, furthermore, can assess the progress of scientific testing and enact or adopt statutes and rules to ensure that only reliable evidence is admitted. Rejecting these commonsense arguments and the concept that reliability is a legitimate concern, the Court today takes a different course. It once more assumes for itself a central role in mandating detailed evidentiary rules, thereby extending and confirming *Melendez-Diaz*'s "vast potential to disrupt criminal procedures."

II

The protections in the Confrontation Clause, and indeed the Sixth Amendment in general, are designed to ensure a fair trial with reliable evidence. But the *Crawford* v. *Washington,* line of cases has treated the reliability of evidence as a reason to exclude it. Today, for example, the Court bars admission of a lab report because it "is formalized in a signed document.". The Court's unconventional and unstated premise is that the State—by acting to ensure a statement's reliability—makes the statement more formal and therefore less likely to be admitted. Park, Is Confrontation the Bottom Line? 19 Regent U. L. Rev. 459, 461 (2007). That is so, the Court insists, because reliability does not animate the Confrontation Clause. Yet just this Term the Court ruled that, in another confrontation context, reliability was an essential part of the constitutional inquiry. See *Michigan* v. *Bryant*.

Like reliability, other principles have weaved in and out of the *Crawford* jurisprudence. Solemnity has sometimes been dispositive, see *Melendez-Diaz*, and sometimes not, see *Davis*. So, too, with the elusive distinction between utterances aimed at proving past events, and those calculated to help police keep the peace. Compare *Davis* and *Bryant*,

It is not even clear which witnesses' testimony could render a scientific report admissible under the Court's approach. *Melendez-Diaz* stated an inflexible rule: Where "analysts' affidavits" included "testimonial statements," defendants were "entitled to be confronted with the analysts" themselves. Now, the Court reveals, this rule is either less clear than it first appeared or too strict to be followed. A report is admissible, today's opinion states, if a "live witness competent to testify to the truth of the statements made in the report" appears.... Such witnesses include not just the certifying analyst, but also any "scientist who ... perform[ed] or observe[d] the test reported in the certification."

Today's majority is not committed in equal shares to a common set of principles in applying the holding of *Crawford*. ... That the Court in the wake of *Crawford* has had such trouble fashioning a clear vision of that case's meaning is unsettling; for *Crawford* binds every judge in every criminal trial in every local, state, and federal court in the Nation. This Court's prior decisions leave trial judges to "guess what future rules this Court will distill from the sparse constitutional text," or to struggle to apply an "amorphous, if not entirely subjective," "highly context-dependent inquiry" involving "open-ended balancing."

The persistent ambiguities in the Court's approach are symptomatic of a rule not amenable to sensible applications. Procedures involving multiple participants illustrate the problem. In *Melendez-Diaz* the Court insisted that its opinion did not require everyone in the chain of custody to testify but then qualified that "what testimony *is* introduced must ... be introduced live." This could mean that a statement that evidence remained in law-enforcement custody is admissible if the statement's maker appears in court. If so, an intern at police headquarters could review the evidence log, declare that chain of custody was retained, and so testify. The rule could also be that that the intern's statement—which draws on statements in the evidence log—is inadmissible unless every officer who signed the log appears at trial. That rule, if applied to this case, would have conditioned admissibility of the report on the testimony of three or more identified witnesses. In other instances, 7 or even 40 witnesses could be required. The court has thus—in its fidelity to *Melendez-Diaz*—boxed itself into a choice of evils: render the Confrontation Clause pro forma or construe it so that its dictates are unworkable.

III

Crawford itself does not compel today's conclusion. It is true, as *Crawford* confirmed, that the Confrontation Clause seeks in part to bar the government from replicating trial procedures outside of public view. *Crawford* explained that the basic purpose of the Clause was to address the sort of abuses exemplified at the notorious treason trial of Sir Walter Raleigh. On this view the Clause operates to bar admission of out-of-court statements obtained through formal interrogation in preparation for trial. The danger is that innocent defendants may be convicted on the basis of unreliable, untested statements by those who observed—or claimed to have observed—preparation for or commission of the crime. And, of course, those statements might not have been uttered at all or— even if spoken—might not have been true.

A rule that bars testimony of that sort, however, provides neither cause nor necessity to impose a constitutional bar on the admission of impartial lab reports like the instant one, reports prepared by experienced technicians in laboratories that follow professional norms and scientific protocols. In addition to the constitutional right to call witnesses in his own defense, the defendant in this case was already protected by checks on potential prosecutorial abuse such as free retesting for defendants; result-blind issuance of reports; testing by an independent agency; routine processes performed en masse, which reduce opportunities for targeted bias; and labs operating pursuant to scientific and professional norms and oversight

In addition to preventing the State from conducting *ex parte* trials, *Crawford*'s rejection of the regime of *Ohio* v. *Roberts*, 448 U. S. 56 (1980), seemed to have two underlying jurisprudential objectives. One was to delink the intricacies of hearsay law from a constitutional mandate; and the other was to allow the States, in their own courts and legislatures and without this Court's supervision, to explore and develop sensible, specific evidentiary rules pertaining to the admissibility of certain statements. These results were to be welcomed, for this Court lacks the experience and day-to-day familiarity with the trial process to suit it well to assume the role of national tribunal for rules of evidence. Yet far from pursuing these objectives, the Court rejects them in favor of their opposites.

Instead of freeing the Clause from reliance on hearsay doctrines, the Court has now linked the Clause with hearsay rules in their earliest, most rigid, and least refined formulations. See, *e.g.*, Mosteller, Remaking Confrontation Clause and Hearsay Doctrine Under the Challenge of Child Sexual Abuse Prosecutions, 1993 U. Ill. L. Rev. 691, 739–740, 742, 744–746; Gallanis, The Rise of Modern Evidence Law, 84 Iowa L. Rev. 499, 502–503, 514–515, 533–537 (1999). In cases like *Melendez-Diaz* and this one, the Court has tied the Confrontation Clause to 18th century hearsay rules unleavened by principles tending to make those rules more sensible. Sklansky, Hearsay's Last Hurrah, 2009 S. Ct. Rev. 1, 5–6, 36. As a result, the Court has taken the Clause far beyond its most important application, which is to forbid sworn, *ex parte*, out-of-court statements by unconfronted and available witnesses who observed the crime and do not appear at trial.

Second, the States are not just at risk of having some of their hearsay rules reviewed by this Court. They often are foreclosed now from contributing to the formulation and enactment of rules that make trials fairer and more reliable. For instance, recent state laws allowing admission of well-documented and supported reports of abuse by women whose abusers later murdered them must give way, unless that abuser murdered with the specific purpose of foreclosing the testimony. *Giles* v. *California*, 554 U.S. 353 (2008); Sklansky, *supra*, at 14–15. Whether those statutes could provide sufficient indicia of reliability and other safeguards to comply with the Confrontation Clause as it should be understood is, to be sure, an open question. The point is that the States cannot now participate in the development of this difficult part of the law.

In short, there is an ongoing, continued, and systemic displacement of the States and dislocation of the federal structure. If this Court persists in applying wooden formalism in order to bar reliable testimony offered by the prosecution—testimony thought proper for many decades in state and federal courts committed to devising fair trial processes—then the States might find it necessary and appropriate to enact statutes to accommodate this new, intrusive federal regime. If they do, those rules could remain on State statute books for decades, even if subsequent decisions of this Court were to better implement the objectives of *Crawford*. This underscores the disruptive, long-term structural consequences of decisions like the one the Court announces today.

States also may decide it is proper and appropriate to enact statutes that require defense counsel to give advance notice if they are going to object to introduction of a report without the presence in court of the technician who prepared it. Indeed, today's opinion relies upon laws of that sort as a palliative to the disruption it is causing. It is quite unrealistic, however, to think that this will take away from the defense the incentives to insist on having the certifying analyst present. There is in the ordinary case that proceeds to trial no good reason for defense counsel to waive the right of confrontation as the Court now interprets it.

Today's opinion repeats an assertion from *Melendez-Diaz* that its decision will not "impose an undue burden on the prosecution." But evidence to the contrary already has begun to mount. New and more rigorous empirical studies further detailing the unfortunate effects of *Melendez-Diaz* are sure to be forthcoming.

In the meantime, New Mexico's experience exemplifies the problems ahead. From 2008 to 2010, subpoenas requiring New Mexico analysts to testify in impaired-driving cases rose 71%, to 1,600—or 8 or 9 every workday. New Mexico Scientific Laboratory Brief 2. In a State that is the Nation's fifth largest by area and that employs just 10 total analysts, each analyst in blood alcohol cases recently received 200 subpoenas per year. The analysts now must travel great distances on most working days. The result has been, in the laboratory's words, "chaotic." And if the defense raises an objection and the analyst is tied up in another court proceeding; or on leave; or absent; or delayed in transit; or no longer employed; or ill; or no longer living, the defense gets a windfall. As a result, good defense attorneys will object in ever-greater numbers to a prosecution failure or inability to produce laboratory analysts at trial. The concomitant increases in subpoenas will further impede the state laboratory's ability to keep pace with its obligations. Scarce state resources could be committed to other urgent needs in the criminal justice system.

* * *

Seven years after its initiation, it bears remembering that the *Crawford* approach was not preordained. This Court's missteps have produced an interpretation of the word "witness" at odds with its meaning elsewhere in the Constitution, including elsewhere in the Sixth Amendment, and at odds with the sound administration of justice. It is time to return to solid ground. A proper place to begin that return is to decline to extend *Melendez-Diaz* to bar the reliable, commonsense evidentiary framework the State sought to follow in this case.

CHAPTER 5

CIRCUMSTANTIAL PROOF: FURTHER PROBLEMS

SECTION 1. EVIDENCE OF OTHER CRIMES

Page 813. Add to Note 2:

See Garceau v. Woodford, 275 F.3d 769, infra. Supp. p. 734.

Page 843. Add new case:

State of Iowa v. Nelson

Supreme Court of Iowa, 2010.
791 N.W. 2d 414.

■ WIGGINS, JUSTICE.

The State seeks further review of a court of appeals decision reversing a defendant's first-degree murder conviction. A jury found the defendant guilty of first-degree murder. On appeal, the court of appeals reversed the conviction because it concluded the district court should not have admitted evidence of the defendant's drug dealing. On further review, we find the evidence is not excludable under Iowa Rule of Evidence 5.404(*b*). Therefore, we vacate the decision of the court of appeals and affirm the judgment of the district court.

. . .

On the evening of June 26, 2007, Michael Collins and his girlfriend, Tracy Lewis, bought some crack and smoked it at a friend's house. Afterwards, Collins and Lewis left to purchase more crack. Eventually, they parked at the intersection of Seventh Street and Hickman Road in Des Moines.

Collins was willing to approach strangers to purchase crack. At approximately midnight, Collins got out of the car, took Lewis's cell phone, and told her he was going to walk to an apartment complex located at the intersection of Eighth Street and Jefferson Avenue where he had previously purchased crack. Accordingly, Collins began to walk south on Seventh Street while Lewis waited in the car. Lewis waited for approximately fifteen to twenty minutes and began to worry. Just as she was about to start the car and go looking for Collins, she heard two "pop

SECTION 1   EVIDENCE OF OTHER CRIMES

pop" sounds. Lewis drove to the intersection of Seventh Street and Franklin Avenue and saw Collins lying in the grass.

... While there, Lester observed a white male talking on a cell phone on the corner of Seventh Street and Franklin Avenue. The white male was Collins.

Nelson finally got in touch with his friend and told him to meet Nelson on Eighth Street. Lester parked their vehicle on Washington Avenue between Seventh and Eighth Street; Nelson got out and waited in the road for his friend to arrive. His friend never arrived, but Collins approached Nelson and the two began to converse. In response to Collins' statements, Lester heard Nelson say twice, "I don't know what you're talking about." Subsequently, Nelson got back into the vehicle with Lester, and they again headed towards Seventh Street and Franklin Avenue.

As they pulled up to Seventh Street and Franklin Avenue, Nelson saw his friend standing outside. Nelson exited the vehicle, while Lester waited inside. Nelson and the friend talked for a few minutes, and then Collins approached Nelson again. Nelson said, "Who are you, dude?" Nelson's friend then said, "I don't know who he is." Nelson pulled a gun out of his pocket and pointed it at Collins. Collins put his hands in the air and said, "I am nobody, I am nobody." Nelson then shot Collins in the face, and he fell to the ground. Collins was on all fours, trying to crawl away. Nelson walked towards Collins and shot him again in the back of the head. Lester witnessed the entire incident between Nelson and Collins. After the shooting, Nelson got back into the vehicle with Lester and drove away. Paramedics rushed Collins to Mercy Medical Center, where he was pronounced dead.

Lester saw Nelson again later the next day. Nelson told her he did not want to kill Collins, but he thought Collins was a police officer trying to apprehend him for drugs and he had to kill Collins because Collins had seen his face. Nelson also threatened to kill Lester if she told anyone about the shooting.

...

... Subsequently, the State notified the court that the police found plastic bags and marijuana in Nelson's vehicle as well as an empty cardboard box for a digital scale in Nelson's home. The State informed the court that it planned to ask Hardy whether these items were consistent with drug dealing. Nelson's counsel argued this evidence was irrelevant and an attempt by the State to improperly show Nelson's bad character. In response, the State argued this evidence corroborated Lester's testimony, explained the context in which the crime took place, and explained why the crime occurred. The court requested the State to make an offer of proof.

After the offer of proof, Nelson's counsel again argued this evidence was not relevant. The court refused to allow Hardy to testify about the marijuana. As for the plastic bags and the empty cardboard digital scale box, the court ruled, "To the extent that the paraphernalia found in the van [and home] could be used in connection with crack sales, I will allow that testimony." Hardy then testified that, based on his experience as an undercover narcotics officer, he was knowledgeable about the items consistently found with crack dealers. Hardy testified plastic bags are consistent with crack sales. He stated that after the crack is weighed, it is placed inside a plastic bag, and a knot is tied so the crack can be kept in a person's pocket or mouth without dissolving. Hardy also testified crack dealers commonly use a gram or digital scale to weigh the drugs before they sell them.

. . .

The jury returned a verdict finding Nelson guilty of first-degree murder. Nelson filed a notice of appeal, and we transferred the case to the court of appeals. Considering Iowa Rule of Evidence 5.404(*b*), the court of appeals concluded the evidence linking Nelson to drug dealing was marginally relevant to complete the story of the crime but not relevant to Nelson's motive or intent because these elements could be inferred from Nelson's use of a deadly weapon to commit the crime. Although determining the evidence was marginally relevant to complete the story of the crime, the court of appeals concluded this evidence primarily served to paint Nelson as a bad person. Therefore, the court of appeals concluded the evidence's probative value was far outweighed by its prejudicial effect. Consequently, the court of appeals held the admission of the drug-dealing evidence was not harmless error, reversed the judgment of the district court, and remanded the case for a new trial. Subsequently, the State sought further review, which we granted.

. . .

The issue we must decide on this further review is whether the admitted testimony of a narcotics officer detailing the sale and distribution of crack as well as the evidence of the plastic bags and the empty digital scale box, which the officer explained are consistently found with crack-drug dealers, requires us to reverse Nelson's conviction.

. . .

A. Admissibility as Intrinsic Evidence that Completes the Story of the Crime. At trial, the State claimed it was not offering the testimony of the narcotics officer and the introduction of the plastic bags and empty scale box as character evidence. Rather, it sought to admit this evidence to give the jury the complete story of the crime and show Collins was in the area to purchase drugs. It was on this basis that the court admitted the testimony of the narcotics officer and permitted the introduction of the plastic bags and empty scale box into evidence.

SECTION 1   EVIDENCE OF OTHER CRIMES

1. *The inextricably intertwined doctrine.* Not all evidence of other crimes, wrongs, or acts falls within the scope of rule 5.404(*b*). One category of other crimes, wrongs, or acts evidence not covered by rule 5.404(*b*) is evidence deemed inextricably intertwined with the crime charged.[1] *See, e.g., United States v. Bowie,* 232 F.3d 923, 927 (D.C.Cir. 2000); *State v. Walters,* 426 N.W.2d 136, 140–41 (Iowa 1988). "Inextricably intertwined evidence is evidence of the surrounding circumstances of the crime in a causal, temporal, or spatial sense, incidentally revealing additional, but uncharged, criminal activity." Jennifer Y. Schuster, *Uncharged Misconduct Under Rule 404(b): The Admissibility of Inextricably Intertwined Evidence,* 42 U. Miami L.Rev. 947, 973 (1988) [hereinafter *Schuster*]; *see also State v. Garren,* 220 N.W.2d 898, 900 (Iowa 1974) (citing Iowa law dating back to 1915 that repeatedly recognized "events and circumstances which immediately surround an offense may be shown even though they may incidentally show commission of another crime"). The inextricably intertwined doctrine bypasses rule 5.404(*b*) because rule 5.404(*b*), by its express terms, is only applicable t evidence of *other* crimes, wrongs, or acts, which is considered to be extrinsic evidence. Edward J. Imwinkelried, *The Second Coming of Res Gestae: A Procedural Approach to Untangling the "Inextricably Intertwined" Theory for Admitting Evidence of an Accused's Uncharged Misconduct,* 59 Cath. U.L.Rev. 719, 724–25 (2010) [hereinafter *Imwinkelried*].

The inextricably intertwined doctrine holds other crimes, wrongs, or acts evidence that is inextricably intertwined with the crime charged is not extrinsic evidence but, rather, intrinsic evidence that is inseparable from the crime charged. *Bowie,* 232 F.3d at 927; Jason M. Brauser, *Intrinsic or Extrinsic?: The Confusing Distinction Between Inextricably Intertwined Evidence and Other Crimes Evidence Under Rule 404(b),* 88 Nw. U.L.Rev. 1582, 1584–85 (1994) [hereinafter *Brauser*]; *Imwinkelried,* 59 Cath. U.L.Rev. at 722, 724–25. Therefore, although there are two separate offenses, the testimony about the two offenses is so closely intertwined and indivisible that the court must admit the evidence of the technically uncharged crime. *Imwinkelried,* 59 Cath. U.L.Rev. at 725. Furthermore, because rule 5.404(*b*) is inapplicable to inextricably intertwined evidence, the court admits the technically uncharged-crime evidence without limitation and irrespective of its unfair prejudice or its bearing on the defendant's bad character. *Brauser,* 88 Nw. U.L.Rev. at

---

1. The inextricably intertwined doctrine developed in the federal circuit courts in relation to Federal Rule of Evidence 404(*b*). However, since its conception, it has gained widespread acceptance in every federal circuit court as well as among the states. Edward J. Imwinkelried, *The Second Coming of Res Gestae: A Procedural Approach to Untangling the "Inextricably Intertwined" Theory for Admitting Evidence of an Accused's Uncharged Misconduct,* 59 Cath. U.L.Rev. 719, 723 (2010). Moreover, we have recognized that Iowa Rule of Evidence 5.404(*b*) is "similar" and "the counterpart to" Federal Rule of Evidence 404(b). *State v. Cox,* 781 N.W.2d 757, 762 (Iowa 2010); *State v. Sullivan,* 679 N.W.2d 19, 23 (Iowa 2004). Thus, for purposes of this opinion, we will generally refer to Iowa Rule of Evidence 5.404(b) when discussing the inextricably intertwined doctrine.

1585; Milton Hirsch, *"This New–Born Babe an Infant Hercules": The Doctrine of "Inextricably Intertwined" Evidence in Florida's Drug Wars,* 25 Nova L.Rev. 279, 289–90 (2000) [hereinafter *Hirsch*]. Instead, the inextricably intertwined evidence is subject to the same general admissibility requirements as other evidence that is used to provide the fact finder with a complete picture of the charged crime. *Schuster,* 42 U. Miami L.Rev. at 973.

In summary, the inextricably intertwined doctrine permits the admission of other crimes, wrongs, or acts evidence based on a special relationship between this evidence and the charged crime, regardless of the strictures of rule 5.404(b). *Imwinkelried,* 59 Cath. U.L.Rev. at 725–26.

2. *History and criticism of the inextricably intertwined doctrine.* The inextricably intertwined doctrine grew out of the inseparable crimes exception. *Brauser,* 88 Nw. U.L.Rev. at 1600. Common law courts generally refused to admit evidence of other crimes, wrongs, or acts because they viewed such evidence as irrelevant and unfair. *Hirsch,* 25 Nova L.Rev. at 281–82. The common law, however, made certain exceptions to this general rule, including the "inseparable crimes" exception. *Brauser,* 88 Nw. U.L.Rev. at 1594. "This exception was invoked [and evidence of an uncharged crime was admitted] whenever a court found that the charged crime could not be proved without mention of another [uncharged] crime." *Id.* at 1594–95. From this exception, courts began to develop a doctrine

> that evidence of uncharged misconduct was admissible when it was "so [closely] blended or connected with the one on trial ... that proof of one incidentally involves the other; or explains the circumstances thereof." This exception broadened the class of admissible other crimes evidence by permitting not only the introduction of uncharged misconduct evidence when it was impossible to prove the crime charged without revealing the uncharged misconduct, but also when the uncharged misconduct evidence explained the circumstances surrounding the charged crime.

Schuster, 42 U. Miami L.Rev. at 955 (quoting *Bracey v. United States,* 142 F.2d 85, 88 (D.C.Cir.1944)). Courts began to refer to other crimes, wrongs, or acts evidence that explained the circumstances of the crime charged, or was necessarily revealed in proving the crime charged, as res gestae. *Id.* at 955–56. Thus, the inseparable crimes exception was enlarged by the courts when they began to use the amorphous phrase res gestae. *Brauser,* 88 Nw. U.L.Rev. at 1600. "The courts developed the res gestae or 'completes the story' doctrine in order to ensure that otherwise relevant evidence would not be excluded when it incidentally involved uncharged criminal activity...." *Schuster,* 42 U. Miami L.Rev. at 971.

Shortly after the passage of Federal Rule of Evidence 404(b), courts began to characterize certain other crimes, wrongs, or acts evidence as inextricably intertwined with the crime charged in order to avoid the limitations of rule 404(b). *Id.* at 970–71. "The inextricably intertwined doctrine is arguably the second coming of the common-law *res gestae* principle." *Imwinkelried,* 59 Cath. U.L.Rev. at 728–29 (arguing the inextricably intertwined doctrine is the "modern de-Latinized" equivalent of res gestae). As one commentator has explained:

> Inextricably intertwined evidence stands in a different relationship to the crime charged than does evidence of wholly independent crimes. The inextricably intertwined evidence is causally, temporally, or spatially connected to the crime charged, and the crime charged and the uncharged acts both involved the defendant. The uncharged misconduct evidence is not offered to prove the defendant's character in order to imply that it was more likely that the defendant committed the crime charged, although in some cases an exact independent theory of relevance may be difficult, if not impossible, to articulate. Rather, the evidence is introduced to facilitate the jury's understanding of the context within which the charged crime occurred, because without this contextual setting the jury would be forced to reach a verdict in a vacuum.

Schuster, 42 U. Miami L.Rev. at 971–72. The federal appellate courts have attempted to define the vague term "inextricably intertwined" in various ways. *Compare United States v. Ramirez,* 45 F.3d 1096, 1102 (7th Cir.1995), *with United States v. Carboni,* 204 F.3d 39, 44 (2d Cir.2000). Moreover, at least one commentator has discovered five broad categories of other crimes, wrongs, or acts evidence, which has been found admissible under the federal inextricably intertwined doctrine. *See Schuster,* 42 U. Miami L.Rev. at 961–62. . . .

Although Iowa has never referred to other crimes, wrongs, or acts evidence as inextricably intertwined, we have long recognized the rule that, "[w]hen acts are so closely related in time and place and so intimately connected that they form a continuous transaction, the whole transaction may be shown *to complete the story of what happened* [even though they may incidentally show the commission of another uncharged crime]." . . .

Although the inextricably intertwined doctrine has gained widespread acceptance, it has also become the target of intense scholarly criticism. *Imwinkelried,* 59 Cath. U.L.Rev. at 723. This doctrine has been criticized for two principal reasons. *Id.* at 728. First, the phrasing "inextricably intertwined" is extremely vague and amorphous. *Id.* at 728–30. Critics argue this vagueness has allowed courts to engage in result-oriented decision-making and invites abuse. *Id.* at 729–30 (stating courts can justify the admission of other crimes, wrongs, or acts evidence by the simple expedient of describing it as inextricably intertwined with the charged offense). Second, critics claim courts have abused the doctrine by applying it in an overly broad manner. *Id.* at 730. "In case after case, the courts have invoked the doctrine even though, on careful scrutiny, the testimony about the charged and uncharged offenses could readily have been separated." *Id.*

. . .

... We agree the inextricably intertwined doctrine should be used infrequently and as a narrow exception to the general rule against admitting evidence of other crimes, wrongs, or acts.

To ensure a court does not admit unnecessary and prejudicial evidence of other crimes, wrongs, or acts, we reaffirm the language from one of our earlier cases and hold we will only allow such evidence to complete the story of what happened when the other crimes, wrongs, or acts evidence is so closely related in time and place and so intimately connected to the crime charged that it forms a continuous transaction. *Oppelt,* 329 N.W.2d at 19. Thus, the charged and uncharged crimes, wrongs, or acts must form a continuous transaction. *Id.* Moreover, we will only allow the admission of other crimes, wrongs, or acts evidence to complete the story of the charged crime when a court cannot sever this evidence from the narrative of the charged crime without leaving the narrative unintelligible, incomprehensible, confusing, or misleading. In this way, we can be sure rule 5.404(*b*) remains the standard for the admission of evidence of other crimes, wrongs, or acts and the inextricably intertwined doctrine is construed as a narrow and limited exception to rule 5.404(*b*). Therefore, under this narrow interpretation of Iowa's inextricably intertwined doctrine that completes the story of the crime, we must analyze the State's argument that the evidence the defendant was a drug dealer is not evidence of other crimes, wrongs, or acts but is, in fact, intrinsic evidence completing the story of the charged crime of murder in the first degree.

It is clear that omitting evidence of the plastic bags, empty digital scale box, and the testimony linking these items to crack-drug dealing would not have left the narrative of this crime unintelligible, incomprehensible, confusing, or misleading. The State argues the story of the murder cannot be intelligibly told without explaining why Nelson would shoot someone who merely approached him and asked him for drugs. However, Lester had already testified that Nelson was in the area where the murder occurred because "somebody wanted some stuff." Lester also testified Nelson told her the day after the murder that he killed Collins because he thought Collins was a police officer trying to apprehend him for selling drugs and because Collins had seen his face. The evidence of the plastic bags, empty digital scale box, and testimony linking these items to drug dealing simply permitted the jury to make the general inference that Nelson was involved in drug trafficking. This evidence did not fill in any gaping holes in the narrative of the story of the crime. Additionally, these items were not so closely related in time and place and so intimately connected to the charged crime that they formed a continuous transaction.

SECTION 1   EVIDENCE OF OTHER CRIMES

At most, the plastic bags, empty digital scale box, and testimony linking these items to drug dealing support the State's proposed motive for the killing—Nelson was a drug dealer who believed Collins was an undercover narcotics officer attempting to apprehend him for selling crack, and he decided to kill Collins because Collins had seen his face. If this evidence was offered for the noncharacter purpose of establishing motive, it must be subjected to a rule 5.404(b) analysis. Accordingly, we hold the evidence of the plastic bags, the empty digital scale box, and the testimony linking these items to crack-drug dealing was not admissible as inextricably intertwined evidence offered to complete the story of the crime.

... At trial, the State did not claim the plastic bags, the empty digital scale box, and the testimony linking these items to crack-drug dealing was admissible under Iowa Rule of Evidence 5.404(b). On appeal, the State claims for the first time the evidence is admissible under rule 5.404(b). Normally, we would not reach this claim because the State failed to preserve error by not arguing this evidence is admissible under rule 5.404(b) in the trial court. *DeVoss v. State*, 648 N.W.2d 56, 60–61 (Iowa 2002). However, we have adopted an exception to the general rule of error preservation when dealing with evidentiary rulings. *Id.* at 62–63. Therefore, we will address the State's claim regarding the admissibility of this evidence under rule 5.404(b).

1. *General legal principles concerning rule 5.404(b).* Iowa Rule of Evidence 5.404(b) governs the admissibility of evidence of other crimes, wrongs, or acts. It provides:

> Evidence of other crimes, wrongs, or acts is not admissible to prove the character of a person in order to show that the person acted in conformity therewith. It may, however, be admissible for other purposes, such as proof of motive, opportunity, intent, preparation, plan, knowledge, identity, or absence of mistake or accident.

Iowa R. Evid. 5.404(b). Rule 5.404(b) is a rule of exclusion. *State v. Sullivan*, 679 N.W.2d 19, 24 (Iowa 2004). The public policy for excluding other crimes, wrongs, or acts evidence is not that the evidence is irrelevant. *Id.* Rather, the public policy for excluding such evidence is based on the premise that a jury will tend to give other crimes, wrongs, or acts evidence excessive weight and the belief that a jury should not convict a person based on his or her previous misdeeds. *Id.*

Other crimes, wrongs, or acts evidence cannot be used to show the defendant has a criminal disposition and, therefore, was more likely to have committed the crime in question. *State v. Reynolds*, 765 N.W.2d 283, 289 (Iowa 2009). However, other crimes, wrongs, or acts evidence is admissible if it is probative of some fact or element in issue other than the defendant's general criminal disposition. *State v. Taylor*, 689 N.W.2d 116, 123 (Iowa 2004). Rule 5.404(b) lists several examples of when prior conduct can be probative of some fact or element in issue other than the defendant's general criminal disposition. The examples included in rule 5.404(b) are "proof of motive, opportunity, intent, preparation, plan, knowledge, identity, or absence of mistake or accident." Iowa R. Evid. 5.404(b). The examples listed in rule 5.404(b) are not exclusive; rather, "[t]he important question is whether the disputed evidence is 'relevant and material to some legitimate issue other than a general propensity to commit wrongful acts.' " *State v. Mitchell,* 633 N.W.2d 295, 298 (Iowa 2001) (quoting *State v. Barrett,* 401 N.W.2d 184, 187 (Iowa 1987)).

To be admissible, the prosecutor must articulate a noncharacter theory of relevance. *Sullivan,* 679 N.W.2d at 28. The court then must determine whether the other crimes, wrongs, or acts evidence is relevant and material to a legitimate issue in the case, other than a general propensity to commit wrongful acts. *State v. Cox,* 781 N.W.2d 757, 761 (Iowa 2010). If the court determines the evidence is relevant to a legitimate issue in dispute, the court must determine whether the probative value of the other crimes, wrongs, or acts evidence is substantially outweighed by the danger of unfair prejudice to the defendant. *Id.* In determining whether the probative value of other crimes, wrongs, or acts evidence is substantially outweighed by the danger of unfair prejudice, the court should consider

> the need for the evidence in light of the issues and the other evidence available to the prosecution, whether there is clear proof the defendant committed the prior bad acts, the strength or weakness of the evidence on the relevant issue, and the degree to which the fact finder will be prompted to decide the case on an improper basis.

Taylor, 689 N.W.2d at 124. If the evidence's probative value is substantially outweighed by its unfair prejudice, it must be excluded. *Mitchell,* 633 N.W.2d at 298–99.

2. *Application of rule 5.404(b).* The State articulates a noncharacter theory of relevance—the evidence of drug dealing is probative to motive and intent. To the extent the challenged evidence tends to support the general inference that Nelson is a crack-drug dealer, it is relevant to the issues of Nelson's motive and intent for killing Collins. The evidence of drug dealing is relevant to motive because a drug dealer would be more inclined to shoot an individual seeking to purchase crack if they believed the person was an undercover narcotics officer. Motive can be relevant to whether a defendant acted with malice aforethought. *See State v. Hoffer,* 383 N.W.2d 543, 549 (Iowa 1986) ("Although motive is not a necessary element of murder, lack of motive may be considered in determining whether an assailant acted with malice aforethought."). Additionally, the evidence is also relevant to intent because a drug dealer would be more inclined to intentionally kill an undercover narcotics officer who could later identify and apprehend him or her. Thus, the challenged evidence is relevant to the legitimate issues of Nelson's motive and intent.

SECTION 1 EVIDENCE OF OTHER CRIMES

The State next claims the probative value of the drug-dealing evidence is not substantially outweighed by the danger of unfair prejudice to Nelson. We agree, the evidence of drug dealing is not substantially outweighed by the danger of unfair prejudice to Nelson.

The record contains sufficient evidence to establish Nelson sold drugs and was in the area on the night in question to engage in a drug deal. Although, the court instructed the jury that it could infer malice aforethought and intent from Nelson's use of a dangerous weapon, the jury was free to accept or reject that inference. On the other hand, the challenged evidence of drug dealing is direct evidence supporting the conclusion that Nelson intentionally and with malice aforethought killed Collins because Nelson thought Collins was an undercover police officer who saw Nelson's face. The State needed this type of evidence to prove its case.

Finally, we doubt the jury decided the case on the basis Nelson was a drug dealer. Lester witnessed the shooting. The next day, Nelson told Lester he shot Collins because Collins saw his face and he thought Collins was a police officer. . . . The evidence was replete with testimony regarding drug dealing in the area where the charged crime took place. In light of all this evidence, the mere fact Nelson was a drug dealer does not lead us to believe the jury decided the case on that basis.

Therefore, the plastic bags, the empty digital scale box, and the testimony linking these items to drug dealing were not excludable under rule 5.404(*b*).

. . .

We vacate the decision of the court of appeals and affirm the judgment of the district court because the plastic bags, the empty digital scale box, and the testimony linking these items to drug dealing were not excludable under rule 5.04(*b*).

Page 851. After Note 1, add:

United States v. Crane

United States District Court for the District of Oregon, 2009.
2009 WL 112942.

■ REDDEN, District Judge:

On May 22, 2008, a grand jury returned an indictment charging Defendant Shawn T. Crane with one count of Felon in Possession of a Firearm, in violation of 18 U.S.C. § 922(g)(1). Before the court is the United States' Motion (doc. 22) for Admission of Rule 404(b) Evidence related to Defendant's 2005 conviction for Felon in Possession of a Firearm. On January 13, 2008, the court held oral argument. For the reasons set forth below, the motion is DENIED.

On April 16, 2005, Portland Police searched Defendant's vehicle after pulling him over for a traffic violation. The officers found a loaded

.45 caliber semi-automatic pistol in the passenger's purse. The passenger told police that the gun was not hers, but could not explain why it was in her bag. On July 26, 2005, Defendant pleaded guilty to being a Felon in Possession of a Firearm and admitted under oath that he possessed the gun found in the passenger's purse.

On September 12, 2007, Portland Police again attempted to pull Defendant over for a traffic violation. After a short pursuit and car crash, Defendant fled the scene.[1] Although police were unable to apprehend Defendant at the scene, the police did locate and detain the other two occupants of the vehicle: Erica Bryant and Deandre Green. During the search of the vehicle, police officers found a loaded .40 caliber semi-automatic pistol in Erica Bryant's purse. She will testify that Defendant handed her the pistol during the police pursuit and said, "just do something with it." Deandre Green, the other individual in the vehicle, told the police that the gun did not belong to him. Some time after the incident, Defendant was arrested on other charges, but denied possession of the firearm found on September 12, 2007. On May 22, 2008, a grand jury returned an indictment charging Defendant with one count of Felon in Possession of a Firearm.

The government seeks to introduce evidence related to the 2005 incident pursuant to Federal Rule of Evidence 404(b). The government contends that the fact that Defendant hid a gun in a passenger's purse during the 2005 traffic stop tends to prove that he was the person who possessed the firearm found in Bryant's purse in this case. The government further suggests that the previous incident should be admitted to demonstrate Defendant's "habit of secreting firearms in female passengers' handbags in order to escape punishment...." Mem. in Supp., at 5. I disagree.

Federal Rule of Evidence 404(b) prohibits the admission of evidence of other crimes, wrongs, or acts "to prove the character of a person in order to show action in conformity therewith." Evidence of other crimes may, however, be admissible for other purposes, such as proof of motive, opportunity, intent, preparation, plan, knowledge, identity, or absence of mistake or accident. Fed.R.Evid. 404(b).

Evidence of prior bad acts may be admitted under Rule 404(b) if: (1) the evidence tends to prove an element of the offense charged; (2) the prior act is not too remote in time; (3) the evidence is sufficient to support a finding that the defendant committed the other act; and (4) where knowledge and intent are at issue, the act is similar to the offense charged. *United States v. Plancarte-Alvarez,* 366 F.3d 1058, 1062 (9th Cir.2004). If the evidence meets those criteria, the court must decide whether the probative value is substantially outweighed by the danger of unfair prejudice under Rule 403. *United States v. Chea,* 231 F.3d 531,

---

1. [Footnote omitted.]

534 (9th Cir.2000). In applying this test, the Ninth Circuit has emphasized that:

> extrinsic acts evidence is not looked upon with favor. We have stated that our reluctance to sanction the use of evidence of other crimes stems from the underlying premise of our criminal justice system, that the defendant must be tried for what he did, not for who he is. Thus, guilt or innocence of the accused must be established by evidence relevant to the particular offense being tried, not by showing that the defendant has engaged in other acts of wrongdoing.

United States v. Mayans, 17 F.3d 1174, 1181 (9th Cir.1994) (citation omitted).

When the other acts evidence is introduced to prove identity, as it is here, "the characteristics of the other crime or act [must] be sufficiently distinctive to warrant an inference that the person who committed the act also committed the offense at issue." *United States v. Perkins,* 937 F.2d 1397, 1400 (9th Cir.1991). "Conversely, if the characteristics of both the prior offense and the charged offense are not in any way distinctive, but are similar to numerous other crimes committed by persons other than the defendant, no inference of identity can arise." *Id.* (quotation omitted).

Here, the evidence of Defendant's prior conduct related to hiding a gun in a passenger's purse is inadmissible as evidence of identity because it is not sufficiently distinctive to warrant the inference that Defendant committed the offense charged in this case. That Defendant once secreted a handgun in another companion's purse does not demonstrate habit. Nor does such an ordinary and common criminal act demonstrate identity under Rule 404(b). Cf. *United States v. Spencer,* 1 F.3d 742, 745 (9th Cir.1992) ("Hiding a gun under a car seat is not a distinctive crime, and cannot be used to satisfy the 'identity' exception to Rule 404(b)"); *United States v. Powell,* 587 F.2d 443, 448 (9th Cir.1978) (excluding evidence of prior marijuana offenses in a prosecution for marijuana trafficking because the offenses were not "sufficiently distinctive"); *United States v. Ezzell,* 644 F.2d 1304, 1306 (9th Cir.1984) (excluding evidence related to previous robberies because the "points of similarity between the ... robberies were ones which are so common to most bank robberies as to be entirely unhelpful). The conduct was not sufficiently peculiar, unique or bizarre, ... nor was it so unusual or distinctive as to constitute" admissible evidence of identity under Rule 404(b) (internal citations and quotations omitted); *United States v. Thomas,* 321 F.3d 627, 634–35 (7th Cir.2003) (holding that defendant's prior conduct in "being met on the street carrying a handgun, dropping it, and then fleeing on foot" was not "sufficiently idiosyncratic to permit an inference of pattern for purposes of proof"). If a pattern of conduct as "generic" as asking a passenger to hide a gun could be used to demonstrate identity or habit, the fairly limited identity exception to Rule 404(b) would gut the rule. *Thomas,* 321 F.3d at 635. Defendant's prior conduct is exactly the kind of improper criminal propensity evidence that Rule 404(b) seeks to exclude. *Id.* It is the kind of evidence that tends to show only that the defendant has engaged in other acts of wrongdoing, rather than the particular offense being tried. As such, I conclude that the minimal probative value of Defendant's previous criminal conduct is far outweighed by the danger of unfair prejudice. Accordingly, the evidence related to Defendant's 2005 conviction for Felon in Possession of a Firearm is inadmissible, and the United States' Motion (doc. 22) for Admission of Rule 404(b) Evidence is DENIED.

Page 851, at end of Note 1:

United States v. Commanche

United States Court of Appeals for the Tenth Circuit.
577 F.3d 1261 (10th Cir. 2009).

■ LUCERO, CIRCUIT JUDGE:

. . .

Although the Rule 404(b) trail has been well marked by our precedent, a critical distinction emerges in this case that requires greater exploration. In some instances, the *permissible* purposes of 404(b) evidence are logically independent from the *impermissible* purpose of demonstrating conformity with a character trait. *See, e.g., Parker,* 553 F.3d at 1315–16. That was the situation in *Tan,* 254 F.3d 1204, in which prior drunk driving convictions were admissible not because they indicated the defendant's propensity for driving drunk but because he had been warned of the risks of his actions. *Id.* at 1207, 1210–11. That is, the defendant's disregard of prior warnings helped to establish malice. Notably, the prior drunk driving convictions were relevant to demonstrate malice without first requiring the jury to conclude that the defendant acted in conformity with an alleged character trait. *Id.* at 1210–11.

In other cases, bad act evidence bears on a permissible purpose only if a jury first concludes that the defendant likely acted in conformity with a particular character trait. Consider a case in which a defendant is accused of murdering his wife using his car but claims that he thought that car was in reverse when it was actually in drive. To demonstrate the absence of mistake, the government attempts to elicit testimony that the defendant twice previously slapped his wife. In such a case, the disparate circumstances between the prior instances and the vehicular killing negate any possibility of directly using the prior instances to show lack of mistake. Rather, a jury could use this evidence to conclude that the defendant was not mistaken as to the status of his transmission only if it first concluded that he had a propensity for violence against his wife and this alleged murder was another such incident. Rule 404(b) does not allow evidence of other bad acts in such a case. If that defendant is to be convicted of murder, it must be based on his allegedly murderous act and not his bad character. We hold that evidence is admissible under Rule 404(b) only if it is relevant for a permissible purpose and that relevance does not depend on a defendant likely acting in conformity with an alleged character trait. *United States v. Himelwright*, 42 F.3d 777, 782 (3d Cir.1994) ("[W]hen evidence of prior bad acts is offered, the proponent must clearly articulate how that evidence fits into a chain of logical inferences, *no link of which may be the inference that the defendant has the propensity to commit the crime charged."* (emphasis added)); Christopher B. Mueller & Laird C. Kirkpatrick, Federal Evidence § 4:28, at 746–47 (3d ed. 2007) ("[P]roof offered [of other bad acts] is not saved from the principle of exclusion by the mere fact that it supports a specific inference to a point like intent if the necessary logical steps include an inference of general character or propensity...."); *see also United States v. Segien*, 114 F.3d 1014, 1022 (10th Cir.1997) (explaining that 404(b) is a rule of inclusion unless evidence is introduced for the impermissible purpose), *overruled on other grounds as recognized in United States v. Hathaway*, 318 F.3d 1001, 1006 (10th Cir.2003).

We so hold based on the structure and purpose of the rule. Rule 404(b) carves out an exception to the general proposition that relevant evidence is admissible, *see* Fed.R.Evid. 402, precluding the use of other bad acts to prove character and demonstrate action in conformity therewith, Fed.R.Evid. 404(b). After explaining the impermissible use of other bad act evidence, Rule 404(b) delineates the boundary of impermissibility by clarifying that such evidence may nonetheless be admissible for nonconformity purposes....

. . .

That Commanche has twice been convicted of battering people in the past using a sharp object has no direct bearing on whether he acted in self defense in this particular instance. Although the government contends that those incidents show that Commanche carried a box cutter knife as a weapon rather than a work tool, thus somehow showing that he intentionally lured a much larger man into a fight to provide himself an excuse to use the box cutter in retaliation, that theory does not wash. The record is undisputed that Commanche was attacked first. Thus it is irrelevant to the self-defense inquiry that Commanche carried a box cutter on at least one other occasion.

. . .

Moreover, the present case is not one in which intent is proven circumstantially based on repeated substantially similar acts. *See Segien*, 114 F.3d at 1023 (allowing prior bad acts evidence to show intent and lack of mistake). There is no indication in the record that Commanche claimed self defense on the two other occasions. Thus, the aggravated battery convictions make it no more likely that Commanche reacted with disproportionate force during this encounter, in which he was not the initial aggressor.

By contrast, the details of Commanche's prior aggravated battery convictions demonstrate nothing about his intent; they simply show that he is violent. It may be that Commanche's violent character would lead a jury to conclude that his fear was unreasonable or that he acted with disproportionate force and thus cannot properly claim self defense. Although this reasoning may have intuitive appeal, it is precisely what Rule 404(b) prohibits—a chain of inferences dependent upon the conclusion that Commanche has violent tendencies and acted consistent with those tendencies during the fight. Because on the facts of this case the 404(b) evidence cannot show that Commanche's self-defense theory was invalid unless the jury impermissibly infers that he acted in conformity with a violent predisposition, the two aggravated battery convictions are inadmissible under Rule 404(b). Accordingly, the district court abused its discretion because it committed an error of law in allowing evidence regarding Commanche's prior convictions under 404(b).[1]

. . .

For the reasons stated, the judgment of the district court is REVERSED. We REMAND for further proceedings consistent with this opinion.

Page 854. Add after Note:

United States v. Mound

United States Court of Appeals, Eighth Circuit, 1998.
149 F.3d 799.[1]

■ Before RICHARD S. ARNOLD, JOHN R. GIBSON, and FAGG, Circuit Judges.

■ RICHARD S. ARNOLD, Circuit Judge.

Alvin Ralph Mound was convicted of two counts of aggravated sexual abuse of a minor, in violation of 18 U.S.C. §§ 2241(c), 2246(2), two counts of aggravated sexual abuse, in violation of 18 U.S.C. §§ 2241(c), 2246(2), two counts of assault resulting in serious bodily injury, in violation of 18 U.S.C. § 113(a)(6), and one count of assault with a dangerous weapon, in violation of 18 U.S.C. § 113(a)(3). On appeal, he challenges the admission at trial of a prior conviction of child sexual abuse under Federal Rule of Evidence 413 (Evidence of Similar Crimes in Sexual Assault Cases). We affirm.

I.

Mound allegedly abused his daughter T.M. physically and sexually from 1993, when she was ten, through January 1997. The alleged abuse

1. [Footnote omitted.]   1. [Footnotes omitted.]

included forced touching and intercourse and beating with an axe handle.

At trial, the government sought to introduce evidence of similar acts committed by Mound in 1987, namely the sexual abuse of two girls, ages 12 and 16. Mound had pleaded guilty to the first offense, in return for which the government dropped its investigation of the second. The District Court admitted the conviction under Rule 413, but excluded evidence of the uncharged offense. The jury convicted Mound of all seven sexual abuse and assault charges. He was sentenced to life imprisonment.

II.

Mound argues first that Federal Rule of Evidence 413 is unconstitutional. . . .

In considering evidence offered under Rules 413, 414, and 415, a trial court must still apply Rule 403, though in such a way as "to allow [the new rules their] intended effect." United States v. LeCompte, 131 F.3d 767, 769 (8th Cir.1997). See also United States v. Sumner, 119 F.3d 658, 661 (8th Cir.1997). The question is thus whether Rule 413, subject to the constraints of Rule 403, is constitutional. We hold that it is.

First, Rule 413 does not violate the Due Process Clause. To determine whether the rule fails "the due process test of fundamental fairness," we consider whether "the introduction of this type of evidence is so extremely unfair that its admission violates fundamental conceptions of justice." Dowling v. United States, 493 U.S. 342, 352, 110 S.Ct. 668, 107 L.Ed.2d 708 (1990) (citation omitted). Mound argues that it does, because it "authorizes the jury to overvalue character evidence, to punish a defendant for past acts and to convict the defendant for who he is, rather than for what he has done." Appellee's Br. at 24.

The Tenth Circuit recently addressed similar arguments in United States v. Enjady, 134 F.3d 1427 (10th Cir.1998), holding that, subject to the protections of Rule 403, Rule 413 did not violate the Due Process Clause. The Court stated, "[t]hat the practice [of excluding prior bad acts evidence] is ancient does not mean it is embodied in the Constitution." Enjady, 134 F.3d at 1432. Discussing the Supreme Court's opinion in Spencer v. Texas, 385 U.S. 554, 87 S.Ct. 648, 17 L.Ed.2d 606 (1967), which rejected a due process challenge to Texas statutes allowing admission of prior convictions for similar offenses, it noted:

> One reason the majority in *Spencer* gave for upholding the validity of the Texas statutes was that "it has never been thought that [the Court's Due Process Clause fundamental fairness] cases establish this Court as a rule-making organ for the promulgation of state rules of criminal procedure." Rule 413 is a federal rule, of course, and most federal procedural rules are promulgated under the auspices of the Supreme Court and the Rules Enabling Act. But we

must recognize that Congress has the ultimate power over the enactment of rules, see 28 U.S.C. § 2074, which it exercised here. Id. at 1432 (citation omitted). We too believe that it was within Congress's power to create exceptions to the longstanding practice of excluding prior-bad-acts evidence.

We also reject Mound's argument that Rule 413 is a violation of his equal-protection rights. Because Rule 413 does not "burden[ ] a fundamental right," and because sex-offense defendants are not a "suspect class," we must "uphold the legislative classification so long as it bears a rational relation to some legitimate end." Romer v. Evans, 517 U.S. 620, 631, 116 S.Ct. 1620, 134 L.Ed.2d 855 (1996). Promoting the effective prosecution of sex offenses is a legitimate end. The legislative history of Rule 413 indicates good reasons why Congress believed that the rule was "justified by the distinctive characteristics of the cases it will affect." 140 Cong. Rec. H8991 (daily ed. Aug. 21, 1994) (statement of Rep. Molinari). These characteristics included the reliance of sex offense cases on difficult credibility determinations that "would otherwise become unresolvable swearing matches," as well as, in the case of child sexual abuse, the "exceptionally probative" value of a defendant's sexual interest in children. Id. "Appellate courts should not and do not try 'to determine whether [the statute] was the correct judgment or whether it best accomplishes Congressional objectives; rather, [courts] determine [only] whether Congress' judgment was rational.' " United States v. Buckner, 894 F.2d 975, 978 (8th Cir.1990) (alterations in original) (citations omitted). We hold that Congress's judgment in enacting Rules 413, 414, and 415, was rational.

III.

We further hold that the District Court's application of Rule 413 and Rule 403 to admit the prior conviction in this case was not an abuse of discretion. See United States v. Ballew, 40 F.3d 936, 941 (8th Cir.1994), cert. denied, 514 U.S. 1091, 115 S.Ct. 1813, 131 L.Ed.2d 737 (1995). The Court first addressed the issue in pretrial proceedings, but deferred ruling until it had heard the testimony of the alleged victim of the uncharged offense, which was the other similar-acts evidence offered, in closed proceedings. At that time, it found that evidence of the uncharged offense was inadmissible under Rule 403, but the prior conviction was admissible.

> [W]hile I find that this evidence is relevant, I find that its probative value is substantially outweighed by the danger of unfair prejudice. And I further find that it would simply confuse the issues in this case, none of which are similar to the case of the witness.... I do find that is not the case with regard to the previous conviction of this defendant and I'm going to allow the government to present that evidence in its case in chief as to the previous conviction which does deal with a child sexual abuse situation.

SECTION 1 EVIDENCE OF OTHER CRIMES

Tr. at 175. Before the conviction was introduced, through the testimony of an FBI agent, the judge issued a cautionary instruction to the jury:

> This defendant was convicted in 1988 of sexual abuse of a minor. This does not mean that he is guilty of any of the charges of aggravated sexual abuse or any other offense as to which he has pled not guilty in this case which you will be deciding. You may give such evidence and the testimony of this witness no weight or such weight as you think it is entitled to receive.... [T]his evidence is being received for a limited purpose only.

Tr. at 338–39.

Clearly, contrary to Mound's assertion, the Court was aware of its duty to apply Rule 403, and performed it. During the resolution of pre-trial motions, the Court said, "going back to ... Rule 413 ... I am clear to the effect that the Court needs to conduct a balancing test under Rule 403." Tr. at 11. After hearing the testimony of the victim of the uncharged offense, it evaluated both this testimony and the prior conviction under Rule 403: though both were admissible evidence under Rule 413, only the conviction survived the Court's Rule 403 balancing.

Nor can we say that the Court erred in determining that the conviction satisfied Rule 403. The 1987 conviction was for sexual abuse of a 12-year-old girl by forced intercourse, conduct that was similar to the aggravated sexual abuse and assault charges against Mound in this case. In comparison, as the Court determined, the risk of unfair prejudice—in light of Rule 413's "underlying legislative judgment ... that [such evidence] is normally not outweighed by any risk of prejudice or other adverse effects," 140 Cong. Rec. H8992—was small. The Court found, "Federal Rule 403 ... defines unfair prejudice as an undue tendency to suggest ... a decision on an improper basis [,] commonly, though not necessarily, an emotional one.... The simple conviction does not go along those lines, whereas a type of incident as to which there was no prosecution and to which the facts are entirely different would, I think, get into that problem...." Tr. at 178. There is no evidence that the prior conviction presented any danger of unfair prejudice beyond that which "all propensity evidence in such trials presents," but is now allowed by Rule 413. LeCompte, 131 F.3d at 770. The Court's cautionary instruction to the jury further guarded against unfair prejudice.

It is true that the Court found the disputed evidence inadmissible under Rule 404(b). However, it was Congress's intent that "[t]he new rules ... supersede in sex offense cases the restrictive aspects of Federal Rule of Evidence 404(b)." 140 Cong. Rec. H8991. Thus, there is no inherent error in admitting under Rule 413 evidence that would be inadmissible under Rule 404(b): that is the rule's intended effect.

We affirm.

CHAPTER 5 CIRCUMSTANTIAL PROOF: FURTHER PROBLEMS

Page 854. Following Note, add:

United States v. Hollow Horn

United States Court of Appeals for the Eighth Circuit, 2008.
523 F.3d 882.

The district court found that Hollow Horn's alleged rape of Laudine was relevant, and that its probative value outweighed the danger of unfair prejudice.[1] Hollow Horn's alleged rape of Laudine occurred approximately 11 and a half years prior to the date of Hollow Horn's alleged abusive sexual contact with R.R.A. and H.C., and the alleged rape was of a 20 year old, not a child. Nonetheless, we agree with the district court that the evidence was relevant and probative. Both offenses involved sexual assaults of defenseless victims. The instant charges involve Hollow Horn's alleged sexual assault of sleeping minor victims, and the earlier alleged rape also involved an unconscious victim. Furthermore, Hollow Horn was related to all three alleged victims. Additionally, in all three instances, the accusers testified that once they realized what Hollow Horn was doing, they took action, either verbally or physically, to make him stop, and he did so. Thus, the district court did not abuse its discretion in ruling that the Rule 413 evidence was relevant.

We must next decide whether the probative value of Laudine's testimony was "substantially outweighed by its potential for unfair prejudice." ... Laudine's testimony was undoubtedly prejudicial to Hollow Horn as evidence admitted under Rule 413 is very likely to be. Rule 403, however, "is concerned only with 'unfair prejudice, that is, an undue tendency to suggest decision on an improper basis.'" *Gabe,* 237 F.3d at 960.... Laudine's testimony is prejudicial to Hollow Horn for the same reason it is probative—it tends to prove his propensity to commit sexual assaults on vulnerable female members of his family when presented with an opportunity to do so undetected. *See Gabe,* 237 F.3d at 960 (finding witness's testimony that defendant sexually molested her 20 years earlier admissible under Rule 414, stating that the "testimony is prejudicial ... for the same reason it is probative—it tends to prove his propensity to molest young children in his family when presented with an opportunity to do so undetected"). Because this specific type of propensity evidence is admissible under Rule 413, Hollow Horn has not shown that its prejudice was *unfair. See id.* (ruling that because Rule 414 evidence is admissible to prove propensity, the result-

---

[1]. In ruling on the admissibility of the Rule 413 evidence, the district court first made a record of the proposed evidence out of the presence of the jury, and then made a clear record of the factors it weighed in reaching its determination. These factors included: (1) Rule 413 did not contain a time limitation; (2) the Rule is intended to be interpreted broadly; (3) the probative value of the evidence was not overcome by its prejudice; and (4) the similarity between the circumstances of assault upon the testifying witness and the alleged assaults upon the present victims, and the factual similarities of the Defendant's actions in the separate assaults. The method employed by the district court was procedurally sound and created a clear record for appellate review.

ing prejudice from the admission of the Rule 414 evidence was not "*unfair* prejudice").

Although the prior sexual assault alleged against Hollow Horn was over 11 years prior to the alleged sexual offenses at issue here, [and committed against an adult rather than minor], "Congress expressly rejected imposing any time limit on prior sex offense evidence," when it enacted Rule 413....

Page 854. Note, following the first two paragraphs of the Note:

Generally the lower Federal courts have held that Rule 413 does not violate the Due Process Clause of the United States Constitution. E.g., Mejia v. Garcia, 534 F.3d 1036 (9th Cir. 2008), cert. denied, 129 S.Ct. 941 (2009); United States v. Rogers, 587 F.3d 816 (7th Cir. 2009) (no Due Process argument raised).

Some states have interpreted their constitutions not to be violated by the admission of propensity evidence in sex cases, see Horn v. State of Oklahoma, 204 P.3d 777 (Ok. CR 2009), but a recent decision of the Iowa Supreme Court holds that an analogue to 413 does violate the due process clause in the Iowa Constitution, even though the Iowa statute allowing its evidence in sex cases expressly made reference to the Balancing Test analogues to Fed.R. of Evid. 403. State v. Cox, 781 N.W. 2d 757 (Sup. Ct. Iowa 2010).

Page 854. Note, following the first two paragraphs of the Note:

In People v. Wilson, 44 Cal. 4th 758, 796–97 (2008), the California Evidence, which is not restricted to children as is Fed.R. of Evid. 414, but makes explicit references to § 352 of the Calif. Evid. Code, which is substantially equivalent to Fed.R. of Evid. 403, the court reaches the Conclusion:

> Defendant raises a number of related arguments challenging the admission of evidence of his uncharged crimes against K.K., but we find none availing because the evidence was admissible under Evidence Code section 1108. At the time of defendant's trial, that section provided in pertinent part: "(a) In a criminal action in which the defendant is accused of a sexual offense, evidence of the defendant's commission of another sexual offense or offenses is not made inadmissible by Section 1101, if the evidence is not inadmissible pursuant to Section 352." (Added by Stats.1995, ch. 439, § 2, p. 3429.) Defendant first argues that Evidence Code section 1108 is unconstitutional because it violates his constitutional right to due process of law. We rejected that precise argument in *People v. Falsetta* (1999) 21 Cal.4th 903, 89 Cal.Rptr.2d 847, 986 P.2d 182 (*Falsetta*), certiorari denied *sub nomine Falsetta v. California* (2000) 529 U.S. 1089, 120 S.Ct. 1723, 146 L.Ed.2d 645, where we explained that although evidence of a criminal's propensity had long been excluded in this state, such "long-standing practice does not necessarily reflect a fundamental, unalterable principle embodied in the Constitution" (*Falsetta*, at p. 914, 89 Cal.Rptr.2d 847, 986 P.2d 182), that a rule permitting admission of such evidence does not offend those fundamental due process principles (*id.* at p. 915, 89 Cal.Rptr.2d 847, 986 P.2d 182), and that "the trial court's discretion to exclude propensity evidence under section 352 saves section 1108 from [the] defendant's due process challenge" (*id.* at p. 917, 89 Cal.Rptr.2d 847, 986 P.2d 182). We have recently endorsed and applied *Falsetta* (*People v. Abilez, supra*, 41 Cal.4th at pp. 501–502, 61 Cal.Rptr.3d 526, 161 P.3d 58; see also *People v. Reliford* (2003) 29 Cal.4th

CHAPTER 5   CIRCUMSTANTIAL PROOF: FURTHER PROBLEMS

1007, 130 Cal.Rptr.2d 254, 62 P.3d 601 [assuming *Falsetta*'s correctness]), as have the Courts of Appeal (*People v. Cabrera* (2007) 152 Cal.App.4th 695, 703–704, 61 Cal.Rptr.3d 373, and cases cited). In addition, the federal courts follow an analogous rule. (See *U.S. v. LeMay* (9th Cir.2001) 260 F.3d 1018, 1022 [upholding constitutionality of Fed. Rules Evid., rule 414, 28 U.S.C.].)

Although defendant invites this court to reconsider the correctness of *Falsetta*, he proffers no persuasive reason to do so. We thus reject his claim that Evidence Code section 1108 violates due process.

Defendant next argues that even if Evidence Code section 1108 is constitutional, the trial court abused its discretion in admitting evidence of his 1992 crimes against K.K. But as respondent argues, Evidence Code section 1108 expressly reserves the trial court's power to exclude evidence as more prejudicial than probative under Evidence Code section 352, a matter over which the trial court exercises broad discretion. (*People v. Cole* (2004) 33 Cal.4th 1158, 1197, 17 Cal.Rptr.3d 532, 95 P.3d 811; *People v. Rodrigues* (1994) 8 Cal.4th 1060, 1124, 36 Cal.Rptr.2d 235, 885 P.2d 1.) On balance, we cannot say the trial court abused its discretion, as the crimes against K.K. occurred only five years before the L.R. rapes and were relevant to proving the charge that defendant twice raped L.R. Significantly, the crimes against K.K. were quickly proven, thus supporting the trial court's decision *798 that, under Evidence Code section 352, presentation of the evidence would not consume an undue amount of time or distract the jury from the present charges.[1]

Page 854. Add to Note:

United States of America v. Batton, 602 F. 3d 1191, 1198–99 (10th Cir. 2010): 403 applies, but it survives the balancing test.

Page 875. Add to Note 1:

Garceau v. Woodford, 275 F.3d 769, 773–78 (9th Cir.2001): In a prosecution for the murder of A and B, evidence was admitted of defendant's conviction for the murder of C. Held: Although there may have been a permissible noncharacter use of the evidence, Due Process was violated by the trial court's positive instructions to the jury that they could use the evidence for any purpose, even to show character and action in accordance therewith on a particular occasion. See also United States v. Mound, supra, Supp. p. 728.

SECTION 2.   EVIDENCE OF A CRIMINAL DEFENDANT'S REPUTATION AND OPINION EVIDENCE OF HIS CHARACTER; EVIDENCE OF VICTIM'S CHARACTER

Page 901. Add Note 1:

Barbe v. McBride

United States Court of Appeals for the Fourth Circuit.
521 F.3d 443 (4th Cir. 2008).

Donald R. Barbe, after unsuccessfully seeking habeas corpus relief under 28 U.S.C. § 2254 in the Northern District of West Virginia,

1. [Footnote omitted.]

appeals from the district court's September 2005 dismissal of his petition. Barbe was convicted in 1999 in the Circuit Court of Ohio County, West Virginia, of eight counts of incest, sexual assault, and sexual abuse by a custodian, for offenses involving his granddaughter (J.M.) and one other victim....[1]

Although the district court rejected Barbe's claims on these two issues, it granted him a certificate of appealability on each of them. As explained below, Barbe was not denied the effective assistance of counsel. His Sixth Amendment confrontation right was indisputably contravened, however, by the state circuit court's application of a per se rule restricting cross-examination of the prosecution's expert under the state rape shield law—a ruling in conflict with what we term the "*Rock–Lucas* Principle" established by the Supreme Court of the United States. *See Michigan v. Lucas,* 500 U.S. 145, 151, 111 S.Ct. 1743, 114 L.Ed.2d 205 (1991) (recognizing that, rather than adopting per se rule for precluding evidence under rape shield statute, state courts must determine, on case-by-case basis, whether exclusionary rule "is 'arbitrary or disproportionate' to the State's legitimate interests") (quoting *Rock v. Arkansas,* 483 U.S. 44, 56, 107 S.Ct. 2704, 97 L.Ed.2d 37 (1987)). Because the circuit court's Sixth Amendment error had a substantial and injurious effect on the jury's verdict as to the offenses involving J.M., we are constrained to deem him entitled to some habeas corpus relief. We therefore affirm in part, vacate in part, and remand for the issuance of a writ that is consistent herewith.

. . .

After J.M. testified, the prosecution called its expert, Ruth Ann Anderson, a licensed clinical counselor, for opinion evidence "in the area of counseling, specifically with regard to adults who have been sexually abused as children." J.A. 990. On direct examination, Anderson testified for the prosecution that she had met with J.M. eleven times over a five-month period and, in those meetings, J.M. had related "three separate incidents of [sexual] abuse" involving Barbe. *Id.* at 997–98. Based on symptoms J.M. exhibited at these meetings, Anderson opined that J.M. had in fact been sexually abused as a child because she fit the diagnostic criteria for post-traumatic stress disorder. In Anderson's view, J.M. "very strongly fit [ ] that criteria." *Id.* at 1002. The defense then sought to cross-examine Anderson about J.M's sexual abuse by men other than Barbe—abuse that might have caused her psychological profile. Before Anderson responded to the defense inquiry, the prosecution objected.

In the ensuing bench conference, the defense advised the state circuit court that it had been informed by Barbe that J M. had previously accused two other men of sexually abusing her. The defense further advised the circuit court that there were witnesses available—in the hallway outside the courtroom—to testify, based on personal knowledge,

---

1. [Some footnotes omitted.]

about J.M.'s sexual abuse accusations against those men. The prosecution argued that the defense was precluded by West Virginia's rape shield law from questioning the prosecution's expert about J.M.'s alleged sexual abuse by other men. *See* W. Va.Code 61–8B–11; W. Va. R. Evid. 404(a)(3). The prosecution relied in this regard on the legal principle established by *State v. Quinn*, 490 S.E.2d at 40 (concluding that, absent showing of falsity, alleged victim's statements about sexual abuse by others constitutes inadmissible evidence under rape shield law). The prosecution asserted that the sole exception to the *Quinn* principle could be satisfied only if Barbe first demonstrated a strong probability that J.M.'s sexual abuse accusations against other men were false.

. . . The defense sought to show that such abuse-and not abuse by Barbe—was the predicate for J.M.'s psychological profile. Accordingly, instead of relying on the falsity exception to the *Quinn* principle, the defense essentially argued for an additional exception to that principle, asserting that *Quinn* "never anticipated us being gagged while [an expert] says that a victim exhibits all the classic signs of being sexually abused." J.A. 1014. The defense also contended that Barbe would not be accorded a fair trial if he was precluded from presenting evidence of J.M.'s sexual abuse accusations against other men, as an alternative explanation for her psychological profile.

. . .

. . . Throughout these proceedings, he has consistently and steadfastly asserted that the trial court's Rape Shield Ruling contravened his Sixth Amendment confrontation right. *See* U.S. Const. amend VI ("In all criminal prosecutions, the accused shall enjoy the right ... to be confronted with the witnesses against him."). Although he explicitly invoked the *Rock–Lucas* Principle by name only in this appeal, he previously raised essentially the same proposition, relying on state authorities. As explained above, under the *Rock-Lucas* Principle, a state court cannot impose a per se rule for disallowing evidence under a rape shield law; rather, it must determine, on a case-by-case basis, whether the exclusionary rule "is 'arbitrary or disproportionate' to the State's legitimate interests." *Michigan v. Lucas*, 500 U.S. 145, 151, 111 S.Ct. 1743, 114 L.Ed.2d 205 (1991) (quoting *Rock v. Arkansas*, 483 U.S. 44, 56, 107 S.Ct. 2704, 97 L.Ed.2d 37 (1987)).

. . .

We review de novo a district court's denial of federal habeas corpus relief on the basis of a state court record. *See Tucker v. Ozmint*, 350 F.3d 433, 438 (4th Cir.2003). Having now conducted such review, we affirm the district court with respect to its denial of relief on the Ineffective Assistance Issue. We deem the Confrontation Issue, however, to be a more troubling and serious constitutional problem, and we thus dedicate the remainder of our decision to it. Based on the following assessment, we vacate the district court's disposition of the Confrontation Issue in part, and remand for the issuance of a writ of habeas corpus that is consistent herewith.

. . .

For the reasons that follow, we conclude that the State Court Decision involves an objectively unreasonable application of federal law, in that the state circuit court either "correctly identifie[d] the governing legal rule"—i.e., the *Rock-Lucas* Principle—"but applie[d] it unreasonably to the facts," or was "unreasonable in refusing to extend the governing legal principle to a context in which it should have controlled." *Conaway,* 453 F.3d at 581 (internal quotation marks omitted). Because of the sparse and cryptic nature of the circuit court's explanation for its denial of habeas corpus relief, we are uncertain if the circuit court failed to assess whether the rape shield law was arbitrary or disproportionate to the State's legitimate interests in the circumstances of Barbe's case, or if it made the relevant assessment and decided against Barbe. Indeed, the court failed to identify or discuss a single state or federal legal authority (including *Rock* or *Lucas*) with particular respect to Barbe's contention that the Rape Shield Ruling contravened his Sixth Amendment confrontation right. In any event, either of these alternative bases for the State Court Decision amounts to an objectively unreasonable application of federal law.

. . .

By its Rape Shield Ruling at Barbe's trial, the state circuit court prohibited the defense from cross-examining the prosecution's expert about J.M.'s sexual abuse accusations against men other than Barbe. The defense had sought to demonstrate that J.M.'s sexual abuse by other men was the predicate for her psychological profile as a victim of child sexual abuse. The defense contended that, if it was prohibited from questioning the expert about J.M.'s sexual abuse accusations against others, Barbe would not be accorded a fair trial. The circuit court sustained the prosecution's objection to the defense's proposed line of inquiry, however, on the ground that it was barred by the West Virginia rape shield law. . . .

. . .

One of our sister circuits recently had occasion to evaluate and apply such an approach to a rape shield issue in a federal habeas corpus case. In *White v. Coplan,* the First Circuit, applying AEDPA principles, reviewed a trial court's decision to bar White, who was accused of sexual assault, from offering evidence that his alleged victim had previously made similar accusations against other persons—notwithstanding evidence of a reasonable probability of the falsity of the other claims—premised on a rape shield law similar to West Virginia's. *See* 399 F.3d 18, 24 (1st Cir.2005). Relying on *Rock* and *Lucas,* the First Circuit concluded that these decisions, "clear although general, call[ ] for a balancing of interests depending on the circumstances of the case." *Id.* The court of appeals also explained that, even if a state rule of exclusion is generally defensible, it can be applied in an unconstitutional manner to a particular set of facts. *Id.* Finally, it recognized that White's Sixth Amendment confrontation right had been contravened at trial, because the state court's failure to admit the excluded evidence was an "unreasonable application" of the controlling *Rock-Lucas* Principle. *Id.* at 25.

We now reiterate that the *Rock-Lucas* Principle constitutes clearly established federal law determined by the Supreme Court of the United States. The *Rock-Lucas* Principle clearly mandates that a state court, in ruling on the admissibility of evidence under a rape shield law, must eschew the application of any per se rule in favor of a case-by-case assessment of whether the relevant exclusionary rule "is 'arbitrary or disproportionate' to the State's legitimate interests." *Lucas,* 500 U.S. at 151, 111 S.Ct. 1743 (quoting *Rock,* 483 U.S. at 56, 107 S.Ct. 2704).

. . .

In this matter, Barbe's effort to cross-examine the prosecution's expert concerning J.M.'s sexual abuse by others was crucial to his presentation of an effective defense. When the expert testified, the defense had already impeached J.M.'s testimony with her previous conflicting versions of her own story, showing that she was a confessed liar. As noted earlier, J.M. initially accused Barbe of sexually assaulting her, then made a tape recording and executed an affidavit swearing that he had never sexually abused her. J.M. thereafter asserted at trial that both her tape recording and affidavit were false and that Barbe had, in fact, sexually abused her. To bolster J.M.'s credibility, the prosecution presented its expert, who opined that J.M. exhibited the psychological profile of an adult who had been sexually abused as a child, and also testified that J.M. had related to her at least three incidents of sexual abuse involving Barbe. That testimony, if left uncontradicted and unimpeached, corroborated the trial testimony of J.M. and created the sole logical inference that her psychological profile resulted from abuse by Barbe.

Thus, Barbe's trial defense on the J.M. offenses—an entirely logical and permissible one—was to show that J.M. was not a credible witness, and that her sexual abuse by other men had caused her psychological profile. When the state circuit court barred Barbe from questioning the prosecution's expert concerning J.M.'s abuse by others, its Rape Shield Ruling undercut and effectively scuttled his defense on the J.M. offenses. The jury was thus left with only one permissible inference—that J.M.'s psychological profile resulted from her abuse by Barbe, and that Barbe, consequently, was guilty of having abused J.M.

. . .

SECTION 2 EVIDENCE OF A CRIMINAL DEFENDANT'S REPUTATION

Pursuant to the foregoing, we affirm the district court's denial of habeas corpus relief on the Ineffective Assistance Issue, vacate its denial of relief on the Confrontation Issue as to the six convictions involving J.M., affirm its denial of relief on the Confrontation Issue as to the two convictions involving B.H., and remand for the issuance of a writ that is consistent herewith.

AFFIRMED IN PART, VACATED IN PART, AND REMANDED

See also the Casebook at pp. 257–71.

Page 901, Add to Note 1:

Gagne v. Booker, 596 F. 3d 335 (6th Cir. 2010) (judgment vacated and rehearing granted, 2010 WL 616436): violated Due Process right to present a complete defense: involved group sex.

Page 901, Add to Note 1:

United States of America v. Pablo

United States Court of Appeals for the Tenth Circuit.
625 F. 3d 1285, 1298 (10th Cir. 2010).

. . .

III. Rule 412 Evidence

Pablo's final argument on appeal asserts that the district court committed reversible error by excluding two pieces of evidence under Federal Rule of Evidence 412: (1) that L.R.H. was seen undressed with two other men on the night of the rape; and (2) that L.R.H. made sexual advances towards Isaac Gordo–Pablo's co-defendant—on the night of the rape. We conclude, however, that the district court did not commit reversible error.

A district court faces a difficult task when confronted with evidence that falls within the scope of Rule 412. Rule 412 pits against each other two exceedingly important values—the need "to safeguard the alleged [sexual assault] victim against the invasion of privacy, potential embarrassment and sexual stereotyping that is associated with public disclosure of intimate sexual details," Fed.R.Evid. 412, cmt. n.1994 amends., and the need to ensure that criminal defendants receive fair trials. The tension between these two values makes it particularly difficult to resolve Rule 412 issues, and we bear that in mind as we address the Rule 412 issues that arose in this case.

. . .

We review a district court's determination regarding the admissibility of evidence under Rule 412 for an abuse of discretion. *See United States v. Ramone*, 218 F.3d 1229, 1234 (10th Cir.2000). To the extent the challenge to the exclusion of evidence proffered by the defendant is based on a constitutional objection, however, we review the district court's ruling excluding that evidence *de novo. See id.; see also United States v. Powell*, 226 F.3d 1181, 1198 (10th Cir.2000) ("[W]e review challenges to rulings excluding evidence proffered by the defense *de novo* where the objections are based on Sixth Amendment confrontation rights.") And to the extent the defendant neglected to raise in the district court an objection to the exclusion of evidence, we review under the plain error standard set forth above. *See James,* 257 F.3d at 1182.

[Quotes Fed. R. of Evid. 412.]

1. Evidence that L.R.H. was partially nude with two other men

In the district court, Pablo proffered that witnesses could testify that, at the dance that preceded the rape, they observed L.R.H. intoxicated and in state of partial undress in the presence of two other men. Pablo now argues for the first time that the district court erred in excluding this evidence under Rule 412 because it falls within Rule 412(b)(1)(A)'s exception to Rule 412(a). Rule 412(b)(1)(A) permits a district court to admit "evidence of specific instances of sexual behavior by the alleged victim offered to prove that a person other than the accused was the source of semen, injury or other physical evidence." Pablo asserts that this evidence could prove that the two other men, not Pablo, were responsible for L.R.H.'s vaginal injuries consistent with a forcible rape. He also argues that the evidence would have shown L.R.H.'s state of intoxication and undermined the reliability of her testimony. Because Pablo concedes that he failed to raise this argument in the district court, we review his claim for plain error. We find no error, plain or otherwise.

Pablo's proffered evidence bears no adequate connection to L.R.H.'s vaginal injuries. The medical professional that examined L.R.H. after the rape testified that she had seen vaginal injuries like those suffered by L.R.H. only in cases of forced vaginal penetration, never in cases of consensual sex. She opined that such injuries would occur in cases of consensual sex, if ever, only in extreme cases of "pretty violent consensual sex." (Supp. R. vol. 3 at 402:18–24.) The evidence Pablo proffered, however, contains no implication that L.R.H. engaged in intercourse with these other two unidentified men nor that any such intercourse was not consensual or was otherwise extremely violent. At most, Pablo describes his proffered evidence as tending to show L.R.H. had engaged in "a *consensual* encounter" with these two men, and that would not explain the injuries that L.R.H. incurred. (Aplt. Br. at 38.) Thus, the district court did not abuse its discretion by excluding the evidence because this evidence bears, at best, only a speculative and tenuous relationship to Pablo's argument that these two men may have caused L.R.H.'s vaginal injuries.

To the extent Pablo further argues that his proffered evidence should have been permitted for the limited purpose of demonstrating L.R.H.'s alleged level of intoxication, we find this argument equally unavailing. Rule 412(a) prohibits the admission of "[e]vidence offered to prove [the] alleged victim engaged in other sexual behavior" or "[e]vidence offered to prove [the] alleged victim's sexual predisposition." And the district court had legitimate reasons to perceive that Pablo sought to introduce this evidence for these impermissible purposes, arguing apparently that her intoxication enhanced her predisposition toward casual sex. Thus, we cannot conclude the district court abused its discretion by excluding the proffered evidence, particularly when the defendant had (and used) other means to prove L.R.H.'s alleged level of intoxication.

. . .

Conviction Affirmed.[1]

Page 901, Note 2A:

Zakrzewska v. New School

United States District Court for the Southern District of New York.
2008 WL 126594 (S.D.N.Y. 2008).

■ Lewis A. Kaplan, District Judge.

Plaintiff moves for a "protective order precluding from discovery material related to Plaintiff's sexual behavior with persons other than the Defendants Pan or related to her sexual predisposition." DI24. Defendant The New School cross-moves to compel discovery from plaintiff. DI28.

Plaintiff's Motion

The focus of plaintiff's motion is portions of plaintiff's diary for the period in which the alleged sexual harassment allegedly occurred, which the Court previously ordered produced.

As plaintiff argues, Fed.R.Evid. 412 generally forecloses evidence offered to prove a victim's predisposition. While this rule does not govern pretrial discovery, the Advisory Committee states that:

> "In order not to undermine the rationale of Rule 412, however, courts should enter appropriate orders pursuant to Fed.R.Civ.P. 26(c) to protect the victim against unwarranted inquiries and to ensure confidentiality. Courts should presumptively issue protective orders barring discovery unless the party seeking discovery makes a showing that the evidence sought to a showing that the evidence to be discovered would be relevant under the facts and theories of the particular case, and cannot be obtained except through discovery. In any action for sexual harassment, for instance, while some evidence of the alleged victim's sexual behavior and/or predisposition in the workplace may perhaps be relevant, non-workplace conduct will usually be irrelevant."

1. [Some footnotes omitted.]

Plaintiff argues therefore that portions of plaintiff's diary that refer to sexual activity with persons other than defendant Pan should not be discoverable.

Defendants disclaim any intent to use the discovery in question to seek to prove plaintiff's sexual predisposition or that plaintiff welcomed any advances that Pan may have made. They point to the fact that plaintiff seeks damage exclusively for emotional distress based on a contention that defendant Pan's alleged unwanted advances changed plaintiff's life markedly for the worse and seriously debilitated her for a substantial period of time.

The New School argues that it should be permitted to see the diaries "in order to explore [plaintiff's] ability to establish or continue in relationships and conduct her daily activities in spite of the allegedly debilitating nature of defendant Pan's conduct." DI27, ¶ 9. It points also to the fact that review of the diaries may yield evidence of intimate relationships in which plaintiff "divulged the sources of any emotional turmoil she claims to have suffered." *Id.*

Defendant Pan makes a broader argument. He notes that plaintiff at the eleventh hour has engaged a psychiatrist who proposes to testify—solely on the basis of an interview with plaintiff, the amended complaint, plaintiffs deposition, and records from The New School's counseling service—that plaintiff is suffering from depression and bulimia as a result of Pan's alleged actions, that "[s]he has lost interest in going out and participating in social activities," that she "has experienced difficulty trusting men since her experience with Mr. Pan," and that these all were results of her experiences at the hands of defendant Pan. Yet there is evidence that plaintiff in May 2006 responded to an ad on the Internet seeking sex with a "non-pro" in return for payment. There is evidence also that she engaged in an instant message dialogue in February 2006 with an unidentified male in which plaintiff arguably offered to engage in sex with someone apparently known to her only by an online pseudonym in exchange for a meal in a "nice and glamorous" restaurant.

Courts quite properly are reluctant to permit discovery into such highly intimate matters. Individuals' privacy interests in such circumstances are important and deserving of protection. Moreover, there is a risk that permitting such discovery would deter some individuals from pursuing meritorious claims. Nevertheless, it would be unfair also to permit a plaintiff claiming emotional distress to block discovery of facts that may shed important light on whether any emotional distress actually was suffered, whether any emotional distress that did occur had a serious impact on the plaintiff's life, and whether any emotional distress was attributable, either in whole or in part, to circumstances other than the alleged conduct of the defendant. Further, where, as here, a plaintiff proposes to offer expert testimony, including testimony that plaintiff has lost interest in social activities and is unable to trust men, it would be quite unfair to foreclose discovery that may well provide material that could seriously undermine the credibility of the expert's opinion....

. . .

This is not to say that plaintiff is entitled to no protection or that defendants are entitled to go on a fishing expedition into her prior history. Appropriate confidentiality protection will be afforded, and the Court will rigorously limit defendants to using the information here in question for their stated purposes.

. . .

Although plaintiff objects to discovery of records relating to the period during which plaintiff was in high school, and such a request in ordinary circumstances might seem far fetched, her argument in the unusual circumstances of this case is not persuasive. Plaintiff's expert has opined that plaintiff suffers from bulimia and that the condition was reactivated as a result of the alleged sexual harassment at issue in this case. Plaintiff completed high school in 2002 and enrolled at The New School. She began working in the computing center, where the alleged sexual harassment is said to have occurred, in April 2003. Thus, this is not a case in which a defendant is seeking records of events many years in the past. Rather, plaintiff had suffered from the eating disorder in high school, possibly as late as June 2002, and claims that the condition was reactivated by defendant Pan's actions that allegedly began only months later. Defendants therefore are entitled to probe the nature and extent of the eating disorder while plaintiff was in high school and, among other things, to seek to challenge the implicit premise of this aspect of plaintiff's expert's opinion, viz. that the eating disorder was inactive when plaintiff arrived at The New School computing center4in April 2003. Records of plaintiff's treatment and health while at high school as late as 2002 are an appropriate subject of interest.

. . .

Plaintiffs motion for a protective order (DI24) is granted to the extent that any portions of her diaries that relate to sexual behavior by the plaintiff with persons other than defendant Pan may be reviewed and copied only by defendants' counsel of record and shall be maintained in confidence by them and used solely for the purpose of this litigation. The motion is denied in all other respects. Counsel shall submit a proposed confidentiality order further elaborating on the treatment of this information, including such matters as reference to it in depositions and in papers filed with the Court.

. . .

Page 907. After Note 8, add Note 9:

9. For a case that considers the relationship between pretrial discovery and Fed. R. of Evid. 412, see Rhodes v. Motion Industries, Inc., 2008 WL 4646110 (E.D. Tenn. 2008).

Page 914. Add to Note 5:

Martinez v. Cui, 608 F. 3d 54, 58–61 (1st Cir. 2010): a civil case in which the district court invoked 403 to exclude another sexual misconduct, affirmed by the Court of Appeals: 403 applies to 415.

SECTION 4. SIMILAR OCCURRENCES

Page 916. Add to Note 2:

Johnson v. Elk Lake School District

United States Court of Appeals, Third Circuit, 2002.
283 F.3d 138.[1]

■ Before BECKER, CHIEF JUDGE, ALITO and BARRY, Circuit Judges.

This case arises out of plaintiff Betsy Sue Johnson's claim that her guidance counselor Wayne Stevens sexually harassed and abused her while she was a high school student in the Elk Lake School District. Johnson sought damages from Stevens in the District Court for the Middle District of Pennsylvania, claiming violations of 42 U.S.C. § 1983 and state tort law....

The principal question arising out of the District Court's denial of the motion for a new trial is whether the Court abused its discretion in refusing to admit the testimony of Karen Radwanski, a former co-worker of Stevens, regarding a bizarre incident in which Stevens allegedly picked her up off the floor in another teacher's office and, in the course of doing so, touched her in the crotch area. Johnson had sought to present this testimony as evidence of Stevens's propensity for sexual abuse under Federal Rule of Evidence 415, which allows for the introduction of evidence of past sexual assaults in civil cases in which the claim for damages is predicated on the defendant's alleged commission of a sexual assault.

. . .

Johnson entered the Elk Lake School District high school as a freshman in September 1991. Sometime in November or December of that year Johnson began making regular visits to Stevens's office to discuss family difficulties. Johnson contends that shortly thereafter, in December 1991, Stevens began sexually harassing and abusing her. She alleges that for the next two years Stevens repeatedly sent her letters, roses, cards, and other suggestive correspondence, attempted on numerous occasions to hug and kiss her without her consent, and at one point fondled her breasts and vagina.

. . .

1. [Some footnotes omitted.]

SECTION 4 SIMILAR OCCURRENCES

During the course of the trial, Johnson attempted to introduce the testimony of Karen Radwanski, a teacher's associate in the high school's restaurant training program and a friend of Stevens, regarding an incident in which Stevens allegedly sexually assaulted her in the office of another teacher, Tony Blaisure. Radwanski had just walked into the office carrying lunch when Stevens allegedly picked her up and threw her over his shoulder. According to Radwanski, who was wearing a skirt at the time, Stevens's hand went up her skirt and touched her in the crotch area while he raised her off the floor. Stevens soon let her down to the floor and the two of them, along with Blaisure, proceeded to sit down and eat lunch together.

Whether Stevens's alleged touching of Radwanski's crotch was intentional or accidental is unclear from the record, as Radwanski offered somewhat inconsistent accounts of the incident....

Federal Rule of Evidence 415 permits the introduction of evidence of a similar "offense ... of sexual assault...." Pursuant to this rule, Johnson sought to introduce Karen Radwanski's testimony as to the alleged touching incident in an effort to establish Stevens's propensity for sexual abuse. The District Court, however, refused to permit Radwanski to testify because it concluded that the touching incident did not qualify as an "offense of sexual assault" under the applicable definition provided by Rule 413(d)....

The precise basis for the District Court's conclusion that the touching incident did not meet Rule 413's definition of an "offense of sexual assault" is not clear, as the Court did not make a formal finding on the issue. Rather, it resolved the matter in several statements that appear in the trial transcript. It appears from these passages and from the opinion accompanying the denial of Johnson's motion for a new trial that the Court was particularly troubled by concerns about the intentionality of Stevens's conduct. In its remarks on the record, the Court stated:

> I think there's insufficient evidence that the touching was in any way intentional.... It was obviously a part of horseplay in the presence of another person, and the conduct of the parties indicated at the time that it was not viewed as an intentional touching of that area.

As further evidence of the lack of intentional conduct on the part of Stevens, the Court considered it important that Radwanski declined to mention the incident to the state police when being interviewed in connection with Johnson's criminal complaint against Stevens. As the Court noted, "I have great uncertainty that [the touching incident] qualifies as a sexual assault under any of [Rule 413's] terms when [Radwanski] didn't think it was sufficiently offensive to tell the state police when she's being interviewed about this conduct."

While it did not do so in terms, our reading of the transcript persuades us that what the Court really did was to engage in a kind of balancing exercise, see Fed.R.Evid. 403, whereby it excluded the evidence because its slight probative value was outweighed by other factors such as the danger of unfair prejudice, confusion of the issues, and waste of time.

. . .

While uncharged conduct is admissible under Rule 415, some limits, of course, need to be placed on its admissibility in order to ensure that the plaintiff may not "parade past the jury a litany of potentially prejudicial similar acts that have been established or connected to the defendant only by unsubstantiated innuendo." Huddleston v. United States, 485 U.S. 681, 689, 108 S.Ct. 1496, 99 L.Ed.2d 771 (1988). At the same time, for reasons of judicial efficiency and economy, the district court cannot be expected to conduct a "trial within a trial" to determine the veracity of the proffered evidence. So exactly what must a district court do before deciding whether to admit or exclude evidence of prior sexual assaults under Rules 413–15? The texts of Rules 413–15 are silent on this issue, and the Supreme Court has never answered this question in the specific context of these rules. The Supreme Court has, however, in Huddleston, considered the same issue in the context of Federal Rule of Evidence 404(b), which allows for the introduction of evidence of "other crimes, wrongs, or acts" to prove issues other than character.

. . .

In part because of the similarity between Rules 404(b) and Rules 413–15—both allow the admission of past acts, including uncharged conduct, albeit for different purposes—the few courts and commentators that have considered the issue have concluded that Huddleston's standard for screening uncharged conduct applies to Rules 413–15. See United States v. Enjady, 134 F.3d 1427, 1433 (10th Cir.1998); 2 Weinstein's Federal Evidence, § 413.03[1], at 413–7. As explained in the margin, we find this position somewhat problematic in light of the difference between the types of evidence that are likely to be introduced under Rules 404(b) and 413–15: the former allows for the introduction of "other crimes, wrongs, or acts," whereas the latter allow evidence of offenses of sexual assault or child molestation.[2] Were it within our power to select the better rule, therefore, we would be inclined to adopt the more exacting standard for the admission of past act evidence rejected by the Court in Huddleston: a preponderance of the evidence finding under

---

2. In our view, because of the severe social stigma attached to crimes of sexual assault and child molestation, evidence of these past acts poses a higher risk, on the whole, of influencing the jury to punish the defendant for the similar act rather than the charged act than the type of evidence that is often introduced under Rule 404(b). See Doe ex rel. Rudy–Glanzer v. Glanzer, 232 F.3d 1258, 1268 (9th Cir.2000) (noting "the strong prejudicial qualities" of evidence submitted under Rule 415) (quoting United States v. Guardia, 135 F.3d 1326, 1330 (10th Cir.1998)). In light of this higher risk of unfair prejudice, we think the need to guard against the introduction of unsubstantiated evidence is greater, and would be best addressed by requiring the trial court to make a finding by a preponderance of the evidence under Rule 104(a).

SECTION 4 SIMILAR OCCURRENCES

Rule 104(a). We find ourselves constrained from doing so, however, by the texts of Rules 413–15 as well as by their legislative history, which indicates that Congress intended that the Huddleston standard apply in this context.

To be sure, certain past acts likely to be introduced under Rule 404(b) are similarly, if not more highly, stigmatized—such as murders or assaults and batteries—and thereby present a significant risk of inappropriate punishment. However, many, if not most, of the past acts introduced under Rule 404(b)—e.g., burglaries, thefts, etc.—are not as potentially inflammatory as offenses of sexual assault or child molestation. On the whole, therefore, we believe that the risk of unfair prejudice is less in the Rule 404(b) context than in the context of Rules 413–15.

As noted above, the texts of Rules 413–15 are silent as to the appropriate standard for admitting evidence of past acts of sexual assault. Following the Court's reasoning in Huddleston, this silence alone is an important reason for not imposing a Rule 104(a) requirement on evidence introduced under Rules 413–15. In interpreting Rule 404(b), the Huddleston Court considered it important that Rule 404(b)'s "text contains no intimation ... that any preliminary showing is necessary," and that such a requirement was "nowhere apparent from the language of" the rule. 485 U.S. at 687–88, 108 S.Ct. 1496. Similarly, Rules 413–15 do not contain any language indicating that a preliminary finding is necessary.

Moreover, just as in Huddleston the Court noted that the legislative history counseled against imposing a Rule 104(a) finding requirement on evidence introduced under Rule 404(b), see 485 U.S. at 688, 108 S.Ct. 1496, the legislative history of Rules 413–15 points to the same conclusion in this context. The principal sponsors of Rules 413–15, Representative Susan Molinari and Senator Robert Dole, declared in their floor statements supporting the new rules that an address delivered to the Evidence section of the Association of American Law Schools by David J. Karp—then Senior Counsel at the Office of Policy Development at the Department of Justice and the drafter of Rules 413–15—was to serve as an "authoritative" part of the Rules' legislative history. 140 Cong. Rec. 23,602 (1994) (statement of Rep. Molinari); 140 Cong. Rec. 24,799 (1994) (statement of Sen. Dole). In the referenced speech, Mr. Karp stated clearly that "the standard of proof with respect to uncharged offenses under the new rules would be governed by the Supreme Court's decision in Huddleston v. United States." Evidence of Propensity, 70 Chi.-Kent L.Rev. at 19.

. . .

[A] trial court considering evidence offered under Rule 415 must decide under Rule 104(b) whether a reasonable jury could find by a preponderance of the evidence that the past act was an "offense of sexual assault" under Rule 413(d)'s definition and that it was committed by the defendant.

Even if a trial court is satisfied that the proffered past act evidence satisfies Rule 104(b), however, it may still exclude it under Federal Rule of Evidence 403....

It appears from the legislative history of Rules 413–15, however, that despite the seemingly absolutist tone of the "is admissible" language, Congress did not intend for the admission of past sexual offense evidence to be mandatory; rather, Congress contemplated that Rule 403 would apply to Rules 413–15. See, e.g., 140 Cong. Rec. 24,799 (1994) (Statement of Sen. Dole) ("[T]he general standards of the rules of evidence will continue to apply [to Rules 413–15], including ... the court's authority under rule 403 to exclude evidence whose probative value is substantially outweighed by its prejudicial effect.").

Having concluded that Rule 403 is applicable to Rules 413–15, we now turn to the manner in which the balancing inquiry ought to be performed. Relying on the legislative history, a number of courts and commentators have concluded that Rule 403 should be applied to Rules 413–15 with a thumb on the scale in favor of admissibility. See United States v. Larson, 112 F.3d 600, 604 (2d Cir.1997) ("With respect to the Rule 403 balancing ... the sponsors [of Rules 413–15] stated that '[t]he presumption is that the evidence admissible pursuant to these rules is typically relevant and probative, and that its probative value is not outweighed by any risk of prejudice.'") (quoting 140 Cong. Rec. S12,990 (daily ed. Sept. 20, 1994) (Statement of Sen. Dole)); see also United States v. LeCompte, 131 F.3d 767, 769 (8th Cir.1997) (noting the "strong legislative judgment that evidence of prior sexual offenses should ordinarily be admissible"). Indeed, in his speech that is referenced as part of the "authoritative" legislative history of Rules 413–15, David Karp observed that there is "an underlying legislative judgment ... that the sort of evidence that is admissible pursuant to proposed Rules 413–15 is typically relevant and probative, and that its probative value is normally not outweighed by any risk of prejudice or other adverse considerations." Evidence of Propensity, 70 Chi.-Kent L.Rev. at 19.

In our view, this characterization of the role of Rule 403 is overly simplified. It makes sense when the past act sought to be introduced under Rules 413–15 is demonstrated with specificity, see Enjady, 134 F.3d at 1433 (identifying "how clearly the prior act has been proved" as a factor to be considered in assessing the probative value of evidence of past sexual assaults), and is sufficiently similar to the type of sexual assault allegedly committed by the defendant. See United States v. Guardia, 135 F.3d 1326, 1331 (10th Cir.1998) (noting that "the similarity of the prior acts" to the acts at issue in the case is a factor to be considered in determining their probative value). In these archetypal cases, where the propensity inference that can be drawn from the past act evidence is greatest, Congress surely intended for the probative value of the evidence to outweigh its prejudicial effect, and, conversely, did not want Rule 403 factors such as undue delay, waste of time, confusion of the issues, etc., to justify exclusion. See, e.g., 140 C.R. 15,209 (1994) (Statement of Rep. Kyl) (recognizing as the archetypal case one in which "there is a clear pattern of conduct by an accused who has been convicted of similar conduct") (emphases added).

In other cases, however, where the past act is not substantially similar to the act for which the defendant is being tried, and/or where the past act cannot be demonstrated with sufficient specificity, the propensity inference provided by the past act is weaker, and no presumption in favor of admissibility is warranted. Where a past act cannot be shown with reasonable certainty, its probative value is reduced and it may prejudice the defendant unfairly, confuse the issues, mislead the jury, and result in undue delay and wasted time—all reasons for excluding evidence under Rule 403. The same can be said of evidence of past acts that are dissimilar to the act for which the defendant is being tried; in particular, the introduction of dissimilar past acts runs the risk of confusing the issues in the trial and wasting valuable time. Also relevant to the Rule 403 balancing analysis are the additional factors recognized by the Tenth Circuit in Guardia: "the closeness in time of the prior acts to the charged acts, the frequency of the prior acts, the presence or lack of intervening events, and the need for evidence beyond the testimony of the defendant and alleged victim." 135 F.3d at 1330 (internal citations omitted).

Finally, it bears repeating that despite these general guidelines, the Rule 403 balancing inquiry is, at its core, an essentially discretionary one that gives the trial court significant latitude to exclude evidence. See Elcock v. Kmart Corp., 233 F.3d 734, 754 (3d Cir.2000).

. . .

In deciding to exclude Radwanski's testimony, the District Court did not indicate what standard for admission it was applying to the evidence. In keeping with Huddleston, the Court was not obliged to hold an in limine hearing, as requested by Johnson, or make a formal finding under Rule 104(a) when excluding the evidence. Under Huddleston, the Court needed only to ask itself whether a jury could reasonably find by a preponderance of the evidence that Stevens committed the act intentionally, provided that the Court was satisfied that the evidence need not be excluded under Rule 403. Although the Court did not say so explicitly, it appears to us that the Court concluded that Radwanski's testimony did not satisfy Rule 403, and it accordingly—and appropriately—bypassed the Huddleston reasonable jury determination.

The basis for the Court's Rule 403 determination seems to have been that Radwanski's equivocal testimony was insufficiently specific as to the intentionality of Stevens's conduct. The District Court stated, "I think there's insufficient evidence that the touching was in any way intentional...." Lacking more specific evidence of intentionality, the Court apparently concluded that the probative value of the evidence was slight and was outweighed by Rule 403's concerns of prejudice, undue delay, waste of time, etc. This judgment appears to us to be sound given the equivocal nature of Radwanski's testimony as regarding the intentionality of Stevens's conduct.

. . .

Additionally, we find the exclusion of the evidence justifiable for a reason not stressed by the District Court: the differences between Stevens's alleged assaults of Radwanski and Johnson. The former occurred in another teacher's office with that teacher present, involved an adult co-worker of Stevens, and consisted of a bizarre incident in which Stevens lifted Radwanski off the ground and placed her on his shoulders. The latter is said to have taken place with no one else present in Stevens's office, involved a minor to whom Stevens served as guidance counselor, and allegedly involved Stevens making more direct sexual advances upon a much younger female. In our view, these dissimilarities reduced significantly the probative value of Radwanski's testimony. The case law is in accord. See, e.g., Doe ex rel. Rudy–Glanzer v. Glanzer, 232 F.3d 1258, 1269–70 (9th Cir.2000) (upholding exclusion of prior sexual assault evidence as too dissimilar because of age difference between victims and the dissimilar circumstances of the alleged misconduct).

. . .

In sum, the uncertainty of the testimony regarding intentionality, the dissimilarities between the similar and alleged acts, and the isolated nature of the Radwanski incident reduced significantly the probative value of Radwanski's testimony. Given this reduced probative value, any presumption in favor of admissibility was unwarranted, and the District Court's exclusion of the evidence can be justified on grounds that its introduction might have prejudiced Stevens unfairly, misled the jury, confused the issues, and wasted valuable trial time. Accordingly, we cannot say that the Court abused its discretion in excluding Radwanski's testimony.

SECTION 6. REPAIRS, LIABILITY INSURANCE

Page 937, Section 6, after Note 5:

"We find that it is reasonable for an engineer to rely upon a warning and alternative safety instruction subsequently issued by the manufacturer in forming an opinion that an earlier service manual fails to provide adequate instructions to automobile technicians." Pineda v. Ford Motor Co., 520 F.3d 237, 247 (3d Cir. 2008) (interpreting both Fed. R. Evid. 407 and Fed. R. Evid. 703.)

SECTION 7. COMPROMISES

Page 940. Add Note 2A:

Hernandez v. State of Arizona, 52 P. 3d 765, 768 (Arizona 2002): A fairly recent decision of the Arizona Supreme Court allows for impeachment purposes if the party takes the stand.

Page 940. Add Note 2B:

Lyondell Chemical Co. v. Occidental Chemical Corp.
United States Court of Appeals for the Fifth Circuit.
608 F. 3d 284, 298–99 (5th Cir. 2010)

. . .

We too decline to adopt any rigid definition of "claim." Our application of Rule 408 has been and remains fact-specific, and tethered to the rationales underlying the rule. And here, we have no trouble concluding the Smythe Reports were created for use in negotiations regarding the "claim" now being litigated. Though separated by time and location, the disputes associated with the Highway 90 and Turtle Bay sites arise out of the same events: the repeated dumping of hazardous waste intended for Highway 90. The disputes involve the same relevant parties, the same waste-generating facilities, the same basic time frame, the same waste hauler, and the same intended disposal site. More to the point, it involves the same primary liability question: What chemicals did each facility ship offsite and in what quantity? And because waste disposal at both sites is inextricably linked, the scope of a party's liability for the Highway 90 Site bears directly on the extent of its liability for Turtle Bayou. The Highway 90 negotiations did not involve circumstances that were merely "similar" to the current dispute over Turtle Bayou. Even El Paso's counsel prudently conceded at oral argument that liability for one site is "germane" to liability for the other.

. . .

Viewed through either lense, the offering of settlement evidence arising out of a shared factual nexus and bearing directly on present issues of liability between many of the same parties falls within Rule 408's prohibition. Effective dispute resolution requires frank and full discussion of relevant evidence. Making the content of such a discussion available for use in related litigation would invite the very situation that Rule 408 is designed to avoid, and worse, in CERCLA litigation, reduce the likelihood that responsible parties would volunteer to right their environmental wrongs. CERCLA only works when that likelihood is high—after all, the entire statutory regime is predicated on the fact that the government has limited resources to find potential polluters, to dictate remedial measures to those polluters it does find, and to pay for those it does not. CERCLA itself protects parties who enter into consent decrees with the government, stating that participation in that process "shall not be considered an admission of liability for any purpose, and the fact of such participation shall not be admissible in any judicial or administrative proceeding."

. . .

We are mindful that Rule 408 should not exclude more than required to effectuate its goals, which, after all, run counter to the overarching policy favoring the admission of all relevant evidence. But we have no difficulty concluding that exclusion of the Smythe Reports fits comfortably within the rule's limitations. The tension between Rule 408 and the policy favoring the admission of relevant evidence is mitigated in the present case: from the general public's standpoint, the need for evidence in a CERCLA contribution case is simply less critical than in a situation in which liability is contested. Here, we know that El Paso and Occidental are responsible for remediating Turtle Bayou; what remains to be determined is how much each private entity will pay.[1]

Page 940, Section 7, insert Note 3A:

United States v. Davis

United States Court of Appeals for the District of Columbia Circuit.
596 F.3d 852 (D.C. Cir. 2010).

■ Opinion by RANDOLPH:

. . .

. . . [T]he court's application of Rule 408 is another matter entirely. Rule 408, which is set out in the margin,[1] excludes evidence of settlement offers and negotiations when the evidence is "offered to prove liability for, invalidity of, or amount of a claim." FED.R.EVID. 408(a).

Invoking Rule 408, Davis made a motion *in limine* to bar Jimmy Hammock from testifying about his second conversation with Davis. The defense motion quoted the following portion of an FBI report of an interview with Hammock in January 2004:

> Sometime between the National Conclave and August 2003, HAMMOCK had a telephone conversation with DAVIS, during which he confronted DAVIS about the checks made payable to cash and DAVIS' explanation [that] the money was deposited to the payroll account. DAVIS said the money had been deposited into the payroll account, but HAMMOCK replied "TERRY, I'm telling you, I've gone through the records and it didn't." DAVIS then unexpectedly said "what will it take to make this go away?" HAMMOCK responded

---

1. [Several footnotes omitted.]   1. [Some footnotes omitted.]

that DAVIS needed to repay "whatever you took." DAVIS asked "what if I split the $29,000?" HAMMOCK told DAVIS the amount of missing money was in excess of $100,000.00, to which DAVIS responded, "Oh, I can't pay that much."

There can be no doubt that Davis offered to compromise a disputed claim. His offer was to split the $29,000 in checks to cash he thought the fraternity had discovered. The claim "was disputed as to validity or amount," FED.R.EVID. 408(a): Davis did not confess to taking the fraternity's money; he said that he had deposited the cash checks into the fraternity's payroll account; and Hammock rejected Davis's explanation. See *Affiliated Mfrs., Inc. v. Alum. Co. of Am.*, 56 F.3d 521, 527–28 (3d Cir.1995). It is also clear that the government intended to introduce Davis's settlement offer in order to prove Davis's guilt, or in the words of Rule 408(a), his "liability." Offers to settle are excluded even if no settlement negotiations follow. FED.R.EVID. 408(a)(1); see, e.g., *Alpex Comp. Corp. v. Nintendo Co., Inc.*, 770 F.Supp. 161, 163–64 (S.D.N.Y. 1991). The Rule is meant to promote settlements. See FED.R.EVID. 408 advisory committee's note (1974). If one party attempts to initiate negotiations with a settlement offer, the offer is excluded from evidence even if the counterparty responds: "I'm not negotiating with you." See FED.R.EVID. 408 advisory committee's note (1972 proposed rule). It makes no sense to force the party who initiates negotiations to do so at his peril.

Rule 408 bars not only evidence of "settlement offers, but also statements made in compromise negotiations." FED.R.EVID. 408(a)(2). Davis's other statements to Hammock during their second conversation were of that sort. Davis asked what it would take to "make this go away"; Hammock said pay back what you took; Davis countered with his offer to split the $29,000; Hammock countered that the missing funds totaled more than $100,000. That Hammock understood this give and take as a compromise negotiation is confirmed by his trial testimony—not before the court *in limine* but cited by the government on appeal—that he told Davis to talk to the fraternity's president or lawyer if he wanted to settle the matter.

. . .

There is, as the government points out, a sentence in the 1972 advisory committee note to Rule 408 stating that an "effort to 'buy off' the prosecution or a prosecuting witness in a criminal case is not within the policy of the rule of exclusion." FED.R.EVID. 408 advisory committee's note (1972 proposed rule). But it would be a mistake to read much into that remark, particularly in cases in which the defendant's actions give rise to potential civil and criminal liability. The 2006 amendment to Rule 408, which made clear that the rule applied to both civil and criminal proceedings,[2] drew a distinction between civil disputes involving

---

2. The circuits had been split on the issue. Compare *United States v. Arias*, 431 F.3d 1327, 1338 (11th Cir.2005), *United States v. Bailey*, 327 F.3d 1131, 1146 (10th

the government and civil disputes involving private parties. Under amended Rule 408, a defendant's statements in settlement negotiations with government agencies may be admitted in a criminal case. FED. R.EVID. 408(a)(2). But if the civil dispute was with a private party, the defendant's offer of settlement and statements in negotiation may not be admitted in a criminal prosecution when "offered to prove liability for, invalidity of, or amount of a claim." FED.R.EVID. 408(a).

This still leaves the example in Rule 408(b) allowing the use of a defendant's settlement offer and statements in negotiation in order to prove the defendant's attempt to obstruct a criminal investigation. This example, and the statement in the 1972 advisory notes, are easy enough to understand when obstruction is one of the criminal charges. 18 U.S.C. §§ 1501 *et seq.*; *see, e.g., Technic Servs.*, 314 F.3d at 1045. But even in such cases there may be difficulties. One problem is that settlement evidence, like other evidence, may be introduced for multiple purposes, some prohibited under Rule 408(a), some permitted under Rule 408(b). *See Old Chief v. United States*, 519 U.S. 172, 187, 190, 117 S.Ct. 644, 136 L.Ed.2d 574 (1997). Another problem is whether the "obstruction" illustration applies only to pending criminal investigations or also to potential investigations. In Davis's case, for instance, there was no date identifying the beginning of a criminal investigation and there was no evidence indicating that Davis knew of any criminal investigation when he talked to Hammock. There may be other difficulties in some cases. One might suppose that if—as in this case—the same acts give rise to potential civil and criminal liability, any settlement of the civil dispute could forestall or influence potential criminal proceedings. Yet to hold that offers of settlement and negotiations in that context amount to obstruction would be contrary to the purpose of Rule 408, *see* 23 C. WRIGHT K. GRAHAM, FEDERAL PRACTICE AND PROCEDURE: EVIDENCE 5313, at 278 (1980), and would contradict the notes of the advisory committee in 2006.

. . .

Cir.2003), *and United States v. Hays*, 872 F.2d 582, 589 (5th Cir.1989) (applying Rule 408 in criminal cases), *with United States v. Logan*, 250 F.3d 350, 367 (6th Cir.2001), *United States v. Prewitt*, 34 F.3d 436, 439 (7th Cir.1994), *and United States v. Baker*, 926 F.2d 179, 180 (2d Cir.1991) (declining to apply Rule 408 in criminal cases).

CHAPTER 6

EXPERT EVIDENCE

SECTION 1. THE NATURE AND FUNCTION OF EXPERT EVIDENCE

Page 955. Following first full paragraph of Note, add:

Trademark Properties, Inc. v. A & E Television Networks

United States District Court, District of South Carolina, 2008.
2008 WL 4811461.

■ C. WESTON HOUCK, District Judge.

The plaintiffs, Trademark Properties, Inc. and Richard C. Davis, have brought this contract case against the defendant, A & E Television Networks ("A & E"). This matter comes before the Court on the defendants' motion in limine (#98) to exclude the testimony of the plaintiffs' damages expert, Mark Halloran.

Mr. Halloran's Expert Witness Report Dated December 14, 2007

The plaintiffs contend that A & E owes them 50% of the net revenues that A & E has earned from the television show "Flip This House." A & E has produced its revenue and expense numbers associated with the show, and the plaintiffs' expert witness, Mark Halloran, has accepted those numbers as true. Mr. Halloran stated during his deposition: "I didn't take an audit of their statement of revenue and expenses but just accepted them to be true." ... Mr. Halloran described his method for calculating the alleged damages as "very simple" or "quite simple." ... He testified that he subtracted expenses from revenues, and then he divided the remainder by two, based on the testimony by plaintiff Richard C. Davis that he had a 50/50 agreement with A & E.... Mr. Halloran explained: "Since this is just revenue, I mean, I can tell you right now I can take a calculator and add this up and split it in half and that would be an additional amount due Mr. Davis." ... As a threshold matter, under Federal Rule of Evidence 401, Mr. Halloran's testimony does not provide "relevant evidence." His testimony is not necessary to prove how to divide in half a sum that is not disputed by the parties.

Mr. Halloran's expert witness report dated December 14, 2007 contains only one opinion: the calculation of 50% of net revenues. The

Federal Rules of Evidence provide the Court with the power to determine any "preliminary questions concerning the qualification of a person to be a witness ... or the admissibility of evidence...." Fed.R.Evid. 104(a). In determining the admissibility of expert testimony, the Court relies on Federal Rule of Evidence 702, which authorizes the admission of expert testimony that "will assist the trier of fact to understand the evidence or to determine a fact in issue[.]" "Although expert testimony is generally presumed helpful to the jury, we have held that Rule 702 excludes expert testimony on matters within the common knowledge of jurors." *Persinger v. Norfolk & Western Railway Co.*, 920 F.2d 1185, 1188 (4th Cir.1990)....

Mr. Halloran's expert witness report and deposition testimony simply state what is well within common knowledge of the jurors: how to divide a sum by two. Mr. Halloran's testimony is of no assistance to the jury, and therefore is not necessary, and shall be excluded from the trial in this case.

. . .

For the foregoing reasons, it is ordered that the defendants' motion in limine (#98) be granted, and that Mr. Halloran's testimony be excluded from the trial in this case.

Page 955. Following first full paragraph, add:

Hynix Semiconductor Inc. v. Rambus Inc.

United States District Court, Northern District of California, 2008.
2008 WL 504098.

■ RONALD M. WHYTE, District Judge.

ORDER REGARDING JOE MACRI AND ILAN KRASHINSKY

This order addresses the scope of the testimony of two "industry" witnesses, Joe Macri and Ilan Krashinsky. The court has reviewed the briefs filed and the court partially grants the motion. Certain aspects of Mr. Krashinsky's intended testimony appear to be improper lay opinions. With respect to the disclosure of Mr. Macri and Mr. Krashinsky's subject areas of testimony and whether Mr. Macri's testimony includes improper lay opinion, the court defers ruling and will decide the issues at trial consistent with this opinion.[1]

. . .

II. THE LIMITS OF LAY OPINION TESTIMONY

A. The Contours of Rule 701

Federal Rule of Evidence ("FRE") 701 imposes three limitations on the admissibility of lay opinion testimony, namely that:

1. [Some footnotes omitted.]

SECTION 1 THE NATURE AND FUNCTION OF EXPERT EVIDENCE

[T]he witness' testimony in the form of opinions or inferences is limited to those opinions or inferences which are:

(a) rationally based on the perception of the witness,

(b) helpful to a clear understanding of the witness' testimony or the determination of a fact in issue, and

(c) not based on scientific, technical, or other specialized knowledge within the scope of Rule 702.

The first two requirements comprise the traditional threshold for lay opinion testimony. The third element, (c), was added in 2000 to prevent litigants from skirting the *Daubert* standard or the expert disclosure guidelines by introducing expert opinion testimony as lay opinion testimony. *See* FRE 701, adv. committee note (2000); 4 WEINSTEIN'S FEDERAL EVIDENCE § 701.03[4][b], at 701–30 (2d ed.2007). Accordingly, the text of Rule 701 contemplates a strict separation between lay and expert testimony that did not exist before 2000.

An illustration of the prior solicitude toward lay opinion testimony is demonstrated in *Union Pacific Resources Co. v. Chesapeake Energy Corp.*, where the court found no reversible error in allowing eight witnesses with industry experience to give lay opinions as to whether a written description enabled a claim. 236 F.3d 684, 692–93 (Fed.Cir.2001) (applying the Fifth Circuit's interpretation of FRE 701 prior to the 2000 amendments). One district court has already disavowed the reasoning in *Union Pacific Resources* as conflicting with the amended text of Rule 701. *Freedom Wireless, Inc. v. Boston Communications Group, Inc.*, 369 F.Supp.2d 155, 157–58 (D.Mass.2005). That court then applied the amended rule to bar lay opinion testimony regarding a patent's obviousness because the opinion was based on the witness' specialized knowledge of telecommunications. *Id.* at 157.[2] The Seventh Circuit has also held that the amended text of Rule 701 implies a strict separation between lay opinion testimony and expert opinion testimony. *United States v. Conn*, 297 F.3d 548, 553–54 (7th Cir.2002).

While the text of Rule 701 appears unflinching in separating lay opinions from expert opinions, the advisory committee note regarding the amendment blinks. The advisory committee note first states that, "[t]he amendment makes clear that any part of a witness' testimony that is based upon scientific, technical, or other specialized knowledge within the scope of Rule 702 is governed by the standards of Rule 702

---

2. Other district courts have also interpreted Rule 701 as barring lay opinion testimony on various issues arising in patent litigation. *Fresenius Medical Care Holdings, Inc. v. Baxter Int'l, Inc.*, 2006 WL 1330002, *3 (N.D.Cal.2006) (Armstrong, J.) (permitting a witness to explain a device's function but forbidding a lay witness from comparing a device to a patent claim); *Laser Design Int'l, LLC v. BJ Crystal, Inc.*, 2007 WL 735763, *2 (N.D.Cal.2007) (White, J.) (striking a declaration opining regarding the nature of laser damage while not striking a declaration explaining how the device worked); *Insight Technology, Inc. v. Sure-Fire, LLC*, 2007 WL 3244092, *1–*2 (D.N.H.2007) (striking opinions regarding animations of prior art).

and the corresponding disclosure requirements of the Civil and Criminal Rules." However, the note goes on to suggest that the amended rule preserves certain prior practices, for example, permitting business owners to opine on expected profits or the value of property:

> For example, most courts have permitted the owner or officer of a business to testify to the value or projected profits of the business, without the necessity of qualifying the witness as an accountant, appraiser, or similar expert. *See, e.g., Lightning Lube, Inc. v. Witco Corp.* 4 F.3d 1153 (3d Cir.1993) (no abuse of discretion in permitting the plaintiff's owner to give lay opinion testimony as to damages, as it was based on his knowledge and participation in the day-to-day affairs of the business). Such opinion testimony is admitted not because of experience, training or specialized knowledge within the realm of an expert, but because of the particularized knowledge that the witness has by virtue of his or her position in the business. The amendment does not purport to change this analysis.

FRE 702, adv. committee note (2000). The note suggests that such testimony is admitted because the witness has "particularized knowledge" regarding the business. This seems irreconcilable with the fact that the witness must have "specialized experience" to be able to offer an opinion based on that particularized knowledge.

Nonetheless, the Manufacturers are able to cite to a variety of cases that support to some degree this "particularized knowledge" exception described in the advisory committee note. Three of the cases were decided after the 2000 amendment to Rule 701. The earliest is *Medforms, Inc. v. Healthcare Management Solutions, Inc.*, 290 F.3d 98 (2d Cir.2002). The Second Circuit there held that a computer programmer could testify regarding the meaning of various terms in a copyright registration because he had personal knowledge of their meaning. 290 F.3d at 110–11. The Second Circuit reasoned that, "[the programmer's] testimony was based on his everyday experience as a computer programmer and specifically on his work on [two computer programs]. Therefore, the testimony did not have to satisfy the requirements for expert testimony under Fed.R.Evid. 702, and the admission of the testimony was not an abuse of discretion." *Id.* at 111.

The second case cited by the Manufacturers is *United States v. Polishan*, 336 F.3d 234 (3d Cir.2003). This opinion does not correctly quote Rule 701, *see id.* at 242, and hence does not address the 2000 amendment's addition of the third element. Accordingly, it is not persuasive regarding the proper scope of lay opinion testimony.

The final case cited by the Manufacturers is *United States v. Munoz–Franco*, 487 F.3d 25 (1st Cir.2007). The First Circuit's opinion correctly quotes the language from the amended Rule 701, then relies on *Medforms* and *Polishan* for their reasoning to conclude that, "Here, [a witness's] testimony was based on knowledge of [a bank's] banking practices that he acquired during his employment there, and thus the opinions he expressed were properly within the scope of Federal Rule of Evidence 701." 487 F.3d at 35.[3]

The court finds these cases persuasive only in the limited context described in the advisory committee note regarding testimony about one's business, and it does not believe they can be read to support a broader "particularized knowledge" exception to the expert disclosure rules. As a general matter, "[l]ay opinion testimony is admissible only to help the jury or the court to understand the facts about which the witness is testifying and not to provide specialized explanations or interpretations that an untrained layman could not make if perceiving the same acts or events." *Conn*, 297 F.3d at 554 (quoting *United States v. Peoples*, 250 F.3d 630, 641 (8th Cir.2001)). The *Conn* case explains the court's general understanding of Rule 701(c). Nonetheless, the rules of evidence have long permitted a person to testify to opinions about their own businesses based on their personal knowledge of their business, as illustrated in the *Medforms* and *Muñoz–Franco* cases discussed above and in the advisory committee note, and the court does not believe that the revised Rule 701 was meant to work a sea change with respect to that form of personal testimony.

B. The Proffered Testimony of Macri and Krashinsky

Rambus's trial motions request the court to bar impermissible lay opinion testimony. The Manufacturers intend to offer lay opinion testimony from Mr. Krashinsky regarding the extent of industry lock-in resulting from the JEDEC DRAM standards and to the potential switching costs industry would incur if forced to use different DRAM technologies. In relying on the cases discussed above, the Manufacturers essentially concede that Mr. Krashinsky's personal knowledge regarding these topics is "specialized" or "technical." *See* Krashinsky Opp'n at 2:28:18–3:8. The Manufacturers emphasize Mr. Krashinsky's vast experience in circuit design and suggest that this experience "more than provides" the necessary foundation for his testimony. That the Manufacturers offer Mr. Krashinsky's qualifications as an engineer as the foundation for his testimony regarding these matters is ample evidence that his opinion testimony is improperly disclosed expert testimony, not a permissible lay opinion. Nevertheless, the court recognizes an exception to the literal language of FRE 701 with respect to testimony by Mr. Krashinsky regarding the types of changes HP would have to make if required to switch technologies. To the extent such opinion testimony is based on Mr. Krashinsky's personal, particularized knowledge, it is admissible.

---

3. The Ninth Circuit has not addressed the paragraph of the advisory committee note endorsing lay opinion testimony based on particularized knowledge. It has, however, favorably relied on a related paragraph of the note about identifying drugs. *See United States v. Durham*, 464 F.3d 976, 982 (9th Cir.2006).

The intended testimony of Joe Macri discussed in the Manufacturers' opposition to the motion regarding him does not appear to be opinion testimony, but instead Mr. Macri's percipient observations regarding votes at JEDEC, requests from JEDEC members, and descriptions of what ATI did and why they did it. To the extent the Manufacturers intend to elicit opinion testimony on industry lock-in, that testimony is prohibited, just as Mr. Krashinsky's.

. . .

IV. ORDER

For the foregoing reasons, the court partially grants the motion. Certain aspects of Mr. Krashinksy's intended testimony appear to be improper lay opinions. With respect to the disclosure of Mr. Macri and Mr. Krashinsky's subject areas of testimony and whether Mr. Macri's testimony includes improper lay opinion, the court defers ruling and will decide the issues at trial consistent with this opinion.

. . .

[After the trial in this case, on a motion for a new trial, the Court observed that "The proper scope of lay opinion and percipient witness testimony was a recurring issue throughout the trial as both parties aggressively offered evidence that stressed the boundaries created by Rule 702." Hynix Semiconductor, Inc. v. Rambus, Inc., 2008 WL 504098.]

Page 955. Following first full paragraph, add:

United States v. Kaplan

United States Court of Appeals for the Second Circuit, 2007.
490 F.3d 110.

■ Before: FEINBERG, LEVAL, and CABRANES, Circuit Judges.

■ FEINBERG, Circuit Judge:

Solomon Kaplan appeals from a judgment of conviction, entered following a jury trial in the United States District Court for the Southern District of New York (Batts, J.), on all seven counts of an indictment charging Kaplan's participation in an insurance fraud scheme (Counts One through Five)....

On appeal, Kaplan's principal contentions are that (I) his conviction on the insurance fraud counts (Counts One through Five) must be vacated because the district court erred in admitting (A) lay opinion testimony regarding his knowledge of the fraud....

For the reasons set forth below, we agree that Kaplan's conviction on Counts One through Five must be vacated because the district court erred in admitting, without adequate foundation, lay opinion testimony regarding Kaplan's knowledge of the fraud....

. . .

I. Counts One through Five: The Insurance Fraud Scheme

Turning first to the insurance fraud counts (Counts One through Five), Kaplan argues on appeal, among other things, that his conviction must be vacated because the district court erred in admitting (A) lay opinion testimony regarding his knowledge of the fraud....

A. Admission of Galkovich's lay opinion testimony

The first issue before us concerns the district court's admission of lay opinion testimony regarding Kaplan's knowledge of the fraud. Kaplan principally objects to two colloquies in which Galkovich recounted a conversation he and Kaplan had as they drove together to the meeting in October 2001 to finalize the sale of the Law Office to Kaplan. After describing the conversation, Galkovich was allowed to offer his lay opinion testimony regarding Kaplan's knowledge of the fraud. First, on direct examination, Galkovich testified as follows:

> [Prosecutor]: Did you have any discussions in the car ride on the way to Davis' office?
>
> [Galkovich]: Yes. It was actually the first time we really talked, me and Solomon Kaplan. And I asked him, What do you do? What kind of work do you do? Are you familiar with car accident cases, with the process of settlement and what it takes to settle? And he explained, yes he has handled cases like this before. Yes, he has settled cases before.
>
> . . . .
>
> He explained that he has experience with these kinds of cases.
>
> [Prosecutor]: What did you understand him to mean when he said "these kinds of cases"?
>
> [Defense Counsel]: Objection.
>
> The Court: I will allow it.
>
> [Galkovich]: That he understood that these were car accident cases where people exaggerated their injuries, where it was crucial to have a narrative report that exaggerated the injuries, that these reports were bought for the best of prices to get the best of reports and that you could settle these cases for very good money in a short period of time.

Joint Appendix ("JA") 104–05. Then, on redirect, Galkovich elaborated:

> [Prosecutor]: What happened in this conversation?
>
> [Galkovich]: I asked him what experience he had with the car accident cases and generally what kind of experience he had, and he

told me that he knew about these car accidents, he knew how to handle these cases, he knew how to maximize potential recoveries, and what is supposed to be in the files, how they are supposed to be worked up.

[Prosecutor]: What was your purpose in asking Kaplan this question?

[Galkovich]: I wanted to know how much he knew about the fraudulent office that he is participating in.

[Prosecutor]: And after you got this answer from Mr. Kaplan, what did you think?

[Galkovich]: I think he knew exactly what he was getting into.

JA 138–39.

We review a district court's decision to admit evidence, including lay opinion testimony, for abuse of discretion. See *United States v. Yuri Garcia*, 413 F.3d 201, 210 (2d Cir.2005) (citing *Old Chief v. United States*, 519 U.S. 172, 174 n. 1, 117 S.Ct. 644, 136 L.Ed.2d 574 (1997)). "A district court 'abuses' or 'exceeds' the discretion accorded to it when (1) its decision rests on an error of law (such as application of the wrong legal principle) or a clearly erroneous factual finding, or (2) its decision— though not necessarily the product of a legal error or a clearly erroneous factual funding—cannot be located within the range of permissible decisions." *Zervos v. Verizon N.Y., Inc.*, 252 F.3d 163, 169 (2d Cir.2001) (footnotes omitted).

The Federal Rules of Evidence, in a sharp departure from the common law, see *Asplundh Mfg. Div. v. Benton Harbor Eng'g*, 57 F.3d 1190, 1195 (3d Cir.1995) (Becker, J.), permit lay witnesses to testify in the form of opinions to address a problem identified by Judge Learned Hand many years ago:

> Every judge of experience in the trial of causes has again and again seen the whole story garbled, because of insistence upon a form with which the witness cannot comply, since, like most men, he is unaware of the extent to which inference enters into his perceptions. He is telling the "facts" in the only way that he knows how, and the result of nagging and checking him is often to choke him altogether, which is, indeed, usually its purpose.

Central R.R. Co. of N.J. v. Monahan, 11 F.2d 212, 214 (2d Cir.1926); see also *Yuri Garcia*, 413 F.3d at 211 ("eyewitnesses sometimes find it difficult to describe the appearance or relationship of persons, the atmosphere of a place, or the value of an object by reference only to objective facts"). Accordingly, Rule 701 of the Federal Rules of Evidence was adopted "to accommodate and ameliorate these difficulties by permitting lay witnesses, in appropriate circumstances, to testify in language with which they are comfortable." 4 Jack B. Weinstein & Margaret A. Berger, Weinstein's Federal Evidence § 701.02 (Joseph M. McLaughlin ed., 2d ed.2004).

But to ensure that lay opinion testimony is reliable and does not usurp the jury's role as fact-finder, Rule 701 imposes certain foundation requirements that must be satisfied if such testimony is to be admitted:

> If the witness is not testifying as an expert, the witness' testimony in the form of opinions or inferences is limited to those opinions or inferences which are (a) rationally based on the perception of the witness, (b) helpful to a clear understanding of the witness' testimony or the determination of a fact in issue, and (c) not based on scientific, technical, or other specialized knowledge within the scope of Rule 702.

Fed.R.Evid. 701 (2001). In interpreting these requirements, we have observed that (a) the rational-basis requirement "is the familiar requirement of first-hand knowledge or observation," *United States v. Rea,* 958 F.2d 1206, 1215 (2d Cir.1992) (quoting Fed.R.Evid. 701 advisory committee's note on 1972 Proposed Rules); (b) the helpfulness requirement is principally "designed to provide assurance[ ] against the admission of opinions which would merely tell the jury what result to reach," *id.* (quoting Fed.R.Evid. 704 advisory committee's note on 1972 Proposed Rules); and (c) the "not based on specialized knowledge" requirement requires that "a lay opinion must be the product of reasoning processes familiar to the average person in everyday life," *Yuri Garcia,* 413 F.3d at 215.[2] See also Fed.R.Evid. 701 advisory committee's note on 2000 amendments.

The government's evidence failed to demonstrate that Galkovich's lay opinion testimony was "rationally based on the perception of the witness." Fed R. Evid. 701(a). We note that Rule 701(a) requires that lay opinion testimony be *both* (a) based on the witness's first-hand perceptions *and* (b) rationally derived from those first-hand perceptions.

As to the first of these requirements, Rule 701(a) reflects, in part, the Rules' more general requirement that "[a] witness may not testify to a matter unless evidence is introduced sufficient to support a finding that the witness has personal knowledge of the matter." Fed.R.Evid. 602; see also *United States v. Durham,* 464 F.3d 976, 982 (9th Cir.2006) ("opinion testimony of lay witnesses must be predicated upon concrete facts within their own observation and recollection—that is facts perceived from their own senses, as distinguished from their opinions or conclusions drawn from such facts" (internal quotation marks omitted)). When Galkovich was asked to articulate the basis for his opinion, he answered, "I based it on the only thing I could base it on, which is my experience there, what people said about [Kaplan], my conversation with [Kaplan], everything that I[had] been involved in. That's what my opinion could be based on." JA 140. Although Galkovich asserts that his

---

2. In 2000, after *Rea* was decided, Rule 701 was amended to include 701(c).

testimony was based in part on first-hand experience—principally his prior experiences at the Law Office and his conversation with Kaplan—his response was extremely vague. Thus, Galkovich's testimony failed to show that his opinion as to Kaplan's knowledge was rationally based on facts he had observed.

We are therefore unable to conclude, as we must under Rule 701, that the opinion he offered was *rationally based* on his own perceptions. See *Rea*, 958 F.2d at 1216 ("When a witness has not identified the objective bases for his opinion, the proffered opinion obviously fails completely to meet the requirements of Rule 701 ... because there is no way for the court to assess whether it is rationally based on the witness's perceptions...."). We applied this requirement to similar facts in *Rea*, and observed that lay opinion testimony regarding a defendant's knowledge will, in most cases, only satisfy the rationally-based requirement if the witness has personal knowledge of one or more "objective factual bases from which it is possible to infer with some confidence that a person knows a given fact ... includ[ing] what the person was told directly, what he was in a position to see or hear, what statements he himself made to others, conduct in which he engaged, and what his background and experience were." 958 F.2d at 1216. Because the Government did not lay an adequate foundation, Galkovich's testimony expressing his opinion as to Kaplan's knowledge was not admissible.

Accordingly, having found that Galkovich's lay opinion testimony does not satisfy Rule 701, we conclude that the district court erred in admitting it.

. . .

Page 955:

United States v. Anchrum

United States Court of Appeals for the Ninth Circuit.
590 F.3d 795 (9th Cir. 2009), cert. denied 2010 WL 1903578 (U.S. 2010).

■ TALLMAN, CIRCUIT JUDGE:

Defendant–Appellant Michael Anchrum ("Anchrum") appeals a jury conviction and sentence for one count of possession of controlled substances with intent to distribute in violation of 21 U.S.C. §§ 841(a)(1) and (b)(1)(C), two counts of assault on federal officers with a deadly or dangerous weapon in violation of 18 U.S.C. §§ 111(a)(1) and (b), and one count of possession of firearms in furtherance of drug trafficking in violation of 18 U.S.C. § 924(c)(1)(A)(i). Anchrum claims (1) that the jury instruction on the assault counts erroneously required the jury to find that he used a "motor vehicle" instead of a "deadly or dangerous weapon," (2) that the government's use of United States Drug Enforcement Administration ("DEA") Special Agent Kenneth Solek ("Agent Solek") as both a lay and expert witness resulted in testimony inconsistent with this court's holding in *United States v. Freeman*, 498 F.3d 893,

904 (9th Cir.2007), as well as Federal Rule of Evidence ("Rule") 704(b), and (3) that the district court erred in applying a six-level official victim enhancement at sentencing under U.S. Sentencing Guidelines ("U.S.S.G.") 3A1.2(c)(1).

. . .

At trial, Agent Solek testified as both a percipient and expert witness. The district court separated the testimony into a first "phase," consisting of Agent Solek's percipient witness testimony regarding the investigation and arrest of Anchrum, and a second "phase," consisting of Agent Solek's expert qualifications as a drug investigator and his opinions that drug dealers usually possess guns for protection, use scales to weigh drugs, and rent cars to avoid detection. A sidebar conference separated the two phases of the agent's testimony. Following the end of the percipient witness portion of testimony and the sidebar, the prosecutor transitioned into the expert phase by stating Agent Solek, I'd like to shift gears here a little bit and talk about some of your education, professional training, and law enforcement experience.

. . .

In *Freeman* we warned of the dangers inherent in permitting investigating police officers—in that case a "case agent"—to testify as both percipient and expert witnesses and we highlighted four "concerns" with the practice. 498 F.3d at 903. First, we expressed concern "that a case agent who testifies as an expert receives 'unmerited credibility' for lay testimony." *Id.* (quoting *United States v. Dukagjini*, 326 F.3d 45, 53 (2d Cir.2003)). Second, we noted that "expert testimony by a fact witness or case agent can inhibit cross-examination" because a "failed effort to impeach the witness as expert may effectively enhance his credibility as a fact witness." *Id.* (internal quotation marks omitted). Third, "there is an increased danger that the expert testimony will stray from applying reliable methodology and convey to the jury the witness's sweeping conclusions about appellants' activities." *Id.* (internal quotation marks omitted). Fourth, there is a danger that some "jurors will find it difficult to discern whether the witness is relying properly on his general experience and reliable methodology, or improperly on what he has learned of the case." *Id.*

Despite these concerns, however, we reasoned that "the use of case agents as both expert and lay witnesses is not so inherently suspect that it should be categorically prohibited." *Id.* at 904. As a result, we advised district courts that "[i]f jurors are aware of the witness's dual roles, the risk of error in these types of trials is reduced." *Id.* Finally, we concluded that the district court in that case had not sufficiently separated the witness's dual roles and that there was a "blurred distinction" between the detective's expert and lay testimony. *Id.*

Here, in careful consideration of our decision in *Freeman,* 498 F.3d at 904, the district court clearly separated Agent Solek's testimony into a first "phase" consisting of his percipient observations, and a second "phase" consisting of his credentials in the field of drug trafficking and expert testimony regarding the modus operandi of drug traffickers.

Defense counsel raised the *Freeman* issue with the court before Agent Solek testified. As a result, the district court agreed to—and actually did—separate the testimony into two distinct phases and gave the jury an instruction that they were the ultimate finders of fact. Defense counsel even conceded, "Judge, if, as my colleague had indicated earlier, she was going to do . . . the fact section, then say, now I'm going to ask you expert questions, then I think that would protect everything. . . ." The prosecutor then developed lay testimony before proceeding to Agent Solek's expert testimony.

When the district court divided Agent Solek's testimony into two separate phases it avoided blurring the distinction between Agent Solek's distinct role as a lay witness and his role as an expert witness. Not only were these two phases separated temporally by a sidebar, but when the prosecutor began the expert phase, she stated, "Agent Solek, I'd like to shift gears here a little bit and talk about some of your education, professional training, and law enforcement experience."

Accordingly, we find that the concerns we expressed in *Freeman* were avoided here and the district court did not exceed the permissible bounds of its discretion in admitting Agent Solek's testimony.

. . .

See also John H. Mansfield, An Embarassing Episode in the History of the Law of Evidence, 34 Seton Hall L. Rev. 77, 85, 87–88 (2003).

Page 977. Note 4. At end of Note 4 add:

United States v. Abu–Jihaad

United States District Court for the District of Connecticut, 2008.
553 F. Supp. 2d 121.

■ MARK R. KRAVITZ, District Judge.

Currently before the Court are Defendant Hassan Abu–Jihaad's MOTION *in Limine* to Conduct *Daubert* Hearing and to Exclude Testimony of Evan Kohlmann [doc. #191]. . . . As Mr. Abu–Jihaad requested in his motion, the Court held a *Daubert* hearing on February 14, 2008, at which Evan Kohlmann testified and was cross-examined by Mr. Abu–Jihaad's counsel. The Government proffered Mr. Kohlmann as an expert in terrorism who would provide testimony regarding the history, structure, and goals of al Qaeda, the recruitment of Muslim fighters, mujahideen activities in Bosnia, Chechnya, and Afghanistan (among other places), and the role of Azzam Publications among the mujahideen. At the conclusion of the testimony, the Court heard arguments on the

Daubert motion as well as on Mr. Abu–Jihaad's other *in limine* motion. The Court orally ruled on both motions, and the purpose of this decision is to memorialize the Court's rulings. The Court assumes familiarity with its previous evidentiary rulings in this case. . . .

1. The *Daubert* Motion

Rule 702 of the *Federal Rules of Evidence* provides as follows:

If scientific, technical, or other specialized knowledge will assist the trier of fact to understand the evidence or to determine a fact in issue, a witness qualified as an expert by knowledge, skill, experience, training, or education, may testify thereto in the form of an opinion or otherwise, if (1) the testimony is based upon sufficient facts or data, (2) the testimony is the product of reliable principles and methods, and (3) the witness has applied the principles and methods reliably to the facts of the case.

In *Daubert v. Merrell Dow Pharmaceuticals, Inc.,* 509 U.S. 579, 113 S.Ct. 2786, 125 L.Ed.2d 469 (1993), the Supreme Court tasked district judges with the responsibility of acting as "gatekeepers" to exclude unreliable expert testimony, and the Court in *Kumho Tire Co., Ltd. v. Carmichael,* 526 U.S. 137, 119 S.Ct. 1167, 143 L.Ed.2d 238 (1999), clarified that the trial court's gatekeeping function applies to all expert testimony, not just to scientific testimony. *See* Fed.R.Evid. 702, Advisory Comm. Notes to 2000 Amendments. Thus, under Rule 702, a district court has "the task of ensuring that an expert's testimony both rests on a reliable foundation and is relevant to the task at hand." *United States v. Williams,* 506 F.3d 151, 160 (2d Cir.2007) (quotation marks omitted).

To decide whether Mr. Kohlmann's proposed testimony is "relevant to the task at hand," the Court must make a "common sense inquiry" into whether the "untrained layman would be qualified to determine intelligently and to the best possible degree the particular issue without enlightenment from those having a specialized understanding of the subject involved in the dispute." *United States v. Locascio* 6 F.3d 924, 936 (2d Cir.1993) (quotation marks omitted). Expert testimony is generally admissible so long as it will assist the trier of fact to understand the evidence or to determine any fact in issue. *See Daubert,* 509 U.S. at 592, 113 S.Ct. 2786; *United States v. Duncan,* 42 F.3d 97, 101 (2d Cir.1994) ("Expert witnesses are often uniquely qualified in guiding the trier of fact through a complicated morass of obscure terms and concepts. Because of their specialized knowledge, their testimony can be extremely valuable and probative.").

It is readily apparent that the testimony Mr. Kohlmann proposes to provide is relevant to the task at hand and will assist the jury. Mr. Abu–Jihaad is charged with supplying classified information to Azzam Publications, and the jury will be required to determine, among other things, whether Mr. Abu–Jihaad provided material support to Azzam Publications knowing or intending that the support be used to kill United States nationals. Therefore, the jury will need to understand the role of Azzam Publications in disseminating information supporting al Qaeda and the mujahideen and its connections to various terrorist groups and leaders. Similarly, background information about the conflicts in Chechnya and Bosnia, and the activities of foreign mujahideen fighters, are also relevant to the Government's case against Mr. Abu–Jihaad since Mr. Abu-Jihaad purchased various videos regarding those conflicts from Azzam Publications.

The Second Circuit has on many occasions approved of the use of experts to provide historical context and structural information to juries in gang and drug conspiracy cases. *See, e.g., United States v. Amuso,* 21 F.3d 1251 (2d Cir.1994); *United States v. Dukagjini,* 326 F.3d 45 (2d Cir.2003); *Locascio,* 6 F.3d at 936. In *Amuso,* the Second Circuit explained that the rationale for permitting such expert testimony is that "[a]side from the probability that the depiction of organized crime in movies and television is misleading, the fact remains that the operational methods of organized crime families are still beyond the knowledge of the average citizen." 21 F.3d at 1264. Thus, the Court of Appeals concluded that "[d]espite the prevalence of organized crime stories in the news and popular media, these topics remain proper subjects for expert testimony." *Id.* So, too, here. Despite the relatively widespread news coverage of al Qaeda and other terrorist organizations, the operations of al Qaeda—and certainly those of Azzam Publications—as well as the conflicts in Bosnia and Chechnya, are still beyond the knowledge of ordinary jurors.

While the Second Circuit has not yet had an opportunity to consider the use of experts in terrorism cases, other circuits have approved of the use of experts to provide historical context and background information in such cases. *See United States v. Damrah,* 412 F.3d 618, 625 (6th Cir.2005); *United States v. Hammoud,* 381 F.3d 316, 337–38 (4th Cir. 2004), *vacated on other grounds by* 543 U.S. 1097, 125 S.Ct. 1051, 160 L.Ed.2d 997 (2005), *relevant portions reinstated by* 405 F.3d 1034 (4th Cir.2005). As the Fourth Circuit explained in *Hammoud,* the expert "testified regarding the structure of Hizballah and identified its leaders. [He] also explained the significance of Hammoud's contact with those leaders ... [a]nd discussed the nature of Hizballah's funding activities with specific reference to Hammoud's activities. This testimony was critical in helping the jury understand the issues before it." *Id.* at 337–38....

Turning next to reliability, the Second Circuit has instructed district courts to consider the indicia of reliability set forth in Rule 702 itself: "namely, (1) that the testimony is grounded on sufficient facts or data; (2) that the testimony is the product of reliable principles and methods; and (3) that the witness has applied the principles and methods reliably to the facts of the case." *Williams,* 506 F.3d at 160 (quotation marks omitted). But these criteria are not exhaustive. *See Wills v. Amerada Hess Corp.,* 379 F.3d 32, 48 (2d Cir.2004). . . .

. . .

Mr. Kohlmann is certainly qualified to provide expert testimony on the issues he proposes to address, and Mr. Abu–Jihaad does not contend otherwise. Mr. Kohlmann's CV was marked as an exhibit at the *Daubert* hearing. He has published a book entitled *Al-Qaida's Jihad in Europe: The Afghan–Bosnian Network,* which was cited as an authoritative source in the 9/11 Commission's Report. It is also used in courses taught at Harvard University and at Johns Hopkins University, among others. Mr. Kohlmann has published peer-reviewed articles on the subjects about which he intends to testify, including articles for *Foreign Affairs.* He also regularly lectures and speaks on these subjects. Mr. Kohlmann has testified as an expert in seven trials held in the United States and in several cases before foreign courts.

. . .

Mr. Abu–Jihaad's principal attack on Mr. Kohlmann's proposed testimony is that it is not based upon sufficient facts or data and is not the product of reliable principles and methods. The Court disagrees. Mr. Kohlmann has conducted first-hand interviews of several leaders of terrorist organizations and has reviewed reams of information about al Qaeda, Azzam Publications, and the other subjects on which he will offer testimony. Indeed, though he is relatively young to be an expert, it is apparent that these subjects are Mr. Kohlmann's life work, and he has, therefore, acquired a considerable amount of information and documentation on these subjects. He testified that he applies to his expert testimony the same social science methodologies that he learned at Georgetown University and that are applied to other subjects that cannot be tested scientifically. Mr. Kohlmann's work receives a considerable amount of peer review from academic scholars and others, and by all accounts, Mr. Kohlmann's work is well regarded.

While Mr. Kohlmann must, perforce, rely often on hearsay, he testified that he gathers information from multiple sources and cross-checks factual information he receives with existing information from other sources. He also works collaboratively with his peers and relies upon original information provided directly by the terrorists organizations themselves. As it relates to Azzam Publications, Mr. Kolhmann has tracked the organization since nearly its founding and has expert knowledge concerning its internet activities and support for jihad. In commenting on an expert's reliance on hearsay in *Locascio,* the Second Circuit explained that the issue is whether the evidence on which the expert relies is "[o]f a type reasonably relied upon by experts in the particular field. Fed.R.Evid. 703. . . . An expert who meets the test of Rule 702 . . . is assumed to have the skill to properly evaluate the hearsay, giving it probative force appropriate to the circumstances."

Locascio, 6 F.3d at 938 (quotation marks and emphasis omitted); *see Damrah,* 412 F.3d at 625 (holding that the district court did not abuse its discretion in allowing expert testimony based on, inter alia, books, press releases, and newspaper articles and quoting the district court's opinion that "[g]iven the secretive nature of terrorists, the Court can think of few other materials that experts in the field of terrorism would rely upon").

[F]or similar reasons [the Court] rejects Mr. Abu–Jihaad's argument that Mr. Kohlmann's testimony is unreliable. Accordingly, in its role as gatekeeper, the Court finds that Mr. Kohlmann's expected testimony meets the requirements of Rule 702.

As the Court explained at the conclusion of the *Daubert* hearing, Mr. Abu–Jihaad retains the right to object to any testimony by Mr. Kohlmann that lacks a proper foundation or that implicates Rule 403's concerns regarding unfair prejudice and confusion. As the Court also cautioned, there are limits to what Mr. Kohlmann may provide by way of testimony. *See, e.g., Dukagjini,* 326 F.3d 45. Mr. Kohlmann may provide the historical context the Government seeks, but he may not testify directly about Mr. Abu–Jihaad or his motivations lest his testimony "usurp[ ] the jury's function." *Id.* at 54 (quotation marks omitted). Thus, Mr. Kohlmann should not testify about why individuals like Mr. Abu–Jihaad would want to order jihadi videos from Azzam Publications or provide information to Azzam Publications. Nor should the Government use Mr. Kohlmann to turn this trial of a single alleged disclosure of classified information into an extended trial that is instead focused on al Qaeda, Bosnia, or Chechnya.

. . .

Page 977. Note 4. At end of Note 4, add:

United States v. Moore

United States Court of Appeals for the Seventh Circuit, 2008.
521 F. 3d 681.

■ EASTERBROOK, Chief Judge.

Michael Sanders arrived in the United States from Nigeria with 3.6 kilograms of heroin in his luggage. When caught, he claimed to be a courier with no interest in the drugs apart from a $3,000 fee for his services; he agreed to participate in a controlled delivery to the next people in the chain, who were to collect the heroin at a bus station in Chicago. Several conversations in Yoruba with "Baba," Sanders's contact, preceded his arrival. Eventually Taofiq Afonja drove up and told Sanders to put his luggage in the trunk of his car. Sanders asked, in Yoruba, whether Afonja was "that person" or "the one" (and surely was not referring to Neo in *The Matrix*). Afonja replied (in translation) that he was, and that "[t]hey have spoken to us. It is them they are talking to on that phone." Afonja then took the suitcase but before he and his passenger, Folashade Moore, could leave, all three were arrested. Another car, presumably carrying Baba, got away; he is a fugitive.

Sanders pleaded guilty to conspiring to possess the heroin with intent to distribute it and has been sentenced to 120 months' imprisonment, the statutory minimum. Moore confessed that she had gone to the bus station to pick up a drug courier for Baba, her boyfriend. Nonetheless she pleaded not guilty. A jury convicted her of attempted possession of the heroin. She has been sentenced to 121 months' imprisonment. Afonja, who did not confess, was tried separately to avoid *Bruton* problems and convicted of conspiracy and attempt. His sentence, too, is 121 months. All three have appealed, but counsel for Moore and Sanders have filed *Anders* briefs. Sanders does not want to withdraw his guilty plea and received the lowest available sentence; he has no conceivable appellate issue....

Afonja has a non-frivolous argument: that a witness testifying as an expert for the prosecution did not satisfy the requirements of Fed. R.Evid. 702. Afonja maintained that he didn't know what was in Sanders's suitcase. Robert Coleman, a police officer employed by Will County, Illinois, and assigned to a drug task force, testified for the prosecution as an expert about drug transactions. One of the questions he addressed was whether innocent persons participate in drug transactions. Over Afonja's objection, Coleman testified that, except for children, only "people that are involved in the drug deal" will be present—and by "involved" Coleman meant people who "have knowledge as to what's taking place, the illegal activity". Afonja maintains that the district judge should have prevented Coleman from giving this testimony.

The district judge concluded that Coleman's training and experience make him an expert on drug transactions. The prosecutor repeats this theme, and we may assume that Coleman indeed knows much more about these transactions than do jurors and so is well situated to provide information about them. But Rule 702 does not say that any testimony within the scope of a witness's expertise is admissible. It provides:

> If scientific, technical, or other specialized knowledge will assist the trier of fact to understand the evidence or to determine a fact in issue, a witness qualified as an expert by knowledge, skill, experience, training, or education, may testify thereto in the form of an opinion or otherwise, if (1) the testimony is based upon sufficient facts or data, (2) the testimony is the product of reliable principles and methods, and (3) the witness has applied the principles and methods reliably to the facts of the case.

The district judge did not address any of the Rule's three questions: (1) whether Coleman's view "is based upon sufficient facts or data"; (2) whether it is "the product of reliable principles and methods"; and (3) whether the "witness has applied the principles and methods reliably to the facts of the case."

Both the judge and the prosecutor stopped with the proposition that Coleman is an expert; for its part, the defense also bypassed the Rule's requirements in favor of the assertion that an expert should not be allowed to testify unless his experience includes a transaction just like this one (presumably, one in which several Yoruba-speaking people exchange a suitcase outside a bus station in Chicago). The defense position is anti-intellectual and has nothing to do with Rule 702; the point of good data and reliable analysis is to find patterns that transcend details such as which bus station is used or what language people speak.

Both the judge and the prosecutor supposed that decisions in this circuit make it unnecessary to address the questions posed by Rule 702. We have held that an agent's field experience can provide "specialized knowledge" that supports expert testimony. See, e.g., *United States v. Ceballos,* 302 F.3d 679, 686–88 (7th Cir.2002); *United States v. Allen,* 269 F.3d 842, 846 (7th Cir.2001). And we have twice held that district judges did not err in admitting testimony of the kind that Coleman gave here. See *United States v. Garcia,* 439 F.3d 363, 367–68 (7th Cir.2006); *United States v. Love,* 336 F.3d 643, 646–47 (7th Cir.2003). But neither *Garcia* nor *Love* dealt with Rule 702. *Garcia* held that testimony (by Coleman himself) did not deprive the accused of the presumption of innocence, and *Love* that testimony about the probability of innocents participating in drug deals did not violate Fed.R.Evid. 704(b), which forbids expert testimony about whether the defendant had the mental state required for conviction. Neither *Garcia* nor *Love* holds that district judges must admit testimony of the sort that Coleman proffered or excuses judges from conducting the inquiry required by Rule 702 every time any expert proposes to testify. See *Kumho Tire Co. v. Carmichael,* 526 U.S. 137, 153–57, 119 S.Ct. 1167, 143 L.Ed.2d 238 (1999).

On what "facts or data" does Coleman's opinion rest? Are his inferential methods reliable? Coleman did not describe either the facts he considered or the methods of analysis used to get from facts to a conclusion. All he said is that drug dealers don't want extra witnesses, which leads them to include in any given transaction only a circle of knowledgeable operatives. That *a priori* proposition may be sound, but an incentive ("avoid conducting drug deals where people who may talk to the police can see you") operates at the margin. The existence of this incentive implies that there will be fewer strangers at drug deals than at sales of antique chairs or swaps of baseball cards, but it does not imply that the number of innocent adults on the scene will be zero. And there are contrary incentives. Dealers may use stooges because they are cheap and reliable; people who know that they are picking up drugs must be paid for the risk that they are taking, and they may be tempted to steal the drugs. Dupes have no reason to demand payment or make off with the inventory. How do these contrary incentives balance out? Coleman did not even mention the potential benefits to drug dealers of using ignorant participants.

SECTION 1 THE NATURE AND FUNCTION OF EXPERT EVIDENCE

How these and other incentives play out cannot be determined by *a priori* reasoning. Facts are essential to testimony based on "specialized knowledge" as well as to scientific and technical expertise. Yet Coleman did not describe any data, and his evaluation does not seem to be falsifiable. Coleman is certain that every adult involved in every drug transaction knows what is going on. Thus if Afonja protests ignorance of what was in the suitcase, Coleman will not believe him. He will treat this as one more "proof" that only knowledgeable participants come to an exchange of drugs. Coleman does not have—or at least did not explain—any way to avoid the GIGO problem. (Garbage in, garbage out.) He *assumes* that everyone present is culpable and uses that assumption as the "proof" of culpability. That's not a reliable way to proceed.

Now maybe Coleman has done some data collection and evaluation, or maybe such work has been done by others—though we could not find any published literature on the subject. Perhaps Coleman knows what portion of people found at drug transactions can be identified as culpable on the basis of evidence *other than* their presence at the transactions, and what portion can be ruled out as knowledgeable participants (again on the basis of other evidence). But no one—not the prosecutor, not defense counsel, and not the judge—asked whether such empirical work had been conducted. No one tried to apply the three criteria in Rule 702 to Coleman's testimony. Defense counsel's attention was elsewhere: on the theme that Coleman had not encountered a drug transaction exactly like this one.

The prosecutor's brief and oral argument rest on the proposition that testimony by any genuine expert is admissible under Rule 702. That's not so. Most junk science is the work of people with Ph.D. degrees and academic positions. For example, in *Emerald Investments L.P. v. Allmerica Financial Life Insurance & Annuity Co.*, 516 F.3d 612 (7th Cir.2008), a professor of finance at a respectable university gave irresponsible testimony that "demonstrated a willingness to abandon the norms of his profession in the interest of his client." In other cases we have excluded analysis that scholars would not have accepted in their undergraduates' term papers....

Because the right questions were not asked, we cannot know whether Coleman should have been allowed to testify. It is difficult to say that the district judge abused his discretion—that's the standard, see *General Electric Co. v. Joiner*, 522 U.S. 136, 118 S.Ct. 512, 139 L.Ed.2d 508 (1997)—when the information on which a sound exercise of discretion depends was never placed before the judge. A judge is not obliged to look into the questions posed by Rule 702 when neither side either requests or assists. So there was no error; the judge answered correctly the only question that the parties posed (whether Coleman qualified as an expert).

Afonja contends that the evidence was insufficient to support his conviction, but the conversation between Afonja and Sanders is damning. Sanders asks "[a]re you that person" and explains that he needs to know "[s]o that I don't go and give the thing to somebody else." Afonja answers that he is the one, that "[i]t is us. It is us." There is more in the same vein. Afonja's statements are not those of a person who was just coming along to spare Moore the need to move a friend's heavy suitcase. Moreover, the car bearing Afonja and Moore (and the second car believed to contain Baba) had been at the station before Sanders's bus arrived. When a police cruiser arrived serendipitously, these two cars hightailed it out of there and did not return until Sanders called to announce his arrival. (They tried to get Sanders to use a taxi and appeared themselves only when he balked.) This behavior bespeaks guilty knowledge.

Afonja's conviction is affirmed. The appeals of Sanders and Moore are dismissed as frivolous, and we grant their lawyers' motions to withdraw.

Page 979, at the end of Note 5, add Note 5A:

United States v. Lee

United States District Court for the District of Pennsylvania.
2008 U.S. Dist. LEXIS 45366.

■ MEMORANDUM OPINION and ORDER OF COURT, by DONETTA W. AMBROSE, DISTRICT JUDGE:

In document numbers 93 and 94, which appear to be identical except for the addition of Exhibit A to document number 94, Defendant seeks a *Daubert* hearing on the question of whether the Government's bloodhound evidence fits within the requirements of *Daubert* and, further, seeks exclusion of the bloodhound evidence under Federal Rules of Evidence 401, 402, 403 and 702.

The facts are the following: On June 27, 2006, Lt. Kraus, a Pittsburgh Police Officer, attempted to make a traffic stop of a Jeep. As Lt. Kraus approached the Jeep, he saw the Defendant, the driver and sole occupant of the vehicle, removing a bullet-proof vest, a black semi-automatic pistol lying on the right side of Defendant's lap, and a black coat draped across a long object in the back seat. The Defendant sped away before Lt. Kraus could make an arrest and Lt. Kraus lost sight of the Jeep.

A short time later, the abandoned Jeep was found not far from where the attempted stop occurred. The bullet-proof vest was on the front seat; the pistol and coat were missing. The coat and an AK–47 rifle were found on a nearby pathway.

A K–9 officer was called to the scene. The K–9 bloodhound, Digger, and his handler, Rudy Harkins, led police from the front seat of the Jeep to the pathway where the coat and AK–47 had been found and then on to an apartment complex where Digger lost the scent.

Later that day, Lt. Kraus talked to Defendant on the telephone at which time Defendant told Lt. Kraus he was somewhere in the aforementioned apartment complex. Defendant was not arrested until July 12, 2006.

Defendant contends that all evidence relating to Digger must be excluded under Rules 401 and 402 as irrelevant; under Rule 403 as unfairly prejudicial; and, under Rule 702 for failing to comply with *Daubert* and as inadmissible expert evidence.

A pretrial hearing was conducted and the reliability of Digger and his handler were addressed. As defense counsel learned from pre-hearing conversations and from the hearing, Digger is a bloodhound successfully used by the Pittsburgh police to locate people and evidence in the past. Digger's handler, Rudy Harkins, is a well-trained and experienced dog trainer and handler.

The evidence introduced at the pre-trial hearing established the reliability of Digger and Harkins. Harkins testified as to the training he and Digger received both separately and together and as to the certifications received by both, as well as Digger's performance in other cases.

Furthermore, the evidence is clearly probative and relevant as it tends to prove that Defendant, who had occupied the front seat of the Jeep, had traveled along the pathway where the coat and rifle were found and then on to the apartment complex. This is circumstantial evidence that Defendant possessed and removed the coat and rifle from the Jeep. The evidence is, therefore, admissible under Rules 401 and 402.

It is also admissible evidence under Rule 403, as the bloodhound evidence makes it more likely that Defendant had possessed the rifle. This evidence has more substantial probative value than it has prejudicial effect.

I note, also, that the Government has agreed to eliminate any reference in the testimony that Digger paused at the coat and rifle, thus, further reducing any unfair prejudice to Defendant.

Finally, with respect to Defendant's *Daubert* argument, I find that the Government has met its burden at the pretrial hearing as to the reliability of Digger and his handler and that the *Daubert* tests do not apply to the admission of dog tracking evidence. Neither the Government nor Defendant have submitted any case law requiring a *Daubert* hearing under these circumstances. Defendant has had, and will have at trial, sufficient opportunities to challenge Digger's reliability....

Would the dog tracking evidence be relevant without the expert testimony?

CHAPTER 6 EXPERT EVIDENCE

Page 980. Note 9. Substitute:

General Electric Co. v. Joiner

Supreme Court of the United States, 1997.
522 U.S 136, 118 S.Ct. 512, 139 L.Ed.2d 508.

■ CHIEF JUSTICE REHNQUIST delivered the opinion of the Court.

We granted certiorari in this case to determine what standard an appellate court should apply in reviewing a trial court's decision to admit or exclude expert testimony under Daubert v. Merrell Dow Pharmaceuticals, Inc., 509 U.S. 579, 113 S.Ct. 2786, 125 L.Ed.2d 469 (1993). We hold that abuse of discretion is the appropriate standard. We apply this standard and conclude that the District Court in this case did not abuse its discretion when it excluded certain proffered expert testimony.

I

Respondent Robert Joiner began work as an electrician in the Water & Light Department of Thomasville, Georgia (City) in 1973. This job required him to work with and around the City's electrical transformers, which used a mineral-based dielectric fluid as a coolant. Joiner often had to stick his hands and arms into the fluid to make repairs. The fluid would sometimes splash onto him, occasionally getting into his eyes and mouth. In 1983 the City discovered that the fluid in some of the transformers was contaminated with polychlorinated biphenyls (PCBs). PCBs are widely considered to be hazardous to human health. Congress, with limited exceptions, banned the production and sale of PCBs in 1978. See 90 Stat.2020, 15 U.S.C. § 2605(e)(2)(A).

Joiner was diagnosed with small cell lung cancer in 1991. He sued petitioners in Georgia state court the following year. Petitioner Monsanto manufactured PCBs from 1935 to 1977; petitioners General Electric and Westinghouse Electric manufactured transformers and dielectric fluid. In his complaint Joiner linked his development of cancer to his exposure to PCBs and their derivatives, polychlorinated dibenzofurans (furans) and polychlorinated dibenzodioxins (dioxins). Joiner had been a smoker for approximately eight years, his parents had both been smokers, and there was a history of lung cancer in his family. He was thus perhaps already at a heightened risk of developing lung cancer eventually. The suit alleged that his exposure to PCBs "promoted" his cancer; had it not been for his exposure to these substances, his cancer would not have developed for many years, if at all.

Petitioners removed the case to federal court. Once there, they moved for summary judgment. They contended that (1) there was no evidence that Joiner suffered significant exposure to PCBs, furans, or dioxins, and (2) there was no admissible scientific evidence that PCBs promoted Joiner's cancer. Joiner responded that there were numerous disputed factual issues that required resolution by a jury. He relied largely on the testimony of expert witnesses. In depositions, his experts had testified that PCBs alone can promote cancer and that furans and dioxins can also promote cancer. They opined that since Joiner had been exposed to PCBs, furans, and dioxins, such exposure was likely responsible for Joiner's cancer.

The District Court ruled that there was a genuine issue of material fact as to whether Joiner had been exposed to PCBs. But it nevertheless granted summary judgment for petitioners because (1) there was no genuine issue as to whether Joiner had been exposed to furans and dioxins, and (2) the testimony of Joiner's experts had failed to show that there was a link between exposure to PCBs and small cell lung cancer. The court believed that the testimony of respondent's experts to the contrary did not rise above "subjective belief or unsupported speculation." 864 F.Supp. 1310, 1326 (N.D.Ga.1994). Their testimony was therefore inadmissible.

The Court of Appeals for the Eleventh Circuit reversed. 78 F.3d 524 (1996). It held that "[b]ecause the Federal Rules of Evidence governing expert testimony display a preference for admissibility, we apply a particularly stringent standard of review to the trial judge's exclusion of expert testimony." Id. at 529. Applying that standard, the Court of Appeals held that the District Court had erred in excluding the testimony of Joiner's expert witnesses. The District Court had made two fundamental errors. First, it excluded the experts' testimony because it "drew different conclusions from the research than did each of the experts." The Court of Appeals opined that a district court should limit its role to determining the "legal reliability of proffered expert testimony, leaving the jury to decide the correctness of competing expert opinions." Id. at 533. Second, the District Court had held that there was no genuine issue of material fact as to whether Joiner had been exposed to furans and dioxins. This was also incorrect, said the Court of Appeals, because testimony in the record supported the proposition that there had been such exposure.

We granted petitioners' petition for a writ of certiorari, 520 U.S. 1114, 117 S.Ct. 1243, 137 L.Ed.2d 325 (1997), and we now reverse.

II

Petitioners challenge the standard applied by the Court of Appeals in reviewing the District Court's decision to exclude respondent's experts' proffered testimony. They argue that that court should have applied traditional "abuse of discretion" review. Respondent agrees that abuse of discretion is the correct standard of review. He contends, however, that the Court of Appeals applied an abuse of discretion standard in this case. As he reads it, the phrase "particularly stringent" announced no new standard of review. It was simply an acknowledgement that an appellate court can and will devote more resources to analyzing district court decisions that are dispositive of the entire litigation. All evidentiary decisions are reviewed under an abuse of discretion standard. He argues, however, that it is perfectly reasonable for appellate courts to give particular attention to those decisions that are outcome-determinative.

We have held that abuse of discretion is the proper standard of review of a district court's evidentiary rulings. Old Chief v. United States, 519 U.S. 172, 174 n. 1, 117 S.Ct. 644, 647 n. 1, 136 L.Ed.2d 574 (1997), United States v. Abel, 469 U.S. 45, 54, 105 S.Ct. 465, 470, 83 L.Ed.2d 450 (1984). Indeed, our cases on the subject go back as far as Spring Co. v. Edgar, 99 U.S. 645, 658, 25 L.Ed. 487 (1878) where we said that "cases arise where it is very much a matter of discretion with the court whether to receive or exclude the evidence; but the appellate court will not reverse in such a case, unless the ruling is manifestly erroneous." The Court of Appeals suggested that Daubert somehow altered this general rule in the context of a district court's decision to exclude scientific evidence. But Daubert did not address the standard of appellate review for evidentiary rulings at all. It did hold that the "austere" Frye standard of "general acceptance" had not been carried over into the Federal Rules of Evidence. But the opinion also said:

> That the Frye test was displaced by the Rules of Evidence does not mean, however, that the Rules themselves place no limits on the admissibility of purportedly scientific evidence. Nor is the trial judge disabled from screening such evidence. To the contrary, under the Rules the trial judge must ensure that any and all scientific testimony or evidence admitted is not only relevant, but reliable. 509 U.S., at 589, 113 S.Ct., at 2794–2795 (footnote omitted).

Thus, while the Federal Rules of Evidence allow district courts to admit a somewhat broader range of scientific testimony than would have been admissible under Frye, they leave in place the "gatekeeper" role of the trial judge in screening such evidence. A court of appeals applying "abuse of discretion" review to such rulings may not categorically distinguish between rulings allowing expert testimony and rulings which disallow it. Compare Beech Aircraft Corp. v. Rainey, 488 U.S. 153, 172, 109 S.Ct. 439, 451, 102 L.Ed.2d 445 (1988) (applying abuse of discretion review to a lower court's decision to exclude evidence) with United States v. Abel, supra, at 54, 105 S.Ct., at 470 (applying abuse of discretion review to a lower court's decision to admit evidence). We likewise reject respondent's argument that because the granting of summary judgment in this case was "outcome determinative," it should have been subjected to a more searching standard of review. On a motion for summary judgment, disputed issues of fact are resolved against the moving party—here, petitioners. But the question of admissibility of expert testimony is not such an issue of fact, and is reviewable under the abuse of discretion standard.

We hold that the Court of Appeals erred in its review of the exclusion of Joiner's experts' testimony. In applying an overly "stringent" review to that ruling, it failed to give the trial court the deference

SECTION 1 THE NATURE AND FUNCTION OF EXPERT EVIDENCE

that is the hallmark of abuse of discretion review. See, e.g., Koon v. United States, 518 U.S. 81, 97–100, 116 S.Ct. 2035, 2046–2047, 135 L.Ed.2d 392 (1996).

III

We believe that a proper application of the correct standard of review here indicates that the District Court did not abuse its discretion. Joiner's theory of liability was that his exposure to PCBs and their derivatives "promoted" his development of small cell lung cancer. In support of that theory he proffered the deposition testimony of expert witnesses. Dr. Arnold Schecter testified that he believed it "more likely than not that Mr. Joiner's lung cancer was causally linked to cigarette smoking and PCB exposure." App. at 107. Dr. Daniel Teitelbaum testified that Joiner's "lung cancer was caused by or contributed to in a significant degree by the materials with which he worked." Id. at 140.

Petitioners contended that the statements of Joiner's experts regarding causation were nothing more than speculation. Petitioners criticized the testimony of the experts in that it was "not supported by epidemiological studies ... [and was] based exclusively on isolated studies of laboratory animals." Joiner responded by claiming that his experts had identified "relevant animal studies which support their opinions." He also directed the court's attention to four epidemiological studies on which his experts had relied.

The District Court agreed with petitioners that the animal studies on which respondent's experts relied did not support his contention that exposure to PCBs had contributed to his cancer. The studies involved infant mice that had developed cancer after being exposed to PCBs. The infant mice in the studies had had massive doses of PCBs injected directly into their peritoneums or stomachs. Joiner was an adult human being whose alleged exposure to PCBs was far less than the exposure in the animal studies. The PCBs were injected into the mice in a highly concentrated form. The fluid with which Joiner had come into contact generally had a much smaller PCB concentration of between 0–500 parts per million. The cancer that these mice developed was alveologenic adenomas; Joiner had developed small-cell carcinomas. No study demonstrated that adult mice developed cancer after being exposed to PCBs. One of the experts admitted that no study had demonstrated that PCBs lead to cancer in any other species.

Respondent failed to reply to this criticism. Rather than explaining how and why the experts could have extrapolated their opinions from these seemingly far-removed animal studies, respondent chose "to proceed as if the only issue [was] whether animal studies can ever be a proper foundation for an expert's opinion." Joiner, 864 F.Supp., at 1324. Of course, whether animal studies can ever be a proper foundation for an expert's opinion was not the issue. The issue was whether these experts' opinions were sufficiently supported by the animal studies on which they purported to rely. The studies were so dissimilar to the facts presented in this litigation that it was not an abuse of discretion for the District Court to have rejected the experts' reliance on them.

The District Court also concluded that the four epidemiological studies on which respondent relied were not a sufficient basis for the experts' opinions. The first such study involved workers at an Italian capacitor plant who had been exposed to PCBs. Bertazzi, Riboldi, Pesatori, Radice, & Zocchetti, Cancer Mortality of Capacitor Manufacturing Workers, 11 American Journal of Industrial Medicine 165 (1987). The authors noted that lung cancer deaths among ex-employees at the plant were higher than might have been expected, but concluded that "there were apparently no grounds for associating lung cancer deaths (although increased above expectations) and exposure in the plant." Id. at 172. Given that Bertazzi et al. were unwilling to say that PCB exposure had caused cancer among the workers they examined, their study did not support the experts' conclusion that Joiner's exposure to PCBs caused his cancer.

The second study followed employees who had worked at Monsanto's PCB production plant. J. Zack & D. Munsch, Mortality of PCB Workers at the Monsanto Plant in Sauget, Illinois (Dec. 14, 1979) (unpublished report), 3 Rec., Doc. No. 11. The authors of this study found that the incidence of lung cancer deaths among these workers was somewhat higher than would ordinarily be expected. The increase, however, was not statistically significant and the authors of the study did not suggest a link between the increase in lung cancer deaths and the exposure to PCBs.

The third and fourth studies were likewise of no help. The third involved workers at a Norwegian cable manufacturing company who had been exposed to mineral oil. Ronneberg, Andersen, Skyberg, Mortality and Incidence of Cancer Among Oil–Exposed Workers in a Norwegian Cable Manufacturing Company, 45 British Journal of Industrial Medicine 595 (1988). A statistically significant increase in lung cancer deaths had been observed in these workers. The study, however, (1) made no mention of PCBs and (2) was expressly limited to the type of mineral oil involved in that study, and thus did not support these experts' opinions. The fourth and final study involved a PCB-exposed group in Japan that had seen a statistically significant increase in lung cancer deaths. Kuratsune, Nakamura, Ikeda, & Hirohata, Analysis of Deaths Seen Among Patients with Yusho—A Preliminary Report, 16 Chemosphere, Nos. 8/9, 2085 (1987). The subjects of this study, however, had been exposed to numerous potential carcinogens, including toxic rice oil that they had ingested.

Respondent points to Daubert's language that the "focus, of course, must be solely on principles and methodology, not on the conclusions that they generate." 509 U.S., at 595, 113 S.Ct., at 2797. He claims that because the District Court's disagreement was with the conclusion that the experts drew from the studies, the District Court committed legal error and was properly reversed by the Court of Appeals. But conclusions and methodology are not entirely distinct from one another. Trained experts commonly extrapolate from existing data. But nothing in either Daubert or the Federal Rules of Evidence requires a district court to admit opinion evidence which is connected to existing data only by the ipse dixit of the expert. A court may conclude that there is simply too great an analytical gap between the data and the opinion proffered. See Turpin v. Merrell Dow Pharmaceuticals, Inc., 959 F.2d 1349, 1360 (C.A.6), cert. denied, 506 U.S. 826, 113 S.Ct. 84, 121 L.Ed.2d 47 (1992). That is what the District Court did here, and we hold that it did not abuse its discretion in so doing.

We hold, therefore, that abuse of discretion is the proper standard by which to review a district court's decision to admit or exclude scientific evidence. We further hold that, because it was within the District Court's discretion to conclude that the studies upon which the experts relied were not sufficient, whether individually or in combination, to support their conclusions that Joiner's exposure to PCBs contributed to his cancer, the District Court did not abuse its discretion in excluding their testimony. These conclusions, however, do not dispose of this entire case.

Respondent's original contention was that his exposure to PCBs, furans, and dioxins contributed to his cancer. The District Court ruled that there was a genuine issue of material fact as to whether Joiner had been exposed to PCBs, but concluded that there was no genuine issue as to whether he had been exposed to furans and dioxins. The District Court accordingly never explicitly considered if there was admissible evidence on the question whether Joiner's alleged exposure to furans and dioxins contributed to his cancer. The Court of Appeals reversed the District Court's conclusion that there had been no exposure to furans and dioxins. Petitioners did not challenge this determination in their petition to this Court. Whether Joiner was exposed to furans and dioxins, and whether if there was such exposure, the opinions of Joiner's experts would then be admissible, remain open questions. We accordingly reverse the judgment of the Court of Appeals and remand this case for proceedings consistent with this opinion.

It is so ordered.

■ JUSTICE BREYER, concurring.

The Court's opinion, which I join, emphasizes Daubert's statement that a trial judge, acting as "gatekeeper," must " 'ensure that any and all scientific testimony or evidence admitted is not only relevant, but reliable.' " Ante, at 517 (quoting Daubert v. Merrell Dow Pharmaceuticals, Inc., 509 U.S. 579, 589, 113 S.Ct. 2786, 2795, 125 L.Ed.2d 469 (1993)). This requirement will sometimes ask judges to make subtle and sophisticated determinations about scientific methodology and its relation to the conclusions an expert witness seeks to offer—particularly when a case arises in an area where the science itself is tentative or uncertain, or where testimony about general risk levels in human beings or animals is offered to prove individual causation. Yet, as amici have pointed out, judges are not scientists and do not have the scientific training that can facilitate the making of such decisions. See, e.g., Brief for Trial Lawyers for Public Justice as Amicus Curiae 15; Brief for The New England Journal of Medicine et al. as Amici Curiae 2 ("Judges ... are generally not trained scientists").

Of course, neither the difficulty of the task nor any comparative lack of expertise can excuse the judge from exercising the "gatekeeper" duties that the Federal Rules impose—determining, for example, whether particular expert testimony is reliable and "will assist the trier of fact," Fed. Rule Evid. 702, or whether the "probative value" of testimony is substantially outweighed by risks of prejudice, confusion or waste of time. Fed. Rule Evid. 403. To the contrary, when law and science intersect, those duties often must be exercised with special care.

Today's toxic tort case provides an example. The plaintiff in today's case says that a chemical substance caused, or promoted, his lung cancer ... Yet modern life, including good health as well as economic well-being, depends upon the use of artificial or manufactured substances, such as chemicals. And it may, therefore, prove particularly important to see that judges fulfill their Daubert gatekeeping function, so that they help assure that the powerful engine of tort liability, which can generate strong financial incentives to reduce, or to eliminate, production, points towards the right substances and does not destroy the wrong ones. It is, thus, essential in this science-related area that the courts administer the Federal Rules of Evidence in order to achieve the "end[s]" that the Rules themselves set forth, not only so that proceedings may be "justly determined," but also so "that the truth may be ascertained." Fed. Rule Evid. 102.

I therefore want specially to note that, as cases presenting significant science-related issues have increased in number, see Judicial Conference of the United States, Report of the Federal Courts Study Committee 97 (Apr. 2, 1990) ("Economic, statistical, technological, and natural and social scientific data are becoming increasingly important in both routine and complex litigation"), judges have increasingly found in the Rules of Evidence and Civil Procedure ways to help them overcome the inherent difficulty of making determinations about complicated scientific or otherwise technical evidence. Among these techniques are an increased use of Rule 16's pretrial conference authority to narrow the scientific issues in dispute, pretrial hearings where potential experts are subject to examination by the court, and the appointment of special masters and specially trained law clerks. See J. Cecil & T. Willging, Court–Appointed Experts: Defining the Role of Experts Appointed Under Federal Rule of Evidence 706, pp. 83–88 (1993); J. Weinstein, Individual

Justice in Mass Tort Litigation 107–110 (1995); cf. Kaysen, In Memoriam: Charles E. Wyzanski, Jr., 100 Harv.L.Rev. 713, 713–715 (1987) (discussing a judge's use of an economist as a law clerk in United States v. United Shoe Machinery Corp., 110 F.Supp. 295 (D.Mass.1953), aff'd, 347 U.S. 521, 74 S.Ct. 699, 98 L.Ed. 910 (1954)).

In the present case, the New England Journal of Medicine has filed an amici brief "in support of neither petitioners nor respondents" in which the Journal writes:

> [A] judge could better fulfill this gatekeeper function if he or she had help from scientists. Judges should be strongly encouraged to make greater use of their inherent authority ... to appoint experts.... Reputable experts could be recommended to courts by established scientific organizations, such as the National Academy of Sciences or the American Association for the Advancement of Science.

Brief for The New England Journal of Medicine 18–19; cf. Fed. Rule Evid. 706 (court may "on its own motion or on the motion of any party" appoint an expert to serve on behalf of the court, and this expert may be selected as "agreed upon by the parties" or chosen by the court); see also Weinstein, supra, at 116 (a court should sometimes "go beyond the experts proffered by the parties" and "utilize its powers to appoint independent experts under Rule 706 of the Federal Rules of Evidence"). Given this kind of offer of cooperative effort, from the scientific to the legal community, and given the various Rules—authorized methods for facilitating the courts' task, it seems to me that Daubert's gatekeeping requirement will not prove inordinately difficult to implement; and that it will help secure the basic objectives of the Federal Rules of Evidence; which are, to repeat, the ascertainment of truth and the just determination of proceedings. Fed. Rule Evid. 102.

■ JUSTICE STEVENS, concurring in part and dissenting in part.

The question that we granted certiorari to decide is whether the Court of Appeals applied the correct standard of review. That question is fully answered in Parts I and II of the Court's opinion. Part III answers the quite different question whether the District Court properly held that the testimony of plaintiff's expert witnesses was inadmissible. Because I am not sure that the parties have adequately briefed that question, or that the Court has adequately explained why the Court of Appeals' disposition was erroneous, I do not join Part III. Moreover, because a proper answer to that question requires a study of the record that can be performed more efficiently by the Court of Appeals than by the nine members of this Court, I would remand the case to that court for application of the proper standard of review.

One aspect of the record will illustrate my concern. As the Court of Appeals pointed out, Joiner's experts relied on "the studies of at least thirteen different researchers, and referred to several reports of the World Health Organization that address the question of whether PCBs cause cancer." 78 F.3d 524, 533 (C.A.11 1996). Only one of those studies is in the record, and only six of them were discussed in the District Court opinion. Whether a fair appraisal of either the methodology or the conclusions of Joiner's experts can be made on the basis of such an incomplete record is a question that I do not feel prepared to answer.

It does seem clear, however, that the Court has not adequately explained why its holding is consistent with Federal Rule of Evidence 702, as interpreted in Daubert v. Merrell Dow Pharmaceuticals, Inc., 509 U.S. 579, 113 S.Ct. 2786, 125 L.Ed.2d 469 (1993). In general, scientific testimony that is both relevant and reliable must be admitted and testimony that is irrelevant or unreliable must be excluded. Id., at 597, 113 S.Ct., at 2798–2799. In this case, the District Court relied on both grounds for exclusion.

The relevance ruling was straightforward. The District Court correctly reasoned that an expert opinion that exposure to PCBs, "furans" and "dioxins" together may cause lung cancer would be irrelevant unless the plaintiff had been exposed to those substances. Having already found that there was no evidence of exposure to furans and dioxins, 864 F.Supp. 1310, 1318–1319 (N.D.Ga.1994), it necessarily followed that this expert opinion testimony was inadmissible. Correctly applying Daubert, the District Court explained that the experts' testimony "manifestly does not fit the facts of this case, and is therefore inadmissible." 864 F.Supp., at 1322. Of course, if the evidence raised a genuine issue of fact on the question of Joiner's exposure to furans and dioxins—as the Court of Appeals held that it did—then this basis for the ruling on admissibility was erroneous, but not because the district judge either abused her discretion or misapplied the law.

The reliability ruling was more complex and arguably is not faithful to the statement in Daubert that "[t]he focus, of course, must be solely on principles and methodology, not on the conclusions that they generate." 509 U.S., at 595, 113 S.Ct., at 2797–2798. Joiner's experts used a "weight of the evidence" methodology to assess whether Joiner's exposure to transformer fluids promoted his lung cancer.[1] They did not suggest that any one study provided adequate support for their conclusions, but instead relied on all the studies taken together (along with

1. Dr. Daniel Teitelbaum elaborated on that approach in his deposition testimony: "[A]s a toxicologist when I look at a study, I am going to require that that study meet the general criteria for methodology and statistical analysis, but that when all of that data is collected and you ask me as a patient, Doctor, have I got a risk of getting cancer from this?' That those studies don't answer the question, that I have to put them all together in my mind and look at them in relation to everything I know about the substance and everything I know about the exposure and come to a conclusion. I think when I say, 'To a reasonable medical probability as a medical toxicologist, this substance was a contributing cause,' . . . to his cancer, that that is a valid conclusion based on the totality of the evidence presented to me. And I think that that is an appropriate thing for a toxicologist to do, and it has been the basis of diagnosis for several hundred years, anyway." Supp.App. to Brief for Respondents 19. [The footnote is in the dissent and has been renumbered. Other footnotes to the opinions have been omitted.]

their interviews of Joiner and their review of his medical records). The District Court, however, examined the studies one by one and concluded that none was sufficient to show a link between PCBs and lung cancer. 864 F.Supp., at 1324–1326. The focus of the opinion was on the separate studies and the conclusions of the experts, not on the experts' methodology. Id., at 1322 ("Defendants ... persuade the court that Plaintiffs' expert testimony would not be admissible ... by attacking the conclusions that Plaintiffs' experts draw from the studies they cite").

Unlike the District Court, the Court of Appeals expressly decided that a "weight of the evidence" methodology was scientifically acceptable.... Petitioners' own experts used the same scientific approach as well. And using this methodology, it would seem that an expert could reasonably have concluded that the study of workers at an Italian capacitor plant, coupled with data from Monsanto's study and other studies, raises an inference that PCBs promote lung cancer.

The Court of Appeals' discussion of admissibility is faithful to the dictum in Daubert that the reliability inquiry must focus on methodology, not conclusions. Thus, even though I fully agree with both the District Court's and this Court's explanation of why each of the studies on which the experts relied was by itself unpersuasive, a critical question remains unanswered: when qualified experts have reached relevant conclusions on the basis of an acceptable methodology, why are their opinions inadmissible?

Daubert quite clearly forbids trial judges from assessing the validity or strength of an expert's scientific conclusions, which is a matter for the jury. Because I am persuaded that the difference between methodology and conclusions is just as categorical as the distinction between means and ends, I do not think the statement that "conclusions and methodology are not entirely distinct from one another," ante, at 519, is either accurate or helps us answer the difficult admissibility question presented by this record.

In any event, it bears emphasis that the Court has not held that it would have been an abuse of discretion to admit the expert testimony. The very point of today's holding is that the abuse of discretion standard of review applies whether the district judge has excluded or admitted evidence. Ante, at 517. And nothing in either Daubert or the Federal Rules of Evidence requires a district judge to reject an expert's conclusions and keep them from the jury when they fit the facts of the case and are based on reliable scientific methodology.

Kumho Tire Co., Ltd. v. Carmichael

Supreme Court of the United States, 1999.
526 U.S. 137, 119 S.Ct. 1167, 143 L.Ed.2d 238.

■ JUSTICE BREYER delivered the opinion of the Court.

In Daubert v. Merrell Dow Pharmaceuticals, Inc., 509 U.S. 579, 113 S.Ct. 2786, 125 L.Ed.2d 469 (1993), this Court focused upon the admissibility of scientific expert testimony. It pointed out that such testimony is admissible only if it is both relevant and reliable. And it held that the Federal Rules of Evidence "assign to the trial judge the task of ensuring that an expert's testimony both rests on a reliable foundation and is relevant to the task at hand." Id., at 597, 113 S.Ct. 2786. The Court also discussed certain more specific factors, such as testing, peer review, error rates, and "acceptability" in the relevant scientific community, some or all of which might prove helpful in determining the reliability of a particular scientific "theory or technique." Id., at 593–594, 113 S.Ct. 2786.

This case requires us to decide how Daubert applies to the testimony of engineers and other experts who are not scientists. We conclude that Daubert's general holding—setting forth the trial judge's general "gatekeeping" obligation—applies not only to testimony based on "scientific" knowledge, but also to testimony based on "technical" and "other specialized" knowledge. See Fed. Rule Evid. 702. We also conclude that a trial court may consider one or more of the more specific factors that Daubert mentioned when doing so will help determine that testimony's reliability. But, as the Court stated in Daubert, the test of reliability is "flexible," and Daubert's list of specific factors neither necessarily nor exclusively applies to all experts or in every case. Rather, the law grants a district court the same broad latitude when it decides how to determine reliability as it enjoys in respect to its ultimate reliability determination. See General Electric Co. v. Joiner, 522 U.S. 136, 143, 118 S.Ct. 512, 139 L.Ed.2d 508 (1997) (courts of appeals are to apply "abuse of discretion" standard when reviewing district court's reliability determination). Applying these standards, we determine that the District Court's decision in this case—not to admit certain expert testimony—was within its discretion and therefore lawful.

I

On July 6, 1993, the right rear tire of a minivan driven by Patrick Carmichael blew out. In the accident that followed, one of the passengers died, and others were severely injured. In October 1993, the Carmichaels brought this diversity suit against the tire's maker and its distributor, whom we refer to collectively as Kumho Tire, claiming that the tire was defective. The plaintiffs rested their case in significant part upon deposition testimony provided by an expert in tire failure analysis, Dennis Carlson, Jr., who intended to testify in support of their conclusion.

Carlson's depositions relied upon certain features of tire technology that are not in dispute. A steel-belted radial tire like the Carmichaels' is made up of a "carcass" containing many layers of flexible cords, called "plies," along which (between the cords and the outer tread) are laid steel strips called "belts." Steel wire loops, called "beads," hold the cords together at the plies' bottom edges. An outer layer, called the "tread," encases the carcass, and the entire tire is bound together in rubber, through the application of heat and various chemicals. See generally, e.g., J. Dixon, Tires, Suspension and Handling 68–72 (2d ed.1996). The bead of the tire sits upon a "bead seat," which is part of the wheel assembly. That assembly contains a "rim flange," which extends over the bead and rests against the side of the tire. See M. Mavrigian, Performance Wheels & Tires 81, 83 (1998) (illustrations).

Carlson's testimony also accepted certain background facts about the tire in question. He assumed that before the blowout the tire had traveled far. (The tire was made in 1988 and had been installed some time before the Carmichaels bought the used minivan in March 1993; the Carmichaels had driven the van approximately 7,000 additional miles in the two months they had owned it.) Carlson noted that the tire's tread depth, which was 11/32 of an inch when new, App. 242, had been worn down to depths that ranged from 3/32 of an inch along some parts of the tire, to nothing at all along others. Id., at 287. He conceded that the tire tread had at least two punctures which had been inadequately repaired. Id., at 258–261, 322.

Despite the tire's age and history, Carlson concluded that a defect in its manufacture or design caused the blow-out. He rested this conclusion in part upon three premises which, for present purposes, we must assume are not in dispute: First, a tire's carcass should stay bound to the inner side of the tread for a significant period of time after its tread depth has worn away. Id., at 208–209. Second, the tread of the tire at issue had separated from its inner steel-belted carcass prior to the accident. Id., at 336. Third, this "separation" caused the blowout. Ibid.

Carlson's conclusion that a defect caused the separation, however, rested upon certain other propositions, several of which the defendants strongly dispute. First, Carlson said that if a separation is not caused by a certain kind of tire misuse called "overdeflection" (which consists of underinflating the tire or causing it to carry too much weight, thereby generating heat that can undo the chemical tread/carcass bond), then, ordinarily, its cause is a tire defect. Id., at 193–195, 277–278. Second, he said that if a tire has been subject to sufficient overdeflection to cause a separation, it should reveal certain physical symptoms. These symptoms include (a) tread wear on the tire's shoulder that is greater than the tread wear along the tire's center, id., at 211; (b) signs of a "bead groove," where the beads have been pushed too hard against the bead seat on the inside of the tire's rim, id., at 196–197; (c) sidewalls of the tire with physical signs of deterioration, such as discoloration, id., at 212; and/or (d) marks on the tire's rim flange, id., at 219–220. Third, Carlson said that where he does not find at least two of the four physical signs just mentioned (and presumably where there is no reason to suspect a less common cause of separation), he concludes that a manufacturing or design defect caused the separation. Id., at 223–224.

Carlson added that he had inspected the tire in question. He conceded that the tire to a limited degree showed greater wear on the shoulder than in the center, some signs of "bead groove," some discoloration, a few marks on the rim flange, and inadequately filled puncture holes (which can also cause heat that might lead to separation). Id., at 256–257, 258–261, 277, 303–304, 308. But, in each instance, he testified that the symptoms were not significant, and he explained why he believed that they did not reveal overdeflection. For example, the extra shoulder wear, he said, appeared primarily on one shoulder, whereas an overdeflected tire would reveal equally abnormal wear on both shoulders. Id., at 277. Carlson concluded that the tire did not bear at least two of the four overdeflection symptoms, nor was there any less obvious cause of separation; and since neither overdeflection nor the punctures caused the blowout, a defect must have done so.

Kumho Tire moved the District Court to exclude Carlson's testimony on the ground that his methodology failed Rule 702's reliability requirement. The court agreed with Kumho that it should act as a Daubert-type reliability "gatekeeper," even though one might consider Carlson's testimony as "technical," rather than "scientific." See Carmichael v. Samyang Tires, Inc., 923 F.Supp. 1514, 1521–1522 (S.D.Ala. 1996). The court then examined Carlson's methodology in light of the reliability-related factors that Daubert mentioned, such as a theory's testability, whether it "has been a subject of peer review or publication," the "known or potential rate of error," and the "degree of acceptance ... within the relevant scientific community." 923 F.Supp., at 1520 (citing Daubert, 509 U.S., at 592–594, 113 S.Ct. 2786). The District Court found that all those factors argued against the reliability of Carlson's methods, and it granted the motion to exclude the testimony (as well as the defendants' accompanying motion for summary judgment).

The plaintiffs, arguing that the court's application of the Daubert factors was too "inflexible," asked for reconsideration. And the Court granted that motion. Carmichael v. Samyang Tires, Inc., 923 F.Supp. 1514 (S.D.Ala.1996), App. to Pet. for Cert. 1c. After reconsidering the matter, the court agreed with the plaintiffs that Daubert should be applied flexibly, that its four factors were simply illustrative, and that other factors could argue in favor of admissibility. It conceded that there may be widespread acceptance of a "visual-inspection method" for some relevant purposes. But the court found insufficient indications of the reliability of "the component of Carlson's tire failure analysis which most concerned the Court, namely, the methodology employed by the expert in analyzing the data obtained in the visual inspection, and the scientific basis, if any, for such an analysis." Id., at 6c.

It consequently affirmed its earlier order declaring Carlson's testimony inadmissable and granting the defendants' motion for summary judgment.

SECTION 1 THE NATURE AND FUNCTION OF EXPERT EVIDENCE

The Eleventh Circuit reversed. See Carmichael v. Samyang Tire, Inc., 131 F.3d 1433 (1997). It "review[ed] ... de novo" the "district court's legal decision to apply Daubert." Id., at 1435. It noted that "the Supreme Court in Daubert explicitly limited its holding to cover only the 'scientific context,'" adding that "a Daubert analysis" applies only where an expert relies "on the application of scientific principles," rather than "on skill- or experience-based observation." Id., at 1435–1436. It concluded that Carlson's testimony, which it viewed as relying on experience, "falls outside the scope of Daubert," that "the district court erred as a matter of law by applying Daubert in this case," and that the case must be remanded for further (non-Daubert-type) consideration under Rule 702. Id., at 1436.

Kumho Tire petitioned for certiorari, asking us to determine whether a trial court "may" consider Daubert's specific "factors" when determining the "admissibility of an engineering expert's testimony." Pet. for Cert. i. We granted certiorari in light of uncertainty among the lower courts about whether, or how, Daubert applies to expert testimony that might be characterized as based not upon "scientific" knowledge, but rather upon "technical" or "other specialized" knowledge. Fed. Rule Evid. 702; compare, e.g., Watkins v. Telsmith, Inc., 121 F.3d 984, 990–991 (C.A.5 1997), with, e.g., Compton v. Subaru of America, Inc., 82 F.3d 1513, 1518–1519 (C.A.10), cert. denied, 519 U.S. 1042, 117 S.Ct. 611, 136 L.Ed.2d 536 (1996).

II

A

In Daubert, this Court held that Federal Rule of Evidence 702 imposes a special obligation upon a trial judge to "ensure that any and all scientific testimony ... is not only relevant, but reliable." 509 U.S., at 589, 113 S.Ct. 2786. The initial question before us is whether this basic gatekeeping obligation applies only to "scientific" testimony or to all expert testimony. We, like the parties, believe that it applies to all expert testimony. See Brief for Petitioners 19; Brief for Respondents 17.

For one thing, Rule 702 itself says:

"If scientific, technical, or other specialized knowledge will assist the trier of fact to understand the evidence or to determine a fact in issue, a witness qualified as an expert by knowledge, skill, experience, training, or education, may testify thereto in the form of an opinion or otherwise."

This language makes no relevant distinction between "scientific" knowledge and "technical" or "other specialized" knowledge. It makes clear that any such knowledge might become the subject of expert testimony. In Daubert, the Court specified that it is the Rule's word "knowledge," not the words (like "scientific") that modify that word, that "establishes a standard of evidentiary reliability." 509 U.S., at 589–590, 113 S.Ct.

2786. Hence, as a matter of language, the Rule applies its reliability standard to all "scientific," "technical," or "other specialized" matters within its scope. We concede that the Court in Daubert referred only to "scientific" knowledge. But as the Court there said, it referred to "scientific" testimony "because that [wa]s the nature of the expertise" at issue. Id., at 590, n. 8, 113 S.Ct. 2786.

Neither is the evidentiary rationale that underlay the Court's basic Daubert "gatekeeping" determination limited to "scientific" knowledge. Daubert pointed out that Federal Rules 702 and 703 grant expert witnesses testimonial latitude unavailable to other witnesses on the "assumption that the expert's opinion will have a reliable basis in the knowledge and experience of his discipline." Id., at 592, 113 S.Ct. 2786 (pointing out that experts may testify to opinions, including those that are not based on firsthand knowledge or observation). The Rules grant that latitude to all experts, not just to "scientific" ones.

Finally, it would prove difficult, if not impossible, for judges to administer evidentiary rules under which a gatekeeping obligation depended upon a distinction between "scientific" knowledge and "technical" or "other specialized" knowledge. There is no clear line that divides the one from the others. Disciplines such as engineering rest upon scientific knowledge. Pure scientific theory itself may depend for its development upon observation and properly engineered machinery. And conceptual efforts to distinguish the two are unlikely to produce clear legal lines capable of application in particular cases. Cf. Brief for National Academy of Engineering as Amicus Curiae 9 (scientist seeks to understand nature while the engineer seeks nature's modification); Brief for Rubber Manufacturers Association as Amicus Curiae 14–16 (engineering, as an "applied science," relies on "scientific reasoning and methodology"); Brief for John Allen et al. as Amici Curiae 6 (engineering relies upon "scientific knowledge and methods").

Neither is there a convincing need to make such distinctions. Experts of all kinds tie observations to conclusions through the use of what Judge Learned Hand called "general truths derived from ... specialized experience." Hand, Historical and Practical Considerations Regarding Expert Testimony, 15 Harv. L.Rev. 40, 54 (1901). And whether the specific expert testimony focuses upon specialized observations, the specialized translation of those observations into theory, a specialized theory itself, or the application of such a theory in a particular case, the expert's testimony often will rest "upon an experience confessedly foreign in kind to [the jury's] own." Ibid. The trial judge's effort to assure that the specialized testimony is reliable and relevant can help the jury evaluate that foreign experience, whether the testimony reflects scientific, technical, or other specialized knowledge.

We conclude that Daubert's general principles apply to the expert matters described in Rule 702. The Rule, in respect to all such matters, "establishes a standard of evidentiary reliability." 509 U.S., at 590, 113

S.Ct. 2786. It "requires a valid ... connection to the pertinent inquiry as a precondition to admissibility." Id., at 592, 113 S.Ct. 2786. And where such testimony's factual basis, data, principles, methods, or their application are called sufficiently into question, see Part III, infra, the trial judge must determine whether the testimony has "a reliable basis in the knowledge and experience of [the relevant] discipline." 509 U.S., at 592, 113 S.Ct. 2786.

B

The petitioners ask more specifically whether a trial judge determining the "admissibility of an engineering expert's testimony" may consider several more specific factors that Daubert said might "bear on" a judge's gate-keeping determination. These factors include:

— Whether a "theory or technique ... can be (and has been) tested";

— Whether it "has been subjected to peer review and publication";

— Whether, in respect to a particular technique, there is a high "known or potential rate of error" and whether there are "standards controlling the technique's operation"; and

— Whether the theory or technique enjoys "general acceptance" within a "relevant scientific community." 509 U.S., at 592–594, 113 S.Ct. 2786.

Emphasizing the word "may" in the question, we answer that question yes.

Engineering testimony rests upon scientific foundations, the reliability of which will be at issue in some cases. See, e.g., Brief for Stephen Bobo et al. as Amici Curiae 23 (stressing the scientific bases of engineering disciplines). In other cases, the relevant reliability concerns may focus upon personal knowledge or experience. As the Solicitor General points out, there are many different kinds of experts, and many different kinds of expertise. See Brief for United States as Amicus Curiae 18–19, and n. 5 (citing cases involving experts in drug terms, handwriting analysis, criminal modus operandi, land valuation, agricultural practices, railroad procedures, attorney's fee valuation, and others). Our emphasis on the word "may" thus reflects Daubert's description of the Rule 702 inquiry as "a flexible one." 509 U.S., at 594, 113 S.Ct. 2786. Daubert makes clear that the factors it mentions do not constitute a "definitive checklist or test." Id., at 593, 113 S.Ct. 2786. And Daubert adds that the gatekeeping inquiry must be " 'tied to the facts' " of a particular "case." Id., at 591, 113 S.Ct. 2786 (quoting United States v. Downing, 753 F.2d 1224, 1242 (C.A.3 1985)). We agree with the Solicitor General that "[t]he factors identified in Daubert may or may not be pertinent in assessing reliability, depending on the nature of the issue, the expert's particular expertise, and the subject of his testimony." Brief for United States as Amicus Curiae 19. The conclusion, in our view, is that we can neither rule out, nor rule in, for all cases and for all time the applicability of the factors mentioned in Daubert, nor can we now do so for subsets of cases categorized by category of expert or by kind of evidence. Too much depends upon the particular circumstances of the particular case at issue.

Daubert itself is not to the contrary. It made clear that its list of factors was meant to be helpful, not definitive. Indeed, those factors do not all necessarily apply even in every instance in which the reliability of scientific testimony is challenged. It might not be surprising in a particular case, for example, that a claim made by a scientific witness has never been the subject of peer review, for the particular application at issue may never previously have interested any scientist. Nor, on the other hand, does the presence of Daubert's general acceptance factor help show that an expert's testimony is reliable where the discipline itself lacks reliability, as, for example, do theories grounded in any so-called generally accepted principles of astrology or necromancy.

At the same time, and contrary to the Court of Appeals' view, some of Daubert's questions can help to evaluate the reliability even of experience-based testimony. In certain cases, it will be appropriate for the trial judge to ask, for example, how often an engineering expert's experience-based methodology has produced erroneous results, or whether such a method is generally accepted in the relevant engineering community. Likewise, it will at times be useful to ask even of a witness whose expertise is based purely on experience, say, a perfume tester able to distinguish among 140 odors at a sniff, whether his preparation is of a kind that others in the field would recognize as acceptable.

We must therefore disagree with the Eleventh Circuit's holding that a trial judge may ask questions of the sort Daubert mentioned only where an expert "relies on the application of scientific principles," but not where an expert relies "on skill- or experience-based observation." 131 F.3d, at 1435. We do not believe that Rule 702 creates a schematism that segregates expertise by type while mapping certain kinds of questions to certain kinds of experts. Life and the legal cases that it generates are too complex to warrant so definitive a match.

To say this is not to deny the importance of Daubert's gatekeeping requirement. The objective of that requirement is to ensure the reliability and relevancy of expert testimony. It is to make certain that an expert, whether basing testimony upon professional studies or personal experience, employs in the courtroom the same level of intellectual rigor that characterizes the practice of an expert in the relevant field. Nor do we deny that, as stated in Daubert, the particular questions that it mentioned will often be appropriate for use in determining the reliability of challenged expert testimony. Rather, we conclude that the trial judge must have considerable leeway in deciding in a particular case how to go about determining whether particular expert testimony is reliable. That is to say, a trial court should consider the specific factors identified in

Daubert where they are reasonable measures of the reliability of expert testimony.

C

The trial court must have the same kind of latitude in deciding how to test an expert's reliability, and to decide whether or when special briefing or other proceedings are needed to investigate reliability, as it enjoys when it decides whether or not that expert's relevant testimony is reliable. Our opinion in Joiner makes clear that a court of appeals is to apply an abuse-of-discretion standard when it "review[s] a trial court's decision to admit or exclude expert testimony." 522 U.S., at 138–139, 118 S.Ct. 512. That standard applies as much to the trial court's decisions about how to determine reliability as to its ultimate conclusion. Otherwise, the trial judge would lack the discretionary authority needed both to avoid unnecessary "reliability" proceedings in ordinary cases where the reliability of an expert's methods is properly taken for granted, and to require appropriate proceedings in the less usual or more complex cases where cause for questioning the expert's reliability arises. Indeed, the Rules seek to avoid "unjustifiable expense and delay" as part of their search for "truth" and the "jus[t] determin[ation]" of proceedings. Fed. Rule Evid. 102. Thus, whether Daubert's specific factors are, or are not, reasonable measures of reliability in a particular case is a matter that the law grants the trial judge broad latitude to determine. See Joiner, supra, at 143, 118 S.Ct. 512. And the Eleventh Circuit erred insofar as it held to the contrary.

III

We further explain the way in which a trial judge "may" consider Daubert's factors by applying these considerations to the case at hand, a matter that has been briefed exhaustively by the parties and their 19 amici. The District Court did not doubt Carlson's qualifications, which included a masters degree in mechanical engineering, 10 years' work at Michelin America, Inc., and testimony as a tire failure consultant in other tort cases. Rather, it excluded the testimony because, despite those qualifications, it initially doubted, and then found unreliable, "the methodology employed by the expert in analyzing the data obtained in the visual inspection, and the scientific basis, if any, for such an analysis." Civ. Action No. 93–0860–CB–S (S.D.Ala., June 5, 1996), App. to Pet. for Cert. 6c. After examining the transcript in "some detail," 923 F.Supp., at 1518–519, n. 4, and after considering respondents' defense of Carlson's methodology, the District Court determined that Carlson's testimony was not reliable. It fell outside the range where experts might reasonably differ, and where the jury must decide among the conflicting views of different experts, even though the evidence is "shaky." Daubert, 509 U.S., at 596, 113 S.Ct. 2786. In our view, the doubts that triggered the District Court's initial inquiry here were reasonable, as was the court's ultimate conclusion.

CHAPTER 6 EXPERT EVIDENCE

For one thing, and contrary to respondents' suggestion, the specific issue before the court was not the reasonableness in general of a tire expert's use of a visual and tactile inspection to determine whether overdeflection had caused the tire's tread to separate from its steel-belted carcass. Rather, it was the reasonableness of using such an approach, along with Carlson's particular method of analyzing the data thereby obtained, to draw a conclusion regarding the particular matter to which the expert testimony was directly relevant. That matter concerned the likelihood that a defect in the tire at issue caused its tread to separate from its carcass. The tire in question, the expert conceded, had traveled far enough so that some of the tread had been worn bald; it should have been taken out of service; it had been repaired (inadequately) for punctures; and it bore some of the very marks that the expert said indicated, not a defect, but abuse through overdeflection. See supra, at 1172; App. 293–294. The relevant issue was whether the expert could reliably determine the cause of this tire's separation.

Nor was the basis for Carlson's conclusion simply the general theory that, in the absence of evidence of abuse, a defect will normally have caused a tire's separation. Rather, the expert employed a more specific theory to establish the existence (or absence) of such abuse. Carlson testified precisely that in the absence of at least two of four signs of abuse (proportionately greater tread wear on the shoulder; signs of grooves caused by the beads; discolored sidewalls; marks on the rim flange) he concludes that a defect caused the separation. And his analysis depended upon acceptance of a further implicit proposition, namely, that his visual and tactile inspection could determine that the tire before him had not been abused despite some evidence of the presence of the very signs for which he looked (and two punctures).

For another thing, the transcripts of Carlson's depositions support both the trial court's initial uncertainty and its final conclusion. Those transcripts cast considerable doubt upon the reliability of both the explicit theory (about the need for two signs of abuse) and the implicit proposition (about the significance of visual inspection in this case). Among other things, the expert could not say whether the tire had traveled more than 10, or 20, or 30, or 40, or 50 thousand miles, adding that 6,000 miles was "about how far" he could "say with any certainty." Id., at 265. The court could reasonably have wondered about the reliability of a method of visual and tactile inspection sufficiently precise to ascertain with some certainty the abuse-related significance of minute shoulder/center relative tread wear differences, but insufficiently precise to tell "with any certainty" from the tread wear whether a tire had traveled less than 10,000 or more than 50,000 miles. And these concerns might have been augmented by Carlson's repeated reliance on the "subjective[ness]" of his mode of analysis in response to questions seeking specific information regarding how he could differentiate between a tire that actually had been overdeflected and a tire that merely

SECTION 1 THE NATURE AND FUNCTION OF EXPERT EVIDENCE

looked as though it had been. Id., at 222, 224–225, 285–286. They would have been further augmented by the fact that Carlson said he had inspected the tire itself for the first time the morning of his first deposition, and then only for a few hours. (His initial conclusions were based on photographs.) Id., at 180.

Moreover, prior to his first deposition, Carlson had issued a signed report in which he concluded that the tire had "not been ... overloaded or underinflated," not because of the absence of "two of four" signs of abuse, but simply because "the rim flange impressions ... were normal." Id., at 335–336. That report also said that the "tread depth remaining was 3/32 inch," id., at 336, though the opposing expert's (apparently undisputed) measurements indicate that the tread depth taken at various positions around the tire actually ranged from .5/32 of an inch to 4/32 of an inch, with the tire apparently showing greater wear along both shoulders than along the center, id., at 432–433.

Further, in respect to one sign of abuse, bead grooving, the expert seemed to deny the sufficiency of his own simple visual-inspection methodology. He testified that most tires have some bead groove pattern, that where there is reason to suspect an abnormal bead groove he would ideally "look at a lot of [similar] tires" to know the grooving's significance, and that he had not looked at many tires similar to the one at issue. Id., at 212–213, 214, 217.

Finally, the court, after looking for a defense of Carlson's methodology as applied in these circumstances, found no convincing defense. Rather, it found (1) that "none" of the Daubert factors, including that of "general acceptance" in the relevant expert community, indicated that Carlson's testimony was reliable, 923 F.Supp., at 1521; (2) that its own analysis "revealed no countervailing factors operating in favor of admissibility which could outweigh those identified in Daubert," App. to Pet. for Cert. 4c; and (3) that the "parties identified no such factors in their briefs," ibid. For these three reasons taken together, it concluded that Carlson's testimony was unreliable.

Respondents now argue to us, as they did to the District Court, that a method of tire failure analysis that employs a visual/tactile inspection is a reliable method, and they point both to its use by other experts and to Carlson's long experience working for Michelin as sufficient indication that that is so. But no one denies that an expert might draw a conclusion from a set of observations based on extensive and specialized experience. Nor does anyone deny that, as a general matter, tire abuse may often be identified by qualified experts through visual or tactile inspection of the tire. See Affidavit of H.R. Baumgardner 1–2, cited in Brief for National Academy of Forensic Engineers as Amici Curiae 16 (Tire engineers rely on visual examination and process of elimination to analyze experimental test tires). As we said before, supra, at 1977, the question before the trial court was specific, not general. The trial court had to decide whether this particular expert had sufficient specialized knowledge to assist the jurors "in deciding the particular issues in the case." 4 J. McLaughlin, Weinstein's Federal Evidence ¶ 702.05[1], p. 702–33 (2d ed.1998); see also Advisory Committee's Note on Proposed Fed. Rule Evid. 702, Preliminary Draft of Proposed Amendments to the Federal Rules of Civil Procedure and Evidence: Request for Comment 126 (1998) (stressing that district courts must "scrutinize" whether the "principles and methods" employed by an expert "have been properly applied to the facts of the case").

The particular issue in this case concerned the use of Carlson's two-factor test and his related use of visual/tactile inspection to draw conclusions on the basis of what seemed small observational differences. We have found no indication in the record that other experts in the industry use Carlson's two-factor test or that tire experts such as Carlson normally make the very fine distinctions about, say, the symmetry of comparatively greater shoulder tread wear that were necessary, on Carlson's own theory, to support his conclusions. Nor, despite the prevalence of tire testing, does anyone refer to any articles or papers that validate Carlson's approach. Compare Bobo, Tire Flaws and Separations, in Mechanics of Pneumatic Tires 636–637 (S. Clark ed.1981); C. Schnuth et al., Compression Grooving and Rim Flange Abrasion as Indicators of Over–Deflected Operating Conditions in Tires, presented to Rubber Division of the American Chemical Society, Oct. 21–24, 1997; J. Walter & R. Kiminecz, Bead Contact Pressure Measurements at the Tire–Rim Interface, presented to Society of Automotive Engineers, Feb. 24–28, 1975. Indeed, no one has argued that Carlson himself, were he still working for Michelin, would have concluded in a report to his employer that a similar tire was similarly defective on grounds identical to those upon which he rested his conclusion here. Of course, Carlson himself claimed that his method was accurate, but, as we pointed out in Joiner, "nothing in either Daubert or the Federal Rules of Evidence requires a district court to admit opinion evidence that is connected to existing data only by the ipse dixit of the expert." 522 U.S., at 146, 118 S.Ct. 512.

Respondents additionally argue that the District Court too rigidly applied Daubert's criteria. They read its opinion to hold that a failure to satisfy any one of those criteria automatically renders expert testimony inadmissible. The District Court's initial opinion might have been vulnerable to a form of this argument. There, the court, after rejecting respondents' claim that Carlson's testimony was "exempted from Daubert-style scrutiny" because it was "technical analysis" rather than "scientific evidence," simply added that "none of the four admissibility criteria outlined by the Daubert court are satisfied." 923 F.Supp., at 1522. Subsequently, however, the court granted respondents' motion for reconsideration. It then explicitly recognized that the relevant reliability inquiry "should be 'flexible,'" that its "'overarching subject [should be] ... validity' and reliability," and that "Daubert was intended neither to be exhaustive nor to apply in every case." App. to Pet. for Cert. 4c (quoting Daubert, 509 U.S., at 594–595, 113 S.Ct. 2786). And the court ultimately based its decision upon Carlson's failure to satisfy either Daubert's factors or any other set of reasonable reliability criteria. In light of the record as developed by the parties, that conclusion was within the District Court's lawful discretion.

In sum, Rule 702 grants the district judge the discretionary authority, reviewable for its abuse, to determine reliability in light of the particular facts and circumstances of the particular case. The District Court did not abuse its discretionary authority in this case. Hence, the judgment of the Court of Appeals is

Reversed.

■ JUSTICE SCALIA, with whom JUSTICE O'CONNOR and JUSTICE THOMAS join, concurring.

I join the opinion of the Court, which makes clear that the discretion it endorses—trial-court discretion in choosing the manner of testing expert reliability—is not discretion to abandon the gatekeeping function. I think it worth adding that it is not discretion to perform the function inadequately. Rather, it is discretion to choose among reasonable means of excluding expertise that is fausse and science that is junky. Though, as the Court makes clear today, the Daubert factors are not holy writ, in a particular case the failure to apply one or another of them may be unreasonable, and hence an abuse of discretion.

■ JUSTICE STEVENS, concurring in part and dissenting in part.

The only question that we granted certiorari to decide is whether a trial judge "[m]ay . . . consider the four factors set out by this Court in Daubert v. Merrell Dow Pharmaceuticals, Inc., 509 U.S. 579, 113 S.Ct. 2786, 125 L.Ed.2d 469 (1993), in a Rule 702 analysis of admissibility of an engineering expert's testimony." Pet. for Cert. i. That question is fully and correctly answered in Parts I and II of the Court's opinion, which I join.

Part III answers the quite different question whether the trial judge abused his discretion when he excluded the testimony of Dennis Carlson. Because a proper answer to that question requires a study of the record that can be performed more efficiently by the Court of Appeals than by the nine Members of this Court, I would remand the case to the Eleventh Circuit to perform that task. . . .

Page 980. Add new case on Expert Testimony:

Primiano v. Yan Cook

United States Court of Appeals, Ninth Circuit, 2010.
598 F. 3d 558 (2010).

■ KLEINFELD, CIRCUIT JUDGE:

We address admissibility under *Daubert* of medical testimony.

CHAPTER 6 EXPERT EVIDENCE

. . .

Marylou Primiano has suffered a miserable ordeal since she had elbow surgery. The question raised by her litigation is whether her ordeal resulted from a defective product, the artificial elbow Howmedica Osteonics Corporation manufactured. The district court granted summary judgment against her and dismissed her case, but that result could not have occurred had her medical expert's testimony been considered. His testimony would have established a genuine issue of material fact, because he thought the plastic bearing between the metal parts of the artificial elbow wore out so quickly that it must have been defective. The district court ruled that his testimony was inadmissible, leaving Primiano with inadequate evidence to establish a genuine issue of fact. The question before us is whether excluding Primiano's expert's testimony was an abuse of discretion.

. . .

Primiano's expert witness, Arnold–Peter Weiss, M.D., declared that the polyethylene bushing had worn through in less than eight months, "not a usual or expected circumstance." Though finite, the typical lifespan of elbow prostheses "far exceeds" how long this one lasted. Dr. Weiss testified in his deposition that although wear starts immediately, elbow prostheses last as long as ten or fifteen years, even twenty, and the earliest he had seen them wear out was around five to eight years, varying with the patient's activity level. Though misalignment could cause excessive wear, he had looked at the x-rays and found no significant misalignment. Nor would ordinary daily activity produce such extraordinarily rapid wear. Nor could he find technically inappropriate use of the prosthesis by Dr. Tait. His opinion was that the extraordinarily rapid wear was caused by abrasive wear and generation of debris from movement of the titanium against the polyethylene. And he concluded that the prosthesis failed to perform in a manner reasonably to be expected by a surgeon using it, because it failed too early.

The district court granted defendants' motion to exclude Dr. Weiss's testimony as not meeting the *Daubert* standard and granted summary judgment. The court concluded that Dr. Weiss's testimony would not be helpful to the jury. The judge reasoned: "Well, I mean it's like res ipsa loquitur, the elbow failed. Now, why did it fail? Maybe it was malpractice, maybe it was Dr. Tait." The evidence of rapid wear "doesn't make it defective." "I think [Dr. Weiss's] opinion is weakened by the fact that he didn't see the plaintiff. He didn't examine her. He didn't talk to her." "[T]here's no peer review … no publication … there's got to be an objective source that he relies on." The court rejected plaintiff's argument, that testimony that the premature failure was not attributable to overuse, medical malpractice, "her physiology," or other factors external to the device, would assist the jury.

. . .

Federal Rule of Evidence 702 controlled admissibility of Dr. Weiss's opinion. That rule establishes several requirements for admissibility: (1) the evidence has to "assist the trier of fact" either "to understand the evidence" or "to determine a fact in issue"; (2) the witness has to be sufficiently qualified to render the opinion:

. . .

Testimony by physicians may or may not be scientific evidence like the epidemiologic testimony at issue in *Daubert*. The classic medical school texts, *Cecil* and *Harrison,* explain that medicine is scientific, but not entirely a science. "[M]edicine is not a science but a learned profession, deeply rooted in a number of sciences and charged with the obligation to apply them for man's benefit." "Evidence-based medicine" is "the conscientious, explicit and judicious use of current best evidence in making decisions about the care of individual patients." "Despite the importance of evidence-based medicine, much of medical decision-making relies on judgment—a process that is difficult to quantify or even to assess qualitatively. Especially when a relevant experience base is unavailable, physicians must use their knowledge and experience as a basis for weighing known factors along with the inevitable uncertainties" to "mak[e] a sound judgment."

. . .

When considering the applicability of *Daubert* criteria to the particular case before the court, the inquiry must be flexible. Peer reviewed scientific literature may be unavailable because the issue may be too particular, new, or of insufficiently broad interest, to be in the literature. Lack of certainty is not, for a qualified expert, the same thing as guesswork. "Expert opinion testimony is relevant if the knowledge underlying it has a valid connection to the pertinent inquiry. And it is reliable if the knowledge underlying it has a reliable basis in the knowledge and experience of the relevant discipline." "[T]he factors identified in *Daubert* may or may not be pertinent in assessing reliability, depending on the nature of the issue, the expert's particular expertise, and the subject of his testimony." Reliable expert testimony need only be relevant, and need not establish every element that the plaintiff must prove, in order to be admissible.

We have some guidance in the cases for applying *Daubert* to physicians' testimony. "A trial court should admit medical expert testimony if physicians would accept it as useful and reliable," but it need not be conclusive because "medical knowledge is often uncertain." "The human body is complex, etiology is often uncertain, and ethical concerns often prevent double-blind studies calculated to establish statistical proof."

CHAPTER 6 EXPERT EVIDENCE

Where the foundation is sufficient, the litigant is "entitled to have the jury decide upon[the experts'] credibility, rather than the judge." We held in *United States v. Smith* that even a physician's assistant was qualified based on experience to offer his opinion.

Other circuits have taken similar approaches focusing especially on experience. The Sixth Circuit held that a district court abused its discretion by excluding a physician's testimony based on extensive, relevant experience even though he had not cited medical literature supporting his view. Likewise the Third Circuit pointed out that a doctor's experience might be good reason to admit his testimony. Thus under our precedents and those of other circuits, the district court in this case was pushing against the current, but that alone does not imply an abuse of discretion.

A close look at the foundation for Dr. Weiss's opinion, the nature of medical opinion, and the question posed by Nevada law does. Dr. Weiss is a board certified orthopedic surgeon and a professor at Brown University School of Medicine in the Division of Hand, Upper Extremity and Microvascular Surgery, department of Orthopedics. He has published over a hundred articles in peer-reviewed medical journals including several specifically on the elbow and at least one somewhat related to this case, "Capitellocondylar Total Elbow Replacement: A Long–Term Follow-up Study." He has years of experience implanting various elbow prostheses and has performed five to ten revisions of total elbow replacements that had been performed by other physicians. He has examined the various types of prosthetics available, and has maintained familiarity with the peer-reviewed literature. He testified that the very short lifespan of Ms. Primiano's artificial elbow is "outside of my review of the known literature." ...

A court would have to find that Dr. Weiss is "qualified as an expert by knowledge, skill, experience, training, or education" to render an opinion on elbow replacements. The district court appears to have rejected the opinion based in part on two elements of Rule 702, whether his opinion would assist the trier of fact, and whether it was based upon sufficient facts or data.

The district court thought Dr. Weiss's opinion would not assist the jury because Dr. Weiss could not say why the plastic part of the artificial elbow failed so quickly. The "will assist" requirement, under *Daubert*, "goes primarily to relevance." What is relevant depends on what must be proved, and that is controlled by Nevada law. Nevada law establishes that "those products are defective which are dangerous because they fail to perform in the manner reasonably to be expected in light of their nature and intended function." In Nevada, a plaintiff need not "produce direct evidence of a specific product defect [or] negate any alternative causes of the accident." An "unexpected, dangerous malfunction" suffices. Since Dr. Weiss, with a sufficient basis in education and experience, testified that the artificial joint "fail[ed] to perform in the manner reasonably to be expected in light of [its] nature and intended function," that was enough to assist the trier of fact. He did not have to know why it failed.

. . .

Reversed.[1]

SECTION 2. THE BASIS OF EXPERT TESTIMONY

Page 1053:

It would appear from United States v. Smith, 566 F.3d 410 (4th Cir. 2009), cert. denied, 130 S.Ct. 1100 (2010), that an expert when testifying is exempt from both the hearsay rule and the best evidence rule.

Page 1060, following Note 3:

United States v. Mejia

United States Court of Appeals for the Second Circuit.
545 F.3d 179 (2d Cir. 2008).

■ HALL, CIRCUIT JUDGE:

Appeal from judgment of conviction entered in the United States District Court for the Eastern District of New York (Wexler, J.) for conspiracy to commit assaults with a dangerous weapon in aid of racketeering activity, 18 U.S.C. § 1959(a)(6), three counts of assault with a dangerous weapon in aid of racketeering activity, id. § 1959(a)(3), and three counts of discharge of a firearm during a crime of violence, id. § 924(c)(1). We vacate the judgment after finding that the admission of expert witness Hector Alicea's testimony violated the Federal Rules of Evidence and the Sixth Amendment Confrontation Clause, and that the error was not harmless. We remand for retrial.

. . .

On June 18, 2003, Ledwin Castro and David Vasquez (collectively, "Appellants"), along with several others, participated in two drive-by shootings on Long Island, New York. At the time, Appellants were members of the MS–13 gang. MS–13 is a nationwide criminal gang organized into local subunits known as "cliques." At the time, to become a full member of MS–13, an individual was required to "make his quota," which meant to engage in acts of violence against members of rival gangs, such as the SWP and the Bloods. MS–13 had local cliques on Long Island, and Castro[1] was the leader of the "Freeport clique (the Freeport Locos Salvatruchas," or "FLS").

. . .

1. [Many footnotes omitted.]   1. [Some footnotes omitted.]

CHAPTER 6   EXPERT EVIDENCE

In February 2004, a federal grand jury indicted Vasquez, Castro, and twelve others for various offenses stemming from a series of violent incidents on Long Island between August 2000 and September 13, 2003. A superseding indictment ("the Indictment") was returned on June 23, 2005. The Indictment described MS–13, or "La Mara Salvatrucha," as a gang that originated in El Salvador but had members throughout the United States. It accused all of the defendants of being members of MS–13, and it alleged that MS–13 members "engaged in criminal" activity in order to increase their position within the organization. According to the Indictment, MS–13 constituted an enterprise under 18 U.S.C. § 1959(b)(2) because it was an ongoing organization the activities of which affected interstate commerce. The Indictment furthermore stated that MS–13 engaged in two forms of racketeering activity under 18 U.S.C. § 1961(1): (1) acts and threats involving murder as defined by New York State law, and (2) narcotics trafficking as defined by federal law.

. . .

... During the course of the trial, which took place between July 19 and July 26, 2005, the Government called Hector Alicea, an officer with the New York State Police, as an expert witness....

... Alicea testified about MS–13's history and structure, and he also explained MS–13's activities on Long Island. Because the nature of Alicea's testimony is an important and disputed issue on appeal, the subjects about which he testified are discussed further in our analysis of Appellants' challenge to the admission of his testimony.

. . .

On July 26, 2005, the jury found Appellants guilty on all ten counts. In a special verdict, the jury further found that MS–13 was an enterprise that affected interstate commerce; that MS–13 engaged in acts and threats of murder; that Appellants were members of the MS–13 enterprise; and that Appellants had participated in the conspiracy to assault and in the charged assaults in order to maintain or increase their positions within MS–13....

. . .

On appeal, Appellants challenge their convictions and sentences on multiple grounds. With one exception, Appellants bring these challenges jointly. They devote the bulk of their argument to their claim that the district court erred in allowing the Government to call Alicea as an expert witness and to their further claim that Alicea's testimony violated the Federal Rules of Evidence and *Crawford v. Washington,* 541 U.S. 36, 124 S.Ct. 1354, 158 L.Ed.2d 177 (2004)....

. . .

SECTION 2 The Basis of Expert Testimony

The Government called Hector Alicea, an investigator with the New York State Police, to testify regarding MS–13's "enterprise structure and the derivation, background and migration of the MS–13 organization, its history and conflicts," as well as MS–13's "hierarchy, cliques, methods and activities, modes of communication and slang." Alicea had been an officer of the New York State Police for eighteen years, and he had been an investigator since 1992. In June 2000, five years before the trial, Alicea had been assigned to the FBI Long Island Gang Task Force. He was also the Chair of the Intelligence Committee of the East Coast Gang Investigators Association.

Prior to trial, Appellants objected to the Government's stated plan to call Alicea on the ground that Alicea would rely on "impermissible hearsay" to reach his conclusions. The accompanying memorandum of law cited to this Court's opinion in *United States v. Dukagjini*, 326 F.3d 45 (2d Cir.2003). The parties argued the motion before the district court, and the district court reserved its decision. Defense counsel continued to press the issue at trial, and Vasquez's attorney was permitted to conduct a voir dire examination of Alicea prior to direct examination by the Government. In response to defense counsel's questioning, Alicea stated that he had participated in somewhere between fifteen and fifty custodial interrogations of MS–13 members. When asked whether he could distinguish between information he had learned during custodial interrogations and information he had learned elsewhere, Alicea responded that his knowledge was based on a "combination of both." At the conclusion of the voir dire, defense counsel again argued that Alicea was not qualified as an expert and that his testimony would introduce testimonial evidence in violation of *Crawford*. See 541 U.S. 36, 124 S.Ct. 1354, 158 L.Ed.2d 177. The district court then denied the motion.

Much of Alicea's testimony concerned MS–13's background. He testified about MS–13's history, its presence on Long Island, and its national and international presence; about the gang's colors, hand signs, graffiti use, naming practices, and tattoos; and about its local subunit structure, leadership structure, division of responsibilities, and membership rules. In addition, Alicea testified to more specific details about MS–13's operations. He stated that when MS–13 members fled from prosecution or needed to travel for "gang business reasons," such as "to transport narcotics," "to transport weapons," or "to commit crimes in other areas," they traveled "on a Greyhound bus" or by car. . . .

With respect to MS–13's activities on Long Island, Alicea testified that since he had joined the Task Force in June 2000, the Task Force had seized "[p]robably between 15 and 25" firearms from MS–13 members. He further testified that Task Force members had seized ammunition, manufactured outside of New York State, from MS–13 members on Long Island. Moving on to MS–13's narcotics-related operations, Alicea told the jury that MS–13 members on Long Island had been arrested for dealing narcotics, primarily cocaine, and that the gang also occasionally dealt marijuana. Alicea also stated that MS–13 "tax[ed]" non-gang drug dealers who wished to deal drugs in bars controlled by MS–13. Most importantly, Alicea attested that MS–13 had committed "between 18 and 22, 23" murders on Long Island between June 2000 and the trial.

On cross-examination, defense counsel probed the sources of Alicea's information. Because of the importance of Alicea's answers, we quote from his testimony at length:

Q. .... I thought you mentioned FLS ... funded itself at the beginning from the sale of marijuana?

A. No. I was referring to the MS–13 gang as a whole.

Q. *Is it fair to say that somebody told you that?*

A. *I had read that from some of the articles that I had researched.*

Q. *Newspaper articles?*

A. *Reports from other law enforcement personnel.*

...

Q. You also told us that MS members ... put a tax on narcotics sales in certain bars; is that correct?

...

A. *I was told that by a gang member, yes.*[2]

In other words, Alicea learned about the drug tax from an MS–13 member in custody during the course of this very investigation. The interrogation took place at the U.S. Attorney's Office. The record does not reflect whether the Assistant United States Attorney in charge of this case was present.

. . .

Under Federal Rule of Evidence 702, in those situations where "scientific, technical, or other specialized knowledge will assist the trier of fact to understand the evidence or to determine a fact in issue," testimony by "a witness qualified as an expert by knowledge, skill, experience, training, or education" is permissible so long as "(1) the testimony is based upon sufficient facts or data, (2) the testimony is the product of reliable principles and methods, and (3) the witness has applied the principles and methods reliably to the facts of the case." Fed.R.Evid. 702. The broad phrasing of the description "scientific, tech-

---

2. After initially characterizing how he learned about the drug tax as a casual conversation with an MS–13 member, Alicea later clarified that he learned about the drug tax during a custodial interrogation of an MS–13 member. Upon further questioning, Alicea stated that this "conversation" had taken place "at the United States Attorney's Office." The MS–13 member with whom Alicea had been "conversing" had been indicted and had not been released on bail, and he had been escorted to the "conversation" by "the U.S. marshals." When asked why that MS–13 member had been arrested, Alicea answered that the individual was "[p]art of this investigation as well, yes."

SECTION 2 The Basis of Expert Testimony

nical, or other specialized knowledge" brings within the scope of the Rule both "experts in the strict sense of the word," such as scientists, and "the large group sometimes called 'skilled' witnesses, such as bankers or landowners testifying to land values." *Id.* advisory committee's note. On the question of when expert testimony is appropriate, the Advisory Committee Notes refer to the traditional common law rule that expert testimony is called for when the "untrained layman" would be unable intelligently to determine "the particular issue" in the absence of guidance from an expert. *Id.* advisory committee's note (quoting Mason Ladd, *Expert Testimony,* 5 Vand. L.Rev. 414, 418 (1952)) (internal quotation marks omitted).

In the 1980s, a new type of "skilled witness" began emerging: the law enforcement officer. In criminal cases, the Government began calling law enforcement officers to testify as experts on what we referred to as "the nature and structure of organized crime families." *United States v. Daly,* 842 F.2d 1380, 1388 (2d Cir.1988). This Court first reviewed a challenge to the use of such an expert in *United States v. Ardito,* 782 F.2d 358 (2d Cir.1986). The Government had called an FBI agent to testify as an expert about terms such as "captain," "capo," "regime," and "crew." *Id.* at 363. We upheld the admission of that expert testimony because it "aided the jury in its understanding of" recorded conversations between the two defendants. *Id.* Furthermore, we noted, the district court had reminded the jury that the defendants there had not been charged with any conduct relating to organized crime. *Id.*

One year later, we upheld the admission of expert testimony by a law enforcement officer on the related matter of the meaning of messages written in code. *United States v. Levasseur,* 816 F.2d 37, 45 (2d Cir.1987). Upholding such testimony was consistent with pre-*Ardito* cases where we and other Circuits had allowed law enforcement officers to testify as experts about the meaning of jargon relating to narcotics trafficking....

In subsequent years, we have encountered novel uses of these "officer experts" and approved of their testifying on a broader range of issues. For example, in *United States v. Daly,* 842 F.2d 1380 (2d Cir.1988), where the defendants were charged with "various crimes arising out of activities of the Gambino crime family," we upheld the expert testimony of an FBI agent who "identified the five organized crime families that operate in the New York area" and "described their requirements for membership, their rules of conduct and code of silence, and the meaning of certain jargon." *Id.* at 1383, 1388. After the Government had played surveillance tapes for the jury, the agent interpreted the jargon the speakers had used. *Id.* at 1384. This Court upheld the district court's decision to admit the agent's testimony, finding that the agent had testified about "much that was outside the expectable realm of knowledge of the average juror." *Id.* at 1388. The district court's judgment that the agent's testimony would be helpful to the juror "was not unreasonable." *Id.* Finally, the agent had not testified about the defendants or any of the charged offenses. *Id.* The only offense element to which the agent had testified "was the existence of a RICO enterprise, as he gave his understanding of the existence of organized crime and the Gambino family." *Id.*

Since *Daly,* we have repeatedly upheld the admission of similar testimony. *See, e.g., United States v. Locascio,* 6 F.3d 924, 936 (2d Cir.1993) (upholding an FBI agent's expert testimony about the internal operating rules of organized crime families, the meaning of recorded conversations, and the identification of members of the Gambino crime family); *United States v. Feliciano,* 223 F.3d 102, 109 (2d Cir. 2000) (upholding an FBI agent's expert testimony about "the structure, leadership, practices, terminology, and operations of [a street gang, Los Solidos]"); *United States v. Matera,* 489 F.3d 115, 121 (2d Cir.2007) (upholding the admission of an officer's expert testimony "about the composition and structure of New York organized crime families" and observing that the district court had limited the expert's testimony to general information rather than information about the defendants themselves). Our decision to permit such expert testimony reflects our understanding that, just as an anthropologist might be equipped by education and fieldwork to testify to the cultural mores of a particular social group, *see Dang Vang v. Toyed,* 944 F.2d 476, 481–82 (9th Cir.1991) (upholding the district court's admission of expert testimony on Hmong culture), law enforcement officers may be equipped by experience and training to speak to the operation, symbols, jargon, and internal structure of criminal organizations. Officers interact with members of the organization, study its operations, and exchange information with other officers. As a result, they are able to break through the group's antipathy toward outsiders and gain valuable knowledge about its parochial practices and insular lexicon. Allowing law enforcement officers to act as experts in cases involving these oft-impenetrable criminal organizations thus responds to the same concerns that animated the enactment of the criminal laws that such organizations (and their members) are typically charged with violating, such as the Racketeer Influenced and Corrupt Organizations Act, 18 U.S.C. §§ 1961–68, and the more recent Violent Crimes in Aid of Racketeering Act, *id.* § 1959. *See* Organized Crime Control Act of 1970, Pub.L. 91–452 pmbl., 84 Stat. 922, 923 (1970) ("[O]rganized crime continues to grow because of defects in the evidence-gathering process of the law inhibiting the development of the legally admissible evidence necessary to bring criminal ... sanctions ... to bear on the unlawful activities of those engaged in organized crime....").

Yet despite the utility of, and need for, expertise of this sort, its use must be limited to those issues where sociological knowledge is appropriate. An increasingly thinning line separates the legitimate use of an officer expert to translate esoteric terminology or to explicate an organization's hierarchical structure from the illegitimate and impermissible substitution of expert opinion for factual evidence. If the officer expert strays beyond the bounds of appropriately "expert" matters, that officer becomes, rather than a sociologist describing the inner workings of a closed community, a chronicler of the recent past whose pronouncements on elements of the charged offense serve as shortcuts to proving guilt. As the officer's purported expertise narrows from "organized crime" to "this particular gang," from the meaning of "capo" to the criminality of the defendant, the officer's testimony becomes more central to the case, more corroborative of the fact witnesses, and thus more like a summary of the facts than an aide in understanding them. The officer expert transforms into the hub of the case, displacing the jury by connecting and combining all other testimony and physical evidence into a coherent, discernible, internally consistent picture of the defendant's guilt.

In such instances, it is a little too convenient that the Government has found an individual who is expert on precisely those facts that the Government must prove to secure a guilty verdict—even more so when that expert happens to be one of the Government's own investigators. Any effective law enforcement agency will necessarily develop expertise on the criminal organizations it investigates, but the primary value of that expertise is in facilitating the agency's gathering of evidence, identification of targets for prosecution, and proving guilt at the subsequent trial. When the Government skips the intermediate steps and proceeds directly from internal expertise to trial, and when those officer experts come to court and simply disgorge their factual knowledge to the jury, the experts are no longer aiding the jury in its factfinding; they are instructing the jury on the existence of the facts needed to satisfy the elements of the charged offense. *See United States v. Nersesian,* 824 F.2d 1294, 1308 (2d Cir.1987) ("In the past, we have upheld the admission of expert testimony to explain the use of narcotics codes and jargon.... We acknowledge some degree of discomfiture [when] this practice is employed, since, uncontrolled, such use of expert testimony may have the effect of providing the government with an additional summation by having the expert interpret the evidence."). It is as though the law enforcement agency in question is a standing master for the criminal court, and the officer expert its representative charged with reporting that master's findings of fact. Not only are masters a creature of civil rather than criminal courts, *see* Amalia D. Kessler, *Our Inquisitorial Tradition: Equity Procedure, Due Process, and the Search for an Alternative to the Adversarial,* 90 Cornell L.Rev. 1181, 1200, 1204 (2005) (describing the advent of masters in fifteenth-century English courts of equity), that sort of usurpation of the jury's role is unacceptable even in the civil context, *see* James Wm. Moore, 9 *Moore's Federal Practice* § 53.13[1], at 53–78 (3d ed. 2005) ("The 2003 amendments [to the Federal Rules of Civil Procedure] abolish the authority of trial courts to appoint trial masters respecting matters to be decided by a jury unless a statute provides otherwise."). The Government cannot satisfy its burden of proof by taking the easy route of calling an "expert" whose expertise happens to be the defendant. Our occasional use of abstract language to describe the subjects of permissible officer expert testimony, *e.g., Locascio,* 6 F.3d at 936 ("We have ... previously upheld the use of expert testimony to help explain the operation, structure, membership, and terminology of organized crime families."); *United States v. Lombardozzi,* 491 F.3d 61, 78 (2d Cir.2007) ("This Court has also permitted expert testimony regarding the organization and structure of organized crime families in [RICO] prosecutions...."), cannot be read to suggest otherwise.

This Court has not been blind to these risks. More than fifteen years ago, we observed that although "the operations of narcotics dealers are a proper subject for expert testimony under Fed.R.Evid. 702, we have carefully circumscribed the use of such testimony to occasions where the subject matter of the testimony is beyond the ken of the average juror." *United States v. Castillo,* 924 F.2d 1227, 1232 (2d Cir.1991) (citations omitted); *see also United States v. Tapia–Ortiz,* 23 F.3d 738, 740 (2d Cir.1994) (cautioning that expert testimony relating to "the operations of narcotics dealers ... should normally be used only for subjects that have esoteric aspects reasonably perceived as beyond the ken of the jury" (internal quotation marks omitted)). Two years later, in *Locascio,* after approving of an FBI agent's expert testimony on the structure of the Gambino family, we nonetheless "remind[ed] the district courts ... that they are not required to admit such testimony, and when they do the testimony should be carefully circumscribed to ensure that the expert does not usurp either the role of the judge in instructing on the law, or the role of the jury in applying the law to the facts before it." *Locascio,* 6 F.3d at 939. In most cases, of course, no reminder was needed, often because the district court had taken affirmative steps on its own to prevent such usurpation. *See, e.g., Ardito,* 782 F.2d at 363 (noting that the district court had "specifically cautioned the jury as to the limited purpose of the agent's testimony"); *Daly,* 842 F.2d at 1389 ("[T]he final [jury] instructions made clear that it was the jury's province to determine whether or not the individuals named in the indictment functioned as an 'enterprise'...."); *Matera,* 489 F.3d at 121 ("Immediately after [the officer expert's] testimony, the district court gave a limiting instruction....").

We more recently cautioned the Government of our concern about these risks in *United States v. Dukagjini,* 326 F.3d 45 (2d Cir.2003), and *Lombardozzi,* 491 F.3d 61. In *Dukagjini,* the Government called the case agent, a DEA officer, as an expert witness for the purpose of interpreting recorded conversations. 326 F.3d at 49–50. The district court allowed the agent to testify, but it "cautioned the prosecutor to limit [the agent's] testimony to 'words of the trade, jargon,' and general practices of drug dealers." *Id.* at 50. During his testimony, the agent interpreted various terms, such as "dry" and "cooked." *Id.* The agent also addressed specific exchanges in recorded conversations and explained their meaning to the jury. *Id.* In doing so, the agent relied on both his experience and his knowledge of the case. *Id.*

After reviewing the agent's testimony, we concluded that the agent had "stray[ed] from his proper expert function" by "act[ing] at times as a summary prosecution witness." *Id.* at 55. The Government's decision to call the case agent as an expert witness, we observed, had "increase[d] the likelihood that inadmissible and prejudicial testimony [would] be proffered." *Id.* at 53. The officer expert's status, we suggested, was likely to give his factual testimony an "unmerited credibility" before the jury. *Id.*; *see also United States v. Alvarez*, 837 F.2d 1024, 1030 (11th Cir. 1988) ("When the expert is a government law enforcement agent testifying on behalf of the prosecution about participation in prior and similar cases, the possibility that the jury will give undue weight to the expert's testimony is greatly increased."). The defense's inability to meaningfully challenge the case agent's expert opinions inadvertently reinforces the agent's credibility on questions of fact. *Dukagjini*, 326 F.3d at 53–54. In addition, case agents testifying as experts are particularly vulnerable to making "sweeping conclusions" about the defendants' activities. *Id.* at 54.

We have identified two distinct ways in which the officer expert might "stray from the scope of his expertise." *Id.* at 55. The expert might, as did the agent in *Dukagjini*, "testif[y] about the meaning of conversations in general, beyond the interpretation of code words." *Id.*; *see also United States v. Freeman*, 488 F.3d 1217, 1227 (9th Cir.2007) ("The fact that [the officer expert] possessed specialized knowledge of the particular language of drug traffickers did not give him carte blanche to testify as to the meaning of other words in recorded telephone calls without regard to reliability or relevance."). Or, we noted, the expert might "interpret[ ] ambiguous slang terms" based on knowledge gained through involvement in the case, rather than by reference to the 'fixed meaning' of those terms 'either within the narcotics world or within this particular conspiracy.' " *Dukagjini*, 326 F.3d at 55.

We went on to find that, because the officer expert had relied on hearsay and custodial interrogations when forming his opinions, his testimony that went outside the scope of his expertise violated the Federal Rules of Evidence and the Confrontation Clause of the Sixth Amendment. *Id.* at 58–59. When the agent "departed from the bounds of Rules 702 and 703" by "repeatedly deviat[ing] from his expertise on drug jargon," he thereby "crossed [the] line" between "permissible and impermissible reliance on hearsay." *Id.* at 58–59. We held that the agent's testimony violated the rules governing expert witnesses, *id.* at 55, the hearsay rules, *id.* at 59, and the Confrontation Clause, *id.* We affirmed the convictions nonetheless because the Confrontation Clause violation had not been plain error, *id.* at 61, and the hearsay violation had been harmless, *id.* at 62.

Similar concerns arose in *Lombardozzi,* 491 F.3d 61. There, the defendant had been charged with loan sharking, and the Government called an investigator with the U.S. Attorney's Office for the Southern District of New York "as an expert who testified as to, inter alia, the general structure of La Cosa Nostra in New York and Lombardozzi's affiliation with organized crime." *Id.* at 72. In addition to testifying about the structure of La Cosa Nostra, the officer told the jury that the defendant was "a soldier in the Gambino crime family." *Id.* When questioned by defense counsel as to his basis for that opinion, the witness testified that his knowledge of the defendant's position in the Gambino family "was based on conversations with cooperating witnesses and confidential informants." *Id.* He added that "he personally observed Lombardozzi's activities approximately two dozen times since 1985." *Id.* Because the defendant had failed to raise a Confrontation Clause challenge to the officer expert's testimony, we reviewed that testimony for plain error and found that it did not affect the defendant's substantial rights. *Id.* We commented, however, that "the record indicate[d] that" the expert may have "communicated out-of-court testimonial statements of cooperating witnesses and confidential informants directly to the jury in the guise of an expert opinion." *Id.*

It is in light of these concerns that we now turn to Appellants' specific challenges to Alicea's testimony. In doing so, we review the district court's admission of expert testimony for abuse of discretion, and we will not find error unless the district court's ruling was "manifestly erroneous." *Dukagjini,* 326 F.3d at 52 (quoting *Locascio,* 6 F.3d at 936).

. . .

Appellants' first challenge to Alicea's testimony is a claim that he was unqualified to testify as an expert. They argue that because much of Alicea's background is in the area of narcotics rather than gangs, he is not qualified to testify about the operations and structure of MS–13.

Under Rule 702, the district court may admit expert testimony if the witness is "qualified as an expert by knowledge, skill, experience, training, or education." Fed.R.Evid. 702. At trial, Alicea testified that he had been an officer with the New York State Police for eighteen years and that he had been an investigator since 1992. He had been trained at the New York State Police academy, and he had received additional training in the field and through refresher courses. In addition, he had been a member of the FBI Gang Task Force on Long Island since 2000 and served as Chair of the Intelligence Committee of the East Coast Gang Investigators' Association. Alicea also had extensive experience relating to MS–13 in particular. He testified that he had "listened to many conversations on tape," performed surveillance in the course of investigations of MS–13, executed search warrants, debriefed MS–13 members, and trained other police departments on MS–13. Since joining the Task Force, he had arrested "between 50 and a hundred" and interviewed "[o]ver a hundred" MS-13 members. He said that he had also "read a lot of documents related to MS, either on the internet or the media or from our instructors or other people from the conferences I have gone to," and that he read "a web site" dealing with MS-13 on a daily basis.

Alicea's qualifications are quite similar to those of experts whose qualifications we have upheld in the past. In *Locascio,* for example, the officer expert "had been an FBI agent for seventeen years, and for five years had been on the FBI's Organized Crime Program, a squad that investigated only organized crime cases." 6 F.3d at 937. Similarly, Alicea had been an investigator with the New York State Police for thirteen years and a member of the Task Force for five. Likewise, in *Matera,* the officer expert had "extensive experience investigating organized crime as a New York Police Department Detective and later as an Investigator for the United States Attorney's Office." 489 F.3d at 122. And in *Feliciano,* we described an officer expert as having "extensive experience" with a particular criminal gang based on the officer's participation in a joint task force for approximately five years, "execution of federal and state search warrants at [gang] locations," participation in electronic surveillance, and review of reports by other agents. 223 F.3d at 109. Alicea's work experience, training, and involvement in investigations of MS-13 are at least as "extensive." The district court did not err in finding that Alicea was qualified to testify as an expert.

The problem was not Alicea's qualifications. It was the subjects about which he testified and the sources on which he relied. We address those concerns below.

. . .

Appellants argue that some of the matters about which Alicea testified were outside the scope of his expertise. Rule 702 requires that expert testimony concern "scientific, technical, or other specialized knowledge." Fed.R.Evid. 702. Testimony is properly characterized as "expert" only if it concerns matters that the average juror is not capable of understanding on his or her own. *See United States v. Amuso,* 21 F.3d 1251, 1263 (2d Cir.1994) ("A district court may commit manifest error by admitting expert testimony where the evidence impermissibly mirrors the testimony offered by fact witnesses, or the subject matter of the expert's testimony is not beyond the ken of the average juror."); *Locascio,* 6 F.3d at 936 (applying the "untrained layman" standard articulated in the Advisory Committee Notes to Rule 702).

Much of Alicea's testimony concerned material well within the grasp of the average juror. A few examples are particularly striking: Alicea's testimony that the FBI gang task force had seized "[p]robably between 15 and 25" firearms, as well as ammunition, from MS-13 members; his statement that MS-13 members on Long Island had been arrested for dealing narcotics; and his statement that MS-13 had committed "between 18 and 22, 23" murders on Long Island between June 2000 and the trial. No expertise is required to understand any of these facts. Had the Government introduced lay witness testimony, arrest records, death certificates, and other competent evidence of these highly specific facts, the jury could have "intelligently" interpreted and understood it. For example, in *United States v. Feliz,* 467 F.3d 227 (2d Cir.2006), where the defendant was charged with RICO murder, "[i]n order to establish the manner and cause of death for each of [the defendant's] victims in the charged homicides, the Government offered nine autopsy reports through the testimony of [a medical examiner]," *id.* at 229. The Government could have done the same here. Expert testimony might have been helpful in establishing the relationship between these facts and MS–13, but it was not helpful in establishing the facts themselves.

In addition to these stark examples, much of the remainder of Alicea's testimony also addressed matters that the average juror could have understood had such factual evidence been introduced. Alicea's testimony about the ways that MS–13 members traveled when fleeing from prosecution or when transporting contraband, his assertion that MS–13 members from Virginia, California, and El Salvador had attended organizational meetings in New York State, and his statement that MS–13 leaders communicated by telephone all fall into this category. So, too, did his testimony about the use of MS–13 treasury funds to buy firearms and narcotics, his statement that the gang occasionally dealt narcotics, and his statement that MS–13 taxed non-member drug dealers.

This testimony, which ranged from MS–13's activities on Long Island to aspects of the gang's operations more generally, went far beyond interpreting jargon or coded messages, *Ardito,* 782 F.2d at 363; *Levasseur,* 816 F.2d at 45, describing membership rules, *Daly,* 842 F.2d at 1388, or explaining organizational hierarchy, *Locascio,* 6 F.3d at 936. We find especially disturbing the portion of Alicea's testimony that essentially summarized the results of the Task Force investigation on Long Island, and in particular Alicea's testimony that MS–13 had committed between eighteen and twenty-three murders since 2000.

We recognize that expertise may have been necessary to connect specific murders to MS–13. An appropriate (admissible) example of such expertise would have been an expert's explanation of how the graffiti near a body indicated that the murderer was a member of MS–13, or an expert's testimony that the gang used a particular method to kill enemies and that as a result of his review of the autopsy reports (which would have been in evidence before the jury), he had concluded that MS–13 committed those murders. The acceptable use of expert testimony for this limited purpose, however, does not make it acceptable to substitute expert testimony for factual evidence of murder in the first instance (a fact, as we must remember, that is an element of the charged offense). If the Government is going to use the fact of murders as a way of proving that the gang engaged in a pattern of racketeering activity involving murder, that an individual was murdered remains a *fact* that must be proven by competent *evidence*. Only then does expertise of the sort proffered by Alicea become necessary to help the jury understand the particular evidence and to show a connection between MS–13 and the murder. The Government cannot take a shortcut around its obligation to prove murder beyond a reasonable doubt just by having an expert pronounce that unspecified deaths of eighteen to twenty-three persons have been homicides committed by members of MS–13. Alicea's testimony in this regard went beyond those issues on which his "expert" testimony would have been helpful and appropriate.

In *Feliciano*, the one case where we have approved of testimony that even arguably approached the scope of Alicea's testimony here, the officer was testifying as both a fact witness and an expert witness. 223 F.3d at 121. Like Appellants, the defendants in *Feliciano* had been charged with offenses under the Violent Crimes in Aid of Racketeering Act. *Id.* at 107. The racketeering enterprise of which those defendants were members was the Los Solidos gang. *Id.* At trial, the Government called the coordinator of a joint task force on gang activity in Hartford, Connecticut, as both an expert witness and a fact witness. *Id.* at 109–10. As an expert, the agent testified about "the structure, leadership, practices, terminology, and operations of Los Solidos." *Id.* at 109. As a fact witness, he testified about his involvement in the task force investigation of Los Solidos. *Id.* at 109–10. On appeal, the defendants argued that the agent had testified to legal conclusions. *Id.* at 120–21. They did not challenge the agent's testimony as outside the scope of his expertise. We upheld the district court's admission of the testimony after finding that the agent had not testified to any legal conclusions. *Id.* at 121. Even as we affirmed the convictions, however, we expressed concern that "the line between [the agent's] opinion and fact witness testimony [was] often hard to discern, and the 'facts' testified to are often stated very broadly and generally." *Id.* Nonetheless, because the defense had had ample opportunity to cross-examine the agent as to the basis for those broadly stated facts, we found that the district court had not manifestly erred in admitting the testimony.

Feliciano thus reinforces our conclusion that it would be improper for the Government to rely on an officer expert's testimony about matters outside the scope of any conceivable expertise and that the district court errs in allowing it to do so. There, the Government correctly realized that it could not call the task force coordinator to testify as an expert about the precise operations of the racketeering enterprise charged in the indictment, and it had the agent testify in dual roles: as a fact witness and as an expert witness. Alicea, in contrast, was proffered and testified in the case before us only as an expert. Those parts of his testimony that involved purely factual matters, as well as those in which Alicea simply summarized the results of the Task Force investigation, fell far beyond the proper bounds of expert testimony. Alicea was acting as a de facto "case agent" in providing this summary information to the jury (the case being the ongoing investigation into MS–13's activities on Long Island).

Testifying as he did, Alicea's evidence runs afoul of our admonition in *Dukagjini*. When case agents testify as experts, they gain "unmerited credibility when testifying about factual matters from first-hand knowledge." *Dukagjini*, 326 F.3d at 53. The testimony loses its expert character and the entire process transforms into "the grand jury practice, improper at trial, of a single agent simply summarizing an investigation by others that is not part of the record." *Id.* at 54. Alicea's factual testimony about matters that required no specialized knowledge clearly implicates these concerns, and the district court erred in allowing him to testify beyond the bounds for which expert testimony would have assisted the jury in understanding the evidence.

. . .

At trial and on appeal, Appellants also claim that Alicea impermissibly relied on inadmissible hearsay in forming his conclusions.

Under Rule 703, experts can testify to opinions based on inadmissible evidence, including hearsay, if "experts in the field reasonably rely on such evidence in forming their opinions." *Locascio*, 6 F.3d at 938; *accord* Fed.R.Evid. 703. Alicea unquestionably relied on hearsay evidence in forming his opinions. This hearsay evidence took the form of statements by MS–13 members given in interviews, both custodial and noncustodial, as well as statements made by other law enforcement officers, statements from intercepted telephone conversations among MS–13 members (which may or may not have been hearsay, depending on whether the conversations were in the course of and in furtherance of the charged conspiracies, *see* Fed.R.Evid. 801(d)(2)(E)), and printed and online materials. Alicea's reliance on such materials was consistent with the ordinary practices of law enforcement officers, who "routinely and reasonably rely upon hearsay in reaching their conclusions," *Dukagjini*, 326 F.3d at 57.

The expert may not, however, simply transmit that hearsay to the jury. *Id.* at 54 ("When an expert is no longer applying his extensive experience and a reliable methodology, *Daubert* teaches that the testimony should be excluded."). Instead, the expert must form his own opinions by "applying his extensive experience and a reliable methodology" to the inadmissible materials. *Id.* at 58. Otherwise, the expert is simply "repeating hearsay evidence without applying any expertise whatsoever," a practice that allows the Government "to circumvent the rules prohibiting hearsay." *Id.* at 58–59.

At trial, Alicea was unable to separate the sources of his information, stating that his testimony was based on "a combination of both" custodial interrogations and other sources. On cross-examination, however, Alicea identified hearsay as the source of much of his information. For example, his testimony that the Freeport clique initially funded itself through drug sales was based on "some of the articles that [he] had researched" and "[r]eports from law enforcement personnel." His testimony about MS–13's taxation of drug sales by non-members was based on a gang member having told him so during a custodial interrogation in this case. Alicea had learned about MS–13 treasury funds from about a dozen MS–13 members both in and out of custody. Additionally, Alicea discovered his information about MS–13's involvement in Mexican immigrant smuggling through "research on the Internet," and more specifically from a website containing a media report and an interview with a law enforcement official. And although Alicea did not identify the source of his statements about the number of firearms the Task Force had seized and the number of murders on Long Island that MS–13 members had committed, we cannot imagine any source for that information other than hearsay (likely consisting of police reports, Task Force meetings, conversations with other officers, or conversations with members of MS–13).

Not all of Alicea's testimony was flawed, and some of the information that he provided to the jury resulted from his synthesis of various source materials. As a review of his testimony shows, however, at least some of his testimony involved merely repeating information he had read or heard-information he learned from witnesses through custodial interrogations, newspaper articles, police reports, and tape recordings. When asked how he learned particular facts, Alicea did not explain how he had pieced together bits of information from different sources and reached a studied conclusion that he then gave to the jury. Instead, he testified that he had read an article, or had talked to gang members in custody (including, on at least one occasion, a gang member arrested as part of this investigation), or listened to a recording (evidence that could have been played to the jury in its original form, notwithstanding that some informants may have been identified in the process). This testimony strongly suggests that Alicea was acting not as an expert but instead as a case agent, thereby implicating our warning in *Dukagjini*—a warning the Government appears not to have heard or heeded. Alicea did not analyze his source materials so much as repeat their contents. Alicea thus provided evidence to the jury without also giving the jury the information it needed "to factor into its deliberations the reliability (or unreliability) of the particular source," *Dukagjini*, 326 F.3d at 57 n. 7. These statements therefore violated Rule 703.

. . .

For similar reasons, some of Alicea's testimony also violated *Crawford*. In *Crawford*, 541 U.S. 36, 124 S.Ct. 1354, 158 L.Ed.2d 177, the Supreme Court held that the Confrontation Clause of the Sixth Amendment prohibits the introduction into evidence of the out-of-court testimonial statements made by an absent witness unless that witness is unavailable and the defendant had a prior opportunity for cross-examination. *Id.* at 54, 124 S.Ct. 1354. While the Court did not provide a comprehensive definition for the term "testimonial," it placed custodial interrogations within the "core class" covered by the rule it had just announced. *Id.* at 51, 124 S.Ct. 1354; *see also Davis v. Washington,* 547 U.S. 813, 822, 126 S.Ct. 2266, 2273, 165 L.Ed.2d 224 (2006) (explaining that a custodial police interrogation after a *Miranda* warning " 'qualifies under any conceivable definition' of an 'interrogation' " (quoting *Crawford,* 541 U.S. at 53, 124 S.Ct. 1354)).

When faced with the intersection of the *Crawford* rule and officer experts, we have determined that an officer expert's testimony violates *Crawford* "if [the expert] communicated out-of-court testimonial statements of cooperating witnesses and confidential informants directly to the jury in the guise of an expert opinion." *Lombardozzi,* 491 F.3d at 72. As with a Rule 703 challenge to the expert's reliance on hearsay, the question under *Crawford* is whether the expert "applied his expertise to those statements but did not directly convey the substance of the statements to the jury," *id.* at 73. In fact, when the inadmissible hearsay at issue is a testimonial statement, the Supreme Court has recognized that Rule 703 hearsay claims and Sixth Amendment *Crawford* claims are "are generally designed to protect similar values." *Dukagjini,* 326 F.3d at 56 n. 6 (citing *Idaho v. Wright,* 497 U.S. 805, 814, 110 S.Ct. 3139, 111 L.Ed.2d 638 (1990)) (remarking that "[i]n this case, the appellants' hearsay and Confrontation Clause claims are coextensive," but noting that the Supreme Court has "been careful not to equate" the two types of claims). Because it is a question of law whether an expert witness's testimony violated *Crawford,* our review is de novo. *United States v. Wallace,* 447 F.3d 184, 186 (2d Cir.2006).

Alicea's reliance on hearsay is beyond doubt; a more difficult question is the extent to which that hearsay took the form of custodial statements and was thus testimonial. At trial, he testified that he had participated in between fifteen and fifty custodial interrogations of Long Island MS–13 members. He also testified that he had learned through a custodial interrogation that MS–13 taxed non-member drug dealers. The interrogation was one that he conducted as part of the same investigation that resulted in the convictions being appealed here. Among the other facts that he learned at least partially from custodial interrogations were that MS–13 treasury funds were used to purchase narcotics and that MS–13 members used interstate telephone calls to coordinate activities.

We are at a loss in understanding how Alicea might have "applied his expertise" to these statements before conveying them to the jury, such that he could have avoided "convey[ing] the substance of [those] statements to the jury." *Lombardozzi,* 491 F.3d at 73. Although the exact source of much of his information remains unclear, there was at least one fact to which Alicea testified—the drug tax—that was based directly on statements made by an MS–13 member in custody (*during the course of this very investigation*). This impugns the legitimacy of all of his testimony and strongly suggests to us that Alicea was "simply summarizing an investigation by others that [was] not part of the record," *Dukagjini*, 326 F.3d at 54, and presenting it "in the guise of an expert opinion," *Lombardozzi*, 491 F.3d at 72. We hold, therefore, that Alicea's reliance on and repetition of out-of-court testimonial statements made by individuals during the course of custodial interrogations violated Appellants's rights under the Confrontation Clause of the Sixth Amendment.

. . .

Because the result in this case is the same whether or not we draw inferences in favor of the defendants, we need not resolve any such conflict here. We take this opportunity, however, to flag for the Court our concern that our approach to harmless error analysis proceed consistently.

CHAPTER 7

PROCEDURAL CONSIDERATIONS

SECTION 1. BURDENS OF PROOF

C. ALLOCATING BURDENS

Page 1114. Add at end of Note 4:

Dixon v. United States, 126 S.Ct. 2437 (2006): The Due Process Clause requires the prosecution to establish beyond a reasonable doubt all the elements of an offense, but it is for the legislature to say what are the elements of an offense. If the issue is not an element of an offense, but an affirmative defense, the burden of proof may be placed upon the defendant without violating the Constitution. When Congress has created a crime—in the litigated case, the purchase of a weapon by a person under indictment and making false statements in connection with the purchase—without expressly addressing the questions of whether a particular affirmative defense should be recognized and who has the burden of proof on that defense—these questions should be answered from the perspective of what "Congress may have contemplated" and in an "offense specific context." In the litigated case, it was correct as a matter of federal common law to place the burden on the defendant to establish the defense of duress more probably than not.

2. PRESUMPTIONS AND RELATED SUBJECTS

Page 1173. Add to Note 1:

Theriault v. Burnham, 2 A. 3d 324 (Maine 2010), is a recent case involving presumptions.

CHAPTER 8

JUDICIAL NOTICE

SECTION 2. FACTS

A. ADJUDICATIVE

Page 1248. Add Note 4A:

State of Vermont v. Gokey, 14 A. 3d 243, 249 (Vt. 2010): When judge called a neighborhood pharmacy without the parties present to determine the effect of some anti-seizure medication on his competency, prejudice is presumed.

CHAPTER 9

PRIVILEGES

SECTION 2. PRIVILEGE BELONGING TO THE INDIVIDUAL: THE PRIVILEGE AGAINST SELF-INCRIMINATION

B. HISTORY AND RATIONALE

Page 1321. Add before C:

In Chavez v. Martinez, below, the Supreme Court addresses some basic questions regarding the scope and application of the privilege against self incrimination and how it relates to Fourteenth Amendment substantive due process. A sharply divided Court in its several opinions touches upon and characterizes many of the doctrinal issues and cases treated in this Section of the Casebook. In your subsequent examination of these issues and cases, you will want to consider the implications of the various Chavez opinions for each of these specific doctrinal areas. As you study the various doctrines, you may also wish to revisit Chavez and reassess it. Query: Are there any doctrinal issues treated in this Section of the Casebook for which Chavez might have implications but that are not mentioned therein?

Chavez v. Martinez
Supreme Court of the United States, 2003.
538 U.S. 760, 123 S.Ct. 1994, 155 L.Ed.2d 984.

■ JUSTICE THOMAS announced the judgment of the Court and delivered an opinion.*

This case involves a § 1983 suit arising out of petitioner Ben Chavez's allegedly coercive interrogation of respondent Oliverio Martinez. The United States Court of Appeals for the Ninth Circuit held that Chavez was not entitled to a defense of qualified immunity because he violated Martinez's clearly established constitutional rights. We conclude that Chavez did not deprive Martinez of a constitutional right.

I

On November 28, 1997, police officers Maria Peã and Andrew Salinas were near a vacant lot in a residential area of Oxnard, California,

---

* The Chief Justice joins this opinion in its entirety. Justice O'Connor joins Parts I and II-A of this opinion. Justice Scalia joins Parts I and II of this opinion.

SECTION 2 PRIVILEGE BELONGING TO THE INDIVIDUAL

investigating suspected narcotics activity. While Peã and Salinas were questioning an individual, they heard a bicycle approaching on a darkened path that crossed the lot. They ordered the rider, respondent Martinez, to dismount, spread his legs, and place his hands behind his head. Martinez complied. Salinas then conducted a patdown frisk and discovered a knife in Martinez's waistband. An altercation ensued.

There is some dispute about what occurred during the altercation. The officers claim that Martinez drew Salinas' gun from its holster and pointed it at them; Martinez denies this. Both sides agree, however, that Salinas yelled, " 'He's got my gun!' " Peã then drew her gun and shot Martinez several times, causing severe injuries that left Martinez permanently blinded and paralyzed from the waist down. The officers then placed Martinez under arrest.

Petitioner Chavez, a patrol supervisor, arrived on the scene minutes later with paramedics. Chavez accompanied Martinez to the hospital and then questioned Martinez there while he was receiving treatment from medical personnel. The interview lasted a total of about 10 minutes, over a 45–minute period, with Chavez leaving the emergency room for periods of time to permit medical personnel to attend to Martinez.

At first, most of Martinez's answers consisted of "I don't know," "I am dying," and "I am choking." Later in the interview, Martinez admitted that he took the gun from the officer's holster and pointed it at the police. He also admitted that he used heroin regularly. At one point, Martinez said "I am not telling you anything until they treat me," yet Chavez continued the interview. At no point during the interview was Martinez given *Miranda* warnings....

Martinez was never charged with a crime, and his answers were never used against him in any criminal prosecution. Nevertheless, Martinez filed suit under Rev. Stat. § 1979, 5 42 U.S.C. § 1983, maintaining that Chavez's actions violated his Fifth Amendment right not to be "compelled in any criminal case to be a witness against himself," as well as his Fourteenth Amendment substantive due process right to be free from coercive questioning.... [T]he Ninth Circuit first concluded that Chavez's actions, as alleged by Martinez, deprived Martinez of his rights under the Fifth and Fourteenth Amendments. The Ninth Circuit did not attempt to explain how Martinez had been "compelled in any criminal case to be a witness against himself." Instead, the Ninth Circuit reiterated the holding of an earlier Ninth Circuit case, Cooper v. Dupnik, 963 F.2d 1220, 1229 (C.A.9 1992) (en banc), that "the Fifth Amendment's purpose is to prevent coercive interrogation practices that are destructive of human dignity," 270 F.3d, at 857, and found that Chavez's "coercive questioning" of Martinez violated his Fifth Amendment rights, "[e]ven though Martinez's statements were not used against him in a criminal proceeding," As to Martinez's due process claim, the Ninth Circuit held that "a police officer violates the Fourteenth Amendment when he obtains a confession by coercive conduct, regardless of whether the confession is subsequently used at trial."

The Ninth Circuit then concluded that the Fifth and Fourteenth Amendment rights asserted by Martinez were clearly established by federal law, explaining that a reasonable officer "would have known that persistent interrogation of the suspect despite repeated requests to stop violated the suspect's Fifth and Fourteenth Amendment right to be free from coercive interrogation."

We granted certiorari....

II

In deciding whether an officer is entitled to qualified immunity, we must first determine whether the officer's alleged conduct violated a constitutional right. If not, the officer is entitled to qualified immunity, and we need not consider whether the asserted right was "clearly established." We conclude that Martinez's allegations fail to state a violation of his constitutional rights.

A.

... We fail to see how, based on the text of the Fifth Amendment, Martinez can allege a violation of this right, since Martinez was never prosecuted for a crime, let alone compelled to be a witness against himself in a criminal case.

Although Martinez contends that the meaning of "criminal case" should encompass the entire criminal investigatory process, including police interrogations, Brief for Respondent 23, we disagree. In our view, a "criminal case" at the very least requires the initiation of legal proceedings.... We need not decide today the precise moment when a "criminal case" commences; it is enough to say that police questioning does not constitute a "case" any more than a private investigator's precomplaint activities constitute a "civil case." Statements compelled by police interrogations of course may not be used against a defendant at trial, see Brown v. Mississippi, 297 U.S. 278, 286, 56 S.Ct. 461, 80 L.Ed. 682 (1936), but it is not until their use in a criminal case that a violation of the Self–Incrimination Clause occurs....

Here, Martinez was never made to be a "witness" against himself in violation of the Fifth Amendment's Self–Incrimination Clause because his statements were never admitted as testimony against him in a criminal case. Nor was he ever placed under oath and exposed to " 'the cruel trilemma of self-accusation, perjury or contempt.' " The text of the Self–Incrimination Clause simply cannot support the Ninth Circuit's view that the mere use of compulsive questioning, without more, violates the Constitution.

Nor can the Ninth Circuit's approach be reconciled with our case law. It is well established that the government may compel witnesses to testify at trial or before a grand jury, on pain of contempt, so long as the witness is not the target of the criminal case in which he testifies. See Minnesota v. Murphy, 465 U.S. 420, 427, 104 S.Ct. 1136, 79 L.Ed.2d 409 (1984); Kastigar v. United States, 406 U.S. 441, 443, 92 S.Ct. 1653, 32 L.Ed.2d 212 (1972). Even for persons who have a legitimate fear that their statements may subject them to criminal prosecution, we have long permitted the compulsion of incriminating testimony so long as those statements (or evidence derived from those statements) cannot be used against the speaker in any criminal case. See Brown v. Walker, 161 U.S. 591, 602–604, 16 S.Ct. 644, 40 L.Ed. 819 (1896); Kastigar, supra, at 458, 92 S.Ct. 1653; United States v. Balsys, 524 U.S. 666, 671–672, 118 S.Ct. 2218, 141 L.Ed.2d 575 (1998). We have also recognized that governments may penalize public employees and government contractors (with the loss of their jobs or government contracts) to induce them to respond to inquiries, so long as the answers elicited (and their fruits) are immunized from use in any criminal case against the speaker. See Lefkowitz v. Turley, 414 U.S. 70, 84–85, 94 S.Ct. 316, 38 L.Ed.2d 274 (1973) ("[T]he State may insist that [contractors] ... either respond to relevant inquiries about the performance of their contracts or suffer cancellation"); Lefkowitz v. Cunningham, 431 U.S. 801, 806, 97 S.Ct. 2132, 53 L.Ed.2d 1 (1977) ("Public employees may constitutionally be discharged for refusing to answer potentially incriminating questions concerning their official duties if they have not been required to surrender their constitutional immunity" against later use of statements in criminal proceedings). By contrast, no "penalty" may ever be imposed on someone who exercises his core Fifth Amendment right not to be a "witness" against himself in a "criminal case...." Our holdings in these cases demonstrate that, contrary to the Ninth Circuit's view, mere coercion does not violate the text of the Self–Incrimination Clause absent use of the compelled statements in a criminal case against the witness.

The government may not, however, penalize public employees and government contractors to induce them to waive their immunity from the use of their compelled statements in subsequent criminal proceedings. See Uniformed Sanitation Men Assn., Inc. v. Commissioner of Sanitation of City of New York, 392 U.S. 280, 88 S.Ct. 1917, 20 L.Ed.2d 1089 (1968); Lefkowitz v. Turley, 414 U.S. 70, 94 S.Ct. 316, 38 L.Ed.2d 274 (1973), and this is true even though immunity is not itself a right secured by the text of the Self–Incrimination Clause, but rather a prophylactic rule we have constructed to protect the Fifth Amendment's right from invasion. Once an immunity waiver is signed, the signatory is unable to assert a Fifth Amendment objection to the subsequent use of his statements in a criminal case, even if his statements were in fact compelled. A waiver of immunity is therefore a prospective waiver of the core self-incrimination right in any subsequent criminal proceeding, and States cannot condition public employment on the waiver of constitutional rights, Lefkowitz, supra, at 85, 97 S.Ct. 2132.

We fail to see how Martinez was any more "compelled in any criminal case to be a witness against himself" than an immunized witness forced to testify on pain of contempt. One difference, perhaps, is that the immunized witness knows that his statements will not, and may not, be used against him, whereas Martinez likely did not. But this does not make the statements of the immunized witness any less "compelled" and lends no support to the Ninth Circuit's conclusion that coercive police interrogations, absent the use of the involuntary statements in a criminal case, violate the Fifth Amendment's Self-Incrimination Clause. Moreover, our cases provide that those subjected to coercive police interrogations have an automatic protection from the use of their involuntary statements (or evidence derived from their statements) in any subsequent criminal trial. This protection is, in fact, coextensive with the use and derivative use immunity mandated by Kastigar when the government compels testimony from a reluctant witness.... [T]he fact that Martinez did not know his statements could not be used against him does not change our view that no violation of Fifth Amendment's Self-Incrimination Clause occurred here.

Although our cases have permitted the Fifth Amendment's self-incrimination privilege to be asserted in non-criminal cases, see id., at 444–445, 92 S.Ct. 1653 (recognizing that the "Fifth Amendment privilege against compulsory self-incrimination ... can be asserted in any proceeding, civil or criminal, administrative or judicial, investigatory or adjudicatory ..."); Lefkowitz v. Turley, supra, at 77, 94 S.Ct. 316 (stating that the Fifth Amendment privilege allows one "not to answer official questions put to him in any other proceeding, civil or criminal, formal or informal, where the answers might incriminate him in future criminal proceedings"), that does not alter our conclusion that a violation of the constitutional right against self-incrimination occurs only if one has been compelled to be a witness against himself in a criminal case.

In the Fifth Amendment context, we have created prophylactic rules designed to safeguard the core constitutional right protected by the Self Incrimination Clause.... Among these rules is an evidentiary privilege that protects witnesses from being forced to give incriminating testimony, even in noncriminal cases, unless that testimony has been immunized from use and derivative use in a future criminal proceeding before it is compelled.... By allowing a witness to insist on an immunity agreement before being compelled to give incriminating testimony in a noncriminal case, the privilege preserves the core Fifth Amendment right from invasion by the use of that compelled testimony in a subsequent criminal case.... Because the failure to assert the privilege will often forfeit the right to exclude the evidence in a subsequent "criminal case," see *Murphy,* 465 U.S., at 440, 104 S.Ct. 1136; Garner v. United States, 424 U.S. 648, 650, 96 S.Ct. 1178, 47 L.Ed.2d 370 (1976) (failure to claim privilege against self-incrimination before disclosing incrimina-

SECTION 2   PRIVILEGE BELONGING TO THE INDIVIDUAL

ting information on tax returns forfeited the right to exclude that information in a criminal prosecution); United States v. Kordel, 397 U.S. 1, 7, 90 S.Ct. 763, 25 L.Ed.2d 1 (1970) (criminal defendant forfeited his right to assert Fifth Amendment privilege with regard to answers he gave to interrogatories in a prior civil proceeding), it is necessary to allow assertion of the privilege prior to the commencement of a "criminal case" to safeguard the core Fifth Amendment trial right. If the privilege could not be asserted in such situations, testimony given in those judicial proceedings would be deemed "voluntary," see Rogers v. United States, 340 U.S. 367, 371, 71 S.Ct. 438, 95 L.Ed. 344 (1951); United States v. Monia, 317 U.S. 424, 427, 63 S.Ct. 409, 87 L.Ed. 376 (1943); hence, insistence on a prior grant of immunity is essential to memorialize the fact that the testimony had indeed been compelled and therefore protected from use against the speaker in any "criminal case."

Rules designed to safeguard a constitutional right, however, do not extend the scope of the constitutional right itself, just as violations of judicially crafted prophylactic rules do not violate the constitutional rights of any person.... The Ninth Circuit's view that mere compulsion violates the Self–Incrimination Clause, finds no support in the text of the Fifth Amendment and is irreconcilable with our case law. Because we find that Chavez's alleged conduct did not violate the Self–Incrimination Clause, we reverse the Ninth Circuit's denial of qualified immunity as to Martinez's Fifth Amendment claim.

That the privilege is a prophylactic one does not alter our penalty cases jurisprudence, which allows such privilege to be asserted prior to, and outside of, criminal proceedings.

Our views on the proper scope of the Fifth Amendment's Self–Incrimination Clause do not mean that police torture or other abuse that results in a confession is constitutionally permissible so long as the statements are not used at trial; it simply means that the Fourteenth Amendment's Due Process Clause, rather than the Fifth Amendment's Self–Incrimination Clause, would govern the inquiry in those cases and provide relief in appropriate circumstances.

B

The Fourteenth Amendment provides that no person shall be deprived "of life, liberty, or property, without due process of law." Convictions based on evidence obtained by methods that are "so brutal and so offensive to human dignity" that they "shoc[k] the conscience" violate the Due Process Clause. Rochin v. California, 342 U.S. 165, 172, 174, 72 S.Ct. 205, 96 L.Ed. 183 (1952) (overturning conviction based on evidence obtained by involuntary stomach pumping). See also Breithaupt v. Abram, 352 U.S. 432, 435, 77 S.Ct. 408, 1 L.Ed.2d 448 (1957) (reiterating that evidence obtained through conduct that "shock[s] the conscience" may not be used to support a criminal conviction). Although Rochin did not establish a civil remedy for abusive police behavior, we recognized in

County of Sacramento v. Lewis, 523 U.S. 833, 846, 118 S.Ct. 1708, 140 L.Ed.2d 1043 (1998), that deprivations of liberty caused by "the most egregious official conduct," may violate the Due Process Clause.

We are satisfied that Chavez's questioning did not violate Martinez's due process rights. Even assuming, arguendo, that the persistent questioning of Martinez somehow deprived him of a liberty interest, we cannot agree with Martinez's characterization of Chavez's behavior as "egregious" or "conscience shocking." As we noted in Lewis, the official conduct "most likely to rise to the conscience-shocking level," is the "conduct intended to injure in some way unjustifiable by any government interest." Here, there is no evidence that Chavez acted with a purpose to harm Martinez by intentionally interfering with his medical treatment. Medical personnel were able to treat Martinez throughout the interview, and Chavez ceased his questioning to allow tests and other procedures to be performed. Nor is there evidence that Chavez's conduct exacerbated Martinez's injuries or prolonged his stay in the hospital. Moreover, the need to investigate whether there had been police misconduct constituted a justifiable government interest given the risk that key evidence would have been lost if Martinez had died without the authorities ever hearing his side of the story.

The Court has held that the Due Process Clause also protects certain "fundamental liberty interest[s]" from deprivation by the government, regardless of the procedures provided, unless the infringement is narrowly tailored to serve a compelling state interest. Washington v. Glucksberg, 521 U.S. 702, 721, 117 S.Ct. 2258, 138 L.Ed.2d 772 (1997). Only fundamental rights and liberties which are "deeply rooted in this Nation's history and tradition" and "implicit in the concept of ordered liberty" qualify for such protection. Ibid. Many times, however, we have expressed our reluctance to expand the doctrine of substantive due process.

Glucksberg requires a "careful description" of the asserted fundamental liberty interest for the purposes of substantive due process analysis; vague generalities, such as "the right not to be talked to," will not suffice. We therefore must take into account the fact that Martinez was hospitalized and in severe pain during the interview, but also that Martinez was a critical nonpolice witness to an altercation resulting in a shooting by a police officer, and that the situation was urgent given the perceived risk that Martinez might die and crucial evidence might be lost. In these circumstances, we can find no basis in our prior jurisprudence, see, e.g., Miranda, 384 U.S., at 477–478, 86 S.Ct. 1602 ("It is an act of responsible citizenship for individuals to give whatever information they may have to aid in law enforcement"), or in our Nation's history and traditions to suppose that freedom from unwanted police questioning is a right so fundamental that it cannot be abridged absent a "compelling state interest." Flores, supra, at 302, 113 S.Ct. 1439. We have never required such a justification for a police interrogation, and we decline to do so here. The lack of any "guideposts for responsible decisionmaking" in this area, and our oft-stated reluctance to expand the doctrine of substantive due process, further counsel against recognizing a new "fundamental liberty interest" in this case.

We conclude that Martinez has failed to allege a violation of the Fourteenth Amendment, and it is therefore unnecessary to inquire whether the right asserted by Martinez was clearly established.

III

Because Chavez did not violate Martinez's Fifth and Fourteenth Amendment rights, he was entitled to qualified immunity. The judgment of the Court of Appeals for the Ninth Circuit is therefore reversed and the case is remanded for further proceedings.

It is so ordered.

■ JUSTICE SOUTER, delivered an opinion, Part II of which is the opinion of the Court, and Part I of which is an opinion concurring in the judgment.**

I

Respondent Martinez's claim under 42 U.S.C. § 1983 for violation of his privilege against compelled self-incrimination should be rejected and his case remanded for further proceedings. I write separately because I believe that our decision requires a degree of discretionary judgment greater than Justice Thomas acknowledges. As he points out, the text of the Fifth Amendment (applied here under the doctrine of Fourteenth Amendment incorporation) focuses on courtroom use of a criminal defendant's compelled, self-incriminating testimony, and the core of the guarantee against compelled self-incrimination is the exclusion of any such evidence.... But Martinez claims more than evidentiary protection in asking this Court to hold that the questioning alone was a completed violation of the Fifth and Fourteenth Amendments subject to redress by an action for damages under § 1983.

To recognize such a constitutional cause of action for compensation would, of course, be well outside the core of Fifth Amendment protection, but that alone is not a sufficient reason to reject Martinez's claim.... I do not, however, believe that Martinez can make the "powerful showing," subject to a realistic assessment of costs and risks, necessary to expand protection of the privilege against compelled self-incrimination to the point of the civil liability he asks us to recognize here. The most obvious drawback inherent in Martinez's purely Fifth Amendment claim to damages is its risk of global application in every instance of interrogation producing a statement inadmissible under Fifth and Fourteenth Amendment principles, or violating one of the complementary

---

** Justice BREYER joins this opinion in its entirety. Justice STEVENS, Justice KENNEDY, and Justice GINSBURG join Part II of this opinion.

rules we have accepted in aid of the privilege against evidentiary use. If obtaining Martinez's statement is to be treated as a stand-alone violation of the privilege subject to compensation, why should the same not be true whenever the police obtain any involuntary self-incriminating statement, or whenever the government so much as threatens a penalty in derogation of the right to immunity, or whenever the police fail to honor *Miranda*? Martinez offers no limiting principle or reason to foresee a stopping place short of liability in all such cases.

Recognizing an action for damages in every such instance not only would revolutionize Fifth and Fourteenth Amendment law, but would beg the question that must inform every extension or recognition of a complementary rule in service of the core privilege: why is this new rule necessary in aid of the basic guarantee? Martinez has offered no reason to believe that the guarantee has been ineffective in all or many of those circumstances in which its vindication has depended on excluding testimonial admissions or barring penalties. And I have no reason to believe the law has been systemically defective in this respect.

But if there is no failure of efficacy infecting the existing body of Fifth Amendment law, any argument for a damages remedy in this case must depend not on its Fifth Amendment feature but upon the particular charge of outrageous conduct by the police, extending from their initial encounter with Martinez through the questioning by Chavez. That claim, however, if it is to be recognized as a constitutional one that may be raised in an action under § 1983, must sound in substantive due process. ("[C]onduct intended to injure in some way unjustifiable by any government interest is the sort of official action most likely to rise to the conscience-shocking level"). Here, it is enough to say that Justice STEVENS shows that Martinez has a serious argument in support of such a position.

II

Whether Martinez may pursue a claim of liability for a substantive due process violation is thus an issue that should be addressed on remand, along with the scope and merits of any such action that may be found open to him.

■ JUSTICE SCALIA, concurring in part in the judgment.

I agree with the Court's rejection of Martinez's Fifth Amendment claim, that is, his claim that Chavez violated his right not to be compelled in any criminal case to be a witness against himself. And without a violation of the right protected by the text of the Self–Incrimination Clause, (what the plurality and Justice SOUTER call the Fifth Amendment's "core"), Martinez's 42 U.S.C. § 1983 action is doomed. Section 1983 does not provide remedies for violations of judicially created prophylactic rules, such as the rule of Miranda v. Arizona, as the Court today holds, nor is it concerned with "extensions" of constitutional provisions designed to safeguard actual constitutional rights. Rather, a plaintiff seeking redress through § 1983 must establish the violation of a federal constitutional or statutory right.

My reasons for rejecting Martinez's Fifth Amendment claim are those set forth in Justice THOMAS's opinion. I join Parts I and II of that opinion, including Part II–B, which deals with substantive due process. Consideration and rejection of that constitutional claim is absolutely necessary to support reversal of the Ninth Circuit's judgment. . . .

■ JUSTICE STEVENS, concurring in part and dissenting in part.

As a matter of fact, the interrogation of respondent was the functional equivalent of an attempt to obtain an involuntary confession from a prisoner by torturous methods. As a matter of law, that type of brutal police conduct constitutes an immediate deprivation of the prisoner's constitutionally protected interest in liberty. Because these propositions are so clear, the District Court and the Court of Appeals correctly held that petitioner is not entitled to qualified immunity.

I

What follows is an English translation of portions of the tape-recorded questioning in Spanish that occurred in the emergency room of the hospital when, as is evident from the text, both parties believed that respondent was about to die:

"Chavez: What happened? Olivero, tell me what happened.

"O[liverio] M[artinez]: I don't know

"Chavez: I don't know what happened (sic)?

"O. M.: Ay! I am dying.

Ay! What are you doing to me?

No, . . . ! (unintelligible scream).

"Chavez: What happened, sir?

"O. M.: My foot hurts . . .

"Chavez: Olivera. Sir, what happened?

"O. M.: I am choking.

"Chavez: Tell me what happened." O. M.: I don't know.

"Chavez: 'I don't know.'

"O. M.: My leg hurts." Chavez: I don't know what happened (sic)?

"O. M.: It hurts . . .

"Chavez: Hey, hey look,

"O. M.: I am choking.

"Chavez: Can you hear? look listen, I am Benjamin Chavez with the police here in Oxnard, look.

"O. M.: I am dying, please.

"Chavez: OK, yes, tell me what happened. If you are going to die, tell me what happened. Look I need to tell (sic) what happened.

"O. M.: I don't know.

"Chavez: You don't know, I don't know what happened (sic)? Did you talk to the police?

"O. M.: Yes.

"Chavez: What happened with the police?

"O. M.: We fought.

"Chavez: Huh? What happened with the police?

"O. M.: The police shot me.

"Chavez: Why?

"O. M.: Because I was fighting with him.

"Chavez: Oh, why were you fighting with the police?" O. M.: I am dying . . .

"Chavez: OK, yes you are dying, but tell me why you are fighting, were you fighting with the police?

. . . .

"O. M.: Doctor, please I want air, I am dying.

"Chavez: OK, OK. I want to know if you pointed the gun [to yourself] at the police.

"O. M.: Yes.

"Chavez: Yes, and you pointed it [to yourself]? (sic) at the police pointed the gun? (sic) Huh?

"O. M.: I am dying, please . . .

. . . .

"Chavez: OK, listen, listen I want to know what happened, ok?

"O. M.: I want them to treat me.

"Chavez: OK, they are do it (sic), look when you took out the gun from the tape (sic) of the police . . .

"O. M.: I am dying . . .

"Chavez: Ok, look, what I want to know if you took out (sic) the gun of the police?

"O. M.: I am not telling you anything until they treat me." Chavez: Look, tell me what happened, I want to know, look well don't you want the police know (sic) what happened with you?

"O. M.: Uuuggghhh! my belly hurts . . .

. . . .

SECTION 2   PRIVILEGE BELONGING TO THE INDIVIDUAL

"Chavez: Nothing, why did you run (sic) from the police?"

"O. M.: I don't want to say anything anymore.

"Chavez: No?" O. M.: I want them to treat me, it hurts a lot, please.

"Chavez: You don't want to tell (sic) what happened with you over there?

"O. M.: I don't want to die, I don't want to die.

"Chavez: Well if you are going to die tell me what happened, and right now you think you are going to die?

"O. M.: No.

"Chavez: No, do you think you are going to die?

"O. M.: Aren't you going to treat me or what?

"Chavez: Look, think you are going to die, (sic) that's all I want to know, if you think you are going to die? Right now, do you think you are going to die?

"O. M.: My belly hurts, please treat me.

"Chavez: Sir?" O. M.: If you treat me I tell you everything, if not, no.

"Chavez: Sir, I want to know if you think you are going to die right now?

"O. M.: I think so.

"Chavez: You think (sic) so? Ok. Look, the doctors are going to help you with all they can do, Ok? That they can do.

"O. M.: Get moving, I am dying, can't you see me? come on.

"Chavez: Ah, huh, right now they are giving you medication." App. 8–22.

The sound recording of this interrogation, which has been lodged with the Court, vividly demonstrates that respondent was suffering severe pain and mental anguish throughout petitioner's persistent questioning....

I respectfully dissent, but for the reasons articulated by Justice KENNEDY, concur in Part II of Justice SOUTER's opinion.

■ JUSTICE KENNEDY, with whom JUSTICE STEVENS joins, and with whom JUSTICE GINSBURG joins as to Parts II and III, concurring in part and dissenting in part.

A single police interrogation now presents us with two issues: first, whether failure to give a required warning under Miranda v. Arizona, 384 U.S. 436, 86 S.Ct. 1602, 16 L.Ed.2d 694 (1966), was itself a completed constitutional violation actionable under 42 U.S.C. § 1983; and second, whether an actionable violation arose at once under the Self-Incrimination Clause (applicable to the States through the Fourteenth Amendment) when the police, after failing to warn, used severe compulsion or extraordinary pressure in an attempt to elicit a statement or confession.

I agree with Justice THOMAS that failure to give a *Miranda* warning does not, without more, establish a completed violation when the unwarned interrogation ensues. As to the second aspect of the case, which does not involve the simple failure to give a *Miranda* warning, it is my respectful submission that Justice SOUTER and Justice THOMAS are incorrect. They conclude that a violation of the Self–Incrimination Clause does not arise until a privileged statement is introduced at some later criminal proceeding.

A constitutional right is traduced the moment torture or its close equivalents are brought to bear. Constitutional protection for a tortured suspect is not held in abeyance until some later criminal proceeding takes place. These are the premises of this separate opinion.

Justice SOUTER and Justice THOMAS are wrong, in my view, to maintain that in all instances a violation of the Self–Incrimination Clause simply does not occur unless and until a statement is introduced at trial, no matter how severe the pain or how direct and commanding the official compulsion used to extract it.

. . .

The conclusion that the Self–Incrimination Clause is not violated until the government seeks to use a statement in some later criminal proceeding strips the Clause of an essential part of its force and meaning. This is no small matter. It should come as an unwelcome surprise to judges, attorneys, and the citizenry as a whole that if a legislative committee or a judge in a civil case demands incriminating testimony without offering immunity, and even imposes sanctions for failure to comply, that the witness and counsel cannot insist the right against compelled self-incrimination is applicable then and there. Justice SOUTER and Justice THOMAS, I submit, should be more respectful of the understanding that has prevailed for generations now. To tell our whole legal system that when conducting a criminal investigation police officials can use severe compulsion or even torture with no present violation of the right against compelled self-incrimination can only diminish a celebrated provision in the Bill of Rights. A Constitution survives over time because the people share a common, historic commitment to certain simple but fundamental principles which preserve their freedom. Today's decision undermines one of those respected precepts. . . .

In my view the Self–Incrimination Clause is applicable at the time and place police use compulsion to extract a statement from a suspect. The Clause forbids that conduct. A majority of the Court has now concluded otherwise, but that should not end this case. It simply implicates the larger definition of liberty under the Due Process Clause of the Fourteenth Amendment. . . . Turning to this essential, but less specific, guarantee, it seems to me a simple enough matter to say that use of torture or its equivalent in an attempt to induce a statement violates an individual's fundamental right to liberty of the person. Brown, supra, at 285, 56 S.Ct. 461; Palko v. Connecticut, 302 U.S. 319, 58 S.Ct. 149, 82 L.Ed. 288 (1937); see also Rochin v. California, 342 U.S. 165, 72 S.Ct. 205, 96 L.Ed. 183 (1952). The Constitution does not countenance the official imposition of severe pain or pressure for purposes of interrogation. This is true whether the protection is found in the Self–Incrimination Clause, the broader guarantees of the Due Process Clause, or both....

Accordingly, I would affirm the decision of the Court of Appeals that a cause of action under § 1983 has been stated. The other opinions filed today, however, reach different conclusions as to the correct disposition of the case. Were Justice STEVENS, Justice GINSBURG, and I to adhere to our position, there would be no controlling judgment of the Court. In these circumstances, and because a ruling on substantive due process in this case could provide much of the essential protection the Self–Incrimination Clause secures, I join Part II of Justice SOUTER's opinion and would remand the case for further consideration.

■ JUSTICE GINSBURG, concurring in part and dissenting in part.

I join Parts II and III of Justice KENNEDY's opinion. For reasons well stated therein, I would hold that the Self–Incrimination Clause applies at the time and place police use severe compulsion to extract a statement from a suspect. The evidence in this case, as Justice KENNEDY explains, supports the conclusion "that the suspect thought his treatment would be delayed, and thus his pain and condition worsened, by refusal to answer questions." I write separately to state my view that, even if no finding were made concerning Martinez's belief that refusal to answer would delay his treatment, or Chavez's intent to create such an impression, the interrogation in this case would remain a clear instance of the kind of compulsion no reasonable officer would have thought constitutionally permissible.

. . .

Convinced that Chavez's conduct violated Martinez's right to be spared from self-incriminating interrogation, I would affirm the judgment of the Court of Appeals. To assure a controlling judgment of the Court, however, I join Part II of Justice SOUTER's opinion.

C. BASIC ELEMENTS

1. THE TEST FOR SELF–INCRIMINATION

a. The Evidentiary Dimension

Page 1324. Add as Note 3, before b:

3. Is it a fair inference to draw from invocation of the privilege that the person claiming the privilege is guilty of a crime? Can a person who testifies to entirely

innocent conduct validly claim the privilege? In Ohio v. Reiner, 532 U.S. 17, 121 S.Ct. 1252 (2001), the Supreme Court ruled that the privilege could be validly asserted by someone who testified to innocent conduct. In a prosecution of a father for causing the death of his child through physical abuse, the defense was that the baby sitter had perpetrated the crime. The baby sitter declined to testify, claiming the privilege, and, at the prosecution's request, the trial court granted her transactional immunity. (Regarding grants of immunity, see text at p. 1367, infra.) The Supreme Court of Ohio ruled that the grant of immunity was unlawful because the baby sitter could not validly assert the privilege: "[Her] ... testimony did not incriminate her, because she denied any involvement in the abuse." The U.S. Supreme Court reversed:

> "... [W]e [have] recognized that truthful responses of an innocent witness, as well as those of a wrongdoer, may provide the government with incriminating evidence from the speaker's own mouth.... [The baby sitter] spent extended periods of time alone with Alex ... in the weeks immediately preceding discovery of ... [the] injuries. She was with Alex within the potential timeframe of the fatal trauma. The defense's theory of the case was that ... [the baby sitter], not respondent, was responsible for Alex's death.... In this setting, it was reasonable for ... [the baby sitter] to fear that answers to possible questions might tend to incriminate her." (121 S.Ct. 1252, 1254).

On remand from Ohio v. Reiner, supra, the Supreme Court of Ohio, responding to the U.S. Supreme Court's decision, reversed its earlier ruling that the baby sitter could not validly assert the privilege but nevertheless affirmed its ruling that it was error to immunize her because the grant of immunity severely prejudiced the rights of the defendant and did not further the administration of justice. See State v. Reiner, 93 Ohio St.3d 601, 757 N.E.2d 1143 (2001) cert. denied, 536 U.S. 940 (2002), described supra this Supplement, at Note 2(e) for page 270 of the main volume.

c. The Jurisdictional Dimension

Pages 1324–1326. Substitute for Notes beginning at bottom of p. 1324:

United States v. Balsys

Supreme Court of the United States, 1998.
524 U.S. 666, 118 S.Ct. 2218, 141 L.Ed.2d 575.

■ [SOUTER, J., delivered the opinion of the Court, in which REHNQUIST, C.J., and STEVENS, O'CONNOR, and KENNEDY, JJ., joined, and in which SCALIA, and THOMAS, JJ., joined as to Parts I, II, and III. STEVENS, J., filed a concurring opinion. GINSBURG, J., filed a dissenting opinion. BREYER, J., filed a dissenting opinion, in which GINSBURG, J., joined.]

■ JUSTICE SOUTER delivered the opinion of the Court.

By administrative subpoena, the Office of Special Investigations of the Criminal Division of the United States Department of Justice (OSI) sought testimony from the respondent, Aloyzas Balsys, about his wartime activities between 1940 and 1944 and his immigration to the United States in 1961. Balsys declined to answer such questions, claiming the Fifth Amendment privilege against self-incrimination, based on his fear of prosecution by a foreign nation. We hold that concern with foreign prosecution is beyond the scope of the Self–Incrimination Clause.

I

Respondent Aloyzas Balsys is a resident alien living in Woodhaven, New York, having obtained admission to this country in 1961 under the Immigration and Nationality Act, 8 U.S.C. § 1201, on an immigrant visa and alien registration issued at the American Consulate in Liverpool. In his application, he said that he had served in the Lithuanian army between 1934 and 1940, and had lived in hiding in Plateliai, Lithuania, between 1940 and 1944. Balsys swore that the information was true, and signed a statement of understanding that if his application contained any false information or materially misleading statements, or concealed any material fact, he would be subject to criminal prosecution and deportation.

OSI, which was created to institute denaturalization and deportation proceedings against suspected Nazi war criminals, is now investigating whether, contrary to his representations, Balsys participated in Nazi persecution during World War II. Such activity would subject him to deportation for persecuting persons because of their race, religion, national origin, or political opinion under §§ 1182(a)(3)(E), 1251(a)(4)(D) as well as for lying on his visa application under §§ 1182(a)(6)(C)(i), 1251(a)(1)(A).

When OSI issued a subpoena requiring Balsys to testify at a deposition, he appeared and gave his name and address, but he refused to answer any other questions, such as those directed to his wartime activities in Europe between 1940–1945 and his immigration to the United States in 1961. In response to all such questions, Balsys invoked the Fifth Amendment privilege against compelled self-incrimination, claiming that his answers could subject him to criminal prosecution. He did not contend that he would incriminate himself under domestic law,[1] but claimed the privilege because his responses could subject him to criminal prosecution by Lithuania, Israel, and Germany.

[T]he Court of Appeals for the Second Circuit vacated the District Court's order, holding that a witness with a real and substantial fear of prosecution by a foreign country may assert the Fifth Amendment privilege to avoid giving testimony in a domestic proceeding, even if the witness has no valid fear of a criminal prosecution in this country. 119 F.3d 122 (1997). We granted certiorari to resolve a conflict among the Circuits on this issue and now reverse.

II

The Self–Incrimination Clause of the Fifth Amendment provides that "[n]o person . . . shall be compelled in any criminal case to be a

---

1. The Government advises us that the statute of limitation bars criminal prosecution for any misrepresentation. Tr. of Oral Arg. 4. [Some footnotes omitted.]

witness against himself." U.S. Const., Amdt. 5. Resident aliens such as Balsys are considered "persons" for purposes of the Fifth Amendment and are entitled to the same protections under the Clause as citizens. See Kwong Hai Chew v. Colding, 344 U.S. 590, 596, 73 S.Ct. 472, 477, 97 L.Ed. 576 (1953). The parties do not dispute that the Government seeks to "compel" testimony from Balsys that would make him "a witness against himself." The question is whether there is a risk that Balsys's testimony will be used in a proceeding that is a "criminal case."

III

Balsys relies in the first instance on the textual contrast between the Sixth Amendment, which clearly applies only to domestic criminal proceedings, and the compelled self-incrimination Clause, with its facially broader reference to "any criminal case." The same point is developed by Balsys's amici, who argue that "any criminal case" means exactly that, regardless of the prosecuting authority. According to the argument, the Framers' use of the adjective "any" precludes recognition of the distinction raised by the Government, between prosecution by a jurisdiction that is itself bound to recognize the privilege and prosecution by a foreign jurisdiction that is not. But the argument overlooks the cardinal rule to construe provisions in context. In the Fifth Amendment context, the Clause in question occurs in the company of guarantees of grand jury proceedings, defense against double jeopardy, due process, and compensation for property taking. Because none of these provisions is implicated except by action of the government that it binds, it would have been strange to choose such associates for a Clause meant to take a broader view, and it would be strange to find such a sweep in the Clause now.... The oddity of such a reading would be especially stark if the expansive language in question is open to another reasonable interpretation, as we think it is. Because the Fifth Amendment opens by requiring a grand jury indictment or presentment "for a capital, or otherwise infamous crime," the phrase beginning with "any" in the subsequent Self–Incrimination Clause may sensibly be read as making it clear that the privilege it provides is not so categorically limited. It is plausible to suppose the adjective was inserted only for that purpose, not as taking the further step of defining the relevant prosecutorial jurisdiction internationally. We therefore take this to be the fair reading of the adjective "any," and we read the Clause contextually as apparently providing a witness with the right against compelled self-incrimination when reasonably fearing prosecution by the government whose power the Clause limits, but not otherwise. Since there is no helpful legislative history, and because there was no different common law practice at the time of the Framing ... there is no reason to disregard the contextual reading. This Court's precedent has indeed adopted that so-called same-sovereign interpretation.

SECTION 2   PRIVILEGE BELONGING TO THE INDIVIDUAL

A

The precursors of today's case were those raising the question of the significance for the federal privilege of possible use of testimony in state prosecution. Only a handful of early cases even touched on the problem....

A holding to this effect came when United States v. Murdock, 284 U.S. 141, 52 S.Ct. 63, 76 L.Ed. 210 (1931), "definitely settled" the question whether in a federal proceeding the privilege applied on account of fear of state prosecution, concluding "that one under examination in a federal tribunal could not refuse to answer on account of probable incrimination under state law." United States v. Murdock, 290 U.S. 389, 396, 54 S.Ct. 223, 226, 78 L.Ed. 381 (1933).

> "The English rule of evidence against compulsory self-incrimination, on which historically that contained in the Fifth Amendment rests, does not protect witnesses against disclosing offenses in violation of the laws of another country. King of the Two Sicilies v. Willcox, 7 State Trials (N.S.) 1050, 1068. Queen v. Boyes, 1 B. & S., at 330[, 121 Eng. Rep., at 738]. This court has held that immunity against state prosecution is not essential to the validity of federal statutes declaring that a witness shall not be excused from giving evidence on the ground that it will incriminate him, and also that the lack of state power to give witnesses protection against federal prosecution does not defeat a state immunity statute. The principle established is that full and complete immunity against prosecution by the government compelling the witness to answer is equivalent to the protection furnished by the rule against compulsory self-incrimination. Counselman v. Hitchcock, 142 U.S. 547, 12 S.Ct. 195, 35 L.Ed. 1110. Brown v. Walker, 161 U.S. 591, 606, 16 S.Ct. 644, 650, 40 L.Ed. 819; Jack v. Kansas, 199 U.S. 372, 381, 26 S.Ct. 73, 75–76, 50 L.Ed. 234. Hale v. Henkel, 201 U.S. 43, 68, 26 S.Ct. 370...."

. . .

C

In 1964 our precedent took a turn away from the unqualified proposition that fear of prosecution outside the jurisdiction seeking to compel testimony did not implicate a Fifth or Fourteenth Amendment privilege, as the case might be. In Murphy v. Waterfront Comm'n of N.Y. Harbor, 378 U.S. 52, 84 S.Ct. 1594, 12 L.Ed.2d 678 (1964), we reconsidered the converse of the situation in Murdock, whether a witness in a state proceeding who had been granted immunity from state prosecution could invoke the privilege based on fear of prosecution on federal charges. In the course of enquiring into a work stoppage at several New Jersey piers, the Waterfront Commission of New York Harbor subpoenaed the defendants, who were given immunity from prosecution under the laws of New Jersey and New York. When the witnesses persisted in refusing to testify based on their fear of federal prosecution, they were held in civil contempt, and the order was affirmed by New Jersey's highest court.... This Court held the defendants could be forced to testify not because fear of federal prosecution was irrelevant but because the Self-Incrimination Clause barred the National Government from using their state testimony or its fruits to obtain a federal conviction. We explained "that the constitutional privilege against self-incrimination protects a state witness against incrimination under federal as well as state law and a federal witness against incrimination under state as well as federal law." 378 U.S., at 77–78, 84 S.Ct., at 1609.

Murphy is a case invested with two alternative rationales. Under the first, the result reached in Murphy was undoubtedly correct, given the decision rendered that very same day in Malloy v. Hogan, 378 U.S. 1, 84 S.Ct. 1489, 12 L.Ed.2d 653 (1964), which applied the doctrine of Fourteenth Amendment due process incorporation to the Self-Incrimination Clause, so as to bind the States as well as the National Government to recognize the privilege. Id., at 3, 84 S.Ct., at 1490–1491. Prior to Malloy, the Court had refused to impose the privilege against self-incrimination against the States through the Fourteenth Amendment, see Twining v. New Jersey, 211 U.S. 78, 29 S.Ct. 14, 53 L.Ed. 97 (1908), thus leaving state-court witnesses seeking exemption from compulsion to testify to their rights under state law, as supplemented by the Fourteenth Amendment's limitations on coerced confessions. Malloy, however, established that "[t]he Fourteenth Amendment secures against state invasion the same privilege that the Fifth Amendment guarantees against federal infringement—the right of a person to remain silent unless he chooses to speak in the unfettered exercise of his own will, and to suffer no penalty ... for such silence." 378 U.S., at 8, 84 S.Ct., at 1493–1494.

As the Court immediately thereafter said in Murphy, Malloy "necessitate[d] a reconsideration" of the unqualified Murdock rule that a witness subject to testimonial compulsion in one jurisdiction, state or federal, could not plead fear of prosecution in the other. 378 U.S., at 57, 84 S.Ct., at 1597–1598. After Malloy, the Fifth Amendment limitation could no longer be seen as framed for one jurisdiction alone, each jurisdiction having instead become subject to the same claim of privilege flowing from the one limitation. Since fear of prosecution in the one jurisdiction bound by the Clause now implicated the very privilege binding upon the other, the Murphy opinion sensibly recognized that if a witness could not assert the privilege in such circumstances, the witness could be "whipsawed into incriminating himself under both state and federal law even though the constitutional privilege against self-incrimination is applicable to each." 378 U.S., at 55.... The whipsawing was possible owing to a feature unique to the guarantee against self-incrimination among the several Fifth Amendment privileges. In the absence of waiver, the other such guarantees are purely and simply binding on the government. But under the Self-Incrimination Clause, the government has an option to exchange the stated privilege for an immunity to prosecutorial use of any compelled inculpatory testimony.... The only condition on the government when it decides to offer immunity in place of the privilege to stay silent is the requirement to provide an immunity as broad as the privilege itself.... After Malloy had held the privilege binding on the state jurisdictions as well as the National Government, it would therefore have been intolerable to allow a prosecutor in one or the other jurisdiction to eliminate the privilege by offering immunity less complete than the privilege's dual jurisdictional reach. Murphy accordingly held that a federal court could not receive testimony compelled by a State in the absence of a statute effectively providing for federal immunity, and it did this by imposing an exclusionary rule prohibiting the National Government "from making any such use of compelled testimony and its fruits"....

This view of Murphy as necessitated by Malloy was adopted in the subsequent case of Kastigar v. United States, 406 U.S., at 457, n. 42, 92 S.Ct., at 1663, n. 42.... Read this way, Murphy rests upon the same understanding of the Self–Incrimination Clause that Murdock recognized and to which the earlier cases had pointed. Although the Clause serves a variety of interests in one degree or another, see Part IV, infra, at its heart lies the principle that the courts of a government from which a witness may reasonably fear prosecution may not in fairness compel the witness to furnish testimonial evidence that may be used to prove his guilt. After Murphy, the immunity option open to the Executive Branch could only be exercised on the understanding that the state and federal jurisdictions were as one, with a federally mandated exclusionary rule filling the space between the limits of state immunity statutes and the scope of the privilege. As so understood, Murphy stands at odds with Balsys's claim.

There is, however, a competing rationale in Murphy, investing the Clause with a more expansive promise. The Murphy majority opened the door to this view by rejecting this Court's previous understanding of the English common-law evidentiary privilege against compelled self-incrimination, which could have informed the Framers' understanding of the Fifth Amendment privilege. See, e.g., Murphy, 378 U.S., at 67, 84 S.Ct., at 1603 (rejecting Murdock's analysis of the scope of the privilege under English common law). Having removed what it saw as an unjustified, historically derived limitation on the privilege, the Murphy Court expressed a comparatively ambitious conceptualization of personal privacy underlying the Clause, one capable of supporting, if not demanding, the scope of protection that Balsys claims. As the Court of Appeals recognized, if we take the Murphy opinion at face value, the expansive rationale can be claimed quite as legitimately as the Murdock–Malloy–Kastigar understanding of Murphy's result, and Balsys's claim accordingly requires us to decide whether Murphy's innovative side is as sound as its traditional one. We conclude that it is not.

[The Court here reviewed the early English cases, concluding that they did not support the Murphy court's reading of them.]

In sum, to the extent that the Murphy majority went beyond its response to Malloy and undercut Murdock's rationale on historical grounds, its reasoning cannot be accepted now. Long before today, indeed, Murphy's history was shown to be fatally flawed.

IV

There remains, at least on the face of the Murphy majority's opinion, a further invitation to revise the principle of the Clause from what Murdock recognized. The Murphy majority opens its discussion with a catalog of "Policies of the Privilege," 378 U.S., at 55....:

> "It reflects many of our fundamental values and most noble aspirations: our unwillingness to subject those suspected of crime to the cruel trilemma of self-accusation, perjury or contempt; our preference for an accusatorial rather than an inquisitorial system of criminal justice; our fear that self-incriminating statements will be elicited by inhumane treatment and abuses; our sense of fair play which dictates a fair state-individual balance by requiring the government to leave the individual alone until good cause is shown for disturbing him and by requiring the government in its contest with the individual to shoulder the entire load; our respect for the inviolability of the human personality and of the right of each individual to a private enclave where he may lead a private life, our distrust of self-deprecatory statements; and our realization that the privilege, while sometimes a shelter to the guilty, is often a protection to the innocent."

Some of the policies listed would seem to point no further than domestic arrangements and so raise no basis for any privilege looking beyond fear of domestic prosecution. Others, however, might suggest a concern broad enough to encompass foreign prosecutions and accordingly to support a more expansive theory of the privilege than the Murdock understanding would allow.

The adoption of any such revised theory would, however, necessarily rest on Murphy's reading of preconstitutional common-law cases as support for (or at least as opening the door to) the expansive view of the Framer's intent, which we and the commentators since Murphy have found to be unsupported. Once the Murphy majority's treatment of the English cases is rejected as an indication of the meaning intended for the Clause, Murdock must be seen as precedent at odds with Balsys's claim. That precedent aside, however, we think there would be sound reasons to stop short of resting an expansion of the Clause's scope on the highly general statements of policy expressed in the foregoing quotation from Murphy. While its list does indeed catalog aspirations furthered by the Clause, its discussion does not even purport to weigh the host of competing policy concerns that would be raised in a legitimate reconsideration of the Clause's scope.

A

The most general of Murphy's policy items ostensibly suggesting protection as comprehensive as that sought by Balsys is listed in the opinion as "the inviolability of the human personality and ... the right of each individual to a private enclave where he may lead a private life." 378 U.S., at 55.... Whatever else those terms might cover, protection of personal inviolability and the privacy of a testimonial enclave would necessarily seem to include protection against the Government's very intrusion through involuntary interrogation. If in fact these values were reliable guides to the actual scope of protection under the Clause, they would be seen to demand a very high degree of protection indeed: "inviolability" is, after all, an uncompromising term, and we know as well from Fourth Amendment law as from a layman's common sense that breaches of privacy are complete at the moment of illicit intrusion, whatever use may or may not later be made of their fruits....

The Fifth Amendment tradition, however, offers no such degree of protection. If the Government is ready to provide the requisite use and derivative use immunity, ... the protection goes no further: no violation of personality is recognized and no claim of privilege will avail. One might reply that the choice of the word "inviolability" was just unfortunate; while testimonial integrity may not be inviolable, it is sufficiently served by requiring the Government to pay a price in the form of use (and derivative use) immunity before a refusal to testify will be overruled. But that answer overlooks the fact that when a witness's response will raise no fear of criminal penalty, there is no protection for testimonial privacy at all....

Thus, what we find in practice is not the protection of personal testimonial inviolability, but a conditional protection of testimonial privacy subject to basic limits recognized before the framing and refined through immunity doctrine in the intervening years. Since the Judiciary could not recognize fear of foreign prosecution and at the same time preserve the Government's existing rights to seek testimony in exchange for immunity (because domestic courts could not enforce the immunity abroad), it follows that extending protection as Balsys requests would change the balance of private and governmental interests that has seemingly been accepted for as long as there has been Fifth Amendment doctrine....

B

Murphy's policy catalog would provide support, at a rather more concrete level, for Balsys's argument that application of the privilege in situations like his would promote the purpose of preventing government overreaching, which on anyone's view lies at the core of the Clause's purposes. This argument begins with the premise that "cooperative internationalism" creates new incentives for the Government to facilitate foreign criminal prosecutions. Because crime, like legitimate trade, is increasingly international, a corresponding degree of international cooperation is coming to characterize the enterprise of criminal prosecution. The mission of the OSI as shown in this case exemplifies the international cooperation that is said to undermine the legitimacy of treating separate governmental authorities as separate for purposes of liberty protection in domestic courts. Because the Government now has a significant interest in seeing individuals convicted abroad for their crimes, it is subject to the same incentive to overreach that has required application of the privilege in the domestic context. Balsys says that this argument is nothing more than the reasoning of the Murphy Court when it justified its recognition of a fear of state prosecution by looking to the significance of " 'cooperative federalism,' " the teamwork of state and national officials to fight interstate crime....

But Balsys invests Murphy's "cooperative federalism" with a significance unsupported by that opinion. We have already pointed out that Murphy's expansion upon Murdock is not supported by Murphy's unsound historical reexamination, but must rest on Murphy's other rationale, under which its holding is a consequence of Malloy. That latter reading is essential to an understanding of "cooperative federalism." For the Murphy majority, "cooperative federalism" was not important standing alone, but simply because it underscored the significance of the Court's holding that after Malloy it would be unjustifiably formalistic for a federal court to ignore fear of state prosecution when ruling on a privilege claim. Thus, the Court described the "whipsaw" effect that the decision in Malloy would have created if fear of state prosecution were not cognizable in a federal proceeding:

> "[The] policies and purposes [of the privilege] are defeated when a witness can be whipsawed into incriminating himself under both state and federal law even though the constitutional privilege against self-incrimination is applicable to each. This has become especially true in our age of 'cooperative federalism,' where the Federal and State Governments are waging a united front against many types of criminal activity." 378 U.S., at 55–56, 84 S.Ct., at 1597.

Since in this case there is no analog of Malloy, imposing the Fifth Amendment beyond the National Government, there is no premise in Murphy for appealing to "cooperative internationalism" by analogy to "cooperative federalism." Any analogy must, instead, be to the pre-Murphy era when the States were not bound by the privilege. Then, testimony compelled in a federal proceeding was admissible in a state prosecution, despite the fact that shared values and similar criminal statutes of the state and national jurisdictions presumably furnished incentive for overreaching by the Government to facilitate criminal prosecutions in the States.

But even if Murphy were authority for considering "cooperative federalism" and "cooperative internationalism" as reasons supporting expansion of the scope of the privilege, any extension would depend ultimately on an analysis of the likely costs and benefits of extending the privilege as Balsys requests. If such analysis were dispositive for us, we would conclude that Balsys has not shown that extension of the protection would produce a benefit justifying the rule he seeks.

The Court of Appeals directed careful attention to an evaluation of what would be gained and lost on Balsys's view. It concluded, for example, that few domestic cases would be adversely affected by recognizing the privilege based upon fear of foreign prosecution, 119 F.3d, at 135–137, that American contempt sanctions for refusal to testify are so lenient in comparison to the likely consequences of foreign prosecution that a witness would probably refuse to testify even if the privilege were unavailable to him, id., at 142 (Block, J., concurring); that by statute and treaty the United States could limit the occasions on which a reasonable fear of foreign prosecution could be shown, as by modifying extradition and deportation standards in cases involving the privilege, id., at 138–139; and that because a witness's refusal to testify may be used as evidence in a civil proceeding, deportation of people in Balsys's position would not necessarily be thwarted by recognizing the privilege as he claims it, id., at 136.

The Court of Appeals accordingly thought the net burden of the expanded privilege too negligible to justify denying its expansion. We remain skeptical, however. While we will not attempt to comment on every element of the Court of Appeals's calculation, two of the points just noted would present difficulty. First, there is a question about the standard that should govern any decision to justify a truly discretionary ruling by making the assumption that it will induce the Government to adopt legislation with international implications or to seek international agreements, in order to mitigate the burdens that the ruling would otherwise impose. Because foreign relations are specifically committed by the Constitution to the political branches, U.S. Const., Art II, § 2, cl. 2, we would not make a discretionary judgment premised on inducing them to adopt policies in relation to other nations without squarely confronting the propriety of grounding judicial action on such a premise.

Second, the very assumption that a witness's silence may be used against him in a deportation or extradition proceeding due to its civil nature, 119 F.3d, at 136 ... raises serious questions about the likely gain from recognizing fear of foreign prosecution. For if a witness claiming the privilege ended up in a foreign jurisdiction that, for whatever reason, recognized no privilege under its criminal law, the recognition of the privilege in the American courts would have gained nothing for the witness. This possibility, of course, presents a sharp contrast with the consequences of recognizing the privilege based on fear of domestic prosecution. If testimony is compelled, Murphy itself illustrates that domestic courts are not even wholly dependent on immunity statutes to see that no use will be made against the witness; the exclusionary principle will guarantee that. See Murphy, 378 U.S., at 79, 84 S.Ct., at 1609–1610. Whatever the cost to the Government may be, the benefit to the individual is not in doubt in a domestic proceeding.

Since the likely gain to the witness fearing foreign prosecution is thus uncertain, the countervailing uncertainty about the loss of testimony to the United States cannot be dismissed as comparatively unimportant. That some testimony will be lost is highly probable, since the United States will not be able to guarantee immunity if testimony is compelled (absent some sort of cooperative international arrangement that we cannot assume will occur). While the Court of Appeals is doubtless correct that the expected consequences of some foreign prosecutions may be so severe that a witness will refuse to testify no matter what, not every foreign prosecution may measure up so harshly as against the expectable domestic consequences of contempt for refusing to testify. We therefore must suppose that on Balsys's view some evidence will in fact be lost to the domestic courts, and we are accordingly unable to dismiss the position of the United States in this case, that domestic law enforcement would suffer serious consequences if fear of foreign prosecution were recognized as sufficient to invoke the privilege.

In sum, the most we would feel able to conclude about the net result of the benefits and burdens that would follow from Balsys's view would be a Scotch verdict. If, then, precedent for the traditional view of the scope of the Clause were not dispositive of the issue before us, if extending the scope of the privilege were open to consideration, we still would not find that Balsys had shown that recognizing his claim would be a sound resolution of the competing interests involved.

V

This is not to say that cooperative conduct between the United States and foreign nations could not develop to a point at which a claim could be made for recognizing fear of foreign prosecution under the Self–Incrimination Clause as traditionally understood. If it could be said that the United States and its allies had enacted substantially similar criminal codes aimed at prosecuting offenses of international character, and if it could be shown that the United States was granting immunity from domestic prosecution for the purpose of obtaining evidence to be delivered to other nations as prosecutors of a crime common to both countries, then an argument could be made that the Fifth Amendment should apply based on fear of foreign prosecution simply because that prosecution was not fairly characterized as distinctly "foreign." The point would be that the prosecution was as much on behalf of the United States as of the prosecuting nation, so that the division of labor between evidence-gatherer and prosecutor made one nation the agent of the other, rendering fear of foreign prosecution tantamount to fear of a criminal case brought by the Government itself.

Whether such an argument should be sustained may be left at the least for another day, since its premises do not fit this case. It is true that Balsys has shown that the United States has assumed an interest in foreign prosecution, as demonstrated by OSI's mandate and American treaty agreements requiring the Government to give to Lithuania and Israel any evidence provided by Balsys. But this interest does not rise to the level of cooperative prosecution. There is no system of complementary substantive offenses at issue here, and the mere support of one nation for the prosecutorial efforts of another does not transform the prosecution of the one into the prosecution of the other. Cf. Bartkus v. Illinois, 359 U.S. 121, 122–124, 79 S.Ct. 676, 677–679, 3 L.Ed.2d 684 (1959) (rejecting double jeopardy claim where federal officials turned over all evidence they had gathered in connection with federal prosecution of defendant for use in subsequent state prosecution of defendant). In this case there is no basis for concluding that the privilege will lose its meaning without a rule precluding compelled testimony when there is a real and substantial risk that such testimony will be used in a criminal prosecution abroad.

Accordingly, the judgment of the Court of Appeals is reversed, and the case is remanded for further proceedings consistent with this opinion.

It is so ordered. [Concurring and dissenting opinions omitted.]

Page 1326. Insert under heading, 2. COMPELLED DISCLOSURE AND WAIVER and before Notes. Also consider in connection with Notes beginning at page 1384:

Mitchell v. United States

Supreme Court of the United States, 1999.
526 U.S. 314, 119 S.Ct. 1307, 143 L.Ed.2d 424.

■ JUSTICE KENNEDY delivered the opinion of the Court.

Two questions relating to a criminal defendant's Fifth Amendment privilege against self-incrimination are presented to us. The first is whether, in the federal criminal system, a guilty plea waives the privilege in the sentencing phase of the case, either as a result of the colloquy preceding the plea or by operation of law when the plea is entered. We hold the plea is not a waiver of the privilege at sentencing. The second question is whether, in determining facts about the crime which bear upon the severity of the sentence, a trial court may draw an adverse inference from the defendant's silence. We hold a sentencing court may not draw the adverse inference.

CHAPTER 9 PRIVILEGES

I

Petitioner Amanda Mitchell and 22 other defendants were indicted for offenses arising from a conspiracy to distribute cocaine in Allentown, Pennsylvania, from 1989 to 1994. According to the indictment, the leader of the conspiracy, Harry Riddick, obtained large quantities of cocaine and resold the drug through couriers and street sellers, including petitioner. Petitioner was charged with one count of conspiring to distribute five or more kilograms of cocaine, in violation of 21 U.S.C. § 846, and with three counts of distributing cocaine within 1,000 feet of a school or playground, in violation of § 860(a). In 1995, without any plea agreement, petitioner pleaded guilty to all four counts. She reserved the right to contest the drug quantity attributable to her under the conspiracy count, and the District Court advised her the drug quantity would be determined at her sentencing hearing.

Before accepting the plea, the District Court made the inquiries required by Rule 11 of the Federal Rules of Criminal Procedure. Informing petitioner of the penalties for her offenses, the District Judge advised her, "the range of punishment here is very complex because we don't know how much cocaine the Government's going to be able to show you were involved in." The judge told petitioner she faced a mandatory minimum of one year in prison under § 860 for distributing cocaine near a school or playground. She also faced "serious punishment depending on the quantity involved" for the conspiracy, with a mandatory minimum of 10 years in prison under § 841 if she could be held responsible for at least 5 kilograms but less than 15 kilograms of cocaine. By pleading guilty, the District Court explained, petitioner would waive various rights, including "the right at trial to remain silent under the Fifth Amendment."

After the Government explained the factual basis for the charges, the judge, having put petitioner under oath, asked her, "Did you do that?" Petitioner answered, "Some of it." She indicated that, although present for one of the transactions charged as a substantive cocaine distribution count, she had not herself delivered the cocaine to the customer. The Government maintained she was liable nevertheless as an aider and abettor of the delivery by another courier. After discussion with her counsel, petitioner reaffirmed her intention to plead guilty to all the charges. The District Court noted she might have a defense to one count on the theory that she was present but did not aid or abet the transaction. Petitioner again confirmed her intention to plead guilty, and the District Court accepted the plea.

In 1996, nine of petitioner's original 22 codefendants went to trial. Three other co-defendants had pleaded guilty and agreed to cooperate with the Government. They testified petitioner was a regular seller for ringleader Riddick. At petitioner's sentencing hearing, the three adopted their trial testimony, and one of them furnished additional information on the amount of cocaine petitioner sold. According to him, petitioner worked two to three times a week, selling 1 1/2 to 2 ounces of cocaine a day, from April 1992 to August 1992. Then, from August 1992 to December 1993 she worked three to five times a week, and from January 1994 to March 1994 she was one of those in charge of cocaine distribution for Riddick. On cross-examination, the codefendant conceded he had not seen petitioner on a regular basis during the relevant period.

Both petitioner and the Government referred to trial testimony by one Alvitta Mack, who had made a series of drug buys under the supervision of law enforcement agents, including three purchases from petitioner totaling two ounces of cocaine in 1992. Petitioner put on no evidence at sentencing, nor did she testify to rebut the Government's evidence about drug quantity. Her counsel argued, however, that the three documented sales to Mack constituted the only evidence of sufficient reliability to be credited in determining the quantity of cocaine attributable to her for sentencing purposes.

After this testimony at the sentencing hearing the District Court ruled that, as a consequence of her guilty plea, petitioner had no right to remain silent with respect to the details of her crimes. The court found credible the testimony indicating petitioner had been a drug courier on a regular basis. Sales of 1 1/2 to 2 ounces twice a week for a year and a half put her over the 5-kilogram threshold, thus mandating a minimum sentence of 10 years. "One of the things" persuading the court to rely on the testimony of the codefendants was petitioner's "not testifying to the contrary."

. . .

The District Court sentenced petitioner to the statutory minimum of 10 years of imprisonment, 6 years of supervised release, and a special assessment of $200.

The Court of Appeals for the Third Circuit affirmed the sentence. According to the Court of Appeals, "By voluntarily and knowingly pleading guilty to the offense Mitchell waived her Fifth Amendment privilege." The court acknowledged other Circuits have held a witness can "claim the Fifth Amendment privilege if his or her testimony might be used to enhance his or her sentence," . . .

We granted certiorari to resolve the apparent circuit conflict created by the Court of Appeals' decision, and we now reverse.

II

The Government maintains that petitioner's guilty plea was a waiver of the privilege against compelled self-incrimination with respect to all the crimes comprehended in the plea. We hold otherwise and rule that petitioner retained the privilege at her sentencing hearing.

A

It is well established that a witness, in a single proceeding, may not testify voluntarily about a subject and then invoke the privilege against self-incrimination when questioned about the details. See Rogers v. United States, 340 U.S. 367 (1951). The privilege is waived for the matters to which the witness testifies, and the scope of the "waiver is determined by the scope of relevant cross-examination," Brown v. United States, 356 U.S. 148 (1958) ... Nice questions will arise, of course, about the extent of the initial testimony and whether the ensuing questions are comprehended within its scope, but for now it suffices to note the general rule.

The justifications for the rule of waiver in the testimonial context are evident: A witness may not pick and choose what aspects of a particular subject to discuss without casting doubt on the trustworthiness of the statements and diminishing the integrity of the factual inquiry. As noted in Rogers, a contrary rule "would open the way to distortion of facts by permitting a witness to select any stopping place in the testimony," 340 U.S. at 371. It would, as we said in Brown, "make of the Fifth Amendment not only a humane safeguard against judicially coerced self-disclosure but a positive invitation to mutilate the truth a party offers to tell," 356 U.S. at 156. The illogic of allowing a witness to offer only self-selected testimony should be obvious even to the witness, so there is no unfairness in allowing cross-examination when testimony is given without invoking the privilege.

We may assume for purposes of this opinion, then, that if petitioner had pleaded not guilty and, having taken the stand at a trial, testified she did "some of it," she could have been cross-examined on the frequency of her drug deliveries and the quantity of cocaine involved. The concerns which justify the cross-examination when the defendant testifies are absent at a plea colloquy, however. The purpose of a plea colloquy is to protect the defendant from an unintelligent or involuntary plea. The Government would turn this constitutional shield into a prosecutorial sword by having the defendant relinquish all rights against compelled self-incrimination upon entry of a guilty plea, including the right to remain silent at sentencing.

There is no convincing reason why the narrow inquiry at the plea colloquy should entail such an extensive waiver of the privilege. Unlike the defendant taking the stand, who "cannot reasonably claim that the Fifth Amendment gives him ... an immunity from cross-examination on the matters he has himself put in dispute," 356 U.S. at 155-156, the defendant who pleads guilty puts nothing in dispute regarding the essentials of the offense. Rather, the defendant takes those matters out of dispute, often by making a joint statement with the prosecution or confirming the prosecution's version of the facts. Under these circumstances, there is little danger that the court will be misled by selective disclosure. In this respect a guilty plea is more like an offer to stipulate

SECTION 2 PRIVILEGE BELONGING TO THE INDIVIDUAL

than a decision to take the stand. Here, petitioner's statement that she had done "some of" the proffered conduct did not pose a threat to the integrity of factfinding proceedings, for the purpose of the District Court's inquiry was simply to ensure that petitioner understood the charges and that there was a factual basis for the Government's case.

. . .

Treating a guilty plea as a waiver of the privilege at sentencing would be a grave encroachment on the rights of defendants. At oral argument, we asked counsel for the United States whether, on the facts of this case, if the Government had no reliable evidence of the amount of drugs involved, the prosecutor "could say, well, we can't prove it, but we'd like to put her on the stand and cross-examine her and see if we can't get her to admit it." Counsel answered: "The waiver analysis that we have put forward suggests that at least as to the facts surrounding the conspiracy to which she admitted, the Government could do that." Ibid. Over 90% of federal criminal defendants whose cases are not dismissed enter pleas of guilty or nolo contendere. U.S. Dept. of Justice, Bureau of Justice Statistics, Sourcebook of Criminal Justice Statistics 1996, p. 448 (24th ed. 1997). Were we to accept the Government's position, prosecutors could indict without specifying the quantity of drugs involved, obtain a guilty plea, and then put the defendant on the stand at sentencing to fill in the drug quantity. The result would be to enlist the defendant as an instrument in his or her own condemnation, undermining the long tradition and vital principle that criminal proceedings rely on accusations proved by the Government, not on inquisitions conducted to enhance its own prosecutorial power.

We reject the position that either petitioner's guilty plea or her statements at the plea colloquy functioned as a waiver of her right to remain silent at sentencing.

B

The centerpiece of the Third Circuit's opinion is the idea that the entry of the guilty plea completes the incrimination of the defendant, thus extinguishing the privilege. Where a sentence has yet to be imposed, however, this Court has already rejected the proposition that "incrimination is complete once guilt has been adjudicated," Estelle v. Smith, 451 U.S. 454 (1981), and we reject it again today.

The Court of Appeals cited Wigmore on Evidence for the proposition that upon conviction "criminality ceases; and with criminality the privilege." (citing 8 J. Wigmore, Evidence § 2279, p. 481 (J. McNaughton rev. 1961)). The passage relied upon does not support the Third Circuit's narrow view of the privilege. The full passage is as follows: "Legal criminality consists in liability to the law's punishment. When that liability is removed, criminality ceases; and with the criminality the privilege." It could be argued that liability for punishment continues until sentence has been imposed, and so does the privilege. Even if the Court of Appeals' interpretation of the treatise were correct, however, and it means the privilege ceases upon conviction but before sentencing, we would respond that the suggested rule is simply wrong. A later supplement to the treatise, indeed, states the proper rule that, "although the witness has pleaded guilty to a crime charged but has not been sentenced, his constitutional privilege remains unimpaired." J. Wigmore, Evidence § 2279, p. 991, n. 1 (A. Best ed. Supp. 1998).

It is true, as a general rule, that where there can be no further incrimination, there is no basis for the assertion of the privilege. We conclude that principle applies to cases in which the sentence has been fixed and the judgment of conviction has become final. If no adverse consequences can be visited upon the convicted person by reason of further testimony, then there is no further incrimination to be feared.

Where the sentence has not yet been imposed a defendant may have a legitimate fear of adverse consequences from further testimony. As the Court stated in Estelle: "Any effort by the State to compel [the defendant] to testify against his will at the sentencing hearing clearly would contravene the Fifth Amendment." 451 U.S. at 463. Estelle was a capital case, but we find no reason not to apply the principle to noncapital sentencing hearings as well. . . .

The Fifth Amendment by its terms prevents a person from being "compelled in any criminal case to be a witness against himself." U.S. Const., Amdt. 5. To maintain that sentencing proceedings are not part of "any criminal case" is contrary to the law and to common sense. As to the law, under the Federal Rules of Criminal Procedure, a court must impose sentence before a judgment of conviction can issue. See Rule 32(d)(1) ("A judgment of conviction must set forth the plea . . . and the sentence"). As to common sense, it appears that in this case, as is often true in the criminal justice system, the defendant was less concerned with the proof of her guilt or innocence than with the severity of her punishment. Petitioner faced imprisonment from one year upwards to life, depending on the circumstances of the crime. To say that she had no right to remain silent but instead could be compelled to cooperate in the deprivation of her liberty would ignore the Fifth Amendment privilege at the precise stage where, from her point of view, it was most important.

III

The Government suggests in a footnote that even if petitioner retained an unwaived privilege against self-incrimination in the sentencing phase of her case, the District Court was entitled, based on her silence, to draw an adverse inference with regard to the amount of drugs attributable to her. The normal rule in a criminal case is that no negative inference from the defendant's failure to testify is permitted. Griffin v. California, 380 U.S. 609, 614, 14 L.Ed.2d 106 (1965). We decline to adopt an exception for the sentencing phase of a criminal case with regard to factual determinations respecting the circumstances and details of the crime.

This Court has recognized "the prevailing rule that the Fifth Amendment does not forbid adverse inferences against parties to civil actions when they refuse to testify in response to probative evidence offered against them," Baxter v. Palmigiano, 425 U.S. 308, 318, at least where refusal to waive the privilege does not lead "automatically and without more to [the] imposition of sanctions," Lefkowitz v. Cunningham, 431 U.S. 801, 808 (1977). In ordinary civil cases, the party confronted with the invocation of the privilege by the opposing side has no capacity to avoid it, say, by offering immunity from prosecution. The rule allowing invocation of the privilege, though at the risk of suffering an adverse inference or even a default, accommodates the right not to be a witness against oneself while still permitting civil litigation to proceed. Another reason for treating civil and criminal cases differently is that "the stakes are higher" in criminal cases, where liberty or even life may be at stake, and where the Government's "sole interest is to convict." Baxter, 425 U.S. at 318–319.

Baxter itself involved state prison disciplinary proceedings which, as the Court noted, "are not criminal proceedings" and "involve the correctional process and important state interests other than conviction for crime." 425 U.S. at 316, 319. Unlike a prison disciplinary proceeding, a sentencing hearing is part of the criminal case—the explicit concern of the self-incrimination privilege. In accordance with the text of the Fifth Amendment, we must accord the privilege the same protection in the sentencing phase of "any criminal case" as that which is due in the trial phase of the same case.

The concerns which mandate the rule against negative inferences at a criminal trial apply with equal force at sentencing. Without question, the stakes are high: Here, the inference drawn by the District Court from petitioner's silence may have resulted in decades of added imprisonment. The Government often has a motive to demand a severe sentence, so the central purpose of the privilege—to protect a defendant from being the unwilling instrument of his or her own condemnation— remains of vital importance.

The rule against adverse inferences from a defendant's silence in criminal proceedings, including sentencing, is of proven utility. Some years ago the Court expressed concern that "too many, even those who should be better advised, view this privilege as a shelter for wrongdoers. They too readily assume that those who invoke it are either guilty of crime or commit perjury in claiming the privilege." Ullmann v. United States, 350 U.S. 422, 426 (1956). Later, it quoted with apparent approval Wigmore's observation that "the layman's natural first suggestion would probably be that the resort to privilege in each instance is a clear confession of crime," Lakeside v. Oregon, 435 U.S. 333, 340 (1978) (quoting 8 [*1316] Wigmore, Evidence § 2272, p. 426 (J. McNaughton rev.1961)). It is far from clear that citizens, and jurors, remain today so skeptical of the principle or are often willing to ignore the prohibition against adverse inferences from silence. Principles once unsettled can find general and wide acceptance in the legal culture, and there can be little doubt that the rule prohibiting an inference of guilt from a defendant's rightful silence has become an essential feature of our legal tradition. This process began even before Griffin. When Griffin was being considered by this Court, some 44 States did not allow a prosecutor to invite the jury to make an adverse inference from the defendant's refusal to testify at trial. See Griffin, supra, at 611, n. 3. The rule against adverse inferences is a vital instrument for teaching that the question in a criminal case is not whether the defendant committed the acts of which he is accused. The question is whether the Government has carried its burden to prove its allegations while respecting the defendant's individual rights. The Government retains the burden of proving facts relevant to the crime at the sentencing phase and cannot enlist the defendant in this process at the expense of the self-incrimination privilege. Whether silence bears upon the determination of a lack of remorse, or upon acceptance of responsibility for purposes of the downward adjustment provided in § 3E1.1 of the United States Sentencing Guidelines (1998), is a separate question. It is not before us, and we express no view on it.

By holding petitioner's silence against her in determining the facts of the offense at the sentencing hearing, the District Court imposed an impermissible burden on the exercise of the constitutional right against compelled self-incrimination. The judgment of the Court of Appeals is reversed, and the case is remanded for further proceedings consistent with this opinion.

It is so ordered.

■ [JUSTICE SCALIA, with whom THE CHIEF JUSTICE, JUSTICE O'CONNOR, and JUSTICE THOMAS joined, dissented. JUSTICE THOMAS also wrote a separate dissent.]

3. THE TESTIMONIAL COMMUNICATION REQUIREMENT

b. Subpoenaed Documents

Page 1344. Add as Note 8, before D:

8. In United States v. Hubbell, 530 U.S. 27, 120 S.Ct. 2037 (2000), a case growing out of the Independent Counsel's investigation of matters relating to President Clinton. Webster Hubbell first pleaded guilty to charges of mail fraud and tax evasion arising out of his billing practices as a member of an Arkansas law firm and then was prosecuted a second time after having produced 13,120 pages of documents in response to a subpoena and having responded to a series of questions that established that those were all of the documents in his custody or control that were responsive to the commands in the subpoena. Initially he had claimed the privilege against self incrimination in response to the subpoena,

SECTION 2   PRIVILEGE BELONGING TO THE INDIVIDUAL

but he was then granted immunity and produced the documents. The contents of the documents provided the Independent Counsel with the information that led to the second prosecution. The court of appeals vacated the judgment dismissing the indictment and remanded for further proceedings. The Supreme Court affirmed the judgement of the court of appeals, but also dismissed the indictment, stating:

> "The Government correctly emphasizes that the testimonial aspect of a response to a subpoena ... does nothing more than establish the existence, authenticity, and custody of items that are produced. We assume that the Government is also entirely correct in its submission that it would not have to advert to respondent's act of production in order to prove the existence, authenticity, or custody of any documents that it might offer in evidence at a criminal trial....
>
> "The question, however, is not whether the response to the subpoena may be introduced into evidence at his criminal trial. That would surely be a prohibited 'use' of the immunized act of production.... But the fact that the Government intends no such use of the act of production leaves open the separate question whether it has already made 'derivative use' of the testimonial aspect of that act in obtaining the indictment against respondent and preparing its case for trial. It clearly has.
>
> "It is apparent from the text of the subpoena itself that the prosecutor needed respondent's assistance both to identify potential sources of information and to produce those sources.... Entirely apart from the contents of the 13,120 pages of materials that respondent produced in this case, it is undeniable that providing a catalog of existing documents fitting within any of the 11 broadly worded subpoena categories could provide a prosecutor with a lead to incriminating evidence.
>
> ".... It is abundantly clear that the testimonial aspect of respondent's act of producing subpoenaed documents was the first step in a chain of evidence that led to this prosecution....
>
> "It was unquestionably necessary for respondent to make extensive use of 'the contents of his own mind' identifying the hundreds of documents responsive to the requests in the subpoena.... The assembly of those documents was like telling an inquisitor the combination to a wall safe, not like being forced to surrender the key to a strongbox.
>
> "... [T]he Government has argued that the communicative aspect of respondent's act of producing ordinary business records is insufficiently 'testimonial' to support a claim of privilege because the existence and possession of such records by a businessman is a 'foregone conclusion', [citing Fisher]....
>
> "Whatever, the scope of this 'foregone' conclusion rationale, the facts of this case plainly fall outside of it. While in Fisher the Government already knew that the documents were in the attorney's possession and could independently confirm their existence and authenticity through the accountants who created them, here the Government has not shown that it had any prior knowledge of either the existence or the whereabouts of the 13,120 pages of documents ultimately produced by respondent. The Government cannot cure this deficiency through the overbroad argument that a businessman such as

CHAPTER 9 PRIVILEGES

respondent will always possess general business and tax records that fall within the broad categories described in this subpoena."

E. IMMUNITY

Page 1376. Add the following paragraphs to Note 11:

In McKune v. Lile, 536 U.S. 24, 122 S.Ct. 2017, 153 L.Ed. 2d 47 (2002), a prison inmate, convicted of rape, sodomy, and kidnapping refused to participate in a Sexual Abuse Treatment Program, designed to be rehabilitative, that would require him to admit responsibility for the crime for which he was sentenced and disclose details of his sexual history including activities that might constitute uncharged criminal offenses. The information thus provided would be treated as not privileged and there would be the possibility that the State might use the evidence against the inmate in future criminal proceedings. As a result of his refusal to participate in the Program, prison officials indicated that his privileges status would be reduced which meant that his visitation rights, earnings, work opportunities, ability to send money to his family, canteen expenditures, access to personal television and other privileges would be curtailed; also he would be transferred to a different maximum security unit "where his movement would be more limited, he would be moved from a two-person to a four-person cell, and he would be in a potentially more dangerous environment." The inmate, relying on his privilege against self-incrimination brought an injunction action against the warden under 42 U.S.C. § 1983.

A five person majority of the Supreme Court ruled that the denial of prison privileges in this context did not amount to unconstitutional compulsion. The plurality opinion noted that the transfer to a different maximum security unit was not intended as a punishment but rather had a "legitimate penological reason"—to make room for inmates willing to participate in the Program. Regarding the loss of other privileges, the plurality wrote:

> An essential tool of prison administration ... is the authority to offer inmates various incentives to behave. The Constitution accords prison officials wide latitude to bestow or revoke these perquisites as they see fit.

Justice O'Connor wrote a separate opinion concurring in the result: She agreed with the plurality opinion of Justice Kennedy that the change in the inmate's prison conditions were not so great as to constitute compulsion, but she also agreed with Justice Stevens writing for the dissenters that "Fifth Amendment compulsion standard is broader than the 'atypical and significant hardship' standard ... adopted for evaluating due process claims in prison," citing Meachum v. Fano, 427 U.S. 215 (1976).

Compare the denial of privileges in McKune with the compulsion exerted against public employees by the threat of dismissal under the Garrity doctrine,

SECTION 3. THE ATTORNEY-CLIENT PRIVILEGE

B. BASIC ELEMENTS

Page 1409. Add following Note 17 and before Section C:

Swidler & Berlin and Hamilton v. United States
Supreme Court of the United States, 1998.
524 U.S. 399, 118 S.Ct. 2081, 141 L.Ed.2d 379.

■ [REHNQUIST, C. J., delivered the opinion of the Court, in which STEVENS, KENNEDY, SOUTER, GINSBURG, and BREYER, JJ., joined. O'CONNOR, J., filed a dissenting opinion, in which SCALIA and THOMAS, JJ., joined.][1]

■ CHIEF JUSTICE REHNQUIST delivered the opinion of the Court.

Petitioner, an attorney, made notes of an initial interview with a client shortly before the client's death. The Government, represented by the Office of Independent Counsel, now seeks his notes for use in a criminal investigation. We hold that the notes are protected by the attorney-client privilege.

This dispute arises out of an investigation conducted by the Office of the Independent Counsel into whether various individuals made false statements, obstructed justice, or committed other crimes during investigations of the 1993 dismissal of employees from the White House Travel Office. Vincent W. Foster, Jr., was Deputy White House Counsel when the firings occurred. In July, 1993, Foster met with petitioner James Hamilton, an attorney at petitioner Swidler & Berlin, to seek legal representation concerning possible congressional or other investigations of the firings. During a 2-hour meeting, Hamilton took three pages of handwritten notes. One of the first entries in the notes is the word "Privileged." Nine days later, Foster committed suicide.

In December 1995, a federal grand jury, at the request of the Independent Counsel, issued subpoenas to petitioners Hamilton and Swidler & Berlin for, inter alia, Hamilton's handwritten notes of his meeting with Foster. Petitioners filed a motion to quash, arguing that the notes were protected by the attorney client privilege and by the work product privilege. The District Court, after examining the notes in camera, concluded they were protected from disclosure by both doctrines and denied enforcement of the subpoenas.

The Court of Appeals for the District of Columbia Circuit reversed. In re Sealed Case, 124 F.3d 230 (1997). While recognizing that most courts assume the privilege survives death, the Court of Appeals noted

1. [Footnotes omitted.]

that holdings actually manifesting the posthumous force of the privilege are rare. Instead, most judicial references to the privilege's posthumous application occur in the context of a well recognized exception allowing disclosure for disputes among the client's heirs. Id., at 231–232. It further noted that most commentators support some measure of posthumous curtailment of the privilege. Id., at 232. The Court of Appeals thought that the risk of posthumous revelation, when confined to the criminal context, would have little to no chilling effect on client communication, but that the costs of protecting communications after death were high. It therefore concluded that the privilege was not absolute in such circumstances, and that instead, a balancing test should apply. Id., at 233–234. It thus held that there is a posthumous exception to the privilege for communications whose relative importance to particular criminal litigation is substantial. Id., at 235. While acknowledging that uncertain privileges are disfavored, Jaffee v. Redmond, 518 U.S. 1, 17–18, 116 S.Ct. 1923, 1932, 135 L.Ed.2d 337 (1996), the Court of Appeals determined that the uncertainty introduced by its balancing test was insignificant in light of existing exceptions to the privilege. 124 F.3d, at 235. The Court of Appeals also held that the notes were not protected by the work product privilege.

The attorney client privilege is one of the oldest recognized privileges for confidential communications. Upjohn Co. v. United States, 449 U.S. 383, 389, 101 S.Ct. 677, 682, 66 L.Ed.2d 584 (1981); Hunt v. Blackburn, 128 U.S. 464, 470, 9 S.Ct. 125, 127, 32 L.Ed. 488 (1888). The privilege is intended to encourage "full and frank communication between attorneys and their clients and thereby promote broader public interests in the observance of law and the administration of justice." Upjohn, supra, at 389, 101 S.Ct. at 682. The issue presented here is the scope of that privilege; more particularly, the extent to which the privilege survives the death of the client. Our interpretation of the privilege's scope is guided by "the principles of the common law ... as interpreted by the courts ... in the light of reason and experience." Fed.Rule Evid. 501; Funk v. United States, 290 U.S. 371, 54 S.Ct. 212, 78 L.Ed. 369 (1933).

The Independent Counsel argues that the attorney-client privilege should not prevent disclosure of confidential communications where the client has died and the information is relevant to a criminal proceeding. There is some authority for this position. One state appellate court, Cohen v. Jenkintown Cab Co., 238 Pa.Super. 456, 357 A.2d 689 (1976), and the Court of Appeals below have held the privilege may be subject to posthumous exceptions in certain circumstances. In Cohen, a civil case, the court recognized that the privilege generally survives death, but concluded that it could make an exception where the interest of justice was compelling and the interest of the client in preserving the confidence was insignificant. Id., 462–464, 357 A.2d, at 692–693.

But other than these two decisions, cases addressing the existence of the privilege after death—most involving the testamentary exception—uniformly presume the privilege survives, even if they do not so hold....

Such testamentary exception cases consistently presume the privilege survives. See, e.g., United States v. Osborn, 561 F.2d 1334, 1340 (C.A.9 1977); DeLoach v. Myers, 215 Ga. 255, 259–260, 109 S.E.2d 777, 780–781 (1959); Doyle v. Reeves, 112 Conn. 521, 152 A. 882 (1931); Russell v. Jackson, 9 Hare. 387, 68 Eng. Rep. 558 (V.C.1851). They view testamentary disclosure of communications as an exception to the privilege: "[T]he general rule with respect to confidential communications ... is that such communications are privileged during the testator's lifetime and, also, after the testator's death unless sought to be disclosed in litigation between the testator's heirs." Osborn, 561 F.2d, at 1340. The rationale for such disclosure is that it furthers the client's intent. Id., at 1340, n. 11.

The great body of this caselaw supports, either by holding or considered dicta, the position that the privilege does survive in a case such as the present one. Given the language of Rule 501, at the very least the burden is on the Independent Counsel to show that "reason and experience" require a departure from this rule.

The Independent Counsel contends that the testamentary exception supports the posthumous termination of the privilege because in practice most cases have refused to apply the privilege posthumously. He further argues that the exception reflects a policy judgment that the interest in settling estates outweighs any posthumous interest in confidentiality. He then reasons by analogy that in criminal proceedings, the interest in determining whether a crime has been committed should trump client confidentiality, particularly since the financial interests of the estate are not at stake.

But the Independent Counsel's interpretation simply does not square with the caselaw's implicit acceptance of the privilege's survival and with the treatment of testamentary disclosure as an "exception" or an implied "waiver." And the premise of his analogy is incorrect, since cases consistently recognize that the rationale for the testamentary exception is that it furthers the client's intent, see, e.g., Glover, supra. There is no reason to suppose as a general matter that grand jury testimony about confidential communications furthers the client's intent.

Commentators on the law also recognize that the general rule is that the attorney-client privilege continues after death. See, e.g., 8 Wigmore, Evidence § 2323 (McNaughton rev. 1961); Frankel, The Attorney–Client Privilege After the Death of the Client, 6 Geo.J.Legal Ethics 45, 78–79 (1992); 1 J. Strong, McCormick on Evidence § 94, p. 348 (4th ed. 1992). Undoubtedly, as the Independent Counsel emphasizes, various commentators have criticized this rule, urging that the privilege should be abrogated after the client's death where extreme injustice would result, as long as disclosure would not seriously undermine the privilege by deterring client communication. See, e.g., C. Mueller & L. Kirkpatrick, 2 Federal Evidence § 199, at 380–381 (2d ed. 1994); Restatement (Third) of the Law Governing Lawyers § 127, Comment d (Proposed Final Draft No. 1, Mar. 29, 1996). But even these critics clearly recognize that established law supports the continuation of the privilege and that a contrary rule would be a modification of the common law. See, e.g., Mueller & Kirkpatrick, supra, at 379; Restatement of the Law Governing Lawyers, supra, § 127, Comment c; 24 C. Wright & K. Graham, Federal Practice and Procedure § 5498, p. 483 (1986).

Despite the scholarly criticism, we think there are weighty reasons that counsel in favor of posthumous application. Knowing that communications will remain confidential even after death encourages the client to communicate fully and frankly with counsel. While the fear of disclosure, and the consequent withholding of information from counsel, may be reduced if disclosure is limited to posthumous disclosure in a criminal context, it seems unreasonable to assume that it vanishes altogether. Clients may be concerned about reputation, civil liability, or possible harm to friends or family. Posthumous disclosure of such communications may be as feared as disclosure during the client's lifetime.

The Independent Counsel suggests, however, that his proposed exception would have little to no effect on the client's willingness to confide in his attorney. He reasons that only clients intending to perjure themselves will be chilled by a rule of disclosure after death, as opposed to truthful clients or those asserting their Fifth Amendment privilege. This is because for the latter group, communications disclosed by the attorney after the client's death purportedly will reveal only information that the client himself would have revealed if alive.

The Independent Counsel assumes, incorrectly we believe, that the privilege is analogous to the Fifth Amendment's protection against self-incrimination. But as suggested above, the privilege serves much broader purposes. Clients consult attorneys for a wide variety of reasons, only one of which involves possible criminal liability. Many attorneys act as counselors on personal and family matters, where, in the course of obtaining the desired advice, confidences about family members or financial problems must be revealed in order to assure sound legal advice. The same is true of owners of small businesses who may regularly consult their attorneys about a variety of problems arising in the course of the business. These confidences may not come close to any sort of admission of criminal wrongdoing, but nonetheless be matters which the client would not wish divulged.

The contention that the attorney is being required to disclose only what the client could have been required to disclose is at odds with the basis for the privilege even during the client's lifetime. In related cases, we have said that the loss of evidence admittedly caused by the privilege is justified in part by the fact that without the privilege, the client may not have made such communications in the first place.... This is true of disclosure before and after the client's death. Without assurance of the privilege's posthumous application, the client may very well not have made disclosures to his attorney at all, so the loss of evidence is more apparent than real. In the case at hand, it seems quite plausible that Foster, perhaps already contemplating suicide, may not have sought legal advice from Hamilton if he had not been assured the conversation was privileged.

The Independent Counsel additionally suggests that his proposed exception would have minimal impact if confined to criminal cases, or, as the Court of Appeals suggests, if it is limited to information of substantial importance to a particular criminal case. However, there is no case authority for the proposition that the privilege applies differently in criminal and civil cases, and only one commentator ventures such a suggestion, see Mueller & Kirkpatrick, supra, at 380–381. In any event, a client may not know at the time he discloses information to his attorney whether it will later be relevant to a civil or a criminal matter, let alone whether it will be of substantial importance. Balancing ex post the importance of the information against client interests, even limited to criminal cases, introduces substantial uncertainty into the privilege's application. For just that reason, we have rejected use of a balancing test in defining the contours of the privilege....

In a similar vein, the Independent Counsel argues that existing exceptions to the privilege, such as the crime-fraud exception and the testamentary exception, make the impact of one more exception marginal. However, these exceptions do not demonstrate that the impact of a posthumous exception would be insignificant, and there is little empirical evidence on this point. The established exceptions are consistent with the purposes of the privilege ... while a posthumous exception in criminal cases appears at odds with the goals of encouraging full and frank communication and of protecting the client's interests. A "no harm in one more exception" rationale could contribute to the general erosion of the privilege, without reference to common law principles or "reason and experience."

Finally, the Independent Counsel, relying on cases such as United States v. Nixon, 418 U.S. 683, 710, 94 S.Ct. 3090, 3108, 41 L.Ed.2d 1039 (1974), and Branzburg v. Hayes, 408 U.S. 665, 92 S.Ct. 2646, 33 L.Ed.2d 626 (1972), urges that privileges be strictly construed because they are inconsistent with the paramount judicial goal of truth seeking. But both Nixon and Branzburg dealt with the creation of privileges not recognized by the common law, whereas here we deal with one of the oldest recognized privileges in the law. And we are asked, not simply to "construe" the privilege, but to narrow it, contrary to the weight of the existing body of caselaw.

It has been generally, if not universally, accepted, for well over a century, that the attorney-client privilege survives the death of the client in a case such as this. While the arguments against the survival of the privilege are by no means frivolous, they are based in large part on speculation—thoughtful speculation, but speculation nonetheless—as to whether posthumous termination of the privilege would diminish a client's willingness to confide in an attorney. In an area where empirical information would be useful, it is scant and inconclusive.

Rule 501's direction to look to "the principles of the common law as they may be interpreted by the courts of the United States in the light of reason and experience" does not mandate that a rule, once established, should endure for all time.... But here the Independent Counsel has simply not made a sufficient showing to overturn the common law rule embodied in the prevailing caselaw. Interpreted in the light of reason and experience, that body of law requires that the attorney client privilege prevent disclosure of the notes at issue in this case. The judgment of the Court of Appeals is

Reversed.

[Dissenting opinion omitted.]

I. The Sixth Amendment Right to Counsel and the Attorney-Client Privilege

Page 1493. Add as Note e. before 2:

In the wake of the September 11th terrorist attacks on the World Trade Center, Attorney General Ashcroft issued a new federal rule, excerpted below, dealing with the monitoring of prison inmate communications with attorneys, "To Deter Acts of Terrorism." This new provision was issued as an interim rule, effective immediately, with provision for post-promulgation public comment, invoking certain exceptions to the usual requirement of pre-implementation public comment. See 5 U.S.C. 553 (a), (b)B, and (d).

Regarding this new rule, the Chairman of the Senate Judiciary Committee, describing himself as "deeply troubled at what appears to be an executive effort to exercise new powers without judicial scrutiny or statutory authorization," sent a letter to the Attorney General asking for explanations regarding the statutory basis for the rule and its constitutionality. 70 U.S. Law Week 2306 (Nov. 20, 2001). In response, the Attorney General testified at a hearing of the Senate Judiciary Committee, defending the new rule and insisting that its intent is not to disrupt communications with counsel but rather to prevent inmates who were plotting terrorist acts from using their attorneys as conduits. 70 U.S. Law Week 2352 (December 11, 2001).

Is this new rule consistent with the attorney-client privilege? Is its constitutionality likely to be upheld? Is it sound as a matter of policy?

66 Fed. Reg. 55062, amending 28 CFR 501:

§ 501.3—Prevention of acts of violence and terrorism.

* * *

SECTION 3   THE ATTORNEY-CLIENT PRIVILEGE

(c) Initial placement of an inmate in administrative detention and/or any limitation of the inmate's privileges in accordance with paragraph (a) of this section may be imposed for up to 120 days or, with the approval of the Attorney General, a longer period of time not to exceed one year. Special restrictions imposed in accordance with paragraph (a) of this section may be extended thereafter by the Director, Bureau of Prisons, in increments not to exceed one year, upon receipt by the Director of an additional written notification from the Attorney General, or, at the Attorney General's direction, from the head of a federal law enforcement agency or the head of a member agency of the United States intelligence community, that there continues to be a substantial risk that the inmate's communications or contacts with other persons could result in death or serious bodily injury to persons, or substantial damage to property that would entail the risk of death or serious bodily injury to persons. The authority of the Director under this paragraph may not be delegated below the level of Acting Director.

(d) In any case where the Attorney General specifically so orders, based on information from the head of a federal law enforcement or intelligence agency that reasonable suspicion exists to believe that a particular inmate may use communications with attorneys or their agents to further or facilitate acts of terrorism, the Director, Bureau of Prisons, shall, in addition to the special administrative measures imposed under paragraph (a) of this section, provide appropriate procedures for the monitoring or review of communications between that inmate and attorneys or attorneys' agents who are traditionally covered by the attorney-client privilege, for the purpose of deterring future acts that could result in death or serious bodily injury to persons, or substantial damage to property that would entail the risk of death or serious bodily injury to persons.

(1) The certification by the Attorney General under this paragraph (d) shall be in addition to any findings or determinations relating to the need for the imposition of other special administrative measures as provided in paragraph (a) of this section, but may be incorporated into the same document.

(2) Except in the case of prior court authorization, the Director, Bureau of Prisons, shall provide written notice to the inmate and to the attorneys involved, prior to the initiation of any monitoring or review under this paragraph (d). The notice shall explain:

(i) That, notwithstanding the provisions of part 540 of this chapter or other rules, all communications between the inmate and attorneys may be monitored, to the extent determined to be reasonably necessary for the purpose of deterring future acts of violence or terrorism;

(ii) That communications between the inmate and attorneys or their agents are not protected by the attorney-client privilege if they would facilitate criminal acts or a conspiracy to commit criminal acts, or if those communications are not related to the seeking or providing of legal advice.

(3) The Director, Bureau of Prisons, with the approval of the Assistant Attorney General for the Criminal Division, shall employ appropriate procedures to ensure that all attorney-client communications are reviewed for privilege claims and that any properly privileged materials (including, but not limited to, recordings of privileged communications) are not retained during the course of the monitoring. To protect the attorney-client privilege and to ensure that the investigation is not compromised by exposure to privileged material relating to the investigation or to defense strategy, a privilege team shall be designated, consisting of individuals not involved in the underlying investigation. The monitoring shall be conducted pursuant to procedures designed to minimize the intrusions into privileged material or conversations. Except in cases where the person in charge of the privilege team determines that acts of violence or terrorism are imminent, the privilege team shall not disclose any information unless and until such disclosure has been approved by a federal judge.

* * *

(f) Other appropriate officials of the Department of Justice having custody of persons for whom special administrative measures are required may exercise the same authorities under this section as the Director of the Bureau of Prisons and the Warden.

Dated: October 26, 2001.

John Ashcroft,

Attorney General.

[FR Doc. 01–27472 Filed 10–30–01; 9:35 am]

Page 1494. Add as new subsection J. before Section 4:

J. INTERLOCUTORY APPEALS? DISCLOSURE ORDER ADVERSE TO ATTORNEY-CLIENT PRIVILEGE

Mohawk Industries, Inc. v. Carpenter

Supreme Court of the United States, 2009.
___ U.S. ___, 130 S.Ct. 599, 175 L.Ed.2d 458.

■ [SOTOMAYOR, J., delivered the opinion of the Court, in which ROBERTS, C. J., and STEVENS, SCALIA, KENNEDY, GINSBURG, BREYER, and ALITO, JJ., joined, and in which THOMAS, J., joined, as to Part II-C. THOMAS, J., filed an opinion concurring in part and concurring in the judgment.]

■ JUSTICE SOTOMAYOR delivered the opinion of the Court.

Section 1291 of the Judicial Code confers on federal courts of appeals jurisdiction to review "final decisions of the district courts." 28

U.S.C. § 1291. Although "final decisions" typically are ones that trigger the entry of judgment, they also include a small set of prejudgment orders that are "collateral to" the merits of an action and "too important" to be denied immediate review. In this case, petitioner Mohawk Industries, Inc., attempted to bring a collateral order appeal after the District Court ordered it to disclose certain confidential materials on the ground that Mohawk had waived the attorney-client privilege. The Court of Appeals dismissed the appeal for want of jurisdiction.

The question before us is whether disclosure orders adverse to the attorney-client privilege qualify for immediate appeal under the collateral order doctrine. Agreeing with the Court of Appeals, we hold that they do not. Postjudgment appeals, together with other review mechanisms, suffice to protect the rights of litigants and preserve the vitality of the attorney-client privilege.

I

In 2007, respondent Norman Carpenter, a former shift supervisor at a Mohawk manufacturing facility, filed suit in the United States District Court for the Northern District of Georgia, alleging that Mohawk had terminated him in violation of 42 U.S.C. § 1985(2) and various Georgia laws. According to Carpenter's complaint, his termination came after he informed a member of Mohawk's human resources department in an e-mail that the company was employing undocumented immigrants. At the time, unbeknownst to Carpenter, Mohawk stood accused in a pending class-action lawsuit of conspiring to drive down the wages of its legal employees by knowingly hiring undocumented workers in violation of federal and state racketeering laws. Company officials directed Carpenter to meet with the company's retained counsel in the Williams case, and counsel allegedly pressured Carpenter to recant his statements. When he refused, Carpenter alleges, Mohawk fired him under false pretenses.

After learning of Carpenter's complaint, the plaintiffs in the Williams case sought an evidentiary hearing to explore Carpenter's allegations. In its response to their motion, Mohawk described Carpenter's accusations as "pure fantasy" and recounted the "true facts" of Carpenter's dismissal.... According to Mohawk, Carpenter himself had "engaged in blatant and illegal misconduct" by attempting to have Mohawk hire an undocumented worker. The company "commenced an immediate investigation," during which retained counsel interviewed Carpenter. Because Carpenter's "efforts to cause Mohawk to circumvent federal immigration law" "blatantly violated Mohawk policy," the company terminated him.

As these events were unfolding in the Williams case, discovery was underway in Carpenter's case. Carpenter filed a motion to compel Mohawk to produce information concerning his meeting with retained counsel and the company's termination decision. Mohawk maintained that the requested information was protected by the attorney-client privilege.

The District Court agreed that the privilege applied to the requested information, but it granted Carpenter's motion to compel disclosure after concluding that Mohawk had implicitly waived the privilege through its representations in the Williams case. The court declined to certify its order for interlocutory appeal under 28 U.S.C. § 1292(b). But, recognizing "the seriousness of its [waiver] finding," it stayed its ruling to allow Mohawk to explore other potential "avenues to appeal ..., such as a petition for mandamus or appealing this Order under the collateral order doctrine."

Mohawk filed a notice of appeal and a petition for a writ of mandamus to the Eleventh Circuit. The Court of Appeals dismissed the appeal for lack of jurisdiction under 28 U.S.C. § 1291, holding that the District Court's ruling did not qualify as an immediately appealable collateral order within the meaning of Cohen [v. Beneficial Industrial Loan Corp.,] 337 U.S. 541 [(1949)]. "Under Cohen," the Court of Appeals explained, "an order is appealable if it (1) conclusively determines the disputed question; (2) resolves an important issue completely separate from the merits of the action; and (3) is effectively unreviewable on appeal from a final judgment." According to the court, the District Court's waiver ruling satisfied the first two of these requirements but not the third, because "a discovery order that implicates the attorney-client privilege" can be adequately reviewed "on appeal from a final judgment." The Court of Appeals also rejected Mohawk's mandamus petition, finding no "clear usurpation of power or abuse of discretion" by the District Court. . . . We granted certiorari, to resolve a conflict among the Circuits concerning the availability of collateral appeals in the attorney-client privilege context.

II

A

... [A]s we held in Cohen, the statute encompasses not only judgments that "terminate an action," but also a "small class" of collateral rulings that, although they do not end the litigation, are appropriately deemed "final." ...

In applying Cohen's collateral order doctrine, we have stressed that it must "never be allowed to swallow the general rule that a party is entitled to a single appeal, to be deferred until final judgment has been entered." Our admonition reflects a healthy respect for the virtues of the final-judgment rule. Permitting piecemeal, prejudgment appeals, we have recognized, undermines "efficient judicial administration" and encroaches upon the prerogatives of district court judges, who play a "special role" in managing ongoing litigation.

. . .

B

In the present case, the Court of Appeals concluded that the District Court's privilege-waiver order satisfied the first two conditions of the collateral order doctrine—conclusiveness and separateness—but not the third-effective unreviewability. Because we agree with the Court of Appeals that collateral order appeals are not necessary to ensure effective review of orders adverse to the attorney-client privilege, we do not decide whether the other Cohen requirements are met.

Mohawk does not dispute that "we have generally denied review of pretrial discovery orders." Mohawk contends, however, that rulings implicating the attorney-client privilege differ in kind from run-of-the-mill discovery orders because of the important institutional interests at stake. According to Mohawk, the right to maintain attorney-client confidences—the sine qua non of a meaningful attorney-client relationship—is "irreparably destroyed absent immediate appeal" of adverse privilege rulings.

We readily acknowledge the importance of the attorney-client privilege, which "is one of the oldest recognized privileges for confidential communications." By assuring confidentiality, the privilege encourages clients to make "full and frank" disclosures to their attorneys, who are then better able to provide candid advice and effective representation. This, in turn, serves "broader public interests in the observance of law and administration of justice."

The crucial question, however, is not whether an interest is important in the abstract; it is whether deferring review until final judgment so imperils the interest as to justify the cost of allowing immediate appeal of the entire class of relevant orders. We routinely require litigants to wait until after final judgment to vindicate valuable rights, including rights central to our adversarial system. . . .

. . . In our estimation, postjudgment appeals generally suffice to protect the rights of litigants and assure the vitality of the attorney-client privilege. Appellate courts can remedy the improper disclosure of privileged material in the same way they remedy a host of other erroneous evidentiary rulings: by vacating an adverse judgment and remanding for a new trial in which the protected material and its fruits are excluded from evidence.

Dismissing such relief as inadequate, Mohawk emphasizes that the attorney-client privilege does not merely "prohibi[t] use of protected information at trial"; it provides a "right not to disclose the privileged information in the first place." Mohawk is undoubtedly correct that an order to disclose privileged information intrudes on the confidentiality of attorney-client communications. But deferring review until final judgment does not meaningfully reduce the *ex ante* incentives for full and frank consultations between clients and counsel.

One reason for the lack of a discernible chill is that, in deciding how freely to speak, clients and counsel are unlikely to focus on the remote prospect of an erroneous disclosure order, let alone on the timing of a possible appeal. Whether or not immediate collateral order appeals are available, clients and counsel must account for the possibility that they will later be required by law to disclose their communications for a variety of reasons—for example, because they misjudged the scope of the privilege, because they waived the privilege, or because their communications fell within the privilege's crime-fraud exception. Most district court rulings on these matters involve the routine application of settled legal principles. They are unlikely to be reversed on appeal, particularly when they rest on factual determinations for which appellate deference is the norm. ... The breadth of the privilege and the narrowness of its exceptions will thus tend to exert a much greater influence on the conduct of clients and counsel than the small risk that the law will be misapplied.

Moreover, were attorneys and clients to reflect upon their appellate options, they would find that litigants confronted with a particularly injurious or novel privilege ruling have several potential avenues of review apart from collateral order appeal. First, a party may ask the district court to certify, and the court of appeals to accept, an interlocutory appeal pursuant to 28 U.S.C. § 1292(b). The preconditions for § 1292(b) review—"a controlling question of law," the prompt resolution of which "may materially advance the ultimate termination of the litigation"—are most likely to be satisfied when a privilege ruling involves a new legal question or is of special consequence, and district courts should not hesitate to certify an interlocutory appeal in such cases. Second, in extraordinary circumstances—*i.e.,* when a disclosure order "amount[s] to a judicial usurpation of power or a clear abuse of discretion," or otherwise works a manifest injustice—a party may petition the court of appeals for a writ of mandamus. While these discretionary review mechanisms do not provide relief in every case, they serve as useful "safety valve[s]" for promptly correcting serious errors.

Another long-recognized option is for a party to defy a disclosure order and incur court-imposed sanctions. District courts have a range of sanctions from which to choose, including "directing that the matters embraced in the order or other designated facts be taken as established for purposes of the action," "prohibiting the disobedient party from supporting or opposing designated claims or defenses," or "striking pleadings in whole or in part." Fed. Rule Civ. Proc. 37(b)(2)(i)–(iii). Such sanctions allow a party to obtain postjudgment review without having to reveal its privileged information. Alternatively, when the circumstances warrant it, a district court may hold a noncomplying party in contempt. The party can then appeal directly from that ruling, at least when the contempt citation can be characterized as a criminal punishment. See, e.g., Church of Scientology of Cal. v. United States, 506 U.S. 9, 18, n. 11, 113 S.Ct. 447, 121 L.Ed.2d 313 (1992); . . . .

These established mechanisms for appellate review not only provide assurances to clients and counsel about the security of their confidential communications; they also go a long way toward addressing Mohawk's concern that, absent collateral order appeals of adverse attorney-client privilege rulings, some litigants may experience severe hardship. Mohawk is no doubt right that an order to disclose privileged material may, in some situations, have implications beyond the case at hand. But the same can be said about many categories of pretrial discovery orders for which collateral order appeals are unavailable. As with these other orders, rulings adverse to the privilege vary in their significance; some may be momentous, but others are more mundane. Section 1292(b) appeals, mandamus, and appeals from contempt citations facilitate immediate review of some of the more consequential attorney-client privilege rulings. Moreover, protective orders are available to limit the spillover effects of disclosing sensitive information. That a fraction of orders adverse to the attorney-client privilege may nevertheless harm individual litigants in ways that are "only imperfectly reparable" does not justify making all such orders immediately appealable as of right under § 1291.

In short, the limited benefits of applying "the blunt, categorical instrument of § 1291 collateral order appeal" to privilege-related disclosure orders simply cannot justify the likely institutional costs. Permitting parties to undertake successive, piecemeal appeals of all adverse attorney-client rulings would unduly delay the resolution of district court litigation and needlessly burden the Courts of Appeals. . . . Attempting to downplay such concerns, Mohawk asserts that the three Circuits in which the collateral order doctrine currently applies to adverse privilege rulings have seen only a trickle of appeals. But this may be due to the fact that the practice in all three Circuits is relatively new and not yet widely known. Were this Court to approve collateral order appeals in the attorney-client privilege context, many more litigants would likely choose that route. They would also likely seek to extend such a ruling to disclosure orders implicating many other categories of sensitive information, raising an array of line-drawing difficulties.[4]

C

In concluding that sufficiently effective review of adverse attorney-client privilege rulings can be had without resort to the Cohen doctrine,

---

4. Participating as amicus curiae in support of respondent Carpenter, the United States contends that collateral order appeals should be available for rulings involving certain governmental privileges "in light of their structural constitutional grounding under the separation of powers, relatively rare invocation, and unique importance to governmental functions." We express no view on that issue.

CHAPTER 9   PRIVILEGES

we reiterate that the class of collaterally appealable orders must remain "narrow and selective in its membership." . . .

Indeed, the rulemaking process has important virtues. It draws on the collective experience of bench and bar, see 28 U.S.C. § 2073, and it facilitates the adoption of measured, practical solutions. We expect that the combination of standard postjudgment appeals, § 1292(b) appeals, mandamus, and contempt appeals will continue to provide adequate protection to litigants ordered to disclose materials purportedly subject to the attorney-client privilege. Any further avenue for immediate appeal of such rulings should be furnished, if at all, through rulemaking, with the opportunity for full airing it provides.

. . .

In sum, we conclude that the collateral order doctrine does not extend to disclosure orders adverse to the attorney-client privilege. Effective appellate review can be had by other means. Accordingly, we affirm the judgment of the Court of Appeals for the Eleventh Circuit.

It is so ordered.

■ [JUSTICE THOMAS, wrote a separate opinion concurring in part and concurring in the judgment.]

SECTION 6.   OTHER RELATIONSHIP PRIVILEGES

A.   CLERGY-PENITENT

Page 1534. Add as Note to be considered in connection with materials in Section 6 (as well as in connection with earlier materials in this Chapter):

Note on the Privileges Invoked in the Investigation of President Clinton by the Independent Counsel

In 1997 and 1998, Kenneth Starr, an Independent Counsel, investigating, inter alia, the possibility of perjury and obstruction of justice on the part of President Clinton, the First Lady, assistants to the President and others, called before the grand jury a wide array of witnesses. The setting produced an unusually diverse set of evidentiary privilege issues arising out of a single investigation.

The factual background: A civil suit in the nature of a sexual harassment claim had been filed against the President by Paula Jones based on his alleged actions while he had been Governor of Arkansas. In connection with that suit, both the President and a White House intern, Monica Lewinsky, gave separate sworn statements to the effect that they had not had a sexual relationship. Subsequently, the Independent Counsel began investigating whether the President and Lewinsky had perjured themselves in providing such statements and ether the President or anyone connected with him had obstructed justice by ging Lewinsky to lie about their relationship.

SECTION 6   OTHER RELATIONSHIP PRIVILEGES

1. Executive privilege

   a. Deputy White House counsels to the President invoked executive privilege in connection with conversations with the President relating to the Independent Counsel's above-described investigation. The official matters asserted to have been involved in these conversations included possible impeachment proceedings and assertions of official privileges. The U.S. District Judge hearing the assertion of privilege ruled that although executive privilege applied, it was outweighed by the need for the testimony of the presidential aides because the information might involve criminal conduct and could not be obtained from other sources. The decision was appealed, and the Independent Counsel sought expedited direct review by the Supreme Court. In the wake of that request, the White House dropped the executive privilege claim and relied solely on the attorney-client privilege with respect to the President's conversations with his aides. The Court rejected the request for expedited review, and the case was reviewed by the U.S. Court of Appeals for the District of Columbia. See 2.c. below for a description of the issues involved.

   b. In an unrelated Independent Counsel investigation, the U.S. Court of Appeals for the District of Columbia expanded the protection afforded to presidential communications to cover communications in which the President is not personally involved but the communications involve immediate advisors to the President and their staff "who have broad and significant responsibility for investigating and formulating the advice to be given to the President on the particular matter to which the communications relate." In re Sealed Case, 121 F.3d 729 (D.C.Cir.1997).

   c. The Independent Counsel served a subpoena summoning President Clinton to testify before the grand jury. The President had available a number of possible options, each of which had a significant political as well as legal dimension, including the following: Move to quash the subpoena claiming that the separation of powers doctrine barred the judicial branch from summoning a sitting President; decline to respond to the subpoena (its direct enforcement would be problematic); testify before the grand jury; or negotiate with the Independent Counsel to furnish his testimony in videotaped form (elements in the negotiation might include the scope of the questions to be put to the President, whether he would receive written questions in advance, whether the testimony would be given in the White House, and whether the President's lawyer would be present). The President chose to give his testimony in videotaped session in the White House.

2. Attorney-client privilege

   a. Lewinsky was represented by a series of attorneys. The first lawyer, Francis Carter, was called before the grand jury and declined to testify. Eventually he was required to testify as to his conversations and dealings with Lewinsky, apparently on the ground that the crime-fraud exception to the attorney-client privilege was applicable.

   b. The second attorney representing Lewinsky, William Ginsburg, carried on unsuccessful negotiations with the Independent Counsel to enter into an immunity arrangement in exchange for Lewinsky's testimony. During this period, Ginsburg was interviewed frequently on national television regarding the matter, was quoted in the national press and wrote a bar magazine article regarding the investigation. There were published criticisms by other lawyers of Ginsburg's handling of the case on various grounds, including the suggestion that he was making statements in his public utterances that might be vicariously attributed to her. It was also suggested that his statements created a risk that the protections of the attorney client privilege would be deemed to have been waived.

c. Attorneys who were also assistants to the President were summoned to the grand jury to testify regarding their conversations with the President and others. Several issues were raised in connection with the invocation of the attorney-client privilege in this context. Was the assistant functioning as a lawyer and was the President his client? Was legal or political advice being sought or provided in connection with the conversations to which the grand jury questions were directed? Can the attorney-client privilege be invoked with respect to conversations with a government lawyer that are being sought by a federal prosecutor? Is a government lawyer under special obligations in relation to a criminal investigation? Were the conversations at issue in furtherance of criminal conduct? The U.S. Court of Appeals for the District of Columbia in a 2–1 decision, while recognizing the existence of a government attorney-client privilege, ruled that a government attorney may not invoke the attorney-client privilege in response to grand jury questions seeking information relating to the possible commission of a federal crime. "Thus, although the traditional privilege between attorneys and clients shields private relationships from inquiry in either civil litigation or criminal prosecution, competing values arise when the Office of the President resists demands for information from a federal grand jury and the nation's chief law enforcement officer." In re Bruce R. Lindsey (Grand Jury Testimony), 158 F.3d 1263, 1271 (D.C. Cir.1998). The Supreme Court denied the petition for certiorari, with two justices dissenting. 119 S.Ct. 466 (1998).

d. See the 1997 Eighth Circuit decision, described in the Casebook at p. 1553, regarding the application of the attorney client privilege to conversations of the White House counsel with the President's wife.

e. Also to be mentioned here is a case, growing out of the Independent Counsel's investigations although not involving the Lewinsky matter, that was decided by the Supreme Court in late June, 1998, Swidler & Berlin and Hamilton v. United States. The Swidler decision is reproduced in this Supplement supra at p. 528. In Swidler, the issue was whether the attorney-client privilege survives the death of the client where the information is sought by a grand jury in the course of a criminal investigation.

3. Protective function privilege (Secret Service privilege)

Mr. Starr called several Secret Service agents to testify before the grand jury regarding what they observed relating to the President and Ms Lewinsky while the agents were in the White House on duty guarding the President. The agents declined to testify, claiming a new "protective function" privilege. The district judge rejected the claim, and the case was appealed to the U.S. Court of Appeals District of Columbia. Statements by several former Presidents were both appellants and respondent in support of and opposed to the recognition of a new privilege in this area. The Court of Appeals ruled against creation of a new privilege:

> ... [J]udicial recognition of the privilege depends entirely upon the Secret Service's ability to establish clearly and convincingly both the need for and efficacy of the proposed privilege. In other words, the Secret Service must demonstrate that recognition of the privilege in its proposed form will materially enhance presidential security by lessening any tendency of the President to "push away" his protectors in situations where there is some risk to his safety.

After examining a series of arguments on the issue, the court concluded that the Secret Service had not met its burden under Rule 501. The court therefore left to the Congress the question whether to establish such a privilege in order to ensure the safety of the President. In re: Sealed Case, 148 F.3d 1079 (D.C.Cir. 1998).

The Secretary of the Treasury petitioned for certiorari in the Supreme Court and applied for a stay of the subpoenas issued to the secret service agents, pending decision on the petition. Chief Justice Rehnquist, sitting as a Circuit Justice, denied the stay holding that the applicant had failed to show irreparable harm. The Chief Justice also indicated that he assumed, without deciding, that the Court was likely to grant certiorari but concluded that there was not a likelihood that the Court would reverse the judgment of the Court of Appeals: "The opinion of the Court of Appeals seems to me cogent and correct." Rubin v. United States Acting Through the Independent Counsel, 119 S.Ct. 1 (1998). Subsequently, several Secret Service bodyguards of the President testified before the grand jury.

If Congress were to consider enacting legislation creating such a privilege, a number of questions would arise. Who is the holder of the privilege? Is the privilege the President's or the Secret Service's to invoke or not? Note that in the Court of Appeals, the Secretary of the Treasury (the cabinet officer who oversees the Secret Service) took the position that his office was the holder of the privilege and not the President, and the White House Counsel wrote that "the privilege is not the [President's] to assert or waive." The Court of Appeals stated: "We know of no other privilege that works that way."

Should the privilege be primarily designed to protect presidential privacy or the effective performance of the Secret Service's protective function? To what kind of information should the privilege be applicable: observations of presidential activities; conversations; any testimony that is adverse to President's personal interests; evidence of non-felonious as opposed to felonious conduct?

Should the privilege be applicable after the President leaves office? Be applicable to the testimony of a former Secret Service agent? To which of the existing recognized privileges would such a new privilege be most similar?

4. Parent-child privilege

Monica Lewinsky's mother was called to testify before the grand jury, probably to answer questions about what her daughter had told her regarding her relationship with the President. Should there be a parent-child confidential communication privilege applicable in that situation? Such a privilege, of course, has only been recognized in a very few jurisdictions.

5. Privilege against self-incrimination

   a. Immunity—As mentioned above, Lewinsky's attorneys negotiated with Mr. Starr in order to obtain immunity for their client in exchange for her testimony. According to newspaper reports, Starr was pressing for testimony that would incriminate the President for obstruction of justice while Lewinsky was only willing to provide testimony that, if true, would indicate that the President had committed perjury in his sworn statement. Is it proper for a prosecutor to condition his willingness to grant immunity on the witness being willing to provide testimony of a specified type. At one point, Lewinsky's attorney made a claim that the Independent Counsel had in a letter in fact provided immunity to his client, but the district judge rule against him on this claim. Subsequently it was reported in the newspapers that Lewinsky had been given transactional immunity in exchange for her testimony.

   b. Lewinsky was ordered to provide fingerprints, hair samples and a recording of her voice, evidentiary items which did not fall within the protections of the privilege against self incrimination.

6. Reporter's privilege

There were charges and counter-charges between the Independent Counsel and the White House regarding leaks of information relating to the Lewinsky matter. At one point, the Independent Counsel called presidential assistants to testify regarding their communications with the media. Although apparently not directly raised, the reporter's privilege was a backdrop to these proceedings.

Page 1535. Substitute the following for the first paragraph under A:

Every state by statute has some form of the clergy-penitent privilege. The general form of the privilege varies among the states. There are three principal statutory versions: a privilege that covers confidential communications seeking spiritual advice from a clergy person; a privilege that covers only confessional communications pursuant to church discipline; and a privilege that expressly covers both of the two foregoing categories. For a brief history of the transition to the modern form of the statutes and a survey of the different state statutory approaches, see Abrams, Addressing the Tension Between the Clergy–Communicant Privilege and the Duty to Report Child Abuse in State Statutes, 44 Boston Coll. L.Rev. 1127, 1130–1138 (2003).

Page 1536. Delete two paragraphs immediately preceding B. and add in their place:

Note on Evidentiary Privilege Issues Arising out of Molestation and Child Abuse Charges against Church Personnel

the course of the past half dozen years or more, numerous allegations tation and child abuse have been made against church personnel.

SECTION 6 OTHER RELATIONSHIP PRIVILEGES

A number of different evidentiary privilege issues arise with some frequency in such instances, and the number of cases in which such issues have reached the courts has increased.

1. The clergy-penitent privilege may, of course, be involved where a priest who has engaged in molestation or abuse confides to his superior or another priest in a context that presents a basis for claiming that privilege, and the authorities seek to obtain evidence regarding the communication.

2. Every state has enacted some kind of statute requiring the reporting of child abuse. Where the statute imposes such a reporting obligation on clergy persons and a priest-perpetrator has confided to another priest in a context covered by the privilege, a significant tension is created between the obligation to report and the confidentiality requirements of the privilege. For a survey of the statutes requiring the reporting of the child abuse and for a set of proposals for resolving this tension, see Abrams, Addressing the Tension Between the Clergy-Communicant Privilege and the Duty to Report Child Abuse in State Statutes, 44 Boston Coll. L.Rev. 1127, 1130–1138 (2003). Also see Mitchell, Must Clergy Tell? Child Abuse Reporting Requirements Versus the The Clergy Privilege and Free Exercise of Religion, 71 Minn. L.Rev. 723 (1987).

3. In a number of instances, in connection with accusations of molestation or abuse, or where there is concern that church officials have not acted appropriately in responding to complaints, state or local authorities have sought church records such as personnel files or other church documents. In many instances, the archdiocese has raised legal objections, claiming that the records are confidential that they may contain priest-penitent communications; and that as confidential church documents, they are protected by the First Amendment Free Exercise Clause and that requiring production of such records interferes with "church autonomy." Generally, the courts have rejected such claims. See, e.g., Society of Jesus of New England v. Commonwealth, 441 Mass. 662, 808 N.E. 2d 272 (2004) (4–3 decision upholding subpoena against First Amendment challenges); People v. Campobello, 810 N.E.2d 307 (Ill. App.2 Dist.) (same). See Eck, Discovery of Church Records, 35 Cath. Law.229 (1994).

4. A set of issues related to those treated in note 3. supra, may be posed as the Catholic Church undertakes church trials of Roman Catholic priests accused of sexual misconduct. It has been reported that some time early in 2004, in a case arising out of the Chicago archdiocese, a special tribunal of three canon law judges began conducting the trial of a priest charged with sexual abuse. Chicago Sun–Times, Metro section, May 21, 2004, at p. 15. The same article indicated that this may be the first of as many as 12 such church trials. The article reported that the "pontifical secret," an order emanating from the Vatican forbade anyone involved from disclosing any details about the trial, including the name of the accused priest. What result if state or local authorities subpoena records of the trial, or, in the alternative, individuals who have information about it? What practical obstacles are there to obtaining such records or individuals by subpoena? Consider how you would proceed if you were a local prosecutor seeking such information, or, if you represented the archdiocese. Note

that the Chicago Sun–Times article, supra, reported that for such trials, "There is no set location, and it can move from place to place."

Section 7. Institutional and Institutional Process Privileges

B. Government Information—Executive Privilege

1. STATE SECRETS

Page 1553. Add at end of Section 2. PRESIDENTIAL COMMUNICATIONS:

Cheney v. United States District Court for the District of Columbia

Supreme Court of the United States, 2004.
542 U.S. 367.

■ [KENNEDY, J., delivered the opinion of the Court, joined by REHNQUIST, C. J., and STEVENS, O'CONNOR, and BREYER, JJ. SCALIA and THOMAS, JJ., joined as to Parts I, II, III, and IV. STEVENS, J., filed a concurring opinion. THOMAS, J., joined by SCALIA, J. filed an opinion concurring in part and dissenting in part. GINSBURG, J., filed a dissenting opinion, in which SOUTER, J., joined.]

[President Bush established a National Energy Policy Development Group (NEPDG) to develop a national energy policy designed to help the private sector and government at all levels. The members of the NEPDG were government agency heads or their assistants with Vice President Cheney as the chairman. After the NEPDG issued its final report and terminated all operations, Judicial Watch and the Sierra Club filed actions alleging that the NEPDG had failed to comply with the procedural and disclosure requirements of the Federal Advisory Committee Act (FACA). FACA imposes various open meeting and disclosure requirements on groups that meet the definition of an "advisory committee." Committees composed entirely of government employees are excluded from the definition of "advisory committee." The plaintiffs alleged, however, that the regular participation in meetings of the NEPDG of non-government individuals including private lobbyists made them de facto members of the NEPDG and therefore it was not exempt from the requirements of FACA.

The district court ruled that the FACA requirements could be enforced against the Vice President and other government defendants under the Mandamus Act and allowed the plaintiffs to conduct a "tightly ~ined" discovery to ascertain the NEPDG's structure and membership ~ to determine whether the de facto membership doctrine applies. ~ourt also explained that the government could assert executive privilege to protect sensitive materials from disclosure. The Vice President and other officials sought a writ of mandamus to vacate the discovery orders, to direct the district court to rule based on the administrative record and to dismiss the Vice President from the suit. A divided panel of the Court of Appeals dismissed the writ of mandamus on the ground that alternative avenues of relief were available; that the plaintiffs must first assert privilege, "with particularity," and if the claims of privilege are denied, mandamus might well be appropriate. The Vice President et al. sought review in the Supreme Court, and the Court granted certiorari.]

■ JUSTICE KENNEDY delivered the opinion of the Court.

The United States District Court for the District of Columbia entered discovery orders directing the Vice President and other senior officials in the Executive Branch to produce information about a task force established to give advice and make policy recommendations to the President. This case requires us to consider the circumstances under which a court of appeals may exercise its power to issue a writ of mandamus to modify or dissolve the orders when, by virtue of their overbreadth, enforcement might interfere with the officials in the discharge of their duties and impinge upon the President's constitutional prerogatives.

. . .

III

We now come to the central issue in the case—whether the Court of Appeals was correct to conclude it "had no authority to exercise the extraordinary remedy of mandamus," on the ground that the Government could protect its rights by asserting executive privilege in the District Court.

. . .

Were the Vice President not a party in the case, the argument that the Court of Appeals should have entertained an action in mandamus, notwithstanding the District Court's denial of the motion for certification, might present different considerations. Here, however, the Vice President and his comembers on the NEPDG are the subjects of the discovery orders. The mandamus petition alleges that the orders threaten "substantial intrusions on the process by which those in closest operational proximity to the President advise the President." These facts and allegations remove this case from the category of ordinary discovery orders where interlocutory appellate review is unavailable, through mandamus or otherwise. It is well established that "a President's communications and activities encompass a vastly wider range of sensitive material than would be true of any 'ordinary individual.'" ... As United States v. Nixon explained, these principles do not mean that the "President is above the law." Rather, they simply acknowledge that the public interest requires that a coequal branch of Government "afford Presidential confidentiality the greatest protection consistent with the fair administration of justice," and give recognition to the paramount necessity of protecting the Executive Branch from vexatious litigation that might distract it from the energetic performance of its constitutional duties.

These separation-of-powers considerations should inform a court of appeals' evaluation of a mandamus petition involving the President or the Vice President. Accepted mandamus standards are broad enough to allow a court of appeals to prevent a lower court from interfering with a coequal branch's ability to discharge its constitutional responsibilities.

IV

The Court of Appeals dismissed these separation-of-powers concerns. Relying on United States v. Nixon, it held that even though respondents' discovery requests are overbroad and "go well beyond FACA's requirements," the Vice President and his former colleagues on the NEPDG "shall bear the burden" of invoking privilege with narrow specificity and objecting to the discovery requests with "detailed precision." In its view, this result was required by Nixon's rejection of an "absolute, unqualified Presidential privilege of immunity from judicial process under all circumstances." If Nixon refused to recognize broad claims of confidentiality where the President had asserted executive privilege, the majority reasoned, Nixon must have rejected, a fortiori, petitioners' claim of discovery immunity where the privilege has not even been invoked. According to the majority, because the Executive Branch can invoke executive privilege to maintain the separation of powers, mandamus relief is premature.

This analysis, however, overlooks fundamental differences in the two cases. Nixon cannot bear the weight the Court of Appeals puts upon it. First, unlike this case, which concerns respondents' requests for information for use in a civil suit, Nixon involves the proper balance between the Executive's interest in the confidentiality of its communications and the "constitutional need for production of relevant evidence in a criminal proceeding." The Court's decision was explicit that it was "not . . . concerned with the balance between the President's generalized interest in confidentiality and the need for relevant evidence in civil litigation. . . . We address only the conflict between the President's assertion of a generalized privilege of confidentiality and the constitutional need for relevant evidence in criminal trials."

The distinction Nixon drew between criminal and civil proceedings is not just a matter of formalism. As the Court explained, the need for information in the criminal context is much weightier because "our ⸺torical commitment to the rule of law . . . is nowhere more profoundly ⸺ than in our view that 'the twofold aim [of criminal justice] is ⸺ not escape or innocence suffer.' " In light of the "fundamental" and "comprehensive" need for "every man's evidence" in the criminal justice system, not only must the Executive Branch first assert privilege to resist disclosure, but privilege claims that shield information from a grand jury proceeding or a criminal trial are not to be "expansively construed, for they are in derogation of the search for truth," The need for information for use in civil cases, while far from negligible, does not share the urgency or significance of the criminal subpoena requests in Nixon. As Nixon recognized, the right to production of relevant evidence in civil proceedings does not have the same "constitutional dimensions."

The Court also observed in Nixon that a "primary constitutional duty of the Judicial Branch [is] to do justice in criminal prosecutions." Withholding materials from a tribunal in an ongoing criminal case when the information is necessary to the court in carrying out its tasks "conflicts with the function of the courts under Art. III." Such an impairment of the "essential functions of [another] branch," is impermissible. Withholding the information in this case, however, does not hamper another branch's ability to perform its "essential functions" in quite the same way. The District Court ordered discovery here, not to remedy known statutory violations, but to ascertain whether FACA's disclosure requirements even apply to the NEPDG in the first place. Even if FACA embodies important congressional objectives, the only consequence from respondents' inability to obtain the discovery they seek is that it would be more difficult for private complainants to vindicate Congress' policy objectives under FACA.... The situation here cannot, in fairness, be compared to Nixon, where a court's ability to fulfill its constitutional responsibility to resolve cases and controversies within its jurisdiction hinges on the availability of certain indispensable information.

A party's need for information is only one facet of the problem. An important factor weighing in the opposite direction is the burden imposed by the discovery orders. This is not a routine discovery dispute. The discovery requests are directed to the Vice President and other senior Government officials who served on the NEPDG to give advice and make recommendations to the President. The Executive Branch, at its highest level, is seeking the aid of the courts to protect its constitutional prerogatives. As we have already noted, special considerations control when the Executive Branch's interests in maintaining the autonomy of its office and safeguarding the confidentiality of its communications are implicated. This Court has held, on more than one occasion, that "the high respect that is owed to the office of the Chief Executive ... is a matter that should inform the conduct of the entire proceeding, including the timing and scope of discovery," and that the Executive's "constitutional responsibilities and status [are] factors counseling judicial deference and restraint" in the conduct of litigation against it.

Respondents' reliance on cases that do not involve senior members of the Executive Branch is altogether misplaced.

Even when compared against United States v. Nixon's criminal subpoenas, which did involve the President, the civil discovery here militates against respondents' position. The observation in Nixon that production of confidential information would not disrupt the functioning of the Executive Branch cannot be applied in a mechanistic fashion to civil litigation. In the criminal justice system, there are various constraints, albeit imperfect, to filter out insubstantial legal claims. The decision to prosecute a criminal case, for example, is made by a publicly accountable prosecutor subject to budgetary considerations and under an ethical obligation, not only to win and zealously to advocate for his client but also to serve the cause of justice. The rigors of the penal system are also mitigated by the responsible exercise of prosecutorial discretion. In contrast, there are no analogous checks in the civil discovery process here. Although under Federal Rule of Civil Procedure 11, sanctions are available, and private attorneys also owe an obligation of candor to the judicial tribunal, these safeguards have proved insufficient to discourage the filing of meritless claims against the Executive Branch. "In view of the visibility of" the Offices of the President and the Vice President and "the effect of their actions on countless people," they are "easily identifiable targets for suits for civil damages."

Finally, the narrow subpoena orders in United States v. Nixon stand on an altogether different footing from the overly broad discovery requests approved by the District Court in this case. The criminal subpoenas in Nixon were required to satisfy exacting standards of "(1) relevancy; (2) admissibility; (3) specificity." . . . The burden of showing these standards were met, moreover, fell on the party requesting the information. ("In order to require production prior to trial, the moving party must show that the applicable standards are met"). In Nixon, the Court addressed the issue of executive privilege only after having satisfied itself that the special prosecutor had surmounted these demanding requirements. . . . The very specificity of the subpoena requests serves as an important safeguard against unnecessary intrusion into the operation of the Office of the President.

In contrast to Nixon's subpoena orders that "precisely identified" and "specifically . . . enumerated" the relevant materials, the discovery requests here, as the panel majority acknowledged, ask for everything under the sky:

"1. All documents identifying or referring to any staff, personnel, contractors, consultants or employees of the Task Force.

"2. All documents establishing or referring to any Sub–Group.

All documents identifying or referring to any staff, personnel, consultants or employees of any Sub–Group.

"4. All documents identifying or referring to any other persons participating in the preparation of the Report or in the activities of the Task Force or any Sub–Group.

"5. All documents concerning any communication relating to the activities of the Task Force, the activities of any Sub–Groups, or the preparation of the Report. . . .

"6. All documents concerning any communication relating to the activities of the Task Force, the activities of the Sub–Groups, or the preparation of the Report between any person . . . and [a list of agencies]." App. 220–221.

. . . Given the breadth of the discovery requests in this case compared to the narrow subpoena orders in United States v. Nixon, our precedent provides no support for the proposition that the Executive Branch "shall bear the burden" of invoking executive privilege with sufficient specificity and of making particularized objections. To be sure, Nixon held that the President cannot, through the assertion of a "broad [and] undifferentiated" need for confidentiality and the invocation of an "absolute, unqualified" executive privilege, withhold information in the face of subpoena orders. It did so, however, only after the party requesting the information—the special prosecutor—had satisfied his burden of showing the propriety of the requests. Here, as the Court of Appeals acknowledged, the discovery requests are anything but appropriate. They provide respondents all the disclosure to which they would be entitled in the event they prevail on the merits, and much more besides. In these circumstances, Nixon does not require the Executive Branch to bear the onus of critiquing the unacceptable discovery requests line by line. Our precedents suggest just the opposite.

The Government, however, did in fact object to the scope of discovery and asked the District Court to narrow it in some way. Its arguments were ignored. . . . In addition, the Government objected to the burden that would arise from the District Court's insistence that the Vice President winnow the discovery orders by asserting specific claims of privilege and making more particular objections. . . . These arguments, too, were rejected.

Contrary to the District Court's and the Court of Appeals' conclusions, Nixon does not leave them the sole option of inviting the Executive Branch to invoke executive privilege while remaining otherwise powerless to modify a party's overly broad discovery requests. Executive privilege is an extraordinary assertion of power "not to be lightly invoked." Once executive privilege is asserted, coequal branches of the Government are set on a collision course. The Judiciary is forced into the difficult task of balancing the need for information in a judicial proceeding and the Executive's Article II prerogatives. This inquiry places courts in the awkward position of evaluating the Executive's claims of confidentiality and autonomy, and pushes to the fore difficult questions of separation of powers and checks and balances. These "occasions for constitutional confrontation between the two branches" should be avoided whenever possible

In recognition of these concerns, there is sound precedent in the District of Columbia itself for district courts to explore other avenues, short of forcing the Executive to invoke privilege, when they are asked to enforce against the Executive Branch unnecessarily broad subpoenas. In United States v. Poindexter, 727 F. Supp. 1501 (1989), defendant Poindexter, on trial for criminal charges, sought to have the District Court enforce subpoena orders against President Reagan to obtain allegedly exculpatory materials. The Executive considered the subpoenas "unreasonable and oppressive." Rejecting defendant's argument that the Executive must first assert executive privilege to narrow the subpoenas, the District Court agreed with the President that "it is undesirable as a matter of constitutional and public policy to compel a President to make his decision on privilege with respect to a large array of documents." The court decided to narrow, on its own, the scope of the subpoenas to allow the Executive "to consider whether to invoke executive privilege with respect to . . . a smaller number of documents following the narrowing of the subpoenas." This is but one example of the choices available to the District Court and the Court of Appeals in this case.

As we discussed at the outset, under principles of mandamus jurisdiction, the Court of Appeals may exercise its power to issue the writ only upon a finding of "exceptional circumstances amounting to a judicial 'usurpation of power,' " or "a clear abuse of discretion." As this case implicates the separation of powers, the Court of Appeals must also ask, as part of this inquiry, whether the District Court's actions constituted an unwarranted impairment of another branch in the performance of its constitutional duties. This is especially so here because the District Court's analysis of whether mandamus relief is appropriate should itself be constrained by principles similar to those we have outlined, that limit the Court of Appeals' use of the remedy. The panel majority, however, failed to ask this question. Instead, it labored under the mistaken assumption that the assertion of executive privilege is a necessary precondition to the Government's separation-of-powers objections.

V

. . . [W]e decline petitioners' invitation to direct the Court of Appeals to issue the writ against the District Court. Moreover, this is not a case where, after having considered the issues, the Court of Appeals abused its discretion by failing to issue the writ. Instead, the Court of Appeals, relying on its mistaken reading of United States v. Nixon, prematurely terminated its inquiry after the Government refused to ⁀rt privilege and did so without even reaching the weighty separation- ⁀ objections raised in the case, much less exercised its discretion ⁀hether "the writ is appropriate under the circumstances."

SECTION 7 INSTITUTIONAL AND INSTITUTIONAL PROCESS PRIVILEGES

Because the issuance of the writ is a matter vested in the discretion of the court to which the petition is made, and because this Court is not presented with an original writ of mandamus, we leave to the Court of Appeals to address the parties' arguments with respect to the challenge to ... the discovery orders. Other matters bearing on whether the writ of mandamus should issue should also be addressed, in the first instance, by the Court of Appeals after considering any additional briefs and arguments as it deems appropriate. We note only that all courts should be mindful of the burdens imposed on the Executive Branch in any future proceedings. Special considerations applicable to the President and the Vice President suggest that the courts should be sensitive to requests by the Government for interlocutory appeals to reexamine, for example, whether the statute embodies the de facto membership doctrine.

The judgment of the Court of Appeals for the District of Columbia is vacated, and the case is remanded for further proceedings consistent with this opinion.

It is so ordered.

†